ITIL® Inter
Certification
Study Guide

ITIL® Intermediate
Certification Companion
Study Guide

Service Lifecycle Exams

Helen Morris

Liz Gallacher

SYBEX®
A Wiley Brand

Senior Acquisitions Editor: Kenyon Brown
Development Editor: Kim Wimpsett
Technical Editors: Jane Holmes and Jim Tebby
Production Editor: Dassi Zeidel
Copy Editor: Judy Flynn
Editorial Manager: Mary Beth Wakefield
Production Manager: Kathleen Wisor
Associate Publisher: Jim Minatel
Supervising Producer: Rich Graves
Book Designers: Judy Fung and Bill Gibson
Proofreader: Kathy Pope, Word One New York
Indexer: Ted Laux
Project Coordinator, Cover: Brent Savage
Cover Designer: Wiley
Cover Image: © Getty Image, Inc./Jeremy Woodhouse

We dedicate this book to our long-suffering partners, Gary Cleaver and John Callaghan, who kept us supplied with food, drink, and encouragement while we slaved over our laptops every evening and weekend writing this book.

Acknowledgments

We thank our colleagues across many organizations over the years who have assisted us in our attempts to put best practices into practice. In particular, Liz Gallacher would like to thank Dave Cousin, who encouraged her to follow her instincts and gave her the opportunity to do just that in two major projects.

We both had teachers who shared their passion for service management during our ITIL® V2 Manager courses all those years ago: Helen would like to thank Ben Weston, Andrew Jacobs, and Mark Haddad, and Liz would like to thank Dave Wheeldon and Lloyd Robinson. Our commitment to focusing our careers in IT service management can be traced back to those few intense weeks.

We thank all the students we have taught for sharing their experiences with us and the clients who have had faith in us and our ability to put theory into practice. Our understanding of service management grows and develops with every organization we work with.

We thank all the ITIL® trainers, wherever they are, spreading the service management message every week of the year.

We thank Jane Holmes and Jim Tebby for checking the content of this book and for the helpful suggestions they made.

About the Authors

Liz Gallacher is a service management consultant and trainer with 30 years of practical experience. She placed in the top 5 percent of candidates in the ITIL Manager Certificate and was invited to join the ISEB V2 Managers Certificate Examiners panel. She holds the ITIL Expert certification and is a certified ISO/IEC 20000 consultant.

Liz provides consultancy and training on all aspects of IT service management, focusing on the ITIL framework and the ISO/IEC 20000 standard. She has designed and implemented improvement initiatives covering many areas of service management for a variety of organizations, large and small. Her experience over the past 30 years has been a mixture of consultancy, training, and implementation, including setting up service desks for many large organizations, working with clients to design their service management processes, and evaluating and implementing service management toolsets that met their requirements. She also advises organizations seeking certification against the ISO/IEC 20000 standard, performing gap analyses advising and mentoring improvement plans.

Liz has worked for several global businesses, central and local government departments, the UK National Health Service, and many other organizations. She has set up several service management organizations from scratch. In each case, she designed and documented the processes, procured the service management toolset, recommended the organizational structure, drafted job descriptions, and recruited several hundred staff over a number of projects. She then trained the staff and devised appropriate marketing campaigns to publicize the new service desks to the customer base.

She has implemented service improvement initiatives for several clients, combining improvements in processes and tools with customer awareness coaching for IT staff. For a national railway infrastructure organization, she implemented a 24/7/365 service desk to replace 18 other sources of support, delivering a service that was assessed by the Gartner and Maven organizations to be "world class" and "highly efficient."

She has provided consultancy on many aspects of service management, including service level management, change management, request fulfilment, and incident and problem management. She has compiled detailed service catalogs.

For many clients, Liz gathered toolset requirements, evaluated products, and recommended the purchase of products that matched the requirements. She also specified the tool configuration to support the processes, delivered the required reporting, and oversaw the implementation in addition to delivering user training.

Liz has developed and delivered bespoke training for clients covering particular aspects of service management. She has also coauthored classroom and distance-learning courses covering the ITIL framework. She delivers ITIL Foundation and Intermediate training and consultancy worldwide, with courses in the United Kingdom as well as 22 other countries so far. With Helen Morris, she has devised an innovative blended approach to mentoring and supporting clients remotely.

Helen Morris provides quality training and consultancy to organizations, assisting with delivery of IT service management. She specializes in providing cultural change support and training to organizations to enable the full exploitation of the benefits from implementing service management best practices.

Helen has 20+ years of experience in service management, including operational management of service desks and technical support teams and service level management. She holds the ITIL Expert qualification and has delivered service management training for many years. She now delivers ITIL Foundation and Intermediate training in the United Kingdom, Europe, and the United States. She has coauthored and recorded distance-learning courses covering the ITIL framework. Helen is also a certified ISO/IEC 20000 consultant.

Helen is an experienced trainer, consultant, and service delivery manager focused on providing customer satisfaction and business benefits. Many of her assignments involve an initial assessment against best practices, recommendations for improvement, and target setting. She leads programs to achieve significant improvements in customer satisfaction, quality of service, reduced costs, and better control.

Helen has presented at a number of international service management conferences, and she blogs regularly on service management topics. With Liz Gallacher, she has devised a unique approach to mentoring, providing assistance and resources to clients while encouraging them to develop the skills they need without expensive onsite consultancy.

As an experienced consultant, Helen has led a number of successful service management improvement programs, working with organizations to develop their service management strategy and being a key player in the implementation of the strategy within the organizations. She has delivered strategic improvements in customer satisfaction, service delivery, and regulatory standards.

Helen managed the support environment for a Microsoft partner and supported the launch of Windows 95, implementing an improvement initiative to achieve the required customer satisfaction targets. Throughout this period, she was also leading a team to achieve and maintain successful ISO 9001 compliance within the division. This included extensive process reengineering in the support division to ensure efficient and effective processes were implemented to support the customer satisfaction targets.

An assignment with a blue-chip telecommunications company allowed Helen to implement strategies for introducing best practices into the service delivery management team as the lead for the rollout of ITIL. This formed part of the company initiative to achieve BS15000 (a precursor to ISO 20000), in which Helen was a key player, specializing in incident and problem management.

Many of Helen's assignments have involved assessing and restructuring the support environment to provide improvements in cost efficiency and customer satisfaction. This has often required working across a broad spectrum of the business to achieve an agreed-on approach within the organization. Helen was the lead consultant in delivering the service improvement program for an outsource provider; she provided support services and networks for a large number of blue-chip and financial institutions, delivered by a service support function of more than 120 personnel. Helen achieved and maintained an improvement in service levels from 80 percent to 95 percent (target) within three months across all service areas.

Helen and Liz cowrote the successful *ITIL Foundation Study Guide* from Sybex.

Contents at a Glance

Contents

Chapter 40   Technology Considerations   905

Introduction

IT service management is an increasingly important area of study for all IT professionals. IT managers are realizing that whatever the technology in use, the requirements to manage it efficiently and effectively and to deliver services that are aligned to the business requirements have never been more important.

The internationally recognized ITIL framework is the best-known approach to IT service management. The popularity of ITIL has spread around the world, with an enthusiastic take-up in the USA, India, the Middle East, and China in particular. For most IT staff members, the certification is now regarded as an essential addition to their resumes, with many job ads specifying the foundation certification as a mandatory requirement. In this book, we take the next step, from the foundation level to the intermediate level. IT managers, and those aspiring to become IT managers, will find the examination of management-level concepts and core information of the supporting activities within each lifecycle stage invaluable. (It should be noted that the intermediate lifecycle syllabi do not include specific details about each of the supporting processes.)

The foundation certificate is a prerequisite to achieving intermediate-level ITIL certification, whether in the Lifecycle or Capability certification areas. An accredited course provided by an accredited training organization is also mandatory; this may be a classroom course or an accredited e-learning course. This book is intended to supplement such a course, not replace it. As experienced classroom tutors and authors of several e-learning courses, we support this mandatory requirement. However, we believe that a real need exists for material beyond what these courses provide. Those who do attend classes often comment that there is too much material to cover in the time allowed. The syllabus guidance specifies that students should complete 21 hours of reading for each examination in addition to attending an accredited course. Purchasing the official core volumes is a considerable investment that may be unaffordable for many. By providing all of the key aspects of the intermediate lifecycle syllabuses, this book is an economical alternative, and it provides more depth than slides or videos. Concepts that were confusing in the course can be studied in depth at the student's own pace. The many practice questions help reinforce understanding.

ITIL Certification Companion Study Guide: Intermediate Lifecycle Exams provides intermediate-level training for IT managers. Readers will gain a management-level overview of the ITIL service lifecycle stages and the ITIL processes, roles, and functions. They will learn how to design, develop, and implement service management. They will also gain an understanding of how the service lifecycle provides effective and efficient IT services that are aligned to and underpin business processes and the critical success factors and key performance indicators required. The book covers the full syllabus for each of the five lifecycle courses.

The book covers all five of the ITIL intermediate lifecycle syllabi. The five examinations are as follows:

Service Strategy   The design, development, and implementation of service management as a strategic asset to align with business processes

Service Design   The design and development of services and service management processes

Service Transition   Building, testing, authorizing, documenting, and implementing new and changed services into live operation

Service Operation   The day-to-day support and management of live services

Continual Service Improvement   Creating and maintaining value for customers through monitoring and improving services, processes, and technology throughout the lifecycle

Interactive Online Learning Environment and Test Bank

The interactive online learning environment and test bank that accompanies *ITIL Certification Companion Study Guide: Intermediate ITIL Service Lifecycle Exams* provides a test bank with study tools to help you prepare for the certification exam—and increase your chances of passing it the first time! The test bank includes the following:

Sample Tests   All the questions in this book are provided, including the **Assessment Test**, which you'll find at the end of this introduction, and the **Chapter Tests** that include the review questions at the end of each chapter. Use these questions to test your knowledge of the study guide material. The online test bank runs on multiple devices.

Flashcards   Questions are provided in digital flashcard format (a question followed by a single correct answer). You can use the flashcards to reinforce your learning and provide last-minute test prep before the exam.

Other Study Tools   A glossary of key terms from this book and their definitions are available as a fully searchable PDF.

 Go to http://sybextestbanks.wiley.com to register and gain access to this interactive online learning environment and test bank with study tools.

How to Contact the Authors

We are experienced trainers and consultants and use practical examples and explanations to help students grasp the material and understand the concepts being explained. We provide support to all our students and readers; emails seeking further explanation or clarification will be answered within 24 hours in most cases. You can contact us at enquiry@helix-services.com.

ITIL Lifecycle Intermediate Exam Objectives

The following tables map each of your study requirements to the chapters of this book. We organized the contents of each chapter to be read in an order that will make it easy for you to study for the exams. The syllabus for each intermediate lifecycle exam examines the corresponding lifecycle stage in terms of its principles and processes, organizational aspects, technology considerations, the approach to its implementation, and its challenges, critical success factors, and risks.

 Mock exams are not included in this book. The complex multiple-choice format of the certification exams means that exam guidance is difficult to convey in a purely written format. Students should use their classroom tutor or the "ask-the-tutor" function of their e-learning course provider to obtain guidance as to the most effective approach to these exams and to explore any difficulties they may experience in choosing the best answers.

Part 1: Service Strategy

Topic	Chapter
Introduction to the Service Strategy Lifecycle Stage	1
Service Strategy Principles	2
Service Strategy Processes: Strategy Management for IT Services, Service Portfolio Management and Financial Management for IT Services	3
Service Strategy Processes: Demand Management and Business Relationship Management	4
Governance	5
Organizing for Service Strategy	6
Technology Considerations	7
Implementing Service Strategy	8
Challenges, Critical Success Factors, and Risks	9

Part 2: Service Design

Part 3: Service Transition

Part 4: Service Operation

Part 5: Continual Service Improvement

Exam units are subject to change at any time without prior notice and at ITIL's sole discretion. Please visit ITIL's website (www.axelos.com/best-practice-solutions/itil) for the most current listing of units.

Assessment Test

1. What types of changes are NOT usually included within the scope of change management?
   A. Changes to a mainframe computer
   B. Changes to business strategy
   C. Changes to a service level agreement (SLA)
   D. The retirement of a service

2. Which of the following is NOT a purpose of service operation?
   A. To undertake testing to ensure that services are designed to meet business needs
   B. To deliver and manage IT services
   C. To manage the technology used to deliver services
   D. To monitor the performance of technology and processes

3. What does the term *IT operations control* refer to?
   A. Managing the technical and application management functions
   B. Overseeing the execution and monitoring of operational activities and events
   C. A set of tools used to monitor and display the status of the IT infrastructure and applications
   D. A service desk monitoring the status of the infrastructure when operators are not available

4. Which process is responsible for recording relationships between service components?
   A. Service level management
   B. Service portfolio management
   C. Service asset and configuration management (SACM)
   D. Incident management

5. What is the RACI model used for?
   A. Documenting the roles and responsibilities of stakeholders in a process or activity
   B. Defining requirements for a new service or process
   C. Analyzing the business impact of an incident
   D. Creating a balanced scorecard showing the overall status of service management

6. Which of the following is the BEST description of an operational level agreement (OLA)?
   A. An agreement between an IT service provider and another part of the same organization that assists in the provision of services
   B. A written agreement between the IT service provider and its customer(s) defining key targets and responsibilities of both parties

   C. An agreement between two service providers about the levels of service required by the customer

   D. An agreement between a third-party service desk and the IT customer about fix and response times

7. What is the MAIN purpose of availability management?

   A. To monitor and report availability of components

   B. To ensure that all targets in the service level agreements (SLAs) are met

   C. To guarantee availability levels for services and components

   D. To ensure that service availability meets the agreed needs of the business

8. For which of the following does service transition provide guidance?

   1. Introducing new services

   2. Decommissioning services

   3. Transfer of services between service providers

      A. 1 and 2 only

      B. 2 only

      C. All of the above

      D. 1 and 3 only

9. Which one of the following is NOT a stage of the service lifecycle?

   A. Service optimization

   B. Service transition

   C. Service design

   D. Service strategy

10. Which one of the following statements about a configuration management system (CMS) is CORRECT?

   A. The CMS should not contain corporate data about customers and users.

   B. There may be more than one CMS.

   C. There should not be more than one configuration management database (CMDB).

   D. If an organization outsources its IT services, there is still a need for a CMS.

11. What are the three subprocesses of capacity management?

   A. Business capacity management, service capacity management, and component capacity management

   B. Supplier capacity management, service capacity management, and component capacity management

   C. Supplier capacity management, service capacity management, and technology capacity management

   D. Business capacity management, technology capacity management, and component capacity management

12. Which of the following would be stored in the definitive media library (DML)?

    1. Copies of purchased software

    2. Copies of internally developed software

    3. Relevant license documentation

    4. The change schedule

        A. All of the above

        B. 1 and 2 only

        C. 3 and 4 only

        D. 1, 2, and 3 only

13. Which process is responsible for reviewing operational level agreements (OLAs) on a regular basis?

    A. Supplier management

    B. Service level management

    C. Service portfolio management

    D. Demand management

14. Which role should ensure that process documentation is current and available?

    A. The service owner

    B. The chief information officer

    C. Knowledge management

    D. The process owner

15. Which of the following does the release and deployment management process address?

    1. Defining and agreeing on release and deployment plans

    2. Ensuring that release packages can be tracked

    3. Authorizing changes to support the process

        A. 1 and 2 only

        B. All of the above

        C. 2 and 3 only

        D. 1 and 3 only

16. Which of the following are characteristics of every process?

    1. It is measurable.

    2. It delivers a specific result.

    3. It delivers its primary results to a customer or stakeholder.

        A. 1 and 3 only

        B. 1 and 2 only

        C. 2 and 3 only

        D. All of the above

17. Which of the following are key ITIL characteristics that contribute to its success?

    1. It is vendor neutral.

    2. It is nonprescriptive.

    3. It is best practice.

    4. It is a standard.

        A. 3 only

        B. 1, 2, and 3 only

        C. All of the above

        D. 2, 3, and 4 only

18. Who should be granted access to the information security policy?

    A. Senior business managers and IT staff

    B. Senior business managers, IT executives, and the information security manager

    C. All customers, users, and IT staff

    D. Information security management staff only

19. Which of the following are valid elements of a service design package (SDP)?

    1. Agreed and documented business requirements

    2. A plan for transition of the service

    3. Requirements for new or changed processes

    4. Metrics to measure the service

        A. 1 only

        B. 2 and 3 only

        C. 1, 2, and 4 only

        D. All of the above

20. Which of the following are examples of tools that might support the service transition stage of the service lifecycle?

    1. A tool to store definitive versions of software

    2. A workflow tool for managing changes

    3. An automated software distribution tool

    4. Testing and validation tools

        A. 1, 3, and 4 only

        B. 1, 2, and 3 only

        C. All of the above

        D. 2, 3, and 4 only

21. Which of the following statements about problem management is/are CORRECT?

    1. It ensures that all resolutions or workarounds that require a change to a configuration item (CI) are submitted through change management.

2. It provides management information about the cost of resolving and preventing problems.

   A. 1 only

   B. 2 only

   C. Both of the above

   D. Neither of the above

22. What is the purpose of the request fulfilment process?

   A. Dealing with service requests from users

   B. Making sure all requests within an IT organization are fulfilled

   C. Ensuring fulfilment of change requests

   D. Making sure the service level agreement (SLA) is met

23. Which statement about value creation through services is CORRECT?

   A. The customer's perception of the service is an important factor in value creation.

   B. The value of a service can only ever be measured in financial terms.

   C. Delivering service provider outcomes is important in the value of a service.

   D. Service provider preferences drive the value perception of a service.

24. Which one of the following statements about internal and external customers is most CORRECT?

   A. External customers should receive better customer service because they pay for their IT services.

   B. Internal customers should receive better customer service because they pay employee salaries.

   C. The best customer service should be given to the customer that pays the most money.

   D. Internal and external customers should receive the agreed level of customer service.

25. Which one of the following should IT services deliver to customers?

   A. Capabilities

   B. Cost

   C. Risk

   D. Value

26. Which one of the following activities is part of the service level management (SLM) process?

   A. Designing the configuration management system from a business perspective

   B. Creating technology metrics to align with customer needs

   C. Monitoring service performance against service level agreements (SLAs)

   D. Training service desk staff on how to deal with customer complaints about service

27. Which one of the following BEST summarizes the purpose of event management?

   A. Detect events, make sense of them, and determine the appropriate control action.

   B. Detect events, restore normal service as soon as possible, and minimize the adverse impact on business operations.

    C. Monitor and control the activities of technical staff.

    D. Report on the successful delivery of services by checking the uptime of infrastructure devices.

28. Which one of the following should a service catalog contain?

    A. The version information of all software

    B. The organizational structure of the company

    C. Asset information

    D. Details of all operational services

29. What does *warranty of a service* mean?

    A. The service is fit for purpose.

    B. There will be no failures in applications and infrastructure associated with the service.

    C. All service-related problems are fixed free of charge for a certain period of time.

    D. Customers are assured of certain levels of availability, capacity, continuity, and security.

30. Which is the first activity of the continual service improvement (CSI) approach?

    A. Understand the business vision and objectives.

    B. Carry out a baseline assessment to understand the current situation.

    C. Agree on priorities for improvement.

    D. Create and verify a plan.

31. Which one of the following is a benefit of using an incident model?

    A. It will make problems easier to identify and diagnose.

    B. It means known incident types never recur.

    C. It provides predefined steps for handling particular types of incidents.

    D. It ensures all incidents are easy to solve.

32. Which one of the following is the CORRECT sequence of activities for handling an incident?

    A. identification, logging, categorization, prioritization, initial diagnosis, escalation, investigation and diagnosis, resolution and recovery, closure

    B. prioritization, identification, logging, categorization, initial diagnosis, escalation, investigation and diagnosis, resolution and recovery, closure

    C. identification, logging, initial diagnosis, categorization, prioritization, escalation, resolution and recovery, investigation and diagnosis, closure

    D. identification, initial diagnosis, investigation, logging, categorization, escalation, prioritization, resolution and recovery, closure

33. Which service lifecycle stage ensures that measurement methods will provide the required metrics for new or changed services?

    A. Service design

    B. Service operation

C. Service strategy

D. Service delivery

34. Which of the following processes are concerned with managing risks to services?

   1. IT service continuity management

   2. Information security management

   3. Service catalog management

       A. All of the above

       B. 1 and 3 only

       C. 2 and 3 only

       D. 1 and 2 only

35. Which one of the following is NOT a type of metric described in continual service improvement (CSI)?

   A. Process metrics

   B. Service metrics

   C. Personnel metrics

   D. Technology metrics

36. Which statement about the relationship between the configuration management system (CMS) and the service knowledge management system (SKMS) is CORRECT?

   A. The SKMS is part of the CMS.

   B. The CMS is part of the SKMS.

   C. The CMS and SKMS are the same thing.

   D. There is no relationship between the CMS and the SKMS.

37. What is the role of the emergency change advisory board (ECAB)?

   A. To assist the change manager in ensuring that no urgent changes are made during particularly volatile business periods

   B. To assist the change manager by implementing emergency changes

   C. To assist the change manager in evaluating emergency changes and to decide whether they should be authorized

   D. To assist the change manager in speeding up the emergency change process so that no unacceptable delays occur

38. Which of the following statements about the service desk is/are CORRECT?

   1. The service desk is a function that provides a means of communication between IT and its users for all operational issues.

   2. The service desk should be the owner of the problem management process.

       A. 2 only

       B. 1 only

C. Both of the above

D. Neither of the above

39. Which one of the following is the CORRECT list of the four *P*s of service design?

    A. Planning, products, position, processes

    B. Planning, perspective, position, people

    C. Perspective, partners, problems, people

    D. People, partners, products, processes

40. Which one of the following represents the BEST course of action to take when a problem workaround is found?

    A. The problem record is closed.

    B. The problem record remains open and details of the workaround are documented within it.

    C. The problem record remains open, and details of the workaround are documented on all related incident records.

    D. The problem record is closed, and details of the workaround are documented in a request for change (RFC).

Answers to Assessment Test

1. **B.** A change request is a formal communication seeking an alteration to one or more configuration items (CIs). Services, SLAs, and computers are examples of CIs. A business strategy is not normally a CI and would be out of scope for change management.

2. **A.** Each option describes a purpose of service operation except for Option A. Undertaking testing to ensure that services are designed to meet business needs is part of service transition.

3. **B.** IT operations control oversees the execution and monitoring of the operational activities and events in the IT infrastructure.

4. **C.** Part of SACM's purpose is to maintain accurate information about assets, including the relationship between assets.

5. **A.** RACI (which stands for responsible, accountable, consulted, informed) is a responsibility model used by ITIL to help define roles and responsibilities.

6. **A.** Option A describes an OLA. Option B is the definition of an SLA, Option C doesn't correspond to an ITIL definition, and Option D describes a contract that involves a third party.

7. **D.** Option A is a supporting element of availability management, not a main purpose. Option B relates to service level management. Availability management does not offer guarantees as identified in Option C. Option D is the main purpose of availability management described in the *ITIL Service Design* core volume: "to ensure that the level of availability delivered in all IT services meets the agreed availability needs of the business."

8. **C.** All three are in scope for service transition because all three involve major change.

9. **A.** Service optimization is not a stage of the service lifecycle.

10. **D.** A CMS can contain corporate data about users and customers such as location or department. There may be more than one CMDB, but they will be part of a single CMS. Option D is correct because a CMS still helps to control and report on the infrastructure when IT services are outsourced.

11. **A.** Business, service, and component capacity management are the three subprocesses of capicity management.

12. **D.** The DML contains master copies of all controlled software in an organization along with license documents or information. The change schedule would not be included.

13. **B.** Service level management is responsible for negotiating and agreeing on OLAs.

14. **D.** A process owner should ensure that process documentation is current and available.

15. **A.** Defining and agreeing on release and deployment plans and ensuring that release packages can be tracked are included in release and deployment objectives. Authorizing changes to support the process is addressed by change management.

16. D. Measurability, delivery of specific results, and delivery of results to a customer or stakeholder are all characteristics of a process.

17. B. Statement 4 is incorrect; ITIL guidance does not constitute a standard, which is prescriptive and subject to audits to check adherence. ISO/IEC 20000 is an example of a standard. ITIL is vendor neutral, nonprescriptive, and provides a best-practice framework.

18. C. In most cases, the policies should be widely available to all customers and users and referenced in service level agreements (SLAs), operational level agreements (OLAs), and underpinning contracts (UCs).

19. D. All of the elements identified are included in the service design package passed to service transition.

20. C. A tool to store definitive versions of software would be used to support a DML. A workflow tool for managing changes helps change management. An automated software distribution tool is a release and deployment tool. Along with testing and validation tools, they all support service transition.

21. C. They are both valid activities for problem management.

22. A. Request fulfilment is the process responsible for dealing with service requests from users. "All requests" (Option B) is too wide a scope for the process. Change management looks after change requests (Option C). Service level management is responsible for making sure the SLA is met (Option D).

23. A. Option A is correct; customer perception is a vital element in defining how much a customer values a service. Option B is incorrect because although the value of a service can be measured in financial terms, other factors are also relevant. Option C is incorrect because delivering on customer outcomes (instead of service provider outcomes) is vital. Option D is incorrect because customer preferences drive value perception.

24. D. Option D is the correct response. Both internal and external customers should be provided with the agreed level of service and with the same level of customer service.

25. D. A service is a means of delivering value to customers. IT needs capabilities to deliver services. Cost and risk are what IT helps to manage.

26. C. Option C is correct; monitoring service performance against SLAs is a vital part of the service level management process. Designing the CMS is a service asset and configuration management activity (Option A). Technology metrics are likely to be created within capacity management or other design processes (Option B). Training the service desk is a service desk role (Option D).

27. A. The purpose of event management is to detect events, make sense of them, and determine the appropriate control action. Option B includes some incident management responsibilities. Option C describes a technical management task. Option D is likely to be shared between availability management and service level management.

28. D. The service catalog should contain details of all operational services.

29. D. Option A is part of the definition of utility. Option B is unrealistic. Option C could be feasible as a warranty statement from another industry but is not the definition of warranty according to ITIL. Option D is a good summary of warranty as defined by ITIL.

30. A. The improvement approach begins with embracing the vision by understanding the high-level business objectives.

31. C. Incident models are designed to provide reusable steps that can be used to restore service after known incident types.

32. A. The correct order is given in the diagram in the incident management process.

33. A. Measurements and metrics should be included in the design for a new or changed service.

34. D. IT service continuity management carries out risk assessment as part of defining the requirements and strategy. Information security also needs to analyze security risks before taking action to mitigate them. Service catalog management does not carry out these assessments.

35. C. Personnel metrics are not one of the three types of metrics described in CSI.

36. B. A is the wrong way round. C is incorrect as the SKMS contains more information than the CMS. D is incorrect as the CMS is part of the SKMS.

37. C. The emergency change advisory board (ECAB) provides assistance in the authorization of emergency changes.

38. B. The service desk should be the single point of contact for IT users on a day-by-day basis. The service desk manager may also be the incident management process owner but would not normally be the owner of problem management.

39. D. People, processes, products (services, technology and tools) and partners (suppliers, manufacturers and vendors).

40. B. A is incorrect; the problem record must remain open as it hasn't yet been resolved. B is correct to document the workaround on the problem record, not on each incident record (C), nor on an RFC (D).

ITIL® Intermediate
Certification Companion
Study Guide

Service Strategy

PART

I

Chapter

1

Introduction to the Service Strategy Lifecycle Stage

THE FOLLOWING ITIL INTERMEDIATE EXAM OBJECTIVES ARE DISCUSSED IN THIS CHAPTER:

✓ The main purpose of service strategy

✓ The objectives of service strategy

✓ The scope of service strategy

✓ Service strategy's value to the business

✓ The context of service strategy and the service lifecycle

This chapter covers the purpose, objectives, and scope of this lifecycle stage and the value it provides to the business. We also examine the context of service strategy within the service lifecycle.

The Main Purpose of Service Strategy

Service strategy is the first stage of the service lifecycle, and in Figure 1.1, it is shown as being at the core.

FIGURE 1.1   The service lifecycle

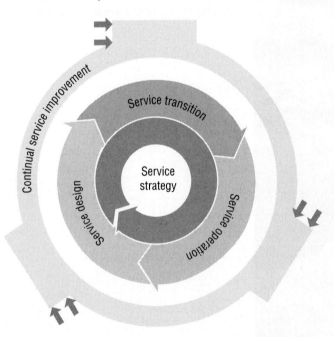

This is because if the wrong strategy is adopted, everything that follows from that strategy will also be wrong. However well realized a product, for example, it will not sell successfully if it is not the product customers want. One such example is the development of mini-disk players; these were meant to replace portable CD players and worked exactly as designed. However, the rise in popularity of MP3 players such as iPods meant that no one wanted to have to use disks, no matter how small, so the product was a failure.

The primary purpose of the service strategy stage of the service lifecycle is to set and manage the correct overall strategy for IT service management. The IT strategy must be based on an understanding of the organization's overall business strategy. For the business strategy to be successful, IT needs to provide the correct IT services to meet the current and future needs of the business. The successful management of IT services is thus important to the success of the organization.

The purpose of the service strategy stage of the service lifecycle, therefore, is to define the perspective, position, plans, and patterns that a service provider needs to be able to execute to meet an organization's business outcomes. We will look at these in detail in the next chapter, but first we will quickly discuss what these terms mean.

The Four *P*s of Service Strategy

The four *P*s are the four forms of strategy that should be present whenever a strategy is defined:

- The first is *perspective*. By this we mean the vision and direction of the organization. Without knowing what it is, we cannot help achieve the vision.

- The next is *position*. This describes how the service provider intends to compete against other service providers in the market.

- The third aspect is *plans*. The service provider must plan how to move from its current situation to its desired situation.

- The final aspect is *patterns*. Patterns describe the ongoing, repeatable actions that a service provider will have to perform in order to continue to meet its strategic objectives.

It is important to understand why we need the four *P*s—it is to enable the service provider to provide the services required to enable the organization to achieve its business outcomes. This means that the focus is on what the organization is trying to achieve and how the IT service provider helps the organization to do so. This is important because IT departments often ignore the business objectives and do not consider the business benefits when choosing a particular technology.

The Objectives of Service Strategy

Let's now consider the objectives of service strategy. The first objective is to provide an understanding of what strategy is. The dictionary definition of *strategy* is "a carefully devised plan of action to achieve a goal, or the art of developing or carrying out such a plan."

So a strategy does not just happen; you need to consider what is required and your options for providing it. It is focused on an understood defined goal, and every aspect of your strategy should be able to be linked to the achievement of the goal.

The second objective is to provide a clear identification of the definition of services and the customers who use them. You need to identify the services you provide. IT staff are inclined to think in terms of technology or systems rather than services. Remember ITIL's definition of a service; it is "a means of delivering *value* to customers by facilitating outcomes customers want to achieve without the ownership of specific costs and risks." Every service provided is there to help the customer achieve their business outcomes. As such, you need to know who your customers are and what it is that they are trying to achieve. You can then base your service provider strategy on that.

Another objective of service strategy is to provide the ability to define how value is created and delivered. This means understanding what we can provide and how this will help the customers achieve their goals. As a service provider, you must be able to spot opportunities where you can provide the services the customer needs and be able to respond quickly to them.

A service provider's strategy must include the development of a clear service provision model, which spells out how services will be delivered and funded and to whom they will be delivered and for what purpose. Service providers must understand what is required from them as an organization if they are to deliver the strategy successfully.

The final objective of service strategy includes the development of a plan that first shows how the service provider's resources and capabilities can be used to deliver the required service effectively and efficiently and that additionally specifies the processes that define the strategy of the organization. The processes would include deciding which services will achieve the strategy, what level of investment will be required and at what levels of demand, and the means to ensure that a working relationship exists between the customer and service provider.

The processes that deliver each of these objectives are as follows:

- The strategy of the organization is defined through the strategy management for IT services process.

- The services that will be used to achieve the strategy are defined using service portfolio management.

- What level of investment will be required is calculated using financial management for IT services.

- Demand management decides how to manage the demand for services.

- Business relationship management ensures a good working relationship between customer and service provider, at the strategic level.

The Scope of Service Strategy

Next we'll cover the scope of service strategy. All service providers need to develop their service strategy, whether they are internal providers offering IT services to other business units within the same organization or external providers offering IT services to other organizations as a profitable business.

Two aspects of strategy are covered in the guidance contained within the *ITIL Service Strategy* publication:

- Defining a strategy whereby a service provider will deliver services to meet a customer's business outcomes
- Defining a strategy for how to manage those services.

The Value Service Strategy Delivers to the Business

By following the best-practice guidelines outlined in the ITIL framework and developing a coherent service strategy, a service provider will ensure that the business benefits in a number of important ways:

- The service provider will be able to link its activities to the achievement of outcomes that are critical to customers. This ensures that the customer appreciates the value of the provider's contribution rather than seeing it as overhead expense. The service provider will develop a clear understanding of what types and levels of service are required to make its customers successful. This then helps the provider to organize itself in the best way to deliver and support those services. Over time, the strategy will deliver a consistent, repeatable approach to defining how value will be built and delivered through the provision of appropriate services.
- The service provider will be aware of changes in the business environment and will therefore be able to adapt quickly to meet the new challenge.
- The provider will be able to develop a range of services that help the business achieve a return on its investment in services.
- The relationship between the service provider and customer will ensure open and honest communication between them, enabling a joint understanding of what is to be delivered and how.
- Through understanding the business requirements, the service provider can ensure that it is structured in the most helpful and efficient way to ensure the delivery of those requirements.

We have covered the purpose and objectives of service strategy and its value to the business. In the remaining sections of this chapter, we will look at the context of service strategy in relation to the other lifecycle stages of service design, service transition, service operation, and continual service improvement.

The Context of Service Strategy within the Service Lifecycle

Service strategy needs to be considered within the context of the whole service lifecycle. Each area of the lifecycle addresses a particular set of challenges that need to be addressed for successful service management, and each stage has an impact on all of the others. Let's look again at the service lifecycle diagram, shown earlier in Figure 1.1.

Service Strategy

Service strategy, the subject of this section, is at the core of the service lifecycle. It is the role of service strategy to understand the organizational objectives and customer needs. People, processes, and products should support the strategy. ITIL service strategy asks *why* something is to be done before thinking of *how*. It helps service providers to set objectives; set expectations of performance serving customers and markets; and identify, select, and prioritize opportunities. Service strategy ensures that providers understand and can handle the costs and risks associated with their service portfolios.

The following is the complete list of service strategy processes:

- Strategy management for IT services
- Service portfolio management
- Financial management for IT services
- Demand management
- Business relationship management

We'll cover each of these later in the book.

Service Design

For services to provide true value to the business, they must be designed with the business objectives in mind. Service design turns strategic ideas into deliverables. The design must always consider the strategy to ensure that services are designed with the business objectives in mind. Design considers the whole IT organization and how it will deliver and support the services, turning the service strategy into a plan for delivering the business objectives. Remember, design includes changes to existing services.

Service design provides guidance for the design and development of both services and the service management practices that will be required. It covers new services and the changes that will be required to existing services over their lifetime to ensure that they adapt to fit changing business requirements, including the retirement of services.

Service design includes ensuring that the service is designed to deliver the continuity and service levels required and that the requirements of any standards or regulations are also considered at the design stage.

This is the complete list of service design processes:

- Design coordination
- Service catalog management
- Service level management
- Availability management
- Capacity management

- IT service continuity management
- Information security management
- Supplier management

Through these processes, service design ensures that both the utility and the warranty of the new or changed service is considered in design, covering the continuity of the service, its achievement of service levels, and conformance to security standards and regulations.

Service Transition

Service transition provides guidance for developing and improving capabilities for introducing new and changed services into supported environments and retiring those services no longer needed. The value of a service is identified in strategy, and the service is designed to deliver that value. Service transition ensures that the value is realized by enabling the necessary changes to take place without unacceptable risks to existing services. Service transition enables the implementation of new services and the modification of existing services along with the retirement of obsolete services to ensure that the services provided deliver the service strategy of achieving the business objectives and that the benefits of the service design are fully realized.

Service transition also introduces the service knowledge management system, which ensures that knowledge is stored and made available to all stages of the service lifecycle, making sure lessons are learned and decisions are backed with factual data, leading to improved efficiency and effectiveness over time.

This is the complete list of service transition processes:

- Transition planning and support
- Change management
- Service asset and configuration management
- Release and deployment management
- Service validation and testing
- Change evaluation
- Knowledge management

Each process has a role to play to ensure that beneficial changes can take place and, as a consequence, the service can be introduced and will work as transitioned.

Service Operation

Service operation describes best practices for managing services in supported environments. It includes guidance on achieving effectiveness, efficiency, stability, and security in the delivery and support of services to ensure value for the customer, the users, and the service provider. Without this, the services would not deliver the value required, and the achievement of business objectives would become difficult or impossible.

The service operation stage is critical to delivering the design and, in doing so, achieving the service strategy. Service operation provides detailed guidance for delivering the service within the agreed service levels by tackling issues both proactively through problem management and reactively through incident management. It provides those delivering the service with guidance for managing the availability of services, controlling demand, optimizing capacity utilization, scheduling operations, and avoiding or resolving service incidents and managing problems. It includes advice on shared services, utility computing, web services, and mobile commerce. By delivering the services to the agreed levels, service operation enables the business to use the services to achieve its business objectives.

This is the complete list of service operation processes:

- Event management
- Incident management
- Request fulfilment
- Problem management
- Access management

Each process has a role to play to ensure the delivery of services within the agreed service levels. The service operation core volume also describes the four service management functions:

- The service desk
- Technical management
- IT operations management
- Application management

Each function is responsible for managing its own area of delivery. Technical and application management will be involved across the lifecycle. Operations management and the service desk are more rooted in service operations but will liaise with service transition, have input into continual service improvement, and carry out tasks for processes from other lifecycle stages, such as updating the configuration management system, producing service reports for service level management, and testing service continuity plans.

Continual Service Improvement

Continual service improvement (CSI) ensures that the service provider continues to provide value to customers by ensuring that the strategy, design, transition, and operation of the services is under constant review. Feedback from any stage of the service lifecycle can be used to identify improvement opportunities for any other stage of the lifecycle. It ensures that opportunities for improvement are recognized, evaluated, and implemented when justified. These may include improvements in the quality of the service or the capabilities of the service provider. It may be developing ways of doing things better or doing them to the same level but more efficiently. Improvements may be major or small and incremental.

CSI enables every new operation to incorporate lessons from previous operations. Deciding which improvements should be undertaken, especially if funding is required, will involve input from service strategy.

CSI ensures that feedback from every lifecycle stage is captured, analyzed, and acted upon. The CSI approach to improvement is based on establishing a baseline, and checking to see whether the improvement actions have been effective. It uses the Plan-Do-Check-Act (PDCA) cycle together with service measurement, demonstrating value with metrics, and conducting maturity assessments. The seven-step improvement process provides a framework for these approaches.

Summary

This chapter covered module 1 of the syllabus, the introduction to service strategy. The chapter covered the purpose, objectives, and scope of service strategy and how this lifecycle stage delivers value to the organization. We looked at service strategy within the context of the service lifecycle, its relationship to the other lifecycle stages of service design, service transition, service operation, and continual service improvement.

In the next chapter, we will cover service strategy principles.

Exam Essentials

Understand the purpose of service strategy: to set and manage the correct overall strategy for IT and IT service management. The IT and IT service management strategy must be based on an understanding of the organization's overall business strategy. For the business strategy to be successful, IT needs to provide the correct IT services to meet the current and future needs of the business.

Understand the meaning of the four *P*s defined by service strategy. The purpose of the service strategy stage of the service lifecycle is to define the perspective, position, plans, and patterns that a service provider needs to be able to execute to meet an organization's business outcomes.

Be able to list the service strategy processes. Know the names of each of the service strategy processes.

- Strategy management for IT services
- Service portfolio management
- Financial management for IT services
- Demand management
- Business relationship management

Understand the value that service strategy delivers to the business.   Be able to explain how service strategy ensures that the service provider is able to link its activities to the achievement of outcomes that are critical to customers and how it develops a clear understanding of what types and levels of service are required to make its customers successful.

Review Questions

You can find the answers to the review questions in the appendix.

1. ITIL guidance describes the purpose of one of the lifecycle stages as to ensure that "any modifications or transitions to the live operational environment meet the agreed expectations of the business, customers, and users." Which stage is being referred to?

    A. Service strategy

    B. Service design

    C. Service transition

    D. Service operation

2. Service strategy talks about *perspective*. What does *perspective* mean?

    A. How the service provider will transition from their current situation to their desired situation

    B. Ongoing, repeatable actions that a service provider will have to perform in order to continue to meet its strategic objectives

    C. How the service provider intends to compete against other service providers in the market

    D. The vision and direction of the organization

3. Which of the items in the following list are included in the four *P*s of service strategy? (Choose all that apply.)

    A. Perspective

    B. Processes

    C. Plans

    D. Position

    E. People

    F. Patterns

4. Which stage of the lifecycle "considers the whole IT organization and how it will deliver and support the services"?

    A. Service strategy

    B. Service design

    C. Service transition

    D. Service operation

5. Which of the following processes is part of service strategy for IT services?

    A. Availability management

    B. Knowledge management

    C. Financial management

    D. The seven-step process

6. Which stage of the lifecycle "includes advice on shared services, utility computing, web services, and mobile commerce"?

   A. Service strategy

   B. Service design

   C. Service transition

   D. Service operation

7. Which of the following processes is part of the service design lifecycle stage?

   A. Problem management

   B. Service asset and configuration management

   C. Service catalog management

   D. Service portfolio management

8. Which stage of the lifecycle ensures that the value is realized by enabling the necessary changes to take place without unacceptable risks to existing services?

   A. Service strategy

   B. Service design

   C. Service transition

   D. Service operation

9. Which concept is primarily discussed in the ITIL core guidance for the service operation lifecycle stage?

   A. SKMS

   B. PDCA

   C. ROI

   D. SLA

   E. Function

10. True or False? Improvements implemented as a result of CSI should always result in financial cost savings.

   A. True

   B. False

Chapter

2

Service Strategy Principles

THE FOLLOWING ITIL INTERMEDIATE EXAM OBJECTIVES ARE DISCUSSED IN THIS CHAPTER:

✓ **Service strategy basics**

    ▪ Basic approach to deciding a strategy

    ▪ Strategy and opposing dynamics

    ▪ Outperforming competitors

    ▪ The four Ps of service strategy

✓ **Services and value**

    ▪ Services

    ▪ Value

    ▪ Utility and warranty

✓ **Assets and service providers**

✓ **Defining services**

    ▪ Eight steps to define services

✓ **Strategies for customer satisfaction**

    ▪ Kano model

✓ **Service economics**

    ▪ Return on investment

    ▪ Business impact analysis

✓ **Sourcing strategy**

✓ **Strategy inputs and outputs within the service lifecycle**

To do well on the exam, you must ensure that you understand the basic principles of service strategy. These principles include the concepts of utility and warranty, service value and service economics. You will need to demonstrate that you can apply these concepts to the scenarios by analyzing the information provided in the exam questions.

Service Strategy Basics

This chapter covers the elements of service strategy that are necessary to understand, use, and apply the processes within service strategy to create business value. These concepts apply across the service lifecycle, but in this chapter we consider their relevance in service strategy. It will enable the use of the knowledge, interpretation, and analysis of service strategy principles, techniques, and relationships and the application for creation of effective service strategies.

Deciding on a Strategy

A strategy is a plan that enables an organization to meet a set of agreed objectives. It is important to establish the IT service management strategy for an organization so that the IT department is focused on meeting the needs and objectives of the organization as a whole and is not working in isolation.

To derive a successful IT service management strategy for the IT department, it is important to consider some key factors.

There are many sources for organizations to obtain their IT needs, and any strategic approach needs to recognize the potential competition. It should ensure that the IT department is in a position to exceed the performance of any outsourced suppliers or to be seen as delivering better value.

Objective Approach

Deriving a successful IT service management strategy will require an objective approach that differentiates the department from other providers. It may be described financially, or by social factors, such as reputation.

Some fundamental aspects that will be important to the organization as a whole should be considered.

What are the barriers to entry into the organizational marketplace? Are there specific regulatory requirements? Perhaps the barriers and the requirements are associated with the industry sector.

How broad is the scope for the service offerings? Can the internal service provider deliver according to the requirements? How much interaction will be required with suppliers, and does the internal provider have the controls to manage the delivery of service effectively?

Will the strategy be to transfer costs within the organization, such as lowering cost structures through specialization or service sourcing?

Whichever approach is adopted, it is all about being better by being different. This is expressed by vision and the mission for the department.

Whatever the desired objectives of the organization, the service provider should develop a strategy that recognizes the constraints under which it must operate.

This will enable the provider to establish the services that are required and the areas of the organization where they will be most effective. This can be expressed as the services offered and the markets served.

Strategy and Opposing Dynamics

It is necessary to understand the limitations of any strategic plan. These are often referred to as the opposing dynamics. In Figure 2.1, you can see a depiction of opposing dynamics.

FIGURE 2.1   Achieving a balance between opposing strategic dynamics

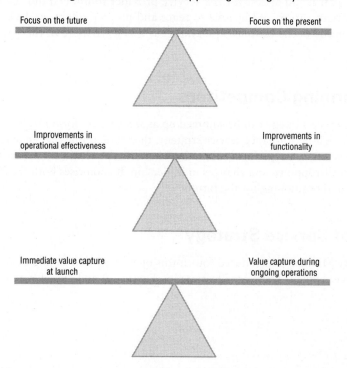

Future vs. Present

This requires that we accommodate the pace of business change as business opportunities arise and disappear. The strategy has to be more than a plan and be able to adapt to the unforeseen.

Operational Effectiveness vs. Improvements in Functionality

Operational effectiveness should not be delivered at the expense of distinctiveness or the service provider may lose its customer base. There is a balance to be achieved here because although improvements increase competitive advantage, it is still important to deliver and provide the required functionality.

Value Capture

In the third dynamic, we are considering value capture. This refers to the value gained when innovations are launched versus the value captured during ongoing operations. Value capture is the portion of value creation a provider is able to keep. There is a very small window between the time an innovative feature is launched and the time the next competitor has the same capability. The service provider needs to be able to achieve a balance between introducing new functionality and maintaining normal practice.

Managing the balance between these opposing dynamics is critical for a successful service strategy. It is important for the service provider to understand the requirements of the organization and be able to react and predict, adapt, and plan to meet the changing needs of the business. Flexibility is a key attribute of the strategic approach.

Outperforming Competitors

The goal of a service strategy can be summed up as *superior performance versus competing alternatives*. A high-performance service strategy, therefore, is one that enables a service provider to consistently outperform competing alternatives over time and across business cycles, industry disruptions, and changes in leadership. It comprises both the ability to succeed today and positioning for the future.

Four *P*s of Service Strategy

In 1994, Henry Mintzberg introduced four forms of strategy that should be present whenever a strategy is defined. These are illustrated in Figure 2.2 and are referred to as the four *P*s of strategy.

FIGURE 2.2   Perspective, positions, plans, and patterns

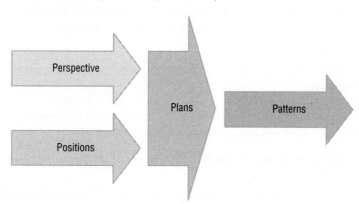

We will consider each of these in turn.

Perspective

Perspective is the vision and direction of the organization. A strategic perspective articulates what the business of the organization is, how it interacts with the customer, and how its services or products will be provided. A perspective cements a service provider's distinctiveness in the minds of the employees and customers.

Perspective Statements

Here are some examples of strategic perspective statements, which you may recognize as directives in your own or other organizations:

"Focus on the user and all else will follow."

"It's all about growth, innovation, and the deployment of technology, led by the greatest people anywhere."

"Consumer connectivity first—anytime, anywhere."

"[Our] purpose is to improve the quality of life of the communities we serve."

Positions

When we consider the position of a strategy, it should describe how the service provider intends to compete against other service providers in the market. The position refers to the attributes and capabilities that set the service provider apart from its competitors. Positions could be based on value or low cost, specialized services or providing an inclusive range of services, knowledge of a customer environment, or industry variables.

Position Statements

Here are some examples of position statements that differentiate the provider from competitors by emphasizing the value created to the customer:

> "We differentiate ourselves through our attorney-centric service offerings and legal industry know-how."

> "We provide high-speed high-quality Internet services to rural locations in the UK."

The framework considers a number of different types of positioning.

First, we look at *variety-based positioning*. This is where the service provider differentiates itself by offering a narrow range of services to a variety of customers with varied needs. For example, a cell phone company offers a range of predefined packages based on time and type of usage. Customers choose the package that suits them, even though they and other customers may use the same package differently.

Another option is that of *needs-based positioning*. The service provider differentiates itself by offering a wide range of services to a small number of customers. This type of positioning may also be called "customer intimacy." The service provider identifies opportunities in a customer, develops services for them, and then continues to develop services for new opportunities or simply continues to provide valuable services that keep other competitors out. The relationship between the service provider and the customer is key in needs-based positioning. Examples here might be specialist service providers of medical systems in the pharmaceutical industry.

When a service provider targets a particular market and offers tailored services commonly based on a special interest or location, this is known as *access-based positioning*. Typically, only people in that group will have access to the service. For example, a service provider might offer branded items that can be bought in only a specific store or through a particular outlet, such as Harrods (London).

Last we consider *demand-based positioning*. As the name suggests, this is a type of positioning in which the service provider meets the demands of a customer by using a variety-based approach to appeal to a broad range of customers. The difference from variety-based positioning is that they allow each customer to customize exactly which components of the service they will use and how much of it they will use. This is an approach that is being explored by online service providers like Dropbox, which allows its customers to choose from different packages.

Plans

A strategy should be documented so that it is formally communicated throughout the organization. This is often the most tangible form of a strategy, a set of documents referred to as the strategic plan, and in many organizations this may be referred to as "the strategy." The plan contains details about how the organization will achieve its strategic objectives and how much it is prepared to invest in order to do so.

To provide for an uncertain future, plans usually contain several scenarios, each one covering a strategic response and level of investment. Throughout the year, the plans are compared with actual events. This allows for adjustments to be made to adapt to any changes in the organizational requirements.

Some plans are high-level plans, such as the overall strategy, while others are more detailed, such as the execution plans for a particular new service or process. All plans should be coordinated and follow the same strategic framework.

Patterns

When we talk about patterns in service strategy, we are describing the ways in which an organization organizes itself to meet its objectives. The patterns could be organizational hierarchies, processes, interdepartmental collaboration, or services. Some patterns involve the way the organization works internally, whereas others involve the way in which the organization interacts with its customers and suppliers.

Recognizing patterns is important because they ensure that the service provider does not continuously react to demand in a new way every time. A pattern will enable the service provider to predict how a strategy will be met and forecast the investment that will be required.

There are two ways in which patterns can be formed. In some cases the organization will define the patterns it needs in its strategy. It will then define the way in which everyone complies with the patterns. In other cases, patterns that have been successful in the past will be formalized into the strategy of the organization. These are often referred to as emergent strategies.

Relationship between the Four *P*s

We have already explored the way in which a service provider's perspective and position will allow it to develop plans that, if executed, will ensure that the service provider achieves its strategic objectives.

However, planning involves the future, and even with the best intent, no plan can be fully reliable. Changes to the organization, its customers, and their respective environments can impact the successful execution of a plan. It is important that the service provider be flexible and not stick rigidly to a plan that is no longer valid. It may be necessary to alter the plan, defer it, or abandon it. In some cases, a service provider may have to merge plans or even create new ones. This is shown in Figure 2.3.

FIGURE 2.3   Strategic plans result in patterns.

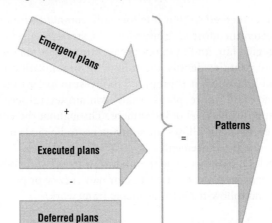

It is necessary to ensure that a strategy is not a rigid application of plans in a changing environment but is instead a continually adapting process, ensuring that the business and service provider stay relevant to a changing environment.

Services and Value

We are going to explore how the strategy for delivery of services is managed and what service management means for an organization.

Service

To refresh your memory, consider the definition of a service, as described in the framework.

A *service* is a means of delivering value to customers. Remember, customers are the people in an organization who pay for, or have financial authority over, what is delivered. The value is expressed in business terms, and it is the service provider's responsibility to ensure that it enables the value to be realized. This is the facilitation of the outcomes while managing the costs and risks on the customers' behalf.

When working on strategy, it is important to remember this definition because it should guide the thinking and decisions made by the service provider. Let's continue to examine this definition.

It is important to remember that what we deliver in IT is not the same as something manufactured, like a physical product. There is a big difference between a service and a product.

Products are delivered as a fixed output, by a repeatable route. Consider the production environment of a factory. The output is produced by the application of a repeatable set of actions, taking raw materials and converting them to a physical end state. Value is created and realized through the exchange of the product between different parties—in other words, when the item is bought and sold.

A production environment also allows for stockpiling of products, which can be used at a later date. The value is maintained in the product itself, not its manufacture.

In contrast to products, services are dynamic interactions between customers and service providers reacting and responding to a real-time demand for a service. The output generated by a service is often variable, dependent on the scale and importance of the input. Think of the different transactions that can be generated by a single user, anything from a minor service request for a replacement of simple technology to the request for a complete new service.

This diversity of output means that we have to accommodate many different ways of delivering service. Consider the difference between a virtual transaction through a self-service portal and the human intervention still required for the physical repair of equipment.

The success of a service is based on the achievement of the customer's desired outcome, not on whether or not the output of the service has been delivered. The value of a service is established only by its use to a customer. It is not the output of a service that is considered valuable but the customer's ability to use its output to achieve their ends.

The result of this is that value can only be present in the relationship between customer and service provider. If there is no relationship, there is nothing to deliver, and there will therefore be no value.

This is often measured in terms of customer satisfaction, showing the importance of the relationship rather than a tangible product.

It is important to understand what we mean by an outcome—the ITIL guidance defines an outcome as "the result of carrying out an activity, following a process, or delivering an IT service."

Outcomes are often described as either business outcomes or customer outcomes. Business and customer outcomes are differentiated by their context. Business outcomes represent the business objectives of both the business unit and the service provider and involve internal customers.

Customer outcomes are usually based on external service providers. For example, the external service provider may be focused on the outcome of delivering a profit, while the customer's business outcomes will make use of the service to deliver their own requirements. Each will be able to fulfil their desired outcomes, but they do not have the same overall goal.

When we consider the difference between an outcome and an output, it's important to remember that the definition of a service refers to an outcome, not an output. An output can be achieved, such as meeting service levels, but it may still result in customer dissatisfaction if the customer's outcome is not met. Delivering a service requires the service provider to focus on the outcome desired by the customer and to track changes and adjust service accordingly.

Business outcomes are achieved when the business is able to perform activities that meet business objectives. They are defined in practical, measurable terms, as in the following examples:

- A product or service is delivered to a customer.
- An employee's salary is paid.
- A financial report is submitted to a regulatory body.
- Taxes are collected.
- Cargo is shipped on a ship or airplane.

When we consider the responsibilities for specific costs and risks, it is important to remember that the focus for the customer is on outcomes and how the service will meet the needs. Customers are concerned about what a service will cost and how reliable it will be. The relationship between the service provider and the customer does not depend on knowing every expenditure item and risk mitigation measure that the service provider employs to deliver the service. The customer will assess value by comparing price and reliability with the desired outcome.

The service triangle (which associates the concepts of utility, warranty, and price to demonstrate value) shows the criteria that the customer will use to judge value and the service provider will use to deliver service. It is important that the service provider and the customer understand that the increase or decrease of any of these criteria will have an impact on the others. Delivering a lower-cost service will mean there is less capability for functionality and performance. The balance has to be achieved between the customer requirements and price, functionality, and performance. It is the responsibility of the service provider to capture the customer requirements while it determines the optimal approach for delivery. This includes the approach to risk and risk mitigation and the technology adopted to deliver the service.

In this way, the customer receives value, without the ownership of specific costs and risks.

Internal and External Customers

Services are delivered to both internal and external customers.

Internal vs. External Customers

Internal customers are those within the same organization as the service provider, and an external customer is one that is outside of the organization.

Internal services are delivered between departments or business units within the same organization, whereas external services are delivered to external customers.

To deliver value, the service provider must be able to differentiate between services that support an internal activity and those that achieve business outcomes, and understand the prioritization of each from the customer's perspective. The activity to deliver the services may be similar, but internal services must be linked to external services before their contribution to business outcomes can be understood, measured, and prioritized. For example, email is important to an organization even though the organization manufactures cars as its main business. How well would the organization be able to function without this element of the desktop service? It may be the most important communication device for the entire organization and therefore should be prioritized accordingly.

Service Categorization

Services can be categorized according to how they are used in the organization.

A supporting service (sometimes known as an infrastructure service) is a service that is not directly used by the business but required by the IT service provider to provide other IT services (e.g., directory services, network). It Identifies interdependencies between components and enables a customer-facing service but is not directly visible to the customer. It may be combined with other components to produce customer-facing services or have no value when viewed alone. These types of services may be sourced from outside the organization.

Internal customer-facing services are IT services that directly support a business process managed by another business unit (e.g., sales reporting service). Identified and defined by the business, they are managed according to SLAs.

An external customer-facing service is an IT service that is directly provided by IT to an external customer (e.g., airport Internet access). It is a business service in its own right.

The service provider can differentiate the types of service it delivers as described in the following sections.

Core Service

A core service is one that is fundamental to the delivery of a basic outcome required by a customer. It will deliver the value that the customer needs and is prepared to pay for. An example of this is the delivery of Internet banking functionality.

Enabling Service

An enabling service is a service that is needed in order for a core service to be delivered. Using the Internet banking example, an enabling service would be the network or the ISP provision. It is not normally something that an Internet banking user would consider or be aware of, but without it, the service could not be delivered.

Enhancing Service

An enhancing service is a service that is added to a core service to make it more exciting or enticing to the customer. Using the Internet banking example, this would be the provision of an additional feature such as the inclusion of a savings management program or the purchase of a financial savings package. It is not vital to the delivery of the core service, but it may make the service more attractive.

Value

Value can be expressed as the level to which a service will meet the customer's expectations and is measured by how much the customer is willing to pay rather than the specific cost of the service.

The characteristics of value are that it is defined by the customer and delivers an affordable mix of features to meet the business requirements. It should enable the customer to meet its objectives and should be flexible to the changes that may take place within an organization over time. No organization will remain static in its requirements and objectives, and an IT service will cease to be perceived as valuable unless it can adapt to changing requirements.

In order to attribute value, the service provider needs to understand three specific inputs:

- What services were provided?

- What did the services achieve?

- What was their cost, or the price that was paid?

The answer to these questions will enable the service provider to demonstrate value to the customer. But the service provider will always be subject to the customer's perception of value.

If we consider value from the perspective of the customer, then there are a number of factors that contribute to the understanding of value. This is shown in Figure 2.4.

FIGURE 2.4   How customers perceive value

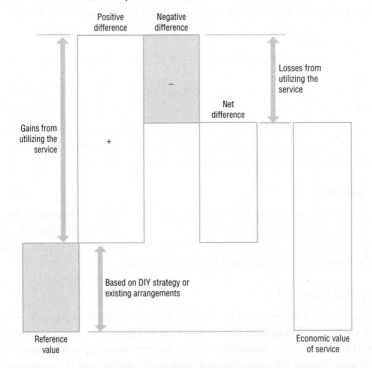

Calculating value can sometimes be a straightforward financial calculation: Does the service achieve what is required for an appropriate cost? If the cost does not impact profitability and the price remains competitive, then the service will be valuable.

As you can see, value is defined in terms of the business outcomes achieved and the customer preferences and perception of what was delivered.

Customers' perceptions are influenced by the attributes of the service, their present or prior experiences, and the image or market position of the organization.

Preferences and perceptions are the basis for selecting one service provider over another, and often the more intangible the value, the more important the definitions and differentiation of value becomes.

Customers must have a value on which they will base their perception of value. This is known as the reference value. It is the perception mentioned previously, based on present or prior experience. The gains that are made from utilizing the service are perceived as a positive difference, an addition to the reference value. In an ideal situation, this would form the perception of value for the customer. But utilizing the service is not always perceived as a positive experience. An outage will create a negative difference, which detracts from the existing positive perception. This is shown as the net difference.

So in the final analysis, the perception of the economic value of a service will be the original reference value and the net difference. Any negative perception may have a significant impact on the overall perception of the service.

When developing the strategy for an IT service provider, it is useful to have a "marketing mind-set." *Marketing* in this context refers not only to advertising services to influence customer perception, but also to understanding the customer's context and requirements and ensuring that services are geared to meeting the outcomes that are important to the customer. Rather than focusing inward on the production of services, there is a need to look from the outside in, from the customer's perspective.

A marketing mind-set begins with simple questions:

- What is our business?
- Who is our customer?
- What does the customer value?
- Who depends on our services?
- How do they use our services?
- Why are our services valuable to them?

To understand value chains and value realization, it is necessary to recognize that to be delivered, a service comprises multiple components. Each component is managed by a department within IT. Money is spent to procure, develop, and maintain each component, and each department manages their components to make sure they are operating correctly and therefore adding value to the service. Each piece of the jigsaw needs to make a positive contribution in terms of value added. The amount spent on the component should be less than the value it adds to the service.

Unfortunately, the true value can be calculated only after the value has been realized. This will only occur when the customer achieves its desired outcome.

If the value realized is not greater than the money spent, then the service provider has not added any value. It has spent money and in effect made a loss.

If IT wants to show it is adding value, it needs to link its activities to where the business realizes value. If it cannot do this, it will be perceived as a money spending organization. The IT money pit!

The only way to improve IT's position is to reduce the amount of money thrown into the pit and cut costs! This will result in IT's value reducing further.

The only way out of this destructive loop is to link services to business outcomes and show how each activity within IT helps to achieve each business outcome.

It is difficult to prove the value that has been added, particularly if there is no baseline or experience to benchmark against. Attempts can be made to explain what is being done to achieve the outcome, but a customer may simply view this as a way to drive up the price.

Ideally, the provider should focus on building a model where the contribution of each internal service can be measured and then link this to the achievement of the customer's business outcome.

Example of an Internal Service

Understanding the contribution of an internal service can present some surprises. Let's consider an example outside of IT.

It was once the case that Formula One cars would be stripped down after practice and every component examined. The purpose was to try to ensure that as reliable a car as possible could be put on the starting grid the following day.

A change in the rules of Formula One dictated that the cars would be put into a secure compound overnight and the mechanics would not have access to them. There were many predictions of mayhem, of many cars failing to finish the race. In fact, the opposite happened. Car failure during the race became a much rarer event.

The activity of stripping the cars down and rebuilding them was simply money spent rather than value added.

It is important that the IT provider understands the contribution provided by the internal service in terms of the utility or warranty it provides. This needs to be recognized in the context of the output the customer will receive and therefore the outcome they can achieve. Their perception of the value of the service will be positively influenced.

Capturing value will be the basis for effective communication of utility and warranty to improve customer perception of value and to provide a structure for the definition of service packages.

Utility and Warranty

Utility and warranty define services and work together to create value for the customer.

Utility and Warranty Definitions

Utility:

- What does the service do?
- The features, inputs, outputs... is the feature "fit for purpose"?
- This leads to functional requirements.

Warranty:

- How well does the service do it?
- Capacity, performance, availability... is the service "fit for use"?
- This leads to nonfunctional requirements.

Customers cannot benefit from something that is fit for purpose but not fit for use and vice versa. The value of a service is therefore only delivered when both utility and warranty are designed and delivered.

Utility

Utility affects the increase of possible gains from the performance of customer assets and the probability of achieving desirable business outcomes.

Figure 2.5 illustrates an example of an airline baggage handling service, which is able to load baggage onto an aircraft within 15 minutes 80 percent of the time. This is shown by the light-colored curve. With new security legislation, they will be required to perform additional security checks and to record the location of each bag in the aircraft hold. These additional activities require changes to the utility of the services.

In response to these new requirements, the airline changes the service to be able to do the additional work and is still able to load baggage onto the aircraft within 15 minutes 80 percent of the time. This new level of utility is shown by the dark-colored curve. The standard deviation remains the same since the warranty has not changed.

FIGURE 2.5   Utility increases the performance average.

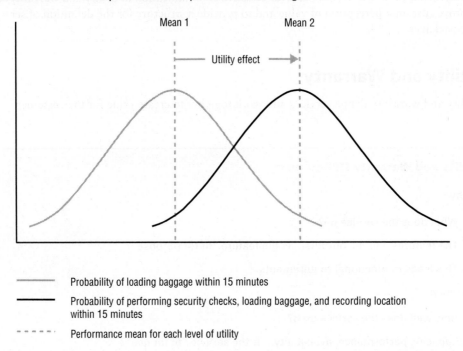

Probability of loading baggage within 15 minutes

Probability of performing security checks, loading baggage, and recording location within 15 minutes

Performance mean for each level of utility

Warranty does not automatically stay the same when utility is increased. In fact, maintaining consistent levels of warranty when increasing utility usually requires good planning and increased investment. More investment is required for making changes to existing processes and tools, training, hiring additional employees to do the increased work, obtaining additional tools to perform newly automated activities, and so on.

Thus, the utility effect means that, although the customer assets perform better and the range of outcomes is increased, the probability of achieving those outcomes remains the same. This can be seen in the diagram; the shape of the graph and the space under the line remain the same.

Warranty

The effect of improving warranty of a service means that the service will continue to do the same things but more reliably. Therefore, there is a higher probability that the desired outcomes will be achieved, along with a decreased risk that the customer will suffer losses due to variations in service performance. Improved warranty also results in an increase in the number of times a task can be performed within an acceptable level of cost, time, and activity. Customers are interested in reliability and the impact of losses rather than the possible gains from receiving the promised utility.

Figure 2.6 shows how the standard deviation of the performance of a service changes when warranty is improved.

FIGURE 2.6 Warranty reduces the performance average.

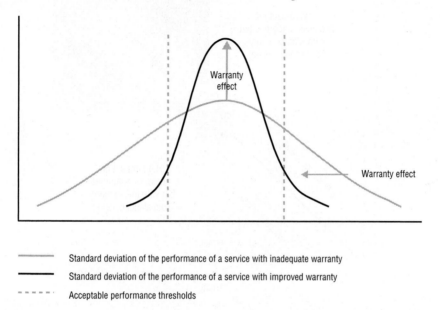

Standard deviation of the performance of a service with inadequate warranty

Standard deviation of the performance of a service with improved warranty

Acceptable performance thresholds

The lighter line shows that a significant percentage of service delivery is outside of the acceptable range. By making various improvements (e.g., training, process, and tool improvement; new tools or processes; automation), the service provider is able to increase the probability that the service will be performed within an acceptable range.

Using the airline baggage handling example, suppose that one year after adding the new utility, the airline would like to increase its "on-time departure" rate. Achieving this means that baggage handling needs to improve its performance. Without adding any new utility, the baggage handling service finds a better way of scanning and recording the location of bags. As a result, the baggage handling service is able to complete the loading of baggage onto the aircraft within 15 minutes 90 percent of the time—a significant improvement.

Combined Utility and Warranty

In Figure 2.7, you can see the impact of utility and warranty and how investment can be allocated according to the importance of the utility and warranty provided.

FIGURE 2.7   Combined effects of utility and warranty on customer assets

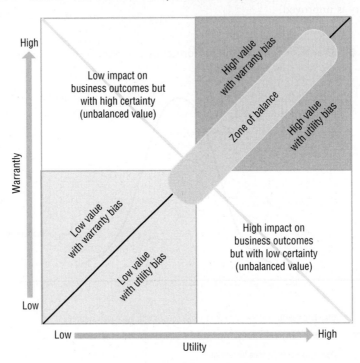

In the bottom-left quadrant, you can see low business impact with variable utility and warranty bias:

- This is showing assets with little value even with utility and warranty.
- This shows that minimal investment in the asset and the utility and warranty is justified, or there is an option to retire the service.

In the top-left quadrant, the diagram shows low business impact with low utility and high warranty:

- This shows the asset deriving little value because service does not meet needs regardless of the high level of warranty.
- It shows that investment should be reallocated to improve utility.

In the bottom-right quadrant, the diagram shows high business impact with high utility and low warranty:

- Again, the value is low because the service does not perform well even with high utility.
- This time the investment needed will be to improve the warranty of service.

In the top-right quadrant, you can see high business impact with balanced utility and warranty:

- Any bias to utility or warranty will be highly visible because the outcomes are valuable to the business.

- This justifies optimum investment in the "zone of balance."

Once we reach an appropriate balance between utility and warranty, customers will see a strong link between the utilization of a service and the positive effect on the performance of their own assets, leading to higher return on assets. This is shown in Figure 2.8.

FIGURE 2.8   Value of a service in terms of return on assets for the customer

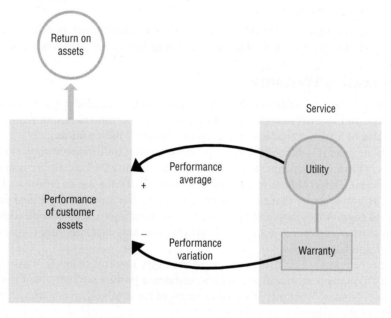

The arrow marked with a + (plus sign) in the diagram indicates a directly proportional relationship; here, the higher the utility, the higher the performance average. The arrow with a − (minus sign) indicates an inversely proportional relationship; here, the higher the level of warranty, the lower the performance variation.

In the diagram, services with a balance between utility and warranty increase the average performance of the customer assets. We could say that they will result in higher-value outcomes. This will also have the effect of reducing the performance variation, increasing the reliability of the service.

The combined effects of utility and warranty will enable the customer assets to achieve the customer's business outcomes and result in a return on their assets. In other words, value is realized.

Communicating both utility and warranty is important for customers to be able to calculate the value of a service.

Communicating Utility

Communicating utility will enable the customer to determine the extent to which utility is matched to their functionality requirements.

Communicating utility in terms of ownership costs and risks avoided means that the service provider should be able to articulate the following points:

- That the service enables the business to achieve the desired outcomes more efficiently. This allows the business to reduce its costs (and in commercial organizations, to increase its profit margins).

- That the service improves the reliability of outcome achievement. In other words, the service mitigates the risk of the business not being able to achieve its outcomes.

Communicating Warranty

Warranty ensures that the utility of the service is available as needed with sufficient capacity, continuity, and security—at the agreed cost or price. Customers cannot realize the promised value of a service that is fit for purpose when it is not fit for use.

Warranty in general is part of the value proposition that influences customers to buy. For customers to realize the expected benefits of manufactured goods, utility is necessary but not sufficient. Defects either make a product unavailable for use or reduce its functional capacity. Warranties assure that the products will retain function for a specified period under certain conditions of use and maintenance. Warranties are void outside such conditions; normal wear and tear is not covered. Most important, customers are owners and operators of purchased goods.

Service providers communicate the value of warranty in terms of levels of assurance. Their ability to manage service assets instills confidence in the customer about the support for business outcomes. Warranty is stated in terms of the availability, capacity, continuity, and security of the utilization of services.

Usability refers to whether users can actually perform the required actions and access the information they need in order to be able to achieve the desired outcomes. For example, factors of usability may include readability of text, whether data entry is straightforward and logical, and so on.

The ability to deliver a certain level of warranty to customers by itself is a basis of competitive advantage for service providers. This is particularly true where services are commoditized or standardized. In such cases, it is hard to differentiate value largely in terms of utility for customers. When customers have a choice between service providers whose services provide more or less the same utility but different levels of warranty, they prefer the greater certainty in the support of business outcomes, provided it is offered at a competitive price and by a service provider with a reputation for being able to deliver what is promised.

One point to bear in mind when defining both utility and warranty is the affordability of the service. A service provider can build a perfect service, but the utility and warranty need to be balanced against what the customer can afford to pay. Affordability is a good way for customers to prioritize the elements of warranty and utility, given the outcomes they want to achieve.

Strategic Assets and Service Providers

We have explored the concept of value and begun to relate this to the customer, service, and assets. The following sections consider the way IT services are created and how value is delivered to the customers through the use of assets, resources, and capabilities.

How do the assets that make up an IT service relate to resources and capabilities, and what relevance does this have to the service management strategy?

Resources and Capabilities

Capabilities represent an organization's ability to coordinate, control, and deploy resources to produce value. Capabilities are typically experience driven, knowledge intensive, information based, and firmly embedded within an organization's people, systems, processes, and technologies. It is relatively easy to acquire resources compared to capabilities. Resources are direct inputs for production. Capabilities can be a major differentiator for competing service providers even though their resources may be the same or similar.

Remember that people appear in both categories, resources and capabilities. All of the items identified as resources and capabilities are service assets.

Business Units and Service Providers

We will now examine the relationship between the assets used by business units and those used by service providers. Specifically, we are going to look at how these assets are related to services and the creation of value.

Business Unit

ITIL describes a business unit as an organizational entity, led by a manager, that performs a defined set of business activities that create value for customers in the form of goods and services.

The goods or services are produced and delivered using a set of assets, referred to as customer assets. Customers pay for the value they receive, which ensures that the business unit maintains an adequate return on assets. The relationship is good as long as the customer receives value and the business unit recovers costs and receives some form of compensation or profit.

It is the responsibility of the business unit to create value, which is determined in the context of the customer and the customer's assets.

Service Provider

While some organizational units are business units, some are clearly service providers. A service provider is an organizational entity, led by a manager, that performs a defined set of activities to create and deliver services that support the activities of business units.

Service providers use service assets to deliver services to business units, and these service assets are used to enhance the performance of business assets to achieve business outcomes.

If there are constraints that affect the ability to deliver services, an investment in both resources and capabilities may be required to overcome them.

Suppliers may be included in this value chain, and they will need to invest in their own resources and capabilities to deliver according to the service provider's requirements. But in service strategy, the focus for the service provider is the business outcome and how this can be established.

Service Asset

In Figure 2.9, you can see the representation of service assets driving services.

FIGURE 2.9 Service assets drive services to achieve business outcomes.

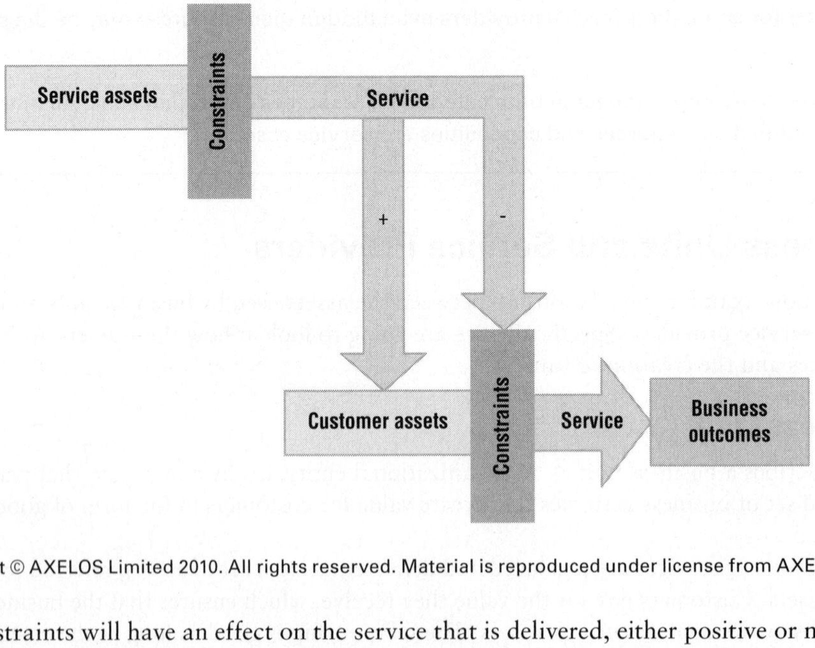

Constraints will have an effect on the service that is delivered, either positive or negative, and this in turn will have an impact on customer assets and the ability to achieve business outcomes.

All organizations have some restrictions on the use of their assets. No organization has unlimited resource, and this will necessarily have an impact on the capability of delivery.

Other constraints may force the use of better-quality components—an example here would be security or regulatory requirements driving an improved capability in service.

IT Service Management

When we consider IT service management in the context of customer and service assets, it is the management of the service assets (resources and capabilities) used to deliver services that support the achievement of the customer's business outcomes. Customers could be external or internal.

Service management enables the service assets to perform according to customer requirements while identifying and reducing the impact of constraints on the service assets. IT service management does this by managing IT's capabilities and resources. This is done either internally or through the support of external service providers and technology vendors.

Achieving this is not straightforward and often takes several years of hard work and cultural change. Changes in the capability of staff and the resultant experience that they will gain takes time to develop.

Most IT service providers start out by organizing their departments according to technical specialization. This is an important principle because each type of technology is very specialized and requires people with specialized skills to manage it.

But this means that goals are accomplished and reporting is done in silos, and the selection of staff is based on expertise, not any strategic plans. Often functional managers compete with each other rather than act in partnership, and as a consequence, issues that affect the organization across the functions are not addressed.

Processes are used as a means for managing silos, to bridge the gaps between the departments. Processes can be self-contained or cross-functional, dependent on the outcome that is required. They should enable thinking of IT as a set of cohesive resources and capabilities, not just as a set of individual departments or specialisms.

It is important that the processes focus on outcomes, not just outputs. Otherwise, the individual departments will simply focus on their specific output and ignore the fact that the outputs produced by all are used to deliver the overall outcome required by the business.

To achieve this successfully, IT priorities must be aligned to the drivers of business value, otherwise the IT department will be entirely inwardly focused.

IT Service Provider

The logical conclusion of this engagement between business units, service management, processes, and IT departments is that the IT department models itself as a service provider, with the goal of meeting business outcomes.

As can be seen in Figure 2.10, the resources and capabilities of the service provider are utilized to support the service (in the context of utility and warranty), and these in turn support and enable the business unit. Use of customer assets in the form of resources and capabilities will deliver the business outcomes.

FIGURE 2.10   How a service provider enables a business unit's outcomes

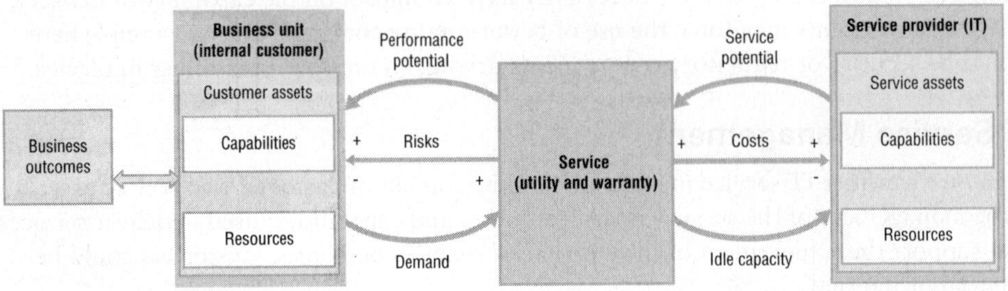

This is a direct connection from the service provider on the right of the image to the business outcomes on the left. Management of service assets by the service provider is used to deliver the utility and warranty, with the positive and negative effects of risks and costs driving the use of assets, both for the service provider and the customer.

This is often viewed as an end-to-end approach for the delivery of service.

Working backwards from the service potential ensures that any strategic decisions are based on customer value.

Here are some key questions to ask to ensure that the service provider will deliver the business outcomes:

- Who are our customers?
- What do those customers want?
- Can we offer anything unique to those customers?
- Are the opportunities already saturated with good solutions?
- Do we have the right portfolio of services developed for given opportunities?
- Do we have the right catalog of services offered to a given customer?
- Is every service designed to support the required outcomes?
- Is every service operated to support the required outcomes?
- Do we have the right models and structures to be a service provider?
- What we are trying to achieve as a service provider? Are our customers happy?
- Do they view our services as strategic assets?

We know that assets are resources and capabilities that are used to deliver services. A strategic asset is any asset (customer or service) that provides the basis for core competence, distinctive performance, or sustainable competitive advantage or that qualifies a business unit to participate in business opportunities. It is an asset that makes a significant difference to the organization.

Strategic assets are dynamic in nature. They are expected to continue to perform well under changing business conditions and objectives of their organization. That requires strategic assets to have learning capabilities, and that means being able to learn from past experience.

Part of service strategy is to identify how IT and IT service management can be viewed as strategic assets rather than an internal administrative function. It is important that IT is able to link its services to business outcomes, which in turn will contribute to the organization's competitive advantage and market differentiation.

We begin to grow service management into a strategic asset by building on our capabilities. This perception of IT as a valuable and trusted strategic part of the business does not happen overnight. It takes a concerted and formal effort in which IT demonstrates its contribution one area at a time.

Each new challenge that IT enables the business to overcome allows IT to develop additional credibility and enables the business to see IT as a strategic service provider. The more trusted IT becomes, the more services the business will ask it to provide, and at higher service levels. This increase in credibility and trust will justify more investment in the IT department, which in turn will allow for investment in greater capability.

Confidence and credibility in a provider have to be earned. Figure 2.11 represents cycles of earning trust. In practice there will be many more. It is of course possible for the cycle to run backwards if you fail to provide the service the business expects.

FIGURE 2.11   Growing service management into a trusted strategic asset

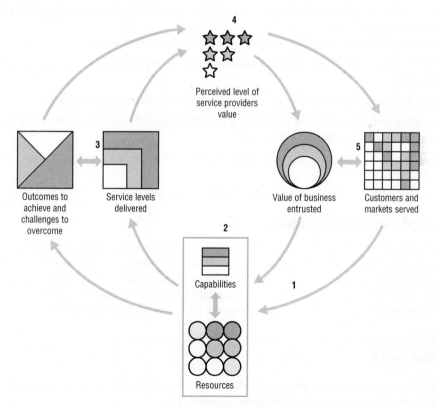

The sequence of activity is as follows:

- Within an existing IT service provider, the cycle begins when the service provider and business have selected an opportunity—which could be an existing service or an initiative that has already been defined. The value of this opportunity is defined in terms of outcomes that need to be achieved and the investment required to meet them. The opportunity will also specify which customers and market spaces the opportunity addresses.

- The service provider ensures that the capabilities and resources are in place to deliver the service(s).

- When delivered at the agreed levels, these services enable the business to achieve its objectives or overcome the defined challenge. It is important that these achievements are documented and reported to the stakeholders.

- The customer recognizes the IT service provider's contribution to their success (the value of the service).

- As a result, the customer is willing to entrust even more opportunities to the service provider.

Service management is viewed as a strategic asset (rather than a set of purely operational processes) when it can demonstrate how it enables the service provider to compete and differentiate itself effectively.

Service management does this by performing the following actions:

- Establishing a catalog of services that contribute to strategic business objectives and outcomes

- Identifying the market spaces in which IT enables the business to compete

- Defining how these services meet business challenges and then measuring them to ensure that this is achieved

- Building capabilities and resources to deliver these services and overcome identified challenges

- Communicating with the business about delivery achievements

Types of Service Providers

There are many options in the market place for the type of service provider an organization might use, and each has its own risks, costs, and benefits. This means that any choices made in sourcing IT from a service provider will need to align to the overall business strategy.

We will need to consider resources and capabilities and the overall outcomes that are required from the service provider, just as we do for a service that they deliver.

Provider Types

The ITIL framework defines a service provider as an organization supplying services to one or more internal customers or external customers.

There are three types of service providers:

- Type I, the internal service provider, which is embedded in the business unit it supports

- Type II, the shared services unit, which provides services to multiple business units throughout an organization

- Type III, the external service provider, which provides services to many customers across potentially multiple organizations

Type I Service Provider

The example in Figure 2.12 shows the Type I service provider. Type I providers are service providers that are dedicated to, and often embedded within, an individual business unit. The business units themselves are usually a part of an organization. They are funded by overheads and are required to operate strictly within the mandates of the business. Type I providers have the benefit of working closely with their customers, and are able to avoid certain costs and risks associated with conducting business with external providers. The control of all services remains within one organization.

FIGURE 2.12   Type I providers

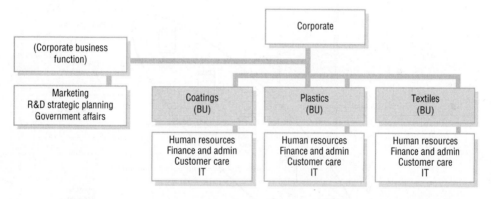

Because Type I service providers are dedicated to specific business units, they are required to have an in-depth knowledge of the business. They are usually highly special-ized, often focusing on designing, customizing, and supporting specific applications or on supporting a specific type of business process.

The diagram shows three business units with Type I service providers. Each IT unit is dedicated to a single business unit and delivers specialized services to that business unit only. A disadvantage of this approach is that there may be duplication and waste when Type I providers are replicated within the organization.

Competition for Type I providers is from providers outside the business unit, such as corporate business functions, who may be able to utilize advantages such as scale, scope, and autonomy.

Type II Service Provider

Functions such as finance, IT, human resources, and logistics are not always at the core of an organization's competitive advantage. Instead, the services of such shared functions are consolidated into an independent special unit called a shared services unit as shown in Figure 2.13. IT is shown as a single department with a service catalog that is available to multiple business units.

FIGURE 2.13   Common Type II providers

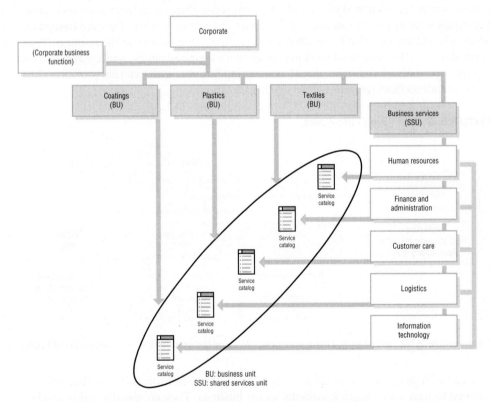

Shared service units can create, grow, and sustain an internal market for their services and model themselves along the lines of service providers in the open market. Often they can leverage opportunities across the organization and spread their costs and risks across a wider base. They are subject to comparisons with external service providers whose performance they should match, if not exceed.

Type II providers can offer lower prices compared to external service providers by leveraging internal agreements and accounting policies. They can standardize their service offerings across business units and use techniques such as market-based pricing to influence demand patterns. Market-based pricing is the approach where the service provider compares itself to an external provider for its pricing model. This makes comparison easier for the customer and may highlight internal economies. A successful Type II service provider can find itself in a position where it is able to provide its services externally as well as internally.

It is possible to combine Type I and Type II within an organization where there is a mix of requirements for IT services—for example, some specialists and dedicated service provisions and some shared services.

Type III Service Provider

A Type III service provider is a service provider that provides IT services to external customers. In Figure 2.14, you can see an example of a Type III provider.

FIGURE 2.14   Type III providers

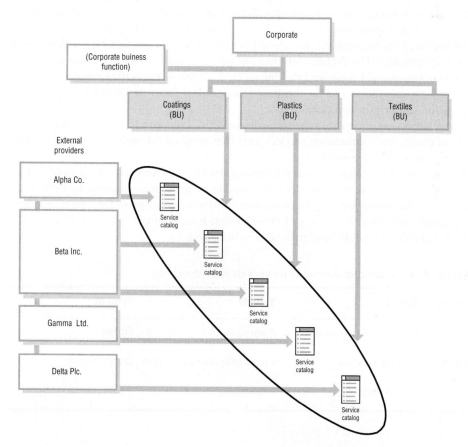

The business strategies of customers sometimes require capabilities more readily available from a Type III provider. Type III providers assume additional risk because their core business is the delivery of service and they are competing against internal Type I and Type II providers. Type III providers can offer competitive prices and drive down unit costs by consolidating demand from a range of clients. They may have the economies of scale to be able to deliver against specialisms that are too expensive for an individual customer by offering the capability to a wider range of customers. A further aspect of Type III service providers is that they provide specific capabilities or activities that are used by a Type I or II service provider to support their services.

Although this is not shown in the diagram, it should be noted that organizations using Type III service providers will still need an internal IT function or functions to manage the specification of services, coordinate the contracts, and ensure that business outcomes are met.

Evaluation of Service Providers

An organization needs to understand the advantages and disadvantages of each provider type. The choice of provider will be influenced by a number of factors, including the cost per transaction with the service provider, the best practice in a particular industry sector, and any specific requirements that can be met by only a particular type.

Of course, a major consideration should be the core competencies that are delivered by the service provider. The decision will need to take into consideration the service provider's risk management capabilities and the impact that the use of a specific provider type might have on the organization and the resultant risk. Another factor to consider is the economy of scale the service provider can deliver.

The tendency is for core services to be delivered by Type I or Type II providers (or indeed a mix of these), while enhancing services are often supplied through Type II or Type III providers (or a mix, as before).

It is important to remember that the organizational requirements may change over time, and this may have an impact on the sourcing model that is required. In Table 2.1, we have an organizational view of the movement from one service provider type to another. For example, changing from a Type I provider (left-hand column) to a Type III provider (right-hand column) would be classified as outsourcing.

TABLE 2.1   Customer decisions on service provider types

From/to	Type I	Type II	Type III
Type I	Functional reorganization	Aggregation	Outsourcing
Type II	Disaggregation	Corporate reorganization	Outsourcing
Type III	Insourcing	Insourcing	Value net reconfiguration

Evaluation of the service provider types depends on the nature of the provision, and whether customers keep a business activity in-house (aggregate), separate it out for dedicated management (disaggregate), or source it from outside (outsource) will depend on the answers to the following questions:

- Does the activity require assets that are highly specialized? Will those assets be idle or obsolete if that activity is no longer performed?
    - If yes, then disaggregate and/or outsource.
- How frequently is the activity performed within a period or business cycle? Is it infrequent or sporadic?
    - If yes, then outsource.
- Does the activity require knowledge specific to a particular business unit, even if the activity is infrequent and/or specialized?
    - If yes, then disaggregate or insource.
- How complex is the activity? Is it simple and routine? Is it stable over time with few changes?
    - If it's stable over time, then outsource. If it is complex and volatile, it might need to be disaggregated.
- Is it hard to define good performance?
    - If yes, then aggregate.
- Is it hard to measure good performance?
    - If yes, then aggregate.
- Is it tightly coupled with other activities or assets in the business? Would separating it increase complexity and cause problems of coordination?
    - If yes, then aggregate.

Organizations learn and improve over time during lasting relationships with customers. Fewer errors are made, investments are recovered, and the resulting cost advantage can be leveraged to increase the gap with competition. This is the same for the relationship between the service provider and their customers.

It is a fact that customers find it less attractive to turn away from well-performing incumbents, simply because of the costs relating to switching to a new provider. Experience can be used to improve assets over time and therefore improve the service delivery.

Service providers must therefore focus on providing the basis for a lasting relationship with customers. It is important for the service provider to carry out strategic planning and control to ensure that common objectives drive everything that is delivered. This requires knowledge to be shared effectively between units and the results of experience fed back into future plans and actions.

Defining Services

ITIL suggests eight steps that are needed for the service provider to be able to define a service. These steps outline how to identify customers and their requirements and whether there is an opportunity that a service provider can fulfil.

1. Define the market and identify customers.
2. Understand the customer.
3. Quantify the outcomes.
4. Classify and visualize the service.
5. Understand the opportunities (market spaces).
6. Define services based on outcomes.
7. Service models.
8. Define service units and packages.

Step 1: Define the Market and Identify Customers

When we talk about markets in this context, we mean the group of customers to whom the service provider is going to deliver services. So the first step has to be understanding the nature of the customer we are going to serve, as this will help us understand the options available.

For example, a Type I service provider will typically serve only one business unit. Their entire market consists of a single internal customer.

Markets can be defined by one or more criteria:

Industry Sector   For example manufacturing, retail, financial services, healthcare, or transportation.

Geographically   By a specific country or region. A service provider may provide a best-in-class service but decide to limit its availability to a single geographical region. A different service provider may provide a lower standard of service but deliver it consistently across multiple regions. This would make it easier for a customer to standardize its services across multiple regions.

Demographic   The service provider may deliver a service geared toward a specific cultural group (e.g., television programming for a Spanish-speaking customer in the United States) or a group of customers with similar incomes (e.g., luxury or economy services).

Corporate Relationships   Some service providers have specifically been set up to provide services to a group of companies with common shareholders and may not market those services to competitors of those companies.

Whatever the criteria, identifying the markets in which the service provider will operate is an important part of identifying which services the service provider will deliver and to which customers.

Step 2: Understand the Customer

For internal service providers, understanding the customer means understanding the overall business strategies and objectives of the organization and how each business unit meets them. It also means understanding the business outcomes that each business unit needs to achieve.

For an external service provider, understanding the customer means recognizing why they need the service they are purchasing. The service provider does not have to comprehend the detailed strategy, tactics, and operations of the customer, but they do need to understand the reasons the customer needs the service and what features are important.

Understanding customers involves understanding their desired business outcomes, their assets and constraints, and how they will perceive and measure value.

Desired Business Outcomes

The customers use their assets to achieve specific outcomes. Understanding what these outcomes are will help the service provider define the warranty and utility of the services and prioritize service needs.

Customer Assets

Services enable and support the performance of the assets the customer uses to achieve its business outcomes. Therefore, it is necessary when defining services to understand the linkage between the service and the customer assets.

Constraints

Customer assets will be limited by some form of constraint, such as lack of funding, lack of knowledge, regulations, and legislation. Understanding those constraints will enable the service provider to define boundaries for the service and also help the customer overcome, or work within, many of them.

How Value Will Be Perceived and Measured

Customers always measure performance, quality, and value. It is vital that the service provider understands how the customer measures the service—even if the service provider is not able to measure the service the same way.

The value of a service is best measured in terms of the improvement in business outcomes. These should be attributable to the impact of the service on the performance of business assets. Some services increase the performance of customer assets, some maintain performance, and others restore performance following an incident. A major aspect of providing value is preventing or reducing the variation in the performance of customer assets.

Step 3: Quantify the Outcomes

In this step, the service provider will work with the customer to identify its desired outcomes. These definitions need to be clear and measurable, and they need to be something that can be linked to the service.

Defining outcomes is an important part of defining services, but customers may take it for granted that everyone understands their particular outcomes because they are part of their normal routine. It is therefore important that the service provider work with the customer to quantify each outcome and document it.

Understanding how services impact outcomes, and therefore what type and level of service is needed, will require the service provider to map the services and outcomes. A good business relationship management process will help the service provider define and document the outcomes in terms that can be measured by the service provider. Mapping of outcomes to services and service assets can be accomplished as part of a configuration management system (CMS) and the service portfolio. Information on services is captured in the service portfolio, particularly the service catalog and service pipeline. Service level agreements also contain service information about how the service is linked to the business outcome.

Gaining insight into the customer's business and having good knowledge of customer outcomes is essential to developing a strong business relationship with customers. This is a key activity within business relationship management.

An outcome-based definition of services ensures that managers plan and execute all aspects of service management entirely from the perspective of what is valuable to the customer. Such an approach ensures that services not only create value for customers but also capture value for the service provider.

Step 4: Classify and Visualize the Service

Every service is unique, but many have similar characteristics. If a new service shares common characteristics with an existing service, it will be easier to determine what it will take to deliver the new service. If it has no characteristics in common with existing services, it will need to be evaluated and designed from the beginning.

Creating a way to classify services and represent them visually can help in identifying whether a new service requirement fits within the current strategy or whether it will represent an expansion of that strategy. It might also assist the service provider in deciding not to make an investment in a service that moves it away from its strategy.

One way to carry out this classification of services is to use service archetypes, or basic building blocks for services.

Archetype

The definition given to an archetype by the ITIL publication is the original pattern or model from which all things of the same kind are copied or on which they are based; a model or first form; prototype

Figure 2.15 visualizes the interaction of service archetypes and customer assets as they may be captured in the service catalog.

FIGURE 2.15   Classifying services using service archetypes and customer assets

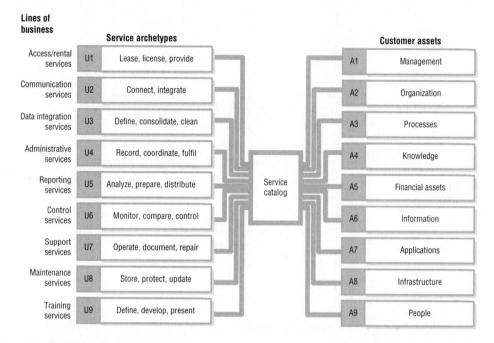

Services are based on service archetypes, such as lease, license, manage, operate, repair, audit, and design. In Figure 2.15, you can see these linked to the customer assets.

Mapping service archetypes and customer assets can also be useful to define strategies or to reveal patterns of demand or competence that have been built over time.

This is especially helpful for those service providers who were required to deliver whatever services the business demanded in the past without having a clear strategy. This is a common experience because organizations often grow organically rather than to a specific or strict strategy. This type of mapping will provide a baseline from which a service provider can identify future opportunities and services.

For example, the service provider may learn that many services are based on the same service archetype. They may learn that their resources and capabilities are mainly targeted at supporting business processes. This would be an asset-based service strategy—represented by the vertical arrow in Figure 2.16.

FIGURE 2.16   Asset-based and utility-based strategies

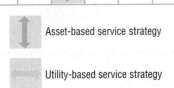

	A1	A2	A3	A4	A5	A6	A7	A8	A9
U1									
U2									
U3									
U4									
U5									
U6									
U7									
U8									
U9									

Asset-based service strategy

Utility-based service strategy

Alternatively, the service provider may learn that what differentiates it is the ability to provide administrative services that support a wide range of customer assets. This is shown by the horizontal arrow in the diagram, which represents a utility-based strategy.

Most organizations have a combination of utility- and asset-based service patterns. Visualization of services helps them to understand where they are strongest and where they need to strengthen their portfolio, resources, or capabilities.

This combination of service archetypes and customer assets often results in a series of patterns that indicate the positions where the service provider is strong.

Services with closely matching patterns indicate that there is an opportunity for consolidation or perhaps packaging them as shared services.

If the applications asset type appears in many patterns, then service providers can focus more investments in capabilities and resources that support services related to applications.

The same can be seen if many patterns include the support archetype. It can be taken as an indication that support has emerged as a core capability.

These are just simple examples of how the service catalog can be visualized as a collection of useful patterns. Service strategy can result in a particular collection of patterns, which is known as an intended strategy. A collection of patterns can make a particular service strategy attractive, and this is known as an emergent strategy.

Figure 2.17 shows examples of patterns of services as just described.

FIGURE 2.17   Visualization of services as value-creating patterns

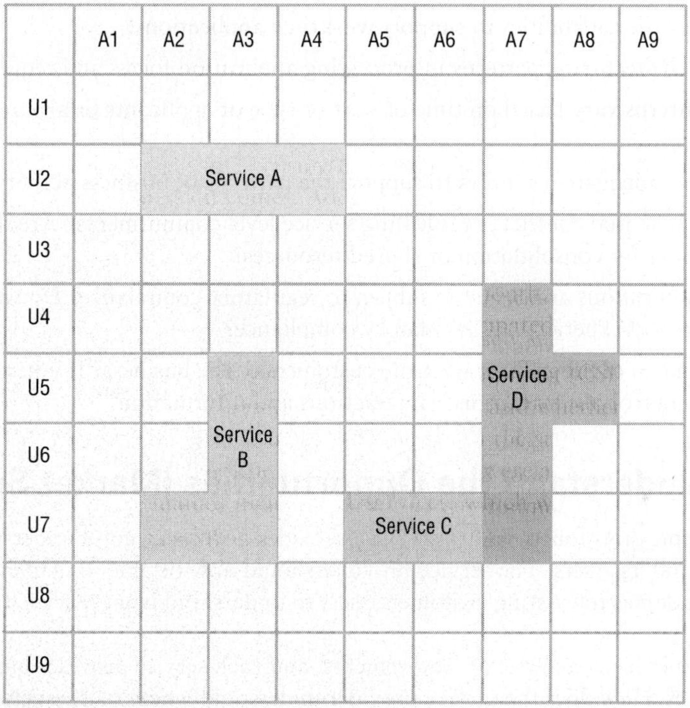

In this diagram, a single service may be constructed from one or more service archetypes and may support one or more customer assets, as follows:

- Service A is a utility-based communication service, which supports three types of customer assets: organization, processes, and knowledge.

- Service B is largely an asset-based process service, in which processes are supported by reporting, control, and support service archetypes. In this service, support services are also provided to support the organization asset.

- Service C is a support service archetype that supports financial assets, information, and applications.

- Service D is a range of service archetypes (administrative, reporting, control, and support) that support application assets. It also includes reporting support for infrastructure assets.

This visual method can be useful in communication and coordination between functions and processes of service management. The visualizations can be used as the basis of more formal definitions of services.

Proper matching of the value-creating context (customer assets) with the value-creating concept (service archetype) can avoid shortfalls in performance.

Questions of the following type can be useful:

- Do we have the capabilities to support workflow applications?

- What are the recurring patterns in processing application forms and requests?

- Do the patterns vary based on time of year or type of applicants or around specific events?

- Do we have adequate resources to support the patterns of business activity?

- Are there potential conflicts in fulfilling service level commitments? Are there opportunities for consolidation or shared resources?

- Are the applications and requests subject to regulatory compliance? Do we have knowledge and experience of regulatory compliance?

- Do we come in direct contact with the customers of the business? If yes, are there adequate controls to manage user interactions and information?

Step 5: Understand the Opportunities (Market Spaces)

Following the previous four steps, the service provider now has a good understanding of the customer and its assets. The service provider should now be able to map existing capabilities and resources to existing customer assets to understand what service it is able to provide.

Each customer has a number of requirements, and each service provider has a number of competencies. How does the service provider understand where its competencies will be able to meet the customer's requirements? These interactions between the service provider's competencies and the customer's requirements are called market spaces. Market spaces identify the possible IT services that an IT service provider may wish to consider delivering.

In this way, a market space is defined by a set of business outcomes, which can be facilitated by a service. The opportunity to facilitate those outcomes defines a market space for a service provider.

The following are examples of business outcomes that can be the basis of one or more market spaces:

- Sales teams are productive with a sales management system on wireless computers.

- An e-commerce website is linked to the warehouse management system.

- Key business applications are monitored and secure.

Each of the outcomes is related to one or more categories of customer assets, such as people, infrastructure, information, accounts receivables, and purchase orders. These can then be linked to the services that make them possible. Each outcome can be met in multiple ways, but customers normally prefer those with lower costs and risks. Service providers need to use this information to ensure that they provide the services that are required by the customer and are profitable for themselves.

Step 6: Define Services Based on Outcomes

Defining services based on outcomes ensures that the customer's requirements and value definitions drive the planning, delivery, and execution of the services. This means that not only does the customer receive the value it requires from the services, but that the service provider is able to capture value as well.

It is important to capture and understand value from the customer's perspective. Customers may express dissatisfaction with a service provider even if the service targets are met if they do not fully understand the value the service is providing to their business outcomes. Defining a service based on customer outcomes ensures that this is less likely to happen.

Ensuring that the design is robust and that the operational requirements are delivered in the service will address both utility and warranty for the customer. This will allow the service provider to identify where improvements can be made.

Clarification of the service delivery will support the perception of the customer in determining the value of the service. It will also enable both the customer and service provider to more easily visualize any patterns to be found across service catalogs and portfolios. This will be useful in determining the coordination efforts required to deliver service. It will remove any ambiguity and avoids any misalignment with the customer requirements.

Figure 2.18 is one of two examples of outcome-based service definitions. The other is in Figure 2.19. In the diagrams, you can see that the service archetypes and specific customer assets from step 4 are used in these definitions.

FIGURE 2.18   Defining services with utility components

FIGURE 2.19 Defining services with warranty components

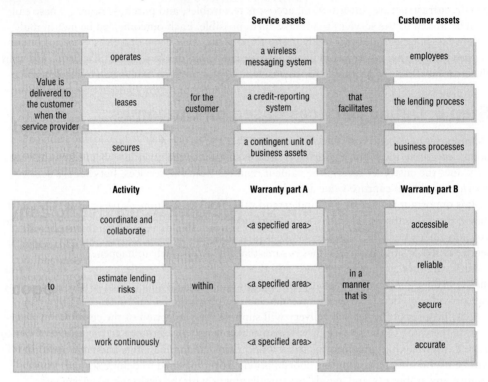

Figure 2.18 shows outcomes based on the utility of three different lines of service. In this case, the outcomes are expressed in terms of the outcomes achieved and the constraints removed (please note that utility can be achieved without having both outcomes achieved *and* constraints removed).

In the diagrams in Figures 2.18 and 2.19, you can see that the service archetypes and specific customer assets from step 4 are used in these definitions, which shows outcomes based on the warranty of the same three different lines of service.

Well-constructed definitions make it easier to visualize patterns across service catalogs and portfolios that earlier were hidden due to unstructured definitions. Patterns help to bring clarity to decisions across the service lifecycle.

Actionable service definitions are useful when they are broken down into discrete elements that can then be assigned to different groups. These groups will manage them in a coordinated manner to control and contribute to the overall effect of delivering value to customers.

Being able to define services in an actionable manner has advantages from a strategic perspective. It removes ambiguity from decision-making and avoids misalignment between what customers want and what service providers are capable of delivering.

Without the context in which the customers use services, it is difficult to completely define value.

But it is possible to ask questions that assist with the definition of a service. Questions that can be helpful in defining the services in an actionable manner are listed in Table 2.2. These types of questions are crucial for an organization to consider in the implementation of a strategic approach to service management. They are applied by all types of service providers, internal and external.

TABLE 2.2   Defining actionable service components

Service type	Utility (Part A and B)
What services do we provide? Who are our customers?	What business outcomes do we support? How do they create value for the business's customers? What constraints do our customers face?
Customer assets	**Service assets**
Which customer assets do we support? Who are the users of our services?	What assets do we deploy to provide value? How do we deploy our assets?
Activity or task	**Warranty**
What type of activity do we support? How do we track performance?	How do we create value for the business's customers? What assurances do we provide?

Step 7: Service Models

Service models can take many forms, from a simple logical chart showing the different components and their dependencies to a complex analytical model analyzing the dynamics of a service under different configurations and demand patterns.

Service Model

The ITIL framework defines a service model as "a model that shows how service assets interact with customer assets to create value. Service models describe the structure of a service (how the configuration items fit together) and the dynamics of the service (activities, flow of resources, and interactions). A service model can be used as a template or blueprint for multiple services."

Service models have a number of uses, especially in service portfolio management:

- Understanding what it will take to deliver a new service

- Identifying critical service components, customer assets, or service assets—and then ensuring that they are designed to cope with the required demand

- Illustrating how value is created

- Mapping the teams and assets that are involved in delivering a service, and ensuring that they understand their impact on the customer's ability to achieve their business outcomes

- As a starting point for designing new services

- As an assessment tool for understanding the impact of changes to existing services

- As a means of identifying whether new services can be delivered using existing assets

- If not, then assessing what type of investment would be required to deliver the service

- Identifying the interface between technology, people, and processes required to develop and deliver the service.

Figure 2.20 provides an example of how the dynamics of a service can be represented in a service model.

FIGURE 2.20 Dynamics of a service model

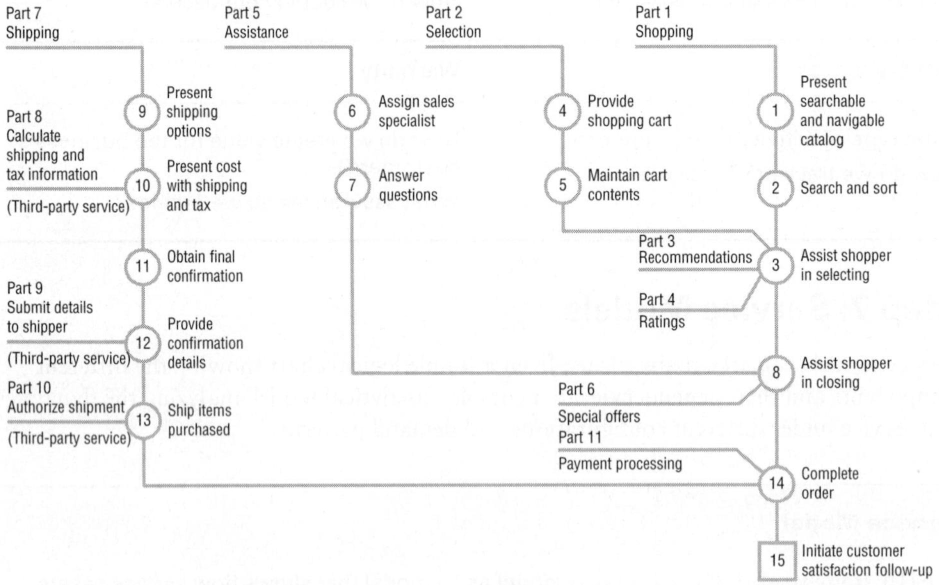

In this diagram, a retail service is illustrated. In this example, each component of the service is listed on a separate leg (or part), and the activities are numbered in the sequence in which the service is normally delivered.

Each component of the service is listed in relation to the other components, the dependencies identified, and the flows of communication and data indicated.

Step 8: Define Service Units and Packages

Services may be as simple as allowing a user to complete a single transaction, but most services are complex. They consist of a range of deliverables and functionality. If each individual aspect of these complex services were defined independently, the service provider would soon find it impossible to track and record all services.

Some services can be delivered on their own, but others require additional services to make them work. Consider buying a book. This is simple and straightforward, but if you purchase an e-book, then there are a number of supporting services and requirements, such as a reading device, an Internet connection, and licensing of the intellectual property.

A single service delivered to a customer is viewed by the service provider as a service. When two or more services are bundled and sold or delivered together, they are viewed by the service provider as a service package.

Service packages are created for two main reasons:

- If the core service requires enabling services to be present

- To create additional value for the customer, which equates to additional revenue and customer loyalty for the service provider

Packaging services requires an understanding of the different types of services. The service provider needs to understand how the services can be marketed and sold. The three basic types of services that can be delivered are core services, enabling services, and enhancing services.

Service Types

Core services deliver the basic outcomes desired by one or more customers. For example, a satellite TV provider sells a core service of a dish, set-top box, and a package of channels.

Enabling services are needed for a core service to be delivered but will often not be visible to the user. Without them, however, the core services cannot be delivered. The satellite TV provider requires an infrastructure of satellite dishes, transmission equipment, and so on.

Enhancing services are added to a core service to make it more attractive to the customer. The satellite provider offers additional services such as premium channels, interactive TV services, and on-demand films to win or keep customers.

An example of a core IT service is email. The enabling services would cover the infrastructure and network to enable the service to work effectively. An enhancing service associated to the core might be the ability to access the email service remotely, through a web-based portal. It is not an essential element of the core service functionality, but it adds something that provides value and customer satisfaction.

Following on from our previous examples of service types, let us now consider them in terms of service packages. Customers buy the provision of satellite TV as a service package from a particular supplier. It consists of the core services, a decoder, satellite dish, cabling, and access to content. The enabling service is the installation, and the enhancing services are the capability for email and Internet access with online storage.

Services and Service Packages Can Include Options

Service providers need to differentiate between service packages to allow for different customers to receive their individual service requirements. Potentially, each type of consumer will require a different level of warranty and utility.

Where a service or service package needs to be differentiated for different types of customer, one or more components of the package can be changed, or offered at different levels of utility and warranty, to create service options. These different service options can then be offered to customers and are sometimes called service level packages.

For example, when considering a core service of satellite television channels:

- Option A includes 100 channels.

- Option B includes 200 channels.

- Option C includes only channels appropriate for families with young children.

- Option D includes 300 channels and 5 pay-per-view sporting events per month.

Each of these services has a defined level of utility and warranty.

Service packages may be created to offer a number of different options to the customer. Each of these options will be documented in the service catalog, allowing the customer to choose the option that best suits its requirements.

Cloud Computing

In the case of cloud computing, the customer is able to pick and choose combinations of services and service levels. The customer is choosing its own packages and options.

Segmentation

An organization may choose to categorize its customers. This enables them to package services targeted to the needs of the categories.

In its simplest form, this could, for example, be a golf club or leisure center offering different membership packages (e.g., individual, family, junior, senior), but it could be more sophisticated, such as the example of the media company offering entertainment and communication packages, mentioned previously.

Segmentation can be extremely valuable for targeting marketing and sales campaigns, for example, as well as for defining service packages aimed at different segments. IT providers can use the same technique to segment IT users.

This will allow service packages to be developed to meet the needs of each user type while giving the following advantages:

- Maximization of standardization

- Minimization of different and diverse services

- Easier distribution
- Simplification of support issue

Designing and Transitioning Service Packages

The design and transition of service packages follows exactly the same process as any other service. A suggestion or request for a new service package (or change to an existing service package) is submitted through service portfolio management. The service package is modeled and assessed, and a change proposal submitted. Once the change proposal is authorized, the required levels of utility and warranty for the service package and its options will be documented in the service charter and submitted to design coordination.

A service design package (SDP) will be created to support the design, transition, and operation of the service package throughout the service lifecycle. The service transition processes will build, test, and deploy the service packages, just as they would any individual service, using the service charter and SDP as a basis for this activity.

The service package and its options will be documented in the service catalog.

Strategies for Customer Satisfaction

Customer satisfaction is very important in a competitive environment. Meeting business outcomes may not be enough to differentiate a service provider. Customers need to feel confident in the ability of the service provider to continue providing that level of service—or even improving it over time.

Customer expectations keep shifting, and a service provider that does not track this will soon lose business.

Kano Model

The Kano evaluation model assists with the understanding of customer expectations and how a service provider can adapt its services to meet the changing customer environment.

Attributes of a service are the characteristics that provide form and function to the service from a utilization perspective. The attributes are traced from business outcomes to be supported by the service. Certain attributes must be present for value creation to begin. Others add value on a sliding scale determined by how customers evaluate increments in utility and warranty. Service level agreements commonly provide for differentiated levels of service quality for different sets of users.

Some attributes are more important to customers than others. They have a direct impact on the performance of customer assets and therefore the realization of basic outcomes. Table 2.3 provides descriptions of the attributes referred to in the Kano model.

TABLE 2.3 The Kano model and service attributes (Kano 1984)

Type of attribute	Fulfilment and perceptions of utility (gain/loss)
Basic factors (B) (must-have, nonlinear)	Attributes of the service expected or taken for granted. Not fulfilling these will cause perceptions of utility loss. Fulfilling them results in utility gain, but only until the neutral zone, after which there is no gain.
Excitement factors (E) (attractive utility, nonlinear)	Attributes of the service that drive perceptions of utility gain but, when not fulfilled, do not cause perceptions of utility loss.
Performance factors (P) (attractive utility, linear)	Attributes of the service that result in perceptions of utility gain when fulfilled and utility loss when not fulfilled in an almost linear, one-dimensional pattern.
Indifferent attributes (I)	Cause neither gains nor losses in perceptions of utility regardless of whether they are fulfilled or not.
Reversed attributes (R)	Cause gains in perceptions of utility when not fulfilled and losses when fulfilled. Assumptions need to be reversed.
Questionable response (Q)	Responses are questionable possibly because questions were not clear or were misinterpreted.

In the Kano model, as shown in Figure 2.21, you can see the three types of factors that are involved in customer satisfaction:

▪ Basic factors are expected or taken for granted.

▪ Performance factors enhance the offering. Customers will pay more for more of these (e.g., amount of storage).

▪ Excitement factors are those that customers do not expect, but they increase satisfaction.

Excitement factors and performance factors are the basis for segmentation and differentiated service levels. They are used to fulfil the needs of particular types of customers. These attributes are necessary for any strategy that involves segmenting of customers into groups and serving them with an appropriate utility package.

Basic factors are necessary for the service provider to enter the market space. Something innovative and new will become commonplace over time, so excitement factors will lose their ability to act as a differentiator. Competition, changes in customer perceptions, and innovations can cause excitement factors to drift toward becoming performance or basic factors.

FIGURE 2.21   Perceptions of utility and customer satisfaction

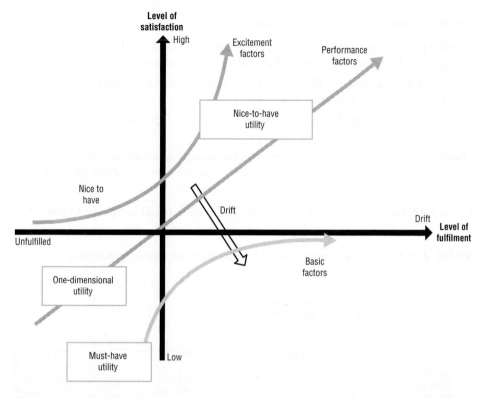

A well-designed service provides a combination of basic, performance, and excitement attributes to deliver the appropriate level of utility for a customer.

Different customers will place different importance on the same combination of attributes. But even if a particular type of customer values a particular combination, the customer may not be able to justify the potential additional charges.

Service Economics

Service economics relate to the balance between the cost of providing services, the value of the outcomes achieved, and the returns that the services enable the service provider to achieve.

The dynamics of service economics for external service providers are different from those for internal service providers. This is because the returns of internal service providers are mainly measured by their internal customers and do not accrue directly to the service provider.

Service economics relies on four main areas:

Service portfolio management is the process that defines the outcomes the business desires to achieve and the services that will be used to achieve them.

Financial management for IT services is the process used to calculate, forecast, and track costs and income related to services.

Return on investment (ROI) is the measurement of the expected or actual benefit of an investment.

Business impact analysis (BIA) allows an organization to establish the relative priorities of service based on their effect on the business if it is not available for a period of time.

Figure 2.22 shows the service economic dynamics for external service providers.

FIGURE 2.22 Service economic dynamics for external service providers

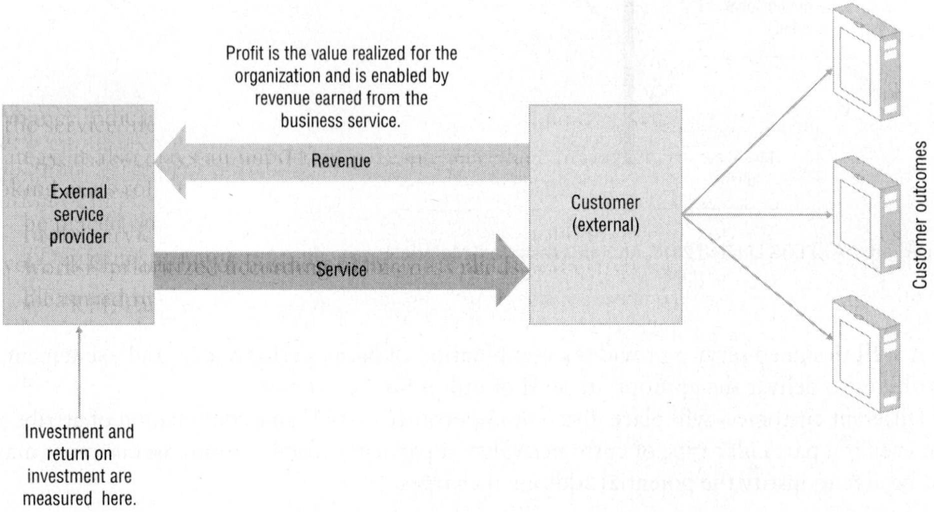

A Type III service provider delivers a service to an external customer for payment. The service provider calculates the total investment required to deliver that service and measures it against the total revenue obtained from delivering the service. The success of the service provider is measured by the return on its investment (ROI).

Figure 2.23 shows the service economic dynamics for internal service providers. It is significantly different than the previous diagram relating to external service providers.

FIGURE 2.23   Service economic dynamics for internal service providers

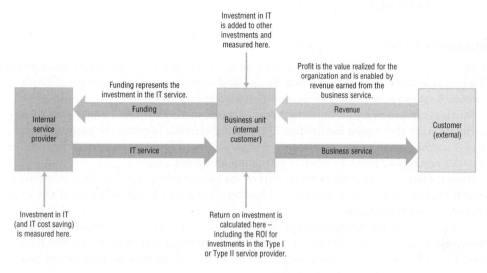

Return on Investment

The return on investment cannot be measured by an internal service provider in isolation from its internal customers. In the diagram in Figure 2.23, the IT service provider delivers a service to another business unit, which covers the costs of the IT service.

The investment in the IT service is carried by the business unit and not the service provider. This means that the funding provided to the IT service provider cannot be viewed as a return on investment; the investment is being made by the business unit. The return has to be calculated based on the profitability generated by the business unit, and the ROI calculation is carried out by the business unit.

Return on investment (ROI) is a recognized concept for quantifying the value of an investment. The calculation is normally performed by financial management. The term is not always used consistently, sometimes being used to refer to business performance. In service management, ROI is used as a measure of the ability to use assets to generate additional value.

In the simplest sense, it is the increase in profit resulting from the service divided by the total investment in the service. This calculation is overly simplistic because there are a number of subjective factors to be considered in service management value for a customer.

To cover this subjectivity, ITIL covers three main areas in ROI:

- The business case, which is a means to identify business imperatives that depend on service management

- Pre-program ROI, which includes techniques for quantitatively analyzing an investment in service management

▪   Post-program ROI, which includes techniques for retroactively analyzing an investment in service management

Business Case

A business case is a decision support and planning tool that projects the likely consequences of a business action. The outcome may be assessed on both qualitative and quantitative criteria. A financial analysis is often central to a good business case.

Business objectives are an important part of the business case because they will be the justification for the request for funding. There is a difference between the business objectives of a profit organization and nonprofit organization. This must be part of the consideration for any service provider when constructing a business case.

Business impact is another essential part of the business case, but it is often only based on cost analysis. If there is a nonfinancial business impact, it should be linked to a business objective to provide a value.

A minimum sample business case structure includes an introduction, presenting the business objectives to be addressed, followed by the methods and assumptions that have been used. This defines the boundaries of the business case, such as the time period and how benefits and costs are being calculated.

The business impacts section of the business case covers the financial and nonfinancial results that are expected. This often includes expressing nonfinancial results in financial terms, such as translating staff improvements as a reduction in expenditure on training and hiring.

Risks and contingencies will be important for the decision-making process and must be included in the business case.

The final section should cover the recommendations and specific actions.

Pre-program ROI

The term *capital budgeting* is used to describe how managers plan significant outlays on projects that have long-term implications. A service management initiative may sometimes require capital budgeting to fund the project or service.

An additional factor to remember when performing pre-program ROI is the relative value of the investment over time. An investment typically occurs early, while returns do not occur until sometime later.

Capital budgeting falls into two broad categories:

▪   Screening decisions relate to whether a proposed service management initiative passes a predetermined requirement—for example, a minimum return. Screening decisions are usually made using a discounted cash flow method of net present value (NPV).

▪   Preference decisions relate to choosing from among several competing alternatives—for example, electing between an internal service improvement plan (SIP) and a service sourcing program. Preference decisions are usually made using a discounted cash flow method of internal rate of return (IRR).

In screening decisions (using net present value), the program's cash inflows are compared to the cash outflows over time. The value of the money spent today will probably change over time due to inflation, currency fluctuations, and so on. This fluctuation in the value of income and expenditure over a period of time is called the *discounted cash flow*.

These discounted cash flows need to be taken in account when ROI calculations are used to calculate the return over a period of time. The difference, called net present value, determines whether or not the investment is suitable. If the NPV is positive, the return is greater than the minimal rate of term, and the program is considered acceptable. If the NPV is zero, this means that the return is equal to the minimal rate of return, which again, may be acceptable. Whenever the net present value is negative, the investment is unlikely to be suitable. This is shown in Table 2.4.

TABLE 2.4 NPV decisions

If the NPV is:	Then the program is:
Positive	Acceptable. It promises a return greater than the required rate of return.
Zero	Acceptable. It promises a return equal to the required rate of return.
Negative	Unacceptable. It promises a return less than the required rate of return.

Table 2.5 shows an example of the calculation of the net present value.

TABLE 2.5 Example of NPV

Initial investment	$70,000
Investment window	5 years
Annual cost savings	$20,000
Required rate of return (i)	10%

You can see the initial investment value, the time frame (5 years), and the annual cost savings being achieved, along with the required rate of return (10%).

In Table 2.6, you can see the application of the discounted cash flow to show the final total, which shows that the NPV is positive, producing a return of over five thousand dollars at the end of the five-year period.

TABLE 2.6   Example of NPV of a proposed service management program

	Years	Amount of cash flow ($)	Discount of 20%	Present value of cash flow (S)
	1 to 5	16,500	2.991*	49,352
Initial investment	Now	(50,000)	1	−50,000
Net present value				−648

Initial investment: $50,000; investment window: 5 years; annual cost savings: $16,500; salvage value: 0; required rate of return: 20%

*Present value of an annuity of $1 in 5 years' arrears.

Preference Decisions (Using Internal Rate of Return)

While many opportunities pass the screening decision process, not all can be acted on. Financial or resource constraints may require comparison of alternatives. Preference decisions, sometimes called rationing or ranking decisions, must be made. The competing alternatives are ranked.

Simply calculating and comparing the NPV of one project with that of another does not compare the actual size of the investment and returns. As a result, the internal rate of return (IRR) is widely used for preference decisions. The higher the internal rate of return, the more desirable the initiative.

The IRR, sometimes called the yield, is the rate of return over the life of an initiative. IRR is computed by finding the discount rate that equates the present value of a project's cash outflows with the present value of its inflows. That is, the IRR is the discount rate resulting when an NPV of zero is achieved (or the exact time when the project will break even and start producing a positive contribution).

In Table 2.7, the calculation of IRR is based on the previous example we used for NPV.

TABLE 2.7   Example of the IRR of a proposed service management program

	Years	Amount of cash flow ($)	Discount of 19–20%	Present value of cash flow (S)
Annual cost savings	1 to 5	16,500	3.0303	50,000
Initial investment	Now	(50,000)	1	−50,000
Net present value				0

Initial investment: $50,000; investment window: 5 years; annual cost savings: $16,500; salvage value: 0; required rate of return: 20%

Both of the project options have a positive NPV, but project 2 (Table 2.7) shows a greater internal rate of return than project 1 (Table 2.6). This conclusion is based only on financial return and does not include any nonfinancial returns that may be achieved from the projects.

Post-program ROI

Many companies successfully justify service management implementations through qualitative arguments, without a business case or plan, often ranking cost savings as a low business driver.

But without clearly defined financial objectives, companies cannot measure the added value brought about by service management, thereby introducing future risk in the form of strong opposition from business leaders.

Stakeholders may question the value of a service management program. Without proof of value, executives may cease further investments. Therefore, all significant projects should be subjected to a post-program ROI analysis. However, if service management is initiated without prior ROI analysis, it is even more important that an analysis be conducted at an appropriate time after (when the anticipated returns can reasonably be measured).

Figure 2.24 illustrates the model for a post-program ROI.

FIGURE 2.24   Post-program ROI approach

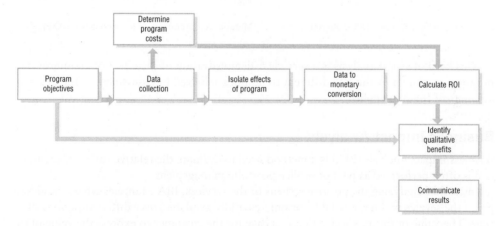

Once the objectives of the program have been identified, data collection takes place to determine the program costs. Understanding the effects of the program, and how they will be expressed in a suitable monetary format, will lead to the calculation of the ROI based on the program costs and expected returns.

The forecast analysis (Figure 2.25) for the success of a program shows a trend-line analysis (or another forecasting model), which is used to project data points had the program not taken place.

FIGURE 2.25   Forecast analysis

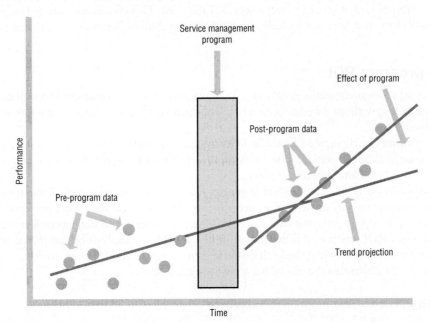

Service management program

Effect of program

Post-program data

Performance

Pre-program data

Trend projection

Time

This kind of visual analysis is a very clear demonstration of the effect of an improvement program, as shown by the two different trend lines achieved by assessment of the different amounts of funding applied.

Business Impact Analysis

Business impact analysis (BIA) is a method used to evaluate the relative value of services and is often performed as part of service portfolio management.

Instead of analyzing the positive returns of the services, BIA examines what would happen if the service was not available, or only partially available, over different periods of time. The value of this method is that it is easy for the customer to express the value of the service in terms that are meaningful to it—both financial and nonfinancial.

An advantage of this approach for internal service providers is that it is an excellent communication tool, demonstrating to their customers that they have understood their priorities and how they have allocated their resources.

This focus on assessing the outages of services, combined with assessing the severity of the outage, makes it a useful method for IT service continuity management and other related service management processes and functions. It will help to answer useful questions about the organization and to support the choices that need to be made to support the required business outcomes.

The BIA high-level activities are as follows:

- Arrange resources from business and IT for the analysis.
- Prioritize candidate services.
- Identify core analysis points for risk and impact assessment.
- Weight the risk and impact elements from a business perspective.
- Score services against weighted risk elements.
- List services in order of risk profile.
- Agree on standard time period for comparing outage costs.
- Calculate the financial impact of each service.
- List services in order of financial impact.
- Generate charts showing company's risk and financial impact for specific services.

Using the results of business impact analysis enables the business to decide on the priorities of service provision in a meaningful way—by comparing the investment in the service with the cost of not having it (or having access at a reduced level). This is an important aspect of strategy.

Sourcing Strategy

Sourcing is about analyzing how to most effectively source and deploy the resources and capabilities required to deliver outcomes to customers. The sourcing strategy should enable a decision about the best combination of supplier types to support the objectives of the organization and the effective and efficient delivery of services.

A service strategy should enhance an organization's special strengths and core competencies. Each component should reinforce the other; change one and the whole model changes.

As organizations seek to improve their performance, they should consider which competencies are essential. Partnering in areas both inside and outside the organization will enhance these core competencies.

Outsourcing moves a value-creating activity from inside the organization to outside the organization, where it will be performed by another company. The decision to outsource is based on a comparison. Does the extra value generated from performing an activity inside the organization outweigh the costs of managing it internally? This decision can change over time.

IT services are increasingly delivered by service providers outside the enterprise. Making an informed service sourcing decision requires finding a balance between thorough qualitative and quantitative considerations. Deciding to outsource is about finding ways to improve the competitive differentiation of the organization by redeploying resources and capabilities outside of the organization.

Any capabilities and resources that are only marginally related to the organization's core strategy and differentiation should be considered for outsourcing. Once potential candidates for sourcing are identified, the following questions can be used to clarify matters:

- Do the candidate services improve the business's resources and capabilities?

- How closely are the candidate services connected to the business's competitive and strategic resources and capabilities?

- Do the candidate services require extensive interactions between the service providers and the business's competitive and strategic resources and capabilities?

If the responses reveal minimal dependencies and infrequent interactions between the sourced services and the business's competitive and strategic positioning, then the candidates are strong contenders.

If candidates for sourcing are closely related to the business's competitive or strategic positioning, then care must be taken. The sourcing risks must be considered:

Substitution   "Why do I need the service provider when its supplier can offer the same services?" The sourced vendor develops competing capabilities and replaces the sourcing organization.

Disruption   The sourced vendor has a direct impact on the quality or reputation of the sourcing organization.

Distinctiveness   The sourced vendor is the source of distinctiveness for the sourcing organization. The sourcing organization then becomes particularly dependent on the continued development and success of the sourced organization.

Care should be taken to distinguish between distinctive activities and critical activities. Critical activities do not necessarily refer to activities that may be distinctive to the service provider. For example, although customer service is most likely critical, if it does not differentiate the provider from competing alternatives, then it is not distinctive, referred to here as *context*.

Regardless of where services, capabilities, or resources are sourced from, the organization retains accountability for their adequacy. Outsourcing does not mean that a service or its performance are no longer important. Outsourcing a capability, resource, or service does not mean outsourcing the governance of what that item does. The organization should adopt a formal governance approach to manage its outsourced services in addition to assuring the delivery of value.

Sourcing Structures

The following sections present an overview of the predominant sourcing structures. These sourcing structures also represent the strategy that the organization is using to deliver its services.

Insourcing

This approach relies on utilizing internal organizational resources in the design, development, transition, maintenance, operation, and/or support of new, changed, or revised services.

Outsourcing

This approach utilizes the resources of an external organization or organizations in a formal arrangement to provide a well-defined portion of a service's design, development, maintenance, operations, and/or support. This includes the consumption of services from application service providers (ASPs), described later.

Co-sourcing or Multi-sourcing

Co-sourcing or multi-sourcing is often a combination of insourcing and outsourcing, using a number of organizations working together to co-source key elements within the lifecycle. This generally involves using a number of external organizations working together to design, develop, transition, maintain, operate, and/or support a portion of a service.

Partnership

A partnership is a formal arrangement between two or more organizations to work together to design, develop, transition, maintain, operate, and/or support IT service(s). The focus here tends to be on strategic partnerships that leverage critical expertise or market opportunities.

Business Process Outsourcing

Business process outsourcing (BPO) is an increasing trend of relocating entire business functions using formal arrangements between organizations. One organization provides and manages the other organization's entire business process(es) or function(s) in a low-cost location. Common examples are accounting, payroll, and call center operations.

Application Service Provision

This involves formal arrangements with an application service provider (ASP) organization that will provide shared computer-based services to customer organizations over a network from the service provider's premises. Applications offered in this way are also sometimes referred to as on-demand software/applications. Through ASPs, the complexities and costs of such shared software can be reduced and provided to organizations that could otherwise not justify the investment. For example, Google now provides Gmail and Google Docs as additional service functionality for users.

Knowledge Process Outsourcing

Knowledge process outsourcing (KPO) is a step ahead of BPO in one respect. KPO organizations provide domain-based processes and business expertise rather than just process expertise. In other words, the organization is required to not only execute a process, but also to make certain low-level decisions based on knowledge of local conditions or industry-specific information. For example, when credit risk assessment is outsourced, the outsourcing organization has historical information that it has analyzed to create knowledge, which in turn enables it to provide a service. Every credit card company collecting and analyzing this data for themselves would not be as cost effective as using KPO.

Cloud

Cloud service providers offer specific predefined services, usually on demand. Services are usually standard, but they can be customized to a specific organization if there is enough demand for the service. Cloud services can be offered internally but generally refer to outsourced service provision.

Multi-vendor Sourcing

This type of sourcing involves sourcing different services from different vendors, often representing different sourcing options from the options we have just explored.

Sourcing Responsibilities

The responsibilities associated with sourcing include monitoring both the performance of agreements and the relationship with service providers. It is still important to manage the sourcing agreements, whether they are in-house or outsourced. Provision of an escalation point for issues and problems is a key part of the management strategy, and it is necessary to ensure that providers understand the organization's priorities.

There will be specific dependencies to achieve the outcomes that the customer requires. It is important to focus on what the service provider is expected to do, including the resource alignment and organizational structures. Understanding the dynamics of the services will affect the way the resources are distributed across the organization. It will drive the management and introduction of new skills, including business, technical, and behavioral requirements.

In this environment, sourcing services from multiple providers has become the norm rather than the exception. The organization maintains a strong relationship with each provider, spreading the risk and reducing costs. It should also be noted that providers may represent different types of sourcing options from the options we explored earlier.

Governing and managing multiple providers, who often have little to do with each other outside of the common customer, can be challenging. When sourcing multiple providers, the following issues should be carefully evaluated:

Technical Complexity   Sourcing services from external service providers is useful for standardized service processes (although as customization increases, it is more difficult to achieve the desired efficiencies).

Organizational Interdependencies   Contracts should be carefully structured to address the dynamics of multiple organizations, ensuring that all providers undergo consistent training in the customer organization's processes. Also, contracts should include incentives designed to encourage consistency in contractual performance between providers.

Integration Planning   The processes, data, and tools of each organization may be different or they may be duplicated. Either case will require the integration of certain processes, data, and tools. In addition, it is critical that the reporting of each organization is integrated, so that governance can be performed consistently across each organization.

Managed Sourcing   This refers to the need for a single interface to the multiple vendors wherever appropriate. A sure recipe for failure in a multi-sourced environment that requires collaboration between service providers is to have each contract negotiated and managed by different groups within the organization.

There are multiple approaches and varying degrees in sourcing. How far up an organization is willing to go with sourcing depends on the business objectives to be achieved and constraints to overcome. Figure 2.26 illustrates the limitations (expressed as the capability and scale ceilings) experienced at each of three levels of sourcing and then indicates the additional benefits or features that can be gained by moving to the next level.

FIGURE 2.26   The service sourcing staircase

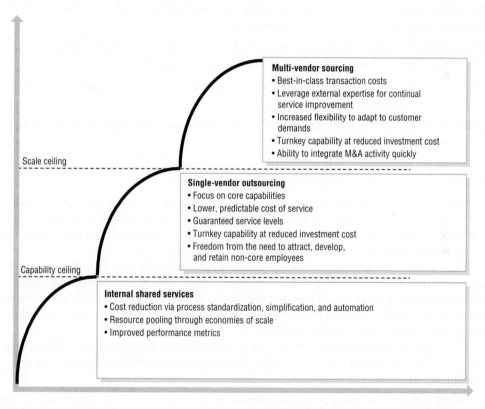

It is important to note that this figure does not imply that any single form of sourcing is better than another, merely that there are different potential benefits as the organization moves up the staircase. Whether or not these benefits can be achieved by each organization for each service will need to be assessed.

In the figure, an organization with limitations in internal capability might move to an outsourcing model where a single outsourcing organization is used to augment current capabilities through economies of scale (for example, specialized, expensive capabilities can be shared across more than one customer, making them available at a lower overall cost to all customers).

A single-vendor outsourcing contract will eventually be limited in what it can provide to a large, complex customer base, requiring customers to source services from multiple providers.

Regardless of the sourcing approach, senior executives must carefully evaluate provider attributes. The following is a useful checklist:

Demonstrated Competencies   In terms of staff, use of technologies, innovation, industry experience, and certifications (for example, ISO/IEC 20000)

Past Achievements   In terms of service quality attained, financial value created, and demonstrated commitment to continual improvement

Relationship Dynamics   In terms of vision and strategy, the cultural fit, relative size of contract in their portfolio, and quality of relationship management

Quality of Solutions   Relevance of services to your requirements, risk management, and performance benchmarks

Overall Capabilities   In terms of financial strength, resources, management systems, and scope and range of services

Commitment to Transferred Personnel   In terms of their longer-term retention, personal development, and career opportunities

In a complex multi-vendor environment, there needs to be good relationships between the various service providers. Guidelines and reference points are needed to refer to technology, procedures, or organization structures. One method of formalizing these reference points is through the use of service provider interfaces (SPIs).

A service provider interface is a formally defined reference point that identifies some interaction between a service provider and a user, customer, process, or one or more suppliers. SPIs are generally used to ensure that multiple parties in a business relationship have the same points of reference for defining, delivering, and reporting services. They also help to coordinate end-to-end management of critical services.

The service catalog drives the service specifications, which are part of standard process definitions. Responsibilities and service levels are negotiated at the time the sourcing relationship is established and include the following:

- Identification of integration points between various management processes of the client and service provider

- Identification of specific roles and responsibilities for managing the ongoing systems management relationship with both parties

- Identification of relevant systems management information that needs to be communicated to the customer on an ongoing basis

The SPIs also have to consider more than live services. There is a need for management, strategy, and transition activities as well as live services. This is especially true if the outsourced service provider is seen as a strategic partner in transforming the client's business or business model.

In Figure 2.27, you can see how SPIs can be used.

FIGURE 2.27   Using service provider interfaces

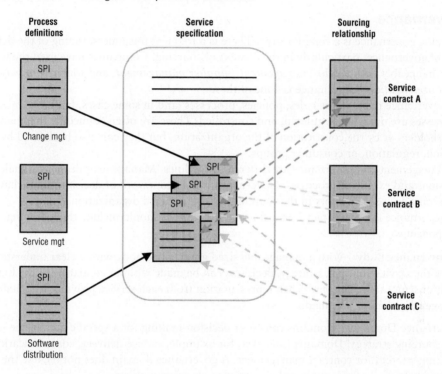

Process SPI definitions consist of the following elements:

- Technology prerequisites (e.g., management tool standards or prescribed protocols)
- Data requirements (e.g., specific events or records), formats (i.e., data layouts), interfaces (e.g., APIs, firewall ports), and protocols (e.g., SNMP, XML)
- Nonnegotiable requirements (e.g., practices, activities, operating procedures)
- Required roles/responsibilities within the service provider and customer organizations
- Response times and escalations

SPIs are defined, maintained, and owned by process owners. Others involved in the definition are as follows:

- Business representatives, who negotiate the SPI requirements and are responsible for managing the strategic relationships with and between service providers
- Service provider process coordinator(s), who take operational responsibility for ensuring that operational processes are synchronized

Governance

Sourcing governance is a complex area. There is a frequent misunderstanding of the definition of governance, particularly in the context of sourcing. Companies have used the word interchangeably with *vendor management*, *supplier management*, and *sourcing management organization*. Governance is none of these.

Governance refers to the rules, policies, processes (and in some cases, laws) by which businesses are operated, regulated, and controlled. These are often defined by the board or shareholders or by the constitution of the organization, but they can also be defined by legislation, regulation, or consumer groups.

Management and governance are different disciplines. Management deals with making decisions and executing processes. Governance is the framework of decision rights that encourage desired behaviors in the sourcing and the sourced organization.

Governance is a major factor in a sourcing strategy. It should include the following components:

A Governance Body   With a manageably sized governance body with a clear understanding of the service sourcing strategy, decisions can be made without escalating to the highest levels of senior management. When representation from each service provider is included, stronger decisions can be made.

Governance Domains   Domains can cover decision-making for a specific area of the service sourcing strategy. Domains can cover, for example, service delivery, communication, sourcing strategy, or contract management. A governance domain does not include the responsibility for its execution, only its strategic decision-making.

Creation of a Decision-Rights Matrix   This ties all three recommendations together. RACI charts are common forms of a decision-rights matrix.

Supplier Management   This ensures that contracts and external service providers are managed according to the organization's governance policies, standards, and controls.

It is important to understand the costs and risks associated with changing from one sourcing model to another. The costs of change can sometimes overshadow any benefit, and the additional management of an outsourced contract can eat into expected savings.

In addition, the risk of moving critical operational activities from one entity to another can be disruptive, and can be irrevocably damaging if this disruption is felt over an extended time. It is important to consider the following critical success factors when making the decision to ensure a successful sourcing strategy:

- Desired outcomes, such as cost reduction, improved service quality, and diminished business risk
- The optimal model for delivering the service
- The best location to deliver the service, such as local, onshore, nearshore, or offshore

The recommended approach to deciding on a strategy includes these three points:

- Ensuring that there is analysis of the organization's internal service management competencies
- Comparison of those findings with industry benchmarks
- Assessment of the organization's ability to deliver strategic value

When the results of the strategic assessment are considered, the sourcing strategy will depend on the levels of competence of service management within the organization.

If the organization's internal service management competence is high and also provides strategic value, then an internal or shared services strategy is the most likely option. The organization should continue to invest internally, leveraging high-value expert providers to refine and enhance the service management competencies.

If the organization's internal service management competence is low but provides strategic value, then outsourcing is an option, provided services can be maintained or improved through the use of high-value providers.

If the organization's internal service management competence is high but does not provide strategic value, then there are multiple options. The business may want to invest in its service capabilities so that they do provide strategic value, or it may sell off these service capabilities because they may be of greater value to a third party.

If the organization's internal service management competence and strategic value are low, then they should be considered candidates for outsourcing.

Prior to any implementation, an organization should establish and maintain a baseline of its performance metrics. Without such metrics, it will be difficult to assess the true impact and trends of a service sourcing implementation.

Measurements can take on two forms:

Business Metrics   Financial savings, service level improvements, business process efficiency

Customer Metrics   Availability and consistency of services, increased offerings, quality of service

Service Strategy Inputs and Outputs

The main outputs from service strategy are the vision and mission, strategies and strategic plans, the service portfolio, change proposals, patterns of business activity, and financial information.

Table 2.8 looks at the major service strategy inputs and outputs by lifecycle stage. Spend some time reviewing these inputs and outputs because they provide important information about the interaction of service strategy across the service lifecycle.

TABLE 2.8   Service strategy inputs and outputs by lifecycle stage

Lifecycle stage	Service strategy inputs (from the lifecycle stages in the first column)	Service strategy outputs (to the lifecycle stages in the first column)
Service design	Input to business cases and the service portfolio Service design packages Updated service models Service portfolio updates, including the service catalog Financial estimates and reports Design-related knowledge and information in the service knowledge management system (SKMS) Designs for service strategy processes and procedures	Vision and mission Service portfolio Policies Strategies and strategic plans Priorities Service charters, including service packages and details of utility and warranty Financial information and budgets Documented patterns of business activity and user profiles Service models
Service transition	Transitioned services Information and feedback for business cases and the service portfolio Response to change proposals Service portfolio updates Change schedule Feedback on strategies and policies Financial information for input to budgets Financial reports Knowledge and information in the SKMS	Vision and mission Service portfolio Policies Strategies and strategic plans Priorities Change proposals, including utility and warranty requirements and expected timescales Financial information and budgets Input to change evaluation and change advisory board (CAB) meetings
Service operation	Operating risks Operating cost information for total cost of ownership (TCO) calculations Actual performance data	Vision and mission Service portfolio Policies Strategies and strategic plans Priorities Financial information and budgets Demand forecasts and strategies Strategic risks

Lifecycle stage	Service strategy inputs (from the lifecycle stages in the first column)	Service strategy outputs (to the lifecycle stages in the first column)
Continual service improvement	Results of customer and user satisfaction surveys Input to business cases and the service portfolio Feedback on strategies and policies Financial information regarding improvement initiatives for input to budgets Data required for metrics, key performance indicators (KPIs), and critical success factors (CSFs) Service reports Requests for change (RFCs) for implementing improvements	Vision and mission Service portfolio Policies Strategies and strategic plans Priorities Financial information and budgets Patterns of business activity Achievements against metrics, KPIs, and CSFs Improvement opportunities logged in the CSI register

As part of the interaction with service design, there are inputs from service design to service strategy, with examples such as information for business cases, the service design package, and information in the service knowledge management system (SKMS).

Example outputs from service strategy to service design include the vision and mission, the service portfolio, policies and priorities, and financial information.

Example inputs from service transition include transitioned services, response to change proposals, change schedule, and knowledge and information in the SKMS.

Example outputs from service strategy include the service portfolio, policies, priorities, and financial information and budgets.

Input examples from service operation include operating risks, cost information, total cost of ownership, and actual performance data.

Output examples from service strategy service operation include the vision and mission, service portfolio, priorities, and strategic risks.

All lifecycle stages are subject to and interact with continual service improvement, and strategy is no different. Examples here include inputs of the results from customer satisfaction survey, financial information on improvement initiatives, and service reports. Output examples include the vision and mission, service portfolio, priorities, and patterns of business activity.

Summary

This chapter covered the elements of service strategy that are necessary to understand, use, and apply the processes within service strategy to create business value. We discussed the use of the knowledge, interpretation, and analysis of service strategy principles, techniques, and relationships and the application for creation of effective service strategies.

We explored the basics of service strategy, including how to decide on a strategy, and the impact the strategy may have, such as being able to outperform competitors. We reviewed the four Ps of service strategy and then went on to describe the terms and concepts for service value, including utility and warranty.

We considered the concepts relating to service assets and service providers, including the steps to define a service. We reviewed the Kano model, used to ensure customer satisfaction, and service economics, to understand the importance of return on investment and business impact analysis on service strategy.

Finally, we looked at the sourcing strategy and how service strategy relates to the rest of the service lifecycle.

Exam Essentials

Understand the importance of a service strategy.   Without a specific strategy to guide the approach to IT, there is a serious risk of mismanagement or not providing what the customer requires.

Know the basic approaches to choosing a strategy.   Understand the organizational requirements and constraints that are present when choosing a strategy.

Understand and expand on the features of opposing dynamics.   Be able to explain the concept of opposing dynamics—future versus present requirements, and operational effectiveness versus improvements.

Explain the four Ps of service strategy.   The four Ps of service strategy are *perspective* and vision of the customer, *position* relating to other providers, *plans* to meet business requirements, and *patterns* of business.

Understand and explain service value in the context of the organization.   Explain the use of the terms *utility* and *warranty* in the development of service value, when agreeing on a strategy.

Understand the use of assets and service providers.   Be able to explain how assets are allocated and used as part of the service strategy. Understand the types of service providers and how to select the most appropriate for the strategy.

Be able to explain the eight steps of defining a service.   Understand and explain the use of the eight steps in defining a service, from step 1, "Define the market and identify customers," through step 8, "Define service units and packages."

Understand and explain the Kano model.   The Kano evaluation model assists with the understanding of customer expectations and how a service provider can adapt its services to meet the changing customer environment.

Understand the use of service economics.   Understand the use of financial management and the approach to service economics as defined in the service lifecycle. It will not be necessary to be able to calculate return on investment as part of the examination.

Explain and justify the use of sourcing strategies.   Be able to explain and rationalize the use of the various sourcing strategies in given circumstances.

Recognize and explain the inputs and outputs of service strategy.   Be able to explain the position of the service strategy in relation to the other service lifecycle stages.

Review Questions

You can find the answers to the review questions in the appendix.

1. Which of these options represents the correct connection of concepts in the opposing dynamics of service strategy?

    1. Operational effectiveness versus improvement in functionality
    2. Future versus present
    3. Launch versus ongoing

    A. Only option 1
    B. Only option 2
    C. Options 1 and 2
    D. Options 1, 2, and 3

2. What is the definition of a business outcome?

    A. The result of carrying out an activity, following a process, or delivering an IT service
    B. Usually external service providers, where the service provider's outcomes are based on the customer's outcomes but are different
    C. Internal customers, where the outcome for the customer represents the overall business objectives of both the business unit and the service provider

3. Which of these is the correct set of service types as described in service strategy?

    A. Core, specialist, additional
    B. Core, specialist, enhancing
    C. Core, enabling, enhancing
    D. Key, enabling, enhancing

4. On what elements do customers calculate the economic value of a service?

    A. Value and financial reports
    B. Reference value and net difference
    C. Net difference and negative difference
    D. Reference value and positive difference

5. True or False? Utility means fit for purpose, and warranty means fit for use.

    A. True
    B. False

6. Which is the correct combination of concepts for the Type I service provider ? (Choose all that apply.)

    A. Shared services unit
    B. Provide services to many customers

    C. Embedded in the business unit it serves

    D. External service provider

    E. Internal service provider

    F. Provide services to multiple business units

7. Put these steps in the correct order to successfully define a service: Define services based on outcomes. Quantify the outcomes. Understand the opportunities. Agree service models. Understand the customer. Define the market and identify customers. Define service units and packages. Classify and visualize the service.

    A. Define service units and packages. Agree service models. Define the market and identify customers. Understand the customer. Quantify the outcomes. Classify and visualize the service. Understand the opportunities. Define service units and packages.

    B. Define the market and identify customers. Understand the customer. Quantify the outcomes. Classify and visualize the service. Understand the opportunities. Define services based on outcomes. Agree service models. Define service units and packages.

    C. Agree service models. Define the market and identify customers. Understand the customer. Quantify the outcomes. Classify and visualize the service. Understand the opportunities. Define service units and packages. Define services based on outcomes.

    D. Understand the customer. Define the market and identify customers. Quantify the outcomes. Classify and visualize the service. Understand the opportunities. Define services based on outcomes. Agree service models. Define service units and packages.

8. ROI is composed of three activities in ITIL. Which activity is performed during post-program ROI?

    A. Techniques for retroactively analyzing results of an investment

    B. Techniques for quantitatively analyzing a future investment

    C. Using a decision support and planning tool that projects the likely consequences of a business action

9. Which of these elements comprise the minimum requirements in a business case? (Choose all that apply.)

    A. Introduction

    B. Measurements

    C. Methods and assumptions

    D. Service targets

    E. Business impacts

    F. Availability requirements

    G. Risks and contingencies

    H. Geographic locations

    I. Recommendations

10. Which of these are valid sourcing structures described in ITIL? (Choose all that apply.)

    A. Cooperative working

    B. Multi-vendor sourcing

    C. Repeated vendor interaction

    D. Cloud

    E. Interactive sourcing

    F. Insourcing

    G. Co-sourcing

    H. Partnership

Chapter 3

Service Strategy Processes: Part 1

THE FOLLOWING ITIL INTERMEDIATE EXAM OBJECTIVES ARE DISCUSSED IN THIS CHAPTER:

✓ **The managerial and supervisory aspects of each of the service strategy processes. The processes examined include**

- Strategy management for IT services
- Service portfolio management
- Financial management for IT services

✓ **Each process is discussed in terms of**

- Purpose
- Objectives
- Scope
- Value
- Policies
- Principles and basic concepts
- Process activities, methods, and techniques
- Triggers, inputs, outputs, and interfaces
- Critical success factors and key performance indicators
- Challenges
- Risks

This chapter covers the managerial and supervisory aspects of service strategy processes. It excludes the day-to-day operation of each process, the detail of its activities, methods, techniques, and its information management. Strategy management is the process of defining and maintaining an organization's perspective, position, plans, and patterns with regard to its services and the management of those services. Service portfolio management ensures that we have the appropriate mix of services delivered by the service provider to meet the requirements of the customer. Financial management is concerned with the understanding of costs for IT services, including justification of expenditure of those services.

The two other processes in service strategy, business relationship management and demand management, are described in the next chapter.

Understanding Strategy Management for IT Services

We start by looking at the definition of this process.

Strategy management for IT services is the process of defining and maintaining an organization's perspective, position, plans, and patterns with regard to its services and the management of those services. We discussed the four *P*s of service strategy in the previous chapter, so you should be familiar with what they mean. Here they are applied to deciding what services are to be offered and how these services will be managed. Strategy management is an important process because it ensures that the service provider defines a strategy and then takes action to ensure that it achieves its purpose. Without this process, a service provider may miss opportunities or "drift" without a clear direction and may offer services without evaluating whether they are appropriate.

Purpose

The purpose of a service strategy is to devise and describe how a service provider enables an organization to achieve its business outcomes; it describes how to decide which services to offer and how these services should be managed. Strategy management for IT services ensures that there is such a strategy and defines, maintains, and periodically evaluates the strategy to ensure that it is achieving its purpose.

Objectives

The objectives of service strategy management are as follows:

- To consider the environments (both internal and external) in which the service provider operates. The aim is to identify opportunities that could be of benefit to the organization.

- To identify any constraints that would impact the ability of the business to achieve its desired outcomes or hamper the delivery or management of services and to identify how those constraints could be removed or their effects reduced.

- To agree on the perspective of the service provider and to ensure it remains relevant so that a clear statement of the vision and mission of the service provider can be defined.

- To understand the position of the service provider relative to its customers and other service providers, enabling the definition of the services to be delivered to each of the market spaces. The service provider will also understand how to maintain a competitive advantage over other providers.

- The final objectives cover the strategic plans. A library of critical documents should be produced, maintained, and distributed to relevant stakeholders. These should include the IT strategy document, the service management strategy document, and strategy plans for each service.

It is essential that these strategic plans are translated into tactical and operational guidance that is practical for the relevant department or group responsible for delivery. As with all key documents, processes should be in place to ensure that the documents are updated as circumstances change.

Scope

Now let's consider the scope of service strategy management. Strategy management for an organization is the responsibility of the executives who set the objectives of the organization and prioritize the necessary investments to enable these objectives to be met. Large organizations will have a dedicated strategy and planning manager who reports directly to the board of directors and is responsible for the assessments, the strategy documents, and the execution of the strategy.

It is important to realize that an organization's strategy is not limited to a single document but is more likely to be broken down into a strategy for each unit of the business. You can see an example of how a business strategy might be broken down into strategies for IT and for manufacturing in Figure 3.1. The achievement of each of these enables the overall strategy to be met.

Strategy management for IT services has to ensure that the services and the way they are managed support the overall enterprise strategy.

FIGURE 3.1 Overall business strategy and the strategies of business units

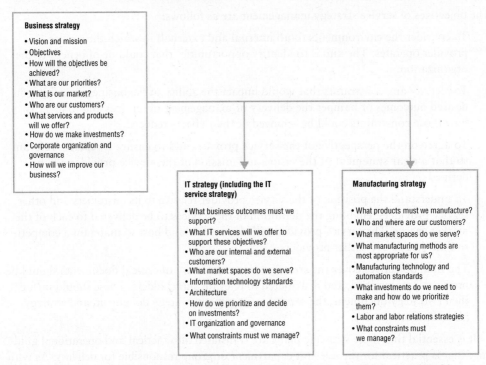

Strategy management can be a generic process that could be applied to the business as a whole or to any of the business units. However, ITIL is specifically concerned with how this process is applied to IT as a service provider. You should note that for an external service provider, the business strategy might be related to IT services delivered to an external customer and the IT strategy would be related to how those services will be delivered and supported. At the same time, external service providers do not just provide IT services to customers. They are also consumers of their own (and potentially other third-party) IT services. External service providers also have internal IT service requirements that must be met to enable them to survive.

A service strategy is a subset of the overall strategy for the organization. In the case of an IT organization, the IT strategy will encompass the IT service strategy.

The scope of strategy management in ITIL is shown in the diagram in Figure 3.2. You can see how a business strategy is used to develop a set of tactics (a set of detailed approaches, processes, and techniques to be used to achieve the strategic objectives) and operations (the specific procedures, technologies, and activities that will be executed by individuals and teams).

FIGURE 3.2   The scope of strategy management

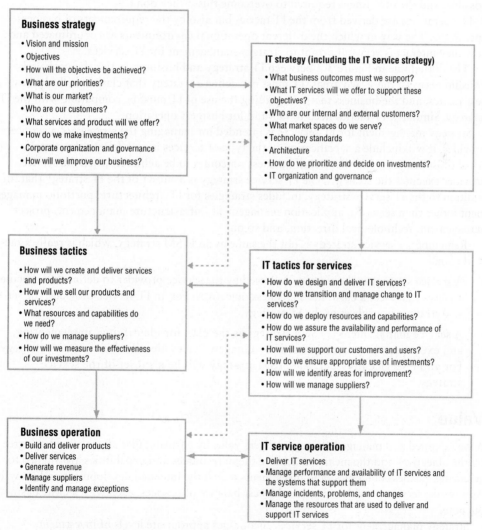

The IT strategy (and therefore also the strategy for IT services) (the top box in the column on the right) is derived from the requirements of the business strategy. The IT strategy can determine whether a strategic objective is technologically possible, and the level of investment required, so that the business has the information upon which to base a decision on whether the objective should be included and at what priority.

IT tactics are influenced by both IT strategy and the business tactics. If a business tactic requires compliance with a regulation, IT will have to ensure that the IT tactics make this possible, and the investment required to overcome this if they don't.

IT operations are derived from the IT tactics but also by the requirements of business operations. The way in which the different operational environments are coordinated and how they interact is very important to strategy management for IT services.

The dotted line in Figure 3.2 between IT strategy and business tactics shows the relationship between these two areas. IT must not define a strategy that clashes with the business tactics, and the business tactics regarding the use of IT must be compatible with the IT strategy. Similarly, IT tactics need to be valid for business operation.

Strategy management for IT services is intended for managing the strategy of a service provider. It will include a specification of the type of services it will deliver, the customers of those services, and the overall business outcomes to be achieved when the service provider executes the strategy. The IT service strategy is a subset of the IT strategy that, in addition to the IT service strategy, includes strategies for IT architecture, portfolio management (other than services), application management, infrastructure management, project management, technological direction, and so on.

Remember, a service strategy is not the same as an ITSM strategy, which is really a tactical plan.

- A service strategy is the strategy followed by the service provider to define and execute services that meet a customer's business objectives. For an IT service provider, the service strategy is a subset of the IT strategy.

- A service management (ITSM) strategy is the plan for identifying, implementing, and executing the processes used to manage services identified in a service strategy. For an IT service provider, the ITSM strategy will be a subset of the service strategy.

Value

A well-defined and managed strategy delivers value by ensuring that all stakeholders agree on the objectives and the means to achieve them; resources and capabilities are aligned to achieving business outcomes, and investments match the intended development and growth. As a result, service providers provide the best balance of services, each with a clear business purpose.

Strategy management for IT services encourages appropriate levels of investment, resulting in the following outcomes:

- Cost savings; investments and expenditure are matched to achievement of validated business objectives rather than unsubstantiated demands.

- Increased levels of investment for key projects or service improvements.
- Shifting investment priorities.

Without a strategy, there is a real danger that whoever shouts loudest gets to decide what happens and services (and expenditure) are matched to unproven demand.

Sometimes, what the customer is asking for requires a departure from the service provider's strategy. An external service provider needs to decide whether to change its strategy or to turn down the business. An internal provider does not usually have the second option, and in these cases, strategy management for IT services will enable the internal provider to work with the business units to make them aware of the impact of their demand on the current strategy. In some cases, customer demands do not change the overall strategy but may involve a change in priorities.

Policies, Principles, and Basic Concepts

The previous chapter defined and explained service strategy in detail. This chapter includes a generic model for defining, executing, and measuring service strategy, which can be applied at the most senior level or as the strategy for just a part of the organization.

The role of the service strategy will differ between different types of service provider; for external service providers, whose core business is providing services, the service strategy will be the central component of the organization's overall strategy.

In contrast, for internal service providers, the service strategy supports the overall enterprise strategy. It forms one of a number of tactical plans for the achievement of the organization's overall strategy. The organization's overall strategy may be at risk of failing if the IT strategy fails to support it. The issue causing the IT strategy failure must be addressed or the strategy must be altered to what is achievable.

The first use of the process must be correctly scoped, and it is particularly important that senior executives are seen to be behind the initiative. Over time, incremental improvements can be made.

Process Activities, Methods, and Techniques

In Figure 3.3, you can see the high-level strategy management process, which we are going to examine in depth. The process is divided into three areas:

- Strategic assessment
- Strategy generation
- Strategy execution

Each area covers a number of steps.

Strategic Assessment

Let's start with looking at the strategic assessment area. Organizations exist in ever-changing environments. The changes have to be assessed for their impact, and the strategy has to be adjusted if required. This stage establishes the current situation and identifies possible changes that could impact service provision. The assessment identifies constraints that could limit the service provider in achieving its current goals.

FIGURE 3.3   The strategy management process

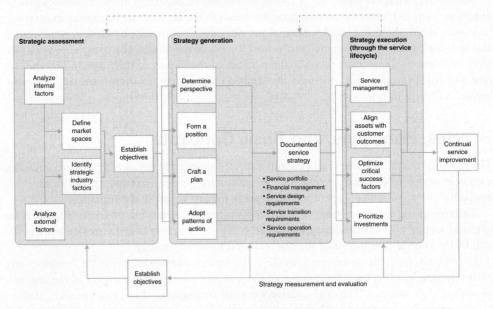

The strategic assessment analyses both the internal environment (the service provider's own organization) and the external environment (the world with which the service provider's organization interacts) and then arrives at a set of objectives that will be used to define the actual strategy. There are five steps to this process:

1. Analyze the internal environment.

2. Analyze the external environment.

3. Define market spaces.

4. Identify strategic industry factors.

5. Establish objectives.

The starting point is to identify the service provider's strengths and weaknesses through an internal analysis. Strengths that can be exploited need to be identified, and consideration should be given to how any weaknesses might be tackled. A service provider would address the following typical categories when analyzing strengths and weaknesses:

Existing Services   Identify what differentiates you from other service providers. What are your distinctive capabilities and core competencies?

Financial Analysis   How much do your services cost, and what is the return on investment?

Human Resources   What skills and capabilities do you have as a service provider? Do you use contract staff who may leave, or do you develop skills in-house?

Operations   How efficient and effective are you at actually supporting and delivering services and managing the technology?

Relationship with the Business Units (for Internal Service Providers)   Is there a good understanding of the customer strategy and requirements? How effectively are you enabling that strategy?

Resources and Capabilities   What resources and capabilities exist, and how are they currently used?

Existing Projects   Are there any current projects addressing any of these areas?

The next step is to analyze the external environment. The diagram in Figure 3.3 shows the most important external factors for a service provider to consider. Internal analysis focuses on strengths and weaknesses, while external analysis focuses on opportunities and threats.

The following external factors should be considered:

Industry and Market Analysis   This analysis focuses on trends in the service provider's industry. For example, are organizations investing more in e-commerce than retail stores? Is there a move toward a new type of technology?

Customers   Who are the customers? What are their challenges and opportunities? What are their strategies? How good is the service provider's relationship with them? What services are they using and why, and will this change?

Suppliers   Who are the suppliers? What changes are they forecasting for their products and services? What will the impact of this be on the service provider's services?

Partners   Is the service provider in a partnership with another organization? What benefits and risks does this bring?

Competitors   How does the service provider compare with its competitors? Is there anything to be learned from their success? Are they gaining or losing ground?

Legislation and Regulation   What legislation or standard will impact the way the service provider works (for example, Sarbanes-Oxley, ISO/IEC 27001)? Could the service provider use its compliance with these as differentiators?

Political   Could political changes have an impact? For example, increased or reduced public expenditure could affect demand, and changes in taxation could impact profitability. Does the service provider provide services in politically unstable areas?

Socioeconomic   Will cyclical changes in the economy affect demand for the services? Will the service provider have to reduce headcount, find efficiencies, and so on should demand fall in a recession?

Technology   How will new technology change how services are delivered or the services themselves?

The technique used here that assesses the organization's relationship to both internal and external factors is called SWOT analysis (which stands for strengths, weaknesses, opportunities, and threats). This is discussed in detail later in the chapters covering ITIL guidance for continual service improvement.

Next we define market spaces. These were described in the previous chapter. Market spaces offer opportunities where a service provider can deliver value to its customer(s). As part of strategy management, current and potential market spaces should be documented. A service provider may want to move away from some existing spaces because they are no longer desirable or profitable or competition is too strong. For each market space, the service provider should decide the following:

- Which services to offer and to whom
- Critical success factors (CSFs)
- Service models, service assets
- The service pipeline and catalog

Internal and external providers will be influenced differently by priorities and strategic value, the investments required, the differing financial objectives, the risks involved, and any policy constraints.

Identifying strategic industry factors is the next step. Every market space has critical factors that determine the success or failure of the strategy. These are influenced by customer needs, business trends, competition, regulatory environment, suppliers, standards, industry best practices, and technologies. From these influences, the service provider can identify CSFs. The CSFs determine the service assets required to implement the strategy successfully.

The final step in the strategic assessment stage is to establish objectives. These are the results the service provider expects to achieve by pursuing a strategy. Once the objectives have been defined, the service provider will need to define how it will achieve the anticipated results. This is the strategy. Clear objectives facilitate consistent decision-making, minimizing later conflicts. They set forth priorities and serve as standards.

Meaningful objectives are based on the outcomes customers desire to achieve. Objectives must provide the service provider with the capability to determine how best to satisfy these outcomes, especially those that are currently underserved. It is therefore important that objectives are not only derived from the overall strategic assessments, they must also take into account specific input from customers. Customer input for creating objectives consists of three distinct types of data and will help the service provider to identify exactly how it creates value:

Customer Tasks   What task or activity is the service to carry out? What job is the customer seeking to execute?

Customer Outcome   What outcomes is the customer attempting to obtain? What is the desired outcome?

Customer Constraints   What constraints may prevent the customer from achieving the desired outcome? How can the provider remove these constraints?

Organizations without clear objectives suffer from the following:

- Managing by crisis. This is based on the belief that the ability to solve problems effectively is a good strategy. The service provider is reactive, driven by events without a plan.

- Managing by reacting to customer demand without questioning if this is the right approach.

- Managing by extrapolation (keep doing what you are doing because it seems to work, but for no other reason, and you may be caught unaware of changes in the industry until too late).

- Managing by hope. Making decisions on the belief they will ultimately work out.

- Managing by best effort, that is, doing one's best to accomplish what should be done. There is no plan or understanding and no way to show the value.

Objectives should be SMART, meaning they should have the following characteristics:

Specific   Objectives should clearly state what the strategy is or is not going to achieve.

Measurable   Managers should be able to assess whether the objective has been met.

Achievable   It must be possible to meet the objective.

Relevant   The objective must be consistent with the culture, structure, and direction of the organization.

Time-bound   The overall timing for achieving the strategy is contained in the vision statement. Each individual objective could have different timing, and if this is the case, these should be clearly stated.

The following list includes some other good advice in this area:

- Don't have too many objectives.

- Use a hierarchy of primary and secondary objectives, with each high-level objective incorporating up to three secondary objectives.

- Keep them simple. Each objective should be easy to read and understand. This will help keep the service provider focused and will also make it easier to sell the strategy to other stakeholders.

- Avoid ambiguity. The objectives should be simply stated but clear.

- Be positive, but state the negative. Objectives will state what the strategy is going to achieve, but it is sometimes clearer and less ambiguous to state what the organization is not going to achieve. This will help in setting expectations.

There are many reasons objectives are not achieved. The following are among the most common:

- The objective is not well designed.

- Different groups had differing expectations.

- There is lack of ownership of the objectives.

- Organizational changes, politics, environmental changes, and other internal or external factors are present.

Some of these, such as differing expectations, can be prevented by stating objectives without ambiguity. This chapter has included guidance on how to design objectives effectively; some factors are outside the service provider's control.

Strategy Generation

Once the assessment has been completed and the service provider has defined the objectives of the strategy, it is possible to generate the actual strategy in terms of the four Ps described in Chapter 2, "Service Strategy Principles":

- *Perspective* clarifies the direction, making it easier to motivate people, coordinate actions, and ensure that all views are represented.

- *Position* is about what differentiates the provider from other providers. It details which services are to be provided, at what level, and to whom.

- *Plans* are deliberate courses of action toward strategic objectives, and describe how the organization will move from one point to another.

- Finally, *patterns* include the management systems, organizational structures, policies, processes, procedures, budgets, and formal interactions between service provider staff and their customers.

Strategy Execution

The agreed strategy now needs to be executed. Detailed tactical plans will define how this is done. These plans describe how the strategy will be achieved,

All service management processes have a role to play in executing a strategy because they are all about achieving the vision, objectives, and plans defined in strategy management. In a very real sense, the other stages of the service lifecycle all have to do with strategy execution. It is usual for a strategy to be linked to a set of formal projects.

Part of executing the strategy is communicating it. Typically, this communication would include the following:

- Distributing a copy of the plan to every executive and key stakeholder. This may just be a summary, excluding any confidential areas.

- Providing board members or IT steering group members with "talking points" guidance on the key points to be communicated and how to ensure compliance in their area of the organization.

- Publicizing key aspects of the strategy, such as vision, mission, and main objectives, through posters, screen savers, and so on.

- Including the strategy in policies, procedures, and employee manuals where relevant and using the strategic objectives to decide upon the KPIs to be used when assessing staff performance.

- Providing key strategic partners, such as vendors and investors, with a summary of plans and a briefing about how they are expected to use them.

Service management processes enable the service provider to achieve alignment between the services and the desired outcomes on an ongoing basis. Other service management processes contribute to strategy execution in three ways:

- They provide a management system that formalizes how the service provider will manage services.
- The strategy defines a number of opportunities, and the service management processes define the services to meet those opportunities.
- They define an action plan for how services will be managed.

Where other components of service management are absent or incomplete, the strategy must include a formal project to rectify the situation. Strategy execution relies on the ability of the service provider to know what service assets they have, where they are located, and how they are deployed. Service assets must be coordinated, controlled, and deployed so that they can provide the appropriate levels of service while ensuring that assets are being used efficiently.

The service provider needs to be able to describe the services, how they are being provided, and to which customers. This information is held in the service portfolio, along with information about which business outcomes each service enables. The service portfolio also identifies who the service owner is and who is involved in delivering and supporting the service. We look at the service portfolio later in this chapter in the section "Understanding Service Portfolio Management."

Triggers, Inputs, Outputs, and Interfaces

Next, we consider the triggers for the process, the inputs used, and the outputs that result from it. We will also examine how this process interfaces with others.

Triggers

Triggers for strategy management for IT services are as follows:

Annual Planning Cycles   Strategy management for IT services is used to review and plan on an annual basis.

New Business Opportunities   Strategy management for IT services is used to analyze and set objectives, perspectives, positions, plans, and patterns for new business or service opportunities.

Changes to Internal or External Environments   Strategy management for IT services will assess the impact of environmental changes on the existing strategic and tactical plans.

Mergers or Acquisitions   The merger with or acquisition of another company will trigger a detailed analysis and definition of the strategy of the new organization.

Inputs

Strategy management for IT services has the following inputs:

- Existing plans and any research on aspects of the environment by specialized research organizations
- Vendor strategies and product road maps that indicate the impact (and possible opportunities) of new or changing technology

- Customer interviews and strategic plans to indicate potential future requirements and the service portfolio to indicate the current and planned future service commitments

- Service reporting to indicate the effectiveness of the strategy and audit reports that indicate compliance with (or deviation from) the organization's strategy

Outputs

The following lists include the outputs of strategy management for IT services:

- Strategic plans—in this context, especially the service strategy and tactical plans that identify how the strategy will be executed.

- Strategy review schedules and documentation, along with any mission and vision statements.

- Another output is a set of policies that show how the plans should be executed and how services will be designed, transitioned, operated, and improved.

- The final output is a list of strategic requirements for new services and input into which existing services need to be changed. Strategy management for IT services will also articulate what business outcomes need to be met and how services will accomplish this.

Interfaces

Strategy management for IT services interfaces and directs all service management processes, either directly or indirectly:

Service Portfolio Management   Strategy management provides the guidelines and framework within which the service portfolio will be defined and managed. Specifically, it provides the objectives, policies, and limits that must be used to evaluate every new service or strategic change to an existing service. The service portfolio provides strategy management for IT services with important information about the type of services currently in the service pipeline or service catalog and what strategic objectives they have been designed to meet. This will assist in the strategic assessment and also in evaluating current and future market spaces.

Financial Management   Strategy management for IT services provides input to financial management to indicate what types of returns are required and where investments need to be made. Financial management, in turn, provides the financial information and tools to enable strategy management for IT services to prioritize actions and plans.

Service Design   Although strategy management for IT services does not define detailed service design requirements, it does provide input to service design. Specifically, it identifies any policies that must be taken into account when designing services, any constraints within which the design teams must work, and a clear prioritization of work. Service design processes will provide feedback into strategy management for IT services to enable measurement and evaluation of the services being designed.

Service Transition   Strategy management for IT services enables service transition to prioritize and evaluate the services that are built to ensure that they meet their original intent and strategic requirements. If any variation is detected during service transition, it will need to be fed back to strategy management for IT services so that the existing strategy can be reviewed or a decision can be made about the priority and validity of the service.

Knowledge Management   Knowledge management plays an important part in structuring information that is used to make strategic decisions. It allows strategic planners to understand the existing environment and its history and its dynamics and to make informed decisions about the future.

Service Operation   Although strategy management for IT services is quite far removed from daily operations, there are some important linkages, especially in terms of the execution of strategic priorities and in the ability to measure whether the strategy is being met. Operational tools and processes must ensure that they have been aligned to the strategic objectives and desired business outcomes. Additionally, the monitoring of operational environments should be instrumented so that the execution of operational activities indicates whether or not the strategy is effective. For example, if a strategic objective is that a new opportunity can result in 10,000 new customers per month, the operational activity required to meet this demand should match what was anticipated.

Continual Service Improvement   Continual service improvement (CSI) will help to evaluate whether the strategy has been executed effectively and whether it has met its objectives (i.e., CSI activities will measure compliance with the strategic plans and policies, and they will also measure whether the anticipated results were achieved). Any deviation will be reported to strategy management for IT services, which will work on improving the process or on adjusting the strategy.

Critical Success Factors and Key Performance Indicators

We now cover CSFs and KPIs and look at some examples for strategy management.

- Critical success factors (CSFs) are the conditions that need to be in place, or things that need to happen, if the process is to be considered successful. Each CSF will include examples of key performance indicators (KPIs).

- KPIs are metrics that are used to evaluate factors that are crucial to the success of the process. KPIs should be related to CSFs.

- CSFs should be based on the organization's objectives for the process, and the KPIs should be appropriate for its level of maturity, its CSFs, and its particular circumstances.

- Achievement against KPIs should be monitored and used to identify opportunities for improvement, which should be logged in the CSI register for evaluation and possible implementation.

We will cover some examples; the full list is available in the *ITIL Service Strategy* publication. Here are some sample CSFs for strategy management for IT services and some associated KPIs:

- CSF: "The ability to identify constraints on the ability of the service provider to meet business outcomes and to deliver and manage services, and the ability to eliminate these constraints or reduce their impact."
    - KPI: Number of corrective actions taken to remove constraints, and the result of those actions on the achievement of strategic objectives.
- CSF: "The service provider has a clear understanding of their perspective, and it is reviewed regularly to ensure ongoing relevance."
    - KPI: Vision and mission statements have been defined, and all staff members have been trained on what they mean in terms of their roles and jobs within the organization.
    - KPI: Each business unit has a strategic plan that clearly shows how the business unit's activities are linked to the objectives, vision, and mission of the organization.

Challenges

The following challenges exist for strategy management for IT services:

- Conducted at the wrong level; should be driven by senior executives
- Lack of accurate information about the external environment
- Lack of support by stakeholders
- Lack of the appropriate tools or a lack of understanding of how to use the tools and techniques identified in this chapter
- Lack of the appropriate document control mechanisms and procedures
- Operational targets that are not matched to the strategic objectives, leading to operational managers striving to achieve targets that are not in support of the strategy

Risks

The risks to strategy management for IT services are as follows:

- A flawed governance model allows managers to decide which aspects of a strategy to implement or to deviate from the strategy for shorter-term goals.
- Short-term priorities override the directives of the strategy.
- Strategic decisions are made based on information that has not been validated and is incomplete, incorrect, or misleading.
- The wrong strategy is chosen; it is important that incorrect decisions are detected early and corrected.
- Deciding upon strategies is seen as an exercise that happens once a year and that has no bearing on what happens for the rest of the year.

- The metrics of each organizational unit must be aligned to those of the strategies.
- Managers and staff alike must be educated about the contents and objectives of the strategies at the appropriate level of detail.

Once a strategy has been finalized, it needs to be communicated. Typically this communication would include the following:

- Distributing a copy of the plan to every executive and key stakeholder. A summary, excluding any confidential areas that might be necessary, should be distributed rather than the full plan.
- Providing board members or IT steering group members with "talking points" guidance on the key points to be communicated, what points to emphasize, and how to ensure compliance in their area of the organization.
- Publicizing key aspects of the strategy, such as vision, mission, and main objectives, through posters, screen savers, and so on.
- The strategy including the goals and KPIs should be included in policies, procedures, and employee manuals where relevant.
- Providing key strategic partners, such as vendors and investors, with a summary of plans and briefing them about how they are expected to use them.

Understanding Service Portfolio Management

The following sections look at the service portfolio management process, which provides an important source of information for the management of services across the lifecycle.

Purpose

The purpose of this process is to ensure that the appropriate mix of services is delivered by the service provider to meet the requirements of the customer. The process enables us to track a number of important items of information about our services, including the investment that has been made and the interaction with other services.

The information captured in the service portfolio links the services being provided to the business outcomes they support. This ensures that activities across the whole of the lifecycle are aligned to ensure value is delivered to customers.

Objectives

The objectives of service portfolio management are as follows:

- Provide a process that allows an organization to manage its overall service provision. Through this process, the service provider develops mechanisms to investigate and decide which services to provide to its customers. This decision is based on the analysis of the potential return that could be generated and acceptable levels of risk.

- Maintain the definitive managed portfolio of services provided by the service provider. Each service should be identified, along with the business need and outcome it supports.

- Provide an information source that allows the organization to understand and evaluate how the IT services provided enable the organization to achieve its desired outcomes. It will also be a mechanism for tracking how IT can respond to organizational changes in the internal or external environments.

- Provide control over which services are offered, to whom, with what level of investment, and under what conditions.

- Track the organizational spend on IT services throughout their lifecycle, allowing for regular reviews of the strategy to ensure that the appropriate investment is being made for the chosen strategic approach.

- Provide information to enable decision-making regarding the viability of services and when they should be retired.

Scope

Service portfolio management has a very broad scope because it covers all the services a service provider delivers as well as those it is planning to deliver and those that have been retired from live operation.

Because the primary concern of the service portfolio management process is to understand if the services being provided are delivering value, the process should cover the ability to track investment and expenditure on services. This can then be compared to the desired business outcomes.

Internal and external service providers may have a different approach to the way they connect services to business outcomes. For an internal service provider, it will be necessary to work closely with the business units in the organization to compare the outcomes with the investment. External service providers are more likely to have this information captured as part of the agreement or contract that defines the relationship with the business. The services they provide are also more likely to be directly associated to revenue generation or support revenue generation services.

Service portfolio management should be responsible for evaluating the value of the services provided throughout the whole of their lifecycle. It is also important to be able to compare the merits of the existing services against those that are being planned or the benefits they provide in replacing retired services. In this way, we can be certain that the services provided meet the required business needs.

The Service Portfolio

We are now going to review the service portfolio itself, which is the output from the process. Figure 3.4 illustrates the components of the service portfolio. You should remember these from your foundation course; they are the service pipeline, service catalog, and retired services.

FIGURE 3.4   The service portfolio

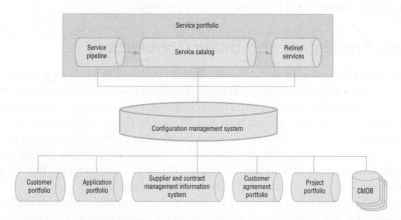

The service portfolio is the complete set of services managed by a service provider. This includes the contractual and financial commitments across internal, external, or third-party providers, new service development activity, and improvement initiatives. All services should be included, whether they are visible, customer-facing services such as the core or the enhancing services or the enabling services that support them.

The service portfolio also covers the services that are currently only in a conceptual stage, potentially the services that would be developed if there were no limit on budget, resources, or capabilities. The service portfolio shows the allocation of all the resources in use across the whole service lifecycle. Each stage of the lifecycle will be making demands on the available resources and capabilities, and the service portfolio allows us to see those allocations and resolve any potential conflicts according to the importance of the business outcomes.

Any new project or development should have an approved financial plan and allocated budget demonstrating the cost recovery or return on investment, and this will be captured in the service portfolio. By ensuring that we have the right mix of services across the pipeline and catalog, we can make sure we have the correct funding for all of the IT service provider activities across the service lifecycle.

As you will see later, the service catalog is the only part of the service portfolio that is customer facing, although the information it contains may be used as part of customer-facing reports, presentations, and business cases. The live operational services, as captured in the service catalog, are the only services that will recover costs or earn profits.

Value

Service portfolio management helps the business to decide where to invest. Services are implemented not just because they are a good idea or because they are an industry standard, but because there is a good business case. The expected outcomes are compared with the investment required to build and deliver a service. This means that customers understand what will be delivered and under what conditions; they can then decide whether the service is a good or bad investment.

The service provider, through the decisions made as part of service portfolio management, can help its customers achieve their business strategies.

Policies, Principles, and Basic Concepts

The service portfolio represents the commitments and investments made by a service provider across all customers and market spaces. It shows any contractual commitments and which new services are being developed. It will also include current service improvement plans initiated by CSI. Some services are not provided directly by the service provider, but bought in from suppliers. The service provider remains responsible for these third-party services, as they form an integral part of the customer service offering. An example of such a service would be the wide area networking service. It is important to note, therefore, that the portfolio includes the complete set of services that are managed by a service provider.

Service portfolio management ensures that the service provider understands all the services it provides, the investment that has been made in these services, and the objectives and required returns for each one. This knowledge is necessary before tactical plans for management of the services are made. The process plays a role in strategy generation, ensuring that the agreed strategy is appropriately executed at each stage. This prevents common mistakes such as choosing a new tool before optimizing processes. It also ensures what is actually done matches what was intended. The service portfolio management approach also helps managers to allocate resources in line with priorities.

The service portfolio also identifies the services that the organization would provide if it had unlimited resources, capabilities, and funding. This helps to identify what can and cannot be done. Every decision to provide a service uses resources that could have been spent on providing a different service, so the choice of what to prioritize and the implications of that choice in terms of the allocation of resources and capabilities are understood. It also ensures that the approval to develop potential services in the pipeline into catalog services is granted only with approved funding and a financial plan for recovering costs (internal) or showing profit (external).

The Service Pipeline

The service pipeline lists all services that are being evaluated as potential offerings or are actually being developed. The services in the pipeline are not yet available to customers, and the pipeline is not normally visible to customers. Investment opportunities are assessed in the pipeline. Services enter the pipeline under a number of circumstances:

- As a result of a customer request
- When the service provider identifies an opportunity, such as when a business outcome is underserved by current services
- As a result of new technology becoming available that could create new business opportunities
- When service management processes identify a better solution to the services that are currently offered
- When continual service improvement processes identify a gap in the current service portfolio

The service pipeline ensures that all of these opportunities are properly evaluated so that the potential returns can be judged against the investment required.

Service Catalog

The catalog is a database of information regarding the services available to customers—these may be already live, or those that are available for deployment. This part of the service portfolio is published to customers, and it includes information about deliverables, prices, contact points, and ordering and request processes. It is essential that due diligence is undertaken before a service is added to the catalog, so that the service provider understands how to deliver it successfully, and at the expected cost. The service catalog also contains details about standard service requests, enabling users to request those services using the appropriate channels. These requests may be channeled through a web portal and then routed to the appropriate request fulfilment procedure.

The service catalog also informs service portfolio management decisions, as it identifies the linkage between service assets, services, and business outcomes and any potential gaps in the service portfolio.

Take a look at Figure 3.5, which shows linkages between service assets, the services they support, and the business outcomes they facilitate:

- The boxes on the left are service assets used by the service provider to provide services. These could be assets such as servers, databases, applications, and network devices.

- The box in the middle shows the services in the service catalog. There are two layers of services shown. The layer on the left shows supporting services, which are usually not seen by the customer directly, such as application hosting (contained in a view of the service catalog called the technical or supporting service catalog). The second layer of services includes customer-facing services.

- The boxes on the right are business outcomes, which the business achieves when it uses these services.

FIGURE 3.5   The service catalog and linkages between services and outcomes

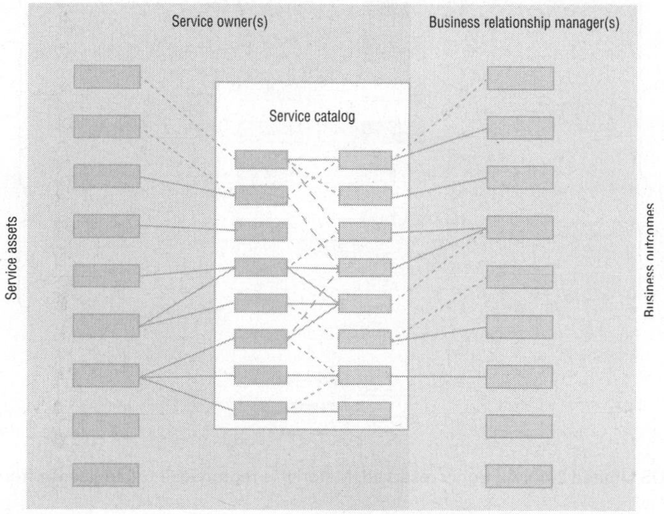

Services that are performing well and are popular are identified. They may be allocated additional resources to ensure that they continue to perform as required, and will be able to satisfy increased demand.

Services that are performing in an acceptable manner but could be improved in terms of efficiencies or functionality are deemed viable services. Introducing new attributes, addressing warranty or utility issues, improving how well they match demand, or setting new pricing policies are all approaches that may be used to make the services more popular.

 Services that are unpopular or which consistently perform badly are marked for retirement.

A subset of the service catalog may be third-party or outsourced services. These extend the range of the service catalog in terms of customers and market spaces. Figure 3.6 shows how these third-party services may be used as a stopgap to address underserved or unserved demand until items in the service pipeline are phased into operation. They may also be used to replace services being retired from the service catalog.

FIGURE 3.6   Service catalog and demand management

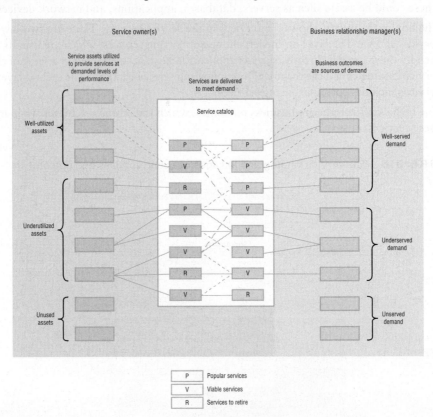

A comparison of the typical content and purpose of the service portfolio and service catalog is illustrated in Figure 3.7.

FIGURE 3.7 Service portfolio and service catalogs

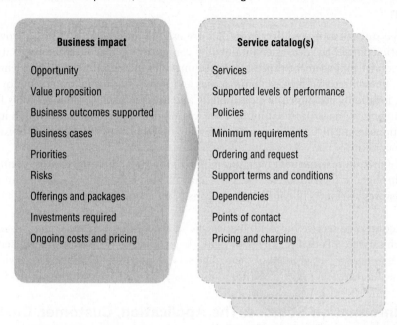

Business impact	Service catalog(s)
Opportunity	Services
Value proposition	Supported levels of performance
Business outcomes supported	Policies
Business cases	Minimum requirements
Priorities	Ordering and request
Risks	Support terms and conditions
Offerings and packages	Dependencies
Investments required	Points of contact
Ongoing costs and pricing	Pricing and charging

Retired Services

Some services in the service portfolio are phased out or retired. Each organization should periodically review services to decide when to move a service from the catalog to retired. A decision may be made to phase out the provision of a service by ceasing to offer it to new customers, even though the service is still being delivered to existing customers. Other organizations will wait until there are no users for the service to move the service out of the catalog.

Retired services are maintained in the service portfolio for a number of reasons:

- If the replacement service fails to meet all requirements, it may be necessary to be able to fall back to the previous service.

- When defining a new service, service portfolio management might realize that some functionality is available from a retired service. This could result in the service being reinstated to the service catalog.

- Regulatory requirements to maintain archived data may mean that the service required to access that data needs to remain available. In this case the information is exported to a read-only database for future use.

The retirement of a service should be managed through service transition to ensure that all customer commitments are fulfilled and service assets are released from contracts.

Other Information Sources: The Configuration Management System

The CMS is a set of tools and databases that are used to manage an IT service provider's configuration data. The CMS is maintained by configuration management and is used by all IT service management processes. It also includes information about incidents, problems, known errors, changes, and releases and may contain data about employees, suppliers, locations, business units, customers, and users. The CMS includes tools for collecting, storing, managing, updating, and presenting data about all configuration items and their relationships. The CMS is examined in more detail in the *ITIL Service Transition* publication.

A configuration management database (CMDB) is a database used to store configuration records throughout their lifecycle. The CMS may include one or more CMDBs, and each database stores attributes of configuration items (CIs) and their relationships with other CIs.

In the context of service portfolio management, the CMS records and controls data about each service, CIs that make up services, the people and tools that support services, and the relationships between all of them. The service portfolio is part of the service knowledge management system (SKMS) and is based on data from sources in the CMS.

Other Information Sources: The Application, Customer, Customer Agreement, and Project Portfolios

Next we cover some other information repositories that are used as part of service portfolio management. They are the application portfolio, the customer portfolio, the customer agreement portfolio, and the project portfolio:

- The application portfolio is a database or structured document used to manage applications throughout their lifecycle. It contains key attributes of all applications. Remember, applications and services are not the same thing. A single service like an online shop might use several applications, or an application might provide a number of services. It is important, therefore, to keep the application portfolio and the service portfolio as two distinct items.

  The application portfolio is usually an output from application development, which uses it for tracking investment in the applications. Having the information gathered into the application portfolio helps to prevent duplication—when a new request is made, existing applications can be checked to see if they could satisfy the requirement or be amended to do so. It is also helpful when tracking who is responsible for a specific application. It identifies which customers and which services use each application. It plays a very important role in service portfolio management, firstly because it links strategic service requirements and requests to specific applications or projects within application development. Secondly, it enables the organization to track investments in a service at all stages of the service lifecycle. Finally, it enables application development and IT operations to coordinate their efforts and facilitates greater cooperation throughout the service lifecycle.

Everything in the application portfolio should have gone through the service portfolio management process, and so every entry in the application portfolio should be linked to one or more entries in the service portfolio.

- The customer portfolio is a database or structured document maintained by the business relationship management process; we will look at it in more detail when considering that process in Chapter 4 "Service Strategy Processes: Part 2." It is the business relationship manager's view of the customers who receive services from the IT service provider. Service portfolio management uses the customer portfolio to capture the relationship between business outcomes, customers, and services. The service portfolio shows these linkages and is validated with customers through business relationship management.

- The customer agreement portfolio is another database or structured document. It is used to manage service contracts or agreements between an IT service provider and its customers. Each IT service delivered to a customer should have a contract or other agreement that is listed in the customer agreement portfolio. Even where SLAs are not being used, customer expectations regarding the services provided should be formally documented. The customers should agree to what has been documented.

  - External service providers track the legal contractual requirements using the customer agreement portfolio. This will link the requirements to the service portfolio and customer portfolio.

  - Internal service providers will use the customer agreement portfolio to track SLAs and less formal agreements. They can then ensure that they are able to meet customer expectations. By documenting the customer expectations, any "creep" in requirements can be prevented unless there is a justified (and funded) need.

- The project portfolio is a database or structured document used to manage projects that have been chartered. A charter is a document authorizing the project and stating its scope, terms, and references. The project portfolio is used to coordinate projects, ensuring that objectives are met within time and cost and to specification. It prevents duplication and scope creep, and ensures that resources are available for each project. The project portfolio can be used to manage both single projects and large-scale multiple-project programs. The project portfolio is usually maintained by a project management office (PMO) in larger organizations. Most organizations will use a separate project portfolio for IT projects, but some include both business and IT projects. The project portfolio helps service portfolio management to track the status of these projects, to compare expenditure against what was expected, and ensure that the services are being built and designed as intended. The project portfolio will align and coordinate activities where several different projects relate to a single service.

Service Models

The concept of service models was discussed in detail in Chapter 2, but we'll look at it again now because it is an integral part of service portfolio management. Service portfolio management uses service models to analyze the impact of new services or changes to existing services. Service portfolio management will ensure that a service model is defined for every service in the pipeline. Service models are also valuable in assessing which existing service assets can support new services, thus enabling more efficiency through the use of the principle of "create once, use many times."

Service portfolio plays an important role in how assets are allocated, deployed, and managed. As you saw earlier, successful strategy execution depends on effectively aligning service assets to customer outcomes. The service portfolio and configuration management systems document the relationship between service assets, services, and business outcomes; each service in the service portfolio is expressed in the configuration management system as a set of service assets, performance requirements, standard operating procedures, functions, and SLAs.

Service Portfolio Management through the Service Lifecycle

Here we'll look briefly at the role played by service portfolio management across the rest of the service lifecycle. Although service portfolio management is a process within service strategy, it also plays an important part in every stage in the service lifecycle. We start by looking at its role in service design.

- In the service design lifecycle stage, service portfolio management ensures that design work is prioritized according to business needs and clarifies how the service will be measured by the business. It ensures that each service is clearly linked to the agreed business outcomes and that the service assets used and performance levels required of the service are documented. Together with demand management information, this gives a clear picture of when service will be required and the expected levels of demand. Service portfolio management helps the design team to focus on objectives, outcomes, and priorities. It also works with the PMO or project manager, ensuring that the services are built on time, to specification, and to budget.

- Service transition builds and tests the services that will be placed into the service catalog. Service portfolio management provides guidance to service transition on building, testing, and evaluating the service. Change management is used to authorize the move of a service into the service catalog. This authorization ensures that the final product is ready and can be supported, that it is technically feasible and financially viable, and that there is sufficient operational capability in place. Before adding items to the catalog, the impact on commitments made to customers needs to be assessed and sufficient resources and capabilities set aside to provide the service. If resources cannot be made available, the service may be prevented from going live.

- Service operation delivers the service in the service catalog part of the service portfolio. Service portfolio management provides operations with an understanding of the services and how and why they need to be delivered. This is an important input to defining standard operating procedures, event management, incident management priorities, and escalation procedures.

- Continual service improvement evaluates whether the services in the portfolio met the stated objectives, and if not, it identifies ways in which the situation can be rectified. Continual service improvement also evaluates the business cases and objectives to ensure that they are still valid and therefore that service portfolio management continues to prioritize services appropriately.

Process Activities, Methods, and Techniques

Service portfolio management consists of four main phases of activity. We are going to examine these one by one. The four stages are Define, Analyze, Approve, and Charter:

- The first stage is the Define stage. This phase focuses on documenting and understanding existing services and new services. Each service must have a documented business case. Data for each service, such as which service assets are required and where investments are made, needs to be validated.

- The second stage is the Analyze stage. The analysis of services in the portfolio will indicate whether the service is able to optimize value and how supply and demand can be prioritized and balanced.

- The third stage is the Approve stage. Every service needs to be approved, and the level of investment needs to be authorized to ensure sufficient resources to deliver the anticipated levels of service.

- The final stage is the Charter stage. A charter is a document authorizing the project and stating its scope, terms, and references. Services are not just built on request from anyone in the organization. They have to be formally chartered, and stakeholders need to be kept up-to-date with information about decisions, resource allocation, and actual investments made.

Before we look at the process in detail, it is important to remember how we define the service portfolio itself. We begin by collecting information from all existing services as well as every proposed service. However, the portfolio is not static, and so the data must be refreshed and validated on a recurring basis. How often this happens will depend on the portfolio itself: does it include stable, legacy systems with few changes or a fast-changing area? A reevaluation of the portfolio may be triggered by external events; for example, a merger with or acquisition of another company would require a thorough reevaluation to spot possible duplications.

New and changed service proposals can be initiated from a number of sources as a result of, for example, changes to plans or the identification of a service improvement plan. They need to be formally assessed and approved. Service portfolio management maintains a central record of all plans, requests, and submissions that are submitted. In some organizations, they are simply called requests, but they are *not* the same as standard service requests submitted for request fulfilment, which could lead to confusion. Inputs to service portfolio management may come from the following processes:

- Strategy management is the primary input to service portfolio management. It presents strategic plans outlining initiatives for business opportunities and outcomes along with the services these require. The plans are evaluated by service portfolio management for technical and financial feasibility and ROI.

- Business relationship management receives requests from customers. These may be dealt with through change management, request fulfilment, or incident management, but some will need to be submitted to service portfolio management. They include requests for new services or added functionality or performance improvements to existing services.

- CSI initiates three types of input to service portfolio management. They may include possible improvements to service levels of existing services. Each will be assessed in terms of the investment and the projected return. CSI may also identify new opportunities or gaps in the current portfolio of services or opportunities for improvements in cost, mitigation of risks, and so on, affecting one or several existing services or even the entire operation of the service provider. Note that any opportunities identified by CSI that would require a change in the organization's strategy are submitted to strategy management.

- Some service management processes involve managing changes to services or modeling warranty and utility options that can be presented to the customer. Many of these would have an impact on investment, so service portfolio management should evaluate these suggested changes before they are initiated.

 The change management process may be sufficient for some requests. Those with a significant impact on the existing levels of investment or achievement of business outcomes should be considered strategic and should be immediately referred to service portfolio management. This requires that service portfolio management and change management define thresholds for what constitutes a strategic issue.

Define the Portfolio

Before we examine the four phases of service portfolio management activity, we need to discuss the existing service portfolio. The existing services and new services need to be documented. This provides an initial inventory of services, which will need to be validated on a recurring basis, especially if the business requirements are changing quickly. Each service in the pipeline must have a documented business case and validated information showing which service assets are required and where investments are made. The desired business outcomes should be defined, with opportunities, utility and warranty requirements, and the services themselves as well as the anticipated investment required to achieve the outcomes.

If the case for approval is compelling, the proposed service will be approved and moved into the service design stage for design and development.

Changes to the portfolio may result from a new or changed strategy. Service portfolio management should consider the strategy to identify specific service opportunities and identify the stakeholders that will be consulted in defining the services. Another reason for changes to the portfolio may be a request from the business. Business relationship management is responsible for documenting these requests on behalf of the customer. Requests may come in different formats, from detailed proposals to informal ideas that can be formalized into standardized formats later. The requests are registered and customers kept updated on their status.

Another source of change to the service portfolio is a request for service improvement. CSI identifies improvement opportunities and builds service improvement plans (SIPs). These opportunities may concern changes to the services themselves, or the processes, people, and tools that support or deliver the services. They are submitted to service portfolio management because they impact the overall investment in providing services and will need to be allocated to the services at some stage.

Next we look at each of the four stages of service portfolio management in some more detail.

Define

The Define stage consists of the following:

- Any service suggestions that require significant investment or impact on the agreed utility and the warranty of a service are submitted to service portfolio management. Here are some examples:

    - New technology to improve performance, suggested by capacity management

    - A new recovery plan from IT service continuity management following the identification of a new business impact

    - Significant modification to the data center to improve availability

    - A suggested resolution to an intermittent problem that requires migration to a new platform

    - Changes to third-party services that could affect the service

 Changes to existing services are treated differently from new services. The existence of a service catalog will help determine if this is actually a new service to avoid duplication. When in doubt, the service should be treated as new.

- New services will be defined based on the information provided. At this stage, a detailed architecture or technical design is not necessary. Instead what is needed are definitions of the service's purpose, customers, consumers, inputs, outputs, high-level requirements, and the business activity it supports. Other requirements may include regulatory or legal requirements, standards to which it must conform, business outcomes, stakeholders, and the anticipated level of investments and returns. Finally, any constraints that need to be considered will be included.

- The service model will be defined. This is a high-level view of all of the components of the service, both customer assets and service assets, and how they fit together. The impact of a new service is assessed in terms of the current business outcomes, investment levels, service level agreements, existing warranty and utility levels, contractual obligations, patterns of business activity, and levels of demand. The impact of changes to an existing service is similarly assessed, especially the impact on the current service model.

Analyze

Each service is analyzed by linking it to the service strategy. Service portfolio management articulates how the perspective, position, plan, and patterns will be translated into actual services. The analysis to be carried out needs to be defined and understood to ensure that the correct data is collected. It will require input from multiple specialized areas.

Service portfolio management regularly reviews existing services to determine whether they still meet their objectives and the strategy of the organization. The review will also ensure that services in the service pipeline are properly defined, analyzed, approved, and chartered.

The output of this review feeds into the analysis of investments, value, and priorities. Sometimes service portfolio management discovers a new opportunity to be presented during the strategy management cycle as part of the strategy assessment stage. Financial management helps to quantify the investment and value of each service so they can be prioritized. Exact costs require a detailed service design, but the feasibility of the service can be assessed. The investment analysis and prioritization results are documented in the business case, which describes the opportunity, the potential business outcomes, and the investment the organization is prepared to make in the service; this information will be used to calculate ROI. The business case is the justification for pursuing a course of action to meet stated organizational goals; it assesses investment in terms of potential benefits and the resources and capabilities required.

Following the analysis, a decision is made regarding the feasibility of the service and whether it should be approved. This requires authorization for expenditure. (At this stage, this is outline approval only, because without a detailed design, the anticipated level of investment may be inaccurate.) There are six possible decisions:

- Retain/build
- Replace
- Rationalize
- Refactor
- Renew
- Retire

If the customer disagrees with the decision, it may want the service provider to move ahead anyway. Possible responses are likely to include a combination of the following:

- Explaining to the customer why the need cannot be fulfilled

- Explaining what is needed of the customer in terms of commitment, sponsorship, or funding for new service development

- Developing the service if the customer makes the necessary commitment

- Declining the opportunity if the customer cannot commit

- Considering supporting the customer in partnership with third parties

Approve

New services, or changes to existing services judged to be feasible, are submitted to change management for approval in the form of a change proposal; this will allow change management to coordinate the activities of all resources required to investigate the customer and infrastructure requirements before the change is approved or rejected. The change proposal should include the following:

- A high-level description

- Business outcomes

- The utility and warranty to be provided

- A full business case including risks, issues, and alternatives as well as budget and financial expectations

- The expected implementation schedule

The change proposal is submitted to change management, who investigates what the new or changed service will look like and what it will take to design, build, and deploy it. If feasible, the detailed design and deployment begins and service portfolio management drafts a service charter. Following a rejection, service portfolio management notifies all stakeholders and updates the service portfolio with the status.

Charter

The final activity in service portfolio is to charter new services. *Charter* has two meanings:

- The new service (or changes to the existing service) is said to be chartered once it has been commissioned by the customer or business executives.

- A document to authorize work to meet defined objectives, outputs, schedules, and expenditure may be called a charter. In service portfolio management, services are chartered using a service charter.

The service charter ensures that all stakeholders and staff have a common understanding of what will be built, by when, and at what cost. It will be an input into the project management process and will be entered into the project portfolio. It is important to ensure that stakeholders are kept informed of the progress of the project from charter to deployment; this helps to ensure their continued support and informs them of any delays or exceptions.

Updates to service portfolio management allow the process to monitor the levels of investment and capability. If cost significantly exceeds the estimate, service portfolio management will escalate the situation to the stakeholders.

Following deployment, the service will be reviewed to confirm that the service has met the requirements of the strategy and is contributing to the achievement of business outcomes as specified by the stakeholders. The services and investments in the portfolio should be held at least quarterly to ensure that they continue to meet the IT and overall organizational strategies. A disconnect between these may have arisen as a result of the following scenarios:

- Conditions and markets changing, invalidating prior ROI calculations
- Services becoming less optimal due to compliance or regulatory concerns
- Events occurring such as mergers and acquisitions, divestitures, new public legislation, or redeployed missions

Note that not all services need be low risk or high reward; an efficient portfolio with optimal levels of ROI and risk maximizes value.

Triggers

Triggers for service portfolio management are as follows:

- A new or changed strategy. A change to a perspective, position, or pattern of action might impact existing services or service models.
- Business relationship management receives a request for a new or changed service; service portfolio management would help define and formalize this request before submitting it to change management as a change proposal.
- Service improvement opportunities from CSI could involve service portfolio management. Any reported deviation from the specifications, cost, or release time from design, build, and transition teams during the charter stage of the process would involve service portfolio management in estimating the impact and defining corrective action.
- Service level management reviews identify a service failing to deliver its expected outcomes or being used in a different way from how it was intended; service portfolio management would be involved in defining corrective actions.
- Financial management reports that the costs for a service vary significantly from the expectation, thus impacting the potential return on investment for that service; again, service portfolio management would be involved in defining corrective actions.

Inputs

Service portfolio management has the following inputs:

- Strategy plans
- Service improvement opportunities

- Financial reports
- Requests, suggestions, or complaints from the business
- Project updates for services in the charter stage of the process

Outputs

The following list includes the outputs of service portfolio management:

- An up-to-date service portfolio
- Service charters authorizing the work for designing and building new services or changes to existing services
- Reports on the status of new or changed services
- Reports on the investment made in services in the service portfolio and the returns on that investment
- Change proposals to allow change management to assess and schedule the work and resources required to charter services
- Strategic risks that could be added to a central risk register

Interfaces

Interfaces include those with the following processes:

- Service catalog management. Service portfolio management determines which services will be placed into the service catalog, while service catalog management ensures that this is done.
- Strategy management for IT services defines the overall strategy of services; this determines what type of services should be included in the portfolio. It determines the objectives for investments in terms of anticipated returns and the ideal market spaces that will be targeted.
- Financial management for IT services provides information and tools to enable service portfolio management to perform return on investment calculations; it also helps to track the actual costs of services. This is used to improve the analysis of services and forecasts in the future.
- Demand management provides information about the patterns of business activity that is used to determine the utilization and expected return on investment for the service.
- Business relationship management initiates requests and obtains business information and requirements used in defining services and evaluating whether they would provide a sufficient return on investment. It keeps customers informed about the status of services in service portfolio management.
- Service level management ensures that services are able to achieve the levels of performance defined in service portfolio management and provides feedback when this is not the case.

- Capacity management and availability management ensure that the capacity and availability requirements of chartered services are designed and built.

- IT service continuity management identifies the business impact of risks associated with delivering the service and designs countermeasures and recovery plans to ensure that the service can achieve the objectives defined during service portfolio management.

- Information security management ensures that the confidentiality, integrity, and availability objectives defined during service portfolio management are met.

- The supplier management process identifies situations in which a supplier cannot continue to supply services or a supplier relationship is at risk.

- Change management evaluates the resources required to introduce new services or changes to existing services, thus enabling the service to be chartered. It ensures that all changes involved in designing, building, and releasing the service are controlled and coordinated.

- Service validation and testing ensures that the anticipated functionality and returns of each service can be achieved.

- Knowledge management enables IT managers and architects to make informed decisions about the best service options to meet the organization's objectives.

- Continual service improvement provides feedback about the actual use and return of services against their anticipated use and return. This information is used to improve services and make changes to the mix and availability of services in the service portfolio.

Critical Success Factors and Key Performance Indicators

Finally, we cover the CSFs and KPIs for this process. (Remember the explanation of these in the strategy management section.) We will cover some examples, but for the full list, see the *ITIL Service Strategy* publication:

- Critical success factor: "The existence of a formal process to investigate and decide which services to provide."
  - KPI: A formal service portfolio management process exists under the ownership of the service portfolio management process owner.
  - KPI: The service portfolio management process is audited and reviewed annually and meets its objectives.
- Critical success factor: "The ability to document each service provided, together with the business need it meets and the business outcome it supports."
  - KPI: A service portfolio exists and is used as the basis for deciding which services to offer. An audit shows that every service is documented in the service portfolio.
  - KPI: There is a documented process for defining the business need and business outcome, which is formally owned by the service portfolio management process owner.

- KPI: Each service in the service portfolio is linked to at least one business outcome. This is verified through a regular review of the service portfolio.

Challenges

Service portfolio management is presented with the following challenges:

- The lack of access to customer business information required to enable service portfolio management to understand the desired business outcomes and strategies
- The absence of a formal project management approach, which makes chartering and tracking services through the design and transition stages more difficult
- The absence of a project portfolio, which makes assessing the impact of new initiatives on new services or proposed changes to services difficult
- Difficulty in identifying objectives, use, and return on investment of services due to the lack of a customer portfolio and customer agreement portfolio
- A service portfolio focusing purely on the service provider aspects of services, which makes it difficult to calculate the value of services, to model future utilization, or to validate the customer requirements for the service
- The lack of a formal change management process to control the introduction of new services and manage changes to existing services

Risks

There are a number of risks to service portfolio management:

- Responding to customer pressure and offering services without validated or complete information and without a full investigation into the risks involved. Service portfolio management is concerned with reducing risks by having a complete understanding of the service being offered; a hurried response negates the whole process.
- Offering services without defining how they will be measured. Without agreeing to this, we cannot calculate the return on investment. A service may be delivering value, but this cannot be proved, making the service vulnerable to being discontinued due to cost cutting.

Understanding Financial Management for IT Services

In the following sections, we cover the financial management process in terms of its purpose, objectives, scope, business value, policies, principles, and basic concepts. We then look at the high-level process activities, methods and techniques, triggers, inputs, outputs, and interfaces for the process and its critical success factors and key performance indicators. Finally, we examine its challenges and risks.

Organizations have to be able to manage their finances, but it is a complex process used across an entire organization. It is normally owned by a very senior executive and managed as a separate business function. It is an extremely important area that allows organizations to manage resources and ensure that their objectives are being achieved.

The IT service provider, as part of the overall organization, must be involved in the financial management process. It is important to make sure all financial practices are aligned; although a separate process may be used for IT financial management, this process should follow the overall organizational principles and requirements.

Purpose of Financial Management

In order to design, develop, and deliver the services that meet the organizational requirements, we must secure an appropriate level of funding. This is the main purpose of financial management for IT services. At the same time, the financial management process should act as a gatekeeper for the expenditure on IT services and ensure that the service provider is not overextended financially for the services it is required to deliver. This will require a balance between the cost and quality of the service.

Cost and quality are key factors in the provision of services, and the only way we can allocate and understand the cost of service provision is through sound financial practices.

Objectives of Financial Management

The objectives of the financial management process are as follows:

- Defining and maintaining a financial framework that allows the service provider to identify, manage, and communicate the actual cost of service delivery.

- Understanding and evaluating the financial impact and implications of any new or changed organizational strategies on the service provider.

- Securing the funding that is required for the provision of the agreed services. This will require significant input from the business and will naturally be dependent on the overall approach to financial management and cross-charging within the organization.

- Facilitating good stewardship of service and customer assets to ensure that the organization meets its objectives. This should be done by working with service asset and configuration management and knowledge management.

- Performing basic financial accounting in respect to the relationship between expenses and income, and ensuring that these are balanced according to the overall organizational financial policies.

- Reporting on and managing expenditure for service provision on behalf of the stakeholders.

- Managing and executing the organization's policies and practices relating to financial controls.

- Ensuring that financial controls and accounting practices are applied to the creation, delivery, and support of services.

- Understanding the future financial requirements of the organization, and providing financial forecasts for service commitments and any required compliance for legislative and regulatory controls.

- If appropriate, defining a framework that allows for the recovery of the costs of service provision from the customer.

Scope of Financial Management

Financial management is normally a well-recognized activity in any organization, but the specific requirement to manage funding related to the provision of IT services may not be so well established.

It is important to understand the strategic approach that is adopted in relation to IT service provision. How will it be managed? Is it internally or externally sourced? If it's internally sourced, is there a requirement to cross-charge for services, or is there some other mechanism of cost recovery in place?

In the majority of organizations, there will be qualified accountants in charge of the corporate finances, usually as part of the finance department. They will set the policies, standards, and accounting practices for the business. The strategy relating to IT funding will be part of the overall accounting approach, but the specifics may be managed locally as part of the IT department.

Those engaged in financial management for IT services must ensure that the practices are consistent with the corporate controls and that reporting and accounting activities meet with the governance standards as defined for the whole organization. This will also assist with general understanding by the various business units of how IT is funded. Communication and reporting of internal funding practices across an organization is extremely important for enabling a true understanding of the costs of IT services.

Using a service management approach to delivering services should mean that the accounting for IT services is more effective, detailed, and efficient. For an internal service provider, this will enable a translation of the information between service provider and business.

Financial management consists of three main processes, budgeting, accounting, and charging.

Budgeting   This is the process of predicting and controlling the income and expenditure of money within an organization. Budgeting consists of a periodic cycle (usually annually) of negotiation to set budgets and the monthly monitoring of the same.

Accounting   This is the process that enables the IT organization to account fully for the way its money has been spent. It should enable a cost breakdown by customer, service, activity, or other factor to demonstrate the allocation of funds. It will normally require some form of accounting system (ledgers, charts of accounts, journal, etc.) and should be managed and overseen by someone with an accountancy qualification or skills.

Charging   This is the process required to bill customers for use of the services, and it will only be applicable where the organizational accounting model requires it to take place. It requires sound accounting practices and supporting systems so that any cross-charging is accurate and traceable.

The cycles associated with financial management are shown in Table 3.1. There are two cycles:

- A planning cycle (annual), where cost projections and workload forecasting form a basis for cost calculations and price setting
- An operational cycle (monthly or quarterly), where costs are monitored and checked against budgets, bills are issued, and revenue is collected

TABLE 3.1   Budgeting, IT Accounting and Charging cycles

Frequency	Budgeting	IT accounting	Charging
Planning (annual)	Agree on overall expenditure.	Establish standard unit costs for each IT resource.	Establish pricing policy and publish price list.
Operational (monthly)	Take actions to manage budget exceptions or changed costs.	Monitor expenditure by cost center.	Compile and issue bills.

Value

Many internal IT organizations now realize that they share several characteristics with external service providers. Both internal and external providers need to analyze, package, market, and then deliver services. Both need to understand and control supply and demand and ensure that their services are delivered as cost-effectively as possible.

Sound financial management for IT services provides the information the service provider needs to achieve:

- Enhanced decision-making
- Speed of change
- Service portfolio management
- Financial compliance and control
- Operational control
- Value capture and creation

Financial management provides the information needed to generate strategies or to devise new ways of using assets to achieve goals. It enables the business to understand the financial results of current strategies, as in the following examples:

- Has cutting our prices resulted in more business?
- Is that business profitable?
- Which services cost us the most, and why?
- How efficient are we compared to alternatives?
- Where could we improve?
- Which areas should we prioritize for CSI?

Good financial management results in a number of specific benefits to the business. It enables the business to comply with regulatory and legislative requirements and generally accepted accounting principles. This ensures that the business is operating legally and is not at risk of being fined for noncompliance. By understanding costs, a realistic budget can be prepared so that the money available is sufficient to cover the cost of service. Finally, the business has the information it needs to make sound business decisions regarding the use of and investment in IT.

Sound financial management also ensures that when it comes to charging for IT services, internal service providers can recover the full cost of service from the business if required. The business units will also have the information regarding the charges they need for preparing their own budgets. External providers can ensure that they charge customers a sufficient amount to cover costs and make a profit. Most fundamentally, by linking IT services to business outcomes, it ensures that all IT spending has a business justification.

Policies, Principles, and Basic Concepts

Financial management for IT services applies the financial management policies of the organization. It must therefore follow the policies and practices of the organization as a whole. It is a policy decision by the organization's executives whether IT is a profit center or a cost center. A cost center is a business unit or department to which costs are assigned, but it does not charge for services provided. It must account for expenditure. A profit center is a business unit that charges for providing services. A profit center can be created with the objective of making a profit, recovering costs, or running at a loss.

Funding

Funding is the sourcing and allocation of money for a specific purpose or project. For IT service management, funding is the means whereby an IT service provider obtains financial resources that pay for the design, transition, operation, and improvement of IT services.

Funding comes from two sources, external and internal:

- External funding comes from revenue that is received from selling services to external customers.
- Internal funding comes from other business units inside the same organization.

The funding models are as follows:

- Rolling plan funding. A rolling plan is a plan for a fixed number of months, years, or other cycles. At the end of the first cycle, the plan is simply extended by one more cycle.

- Trigger-based funding. In this model, a plan is initiated and funding is provided when a specific situation or event occurs.

- Zero-based funding. Most internal service providers are funded using this model because it is based on ensuring that IT breaks even. IT is allowed to spend up to the agreed budget amount, and at the end of the financial period (monthly, quarterly, or annually), the money is recovered from the other business units through cost transfers.

Value

The value of services can only be determined with clearly defined and properly executed practices for financial management for IT services. The calculation of value is a joint responsibility of both the service provider and the customer. They need to have a shared understanding of how costs and returns are calculated in order to be able to demonstrate the value of IT services.

We looked at value, calculating value, and the roles of the service provider and customer in defining value in more detail in Chapter 2.

Compliance

Compliance relates to the ability to demonstrate that proper and consistent accounting methods and/or practices are being employed. It is essential that enterprise financial management policies should clearly outline what legislative and other regulatory requirements apply to the service provider and the customer's organizations. Regulations such as Basel II and Sarbanes-Oxley have had enormous impact on financial audit and compliance activities.

Although this increases costs, regulatory compliance tends to improve data security and quality processes.

Process Activities, Methods, and Techniques

In Figure 3.8, you can see the financial management process. We are going to examine the high-level process steps of accounting, budgeting, and charging.

Accounting

First we will look at accounting. This is the process responsible for identifying the actual costs of delivering IT services, comparing the actual costs with budgeted costs, and managing variance from the budget. Accounting is also responsible for tracking any income earned by services. Accounting enables the service provider to do the following:

- Track actual costs against budget

- Support the development of a sound investment strategy that recognizes and evaluates the options and flexibility available from modern technology

- Provide cost targets for service performance and delivery

- Facilitate prioritization of resource usage

- Make decisions with full understanding of the cost implications and hence minimum risk
- Support the introduction, if required, of charging for IT services
- Review the financial consequences of previous strategic decisions to enable the organization to learn and improve

FIGURE 3.8   Major inputs, outputs, and activities of financial management for IT services

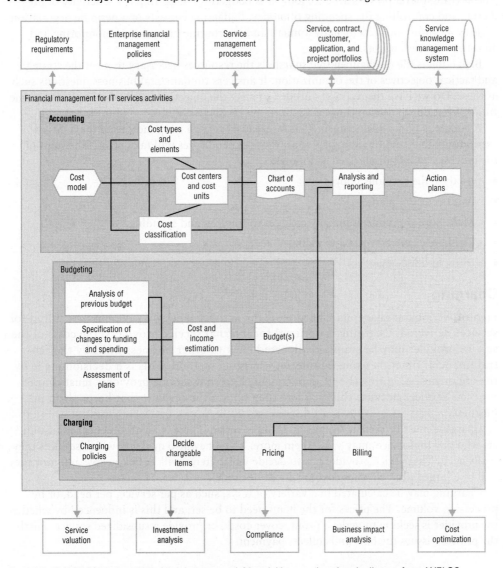

An important accounting activity is the creation of cost models. A cost model is a framework that allows the service provider to determine the costs of providing services and ensure that those costs are allocated correctly. It helps the provider understand the impact of proposed changes to the current service, customer, and customer agreement portfolios.

Budgeting

The next high-level process area we look at is budgeting. Budgeting is the activity of predicting and controlling the spending of money. Budgeting consists of a periodic negotiation cycle to set future budgets (usually annual) and the routine processes of monitoring and adjusting current budgets.

Budgeting is the mechanism that marshals the resources necessary to meet the strategic and tactical objectives of the organization. It answers fundamental business questions such as these: Do we have the resources needed to meet the objectives, and where will they come from? What do we need and when?

A budget is typically documented as a spreadsheet with rows indicating the items of expenditure and columns showing when those expenditures will take place. The steps of the process can be summarized as follows:

- Analyze the previous budget.
- Assess current plans.
- Make sure you understand any changes to funding and spending.
- Estimate expected costs and income.
- Draw up the budget.

Charging

Finally, we look at charging. Charging is the activity whereby payment is required for services delivered. Charging is optional for internal service providers; the costs of the service provider may be simply reallocated back to other business units by the central financial function using an internal charging method. This is a decision made by the organization, not by the IT department. External service providers must charge for their services because this is where they obtain the revenue that keeps them in business.

Charging must be seen as simple, fair, and realistic. There is an argument that customers who pay for services may value them more. They may also question which services they really need. The service provider has to decide which items will be chargeable and how they will be charged (that is, what cost units will be used?).

Charging may be calculated in a variety of ways, such as per service, per head, or by processing volume. The prices for the items need to be set, and this is influenced by whether the provider is seeking to make a profit, cover costs, or provide a subsidized service. Finally, the provider issues the bills and collects payment.

Triggers

The following triggers are associated with financial management for IT services:

- The organization will have its own monthly, quarterly, and annual financial reporting cycles for activities such as budgeting. Preparing these mandatory reports on IT expenditure would trigger the process.

- Audits may suggest or mandate improvement actions which would need to be implemented.

- Other service management processes may request financial information regarding return on investment data, for example.

- An investigation into a new service opportunity would trigger a financial assessment.

- The introduction of charging for IT services for an internal service provider or the need to determine the price of a service for an external service provider would trigger the accounting and charging processes.

- Finally, a request for change will trigger the need for financial information about the cost of making changes and the ongoing financial impact of the change.

Inputs

We looked at the financial management activities shown on Figure 3.8. This diagram also shows the inputs and outputs of the process. The typical inputs shown on the diagram include the following:

- The policies, standards, and practices that are laid down by legislation or regulators and those imposed by the organization's financial managers.

- The generally accepted accounting principles (GAAP) and local variations is another input.

- All data sources in which financial information is stored, including the supplier database, configuration management system, the service portfolio, customer agreement portfolio, application portfolio, and project portfolio, may input into financial management.

- Finally, the service portfolio provides the structure of services that will be provided. These services will be the basis for the accounting system because all costs (and returns) will ultimately be expressed in terms of the services provided.

Outputs

Next we look at the outputs of financial management. These were also shown on Figure 3.8, in addition to the inputs and activities discussed previously. The outputs are as follows:

- Service valuation. This is the ability to understand the costs of a service relative to its business value.

- Service investment analysis. Financial management provides the information and history to enable the service provider to determine the value of the investment in a service.

- Compliance. Regardless of the location of a service provider, or whether it is internal or external, financial data is subject to regulation and legislation. Financial management for IT services helps implement and enforce policies that ensure that the organization is able to store and archive financial data, secure and control it, and make sure it is reported to the appropriate people.

- Cost optimization. The goal of cost optimization is to make sure investments are appropriate for the level of service that the customers demand and the level of returns that are being projected. Business impact analysis (BIA) involves understanding the effect on the business if a service were not available. This enables the business to prioritize investments in services and service continuity.

- Planning confidence. This is not a tangible output; it refers to the level of confidence that service stakeholders have in the service provider being able to accurately forecast costs and returns.

Interfaces

All service management processes use financial management to determine the costs and benefits of the process itself. Some also use it to support the execution of their process activities. The following list includes the major interfaces with financial management for IT services:

- Strategy management works with enterprise financial management to determine the financial objectives for the organization. It defines expected returns on investment based on information provided by financial management. Financial management will track and report on the achievement of ROI.

- Service portfolio management provides the service structure that will be used to define cost models, accounting and budgeting systems, and the basis for charging.

- Business relationship management provides information to financial management regarding how the business measures the value of services and what they are prepared to pay for services.

- Capacity and availability management are able to provide valuable information to financial management for IT services about the various options of technology and service performance. This in turn will be used to calculate costs.

- Change management uses financial management for IT services to help determine the financial impact or requirements of changes.

- Service asset and configuration management documents financial data about assets and configuration items. This data is used as the basis for financial analysis and reporting. Enterprise financial management also provides the policies that are used as the basis for managing financial assets of the organization (such as depreciation).

- Continual service improvement uses financial management for IT services to determine whether the return of a proposed improvement is worth the investment required to make the improvement.

Critical Success Factors and Key Performance Indicators

Finally, we cover the CSFs and KPIs for this process. (Remember the explanation of these in the section on strategy management for IT services.) We will provide some examples, but as with the other processes, the full list is available in the *ITIL Service Strategy* publication. Here are examples of CSFs and KPIs for financial management for IT services:

- Critical success factor: "The existence of an enterprise-wide framework to identify, manage, and communicate financial information, including the cost and associated return of services."

  - KPI: The existence of established standards, policies, and charts of accounts, which enterprise financial management requires all business units to use and comply with. Audits will indicate the extent of compliance.

  - KPI: The financial management for IT services framework specifies how services will be accounted for; regular reports are submitted and used as a basis for measuring the service provider's performance.

  - KPI: The production of timely and accurate submission of financial reports by each organizational unit.

- Critical success factor: "The requirement for the service provider to be able to account for the money spent on the creation, delivery, and support of services."

  - KPI: The service provider uses an accounting system, and this is configured to report on its costs by service.

  - KPI: The provision of regular reports on the costs of services in design, transition, and operation.

Challenges

Challenges for financial management for IT services are as follows:

- Financial reporting and cost models that focus on the cost of infrastructure and applications rather than the cost of services make it difficult to communicate the value of services.

- While financial management for IT services must comply with enterprise standards and policies, its chart of accounts and reporting should be appropriate for an IT service provider.

- An organizational focus on cost saving rather than cost optimization leads to cost-cutting rather than demonstrating return on investment and value.

- When the process is first introduced, it may be difficult to find where financial data is located and how it is controlled.

- The process is reliant upon planning information provided by other processes.

- Difficulties can be experienced by internal service providers when introducing charging. This requires a change in culture and in how its success is measured, especially the need to articulate value in relation to alternative service providers. There is a possibility that the users may become more demanding as a result of being charged.

- There is a need for external service providers to balance the cost of services with the perceived value of those services to ensure the correct pricing models. The correct price must be higher than the cost, but it must also reflect the value to the customer (what the customer is prepared to pay for the service).

Risk

There are a number of risks to financial management for IT services:

- The introduction of dedicated financial management processes for an internal service provider may be viewed as unnecessary, even though the cost of a bad investment decision about the type and level of services offered can far outweigh the costs of implementing the process.

- A lack of adequate financial management processes for IT services may lead to penalties for noncompliance.

- There may be no staff in the organization who understand both IT and finance.

Summary

In this chapter, we began our examination of the service strategy processes. Although you may not have the opportunity to see these processes in action within your own organization, they are critical to successful service provision. These processes ensure that the service provider takes a strategic view of the services to be offered or retired and is able to prove the financial benefit of the agreed course of action.

Exam Essentials

Understand the principles and techniques of service strategy.   You will need to be able to understand service strategy principles, techniques, and relationships and their application for the creation of effective service strategies.

Understand the service strategy processes of strategy management, service portfolio management, and financial management for IT services.   You need to understand, from a management-level viewpoint, the purpose, objectives, scope, principles, and activities of strategy management for IT services, service portfolio management, and financial management for IT services.

Be able to describe the contents of the service portfolio and their relationship to the lifecycle.   It is important to be able to identify the various components of the service portfolio. It comprises the service pipeline, the service catalog, and retired services. You need to be able to describe how each of these interfaces with the rest of the service lifecycle and the processes from the other lifecycle stages.

Understand the business value, challenges, and risks of each process.   You should be able to explain the value the business derives from each process and the challenges and risks involved in running the process.

Understand the key activities of financial management.   You will need to be able to identify the purpose, objectives, and scope for financial management. Remember the three main areas: budgeting, IT accounting, and charging. Financial management is crucial for the calculation of value for services.

Review Questions

You can find the answers to the review questions in the appendix.

1. Which of the following is NOT an objective of strategy management for IT services?

    A.   To analyse the internal and external environments in which the service provider exists, to identify opportunities that will benefit the organization

    B.   To secure the funding that is required for the provision of the agreed services

    C.   To identify constraints that might prevent the delivery or management of services, and define how those constraints could be removed or their effects reduced

    D.   To define which services will be delivered to which market spaces, and how to maintain a competitive advantage

2. What is the definition of *service valuation*?

    A.   The process responsible for identifying the actual costs of delivering IT services, comparing them with budgeted costs, and managing variance from the budget

    B.   A framework that allows the service provider to determine the costs of providing services

    C.   The activity of predicting and controlling the spending of money

    D.   The ability to understand the costs of a service relative to its business value

3. Which of the following statements about the activities of financial management for IT services, namely accounting, budgeting, and charging, is CORRECT?

    A.   All three activities must be carried out by all types of service provider.

    B.   The decision on whether to carry out the accounting activity will depend on the type of service provider.

    C.   The decision on whether to carry out the budgeting activity will depend on the type of service provider.

    D.   The decision on whether to carry out the charging activity will depend on the type of service provider.

4. Which of the following responsibilities does NOT fit into business relationship management?

    A.   Identifying customer needs (utility and warranty) and ensuring that the service provider is able to meet these needs

    B.   Ensuring that all service management processes, operational level agreements, and underpinning contracts are appropriate for the agreed service

    C.   Maintaining a strategic focus

    D.   Deciding which services the service provider will deliver to meet customer needs

5. With which stages of the service lifecycle does the service portfolio interact?

    A.   Service strategy, service design

    B. Service strategy, service transition, continual service improvement

    C. Service strategy, service design, service operation, continual service improvement

    D. Service strategy, service design, service transition, service operation, continual service improvement

6. One of the objectives of strategy management for IT services is to produce and maintain a library of critical documents and distribute these documents to relevant stakeholders. Which of the following documents should always be included?

    1. Business strategy document

    2. IT strategy document

    3. Service asset strategy document

    4. Communications strategy document

    5. Service management strategy document

    6. Strategy plans for each service

    7. Human resources strategy document

    8. Marketing strategy document

        A. All of the above

        B. 1, 4, 5, and 7 only

        C. 2, 5, and 6 only

        D. 1, 2, 3, 5, and 6 only

7. According to the *ITIL Service Strategy* publication, organizations without clear objectives may suffer from which of the following?

    1. Managing by crisis

    2. Managing by hierarchy

    3. Managing by reacting to customer demand

    4. Managing by extrapolation

    5. Managing by least resistance

    6. Managing by hope

    7. Managing by best effort

        A. 1, 2, 4, 5, and 7 only

        B. 1, 2, 5, 6, and 7 only

        C. All of the above

        D. 1, 3, 4, 6, and 7 only

8. Which of the following statements is correct?

    A. IT financial management is quite separate from the enterprise's financial management.

    B. All IT service providers must carry out the three core financial processes of accounting, budgeting, and charging.

C. The cost of the provision of IT services should always be visible to the customer.

D. IT spending needs a business justification.

9. Which of the following is an objective of financial management?

   A. Ensuring that customer expectations do not exceed what it is willing to pay for

   B. Helping the business to articulate the value of a service

   C. Ensuring that the service provider does not commit to services that it is not able to provide

   D. Ensuring that the service provider understands and is able to meet customer needs

10. Which of these statements reflects the purpose of service portfolio management?

   A. Ensures sufficient capacity for the current and future needs of the business

   B. Ensures that the service delivered by the service providers will align with business requirements

   C. Ensures sufficient availability to meet the current and future needs of the business

   D. Ensures that the service provider has the right mix of services to balance the investment in IT with the ability to meet business outcomes

Chapter 4

Service Strategy Processes: Part 2

THE FOLLOWING ITIL INTERMEDIATE EXAM OBJECTIVES ARE DISCUSSED IN THIS CHAPTER:

✓ **The managerial and supervisory aspects of the two remaining service strategy processes. The processes examined are**

- Demand management
- Business relationship management

✓ **Each process is discussed in terms of its**

- Purpose
- Objectives
- Scope
- Value
- Policies
- Principles and basic concepts
- Process activities, methods, and techniques
- Triggers, inputs, outputs, and interfaces
- Critical success factors and key performance indicators
- Challenges
- Risks

As stated previously, the syllabus for this qualification covers the managerial and supervisory aspects of the service strategy processes. It excludes the day-to-day operation of each process and the detail of the process activities, its methods and techniques, and its information management.

Demand management is the process that seeks to understand, anticipate, and influence customer demand for services and the provision of capacity to meet these demands.

Business relationship management is crucial to ensuring that we have an integrated approach to the delivery of services to meet organizational needs.

Understanding Business Relationship Management

Business relationship management has matured as a process over time. Initially, it was simply a role that was filled to ensure that a business had a named contact within the IT service provider's organization. But now, as part of a mature service management approach, we recognize the need for business relationship management as a strategic process in its own right, not just as a role supporting service level management at an executive level.

The process of business relationship management provides a connection between organizational executives and the strategic management of the service provider.

Purpose of Business Relationship Management

This process has a very important part to play in the alignment of the IT service provider and the customer.

The purpose of the process is twofold:

- Establish a relationship between the service provider and the customer, and maintain it by a continued review of business and customer needs. This relationship is extremely important for building a business rapport between service provider and customer.

- Identify customer needs and ensure that the service provider can meet those needs, both now and in the future. Business relationship management is the process that ensures that the service provider is able to understand the changing needs of the business over time. The relationship also allows the customer to articulate the value of the services to the service provider.

One of the most important concepts in this relationship is that of expectation: the customer's expectation of the service provider's capability and the service provider's expectation of the customer's needs. It is critical that the expectation of the customer does not exceed what it is prepared to pay for, and business relationship management is instrumental in the management of this communication.

Objectives of Business Relationship Management

The objectives of business relationship management are as follows:

- Ensure that the service provider has a clear understanding of the customer's perspective of the service so that it is able to prioritize the services and assets accordingly.

- Ensure that customer satisfaction remains high, which will demonstrate that the service is achieving the needs of the customer.

- Establish and maintain a relationship between the customer and service provider that enables understanding of the business drivers and the customer.

- Ensure that the organization and the service provider communicate effectively so that the service provider will be aware of any changes to the customer environment. Changes to the customer environment may have an impact on the services provided.

- Identify technology changes or trends that may impact the type, level, or utilization of the service provided.

- Ensure that the service provider is able to articulate the business requirements for new or changed services and that services continue to meet the needs of the business and continue to deliver value.

- Provide mediation where there is conflict on the use of services between business units. This may be a conflict of resource allocation, or perhaps the requirement to utilize or change functionality differs for specific departments.

- Establish a formal procedure for managing complaints and escalations with the customer.

Scope of Business Relationship Management

The scope of business relationship management will vary dependent on the nature and culture of the organization. If the organization works with an internal service provider, it is likely that business relationship management will be carried out between senior management representatives in both the IT department and business units. Often in larger organizations, you will be able to find dedicated business relationship managers (BRMs), but in smaller organizations, the role may be combined with other managerial responsibility. The BRM will work with the customer representatives to understand the objectives of the business and ensure that the services provided are in alignment and supportive of those objectives.

If an external service provider supports the organization, you will commonly find that a dedicated account manager carries out the process, with an individual allocated to a customer or to a group of smaller customers with similar requirements. As the external service provider relationship with the business is captured in a contract, the focus will be on maximizing contractual value through customer satisfaction.

One of the major requirements for business relationship management is to focus on understanding how the services we provide meet the requirements of our customers. The process needs to ensure that we can communicate effectively with our customers so that we can understand their needs. There are a number of key areas we should consider:

- Business outcomes, so that we understand what the customer wants to achieve.

- How customers use our services, and which services are being offered to them.

- How we manage the services that are being offered, in terms of responsibility for the provision, the service levels we deliver, and the quality of service that is being achieved. We should also consider any changes that may be required in response to business and IT plans.

- As IT service providers, it is vital that we keep track of technology trends and advances that may have an impact on our service delivery. All too often, customers will hear about new technologies but not understand their impact. It is the responsibility of business relationship management to ensure that we communicate and advise on the best use of technology to deliver service value.

- We need to measure the levels of customer satisfaction and respond to any drop in satisfaction with suitable action plans. The BRM will be a key figure in the communication and management of any such plans.

- We need to consider how we can optimize the service we provide for the future.

- The business relationship management process should be concerned with the way the service provider is represented to the customer. This may mean engaging with the business to ensure that commitments from both sides have been fulfilled.

To successfully carry out the process of business relationship management and make sure all of the factors in the preceding list can be taken into consideration, it is necessary to work with other service management processes and functions. For example, the ability to associate business outcomes with services is part of service portfolio management; service level management provides information about service levels and their achievements; service asset and configuration management maps customers and service owners to the infrastructure, applications, and services.

Often other activities such as project management will use the BRM when they need someone to communicate with the customer. The communication is the responsibility of the business relationship manager, but it remains part of the project. The business relationship manager role is discussed further in Chapter 6, "Organizing for Service Strategy."

This will require the identification of clear boundaries, relationships, and responsibilities between business relationship management and other service management processes because there is a strong potential for confusion. Business relationship management should focus on the relationship between the customer and service provider and the achievement of customer satisfaction, but the other service management processes should focus on the services themselves and how well they meet the agreed requirements.

Business relationship management does not ignore the services, but it should be focused on the high-level perspective of whether or not a service is meeting the business needs rather than focusing on specific targets for delivery. Equally, the other service management processes do not ignore this aspect of customer satisfaction, but they should be focused on the quality of the services and how customer expectations can be met.

An example of this is the difference between the service level management and business relationship management processes. They both have regular interaction with customers and are concerned with the ongoing review and management of service and service quality. But each has a different purpose, and the nature of the interface with the customer differs in content and responsibility.

This is clearly shown in Table 4.1, which is an extract from the *ITIL Service Strategy* publication.

TABLE 4.1   Differences between business relationship management and service level management

	Business relationship management	**Service level management**
Purpose	To establish and maintain a business relationship between the service provider and the customer based on understanding the customer and its business needs. To identify customer needs (utility and warranty) and ensure that the service provider is able to meet these needs.	To negotiate service level agreements (warranty terms) with customers and ensure that all service management processes, operational level agreements, and underpinning contracts are appropriate for the agreed service level targets.
Focus	Strategic and tactical. The focus is on the overall relationship between the service provider and its customer and which services the service provider will deliver to meet customer needs.	Tactical and operational. The focus is on reaching agreement on the level of service that will be delivered for new and existing services and whether the service provider was able to meet those agreements.
Primary measure	Customer satisfaction. Also an improvement in the customer's intention to better use and pay for the service. Another metric is whether customers are willing to recommend the service to other (potential) customers.	Achieving agreed levels of service (which leads to customer satisfaction).

Business relationship management is also concerned with the design of services, which makes it the ideal contact for strategic communication with customers for all of the service provider's departments. There is a potential connection for business relationship management with application development as well as other development and design areas.

There are many connections and similarities between business relationship management and service level management and other service management processes, and the roles are often combined. But as you can see from Table 4.2, there are distinct differences in the activities for the processes, and there needs to be a clear understanding that when carrying out business relationship management, an individual needs to be aware when they are working on a strategic business relationship and when they are working tactically.

TABLE 4.2   Business relationship management process and other service management processes

Scenario	Primary process being executed	Other processes involved
Developing high-level customer requirements for a proposed new service	Business relationship management	Service portfolio management
Building a business case for a proposed new service	Business relationship management	Service portfolio management
Confirming customer's detailed functionality requirements for a new service	Design coordination	Business relationship management
Confirming a customer requirement for service availability for a new service	Service level management	Business relationship management, availability management
Establishing patterns of business activity	Demand management	Business relationship management
Evaluating business case for new service request from customer and deciding go/no go	Service portfolio management	Business relationship management, financial management for IT services
Report service performance against service level	Service level management	Business relationship management

When revising for this exam, make sure you are aware of the differences between business relationship management and the other service management processes, especially service level management. Remember, business relationship management is concerned with a strategic relationship with the customer, whereas other processes are more tactically based.

Value

The value of business relationship management is that it provides structured ongoing communication with customers, enabling the service provider to articulate and meet the current and future business needs of its customers. Each party gains a better understanding of the other so that customer expectations are realistic. Business relationship management mediates in disagreements and builds trust between the parties so they work together as strategic partners.

Business relationship management measures customer satisfaction and compares service provider performance with customer satisfaction targets and previous scores, usually through a regular survey. Business relationship management surveys are concerned with whether the service achieves its objectives at every level rather than day-to-day handling of individual incidents.

Significant variations in satisfaction levels or downward trends should be investigated and discussed with customers so that the reasons are understood. Any opportunities for improvement should be logged in the CSI register in conjunction with service level management for later review and prioritization. Care should be taken to ensure consistent measurements and to validate anomalous results that may have other causes.

The focus on customer satisfaction enables the service provider and customer to understand if the business objectives are being met. Although service provision without business relationship management is possible, it is potentially costly, erratic, and filled with mistrust.

Policies, Principles, and Basic Concepts

Next we consider some of the policies, principles, and basic concepts of business relationship management.

The process of business relationship management is often confused with the business relationship manager role. This is because the role of many BRMs is broader than just the business relationship management process. The BRM often represents other processes when engaged in business relationship management—for example, when obtaining information about customer requirements and business outcomes for use by service portfolio management, demand, and capacity management.

Among the key concepts are a number of data repositories. You saw these earlier when we discussed the service portfolio in Chapter 3, "Service Strategy Processes: Part 1."

- The customer portfolio is a database or structured document used to record all customers of the IT service provider. It is business relationship management's view of the customers who receive services from the IT service provider. Although used in several processes, especially service portfolio management, it is defined and maintained in the business relationship management process. The customer portfolio allows the service provider to quantify its commitments, investments, and risks relative to each customer.

- The customer agreement portfolio is a database or structured document used to manage service contracts or agreements between an IT service provider and its customers. Each IT service delivered to a customer should have a contract or other agreement that is listed in this portfolio. It is an important tool for business relationship management, but it is usually defined and maintained as part of service level management.

- Contracts or SLAs are negotiated and managed separately for each customer. For internal service providers, SLAs are negotiated and maintained by service level management, involving BRMs where these exist, whereas for external service providers, the process involves legal specialists, service level management, and dedicated BRMs.

Business relationship management works throughout the service lifecycle to understand customer requirements and expectations and ensure that they are being met or exceeded:

- In service strategy, business relationship management ensures that the service provider understands the customer's objectives and overall requirements.

- In service design, business relationship management ensures that the service provider has properly understood the customer's detailed requirements and initiates corrective action if this is not the case. In addition, business relationship management will work with service level management to ensure that the customer's expectations of the new service are set at the appropriate level.

- In service transition, business relationship management ensures that the customer is involved in change, release, and deployment activities that impact its services, ensuring that its feedback has been taken into due consideration. The BRM may represent the customer on the change advisory board (CAB), or they may arrange for the customer to be at CAB meetings and change evaluation meetings when appropriate.

- In service operation, business relationship management works with service level management, incident management, and the service desk to ensure that services have been delivered according to the contract or SLA and may well be part of the escalation procedures.

- In continual service improvement, business relationship management monitors service reports and is given frequent updates about levels of customer satisfaction, exceptions to service levels, or specific requests or complaints from the customer. Working together with other processes and functions, business relationship management will help to identify appropriate remedial action in agreement with the customer.

Business relationship management is involved in defining and clarifying requirements for service. Customers may present solutions, specifications, needs, or benefits when what is required is a statement of the value the customer is trying to achieve. Business relationship management should focus on the outcome and work back to defining the service.

Some service providers are included in strategic discussions about the customer's business. Business relationship management is the process that facilitates this and ensures that the right person is included in these meetings. It also ensures that relevant information about the strategic direction of the customer is communicated back into the appropriate processes and to the people within the service provider organization.

Process Activities, Methods, and Techniques

Figure 4.1 shows the business relationship management activities. We are going to look at them in more detail.

The business relationship management process itself consists of activities in every stage of the service lifecycle, but it is rarely executed as a single end-to-end process. The exact activities that are executed will depend on the situation that has caused the service provider or customer to initiate the process. The process also interfaces with a number of other service management processes throughout the service lifecycle. Business relationship management is not a single end-to-end process with a single beginning and end. Rather, it consists of a number of key activities that are linked together.

The business relationship management process is initiated either by the customer or by service management processes and functions, usually by contacting the business relationship manager. For customers, business relationship management provides a way to communicate with the service provider about their needs, opportunities, and requirements and to have these taken care of in a formal, organized manner. The business relationship manager must maintain a register of all opportunities, requests, complaints, and compliments to track them and ensure that they do not fall between different processes and functions. The service provider is also able to initiate the business relationship management process if it needs input from customers or if it needs to initiate the creation of a new service or changes to an existing service.

Service Strategy

In business relationship management, the business relationship manager works to apply strategies, policies, and plans to coordinate the service provider's processes with customer requirements and opportunities. Strategy management will have identified the key market spaces and business opportunities. The BRM will ensure that these are appropriately defined and executed from a customer perspective.

Business relationship management will work with the other service strategy processes:

- With IT strategy management to understand if the request is in line with strategy
- With service portfolio management to decide if a new service is required or whether existing services can be leveraged
- With financial management for IT services to understand how it is to be funded
- With demand management to understand the PBAs

FIGURE 4.1   Business relationship management activities

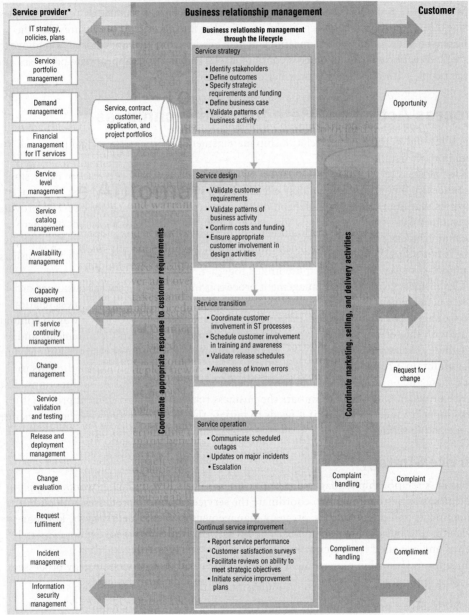

* Only a sample of activities and processes are illustrated.

Service Design

In the service design stage, business relationship management will work to ensure that the detailed design and development of services continue to meet the requirements of the customer and that they are valid for the business outcomes that have been identified.

The main activities and processes the business relationship manager will work with are as follows:

- Project management (by liaising with the customer)
- Financial management (The BRM ensures that costs are in line with the investment anticipated.)
- Service level management (The BRM will help in obtaining the agreement of the customer to the SLAs.)
- Demand management (The BRM will confirm patterns of business activity.)
- Service catalog management (The BRM will help to define the catalog entry.)
- Availability management (The BRM will verify exactly when the service needs to be available.)
- Capacity management (The BRM will verify performance requirements.)
- IT service continuity management (The BRM will identify business impacts and recovery objectives with the customer.)

Service Transition

The BRM will coordinate customer involvement in the processes active during service transition. They will also ensure that all changes and releases meet the requirements set by the customer.

The BRM will work with the following main processes:

- Change management (The BRM's role is to represent the customer.)
- Knowledge management (The BRM will ensure that knowledge management plans includes the customer requirements for knowledge and information and that the knowledge and information about the customer and their business processes are made available in the service knowledge management system.)
- Service testing and validation (The BRM coordinates user acceptance testing.)
- Release and deployment management (The BRM ensures that the customer experiences minimum disruption.)
- Change evaluation (The BRM is responsible for logging and coordinating any action arising from the evaluation.)

Service Operations

In service operations, business relationship management is still required. First, customers use of services changes over time. The BRM will feed this back to the service provider. Second, although the service desk is able to deal with most incidents and requests, some require a higher level of involvement and communication, which the business relationship manager provides.

The BRM will work with the following main processes:

- Request fulfilment (The BRM may be the point of contact for requesting some services.)
- Incident management (The BRM is usually involved during major incidents to provide focused communication to the customer. Business relationship management provides incident management with business information that will help in evaluating the relative priority of incidents.)

Continual Service Improvement

The BRM facilitates CSI by identifying improvement opportunities and then coordinating both service provider and customer activities to achieve this improvement. The BRM also conducts customer satisfaction surveys, which are instrumental in identifying areas for improvement and new opportunities.

Business relationship management will work with the following main activities and processes:

Service Reporting   Business relationship management is key to identifying what will be reported to the customer and what the customer will be expected to do with the reports they receive.

Service Level Management   Any actions agreed on at service reviews with the customers will be coordinated and monitored by the BRM, whether the actions apply to customers or the service provider.

The Seven-Step Improvement Process   Business relationship management helps to identify and communicate proposed improvement to services or to the service strategy, design, transition, and operation processes of the supplier.

Triggers

Business relationship management includes the following triggers:

- A new strategic initiative or a new service, or a change to an existing service, has been initiated.
- A new opportunity has been identified or a service has been chartered by service portfolio management.
- Other triggers could be customer requests, suggestions, or complaints or the fact that a customer meeting or customer satisfaction survey has been scheduled.

Inputs

Inputs to business relationship management are as follows:

- Customer requirements, requests, complaints, escalations or compliments
- The service strategy and, where possible, the customer's strategy

- The service and project portfolios, SLAs, and RFCs
- A request to validate patterns of business activity or user profiles defined by demand management

Outputs

Business relationship management has the following outputs:

- Stakeholder definitions, defined business outcomes, and an agreement to fund (internal) or pay for (external) services
- The customer portfolio and service requirements for strategy, design, and transition
- Customer satisfaction surveys and their results
- Schedules of customer activity in various service management process activities and of training and awareness events
- Reports on the customer perception of service performance

Interfaces

The following list includes major interfaces with business relationship management:

- Strategy management for IT services, which works closely with the BRM to identify market spaces with information gleaned from customers. The BRM also gathers strategic requirements and desired business outcomes and secures funding (internal) or pursues deals (external).
- Service portfolio management, which works with BRM to identify more detailed requirements and information about the customer environment required to create service models and assess proposed services.
- Financial management for IT services obtains information about the financial objectives of the customer and helps the service provider to understand what level of funding or pricing the customer is prepared to accept.
- Demand management works with business relationship management to identify and validate patterns of business and user profiles. The BRM will also identify changes to those patterns or the priorities of specific business activities.
- Service level management uses customer information and service requirements gathered by the BRM to understand the customer's priorities regarding service performance and deliverables.
- Capacity and availability management, which rely on information about business outcomes and service requirements gathered through business relationship management. The BRM will also validate whether proposed levels of performance and availability will be acceptable to customers.
- The BRM provides information on business priorities and outcomes for IT service continuity management and ensures that countermeasures, recovery plans, and tests accurately represent the world of the customer.

- Service catalog management provides the basis for many discussions, reviews, and requests that are initiated through business relationship management.

- Change management, because business relationship management is often the initiating point for requests for change and will also be involved with assessing the impact and priority of changes.

- The BRM also ensures the appropriate level of customer involvement in release and deployment management and service validation and testing processes.

- Continual service improvement, with which business relationship management has a strong interface because service improvements and the seven-step improvement process are important parts of business relationship management. The BRM validates, prioritizes, and communicates improvement opportunities and plans with the customer in conjunction with service level management.

Critical Success Factors and Key Performance Indicators

Finally we consider the CSFs and KPIs for this process. (Remember the explanation of these in Chapter 3 in the section on strategy management for IT services.) We shall consider the following examples, but for the full list, see the *ITIL Service Strategy* publication:

- Critical success factor: "The ability to document and understand customer requirements of services and the business outcomes they wish to achieve."

  - KPI: That business outcomes and customer requirements are documented and signed off by the customer as input into the service portfolio management and service design processes. If this KPI is present and achieved, the CSF will be achieved.

- Critical success factor: "The ability to establish and articulate business requirements for new services or changes to existing services."

  - KPI: Every new service has a comprehensive set of requirements defined by business managers and staff, and these have been signed off by both business and IT leadership at the strategy, design, and transition stage.

  - KPI: The reasons for expected results and detailed requirements for changes to services are documented and signed off at the strategy, design, and transition stages.

Challenges

Business relationship management faces the following challenges:

- Moving beyond using business relationship management purely as a means of working on levels of customer satisfaction. The BRM needs to be involved in defining services and tracking that they are delivered according to the agreed levels of service.

- Another challenge can be that a history of poor service causes the BRM to struggle to have any credibility. This sometimes results in customers not being willing to share requirements, feedback, and opportunities.

- There may be confusion between the role of business relationship manager (BRM) and the process of business relationship management. Although the BRMs are often required to execute activities from other processes simply because of their customer-facing position, this does not make those activities part of the business relationship management process.

Risks

Business relationship management risks are as follows:

- Confusion regarding the boundaries between business relationship management and other processes. This may lead to duplication of effort, or alternatively, some activities may be neglected. An example of this would be during a major incident the incident manager may receive multiple calls from business relationship management and service level management. It is important that these boundaries are clearly defined.

- A disconnect between the customer-facing processes, such as business relationship management, and those focusing on technology, such as capacity management. Both are critical for success, and they need to be properly integrated.

Understanding Demand Management

The final service strategy process we'll examine is demand management. As we have done with the processes, we'll consider the demand management process in terms its:

- Purpose
- Objectives
- Scope
- Business value
- Policies, principles, and basic concepts
- Process activities, methods, and techniques
- Triggers
- Inputs
- Outputs
- Critical success factors and key performance indicators
- Challenges
- Risks

So let's start with a reminder of what demand management is. Demand management is the process that seeks to understand, anticipate, and influence customer demand for services and the provision of capacity to meet these demands. It is a critical aspect of service management. Poorly managed demand is a source of risk for service providers because of the uncertainty in demand. Excess capacity generates cost without creating value.

Purpose

The purpose of demand management is to understand, anticipate, and influence customer demand for services and to work with capacity management to ensure that the service provider has capacity to meet this demand. Demand management works at every stage of the lifecycle to ensure that services are designed, tested, and delivered to support the achievement of business outcomes at the appropriate levels of activity.

Objectives

The objectives of demand management are as follows:

- The first objective is about understanding the demands that will be placed on the service by identifying and analyzing patterns of business activity.

- The second objective is concerned with understanding the different types of user profiles that will use the service and how the demand from each type differs from the others. An example of this would be a cell phone supplier who offers different tariffs to business users and schoolchildren because they put very different demands on the service provided.

- The third objective is to ensure that services are designed to meet the patterns of business activity that have been identified and are therefore able to meet the business outcomes.

- Another objective of demand management is to work with capacity management to ensure that there are adequate resources to meet the demand for services, maintaining a balance between the cost of service and the value that it achieves. Unused resources are an additional cost.

- Demand management seeks to anticipate and prevent or manage situations in which demand for a service exceeds the capacity to deliver it. Insufficient resources have an impact on the achievement of the business objectives.

- The process aims to gear the utilization of resources that deliver services to meet the fluctuating levels of demand for those services.

Scope

The scope of the demand management process is to identify and analyze the patterns of business activity that initiate demand for services and to identify and analyze how different types of user influence the demand for services.

Value

The main value of demand management is to achieve a balance between the cost of a service and the value of the business outcomes it supports. The other service strategy processes define the linkage between (and the investment required for) business outcomes, services, resources, and capabilities. Demand management refines the understanding of how, when, and to what level these elements interact.

Policies, Principles, and Basic Concepts

Demand management is about matching supply to demand. Unlike a factory that produces products, which can continue to be produced and stockpiled in anticipation of increased demand later, when we supply a service, the demand has to be met immediately, not later. A call center that receives few calls on a Friday afternoon cannot start answering the following Monday morning's calls! Monday morning will be busy, but there is no way to use the quiet times to balance out that busy morning. Another way of saying this is that consumption produces demand and production consumes demand in a highly synchronized pattern. There is a real risk that insufficient capacity will mean that the demand cannot be met at the time it is needed.

Supply and Demand

A major part of demand management is to understand the potential demand and the impact of the demand on the service assets. This allows capacity management to manage service assets (and investments) toward optimal performance and cost. The aim is to adjust the productive capacity to meet the demand forecasts and patterns. Some types of capacity can be quickly increased as required and released when not in use. Offering price incentives to customers to use services at quieter times means that the arrival of demand can be influenced to some extent. However, we cannot stockpile the service output before demand actually materializes. This cycle of demand, which is then supplied, will function only while there is available capacity; as soon as capacity is no longer available, the service provider will not be able to supply enough of the services to satisfy customer demand.

This highly synchronized pattern of supply and demand can be seen in Figure 4.2. Each time a user consumes a service, demand is presented to the service provider, and this consumes capacity of the service assets. This, in turn, results in the service being supplied to meet the consumer's demand. The greater the consumption of the service, the higher the demand, the higher the consumption of capacity, and the more the service is supplied.

FIGURE 4.2   Tight coupling between demands, capacity, and supply

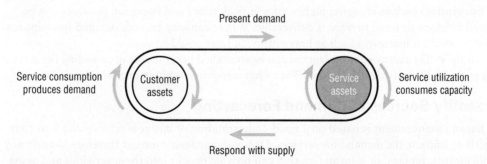

Gearing Service Assets

The balance of supply and demand is achieved by gearing the service assets to meet the dynamic patterns of demand on services. This means that the service provider does not just react to demand but proactively anticipates it, identifying the signals of increasing or decreasing demand and defining a mechanism to scale investment and supply as required.

This involves identifying the services using service portfolio management and quantifying the patterns of business activity. Next, the appropriate architecture to deal with the type and quantity of demand is chosen, and the capacity and availability planning processes ensure that the right service assets are available at the right time and are performing at the right levels. Performance management and tuning are carried out as required to deal with variations in demand. Gearing of service assets like this requires input from across the service lifecycle:

Service Strategy   Identifies the services, outcomes, and patterns of business activity and communicates the forecast demand to design teams.

Service Design   Service design confirms the availability and capacity requirements and validates that the service assets are designed to meet those requirements.

Service Transition   Service transition ensures that the new or changed service is tested and validated for the forecast utilization and patterns of business activity. Tests should also be carried out to check the ability to influence and manage demand.

Service Operation   The service operation functions should monitor service assets and service utilization levels to ensure that demand is within normal levels and, if not, initiate performance tuning or corrective action.

Continual Service Improvement   Continual service improvement will work with demand management to identify trends in patterns of business activity and to initiate changes to the capabilities of the service provider or changes to the behavior of customers where appropriate.

Process Activities, Methods, and Techniques

Demand management activities include identifying and implementing measures to influence and manage demand together with capacity management. This could be in situations where service demand exceeds capacity and where capacity increases are not feasible. Disincentives such as charging higher rates at peak times and imposing penalties can be used to lessen demand to what is deliverable. Where capacity exceeds demand (perhaps for a new service), incentives such as lower off-peak rates could be used.

If the peaks and troughs of demand can be smoothed out, the cost of providing the service is optimized because it can always deliver what is required without excessive wasted capacity.

Identify Sources of Demand Forecasting

Demand management is based on a good understanding of business activity and how that activity impacts the demand for services. Demand management must therefore identify any documents, reports, or information that can provide insight into these activities and assist in forecasting the levels of demand. These sources will be used to define, monitor, and refine the other components of demand management described in the following section.

The following potential sources of information can assist demand management in forecasting demand:

- Business plans
- Marketing plans and forecasts
- New product launch plans
- Sales forecasts

Patterns of Business Activity

Services are designed to enable business activities, which in turn achieve business outcomes. So every time a business activity is performed, it generates demand for services. Customer assets such as people, processes, and applications all perform business activities, and because of the way these assets are organized or because of the tasks they are completing, there will tend to be noticeable patterns in the way the activities are performed. These patterns of business activity (PBAs) represent the dynamics of the business and include interactions with customers, suppliers, partners, and other stakeholders.

PBAs must be properly understood, defined, and documented, and any changes to them must be properly controlled. Each PBA needs to have a documented PBA profile containing the following details:

Classification   PBAs are classified by type, which could refer to where they originate (user or automated), the type and impact of outcomes supported, and the type of workload supported.

Attributes   These may include frequency, volume, location, and duration.

Requirements   These could be performance, security, availability, privacy, latency, or tolerance for delays.

Service Asset Requirements   Design teams will draft a utilization profile for each PBA in terms of what resources it uses, when the resources are used, and how much of each resource is used. If the quantity of resources is known and the pattern of utilization is known, the capacity management process will be able to ensure that resources are available to meet the demand, provided it stays within the forecast range.

Figure 4.3 shows a number of different examples of patterns of business activity. Take a moment to look at them.

Example A shows the pattern of sales for a greeting card company in the United States. The pattern of card sales varies in line with major holidays or events; this in turn will lead to different levels of IT service utilization. The IT service provider must anticipate the business activity before each major holiday so the company can be sure to prepare and ship the greeting cards in time. In addition, the online ordering systems will be in high demand in the two weeks prior to the holiday. This high demand is not typical, so either the service provider will need to invest in spare capacity that will be idle at other times of the year or they will need to be able to balance the workload across multiple resources. In this way, processing lower-priority services will make way for the volumes of the higher-priority seasonal activity.

FIGURE 4.3   Examples of patterns of business activity

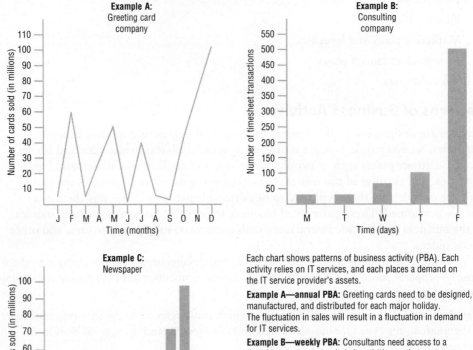

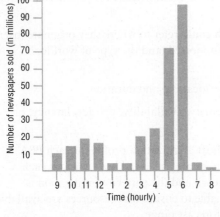

Each chart shows patterns of business activity (PBA). Each activity relies on IT services, and each places a demand on the IT service provider's assets.

Example A—annual PBA: Greeting cards need to be designed, manufactured, and distributed for each major holiday.
The fluctuation in sales will result in a fluctuation in demand for IT services.

Example B—weekly PBA: Consultants need access to a timesheet system to track their activities so that customers can be billed. Most consultants wait until the end of the week to complete their timesheets. Some consultants record their activities daily.

Example C—daily PBA: Journalists have to meet the deadline of 6:00 p.m. to submit their stories for publication. After the deadline, only high-impact corrections are made. The later in the day, the more critical the IT services become, and also the more utilized. Most journalists use the lunch hour to interview people for stories.

In example B, a consulting company relies on a timesheet service to bill consultants' time. Since most consultants complete their timesheets for the entire week at the end of the week, the service is more critical and is utilized more later in the week. Consultants may need to be encouraged to log their time at the end of each day or the beginning of the next day.

Example C shows how journalists use a word-processing and editorial service. From a quiet start early in the day, the service gets busier and busier as deadlines approach. This behavior is consistent with the nature of journalism, so trying to change it is unlikely to be successful. In these cases, measures will have to be taken to ensure that resources are available to match the PBA.

User profiles (UPs) are based on roles and responsibilities within organizations and may include business processes and applications. Many processes are automated and can consume services on their own. Processes and applications can have user profiles. Each UP can be associated with one or more PBAs.

Activity-Based Demand Management

Business processes are the primary source of demand for services. Patterns of business activity (PBAs) influence the demand patterns seen by the service providers. It is important to study the customer's business to identify, analyze, and classify such patterns to provide sufficient basis for capacity management. The service provider must visualize the customer's business activity and plans in terms of the demand for supporting services, as shown in Figure 4.4. Analyzing and tracking the activity patterns of the business process make it possible to predict demand patterns for services in the catalog that support the process. It is also possible to predict demand for underlying service assets that support those services.

FIGURE 4.4   Business activity influences patterns of demand for services.

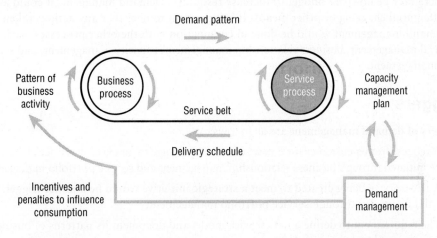

Some of the benefits for analyzing PBAs are in the form of inputs to service management functions and processes:

- Service design can optimize designs to suit demand patterns.
- Capacity management translates the PBAs into workload profiles so that the appropriate resources can be made available to support the levels of service utilization.
- The service catalog can map demand patterns to appropriate services.
- Service portfolio management can approve investments in additional capacity, new services, or changes to services.
- Service operation can adjust allocation of resources and scheduling.

- Service operation can identify opportunities to consolidate demand by grouping closely matching demand patterns.

- Financial management for IT services can approve suitable incentives to influence demand.

Develop Differentiated Offerings

The PBAs may show that different levels of performance are required at different times or with different combinations of utility. In these cases, demand and service portfolio management can work together to define service packages that meet the variations in PBAs.

One of the activities of demand management during service operation is to manage or influence the demand where services or resources are being overutilized. Typically this would occur in the following situations:

- Inaccurate patterns of business activity

- A change to the business environment

- An inaccurate resource forecast

There may be no spare budget to increase resources. Demand management could assist by differential charging or other means. It is important to note that any actions taken by demand management would be done in conjunction with the other processes, such as financial management, business relationship management, capacity management, and service level management.

Triggers

Triggers of demand management are as follows:

- A request from a customer for a new service or a change to an existing service. This will be initiated through business relationship management and service portfolio management.

- A new service being created to meet a strategic initiative would be another trigger. This will be initiated through service portfolio management.

- The requirement to define a new service model and document its patterns of business activity and/or user profiles.

- Demand management would also be invoked if utilization rates are causing potential performance issues or a potential breach to an SLA.

- An exception has occurred to forecast patterns of business activity.

Inputs

Demand management has the following inputs:

- Initiatives to create a new service or to change an existing service. These inputs can come from service portfolio management or from change management.

- Service models need to be validated, and patterns of business activity associated with each service model will need to be defined. The customer portfolio, service portfolio, and customer agreement portfolio, all of which will contain information about supply and demand for services, are also inputs to demand management.

- Charging models will be assessed to ensure that under- or over-recovery does not occur with internal service providers or that pricing will be profitable for external service providers. Chargeable items will need to be validated to ensure that customers actually perceive them and use them as defined.

- Service improvement opportunities and plans will need to be assessed in terms of their impact on demand.

Outputs

The outputs of demand management include user profiles and documented patterns of business activity to be included in the service and customer portfolios. Other outputs are policies for management of demand when resources are overutilized and policies for how to deal with situations in which service utilization is higher or lower than anticipated by the customer. Finally, demand management will agree on and document the various options for differentiated offerings that can be used to create service packages.

Interfaces

Major interfaces with demand management are as follows:

- Strategy management for IT services will identify the key business outcomes and business activities that will be used to establish patterns of business activity and user profiles.

- Service portfolio management uses information from demand management to create and evaluate service models, to establish and forecast utilization requirements, and to identify the different types of users of the service. In addition, it will develop service packages based on the information about patterns of business activity and user profiles.

- Financial management for IT services forecasts the cost of providing the capacity to satisfy the demand and helps to identify charging measures to regulate demand in the event of overutilization.

- Business relationship management is the primary source of information about the business activities of the customer. Business relationship management will also be useful in validating the user profiles and differentiated service offerings before they are confirmed in the customer and service portfolios.

- Service level management will help to formalize agreements in which the customer commits to levels of utilization and the service provider commits to levels of performance. Actual levels of performance and utilization will be reviewed at the regular service level review meetings (using information from demand management and capacity management) and any deviations noted. Demand management will work with service level management to define policies for how to deal with variances in supply and demand.

- Capacity management works closely with demand management to define how to match supply and demand in the design and operation of services and to understand trends of utilization and how the services might be adjusted for future use. It also monitors the actual utilization of services.

- Availability management identifies the times when availability is the most important through analyzing patterns of business activity.

- IT service continuity management uses demand management information to analyze business impact and size recovery options.

- Change management works with demand management and capacity management to assess the impact of changes on how the business uses services.

- Service asset and configuration management identifies the relationship between the demand placed on services and the demand placed on systems and devices.

- Service validation and testing ensures that services deal with patterns of demand and validates the effectiveness of measures taken to prevent overutilization.

- Finally, event management provides information about actual patterns of service utilization versus the anticipated patterns of business activity for a service.

Critical Success Factors and Key Performance Indicators

You'll recall from earlier discussions the definitions of critical success factors and key performance indicators. Here are some examples for demand management.

- Critical success factor: "The service provider has identified and analyzed the patterns of business activity and is able to use these to understand the levels of demand that will be placed on a service."

  - KPI: Patterns of business activity are defined for each relevant service.

  - KPI: Patterns of business activity have been translated into workload information by capacity management.

- Critical success factor: "The existence of a means to manage situations where demand for a service exceeds the capacity to deliver it."

  - KPI: Techniques to manage demand have been documented in capacity plans and, where appropriate, in service level agreements.

  - KPI: Differential charging (as an example of one such technique) has resulted in a more even demand on the service over time.

Challenges

Demand management faces the following challenges:

- Information about business activities may be hard to obtain if demand management was not included in the set of requirements.

- Customers may struggle to break down individual activities that make sense to the service provider. Business relationship management should be able to help.

- Lack of a formal service portfolio management process or service portfolio will hamper the understanding of the business requirements, relative value, and priority of services. This may mean that demand management information is only recorded on an ad hoc basis.

Risks

The risks of demand management are as follows:

- Lack of, or inaccurate, configuration management information makes it difficult to estimate the impact of changing demand on the service provider's infrastructure and applications.

- Service level management may be unable to obtain commitments from the business for minimum or maximum utilization levels. Without this commitment on utilization, it is difficult for demand management to commit to levels of service. As a result, higher levels of investments than are actually required are made to enable the service provider to keep ahead of demand, even when the service is not essential.

Summary

In this chapter, we completed our examination of the service strategy processes by looking at business relationship management and demand management. Business relationship management ensures that the services provided meet the needs of the organization in both the short and long term by working with senior business management to align the services provided to the business strategic requirements.

Through demand management, the service provider is able to anticipate and influence customer demand for services. Demand management techniques can moderate excessive demand or stimulate demand where there is overcapacity. Demand management endeavors to ensure that demand does not exceed the capacity to deliver and that there is no expensive unused capacity.

Exam Essentials

Understand the principles and techniques of service strategy.   You will need to understand service strategy principles, techniques, and relationships and their application for the creation of effective service strategies.

Know the service strategy processes of demand management and business relationship management.   From a management-level viewpoint, know the purpose objectives, scope, principles, and activities of business relationship management and demand management.

Understand the interfaces with other processes.   You need to be able to describe how the business relationship management and demand management processes interface with the rest of the service lifecycle and the processes from the other lifecycle stages.

Understand the business value, challenges, and risks of each process.   You should be able to explain the value the business derives from the business relationship management and demand management processes and the challenges and risks involved in running them.

Understand how business relationship management works with the senior business management.   Make sure you understand how the business relationship manager(s) work to ensure that the service provider understands the business strategy and provides the services required to further that strategy. Know that this process also involves explaining to the business what the service provider can and cannot do.

Be able to describe the key differences between business relationship management and service level management.   You should be able to list and explain the differences in activities and focus between business relationship management and service level management.

Understand the key activities of demand management.   Make sure you understand how demand management anticipates the level of demand and works with capacity management and other processes to meet it.

Review Questions

You can find the answers to the review questions in the appendix.

1. Patterns of business activity are used to track what?
    A. Usage of individual IT services by users
    B. Usage of individual IT services by departments
    C. Activity of the business to deliver business outcomes
    D. Value of services to the business

2. Demand management is about matching what to demand?
    A. Services
    B. Supply
    C. Strategy
    D. Service level agreements

3. Which of these information sources should be used by demand management?
    1. Business plans
    2. Marketing plans and forecasts
    3. Production plans (in manufacturing environments)
    4. Sales forecasts
    5. New product launch plans
        A. 1, 2, 3, 4, 5
        B. 1, 3, 5
        C. 2, 4
        D. 1, 2, 3, 4

4. User profiles (UPs) are based on what?
    A. Roles and responsibilities within organizations
    B. Processes within organizations
    C. Service level agreements
    D. Operational level agreements

5. Which of the following statements is incorrect?
    A. From a strategic perspective, demand management is about matching supply to demand.
    B. Demand management may use differential charging to try to influence the demand where services or resources are being overutilized.

    C. Unlike goods, services cannot be manufactured in advance and stocked in a finished goods inventory in anticipation of demand.

    D. Consumption consumes demand and production produces demand in a highly synchronized pattern.

6. Every _____ should be documented with the following details: classification, attributes, requirements, and service asset requirements.

    A. User profile

    B. Service

    C. SLA

    D. Pattern of business activity

7. Which of the following responsibilities is NOT a responsibility of BRM?

    A. Identifying customer needs (utility and warranty) and ensuring that the service provider is able to meet these needs

    B. Strategic focus

    C. Deciding which services the service provider will deliver to meet customer needs

    D. Operational focus

8. Which of the following responsibilities is NOT a responsibility of service level management?

    A. Building a business case for a proposed new service

    B. Agreeing on the level of service that will be delivered for new and existing services

    C. Monitoring whether the service provider is able to meet the agreements

    D. Ensuring that all operational level agreements and underpinning contracts are appropriate for the agreed service

9. True or False? The customer portfolio is a database or structured document used to record all customers of the IT service provider. The customer agreement portfolio is a database or structured document used to manage service contracts or agreements between an IT service provider and its customers.

    A. True

    B. False

10. Which of the following is NOT a trigger for BRM?

    A. A new strategic initiative or a new service, or a change to an existing service, has been initiated.

    B. The service provider's ROI is less than predicted in the business case.

    C. A new opportunity has been identified or a service has been chartered by service portfolio management.

    D. A customer complains about the service being delivered.

Chapter

5

Governance

THE FOLLOWING ITIL INTERMEDIATE EXAM OBJECTIVES ARE DISCUSSED IN THIS CHAPTER:

✓ **Governance**

✓ **Setting the strategy for governance**

  ▪ Evaluate, direct, and monitor

✓ **Governance framework**

✓ **What is IT governance?**

✓ **Governance bodies**

  ▪ How service strategy relates to governance

To do well on the exam, you must ensure that you understand the concepts associated with governance. You will need to demonstrate that you can apply these concepts to the scenarios by analyzing the information provided in the exam questions.

Understanding Governance

Governance is the single overarching area that ties IT and the business together. It is what defines the common directions, policies, and rules that both the business and IT use to conduct business. Many IT service management strategies fail because they try to build a structure or processes according to how they would like the organization to work instead of working within existing governance structures.

Corporate governance refers to the rules, policies, and processes (and in some cases, laws) by which businesses are operated, regulated, and controlled. These are often defined by a board of directors or shareholders or the constitution of the organization, but they can also be defined by legislation, regulation, standards bodies, or consumer groups.

Setting the Strategy for Governance

Governance is important in the context of service strategy because the strategy of the organization forms a foundation for how the organization is governed and managed. The standard for corporate governance of IT is ISO/IEC 38500. ITIL references the concepts of this standard and how it has been applied. Governance is expressed in a set comprising strategy, policies, and plans (Figure 5.1).

Figure 5.1 shows how governance works to apply a consistently managed approach at all levels of the organization—first by ensuring that a clear strategy is set, then by defining the policies whereby the strategy will be achieved. The policies also define boundaries, or what the organization may not do as part of its operations. For example, there may be a policy stating that IT services will be delivered to internal business units only and will not be sold externally as an outsourcing company would.

The policies should also clearly identify the authority structures of the organization. This is indicated in how decisions are made, and what the limits of decision-making will be for each level of management. The plans ensure that the strategy can be achieved within the boundaries of the policies.

FIGURE 5.1   Strategy, policy, and plan

It is important to remember that although plans are part of governance, governors themselves will not produce or define the plans. Managers will use governance to define plans that are consistent with, and approved by, the organization's executives and governors. However, governors will review the progress and implementation of plans.

Defining strategy, policies, and plans is a rigorous process, consisting of three main activities: evaluate, direct, and monitor. We will look at an overview of the process and show the links between service strategy and governance in the following sections.

Evaluate

Evaluate refers to the ongoing evaluation of the organization's performance and its environment. This evaluation will include a detailed knowledge of the industry, including its trends, regulatory environment, and the markets the organization serves. A strategic assessment is typical of the type of input that is used in this evaluation.

The following items are used to evaluate the organization:

- Financial performance
- Service and project portfolios
- Ongoing operations
- Escalations
- Opportunities and threats
- Proposals from managers, shareholders, customers, and so on
- Contracts
- Feedback from users, customers, and partners

Direct

The direct activity relates to communicating the strategy, policies, and plans to, and through, management. It also ensures that management is given the appropriate guidelines to be able to comply with governance.

This activity includes the following:

- Delegation of authority and responsibility

- Steering committees to communicate with management and to discuss feedback (also used during the evaluate activity)

- Vision, strategy, and policies that are communicated to managers, who are expected to communicate and comply with them

- Decisions that have been escalated to management or where governance is not clear

Monitor

In the monitor activity, the governors of the organization are able to determine whether governance is being fulfilled effectively. It will also highlight whether there are any exceptions. This enables them to take action to rectify the situation and also provides input to further evaluate the effectiveness of current governance measures.

Monitoring requires the following areas to be established:

- A measurement system, often a balanced scorecard

- Key performance indicators

- Risk assessment

- Compliance audit

- Capability analysis, which will ensure that management has what it needs to comply with governance

Governance Framework

A governance framework is a categorized and structured set of documents that clearly articulate the strategy, policies, and plans of the organization.

The ISO/IEC 38500 standard outlines the following six principles that are used to define domains of governance (or areas that need to be governed):

- Establish responsibilities.

- Agree on a strategy to set and meet the organization's objectives.

- Acquire for valid reasons.

- Ensure performance when required.

- Ensure conformance with rules.

- Ensure respect for human factors.

Each of these domains will have high-level policies that form part of the framework and will be used by managers to build procedures, services, and operations that meet the organization's objectives.

What Is IT Governance?

IT governance does not exist as a separate area. Because IT is part of the organization, it cannot be governed in a different way from the rest of the organization. ISO/IEC 38500 refers to "corporate governance of IT," not IT governance. This implies that IT complies with and fulfils the policies and rules of the organization and does not create a separate set for itself.

IT and the other business units share the same objectives and corporate identity and are required to follow the same governance rules.

What is normally called IT governance is usually a matter of the chief information officer (CIO), or senior IT manager, enforcing corporate governance through a set of applied corporate strategies, policies, and plans. Nevertheless, as a member of the executive team, the CIO participates in how governance is defined and translated for management.

Let's consider how this governance framework is managed through the organization by reviewing the suggested governance bodies, as shown in Figure 5.2, later in this section.

FIGURE 5.2   Governing bodies

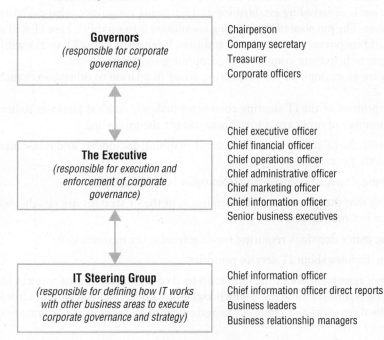

Governors *(responsible for corporate governance)*	Chairperson Company secretary Treasurer Corporate officers
The Executive *(responsible for execution and enforcement of corporate governance)*	Chief executive officer Chief financial officer Chief operations officer Chief administrative officer Chief marketing officer Chief information officer Senior business executives
IT Steering Group *(responsible for defining how IT works with other business areas to execute corporate governance and strategy)*	Chief information officer Chief information officer direct reports Business leaders Business relationship managers

Although IT governance is not separate from corporate governance, it is important that IT executives have input into how corporate governance will specify how IT is governed. This is usually done through an IT steering committee, which also defines IT strategy and is involved in all major decisions regarding IT and its role in the organization.

As a member of the executive group, the CIO will ensure that the corporate strategies, policies, rules, and plans include a high-level overview of how IT will be governed. If the CIO is not a member of the board of directors, it is the responsibility of the member who is responsible for IT to ensure that the CIO is consulted on what needs to be included.

In most cases, the governors will need assistance in defining governance for IT. This can be provided by management consultants or by engagement with senior IT leaders in the organization. In many organizations, the IT department will be heavily involved in defining governance and may even have a dedicated group to work on defining, enforcing, and monitoring governance for IT. It is important to note, however, that the final decision about the strategy, policies, rules, and plans and how they are enforced is made by the governors because they are accountable for governance. This accountability may not be delegated to managers, who are required to comply with governance.

Governance is fulfilled by the leadership of each business unit, including IT. Therefore, the CIO is responsible for ensuring that IT operates according to the strategy, policies, rules, and plans defined in corporate governance. Since IT is an integral part of each business unit, however, it is important that the leaders of other business units are also engaged in defining how governance of IT will be fulfilled and enforced.

This is usually achieved by establishing an IT steering committee, also called an IT steering group. The purpose of the steering committee is to establish how IT will comply with and fulfil corporate governance. In addition, it represents how IT works with other business units to help them comply with corporate governance.

You can see an example of the IT steering group in relation to other governance bodies in Figure 5.2.

The composition of the IT steering committee makes it an ideal platform to discuss and agree on a number of other areas too. These include the following:

- Discussing the IT strategy and IT strategy planning documents and recommending them to the governors

- Clarifying strategic requirements from other business units

- Ensuring that the contents and consequences of the IT strategy are clearly understood by other business leaders

- Making major decisions requiring funding from other business units

- Settling disputes about IT service priorities

- Reaching agreement about the minimum level of service for shared services (usually when one business unit wants a much higher level of service but cannot afford to cover the costs themselves and requires the agreement of all other business units to move to the higher level)

- Discussing IT service issues that require senior management intervention
- Negotiating changes to policies in other business units that impede IT's ability to meet its objectives (for example, when an IT organization is asked to reduce costs but users insist on the most expensive solution)

Service Strategy Relating to Governance

Reviewing the chapter so far, it may appear that all strategy is strictly contained within the role of the governors. This is not the case. Rather, the governors are responsible for the strategy of the organization and for ensuring that all parts of the organization are aligned to that strategy.

Every part of the organization must, however, produce its own strategy that enables it to fulfil the overall corporate strategy. Each strategy must be grounded in the corporate strategy and must be approved by the governors.

Strategy management for an internal IT service provider will be overseen by the CIO and the IT steering committee. In larger organizations, this might be a dedicated function reporting to the CIO.

Key processes for fulfilling governance are as follows:

- The service portfolio is an integral part of fulfilling governance because the nature of services, their content, and the required investment are directly related to whether the strategy is achievable. The current and planned services in the service portfolio are an important part of strategy analysis and execution.

- Financial management for IT services is also a critical element of evaluating what investment is required to execute the service strategy, ensuring that the strategy is executed within the appropriate costs, and then measuring whether this was achieved within the defined limits.

- Demand management provides a mechanism for identifying tolerance levels for effective strategy execution. Each strategy approved by the governors must include the boundaries within which that strategy will be effective. Demand management assists in defining these boundaries in terms of business activity and service performance.

- Business relationship management is instrumental in defining the requirements and performance of services to customers. This makes it possible for those customers to comply with corporate governance in their organizations.

Summary

In this chapter, we reviewed the importance of governance as it applies to the service strategy lifecycle stage. This included an explanation of what ITIL means by governance and how we set the strategy for governance in the strategy lifecycle stage.

We explored the concepts of evaluate, direct, and monitor and their application in the service lifecycle.

We also examined the importance of a governance framework and how IT governance fits into this framework. Finally, we explored the use of governance bodies.

Exam Essentials

Understand the concepts of governance.   You will need to understand the concepts of governance as they relates to service strategy.

Understand the role of governance.   Make sure you comprehend, from a management-level viewpoint, the role of governance in service management.

Describe how the governance process is developed.   You need to be able to describe how the governance process—evaluate, direct, and monitor—is part of service strategy.

Explain the governance framework.   Explain the governance framework and its use in service management.

Describe what IT governance is.   Be able to describe what IT governance is and the governance bodies it consists of.

Understand governance in service strategy.   Understand the role of service strategy processes and governance.

Review Questions

You can find the answers to the review questions in the appendix.

1. What is the key fact about governance that makes it important as a strategic concept?

    A. It connects the service provider to the operational users.

    B. It is an overarching area that ties IT and the business together.

    C. It connects operational functions to the service provider.

    D. It is a concept that reviews all operational activity for process adherence.

2. Match the options to the following governance activities.

    1. Direct

    2. Evaluate

    3. Monitor

        A. Refers to the ongoing assessment of the organization's performance and its environment.

        B. The governors of the organization are able to determine whether governance is being fulfilled effectively.

        C. Relates to communicating the strategy, policies, and plans to, and through, management.

3. Which of these is the ISO standard associated with corporate governance of IT?

    A. ISO 20000

    B. ISO 27001

    C. ISO 15504

    D. ISO 38500

4. Governance is expressed in terms of three elements. Which of these is the correct set?

    A. Strategy, policies, plans

    B. People, process, policy

    C. Plans, process, objectives

    D. Strategy, policy, process

5. True or False? Policies define boundaries, or what the organization may or may not do as part of its operations.

    A. True

    B. False

6. Which of these are the principles covered in the ISO 38500 standard? (Choose all that apply.)

    A. Establish responsibilities.

    B. Agree on a strategy to set and meet the organization's objectives.

    C. Acquire for valid reasons.

    D. Ensure performance when required.

    E. Ensure conformance with rules.

    F. Ensure respect for human factors.

7. Which of these options best reflects the approach to IT and corporate governance?

    A. Corporate governance does not apply to IT.

    B. IT governance is distinct and separate from all other governance approaches in the organization.

    C. Corporate governance applies across the whole organization, and because IT is part of the organization, corporate governance applies.

    D. IT governance is managed by the CIO and is not subject to any oversight by other organizational directors.

8. Who makes the final decision about the strategy, policies, rules, and plans and how they are enforced?

    A. IT steering group

    B. Operational management

    C. Governors of the organization

    D. CIO and finance director

9. Which of these are common topics of discussion for the IT steering group? (Choose all that apply.)

    A. Clarification of strategic requirements from other business units

    B. Agreeing on corporate strategy for all business units

    C. Ensuring that the contents and consequences of the IT strategy are clearly understood by other business leaders

    D. Making major decisions that require funding from other business units

    E. Settling disputes about IT service priorities

10. Which of these are key service strategy processes that assist in fulfilling governance? (Choose all that apply.)

    A. Design coordination

    B. Service portfolio management

    C. IT service continuity management

    D. Financial management for IT services

    E. Demand management

    F. Service level management

    G. Business relationship management

    H. Service asset and configuration management

Chapter

6

Organizing for Service Strategy

THE FOLLOWING ITIL INTERMEDIATE EXAM OBJECTIVES ARE DISCUSSED IN THIS CHAPTER:

✓ Organizational development

✓ Organizational departmentalization

✓ Organizational design

✓ The role of service owner and business relationship manager

✓ Strategy management, service portfolio management, financial management, and demand management roles

To do well on the exam, you must ensure that you understand the concepts associated with organizational development and design. You will also need to understand the roles associated with the service strategy process. You will need to demonstrate that you can apply these concepts to the scenarios by analyzing the information provided in the exam questions.

Organizational Development

There is no one best way to organize. Every organization has its own strategic objectives. The best way to organize is to adopt a structure that maximizes the chances of achievement of these objectives. Elements of an organizational design, such as scale, scope, and structure, will differ according to the strategic objectives, and a design that is suitable may become less effective over time. Each organization has its own culture, and the organizational structure needs to be compatible with this.

Well-performing organizations tend to become more decentralized, with greater autonomy allowed for local managers. Where the organization is not performing well, the tendency is to retain more centralized control. Centralization is the result of a lack of confidence in local decision-making, and a belief that it needs to be controlled from the top. Senior managers can see the "whole picture" but lack the detailed knowledge of local managers.

This moving between centralized and decentralized management can be the source of long-term organizational problems and has been described as "the illusion of being in control." Figure 6.1 shows the advantages and disadvantages of each approach.

FIGURE 6.1 The centralized-decentralized spectrum

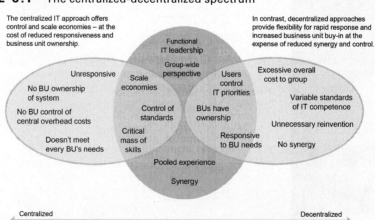

Organizations move through different management styles, known as network, directive, delegative, coordinated, and collaborative. Again, there is no one correct style; at different times, different styles are appropriate—the same style may be inappropriate in a different situation. Over time, there will be challenges that cannot be met successfully with the current management style. Reverting to a previous style is not the answer—the organization must move ahead. The adoption of each style is a stage in the evolving maturity of the organization. Figure 6.2 shows these stages.

FIGURE 6.2   Stages of organizational development

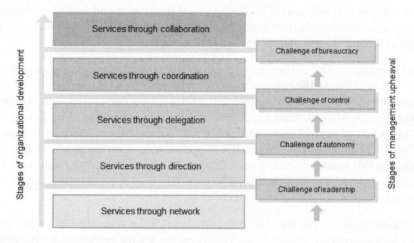

Let's look at each of these stages in turn:

Stage 1: Network   This style has an informal approach to service delivery. The focus may be highly technical and is against having formal organizational structures. Over time, as the organization develops, this approach struggles to cope with increasing demands; the technical skills required for this style are not helpful when trying to manage a growing organization.

A common structure in this stage is called a network. This means actions are coordinated by agreements rather than through a formal hierarchy of authority. Staff complement each other's activities, working together. The organization shares its skills with the customer to allow them to become more efficient, reduce costs, or improve quality.

The key advantages of a network structure are as follows:

- Lack of bureaucracy
- Flat structure, fewer managers required
- Adaptable

The disadvantages are as follows:

- Need for managers to integrate staff activities
- Difficulties coordinating actions
- Difficulties in externally sourcing functional activities

As the organization grows, the network approach is less useful, but moving to the next stage is challenging. The aim is to develop a management team with skill and experience in service management structures to guide the development to the next stage.

Stage 2: Directive   As the stage 1 organization develops, the management team encourages lower-level managers to become responsible for particular functions. Stage 2 is therefore quite hierarchical, with the functions separated and basic processes in place.

Issues can arise when centralization prevents autonomy; this means that actions are carried out in the agreed way but little innovation occurs because any deviation from the standard approach requires authorization. This leads to staff frustration and lack of innovation. In order to prosper, the organization needs to develop to the next stage and encourage delegation, such as having process owners at the lower levels.

Stage 3: Delegation   The challenges of the directive structure are met by encouraging delegation, which allows the organization to strike a balance between technical efficiency and the encouragement of innovation. However, this delegated structure presents its own challenges, such as when functional and process objectives clash. Functional owners feel a loss of control and seek to regain it. Top managers intervene in decision-making only when necessary. The conflict may encourage a return to a centralized approach, but this is not advised; a better approach is to enhance the organization's coordination techniques and solutions. The most common approach is through formal systems and programs.

Stage 4: Coordination   The focus of a stage 4 organization is on the use of formal systems in achieving greater coordination. These systems are the responsibility of senior managers. The solutions lead to planned service management structures that are intensely reviewed and continually improved. Each service and its investment are carefully monitored. Technical functions are centralized while service management processes are decentralized.

The challenge is to respond to business needs in an agile manner. The business may regard IT as bureaucratic and rigid. The emphasis on delivering a good service may prevent innovation, and adherence to procedures may mean a loss of agility.

Stage 5: Collaboration   An organization that has reached stage 5 has a strong collaboration with the business. Managers are used to manage relationships and resolve conflicts in an effective and flexible manner. Cross-functional teams respond to changes in business conditions and strategy. There is an open-minded approach to the adoption of new approaches. Matrix management is common.

A matrix structure is shown as a rectangular grid, as shown in Figure 6.3. Functional responsibility flows vertically; product or customer responsibility flows horizontally. There are basically two (or more) line organizations, with dual lines of authority and a balance of power, and two (or more) bosses in each area, each actively participating in strategy setting and governance.

FIGURE 6.3   Services through collaboration

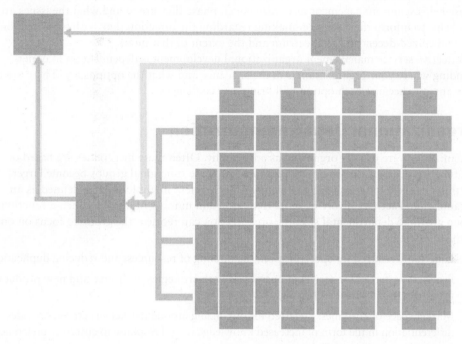

A matrix structure has both advantages and disadvantages. The advantages are as follows:

- Reduces and overcomes functional barriers
- Increases responsiveness to changing needs
- Improves communication between functional specialists
- Provides cross-skilling opportunities
- Uses the skills of specialized employees who move from product to product, or customer to customer, as needed

The disadvantages are as follows:

- Staff not knowing what to expect of each other
- Staff disliking the resulting ambiguity and role conflict
- Potential for conflict between functions and product or customer teams over time

Deciding on a Structure

The descriptions of each stage in the preceding section show how each phase influences the others over time. There is no right or wrong phase, and the progression through phases may not be linear (1, then 2, then 3, for example). Understanding the characteristics of each phase helps senior management recognize which phase they are in and what the issues are; this helps to inform their decision-making regarding the direction they wish to move along the centralized-decentralized spectrum and the extent of that move.

Effective service management organizational development is dependent upon understanding where your organization is in the sequence and what the options are. There are no easy answers because each option will bring new challenges.

Organizational Departmentalization

Organizations are usually organized as a hierarchy. Often these hierarchies are based on the functions carried out by different groups. As these functional groups become larger, we think of them in terms of departments. A department might loosely be defined as an organizational activity involving more than a certain number of people. When a functional group grows to departmental size, the organization can reorient the group to focus on one of the following areas:

- Function: Preferred for specialization, the pooling of resources, and reducing duplication.
- Product: Preferred for servicing businesses with strategies of diverse and new products, usually manufacturing businesses.
- Market space or customer: Preferred for organizing around market structures. Provides differentiation in the form of increased knowledge of and response to customer preferences.
- Geography: The use of geography depends on the industry. By providing services in close geographical proximity, the organization minimizes travel and distribution costs while leveraging local knowledge.
- Process: Preferred for an end-to-end coverage of a process.

This means the organization will organize its departments to suit its strategy. Table 6.1 shows how some structures are particularly suited to some particular strategies.

TABLE 6.1   Basic organizational structures

Basic structure	Strategic considerations
Functional	Specialization
	Common standards
	Small size
Product	Product focus
	Strong product knowledge
Market space or customer	Service unique to segment
	Customer service
	Buyer strength
	Rapid customer service

Basic structure	Strategic considerations
Geography	Onsite services
	Proximity to customer for delivery and support
	Organization perceived as local
Process	Need to minimize process cycle times
	Process excellence

Organizational Design

The first consideration when choosing an organizational design is strategy; this is illustrated in Figure 6.4, showing how we match strategic forces with organizational development. It sets the direction and guides the criteria for each step of the design process.

FIGURE 6.4   Matching strategic forces with organizational development

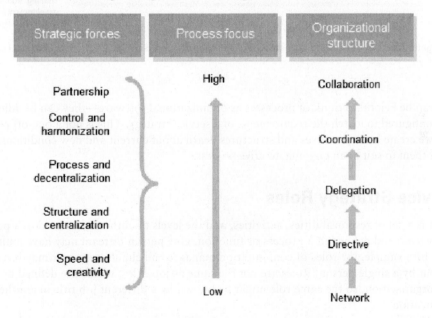

Again, before we start designing our key processes, we should first choose a departmentalization structure. For example, if the provider's organization will be structured by geography or aligned by customers, the process design will be impacted by this decision. Once key processes are understood, we can begin organizational design as shown in Figure 6.5.

FIGURE 6.5 Organizational design steps

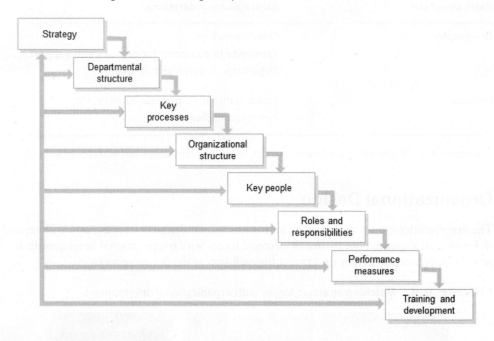

It can be helpful to think of processes as organizational software—they can be adjusted and configured to match the requirements of a service strategy. This is not a one-off process; we create basic processes and structures, learn about current and new conditions, and adjust them to suit in an ongoing iterative process.

Service Strategy Roles

A role is a set of responsibilities, activities, and the levels of authority granted to a person or team and defined in a process or function. One person or team may have multiple roles; for example, the roles of configuration manager and change manager may be carried out by a single person. Roles are not the same as job titles, which are defined by each organization, so the same role might be known by a different job title in another organization.

Roles fall into two main categories—generic roles, such as process manager and process owner, and specific roles that are involved within a particular lifecycle stage or process, such as a change administrator or knowledge management process owner. We will look at both types of role in relation to service strategy.

Service Owner

Large organizations will have many specialist areas, each concerned with its own processes and capabilities. Providing a service to a customer requires many of these specialist departments, or silos, to contribute. The service owner provides an end-to-end view, which ensures consistency across the service.

The service owner understands what the service needs to deliver and how it has been built to satisfy these requirements. As the representative of the service, they are involved in assessment of the impact of changes affecting the service, and when it suffers a major incident, they are involved as an escalation and communication point.

By attending internal and external reviews, the service owner ensures that the service is delivered according to the customer requirements. This allows the role to identify the requirements for improvement and provide input to continual service improvement to work with IT to address any deficiencies.

The service catalog process provides the business with information regarding the service, and maintaining this information with the service catalog process owner is another responsibility for the service owner.

The service owner interfaces with the underlying IT processes. It will have close associations with many of the processes:

Incident Management   Involved in or perhaps chairs the crisis management team for high-priority incidents impacting the service owned

Problem Management   Plays a major role in establishing the root cause and proposed permanent fix for the service being evaluated

Release and Deployment Management   Acts as a key stakeholder in determining whether a new release affecting a service in production is ready for promotion

Change Management   Participates in change advisory board decisions, approving changes to the services they own

Service Asset and Configuration Management   Ensures that all groups that maintain the data and relationships for the service architecture they are responsible for have done so with the level of integrity required

Service Level Management   Acts as the single point of contact for a specific service and ensures that the service portfolio and service catalog are accurate in relation to the service

Availability and Capacity Management   Reviews technical monitoring data from a domain perspective to ensure that the overall needs are being met

IT Service Continuity Management   Understands and is responsible for ensuring that all elements required to restore the service are known and in place in the event of a crisis

Financial Management for IT Services   Assists in defining and tracking the cost models in relation to how the service is costed and recovered

Business Relationship Manager

Many organizations will have a person with the job title business relationship manager (BRM). This job may combine the roles of the business relationship management process owner and the business relationship management process manager and allocate it to one person. There may be several business relationship managers, each focused on different customer segments or groups. The role is sometimes combined with the role of service level manager.

By its nature, the role of business relationship manager often includes tasks from other processes; in the event of a major incident, for example, the BRM might attend major incident reviews to represent the customer. This does not make those activities part of the business relationship management process.

As we have said, the roles of business relationship management process owner and business relationship management process manager are often combined. The business relationship management process owner's responsibilities typically include the generic process owner role of accountability for policy, documentation, auditing, and so on for the process combined with working with other process owners to ensure that there is an integrated approach to the design and implementation of business relationship management.

Now let's consider the business relationship management process manager's responsibilities. Typically they will have the following responsibilities:

- Carrying out the generic process manager role for the business relationship management process
- Identifying customer needs and ensuring that the service provider is able to meet these needs with an appropriate catalog of services
- Ensuring that customer expectations do not exceed what they are willing to pay for and that the service provider is able to meet the customer's expectations before agreeing to deliver the service
- Ensuring high levels of customer satisfaction, indicating that the service provider is meeting the customer's requirements
- Establishing and maintaining a constructive relationship between the service provider and the customer based on understanding the customer and their business drivers

Further responsibilities are as follows:

- Identifying changes to the customer environment that could potentially impact the type, level, or utilization of services provided
- Identifying technology trends that could potentially impact the type, level, or utilization of services provided
- Establishing and articulating business requirements for new services or changes to existing services
- Ensuring that the service provider is meeting the business needs of the customer
- Mediating in cases where there are conflicting requirements for services from different business units

It is important to remember that there are other parties involved in the business relationship management process. The business has a responsibility to play its part in the relationship. So, the customers and users of the IT services need to be involved, state their requirements, and work with the business relationship manager to ensure that these requirements are met so that the required business outcomes are supported.

Strategy Management Roles

Let's look at the roles associated with strategy management for IT services. These include the process owner and process manager.

Strategy Management for IT Services Process Owner

The strategy management for IT services process owner typically has the following responsibilities:

- Carrying out the generic process owner role for the strategy management for IT services process
- Working with other process owners to ensure that the organization's overall IT strategy is effectively reflected in their processes

Strategy Management for IT Services Process Manager

The strategy management for IT services process manager typically has the following responsibilities:

- Carrying out the generic process manager role for the strategy management for IT services process
- Formulating, documenting, and maintaining the organization's overall IT strategy to best underpin the business strategy
- Assisting in informing, publicizing, and marketing the key aspects of the IT strategy so that all stakeholders are aware of the strategy and how it will be implemented
- Being responsible to the IT steering group for the successful implementation and operation of the IT strategy
- Reviewing how well the strategy is working, and making any necessary adjustments to make it more effective
- Ensuring that the appropriate support is in place for any strategy management tools and processes
- Coordinating the interfaces between strategy management for IT services and other processes

Other Roles Involved in Strategy Management for IT Services

In addition to these specific roles and activities, others are performed by the service provider's senior management and the wider organization. Whatever they are called within an organization, the following roles should exist.

- Business strategy manager. This role formulates, documents, and maintains the organization's overall business strategy.

- IT steering group. This role is formed of senior management from the business and IT roles and may include one or more enterprise architects to make decisions on policy.

- IT director or service management director. Larger organizations sometimes appoint an IT director or service management director to be responsible for all of their ITSM processes and to establish a service management office.

Service Portfolio Roles

Now let's consider the roles associated with the service portfolio management process. These include the process owner and the process manager.

Service Portfolio Management Process Owner

The service portfolio management process owner typically has the following responsibilities:

- Carrying out the generic process owner role for the service portfolio management process

- Working with other process owners to ensure that there is an integrated approach to the design and implementation of service portfolio management

Service Portfolio Management Process Manager

The next role is that of the process manager. The service portfolio management process manager typically has the following responsibilities:

- Carrying out the generic process manager role for the service portfolio management process

- Managing and maintaining the service portfolio

- Managing the surrounding processes for keeping the portfolio attractive to customers and up-to-date

- Marketing the portfolio, and in particular the service catalog, so that customers and potential customers are aware of the services available

- Helping to formulate service packages and associated options, which enables the logical grouping of services into products designed to be marketed to, sold to, and consumed by suitable customer groups

Financial Management Roles

We will now look at the roles associated with the financial management process. It is important to remember that although job titles may differ, many organizations will have a person with the job title IT financial manager. This job typically combines the roles of financial management for IT services process owner and financial management for IT services process manager.

Financial Management for IT Services Process Owner

The financial management for IT services process owner typically has the following responsibilities:

- Carrying out the generic process owner role for the financial management for IT services process
- Working with other process owners to develop an integrated approach to the design and implementation of financial management for IT services

Financial Management for IT Services Process Manager

The financial management for IT services process manager typically has the following responsibilities:

- Carrying out the generic process manager role for the financial management for IT services process
- Compiling and formulating the annual IT budgets to be scrutinized by the IT steering group
- Managing the IT budgets on a daily, monthly, and annual basis, ensuring that expenditure is in line with the budgets
- Producing regular statements of accounts to enable relevant managers to manage their own areas of the budgets
- Formulating and managing recharging systems for IT customers
- Reporting on value for money of all major activities, projects, and proposed expenditure items within IT

Budget Holders

Another role associated with financial management is that of budget holder. Individual IT managers may be budget holders responsible for managing the budgets for their own particular area. Their responsibilities typically include the following:

- Submitting an annual budget estimate
- Negotiating and agreeing on their annual budget
- Managing their budget on an ongoing basis
- Reporting budget activities and outcomes

Demand Management Roles

Our final process roles are related to the demand management process. These include the process owner and process manager.

Demand Management Process Owner

The demand management process owner typically has the following responsibilities:

- Carrying out the generic process owner role for the demand management process
- Working with other process owners to ensure that there is an integrated approach to the design and implementation of demand management

Demand Management Process Manager

The demand management process manager typically has the following responsibilities:

- Carrying out the generic process manager role for the demand management process
- Identifying and analyzing patterns of business activity to understand the levels of demand that will be placed on a service
- Defining and analyzing user profiles to understand the typical profiles of demand for services from different types of users
- Helping to design services that meet the patterns of business activity and that have the ability to meet business outcomes
- Ensuring that adequate resources are available at the appropriate levels of capacity to meet the demand for services
- Anticipating and managing potential situations where demand for a service exceeds the capacity to deliver it
- Gearing the utilization of resources that deliver services to meet the fluctuating levels of demand for those services

Summary

This chapter covered the concepts of organizational considerations as they relate to service strategy. We explored organizational development, departmentalization, and design and the roles of service owner and business relationship manager in addition to the roles involved in strategy management, service portfolio management, financial management, and demand management.

Exam Essentials

Understand the development of organizations, in particular the phases of organizing by function, product, market space or customer, geography, or process. Understand the strengths and challenges delivered by each.

Understand the generic role of the service owner.   Be able to describe the role of the service owner.

Be able to explain and expand on the role of process owner for each of the service strategy processes of business relationship management, strategy management, financial management, portfolio management, and demand management.   Each process will have an owner, and each process has slightly different responsibilities allocated to the role to meet the process objectives.

Understand and expand on the role of process manager for each of the service strategy processes of business relationship management, strategy management, financial management, portfolio management, and demand management.   Be aware of the difference between the process owner and process manager. Differentiate between the process managers for each process and the responsibilities associated with each.

Review Questions

You can find the answers to the review questions in the appendix.

1. Which of these are recognized organizational structures in the *ITIL Service Strategy* publication? Select all that apply.

    A. Localized

    B. Virtual

    C. Centralized

    D. Follow the Sun

    E. Decentralized

2. Deciding on an organizational structure requires an understanding of where your organization is in the sequence of management styles. Put these styles in the correct order: coordination, directive, collaboration, delegation, network.

    A. Coordination, directive, collaboration, delegation, network

    B. Network, directive, delegation, collaboration, coordination

    C. Network, coordination, directive, collaboration, delegation

    D. Network, directive, delegation, coordination, collaboration

3. What are the key characteristics of the network management style?

    A. Flexibility, responsiveness, and a matrix approach

    B. Focused on rapid, informal, and adhoc delivery

    C. Promotes a balance between technical efficiency and innovation

    D. Focused on a hierarchic structure with separate functional activities

    E. Characterized by planned IT service management structures that are reviewed and improved

4. Which of the following steps need to be taken before organizational design begins? Select all that apply.

    A. Consider the organizational strategy.

    B. Consider the organizational culture.

    C. Decide on a departmentalization structure.

    D. Design key processes.

5. Which of these is the correct description of a role according to the *ITIL Service Strategy* publication?

    A. A role is a functional group of people carrying out a specific activity.

    B. A role describes an executive in an organization.

    C. A role is a set of responsibilities, activities, and associated levels of authority granted to a person or team.

    D. A role is the supporting discipline for a process and can only be carried out by a member of the organizational executive team.

6. Which of these statements about a service owner is correct?

    1. The service owner is accountable for the delivery of a specific service.

    2. The service owner is critical to service management.

    A. Statement 1 only

    B. Statement 2 only

    C. Both statements

    D. Neither statement

7. According to the *ITIL Service Strategy* publication, which of these is identified as an additional role within financial management for IT services?

    A. Business strategy manager

    B. Budget holder

    C. Service owner

    D. IT director

8. Which of these is the best description of the role of service owner?

    A. Manages the process so that it is performed efficiently and meets the expectation of the business customer.

    B. Ensures that the process produces the correct output.

    C. Represents the service across the service provider and business organization.

    D. Represents the process at the change advisory board.

9. Matching the description to the process role, which of the following statements are correct? (Choose all that apply.)

    A. The process owner ensures that the process can be carried out effectively.

    B. The process manager ensures that the process can be carried out effectively.

    C. The process manager ensures that the process is carried out effectively

    D. The process owner ensures that the process is carried out effectively.

10. Which option best describes the responsibility of a demand management process manager?

    A. Designing services that meet the patterns of business activity and have the ability to meet business outcomes

    B. Performing sizing on all proposed new services and systems

    C. Compiling and formulating the annual IT budgets to be scrutinized by the IT steering group

    D. Establishing and articulating business requirements for new services or changes to existing services

Chapter

7

Technology Considerations

THE FOLLOWING ITIL INTERMEDIATE EXAM OBJECTIVES ARE DISCUSSED IN THIS CHAPTER:

✓ Service automation

✓ Service interfaces

To do well on the exam, you must ensure that you understand the concepts associated with service automation and service interfaces. You will need to demonstrate that you can apply these concepts to the scenarios by analyzing the information provided in the exam questions. We also include a brief look at service analytics.

Service Automation

We automate processes and activities because automation offers significant advantages when compared with doing the same things manually. Automated systems can be much faster, and they can work without breaks or holidays. They are also consistent, performing the same task in exactly the same way over and over, as compared to human operators who may have different approaches, make mistakes, and so on. Automation can therefore have a significant impact on the performance of service assets such as management, organization, people, process, knowledge, and information. Many processes that used to be handled by human operators are now performed by software-based service agents, made possible by advances in technology.

For example, a chatbot is a computer program designed to simulate an intelligent conversation with one or more human users. Chatbots are often integrated into dialog systems for purposes such as offline help. Some chatbots use sophisticated natural language processing systems, but many simply scan for keywords within the input and pull a reply with the most matching keywords, or the most similar wording pattern, from a textual database.

Automation can offer many benefits, improving the utility and warranty of services:

- It is easier to adjust capacity to automated resources in response to variations in demand volumes than to train staff, who may not then be required.

- As stated previously, automated tools help to eradicate human error and have fewer restrictions on time of access; they don't sleep, eat, get sick, or take holidays.

- They present a standardized service, making measurement easier because there are not the variations that humans bring to an interaction. For example, a voice-activated system to confirm identity and then reset a password will take the same time every time. The time to do this by calling a service desk could vary greatly.

- The volume of calculations required for areas such as load balancing in capacity management, and the speed at which these calculations must be done, is beyond the capacity of human agents.

- Automated processes can be used to gather information in a consistent manner and then to distribute it as required. This overcomes the issue of knowledge being lost when employees move within the organization or permanently leave.

Used with care, automation of service processes helps improve the quality of service, reduce costs, and reduce risks by reducing complexity and uncertainty.

Automation and Service Management

The following are some of the areas where service management can benefit from automation:

- Design and modeling
- Service catalog, including self-service request fulfilment
- Pattern recognition and analysis, used in event management to correlate events, for detection, and monitoring of events
- Classification, prioritization, and routing, as used in service desk systems
- Detection and monitoring
- Optimization in capacity management

As we have already remarked, people do not work at a consistent level. Their performance can be affected by the workload, their motivation, and the nature of the task at hand (easy but boring, for example); different staff will have different knowledge, skills, and experience affecting their productivity. These factors can lead to inconsistent processing times, which in turn may result in degradation of service levels, as shown in Figure 7.1. Standardizing processing time by removing the "human factor" will reduce variation and prevent service level degradation.

FIGURE 7.1   Degrading effect of variation in service processes

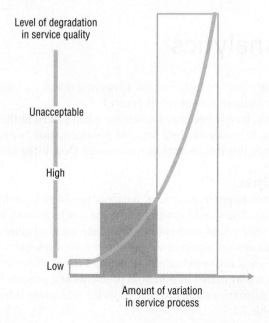

Preparing to Automate

Automation should be introduced with care. Although introduced to improve service, a failed attempt at automating something can be a source of customer dissatisfaction and poor staff morale. The simpler the process, the easier it is to automate and the smaller the chance of error, so processes should be simplified before being automated. Removing unnecessary steps may itself reduce performance variations because there are fewer steps to go wrong. Simplification does not mean degradation; unnecessary steps may be removed, but the process should still deliver the same end result, with the same quality of output.

There are limits to simplification. When the process cannot be simplified any further, it is appropriate to start to consider how to automate it.

When automating a process, ensure that the activities, allocation of tasks, required information, and interactions are all fully understood. All users of the automated service should be clear about the required inputs. Automate, clarify, test, modify, and then automate again.

Self-service can hide the underlying systems and processes from the user; the interface should be simplified so that users see only the attributes needed to present demand and extract utility.

Remember, complex tasks, or those with significant variations in terms of inputs, resources, and outcomes each time, may not be suitable for automation. The greatest advantage in terms of efficiency gains will come with automating simple but frequent tasks; automating a complex task will require more effort, which may not be justified if the task is performed only rarely.

Service Analytics

Information is necessary but not sufficient for answering questions such as, Why is the data as it is? and How is it likely to change in the future?

Information is static. It only becomes knowledge when placed in the context of patterns and their implications. By understanding patterns of information, we can answer questions such as these: How does this incident affect the service? How is the business impacted? How do we respond?

This is service analytics.

To understand means to put it in context. Analysis produces knowledge; then synthesis provides understanding. You should remember the data, information, knowledge, wisdom (DIKW) model from your Foundation course; it is illustrated in Figure 7.2.

Data alone does not answer any questions, but it is a vital resource. Most data collection is carried out by using instrumentation to measure the behavior of the infrastructure elements. These tools report actual or potential problems and provide feedback after adjustments. Most organizations already have tools for measuring infrastructure elements, similar to those in Table 7.1.

FIGURE 7.2   The flow from data to wisdom

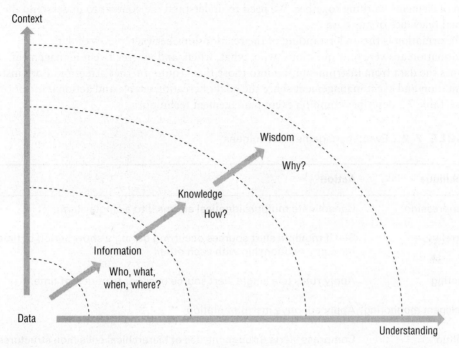

TABLE 7.1   Instrumentation techniques

Technique	Action
Asynchronous capture	Passive listeners scan for alerts.
External source	Compile data from external sources, such as service desk tickets, suppliers, or systems—e.g., enterprise resource planning (ERP).
Manual generation	Manually create or alter an event.
Polling	Monitoring systems actively interrogate functional elements.
Synthetic transactions	Simulate the end user experience through known transactions.

Instrumentation provides raw data, but the behavior of a service is impacted by a combination of elements working together. We need to understand the context to understand the actual relevance of any data.

Information is the understanding of the relationships between pieces of data. Information answers four questions: who, what, when, and where? Event management refines the data from instrumentation into those that require further attention. Both instrumentation and event management share the goal of creating usable and actionable information. Table 7.2 describes common event management techniques.

TABLE 7.2   Event management techniques

Technique	Action
Compression	Consolidate multiple identical alarms into a single alarm.
Correlation	See if multiple alert sources occurring during a short period of time have any relationship with each other.
Filtering	Apply rules to a single alert source over some period of time.
Intelligent monitoring	Apply adaptive instrumentation.
Roll-up	Compress alerts through the use of hierarchical collection structures.
Verification	Actively confirm an actual incident.

A fault is defined as an abnormal condition that requires action to repair, while an error is a single event. A fault is usually indicated by excessive errors. Event management will monitor for thresholds being breached (an alert) or for a significant change of state (an event) of a configuration item.

Performance, however, is a measure of how well something is working. Operations staff will begin with fault management. As it becomes more mature, the function will move from being reactive to becoming proactive. Fault management systems often have difficulties in dealing with complex objects that span multiple object types and geographies. Further context is needed to make this information useful for services. We begin by transitioning from information to knowledge.

Service analytics is useful to model existing infrastructure components and support services and how they relate to the higher-level business services. This model shows the dependencies rather than the design, the chain of events that could cause a negative impact to the business services. The link between specific infrastructure events and corresponding business processes becomes apparent. The component-to-system-to-process linkage—also known as the service model—allows us to clearly identify the business impact of an event. Managers can then understand the behavior of the service as a whole, not just each error.

The correct behavior of the service when it is operating normally can be defined as a baseline against which actual performance can be compared

Service analytics can help an operations group do a better job of identifying and correcting problems from the user's standpoint. It can also predict the impact of changes to the environment. This same model can be turned around to show business demand for IT services. This is a high leverage point when building an on-demand environment.

Automation can therefore help with the early steps of the DIKW model. No computer-based technology can provide wisdom. People are required to provide evaluated understanding, to answer and appreciate the "why" questions. The application of intelligence and experience is more likely to be found in the organizational processes that define and deliver service management than in applied technologies.

Service Interfaces

The design of service interfaces is critical to service management. Service access points are associated with one or more channels of service. User interfaces include those provided for the customer's employees and other agents as well as process-to-process interfaces. Service interfaces are typically present at the point of utilization or service access points (see Figure 7.3).

FIGURE 7.3   The critical role of service interfaces

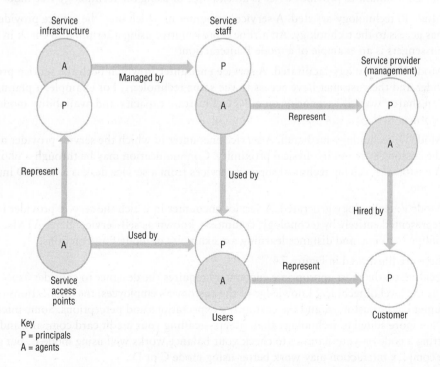

The service interfaces should meet the basic requirements of warranty:

- They should be easily located, ubiquitous, or simply embedded in the immediate environment or business context.

- They should be available in forms that allow choice and flexibility for users.

- They should be available with sufficient capacity to cope with the number of users.

- They should accommodate users with varying levels of skills, competencies, backgrounds, and disabilities.

- Ubiquity should be balanced with the need to keep interfaces low profile and low overhead to avoid undue stress.

- They should be simple and reliable and self-reliant.

Types of Service Technology Encounters

Customers now interact with service providers very differently than they used to; for example, using self-check-in kiosks at airports has replaced the interaction with the check-in staff

There are five modes in which technology interacts with a service provider's customers:

- Mode A: technology-free. Technology is not involved in the service encounter. Employing a consultant to provide advice is an example of using the technology-free model.

- Mode B: technology-assisted. A service encounter in which only the service provider has access to the technology. An airline representative using a terminal to check in passengers is an example of a mode B interaction.

- Mode C: technology-facilitated. A service encounter in which both the service provider and the customer have access to the same technology. For example, a planner can share "what if" scenarios on a PC to illustrate capacity and availability modeling profiles.

- Mode D: technology-mediated. A service encounter in which the service provider and the customer are not in physical proximity. Communication may be through a phone. A customer receiving technical support services from a service desk is a mode D interaction.

- Mode E: technology-generated. A service encounter in which the service provider is represented entirely by technology, commonly known as self-service. Bank ATMs, online banking, and distance learning are examples of mode E interactions.

These are illustrated in Figure 7.4.

Deciding on the most appropriate encounters requires the designer to consider aspects such as the level of technical knowledge of the customer's employees, the implications of the encounter to the customer, and the customer's expectations and perceptions. Some interactions are more suited to technology than others—calling your credit card company and inputting a code on your handset to check your balance works well using mode E, but a more complex interaction may work better using mode C or D.

FIGURE 7.4   Types of service technology encounters

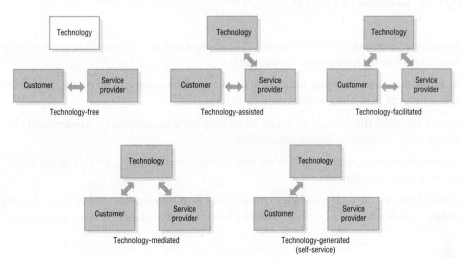

Self-Service Channels

Automation, especially self-service, can be very useful in dealing with peaks of demand. Users are increasingly happy to use such channels because they are used for online shopping, banking, and so on. The Internet browser is a highly familiar service access point. In addition, self-service channels have low marginal cost, can be easily scaled up, provide a consistent service, and are available 24 hours a day. Users may even prefer the consistency of a self-service incident and problem management service rather than human service of variable quality, higher cost, and lower availability.

Poorly designed self-service channels may actually negatively impact the user perception, so the design should ensure usability, efficiency, and ease in interactions through the automated interface.

The level of control users are expected to assume with self-service options should be commensurate with the skill and experience level of the users.

Summary

This chapter covered the technology considerations for service strategy. In particular we looked at service automation, service analytics, and the five types of service interfaces: technology-free, technology-assisted, technology-facilitated, technology-mediated, and technology-generated.

Exam Essentials

Understand the advantages of automating processes and tasks.   This includes understanding when it may not be appropriate to automate.

Be able to list the areas of service management where automation can be useful.   Be able to give examples of how automation could be helpful.

Understand the steps that should be taken when preparing to automate.   Understand the importance of simplification before automation.

Understand the instrumentation and event management techniques.   Be able to list and explain the different techniques.

Understand how service analytics helps convert data into information and helps to develop knowledge.   Understand why service analytics is not useful in the knowledge-to-wisdom step.

Review Questions

You can find the answers to the review questions in the appendix.

1. Which of the following is NOT a benefit of service automation?

   A. Easy to vary capacity

   B. Personalized service

   C. Knowledge retention

   D. Less varied, more standard service

2. Which of the following are event management techniques? (Choose all that apply.)

   1. Compression

   2. Correlation

   3. Service analytics

   4. Filtering

   5. Service automation

   6. Intelligent monitoring

   7. Roll-up

   8. Verification

      A. 1, 2, 4, 5, and 7 only

      B. 1, 2, 4, 6, 7, and 8 only

      C. All of the above

      D. 1, 3, 4, 6, 7, and 8 only

3. Understanding patterns of information is called _____.

   A. DIKW

   B. Service analytics

   C. Service economics

   D. Service knowledge

4. Fill in the blanks in the following sentences: An abnormal condition that requires action to repair is a/an _____. A/an _____ is a single event. We need to apply _____ to determine the relevance of any data. _____ alone can reduce variations in performance.

   A. fault, error, context, simplification

   B. error, context, simplification, fault

   C. context, simplification, fault, error

   D. simplification, fault, error, context

5. Which example fits the term *technology-assisted*?

    A. Consulting services

    B. A planner in consultation with a customer who refers to "what if" scenarios on a personal computer to illustrate capacity and availability modeling profiles

    C. A customer who receives technical support services from a service desk

    D. An airline representative who uses a terminal to check in passengers

6. Which of the following is NOT an instrumentation technique described in the *ITIL Service Strategy* publication?

    A. Asynchronous capture

    B. Synthetic generation

    C. Polling

    D. Synthetic transactions

7. Which of the following are areas where service management may benefit from automation?

    1. Design and modeling

    2. Service catalog

    3. Pattern recognition and analysis

    4. Classification, prioritization, and routing

    5. Optimization

        A. 1, 3, and 4 only

        B. 1, 3, 4, and 5 only

        C. All of the above

        D. 1, 2, 3, and 4 only

8. Which of the following statements about implementing automation is/are incorrect?

    1. Complex tasks may not be suitable for automation.

    2. The greatest benefit will be achieved from automating complex tasks.

    3. Simple tasks are not worth the effort of automating.

    4. Simplification should happen before automation.

        A. All of the above

        B. 2 and 3 only

        C. None of the above

        D. 1 and 4 only

9. Which of the following statements about service analytics is/are TRUE and which is/are FALSE?

    1. Service analytics helps to convert data to information and then to knowledge and finally to wisdom.

2. Service analytics provides the linkage from component to system to process to show the impact of faults on business processes.

   A. Both are TRUE.

   B. 1 is TRUE; 2 is FALSE.

   C. Neither is TRUE.

   D. 1 is FALSE; 2 is TRUE.

10. What is being described in the following statement? "They should be easily located, ubiquitous, or simply embedded in the immediate environment or business context, available in forms that allow choice and flexibility for users and with sufficient capacity to cope with the number of users."

   A. Service catalog entries

   B. Service interfaces

   C. Service analytics

   D. Service technology encounters

Chapter

8

Implementing Service Strategy

THE FOLLOWING ITIL INTERMEDIATE
EXAM OBJECTIVES ARE DISCUSSED IN
THIS CHAPTER:

✓ Implementation of service strategy through the lifecycle

✓ Following a lifecycle approach

✓ The impact of service strategy on other lifecycle stages

To do well on the exam, you must ensure that you understand how to implement service strategy, by following a lifecycle approach, and how this impacts on the other lifecycle stages. You will need to demonstrate that you can apply these concepts to the scenarios by analyzing the information provided in the exam questions.

Implementation through the Lifecycle

In Chapter 2, "Service Strategy Principles," we examined the four Ps of service strategy: perspective, positions, plans, and patterns.

Strategic positions and perspective are converted into strategic plans and patterns with goals and objectives for execution through the service lifecycle. The positions are driven by the need to serve specific customers and market spaces and influenced by strategic perspective as a service provider. Plans are a means of achieving those positions. Plans include projects and programs and result in ongoing revision of the service catalog, service pipeline, customer agreement portfolio, financial budgets and delivery schedules, and the implementation of improvement programs.

Figure 8.1 shows them in action when implementing service strategy through the lifecycle, as described by Simons in 1995.

Plans translate the intent of strategy into action. They identify specific actions that need to be undertaken within each stage of the lifecycle to develop and deploy the capabilities and resources required to reach strategic positions.

These become patterns over time.

Service strategy provides input to each stage of the service lifecycle. CSI provides the feedback and learning mechanism by which the execution of strategy is controlled. In Figure 8.2, you can see the approach of service management driven by strategy.

It is service strategy's job to define which services to offer (the service portfolio) and to whom (the customer portfolio). This in turn determines the customer agreement portfolio that needs to be supported with design, transition, and operation capabilities. By capabilities, we mean the systems, processes, knowledge, skills, and experience required at each stage to effectively support the customer agreement portfolios.

Service design and operation capabilities determine the type of transition capabilities required. They determine the portfolio of service designs and the operating range of the service provider in terms of models and capacities.

FIGURE 8.1   Strategic planning and control process (Simons, 1995)

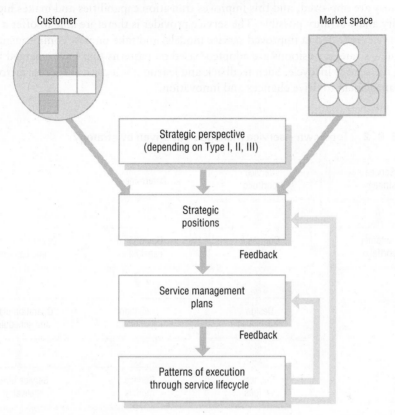

How quickly a service is transitioned from design to operations depends on the capabilities of the service transition stage. Transition capabilities reduce the costs and risks for customers and service providers throughout the lifecycle by maintaining visibility and control over all service management systems and processes. In this manner, transition capabilities act not only as filters, but also as amplifiers that increase the effectiveness of design and operation. They interact with service designs to provide new and improved service models. They interact with operation models and capacity to increase the operational effectiveness of plans and schedules. The net effect is reflected in the service levels delivered to customers in fulfilment of contracts.

Service strategy requires continual service improvement to drive feedback through the lifecycle elements to ensure that improvements are identified, challenges met, and opportunities exploited. This ensures that the services continue to be aligned with the business requirements and strategy. As CSI feeds back possible improvements, the design and operations delivery are improved, and this improves transition capabilities and makes higher levels of utility and warranty possible. The service provider is therefore able to offer a higher level of service (reflected in improved service models) and take on new commitments. In this way, new strategic positions are adopted based on patterns that have emerged from executing the service lifecycle. Such feedback and learning is a critical success factor for service management to drive changes and innovation.

FIGURE 8.2 Top down – service management driven by strategy

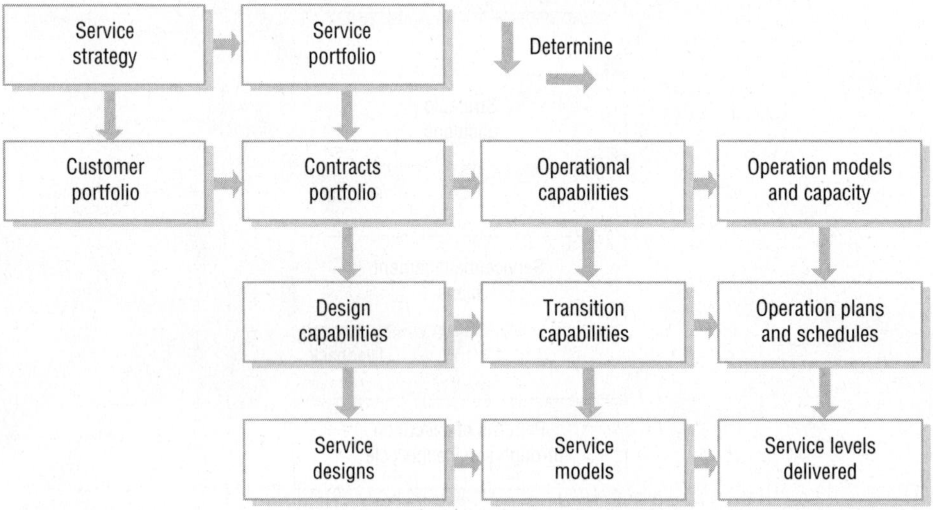

Following a Lifecycle Approach

Strategy is not a static process; it is continually adjusted to meet changing customer requirements.

Service Strategy Approach

Service strategy processes themselves should undergo continual improvement like any process. Both the strategy and its processes are directed by the senior executives of the organization.

Service strategy determines how the service lifecycle functions and how services are designed, transitioned, operated, and improved. It is critical that the implementation of service strategy processes follow the service lifecycle.

Implementing the service strategy processes for the first time is best done using the organization's program and project management approach, and the implementation should be managed as a formal project or series of projects.

The strategy for the implementation should, at a minimum, include the following areas:

- The current state should be assessed and the desired end state defined.

- The gaps between the two states should be analyzed.

- The project should be identified, and activities with specific objectives to close the gaps should be grouped together.

- The scale of the project needs to be sized, so an analysis of the project's scope, scale, interdependencies, risks, costs, and resource requirements is required before it can progress.

- The various projects should then be grouped into logical streams to address key aspects of governance, people, and so on.

- Finally, a road map should be drawn up. This is a time-bound action plan showing the sequence of the initiatives and projects required to close the gaps.

Although a formal service strategy may be absent, every organization has a culture and a way of making decisions. The existing environment must be considered when a service strategy is implemented.

Cultural change like this requires significant organizational change management. A method for gathering feedback during implementation is essential; the plan may need to be deferred or adjusted in light of factors discovered during the design, transition, and operation stages. The importance of executive ownership of the initiative and processes cannot be overemphasized. This is not just an IT project; service strategy is at the heart of the business of the service provider and is a key executive responsibility, which they must appreciate and accept.

Service Design Approach

In service design, the processes, tools, and organizational structure (if required) will be designed. This includes gathering detailed requirements and the actual design of the tools and procedures to be used.

The information that is gathered should include process design of each of the strategy processes, the definition of roles for these processes, and the interfaces between processes, especially between strategy management and business relationship management.

For strategy management, service design should include an agreed assessment method, forecasting and planning tools, document control tools, and identified sources for industry information.

The design should incorporate the policies and processes for the service portfolio, customer portfolio, customer agreement portfolio, and a standard for defining service models and assessing the business impact of new services or changes to existing services.

Financial management tools, policies, charts of accounts (if these do not already exist), cost model definitions, charging strategies and methods, demand management procedures, techniques, and tools will all need to be addressed as part of design.

Service Transition Approach

During transition, the designed service strategy processes and tools will be built or purchased (and customized if necessary) and then tested and deployed.

This stage includes some high-level activities, such as training the project teams and developing or purchasing any tools they need. Tool administrators will need to be trained on how to manage the tools, and process managers should be trained on how to manage the process.

It is important to make sure the tools are tested for utility and warranty, and the processes should be tested to show they can achieve the desired results as planned. Another important factor is running a pilot for the tools and/or processes and training the users of the tools and the staff who will need to comply with the processes. Following the pilot, the tools and/or processes should be deployed. Finally, a postimplementation review should be carried out to ensure that the tools and processes are delivering as they were designed and to provide appropriate feedback.

Service Operation Approach

In service operations, the service strategy processes will actually be executed.
The following generic activities will be included in this stage:

- The execution of process activities as defined in the process documentation and according to the defined policies for the process
- The maintenance of the tools used to support these processes, monitoring the performance and the quality of the output of the processes, and identifying and resolving process exceptions
- Finally, monitoring the overall success of the strategy, services, and customer relationships

Continual Service Improvement Approach

The role of continual service improvement will include the generic CSI activities, applied to service strategy:

- The assessment of the metrics of each process
- Evaluation of the effectiveness and efficiency of each process
- Revision of the requirements for metrics and information as the processes mature
- Identification of opportunities for improvement of processes
- Evaluation of whether the strategy and services are meeting the objectives set
- Plans to address the situation if they are not

Impact of Service Strategy on Lifecycle Stages

Although all lifecycle stages interface with one another, service strategy provides the direction in which services move through the lifecycle and the policies and standards whereby each stage is executed. The following sections highlight the major impact service strategy has on the other four stages.

Service Design Stage

Service strategy sets the direction for the design of services, the objectives the services need to achieve, and the specific outcomes they need to achieve. It defines what is required to ensure both competitiveness and satisfied customers and how this will be achieved.

Service strategy enables design, and it also defines boundaries within which that design must be undertaken.

The design of a service is based on the outcomes the customer desires, expressed in terms of utility and warranty. Determining which attributes of a service are essential, which add value, and which are purely "nice to have" is an important part of designing a service, made clearer by the work done during service strategy. Service strategy will also identify the constraints under which the service needs to be developed. You can see examples of these constraints here in Figure 8.3.

Service Models

Service models provide the basic architecture that is used to develop services during service design. These are the starting point for defining and developing a service design package. Service models will inform the designers about not only the market space that the service is being designed for, but also the type of asset that will need to be put in place to deliver and support the service.

Service models also aid in communicating the intent of the service strategy, and the dynamics of the service, to a broad range of teams involved in the design of the service. This will assist in maintaining consistency of both understanding and design.

Patterns of Business Activity

Design activities related to the utilization, performance, capacity, and availability of the service will rely heavily on the identification and validation of patterns of business activity (PBAs) through demand management. For more information on PBAs, please see Chapter 4, "Service Strategy Processes: Part 2."

Business Impact Analysis

The design teams might be aware of the relative importance of services based on an understanding of the outcomes and their knowledge of the customers. Nevertheless, it is important that the business importance of the service is objectively defined and held as a standard for design prioritization.

FIGURE 8.3 Design constraints driven by strategy

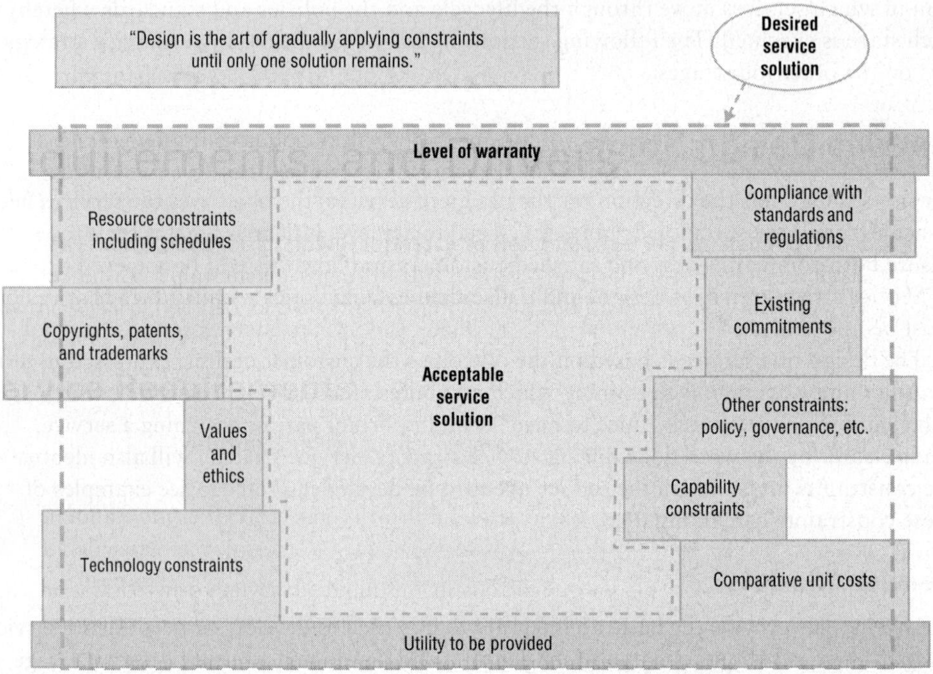

Copyright © AXELOS Limited 2010. All rights reserved. Material is reproduced under license from AXELOS.

This is important from two points of view. Firstly, the design needs to incorporate appropriate levels of availability, service continuity, security, and performance. Business impact analysis (BIA) is an important input for this activity. Secondly, the design teams will need to prioritize their own activities. Business impact analysis will help the teams to be able to judge where their efforts are best spent, especially where there is a resource conflict. For more information on BIA, please see Chapter 2.

Business Relationship Management

Business relationship management is an important source of information about the customer and its objectives, environment, and requirements. It is especially important to continue to validate and clarify customer requirements throughout the service design stage.

Any changes to requirements or design that impact the overall service model, investment, or strategy will need to be validated against the strategy for the service and the service provider. Business relationship management plays an invaluable role in ensuring that this is done.

Service Transition Stage

Service transition is not just a tactical stage in which services are moved into operation; it is critical in achieving a change of strategy. This stage is responsible for the cultural, organizational, and service changes required to meet changing objectives.

Service strategy impacts service transition in three ways:

- Firstly, service strategy assists in deciding how services should be transitioned, considering aspects such as customer involvement, what release and deployment mechanisms are appropriate, and training requirements for the new or changed service.

- Secondly, service strategy defines what needs to change, when, and to what extent.

- Finally, because service transition validates the ability of the new or changed services to achieve the objectives and outcomes defined during service strategy and service design, it is service strategy that provides the basis for the tests and service evaluation.

Service Operation Stage

Service operation is where the value that was anticipated and designed is finally realized. Strategies must consider the limits to operational capabilities, and operations must understand the required outcomes and work to achieve these.

It should be possible to measure how successfully the strategy is being executed and how well it is achieving its objectives by measuring operational activities, but only if these metrics have been anticipated in the design of the service.

Continual Service Improvement Stage

Continual service improvement takes its lead from service strategy; it uses the defined strategies and desired outcomes as a basis for evaluating whether services are successful.

At the same time, continual service improvement acts as an initiator of strategy. Through continual assessment and measurement, it assists in determining where a strategy needs to be changed and how it can be made more effective. It detects changes in the use and outcomes of services and determines the ongoing relevance of services.

Summary

In this chapter, we reviewed what it means to employ a lifecycle approach to strategy and the impact of service strategy on the rest of the service lifecycle stages.

Exam Essentials

Understand how service strategy is implemented.   In order to understand the approach to implementing service strategy, it is important to understand how service strategy is implemented throughout the lifecycle.

Understand the importance of following a lifecycle approach.   You need to comprehend, from a management perspective, the importance of following a lifecycle approach when implementing strategy.

Describe the impact of service strategy.   You need to be able to describe the impact of service strategy on the other lifecycle stages.

Review Questions

You can find the answers to the review questions in the appendix.

1. What are the four *P*s of service strategy?
   - **A.** People, processes, products, and partners
   - **B.** Policies, prospects, processes, and patterns
   - **C.** Perspective, positions, plans, and patterns
   - **D.** Perspective, processes, patterns, and policies

2. Service strategy has an impact on which lifecycle stages?
   - **A.** Service design and service operation only
   - **B.** Service design, service transition, and service operation only
   - **C.** Service design only
   - **D.** Service design, service transition, service operation, and continual service improvement

3. Which of these statements is/are correct?
   1. Strategic positions and perspectives are converted into strategic plans and patterns with goals and objectives for execution through the service lifecycle.
   2. The positions are driven by the need to serve specific customers and market spaces and influenced by the service provider's strategic perspectives.
      - **A.** Statement 1 only
      - **B.** Statement 2 only
      - **C.** Neither statement
      - **D.** Both statements

4. In which document are the defined services captured?
   - **A.** Service portfolio
   - **B.** Customer portfolio
   - **C.** Configuration management system
   - **D.** Customer satisfaction survey

5. In which document are the customers of the portfolio of services stored?
   - **A.** Service level agreement
   - **B.** Operational level agreement
   - **C.** Customer portfolio
   - **D.** Service portfolio

6. Which of these are part of the strategic approach to implementing service strategy?
   1. A current state assessment and definition of the desired end state
   2. An analysis of the gaps between the two states

3. Testing the processes to ensure that they work
    A. 1 only
    B. 1 and 2 only
    C. 1, 2, 3
    D. 1 and 3 only

7. Which of these are valid design constraints driven by strategy?
    1. Ethics and values
    2. Legislation and regulation
    3. Comparative cost units
    4. Copyright and patents
    5. Resourcing constraints
        A. 1, 2, 3, 4
        B. 2, 3, 5
        C. 1, 2, 3, 4, 5
        D. 1, 3, 5

8. Which of these statements is/are correct?
    1. Service models provide the basic architecture that is used to develop services during service design.
    2. Service models are used to deliver strategic operational goals and objectives for the customers and users.
        A. Statement 1 only
        B. Statement 2 only
        C. Both statements
        D. Neither statement

9. Patterns of business activity support the development of strategy. In which strategic process are they explored?
    A. Demand management
    B. Business relationship management
    C. Financial management for IT services
    D. Service portfolio management

10. In which lifecycle stage does business impact analysis have the most significant part to play when implementing strategy?
    A. Service transition
    B. Service design
    C. Continual service improvement
    D. Service operation

Chapter

9

Challenges, Critical Success Factors, and Risks

THE FOLLOWING ITIL INTERMEDIATE EXAM OBJECTIVES ARE DISCUSSED IN THIS CHAPTER:

✓ Service strategy challenges

✓ Service strategy risks

✓ Service strategy critical success factors

This chapter covers the challenges, risks, and critical success factors of service strategy. The learning objective for this chapter is to gain an understanding of these three areas.

Service Strategy Challenges

Service strategy managers face a number of challenges, which fall into four main areas: first, the complexity of the organization; second, the requirement for coordination and control; third, the need to preserve value; and finally, the challenge of effective measurement. We will look at each of these challenges in turn.

Complexity

IT organizations have many components (people, processes, technology, etc.), and each component interacts with other components, resulting in a complex matrix of links and interdependencies. Service providers may focus on trying to maintain stability in the face of such complexity. Although understandable, this focus can result in a reluctance to experiment and a resistance to change, which may mean opportunities to improve effectiveness or efficiency are missed. Organizations often break services down into processes with specialist support teams for each, but such specialization then increases the need for coordination between components.

Another approach is to break services and service management down into specific processes. This can be successful, although there is a danger that their interconnectedness will be lost. All service management processes need to work together in order to produce services that deliver value for the customer. Failure to understand how the output of one process may affect the input to another may result in unforeseen consequences of decisions and actions, which do not become apparent until after major problems and incidents occur. Service strategy must therefore ensure that the bigger-picture perspective is always taken into account.

Coordination and Control

Decision-makers have limited time, so they delegate roles and responsibilities to specialized teams and individuals. Specialization can be beneficial as it allows for development of in-depth knowledge, skills, and experience, which can facilitate innovation and improvement.

However, as the organization develops more specialist teams, there will be a corresponding increase in the need for coordination. This is a major challenge in service management because of the level of specialization needed for various stages of the service lifecycle and the processes and functions. It is important to appreciate this increased need for coordination and to address it through cooperation and control between teams and individuals and with suppliers.

Preserving Value

The value of services to the customer needs to be preserved, together with the customer's perception of this value. This can be achieved through the following methods:

- Eliminating or reducing deviations in performance

- Maintaining operational effectiveness and efficiency

- Reducing hidden costs, such as high transaction costs incurred when changes are made to services, service levels, or demand levels in a trial-and-error manner

- Publicizing and substantiating hidden benefits like reduced lock-in through leasing assets rather than buying

- Reducing the cost of providing services by the use of automation, web-based functionality, support tools, and so on. These will also allow scalability without cost increases.

Effective Measurement

Organizations accept that "if you cannot measure it, you cannot manage it," yet IT organizations are often poor at providing effective measurements. There may be many measurements, but they are meaningless, irrelevant, or presented with no context. Measurements are often inwardly focused on internal goals rather than customer satisfaction.

There are some common rules that are useful in designing effective measurements, as shown in Table 9.1.

TABLE 9.1   Measurement principles

Principle	Guidance
Begin on the outside, not the inside of the service organization.	A service organization should ask itself, "What do customers really want and when?" and "What do the best alternatives give our customers that we do not?"
	Customers, for example, frequently welcome discussion on ways to make better use of their service providers. They may also welcome personal relationships in the building of commitment from providers.

TABLE 9.1   Measurement principles *(continued)*

Principle	Guidance
Responsiveness to customers beats all other measurement goals.	Care is taken not to construct control measures that work against customer responsiveness.
	For example, organizations sometimes measure change management process compliance by the number of RFCs rejected. While this measurement may be useful, it indirectly rewards slow response. An improved measurement strategy would include the number of RFCs authorized in a set period of time as well as the percentage of changes that do not generate unintended consequences. Throughput, as well as compliance, is directly rewarded.
Think of process and service as equals.	Focusing on services is important, but be careful not to do so at the expense of process. It is easy to lose sight of process unless measurements make it equally explicit to the organization. Reward those who fix and improve process.
Numbers matter.	Use a numerical and timescale that can go back far enough to cover the explanation of the current situation.
	Financial metrics are often appropriate. For noncommercial settings, adopt the same principle of measuring performance for outcomes desired (for example, beneficiaries served).
Compete as an organization. Don't let overall goals get lost among the many performance measures.	Be mindful of losing track of overall measures that tell you how the customer perceives your organization against alternatives. Train the organization to think of the service organization as an integrated IT system for the customer's benefit.

Measurements focus the organization on its strategic goals, tracking progress and providing feedback. If strategy changes, what is measured should change to fit. Indeed, adopting new goals without changing what is measured will mean that the new goals are ignored because there is no way of checking whether they are being followed.

Monitoring of discrete failures does not provide a picture of the customer experience. We often talk about "end-to-end" monitoring; however, this is usually still restricted to the technical components and does not include the business processes. IT must move away from measuring components and toward understanding the impact on the business of failures, being able to answer questions such as these:

- Is the delay on the supply chain due to an IT problem, and what is the resultant business impact?

- How long does it take to process procurement orders, and where are the worst delays?

Technology too often focuses on data collection without providing insight into services. This is where data must be translated: data to information to knowledge to wisdom.

Service Strategy Risks

It is essential for organizations to manage risk; without an awareness of possible risks, and actions taken to mitigate them where possible, there is the possibility that the benefits that should accrue from the planning and work that has been carried out will never materialize, or at least they will be reduced.

Definition of Risk

Risk is defined as a possible event that could cause harm or loss or affect an organization's ability to achieve its objectives. A risk is measured by the probability of a threat, the vulnerability of the asset to that threat, and the impact it would have if it occurred. Risk can also be defined as uncertainty of outcome and can be used in the context of measuring the probability of positive outcomes as well as negative outcomes.

Every organization should therefore manage its risk in a way that is visible, repeatable, and consistently applied to support decision-making. By understanding the risks, and their likely impact, the organization and its management can make better decisions. Risk management ensures that an organization makes cost-effective use of a risk framework that has a series of well-defined steps. There are two distinct phases in dealing with risk. First, risk assessment is concerned with gathering information about exposure to risk so that appropriate decisions can be made and the risk managed appropriately. Second, risk management involves having processes in place to do the following:

- Monitor risks
- Provide access to reliable and up-to-date information about risks
- Enforce the right balance of control to deal with those risks
- Implement decision-making processes supported by a framework of risk assessment and evaluation

Inaccurate Information

Inadequate or incomplete information impacts the quality of decision-making. All organizations need to gather and validate the information needed for business decisions to be made. Accurate information is dependent upon good and appropriate measurement, as we have said; it also relies upon building relationships with business units, customers, and suppliers. These relationships will provide a channel of communication concerning business strategy and tactics, customer needs, service and performance requirements, demand patterns and volumetrics, market intelligence, and technical capabilities.

Risk of Taking, or Failing to Take, Opportunities

Risk is normally seen as something to be avoided due to the possible negative consequences, but risks may also present opportunities. For example, underserved market spaces and unfulfilled demand are risks to be avoided, but they can also be exploited. The service portfolio can be mapped to an underlying portfolio of risks that are to be managed. When service management is effective, services in the catalog and pipeline represent opportunities to create value for customers and capture value for stakeholders.

Implementing strategies often requires changes to the service portfolio, which means managing associated risks. Decisions about risk need to be balanced so that potential benefits outweigh the costs to address the risk. Developing a new service might be risky if it is unsuccessful, but there is also the possibility that it could achieve major benefits. The organization needs to take risks but limit exposure to an acceptable level.

Design Risks

There is a risk that services fail to deliver the expected utility benefits; poor design causes poor performance. For example, a change in the pattern of demand for a service could reduce its utility if it has not been designed to be scalable.

Service design should ensure that opportunities and resources are not wasted. Good service design processes and methods reduce the risk of failure by ensuring that the service can deliver the necessary performance and also tolerate limited variations. Good designs also ensure that services are economical and flexible so that they can adapt to changing requirements without a major redesign.

Operational Risks

There are two levels of risk that must be considered from a service management perspective. Both need to be considered because they interact with each other:

- Risks faced by the business and the business services it uses
- Risks to the IT services that underpin the business and its processes

Service transition should filter and negate these risks, and service operation should be able to convert risks into opportunities. Procedures in transition must be robust enough to resist demands for early delivery of a new capability without the agreed level of warranty, which could lead to tensions when the service falls below the agreed quality. Value to customers is realized in the service operation stage of the lifecycle when actual demand for services arrives. Warranty commitments require every unit of demand to be met with a unit of capacity that is available, secure, and continuous.

Market Risks

Sourcing decisions made by customers are potential risks for all service providers. Type I providers face the risk of outsourcing when customers sign contracts with external providers in pursuit of strategic objectives. Customers are willing to make the switch to external providers when benefits outweigh the costs and risks of switching from one type to another. Insourcing continues to be a valuable strategic option for customers who may reject an outsourced service and return to providing the service in house. This possibility represents a risk for Type 3 providers.

Market risks can be reduced by reducing the total cost of utilization (TCU), giving customers financial incentives not to switch to other options, or by differentiation, providing services that are unique, novel, or difficult for competitors to replicate. A third approach is consolidation: concentrating demand from several customers or customer groups onto a single service rather than offering a lot of diverse but similar services, thus reducing costs to help retain customers.

Critical Success Factors

All of the challenges and risks already mentioned can be inverted to become critical success factors (CSFs). For example, achieving accurate measurement is a challenge; lack of accurate measurement is a risk; having accurate measurement in place is a critical success factor—without it successful services are impossible to achieve.

There are a number of other factors critical to the success of a service management organization: Firstly, experienced, skilled, and trained staff with strategic vision and decision-making skills are needed for success. Secondly, there must be adequate support and funding from the business, which must recognize the potential value IT service management can offer. Finally, appropriate and effective support tools allow the processes to be quickly and successfully implemented and operated in a cost-effective way.

Summary

This chapter covered the following:

- Service strategy challenges
- Service strategy risks
- Service strategy critical success factors

We have completed the syllabus for the ITIL Intermediate Service Strategy exam.

Exam Essentials

Understand the challenges faced by service strategy when dealing with complex organizations with many interconnections and interdependencies. Understand the benefits of specialization as organizations become more complex, but also the danger of treating each area as separate and distinct.

Understand the challenge involved in balancing specialization and coordination. Understand the benefits of specialization in terms of in-depth knowledge, skills, and experience and the need to ensure that these specialists work together for the overall benefit of the organization.

Know the different types of risks encountered in the service strategy stage. Be able to list and explain the risks of inaccurate information; the risks of failing to take up opportunities; and design, operational, and market risks.

Understand why there may be resistance to change. In particular, understand why complex organizations emphasize stability and how this can encourage a wariness about change because it might threaten that stability.

Understand the critical success factors that need to be in place if successful service strategy is to take place. Understand the importance of having sufficient staff with necessary skills and vision, the appropriate level of financial support from the business, and the correct tools to implement the strategy.

Review Questions

You can find the answers to the review questions in the appendix.

1. Which of the following statements about measurement is incorrect?

    A. Measurements are meaningless without context.

    B. Measurements should be focused on measuring the achievement of internal goals.

    C. Measurements focus the organization on its strategic goals, tracking progress and providing feedback.

    D. What is measured should change if strategy changes.

2. Which of the following statements about the measurement of risk is false?

    A. A risk is measured by the probability of a threat.

    B. A risk is measured by the vulnerability of the asset to a threat.

    C. A risk is measured by the cost of the asset that would be affected.

    D. A risk is measured by the impact it would have if it occurred.

3. What type of risk is a change in the pattern of demand for a service that reduces its utility?

    A. Design risk

    B. Operational risk

    C. Market risk

    D. Missed opportunity risk

4. Lack of accurate measurement is a _____ .

    A. Challenge

    B. Risk

    C. Critical Success Factor

    D. KPI

5. What are the four types of challenges faced by service strategy managers discussed in the *ITIL Service Strategy* publication?

    1. The complexity of the organization

    2. Low maturity levels of one process, making it impossible to achieve full maturity in other processes

    3. The need to coordinate and prioritize many new or changed services

    4. The requirement for coordination and control

    5. Lack of engagement with development and project staff

6. The need to preserve value

7. The challenge of effective measurement

    A. 1, 4, 5, 7

    B. 1, 2, 3, 4

    C. 1, 4, 6, 7

    D. 2, 4, 6, 7

6. Risk management involves having processes in place to do which of the following? (Choose all that apply.)

    A. Monitor risks

    B. Provide access to reliable and up-to-date information about risks

    C. Enforce the right balance of control to deal with those risks

    D. Implement decision-making processes supported by a framework of risk assessment and evaluation

7. Eliminating or reducing deviations in performance, maintaining operational effectiveness and efficiency, and publicizing and substantiating hidden benefits, like reduced lock-in through leasing assets rather than buying, are all responses to which service strategy challenge?

    A. The complexity of the organization

    B. The requirement for coordination and control

    C. The need to preserve value

    D. The challenge of effective measurement

8. True or False? It is the responsibility of the service provider's management team to identify as many risks as possible and take action to avoid them.

    A. True

    B. False

9. Decisions by the business to insource or outsource IT service provision are risks to IT service providers. Which of the following is NOT an appropriate response to mitigate the risk?

    A. Reducing the total cost of utilization

    B. Differentiation

    C. Specialization

    D. Consolidation

10. Which of the following statements concerning coordination and control is INCORRECT?

    A. Delegation to specialized teams is necessary due to decision-makers having insufficient time.

    B. Specialization encourages development of skills and knowledge.

    C. Specialization inevitably leads to silos within an organization.

    D. The more specialization takes place, the greater the need for coordination.

Service Design

PART

II

Service Design

Chapter

10

Introduction to the Service Design Lifecycle Stage

THE FOLLOWING ITIL INTERMEDIATE EXAM OBJECTIVES ARE DISCUSSED IN THIS CHAPTER:

✓ The main purpose, goals, and objectives of service design

✓ The scope of service design

✓ Service design's value to the business

✓ The context of service design and the service lifecycle

✓ Service design inputs and outputs and the contents and use of the service design package

✓ The contents and use of service acceptance criteria

Introduction to
the Service
Lifecycle 3

This part of the book covers how service design takes the outputs from service strategy, the preceding stage of the service lifecycle, and uses them to ensure that the solution designs that are produced are consistent with the overall IT service provider strategy. We have seen, in the earlier chapters of this book, how service strategy sets the objectives; service design is about providing the services that are required to deliver those objectives. Service design is also concerned with redesigning existing services and retiring services that are no longer needed. This first chapter provides an introduction to this lifecycle stage; we consider the core concepts of service design in terms of its purpose, objectives, and scope and its relationship to the other ITIL lifecycle stages.

The learning objective for this chapter is to achieve a full understanding of service design terms and core concepts. We start by looking at the purpose of service design, its objectives and scope, and how it delivers value to the business.

Service design is a critically important stage of the service lifecycle. It is in design that the intentions behind the service strategy start to be made reality. A poor service design will fail to deliver the strategy, could prevent a worthwhile return on investment, and could potentially damage the performance and reputation of the business. This stage is often rushed, however, in an attempt to meet project deadlines; such a course of action is foolish because it remains true that time spent in design saves time spent in rework later.

The Purpose of Service Design

The purpose of the service design stage of the lifecycle is to design IT services, with the necessary supporting IT practices, processes, and policies, to realize the service provider's strategy. It is important to understand this point—design is not just about the technical design; it also considers the way it will be used and the processes required. Design should also include thinking about how the service will be transitioned; it should facilitate the introduction of the service into the supported environment in such a way as to ensure quality service delivery, customer satisfaction, and cost-effective service provision. So it is the job of design to make the strategy a practical reality. Importantly, design must consider *how* the service will work.

The Goals and Objectives of Service Design

Let's start by considering the goals and objectives of service design. Service design has to design services to satisfy business objectives and align with business needs. This includes consideration of quality, compliance, risk, and security requirements, ensuring the delivery of more effective and efficient IT and business solutions by coordinating all design activities for IT services. Ensuring consistency of service and business focus in the design is a key goal.

Service design activities can be periodic, or they can be triggered by a specific business need or event. (We call these exception-based activities.) In an ideal world, service design would design IT services so effectively that little or no improvement during their lifecycle would be required. However, it is only when services are actually being used in the live environment that we can really understand what is required of them. The use of the services will also change over time. It is essential, therefore, for service design to embed continual improvement in all its activities. This ensures that the solutions and designs become even more effective over time. This will enable changing trends in the business that could provide improvement opportunities to be identified and acted upon.

Additional goals and objectives of service design are as follows:

- Ensuring that the services that are designed are adaptable to future requirements so they can be easily expanded or developed to meet changing requirements

- Aiming to produce a design that reduces, minimizes, or constrains the long-term costs of provision because a service that is too expensive to run has no future

- Designing an efficient and effective service management system, including the processes required for the design, transition, operation, and improvement of high-quality IT services

- Providing the supporting tools, systems, and information, especially the service portfolio, to manage services through their lifecycle

- Identifying and managing risks so that they can be removed or mitigated before the services go live

The final set of goals and objectives of service design are as follows:

- Designing the measurement methods and metrics for assessing the effectiveness and efficiency of the design processes and their deliverables. Design must consider how the effectiveness of a service could be measured and ensure that the service is designed so that these metrics can be gathered.

- Producing and maintaining all the IT plans, processes, policies, architectures, frameworks, and documents needed for the design of quality IT solutions that will meet current and future agreed business needs.

- Assisting in the development of policies and standards in all areas of design and planning of the IT services and processes. By receiving and acting on feedback on design processes from other areas and incorporating this feedback into the processes in the future, design ensures continual improvement of these processes.

- Developing skills and capability within IT by moving strategy and design activities into operational tasks, making effective and efficient use of all IT service resources.

- Contributing to the improvement of the overall quality of IT service within the imposed design constraints. It reduces the need for reworking and enhancing services once they have been implemented in the live environment.

The Scope of Service Design

The scope of ITIL service design includes providing guidance for the design of appropriate and innovative IT services to meet current and future agreed business requirements. The core guidance for this lifecycle stage describes the principles of service design and looks at identifying, defining, and aligning the IT solution with the business requirement. It also introduces the concept of the service design package and looks at selecting the appropriate service design model. We shall look at the contents and use of the service design package later in this chapter, and consider service design models in more depth in Chapter 11, "Service Design Principles."

It is a key principle of ITIL service design that the initial service design should always be driven by factors such as functional requirements, the requirements within service level agreements (SLAs), the business benefits, and the overall design constraints. The service design Intermediate course syllabus covers the methods, practices, and tools to achieve excellence in service design. It discusses the fundamentals of the design processes and attends to what are called the "five aspects of service design."

The Five Aspects of Service Design

These are the five aspects of service design:

- The design of the actual solution itself
- The service management system and tools that will be required to manage the service
- The management and technology architectures that the service will use
- The processes needed to support the service in operation
- The measurement systems, methods, and metrics that will be required

These shall be examined later in Chapter 11, "Service Design Principles."

Also included within the scope of service design are the service design processes:

- Design coordination
- Service catalog management

- Service level management
- Availability management
- Capacity management
- IT service continuity management
- Information security management
- Supplier management

These processes are described in detail later in the book. It should be noted that all of these processes, other than design coordination, are also active throughout the other stages of the service lifecycle and processes in other stages of the service lifecycle will impact service design. All the lifecycle processes should be linked closely together to ensure the successful management, design, support, and maintenance of the services, the IT infrastructure, the environment, the applications, and the data. The interfaces between processes need to be clearly defined when designing a service or improving or implementing a process.

In Figure 10.1, you can see the complete service design stage. It starts with a set of new or changed business requirements and ends with the development of a service solution designed to meet the documented needs of the business. This service solution, together with its service design package, is then passed to service transition to evaluate, build, test, and deploy the new or changed service or to retire the service if this is the change required. On completion of these transition activities, control is transferred to the service operation stage of the service lifecycle.

FIGURE 10.1   The scope of service design

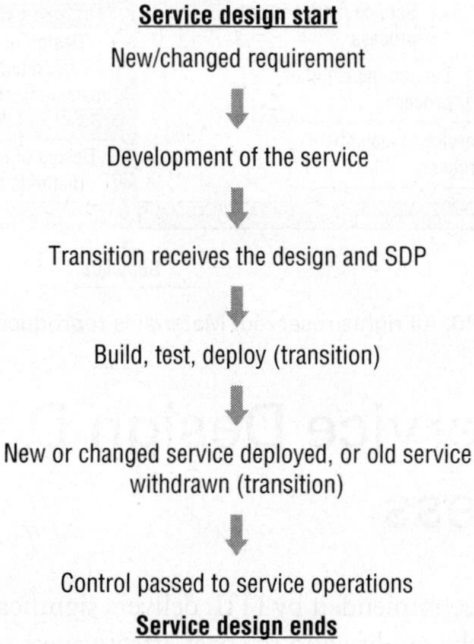

Service design start

New/changed requirement

⬇

Development of the service

⬇

Transition receives the design and SDP

⬇

Build, test, deploy (transition)

⬇

New or changed service deployed, or old service
withdrawn (transition)

⬇

Control passed to service operations

Service design ends

The overall scope of service design and the five aspects of design are illustrated in Figure 10.2, within the context of the IT service provider's relationship to the business. The diagram shows how IT and the business interact through the provision of service and how the work of service design is part of the complete service lifecycle.

FIGURE 10.2 The scope of service design and the five aspects

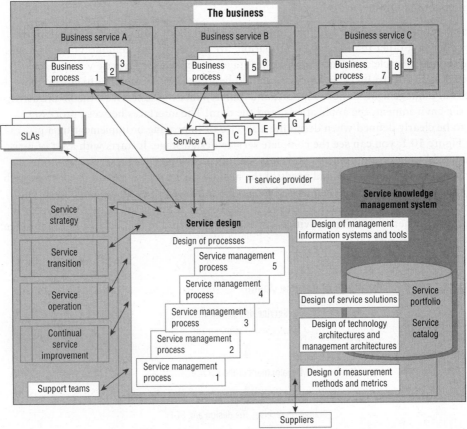

The Value Service Design Delivers to the Business

Adopting the best practice recommended by ITIL delivers significant business benefits. Good service design ensures both the quality and the cost-effectiveness of the service. Both aspects need to be delivered if the service is to be useful to the business. Good service design using a standard, consistent approach delivers a number of benefits, which we will consider in turn:

- A reduced total cost of ownership (TCO). The design will consider the costs of various design options and choose one that delivers what is required, without unnecessary expenditure. In addition, because the design fits the business requirement, there will not be a large volume of changes to try to align it more effectively with the business requirement. Aspects such as the availability and capacity requirements for the service must be considered during the design stage to reduce incidents (and the resulting support costs) when the service is operational.

- Improved quality of service. Services that are well designed and meet the required outcomes of the customer will deliver the quality of service that the business needs.

- Improved consistency of service. Designing services within the corporate strategy, architectures, and constraints will ensure that a consistent level of service is delivered.

- Easier implementation of new or changed services. Well-designed services are easier to transition.

- Improved service alignment. By involving service design from the beginning, we can ensure that the new or changed service is designed to match the business requirement and will be able to support the required service levels.

- Improved service performance. The service will have been designed to meet the specific performance criteria, incorporating capacity, availability, and IT service continuity requirements into the design.

- Improved IT governance. This will be as a result of ensuring that the necessary controls are built into the design.

- Improved effectiveness of service management and IT processes. The design of processes is one of the five aspects of service design; when processes are considered as part of design, it is to be expected that they will be designed to deliver both quality and cost effectiveness.

- Improved information and decision-making. The design includes ensuring that the required measurements and metrics will be produced, enabling the service provider to be confident that they possess accurate information on which to base decisions. These measurements will also form the basis for assessing the service and identifying opportunities for continual improvement of both services and service management throughout the service lifecycle.

- Improved alignment with customer values and strategies. If an organization has a policy of promoting concepts such as green IT or a strategy of using cloud technologies, service design will ensure that the design of the new or changed service is aligned with these values and strategies.

Service design ensures that IT services focus on supporting business processes and goals. This includes the following:

- Prioritizing IT activities based on business impact and urgency so that critical business processes and services receive the most attention

- Increasing business productivity by ensuring that IT processes are efficient and effective

- Supporting corporate governance requirements with appropriate IT governance and controls, ensuring compliance with regulatory and legislative requirements

- Exploiting the IT infrastructure and providing innovative solutions to create competitive advantage
- Improving service quality, customer satisfaction, and user perception
- Ensuring that all IT and information assets are appropriately protected

The Context of Service Design and the Service Lifecycle

Service design needs to be considered within the context of the whole service lifecycle. Each area of the lifecycle addresses a particular set of challenges that need to be addressed for successful service management, and each stage has an impact on all of the others.

FIGURE 10.3   The ITIL service lifecycle

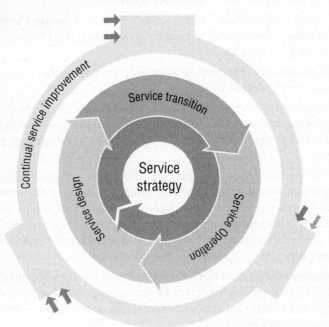

Service Strategy   Service strategy is at the core of the service lifecycle. It is the role of strategy to understand the organizational objectives and customer needs. People, processes, and products should support the strategy. ITIL service strategy asks why something is to be done before thinking of how. It helps service providers to set objectives; to set expectations of performance serving customers and markets; and to identify, select, and prioritize opportunities. Service strategy ensures that providers understand and can handle the costs and risks associated with their service portfolios.

The complete list of service strategy processes is as follows: strategy management for IT services, service portfolio management, financial management for IT services, demand management, and business relationship management.

Service Design　Service design, the subject of Part 2 of this book, turns strategic ideas into deliverables. The design must always consider the strategy to ensure that services are designed with the business objectives in mind. Design considers the whole IT organization and how it will deliver and support the services, turning the service strategy into a plan for delivering the business objectives. Remember, design includes changes to existing services and retiring those services no longer required.

The complete list of service design processes is as follows: design coordination, service catalog management, service level management, availability management, capacity management, IT service continuity management, information security management, and supplier management. These processes ensure that both the utility and the warranty of the new or changed service is considered in design, covering the continuity of the service, its achievement of service levels, and conformance to security standards and regulations.

Service Transition　Service transition provides guidance for developing and improving capabilities for introducing new and changed services into supported environments. The value of a service is identified in strategy, and the service is designed to deliver that value. Service transition ensures that the value is realized by enabling the necessary changes to take place without unacceptable risks to existing services. Service transition enables the implementation of new services, and the modification of existing services, to ensure that the services provided deliver the service strategy of achieving the business objectives and that the benefits of the service design are fully realized. Service transition also introduces the service knowledge management system, which ensures that knowledge is stored and made available to all stages of the service lifecycle, making sure lessons are learned and decisions are backed with factual data, leading to improved efficiency and effectiveness over time.

The complete list of service transition processes is as follows: transition planning and support, change management, service asset and configuration management, release and deployment management, service validation and testing, change evaluation, and knowledge management. Each process has a role to play to ensure that beneficial changes can take place and, as a consequence, the service can be introduced and will work as transitioned.

Service Operation　Service operation describes best practice for managing services in supported environments. It includes guidance on achieving effectiveness, efficiency, stability, and security in the delivery and support of services to ensure value for the customer, the users, and the service provider. Without this, the services would not deliver the value required and the achievement of business objectives would become difficult or impossible.

The service operation stage is therefore critical to delivering the design and, in doing so, achieving the service strategy. Service operation provides detailed guidance for delivering the service within the agreed service levels by tackling issues both proactively, through problem management, and reactively, through incident management. It provides those delivering the service with guidance for managing the availability of services, controlling demand, optimizing capacity utilization, scheduling of operations, and avoiding or resolving service incidents and managing problems. It includes advice on shared services, utility computing, web services, and mobile commerce. By delivering the services to the agreed levels, service operation enables the business to use the services to achieve its business objectives.

The complete list of service operation processes is as follows: event management, incident management, request fulfilment, problem management, and access management. We shall be considering each of these in the service operation section of this book, in the chapters covering service operation processes. Each process has a role to play to ensure the delivery of services within the agreed service levels. Service operation also describes the four service operation functions: the service desk, technical management, IT operations management, and application management. Each function is responsible for managing its own area of delivery across all stages of the lifecycle.

Continual Service Improvement   The final stage of the lifecycle is continual service improvement. CSI ensures that the service provider continues to provide value to customers by making sure the strategy, transition, and operation of the services is under constant review. Feedback from any stage of the service lifecycle can be used to identify improvement opportunities for any other stage of the lifecycle. It ensures that opportunities for improvement are recognized, evaluated, and implemented when justified. These may include improvements in the quality of the service or the capabilities of the service provider. It may be developing ways of doing things better or doing them to the same level but more efficiently. Improvements may be major or small and incremental. It enables every new operation to incorporate lessons from previous operations.

CSI ensures that feedback from every lifecycle stage is captured, analyzed, and acted upon. The CSI approach to improvement is based on establishing a baseline and checking to see whether the improvement actions have been effective. It uses the Plan-Do-Check-Act (PDCA) cycle, together with service measurement, demonstrating value with metrics and conducting maturity assessments. The seven-step improvement process provides a framework for these approaches.

In addition to these long-term improvement initiatives, there are the short-term ongoing improvements; these are the improvements made to working practices within the processes, functions, and technologies that underpin service design. They are generally smaller improvements that are implemented without any change to the fundamental nature of a process or technology. Examples include tuning, workload balancing, personnel redeployment, and training.

Service Design Inputs and Outputs

The main inputs to service design are requirements for new or changed services. The main output of service design is the service design package, which includes all of the information needed to manage the entire lifecycle of a new or changed service. We shall look at the service design package later in this chapter, but first we examine the particular inputs to service design and outputs from design for each lifecycle stage.

Strategy Inputs and Outputs

The inputs from strategy into service design are as follows:

- Vision and mission
- Service portfolio
- Policies
- Strategies and strategic plans
- Priorities
- Service charters, including service packages and details of utility and warranty
- Financial information and budgets
- Documented patterns of business activity and user profiles
- Service models

Strategy provides the vision and mission about what is to be done. The decision regarding what services should form the portfolio is made in the strategy stage of the lifecycle, along with other strategies and plans.

Strategy provides the utility and warranty requirements to design for the new service. It formulates the service packages and service charters (these are covered in detail in the service strategy course). Strategy documents the patterns of business activity and the different user profiles and decides upon the service models. Finally, strategy is in control of the money—design can start its work only when strategy has decided to fund it.

Let's now consider the reverse flow, the outputs from design into strategy:

- Input to business cases and the service portfolio
- Service design packages
- Updated service models
- Service portfolio updates, including the service catalog
- Financial estimates and reports
- Design-related knowledge and information in the service knowledge management system (SKMS)
- Designs for service strategy processes and procedures

Design provides important information that strategy uses in the service portfolio and to draw up business cases. The major output from design is the service design package, and this is an input to the strategy phase as well as to other lifecycle stages. Other outputs to strategy from design include updates to the service models, service catalog, and portfolio. Design will produce new process designs for strategy processes, will update the service knowledge management system, and produce financial reports and estimates to feed back into financial management.

Transition Inputs and Outputs

Following the activities of service design, a number of outputs are passed to the next stage, that of transition:

- Service catalog details
- Service design packages, including the following:
  - Details of utility and warranty
  - Acceptance criteria
  - Service models
  - Designs and interface specifications
  - Transition plans
  - Operation plans and procedures
  - Communication and training plans
  - User and support guides
- RFCs to transition or deploy new or changed services
- Input to change evaluation and CAB meetings
- Designs for service transition processes and procedures
- SLAs, OLAs, and underpinning contracts

The major output is the service design package (SDP), which includes the details of the new or changed service and plans for its transition and operation. We will look at the SDP in more detail shortly. Design will also raise the requests for change to kick off the transition and deployment. In addition, design will provide input to the evaluation process so that it is clear how the service is expected to behave and what benefits it is expected to deliver. Design may also provide information to the change advisory board to help in their deliberations. Finally, the SLAs, OLAs, and underpinning contracts that were drawn up as part of the design process of service level management are passed to transition. It will be the job of transition to ensure that the new or changed service meets the agreed service levels by the time it is accepted into operation.

Service design takes a number of outputs from transition. These are mostly in the form of feedback and potential improvements for the next service design:

- Service catalog updates
- Feedback on all aspects of service design and service design packages

- Input and feedback to transition plans
- Response to requests for change (RFCs)
- Knowledge and information in the SKMS (including the CMS)
- Design errors identified in transition for redesign
- Evaluation reports

Transition will provide feedback on every aspect of service design and on the adequacy of the service design package. Transition will also respond to the proposed transition plan it received from design, with any suggested amendments. Reports from the evaluation stage will be fed back to design, along with details of any design errors that came to light during transition and require redesign.

In addition, transition will respond to the requests for change raised by service design and will update the service knowledge management system and configuration management system as the service is deployed.

Operation Inputs and Outputs

Service design provides the following outputs to the operation stage:

- Service catalog
- Service design package, including these:
    - Details of utility and warranty
    - Operations plans and procedures
    - Recovery procedures
    - Knowledge and information in the SKMS
    - Which services are considered vital business functions
    - Hardware and software maintenance requirements
    - Designs for service operation processes and procedures
    - SLAs, OLAs, and underpinning contracts
    - Security policies

As you may notice, some of these were also outputs to other stages, particularly the service design package. Here, though, the SDP content that is passed to operations is particularly concerned with the operation of the new or changed service, containing details of utility and warranty that should be delivered in operations along with plans, procedures, processes, and security policies for operations to carry out. Again, we can see that the SKMS is updated. The utility and warranty requirements are backed up with the hardware and software maintenance requirements and details of the SLA to be delivered together with the underpinning OLAs and contracts that will be needed to meet the SLA successfully. Finally, details of vital business functions are passed to operations to assist in the assessment of the impact of incidents and their prioritization.

The service operation stage of the lifecycle provides the following inputs into service design:

- Operational requirements
- Actual performance information
- RFCs to resolve operational issues
- Historical incident and problem records

The operational requirements to be incorporated into the design and the actual performance information ensure that design understands how the service is performing. Any operational issues that arise could result in an RFC to have a design change, and the provision of historical incident and problem records will show design the issues to be avoided in the new design.

CSI Inputs and Outputs

Design provides the following outputs to the continual service improvement lifecycle stage:

- Service catalog
- Service design packages, including details of utility and warranty
- Knowledge and information in the SKMS
- Achievements against metrics, KPIs, and CSFs
- Design of services, measurements, processes, infrastructure, and systems
- Design for the seven-step improvement process and procedures
- Improvement opportunities logged in the CSI register

CSI will need the service catalog, the SKMS, and the service design packages with the details of the utility and warranty requirements to identify which services are failing to meet their requirements and need to be improved. The achievements of the different service design processes against key performance indicators will identify which processes need improvement. CSI will also need to understand the design of the services, processes, and so on to identify where improvements can be made. Service design is responsible for the design of the seven-step improvement process and procedures.

Service design will also suggest improvements, which will be logged in the CSI register.

The outputs from continual service improvement to design are as follows:

- Results of customer and user satisfaction surveys
- Input to design requirements
- Data required for metrics, KPIs, and CSFs
- Service reports
- Feedback on service design packages
- RFCs for implementing improvements

The results of customer and user satisfaction surveys, indicating how well the design meets their requirements, will show where it should be improved. Feedback on the service design packages will be used by design to improve future SDPs. CSI will raise the RFCs required to implement design improvements. Finally, service reports and other data required for metrics, KPIs, and CSFs are provided by CSI to service design.

Table 10.1 summarizes service design inputs and outputs by lifecycle stage.

TABLE 10.1   Summary of service design inputs and outputs by lifecycle stage

Lifecycle stage	Service design inputs (from the lifecycle stage in the first column)	Service design outputs (to the lifecycle stage in the first column)
Service strategy	Vision and mission Service portfolio Policies Strategies and strategic plans Priorities Service charters, including service packages and details of utility and warranty Financial information and budgets Documented patterns of business activity and user profiles Service models	Input to business cases and the service portfolio Service design packages Updated service models Service portfolio updates, including updates to the service catalog Financial estimates and reports Design-related knowledge and information in the SKMS Designs for service strategy processes and procedures
Service transition	Service catalog updates Feedback on all aspects of service design and service design packages Input and feedback on transition plans Response to requests for change (RFCs) Knowledge and information in the SKMS (including the CMS) Design errors identified in transition for redesign Evaluation reports	Service catalog Service design packages, including: ■ Details of utility and warranty ■ Acceptance criteria ■ Service models ■ Designs and interface specifications ■ Transition plans ■ Operation plans and procedures ■ RFCs to transition or deploy new or changed services ■ Input to change evaluation and CAB meetings ■ Designs for service transition processes and procedures ■ SLAs, OLAs, and underpinning contracts

TABLE 10.1 Summary of service design inputs and outputs by lifecycle stage *(continued)*

Lifecycle stage	Service design inputs (from the lifecycle stage in the first column)	Service design outputs (to the lifecycle stage in the first column)
Service operation	Operational requirements Actual performance information RFCs to resolve operational issues Historical incident and problem records	Service catalog Service design package, including: ▪ Details of utility and warranty ▪ Operations plans and procedures ▪ Recovery procedures ▪ Knowledge and information in the SKMS ▪ Vital business functions ▪ HW/SW maintenance requirements ▪ Designs for service operation processes and procedures ▪ SLAs, OLAs, and underpinning contracts ▪ Security policies
Continual service improvement	Results of customer and user satisfaction surveys Input to design requirements Data required for metrics, KPIs, and CSFs Service reports Feedback on service design packages RFCs for implementing improvements	Service catalog Service design packages, including details of utility and warranty Knowledge and information in the SKMS Achievements against metrics, KPIs, and CSFs Design of services, measurements, processes, infrastructure, and systems Design for the seven-step improvement process and procedures Improvement opportunities logged in the CSI register

The Contents and Use of the Service Design Package

The service design package is the major output of service design. This is a collection of documents defining all aspects of the service. It could include technical design documents, service level agreements, acceptance criteria, business requirements, testing plans, and so on. Without the service design package pulling all these documents together into one place, there would be no single source of accurate information regarding the service.

The service design package should be produced during the design stage, for each new service, each major change to a service, the removal of a service, or even for changes to the service design package itself. It is passed from service design to service transition and from transition to operations. It details all aspects of the service and its requirements through all of the subsequent stages of its lifecycle.

The Contents and Use of Service Acceptance Criteria

The service acceptance criteria is a set of criteria used to ensure that the service meets its expected functionality and quality and that the service provider is ready to deliver the new service once it has been deployed. It can be used as a checklist to ensure that nothing has been forgotten. Table 10.2 shows typical service acceptance criteria.

TABLE 10.2 Typical service acceptance criteria

Criteria	Responsibility
Have the "go-live" date and the guarantee period been agreed with all concerned parties, together with final acceptance criteria?	Change, service level
Have the deployment project and schedule been documented, agreed, and made public to all affected personnel?	Change, incident
Have the service level agreement (SLA) and service level requirements (SLRs) been reviewed, revised, and agreed with all concerned parties?	Service level
Has the service been entered/updated in the service catalog/ service portfolio within the configuration management system (CMS) and appropriate relationships established for all supporting components?	Service level, configuration

TABLE 10.2 Typical service acceptance criteria *(continued)*

Criteria	Responsibility
Have all customers and other stakeholders been identified and recorded in the CMS?	Service level, business relationship
Have all operational risks associated with running the new service been assessed and mitigation actions completed where appropriate?	Business continuity, availability
Have contingency and fail-over measures been successfully tested and added to the overall resilience test schedule?	Business continuity, availability
Can all SLA/SLR targets be monitored, measured, reported, and reviewed, including availability and performance?	Service level, availability
Have all users been identified/approved and the appropriate accounts created for them?	Account management
Can all workload characteristics, performance, and capacity targets be measured and incorporated into capacity plans?	Capacity
Have all operational processes, schedules, and procedures been agreed, tested, documented, and accepted (e.g., site documentation, backups, housekeeping, archiving, retention)?	Operations, business continuity
Have all batch jobs and printing requirements been agreed, tested, documented, and accepted?	Operations
Have all test plans been completed successfully?	Test manager
Have all security checks and tests been completed successfully?	Security compliance
Are appropriate monitoring and measurement tools and procedures in place to monitor the new service, together with an out-of-hours support rota?	Systems management
Have all ongoing operational workloads and costs been identified and approved?	Operations, IT finance
Are all service and component operational costs understood and incorporated into financial processes and the cost model?	IT finance
Have incident and problem categories and processes been reviewed and revised for the new service, together with any known errors and deficiencies?	Incident, problem reporting

Criteria	Responsibility
Have all new suppliers been identified and their associated contracts drawn up accordingly?	Contract and supplier management
Have all support arrangements been reviewed and revised—SLAs, SLRs, operational level agreements (OLAs)—and contracts agreed, with documentation accepted by all teams (including suppliers, support teams, supplier management, development teams, and application support)?	Project manager
Has appropriate technical support documentation been provided and accepted by incident, problem, and all IT support teams?	Incident, problem
Have all requests for change and release records been authorized and updated?	Change
Have all service, SLA, SLR, OLA, and contract details, together with all applications and infrastructure component details, been entered on the CMS?	Project management, support teams configuration
Have appropriate software licenses been purchased or reallocated licenses used?	Configuration
Have any new hardware components been recorded in the CMS?	Configuration
Have all new software components been lodged in the definitive media library (DML) with details recorded in the CMS?	Configuration
Have all maintenance and upgrade plans been agreed, together with release policies, frequencies, and mechanisms?	Release and deployment
Have all users been trained, and has user documentation been accepted and supplied to all users?	Project manager
Are all relationships, interfaces, and dependencies with all other internal and external systems and services documented, agreed, and supported?	Project manager
Have appropriate business managers signed off on acceptance of new service?	Project manager

Exam Essentials

Understand the purpose of service design   The purpose of service design is to design IT services with the necessary supporting IT practices, processes, and policies to realize the service provider's strategy. Design is not just about the technical design; it also considers the way it will be used and the processes required.

Understand that services must be designed to be adaptable to future requirements.   Services should be designed so that they are able to be easily expanded or developed to meet changing requirements.

Be able to list and explain the five aspects of service design.   The five aspects of service design are the design of service solutions, management information systems and tools, architectures, processes, and measurements.

Understand how good design delivers financial and other benefits to the business.   When the design fits the business requirement and is adaptable to changing requirements, the need to completely redesign the service is avoided, thus minimizing the total cost of ownership.

Summary

This chapter covered the purpose, goals, objectives, and scope of service design and how this lifecycle stage delivers value to the organization. We looked at service design within the context of the service lifecycle. We also discussed service design inputs and outputs and the contents and use of the service design package and the service acceptance criteria.

Review Questions

You can find the answers to the review questions in the appendix.

1. Which of the following is NOT a purpose of service design?

    A. To evaluate the financial impact of new or changed strategies on the service provider

    B. To ensure quality service delivery

    C. To ensure customer satisfaction

    D. To ensure cost-effective service provision

2. Which of the following are goals of service design?

    1. To ensure that services are adaptable and expandable to meet future requirements

    2. To consider the total cost of ownership so that long-term costs are controlled

    3. To develop the required processes and tools for designing, transitioning, operating, and improving services during their life span

    4. To manage risks effectively, ensuring that the design is resilient and secure and meets current and future requirements

    A. 1, 2, and 4 only

    B. 1, 2, and 3 only

    C. All of the above

    D. 1, 3, and 4 only

3. Which of the following is NOT one of the five aspects of service design?

    A. Designing service solutions

    B. Risk management

    C. Management and technology architectures

    D. Measurement systems, methods, and metrics

4. What is being defined here? "Document(s) defining all aspects of an IT service and its requirements through each stage of its lifecycle. A _____ is produced for each new IT service, major change, or IT service retirement."

    A. Statement of requirements (SoR)

    B. Service acceptance criteria (SAC)

    C. Service level requirement (SLR)

    D. Service design package (SDP)

5. Which of the following is NOT a possible service acceptance criteria?

    A. All SLA/SLR targets can be monitored, measured, and reported.

    B. Contingency measures have been successfully tested.

    C. A postimplementation review has been held, and the lessons learned have been documented.

    D. The service has been entered/updated in the service catalog/service portfolio.

6. Which of the following is NOT a service design process?
   A. Service catalog management
   B. Service level management
   C. Service portfolio management
   D. Information security management

7. Which of the following is NOT a benefit of effective service design?
   A. Services that are easier to change when circumstances change
   B. A reduced total cost of ownership (TCO)
   C. Improved IT governance
   D. Improved design of business processes

8. Which of the following are inputs into service design from service strategy?
   1. Vision and mission
   2. Service portfolio
   3. Policies
   4. Strategies and strategic plans
   5. Service design packages
   6. Updated service models
   7. Priorities
   8. Service charters
      A. All of the above
      B. 1, 2, 3, and 4 only
      C. 1, 3 ,4, 5, and 7 only
      D. 1, 2, 3, 4, 7, and 8 only

9. Which stage of the lifecycle provides the following outputs, and to which stage are they an input?
   1. Feedback on all aspects of service design and service design packages
   2. Input and feedback on transition plans
   3. Response to requests for change (RFCs)
   4. Knowledge and information in the SKMS (including the CMS)
      A. Outputs from strategy into transition
      B. Outputs from transition into design
      C. Outputs from design into transition
      D. Outputs from operation into design

10. Which of the following are valid inclusions in a service design package?

  1. Technical design documents

  2. Service level agreements

  3. Change schedule

  4. Acceptance criteria

  5. Business requirements

  6. Testing plans

  7. The CMS

    A. All of the above

    B. 1, 2, 3, 5, and 6 only

    C. 1, 2, 4, 5, and 6 only

    D. 1, 2, 4, and 5 only

Chapter

11

Service Design Principles

THE FOLLOWING ITIL INTERMEDIATE EXAM OBJECTIVES ARE DISCUSSED IN THIS CHAPTER:

✓ Service design principles, techniques, and relationships and their application to the design of effective service solutions

✓ Designing service solutions related to a customer's needs

✓ Designing and utilizing the service portfolio to enhance business value

✓ The measurement systems and metrics required

✓ The use of service design models to accommodate different service solutions

In this chapter, we'll consider the core concepts of service design. We'll start by looking at service design principles and then examine service design in more detail, looking at the principles that underpin good design and considering the various aspects that together make up the overall design. We'll also consider the importance of creating a balanced design. This chapter covers the following topics.

- Holistic and balanced service design
- Service requirements, business requirements and drivers
- Design activities and constraints
- The five aspects of service design
- Service-oriented architecture (SOA) principles
- Design models

The learning objective for this module of the exam syllabus is to gain sufficient knowledge to interpret and analyze service design principles, techniques, and relationships and their application to the design of effective service solutions. In particular, the student should understand the following:

- Designing service solutions related to a customer's needs
- Designing and utilizing the service portfolio to enhance business value
- The measurement systems and metrics
- Service design models to accommodate different service solutions

Holistic and Balanced Service Design

When a design needs to be changed or any of the individual elements of the design need to be amended, consideration must be given to all aspects. This is called having a holistic service design. When a new application is being designed, its impact on the overall service, the management information systems and tools (e.g., service portfolio and service catalog), the architectures, the technology, the service management processes, and the necessary measurements and metrics all need to be considered. This will ensure not only that the design considers the functional elements, but also that all of the management and operational requirements are included. The requirements should be a fundamental part of the design and not added as an afterthought.

The holistic approach and the five aspects of design are important parts of the service provider's overall service management system. Adopting a holistic approach when planning for changes to the service and for its retirement helps prevent unforeseen consequences. Unless carefully planned, the retirement of a service or any aspect of a service could cause avoidable negative effects on the customer or business. A holistic approach ensures integration of all activities and processes, providing the end-to-end functionality and quality that the business requires.

Service Design and Change Management

Not every change will require the same level of service design activity. Although every change needs to be designed, not every change requires a large design overhead. Often changes have been carried out many times before and have an accepted approach, so minimizing the design effort required. It is important to remember that a seemingly small change may have a large potential impact, so each organization needs to define what level of design activity is required for different categories of change. As with all guidelines, the message should be clear and unambiguous and communicated to all staff. An important part of the change management impact assessment is assessing the service design requirements of each change. More information about the change management process, including impact assessment, is described within the *ITIL Service Transition* publication and in Part 3 of this book.

Utility and Warranty

For a service to deliver value, its design must deliver both utility and warranty (see Figure 11.1). Utility is the functionality offered by a product or a service to meet a specific customer need. Warranty provides the assurance that a product or service will meet the agreed requirements. It refers to the ability of the service to be available when needed, to have sufficient capacity to meet the requirements, and to be reliable in terms of both security and continuity.

FIGURE 11.1   Utility and warranty

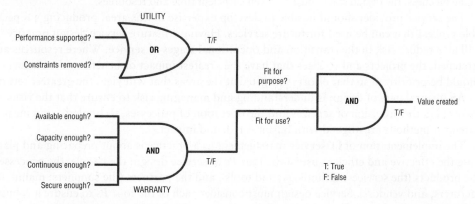

We will look at the particular processes of availability, capacity, security, and service continuity in the next four chapters, which cover service design processes, but we'll consider them briefly here because it is a basic principle of service design that all of these aspects must be considered and delivered in an integrated manner.

Business Focus

It is essential that IT systems and services are designed, planned, implemented, and managed to suit the business requirements.

IT services must be business and customer oriented. The focus must be on delivering the business requirement, and therefore achieving the business strategy, rather than on the technology used. A good service that is too expensive will fail to deliver the business benefit, so the design must also consider cost-effectiveness.

The warranty aspects of the service must be incorporated into the design. This means that the design must meet the customer's security requirements and provide the appropriate availability and capacity for business needs, and it must also offer the required service continuity.

Risk

Service design must deliver services that can be managed and operated with an acceptable level of risk. They must perform well at the point of delivery while also offering flexibility and adaptability. They should be designed to be able to cope with increasing volume and speed of change as needs change. There is a temptation to minimize or ignore the design and planning processes. This is dangerous because the overall quality of the design depends upon the quality of the planning process. Although there may be pressure to deliver in a particular timeframe, the time spent on design should be protected because skimping on this area may cause delays and expense later. This is an important principle that needs to be understood by those carrying out the design and those exerting the pressure for delivery. There may be some circumstances in which meeting the delivery date is critical, even if it means a design that will need rework later, but these situations are rare. In most cases, in order for the service to deliver the required value to the business, the design stage must be given sufficient time and resources.

The service provider should be able to develop expertise in this area, producing a repeatable process that can be used for future services. Having a mature service design practice will also reduce risk in the transition and operational stages of service. Where resources are stretched, the projects and services that have the greatest impact or benefit to the business should be prioritized so that effort is targeted at the areas that will yield the greatest return.

An integral part of design is understanding and managing risk to ensure that the risks involved in the provision of services and the operation of processes, technology, and measurement methods are aligned with business risk and impact.

The implementation of IT service management as a practice is about preparing and planning the effective and efficient use of the four Ps of service design: the people, the processes, the products (the services, technology, and tools), and the partners (the suppliers, manufacturers, and vendors). Service design must consider each of the four Ps to ensure a robust design that meets the requirements, as shown in Figure 11.2.

FIGURE 11.2   The four *P*s of service design

Service design must consider all aspects of the design:

- Products: The new service should be added to the portfolio, and the entry should be updated as it moves through design and transition and into operation.

- Processes: The processes of service level, financial, and capacity management will each play a part in the design.

- People: The technical, application, operations, and service desk staff will need to be aware of what will be required of them as far as operations and support is concerned.

- Partners: Supplier management will need to identify suitable partners/suppliers.

Listed here is a set of questions that need to be answered when undertaking a design for a new or changed service:

- Do you understand the functional requirements? What constraints are you working within (governance, compliance, etc.)?

- Do you understand the service level requirements (SLRs) for the service? Are the operational level agreements (OLAs) and underpinning contracts (UCs) in place?

- Do you understand all the technical components that will be needed?

- Do you know the applications required, and have you verified the data sources?

- Have you considered the environmental requirements and supporting services?

You need to understand the functional requirements and the business process being supported. You need to know how the service being offered supports these. And you need to be aware of any relevant policies or strategy and any governance or compliance requirements. The service requirements must be clear, and the necessary service level agreements (SLAs) need to be in place. The technical design must be understood, and the necessary components need to be available and ready to deliver the service, along with any environmental requirements such as power and air conditioning. You need to understand where the data is going to come from and have it verified for accuracy. The applications required to manipulate the data and provide the functional requirements of the business processes must be designed and validated. The requirements for any supporting services that are necessary to support the operation of the delivered service must be identified. The requirement for support from internal teams or suppliers must be agreed and documented in the OLAs and underpinning contracts. Finally, the service management processes needed to ensure the successful provision of the service must be considered.

Figure 11.3 shows the composition of a service. You can see how the business requirement and the governance and compliance requirement are the inputs into defining what the utility of the service needs to be. The SLAs take these SLRs and define the warranty requirements; each SLA is then underpinned with the appropriate OLAs and underpinning contracts, defining what the support teams and suppliers will deliver. This is the assets and capabilities layer. The service itself is designed in terms of the assets and resources it requires, such as infrastructure, environment, data, and applications. Finally, the service management processes support the management of the resources or products, the people, and the third-party partners.

FIGURE 11.3   Service Composition

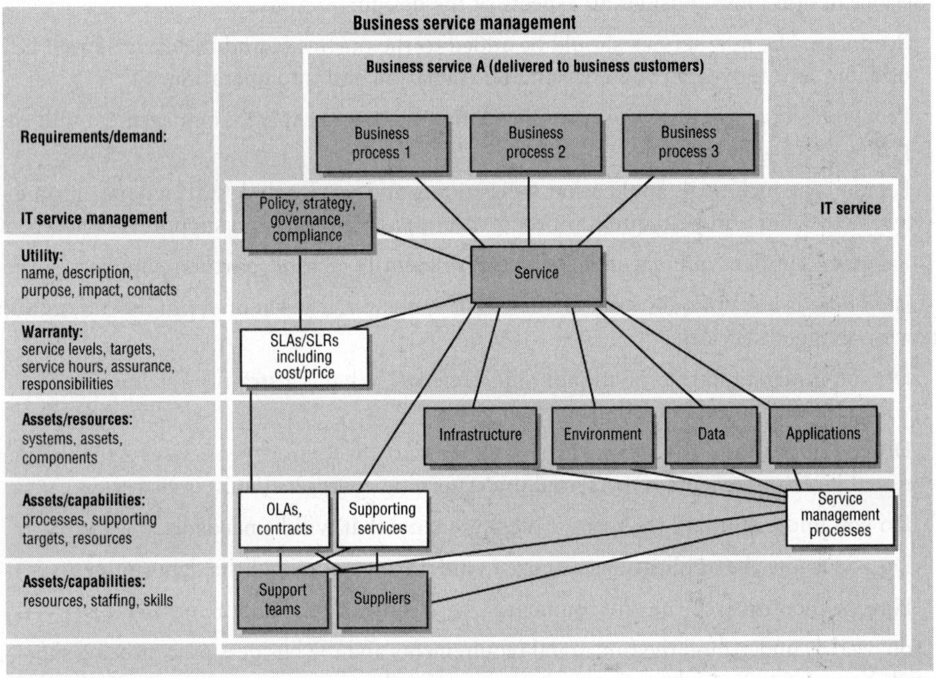

Balanced Design

All service design needs to balance the functional requirements and the performance targets (that is, the functionality of the service with how it will operate). In other words, it needs to ensure that all required utility and warranty can be delivered by the service being designed. This balance must be achieved within the time and cost restraints. Failure to meet the deadline, going over budget, delivering a service without the necessary functionality, or delivering one that fails to perform as required—any of these outcomes will prevent the value of the service from being realized. Design must therefore balance all of these requirements.

Jim McCarthy, author of *Dynamics of Software Development* (Microsoft Press, 2005), states that as a development manager, you are working with only three things:

Functionality   The service or product and everything that is part of the service and its provision

Resources   The people, technology, and money available for the effort

Schedule   The timescales for completion

You should note that throughout service design, the word *functionality* typically refers primarily to the utility of a service—what it does for the customer. In this context, however, McCarthy was using the term to refer to both utility and warranty (what the service will do and how it will do it)—this is what is being designed.

Figure 11.4 shows the three aspects of resources, time (i.e., schedule), and functionality. Changing any one of the three elements will impact the other two; overemphasizing or ignoring one will unbalance the design. You use resources to deliver this functionality to the customer within the schedule required. The service provider must always remember that the customer's business requirements include not only the details of the service itself but also the cost and the schedule.

FIGURE 11.4   Balanced design

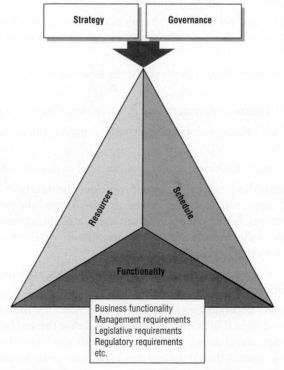

It is likely that business drivers and needs will change during design and delivery. Services should be designed so that they continue to deliver value throughout the lifecycle—often designers fail to consider what happens after the implementation of the service into the live environment. A holistic approach should ensure that not only does the service deliver the agreed requirements of the business, it is designed so that it can be effectively managed and improved throughout its operational life to achieve all of its agreed service targets.

Service Requirements, Business Requirements, and Drivers

We discussed the need for a holistic approach to design earlier in this chapter. When you consider service requirements as part of this holistic approach, you need to understand not only the service, but also its constituent components and their interrelationships.

Service Requirements

There are a number of things that we must ensure:

- The services delivered meet the requirements of the business in all areas, including the scalability of the service to meet future requirements in support of the long-term business objectives.

- The services also deliver the requirements of the business processes and business units it supports:

  - The agreed business requirements for functionality, that is, the utility requirements

  - The service level requirements and service level agreement covering the warranty requirements

- The design also specifies what technology will be used to deploy and deliver the service.

- Other requirements that design must consider include the internally delivered supporting services and components and their associated OLAs, and the externally supplied supporting services and components and their associated underpinning contracts. Design must specify the performance measurements and metrics that will be required and the required security levels.

- There may also be other aspects that the customer requires, such as the service having to meet sustainability requirements.

The relationships and dependencies between these elements are illustrated in Figure 11.5. Services are not designed in isolation. It is essential that the staff of the service provider organization understand the supporting components and supporting services of each service. The targets set within the OLAs and contracts must relate to and underpin those agreed between the service provider and its customers.

FIGURE 11.5   The service relationships and dependencies

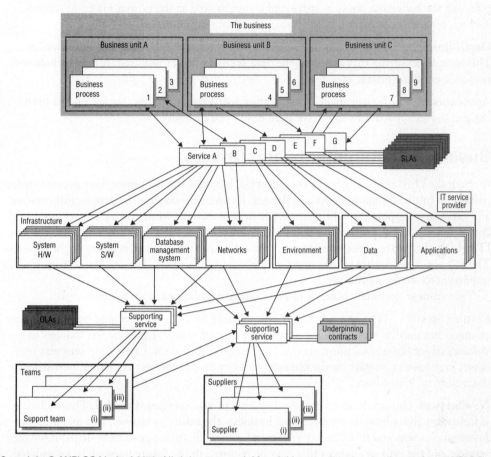

As you have seen, the elements of a service are interrelated. Should any element be changed, the impact of that change on all the other elements must be understood and catered to. So the design of a new or changed service may require numerous changes to the elements that contribute to the service. Because these various elements might be provided by a number of third-party suppliers, such changes need to be coordinated by a central service design authority to ensure that services and processes are fully integrated across all parties.

There are four separate technology domains that support components of every service, and design needs to address all four. The four domains are as follows:

Infrastructure   The management and control of all of the infrastructure elements used by the service, including servers, network equipment, database systems, mass storage systems, systems software, utilities, backup systems, firewalls, development and test environments, management tools, and so on.

Environmental   The management and control of all major equipment rooms. This includes planning the use of the physical space and layout as well as the power, air-conditioning, cabling, physical security, and other environmental requirements.

Data/Information   The means of managing and controlling the data and information. This includes ensuring that access to the data is controlled as required. It may include the management of test data.

Applications   The management of application software, including that which has been bought in and applications that have been developed in-house.

Business Requirements and Drivers

In order for IT to provide services that meet the business needs, it must have accurate information on business requirements and drivers. Business drivers are the people, information, and tasks that support the fulfilment of business objectives. Maintaining the accuracy and completeness of this information requires IT to have a close relationship with the business. IT needs to be aware of the operational, tactical, and strategic requirements of the business. The business relationship management process detailed in *ITIL Service Strategy* is vitally important to achieving this aim.

The business information needs to be obtained and agreed in three main areas:

Existing Services   IT must understand how existing services are used and be aware of any changes that may be required with regard to increased utility requirements, changes in volumes of service transactions, service level targets, and so on. Changes in business processes may have an impact on the criticality and impact of the service, either increasing or decreasing its importance.

New Services   Information on the requirements of new services is needed. This includes information about how they support the business, the utility, warranty, and management information. Seasonal fluctuations in demand, the likely future growth in demand for the service, and the type of changes that may be required in the future must all be considered.

Retiring Services   IT needs information on which services or parts of services are to be retired, when and how this should happen, and what the replacement will be. The disposal and/or reuse requirements for the service assets and configuration items need to be agreed upon, as does the archiving strategy for any business data.

Gathering Business Requirements

Collecting information on the business requirements is the first and most important stage for designing and delivering new services or major changes to existing services. Information must be accurate, and the business must appreciate how important it is to provide the information accurately. Senior business support for this is necessary because a design based on incomplete or inaccurate information will inevitably result in the design of services that do not match the needs of the business. Business requirements may change over time, so there needs to be a formal process for documenting and agreeing on these changes. Requirements should be documented in a clear, concise, and unambiguous manner.

As we said previously, spending time to capture the requirements accurately will prevent issues later and will minimize the likelihood of there being a gap between the business expectation for the service and what is delivered. As part of the gathering business requirements stage, a number of actions should take place:

- The appointment of a project manager, the creation of a project team, and the agreement of project governance by the application of a formal, structured project methodology.

- Identification of all stakeholders and their requirements should be documented, together with the benefits stakeholders should gain from the implementation.

- Requirements should be analyzed, prioritized, agreed on, and documented.

- The business and the service provider need to agree on the outline budgets.

- Any potential conflict between business units and agreement on corporate requirements needs to be identified and resolved.

- Obtain agreement for the mechanism of signing off on requirements and changes to those requirements. While requirements can seldom be fixed early in the project and need to be developed in an iterative manner, there is a danger of "scope creep," so the agreement of changes should be tightly controlled.

- Develop a customer engagement plan (in conjunction with the business relationship management process and in cooperation with design coordination) to ensure that the relationship with all key business stakeholders is managed.

- Carry out a financial assessment to identify which service requirements are too costly to include once the ongoing costs are included. Agree with the business as to which service requirements are to be excluded. Document the agreement to omit these requirements.

Holistic Approach

All design activities are triggered by changes in business needs or service improvements. A structured and holistic approach to the design activities should be adopted to ensure that consistency and integration are achieved within all design activities throughout the IT service provider organization. Too often organizations focus on the functional requirements, almost to the exclusion of other important areas such as manageability and operational requirements. A design or architecture by definition needs to consider all design aspects. It is not a smaller organization that combines these aspects, it is a sensible one.

Design Activities

Once the desired service solution has been designed, service design must carry out three activities before the solution passes into the service transition stage:

- Evaluate alternative solutions
- Procure the preferred solution
- Develop the solution

Evaluate Alternative Solutions

If external supplier services and solutions are involved, choosing a supplier and solution will involve evaluating alternative solutions:

- Compiling a statement of requirements for the suppliers
- Tendering the work
- Compiling a short list from the proposed solutions put forward by the suppliers, excluding any proposed solution that did not fulfil any of the mandatory requirements in the statement of requirements
- Evaluating the proposed solutions against a set of agreed criteria, using an agreed scoring mechanism
- Costing the solutions
- Choosing the winning supplier solution based on the scoring and costings

It is important to remember that costing should include both one-off costs and the ongoing costs of operation and ownership, including support and maintenance. More information about service economics and service costing is covered in Part 1 of this book, "Service Strategy."

Procure the Preferred Solution

Most solutions require some involvement from external suppliers. The following activities are required to procure the solution:

- Completing all necessary due diligence checks on the preferred supplier
- Finalizing the terms and conditions of any new contracts
- Ensuring that all corporate policies are enforced
- Signing the contracts
- Completing the procurement of the selected solution

Develop the Solution

The development phase consists of translating the service design into a plan for the development, reuse, or redevelopment of the components required to deliver the service and the subsequent implementation of the developed service.

Major service changes may need to be developed into a program of plans, each responsible for delivering one or more components. The plans should include the following:

- The needs of the business
- The timescales involved
- The strategy for developing and/or purchasing the solution
- Ensuring that sufficient resources are available in terms of facilities, IT infrastructure, and skills

- Developing the service, including the management, monitoring, and measurement mechanisms
- Service and component test plans

Careful project management should avoid conflict and ensure compatibility of components sourced from different development activities.

Design Constraints

All design activities operate within a number of constraints. These constraints come from the business and service strategy and cover many different areas, as illustrated in Figure 11.6. Designers are not always "free" to design the most desirable solution; they must always take these constraints into consideration.

FIGURE 11.6 Design constraints

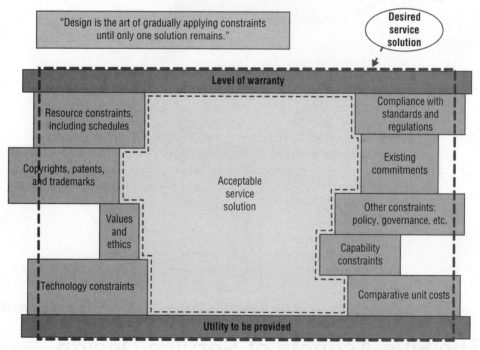

The most important constraints are the utility and warranty requirements because any solution that does not satisfy these will not deliver the required business value. Cost is another obvious constraint; the budget may not stretch to the best technical solution. The designer must either work within the constraints or seek to have them changed, by negotiating a bigger budget, for example.

There may also be many external factors that can influence the design, as shown in Figure 11.7. Many arise from the need for good corporate and IT governance, and others are from the requirement for compliance with regulations, legislation, and international standards. Designers must recognize these constraints and ensure that their design includes all of the necessary controls and capability required by them.

FIGURE 11.7   External influences on solution design

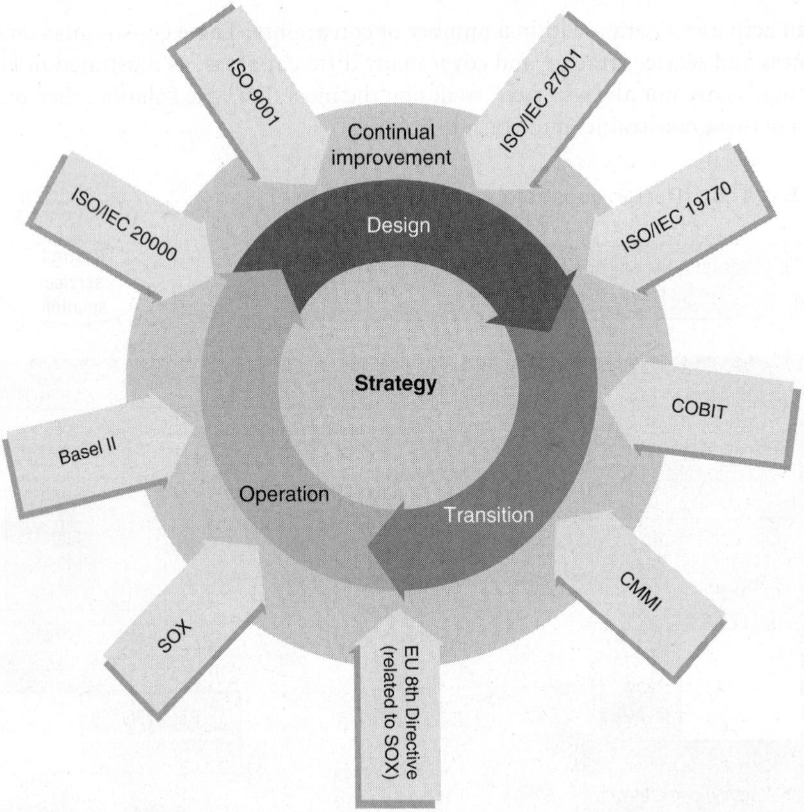

The Five Aspects of Service Design

We are now going to spend some time considering the five aspects of service design. We listed these in Chapter 10, "Introduction to the Service Design Lifecycle Stage." As a reminder, the five aspects are as follows:

- The design of the actual solution itself
- The service management system and tools that will be required to manage the service
- The management and technology architectures that the service will use
- The processes required to operate, support, and maintain the services
- The measurement systems, methods, and metrics that will be required

You should remember studying these five aspects before, as part of the Foundation course. Here you will look at them in more depth. You need to ensure that, for each of the five aspects, the desired business outcomes and planned results are clearly defined. This should help ensure that the final service delivered meets the expectations of the customers and users. Each of the five aspects must focus on this to facilitate quality, consistency, and continual improvement.

The key aspect is the design of new or changed service solutions to meet changing business needs. Every new solution must be checked to ensure that it conforms to the five aspects and will interface with other services successfully.

Service design is responsible for creating plans for the design, transition, and subsequent operation of these five different aspects. The plans should include the following items:

- The approach taken
- The associated timescales
- The organizational impact of the new or changed solution on both the business and IT
- The commercial impact of the solution on the organization, including the funding, costs, and budgets required
- The technical impact of the solution
- The impact on the staff and their roles and responsibilities
- The skills, knowledge, training, and competencies required to deploy, operate, maintain, and optimize the new solution to the business
- The commercial justification assessment of the impact of the solution on existing business—judging the impact on the capacity and performance of IT and service management processes
- The risks identified to services, processes, and activities (documented and mitigated)
- With so much activity taking place and so many different parties involved, a communication plan to ensure that the right information gets to the right people at the right time
- Any modifications required to existing contracts or agreements in light of the new service, including documenting the expected service levels in new or existing SLAs

The plans should result in the production of a service design package containing everything necessary for the subsequent testing, introduction, and operation of the solution or service. This should include the production of a set of service acceptance criteria (SAC) that will be used to ensure that the service provider is ready to deliver and support the new or changed service in the live environment. We looked at the contents and use of service acceptance criteria in Chapter 10.

There are many activities to be completed within service design. Managing them all and meeting the time, budget, and quality criteria is challenging and requires a formal and structured approach. This will facilitate the delivery of the new service at the right cost, utility, and warranty and within the right time frame.

An example of such an approach and its constituent stages is shown in Figure 11.8, together with the other major areas that will need to be involved along the way. This is a complex diagram; take the time to fully understand it.

FIGURE 11.8   Aligning new services to business requirements

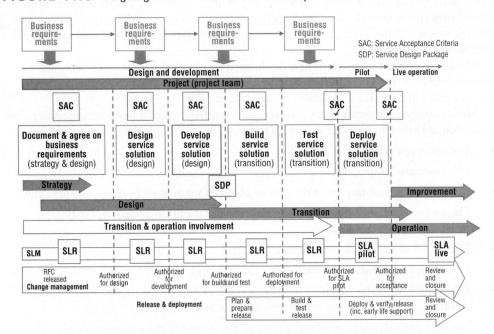

The diagram shows the lifecycle of a service from the initial or changed business requirement through the design, transition, and operation stages of the lifecycle.

First you see how the service moves through a design and development stage, into a pilot, and finally into the live operations stage. The project team is involved during the first two stages, but not in the live operations stage. You can see the involvement of the service level management and change management processes throughout and the release and deployment management processes of service transition.

You can see how the business requirements feed into the service acceptance criteria (SAC). Documented requirements and service level requirements are produced during the strategy and design lifecycle stages.

As the solution is designed, developed, and built, the business requirements continue to feed into the SAC, allowing for any changes to be incorporated (if this is agreed). The SLRs and SAC will be updated to fit the changed requirement. The service is then tested in transition against the criteria and deployed. It is important that knowledge transfer between the operational staff and the project staff takes place at all stages to ensure smooth progression through each of the stages illustrated.

The diagram also shows the role of the project team within this activity of delivering new and changing IT services to the business and its relationship to design activities. This approach must be iterative/incremental to ensure that the service meets the evolving needs of the business as these needs develop during the business process development and the IT service lifecycle. Additional project managers and project teams may need to be allocated to manage the stages within the lifecycle for the deployment of the new service.

Designing Service Solutions

Now we'll begin to look at each of the five aspects of service design in detail. The first of these that we'll examine is designing service solutions. The following areas need to be considered within the design of the service solution:

- Analyze the agreed business requirements.

- Review the existing IT services and infrastructure; this may identify alternative solutions, which can reuse or exploit existing components.

- Design solutions to the new requirements, including their constituent components. The design should include the facilities or features and functionality required (i.e., the utility) and any information required that will enable the performance of the service or process to be monitored.

- The design must address the requirements of the business processes it will support, and so it needs to take into account dependencies, priorities, criticality, and the impact of the service together with the business benefits that will be delivered by the service.

- The design will also need to cater to the business cycles and seasonal variations and the related business transaction levels, service transaction levels, the number and types of users, anticipated future growth, and any business continuity requirements.

- The design of the service has to be in line with the service level requirements and service level targets (i.e., the warranty requirements).

- It also needs to be aware of the service measuring, reporting, and reviewing activities.

- The timescales, planned outcome from the new service, and its impact on existing services must be understood.

- The design must also take into consideration any required testing, including any user acceptance testing (UAT) and how the test results will be managed.

- The new service will need to integrate into the overall service management system.

It is an essential responsibility of design to ensure that the service acceptance criteria are planned into the initial design. Alternative designs should be evaluated and costed to ensure that the final design is the optimum approach:

- The design stage has to have an agreed budget and timeline to design, develop, build, test, and deploy the service.

- The business benefits, especially the required return on investment, should be confirmed.

- All costs and benefits and any increased revenues need to be identified and quantified. The costs should cover the total cost of ownership of the service and include startup costs and all ongoing operational costs, including management, support, and maintenance.

- Finally, all parties can agree on the preferred solution and its planned outcomes and targets (both utility and warranty).

Before commencing on building the solution, a check should be made that it is in line with all corporate and IT strategies, policies, plans, governance and security controls, and architectural documents. If there is any aspect where the design is in conflict with any of these, either the solution will need to be revised or a change will need to be made to the strategic documentation. Any such change to strategy or policies may have repercussions that will need to be taken into account. The changing of strategy will involve a significant amount of work and will be done in conjunction with service strategy.

The best designed service solution will fail if the organization is not ready to use it. An *organizational readiness assessment* should be carried out to ensure that the organization has the appropriate capability to deliver to the agreed level. This will include the following:

- The commercial impact on the business and IT should be assessed, including all of the business benefits and all of the costs involved in the design, development, and ongoing operation and support of the service.

- Risks associated with the new or changed service, particularly to the operation, security, availability, and continuity of the service, need to be assessed and mitigated.

- The business needs to assess its own capability and maturity, ensuring that the right processes, structure, people, roles, responsibilities, and facilities are in place to operate the new service.

- IT must also assess its own capability and maturity and readiness to deliver the service. This should include assessing the impact on the environment, technology, and existing services.

- The IT department itself should be assessed to ensure that the required roles and responsibilities can be delivered, that the IT processes are effective, and that documentation is up-to-date.

- Any gaps in the skills, knowledge, and competence of the staff or in the capabilities of the processes and tools should be addressed.

- Changes to agreements with suppliers to ensure support of the service should be carried out.

- Finally, the service design package should be assembled for the transition, operation, and improvement stages.

The Design of the Management Information Systems and Tools

Next we'll consider the second aspect of service design, the design of the management information systems and tools. These systems and tools will be essential to the management of the service throughout its lifecycle. Management information systems are usually part of a larger framework of policies, processes, functions, standards, guidelines, and tools that are planned and managed together and used to ensure that the desired objectives are achieved. This larger system, or framework, is known as a management system, and examples include a quality management system, an information security management system, or even the overall service management system.

The service management system may include the service portfolio, CMS, capacity management information system (CMIS), availability management information system (AMIS), security management information system (SMIS), and supplier and contract management information system (SCMIS).

The Service Portfolio

The service portfolio (Figure 11.9) is the most critical management information system. It supports all processes and describes a provider's services in terms of business value. It articulates business needs and the provider's response to those needs.

FIGURE 11.9   The service portfolio

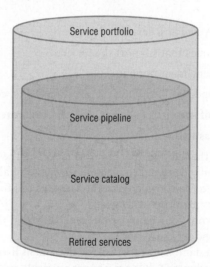

The service portfolio either clarifies or helps to clarify the following strategic questions:

- Why should a customer buy these services?
- Why should they buy these services from us?

- What are the pricing or charge-back models?
- What are our strengths and weaknesses, priorities, and risks?
- How should our resources and capabilities be allocated?

Ideally the service portfolio should form part of a comprehensive service knowledge management system (SKMS) and be registered as a document in the configuration management system (CMS). Further information on both the CMS and the SKMS is provided within *ITIL Service Transition*. Once a strategic decision to charter a service is made, this is the stage in the service lifecycle when service design begins architecting the service, which will eventually become part of the service catalog.

Each organization should choose the content and access allowed to its own service portfolio. The following content is required for each service included in the portfolio:

- Service name
- Version
- Description
- Status
- Classification
- Criticality
- The applications and data used
- Which business processes the service supports and the business and IT owners for these business services
- The warranty and SLA and SLR levels
- The services and resources that support the service
- Which resources are dependent upon it
- How the service is supported, including the relevant OLAs, contracts, and agreements
- The financial aspects of the service—costs, charges, and revenue (if applicable)
- How the service is measured

The service portfolio is the main source of information on the requirements and services and needs to be very carefully designed to meet all the needs of all its users. The design of the service portfolio needs to be considered in the same way as the design of the IT service itself to ensure that it meets all of these needs.

You should remember from your Foundation level study that the portfolio is made up of the pipeline, the catalog, and retired services.

The service pipeline is a database or structured document listing all services that are under consideration or development but are not yet available to customers. It provides a business view of possible future services and is not normally published to customers. The pipeline contains details of all of the business requirements that have not yet been addressed via existing services. It is used to define, analyze, prioritize, and approve all requests for new or changed services to ensure that new and changed services are aligned to business requirements. It is an input to the activities of the service strategy and service design stages of the service lifecycle, but it also provides valuable input to service transition.

The service catalog is another database or structured document. It contains information about all live IT services, including those available for deployment. The service catalog is the only part of the service portfolio published to customers, and it's used to support the sale and delivery of IT services. It includes information about deliverables, prices, contact points, ordering, and request processes. It is essential that all of the details within the overall service portfolio are accurate and updated as a service moves from the pipeline into the catalog. We'll look in more detail at the service catalog and its management in Chapter 12, "Service Design Processes: Design Coordination and Service Catalog Management." The retired services area of the service portfolio represents services that are phased out or retired. The retirement of a service must be carefully planned during service design and is managed through service transition. When services are retired, the related knowledge and information is stored in a knowledge base for future use.

The service portfolio should contain information relating to every service and its current status within the organization. It is recommended that the service portfolio include the following status options:

Requirements   A set of outline requirements have been received from the business or IT for a new or changed service.

Definition   The requirements for the new service are being assessed, defined, and documented, and the SLR is being produced.

Analysis   The requirements for the new service are being analyzed and prioritized.

Approved   The requirements for the new service have been finalized and authorized.

Chartered   The new service requirements are being communicated and resources and budgets allocated.

Design   The new service and its constituent components are being designed and procured, if required.

Development   The service and its constituent components are being developed or harvested, if applicable.

Build   The service and its constituent components are being built.

Test   The service and its constituent components are being tested.

Release   The service and its constituent components are being released.

Operational/Live   The service and its constituent components are operational within the live environment.

Retiring   The service is still being delivered in the live environment to legacy customers but will not be sold to or activated for new customers.

Retired   The service and its constituent components have been retired.

The service portfolio would therefore contain details of all services and their status with respect to the current stage within the service lifecycle, as shown in Figure 11.10.

FIGURE 11.10 The service portfolio, showing service status

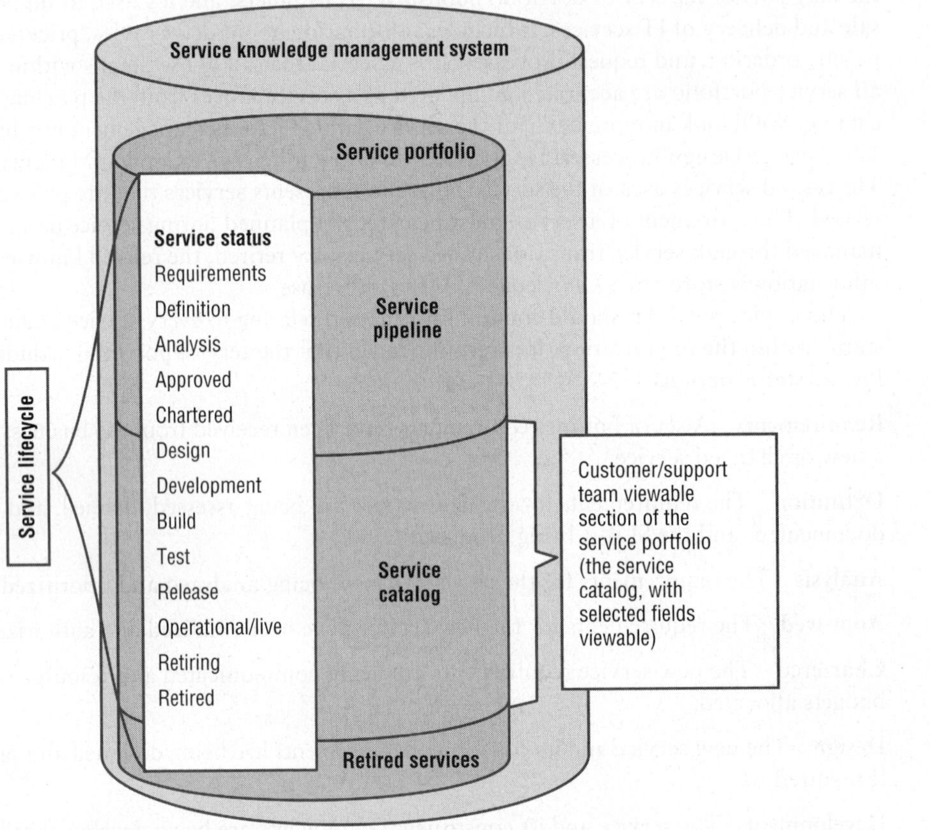

Service knowledge management system

Service portfolio

Service status

Requirements

Definition

Analysis

Approved

Chartered

Design

Development

Build

Test

Release

Operational/live

Retiring

Retired

Service lifecycle

Service pipeline

Service catalog

Customer/support team viewable section of the service portfolio (the service catalog, with selected fields viewable)

Retired services

A service should appear in the service pipeline from the "requirements" status to the "chartered" status. Once a service achieves the "operational" status in the live environment, it should appear in the service catalog. Between "chartered" and "operational," each organization should decide on a clear policy regarding when a service will move from pipeline to catalog. Between "operational" and "retired," each organization should decide upon a clear policy regarding when a service will move from catalog to retired services. The responsibility and accountability for a service at different stages should be clearly defined.

As part of the design of its service portfolio, each organization should define clear policies regarding the service lifecycle and the relationship between each service status and the service's progression through the sections of the service portfolio. The relationship between service status and portfolio shown in Figure 11.10 is one possible approach. In this example, services within the service portfolio between "chartered" and "retiring" appear in the service catalog and are therefore accessible to customers and users.

Each version of a service should be assigned a number or other unique identifier to assist in clearly monitoring the progress of that version of the service throughout its lifecycle. Ideally, each particular version of a service should exist in only one section of the portfolio at a time. Newer versions of a service may be in the pipeline while the current version is in the catalog or in the catalog while an older version is in the retired services.

Clear rules are needed where multiple versions exist in the same portfolio section. There may be two or more versions in the catalog due to a phased rollout. Service strategy and design staff need access to the whole portfolio; other staff need only a subset. It should be noted that the portfolio is designed during service design but managed through strategy.

Management and Technology Architectures

Architectural design can be thought of as the blueprint of the development and deployment of an IT infrastructure to satisfy the current and future needs of the business. In this context, architecture is defined as the fundamental organization of a system—that is, how its components relate to each other and to the environment and the principles guiding its design and evolution.

The system could be, for example, a whole organization, a business function, a product line, or an information system. Each of these systems will have an "architecture" made up of its components; the relationships between the components; the relationships between the system and its environment; and the design principles that inform, guide, and constrain its structure and operation as well as its future development.

Enterprises are complex and usually include the following components:

- Staff
- Business functions and processes
- Organizational structure and physical distribution
- Information resources and systems
- Financial and other resources, including technology
- Strategies, plans, management, policies, and governance structures

We are concerned with the architectures of the business of the organization and the information systems that support it. Each of these architectures calls on distinct architectural disciplines and areas of expertise, as seen in Figure 11.11.

FIGURE 11.11   Enterprise architecture

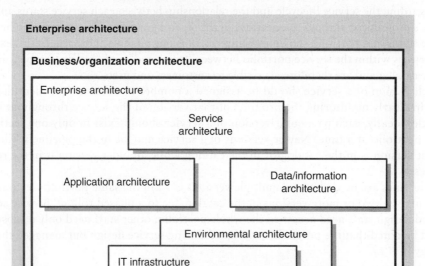

In this diagram you can see enterprise architecture, service architecture, application architecture, and data architecture. The IT infrastructure and environmental architectures are also shown.

Gartner defines enterprise architecture as "the process of translating the business's vision and strategy into effective enterprise change by creating, communicating and improving key requirements, principles and models that describe the enterprise's future state and enable its evolution toward it" (Basualdo, Militza. "Business Value through Enterprise Architecture." Gartner, 2010. Executive Programs Road Notes). This should be an integrated element of the business architecture and should include the major architectures: service, application, data/information, infrastructure, technology, and environmental architectures. Let's consider these different architectures in turn:

▪   Service architecture translates applications and infrastructure, organization, and support activities into a set of services. This means that there may be changes in these architectures without changing the services themselves. It includes the services themselves, their overall integration, and the management of those services.

- Application architecture maps business and functional requirements onto applications and shows the interrelationships between applications.

- Data/information architecture describes the logical and physical data assets of the enterprise and the data management resources. It shows how the information resources are managed and shared for the benefit of the enterprise.

- IT infrastructure architecture describes the structure, functionality, and geographical distribution of the components that underpin the overall architecture and the technical standards applying to them. It includes product and management architecture:

  - A product architecture describes the particular proprietary products and industry standards that the enterprise uses to implement the infrastructure.

  - A management architecture consists of the management tools used to manage the products, processes, and environments.

- Environmental architecture describes all aspects, types, and levels of environmental controls and their management.

- Technology architectures include the following:

  - Applications and systems software

  - Information, data, and databases

  - Infrastructure design, including the design of the following items:

    - Servers

    - LANs

    - WANs

    - Voice networks

    - Internet/intranet/extranet

    - Client systems

    - PDAs

    - Storage area networks (SANs)

    - Network-attached storage (NAS)

    - Environmental systems

Management architectures need to be business aligned, not technology driven. There are two separate approaches to developing a management architecture: either use a proprietary integrated management architecture across the whole infrastructure or adopt a "best of breed" architecture for each requirement.

In Figure 11.12, you can see how these different architectures relate to each other. Take a moment to study it.

FIGURE 11.12 Relationship between architectures

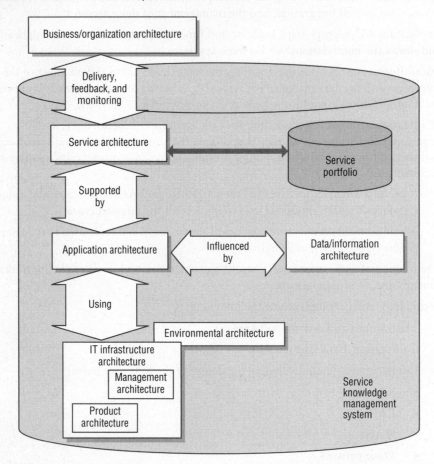

Enterprise architecture frameworks include the following items:

- Descriptions of organizational structure
- Business processes
- Planning and control systems
- Management and governance mechanisms
- Enterprise policies and procedures

They show how these components interoperate and contribute to the achievement of business goals and objectives and provide the basis for identifying the requirements for information systems that support these business processes. The real benefit and return on investment of the enterprise architecture comes from the ability of an organization to design and successfully implement projects and solutions in a rapid and consistent manner.

There are a number of enterprise architecture frameworks that have been widely adopted, including these two:

The Open Group Architecture Framework (TOGAF)   This is a high-level and holistic approach to design. It relies heavily on modularization and standardization and already existing, proven technologies and products.

Architecture of Integrated Information Systems (ARIS)   This is an approach to enterprise modeling; it offers methods for analyzing processes and taking a holistic view of process design, management, work flow, and application processing.

It is possible to identify (at least) three architectural roles. They could all report to a senior "enterprise architect" in the organization. They are the business/organizational architect, the service architect (which may be split into applications and information/data architect), and the IT infrastructure architect.

Processes

Let's now move on to the next aspect of service design, process design. But first, here's a reminder of the definition of a process. A process is a structured set of activities designed to accomplish a specific objective. It takes one or more inputs and turns them into defined outputs. Process definitions should include the roles, responsibilities, tools, and management controls required to reliably deliver the outputs. The definition may also define or revise policies, standards, guidelines, activities, processes, procedures, and work instructions if they are needed.

Figure 11.13 shows the generic process model, which you should recognize from your Foundation studies. It shows how data enters the process, is processed, and is output and how the outcome is measured and reviewed. A process is always organized around a set of objectives, which define what the main outputs should be. Importantly, a process should always include process measurements (metrics), reports, and process improvement.

Each process should be owned by a process owner, who should be accountable for the process and its improvement and for ensuring that a process meets its objectives. Service design should assist in the design of processes to ensure consistency and enable integration between processes.

The output of an effective process conforms to the business objectives. If the activities are carried out with a minimum use of resources, the process can also be considered efficient. Process analysis, results, and metrics should be incorporated in regular management reports and process improvements. Even before starting, it is important to think about what the process outcomes should look like. Outputs from processes should be compared to what is expected ("norms") to assess the quality. Measuring allows comparison of what has actually been done with what the organization set out to do and helps to identify and implement improvements within the process. This integrates with the Plan-Do-Check-Act cycle of continual improvement.

Not all process activities take place within the same organizational unit. The individual activities should therefore be clearly mapped to well-defined roles. The roles and activities are coordinated by process managers. Once detailed procedures and work instructions have been developed, an organization must map the defined roles and the activities of the process to its existing staff. Clear definitions of accountability and responsibility are critical success factors (CSFs) for any improvement activity. Without this, roles and responsibilities within the new process can be confusing, and individuals will revert to "the way we've always done it" before the new procedures were put in place.

FIGURE 11.13 The generic process model

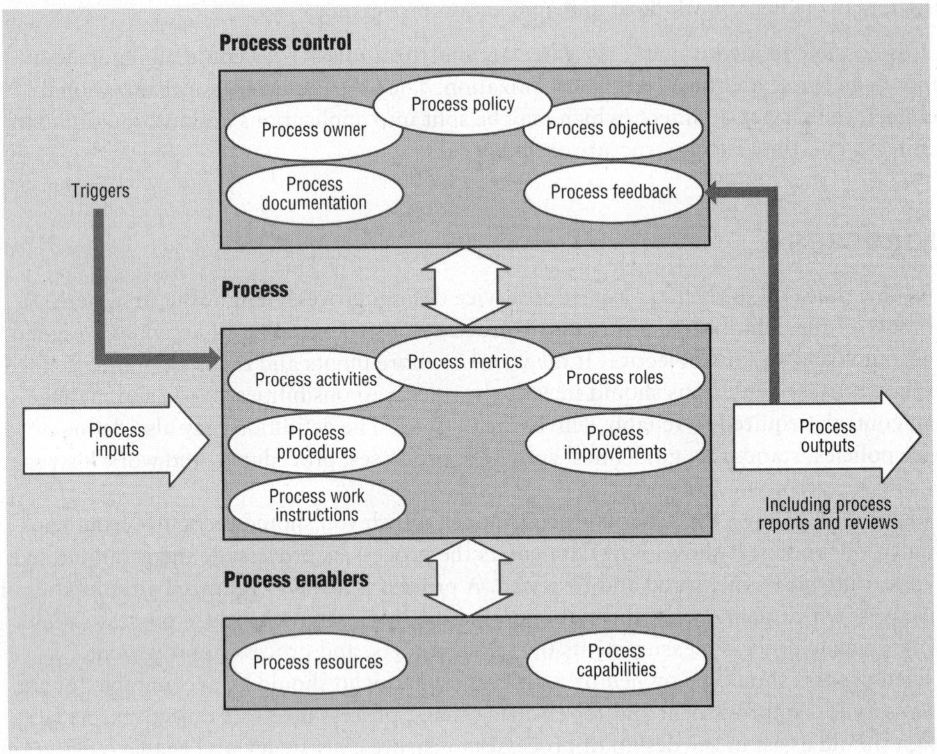

The RACI model should be familiar; you studied it as part of your Foundation course. As a reminder, this is a method of defining who is responsible, accountable, consulted, or informed for each task. The responsible person is the person who actually does the job, whereas the accountable person has ownership of the quality and the end result. Some people may be consulted and input knowledge and information into the process, while others are kept informed on progress.

When the RACI model is applied to a process, only one person should hold end-to-end accountability for the process, typically the process owner. Similarly, there is only one person accountable for any individual activity, although several people may be responsible for executing parts of the activity.

In Figure 11.14, you can see an example of a simple RACI matrix. Remember, there has to be one, and only one, person accountable, and one or more people have to be responsible. Not every task includes people who are consulted or informed.

FIGURE 11.14   An example of a simple RACI matrix

	Director service management	Service level manager	Problem manager	Security manager	Procurement manager
Activity 1	AR	C	I	I	C
Activity 2	A	R	C	C	C
Activity 3	I	A	R	I	C
Activity 4	I	A	R	I	
Activity 5	I	R	A	C	I

Measurement Systems and Metrics

Now we move on to the last of the five aspects of service design, designing measurement systems and metrics. You might be familiar with the Peter Drucker's saying, "If you can't measure it, then you can't manage it." This is very true, and so in order to manage and control processes and services, they have to be monitored and measured.

Care should be exercised when selecting measurements and metrics and the methods used to produce them. This is because the metrics and measurements chosen will actually affect and change the behavior of people being measured, particularly where this relates to objectives, personal and team performance, and performance-related pay schemes. Therefore you should include only measurements that encourage progression toward meeting business objectives or desired behavioral change. For example, measuring first-contact fix rates at the service desk may encourage staff to spend too long on an incident, trying to resolve it rather than passing it on to second line. This may actually impact customer satisfaction because users might wait longer for their call to be answered.

Measurements should have the following characteristics:

- Measurements should be fit for purpose, providing the information required.
- They should be fit for use, not overengineered or underengineered.

- Measurement systems should be right the first time, with minimal rework required. If the basis of measurement is being continually tweaked, it will raise questions about the validity of the results and make it impossible to establish any trends.

- Measurements should reflect the perspective of the business and the customers.

- They need to reflect the ability of the delivered solutions to meet the identified and agreed requirements of the business.

There are four types of metrics that can be used to measure the capability and performance of processes:

- **Progress**, that is, the milestones and deliverables in the capability of the process

- **Compliance** of the process to governance requirements and compliance of people to the use of the process

- **Effectiveness** of the process and its ability to deliver the right result

- **Efficiency**, which means the productivity of the process and its speed, throughput, and resource utilization

Measurements and metrics should develop and change as the maturity and capability of a process develops. Initially, the progress and compliance of the process need to be the main focus. As the process maturity develops, effectiveness and efficiency metrics can also be used.

What to measure and how to measure and report it requires careful design and planning. The primary metrics should always focus on determining the effectiveness and the quality of the solutions provided. Secondary metrics can then measure the efficiency of the processes used to produce and manage the solution. The priority should always be to ensure that the processes provide the correct results for the business. Measurements in individual areas should be aggregated together to give the full picture, but this means that there cannot be gaps in what is being measured or inconsistencies in how it is being measured.

The metrics tree shown in Figure 11.15 is based on a typical balanced scorecard and uses dials to represent metrics results for each level shown. It is important to note the linkage from the lowest level of the tree of individual component metrics all the way up to objectives and metrics of the business itself. Each lower step should be feeding into the step above. For example, individual customer satisfaction scores for particular services feed into overall customer satisfaction measurements.

Measurement systems should ensure that each role is provided with appropriate information so that business managers and customers get a top-level business dashboard, aligned with business needs and processes, while senior IT managers focus on the top-level IT management dashboard.

Service owners will focus on the performance of particular services, and process owners and managers will want to view the performance of their processes. Finally, technical specialists can look at the performance of individual components.

FIGURE 11.15   A metrics tree

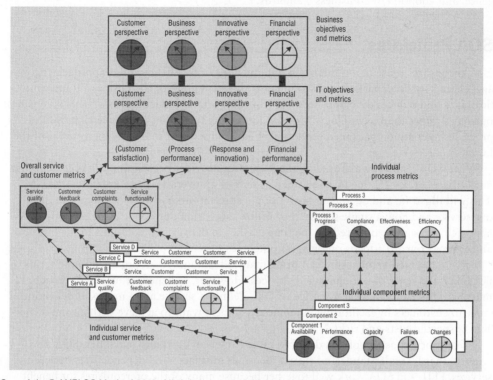

Service-Oriented Architecture

The best-practice approach of a service-oriented architecture (SOA) should be used in
the design of business processes and solutions. This SOA approach is used by many organizations to improve their effectiveness and efficiency in the provision of IT services.
SOA is defined by OASIS (Organization for the Advancement of Structured Information
Standards, www.oasis-open.org) as follows:

> A paradigm for organizing and utilizing distributed capabilities that
> may be under the control of different ownership domains. It provides a
> uniform means to offer, discover, interact with and use capabilities to
> produce desired effects consistent with measurable preconditions and
> expectations.

OASIS is a not-for-profit, international consortium that drives the development, convergence, and adoption of e-business standards.

SOA Principles

SOA encourages reuse of modular self-contained services. This modular approach encourages shared services that can be used in many different areas of the business. It increases flexibility and reduces development time. Most important, it encourages a focus on business outcomes rather than technology. More and more organizations are converting business processes to common packaged services that can be used and shared by many areas of the business.

When SOA principles are used by the IT service provider organization, it is critical that an accurate service catalog is maintained as part of an overall service portfolio and CMS. This will illustrate and document how a single application may form part of more than one service and how a single service may utilize more than one application. Adopting this approach can significantly reduce the time it takes to deliver new solutions to the business and to move toward a focus on business outcomes instead of technology.

Service-oriented architecture can bring many advantages to an organization in terms of flexibility and reuse of self-contained services. However, to benefit from this approach, IT must have first defined what a service is. ITIL defines a service as "a means of delivering value to customers by facilitating outcomes customers want to achieve without the ownership of specific costs and risks."

The important aspect of this definition is the focus of customer outcomes. SOA also requires that IT understands and clearly identifies interfaces and dependencies between services. ITIL and SOA work well together because many of the prerequisites for benefiting from this approach are outputs of ITIL processes. For example, the service catalog and the CMS show the composition of and interfaces and dependencies between services. ITIL also provides a standardized approach for the development and definition of services and encourages the use of common technology and toolsets. ITIL's change management process ensures that the impact of changes to shared services is determined in advance of the change. If the SOA approach is to be adopted, IT must ensure that staff receive training in SOA to enable a common language to be used and to improve the implementation and support of the new or changed services.

Service Design Models

The model selected for the design of IT services will depend mainly on the model selected for the delivery of IT services. Before adopting a design model for a major new service, conduct a review of the current capability and provisions with respect to all aspects of the delivery of IT services. The review should consider all aspects, including the business drivers and requirements and the demands, targets, and requirements of the new service. The scope and capabilities of the existing service provider and the external suppliers should be considered together with the maturity of the processes and the culture of the various organizations currently involved.

The IT infrastructure and all components involved in the service should be reviewed, as should the degree of corporate and IT governance, ownership, and control required. Finally, the financial and staff resources should be assessed. The main sourcing structures are as follows:

- Insourcing. This model describes where the organization uses its own resources to carry out all stages of the service lifecycle for new, changed, or revised services.

- Outsourcing. In this model, the organization uses the resources of one or more third-party organizations to provide some or all of the lifecycle activities for the service. Outsourcers may be used to provide the whole service or just the design or support stages, for example. Using an outsourcer requires a formal agreement or contract in which the services supplied are clearly defined.

- Cosourcing or multisourcing. There is often a combination of insourcing and outsourcing using a number of organizations working together.

- A partnership model is another option. This involves formal arrangements between organizations to work together to design, develop, transition, maintain, operate, and/ or support IT service(s).

- Business process outsourcing, or BPO, is different from the IT sourcing options; with BPO, an entire business function or process is managed by a third party. This is usually to enable the business function to be carried out in a low-cost location. Again, it is important that a formal arrangement between the organizations is negotiated so that expectations and responsibilities are clearly defined.

- The next option is to use an application service provider. ASPs provide shared computer-based services from their own premises to customer organizations over a network. Again, a formal arrangement should be in place to define the service to be provided.

- Knowledge process outsourcing, or KPO, organizations not only execute a process, but also make certain low-level decisions based on knowledge of local conditions or industry-specific information. For example, a KPO organization may handle small claims for an insurer and make decisions over whether these should be paid and how much the settlement should be. This differs from business process outsourcing where the decision will have been made by the organization employing the outsourcer and just processed by the outsourcer.

- The cloud services model is becoming increasingly popular. Cloud services offer specific, predefined services usually provided on demand. Services are usually standard but can be customized if there is enough demand. Cloud services can be offered internally, but they are generally outsourced service provisions.

- Multivendor sourcing involves different sources from different vendors, often representing combined versions of the preceding sourcing options.

For all sourcing solutions requiring external providers, the need for a clear agreement of what is to be provided is essential. The supplier management process should also be used to ensure that the suppliers deliver the agreed service. These delivery strategies are relevant to the design, transition, and operational stages of the service lifecycle. The suppliers themselves may operate offshore, adding to the challenge of maintaining good communications with them.

Another challenge is to ensure that all organizations involved clearly understand their own roles and responsibilities and those of the other organizations involved, especially when different strategies have been adopted for different stages of the lifecycle. Without this understanding, there is a risk to effective acceptance and the handover processes.

Design and Development Approaches

There are a number of different approaches to design and development:

Structured System Development   This is the traditional "waterfall" approach. It involves defining a complete set of requirements early in the lifecycle and then managing changes to them, if necessary.

Rapid Applications Development Approach   This is becoming increasingly popular. There are a number of variants of RAD, of which the most popular is the Agile methodology. The rapid approach involves the introduction of increments and iterations in the development process so that risks associated with uncertainty and changing requirements can be managed.

Commercial Off-the-Shelf (COTS) Solutions   This involves purchasing, implementing, and possibly customizing commercial packaged solutions.

Summary

In this chapter, you studied service design principles. We looked at holistic service design, service composition and the four Ps of service design, and the importance of and approach to balanced design. We also discussed service requirements, business requirements, and drivers. We examined design activities, constraints, and models, including the five aspects of service design and the management of service design processes. Finally, we considered service-oriented architecture principles and service design models.

Exam Essentials

Understand what is meant by the term *holistic service design*.   Give examples of aspects to be considered using this approach.

Be able to explain the four separate technology domains that support components of every service and that design needs to address.   Be able to give examples.

Understand the five aspects of service design.   Be able to list and explain them.

Understand and expand on the concepts of service-oriented architecture.   List the benefits it can deliver and how it relates to ITIL best practice.

Be able to list the typical contents of a service design plan.   You should be able to specify what is in a service design plan.

Review Questions

You can find the answers to the review questions in the appendix.

1. Which of the following statements is correct?

   A. The service portfolio is part of the service catalog, which is part of the service knowledge management system.

   B. The service pipeline is part of the service portfolio, which is part of the service knowledge management system.

   C. The service knowledge management system is part of the CMS, which is part of the service portfolio.

   D. The service knowledge management system is part of the service portfolio, which is part of the CMS.

2. Which of the following are aspects of warranty?

   1. Integration
   2. Security
   3. Capacity
   4. Cost-effectiveness
   5. Removal of constraints
   6. Continuity
   7. Availability
   8. Consistency

      A. 1, 3, 5, and 6 only
      B. All of the above
      C. 2, 3, 5, 6, and 7 only
      D. 2, 3, 6, and 7 only

3. What are the four *P*s of service design?

   A. People, principles, products, policies
   B. Processes, policies, principles, projects
   C. Processes, people, products, policies
   D. Processes, people, partners, products

4. Which three aspects must be balanced in a balanced design?

   A. Schedule, cost, complexity
   B. Resources, schedule, functionality
   C. Resources, utility, warranty
   D. Functionality, consistency, resources

5. Which of the following are domains that need to be addressed by the service design?
    1. Infrastructure
    2. Applications
    3. Networks
    4. Hardware
    5. Environmental
    6. Software
    7. Data/information
    8. Support
        A. 1, 4, 5, and 6 only
        B. 3, 4, 5, and 8 only
        C. 1, 2, 5, and 7 only
        D. 2, 3, 5, and 7 only

6. The Service Portfolio is made up of which three parts?
    1. Service catalog
    2. Service knowledge management system
    3. Service assets
    4. Service pipeline
    5. Retired services
    6. Supporting services
        A. 1, 3, and 6
        B. 2, 4, and 5
        C. 1, 4, and 5
        D. 3, 4, and 5

7. What is meant by holistic service design?
    A. The design can be implemented without the users being affected.
    B. All five aspects of design are taken into account.
    C. The design is balanced between functionality, resources, and the required schedule.
    D. The design has been costed to show the total cost of ownership.

8. Which of the following is NOT a possible risk when designing a service?
    A. The design will be inflexible and therefore unable to adapt to meet changing requirements.
    B. Insufficient time spent on warranty aspects may mean the service is not fit for use.
    C. Insufficient time spent on warranty aspects may mean the service is not fit for purpose.
    D. The delivery date may be missed.

9. The design for a service must include which of the following?

    1. Details of the underpinning contracts that will be required

    2. Details of the technology components required

    3. Details of the skills that support staff will need

    4. Details of the governance requirements for the service

        A. 1, 2, and 4 only

        B. 1 and 2 only

        C. 2 and 4 only

        D. All of the above

10. Once the desired service solution has been designed, service design must carry out three activities before the solution passes into the service transition stage. Which of the following is NOT one of these activities?

    A. Evaluate alternative solutions

    B. Develop the business case

    C. Procure the preferred solution

    D. Develop the solution

Chapter 12

Service Design Processes: Design Coordination and Service Catalog Management

---

THE FOLLOWING ITIL INTERMEDIATE EXAM OBJECTIVES ARE DISCUSSED IN THIS CHAPTER:

✓ Design coordination and service catalog management are discussed in terms of

- Purpose
- Objectives
- Scope
- Value
- Policies
- Principles and basic concepts
- Process activities, methods, and techniques
- Triggers, inputs, outputs, and interfaces
- Information management
- Critical success factors and key performance indicators
- Challenges
- Risks

ITIL service design covers the managerial and supervisory aspects of service design processes. It excludes the day-to-day operation of each process and the details of the process activities, methods, and techniques, and its information management. More detailed process operation guidance is covered in the service capability courses. Each process is considered from the management perspective. That means at the end of this chapter, you should understand those aspects that would be required to understand each process and its interfaces, oversee its implementation, and judge its effectiveness and efficiency.

Design Coordination

Service design involves many different aspects beyond designing a new application to provide new functionality (utility). Consideration must be given to how the service will operate, both now and in the future; what level of availability, security, continuity, and capacity will need to be provided; and the best approach to this (warranty). Other processes will interface with the service design processes. To ensure a successful outcome, the design activities must be coordinated.

The Purpose of Design Coordination

The purpose of the *design coordination* process is to carry out the coordination of the many different activities of service design. The many processes and numerous interfaces involved are all potential sources of conflict. By providing a single point of contact, complications and misunderstandings are avoided.

The Objectives of Design Coordination

The objectives of design coordination are quite straightforward. They are to ensure that there is a consistent approach applied to design across all five aspects of service design. Design is a complex lifecycle stage. Coordination of the design activities is a key objective because the activities will spread across projects, teams, and suppliers as well as across the many conflicting demands, which need to be managed. This will include time, money, and resources related to day-to-day operational activities.

To make sure the design processes are effective, there needs to be coordination of the resources and capabilities in use by each process. A common challenge is that there may be overlapping requirements for the same resources, and this is why it is important to have this coordination capability in place. This is a higher-level or strategic objective—for example, in the long term, what skills and how many designers are needed? Design coordination should not be about individual resource management for specific processes.

The design coordination process is responsible for ensuring the delivery of the service design package (SDP).

 Remember, the SDP is the "blueprint" for the new or changed service that will capture the requirements and plans for the rest of the lifecycle.

This means that the process is also responsible for managing the interfaces between the service lifecycle stages, ensuring the quality of the inputs and outputs.

Design coordination should ensure conformance of designs to policy, architecture and regulatory, legal, security, and other governance requirements.

As with all processes, there will be an element of continual service improvement relating to the management of the service design lifecycle stage and its processes.

The Scope of Design Coordination

The scope of the design coordination process includes all design activity, particularly all new or changed service solutions that are being designed for transition into (or out of, in the case of a service retirement) the live environment.

Design coordination should only be applied as necessary. Some design efforts will be part of a project, whereas others will be managed through the change process alone, without a formally defined project. Some design efforts will be extensive and complex while others will be simple and swift.

Each organization will need to define the criteria that will be used to determine the level of rigor or attention to be applied in design coordination for each design.

When we consider the further scope of the design coordination process, it should include assisting and supporting each project or other significant or major change. The process will also be responsible for maintaining policies, guidelines, standards, budgets, models, resources, and capabilities for all service design processes and activities. At a strategic level, design coordination will be responsible for coordinating, prioritizing, and scheduling service design resources to satisfy conflicting demands from all projects and changes. This is a major challenge for most organizations. It will involve planning and forecasting the resources needed for the future demand for service design activities.

Because the process is responsible for ensuring the output from the design lifecycle stage, it will be engaged in reviewing, measuring, and improving the performance of all service design activities and processes. This will also ensure that all requirements are appropriately addressed in service designs, particularly utility and warranty requirements. The final activity for the service design coordination process is ensuring the production of service designs and/or SDPs and their handover to service transition.

It is important to remember that the design coordination process does not include the following:

- Responsibility for any activities or processes outside of the design stage of the service lifecycle.

- Responsibility for designing the detailed service solutions themselves or the production of the individual parts of the SDPs. These are the responsibility of the individual projects or service management processes that will capture the requirements and plans for the rest of the lifecycle.

The Value of Design Coordination to the Business

The main value of the design coordination process to the business is the production of a set of consistent quality solution designs and SDPs that will provide the desired business outcomes.

Design coordination will improve each of these:

- Achieve the intended business value of services through ensuring that design takes place within acceptable risk and cost levels.

- Minimize the rework and unplanned labor costs associated with reworking design issues during later service lifecycle stages.

- Support the achievement of higher customer and user satisfaction and improved confidence in IT and in the services received.

- Ensure that all services conform to a consistent architecture, allowing integration and data exchange between services and systems.

- Provide improved focus on service value as well as business and customer outcomes.

- Develop improved efficiency and effectiveness of all service design activities and processes, supporting higher volumes of successful change delivered in a timely and cost-effective manner.

- Achieve greater agility and better quality in the design of service solutions within projects and major changes.

Design Coordination Policies

It is important to ensure that the service design lifecycle stage has a structured and holistic approach to design activities. It is the responsibility of the design coordination process to provide guidelines and policies to allow for this holistic approach and the coordination to ensure that the practices are followed.

The service provider should define policies for which service design efforts require which type of attention from design coordination.

For example, the policy might specify that the design portion of all projects, as well as for all changes that meet specific criteria (such as major changes), should be coordinated individually, while other changes must simply adhere to predefined design standards for the corresponding change type. These design standards are likely to be embedded in the change model and associated documented procedures for executing changes of that type.

The level of required documentation should also be established and recorded as a policy. For design efforts that are part of a project or are associated with changes that meet specific criteria (such as major changes), a full SDP will be required. For other changes, if they are in scope, the service design may be documented very simply and may even be prebuilt if a change has been made before.

The following design coordination policies should be included:

- Adherence to corporate standards and conventions
- Explicit attention to governance and regulatory compliance in all design activities
- Standards for elements of a comprehensive design for new or changed services
- Criteria for resolving conflicting demands for service design resources
- Standard cost models

Design coordination policies should provide for appropriate variations within acceptable parameters for designs of different types and scopes. The policies and standards established should result in the most appropriate SDPs, while the least possible time and effort should be expended to produce them. It is important that design coordination does not become a "blocker" to successful and efficient design activity.

Principles and Basic Concepts for Design Coordination

Arguably, the single most important guideline to be followed in design coordination is balance. The goal is a comprehensive design that addresses all aspects of utility and warranty as well as the needs of the service throughout its lifecycle.

It can be easy to set up standards or documentation requirements that create excessive bureaucracy without consistently returning better services to the business and/or customer. The goal should be to put just enough definition, measurement, and control of design activities in place to successfully manage the work and improve results, but no more.

Consider the best approach to integrate with project management in your organization. Each organization will have a different approach, and although it may be based on best practice, all organizations are able to "adopt and adapt" to meet their own requirements. It is important for design coordination to be seen as an enabler in the project lifecycle and to provide a positive influence and principles of best practice.

When implementing a formal design coordination process, a service provider should build on its current practices and leverage the steps of the continual service improvement (CSI) approach as a guide. Consider the examples in Table 12.1.

TABLE 12.1 CSI approach for design coordination implementation

CSI approach step	Guidance
What is the vision?	Consider how, in a perfect world, service design should work at your organization. Come to consensus among the key stakeholders regarding what you would like to create and what the critical success factors for service design should be.
Where are we now?	As objectively as possible, assess the current state of service design activities. How are they performed now? By whom are they performed and under what circumstances? What are the challenges and weaknesses in the current approach? What is working well? Where do the greatest pain points exist in the current approach? What capabilities do we have or will we need to have? What risks exist? To the extent possible, collect baseline measurements of the performance of current practices.
Where do we want to be?	Based on the overall vision for service design and the current state of these activities, agree on priorities for improvement. Improvement opportunities will exist in many processes that are active during service design, but the implementation of the design coordination process should provide for reliable, repeatable, and consistent overall practices for service design. Based on the agreed priorities, select the specific design coordination practices to implement, defining them clearly with SMART objectives (specific, measureable, achievable, realistic, timebound).
How do we get there?	Devise a detailed plan for how to move from the current state to the achievement of the agreed improvements, and then execute the plan.
Did we get there?	Use the metrics associated with the SMART objectives to determine if the improvement (or improvements) to service design practices has been successfully implemented. If a gap still remains between the new current state and the desired state, additional work may be necessary.
How do we keep the momentum going?	Use ongoing monitoring of the performance of service design practices to ensure that new or revised practices become institutionalized. Encourage feedback and suggestions for improvement from all other stages in the lifecycle.

Design Coordination Process Activities, Methods, and Techniques

We will now take a look at each of the activities in design coordination. You will find it helpful to refer to Figure 12.1, which shows the process flow.

FIGURE 12.1   Design coordination process flow

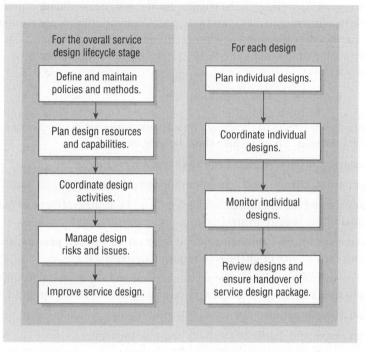

For the overall service design lifecycle stage

Define and maintain policies and methods.

↓

Plan design resources and capabilities.

↓

Coordinate design activities.

↓

Manage design risks and issues.

↓

Improve service design.

For each design

Plan individual designs.

↓

Coordinate individual designs.

↓

Monitor individual designs.

↓

Review designs and ensure handover of service design package.

In the figure, you can see that design coordination activities fall into two categories. It is important to note that the activities are applicable in two different ways.

Activities Relating to Overall Design

The activities relating to the overall service design lifecycle stage include the development, deployment, and continual improvement of appropriate service design practices as well as the coordination of actual design activity across projects and changes. These activities may be performed by design coordination process manager(s).

Activities Relating to Each Individual Design

These activities focus on ensuring that each individual design effort and SDP, whether part of a project or simply associated with a change, conform with defined practices and that they produce a design that will support the required business outcomes. These activities may be performed by a project manager or other individual with direct responsibility for the project or change, with the assistance and guidance of the design coordination process manager(s).

Triggers, Inputs, Outputs, and Interfaces

We will now consider the triggers, inputs, outputs, and interfaces to the lifecycle stages for the process of design coordination.

Triggers

All processes respond to a trigger. The triggers for the design coordination process are changes in the business requirements and services. The main triggers are requests for changes (RFCs) and the creation of new programs and projects. Another major trigger would be the revision of the overall IT strategy, which would require the review of design coordination activities.

Inputs

When we consider the inputs to the design coordination process, a number of sources of information are relevant. These include the following examples:

- Service charters for new or significantly changed services

- Change requests, change records, and authorized changes

- Information about the organization's business and IT strategy, financial plans, and its current and future requirements

- Business impact analysis, providing information on the impact, priority, and risk associated with each service or changes to service requirements

- The service portfolio, including the service catalog and the business requirements for new or changed services in terms of service packages and service options

- Governance requirements

- Corporate, legal, and regulatory policies and requirements

Outputs

The process outputs of design coordination include a comprehensive and consistent set of service designs and service design packages. The output may also require a revision of the enterprise architecture, management systems, processes, and measurement and metrics methods. Design coordination will ensure that the appropriate updates are made to current relevant change records and the service portfolio.

Interfaces

As you would expect, the principal interfaces to the adjacent stages of the lifecycle are using information contained within the IT strategy and service portfolio for service strategy and the handover of the design of service solutions within the SDP for service transition.

The interfaces between design coordination and other individual processes are many because this is a key collaborative process for the lifecycle stage of service design. As a consequence, it is possible to draw a connection between this process and a number of others:

- Service portfolio management

- Change management

- Financial management

- Business relationship management

- Transition planning and support
- Strategy management
- Release and deployment management
- Service validation and testing
- Change evaluation
- Service level management
- Availability, capacity, continuity, and security (the warranty processes)
- Supplier management

Information Management

When we consider the key information generated by the design coordination process, we have to review the material included in the SDP, which contains everything necessary to take the service through all other stages of the service lifecycle. The SDP is likely to consist of multiple documents. These documents should be included in the overall service knowledge management system (SKMS) and described by records about the information held in the configuration management system (CMS).

Critical Success Factors and Key Performance Indicators

This section includes some sample critical success factors (CSFs) for design coordination. Each organization should develop key performance indicators (KPIs) that are appropriate for its level of maturity, its CSFs, and its particular circumstances.

Achievement against KPIs should be monitored and used to identify opportunities for improvement, which should be logged in the CSI register for evaluation and possible implementation.

The examples of critical success factors and key performance indicators are as follows:

- Critical success factor: "The accurate and consistent production of service design packages (SDPs)."
    - KPI: A reduction in the number of subsequent revisions of the content of SDPs.
    - KPI: A reduction (measured as a percentage) in the rework required for new or changed service solutions in subsequent lifecycle stages.
- Critical success factor: "Managing conflicting demands for shared resources."
    - KPI: Increased satisfaction with the service design activities within project and change management staff.
    - KPI: Improved effectiveness and efficiency in the service design processes, activities, and supporting systems.
- Critical success factor: "New and changed services meet customer expectations."
    - KPI: Customer satisfaction score for each new or changed service meets or exceeds a designated rating.

- KPI: Increase (measured as a percentage) in the number of transitioned services that consistently achieve the agreed service level targets.

Additional examples are available in *ITIL Service Design*.

Challenges

The major challenge facing design coordination is maintaining high-quality designs and SDPs consistently across all areas of the business, services, and infrastructure. This requires multiskilled designers and architects. It also requires integration of standards and practices developed by design coordination into the organization's project management methodology wherever appropriate.

It is important to ensure that sufficient time and resources are devoted to design coordination activities and that the roles and responsibilities of the process are assigned appropriately. In most organizations, many of the design coordination activities for an individual design may be assigned to a project manager. Overall lifecycle stage activities may be assigned to the process managers, but key contributions are likely to be made by the service design manager if one exists.

Another significant challenge is developing design practices without introducing unnecessary bureaucracy. It is important that the level of control around design activities be appropriate to the need. Too little control and designs will be inconsistent and fail to meet true required business outcomes. Too much control and creativity may be stifled and inefficiencies introduced. If the processes are too difficult to follow, resistance and noncompliance will result.

Risks

The main risks associated with the provision of the design coordination process are as follows:

- A potential lack of skills and knowledge
- Reluctance of the business to be involved
- Poor direction and strategy
- Lack of information on business priorities and impacts
- Poorly defined requirements and desired outcomes
- Reluctance of project managers to communicate and get involved with design coordination
- Poor communication across IT, business, projects, and stakeholders
- Lack of involvement from all relevant stakeholders, including customers, users, and support and other operations staff
- Insufficient interaction with and input from other lifecycle stages
- Trying to save time and money during the design stage, which will result in poorer designs requiring more changes after the new or changed service goes live

Service Catalog Management

A *service catalog* is defined in the ITIL glossary as follows:

> A database or structured document with information about all live IT services, including those available for deployment. The service catalog is part of the service portfolio and contains information about two types of IT service: customer-facing services that are visible to the business and supporting services required by the service provider to deliver customer-facing services.

Let's examine this definition in more detail:

A database or structured document   The catalog gathers the service information and presents it in a form that is easy for the business to understand.

Information about all live IT services, including those available for deployment   The catalog contains details of services that are available to the business; in this way, it differs from the other components of the service portfolio (the service pipeline and retired services). Gathering and maintaining that information is the job of service catalog management.

Information about two types of IT service   The catalog provides the details that the customers require about the services available, namely deliverables, prices, contact points, ordering, and request processes. There is another view of the service catalog—the view that is visible only to IT, showing the supporting services that must be in place if the customer services are to be delivered.

Let's begin by looking at the purpose of the service catalog management process.

Purpose

The purpose of the service catalog management process is to provide and maintain a single source of consistent information on all operational services. It may also include those that are being prepared to be run operationally. The service catalog management process ensures that the service catalog is widely available to those who are authorized to access it.

Objectives

The objectives of the service catalog management process include managing the information contained within the service catalog. This ensures that the service catalog is accurate and reflects the current details, status, interfaces, and dependencies of all services that are being run, or being prepared to run, in the live environment.

Another objective is that this process should ensure that the service catalog is made available to those approved to access it in a manner that supports their effective and efficient use of its information. This may vary depending on the audience; for example, technical support staff need a different perspective on the services than the users.

Finally, it is important to ensure that the service catalog supports the evolving needs of all other service management processes for service catalog information, including all interface and dependency information.

Scope

The scope of the service catalog management process is to provide and maintain accurate information on all services that are being transitioned or have been transitioned to the live environment. It is up to the organization to define the point at which it is comfortable having services displayed as part of the service catalog. The services presented in the service catalog may be listed individually, or more typically, some or all of the services may be presented in the form of service packages.

The service catalog management process covers the following items:

- Contribution to the definition of services and service packages
- Development and maintenance of service and service package descriptions appropriate for the service catalog
- Production and maintenance of an accurate service catalog
- Interfaces, dependencies, and consistency between the service catalog and the overall service portfolio
- Interfaces and dependencies between all services and supporting services within the service catalog and the configuration management system (CMS)
- Interfaces and dependencies between all services, and supporting components and configuration items (CIs) within the service catalog and the CMS

The service catalog management process does not include the following:

- Detailed attention to capturing, maintaining, and using service asset and configuration data because this is performed through the service asset and configuration management process
- Detailed attention to capturing, maintaining, and fulfilling service requests because this is performed through the request fulfilment process

Value

The service catalog provides a central source of information on the IT services delivered by the service provider organization. It includes a customer-facing view (or views) of the IT services in use, how they are intended to be used, the business processes they enable, and the levels and quality of service the customer can expect for each service.

Through the work of service catalog management, organizations can do the following:

- Ensure a common understanding of IT services and improved relationships between the customer and service provider by utilizing the service catalog as a marketing and communication tool
- Improve service provider focus on customer outcomes by correlating internal service provider activities and service assets to business processes and outcomes
- Improve efficiency and effectiveness of other service management processes by leveraging the information contained in or connected to the service catalog

- Improve knowledge, alignment, and focus on the business value of each service throughout the service provider organization and its activities

Policies

Each organization should develop and maintain a policy with regard to both the overall service portfolio and the constituent service catalog, relating to the services recorded within them and what details are recorded (including what statuses are recorded for each of the services).

The policy should also contain details of responsibilities for each section of the overall service portfolio and the scope of each of the constituent sections. This will include policies regarding when a service is published in the service catalog as well as when it will be removed from the service catalog and appear only in the retired services section of the service portfolio.

Principles and Basic Concepts

There are different types of service delivered by a service provider. In Figure 12.2, you can see the types of service described by the framework.

FIGURE 12.2   Types of service in a service catalog

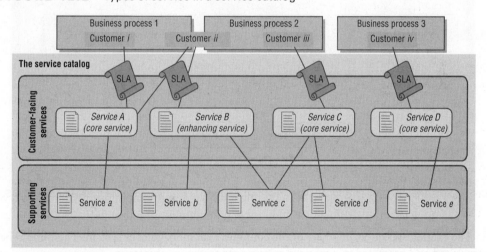

Customer-facing services are IT services that are seen by the customer. They are typically services that support the customer's business units/business processes, directly facilitating some outcome or outcomes desired by the customer.

Supporting services are the IT services that support or "underpin" the customer-facing services. They are typically invisible to the customer but essential to the delivery of customer-facing IT services.

To be most effective, the service catalog views should be tailored to meet the requirements of the audience. The information required from the customer's perspective is different than that required by the technical support teams. In Figure 12.3, you can see the perspective of the service catalog in two views, the business or customer view and the technical view.

FIGURE 12.3 Two-view service catalog

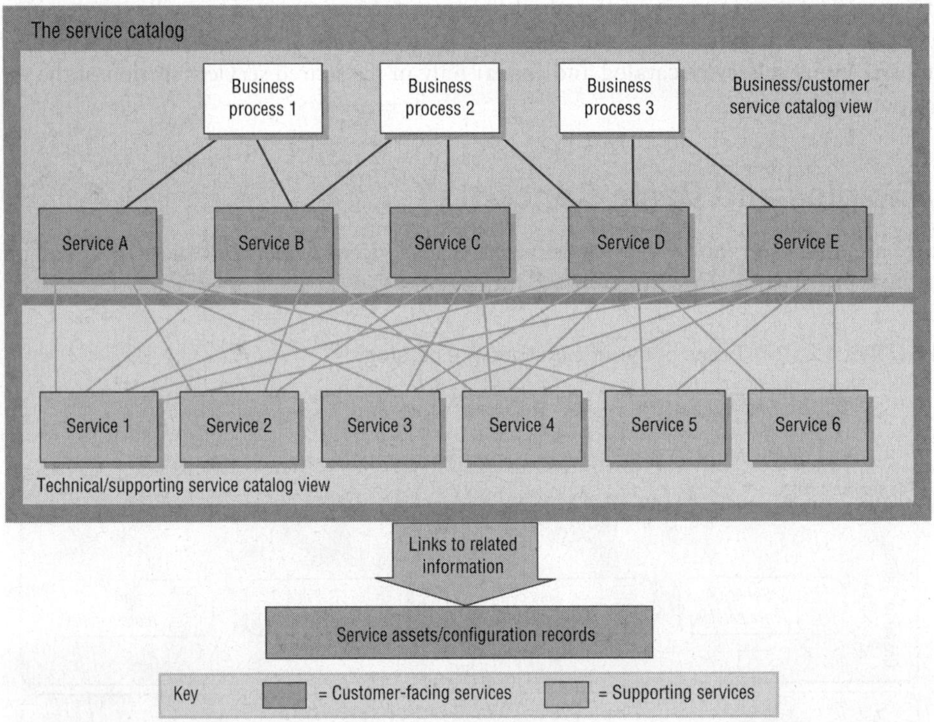

The catalog should form a part of the configuration management system. This should be structured and presented in a manner appropriate to the organization.

In the example in Figure 12.4, the customer-facing catalog has been partitioned such that a business unit has sight of only the services it uses. This might be appropriate for a commercial service provider, where two different customer groups do not need to share visibility across the whole catalog. The two customer groups are generically referred to as either wholesale or retail customers.

FIGURE 12.4   Three-view service catalog

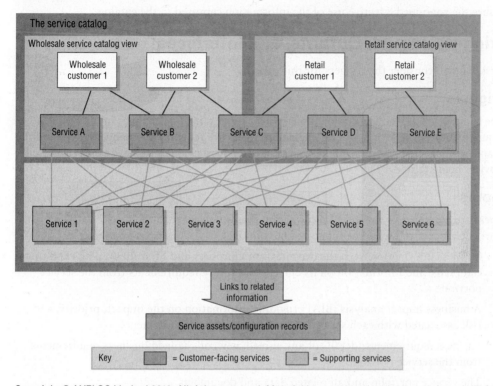

Process Activities, Methods, and Techniques

We will now consider the process activities from a management perspective. There are a number of activities to consider, not least of which is the agreement and documentation of services.

Key activities include ensuring that the services are defined and described appropriately within the documentation.

The service catalog should interface with the service portfolio, so the processes of service catalog management and service portfolio management should be closely linked. This will enable the content of both to remain accurate and up-to-date. The service catalog is a significant information source for the process of IT service continuity and supports business continuity management, ensuring that appropriate services are maintained according to the continuity needs of the business. It also serves to capture the relationships with suppliers and internal service provider teams (such as service asset and configuration management), supporting the understanding of the overall IT estate. The service catalog supports both service level and business relationship management, ensuring alignment to business requirements and processes.

All of these interactions require attention from the service catalog process manager to ensure the continued effective use of the information captured in the catalog.

Triggers, Inputs, Outputs, and Interfaces

First, we will consider the triggers for this process.

Triggers

The triggers for the service catalog management process include changes in the business requirements and services. Among the main triggers are requests for change (RFCs) and the change management process. This includes new services, changes to existing services, and services being retired.

Inputs

There are a number of sources of information that are relevant to the service catalog management process and form the inputs to the catalog:

- Business information from the organization's business and IT strategy, plans and financial plans, and information on its current and future requirements from the service portfolio
- A business impact analysis (BIA) providing information on the impact, priority, and risk associated with each service or changes to service requirements
- Business requirements; details of any agreed, new, or changed business requirements from the service portfolio
- The service portfolio and all related data and documents
- The configuration management system
- Requests for change
- Feedback from all other processes

Outputs

The outputs of the service catalog management process are as follows:

- The documentation and agreement of a definition of the service
- Updates to the service portfolio; should contain the current status of all services and requirements for services
- Updates to requests for change
- The service catalog; should contain the details and the current status of every live service provided by the service provider or every service being transitioned into the live environment, together with the interfaces and dependencies

Interfaces

Every service provider process uses the service catalog, so it could be said that the service catalog management process interfaces with all processes, but the following list includes some of the most prominent interfaces:

Service Portfolio Management   This process determines which services will be chartered and therefore moved forward for eventual inclusion in the service catalog. It also includes critical information regarding each service or potential service, including any agreed service packages and service options.

Business Relationship Management   This process ensures that the relationship between the service and the customer(s) who require it is clearly defined in terms of how the service supports the customer(s) needs.

Service Asset and Configuration Management   This process works collaboratively with service catalog management to ensure that information in the CMS and information in the service catalog are appropriately linked together to provide a consistent, accurate, and comprehensive view of the interfaces and dependencies between services, customers, business processes, service assets, and configuration items (CIs).

Service Level Management   This process negotiates specific levels of service warranty to be delivered, which will be reflected in the service catalog.

Demand Management   In conjunction with service portfolio management, this process determines how services will be composed into service packages for provisioning and assists service catalog management in ensuring that these packages are appropriately represented in the service catalog.

Information Management

The key information for this process is that which is contained within the service catalog itself. Because the service catalog is part of the service portfolio, the main input for this information comes from the business via either the business relationship management or service level management process. It is important to verify the information for accuracy before it is recorded within the service catalog. The information and the service catalog itself need to be maintained using the change management process.

There are many different approaches to managing service catalog information:

- Intranet solutions that are built by the service provider organization and leverage technology already in place
- Commercially available solutions designed for service catalog management
- Solutions that are part of a more comprehensive service management suite

The service catalog data may be held in a single repository or multiple repositories. Some service providers may maintain the data that supports different views of the service catalog in different locations or toolsets.

For example, detailed data for supporting services may be stored in the CMS and presented via the same interface used to access other service asset and configuration data, while data on customer-facing services may be held for presentation to the customers in a browser-based application via the corporate intranet.

Constructing different views of the service catalog should be based on the perspective and requirements of the intended audience. The service provider should consider which services (rows of data) and which data elements or fields (columns of data) should be included in each view. For example, details of relationships of supporting services may be important to include in a view intended for staff members of the service provider, whereas these details are typically of no interest to customers and are likely to be excluded from a customer-facing view.

Integration with the management of the service portfolio is critical here, as is the ability to access other closely related functionality. Customers should be able to view their service level agreement monitoring reports or access a self-help portal for service requests. Some commercially available service catalog tools are maturing to offer management of the full-service portfolio from proposal to retirement.

Each organization will have to understand the solution that will best serve its current and future needs. It is important, however, not to confuse the toolset used to present the service catalog with the catalog itself. An organization with a paper-based catalog and an organization with a robust technical solution both still have a service catalog.

Critical Success Factors and Key Performance Indicators

The following list includes some sample critical success factors and key performance indicators for service catalog management.

- Critical success factor: "An accurate service catalog"
    - KPI: An increase in the number of services recorded and managed within the service catalog as a percentage of those being delivered and transitioned in the live environment
    - KPI: Reduction (measured as a percentage) in the number of variances detected between the information contained within the service catalog and the "real-world" situation
- Critical success factor:: "Business users' awareness of the services being provided"
    - KPI: Increase (measured as a percentage) in completeness of the customer-facing views of the service catalog against operational services
    - KPI: Increase (measured as a percentage) in business user survey responses showing knowledge of services listed in the service catalog
    - KPI: Increase in measured business user access to intranet-based service catalog
- Critical success factor:: "IT staff awareness of the technology supporting the services"
    - KPI: Increase (measured as a percentage) in completeness of supporting services against the IT components that make up those services
    - KPI: Increase in service desk and other IT staff having access to information to support all live services, measured by the percentage of incidents with the appropriate service related information

Challenges

The major challenge facing the process of service catalog management is maintaining an accurate service catalog. This should be managed as part of a service portfolio, incorporating all catalog views as part of an overall CMS and SKMS.

For this to be achieved, the culture of the organization needs to accept that the catalog and portfolio are essential sources of information. It is then important to ensure that everyone within the IT organization understands that all are responsible for supporting the use and helping maintain its accuracy.

Risks

The risks associated with the provision of an accurate service catalog are as follows:

- Inaccuracy of the data in the catalog and it not being under rigorous change control.
- Poor acceptance of the service catalog and its usage in all operational processes. The more active the catalog is, the more likely it is to be accurate in its content.
- Inaccuracy of service information received from the business, IT, and the service portfolio.
- Insufficient tools and resources required to maintain the information.
- Poor access to accurate change management information and processes.
- Poor access to and support of an appropriate and up-to-date CMS and SKMS for integration with the service catalog.
- Circumvention of the use of the service portfolio and service catalog.
- Information that is either too detailed to maintain accurately or at too high a level to be of any value. It should be consistent with the level of detail within the CMS and the SKMS.

Summary

This chapter explored the first two processes in the service design stage, design coordination and service catalog management. It covered the purpose and objectives for each process and the scope. The scope includes all aspects of the design lifecycle stage, which require coordination.

We looked at the value of the processes, particularly for integration with complex projects. Then we reviewed the policies for each process and the activities, methods, and techniques.

Last, we reviewed triggers, inputs, outputs, and interfaces for each process, and the information management associated with the process. We also considered the critical success factors and key performance indicators, challenges, and risks.

We examined how each of these processes supports the other and the importance of these processes to the business and the IT service provider.

Exam Essentials

Understand the purpose and objectives of design coordination. It is important for you to be able to explain the purpose and objectives of the design coordination process. The process is there to ensure that the five aspects of design are carried out successfully and that a service design package is created and published.

Understand how continual service improvement should be used to support design coordination activities. This focus on CSI is important to make sure design coordination remains relevant.

Explain the different approaches of design coordination. Explain the coordination of the overall design effort within the process. Explain the approach to the coordination of the individual processes within the service design lifecycle stage.

Understand the critical success factors and key performance indicators for the process. Measurement of the process is an important part of understanding its success, so it is important to understand the reasoning for the KPIs and CSFs for this process.

Understand the purpose and objectives of service catalog management. Be able to explain how the service catalog supports the overall lifecycle and the requirement to maintain the data accuracy.

Understand the exclusions from the service catalog. Service asset and configuration management is concerned with the management of CIs. Fulfilment of service requests are not managed through the service catalog.

Explain the different views of the service catalog. There are a number of views that can be used to display information in the service catalog. You need to be able to differentiate between technical and business views and explain the purpose for each. It is also important to understand when to provide multiple views of the service catalog to the organization.

Understand the relationship between the service catalog and the service portfolio. Be able to explain the relationship between the service portfolio and the service catalog, and be able to understand when a service moves from the service portfolio pipeline into the service catalog.

Explain the role of information management in service catalog management. Information is key to the service catalog management process. The output from the process is accurate information and its maintenance.

Review Questions

You can find the answers to the review questions in the appendix.

1. What is the purpose of the design coordination process?

   A. Manage the service level management process

   B. Manage the service transition lifecycle stage

   C. Ensure the production of the service design package

   D. Ensure that the strategy is managed throughout the lifecycle

2. Which description (X, Y, or Z) best matches each catalog type (1, 2, and 3)?

   1. Business/customer catalog

   2. Technical catalog

   3. Multiview catalog

   4. View of all services that are used

   5. View of the supporting services used to deliver the customer-facing services

   6. View of the customer-facing services that are directly delivered to the customer

      A. X=3, Y=2, Z=1

      B. X=1, Y=2, Z=3

      C. X=2, Y=1, Z=3

      D. X=2, Y=3, Z=1

3. Which of the following is the correct definition of the service catalog?

   A. A document that describes the IT service, service level targets, and responsibilities of the IT service provider and the customer

   B. The complete set of services managed by a service provider, used to manage the entire lifecycle of all services

   C. A database or document with information about all live IT services

   D. Justification for a particular item of expenditure, including information about costs, benefits, options, and risks

4. Which of the following are included in a service catalog?

   1. Customer-facing services

   2. Strategic services

   3. Supporting services

   4. Retired services

    A. 1 and 2

    B. 1, 2, 3, and 4

    C. 1 and 3

    D. 2 and 3

5. Which of the following statements is true?

    1. The service catalog forms part of the service portfolio.

    2. The service portfolio forms part of the service catalog.

    3. There is no relationship between the service catalog and the service portfolio.

    4. Customer-facing services appear in the service catalog, and supporting services appear in the service portfolio.

        A. 1 and 3

        B. 1 only

        C. 2 and 4

        D. 4 only

6. Which of the following options is NOT a responsibility of design coordination?

    A. To ensure that the goals and objectives of the design stage are met

    B. To design the solution

    C. To provide a single coordination point

    D. To ensure that the design meets the requirements

7. Which of the following are outputs from design coordination?

    1. The service design package

    2. The CMS

    3. The governance requirements

    4. Suggestions for improvements to be made to the design stage

        A. 2, 3, and 4

        B. 1 and 2 only

        C. All of the above

        D. 1 and 4 only

8. Which of the following statements about the service catalog is TRUE?

    A. The service catalog contains information on customer-facing services only.

    B. The service catalog contains information on supporting services only.

    C. The service catalog shows which IT service supports each business process.

    D. The service catalog shows details of services under development.

9. True or False? Service catalog management can be connected to the majority of the lifecycle processes.

   A. True

   B. False

10. True or False? Design coordination is responsible for the management of the service operation processes that have design responsibilities.

   A. True

   B. False

Chapter

13

Service Design Processes: Service Level Management and Availability Management

THE FOLLOWING ITIL INTERMEDIATE EXAM OBJECTIVES ARE DISCUSSED IN THIS CHAPTER:

✓ Service level management and availability management are discussed in terms of

- Purpose
- Objectives
- Scope
- Value
- Policies
- Principles and basic concepts
- Process activities, methods, and techniques
- Triggers, inputs, outputs, and interfaces
- Information management
- Critical success factors and key performance indicators
- Challenges
- Risks

The ITIL service design core volume covers the managerial and supervisory aspects of service design processes. It excludes the day-to-day operation of each process and the details of the process activities, methods, and techniques and its information management. More detailed process operation guidance is covered in the service capability courses. Each process is considered from the management perspective. That means at the end of this chapter, you should understand those aspects that would be required to understand each process and its interfaces, oversee its implementation, and judge its effectiveness and efficiency.

Service Level Management

The service level management (SLM) process requires a constant cycle of negotiating, agreeing, monitoring, reporting on, and reviewing IT service targets and achievements. Improvements and corrections to service levels will be managed as part of continual service improvement and through instigation of actions to correct or improve the level of service delivered.

Purpose of Service Level Management

We will begin by looking at the purpose of the service level management process according the ITIL framework. ITIL states that the purpose of service level management is to ensure that all current and planned IT services are delivered to agreed achievable targets. The key words here are *agreed* and *targets*. Service level management is about discussing, negotiating, and agreeing with the customer about what IT services should be provided and ensuring that objective measures are used to ascertain whether that service has been provided to the agreed level.

Service level management is therefore concerned with defining the services, documenting them in an agreement, and then ensuring that the targets are measured and met, taking action where necessary to improve the level of service delivered. These improvements will often be carried out as part of continual service improvement.

Note also that the definition of service level management talks about current and planned IT services. Service level management's purpose is not only to ensure that all IT services currently being delivered have a *service level agreement (SLA)* in place, but also to ensure that discussion and negotiation takes place regarding the requirements for planned services so that an SLA is agreed on and in place when the service becomes operational.

It is for this latter reason that service level management is one of the service design processes; services must be designed to deliver the levels of availability, capacity, and so on that the customer requires and that service level management documents in the SLA. It is a frequent problem that the SLA is not considered until just before (or even after) the go-live date, when it is realized that the customer's service level requirements are not met by the design. Service level management is concerned primarily with the warranty aspects of the service. The response time, capacity, availability, and so on of the new service will be the subject of the SLA, and it is essential that the service is therefore designed to meet both utility and warranty requirements.

Objectives of Service Level Management

The objectives of service level management are not restricted to "define, document, agree, monitor, measure, report, and review" (how well the IT service is delivered) and undertaking improvement actions when necessary. It also includes working with business relationship management to build a good working relationship with the business customers. The regular meetings held with the business as part of service level management form the basis of a strong communications channel that strengthens the relationship between the customer and IT.

 The distinction between customer and user is important in service level management. Customers are usually senior people within the organization who specify the level of service required, take part in SLM negotiations, and sign the agreed SLA. Users are provided with the service but have no direct input into the service level to be provided.

It is an essential feature of service level management that the customer and IT agree on what constitutes an acceptable level of service. Therefore, one of the objectives of SLM is to develop appropriate targets for each IT service. These targets must be specific and measurable so that there is no debate whether they were achieved. The temptation to use expressions such as "as soon as possible" and "reasonable endeavors" should be resisted because the customer and IT may disagree on what constitutes "as soon as possible" or what is "reasonable." By using such expressions in an SLA, it may be impossible for the IT service provider to fail, but this leads to cynicism from the customer and damages the relationship that the SLM aims to build. Where the IT service provider is an external company, the legal department will inevitably seek to reduce the possibility of the provider being sued for breach of contract, and these phrases may therefore be included; for an internal service provider, there is no such excuse. Using objective success criteria is essential if SLM is to achieve another of its objectives, that of ensuring that both the customer and IT have "clear and unambiguous expectations" regarding the level of service.

A further SLM objective is to ascertain the level of customer satisfaction with the service being provided and to take steps to increase it. There are challenges in this objective, because obtaining an accurate assessment of customer satisfaction is not straightforward. Customer satisfaction surveys may be completed only by a self-selecting minority. Those who are unhappy are more likely to complete such a survey than those who are content. Despite this tendency, the service level manager must still attempt to monitor customer satisfaction as accurately as possible, using whatever methods are appropriate; in addition to surveys, focus groups, and individual interviews, other methods can be employed.

The final objective that ITIL lists for service level management is that of improving the level of service even when the targets are being met. Such improvements must be cost-effective, so an analysis of the return expected for any financial or resource investment must be carried out. SLM actively seeks out opportunities for such cost-effective improvements. Achieving this objective forms part of the continual service improvement that is an essential element in all ITIL processes.

Scope of Service Level Management

The scope of service level management includes the performance of existing services being provided and the definition of required service levels for planned services. It forms a regular communication channel between the business and the IT service provider on all issues concerning the quality of service. SLM therefore has an important role to play in managing customers' expectations to ensure that the level of service they expect and the level of service they perceive they are receiving match. As stated earlier, SLM is concerned with ensuring that the warranty aspects of a service are provided to the expected level. The level of service expected for planned services is detailed in the service level requirements (*SLRs*), and the agreed service levels (following negotiation) are documented in the SLA. SLAs should be written to cover *all* operational services. Through this involvement in the design phase, SLM ensures that the planned services will deliver the warranty levels required by the business.

 SLM does *not* include agreeing on the utility aspects. The negotiation and agreement of requirements for service functionality (utility) are not part of the process, except to the degree that the functionality influences a service level requirement or target. Service level agreements typically describe key elements of the service's utility as part of the service description, but service level management activity does not include agreeing on what the utility will be.

Service Level Management Value to the Business

Each IT service is composed of a number of elements provided by internal support teams or external third-party suppliers. An essential element of successful service level management is the negotiation and agreement with those who provide each element of the level of service they provide. A failure by these providers will translate to a failure to meet the SLA. These agreements are called *operational level agreements (OLAs)* in the case of internal teams and *underpinning contracts* in the case of external suppliers.

Finally, SLM includes measuring and reporting on how all service achievements compare to the agreed targets. The frequency, measurement method, and depth of reporting required is agreed as part of the SLA negotiations.

It is important to understand the relationship between service level management and business relationship management. SLM deals with issues around the quality of service being provided; business relationship management's role is more strategic. The business relationship manager (BRM) works closely with the business, understanding its current and future IT requirements. It is then the responsibility of the BRM to ensure that the service provider understands these needs and is able to meet them. SLM is concerned more about how to meet the targets by ensuring that agreements are in place with internal and external suppliers to provide elements of the service to the required standard.

Service level management cooperates with and complements business relationship management. Similarly, the improvement actions identified by SLM in a *service improvement plan (SIP)* are implemented in conjunction with continual service improvement; they are documented in the CSI register, where they are prioritized and reviewed.

Providers and Suppliers

It is important to understand the difference between providers and suppliers. Suppliers are external organizations that supply an element of the overall service. Customers may have little or no knowledge of the suppliers and the contracts that are held with them. The IT service provider will usually aim to provide a seamless service to the customer.

Providers fall into three categories; they can be embedded in a business unit (Type I), be shared across business units (Type II), or be external to the organization (Type III). Type III service providers will have an SLA with their external customers that will be a legal contract because they are separate organizations.

The critical difference between suppliers and service providers is that suppliers provide only an element of the service and are not visible to the customer, whereas providers (including Type III providers) provide the whole service. A Type III provider will typically use a number of suppliers to provide elements of the service it is providing, but the service level agreement is between the provider and the customer; the provider is responsible for ensuring that the supplier fulfils the contract that the provider has with them.

Service Level Management Policies

The service provider should establish clear policies for the conduct of the service level management process. Policies typically define such things as the minimum required content of service level agreements and operational level agreements; when and how agreements are to be reviewed, renewed, revised, and/or renegotiated and how frequently; and what methods will be used to provide service level reporting.

Priority should be given to the policies that are between SLM and the supplier's management because the performance of suppliers can be the critical element in the achievement of end-to-end service level commitments.

Service level management terminology is expressed from the point of view of the IT service provider, particularly as it relates to underpinning contracts and agreements. You should be familiar with this from your Foundation studies.

The term *underpinning contract* is used here to refer to any kind of agreement or contract between an IT service provider and a supplier that supports the delivery of service to the customer. The term *service level agreement (SLA)* is used to refer to an agreement between only the IT service provider and the customer(s).

Underpinning agreements is a more generic term used to refer to all OLAs and contracts or other agreements that underpin the customer SLAs.

Service Level Management Process Activities, Methods, and Techniques

We are not going to explore the process in detail, but you should make sure you are familiar with all the aspects of the process and the management requirements for each.

Figure 13.1 shows the full scope of the activities in the service level management process.

FIGURE 13.1 The service level management process

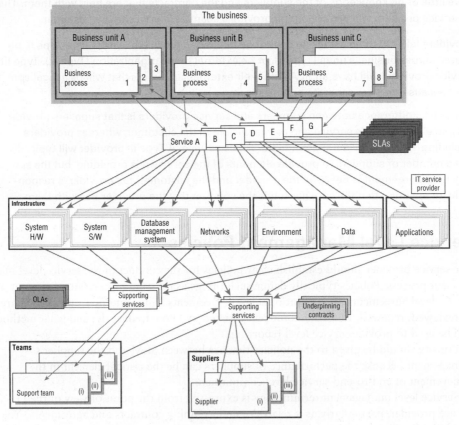

The key activities within the SLM process should include the following:

- Determining, negotiating, documenting, and agreeing on requirements for new or changed services in SLRs, and managing and reviewing them through the service lifecycle to create SLAs for operational services

- Monitoring and measuring service performance achievements of all operational services against targets within SLAs

- Producing service reports

- Conducting service reviews and identifying improvement opportunities

- Collating, measuring, and improving customer satisfaction

- Reviewing and revising SLAs, service scope, and OLAs and contracts

- Providing appropriate management information

- Logging and managing complaints and compliments

These other activities within the SLM process support the successful execution of the key activities:

- Designing SLA frameworks

- Developing, maintaining, and operating SLM procedures, including procedures for logging, actioning, and resolving all complaints and for logging and distributing compliments

- Making available and maintaining up-to-date SLM document templates and standards, including assisting with the service catalog

Service Level Management Triggers, Inputs, and Outputs

Let's consider the triggers, inputs, and outputs for the service level management process. SLM is a process that has many active connections throughout the organization and its processes. It is important that the triggers, inputs, outputs, and interfaces be clearly defined to avoid duplicated effort or gaps in workflow.

Triggers

The following triggers are among the many that instigate SLM activity:

- Changes in the service portfolio, such as new or changed business requirements or new or changed services

- New or changed agreements, service level requirements, service level agreements, operational level agreements, and contracts

- Service review meetings and actions

- Service breaches or threatened breaches

- Compliments and complaints

- Periodic activities such as reviewing, reporting, and customer satisfaction surveys
- Changes in strategy or policy

Inputs

A number of sources of information are relevant to the service level management process:

- Business information from the organization's business strategy, plans and financial plans, and information on its current and future requirements
- Business impact analysis providing information on the impact, priority, risk, and number of users associated with each service
- Details of agreed, new, or changed business requirements
- The strategies, policies, and constraints from service strategy
- The service portfolio and service catalog
- Change information (including RFCs) from the change management process, with a change schedule and an assessment of all changes for their impact on all services
- Configuration management system containing information on the relationships between the business services, the supporting services, and the technology
- Customer and user feedback, including complaints and compliments
- Improvement opportunities from the CSI register

Other inputs are advice, information, and input from any of the other processes (e.g., incident management, capacity management, and availability management) together with the existing SLAs, SLRs, OLAs, and past service reports on the quality of service delivered.

Outputs

The outputs of SLM are as follows:

- Service reports that provide details of the service levels achieved in relation to the targets contained within SLAs
- Service improvement opportunities for inclusion in the CSI register and for later review and prioritization in conjunction with the CSI manager
- Service improvement plans that provide an overall program or plan of prioritized improvement actions, encompassing appropriate services and processes together with associated impacts and risks
- The service quality plan, which should document and plan the overall improvement of service quality
- Document templates for service level requirements capture, service level agreements, operational level agreements, and contracts
- Reports on OLAs and underpinning contracts
- Service review meeting minutes and actions

- SLA review and service scope review meeting minutes
- Updated change information, including updates to RFCs
- Revised requirements for underpinning contracts

Service Level Management Interfaces

SLM interfaces with several other processes to ensure that agreed service levels are being met:

- Problem management will address the causes of any failures that impact targets and work to prevent their recurrence, thus improving the delivery of the service against targets.

- Availability management works to remove any single points of failure that could lead to downtime and addresses the causes of such downtime in order to deliver the agreed level of availability to the customer.

- Capacity management plans ahead to ensure that sufficient capacity is provided and therefore prevent service failures that would otherwise have occurred.

- Incident management focuses on resolving incidents and restoring service as quickly as possible. Performance against targets for incident resolution by identifying agreed priorities is usually a major area within an SLA.

- IT service continuity will plan to ensure that service continues to be provided despite major upheavals; where a break in service cannot be prevented, it will work to ensure that the service is restored in line with the business requirements.

- Information security ensures that the customer's data is protected and will work with the service level manager to educate the customers and users regarding their own responsibilities in this area.

- Supplier management ensures that UCs are in place and are being fulfilled.

- Service catalog management provides information about services to support the SLA.

- Financial management provides cost information.

- Design coordination ensures that the design meets the SLR.

- SLM works with CSI in designing and implementing the SIP.

- SLM works with business relationship management. Business relationship management is more concerned with strategy, identifying customer needs, and ensuring that the objectives are met.

Information Management and Service Level Management

Service level management is a process that provides key information on operational services, their expected targets, and their service achievements and breaches. This means it is an important part of information management across the lifecycle. It assists service catalog management with the management of the service catalog and also provides the information and trends on customer satisfaction, including complaints and compliments.

The service provider organization is reliant on the information that service level management provides on the quality of IT service provided to the customer. This includes information on the customer's expectation and perception of that quality of service. This information should be widely available to all areas of the service provider organization.

Measures, Metrics, and Critical Success Factors for Service Level Management

Key performance indicators and metrics can be used to judge the efficiency and effectiveness of service level management activities and the progress of the service improvement plan.

These metrics should be developed from the service, customer, and business perspective and should be both subjective (qualitative) and objective (quantitative), such as the following examples.

Objective measures include the following:

- The number or percentage of service targets being met

- The number and severity of service breaches

- The number of services with up-to-date SLAs

- The number of services with timely reports and active service reviews

A subjective measure would be an improvement in customer satisfaction.

The following list includes some sample critical success factors and key performance indicators for SLM:

- Critical success factor: "Managing the overall quality of IT services required both in the number and level of services provided and managed."

    - KPI: Reduction (measured as a percentage) in SLA targets threatened

    - KPI: Increase (measured as a percentage) in customer perception and satisfaction of SLA achievements via service reviews and customer satisfaction survey responses

- Critical success factor: "Deliver the service as previously agreed at affordable costs."

    - KPI: Total number and percentage increase in fully documented SLAs in place

    - KPI: Reduction (measured as a percentage) in the costs associated with service provision

    - KPI: Frequency of service review meetings

- Critical success factor: "Manage the interface with the business and users."

    - KPI: Increased percentage of services covered by SLAs

    - KPI: Documented and agreed SLM processes and procedures in place

    - KPI: Documentary evidence that issues raised at service and SLA reviews are being followed up and resolved

    - KPI: Reduction in the number and severity of SLA breaches

- KPI: Effective review and follow-up of all SLA, OLA, and underpinning contract breaches

Challenges for Service Level Management

There are numerous challenges faced when introducing service level management because it requires alignment and engagement across the whole organization.

One challenge faced by service level management is that of identifying suitable customer representatives with whom to negotiate. Who "owns" the service on the customer side?

Another challenge may arise if there has been no previous experience of service level management. In these cases, it is advisable to start with a draft service level agreement.

One difficulty sometimes encountered is that staff at different levels within the customer community may have different objectives and perceptions.

Risks for Service Level Management

Some of the risks associated with service level management are as follows:

- A lack of accurate input, involvement, and commitment from the business and customers
- Lack of appropriate tools and required resources
- The process becoming a bureaucratic, administrative process
- Access to and support of appropriate and up-to-date CMS and SKMS
- Bypassing the use of the service level management processes
- High customer expectations and low perception

Availability Management

The availability of a service is critical to its value. No matter how clever it is or what functionality it offers (its utility), the service is of no value to the customer unless it delivers the warranty expected. Poor availability is a primary cause of customer dissatisfaction. Availability is one of the four warranty aspects that must be delivered if the service is to be fit for use. Targets for availability are often included in service level agreements, so the IT service provider must understand the factors to be considered when seeking to meet or exceed the availability target. The following sections cover how availability is measured; the purpose, objectives, and scope of availability management; and a number of key concepts.

Defining Availability

ITIL defines *availability* as the ability of an IT service or other configuration item to perform its agreed function when required. Any unplanned interruption to a service during its agreed service hours (also called the agreed *service time*, specified in the service level agreement) is defined as *downtime*. The availability measure is calculated by subtracting the downtime from the agreed service time and converting it to a percentage of the agreed service time.

It is important to note the inclusion of *when required* in the definition and the word *agreed* in the calculation. The service may be available when the customer does not require it; including time when the customer does not need the service in the calculation gives a false impression of the availability from the customer perspective. If customer perception does not match the reporting provided, the customer will become cynical and distrust the reports.

Calculating Availability: Two Examples

Example A: A service is available 24 hours a day, 7 days a week. One hour of downtime per week is calculated as follows:

   168 hours − 1 hour downtime = 167/168 * 100 = 99.4% availability

Example B: If the service is available but used only 9 a.m. to 5 p.m., Monday through Friday (and these 40 hours are the service hours agreed in the SLA), then the same 1 hour of downtime results in a different figure:

   40 hours − 1 hour downtime = 39/40 × 100 = 97.5% availability

$$Availability\ (\%) = \frac{Agreed\ service\ time\ (AST) - downtime}{AST} \times 100$$

If the downtime occurred overnight, it would be included in the calculations in Example A but not those in Example B because there was no agreed service after 5 p.m.

It is important, therefore, to agree on exactly what the agreed service hours are; they should be documented in the SLA. The basis for the calculation should be clear to the customer.

Keep in mind that the customer experiences the end-to-end service; the availability delivered depends on all links in the chain being operational when required. The customer will complain that a service is unavailable whether the fault is with the application, the network, or the hardware. The availability management process is therefore concerned with reducing service affecting downtime wherever it occurs. Again, it should be clearly stated in the availability reports whether the calculations are based on the end-to-end service or just the application availability. It is therefore essential to understand the difference between service availability and component availability.

Purpose of Availability Management

The purpose of the availability management process is to take the necessary steps to deliver the availability requirements defined in the SLA. The process should consider both the current requirements and the future needs of the business. All actions taken to improve availability have an accompanying cost, so all improvements made must be assessed for cost-effectiveness.

Availability management considers all aspects of IT service provision to identify possible improvements to availability. Some improvements will be dependent on implementing new technology; others will result from more effective use of staff resources or streamlined processes. Availability management analyzes reasons for downtime and assesses the return on investment for improvements to ensure that the most cost-effective measures are taken. The process ensures that the delivery of the agreed availability is prioritized across all phases of the lifecycle.

Objectives of Availability Management

The objectives of availability management are as follows:

- Producing and maintaining a plan that details how the current and future availability requirements are to be met. This plan should consider requirements 12 to 24 months in advance to ensure that any necessary expenditure is agreed on in the annual budget negotiations and any new equipment is bought and installed before the availability is affected. The plan should be revised regularly to take into account any changes in the business.

- Providing advice throughout the service lifecycle on all availability-related issues to both the business and IT, ensuring that the impact of any decisions on availability is considered.

- Managing the delivery of services to meet the agreed targets. Where downtime has occurred, availability management will assist in resolving the incident by utilizing incident management and, when appropriate, resolving the underlying problem by utilizing the problem management process.

- Assessing all requests for change to ensure that any potential risk to availability has been considered. Any updates to the availability plan required as a result of changes will also be considered and implemented.

- Considering all possible proactive steps that could be taken to improve availability across the end-to-end service, assessing the risk and potential benefits of these improvements, and implementing them where justified.

- Implementing monitoring of availability to ensure that targets are being achieved.

- Optimizing all areas of IT service provision to deliver the required availability consistently to enable the business to use the services provided to achieve its objectives.

Scope of Availability Management

As discussed, the availability management process encompasses all phases of the service lifecycle. It is included in the design phase because the most effective way to deliver availability is to ensure that availability considerations are designed in from the start. Once the service is operational, opportunities are continually sought to remove risks to availability and make the service more robust. The activities for these opportunities are part of pro-active availability management. Throughout the live delivery of the service, availability management analyzes any downtime and implements measures to reduce the frequency and length of future occurrences. These are the reactive activities of availability management. Changes to live services are assessed to understand risks to the service, and measurements are put in place to ensure that downtime is measured accurately. This continues throughout the operational phase until the service is retired.

The scope of availability management includes all operational services and technology. Where SLAs are in place, there will be clear, agreed targets. There may be other services, however, where no formal SLA exists but where downtime has a significant business impact. Availability management should not exclude these services from consideration; it should strive to achieve high availability in line with the potential impact of downtime on the business. Service level management should work to negotiate SLAs for all such services in the future because without them, it is the IT service provider who is assessing the level of availability required, but this should be a business decision. Availability management should be applied to all new IT services and for existing services where SLRs or SLAs have been established. Supporting services must be included because the failures of these services impact the customer-facing services. Availability management may also work with supplier management to ensure that the level of service provided by partners does not threaten the overall service availability.

Every aspect of service provision comes within the scope of availability management; poor processes, untrained staff, and ineffective tools can all contribute to causing or unnecessarily prolonging downtime.

The availability management process ensures that the availability of systems and services matches the evolving agreed needs of the business.

The role of IT within businesses is now critical. The availability and reliability of IT services can directly influence customer satisfaction and the reputation of the business. Availability management is essential in ensuring that IT delivers the levels of service availability required by the business to satisfy its business objectives and deliver the quality of service demanded by its customers.

Customer satisfaction is an important factor for all businesses and may provide a competitive edge for the organization. Dissatisfaction with the availability and reliability of IT service can be a key factor in customers taking their business to a competitor.

Availability can also improve the ability of the business to follow an environmentally responsible strategy by using green technologies and techniques in availability management.

Availability Management Policies

The policies of availability management should state that the process is included as part of all lifecycle stages, from service strategy through to continual service improvement. The appropriate availability and resilience should be designed into services and components from the initial design stages. This will ensure not only that the availability of any new or changed service meets the expected targets, but also that all existing services and components continue to meet all of their targets.

Availability policies should be established by the service provider to ensure that availability is considered throughout the lifecycle. Policies should also be established regarding the criteria to be used to define availability and unavailability of a service or component and how each will be measured.

Availability management is completed at two interconnected levels:

- Service availability involves all aspects of service availability and unavailability. This includes the impact of component availability and the potential impact of component unavailability on service.

- Component availability involves all aspects of component availability and unavailability.

Availability Management Principles and Basic Concepts

Availability management must align its activities and priorities to the requirements of the business. This requires a firm understanding of the business processes and how they are underpinned by the IT service. Information regarding the future business plans and priorities and therefore the future requirements of the business with regard to availability is essential input to the availability plan. Only with this understanding of the business requirement can the service provider be sure that its efforts to improve availability are correctly targeted.

The response of the IT service provider to failure can improve the customer's perception of the service, despite the break in service. The service provider's actions can show an understanding of the impact of the downtime on the business processes, and an eagerness to overcome the issue and prevent recurrences can reassure the business that IT understands its needs.

Additionally, the process requires a strong technical understanding of the individual components that make up each service, their capabilities, and their current performance. Through this combination of business understanding and technical knowledge, the optimal design can be delivered to produce the required level of availability to meet current and future needs.

When designing a new service and discussing its availability requirements, the service provider and the business must focus on the criticality of the service to the business being able to achieve its aims. Expenditure to provide high availability across every aspect of a service is unlikely to be justified. The business process that the IT service supports may be a *vital business function (VBF)*, and identifying which services or parts of services are the most critical is therefore a business decision. For example, the ability for an Internet-based bookshop to be able to process credit card payments would be a vital business function. The ability to display a "customers who bought this book also bought these other books" feature is not vital. It may encourage some increased sales, but the purchaser is able to complete their purchase without it. Once these VBFs are understood, the design of the service to ensure the required availability can commence. Understanding the VBFs informs decisions regarding where expenditure to protect availability is justified.

Determining what the appropriate availability target of a service should be is a business decision, not an IT decision. However, availability comes at a price, and the service provider must ensure that the customer understands the cost implications of too high a target. Customers may otherwise demand a very high availability target (99.99% or greater) and then find the service unaffordable.

Where the cost of very high availability is justified, the design of the service will include highly reliable components, resilience, and minimal or no planned downtime.

Having considered the importance of availability to the business, in the following sections we examine some of the key availability management activities and concepts that the IT service provider may employ to cut downtime and thus deliver the required availability to the business, enabling it to achieve its business objectives.

Availability Concepts

Availability management comprises both reactive and proactive activities, as shown in Figure 13.2. The reactive activities include regular monitoring of service provisions involving extensive data gathering and reporting of the performance of individual components and processes and the availability delivered by them. Event management is often used to monitor components because this speeds up the identification of any issues through the setting of alert thresholds. It may even be possible to restart the failing service automatically, possibly before the break has been noticed by the customers. Instances of downtime are investigated, and remedial actions are taken to prevent a recurrence. The proactive activities include identifying and managing risks to the availability of the service and implementing measures to protect against such an occurrence. Where protective measures have been put in place to provide resilience in the event of component failure, the measures require regular testing to ensure that they actually work as designed to protect the service availability. All new or changed services should be subject to continual service improvement; countermeasures should be implemented wherever they can be cost justified. This cost justification requires an understanding of the vital business functions and the cost to the business of any downtime. It is ultimately a business decision, not a technical decision. Figure 13.2 also shows the availability management information system (AMIS); this is the repository for all availability management reports, plans, risk registers, and so on, and it forms part of the service knowledge management system (SKMS).

Business continuity management and IT service continuity management are outside the scope of availability management. There is a strong relationship between availability management and these processes, however, because every action taken to mitigate a risk to availability or to provide resilience will support ITSCM.

Reliability

The first availability concept we cover is *reliability*. This is defined by ITIL as "a measure of how long a service, component, or CI can perform its agreed function without interruption." We normally describe how reliable an item is by stating how frequently it can be expected to break down within a given time: "My car is very reliable. It has broken down only twice in five years." We measure reliability by calculating the *mean (or average) time between failures (MTBF)* or the *mean (or average) time between service incidents (MTBSI)*.

FIGURE 13.2 The availability management process

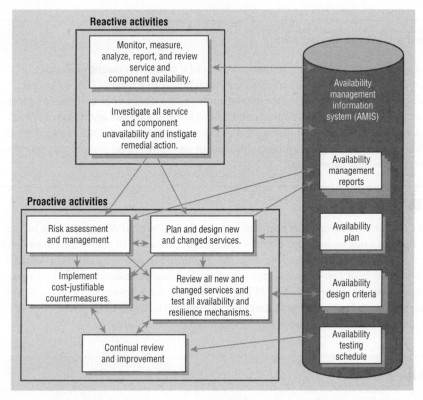

 MTBF is measured from when the configuration item starts working until it next fails. It is therefore a measure of uptime.

 MTBSI is measured from when a system or IT service fails until it next fails. It therefore includes both the MTBF and the time taken to restore the service.

Reliability of a service can be improved first by ensuring that the components specified in the design are of good quality and from a supplier with a good reputation. Even the best components will fail eventually; however, the reliability of the service can be improved by designing the service so that a component failure does not result in downtime. This is another availability concept called *resilience*. By ensuring that the design includes alternate network routes, for example, a network component failure will not lead to service downtime because the traffic will reroute. Carrying out planned maintenance to ensure that all the components are kept in good working order will also help improve reliability.

Resilience through Redundancy

A good example of designing in resilience is that of a modern passenger aircraft. Although the engines are designed to be very reliable, with a long MTBF, an aircraft with a single engine could still suffer catastrophic failure if that engine developed a fault mid-flight. Aircraft are therefore designed to have several engines and to be able to fly and land with only one of them operational. This availability management approach delivers resilience by providing redundancy (the use of one or more additional configuration items to provide fault tolerance).

Maintainability

However reliable the equipment and resilient the design, not all downtime can be prevented. When a fault occurs and there is insufficient resilience in the design to prevent it from affecting the service, the length of the downtime that results can be affected by how quickly the fault can be overcome. This is called *maintainability* and is measured as the *mean time to restore service (MTRS)*. It may be more cost-effective to concentrate resilience measures for those items that have a long service restoration time. To calculate MTRS, divide the total downtime by the total number of failures.

Calculating MTRS

A service suffers four failures in a month. The duration of each was 1 hour, 2 hours, 1.2 hours, and 1.8 hours, resulting in a total downtime of 6 hours.

MTRS = 6 / 4 = 1.5 hours

$$\text{Maintainability (MTRS in hours)} = \frac{\text{Total downtime in hours}}{\text{Number of service breaks}}$$

Simple measures can be taken to reduce MTRS, such as having common spares available on site, and these measures can have a significant impact on availability.

ITIL recommends the use of MTRS rather than mean time to repair (MTTR) because repair may or may not include the restoration of the service following the repair. From the customer perspective, downtime includes all the time between the fault occurring and the service being fully usable again. MTRS measures this complete time and is therefore a more meaningful measurement.

These concepts are illustrated in Figure 13.3, which shows what ITIL calls the *expanded incident lifecycle*. This shows periods of uptime with incidents causing periods of downtime. MTRS is shown as the average of the downtime for the incident. MTBF is shown as the average of the uptime for the incident.

FIGURE 13.3   The expanded incident lifecycle

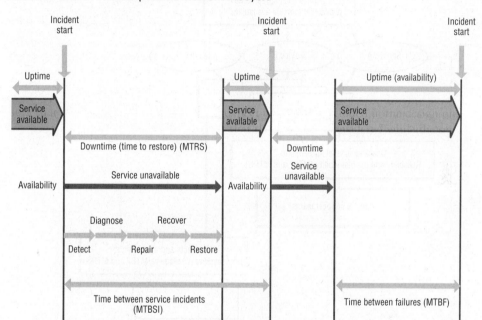

Each incident needs to be detected, diagnosed, and repaired, and the data needs to be recovered and the service restored. Any method of shortening any of these steps—speeding up detection through event management or speeding up diagnosis by the use of a knowledge base, for example—will shorten the downtime and improve availability. The figure also shows another concept, that of MTBSI; this calculates the average time from the start of one incident to the start of the next.

Serviceability

Serviceability is defined as the ability of a third-party supplier to meet the terms of its contract. This contract will include agreed levels of availability, reliability, and/or maintainability for a supporting service or component.

In Figure 13.4, you can see the terms and measures used in availability management, which are combined when applied to suppliers providing serviceability.

FIGURE 13.4   Availability terms and measures

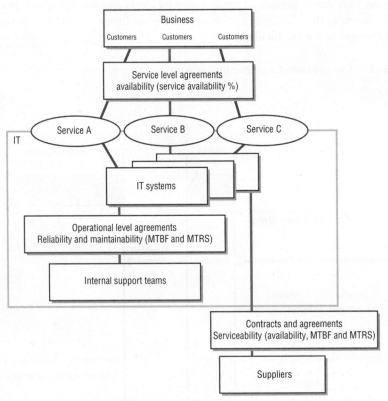

Availability Concepts: Reliability, Maintainability, and Serviceability

A large bakery had used a machine for making bread rolls for 15 years without any downtime. This machine was responsible for the production of all the bread rolls for a major fast-food company and was therefore very important to the business. The long period without failure showed that the machine was very *reliable*, possibly because of a *resilient* design. One day it failed. Because it had never failed before, there was consternation; there was no procedure in place for such an occurrence. Eventually a manual was located, but it was in German. The folks at the bakery tracked down the manufacturer in Germany (this was in the days before Google) and placed a call. An engineer arrived the following day (exactly two days since the fault occurred) and fixed the machine in 15 minutes. The mean time to repair was therefore short (15 minutes), but the mean time to restore service was 2 days and 15 minutes, which had a major impact on the ability of the company to satisfy its external customer, the fast-food chain. The weakness here was in the *serviceability* of the machine; there was no contract in place to ensure a response and fix in an appropriate time.

Measurement of Availability

The term *vital business function (VBF)* is used to reflect the part of a business process that is critical to the success of the business. The more vital the business function generally, the greater the level of resilience and availability that needs to be incorporated into the design of the supporting IT services. The availability requirements for all services, vital or not, should be determined by the business and not by IT.

Certain vital business functions may need special designs; these commonly include the following functions:

High Availability   This is a characteristic of the IT service that minimizes or masks the effects of IT component failure to the users of a service.

Fault Tolerance   This is the ability of an IT service, component, or configuration item to continue to operate correctly after failure of a component part.

Continuous Operation   This is an approach or design to eliminate planned downtime of an IT service. Individual components or configuration items may be down even though the IT service remains available.

Continuous Availability   This is an approach or design to achieve 100 percent availability. A continuously available IT service has no planned or unplanned downtime.

Within the IT industry, many suppliers commit to high availability or continuous availability solutions, but only if specific environmental standards and resilient processes are used. They often agree to such contracts only after additional, sometimes costly, improvements have been made.

The availability management process depends heavily on the measurement of service and component achievements with regard to availability.

The decision on what to measure and how to report it depends on which activity is being supported, who the recipients are, and how the information is to be utilized. It is important to recognize the differing perspectives of availability from the business, users, and service providers to ensure that measurement and reporting satisfies these varied needs.

The business perspective considers IT service availability in terms of its contribution or impact on the vital business functions that drive the business operation.

The user perspective considers IT service availability as a combination of three factors. These are the frequency, the duration, and the scope of impact. For many applications, poor response times for the user are considered at the same level as failures of technology.

The IT service provider perspective considers IT service and component availability with regard to availability, reliability, and maintainability.

It is important to consider the full scope of measures needed to report the same level of availability in different ways to satisfy the differing perspectives of availability. Measurements need to be meaningful and add value. This is influenced strongly by the combination of "what you measure" and "how you report it."

Availability Management Process, Methods, and Techniques

We have explored the concepts and measures used in the availability management process. The diagram in Figure 13.5 shows the key elements of the process, including the availability management information system.

FIGURE 13.5 The availability management process

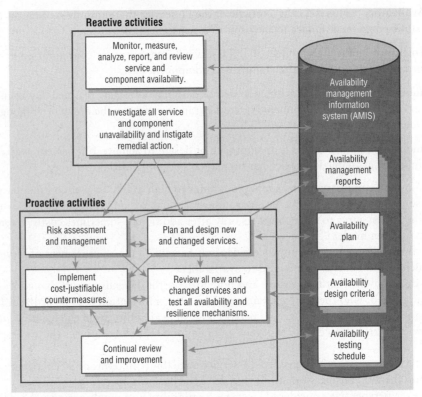

There are a number of different techniques that can be used for availability management. These are explored more fully in the capability course material, but the following provides a brief overview of each technique.

Expanded Incident Lifecycle

This technique requires the analysis of the lifecycle of an incident from start to finish and to the next outage. Throughout this analysis, the perspective of the support environment will be considered in terms of how to improve the management of an incident. Consideration of the expanded incident lifecycle provides valuable insight into the management of availability from an operational perspective, as described earlier as part of the exploration of the concepts of availability.

Fault Tree Analysis

This approach uses Boolean logic, the AND and OR statements, to analyze the sequence of events that lead to a failure. This helps in understanding single points of failure.

Component Failure Impact Analysis

As it sounds, this is a technique that considers the importance of an individual component to the provision of service. Combined with other techniques, this approach can provide useful information for the design of future services.

Service Failure Analysis

This technique is used as a proactive approach to the analysis of an interruption. Each time an interruption takes place, full analysis is undertaken to try to identify a preventative action.

Risk Analysis and Management

This provides an analysis of the likelihood of business impact relating to availability risks (the likelihood of something happening). Business impact analysis and the identification of the potential impact of the business is a vital part of risk management. Identification of mitigation against risk is a key part of the design of services.

Availability Management Triggers, Inputs, and Outputs

We will now review the triggers, inputs, and outputs of availability management.

Triggers

Many events may trigger availability management activity, including the following events:

- New or changed business needs or new or changed services
- New or changed targets within agreements, such as service level requirements, service level agreements, operational level agreements, and contracts
- Service or component breaches, availability events, and alerts, including threshold events and exception reports
- Periodic activities such as reviewing, revising, or reporting against services
- Review of availability management forecasts, reports, and plans
- Review and revision of business and IT plans and strategies
- Review and revision of designs and strategies

- Recognition or notification of a change of risk or impact of a business process, a vital business function, an IT service, or a component
- Request from service level management for assistance with availability targets and explanation of achievements

Inputs

A number of sources of information are relevant as inputs to the availability management process. Some of these are as follows:

- Business information from the organization's business strategy, plans, and financial plans and information on its current and future requirements, including the availability requirements for new or enhanced IT services
- Service information from the service level management process, with details of the services from the service portfolio and the service catalog; from service level targets within service level agreements and service level requirements; and possibly from the monitoring of SLAs, service reviews, and breaches of the SLAs
- Financial information from financial management for IT services, the cost of service provision, and the cost of resources and components
- Change and release information from the change management process with a change schedule, the release schedule from release and deployment management, and an assessment of all changes for their impact on service availability
- Service asset and configuration management containing information on the relationships between the business, the services, the supporting services, and the technology
- Component information on the availability, reliability, and maintainability requirements for the technology components that underpin IT service(s)
- Technology information from the configuration management system
- Past performance from previous measurements, achievements, reports, and the availability management information system (AMIS)
- Unavailability and failure information from incidents and problems

Outputs

Availability management produces the following outputs:

- The availability management information system (AMIS)
- The availability plan for the proactive improvement of IT services and technology
- Availability and recovery design criteria and proposed service targets for new or changed services
- Service availability, reliability, and maintainability reports of achievements against targets, including input for all service reports
- Component availability, reliability, and maintainability reports of achievements against targets

- Revised risk assessment reviews and reports and an updated risk register
- Monitoring, management, and reporting requirements for IT services and components
- An availability management test schedule for testing all availability, resilience, and recovery mechanisms
- The planned and preventive maintenance schedules
- Contributions for the projected service outage (PSO) document to be created by change management in collaboration with release and deployment management
- Details of the proactive availability techniques and measures that will be deployed
- Improvement actions for inclusion within the service improvement plan

Availability Management Interfaces

As you would expect for this process, there are a number of interfaces across the lifecycle. In fact, availability management can be linked to the majority of the service management processes. However, the key interfaces that availability management has with other processes are as follows:

Service Level Management   This process relies on availability management to determine and validate availability targets and to investigate and resolve service and component breaches. It links to both the reactive and proactive elements of availability management.

Incident and Problem Management   As you have seen from the techniques used in availability measurement and management, these processes are assisted by availability management in the resolution of incidents and problems.

Capacity Management   This provides appropriate capacity to support resilience and overall service availability. There are strong connections between the availability of a service and the capacity of the service. Patterns of business activity and user profiles are used to understand business demand for IT for business-aligned availability planning.

Change Management   As a result of investigations into outages, or improvements required by the business, change management supports the management of changes. This in turn is used in the creation of the PSO document to project the availability-related issues during a change, with contributions from availability management.

IT Service Continuity Management   Availability management works collaboratively with this process on the assessment of business impact and risk and the provision of resilience, fail-over, and recovery mechanisms. A continuity invocation is the result of an availability management issue that cannot be resolved within the agreed time frames without additional resources as described in the recovery plan.

Information Security Management   Put simply, if the data becomes unavailable, the service becomes unavailable. Information security management defines the security measures and policies that must be included in the service design for availability and the design for recovery.

Access Management   Availability management provides the methods for appropriately granting and revoking access to services as needed. This should be carefully monitored because unauthorized or uncontrolled access can be a significant risk to service availability.

Information Management and Availability Management

The process talks about and stresses the importance of an availability management information system. Although this is shown in the process diagram (Figure 13.2) as a single database or repository, it is unlikely to be the case in the real world. It is far more likely that the information relating to availability is captured and resides in a number of different tools and systems.

The challenge, for an availability manager, is to make sense of these disparate sources and create a unified information source that enables the production of the availability plan.

There are many tools in the marketplace that make claims about being able to manage availability across an enterprise, but it would be surprising if the unique requirements of a customer were met by a generic toolset.

Customization, adaptation, and configuration to meet the customer requirements will always be required, and the information obtained must be managed so that it is fit for use and purpose. This information, covering services, components, and supporting services, provides the basis for regular, ad hoc, and exception availability reporting and the identification of trends within the data for the instigation of improvement activities.

The availability plan should have aims, objectives, and deliverables and should consider the wider issues of people, processes, tools, and techniques as well as have a technology focus. As the availability management process matures, the plan should evolve to cover the following:

- Actual levels of availability versus agreed levels of availability for key IT services. Availability measurements should always be business and customer focused and report availability as experienced by the business and users.

- Activities being progressed to address shortfalls in availability for existing IT services. Where investment decisions are required, options with associated costs and benefits should be included.

- Details of changing availability requirements for existing IT services. The plan should document the options available to meet these changed requirements. Where investment decisions are required, the associated costs of each option should be included.

- Details of the availability requirements for forthcoming new IT services. The plan should document the options available to meet these new requirements. Where investment decisions are required, the associated costs of each option should be included.

- A forward-looking schedule for the planned SFA assignments.

- Regular reviews of SFA assignments. These reviews should be completed to ensure that the availability of technology is being proactively improved in conjunction with the SIP.

- A technology futures section to provide an indication of the potential benefits and exploitation opportunities that exist for planned technology upgrades. Anticipated availability benefits should be detailed, where possible based on business-focused measures, in conjunction with capacity management. The effort required to realize these benefits where possible should also be quantified.

Covering a period of six months to a year, this plan is often produced as a rolling plan, continually updated to meet the changing needs of the business. At a minimum, it is recommended that publication is aligned with the capacity and business budgeting cycle and that the availability plan is considered complementary to the capacity plan and financial plan. Frequency of updates will depend on the nature of the organization and the rate of technological or business change.

The availability management information system can be utilized to record and store selected data and information required to support key activities such as report generation, statistical analysis, and availability forecasting and planning. It should be the main repository for the recording of IT availability metrics, measurements, targets, and documents, including the availability plan, availability measurements, achievement reports, SFA assignment reports, design criteria, action plans, and testing schedules.

 When considering the use of information in availability management, it is important to be pragmatic. If you define the initial tool requirements and identify what is already deployed and what can be used and shared, this will help to get started as quickly as possible. Where basic tools are not already available, it may be necessary to work with the other IT service and systems management processes to identify common requirements with the aim of selecting shared tools and minimizing costs. The AMIS should address the specific reporting needs of availability management not currently provided by existing repositories and integrate with them and their contents. After all, best practice does not include "reinventing the wheel"—if information is already available, there is no point in recreating it in another form.

Availability Management Critical Success Factors and Key Performance Indicators

This section includes some sample critical success factors for availability management. There are many more, and they can be obtained from the *ITIL Service Design* publication, or from your own experience within your organization.

- Critical success factor: "Manage availability and reliability of IT service."
  - KPI: Reduction (measured as a percentage) in the unavailability of services and components
  - KPI: Increase (measured as a percentage) in the reliability of services and components
  - KPI: Effective review and follow-up of all SLA, OLA, and underpinning contract breaches relating to availability and reliability

- Critical success factor: "Satisfy business needs for access to IT services."
  - KPI: Reduction (measured as a percentage) in the unavailability of services
  - KPI: Reduction (measured as a percentage) of the cost of business overtime due to unavailable IT
- Critical success factor: "Availability of IT infrastructure and applications, as documented in SLAs, provided at optimum costs."
  - KPI: Reduction (measured as a percentage) in the cost of unavailability
  - KPI: Improvement (measured as a percentage) in the service delivery costs

Availability Management Challenges and Risks

We'll begin with looking at the key challenges for the process.

Challenges

The main challenge is to meet and manage the expectations of the customers and the business. The service levels should be publicized to all customers and areas of the business so that when services do fail, the expectation for their recovery is at the right level. It also means that availability management must have access to the right level of quality information on the current business need for IT services and its plans for the future.

Another challenge facing availability management is the integration of all of the availability data into an integrated set of information (AMIS). This can be analyzed in a consistent manner to provide details on the availability of all services and components. This is particularly challenging when the information from the different technologies is provided by different tools in different formats, which often happens.

Yet another challenge facing availability management is the investment needed in proactive availability measures. Availability management should work closely with ITSCM, information security management, and capacity management in producing the justifications necessary to secure the appropriate investment.

Risks

The following major risks are among those associated with availability management:

- A lack of commitment from the business to the availability management process
- A lack of appropriate information on future plans and strategies from the business
- A lack of senior management commitment to or a lack of resources and/or budget for the availability management process
- Labor-intensive reporting processes
- The processes focus too much on the technology and not enough on the services and the needs of the business.
- The availability management information system is maintained in isolation and is not shared or consistent with other process areas, especially ITSCM, information security

management, and capacity management. This interaction is particularly important when considering the necessary service and component backup and recovery tools, technology, and processes to meet the agreed needs.

Summary

This chapter explored the next two processes in the service design stage, service level management and availability management. It covered the purpose, objectives, and scope for both processes.

We also looked at the value of each processes and reviewed their policies, activities, methods, and techniques.

We reviewed triggers, inputs, outputs, and interfaces for the processes and the information management associated with them. We also considered the critical success factors and key performance indicators, the challenges, and the risks for each process.

We examined how each of these processes supports the other and the importance of these processes to the business and to the IT service provider.

Exam Essentials

Understand the purpose and objectives of service level management and availability management.   It is important for you to be able to explain the purpose and objectives of the service level management and availability management processes.

Service level management should ensure that the services are delivered to the customer's satisfaction and in line with their requirements.

Availability management should ensure that the required availability is delivered to meet the targets in the service level agreement.

Understand the scope of service level management.   SLM does *not* include agreeing on the utility aspects. The negotiation and agreement of requirements for service functionality (utility) are not part of the process, except to the degree that the functionality influences a service level requirement or target.

Explain the different categories of service providers.   Providers fall into three categories; they can be embedded in a business unit (Type I), shared across business units (Type II), or external to the organization (Type III). Type III service providers will have an SLA with their external customers that will be a legal contract because they are separate organizations.

Understand the critical success factors and key performance indicators for the processes.   Measurement of the processes is an important part of understanding their success. You should be familiar with the CSFs and KPIs for both service level management and availability management.

Understand the definition of availability.   ITIL defines availability as the ability of an IT service or other configuration item to perform its agreed function when required. Any unplanned interruption to a service during its agreed service hours (also called the agreed service time, specified in the service level agreement) is defined as downtime. The availability measure is calculated by subtracting the downtime from the agreed service time and converting it to a percentage of the agreed service time.

Explain the different concepts of availability management.   You need to be able to differentiate between reliability, maintainability, and serviceability. *Reliability* is defined by ITIL as "a measure of how long a service, component, or CI can perform its agreed function without interruption." *Maintainability* is measured as the mean time to restore service (MTRS). *Serviceability* is defined as the ability of a third-party supplier to meet the terms of its contract. This contract will include agreed levels of availability, reliability, and/or maintainability for a supporting service or component.

Understand and differentiate between the methods and techniques of availability management.   There are a number of different techniques that can be used for availability management. Ensure that you are familiar with each of them and can explain the purpose of each.

Explain the role of information management in availability management.   Information is key to the service lifecycle, so you need to understand the content of the availability management information system and its use throughout the lifecycle.

Review Questions

You can find the answers to the review questions in the appendix.

1. Which of these statements provides the *best* description of the purpose of service level management?

    A. Ensure that all current and planned IT services are delivered to agreed achievable targets.

    B. Ensure that there is a high-level relationship with customers to capture business demands.

    C. Ensure that users have a single point of contact for all operational issues.

    D. Ensure that there is a smooth transition of services to and from service providers.

2. Which of these is an objective of service level management?

    A. Monitor changes throughout their lifecycle.

    B. Define, document, agree, monitor, measure, report, and review services.

    C. Respond to service requests and inquiries promptly.

    D. Establish the root cause of incidents and problems efficiently and cost-effectively.

3. Availability is calculated using the formula AST-DT/AST × 100. What do the abbreviations AST and DT refer to?

    A. AST = assumed service target, DT = delivery time

    B. AST = availability service target, DT = downtime

    C. AST = agreed service time, DT = downtime

    D. AST = agreed service time, DT = delivery time

4. Which of the following concepts are key to availability management?

    1. Reliability

    2. Resilience

    3. Resistance

    4. Attainability

    5. Serviceability

    6. Maintainability

    7. Detectability

    > **A.** 1, 2, 6, 7
    >
    > **B.** 2, 3, 5, 6
    >
    > **C.** 1, 4, 6, 7
    >
    > **D.** 1, 2, 5, 6

5. Service level requirements are related to which of the following?

    A. Utility

    B. Warranty

   C. Change records

   D. Configuration records

6. Which of the following would NOT be part of a service level agreement?

   A. Description of the service

   B. Service hours

   C. Definition of business strategy

   D. Service continuity arrangements

7. Which of the following agreements commonly supports the achievement of a service level agreement?

   1. Operational level agreement

   2. Strategic business plan

   3. Underpinning contract

   4. Internal finance agreement

      A. 1, 2, and 3

      B. 1, 2, and 4

      C. 1 and 3

      D. 2 and 4

8. Which of the following is the best description of an underpinning contract?

   A. An agreement between an IT service provider and another part of the same organization assisting in the provision of services

   B. An agreement between an IT service provider and customer relating to the delivery of services

   C. An agreement between different customers about the requirements of the service

   D. A contract between an IT service provider and an external third-party organization assisting in the delivery of services

9. Availability management considers VBFs. What does VBF stand for?

   A. Viable business factors

   B. Vital business function

   C. Visibility, benefits, functionality

   D. Vital business facilities

10. Which of the following is a common color scheme that's applied to a service level management monitoring chart?

   A. Red, blue, green

   B. Red, amber, green

   C. Blue, green, black

   D. Black, amber, blue

Chapter

14

Service Design Processes: Capacity Management and IT Service Continuity Management

---

THE FOLLOWING ITIL INTERMEDIATE EXAM OBJECTIVES ARE DISCUSSED IN THIS CHAPTER:

✓ Capacity management and IT service continuity management are discussed in terms of

- Purpose
- Objectives
- Scope
- Value
- Policies
- Principles and basic concepts
- Process activities, methods, and techniques
- Triggers, inputs, outputs, and interfaces
- Information management
- Critical success factors and key performance indicators
- Challenges
- Risks

The ITIL service design publication covers the managerial and supervisory aspects of service design processes. It excludes the day-to-day operation of each process and the details of the process activities, methods, and techniques or its information management. More detailed process operation guidance is covered in the service capability courses. Each process is considered from the management perspective. That means that at the end of this chapter, you should understand those aspects that would be required to understand each process and its interfaces, oversee its implementation, and judge its effectiveness and efficiency.

Capacity Management

ITIL states that *capacity management* is responsible for ensuring that the capacity of IT services and the IT infrastructure is able to meet agreed current and future capacity and performance needs in a cost-effective and timely manner. The capacity management process must therefore understand the likely changes in capacity requirements and ensure that the design and ongoing management of a service meet this demand. Sufficient capacity is a key warranty aspect of a service that needs to be delivered if the benefits of the service are to be realized.

Capacity management is considered throughout the lifecycle; as part of strategy, the likely capacity requirements for a new service are considered as part of the service evaluation to ensure that the service is meeting a real need. In design, the service is engineered to cope with that demand and to be flexible enough to be able to adjust to meet changing capacity requirements. Transition ensures that the service, when implemented, is delivering according to its specification. The operational phase of the lifecycle ensures that day-to-day adjustments that are necessary to meet changes in requirements are implemented. Finally, as part of continual service improvement, capacity-related issues are addressed and adjustments are made to ensure that the most cost-effective and reliable delivery of the service is achieved.

Purpose of Capacity Management

The purpose of the capacity management process is to understand the current and future capacity needs of a service and to ensure that the service and its supporting services are able to deliver to this level. The actual capacity requirements will have been agreed upon as part of service level management; capacity management must not only meet these, but also ensure that the future needs of the business, which may change over time, are met.

Objectives of Capacity Management

The objectives of capacity management are met by the development of a detailed plan that states the current business requirement, the expected future requirement, and the actions that will be taken to meet these requirements. This plan should be reviewed and updated at regular intervals (at least annually) to ensure that changes in business requirements are considered. Similarly, any requests to change the current configuration will be considered by capacity management to ensure that they are in line with expectations or, if not, that the capacity plan is amended to suit the changed requirement. Those responsible for capacity management will review any issues that arise and help resolve any incidents or problems that are the result of insufficient capacity. This helps ensure that the service meets its objectives.

An essential objective is to make sure capacity is increased in a timely manner so the business is not impacted.

As part of the ongoing management of capacity and its continual improvement, any proactive measures that may improve performance at a reasonable cost are identified and acted upon. Advice and guidance on capacity and performance-related issues are provided, and assistance is given to service operations with performance- and capacity-related incidents and problems.

Scope of Capacity Management

The capacity management process has responsibility for ensuring sufficient capacity at all times, including both planning for short-term fluctuations, such as those caused by seasonal variations, and ensuring that the required capacity is there for longer-term business expansion. Changes in demand may sometimes actually be reductions in that demand, and this is also within the scope of the process. Capacity management should ensure that as demand for the service falls, the capacity provided for that service is also reduced to ensure that unnecessary expenditure is avoided.

The process includes all aspects of service provision and therefore may involve the technical, applications, and operations management functions. Other aspects of capacity, such as staff resources, are also considered.

 Real World Scenario

Capacity Management

A retail organization that was struggling to maintain its market position decided to expand its online and telephone-ordering service through a major marketing campaign.

As part of this initiative, the telephone-ordering service hours were to be extended to 24 hours, 7 days a week. The business was considering what this would mean in terms of increased call center staff, warehouse staff, and stock levels. The IT director was tasked with ensuring that the IT services would support this business initiative.

The IT director called together his managers involved in the capacity management process. Those in the technical management function had to ensure that the infrastructure would be able to cope with the expected increased demand. This included the telecoms infrastructure capacity, required for the extra call center staff, and the voice traffic that the staff would generate in addition to the increase in data traffic. The website's capacity to handle increased traffic and the ability of the applications to handle a high volume of orders, credit card processing, and so on were investigated by the technical and applications management functions. The technical solutions that were recommended as a result meant more equipment would be purchased. The operations management function investigated the impact on operational processes, such as increased time needed to carry out backups and the impact of 24/7 operations on planned maintenance. Included was the impact of the extra equipment on the UPS, air conditioning, and so on. Finally, the service desk manager calculated what increase in staff would be required to move to a 24/7 support operation and an increased user population during peak hours. This was calculated as requiring two new service desk analysts, and the building services department was asked to provide the extra office space for the new staff.

As the example in the case study "Capacity Management" illustrates, an increase in capacity requirements may have repercussions across the infrastructure and on the IT staff resources required to manage it. Although staffing is a line management responsibility, the calculation of resource requirements in this area is also part of the overall capacity management process.

Capacity management also involves monitoring "patterns of business activity" to understand how well the infrastructure is meeting the demands upon it and making adjustments as required to ensure that the demand is met. Proactive improvements to capacity may also be implemented, where justified, and any incidents caused by capacity issues need to be investigated.

Capacity management may also recommend demand management techniques to smooth out excessive peaks in demand.

Capacity Management Value to the Business

Capacity management provides value to the business by improving the performance and availability of IT services the business needs; it does so by helping to reduce capacity- and performance-related incidents and problems. The process will also ensure that the required capacity and performance are provided in the most cost-effective manner.

All processes should be contributing in some way to the achievement of customer satisfaction, and capacity management does this by ensuring all capacity- and performance-related service levels are met.

Proactive capacity management activities will support the efficient and effective design and transition of new or changed services. This will include the production of a forward-looking capacity plan based on a sound understanding of business needs and plans.

As with availability management, capacity management will have the opportunity to improve the ability of the business to follow an environmentally responsible strategy by using green technologies and techniques.

Capacity Management Policies

Capacity management is essentially a balancing act. It ensures that the capacity and performance of the IT services and systems match the evolving demands of the business in the most cost-effective and timely manner. This requires balancing the costs against the resources needed. Capacity management needs to ensure that the processing capacity that is purchased is cost justifiable in terms of business need. It ensures that the organization makes the most efficient use of those resources.

Capacity management is also about balancing supply against demand. It is important to ensure that the available supply of IT processing power matches the demands made on it by the business, both now and in the future. It may also be necessary to manage or influence the demand for a particular resource.

The policies for capacity management should reflect the need for capacity management to play a significant role across the service lifecycle.

It is important to ensure that capacity management is part of the consideration for all service level and operational level agreements, and of course any supporting contracts with suppliers. These agreements will capture the service requirements of the business, and capacity management should consider these for the current and future business needs.

Capacity Management Process Activities, Methods, and Techniques

We are not going to explore the process in detail, but you should make sure you are familiar with all the aspects of the process and the management requirements for each.

In Figure 14.1, you can see the full scope of the subprocesses, techniques, and activities for the capacity management process.

Capacity management is an extremely technical, complex, and demanding process, and in order to achieve results, it requires three supporting subprocesses: business capacity management, service capacity management, and component capacity management.

FIGURE 14.1 Capacity management subprocesses

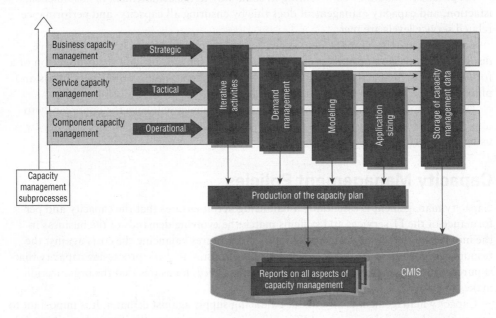

Business capacity management is focused on the current and future business requirements, while service capacity management is focused on the delivery of the existing services that support the business and component capacity management is focused on the IT infrastructure that underpins service provision.

It is important to ensure that the tools used by capacity management conform to the organization's management architecture and also integrate with other tools used for the management of IT systems and automating IT processes.

The monitoring and control activities within service operation should provide a basis for the tools to support and analyze information for capacity management. The IT operations management function and the technical management departments (such as network management and server management) may carry out the bulk of the day-to-day operational duties. They will participate in the capacity management process by providing it with performance information.

Like availability management, capacity management has both reactive and proactive activities. In Figure 14.2, you can see the activities relating to both reactive and proactive capacity management and the interaction between the subprocesses.

FIGURE 14.2   Capacity management overview with subprocesses

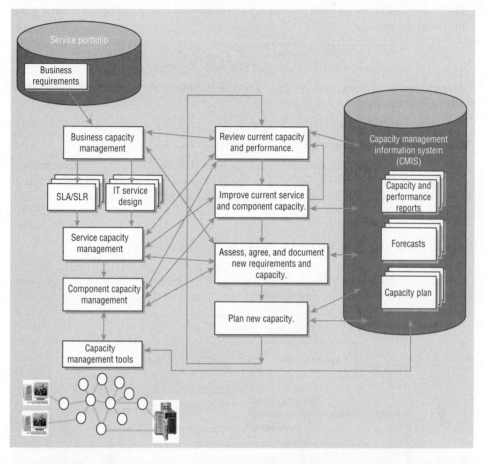

Capacity management should include the following proactive activities:

- Preempting performance issues by taking the necessary actions before the issues occur
- Producing trends of the current component utilization and using them to estimate the future requirements and for planning upgrades and enhancements
- Modeling and trending the predicted changes in IT services (including service retirements)
- Ensuring that upgrades are budgeted, planned, and implemented before service level agreements and service targets are breached or performance issues occur

- Actively seeking to improve service performance wherever the cost is justifiable
- Producing and maintaining a capacity plan addressing future requirements and plans for meeting them
- Tuning (also known as optimizing) the performance of services and components

  Capacity management should include the following reactive activities:

- Monitoring, measuring, reporting, and reviewing the current performance of both services and components
- Responding to all capacity-related "threshold" events and instigating corrective action
- Reacting to and assisting with specific performance issues

There are a number of ongoing activities that form part of the capacity management process. These activities provide the basic historical information and triggers necessary for all of the other activities and processes within capacity management. These can be seen in Figure 14.3.

FIGURE 14.3 Ongoing iterative activities of capacity management

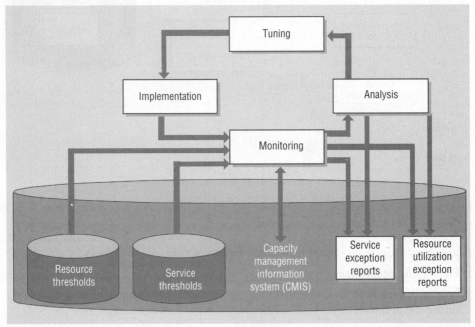

Monitoring should be established on all the components and for each of the services. The data from the monitoring systems should be analyzed using expert systems to compare usage levels against thresholds. The results of the analysis should be included in reports

and used to make recommendations for management of the systems. Control mechanisms should then be put in place to act on the recommendations.

There are many different approaches to managing capacity, including balancing services, balancing workloads, changing concurrency levels, and adding or removing resources. The information accumulated during these activities should be stored in the capacity management information system (CMIS).

This is a cyclic activity, and any changes should be monitored to make sure they deliver a positive benefit. These iterative activities are primarily performed as part of the service operation stage of the service lifecycle.

Capacity Management Triggers, Inputs, and Outputs

Let's consider the triggers, inputs, and outputs for the capacity management process. Capacity management is a process that has many active connections throughout the organization and its processes. It is important that the triggers, inputs, outputs, and interfaces be clearly defined to avoid duplicated effort or gaps in workflow.

Triggers

There are many triggers that will initiate capacity management activities:

- New and changed services requiring additional capacity
- Service breaches, capacity or performance events, and alerts, including threshold events
- Exception reports
- Periodic revision of current capacity and performance and the review of forecasts, reports, and plans
- Periodic trending and modeling
- Review and revision of business and IT plans and strategies
- Review and revision of designs and strategies
- Review and revision of service level agreements, operational level agreements, contracts, or any other agreements
- Requests from service level management for assistance with capacity and/or performance targets and explanation of achievements

Inputs

A number of sources of information are relevant to the capacity management process:

- Business information
- Service and IT information
- Component performance and capacity information
- Service performance issue information
- Service information

- Financial information
- Change information
- Performance information
- CMS
- Workload information

Outputs

The outputs of capacity management are used within the process itself as well as by many other processes and other parts of the organization. The information is often reproduced in an electronic format as visual real-time displays of performance. The outputs are as follows:

- The capacity management information system
- The capacity plan
- Service performance information and reports
- Workload analysis and reports
- Ad hoc capacity and performance reports
- Forecasts and predictive reports
- Thresholds, alerts, and events
- Improvement actions

Capacity Management Interfaces

As we have already explained, capacity management has strong connections across the service lifecycle with a number of other processes. The key interfaces are as follows:

- Availability management works with capacity management to determine the resources needed to ensure the required availability of services and components.
- Service level management provides assistance with determining capacity targets and the investigation and resolution of breaches related to service and component capacity.
- IT service continuity management is supported by capacity management through the assessment of business impact and risk, determining the capacity needed to support risk reduction measures and recovery options.
- Capacity management provides assistance with incident and problem management for the resolution and correction of capacity-related incidents and problems.
- By anticipating the demand for services based on user profiles and patterns of business activity, and by identifying the means to influence that demand, demand management provides strategic decision-making and critical related data on which capacity management can act.

Information Management and Capacity Management

The CMIS is used to provide the relevant capacity and performance information to produce reports and support the capacity management process. The reports provide information to a number of IT and service management processes. These should include the reports described in the following sections.

Component-Based Reports

There is likely to be a team of technical staff responsible for each component, and they should be in charge of their control and management. Reports must be produced to illustrate how components are performing and how much of their maximum capacity is being used.

Service-Based Reports

Service-based reports will provide the basis of SLM and customer service reports. Reports and information must be produced to illustrate how the service and its constituent components are performing with respect to their overall service targets and constraints.

Exception Reports

Exception reports can be used to show management and technical staff when the capacity and performance of a particular component or service becomes unacceptable. Thresholds can be set for any component, service, or measurement within the CMIS. An example threshold may be that processor utilization for a particular server has breached 70 percent for three consecutive hours or that the concurrent number of logged-in users exceeds the agreed limit.

In particular, exception reports are of interest to the SLM process in determining whether the targets in SLAs have been breached. Also, the incident and problem management processes may be able to use the exception reports in the resolution of incidents and problems. Excess capacity should also be identified. Unused capacity may represent an opportunity for cost savings.

Predictive and Forecast Reports

Part of the capacity management process is to predict future workloads and growth. To do this, future component and service capacity and performance must be forecast. This can be done in a variety of ways, depending on the techniques and the technology used. A simple example of a capacity forecast is a correlation between a business driver and component utilization. If the forecasts on future capacity requirements identify a requirement for increased resource, this requirement needs to be input into the capacity plan and included within the IT budget cycle.

Often capacity reports are consolidated and stored on an intranet site so that anyone can access and refer to them.

Measures, Metrics, and Critical Success Factors for Capacity Management

The following list includes some sample critical success factors for capacity management and some key performance indicators for each.

- Critical success factor: "Accurate business forecasts."
    - KPI: Production of workload forecasts on time
    - KPI: Accuracy (measured as a percentage) of forecasts of business trends
- Critical success factor: "Knowledge of current and future technologies."
    - KPI: Timely justification and implementation of new technology in line with business requirements (time, cost, and functionality)
    - KPI: Reduction in the use of old technology, causing breached SLAs due to problems with support or performance
- Critical success factor: "Ability to demonstrate cost effectiveness."
    - KPI: Reduction in last-minute buying to address urgent performance issues
    - KPI: Reduction in the overcapacity of IT
- Critical success factor: "Ability to plan and implement the appropriate IT capacity to match business needs."
    - KPI: Reduction (measured as a percentage) in the number of incidents due to poor performance
    - KPI: Reduction (measured as a percentage) in lost business due to inadequate capacity

Challenges for Capacity Management

One of the major challenges facing capacity management is persuading the business to provide information on its strategic business plans. Without this information, the IT service provider will find it difficult to provide effective business capacity management. Where there may be commercial or confidential reasons this data cannot be shared, it becomes even more challenging for the service provider.

Another challenge is the combination of all of the component capacity management data into an integrated set of information that can be analyzed in a consistent manner. This is particularly challenging when the information from the different technologies is provided by different tools in differing formats.

The amount of information produced by business capacity management, and especially service capacity management and component capacity management, is huge, and the analysis of this information is often difficult to achieve.

It is important that the people and the processes focus on the key resources and their usage, without ignoring other areas. For this to be done, appropriate thresholds must be used, and reliance must be placed on tools and technology to automatically manage the technology and provide warnings and alerts when things deviate significantly from the norm.

Risks for Capacity Management

The following list includes some of the major risks associated with capacity management:

- A lack of commitment from the business to the capacity management process.
- A lack of appropriate information from the business on future plans and strategies.
- A lack of senior management commitment to or a lack of resources and/or budget for the capacity management process.
- Service capacity management and component capacity management performed in isolation because business capacity management is difficult or there is a lack of appropriate and accurate business information.
- The processes become too bureaucratic or manually intensive.
- The processes focus too much on the technology (component capacity management) and not enough on the services (service capacity management) and the business (business capacity management).
- The reports and information provided are too technical and do not give the information required by or appropriate for the customers and the business.

IT Service Continuity Management

It is a fact that a service delivers value only when it is available for use. In addition to the activities carried out under the availability management process, there is a requirement for the IT service provider to ensure that the service is protected from catastrophic events that could prevent it from being delivered at all. Where these cannot be avoided, there is a requirement to have a plan to recover from any such disruption in a timescale and at a cost that meets the business requirement. Ensuring IT service continuity is an essential element of the warranty of the service.

It is important to understand that *IT service continuity management (ITSCM)* is responsible for the continuity of the IT services required by the business. The business should have a business continuity plan to ensure that any potential situations that would impact the ability of the business to function are identified and avoided. Where it is not possible to avoid such an event, the business continuity management process should have a plan, which is appropriate and affordable, to both minimize its impact and recover from it. Thus, ITSCM can be seen as one of a number of elements supporting a business continuity management (BCM) process, along with a human resources continuity plan, a financial management continuity plan, a building management continuity plan, and so on.

Purpose of IT Service Continuity Management

The purpose of the IT service continuity management process is to support the overall business continuity management (BCM) process. It is not a replacement for business continuity, even though many organizations could not survive without their IT service provider. It is important that this process understands the business continuity requirements. The service provider can then support these requirements by ensuring that, through managing the risks that could seriously affect IT services, the IT service provider can always provide the minimum agreed business continuity-related service levels.

To support and align with the BCM process, ITSCM uses formal risk assessment and management techniques to reduce risks to IT services to agreed acceptable levels. The service provider will plan and prepare for the recovery of IT services to meet these agreed levels.

Objectives of IT Service Continuity Management

A key objective of IT service continuity management is to produce and maintain a set of IT service continuity plans that support the overall business continuity plans of the organization. This will require complete and regular business impact analysis exercises to ensure that all continuity plans are maintained in line with changing business impacts and requirements.

A further objective is to conduct regular risk assessment and management exercises to manage IT services within an agreed level of business risk. This should be completed in conjunction with the business and the availability management and information security management processes.

As with all the service design processes, this process has an objective to provide advice and guidance to all other areas of the business and IT on all continuity-related issues.

IT service continuity should also ensure that appropriate continuity mechanisms are put in place to meet or exceed the agreed business continuity targets. This will require the assessment of the impact of all changes on the IT service continuity plans and supporting methods and procedures.

Working with availability management, the process should ensure that cost-justifiable proactive measures to improve the availability of services are implemented.

Service continuity management should also negotiate and agree on contracts with suppliers for the provision of the necessary recovery capability to support all continuity plans in conjunction with the supplier management process.

Scope of IT Service Continuity Management

When we consider the scope of IT service continuity management, it is important to understand that the process focuses on events that the business considers significant enough to be treated as a disaster. Less significant events will be dealt with as part of the incident management process.

Each organization will have its own understanding of what constitutes a disaster. The scope of IT service continuity management within an organization is determined by the organizational structure, culture, and strategic direction (both business and technology) in terms of the services provided and how these develop and change over time.

IT service continuity management first considers the IT assets and configurations that support the business processes. The process is not normally concerned with longer-term risks such as those from changes in business direction or other business-related alterations. Similarly, it does not usually cover minor technical faults (for example, noncritical disk failure) unless there is a possibility that the impact on the business could be major.

The IT service continuity management process includes the agreement of the scope of the ITSCM process and the policies adopted to support the business requirements. The process will also carry out business impact analysis to quantify the impact that the loss of IT service would have on the business.

It is important to establish the likelihood of potential threats taking place by carrying out risk assessment and management. This also includes taking measures to manage the identified threats where the cost can be justified. The approach to managing these threats will form the core of the ITSCM strategy and plans.

Essential to the process is the production of an overall IT service continuity management strategy that must be integrated into the business continuity management strategy. This should be produced by using both risk assessment and management and business impact analysis. The strategy should include cost-justifiable risk reduction measures as well as selection of appropriate and comprehensive recovery options.

As part of the strategy, there should be the requirement to produce an IT service continuity plan, which should integrate with the business continuity plan. These plans should be tested and managed as part of the ongoing operation. This will require regular testing and maintenance to ensure that they are in alignment with business continuity management.

IT Service Continuity Management Value to the Business

IT service continuity management is a vital part of the assurance and management of IT service provision for an organization because it supports the business continuity process. It can often be used to provide the justification for business continuity processes and plans by raising awareness of the impact of failures to the organization.

The process should be driven by business risk as identified by business continuity and ensure that the recovery arrangements for IT services are aligned to identified business impacts, risks, and needs.

IT Service Continuity Management Process, Methods, and Techniques

IT service continuity management is a repeating, cyclic process. As the needs of the organization change, so will the requirements for continuity and recovery, so the process must be continually reviewed and the output verified for effectiveness. The process is shown in Figure 14.4.

FIGURE 14.4   Lifecycle of IT service continuity management

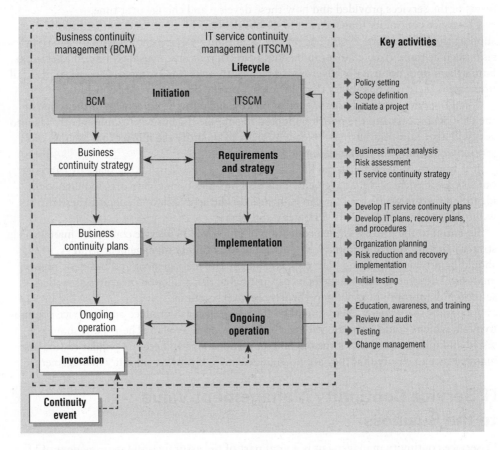

Initiation   The process is structured in four stages. The first is initiation, where the policies and scope of the continuity requirement are established in alignment with the business continuity requirements. It is during this stage that, if the scope requires it, a project management approach will be adopted.

Requirements and Strategy   In the next stage, requirements and strategy, the activities of business impact analysis and risk assessment and management are carried out. This will allow the strategy for continuity to be developed.

Implementation   Implementation of the strategy requires the development of the IT service continuity plans, including the recovery plans and procedures. This stage is where the risk reduction measures are implemented and the initial testing of the plans is carried out. Once these are found to be successful in supporting the business requirements, the operational stage begins.

Ongoing Operation   During the operational stage, it will be important to ensure that there is adequate information delivered to the organization, through education, awareness, and training. The plans should be regularly reviewed and audited to ensure that they meet the ongoing requirements of the business. This will require an association with the change management process, and the plans and procedures for continuity should be subject to change procedures. Regular testing is part of this stage, and the results of testing will be fed back into the process.

Invocation   It is important to ensure that there is a clearly understood mechanism and definition of when to invoke the continuity plans. This is not a stage of the process, as such, but it is a vital part of the process, because the establishment of the trigger for implementing the continuity plan is very important.

IT Service Continuity Management Triggers, Inputs, and Outputs

We will now review the triggers, inputs, and outputs of IT service continuity management.

Triggers

Many events may trigger IT service continuity management activity, including new or changed business needs, new or changed services, and new or changed targets within agreements, such as service level requirements, service level agreements, operational level agreements, and contracts.

Major incidents that require assessment for potential invocation of either business or IT continuity plans are another trigger for the process, as are periodic activities such as the business impact analysis and risk assessment activities; maintenance of continuity plans; and other reviewing, revising, or reporting activities.

Assessment of changes and attendance at change advisory board meetings should be a part of the process scope, because it is here that there will be opportunity to review and revise business and IT plans and strategies in light of altering business needs, which may trigger changes to the process output. This will include the review and revision of designs and strategies, both for the business and IT service provider.

Other triggers will include the recognition or notification of a change in the risk or impact of a business process or vital business function, an IT service, or a component. The results of testing the plans and lessons learned from previous continuity events will also provide triggers for the process.

Inputs

There are many sources of input required by the ITSCM process:

- Business information from the organization's business strategy, plans, and financial plans and information on their current and future requirements

- IT information from the IT strategy and plans and current budgets

- A business continuity strategy and a set of business continuity plans from all areas of the business

- Service information from the SLM process, with details of the services from the service portfolio and the service catalog and service level targets within SLAs and SLRs
- Financial information from financial management for IT services, the cost of service provision, and the cost of resources and components
- Change information from the change management process, with a change schedule and an assessment of all changes for their impact on all ITSCM plans
- A configuration management system (CMS) containing information on the relationships between the business, the services, the supporting services, and the technology
- Business continuity management and availability management testing schedules
- Capacity management information identifying the resources required to run the critical services in the event of a continuity event
- IT service continuity plans and test reports from supplier and partners, where appropriate

Outputs

The outputs from the ITSCM process are as follows:

- A revised ITSCM policy and strategy
- A set of ITSCM plans, including all crisis management plans, emergency response plans, and disaster recovery plans, together with a set of supporting plans and contracts with recovery service providers
- Business impact analysis exercises and reports, in conjunction with business continuity management and the business
- Risk assessment and management reviews and reports, in conjunction with the business, availability management, and information security management
- An ITSCM testing schedule
- ITSCM test scenarios
- ITSCM test reports and reviews
- Forecasts and predictive reports used by all areas to analyze, predict, and forecast particular business and IT scenarios and their potential solutions

IT Service Continuity Management Interfaces

IT service continuity should have interfaces to all other processes across the whole service lifecycle.

Important examples are as follows:

- Change management, because all changes need to be considered for their impact on the continuity plans. The plan itself must be under change management control.
- Incident and problem management require clear criteria that is agreed on and documented for the invocation of the ITSCM plans.

- Availability management undertakes risk assessment, and implementing risk responses should be closely coordinated with the availability process to optimize risk mitigation.

- Recovery requirements will be agreed and documented in the service level agreements. Different service levels that would be acceptable in a disaster situation could be agreed on and documented through the service level management process.

- Capacity management should ensure that there are sufficient resources to enable recovery to replacement systems following a disaster.

- Service asset and configuration management provides a valuable tool for the continuity process. The configuration management system documents the components that make up the infrastructure and the relationship between the components.

- A very close relationship exists between ITSCM and information security management. A major security breach could be considered a disaster, so when the service provider is conducting business impact analysis and risk assessment, security will be a very important consideration.

Information Management

ITSCM needs to record all of the information necessary to maintain a comprehensive set of ITSCM plans. This information base should include the following items:

- Information from the latest version of the BIA
- Comprehensive information on risk within a risk register, including risk assessment and risk responses
- The latest version of the BCM strategy and business continuity plans
- Details relating to all completed tests and a schedule of all planned tests
- Details of all ITSCM plans and their contents
- Details of all other plans associated with ITSCM plans
- Details of all existing recovery facilities, recovery suppliers and partners, recovery agreements and contracts, and spare and alternative equipment
- Details of all backup and recovery processes, schedules, systems, and media and their respective locations

All the preceding information needs to be integrated and aligned with all BCM information and all the other information required by ITSCM. Interfaces to many other processes are required to ensure that this alignment is maintained.

IT Service Continuity Management Critical Success Factors and KPIs

The following list includes some sample critical success factors for ITSCM.

- Critical success factor: "IT services are delivered and can be recovered to meet business objectives."
  - KPI: Increase in success of regular audits of the ITSCM plans to ensure that, at all times, the agreed recovery requirements of the business can be achieved
  - KPI: Regular and comprehensive testing of ITSCM plans achieved consistently
  - KPI: Regular reviews, at least annual, of the business and IT continuity plans with the business areas
  - KPI: Overall reduction in the risk and impact of possible failure of IT services
- Critical success factor: "Awareness throughout the organization of the business and IT service continuity plans."
  - KPI: Increase in validated awareness of business impact, needs, and requirements throughout IT
  - KPI: Increase in successful test results, ensuring that all IT service areas and staff are prepared and able to respond to an invocation of the ITSCM plans

IT Service Continuity Management Challenges and Risks

We'll begin with looking at the key challenges for the process and then look at the risks.

Challenges

A major challenge facing ITSCM is to provide appropriate plans when there is no BCM process. If there is no BCM process, then IT is likely to adopt the wrong continuity strategies and options and make incorrect assumptions about business criticality of business processes. Also, if BCM is absent, then the business may fail to identify inexpensive non-IT solutions and waste money on ineffective, expensive IT solutions.

In some organizations, the perception is that continuity is an IT responsibility, and the business assumes that IT will be responsible for disaster recovery and that IT services will continue to run under any circumstances.

The challenge, if there is a BCM process established, becomes one of alignment and integration. Following that, the challenge becomes one of keeping the ITSCM process and BCM process aligned by management and by controlling business and IT change. All documents and plans should be maintained under the strict control of change management and service asset and configuration management.

Risks

The major risks are among those associated with ITSCM:

- Lack of a business continuity management process
- Lack of commitment from the business to the ITSCM processes and procedures
- Lack of appropriate information on future business plans and strategies

- Lack of senior management commitment to or lack of resources and/or budget for the ITSCM process

- The risk that the processes focus too much on the technology issues and not enough on the IT services and the needs and priorities of the business

- The risk that the process is unlikely to succeed in its objectives if risk assessment and management are conducted in isolation and not in conjunction with availability management and information security management

- ITSCM plans and information becoming out of date and losing alignment with the information and plans of the business and BCM

Summary

This chapter explored the next two processes in the service design stage, capacity management and IT service continuity management. It covered the purpose and objectives for each process in addition to the scope.

We looked at the value of the processes. Then we reviewed the policies for each process and the activities, methods, and techniques.

Last, we reviewed triggers, inputs, outputs, and interfaces for each process and the information management associated with it. We also considered the critical success factors and key performance indicators and the challenges and risks for the processes.

We examined how each of these processes supports the other and the importance of these processes to the business and the IT service provider.

Exam Essentials

Understand the purpose and objectives of capacity management and IT service continuity management. It is important for you to be able to explain the purpose and objectives of the capacity management and IT service continuity management processes.

Capacity management is concerned with the current and future capacity of services to the business.

IT service continuity management should ensure that the required business continuity plan is delivered to meet the business needs.

Understand the iterative activities of capacity management. Capacity management has both proactive and reactive activities. These include monitoring, tuning, and analysis, which may be carried out as part of a proactive or reactive approach.

Understand the subprocesses of capacity management. Business capacity management is concerned with the business requirements and understanding business needs.

Service capacity management is concerned with the capacity of services to fulfil the needs of the business.

Component capacity management is concerned with the technical aspect of capacity management and the capacity of individual service components.

Explain and differentiate between the different stages of IT service continuity management.   Initiation is the start of the process and the trigger received from business continuity management.

Requirements and strategy are where a clear understanding of the business requirements and strategy are developed.

Implementation is where the decisions in the strategy are realized.

Ongoing operation is where the continuity plans are managed as part of the ongoing operation of the services.

Understand the critical success factors and key performance indicators for the processes.   Measurement of the processes is an important part of understanding their success. You should be familiar with the CSFs and KPIs for both capacity management and IT service continuity management.

Review Questions

You can find the answers to the review questions in the appendix.

1. Which of the following are responsibilities of capacity management?
   1. Negotiating capacity requirements to be included in the SLA
   2. Monitoring capacity
   3. Forecasting capacity requirements
   4. Dealing with capacity issues
      A. 2, 3, and 4
      B. 1 and 2 only
      C. All of the above
      D. 1, 2, and 4

2. Capacity management includes three subprocesses. What are they?
   A. Service capacity, business capacity, component capacity
   B. System capacity, business capacity, component capacity
   C. Service capacity, business capacity, configuration capacity
   D. System capacity, business capacity, infrastructure capacity

3. Which of the following are responsibilities of IT service continuity management?
   1. Ensuring that IT services can continue in the event of a disaster
   2. Carrying out risk assessments
   3. Ensuring that the business has contingency plans in place in case of a disaster
   4. Ensuring all IT staff know their role in the event of a disaster
      A. 2, 3, and 4
      B. 1, 2, and 4
      C. 1 and 2 only
      D. All of the above

4. IT service continuity management carries out a BIA in conjunction with the business. What does BIA stand for?
   A. Business integrity appraisal
   B. Business information alternatives
   C. Benefit integration assessment
   D. Business impact analysis

5. Which of the following statements about IT service continuity management (ITSCM) is TRUE?
   A. ITSCM defines the service that can be provided in the event of a major disruption. The business can then plan how it will use the service.
   B. ITSCM and business continuity management (BCM) have no impact on each other.

    C. BCM defines the level of IT service that will be required in the event of a major disruption. ITSCM is responsible for delivering this level of service.

    D. It is the responsibility of ITSCM to deliver a single continuity plan that will fit all situations.

6. Match each subprocess (a, b, and c) to its definition (1, 2, and 3).

    a. Business capacity management

    b. Service capacity management

    c. Component capacity management

    1. View of the future plans and requirements of the organization

    2. View of the detailed information relating to the performance management of technical assets

    3. View of the service performance achieved in the operational environment

7. True or False? Capacity management has both reactive and proactive activities.

    A. True

    B. False

8. Which of these are KPIs relating to IT service continuity management?

    1. KPI: Regular and comprehensive testing of ITSCM plans achieved consistently

    2. KPI: Regular reviews undertaken, at least annually, of the business and IT continuity plans with the business areas

    3. KPI: Overall reduction in the risk and impact of possible failure of IT services

    4. KPI: Number of incidents that result in a major incident

        A. 1, 3, 4

        B. 2, 3, 4

        C. 1, 2, 3

        D. 1, 2, 4

9. Which of these statements is/are correct?

    1. Risk management is a vital part of both capacity and service continuity management.

    2. Both capacity management and service continuity management are cyclic processes.

        A. Statement 1 only

        B. Statement 2 only

        C. Both statements

        D. Neither statement

10. In which stages of the IT service continuity lifecycle does testing take place?

    A. Initiation and ongoing operation

    B. Initiation and implementation

    C. Implementation and ongoing operation

    D. Requirements and strategy and ongoing operation

Chapter

15

Service Design Processes: Information Security Management and Supplier Management

---

THE FOLLOWING ITIL INTERMEDIATE EXAM OBJECTIVES ARE DISCUSSED IN THIS CHAPTER:

✓ Information security management and supplier management are discussed in terms of

- Purpose
- Objectives
- Scope
- Value
- Policies
- Principles and basic concepts
- Process activities, methods, and techniques
- Triggers, inputs, outputs, and interfaces
- Information management
- Critical success factors and key performance indicators
- Challenges
- Risks

The ITIL service design publication covers the managerial and supervisory aspects of service design processes. It excludes the day-to-day operation of each process and the details of the process activities, methods, and techniques as well as its information management. More detailed process operation guidance is covered in the service capability courses. Each process is considered from the management perspective. That means at the end of this chapter, you should understand those aspects that would be required to understand each process and its interfaces, oversee its implementation, and judge its effectiveness and efficiency.

Information Security Management

Another of the key warranty aspects of a service is security, and it is this aspect that we will discuss in this part of the chapter. A service that is insecure will not deliver value to the customer and indeed may not be used by the customer at all.

ITIL defines information security as "the management process within the corporate governance framework, which provides the strategic direction for security activities and ensures objectives are achieved."

Central to *information security management (ISM)* is the identification and mitigation of risks to the security of the organization's information. The ISM process ensures that all security aspects are considered and managed throughout the service lifecycle.

Information includes data stores, databases, and metadata (*metadata* is the term applied to a set of data that describes and provides information about other data).

Organizations operate under an overall corporate governance framework, and information security management forms part of this framework. In accordance with organizational-wide governance, ISM provides guidance as to what is required, ensuring that risks are managed and the objectives of the organization are achieved.

Purpose of Information Security Management

The purpose of the information security management process is to align IT security with business security. IT and business security requires that the confidentiality, integrity, and availability of the organization's assets, information, data, and IT services always match the agreed needs of the business.

Objectives of Information Security Management

The objective of information security management is to protect the interests of those relying on information. It should also ensure that the systems and communications that deliver the information are protected from harm resulting from failures of confidentiality, integrity, and availability.

For most organizations, the security objective is met when the following terms are fulfilled:

- Confidentiality, where information is observed by or disclosed to only those who have a right to know

- Integrity, where information is complete, accurate, and protected against unauthorized modification

- Availability, where information is available and usable when required and the systems that provide it can appropriately resist attacks and recover from or prevent failures

- Business transactions, as well as information exchanges between enterprises or with partners, can be trusted. This is referred to as authenticity and, where there is control of the denial of access, nonrepudiation.

Scope of Information Security Management

The scope of ISM includes all aspects of information security that are important to the business. It is the responsibility of the business to define what requires protection and how strong this protection should be. Risks to security must be recognized, and appropriate countermeasures should be implemented. These may include physical aspects (restricting access to secure areas through swipe cards) as well as technical aspects (password policies, use of biometrics, and so on). Information security is an integral part of corporate governance.

The information security management process should be the focal point for all IT security issues. A key responsibility of the process is the production of an information security policy that is maintained and enforced and covers the use and misuse of all IT systems and services.

Information security management needs to understand the total IT and business security environment. Important aspects that must be included in the policy are the business security policy and plans along with the current business operation and its security requirements. Consideration must also be given to future business plans and requirements. External factors should also be included in the policy, such as legislative and regulatory requirements.

IT's obligations and responsibilities with regard to security should be contained within the service level agreements with their customers. The policy should also include reference to the business and IT risks and their management.

The information security management process should include the production, maintenance, distribution, and enforcement of an information security policy and supporting security policies. This will include understanding the agreed current and future security requirements of the business and the existing business security policy and plans.

The process will be responsible for implementation of a set of security controls that support the information security policy. This will support the management of risks associated with access to services, information, and systems. Information security management is responsible for the documentation of all security controls together with the operation and maintenance of the controls and their associated risks.

In association with supplier management, the process will also address the management of suppliers and contracts regarding access to systems and services.

Operationally, information security management will be involved in the management of all security breaches, incidents, and problems associated with all systems and services. It will also be responsible for the proactive improvement of security controls and security risk management and the reduction of security risks.

Information security management is also responsible for the integration of security aspects within all other IT service management processes. In order to achieve effective information security governance, the process must establish and maintain an information security management system (ISMS).

Information Security Management Value to the Business

Security has become a critical issue for organizations as their reliance on IT systems increases and more electronic media is used for confidential transactions within and between organizations.

Information security management ensures that an information security policy that fulfils the needs of the business security policy and the requirements of corporate governance is maintained and enforced. The information security policy provides assurance of business processes by enforcing appropriate security controls in all areas of IT. The process is responsible for the management of IT risk in line with business and corporate risk management processes and guidelines.

Information Security Management Policies

Information security management activities should be focused on and driven by an overall information security policy and a set of underpinning specific security policies.

The information security policy should have the full support of the top executive IT management. Ideally, the top executive business management should also be in support of and committed to the security policy. The policy should cover all areas of security, be appropriate, and meet the needs of the business.

Email usage policies, antivirus policies, and remote access policies are examples of specific security policies.

The information security process is responsible for creating, managing, and maintaining an information security management system. The elements of the management system are shown in Figure 15.1. It begins with the identification of the customer requirements and business needs.

FIGURE 15.1   Elements of an ISMS for managing IT security

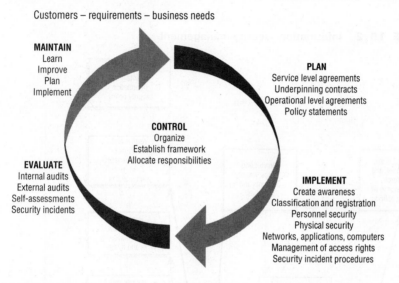

Customers – requirements – business needs

MAINTAIN
Learn
Improve
Plan
Implement

PLAN
Service level agreements
Underpinning contracts
Operational level agreements
Policy statements

CONTROL
Organize
Establish framework
Allocate responsibilities

EVALUATE
Internal audits
External audits
Self-assessments
Security incidents

IMPLEMENT
Create awareness
Classification and registration
Personnel security
Physical security
Networks, applications, computers
Management of access rights
Security incident procedures

Planning the system incorporates use of the details and targets captured in the various agreements and contracts. It also covers use of the various policies agreed between the business and IT.

Implementation of the system requires awareness of the policies and the systems by all who are affected by them. This will need the engagement of all parts of the organization because the policies will cover everything from personnel security to the procedures for security incidents.

The next stage is evaluation, which requires internal and external audits of the state of system security, but there may also be self-assessments. Security incidents will also be evaluated as part of this stage of the management of the system.

Maintaining the system requires that the information security process captures the lessons learned so that improvements can be planned and implemented.

The overall approach is designed to maintain control and establish a framework for managing security throughout the organization. Part of this will be to allocate appropriate responsibilities for ensuring that the information security management system is maintained, within both the IT department and the rest of the organization.

IT Security Management Process Activities, Methods, and Techniques

We are not going to explore the process in detail, but you should make sure you are familiar with all the aspects of the process and the management requirements for each.

In Figure 15.2, you can see the full scope of the information security management process and its techniques and activities.

FIGURE 15.2 Information security management

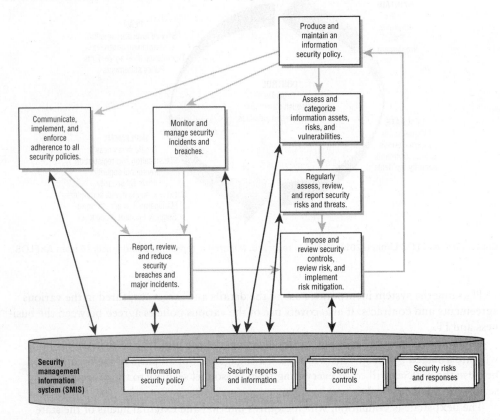

The information security management process ensures that the security aspects are appropriately managed and controlled in line with business needs and risks.

A key activity within the information security management process is the production and maintenance of an overall information security policy and a set of supporting specific policies. The process is also responsible for the communication, implementation, and enforcement of the security policies, including the provision of advice and guidance to all other areas of the business and IT on all issues related to information security.

Information security management is responsible for the assessment and classification of all information assets and documentation. The process covers the implementation, review, revision, and improvement of a set of security controls as well as risk assessment and responses, including assessment of the impact of all changes on information security policies, controls, and measures. Where possible, if it is in the business interest and the cost is justifiable, the process should implement proactive measures to improve information security.

Monitoring and management of all security breaches and major security incidents is a key part of the information security management process. This includes the analysis, reporting, and reduction of the volume and impact of security breaches and incidents.

The process is also responsible for scheduling and completing security reviews, audits, and penetration tests. The outputs from the process will be captured and recorded in the security management information system.

Information Security Management Triggers, Inputs, and Outputs

Let's consider the triggers, inputs, and outputs for the information security management process. Information security management is a process that has many active connections throughout the organization and its processes. It is important that the triggers, inputs, outputs, and interfaces be clearly defined to avoid duplicated effort or gaps in workflow.

Triggers

Information security management activity can be triggered by many events, including these:

- New or changed corporate governance guidelines
- New or changed business security policy
- New or changed corporate risk management processes and guidelines
- New or changed business needs and new or changed services
- New or changed requirements within agreements, such as service level requirements, service level agreements, operational level agreements, and contracts
- Review and revision of business and IT plans and strategies
- Review and revision of designs and strategies
- Service or component security breaches or warnings, events, and alerts, including threshold events and exception reports
- Periodic activities such as reviewing, revising, and reporting, including reviewing and revising information security management policies, reports, and plans

- Recognition or notification of a change of risk or impact of a business process or vital business functions, an IT service, or a component
- Requests from other areas, particularly service level management, for assistance with security issues

Inputs

Information security management will need to obtain input from many areas:

- Business information from the organization's business strategy, plans and financial plans, and information on its current and future requirements
- Governance and security from corporate governance and business security policies and guidelines, security plans, and risk assessment and responses
- IT information from the IT strategy, plans, and current budgets
- Service information from the SLM process with details of the services from the service portfolio
- Risk assessment processes and reports from ISM, availability management, and ITSCM
- Details of all security events and breaches—from all areas of IT and IT service management, especially incident management and problem management
- Change information from the change management process
- The configuration management system containing information on the relationships between the business, the services, supporting services, and the technology
- Details of partner and supplier external access to services and systems from supplier management and availability management

Outputs

The following outputs are produced by the information security management process and used in all areas:

- An overall information security management policy, together with a set of specific security policies
- A security management information system (SMIS) containing all the information related to information security management
- Revised security risk assessment processes and reports
- A set of security controls with details of their operation and maintenance and their associated risks
- Security audits and audit reports
- Security test schedules and plans, including security penetration tests and other security tests and reports
- A set of security classifications and a set of classified information assets
- Reviews and reports of security breaches and major incidents

- Policies, processes, and procedures for managing partners and suppliers and their access to services and information

Information Security Management Interfaces

The key interfaces that information security management has with other processes are as follows:

- Service level management
- Access management
- Change management
- Incident and problem management
- IT service continuity management
- Service asset and configuration management
- Availability management
- Capacity management
- Financial management for IT services
- Supplier management
- Legal and human resources issues

Measures, Metrics, and Critical Success Factors for Information Security Management

The following list includes some sample critical success factors for information security management.

- Critical success factor: "Business is protected against security violations."
  - KPI: Decrease (measured as a percentage) in security breaches reported to the service desk
  - KPI: Decrease (measured as a percentage) in the impact of security breaches and incidents
- Critical success factor: "The determination of a clear and agreed policy, integrated with the needs of the business."
  - KPI: Decrease in the number of nonconformances of the information security management process with the business security policy and process
- Critical success factor: "Effective marketing and education in security requirements, and IT staff awareness of the technology supporting the services."
  - KPI: Increased awareness throughout the organization of the security policy and its contents

- KPI: Increase (measured as a percentage) in completeness of supporting services against the IT components that make up those services
- Critical success factor: "Clear ownership and awareness of the security policies among the customer community."
  - KPI: Increase (measured as a percentage) in acceptable scores on security awareness questionnaires completed by customers and users

Challenges for Information Security Management

One of the biggest challenges is to ensure that there is adequate support from the business, business security, and senior management. It is pointless to implement security policies, procedures, and controls in IT if they cannot be enforced throughout the business. The major use of IT services and assets is outside of IT, and so are the majority of security threats and risks.

If there is a business security process established, then the challenge becomes alignment and integration. Once there is alignment, the challenge becomes keeping them aligned by management and control of changes to business methods and IT systems using strict change management and service asset and configuration management control. Again, this requires support and commitment from the business and from senior management.

Risks for Information Security Management

Information systems can generate many direct and indirect benefits—and as many direct and indirect risks. This means that there are new risk areas that could have a significant impact on critical business operations:

- Increasing requirements for availability and robustness
- Growing potential for misuse and abuse of information systems affecting privacy and ethical values
- External dangers from hackers, leading to denial of service and virus attacks, extortion, industrial espionage, and leakage of organizational information or private data
- A lack of commitment from the business
- A lack of senior management commitment
- The processes focusing too much on the technology issues and not enough on the IT services and the needs and priorities of the business
- Conducting risk assessment and management in isolation and not in conjunction with availability management and ITSCM
- Information security management policies, plans, risks, and information becoming out of date and losing alignment with the corresponding relevant information and plans of the business and business security

- Security policies becoming bureaucratic and/or excessively difficult to follow, discouraging compliance
- Security policies adding no value to business

Supplier Management

ITIL defines *supplier management* as the process responsible for obtaining value for money from suppliers, ensuring that all contracts and agreements with suppliers support the needs of the business and that all suppliers meet their contractual commitments.

The supplier management process describes best practices in managing suppliers to ensure that the services they provide meet expectations. It is included in the design phase of the service lifecycle because it is important that this aspect is considered while the service is being designed. The type of supplier relationship will be part of the strategy phase, and a close relationship with suppliers will be required for a successful service transition. Once the service is operational, the day-to-day delivery against the contract must be monitored and managed, and should there be any issues, the improvement plan will be the responsibility of continual service improvement.

Purpose of Supplier Management

The purpose of supplier management is to ensure that suppliers provide value for money. By managing suppliers, the service provider can ensure the best delivery of service to its customer. Managing suppliers ensures that the necessary contracts are in place and enforced.

Objectives of Supplier Management

The main objectives of the supplier management process are to obtain value for money from suppliers and contracts and ensure that contracts with suppliers are aligned to business needs. These contracts should support and align with agreed targets in service level requirements and service level agreements in conjunction with service level management.

Scope of Supplier Management

The supplier management process should include the management of all suppliers and contracts needed to support the provision of IT services to the business. Each service provider should have formal processes for the management of all suppliers and contracts.

The supplier management process should include implementation and enforcement of the supplier policy, including maintenance of a supplier and contract management information system (SCMIS). It is important to ensure that suppliers and contracts are categorized and a risk assessment is carried out. Suppliers and contracts need to be evaluated and selected so that the appropriate suppliers are engaged.

A key part of the process is developing, negotiating, and agreeing of contracts, including contract review, renewal, and termination. This is part of the management of suppliers and supplier performance.

The process will also identify improvement opportunities for inclusion in the CSI register and the implementation of service and supplier improvement plans.

Supplier management will also manage the maintenance of standard contracts, terms and conditions, contractual dispute resolution, and, where applicable, the engagement of subcontracted suppliers.

IT supplier management often has to comply with organizational or corporate standards, guidelines, and requirements, particularly those of corporate legal, finance, and purchasing.

Supplier Management Value to the Business

The process will manage relationships with suppliers and monitor and manage supplier performance. Supplier management is responsible for the negotiation and agreement of contracts with suppliers and managing them through their lifecycle. This is assisted by the development and maintenance of a supplier policy and a supporting supplier and contract management information system (SCMIS).

This is to ensure the delivery to the business of end-to-end, seamless, quality IT services that are aligned to the business's expectations. The supplier management process should align with all corporate requirements and the requirements of all other IT and service management processes, particularly information security management and IT service continuity management. This ensures that the business obtains value from supporting supplier services and that they are aligned with business needs.

Supplier Management Principles, Policies, and Basic Concepts

The supplier management process attempts to ensure that suppliers meet the terms, conditions, and targets of their contracts while trying to increase the value for money obtained from suppliers and the services they provide.

All supplier management process activity should be driven by a supplier strategy and policy from service strategy. The supplier strategy, sometimes called the sourcing strategy, defines the service provider's plan for how it will leverage the contribution of suppliers in the achievement of the overall service strategy. Some organizations might adopt a strategy that dictates the use of suppliers only in very specific and limited circumstances, while other organizations might choose to make extensive use of suppliers in IT service provision. In Figure 15.3, you can see the engagement of the process with the contracts manager and the various supplier managers in the organization.

FIGURE 15.3   Supplier management roles and interfaces

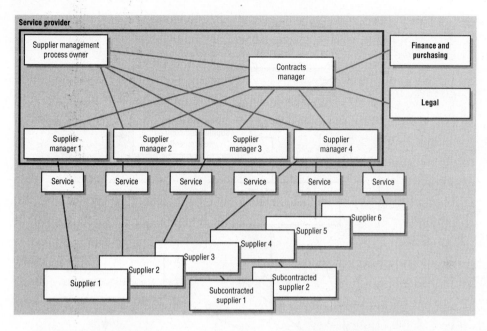

You can also see the interaction with finance and purchasing and the legal department, all of which are important when engaging with third parties outside of the main organization.

You can see the management of the services provided by or supported by the suppliers and their subcontracted partners.

Supplier Management Process, Methods, and Techniques

The process should be subject to the corporate supplier management policy, but an IT supplier strategy should be developed to manage the specific requirements for IT service delivery. Figure 15.4 shows the main activities of the supplier management process.

Once the requirements for suppliers have been defined as part of the overall approach to the delivery of a service, the supplier management process needs to evaluate the appropriate suppliers and ensure that the contracts are fit for purpose and use. It is important to establish relationships with new suppliers and ensure that there are the appropriate measures and management in place to monitor supplier performance. All contracts should have references to renewal and termination, which should be included in regular reviews of the contract.

FIGURE 15.4 Supplier management process

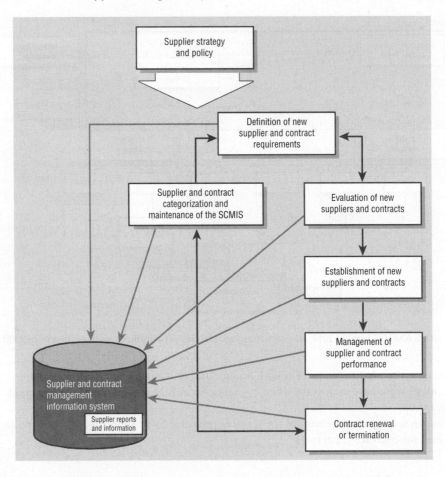

All information, reports, and measures should be stored in the supplier and contract management information system (SCMIS).

It is important for the supplier management process to understand the importance of the suppliers to the organization. This requires that the suppliers are categorized according to their value and importance and according to the risk of the supplier not performing as contracted and the impact to the organization if that happens. There are four layers of categorization:

Strategic For significant "partnering" relationships that involve senior managers sharing confidential strategic information to facilitate long-term plans. These relationships would normally be managed and owned at a senior management level within the service provider organization and would involve regular and frequent contact and performance reviews.

Tactical   For relationships involving significant commercial activity and business interaction. These relationships would normally be managed by middle management and would involve regular contact and performance reviews, often including an ongoing improvement program.

Operational   For suppliers of operational products or services. These relationships would normally be managed by junior operational management and would involve infrequent but regular contact and performance reviews.

Commodity   For suppliers providing low-value and/or readily available products and services, which could be alternatively sourced relatively easily.

Supplier Management Triggers, Inputs, and Outputs

We will now review the triggers, inputs, and outputs of supplier management.

Triggers

There are many events that could trigger supplier management activity:

- New or changed corporate governance guidelines
- New or changed business and IT strategies, policies, and plans
- New or changed business needs and new or changed services
- New or changed requirements within agreements, such as service level requirements, service level agreements, operational level agreements, and contracts
- Review and revision of designs and strategies
- Periodic activities such as reviewing, revising, and reporting, including review and revision of supplier management policies, reports, and plans
- Requests from other areas, particularly SLM and information security management, for assistance with supplier issues
- Requirements for new contracts, contract renewal, or contract termination
- Recategorization of suppliers and/or contracts

Inputs

There are numerous inputs to the supplier management process:

- Business information
- Supplier and contracts strategy
- Supplier plans and strategies
- Supplier contracts, agreements, and targets
- Supplier and contract performance information
- IT information
- Performance issues

- Financial information
- Service information
- CMS

Outputs

The outputs of supplier management are used within all other parts of the process, by many other processes, and by other parts of the organization.

The information provided by supplier management is as follows:

- SCMIS
- Supplier and contract performance information and reports
- Supplier and contract review meeting minutes
- Supplier SIPs
- Supplier survey reports

Supplier Management Interfaces

The following list includes the key interfaces that supplier management has with other processes:

Service Level Management   Supplier management provides assistance with determining targets, requirements, and responsibilities for suppliers. SLM assists supplier management in the investigation of SLA and SLR breaches caused by poor supplier performance. SLM also provides invaluable input into the supplier management review process.

Change Management   Contractual documents should be managed through change control.

Information Security Management   Information security management relies on supplier management for the management of suppliers and their access to services and systems as well as their responsibilities with regard to conformance to the service provider's ISM policies and requirements.

Financial Management for IT Services   This process provides adequate funds to finance supplier management requirements and contracts and provides financial advice and guidance on purchase and procurement matters.

Service Portfolio Management   This process looks to supplier management input to ensure that all supporting services and their details and relationships are accurately reflected within the service portfolio.

IT Service Continuity Management   This process works with supplier management with regard to the management of continuity service suppliers.

Information Management

The information required by supplier management should be stored in the supplier and contract management information system (SCMIS).

All information relating to suppliers and contracts as well as all information relating to the operation of the supporting services provided by suppliers should be held in the system. Information relating to these supporting services should also be contained within the service portfolio, together with information on their relationships to all other services and components. This information should be integrated and maintained in alignment with all other IT management information systems, particularly the service portfolio and the CMS.

Supplier Management Critical Success Factors and KPIs

The following list includes some sample critical success factors for supplier management.

- Critical success factor: "Business protected from poor supplier performance or disruption."
    - KPI: Increase in the number of suppliers meeting the targets within the contract
    - KPI: Reduction in the number of breaches of contractual targets
- Critical success factor: "Supporting services and their targets align with business needs and targets."
    - KPI: Increase in the number of service and contractual reviews held with suppliers
    - KPI: Increase in the number of supplier and contractual targets aligned with SLA and SLR targets
- Critical success factor: "Availability of services is not compromised by supplier performance."
    - KPI: Reduction in the number of service breaches caused by suppliers
    - KPI: Reduction in the number of threatened service breaches caused by suppliers

Supplier Management Challenges and Risks

We'll begin by looking at the key challenges for the process.

Challenges

Supplier management faces many challenges, which could include the following examples:

- Continually changing business and IT needs and managing significant changes in parallel with delivering existing services
- Working with an imposed contract that's not ideal, a contract that has poor targets or terms and conditions, or a contract with a poor or nonexistent definition of service or supplier performance targets, including those that have punitive penalty charges for early exit
- Legacy issues, especially with services recently outsourced
- Insufficient expertise retained within the organization
- Disputes over charges
- Interference by either party in the running of the other's operation
- Being caught in a daily firefighting mode, losing the proactive approach

- Poor communication, such as not interacting often enough or quickly enough or not focusing on the right issues, including personality conflicts and/or cultural conflicts

- One party using the contract to the detriment of the other party, resulting in win-lose changes rather than joint win-win changes

- Losing the strategic perspective, focusing solely on operational issues

Risks

The major areas of risk associated with supplier management are as follows:

- Lack of commitment from the business and senior management to the supplier management process and procedures

- Lack of appropriate information on future business and IT policies, plans, and strategies

- Lack of resources and/or budget for the supplier management process

- Legacy of badly written and agreed contracts that do not underpin or support business needs or SLA and SLR targets

- Supplier personnel or organizational culture that's not aligned to that of the service provider or the business

- Lack of clarity and integration by supplier with service management processes, policies, and procedures of the service provider

- Poor corporate financial processes, such as procurement and purchasing, that do not support good supplier management

Summary

This chapter explored the next two processes in the service design stage, information security management and supplier management. It covered the purpose and objectives for the processes and their scope.

We looked at the value of the processes. Then we reviewed the policies for each process and the activities, methods, and techniques.

Last, we reviewed triggers, inputs, outputs, and interfaces for each process and the information management associated with it. We also considered the critical success factors and key performance indicators, challenges, and risks for the processes.

We examined how each of these processes supports the other and the importance of these processes to the business and the IT service provider.

Exam Essentials

Understand the purpose and objectives of information security management and supplier management. It is important for you to be able to explain the purpose and objectives of the information security management and supplier management processes.

Information security management is concerned with the protection of information and data according to the security requirements of the business.

Supplier management should ensure that value for money is obtained from all contractual relationships with external organizations.

Understand the approach to security management.   Plan, implement, evaluate, maintain, and control—ensure that you can explain how each of these stages supports the approach to the management of information security.

Understand the process of information security management.   Ensure that you are able to explain the various steps of the process and their relationship to the information security management system.

Explain and differentiate between the different stages of supplier management.   Understand the importance of contract negotiation and the implementation of the supplier policy.

Understand the critical success factors and key performance indicators for the processes.   Measurement of the processes is an important part of understanding their success. You should be familiar with the CSFs and KPIs for both information security management and supplier management.

Review Questions

You can find the answers to the review questions in the appendix.

1. Which of the following are responsibilities of information security management?
   1. Defining the protection required for systems and data
   2. Undertaking risk assessments
   3. Producing the information security policy
   4. Implementing security measures to new systems during service transition
      A. 1 and 2 only
      B. All of the above
      C. 1, 2, and 3
      D. 2, 3, and 4

2. Where does information security management keep information about security?
   A. SMIS
   B. IMSS
   C. KEDB
   D. ISDB

3. Which of the following are responsibilities of supplier management?
   1. Negotiating with internal suppliers
   2. Negotiating with external suppliers
   3. Monitoring delivery against the contract
   4. Ensuring value for money
      A. 1 and 2 only
      B. All of the above
      C. 1, 2, and 3
      D. 2, 3, and 4

4. Which of the following are categories of suppliers described in ITIL?
   1. Strategic
   2. Operational
   3. Trusted
   4. Commodity
      A. 1 and 2 only
      B. All of the above
      C. 1, 2, and 4
      D. 2, 3, and 4

5. Which of these is the key purpose of the information security management process?

    A. Create and maintain an information security policy

    B. Deliver guidance to the operational processes on security issues

    C. Support supplier management in maintaining security concerns in contracts

    D. Manage the information security management information system

6. To demonstrate their priority, suppliers are categorized according to which factors?

    A. Risk and importance / value and impact

    B. Cost and importance / risk and value

    C. Risk and impact / value and importance

    D. Value and cost / risk and probability

7. Which of these statements is/are correct?

    1. Plan is a key part of the approach to information security management.

    2. Maintain is a key part of the approach to information security management.

        A. Statement 1 only

        B. Statement 2 only

        C. Both statements

        D. Neither statement

8. True or False? Supplier management has a significant relationship with service level management.

    A. True

    B. False

9. Which of these statements is incorrect about supplier management?

    A. Third-party contracts should contain information about operational level agreements with customers.

    B. Contracts with external third parties should contain information about renewal.

    C. Contracts with external third parties should contain information about penalties and financial benefits.

    D. Third-party contracts should contain information about security requirements for delivery of services.

10. Which of these statements is/are correct?

    1. Information about supplier policies is held in the SCMIS.

    2. Supplier contracts are held in the SCMIS.

        A. Statement 1 only

        B. Statement 2 only

        C. Both statements

        D. Neither statement

Chapter

16

Technology-Related Activities

THE FOLLOWING ITIL INTERMEDIATE EXAM OBJECTIVES ARE DISCUSSED IN THIS CHAPTER:

✓ The service design activities and techniques within requirements engineering

✓ The service design activities and techniques within data and information management

✓ The service design activities and techniques associated with application management

Technology-Related
Activities

This chapter covers the management of technology-related activities commonly performed in the service design stage.

It covers requirements engineering in relation to the activities/techniques associated with data and information management as well as application management. To meet the learning outcomes and examination level of difficulty, you must ensure that you are able to understand, describe, identify, demonstrate, apply, distinguish, produce, decide, and analyze the service design activities and techniques within requirements engineering, within data and information management, and associated with application management.

Service Design Activities and Techniques within Requirements Engineering

Requirements engineering is the name given to the approach by which we ascertain, understand, and document the requirements of the business, users, and other stakeholders. This enables service design to understand what is required and ensures the traceability of changes to each requirement.

This process is made up of three stages. The first is elicitation, when we try and get the business to describe its requirements. The second stage is analysis, when we seek to understand those requirements. This stage may feed back into the elicitation stage as we seek further clarification. The final stage is validation. The aim of these three stages is to be able to produce a rigorous, complete requirements document.

The core of this document is a repository of individual requirements. Some of these requirements are technical and originate from IT to ensure that the new service fits the current architecture. All requirements need to be agreed with the business. This chapter focuses on the requirements for the technology related to a service. There are many other areas where requirements will need to be defined, but we are not considering them here. They could include user and support staff training, marketing and communication related to the service and its deployment, documentation requirements, and organizational and cultural readiness. It is the responsibility of design coordination to set the standards and methods for defining requirements and ensure that they are followed during the service design stage. The design coordination process was covered in Chapter 12, "Service Design Processes: Design Coordination and Service Catalog Management."

Types of Requirement

By analyzing current and required business processes, we can ascertain the functional requirements that are to be met through IT services (comprising applications, data, infrastructure, environment, and support skills). There are commonly said to be three major types of requirements for any system. These are functional, management and operational, and usability requirements. Let's examine the ITIL definitions for them:

- Functional requirements. ITIL defines these as the requirements that directly support a particular business function or business process or remove a customer or user constraint. These requirements describe the utility aspects of a service.

- Management and operational requirements. These are sometimes referred to as non-functional requirements. ITIL defines these as the requirements that address the need for an available and secure service and deal with such issues as operability, management needs, and security. These requirements describe the warranty aspects of a service.

- Usability requirements. ITIL says these requirements are concerned with how easy the service is to use and how easily a user may achieve their desired outcomes. They include the "look and feel" requirements and so can influence user perceptions of a service.

Functional Requirements

Functional requirements describe the things a service is intended to do—in other words, the utility it will provide. There are a number of different methods for documenting these requirements:

- A description of tasks or functions that the service must perform.

- A system context diagram that shows all information exchanges between the IT service and the sources or destinations of data used by the service.

- A use case model that shows the boundary of the system, the interaction with other services, and the scenarios that need to be supported. These scenarios can be expanded later into test cases.

- A data flow or object diagram that describes the different "objects" in the service, their mutual relationships, and their internal structure and shows how the inputs will be transformed into the outputs. Sometimes textual descriptions are used.

Management and Operational Requirements

Management and operational requirements (or nonfunctional requirements) define requirements and constraints. They are useful for sizing the service and estimating cost and so can help when assessing whether the proposed IT service is viable. They are useful in reminding developers to think beyond the purely functional requirements.

These requirements ensure that we consider how the service will perform. Requirements in the following areas need to be clarified:

- Manageability

- Efficiency

- Availability and reliability

- Capacity and performance
- Security
- Installation, automated or otherwise
- Service continuity, including the required levels of resilience and recovery targets
- Monitoring and management requirements
- Maintainability requirements covering how easily the application can be adjusted, corrected, maintained, and changed for future requirements
- Operability requirements to ensure that the application does not impact other applications
- Measurability and reportability requirements defining the measurements and reporting needed

As you know, ITIL says that a service only delivers value when both utility and warranty aspects are delivered to the level required by the business. The functional requirements define the utility, and the management and operational requirements ensure that the warranty of the application or service is sufficient. These aspects must be tested during transition to ensure that the live service will deliver value. At this stage, they can be used to design test plans for testing the applications.

Usability Requirements

These requirements define what users expect in terms of how easy it will be to use the service. This requires setting specific standards against which the service can be evaluated.

In order to establish usability requirements, care must be taken to establish the types of users likely to use the service and to understand their varied needs. For example, users who are color-blind would not find a service that relied heavily on color differentiation easy to use, or users working in a second language may have difficulty with screen terminology that does not translate well. Similarly, the creator of a website used by the public should recognize and take into consideration the literacy level of the general population.

Requirements Investigation Techniques

The following techniques can be used for requirements gathering:

- Interviews
- Workshops
- Observation
- Protocol analysis
- Shadowing
- Scenario analysis
- Prototyping
- Questionnaires
- Activity sampling

Interviews

The interview is a key tool used to gather requirements. It also helps to build a relationship with key stakeholders and facilitates the gathering of information about the business situation, including issues and problems.

There are three areas that are considered during interviews:

- Any requirements for current business processes that the new business system needs to address
- Current problems to be tackled
- New features required

The interviewing process will be most productive if it is thoroughly planned. This helps avoid unnecessary explanations. The classic questions of why, what, who, when, where, and how provide an excellent framework. Formally closing the interview by summarizing the points made and the actions agreed on is also important. Interviewing helps build a relationship with the users, and is an opportunity to gather information from all the stakeholders and may open up new areas for investigation.

Interviews can be time-consuming, and because they are carried out individually, they don't offer any opportunity for resolving disagreements between users and building a consensus.

Workshops

Another requirements-gathering technique is running workshops. They provide a forum for discussion, where requirements can be captured, conflicts resolved, and a consensus reached.

Facilitating workshops can be challenging; it is important to have the correct people attend and then to ensure that different views are heard. It is essential that no one view is allowed to dominate and that, wherever possible, progress is made toward a common view. Figure 16.1 shows some techniques that may be useful for conducting a workshop. The key points of discussion should be recorded, and they should be summarized at the end of the workshop. Any agreed actions should be assigned to an owner.

FIGURE 16.1   Requirements workshop techniques

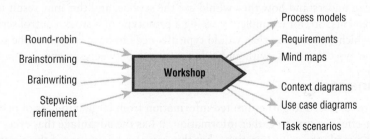

Observation

Observing people at work performing a specific task provides useful information about the business and its work practices. This enables a more complete understanding of business problems and difficulties, which helps when designing solutions because the solutions need to be acceptable to the business.

Conversely, being observed can be rather unnerving, and the old saying "you change when being observed" needs to be factored into your approach and findings.

Protocol Analysis

Protocol analysis is simply getting the users to perform a task and describe each step as they perform it. Users are encouraged to think aloud as they solve a problem or complete a task, and their description of what they are doing and why can then be analyzed.

Shadowing

Shadowing involves understanding how someone works by following them for a period of time, such as one day. This can be extremely helpful in understanding someone's role because the actual activities they carry out may not mirror their job description. Questions can be asked at the time, when the work is being carried out, to validate any assumptions.

Scenario Analysis

Scenario analysis traces a transaction from an initial business trigger through each of the steps needed to achieve a successful outcome. In doing so, alternative approaches may be discovered. This method can be time-consuming. It may be helpful to use graphical methods of documenting the scenario, such as storyboards and decision tree diagrams.

Prototyping

Prototyping is a technique for eliciting, analyzing, demonstrating, and validating requirements. Users may find it hard to envisage what the service will look like and how they might use it. Prototyping shows how a new service will work before it has actually been built. Users can understand how they would use the service, and this may result in additional requirements. So, for example, by seeing a prototype of a stock-control service, users may realize which information they would typically need to have shown on the screen to be able to answer typical queries, without having to switch between screens.

Questionnaires

Questionnaires are used to gather limited information from large numbers of people. This can be a cost-effective way to gather information. It has the advantage that every respondent answers exactly the same questions, but this can also be limiting if the questions do not cover particular areas.

Activity Sampling

Activity sampling can be used to understand how people spend their time. For example, it can be used to see how much time is spent on processing orders, or on invoicing or sorting out queries.

Problems with Requirements Engineering

Gathering requirements accurately is critical and should not be rushed, even if timescales and budgets are tight. Pressure on developers to deliver a service may mean that they start to design the solution before the requirements have been fully understood and defined; there is a risk that the business may not receive the service it wants. Research into IT project failures shows that over 80 percent of errors are introduced at the requirements phase. This is far more than design or development errors. Most project time is taken up with the development and testing phases, but with incomplete or inaccurate requirements, this time may be spent developing a service that will prove unsatisfactory. Such fundamental errors are expensive to fix.

Requirements must be unambiguously described with clear criteria for assessing whether they have been delivered. It is essential to include the nontechnical requirements and to resist requirements creep—the gradual addition of seemingly small requirements that together will have a significant impact on the cost and effort required from the project.

The following list includes some other problems that may be encountered when requirements are gathered:

- Lack of relevance to the objectives of the service
- Lack of clarity or ambiguity in the wording
- Duplication between requirements
- Conflicting requirements
- Requirements without clear delivery criteria
- Users' lack of certainty about what they need
- Inconsistent levels of detail
- Failure to include requirements from stakeholders such as service operations and support staff

Documenting Requirements

Requirements should be documented in two distinct phases: building the requirements list and, later, developing an organized requirements catalog.

- The requirements list is an informal document that includes the requirements, their source, comments, and level of detail. Each requirement in the list must be checked to see whether or not it is well formed and SMART (specific, measurable, achievable, relevant, and time-bound).
- The requirements catalog lists requirements, with each individual requirement documented using a standard template. Requirements are included only after careful

scrutiny to ensure that they are complete and clearly expressed. When completed, the retirements catalog should be signed off on by the business as a true statement of the requirements.

Management of Data and Information

Data is a critical asset type; it must be managed in order to develop, deliver, and support IT services effectively. Key factors for successful data management are as follows:

- Ensuring that all users can access the information they need to do their jobs
- Ensuring that the data is exploited as much as possible by sharing it with others while storing and protecting it from unauthorized access
- Maintaining data quality so that the information used by the business is accurate, reliable, and consistent
- Fulfilling legal requirements regarding privacy, security, confidentiality, and integrity of data
- Handling data effectively and efficiently
- Using an enterprise data model to define the most important entities and their relationships, thus reducing redundancies and ensuring that the data architecture remains effective despite changes over the years

If data is not managed effectively, resources will be wasted collecting and maintaining unnecessary data, or the data that is useful may not be available to those who need it. The quality of data may be improved by using a data management process that establishes policies and standards, provides expertise, and makes it easier to handle the data aspects of new services.

There are four areas of management included within the scope of data/information management.

Management of Data Resources   Management of data resources involves ensuring that all the data resources are known and assigning ownership of data and metadata. This includes responsibility for the following activities:

- Defining information needs
- Constructing a data inventory and an enterprise data model
- Identifying data duplication and deficiencies
- Maintaining a catalog/index of data/information content
- Measuring the cost and value of the organization's data

Management of Data/Information Technology   Management of data/information technology includes the management of the IT that underpins the organization's information systems. This includes processes such as database design and database administration, carried out by specialist staff.

Management of Information Processes   Management of information processes includes the activities of creating, collecting, accessing, modifying, storing, deleting, and archiving data—that is, the data lifecycle.

Management of Data Standards and Policies   Management of data standards and policies includes the following activities:

- Defining policies for procedures

- Defining responsibilities for data management in the organization

- Defining technical policies, architectures, and standards that will apply to the IT infrastructure supporting the organization's information systems

Data Management and the Service Lifecycle

A lifecycle will help in understanding the use of data in business processes. We need to know who will access the data and how and why this will be done. We need to maintain data quality and plan for its eventual disposal.

Classifying Data

Data can be initially classified as operational, tactical, or strategic:

- Operational data is necessary for an organization to function and can be regarded as the lowest, most specific level.

- Tactical data is usually needed by second-line management—or higher—and is typically concerned with summarized data and historical data, typically year-to-year data or quarterly data.

- Strategic data is often concerned with longer-term trends and comparison with the outside world. This involves bringing together the operational and tactical data from many different areas with relevant external data.

Data management requires setting standards for naming conventions, metadata, ownership, and format and the use of appropriate tools for data migration and capture.

Management of Applications

Now we'll consider service design activities and techniques associated with application management. Let's start with a definition for the term *application*.

An application is software that provides functions that are required by an IT service. An application can be part of more than one IT service. An application runs on one or more servers or clients.

Applications are one component of a service, along with the hardware, operating system, and so on. They must meet both the functional and nonfunctional requirements in order to work successfully.

Two alternative approaches are necessary to fully implement management of applications:

- Using the extended service development lifecycle (SDLC) is a systematic approach to problem solving, comprising a feasibility study, analysis, design, testing, implementation, evaluation, and maintenance.

- The other approach takes a global view of all services to ensure the ongoing maintainability and manageability of the applications:

  - Applications are described in an application portfolio maintained to enable alignment with changing business needs.

  - Consistency in development is enforced through using a limited number of application frameworks and adopting a "reuse first" philosophy.

  - Common software components are created or acquired at an organizational level and used by individual systems to support the development of a service.

The Application Portfolio

The portfolio provides a full record of all applications within the organization. The data for each application will include a number of attributes for each service. (As a reminder, an attribute is a piece of information about a CI or service.) Figure 16.2 shows examples of the attributes that may be recorded for specific applications.

FIGURE 16.2   Application portfolio attributes example

Application name	IT operations owner	New-development cost
Application identifier	IT development owner	Annual operational costs
Application description	Support contacts	Annual support cost
Business process supported	Database technologies	Annual maintenance costs
IT services supported	Dependent applications	Outsourced components
Executive sponsor	IT systems supported	Outsource partners
Geographies supported	User interfaces	Production metrics
Business criticality	IT architecture, including network topology	OLA link
SLA link	Application technologies used	Support metrics
Business owner	Number of users	

Linking Application and Service Portfolio

Some organizations choose to have a separate application portfolio with separate attributes, while others store the application portfolio within the configuration management system (CMS) together with the appropriate relationships. Other organizations combine the application portfolio with the service portfolio. There is no one correct approach; it is for each organization to decide the most appropriate strategy for its own needs.

Application Frameworks

An application framework can cover all management and operational aspects, providing solutions for all of an application's management and operational requirements. Implied in the use of application frameworks is the concept of standardization. The service, infrastructure, environment, and data architectures must all be closely integrated with the application architecture and framework. This means a separation between designing applications and designing application frameworks. Application developers should focus on a single application, while application framework developers should focus on more than one application and on the common features of those applications.

The Need for CASE Tools and Repositories

Specialist tools are available that support requirements-gathering processes. These are called computer-aided software engineering (CASE) tools. Application design may use CASE tools to specify requirements, draw design diagrams, or even generate complete applications or nearly complete application skeletons. These tools also provide a central location, generally called a repository, for storing and managing all the elements that are created during application development.

It is not always possible to foresee every aspect of a solution's design ahead of time. The key is to create a flexible design so that making a change does not send developers all the way back to the beginning of the design phase. Using application frameworks, design guidelines, and checklists will help avoid this. It is important to include the management and operational requirements within the service design package and service acceptance criteria as well as the functional requirements. Trade-offs may be required between resources, the project schedule, and features required for quality.

Outputs

Here you can see a list of examples of typical outputs from an application design:

- Input, output, and user interface designs
- A suitable data/object model and a process flow or workflow model
- Detailed specifications for update and read-only processes
- Mechanisms for achieving audit controls, security, confidentiality, and privacy
- A technology-specific physical design

- Test scripts
- Interfaces and dependencies on other applications

Design Patterns

A design pattern is a general, repeatable solution to a commonly occurring problem in software design. Design patterns describe both a problem and a solution for common issues encountered during application development.

An important design principle used as the basis for a large number of design patterns is that of separation of concerns (SoC). Separation of concerns will lead to applications divided into components. The advantage of such an application is that modification can be made to individual components with little or no impact on other components.

Developing Individual Applications

Once the design phase is completed, the application development team will take the designs that have been produced and move on to developing the application. Both the application and the related environment are made ready for deployment. Application components are coded or acquired and then integrated and tested.

To ensure that the application is developed with management at the core, the development team needs to focus on ensuring that the developing phase continues to correctly address the management and operational aspects of the design (e.g., responsiveness, availability, security). All service requirements should be found in the SDP.

Templates and Code Generation

Development tools may provide a variety of templates for creating common application components. Other development tools will generate large pieces of code (skeletons) based on the design models and coding conventions. Developers can then customize the templates to suit, rather than having to design the component from scratch. The more that standard components are designed into the solution, the faster applications can be developed. Although the cost of the development of the templates needs to be considered, reusing them in this way will lead to lower costs in the long term.

Diagnostic Hooks

Diagnostic hooks are of greatest value during testing and when an error has been discovered in the production service. They mainly provide the information necessary to solve problems and application errors rapidly and restore service. They can also be used to provide measurement and management information of applications. There are four main categories:

- System-level information provided by the operating systems and hardware
- Software-level information provided by the application infrastructure components such as databases, web servers, and messaging systems

- Custom information provided by the applications

- Information on component and service performance

Outputs

The major outputs from the development phase are as follows:

- Scripts to check hardware and software configurations of target environments before deployment or installation

- Scripts to start or stop applications

- Specification of metrics and events that indicate the performance status of an application

- Customized scripts used by service operation staff to manage an application

- Access control information for the system resources used by an application

- Specification of the details required to track an application's major transactions

- SLA targets and requirements

- Operational requirements and documentation

- Support requirements

- Application recovery and backups

Summary

This brings us to the end of the chapter. In this chapter we reviewed the management of technology-related activities commonly performed in the service design stage. We considered requirements engineering in relation to the activities/techniques associated with data and information management as well as application management.

Exam Essentials

Understand the difference between types of requirements.   This includes understanding why it is important to gather information regarding each type of requirement.

Be able to list the different requirements-gathering techniques.   Understand when each approach should be used and the advantages and disadvantages of the different approaches.

Understand the two phases involved when documenting requirements.   The two phases are building the requirements list and developing an organized requirements catalog. Understand the difference between the requirements list and the requirements catalog.

Understand the importance of data management.   Be able to list and explain the four areas of management within the scope of data management.

Understand the contents and use of the applications portfolio.   Be able to list typical attributes contained within the applications portfolio.

Review Questions

You can find the answers to the review questions in the appendix.

1. Which of the following is NOT one of the three stages of requirements engineering?
   A. Analysis
   B. Prioritization
   C. Elicitation
   D. Validation

2. Requirements can be categorized into three types. What are they?
   A. Functional, nonfunctional, technical
   B. Warranty, utility, usability
   C. Functional, management/operational, usability
   D. Mandatory, preferred, optional

3. Which of the following are valid methods of gathering requirements?
   1. Protocol analysis
   2. Observation
   3. Shadowing
   4. Market testing
   5. Workshops
   6. Prototyping
   7. Activity sampling
   8. Interviews
   9. Outsourcing
      A. 2, 3, 4, 5, 6, 7, and 9 only
      B. All of the above
      C. 1, 2, 3, 5, and 9 only
      D. 1, 2, 3, 5, 6, 7, and 8 only

4. Which of the following are benefits of data management?
   1. All users have ready access to the information they need.
   2. The value of the data is exploited.
   3. The data assets are adequately protected, secured, and managed.
   4. Time is not wasted collecting data that is not required.
      A. 1, 2, and 3 only
      B. All of the above

    C. 2 and 4 only

    D. 2, 3, and 4 only

5. Match the category of data with its definition.

    1. Operational data

    2. Tactical data

    3. Strategic data

        A. _____ is typically concerned with summarized data and historical data.

        B. _____ is necessary for the ongoing functioning of an organization.

        C. _____ is often concerned with longer-term trends and comparison with the outside world.

6. Which of the following is NOT one of the four areas of management included within the scope of data/information management?

    A. The management of data resources

    B. The management of data/information technology

    C. The management of staff involved in data management

    D. The management of information processes

7. There are four types of information provided by diagnostic hooks. which of the following is NOT one of them?

    A. Customer satisfaction scores

    B. System-level information provided by the operating systems and hardware

    C. Software-level information provided by the application infrastructure components such as databases, web servers, and messaging systems

    D. Information on component and service performance

8. Specialist tools are available that support requirements processes. These are called CASE tools. What does *CASE* stand for?

    A. Centralized activities for support education

    B. Computer associates software engineering

    C. Computer-aided software engineering

    D. Computer-assisted support engineering

9. What is described by using one of the following methods: a system context diagram, a use case model, or a data flow or object diagram?

    A. Business needs

    B. Operational requirements

    C. Warranty requirements

    D. Utility requirements

10. Which of the following statements about requirements gathering is TRUE?

    A. Requirements gathering should not take up too much project time because there is a risk that there will be insufficient time to deliver the end result.

    B. Gathering the functional requirements is paramount; other requirements can be gathered later, when there is more time.

    C. Most errors in systems are due to poor requirements gathering.

    D. Gathering the functional requirements is paramount; other requirements cannot be gathered until later, when the technical design is known.

Chapter

17

Organizing for Service Design

THE FOLLOWING ITIL INTERMEDIATE EXAM OBJECTIVES ARE DISCUSSED IN THIS CHAPTER:

✓ Use of the RACI matrix

✓ Generic process roles

✓ Specific service design lifecycle roles

✓ Service design process roles and responsibilities for:

- Design coordination

- Service catalog management

- Service level management

- Availability management

- Capacity management

- IT service continuity management

- Information security management

- Supplier management

In this chapter, we explore organizing for service design and the process roles. It is important that you are able to explain and demonstrate understanding of the concepts covered in this chapter. You should be able to explain and describe the roles and responsibilities relating to the processes in the service design lifecycle stage.

The RACI Matrix

The RACI model, or authority matrix, is often used by organizations to define roles and responsibilities in relation to processes and activities. You should remember this from your Foundation studies, but here is a reminder. RACI is an acronym for the following four categories:

Responsible   Applied to the person or people responsible for correct execution—for getting the job done.

Accountable   Applied to the person who has ownership of quality and the end result. Only one person can be accountable for each task.

Consulted   Refers to the people who are consulted and whose opinions are sought. They have involvement through input of knowledge and information.

Informed   Refers to the people who are kept up-to-date on progress. They receive information about process execution and quality.

Occasionally an expanded version of RACI is used, called RACI-VS, with two further roles as follows:

Verifies   Refers to the person or group that checks whether the acceptance criteria have been met.

Signs Off   Refers to the person who approves the decision made by the person who verifies that the criteria have been met (V) and authorizes the product handover. This could be the person held accountable (A).

A third variation of the RACI model is RASCI, where the *S* represents *supportive*. This role provides additional resources to conduct the work or plays a supportive role in implementation of the work, for example. This could be beneficial for IT service implementation. It also allows for clear identification of lead responsibility when a number of roles are responsible for an activity, such as where accountability rests with a process owner and responsibility with a number of roles.

Table 17.1 shows the structure and power of RACI modeling. The rows represent a number of required activities, and the columns identify the people who make the decisions, carry out the activities, or provide input.

TABLE 17.1 An example of a simple RACI matrix

	Director service management	Service level manager	Problem manager	Security manager	Procurement manager
Activity 1	AR	C	I	I	C
Activity 2	A	R	C	C	C
Activity 3	I	A	R	I	C
Activity 4	I	A	R	I	
Activity 5	I	R	A	C	I

For example, the first activity shows the director of service management both account-able and responsible for the activity, with both the service level manager and procurement manager being consulted on the activity. This may be where a policy or principle is being prepared and agreed.

To build a RACI chart, the following steps are required:

- Identify the processes/activities
- Identify and define the roles
- Conduct meetings and assign the RACI codes
- Identify any gaps or overlaps—for example, where there are multiple *R*s or no *R*s
- Distribute the chart and incorporate feedback
- Ensure that the allocations are being followed.

Analysis of a RACI chart to identify weaknesses or areas for improvement should include considering both the role and activity perspectives.

Functional Roles in Service Design

For service design to be successful, it is important to clearly define the roles and responsibilities required to undertake the processes. These roles will need to be assigned to individuals, and an appropriate organizational structure of teams, groups, or functions should be established and managed.

The ITIL framework does not define functions for each lifecycle stage, but service design does rely on the technical and application management functions described in the service operation lifecycle stage. These functional areas are where the expertise for technical and application management are provided. They are used to manage the whole service lifecycle, and practitioner roles within service design may be performed by members of these functions.

There are other areas that act as functions and are commonly referred to in most organizations, but that are not covered as part of the ITIL framework. These are application development and project management.

Application Development While it is possible for an IT service provider to design, deploy, deliver, and improve IT services without developing any applications in-house, many organizations perform some of their own software development.

Project Management Another functional unit that may exist within the IT service provider organization is project management, often referred to as the project management office (PMO).

Organizational Structures in Service Design

The ITIL framework provides some suggestions for organizational structures that might be adopted to enable the successful management of service design.

Figure 17.1 shows an example for a small organization.

FIGURE 17.1 Example of a service design organizational structure for a small organization

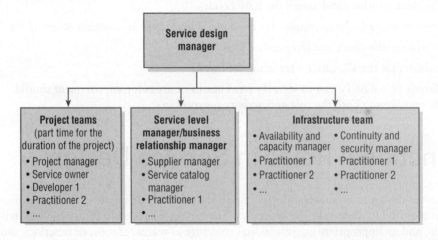

The functional capability is maintained within the infrastructure teams, with service management and project management support.

Figure 17.2 shows an example for a large organization.

FIGURE 17.2   Example of a service design organization structure for a large organization

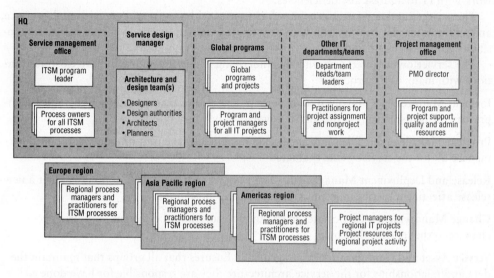

In a larger organization, there is more flexibility in the approach, and the functions may be spread across a number of regional or locational divisions or departments. The challenge then becomes one of coordination to ensure that the service design approach is maintained consistently across the whole organization.

Generic Roles

Throughout the ITIL framework, there is consistent use of some generic roles across all life-cycle stages. The first of these is the service owner.

Service Owner

Large organizations will have many specialist areas, each concerned with its own processes and capabilities. Providing a service to a customer requires many of these specialist silos to contribute part of that service. The service owner provides an end-to-end view, which ensures consistency across the service.

The service owner understands what the service needs to deliver and how it has been built to satisfy these requirements. As the representative of the service, they are involved in assessment of the impact of changes affecting the service and are involved when it suffers a major incident, as an escalation and communication point.

By attending internal and external reviews, the service owner ensures that the service is delivered according to the customer requirements. This allows the role to identify the requirements for improvement and will provide input to continual service improvement to work with IT to address any deficiencies.

The service catalog process provides the business with information regarding the service, and maintaining this information with the service catalog process owner is another responsibility for the service owner.

The service owner interfaces with the underlying IT processes. It will have close associations with many of the processes:

Incident Management   Involved in or perhaps chairs the crisis management team for high-priority incidents impacting the service owned

Problem Management   Plays a major role in establishing the root cause and proposed permanent fix for the service being evaluated

Release and Deployment Management   Is a key stakeholder in determining whether a new release affecting a service in production is ready for promotion

Change Management   Participates in change advisory board decisions, authorizing changes to the services they own

Service Asset and Configuration Management   Ensures that all groups that maintain the data and relationships for the service architecture they are responsible for have done so with the level of integrity required

Service Level Management   Acts as the single point of contact for a specific service and ensures that the service portfolio and service catalog are accurate in relationship to their service

Availability and Capacity Management   Reviews technical monitoring data from a domain perspective to ensure that the needs of the overall service are being met

IT Service Continuity Management   Understands and is responsible for ensuring that all elements required to restore their service are known and in place in the event of a crisis

IT Financial Management   Assists in defining and tracking the cost models in relationship to how their service is costed and recovered

Process Owner

The next generic role we look at is that of process owner. The process owner role is accountable for ensuring that a process is fit for purpose. This role is often assigned to the same person who carries out the process manager role, but the two roles may be separate in larger organizations. The process owner role is accountable for ensuring that the process is performed according to the agreed and documented standard and meets the aims of the process definition.

The process owner has the following accountabilities:

- Sponsoring, designing, and change managing the process and its metrics
- Defining the process strategy
- Assisting with process design
- Defining appropriate policies and standards to be employed throughout the process
- Periodically reviewing the process strategy to ensure that it is still appropriate and change as required
- Communicating process information or changes as appropriate to ensure awareness
- Providing process resources to support activities required throughout the service lifecycle
- Making improvements to the process

Process Manager

Working closely with the process owner, the process manager role is accountable for operational management of a process. There may be several process managers for one process, for example, regional change managers or IT service continuity managers for each data center. The process manager role is often assigned to the person who carries out the process owner role, but the two roles may be separate in larger organizations.

The process manager has the following accountabilities:

- Working with the process owner to plan and coordinate all process activities
- Ensuring that all activities are carried out as required throughout the service lifecycle
- Appointing people to the required roles
- Managing resources assigned to the process
- Working with service owners and other process managers to ensure that services run smoothly
- Monitoring and reporting on process performance
- Identifying improvement opportunities for inclusion in the CSI register
- Working with the CSI manager and process owner to review and prioritize improvements in the CSI register
- Making improvements to the process implementation

Process Practitioner

We have considered the generic roles of process owner and process manager, and now we will review the practitioner role. A process practitioner is responsible for carrying out one or more process activities.

In some organizations, and for some processes, the process practitioner role may be combined with the process manager role. In others, there may be large numbers of practitioners carrying out different parts of the process.

The process practitioner typically has the following responsibilities:

- Carrying out one or more activities of a process
- Understanding how their role contributes to the overall delivery of service and creation of value for the business
- Working with other stakeholders, such as their manager, coworkers, users, and customers, to ensure that their contributions are effective
- Ensuring that inputs, outputs, and interfaces for their activities are correct
- Creating or updating records to show that activities have been carried out correctly

Specific Service Design Roles

There are a number of specific roles that complement and support the service design generic process roles.

Service Design Manager   The job title service design manager typically combines the roles of design coordination process owner and design coordination process manager. It may also include some degree of line management of the people involved in service design.

IT Planner   An IT planner is responsible for the production and coordination of IT plans.

IT Designer/Architect   An IT designer/architect is responsible for the overall coordination and design of the required technology.

Service Design Process Roles

In the following sections, we consider roles and responsibilities within the service design lifecycle stage for each of the service design processes.

Design Coordination Roles

There are additional aspects to the generic roles for each process; first we'll consider the process of design coordination.

Design Coordination Process Owner

The design coordination process owner is responsible for the following activities:

- Carrying out the generic process owner role for the design coordination process
- Setting the scope and policies for service design
- Overseeing the overall design of all service design processes to ensure that they will work together to meet the needs of the business

Design Coordination Process Manager

The design coordination process manager is responsible for the following activities and tasks:

- Carrying out the generic process manager role for the design coordination process
- Coordinating interfaces between design coordination and other processes
- Ensuring that overall service strategies are reflected in the service design practice
- Ensuring the consistent design of appropriate services, service management information systems, architectures, technology, processes, information, and metrics to meet current and evolving business outcomes and requirements
- Coordinating all design activities across projects, changes, suppliers, and support teams, and managing schedules, resources, and conflicts where required
- Planning and coordinating the resources and capabilities required to design new or changed services
- Producing service design packages (SDPs) based on service charters and change requests
- Ensuring that appropriate service designs and/or SDPs are produced and that they are handed over to service transition as agreed
- Managing the quality criteria, requirements, and handover points between the service design stage and service strategy and service transition
- Ensuring that all service models and service solution designs conform to strategic, architectural, governance, and other corporate requirements
- Improving the effectiveness and efficiency of service design activities and processes
- Ensuring that all parties adopt a common framework of standard, reusable design practices in the form of activities, processes, and supporting systems whenever appropriate

Service Catalog Management Roles

Next, we consider the additional aspects to the generic roles for the process of service catalog management.

Service Catalog Management Process Owner

The service catalog management process owner is responsible for the following activities:

- Carrying out the generic process owner role for the service catalog management process
- Working with other process owners to ensure that there is an integrated approach to the design and implementation of service catalog management, service portfolio management, service level management, and business relationship management

Service Catalog Management Process Manager

The service catalog management process manager is responsible for the following activities and tasks:

- Coordinating interfaces between service catalog management and other processes, especially service asset and configuration management and release and deployment management

- Ensuring that all operational services and all services being prepared for operational running are recorded within the service catalog

- Ensuring that all the information within the service catalog is accurate and up-to-date

- Ensuring that appropriate views of the service catalog are maintained and made available to those for whom they are targeted

- Ensuring that all the information within the service catalog is consistent with the information within the service portfolio

- Ensuring that the information within the service catalog is adequately protected and backed up

Service Level Management Roles

In the following sections, we consider additional aspects to the generic roles for the process of service level management.

Service Level Management Process Owner

The service level management process owner is responsible for the following activities:

- Carrying out the generic process owner role for the service level management process

- Liaising with the business relationship management process owner to ensure proper coordination and communication between the two processes

- Working with other process owners to ensure that there is an integrated approach to the design and implementation of service catalog management, service portfolio management, service level management, and business relationship management

Service Level Management Process Manager

The service level management process manager is responsible for the following activities and tasks:

- Carrying out the generic process manager role for the service level management process

- Coordinating interfaces between service level management and other processes, especially service catalog management, service portfolio management, business relationship management, and supplier management

- Keeping aware of changing business needs

- Ensuring that the current and future service level requirements of customers are identified, understood, and documented in service level agreement (SLA) and service level requirements (SLR) documents

- Negotiating and agreeing with the customer on levels of service to be delivered; formally documenting these levels of service in SLAs

- Negotiating and agreeing on operational level agreements (OLAs) and, in some cases, other SLAs and agreements that underpin the SLAs with the customers of the service

- Assisting with the production and maintenance of an accurate service portfolio, service catalog, application portfolio, and the corresponding maintenance procedures

- Ensuring that agreed targets within underpinning contracts are aligned with SLA and SLR targets

- Ensuring that service reports are produced for each customer service and that breaches of SLA targets are highlighted and investigated and actions taken to prevent their recurrence

- Ensuring that service performance reviews are scheduled, carried out with customers regularly, and the actions agreed on at the review documented and progressed.

- Ensuring that improvement initiatives identified in service reviews are acted on and progress reports are provided to customers

- Reviewing service scope, SLAs, OLAs, and other agreements on a regular basis, ideally at least annually

- Ensuring that all changes are assessed for their impact on service levels (such as changes in SLAs, OLAs, and underpinning contracts), including attendance at change advisory board (CAB) meetings if appropriate

- Identifying all customers and other key stakeholders to involve in SLR, SLA, and OLA negotiations

- Developing relationships and communication with customers, key users, and other stakeholders

- Defining and agreeing on complaints, including recording, managing, escalating (where necessary), and resolving them

- Measuring, recording, analyzing, and improving customer satisfaction

Availability Management Process Roles

In the following sections, we consider additional aspects to the generic roles for the process of availability management.

Availability Management Process Owner

The availability management process owner is responsible for the following activities:

- Carrying out the generic process owner role for the availability management process

- Working with managers of all functions to ensure acceptance of the availability management process as the single point of coordination for all availability-related issues regardless of the specific technology involved

- Working with other process owners to ensure that there is an integrated approach to the design and implementation of availability management, service level management, capacity management, IT service continuity management, and information security management

Availability Management Process Manager

The availability management process manager is responsible for the following activities and tasks:

- Carrying out the generic process manager role for the availability management process
- Coordinating interfaces between availability management and other processes, especially service level management, capacity management, IT service continuity management, and information security management
- Ensuring that all existing services deliver the levels of availability agreed on with the business in SLAs
- Ensuring that all new services are designed to deliver the levels of availability required by the business and validation of the final design to meet the minimum levels of availability as agreed by the business for IT services
- Assisting with the investigation and diagnosis of all incidents and problems that cause availability issues or unavailability of services or components
- Participating in the IT infrastructure design, including specifying the availability requirements for hardware and software
- Specifying the requirements for new or enhanced event management systems
- Specifying the reliability, maintainability, and serviceability requirements for components
- Being responsible for monitoring actual IT availability achieved against SLA targets
- Proactively improving service availability
- Creating, maintaining, and regularly reviewing an availability management information system
- Maintaining and completing an availability testing schedule for all availability mechanisms
- Ensuring that all availability tests and plans are tested after every major business change

Capacity Management Process Roles

In the following sections, we consider additional aspects to the generic roles for the process of capacity management.

Capacity Management Process Owner

The capacity management process owner is responsible for the following activities:

- Carrying out the generic process owner role for the capacity management process
- Working with managers of all functions to ensure acceptance of the capacity management process as the single point of coordination for all capacity- and performance-related issues regardless of the specific technology involved
- Working with other process owners to ensure that there is an integrated approach to the design and implementation of capacity management, availability management, IT service continuity management, and information security management

Capacity Management Process Manager

The capacity management process manager is responsible for the following activities and tasks:

- Carrying out the generic process manager role for the capacity management process
- Coordinating interfaces between capacity management and other processes, especially service level management, availability management, IT service continuity management, and information security management
- Ensuring that there is adequate IT capacity to meet required levels of service
- Identifying, with the service level manager, capacity requirements through discussions with the business users
- Understanding the current usage of the infrastructure and IT services and the maximum capacity of each component
- Identifying capacity requirements and current usage of the infrastructure and IT services
- Performing sizing on all proposed new services and systems
- Forecasting future capacity requirements
- Production, regular review, and revision of the capacity plan
- Analysis of usage and performance data
- Raising incidents and problems when breaches of capacity or performance thresholds are detected
- Identifying and initiating any technical tuning to be carried out
- Identifying and implementing initiatives to improve resource usage
- Being familiar with potential future demand for IT services and assessing this on performance service levels
- Ensuring that all changes are assessed for their impact on capacity
- Acting as a focal point for all capacity and performance issues

IT Service Continuity Management Process Roles

In the following sections, we consider additional aspects to the generic roles for the process of IT service continuity management (ITSCM).

ITSCM Process Owner

The IT service continuity management process owner is responsible for the following activities:

- Carrying out the generic process owner role for the IT service continuity management process
- Working with the business to ensure proper coordination and communication between business continuity management and IT service continuity management
- Working with managers of all functions to ensure acceptance of the IT service continuity management process as the single point of coordination for all issues related to IT service continuity regardless of the specific technology involved
- Working with other process owners to ensure that there is an integrated approach to the design and implementation of IT service continuity management, information security management, availability management, and business continuity management

ITSCM Process Manager

The IT service continuity management process manager is responsible for the following activities and tasks:

- Carrying out the generic process manager role for the IT service continuity management process
- Coordinating interfaces between IT service continuity management and other processes, especially service level management, information security management, availability management, capacity management, and business continuity management
- Performing business impact analyses for all existing and new services
- Implementing and maintaining the IT service continuity management process
- Ensuring that all IT service continuity management plans, risks, and activities underpin and align with all business continuity management
- Performing risk assessment and risk management
- Developing and maintaining the organization's continuity strategy
- Assessing potential service continuity issues and invoking the service continuity plan if necessary
- Managing the service continuity plan
- Performing postmortem reviews of service continuity tests and invocations, and instigating corrective actions where required
- Ensuring that all IT service areas are prepared and able to respond to an invocation of the continuity plans

- Maintaining a comprehensive IT testing schedule, including testing all continuity plans in line with business requirements and after every major business change
- Undertaking quality reviews of all procedures
- Communicating and maintaining awareness of IT service continuity management objectives within the business areas
- Undertaking regular reviews of the continuity plans, at least annually
- Negotiating and managing contracts with providers of third-party recovery services
- Assessing changes for their impact on service continuity and continuity plans

Information Security Management Process Roles

In the following sections, we consider additional aspects to the generic roles for the process of information security management.

Information Security Management Process Owner

The information security management process owner is responsible for the following activities:

- Carrying out the generic process owner role for the information security management process
- Working with the business to ensure proper coordination and communication between organizational (business) security management and information security management
- Working with managers of all functions to ensure acceptance of the information security management process as the single point of coordination for all issues related to information security regardless of the specific technology involved
- Working with other process owners to ensure that there is an integrated approach to the design and implementation of information security management, availability management, IT service continuity management, and organizational security management

Information Security Management Process Manager

The information security management process manager is responsible for the following activities and tasks:

- Carrying out the generic process manager role for the information security management process
- Coordinating interfaces between information security management and other processes, especially service level management, availability management, IT service continuity management, and organizational security management
- Developing and maintaining the information security policy and a supporting set of specific policies
- Communicating and publicizing the information security policy
- Ensuring that the information security policy is enforced

- Identifying and classifying IT and information assets
- Assisting with business impact analyses
- Performing security risk assessment and risk management
- Designing security controls and developing security plans
- Developing and documenting procedures for operating and maintaining security controls
- Monitoring and managing all security breaches
- Reporting, analyzing, and reducing the impact and volumes of all security incidents in conjunction with problem management
- Promoting education and awareness of security
- Maintaining a set of security controls and documentation
- Ensuring that all changes are assessed for impact on all security aspects
- Ensuring that security tests are performed as required
- Participating in security reviews arising from security breaches
- Ensuring that the confidentiality, integrity, and availability of the services are maintained at the levels agreed to in the SLAs
- Ensuring that all access to services by external partners and suppliers is subject to contractual agreements and responsibilities

Supplier Management Process Roles

In the following sections, we consider additional aspects to the generic roles for the process of supplier management.

Supplier Management Process Owner

The supplier management process owner is responsible for the following:

- Carrying out the generic process owner role for the supplier management process
- Working with the business to ensure proper coordination and communication between corporate vendor management and/or procurement and supplier management
- Working with other process owners to ensure that there is an integrated approach to the design and implementation of supplier management, service level management, and corporate vendor management and/or procurement processes

Supplier Management Process Manager

The supplier management process manager is responsible for the following activities and tasks:

- Carrying out the generic process manager role for the supplier management process
- Coordinating interfaces between supplier management and other processes, especially service level management and corporate vendor management and/or procurement processes

- Providing assistance in the development and review of SLAs, contracts, agreements, and other documents for third-party suppliers

- Ensuring that value for money is obtained from all IT suppliers and contracts

- Ensuring that all IT supplier processes are consistent and interface to all corporate supplier strategies

- Maintaining and reviewing a supplier and contract management information system

- Ensuring that underpinning contracts, agreements, or SLAs developed are aligned with those of the business

- Ensuring that all roles and relationships between lead and subcontracted suppliers are documented, maintained, and subject to contractual agreement

- Reviewing lead suppliers' processes to ensure that subcontracted suppliers are meeting their contractual obligations

- Performing contract or SLA reviews at least annually

- Updating contracts or SLAs when required

- Maintaining a process for dealing with contractual disputes

- Maintaining a process for dealing with the expected end, early end, or transfer of a service

- Monitoring, reporting, and regularly reviewing supplier performance against targets

- Ensuring that changes are assessed for their impact on suppliers, supporting services, and contracts and attending CAB meetings when appropriate

Summary

This chapter covered service design roles.

We explored the generic ITIL roles and their responsibilities and related them to the service design processes. We also considered the roles specific to the service design lifecycle stage.

Exam Essentials

Understand the generic roles in the service lifecycle.   Know the responsibilities of the service owner, process owner, process manager, and process practitioner.

Be able to explain and expand on the role of process owner for the service design processes.   Each process will have an owner, and each process has slightly different responsibilities allocated to the role to meet the process objectives.

Understand and expand on the role of process manager for the service design processes.   Be aware of the difference between the process owner and process manager. Differentiate between the process managers for each process for service design and the responsibilities associated with each.

Review Questions

You can find the answers to the review questions in the appendix.

1. Which of these is the best description of the role of service owner?

   A. Manage the process so that it is performed efficiently and meets the expectation of the business customer

   B. Ensure that the process produces the correct output

   C. Represent the service across the service provider and business organization

   D. Represent the process at the change advisory board

2. What is the correct description for process owner, process manager, and process practitioner?

   1. Carries out the activity of the process

   2. Ensures that the process can be carried out effectively

   3. Ensures that the process is carried out effectively

3. Which of these is the best description of the role of service design manager?

   A. Often combines design coordination process owner and design coordination process manager

   B. Often combines service level manager and incident manager

   C. Often combines availability manager and capacity manager

   D. Often combines continuity manager and supplier manager

4. The RACI matrix is often expanded to include other potential roles. Which of these describes the additional roles correctly?

   A. RACI-PM: process manager; RASCI: serviceable

   B. RACI-VS: volunteer, supportive; RASCI: signs off

   C. RACI-PM: process, management; RASCI: supplier

   D. RACI-VS: verifies, signs off; RASCI: supportive

5. Which option is the best description of the role of IT planner?

   A. An IT planner delivers the service strategy to the service design lifecycle stage.

   B. An IT planner is responsible for the production and coordination of IT plans.

   C. An IT planner is responsible for the plans for the service transition lifecycle stage only.

   D. An IT planner delivers the contents of the service level agreements and contracts.

6. Which option best describes the responsibility of a service capacity process manager?

   A. Performing sizing on all proposed new services and systems

   B. Producing service design packages (SDPs) based on service charters and change requests

   C. Sizing SDPs for the service portfolio management

   D. Defining the service processes that support availability

7. Which process in service design is responsible for the production of the service design package?

   A. Service level management

   B. Service catalog management

   C. Design coordination

   D. Supplier management

8. Which of these skills would be most useful for a service level manager?

   A. Technical understanding of monitoring systems

   B. Experience of configuring security applications

   C. Business analysis

   D. Negotiating skills and business understanding

9. Which of these best represents the responsibilities of an availability process owner?

   A. Coordination and communication between corporate vendor management and supplier management

   B. Ensuring acceptance of the information security management process as the single point of coordination for all information security

   C. Working with other process owners to ensure that there is an integrated approach to the design and implementation of availability management

   D. Working with the business to ensure proper coordination and communication between business continuity management and IT service continuity management

10. True or False? ITIL suggests that all organizations should adopt the same common service design structure to enable easy integration with other organizations and suppliers regardless of their size.

   A. True

   B. False

Chapter

18

Technology Considerations

THE FOLLOWING ITIL INTERMEDIATE EXAM OBJECTIVES ARE DISCUSSED IN THIS CHAPTER:

✓ The types of tools that would benefit service design

✓ The requirements for service management tools

To meet the learning outcomes and examination level of difficulty, you must ensure that you are able to understand, describe, identify, demonstrate, apply, distinguish, produce, decide, and analyze the service design technology considerations. The syllabus for the ITIL Intermediate Lifecycle service design examination requires that you understand how service design principles and techniques are applied to the choice of service management tools.

Service Design Tools

Most service providers use service management tools. These tools can help in the implementation of various service management processes across the whole service lifecycle. They can help the service design and other processes to work more effectively. They allow large amounts of repetitive work to be carried out quickly and consistently. Tools also provide a wealth of management information, leading to identification of weaknesses and opportunities for improvement. The use of tools will help standardize practices and both centralize and integrate processes.

Process or Tool First?

It is important that the tool being used supports the processes—not the other way around. Although a process should not be modified to fit the tool, there may not be a tool that can support the process as it has been designed. As long as it achieves the desired end result, a tool can be chosen that requires the process to be redesigned to some extent. The benefits of being able to automate the process should outweigh any loss as a result of changing the process.

Often organizations believe that by purchasing or developing a tool, all their problems will be solved, and it is easy to forget that we are still dependent on the process, the function, and most important, the people. Remember, "A fool with a tool is still a fool."

Specifying Requirements

The same attention should be given to choosing any tool for a business. Requirements must be gathered from stakeholders, as described in Chapter 16, "Technology-Related

Activities," in the section "Service Design Activities and Techniques within Requirements Engineering." These requirements will then form the statement of requirements (SoR) for use during the selection process. It is essential that requirements are clearly stated, and they should be subdivided into business requirements, mandatory facilities, and "nice to have." The statement can then be used as a checklist.

There are dozens, if not hundreds, of service management tools available. Details can be found on the Internet, in service management manuals, by asking other organizations, by asking consultants, or by attending seminars and conferences to see what products are available. Consider restricting your consideration to those tools that have been independently assessed.

Evaluation

Consideration must be given to the architectural platform where the tool will reside, and compatibility with the architecture will be a key mandatory requirement. Such mandatory requirements may well restrict which products can be included in the evaluation process, but this is to be expected and ensures that the final choice can meet the requirements. It is also essential to ensure that any tool procurement exercise fits within existing approved budgets.

One simple evaluation method is known as a MoSCoW analysis. It involves creating a detailed list of all requirements and classifying each one as must have, should have, could have, or would like in future.

- *Must have* requirements are mandatory. Any tool that does not satisfy all of the requirements is rejected.
- *Should have* requirements are those that we expect but are not essential.
- *Could have* requirements are useful but not hugely important.
- *Would like in future* requirements are those that we don't need right now but will be needed in future.

As with choosing any tool, functionality (i.e., utility) is not the only requirement. The product's ability to perform in terms of warranty must also be considered; factors such as scalability and security must match the requirement.

The following points should also be considered when evaluating service management tools:

- How data is structured and handled.
- Compatibility with infrastructure components from other vendors. If the tool conforms to international open standards, integration with other tools will be easier.
- Flexibility.
- Ease of use.
- It should be easy to set up the tool to deliver the functionality, such as support for monitoring service levels.
- The technical platform used; does it use a client/server approach?

- How is data protected and backed up?
- If the decision is made to import historical data into the new tool, there should be a simple mechanism to do so.
- The support options provided by the tool vendor should be assessed.

Most organizations find it preferable to use a single integrated tool across the various service management processes, rather than having the overhead of integrating different tools.

Evaluation Process

The diagram in Figure 18.1 shows the standard approach of identifying requirements before identifying products. In reality, looking at products in the market may highlight useful facilities that one had previously been unaware of. These can then be added to the final requirements statement.

FIGURE 18.1   Service management tool evaluation process

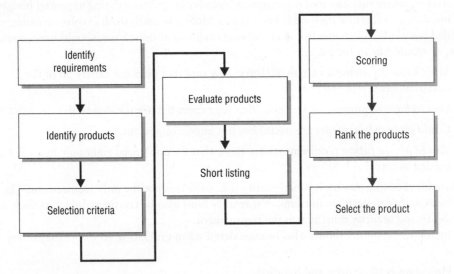

The stages shown here are targeted primarily at the evaluation of packaged software products, but a similar approach could also be used when evaluating custom-built software. The key message is to define what is required, compare available products, discard any that do not meet the mandatory requirements, and then choose the product based on how well it fulfils these requirements. Although cost is an important factor, you may not get the required functionality if you buy a tool because it is cheap, and it would therefore be a waste of money; conversely, most expensive does not necessarily mean best, and buying a tool that has facilities you will never use is also a waste of money.

Choosing the Preferred Option

Tools should be rejected if they fail to meet any of the mandatory requirements. When no tool achieves this, choose the best fit and reconsider how the remaining requirements might be fulfilled—possibly through customization or using additional tools. It is possible that the supplier might make the necessary changes.

When evaluating tools, a 100 percent fit to requirements is unlikely. Use the 80/20 rule. A tool is deemed to be fit for its purpose if it meets 80 percent or more of the business's operational requirements. Whatever tool or type of tool is chosen, the fulfilment of the requirements may be achieved in different ways:

- Some products fulfil the requirement "out of the box" without further work being required.

- Sometimes the requirement can be fulfilled by configuring the tool. The configuration is preserved when the product is upgraded.

- Some tools require customization. Some of the issues to be considered when choosing such a tool include the following:

  - The customization would need to be repeated on every product upgrade.

  - Extensive customization of any product is best avoided because of the high costs incurred when the product is upgraded.

  - There is a risk that the tool may change so much in the future that the customization cannot be carried out on later releases.

  - Vendors may also refuse to support the customized product.

  - Finally, training in the tool would need to be bespoke because the implementation would be unique.

Other considerations when scoring the short-listed products include the background and experience of the vendor in the service management area. Some vendors specialize in service management; others just wish to add a service management tool to their suite of other tools. Are you confident that the supplier will still be supplying and supporting the product in five years? Carrying out the following actions will help you choose the right supplier:

- Consider the support offered. Try telephoning the supplier's service desk to see how easy it is to get through, and ask some test questions to assess their technical competence.

- Arrange a visit to an organization with similar tool requirements to see the tool in use.

- Assess the training needs of your organization, and evaluate the capability of the supplier to provide the appropriate training.

- Confirm whether the integration with telephony or other tools has been carried out successfully elsewhere.

The tool that is finally selected should provide the following benefits:

- An 80 percent fit to all functional and technical requirements
- Meets all mandatory requirements
- Little (if any) product customization required
- Adherence of tool and supplier to service management best practice
- A sound data structure and handling
- Integration with other service management and operational management tools
- Support of open standards and interfaces
- Business-driven rather than technology-driven design
- Administration and maintenance costs within budget
- Acceptable levels of maintenance and release policies
- Security and integrity
- Availability of training and consultancy services
- Good report generation
- Scalability and growth

Implementation

Selecting the tool is just the start. Consideration should be given to its implementation. This includes populating the tool with data. The sources of this data need to be chosen: what, where, how and when? Timing is important to the testing, implementation, and go-live processes. Schedule the implementation when sufficient resources are available to ensure success.

Many organizations now choose to buy Software as a Service (SaaS) products. Several service management tools are available as a service. Using this approach means that hardware and software are not required because these products provide network-based access to and management of commercially available software. These types of products will still require planning and implementation, but the process should be simplified because no dedicated hardware is required.

Summary

In this chapter, we examined the key steps to be carried out when choosing and implementing a new integrated service management tool. This included the gathering requirements, considering other factors, assessing tools against requirements, and implementing the tools.

Exam Essentials

Understand the benefits that an integrated service management tool delivers.   This includes understanding how tools can process large amounts of data and deliver consistency and their ability to link different pieces of information together (such as incidents and problems) and to produce reports on service delivery.

Explain the importance of defining the utility and warranty aspects required from a tool.   Understand the importance of clearly specifying both what the tool needs to do and the performance it needs to deliver in terms of capacity, availability, and security.

Understand the different types of requirements.   Be able to identify the difference between mandatory and desirable requirements.

Explain the selection technique known as MoSCoW   Understand what the acronym stands for (Must/Should/Could/Would) and be able to explain its use in tool selection.

Review Questions

You can find the answers to the review questions in the appendix.

1. Which of the following statements about a statement of requirements is INCORRECT?

    A. An SoR should always contain business requirements.

    B. An SoR should identify the mandatory facilities.

    C. The SoR should always state the maximum budget available.

    D. The SoR should specify the architecture upon which the solution is required to run.

2. Which of the following statements regarding the implementation of a new tool is CORRECT?

    A. Customization will have to be repeated for each upgrade.

    B. Configuration may affect supplier support obligations.

    C. An out-of-the box tool would require bespoke training.

    D. Following configuration, but before deployment, all the new processes should be defined.

3. The MoSCoW approach is often adopted when preparing a request for a new service management tool. What do the uppercase letters in the term MoSCoW stand for?

    A. Might, Should, Could, Wanted

    B. Mandatory, Should, Costed, Wanted,

    C. Must, Should, Could, Would

    D. Mandatory, Should, Customizable, Won't

4. Which of the following shows the correct order of steps to be carried out when selecting a tool?

    A. Agree on selection criteria. Identify requirements. Identify products. Evaluate products. Rank the products. Score each product. Compile short-list of suitable products. Select product.

    B. Identify requirements. Identify products. Agree on selection criteria. Evaluate products. Score each product. Rank the products. Compile short-list of suitable products. Select product.

    C. Identify requirements. Identify products. Agree on selection criteria. Evaluate products. Compile short-list of suitable products. Score the products. Rank the products. Select product.

    D. Identify products. Identify requirements. Agree on selection criteria. Evaluate products. Rank the products. Compile short-list of suitable products. Score each product. Select product.

5. Which of the following is NOT an advantage of using tools during service design?

    A. They allow large amounts of repetitive work to be carried out quickly and consistently.

    B. They will save time because less testing of the solution will be required.

    C. Tools provide a wealth of management information.

    D. The use of tools will help standardize practices and integrate processes.

6. Which of the following statements is untrue?

  A. The tool should be purchased, and then the process should be written to take best advantage of its capabilities.

  B. The process should be written, and then a tool should be found that fits it.

  C. If no tool supports the process, a tool may be chosen that requires the process to be redesigned to some extent as long as it achieves the desired end result.

  D. A tool is deemed to be fit for its purpose if it meets 80 percent or more of the business's operational requirements.

7. Which of the following statements about tool selection is/are correct?

  1. The tool's capabilities and how it matches the process are the only factors to be considered when choosing a tool.

  2. The quality of support offered by the vendor should be assessed; poor support could lead to the product being rejected.

  A. 1 only

  B. 2 only

  C. Both

  D. Neither

8. Which of the following aspects of service design tools should be considered when evaluating different products?

  1. Conformity to international open standards

  2. Flexibility in implementation, usage, and data sharing

  3. Usability—the ease of use permitted by the user interface

  4. Support for monitoring service levels

  5. Conversion requirements for previously tracked data

  6. Data backup, control, and security

  A. 1, 3, 5, and 6 only

  B. 2, 3, 5, and 6 only

  C. All of the above

  D. 3, 4, 5, and 6 only

9. When implementing a new tool, what additional costs should be budgeted for, in addition to the software's purchase costs?

  1. Training of staff in the use of the tool

  2. Cost of time spent setting up web portal

  3. Configuration costs

  4. Cost of time spent setting up reporting

  A. None of the above; these are business-as-usual costs.

  B. 1, 2, and 3 only.

    C.   1, 3, and 4 only.

    D.   All of the above.

10. Which of the following are advantages of implementing a new tool under a Software as a Service arrangement?

    1.   No extra hardware is required.

    2.   No extra software is required.

    3.   No extra training is required.

    4.   Less management overhead.

       A.   All of the above

       B.   1, 2, and 4 only

       C.   1, 2, and 3 only

       D.   1, 3, and 4 only

Chapter

19

Implementation and Improvement of Service Design

THE FOLLOWING ITIL INTERMEDIATE EXAM OBJECTIVES ARE DISCUSSED IN THIS CHAPTER:

✓ **The service design issues relating to:**

- Business impact analysis
- Service level management
- Risks

✓ **The six-stage implementation approach**

✓ **Measurements of service design**

In this chapter we will explore service design in terms of business impact, service level management, and risks, and you will be required to apply your understanding of these concepts in the exams. You will also be required to understand and analyze the use of the six-stage implementation approach. Lastly, we will look at the measurements of service design.

Business Impact Analysis

Business impact analysis (BIA) is a valuable resource when identifying business needs, impacts, and risks. This method is an essential element of the overall business continuity process, which we looked at in the discussion of the IT service continuity process, and influences the risk reduction and disaster recovery strategy. BIA identifies the parts of the organization that would be most affected by a major incident and what effect the incident would have on the overall business. IT provides insight into identifying the most critical business functions; it also highlights when this criticality differs depending on the time of the day, week, month, or year.

Business impact analysis can also be very helpful in other areas because it provides a far better understanding of the service than would otherwise be the case.

Business management may use the results of business impact analysis to ascertain the effect on the business of the complete or partial loss of a business process or function. This would include whether a manual work-around exists, whether the staff are aware of it, and what the cost of using a manual method would be.

Business impact analysis is also useful in service management, where understanding the effects of the loss of an IT service to the business informs processes such as availability management and IT service continuity management. As part of the design phase of a new or changed service, a business impact analysis should be conducted to help define the business continuity strategy and to enable a greater understanding about the function and importance of the service. This helps to define critical services, what constitutes a major incident, and the subsequent impact and disruption caused to the business. It should be taken into consideration that when scheduling changes or planning service outages, IT must understand the important periods to avoid and the cost of loss of service as well as the potential security implications of a loss of service.

Service Level Management

As part of the service level management process, which we considered earlier, service level requirements for all services are gathered from the business. IT's ability to meet these requirements will be assessed and finally agreed on in a formal service level agreement (SLA).

For new services, the requirements must be ascertained at the start of the development process, not after completion. Building the service with service level requirements prioritized as part of the most important factors is essential from a service design perspective.

Risks to the Services and Processes

It is important that normal business operations are not disrupted by the implementation of service design and other IT service management processes.

The risk of service disruption must be considered during the production and selection of the preferred solution to ensure that any adverse impact to operational services is minimized.

This assessment of risk should then be considered in detail in the service transition activities as part of the implementation process.

Implementing Service Design

In order to ensure that the services delivered meet the current and future business requirements, we need to document and use the process, policy, and architecture for service design and implement the other service management processes described in the ITIL service design core volume.

One of the most basic questions is, "So where do we start?"

Organizations often ask, "Which process should we implement first?" Ideally, all of the processes should be implemented, because each process adds to the effectiveness of the others—some processes are dependent on others. Ultimately, organizations require a single, integrated set of processes, providing management and control of a set of IT services throughout their entire lifecycle.

Realistically, organizations cannot do everything at once, and attempting to do so may increase the risk of none of the processes working effectively. The areas of greatest need should be addressed first, and this will vary between organizations.

Ascertaining which areas should be addressed first will require a detailed assessment. This may include conducting customer satisfaction surveys, talking to customers, talking to IT staff, and analyzing the processes in action. If required, formal, process, and organizational maturity can also be assessed using established maturity scales.

From the detailed assessment, short-, medium-, and long-term strategies can be developed.

Quick wins may be needed to improve the current situation, although they may be replaced later with a longer-term solution. Quick wins can be useful in showing the principles in action and may help to build momentum. Improvements always require an element of personal change for those involved, and seeing the result of a quick win is often important for staff morale in changing times.

Every organization's starting point will depend on the maturity of its current service management activities. Implementation priorities should be set against the goals of a service improvement plan (SIP). Throughout the implementation process, key players (both receivers and providers of the service) should be involved in the decision-making process. This will ensure that the correct focus is given to the improvements that will make the most positive impact on the business.

Workshops or focus groups will be beneficial in understanding the requirements and the most suitable process for implementation.

Improving Service Design

The first action is to establish a formal process and method of implementation and improvement of service design, with the appropriate governance in place. This formal process should be based around the six-stage approach illustrated in Figure 19.1.

FIGURE 19.1   Implementation/continual service improvement approach

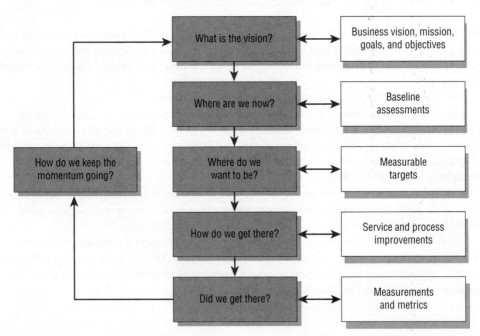

This approach should be familiar to you from the Foundation qualification, as part of the ITIL Continual Service Improvement core volume. It is also important to use a structured project management method when implementing or improving processes.

Stage 1   What is the vision? Understand the vision by ascertaining the high-level business objectives. Doing so should set and align business and IT strategies.

Stage 2   Where are we now? Assess the current situation to identify strengths and weaknesses in terms of the business, organization, people, and process.

Stage 3   Where do we want to be? This builds on the agreed vision, priorities for improvement, and objective targets.

Stage 4   How do we get there? Document the agreed improvement actions in a service improvement plan and carry out the actions.

Stage 5   Did we get there? Measurements and metrics are required to show whether the objective targets have been met.

Stage 6   How do we keep the momentum going? The process starts again by identifying new goals to be achieved to deliver the business vision.

What Is the Vision?

There are some key elements for ensuring that IT is aligned with business objectives.

Vision and leadership are required, with clearly understood goals. IT staff must be open-minded regarding new tools and methods, and IT as a whole must have a thorough understanding of the business, its needs, and its stakeholders, with time set aside for gaining this knowledge. The business, for its part, needs to understand the potential of IT and how it can help the achievement of business objectives. Information should be made available and accessible to everyone who needs it through a communications plan. IT should be continuously tracking technical developments to identify opportunities for the business.

The starting point for all of these activities is the culture and environment of the service provider organization. The people and the culture have to be open to improvement and change. Therefore, before anything else is attempted, the culture within the service provider needs to be reviewed to ensure that it will accept and support the required changes and improvements.

The following key steps need to be completed to achieve this stage of the cycle:

- Establish a vision aligned with the business vision and objectives, and establish the scope of the project/program with a set of high-level objectives.

- Ensure that the necessary governance, senior management commitment, sponsorship, and budget are in place.

- Establish a culture focused on quality, with a focus on the needs of the customer and the business. Develop a learning environment rather than a blame culture, so lessons learned can be fed into the next cycle. Ensure commitment to continual improvement and the improvement cycle. Most important, ensure that ownership and accountability are clearly defined.

Where Are We Now?

Once the vision and high-level objectives have been defined, the service provider needs to review the current situation in terms of what processes are in place and the maturity of the organization. The activities that need to be completed here are a review, an assessment, or a more formal audit of the current situation, using a preferred technique such as an internal review or audit, a maturity assessment, an external assessment, or an audit against a benchmark such as ISO/IEC 20000 or COBIT. A strengths, weaknesses, opportunities, and threats (SWOT) analysis will highlight areas for attention and improvement. Remember, any change carries a potential risk, so a risk assessment and management methodology should be put in place.

The review should include the following:

- The culture and maturity of the service provider and an assessment of the four *P*s (people, processes, products, and partners): the processes in place and their capability, maturity, and adoption; the skills and competence of the people; the services and technology; and the capability of the supplier

- A review of current measurements to ensure that metrics and KPIs are aligned with business goals and objectives

- Finally, a report detailing the findings and recommendations

Baseline measurements are essential. They provide objectivity in assessing the best opportunities for improvement, inform the development of measurable targets for improvement, and provide a basis for later comparison after improvement efforts have been undertaken. Even if the quality of the metrics is poor, they provide a starting point and can be improved later.

When starting out on the implementation or improvement of service design, or any set of processes, it is important to build on the strengths of the existing cultures and processes and rapidly identify and improve the weaknesses.

Where Do We Want to Be?

Based on an assessment of the current state and the vision and high-level objectives, we can define a future desired state, expressed in terms of planned outcomes, including some or all of the following items:

- Improved IT service provision alignment with total business requirements

- Improved quality of service design, achievement of service levels, and quality

- Increases in customer satisfaction and process performance

The future desired state should be defined as specifically as possible to ensure success. The use of SMART objectives (specific, measurable, achievable, relevant, and time-bound) is valuable in building clear and unambiguous expectations for the improvement.

How Do We Get There?

This step requires that we define the improvements required and build an improvement plan, including transition and operation. It should include the improvement actions and the methods to be used, the activities to be undertaken, and the timescales involved. It is important to ensure that risks are managed and identify the resources and budgets required. Another key element is to allocate roles and responsibilities. Part of the plan should be the definition of how monitoring, measurement, and review will be carried out. Improvement plans should also take into consideration challenges, critical success factors, and risks.

Did We Get There?

Often organizations start an improvement initiative without an end goal in mind. It is then difficult to measure its success. The measurement system should be clear from the outset. A defined set of metrics should be used in order to ensure that the desired future state is achieved. This desired future state must be expressed in measurable terms (a central aspect of SMART objectives) such as these:

- $X\%$ reduction in service design nonconformances
- $X\%$ increase in customer satisfaction
- $X\%$ increase in the service availability of critical services

Once the improvement actions and plans have been completed, checks against these measures can be carried out to determine whether the objectives were met, whether lessons were learned, and whether it could be done better next time. It should also be determined whether any other improvement actions have been identified.

How Do We Keep the Momentum Going?

Following the implementation of a successful improvement plan, it is important to consolidate the resulting improvements into business as usual and to move on to the next improvements. As part of continual service improvement, the vision and objectives should be reviewed and more improvement actions identified and logged into the continual service improvement (CSI) register.

The six-stage approach can then be repeated so that the cycle of improvement continues. Establishing a culture of continual service improvement requires a desire to improve throughout the organization, with an appreciation that improvement and a willingness to learn is part of everybody's job.

Measurement of Service Design

It is necessary to ensure that improvements have a baseline and agreed measurable targets if they are to be successful. The success of the service design and the success of the improvement to the processes around the service design must be measured.

Balanced Scorecard

There are many measurement methods available that assist in the analysis of service improvement, and one of these is the balanced scorecard. This is a method developed by Robert Kaplan and David Norton as a concept for measuring a company's activities in terms of its vision and strategies. It gives a comprehensive view of the performance of a business. The system forces managers to focus on the important performance metrics that drive success. The balanced scorecard method is covered in *ITIL Continual Service Improvement* publication.

Six Sigma

Another methodology is Six Sigma. This was developed by Bill Smith at Motorola Inc. in 1986 and was originally designed to systematically work toward managing process variations to eliminate the defects they cause. Six Sigma has now grown beyond defect control and is often used to measure improvement in IT process execution.

Six Sigma DMADV is used to develop new processes and includes these steps:

Define Formally define the goals of the design activity that are consistent with customer demands and organization strategy.

Measure Identify critical success factors, capabilities, process capability, and risk assessment.

Analyze Develop and design alternatives, create high-level designs, and evaluate design capability to select the best design.

Design Develop detailed designs, optimize designs, and plan for design verification.

Verify Set up pilot runs, implement production processes, and hand over the processes to the process owners.

The Six Sigma DMAIC process (define, measure, analyze, improve, control) is an improvement system for existing processes that fall below specification and need incremental improvement.

Measuring Service Design

There are a number of key factors that are important to measuring service design:

- An effective and efficient measurement program for service design is dependent upon having clearly defined goals and objectives for the service design stage and a strong understanding of the processes, procedures, functions, roles, and responsibilities associated with successful service design.

- The interfaces and dependencies between service design elements and the rest of the service lifecycle must be understood and alignment with the needs of the business achieved.

- Appropriate measurements to evaluate service design and identify, implement, and validate improvement are essential, combined with regular reviews to ensure continued alignment with overall requirements.

- Measurement should be automated wherever possible because automation is more consistent and cost-effective. It is necessary to be careful to ensure that the cost of measurement does not outweigh the value of the information gathered. Staff resources should be used for the analysis of the results, and the analysis should be followed by prioritized improvements.

Summary

This chapter covered implementing and improving service design. We explored the following topics:

- The service design issues relating to business impact analysis, service level requirements, and risks
- The six-stage implementation approach
- Measurements of service design as a prerequisite for success

Exam Essentials

Understand the issues related to business impact analysis, service level requirements, and risks.   All lifecycle stages will be impacted by the results of service design, and it is important to ensure that you understand these critical elements.

Be able to explain and expand on the six-stage implementation approach.   Although this is a continual service improvement approach, it is applicable for all lifecycle stages. It is important to understand how this is applied within service design.

Understand and expand on the measurements used for service design.   Service design, as a whole, needs to be measured for success because this is where we are preparing the blueprints for new or changed services. Poor design will have significant impacts in service operation.

Review Questions

You can find the answers to the review questions in the appendix.

1. Identify the stages and the inputs for the six-stage improvement approach so that they are in the right order. The six stages are as follows: How do we get there? What is the vision? Did we get there? Where are we now? How do we keep the momentum going? Where do we want to be?

    The inputs are as follows:

    Business vision, mission, goals, and objectives

    Baseline assessments

    Service and process improvements

    Measurements and metrics

    A. What is the vision? (Business vision, mission, goals, and objectives)
    B. Where do we want to be? (Baseline assessments)
    C. Did we get there? (Measurable targets)
    D. Where are we now? (Service and process improvements)

2. Which of the following statements about business impact analysis (BIA) is/are correct?

    1. BIA is used to ascertain business needs, impacts, and risks for IT service continuity.
    2. BIA is used in service design to ascertain availability requirements.
    3. BIA is used by business management to ascertain the effect on the business of a complete or partial loss of a business process or function.
    4. BIA identifies whether criticality varies at different times or on different days.

        A. None of the above
        B. 1, 2, and 4 only
        C. All of the above
        D. 1, 2, and 3 only

3. Which of the following statements about service level management (SLM) is MOST CORRECT?

    A. SLM is used to inform the customer what levels of availability and capacity will be delivered; the customer can then adjust their working practices to use them most efficiently.
    B. SLM ascertains the service level requirements for new or changed services. Design then ensures that the service is designed to meet them.
    C. SLM is responsible for finalizing the SLA before design can begin.
    D. Following the design of the service, SLM gathers the SLRs from the customer.

4. Which of the following may be carried out to answer the question, Where are we now?

   1. Internal review or audit
   2. External assessment or benchmark
   3. Maturity assessment
   4. ISO/IEC 20000 assessment or audit
   5. Audit against COBIT
   6. Strengths, weaknesses, opportunities, and threats (SWOT) analysis

      A. 1, 2, and 4 only
      B. 1, 2, and 3 only
      C. Any/all of the above
      D. 1, 3, and 6 only

5. The review to answer the question, Where are we now? should include the following: the processes in place and their capability, maturity, and adoption; the skills and competence of the people; the services and technology products; and the suppliers, contracts, and their capability. These are normally known as which of the following?

   A. Risk assessment
   B. Business impact analysis
   C. Organizational readiness assessment
   D. The four *P*s

6. Which is the best description of the use of a balanced scorecard?

   A. The system forces managers to focus on the important performance metrics that drive success.
   B. The system provides an audit trail for the balance of operations.
   C. The system prevents use of unbalanced metrics for technical monitoring.
   D. The system supports the delivery of service transition by focusing solely on financial benefits.

7. What are the steps for the version of Six Sigma used to develop a new process?

   1. Develop
   2. Measure
   3. Define
   4. Verify
   5. Audit
   6. Design
   7. Revision
   8. Analyze

      A.   1, 3, 5, 7, 8

      B.   2, 3, 4, 6, 8

      C.   2, 4, 5, 6, 7

      D.   1, 2, 4, 5, 8

8. The objectives used to ensure that service design is effective must be measurable. What is the acronym commonly used to describe measurability?

      A.   MIRTH

      B.   DMADV

      C.   PPPP

      D.   SMART

9. What does the acronym SWOT stand for?

      A.   Strengths, weaknesses, opportunities, threats

      B.   Strengths, warranties, operations, threats

      C.   Supports, warranties, operations, transitions

      D.   Supports, weaknesses, opportunities, transitions

10. The Six Sigma improvement process includes which of these steps?

      1.   Define

      2.   Measure

      3.   Analyze

      4.   Improve

      5.   Control

          A.   1, 3, 5

          B.   1, 2, 4, 5

          C.   2, 3, 4, 5

          D.   1, 2, 3, 4, 5

Chapter

20

Challenges, Critical Success Factors, and Risks

THE FOLLOWING ITIL INTERMEDIATE EXAM OBJECTIVES ARE DISCUSSED IN THIS CHAPTER:

✓ Service design challenges

✓ Service design critical success factors

✓ Service design risks

This chapter covers the challenges, critical success factors, and risks of service design. The learning objective for this chapter is to gain an understanding of these three areas.

Service Design Challenges

Every new design comes with challenges related to meeting all stakeholders' requirements. The following list includes some examples of service design challenges:

- Organizational resistance to change.

- Difficulty with documentation and adherence to agreed practices and processes.

- Unclear or changing requirements from the business. This may be unavoidable in some cases because business needs are likely to change. The service provider must strive for a close relationship with the business customer. This will ensure that any changing requirements are identified as quickly as possible.

- A lack of awareness and knowledge of service and business targets and requirements. Effective requirements gathering and testing will help ensure that all the required facilities are built into the design.

- A resistance to planning, or a lack of planning leading to unplanned initiatives and unplanned purchases.

- Inefficient use of resources, causing wasted time and money.

- Resistance to work within the agreed strategy.

- Restrictions due to the need to use legacy systems.

- Required tools that are too costly or too complex to implement or maintain with the current staff skills.

- Lack of information, monitoring, and measurements.

- Unreasonable targets and timescales previously agreed to in the SLAs and OLAs.

- Overcommitment of available resources with an associated inability to deliver (e.g., projects always late or over budget).

- Poor supplier management and/or poor supplier performance.

- Lack of focus on service availability.

- The use of diverse and disparate technologies and applications.

- Lack of awareness and adherence to the operational aspects of security policies and procedures.
- Ensuring that normal daily operation or business as usual is considered as part of the design.
- Cost and budgetary constraints.
- Difficulty ascertaining the return on investments and the realization of business benefit.

Meeting the Challenges

Many of the challenges are addressed within the ITIL framework, and adherence to the best practice guidelines contained within ITIL will help to meet or avoid them. To overcome challenges, the service provider must understand the business requirements and the business priorities and ensure that they influence the design of the processes and the services. The people and the organizational culture also need to be understood and taken into account.

Here are some other means of meeting service design challenges:

- Effective communication. It is essential to explain clearly what is happening and what this means for individuals. Additionally, we need to listen if we are to gather requirements effectively.
- Involving as many people as possible in the design. Focus groups can perform a dual role: achieving the right solution as well as building consensus and support.
- Achieving commitment from senior management and all levels of staff.

Critical Success Factors

Let us now consider some of the critical success factors for successful service design. Let's first remind ourselves of the definitions of critical success factors (CSFs) and key performance indicators (KPIs). A CSF describes something that is necessary for an organization or project to achieve its mission.

Key performance indicators are measures that show whether we are meeting our CSFs. There should be KPIs for the overall design and for each of the processes. Achievement against KPIs should be monitored; this will highlight possible opportunities for improvement, which should be logged in the CSI register for evaluation and possible implementation.

Set a small subset of CSFs and KPIs and focus on these. Over time, other areas can become the focus, but having too many CSFs at once risks dissipating effort. These CSFs and KPIs should be set at the beginning of any implementation or improvement activities. It is important that CSFs are agreed on during design so that the design includes the necessary metrics. KPIs should measure both utility and warranty to ensure a complete picture.

It is also important to consider the resources used, not just the quality of the product, when evaluating efficiency. Collect data regularly, especially as part the review for each significant stage to ensure that objectives have been met.

It is vital when designing services or processes that KPIs are designed from the outset and collected regularly and at important milestones. For example, at the completion of each significant stage of the program, a postimplementation review should be conducted to ensure that the objectives have been met. The postimplementation review will include a review of supporting documentation and the general awareness among staff of the refined processes.

Clearly defined objectives with measurable targets should be set in order to assess the quality of the service. These will provide confirmation or otherwise of the success of any improvement initiatives. Carry out a comparison of what has been achieved against the original goals set in the project. Once this has been confirmed, new improvement targets should be defined.

Key Performance Indicators

KPIs need to be constantly monitored. They include customer satisfaction targets, so customers should be surveyed at various stages to confirm that changes made are improving the customer perception of the service quality. It may be that some KPIs have improved (availability, response times, etc.) but customer satisfaction has deteriorated. This would indicate that the improvements carried out did not address the customers' main concerns.

This list includes some possible service design KPIs:

- Percentage of service design requirement specifications produced on time (and on budget).

- Percentage of service design plans produced on time.

- Percentage of service design packs completed on time.

- Percentage of QA and acceptance criteria plans produced on time.

- Accuracy of service design—for example, was the correct infrastructure built to support the service?

- Percentage of cost estimates of the whole service design stage for new or changed services that are within acceptable boundaries, such as "within 2% of actual cost."

- Accuracy of service level agreement(s), operational level agreement(s) and contract(s)— do they really support the required level of service?

Service Design Risks

There are a number of risks directly associated with the service design stage of the service lifecycle:

- Failing to meet a CSF is a risk, especially if this is the result of immature processes; when there are poor processes in one area, there is a risk of other areas or processes being affected. Poor incident management, especially concerning the quality and quantity of data gathered, will affect problem management as well as incident management itself. Poor configuration management makes the impact assessment of a change much more difficult.

- Failure to manage unrealistic business expectations may mean that the design does not meet the requirement.

- Insufficient testing may allow poor-quality services to be launched into the live operational environment.

- Another risk is failing to achieve a balance between innovation, risk, and cost while seeking a competitive edge; this could mean excessive costs or designs that cannot deliver.

- There may be too much focus on IT improvements without a clear understanding of business needs and objectives. There may not be a good enough fit between infrastructures, customers, and partners to meet the overall business requirements, or there may be a poorly implemented interface between IT and business planners.

- The service strategy may not be understood or processes may be over- or underengineered. Insufficient resources, budget, time, or skills available for service design activities are common risks. Services may be developed in isolation for short-term savings but may be much more costly in the long term.

- The approach to CSI may be ad hoc, with no consistent approach to identifying areas most in need of improvement.

- The service provider may fail to carry out sufficient monitoring and analysis to identify the areas of greatest need.

- A lack of commitment to improvement by staff will make success almost impossible.

- Insufficient data to populate a business case for improvement may mean that the importance of the improvement is not realized.

- There may be a lack of ownership or loss of ownership for the improvement initiatives.

Finally, although a culture of continuous improvement is to be encouraged, the organization should not lose sight of the business needs and objectives; improvements should not be carried out for their own sake but only when they further those business aims and objectives.

Summary

In this chapter we discussed the following:

- Service design challenges
- Service design critical success factors
- Service design risks

We have now completed the entire syllabus for the Service Design Lifecycle examination.

Exam Essentials

Understand the challenges faced by service design staff when designing services that meet stakeholder requirements.   Understand the difficulties caused for service design by unclear requirements. Be able to list several other challenges that are commonly encountered.

Understand how service design challenges may be overcome using ITIL guidance regarding best practice.   Understand how the advice contained within ITIL core guidance addresses the challenges, in particular regarding gathering requirements and ensuring buy-in from stakeholders.

Understand the role played by KPIs in relation to CSFs.   Understand that it is through measurement of KPIs that we know whether we are achieving our CSFs.

Understand the critical success factors that need to be in place if successful service design is to take place.   Understand the importance of clearly defined objectives with measurable targets. Be able to list some CSFs and their related KPIs for service design.

Know the risks encountered in the service design stage, in particular the danger that the importance of this stage may not be recognized.   Understand the risk that spending insufficient time or resources on service design in order to save time or money will lead to increased costs and delays later.

Review Questions

You can find the answers to the review questions in the appendix.

1. A _____ is an element that is necessary for an organization or project to achieve its mission.

    A. CSF

    B. KPI

    C. Target

    D. Metric

2. A _____ is a measure that quantifies objectives and enables the measurement of performance.

    A. CSF

    B. Metric

    C. Target

    D. KPI

3. Which of the following would be an appropriate KPI for the service design CSF "Manage conflicting demands for shared resources."

    A. Increased customer satisfaction with the quality of service design output

    B. Reduced number of issues caused by unavailable resources

    C. Increase (measured as a percentage of all new and changed services) in the number of new and changed services delivered ahead of schedule

    D. A decrease in the cost of the service design stage

4. What is "a metric that is used to help manage an IT service, process, plan, project, or other activity"?

    A. A critical success factor

    B. A key performance indicator

    C. An SLR

    D. A gap analysis

5. Which of the following is NOT a common service design risk?

    A. Lack of coordination between IT and business planners

    B. Policies and strategies missing or poorly understood

    C. Processes over- or underengineered

    D. Lack of testing facilities

6. What factors are considered when assessing risk?

    A. Impact and urgency

    B. Vulnerability and probability

    C. Cost and quality

    D. Time and resources

7. What is "unclear or changing requirements from the business"?

   A. Risk

   B. CSF

   C. KPI

   D. Challenge

8. Which of the following is NOT a common service design risk?

   A. Unclear business requirements

   B. Insufficient time given for proper service design

   C. Failure to manage unrealistic business expectations

   D. Market risks

9. It is often said that good design is a competition between three factors, of which only two can be satisfied. What are these three factors?

   A. Accuracy, cost, quality

   B. Speed, quality, cost

   C. Constraints, requirements, functionality

   D. Must have, should have, could have

10. When should KPIs be designed and collected?

   A. Designed at the start of the design stage and collected at the end

   B. Designed and collected throughout the design stage

   C. Designed and collected at the end of the design stage

   D. Designed at the start of design, collected throughout

Service Transition

PART III

Chapter

21

Introduction to Service Transition

THE FOLLOWING ITIL INTERMEDIATE EXAM OBJECTIVES ARE DISCUSSED IN THIS CHAPTER:

✓ **The concepts of service transition relating to**

- ▪ Purpose
- ▪ Objectives
- ▪ Scope
- ▪ Value to the business

✓ **Service transition in relation to the other lifecycle stages**

- ▪ Service strategy
- ▪ Service design
- ▪ Service operation
- ▪ Continual service improvement

In this chapter we will examine the concepts relating to the service transition lifecycle stage, including the purpose, objectives, and scope of the stage. You will be expected to be able to apply your understanding of these concepts in the examination. We will also consider the relationship of service transition to the other lifecycles stages, and you should be able to analyze these relationships and demonstrate your understanding of their importance in the examination.

Service Transition Concepts

Service transition's main aim is to ensure that any modifications or transitions to the live operational environment—affecting new, modified, retiring, or retired services—meet the agreed expectations of the business, customers, and users.

Purpose

The purpose of service transition is to transition new, modified, retiring, or retired services that have been designed to deliver the strategy. Following transition, the services must meet the business expectations as established in the earlier lifecycle stages.

Objectives

The objectives of service transition include ensuring that changes to services happen as seamlessly as possible. The service releases are deployed into the supported live environment, where they can deliver the business value identified in service strategy. The new or changed service should be transitioned into the live environment without disrupting the other services and, as a result, without disrupting the business. Transition must strike a balance between avoiding risk to the live services and ensuring that the business can receive the new or changed service it requires without unnecessary delay or cost. Effective risk management is therefore also a key objective of this lifecycle stage.

A key aspect of service transition is communication. The business must know what to expect from the new or changed service in terms of its performance or use; if the business's expectations are not managed, it may judge a transition to have failed because it did not deliver the benefits or functionality that it was expecting but had never been part of the design.

Having said that, however, transition must ensure that the expected business value is delivered. It is a common mistake to focus on the successful installation of hardware or software and fail to ensure that the business obtains the expected value from these.

An essential part of every transition is the accompanying knowledge transfer. A key objective of service transition is to provide good-quality knowledge and information about services and service assets.

The requirements for successful service transition are as follows:

- Careful planning of resources
- Risk assessment and mitigation
- Control of service assets to ensure that their integrity is maintained
- Efficient repeatable mechanisms for building, testing, and releasing the service to increase the chances of success while reducing the cost and risks of transition

Service transition must understand the constraints under which the service will operate and ensure that the transitioned service can operate and be managed and supported successfully under these constraints.

Scope

The guidance given in the *ITIL Service Transition* volume is focused on improving an organization's capabilities for transferring new and changed services into supported environments. Its scope is wider than change management's scope; it covers planning the release, building and testing it, and then evaluating and deploying it. Included within the scope of service transition are retiring services at the end of their useful life and transferring services between service providers, such as during an outsourcing or insourcing exercise or when a service is moved from one outsourced service provider to another. Service transition is all about ensuring that the requirements from service strategy, which were developed in service design, are effectively realized in service operation while controlling the risks of failure and subsequent disruption. A well-designed service can be damaged in the eyes of the business if it is poorly transitioned. If it fails to deliver the benefits reliably because the planning or testing was insufficient, it may be rejected by the business.

Service transition provides guidance on managing changes to services and service management processes, ensuring that the organization is protected from unplanned consequences of changes, while still enabling successful changes that deliver business benefits. These changes may be new services or improvements to existing services, such as expansion, reduction, change of supplier, acquisition or disposal of user base or suppliers, or changed requirements.

Service transition also covers managing the end of a service being provided, including decommissioning equipment, discontinuing contracts or other service components, and so on.

The scope of service transition also includes managing the introduction of changes to the service provider's people, processes, products, or partners.

Transition includes managing the transfer of services to and from other service providers:

- Transfer to a new supplier by outsourcing the work or transfer between suppliers. Sometimes the transfer is from a supplier to in-house provision. This is called insourcing.

- Moving to a partnership or co-sourcing arrangement for some aspects of the service; this may involve multiple suppliers and is sometimes called multi-sourcing.

Although the service itself may not change, such transfers are not without risk, and careful planning is required to ensure that the transfer appears seamless to the business and nothing is forgotten.

Other transitions may be the result of setting up a joint venture with another organization or restructuring the organization through reducing staff (downsizing) or increasing staff (upsizing). Both of these are known as rightsizing, and the best solution will vary among organizations. Finally, work may be transferred to a location with cheaper labor costs. This is called offshoring. The organization may be involved in a merger or an acquisition.

Of course, in any organization, several of these transitions may be combined, with all present risk as well as opportunity, and so must be carefully planned and executed.

The following two lists include the service transition processes. They can be categorized into two groups, based on the extent to which their activities take place within the service transition stage of the service lifecycle. The first group consists of processes that are critical during the service transition stage but influence and support all stages of the service lifecycle:

- Change management
- Service asset and configuration management
- Knowledge management

The second group consists of processes whose focus is strongly related to service transition:

- Transition planning and support
- Release and deployment management
- Service testing and validation
- Change evaluation

We shall look at all of these processes later in this publication. Remember, almost all transition processes are active in other stages of the lifecycle, and transition is also impacted by processes from other lifecycle stages.

All the lifecycle processes should be linked closely together, and it is important to define the interfaces between processes when designing a service or improving or implementing a process.

Figure 21.1 shows all of the processes described in *ITIL Service Transition*.

FIGURE 21.1   The scope of service transition

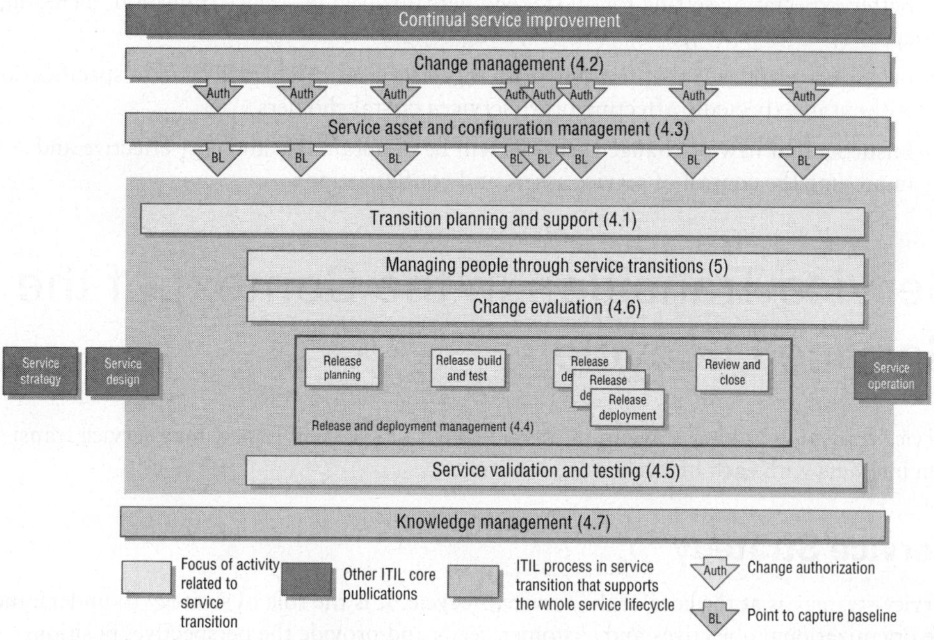

Processes that are largely within the service transition stage of the service lifecycle are shown within the central rectangle; the other stages of the service lifecycle that come before and after these processes are shown in the smaller, darker rectangles. The service transition processes that support the whole lifecycle are shown in the mid-color rectangles.

Value to the Business

Selecting and adopting the best practice as recommended by ITIL will assist organizations in delivering significant benefits. Adopting and implementing standard and consistent approaches for service transition will benefit the business by making it easier for projects to estimate the cost, timing, resource requirement, and risks associated with service transition. This in turn enables a higher volume of successful change because there will be less rework required. Other benefits include clear processes that are easy to adopt and follow and sharing assets across projects while avoiding clashes between transition projects that require the same asset (such as a test environment) at the same time. Avoiding such clashes will also reduce delay. Following the advice will also minimize the effort spent on managing the service transition test and pilot environments.

Good service transition ensures the following benefits:

- Better expectation setting for all stakeholders involved in service transition, including customers, users, suppliers, partners, and projects

- Increased confidence that the new or changed services can be delivered to specification without unexpectedly affecting other services or stakeholders

- Ensuring that new or changed services will be maintainable and cost-effective and improving the control of service assets and configurations

Service Transition in the Context of the Service Lifecycle

Service transition is a key stage in the service lifecycle. We will review how service transition interacts with each lifecycle stage in turn.

Service Strategy

Service strategy is at the core of the service lifecycle. It is the role of strategy to understand the organizational objectives and customer needs and provide the perspective, position, plans, and patterns to support the strategy.

ITIL service strategy asks why something is to be done before thinking of how. Incorporating the processes of service portfolio management, demand management, financial management for IT services, business relationship management, and strategy management for IT services, this stage makes the plans for the IT services.

It helps service providers to set objectives; set expectations of performance serving customers and markets; and identify, select, and prioritize opportunities.

Service strategy ensures that providers understand and can handle the costs and risks associated with their service portfolios.

Service Design

Service design turns strategic ideas into deliverables. The design must always consider the strategy to ensure that services are designed with the business objectives in mind.

Design considers the whole IT organization and how it will deliver and support the services, turning the service strategy into a plan for delivering the business objectives.

Remember, design includes changes to existing services, not just the introduction of new services.

The service design processes include design coordination, service catalog management, service level management, availability management, capacity management, IT service continuity management, information security management, and supplier management.

Through these processes, service design ensures that both the utility and the warranty of the new or changed service is considered in design, covering the continuity of the service, its achievement of service levels, and its conformance to security standards and regulations.

Service Transition

Service transition, the subject of this section of the book, provides guidance for developing and improving capabilities for introducing new and changed services into supported environments.

The value of a service is identified in strategy, and the service is designed to deliver that value. Service transition ensures that the value is realized by enabling the necessary changes to take place without unacceptable risks to existing services.

Service transition enables the implementation of new services, and the modification of existing services, to ensure that the services provided deliver the service strategy of achieving the business objectives and that the benefits of the service design are fully realized.

Service transition also introduces the service knowledge management system, which ensures that knowledge is stored and made available to all stages of the service lifecycle so that lessons are learned and decisions are backed with factual data, leading to improved efficiency and effectiveness over time.

The service transition processes include transition planning and support, change management, service asset and configuration management, release and deployment management, service validation and testing, change evaluation, and knowledge management.

Each process has a role to play to ensure that beneficial changes can take place and, as a consequence, the service can be introduced and will work as transitioned.

Service Operation

Service operation describes best practice for managing services in supported environments. It includes guidance on achieving effectiveness, efficiency, stability, and security in the delivery and support of services to ensure value for the customer, the users, and the service provider. Without this, the services would not deliver the value required and the achievement of business objectives would become difficult or impossible.

The service operation stage is therefore critical to delivering the design and, in doing so, achieving the service strategy and outcomes.

Service operation provides detailed guidance for delivering the service within the agreed service levels by tackling issues both proactively through problem management and reactively through incident management. It provides those delivering the service with guidance in managing the availability of services, controlling demand, optimizing capacity utilization, scheduling operations, and avoiding or resolving service incidents and managing problems. It includes advice on shared services, utility computing, web services, and mobile commerce. By delivering the services to the agreed levels, service operations enable the business to use the services to achieve its business objectives.

The service operation processes include event management, incident management, request fulfilment, problem management, and access management.

Each process has a role to play to ensure the delivery of services within the agreed service levels. The operations functions are the service desk, technical management, IT operations management, and application management. Each function is responsible for managing its own area of delivery across all stages of the lifecycle.

Continual Service Improvement

CSI ensures that the service provider continues to provide value to customers by ensuring that the strategy, design, transition, and operation of the services is under constant review. Feedback from any stage of the service lifecycle can be used to identify improvement opportunities for any other stage of the lifecycle. It ensures that opportunities for improvement are recognized, evaluated, and implemented when justified. These may include improvements in the quality of the service or the capabilities of the service provider. It may be developing ways of doing things better, or doing them to the same level but more efficiently. Improvements may be major or small and incremental. It enables every new transition to incorporate lessons from previous transitions.

CSI ensures that feedback from every lifecycle stage is captured, analyzed, and acted upon. The CSI approach to improvement is based on establishing a baseline and checking to see whether the improvement actions have been effective. It uses the Plan-Do-Check-Act (PDCA) cycle together with service measurement, demonstrating value with metrics, and conducting maturity assessments. The seven-step improvement process provides a framework for these approaches.

Summary

In this chapter we looked at the introduction to service transition. We explored the purpose, objectives, and scope of service transition and its value to the business. We examined the context of service transition in relation to the other four stages of the service lifecycle: service strategy, service design, service operation, and continual service improvement.

Exam Essentials

Understand the purpose of service transition.   All lifecycle stages are important, but the purpose of service transition is to ensure that strategy and design are implemented correctly.

Be able to explain and expand on the objectives of service transition.   Ensure that the implementation of any and all new or changed services is seamless and effective for the business.

Understand and expand on the scope of service transition.   The scope of service transition is to improve an organization's capabilities for transferring new and changed services into supported environments, including all aspects of change, release, evaluation, and testing for new, modified, retiring, or retired services.

Be able to explain and justify the value of service transition to the business.   Transition is a key part of the lifecycle, enabling the services to be integrated seamlessly into the organization. Without this stage, testing and preparation may be overlooked, causing difficulties in delivery and support.

Understand and explain service transition in the context of the service lifecycle.   Transition is responsible for ensuring that the decisions and designs made in strategy and design are implemented successfully so that they can be of value to the business in operation. All lifecycle stages are of course integrated with continual service improvement.

Review Questions

You can find the answers to the review questions in the appendix.

1. Which of the following is NOT an objective of service transition?
   A. Set correct expectations on the performance and use of new or changed services.
   B. Provide good-quality knowledge and information about services and service assets.
   C. Document how service assets are used to deliver services and how to optimize their performance.
   D. Ensure that service changes create the expected business value.

2. Which of the following statements about service transition is/are correct?
   1. Transition turns strategy into deliverables.
   2. It is in the service transition stage that the design is used in the real world and the strategy is realized.
   3. The value of a service is identified in strategy, and the service is transitioned to deliver that value.
   4. Improvements identified by CSI may need to go through transition to be implemented.
      A. All of the above
      B. 1, 2, and 3 only
      C. 3 and 4 only
      D. 2, 3, and 4 only

3. Which of these situations is out of scope for service transition?
   1. Transferring between suppliers
   2. Producing a business case to justify outsourcing the service to an external supplier
   3. Moving to a partnership with several suppliers
   4. Setting up a joint venture with another organization
   5. Terminating a contract with a supplier
      A. None of the above
      B. 1, 3, and 4 only
      C. 1, 2, 3, and 4 only
      D. 1, 3, 4, and 5 only

4. True or False? The purpose of service transition is to ensure that new or changed services are designed according to the strategy.
   A. True
   B. False

5. Which of these options is NOT an aspect of successful service transition?
   A. Developing capacity plans to identify customer needs
   B. Risk assessment and mitigation

C. Controlling service assets to ensure that their integrity is maintained

D. Building efficient repeatable mechanisms for building, testing, and releasing the service

6. Which of these processes is considered to have a focus that is strongly related to service transition rather than in use across the service lifecycle?

A. Change management

B. Change evaluation

C. Knowledge management

D. Service asset and configuration management

7. Which of these statements is/are correct about the scope of service transition?

1. Introduction of a new service is covered under service transition.

2. Transfer of a service between providers is covered under service transition.

A. Statement 1 only

B. Statement 2 only

C. Both statements

D. Neither statement

8. Which of the following approaches are included in the management of transitional activity?

1. Insourcing

2. Outsourcing

3. Co-sourcing

4. Offshoring

A. 1, 2, 3

B. 2, 3, 4

C. 1, 3, 4

D. 1, 2, 3, 4

9. Which of these statements is correct about the service lifecycle?

A. Service strategy describes the needs of the supplier as a priority for delivery.

B. Service design controls the operational environment and optimizes service delivery.

C. Service transition provides guidance for developing capabilities to introduce new services.

D. Service operation exploits the business needs to describe and develop the strategy for improvement.

10. True or False? Service transition integrates with continual service improvement and will apply the PDCA approach to improving the processes in the transition lifecycle stage.

A. True

B. False

Chapter

22

Service Transition Principles

THE FOLLOWING ITIL INTERMEDIATE EXAM OBJECTIVES ARE DISCUSSED IN THIS CHAPTER:

✓ **The concepts of service transition relating to**

- Policies
- Principles
- Best practices

✓ **Optimization of service transition**

✓ **Metrics**

✓ **Inputs and outputs by lifecycle stage**

In this chapter, we will review the policies of service transition and the associated principles and best practices relating to them. We will consider each in turn, and it is important to remember that these should be applied to ensure that service transition is effective and efficient.

Formal Policy for Service Transition

A formal policy is designed to provide structure for the approach to transition across the organization. It should be given full management support and commitment.

Policy

This policy states that "a formal policy for service transition should be defined, documented, and approved by the management team, who ensure that it is communicated throughout the organization and to all relevant suppliers and partners" (*ITIL Service Transition* core volume).

Principles

The formal policy should clearly state the objectives and that any noncompliance with the policy shall be remedied. It is important to ensure that the policy aligns with the overall governance framework, organization, and service management policies. The sponsors and decision-makers involved in developing the policy must demonstrate their commitment to adapting and implementing it. This includes the commitment to deliver predicted outcomes from any change in the services.

Teamwork is an important factor in developing the overall policy for transition, and this stage should use processes that integrate teams. This will allow for a blend of competencies while maintaining clear lines of accountability and responsibility.

It is important for any changes to be delivered in releases. This means that the department should address deployment early in the release design and release planning stages, demonstrating a commitment to engagement with transition.

Best Practice

The best practice example for this policy would be that formal sign-off is obtained from the management team, sponsors, and decision-makers involved in developing the policy. This demonstrates the commitment required from a top-down approach.

Governance Policy for Service Transition

The second key policy is supporting the approach to governance throughout the service life-cycle. This policy declares that all changes to services will be implemented through service transition.

Policy

The governance policy states that "all changes to the service portfolio or service catalog are implemented through change management and the changes that are managed by the service transition lifecycle stage are defined and agreed" (*ITIL Service Transition* core volume).

Principles

This governance approach includes the following requirements or principles:

- That there is a single focal point for changes to the live production services to minimize the probability of conflicting changes and potential disruption to the supported environment. This should include the principle that people who do not have the authority to make a change or release into the supported environment are prevented from having access.
- There should be sufficient familiarity with the service operation organization to enhance mobilization and enable organizational change.
- There should be an increase in knowledge of and experience with the services and supported environments to improve efficiency.
- Each release package will be designed and governed by a request for change raised via the change management process to ensure effective control and traceability.
- Standardized methods and procedures will be used for efficient and prompt handling of all changes in order to minimize the impact of change-related incidents on business continuity, service quality, and rework.
- All updates to changes and releases will be recorded against service assets and/or configuration items in the configuration management system.

Best Practice

Management commitment to the change process should be clear and visible, supporting existing processes through standardization and a top-down management approach.

Changes should be defined in a service design package and supported by a business case to ensure commitment from all areas.

Common Framework for Service Transition

The next policy also highlights some governance controls, this time looking at a structured approach by using a common framework and standards.

Policy

The policy states that service transition should be based on a common framework of standard reusable processes and systems to improve integration of the parties involved in service transition and reduce variations in the processes.

Principles

The principles supporting the policy to adopt a standardized approach include the requirement to implement industry best practices as the basis of standardization. This will enable integration across the supply chain and support seamless transition activity.

Once agreed, it is recommended that the service transition framework and standards are controlled under change and configuration management.

Maintaining the standards is key, so to ensure that processes are adopted consistently, there should be regular, scheduled reviews and audits of the service management processes.

Best Practice

The examples of best practices for standardization include ensuring that the standards and best practices for service transition are published. There is also a need to provide a framework for establishing consistent processes for evaluating the service capability and risk profile and ensuring that it is in place before and after a release is deployed.

To achieve this standardization, it is important to provide supporting systems to automate standard processes in order to reduce resistance to adoption. This will require management understanding the need for standard ways of working so that there is a consistent approach to developing and delivering improvements based on a sound business case.

The engagement and commitment of management and stakeholders will be important, and there should be action taken to close any gaps. This will encourage continual planning of how to improve the buy-in to adopting a common framework and standards.

Maximize Reuse of Established Processes and Systems

The next policy addresses the efficiency of the service transition lifecycle stage by recommending the maximization of the reuse of established processes and systems.

Policy

The policy states that service transition processes should be aligned with the organization's processes and related systems to improve efficiency and effectiveness, and where new processes are required, they are developed with reuse in mind.

This approach supports the continual service improvement of the service lifecycle as well as optimizing efficiency and the use of resources.

Principles

The principles associated with this policy are concerned with the reuse of established processes and systems wherever possible. This will include capturing data and information from the original source to reduce errors and aid efficiency.

The development of reusable standard service transition models to build up experience and confidence in the service transition activities is also key and should support the implementation of industry standards and best practices as the basis of standardization. This should enable the integration of deliverables from many suppliers.

Best Practice

The best practices that demonstrate the policy and principles are the integration of the service transition processes into the quality management system, showing the capability to reuse the processes.

Best practice will also encourage use of the organization's program and project management practices to utilize a repeatable methodology. This includes using the existing communications channels for service transition communication.

It is important to ensure that the service transition approach adopts and follows human resources, training, finance and facilities management processes, and common practices.

Another consideration will be to design the service transition models to enable easy customization to suit specific circumstances but structure models such that a consistent approach is repeated for each target service unit or environment, with local variation as required.

Business Alignment of Service Transition

The next policy concerns the alignment of service transition plans with the business needs.

Policy

The policy states that, in order to maximize the value delivered by a change, service transition plans and new or changed services should be aligned to the customer and business needs.

This policy is a reflection of the overall approach adopted throughout the lifecycle from service strategy to continual service improvement.

Principles

The principles supporting this alignment include setting the customer and user expectations during transition on how the performance and use of the new or changed service can enable business change. This involves the provision of information and establishing processes to enable business change projects and customers to integrate a release into their business processes and services. It should ensure that the service can be used in accordance with the requirements and constraints specified within the service requirements in order to improve customer and stakeholder satisfaction.

The communication and transfer of knowledge to the customers, users, and stakeholders is a vital part of increasing their capability to maximize use of the new or changed service.

Monitoring and measuring the use of the services and underlying applications and technology solutions during deployment and early life support should ensure that the service is well established before transition closure.

Service transition should compare the actual performance of services after a transition against the predicted performance defined in service design, with the aim of reducing variations in service capability and performance.

Best Practice

The best practice approach should be to adopt program and project management best practices to plan and manage the resources required to package, build, test, and deploy a release successfully within the predicted cost, quality, and time estimates.

Any new implementation of a change or new service should provide clear and comprehensive plans that enable the customer and business change projects to align their activities with the service transition plans.

As part of any change or transition of a new or changed service, it will also be important to manage stakeholder commitment and communications.

Establish and Maintain Relationships with Stakeholders

This policy stresses the importance of relationships with key stakeholders during service transition.

Policy

This policy is to establish and maintain relationships with customers, customer representatives, users, and suppliers throughout service transition in order to set their expectations about the new or changed service.

Principles

The principles associated with this policy are as follows:

- Set stakeholder expectations on how the performance and use of the new or changed service can enable business change.
- Communicate changes to all stakeholders in order to improve their understanding and knowledge of the new or changed service.
- Provide good-quality knowledge and information so that stakeholders can find information about the service transition easily—for example, release and deployment plans and release documentation.

Best Practice

The best practices that support this policy are as follows:

- Checking with stakeholders to make sure the new or changed service can be used in accordance with the requirements and constraints specified within the service requirements
- Ensuring that service transition and release plans and any changes are shared with stakeholders
- Working with business relationship management and service level management to build customer and stakeholder relationships during service transition
- Working with supplier management to ensure commitment and support from key suppliers during and following transition

Establish Control and Disciplines

The next policy is to establish effective controls and disciplines.

Policy

The policy states that it is necessary to establish suitable controls and disciplines throughout the service lifecycle to enable the smooth transition of service changes and releases.

This will ensure a seamless transition of new or changed services through the service lifecycle from strategy to continual service improvement.

Principles

The supporting principles for maintenance of suitable controls include service asset and configuration management, which is accomplished by establishing and maintaining the integrity of all identified service assets and configurations as they evolve through the service transition stage.

Where possible and cost effective, audit activities should be automated to increase the detection of unauthorized changes and discrepancies in the configurations.

Roles and responsibilities throughout the transition should be clearly defined to understand who is doing what, when, and where at all handover points. Doing so will increase accountability for delivery against the plans and processes. This will include the definition and communication of roles and responsibilities for handover and acceptance through the service transition activities (e.g., build, test, release, and deployment) to reduce errors resulting from misunderstandings and lack of ownership.

It will also be important to establish transaction-based processes for configuration, change, and problem management to provide an audit trail and the management information necessary to improve the controls.

Best Practice

The best practices for this policy should ensure that roles and responsibilities are well defined, maintained, and understood by those involved and mapped to any relevant processes for current and foreseen circumstances. This will involve the assignment of people to each role and the maintenance of the assignment in the service knowledge management system (SKMS) or configuration management system (CMS) to provide visibility of the person responsible for particular activities.

Implementing integrated incident, problem, change, and configuration management processes with service level management to measure the quality of configuration items throughout the service lifecycle is also important for the support of this policy. This will ensure that the service can be managed, operated, and supported in accordance with the requirements and constraints specified within the service design by the service provider organization.

Ensuring that only competent staff can implement changes to controlled test environments and supported services will provide further protection against errors. Checking and performing configuration audits and process audits to identify configuration discrepancies and nonconformance that may impact service transitions will also support this policy.

Knowledge Transfer and Service Transition

The next policy is concerned with the important practice of knowledge transfer during the service transition lifecycle stage.

Policy

The policy specifies the knowledge transfer that is required in order to support decision-making in the organization. It states that service transition develops systems and processes to transfer knowledge for effective operation of the service and to enable decisions to be made at the right time by competent decision-makers.

It is a key function of the transition lifecycle stage to ensure that sufficient knowledge is transferred to the operational teams so that full understanding of new or changed services is communicated effectively. This will ensure that the decision-makers have the right information at the right time for effective operation of the service.

Principles

One of the principles that supports the transfer of knowledge and decision-making is that the service transition stage provides quality data, information, and knowledge at the right time to the right people to reduce effort spent waiting for decisions and consequent delays. It is important to ensure that there is adequate training and knowledge transfer to users to reduce the number of training calls that the service desk handles.

Service transition should improve the quality of information and data to improve user and stakeholder satisfaction while optimizing the cost of production and maintenance. This will involve improving the quality of documentation to reduce the number of incidents and problems caused by poor-quality user, release, deployment, support, and operational documentation. In addition, service transition should improve the quality of release and deployment documentation between the time changes are implemented and the document is updated.

It is also necessary to provide easy access to quality information to reduce the time spent searching for and finding information, particularly during critical activities such as handling a major incident.

A key principle is to establish the definitive source of information and share information across the service lifecycle and with stakeholders in order to maximize the quality of information and reduce the overhead in maintaining information. This will provide consolidated information to enable change management and release and deployment management to expedite effective decisions about promoting a release through the test environments and into a supported operational environment.

Best Practice

Demonstration of the principles for knowledge transfer include the provision of easy access and presentation and reporting tools for the service knowledge management system (SKMS) and configuration management system (CMS).

Another best practice approach is to provide quality user interfaces and tools to the SKMS and CMS for different people and roles to make decisions at appropriate times. It is important that, during service transition, the change evaluation process summarizes and publishes the predicted and unpredicted effects of change, deviations from actual versus predicted capability and performance, and the risk profile.

Service transition is also responsible for ensuring that service asset and configuration management information is accurate. This will be important to trigger approval and notification transactions for decision-making via workflow tools—for example, changes and acceptance of deliverables.

It is key to this lifecycle stage that there is provision of knowledge, information and data for deployment, service desk, operations, and support teams to resolve incidents and errors.

Plan Release Packages

The next policy relates to the release and deployment process in the service transition lifecycle and the need to plan properly for any and all releases.

Policy

The policy states that release packages are planned and designed to be built, tested, delivered, distributed, and deployed into the live environment in a manner that provides the agreed levels of traceability in a cost-effective and efficient way.

This policy ensures that there is an audit trail and that the environment remains stable and secure.

Principles

The supporting principles ensure that appropriate planning takes place in advance and that a release policy is agreed on with the business and all relevant stakeholders. It is important that all resources are properly utilized to enable costs to be optimized during this lifecycle stage. This will require coordination of resources across release and deployment activities.

To maintain the integrity of release components, release and distribution mechanisms are planned for the installation, handling, packaging, and delivery of releases. If there is a requirement for an emergency release, this should be managed in accordance with the emergency change procedure. Coordinating these processes ensures that the risks of backing out or remediating a failed release can be assessed and managed with minimal disruption to the business.

The success or failure of a release should be measured so that improvements can be made, if required, to effectiveness, efficiency, and cost optimization.

Best Practice

These principles will be evidenced by ensuring that all updates to releases are managed and recorded through the configuration management system. This should include the capture of the definitive versions of electronic media, including software, in a definitive media library prior to release into the service operations readiness test environment.

The planned release and deployment dates and deliverables should be recorded, referencing the related change requests and problems. This should include proven procedures for handling, distribution, and delivery of release and deployment packages, including verification. It is important to ensure that the prerequisites and corequisites for a release (for example, technical requirements for test environment) are documented and communicated to the relevant parties.

Anticipate and Manage Course Corrections

One of the most challenging factors for any service provider is that the businesses it supports often change their requirements to meet new demands from their customers. This is referred to as a course correction. A course correction should not be a radical shift in direction. It should be a minor adjustment to meet changing needs and to recognize where the plans do not match the reality. Successful transition is a journey, from the "as is" state within an organization toward the "required" state. In the dynamic world within which IT service management functions, it is very often the case that factors arise between initial design of a changed or new service and its actual transition. This means there is a need for course corrections to that service transition journey, altering the original service design planned course of action to the destination the customer needs to reach.

Policy

The policy states that the service provider should anticipate and manage course corrections. This will require staff to be trained to recognize the need for course corrections and to empower them to apply necessary variations within prescribed and understood limits.

Principles

The principles supporting the policy include building stakeholder expectations to accept that changes to plans are necessary and encouraged. It is important to learn from previous course corrections to predict future ones and reuse successful approaches.

This can be achieved by ensuring that end-of-transition debriefing sessions take place to propagate knowledge and make conclusions available through the service knowledge management system. All course corrections should be managed through the appropriate change management and baseline procedures.

Best Practice

In order to manage course corrections effectively, it is important to use best practice approaches such as project management practices and the change management process. This will include documenting and controlling changes, but without making the process bureaucratic (it must be easier to do it correctly than to cope with the consequences of doing it wrong).

A key factor will be to provide information on changes that were applied after the configuration baseline was established. This can be demonstrated by involving stakeholders with changes but managing issues and risks within service transition when appropriate.

Proactively Manage Resources

One of the major factors in managing transitions is the availability of specialist resources, and this needs to be part of the planning for service transition.

Policy

The policy states that the service provider should provide and manage shared and specialist resources across service transition activities to eliminate delays.

Principles

It is important to recognize the resources, skills, and knowledge required to deliver service transition within the organization. This will require the development of a team (including externally sourced resources) capable of successful implementation of the service transition strategy, service design package, and release package.

Establishing dedicated resources to perform critical activities to reduce delays is crucial to the management of shared resources to improve the effectiveness and efficiency of service transition. This will involve automating repetitive and error-prone processes to improve the effectiveness and efficiency of key activities such as distribution, build, and installation.

Best Practice

The best practice approach to demonstrate this policy is to work with human resources (HR), supplier management, and so on to identify, manage, and make use of competent and available resources. It is important to recognize and use competent and specialist resources outside the core ITSM team to deliver service transition.

Management of shared resources to minimize the impact that delays in one transition have on another transition is something that should be planned proactively. In this way, it should be possible to measure the impact of using dedicated versus nondedicated resources on delays—for example, using operations staff who get diverted to fix major incidents or resolving scheduling issues with test facilities.

Ensure Early Involvement in Service Lifecycle

A key factor for transition success is to ensure that checks on the new or changed services ability to deliver the proposed benefit are included early in the service lifecycle. Course corrections can be made during transition, but a complete restart is costly and time consuming.

Policy

The policy states that the service provider should establish suitable controls and disciplines to check at the earliest possible stage in the service lifecycle that a new or changed service will be capable of delivering the value required.

Principles

One principle supporting this early engagement is to use a range of techniques to maximize fault detection early in the service lifecycle in order to reduce the cost of rectification. This is because the later in the lifecycle an error is detected, the higher the cost of rectification.

It is also important to identify changes that will not deliver the expected benefits and either change the service requirements or stop the change before resources are wasted. Stopping a change is always a difficult choice because it is a recognition that the time and effort already expended have been wasted. So the earlier these checks can be made, the better for the service provider and customer.

Best Practice

There are a number of ways to ensure that early engagement is taking place, and foremost is to involve customers or customer representatives in service acceptance test planning and test design to understand how to validate that the service will add value to the customer's business processes and services.

Involving users in test planning and design whenever possible is also valuable. This should include base testing on how the users actually work with a service, not just how the designers intended it to be used.

As always, use previous experience to identify errors in the service design.

It is necessary to build in—at the earliest possible stage—the ability to check for and demonstrate that a new or changed service will be capable of delivering the value required of it. This may require an independent evaluation of the service design and internal audits to establish whether the risks of progressing are acceptable.

Quality Assurance

As the transition progresses, it is important to assure the quality of the new or changed service.

Policy

The policy here states that it will be necessary to verify and validate that the proposed changes to the operational services are defined in the service and release definitions, service model, and service design package. This is to assure that it can deliver the required service requirements and business benefits.

Principles

Assurance of quality is an important factor in any change, and service transition is responsible for assuring that the proposed changes to the operational services can be delivered according to the agreements, specifications, and plans within agreed confidence levels.

Customer and user satisfaction will be very important, and it is necessary to ensure that service transition teams understand what the customers and business actually require from a service to improve customer and user satisfaction.

There are many approaches to assuring success, but quality assurance and testing practices provide a comprehensive method for assuring the quality and risks of new or changed services.

There are some obvious requirements for the success of any transition. For example, test environments need to reflect the live environment to the greatest degree possible in order to optimize the testing efforts.

Also, there is the need to manage test design and execution and ensure that testing is delivered independently from the service designer and developer in order to increase the effectiveness of testing and meet any segregation of duty requirements.

Performing independent evaluations of the service design and the new or changed service to identify the risks that need to be managed and mitigated during build, test, deployment, and use of the service is also key. This will require the implementation of problem and configuration management processes across the service lifecycle to measure and reduce the known errors caused by implementing releases into the live environment.

Best Practice

The best practices for testing include ensuring that service transition understands the business's process and priorities. This often requires an understanding of the business's culture, language, customs, and customers.

Comprehensive engagement with, and involvement of, stakeholders is important both for effective testing and to build stakeholder confidence and so should be visible across the stakeholder community.

It is necessary to understand the differences between the build, test, and supported environments in order to manage any differences and improve the ability to predict a service's behavior. This will include ensuring that test environments are maintained under change and configuration management and that their continued relevance is considered directly as part of any change.

The service provider should establish the current service baseline and the service design baseline prior to evaluation of the change. They can then evaluate the predicted capability, quality, and costs of the service design, taking into account the results of previous experience and stakeholder feedback prior to release and deployment.

It is also very important to consider the circumstances that will actually be in place when service transition is complete, not just what was expected at the design stage.

Proactively Improve Quality During Service Transition

As with all lifecycle stages, it is important to proactively improve quality during service transition.

Policy

The resulting policy states that the service provider should proactively plan and improve the quality of the new or changed service during transition.

Principles

The supporting principles include the detection and resolution of incidents and problems during transition to reduce the likelihood of errors occurring during the operational phase and directly affecting business operations adversely. Often service providers apply these processes only during the operational stage of the lifecycle, but they are invaluable in management of transition as well. By proactively managing and reducing incidents, problems, and errors detected during service transition, the service provider will be able to reduce costs, rework, and the impact on the user's business activities. It is therefore important to align the management of incidents, problems, and errors during transition with the service operation processes in order to measure and manage the impact and cost of errors across the service lifecycle easily.

Best Practice

The best practice approaches that support this policy are to perform an independent evaluation of the new or changed service to identify the risk profile and prioritize the risks that need to be mitigated prior to transition closure. Such risks would include, for example, security risks that may impact the warranties.

Service providers should use the risk profile from the evaluation of the service design to develop risk-based tests. They should also encourage cross-fertilization of knowledge (for example, work-arounds and fixes) between transition and operation stages to improve problem diagnoses and resolution time. This should include the establishment of transition incident, problem, error, and resolution procedures and measures that reflect the procedures in use in the live environment. These processes will allow the service provider to fix known errors and resolve incidents in accordance with their priority for resolution, including documenting resolutions such as work-arounds so that the information can be analyzed. With this information, the service provider will be able to proactively analyze the root cause of high-priority and repeat incidents.

As with the live environment, it is important to record, classify, and measure the number and impact of incidents and problems against each release in the test, deployment, and live service stages in order to identify early opportunities to fix errors. This allows the service provider to compare the number and impact of incidents and problems between deployments in order to identify improvements and fix any underlying problems that will improve the user experience for subsequent deployments.

Summary

This chapter explored the 14 policies that ITIL identifies for the service transition lifecycle stage.

They provide the guidance for managing transitions successfully and should be used to ensure that transitions are carried out seamlessly, with minimal disruption to the business.

Exam Essentials

Understand the policies of service transition.   Each of the 14 policies has something specific to contribute to the lifecycle. It is important to be familiar with each of them.

Be able to explain and expand on the principles of service transition.   Supporting the policies, the principles provide further detail on the scope of the policies. Understanding these concepts will support your ability to answer any policy-based exam question.

Understand and expand on the best practices relating to the policies of service transition.   Each policy has a description of the best practice that supports its achievement. It is important that you understand the nature of these best practices.

Review Questions

You can find the answers to the review questions in the appendix.

1. Which group of people should approve the formal service transition policy?
    A. The IT steering group
    B. The service management team
    C. The management team
    D. The service level managers

2. Which of these is a service transition policy concerned with governance?
    A. Establish effective controls and disciplines throughout the service lifecycle.
    B. Review the governance standards periodically throughout a transition.
    C. Deliver the transition into the remaining service lifecycle stages without failures.
    D. Establish the audit requirements in service strategy.

3. Which of these is a service transition policy concerned with changing business requirements during a transition?
    A. Establish a change process that is used throughout the lifecycle.
    B. Anticipate and manage course corrections.
    C. Manage releases and ensure that there is an audit trail.
    D. Deliver services through a planned approach.

4. At what point should service transition ensure that controls are involved in the service lifecycle?
    A. As early as possible in the service lifecycle
    B. Only during the transition lifecycle stage
    C. During continual service improvement only
    D. Only during the design stage of the lifecycle

5. Which of these descriptions fits the term *resource* as used in the framework?
    1. *Resource* is a generic term that includes IT infrastructure, people, money, or anything else that might help to deliver an IT service.
    2. Resources are firmly embedded within an organization's people, systems, processes, and technologies.
        A. Neither statement
        B. Both statements
        C. Statement 1 only
        D. Statement 2 only

6. Which of these descriptions fits the term *capability* as used in the framework?

   1. *Capabilities* are groups of individuals working together to achieve a specific goal.

   2. *Capabilities* are intangible assets of an organization.

     A. Neither statement

     B. Both statements

     C. Statement 1 only

     D. Statement 2 only

7. Which of these are inputs to service transition from the service strategy lifecycle stage?

   A. Service design package, SLAs, OLAs

   B. Service portfolio, financial budget, vision

   C. CSI register, service reports, RFCs

   D. Actual performance data, results of operational testing

8. Which policy is concerned with the management of shared and specialist resources?

   A. Knowledge transfer and service transition

   B. Quality assurance

   C. Plan release packages

   D. Proactively manage resources

9. Which of these statements is correct about the policy relating to service transition efficiency?

   A. The policy recommends the creation of new policies for each transition.

   B. The policy recommends that transitions will be subject to strategic governance.

   C. The policy recommends the reuse of existing processes.

   D. The policy recommends that the service provider proactively plan and improve the quality of the new or changed service.

10. True or False? Service transition policies are important in the management and guidance of the service transition lifecycle stage.

   A. True

   B. False

Chapter

23

Service Transition Processes: Transition Planning and Support and Change Management

THE FOLLOWING ITIL INTERMEDIATE EXAM OBJECTIVES ARE DISCUSSED IN THIS CHAPTER:

✓ **Transition planning and support and change management are discussed in terms of**

- Purpose
- Objectives
- Scope
- Value
- Policies
- Principles and basic concepts
- Process activities, methods, and techniques
- Triggers, inputs, outputs, and interfaces
- Critical success factors and key performance indicators
- Challenges
- Risks

The syllabus covers the managerial and supervisory aspects of service transition processes. It excludes the day-to-day operation of each process and the details of the process activities, methods, and techniques as well as its information management. More detailed process operation guidance is covered in the intermediate service capability courses. More detail on the courses included in the ITIL exam framework can be found at www.axelos.com/qualifications/itil-qualifications. Each process is considered from the management perspective. That means at the end of this section of the book, you should understand those aspects that would be required to understand each process and its interfaces, oversee its implementation, and judge its effectiveness and efficiency.

Transition Planning and Support

The transition process involves many functional and process areas. All activities must be coordinated if the transition is to be successful.

Purpose

It is the job of the transition planning and support process to ensure that the multiple plans that are required for a successful transition are consistent and coordinated; it is also responsible for coordinating resources for which there may be competing demands.

Transition planning and support ensures that the strategy and design as declared in the service design package (SDP) are delivered successfully into operations. Throughout this activity, the goal is to minimize and mitigate against the risk of failure and disruption.

Objectives

The objectives of this process are concerned with ensuring that the purpose and goals are achieved in a consistent and repeatable manner through the production of comprehensive plans that ensure effective and efficient transition into the live environment.

The following list includes specific objectives:

- Planning and coordinating all of the transition resources to ensure that the requirements specified in service strategy and encoded in service design are delivered in service operation; in particular, this involves coordinating activities across projects, suppliers, and service teams where required.

- Coordinating activities across projects, suppliers, and service teams where required.

- Establishing new or changed services into supported environments within the predicted cost, quality, and time estimates.

- Establishing new or modified management information systems and tools, technology and management architectures, service management processes, and measurement methods and metrics to meet requirements established during the service design stage of the lifecycle.

- Ensuring the adoption of a common framework of standard reusable processes and supporting systems.

- Helping customer and business change projects align their activities with service transition by providing clear and comprehensive plans.

Risk management is an important part of transition planning, and process objectives include identifying, managing, and controlling risks to reduce the likelihood of failure and disruption. It ensures that all service transition issues, risks, and deviations are reported to the appropriate stakeholders and decision-makers.

The objectives of the process can be summarized as monitoring and improving the performance of the service transition lifecycle stage.

Scope

The scope of transition planning and support includes the maintenance of service transition policies, standards, and models for use in each transition. Every major change or new service must be guided through all the service transition processes, and transition planning and support ensures that this is carried out successfully. Of course there may be many transitions taking place, so transition planning and support is responsible for prioritizing conflicting resource requirements and coordinating the efforts needed to manage multiple simultaneous transitions.

Other activities within the scope of transition planning and support include planning the transition budget and resources needed and identifying opportunities for improving the performance of transition planning and support activities. It also ensures that service transition is coordinated with program and project management, service design, and service development activities.

It is important to note that transition planning and support is *not* responsible for detailed planning of the build, test, and deployment of individual changes or releases; these are part of change management and release and deployment management.

Value to the Business

Change can be disruptive and get in the way of the business achieving its aims. Properly planned and managed changes, however, will deliver the benefits the business wants, without disruption. This means that a large number of releases can be implemented. Release planning ensures that the IT plans for implementing changes are aligned with the customer, supplier, and business change project plans.

Policies, Principles, and Basic Concepts

Now we turn our attention to the basic concepts that support effective planning for service transition. The first of these is the service design package. You should remember from your foundation or other intermediate studies that the SDP is produced as a key output of service design.

The Service Design Package

The SDP includes a great deal of information required by the service transition team. This includes the service charter, which details the expected utility and warranty, as well as the outline budgets and timescales. The service specification, service models, and architectural design required to deliver the new or changed service are also included, along with details of any constraints. In preparation, each new or changed service release is defined and its design documented. The SDP will contain a detailed description of how the service components will be assembled and integrated into a release package. The release and deployment plans and the service acceptance criteria are also included. Service design packages will be created (or updated) for all major changes.

The Service Transition and Release Policies

Transition planning and support will make use of the service transition and release policies. In Chapter 22, "Service Transition Principles," we looked at transition policies in more detail. We shall look at policies specific to each of the service transition processes in the following chapters.

The release policy should be defined for one or more services and include numbering and naming conventions for different release types, the roles and responsibilities at each stage, and the expected frequency of releases.

The policy will include the requirement to deploy software from the definitive media library and the criteria for choosing and grouping changes into a release. Details of how the build, installation, and release distribution shall be automated will also be part of the policy.

Other elements of a release policy include details of what is required to capture and verify a release configuration baseline. The exit and entry criteria and authority for acceptance of the release into each stage and into each environment should be detailed together with the criteria and authorization to exit the early life support phase and complete the handover of the service to the service operation functions.

An example of a responsibility matrix for an organization that supports client/server applications is shown in Figure 23.1. Such a matrix will help to identify gaps and overlaps, and typical roles can be planned for the future. Study it, and if you can, try to imagine what one for your own organization might look like.

FIGURE 23.1 Example of a responsibility matrix for release points during service transition

	Development	Controlled test	Release to production	Live
Class of object	Released from	Accepted by	Authority to release to live	Accepted and supported by
Purchased package	Application development manager	Test manager	Change manager/ change authority	Operations manager
Customized modules	Application development manager	Test manager	Change manager/ change authority	Operations manager
Physical database changes	Application development manager	Database administrator	Change manager/ change authority	Database administrator
Server	Server builder	Server manager	Change manager/ change authority	Server manager
Desktop build (e.g., a new application)	Desktop development manager	Test manager	Change manager/ change authority	Desktop support manager
Desktop application (already built and within operational constraints)	Desktop development manager	Desktop support manager	Desktop support manager, change manager/ change authority	Desktop support manager
Desktop computers	Logistics	Desktop support	Desktop support manager, change manager/ change authority	Desktop support manager
Desktop service	Service development	Desktop support	Service level management, desktop support manager, change manager/change authority	Service level management, desktop support manager
Release/change authorization	Development manager, change manager/change authority	Test manager, change manager/ change authority	Release manager, test manager, operations manager, desktop support service, desk user at each site, customer stakeholder, change manager/change authority	Service desk users

It is useful to define different types of releases; this helps set expectations. A typical example is categorizing releases as major, minor, and emergency. Typically, major releases may be defined as those containing large areas of new functionality, which may be to replace temporary fixes to problems with a permanent fix. A major release supersedes all preceding minor upgrades, releases, and emergency fixes. Minor releases may be defined as those containing small enhancements and fixes, some of which may replace earlier emergency fixes. A minor upgrade or release usually supersedes all preceding emergency fixes.

Finally, emergency releases would normally contain corrections to a small number of known errors or sometimes a high-priority enhancement.

The release policy will specify the frequency of releases and the criteria for an emergency release. Emergency releases should be kept to a minimum, so the service provider must always balance the need for regular enhancements and the risk and disruption these may cause. However, releases that are too spaced out will lead inevitably to more emergency changes.

All releases should have a unique identifier that can be used by service asset and configuration management.

Here is an example of a naming convention:

- The format is AA_n.n.n.
- Characters before the underscore identify the service.
- Characters after the underscore identify the specific release.
- Each major release will increment the first number.
- Characters to the right of decimal points represent successively minor releases.

Using those conventions, consider the name EW_2.3:

- The service is EW.
- The first number after the underscore is 2, signifying that this is major release 2.
- The next number is 3, meaning this is the third minor release applied to major release 2.
- Another minor release applied to major release 2 would be numbered EW_2.4.
- If instead an emergency release is required, it would be EW_2.3.1.
- A new major release would be numbered EW_3.0.
- A minor release applied to release 3 would be EW_3.1.

Process Activities, Methods, and Techniques

In the following sections, we will consider the high-level management activities, methods, and techniques for the transition planning and support process. You need to understand the basic flow and activities, but you don't need to know the details of these activities or understand the details of specific methods and techniques; these aspects are covered in the Release, Control, and Validation Intermediate Capability course.

Transition Strategy

Each organization should choose an approach to service transition that suits their particular requirements. Organizations vary in the type of services they offer and the size of their operation. Their approach may be flexible or risk averse, and this will influence their choices regarding how frequently they wish to deploy a new release. So each organization needs to develop its own service transition strategy. This will define the overall approach to transition and the allocation of resources.

The strategy will cover the purpose, goals, and objectives of service transition for the organization and the context in which it operates. It will define what is within and outside the scope of transition and include any restrictions under which the organization has to operate (for example, standards or agreements or legal, regulatory, or contractual requirements). It will identify the various organizations and stakeholders involved in transition, such as third parties, strategic partners, suppliers and service providers, customers, and users. The organizational structure of service transition will be explored (we look at this in more detail in Chapter 28, "Organizing for Service Transition").

The transition strategy will define the transition policies, processes, and practices, including interfaces between the process and the service provider. There are other processes and methodologies being used during transition, such as program and project management; the strategy will define how these should interact. The roles and responsibilities of those involved will be defined, together with the methods to be used for resource planning and estimation activities.

The policies and processes will include those for preparing for transition, such as evaluation of training requirements and how changes and releases are to be authorized. The aim is to create a robust, effective reusable process so the organization's experience, expertise, tools, knowledge, and so forth can be reused.

The service transition strategy defines entry and exit criteria for each release stage and for stopping or restarting transition activities. It specifies the criteria for judging the success or failure of the transition.

It also identifies the requirements and content of the new or changed service and where and when the transition is to take place. It defines what is to be in each release, what the contents of the SDP should be, and requirements for environments to be used. It includes the planning and management of environments (for example, commissioning and decommissioning equipment).

The transition strategy will assign roles and responsibilities. This would include who is able to authorize changes, for example. If any training is required, it would be arranged for those needing it, together with any other knowledge transfer activities, such as drawing up FAQs.

The whole approach to service transition will be defined in the transition strategy. This would include a transition model covering each of the service transition lifecycle stages. The approach to managing changes and assets will be defined, including the baseline, evaluation, configuration audit and verification points, and the points where change authorization is needed. Any defined change windows would also be listed.

The strategy should explain the approach to how the estimation of resources and costs should be carried out and the steps that should be taken when preparing for a transition. The methods used to evaluate and authorize changes and plan the various stages of the release—including build, test, deployment, and early life support—should be described, together with a description of how errors should be handled, corrected, and controlled.

The strategy should also cover the management and control aspects of recording, progress monitoring, and reporting. Finally, details should be given regarding how the service performance will be measured, and the KPIs and improvement targets should be described.

The transition strategy should define the deliverables from transition activities, including mandatory and optional documentation for each stage and the expected format for each document. This documentation will include plans and reports and documentation for transition, change management, service asset and configuration management, releases, testing, builds, and so on.

As with any project, the key milestones will be described with the required budget and funding.

Service Transition Lifecycle Stages

The SDP will define the lifecycle stages of the transition. These stages will usually include acquiring and testing CIs and components and carrying out the build and test and service release test stages. The SDP also ensures that everything is in place for the new or changed service through a service operational readiness test. The remaining lifecycle stages will be the deployment and early life support of the service and the postimplementation review and closure. Remember, for each stage there will be exit and entry criteria and a list of mandatory deliverables.

Prepare for Service Transition   The next stage is to prepare for service transition. It is important to ensure that everything required for the transition has been considered prior to the start of the transition process. All of the required input deliverables must be available and complete, and the RFCs must be scheduled for the deployment. The CMS must be updated with the baseline information, and everything must be checked before permission is granted to proceed.

Planning and Coordinating Service Transition   A service transition plan describes the work environment, infrastructure, tasks, and activities required to release and deploy a release into the test environments and into production.

The plan will usually include a schedule of milestones, handover and delivery dates, and a list of the activities and tasks to be performed. The staffing, resource requirements, budgets, and timescales at each stage are detailed, and any issues and risks to be managed are listed in issue and risk registers. Finally, all plans should include lead times and contingency. The plan should be built as information becomes available. Use a service transition model, amended as required, and allocate and schedule the required resources.

Integrated Planning   Good planning and management are essential for successful deployment of a release. In reality, there is not just one plan but a series of interlocking plans, which need to be integrated to be successful. Transition plans need to be linked to lower-level plans such as release build and test plans. The linked plans are then integrated with the change schedule and release and deployment management plans. Careful planning at the start will help with successful resource allocation, utilization, budgeting, and accounting.

The overall service transition plan should include the key activities to acquire the release components and package the release as well as build, test, deploy, evaluate, and proactively improve the service through early life support. It will also include the activities to build and maintain the service and the IT infrastructure, the systems and environments, and the measurement system to support the transition activities.

Adopting Program and Project Management Best Practices   The plans for an individual service transition must be integrated with plans for other transitions taking place at the same time, using industry best practices for project and program management. At this point, it may become apparent that the required date is not feasible; reprioritize other work if required to free up the resources needed. Liaise with change management and release and deployment management throughout because changes made to the plan will impact those areas too.

Multiple releases and deployments should be managed as a program, with each significant deployment run as a project, typically using a framework such as PRINCE2 or the guidance in the *PMBOK Guide*. The actual deployment may be carried out by dedicated operations staff, by a team brought together for the purpose, and/or by external suppliers.

Significant deployments are complex projects in their own right. Planning needs to consider the people, application, hardware, software, documentation, and knowledge elements; this will mean subdeployments for each of these.

Review of the Plan   All service transition and release and deployment plans should be reviewed. A possible checklist of what to review would include the following items:

- A contingency allowance has been made for unplanned costs or delays.
- The plans include an allowance for varying lead times.
- Plans are complete, up-to date, and authorized.
- Release dates and deliverables are defined.
- Cost and other impacts are considered and risks managed.
- CIs have been checked for compatibility.
- Changes in circumstance are reflected in amendments to the plan.
- People are ready for the deployment.
- The release is in line with the SDP.

Transition Process Support   Service transition should provide support for all stakeholders to enable them to understand and follow the service transition framework of processes and supporting systems and tools. Support may be given to all stakeholders and should help them to follow the process correctly. Identifying subject matter experts from outside the service transition team may be helpful in the future. It's important to remember that project managers are not always aware of ITIL best practices, so transition planning and support needs to provide support in this area.

Transition planning and support should provide administrative support for managing service transition changes and work orders, issues, risks, and deviations. It should support the tools and service transition processes and monitor the service transition performance, identifying possible improvements to be input into continual service improvement. Any changes affecting the baseline configuration items will be controlled through change management.

Managing communication throughout a service transition is essential. Communication plans should include a clear definition of the objectives of communication and all the relevant stakeholders. The content and frequency of communication for each type of stakeholder may vary at different stages of the transition. The appropriate communications channel for different stakeholders should be chosen; possible channels include newsletters, posters, emails, reports, and presentations. The plan should also define how successful communication will be measured.

Plans and progress should be communicated and made available to relevant stakeholders. The list of stakeholders is in the SDP; this list should be updated as required.

Service transition activities should be monitored to ensure that the transition is proceeding according to plan. The actual transitions should be compared to the integrated service transition plans and release and change schedules. The progress of each transition should be monitored periodically, especially at milestone or baseline points. Management reports on the status of each transition will identify any significant variances so that action can be taken. As transitions are being deployed into a live and changing environment, it is to be expected that periodic adjustments will be required to the plans to suit the new situation.

Triggers, Inputs, Outputs, and Interfaces

The trigger for planning a single transition is an authorized request for change. Longer-term planning may be triggered by receipt of a change proposal from service portfolio management.

The service design package is the principle input. It contains the release package definition and design specification, the test and deployment plans, and the service acceptance criteria (or SAC). Key inputs to transition planning and support come from the service design stage of the lifecycle in the form of a service design package. It is common for some design work to actually be carried out by personnel who work within service transition teams, especially in the areas of release build and test and release deployment. Key inputs to this SDP will come from service level management, information security management, IT service continuity management, availability management, and capacity management.

The outputs are the transition strategy and an integrated set of service transition plans.

Transition planning and support has interfaces with almost every other area of service management. These include demand management, which should provide long-term information about likely resource requirements. The service portfolio management process should engage transition planning and support to provide input to their planning and decision-making and will also submit a change proposal to trigger longer-term planning within transition planning and support.

Business relationship management will help to manage appropriate two-way communication with customers. Supplier management will work during the service transition to ensure that appropriate contracts are in place. All service transition processes are coordinated by transition planning and support, so service transition planning and support must have interfaces with change management, SACM, release and deployment management, service validation and testing, change evaluation, and knowledge management. Pilots, the handover, and early life support must be coordinated with the service operation functions.

Technical management and application management will provide the personnel needed to carry out many aspects of service transition, for example, to review changes or plan deployments.

There are also interfaces with project and program management teams, which have to work very closely with transition planning and support and with customers who must be involved in many aspects of service transition.

Critical Success Factors and Key Performance Indicators

Here we look at some sample critical success factors (CSFs) for transition planning. Each sample CSF is followed by a small number of typical key performance indicators (KPIs) that support it. Each organization should develop KPIs that are appropriate for its level of maturity, its CSFs, and its particular circumstances.

Achievement against KPIs should be monitored and used to identify opportunities for improvement, which should be logged in the CSI register for evaluation and possible implementation.

The following list includes examples of critical success factors and key performance indicators for transition planning and support:

- Critical success factor: "Understanding and managing the trade-offs between cost, quality, and time."
  - KPI: An increase in the number of implemented releases that meet the customer's agreed requirements in terms of cost, quality, scope, and release schedule (expressed as a percentage of all releases)
  - KPI: A reduced variation of actual versus predicted scope, quality, cost, and time
- Critical success factor: "Understanding and managing risks of failure and disruption."
  - KPI: A reduction in number of issues, risks, and delays
  - KPI: Improved service transition success rates
- Critical success factor: "Managing conflicting demands for shared resources."
  - KPI: Increased project and service team satisfaction with the service transition practices
  - KPI: A reduced number of issues caused by conflicting demands for shared resources

Challenges

Managing and coordinating the many stakeholders involved in a project is the biggest challenge for transition planning and support, especially because these relationships may not be hierarchical and so require careful negotiation.

Delays and test failures may cause delays, leading to the challenge of coordinating and prioritizing many new or changed services.

Finally, there is the challenge of understanding the risks and issues for each project in order to proactively manage resource planning.

Risks

One risk to transition planning is that the process will become entirely reactive. There is also the risk that long-term planning will be insufficient due to poor information from demand management and service portfolio management. Poor relationships with project and program teams may result in sudden and unexpected service transition requirements. There is also the possibility that resource constraints may cause a delay to one transition, therefore causing delays to subsequent transitions. Finally, there may be insufficient information to prioritize conflicting requirements.

Change Management

The one constant we can be sure of in IT management is that there will always be a need to change what we have. IT does not stand still, and whether changes are made to take advantage of new technology or because the business requirement has evolved, effective service management depends on being able to implement changes without disruption to the services being provided. Changes may be proactive, such as just described—improving or expanding the service—or they may be a reaction to errors or changing circumstances. We need to manage these changes to minimize the risk to services while ensuring that users and customers are fully prepared.

ITIL's change management guidance can be scaled to fit organizations of all sizes, and of all types.

The Purpose of Change Management

The purpose of the *change management* process is to control the lifecycle of all changes, enabling beneficial changes to be made with minimum disruption to IT services.

The Objective of Change Management

The objective of change management is to facilitate the changes that the business requires, thus ensuring that services continue to align with the business needs. This means satisfying the customer's changing business requirements while avoiding incidents, disruption, and rework. Change management seeks to optimize overall business risk. Optimizing risk may mean avoiding a risk completely, but it also includes consciously accepting a risk because of the potential benefit.

Responding to requests for change entails an assessment of risk, impact, resource requirements, and business benefit. The risk of not implementing the change should be considered also, as well as any risks that the change might introduce. It is essential to maintain the balance between the need for change and the impact of that change.

This means that the process is also responsible for managing the interfaces between the service lifecycle stages, ensuring the quality of the inputs and outputs.

Another objective of change management is to ensure that all changes are thoroughly understood. This means that they must be recorded, evaluated, prioritized, planned, tested, implemented, documented, and reviewed in a controlled manner. Change management also ensures that all changes to configuration items are recorded in the configuration management system.

The Scope of Change Management

The ITIL definition of a change is "the addition, modification, or removal of anything that could have an effect on IT services." This means that the scope of change management includes changes to all architectures, processes, tools, metrics, and documentation as well as changes to IT services and other configuration items. Changing any of these could have an effect on the IT service, so change management ensures that we understand what we are changing and the potential impact of that change.

Definition of a change: "The addition, modification, or removal of anything that could have an effect on IT services."

The scope of change management is defined by each organization, but it usually includes changes to all CIs across the whole service lifecycle, including both physical and virtual assets. Changes to any of the five aspects of service design are also in scope, including changes to service solutions; management information systems and tools; technology and management architectures required to provide the services; the processes needed to design, transition, operate, and improve the services; and the measurement systems, methods, and metrics used to measure it.

It is for each organization to decide exactly what lies outside the scope of its own change management process, such as changes with wider impact, like those to departmental organization, policies, or business operations, for example. It should be noted that such changes would involve requests for change (RFCs) later to cater to the service changes that would follow as a consequence. Operational changes such as component repairs may also be excluded.

Figure 23.2 illustrates a typical scope for the service change management process for an IT department. It shows how the process interfaces with the business and suppliers at strategic, tactical, and operational levels. It shows the interfaces with internal service providers and also with those external service providers where there are shared assets that need to be under change management.

Service change management interfaces with business change management (to the left in the diagram) and with the supplier's change management (to the right). The supplier in this case may be an external supplier, using its own change management process, or a project team using project change mechanisms.

FIGURE 23.2 Scope of change management and release and deployment management for services

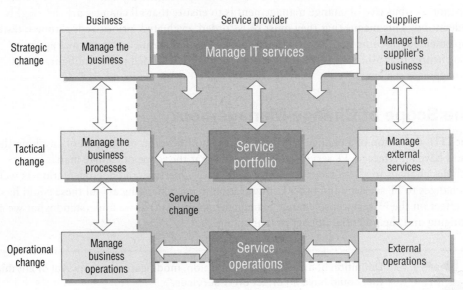

The service portfolio defines current, planned, and retired services, and it therefore helps those involved to understand the potential impact of changes on current services. Changes may originate from different areas of the lifecycle. Strategic changes come as proposals from service strategy and service portfolio management, while changes to a service come from service design, continual service improvement, service level management, and service catalog management. Corrective changes are also implemented to resolve faults and will originate from incident and problem management.

Remember, change management is *not* responsible for coordinating the various service management processes to ensure the smooth implementation of projects. This is carried out by transition planning and support.

The Value of Change Management to the Business

Next, we consider the value that change management provides to the business. Consider your own organization. How would the business be impacted by poor IT change management? What benefits are gained by the introduction of good change management, and how would you explain this to the business?

Availability of a service is a key warranty aspect; without a reliable service, the business will not achieve the benefits the service is designed to deliver. Protecting this aspect, ensuring that changes do not disrupt the service, is a major benefit of implementing change management. Good change management enables the service provider to add value to the business by implementing beneficial changes while protecting existing services. It ensures that changes meet the business requirements while optimizing the costs of change. By providing auditable evidence of how changes are managed, the adherence of the organization to governance, legal, contractual, and regulatory requirements can be shown. This is also helpful where the service provider needs evidence of adherence to best practice processes in order to pass audits for ISO/IEC 20000 or ISO/IEC 38500 standards.

Change management will reduce the number of failed changes, minimizing disruption and rework. When the process is enforced, the number of unauthorized changes should decrease, ensuring that only well-planned and understood changes are implemented. This, in turn, should reduce disruption and time spent resolving change-related incidents. By ensuring that changes are well managed, with the right balance of control without unnecessary bureaucracy, the service provider should be able to deliver accurate estimates of the time and cost required for a change and to track and implement changes promptly to meet business timescales. Change management ensures that risks associated with changes are understood and mitigated where possible. Emergency changes are kept to a minimum and availability is maximized.

Effective change management is essential for any organization as the reliance on complex IT services becomes more widespread. Taking the time to analyze the impact of business change on IT, and an IT change on the business, is essential, as is communication with those affected and accurate records of actions taken. It enables the service provider to meet business needs and costs in a timely and controlled manner and ensures that changes comply with governance standards; by controlling change, service providers are able to accurately predict costs and assess risks.

Despite the effort made, some disruption resulting from changes is inevitable; efficiently handling any incidents or problems caused by the change should keep this to a minimum. Indeed, considerable cost savings and efficiencies can be gained from well-planned changes and releases.

Change Management Policies, Principles, and Basic Concepts

The following sections set out basic concepts within change management that support its effective execution.

Policies

Laying down the principles behind the change process in one or more policy documents will help staff understand the seriousness with which this process is taken by senior management, and this, in turn, will help build a culture where change management is taken seriously and the agreed process is followed. This will increase the success rate of changes and releases, which will help build credibility for the process and reduce attempts to bypass it.

Ensuring adherence to best practice in this area can be challenging because pressure to meet deadlines and to cut costs encourages the cutting of corners by reducing testing and training. The existence of published policies will help such pressures to be resisted; this may even include a decision not to implement a required change due to these policies having been ignored.

Let's look now at some of the possible policies supporting change management that an organization might adopt. The aim of these policies is to encourage zero tolerance for unauthorized changes. The process must align with business, project, and stakeholder change management processes to be effective. IT is not responsible for the business change process but should ensure that the IT process aligns to the business needs. Other policies are as follows:

- All changes must create business value, and the business benefits must be measured and reported.
- Prioritization of changes should follow the guidance laid down regarding innovation versus preventive versus detective versus corrective changes.
- Accountability and responsibilities for changes are laid down throughout the service lifecycle.
- Segregation of duty controls ensures that, for example, the person agreeing, the success of a test is not the person doing the testing.
- A single focal point for changes helps to minimize conflicting changes and potential disruption to supported environments.

Here are some other possible policies supporting change management that an organization might adopt:

- Work with access management to ensure people who are not authorized to make changes do not have access to supported environments.
- Work with other processes such as service asset and configuration management to detect unauthorized changes, and incident management to identify change-related incidents.
- Ensure that changes are implemented at suitable times, by specifying change windows and then enforcing them.
- Evaluate the risk of all changes that impact service.
- Measure the efficiency and effectiveness of the process.

Design and Planning Considerations

The design of a robust change management process should include any legislative or regulatory requirements that may exist within the organization. It should also consider the organizational roles and responsibilities required to ensure effective management of the process, along with the dependencies and relationships with other service management processes. Measurement is a key characteristic of any process, and suitable measures should be included to ensure that the process is working effectively. All of these aspects should be fully documented to ensure understanding of the complete process, including how changes are to be classified and authorized. Identification and classification of changes would include the change document identifiers to be used, the types of change documents required, templates for change documentation, and the expected content. The approach to prioritization of changes using impact and urgency should be specified, including the roles, responsibilities, and accountabilities.

Other design requirements for change management processes are as follows:

- Organizational roles and responsibilities such as those for independent testing and formal evaluation of change

- Change authorization levels and escalation rules and the composition of the CAB and ECAB

- Details of how changes should be planned and communicated to stakeholders

- How changes may be grouped into releases or change windows and the detailed procedures for raising, assessing, evaluating, and verifying changes

- Identification of dependencies and clashes between changes

- The interfaces with other service management processes, especially the provision of information to service asset and configuration management

- The measurement and reporting of changes

The change management process should be planned in conjunction with release and deployment management and service asset and configuration management. This helps the service provider evaluate the impact of the change on the current and planned services and releases.

Types of Change Requests

A change request is a formal communication seeking an alteration to one or more configuration items. This may be a request for change (RFC) document, or the request may be made by a call to the service desk or as a result of a project initiation document. Major changes may require a change proposal, which is created by the service portfolio management process. The procedures for different types of change should be appropriate for each type; minor changes should not require a lot of documentation. Similarly, the levels of authorization required should be appropriate for each level of change.

There are three different types of service changes:

- Many changes can be categorized as standard changes. These are low risk, relatively common, and follow a defined procedure. As a result, they do not need to be assessed each time they are requested; instead these changes are preauthorized.

- Emergency changes must be implemented as soon as possible—for example, to resolve a major incident or implement a security patch. These are normally defined as changes where the risk of *not* carrying out the change is greater than the risk of implementing it.

- All other changes are defined as normal changes.

Changes may be categorized as major, significant, and minor, depending on the cost and risk involved. This categorization may be used to identify an appropriate change authority.

As much use as possible should be made of devolved authorization, both through the standard change procedure and through the authorization of minor changes by change management staff.

Changes, RFCs, and Change Records

The terms *change*, *change record*, and *RFC* are often used inconsistently. The ITIL core guidance defines these terms as follows:

- Change: The addition, modification, or removal of anything that could have an effect on IT services, including changes to architectures, processes, tools, metrics, and documentation as well as changes to IT services and other configuration items.

- Change record: A record containing the lifecycle of a single change and referencing the affected configuration items (CIs). A change record is created for every request received and may be stored in the configuration management system or elsewhere in the service knowledge management system.

- Request for change (RFC): A formal proposal for a change to be made. It may be recorded on paper or electronically.

RFCs are used only to submit requests; they are not used to communicate the decisions of change management or to document the details of the change. A change record contains all the required information about a change, including information from the RFC, and is used to manage the lifecycle of that change.

Change Models and Workflows

A change model predefines how to handle a particular type of change; this can then be programmed into the support tool to manage the change, ensuring that every such change is handled in this way. Models are useful for common changes and also those requiring specialized handling, such as emergency changes that may need different authorization and may have to be documented retrospectively or any changes that require specific sequences of testing and implementation.

Change models are especially useful for standard changes resulting from service requests.

The change model would normally include the steps to be carried out to handle the change, including handling issues and unexpected events. The model would list the steps in chronological order, with dependencies or concurrent steps, and the responsibility for each step would be defined. Timescales and thresholds for completion of the actions and any escalation procedures are also included. The support tools used can then automate many of these aspects.

Change Proposals

Major changes that involve significant cost, risk, or organizational impact will usually be initiated through the service portfolio management process. Before the new or changed service is chartered, it is reviewed for its potential impact. Authorization of the change proposal does not authorize implementation of the change but allows the service to be chartered so that service design activity can commence.

The proposal contains a high-level description of the change, including utility and warranty levels and the business outcomes it supports. The full business case and an outline schedule for design and implementation of the change are the remaining contents.

When the change proposal is authorized, the change schedule is updated to include the proposed change. RFCs will then be used in the normal way to request authorization for specific changes.

Standard Changes (Preauthorized)

As previously discussed, standard changes are preauthorized by change management, and a documented procedure is followed to deliver a specific change. Every standard change should have a change model defining how it should be handled. Many standard changes are triggered by the request fulfilment process and may be directly recorded and passed for action by the service desk.

The crucial elements of a standard change include a defined trigger to initiate the change and a series of tasks that are well known, documented and proven, and preauthorized. Budgetary approval will be preauthorized or within the control of the change requester. Crucially, the risk involved in implementing the change is usually low and always well understood. A change model is usually associated with each standard change.

Standard changes should be identified early on when the change management process is being built. This helps avoid unnecessarily high levels of administration leading to staff resistance to the process.

Remediation

All changes must include a plan for dealing with failure; this plan must itself be tested. Understanding the remediation options helps in the assessment of the risk associated with the change—if a simple back-out is possible, the risk is reduced. Change plans should include decision points for when remediation is required and sufficient time for it to be carried out.

NOTE

Definition of remediation: "Actions taken to recover after a failed change or release. Remediation may include back-out, invocation of service continuity plans, or other actions designed to enable the business process to continue." *ITIL Service Transition*

Change Management Process Activities, Methods, and Techniques

As stated at the start of this chapter, the specific details of the methods and techniques are covered in the intermediate service capability courses, specifically the Release, Control, and

Validation course and syllabus. The Service Transition exam syllabus considers only the management recommendations existing within the workflow. Managing changes effectively requires a number of activities to be addressed:

- Planning and controlling changes, ensuring that the schedule for implementing changes is appropriate
- Communicating the changes to stakeholders with the right information at the right time
- Ensuring that those with authority to authorize or make decisions about changes are the most appropriate people, with the necessary authority levels

We have already mentioned the importance of ensuring that remediation plans are in place. Measuring and controlling change is also essential to protect the live environment, as is understanding the impact of changes. Finally, providing management information through reporting helps to identify weaknesses in the process that may be addressed through continual service improvement.

Typical activities in managing individual changes include creating and recording the RFC and then reviewing it so that incomplete or wrongly routed changes can be identified and filtered out. The change is assessed and evaluated, and the appropriate change authority identified. A decision is made regarding who should be involved in the CAB for this change. The change is evaluated in terms of its business justification, impact, cost, benefits, risks, and predicted performance, and a request is submitted to the change evaluation process. The change is then authorized or rejected and the stakeholders informed, especially the initiator. If the change is approved, the implementation is planned, coordinated, reviewed, and closed. The documentation (for example, baselines and evaluation reports and the document listing the lessons learned) is collated in the SKMS. When all actions are completed, the change is closed.

NB information is gathered throughout the process; it is stored in the SKMS, recorded in the CMS, and reported.

In Figure 23.3, you can see an example of a normal change, such as a change to the service provider's services, applications, or infrastructure. You can see how the status of the change changes. As the change progresses, information about it and the configuration items involved is updated.

In this example, authorization will be required for both the activities of building and testing the change, as well as to separate authorization for the activity of change deployment. For other changes, there may be additional authorization steps, such as to authorize change design or change development.

Change Authorities

Each change must be authorized by a change authority. The change authority could be a particular role, person, or group of people; for example, the security manager role may be required to authorize certain categories of change, or the authorization of each support team leader may be required. The levels of authorization are dependent upon the type, size, risk, and potential business impact of the change. Where changes affecting several sites in a large enterprise are planned, there may need to be authorization by a higher-level change authority such as a global CAB or the board of directors.

FIGURE 23.3 Example of a process flow for a normal change

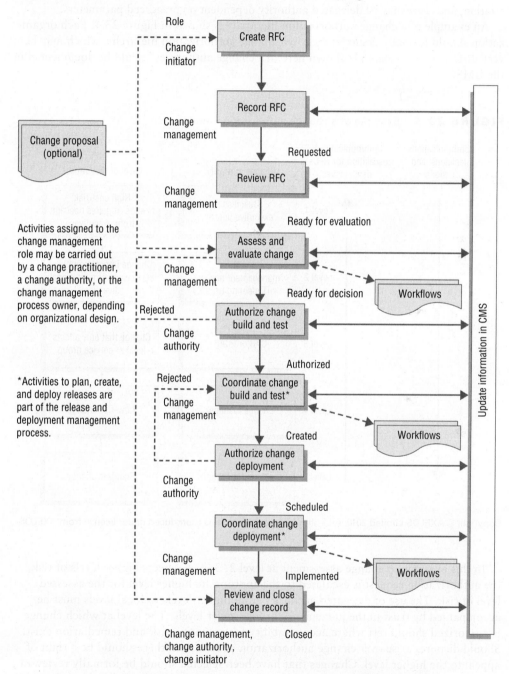

Depending on the culture of the organization, there may be many or few layers of authorization, and there may be delegated authority dependent on preagreed parameters.

An example of a change authorization hierarchy is shown in Figure 23.4. Each organization should formally document its own change authorization hierarchy, which may be very different to the example shown here. All change authorities should be documented in the CMS.

FIGURE 23.4 Example of a change authorization model

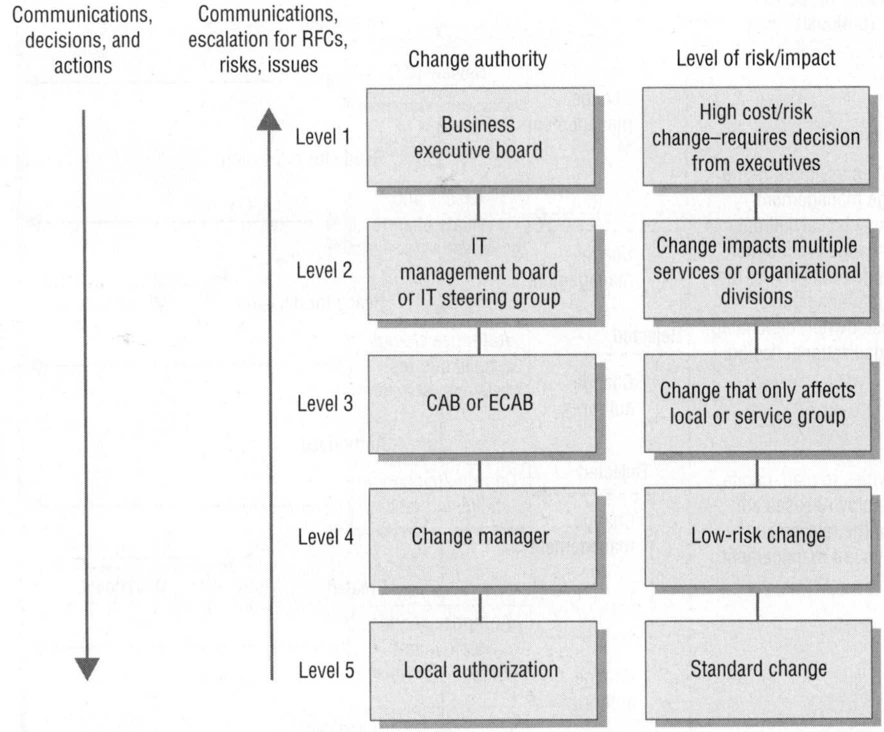

Communications, decisions, and actions	Communications, escalation for RFCs, risks, issues	Change authority	Level of risk/impact
	Level 1	Business executive board	High cost/risk change–requires decision from executives
	Level 2	IT management board or IT steering group	Change impacts multiple services or organizational divisions
	Level 3	CAB or ECAB	Change that only affects local or service group
	Level 4	Change manager	Low-risk change
	Level 5	Local authorization	Standard change

In this example, if change assessment at level 2, 3, or 4 detects higher levels of risk, the authorization request is escalated to the appropriate higher level for the assessed level of risk. The use of delegated authority from higher levels to local levels must be accompanied by trust in the judgement of those lower levels. The level at which change is authorized should rest where accountability for accepting risk and remediation exist. Should disputes arise over change authorization or rejection, there should be a right of appeal to the higher level. Changes that have been rejected should be formally reviewed and closed.

Standard Deployment

Figure 23.5 and Figure 23.6 show the equivalent process flow for some examples of standard changes.

After a change has been built and tested and the deployment procedure has been used successfully one or more times, it may be appropriate to use a standard deployment request change model for future deployments of the same change. This is much simpler than the full change management process flow. You can see an example of a process flow for this kind of standard change in Figure 23.5.

FIGURE 23.5   Example of a process flow for a standard deployment request

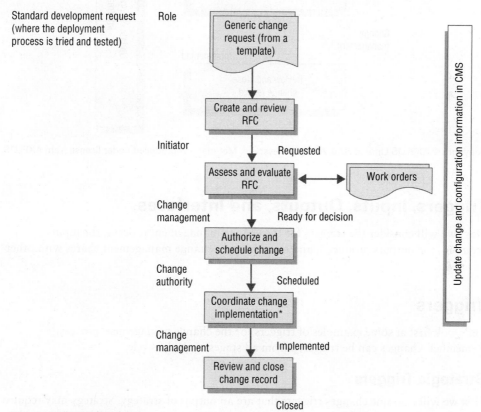

*Includes build and test the change

Some very low-risk changes may be delegated to service desk or other service operation staff as a change authority. The change model for this kind of standard change may be very simple, as shown in Figure 23.6.

FIGURE 23.6   Example of a process flow for a standard operational change request

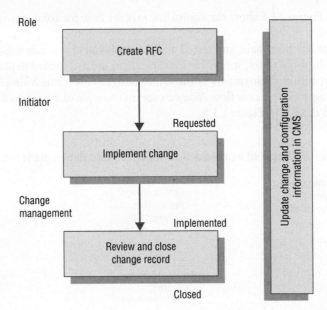

Triggers, Inputs, Outputs, and Interfaces

Next we will consider the triggers for the change management process, the inputs required, the outputs produced, and the interfaces change management shares with other processes.

Triggers

Let's look first at some examples of triggers for the change management process. Remember, changes can be triggered from all stages of the lifecycle.

Strategic Triggers

First we will examine changes triggers that are an output of strategy. Strategy may require changes to achieve specific objectives while minimizing costs and risks. There is no such thing as cost-free and risk-free strategic plans or initiatives; we can only try to minimize these. Let's look at some examples of programs and initiatives that implement strategic changes.

Legal, regulatory, policy, or standards changes may require changes to services, as would organizational changes. Changes may result from an analysis of business, customer, and user activity patterns. Adding new services or updates to the service, customer, or contract portfolios or changing the sourcing model would also require the service provider to carry out changes. Finally, there are always new advancements in technology; the service provider may want to take advantage of them.

Changes to the services to be offered through the service portfolio and changes to the current services in the service catalog will trigger the change management process. These could include changes to service packages, service definitions or characteristics or to utility, warranty, or service levels, or capacity and resource requirements. Any changes to costs, service assets, or acceptance criteria could also trigger the process. Take a minute to consider all of these examples of possible triggers and consider the possible impact of each; it is the responsibility of change management to manage the possible impact while ensuring that the benefits are realized.

Operational Changes

Many requests from users result in operational changes; these could include a request for a password reset, a request for access, or a request to move an IT asset. These types of changes will often be managed as standard changes by the request fulfilment process.

Service operation functions will also implement changes via the normal and standard change procedures. They may be corrective, such as rebooting a server or restarting an application, or preventative, such as applying a service pack, which may prevent possible incidents. In either case, they may impact a shared service.

The final trigger comes from CSI and concerns changes to deliver continual service improvement. As a result of CSI actions, a requirement for a change may be identified. CSI may identify improvements in, for example, technology, processes, and documentation that are required to deliver an improvement in the service. These changes will be raised as RFCs, and their implementation could have unintended negative effects on service provision and on other CSI initiatives. They therefore need to be managed to minimize the risk.

Inputs

Here are some examples of inputs to the change management process:

- Service charters for new or significantly changed services
- Change requests, change proposals, change records, and authorized changes
- Business information from the organization's business and IT strategy, plans and financial plans, and information on the business's current and future requirements
- Business impact analysis, providing information on the impact, priority, and risk associated with each service or changes to service requirements
- The service portfolio, including the service catalog and the business requirements for new or changed services in terms of service packages and service options
- Governance requirements
- Corporate, legal, and regulatory policies and requirements
- Test results, test reports, and evaluation reports

Outputs

Change management has the following outputs:

- Rejected or approved RFCs

- The change to the services, service, or infrastructure resulting from the approved RFCs

- New, changed, or disposed assets or configuration items (for example, baseline, service package, release package)

- A revised change schedule and projected service outage, authorized change plans, decisions, and actions

- Change documents, records, and reports.

Interfaces

There are several interfaces between change management and other individual processes. Any process may be affected by a change, and so a feature of change management is the need for collaboration between diverse areas. It is important to identify clear boundaries, dependencies, and rules on how these interfaces will operate.

Change management works closely with the other transition processes. For example, it works with transition planning and support to ensure that there is a coordinated overall approach to managing service transitions and with service asset and configuration management to ensure that all changes to CIs are logged. The process must also be tightly integrated with change evaluation, with clear agreement on which types of change will be subject to formal change evaluation and the necessary time set aside for this. The evaluation report will be used by the CAB to help decision-making. The implementation of the change may also require an interface with release and deployment management.

When a proposed change could have an impact on other parts of the organization, the change management process must interface with business change processes and business project management. The service portfolio management process will submit change proposals to change management before chartering new or changed services in order to ensure that potential conflicts for resources or other issues are identified. Any process that could affect or be affected by a change must therefore interface with the change management process. The problem management process will be a source of many changes as fixes to faults are implemented. There are several major connections between change management and the following processes:

- Financial management

- Business relationship management

- Strategy management

- Service validation and testing

- Service level management

- Availability, capacity, continuity, and security (the "warranty" processes)

Each of these can be the source of a change or be affected by a change.

Critical Success Factors and Key Performance Indicators

Each organization should develop key performance indicators (KPIs) that are appropriate for its level of maturity, its CSFs, and its particular circumstances.

Achievement against KPIs should be monitored and used to identify opportunities for improvement, which should be logged in the CSI register for evaluation and possible implementation.

KPIs must be meaningful and SMART (that is, specific, measurable, achievable, relevant, and time-bound) and as such, should enable management to make timely and accurate actionable decisions. KPIs show whether the CSF is being achieved. For example, the achievement of the CSF "Responding to business and IT requests for change that will align the services with the business needs while maximizing value" could be measured by KPIs showing an increased percentage of changes that meet the customer's agreed requirements or that deliver benefits of change (measured by the "value of improvements made" and "negative impacts prevented") that exceed the costs of change. Other relevant KPIs would be a reduction in the backlog of change requests and the average time taken to implement a change falling within SLA targets.

Additional examples are available in the *ITIL Service Transition* core volume.

Challenges

The major challenge for change management is ensuring that all changes are recorded and managed so that no change circumvents the process. The challenge of convincing staff of the importance of the process is mitigated if senior management support is visibly present. It can also be difficult to persuade staff that change management facilitates changes rather than hampering or delaying them and adds value by helping changes happen faster and with higher success rates. If these challenges in convincing staff of the value of the process are met, the number of unauthorized changes will be reduced.

Another common challenge for organizations is to move away from simple change authorization, when RFCs are considered only just before changes are about to go live, and toward complete change management, where they are assessed and planned from earlier in the lifecycle. Larger organizations may also find it challenging to obtain agreement for the required levels of change authority and to communicate effectively between these levels.

Risks

Risks to change management include, primarily, a lack of commitment to the change management process. This may be a lack of commitment from the business (such as a lack of business sponsorship), from IT management (such as a lack of IT management sponsorship), or from IT staff (leading to changes circumventing the process).

Other risks include insufficient assessment of changes, with a tick-the-box attitude, which allows changes to be made without a full assessment and unnecessary delays to implementation of changes. This is often due to excessive bureaucracy. These risks, if they occur, encourage the lack of commitment to the process. There may be pressure from the business or projects to cut corners, leading to insufficient time or resources for assessment. Finally, the interfaces with other processes may be poorly defined, causing confusion.

Summary

This chapter explored the first two processes in the service transition stage, transition planning and support and change management. By ensuring that the introduction of a new or changed service is carefully planned and coordinated with any other changes taking place, using the transition planning and support process, service providers can reduce the risk of the change disrupting other operational services. The change management process ensures that the implications of changes are examined to an appropriate level, balancing the need to understand the possible impact and risk, without overburdening the process with unnecessary reviews of repeat low-risk changes. Change management ensures that changes are authorized and agreed, contain a remediation plan, and, in the case of an emergency, can be expedited through the emergency change process.

We examined how these processes interact and the importance of these processes to the business and to the IT service provider.

Exam Essentials

Understand the purpose and objectives of transition planning and support. It is important for you to be able to explain the purpose and objectives of this process. The process is there to ensure a successful transition by ensuring that plans are coordinated and resources are provided as required.

Understand the importance of the transition planning and release policy and typical contents of such a policy. Be able to explain how the release policy helps ensure a successful transition. Make sure you can list the main contents of such a policy, including numbering conventions, roles and responsibilities at each stage, use of the DML, prioritization, baselining, and the frequency of each type of release.

Understand the purpose and objectives of change management. Be able to explain how the change management process controls the lifecycle of all changes, enabling beneficial changes to be made with minimum disruption to the business.

Explain the different types of change and when they would be used. Understand that not all changes require the same level of oversight and that even when change is desirable, it may not be possible. Be able to define and explain the differences between normal, standard, and emergency change.

Be able to explain when a change proposal would be required. A change proposal is needed only if the change has a major impact on the business in terms of risk, cost, or resources.

Be able to explain why the members of the CAB may vary from change to change. Understand the role of the CAB and the importance of having the appropriate stakeholders approve each change.

Understand the critical success factors and key performance indicators for each of the processes. Measurement of each process is an important part of understanding whether it is successful or requires improvement.

Review Questions

You can find the answers to the review questions in the appendix.

1. Which of these activities is out of scope for transition planning and support?

   A. Planning the budget and resources needed

   B. Improving the performance of transition planning and support activities

   C. Detailed planning of the build, test, and deployment of individual changes or releases

   D. Coordinating service activities with program and project management, service design, and service development activities

2. Which of these would be a valid start point for the change management process?

   1. Request for change

   2. Service desk call

   3. Project initiation document

   4. Change proposal

       A. 1, 2, and 4

       B. 1, 3, and 4

       C. All of the above

       D. 1 and 4 only

3. Which of these is NOT a valid type of change, according to ITIL?

   A. Emergency

   B. Urgent

   C. Normal

   D. Standard

4. Which of the following is NOT true about KPIs?

   A. They should be meaningful.

   B. They should be SMART (specific, measurable, achievable, relevant, and time-bound).

   C. They describe an element that is necessary for an organization or project to achieve its mission.

   D. They help management make timely and accurate actionable decisions.

5. Which of the following is the correct definition of a release package?

   A. A set of configuration items that will be built, tested, and deployed together

   B. A group of components of a service that are normally released together

   C. One or more changes to an IT service that are built, tested, and deployed together

   D. A repeatable way of dealing with a particular category of release

6. Which if these is the *best* description of the purpose of the transition planning and support process?

A. To provide overall planning and coordination of resources for service transition

B. To provide coordination for all change management activities

C. To provide planning for all designs in the service lifecycle

D. To provide planning for operational activities during release management

7. Which option is NOT a recommended part of a release policy?

A. A unique identification structure or naming convention to ensure that releases can be easily identified and tracked

B. Definitions of the roles and responsibilities required for the management of the release throughout all its stages

C. Definition of the configuration management database naming convention

D. Use of the definitive media library for all software asset releases

8. The change advisory board (CAB) should contain relevant stakeholders; the membership of the ECAB is different from the CAB. Which of the following stakeholders would be appropriate members of an ECAB?

1. Customer

2. Representative of application support team

3. Senior IT manager

4. Representative of desktop support team

5. Senior technical manager

6. Representative of network support team

7. Service desk manager

    A. All of the above

    B. 2, 4, and 6 only

    C. 3, 5, and 7 only

    D. 1, 3, and 5 only

9. Which of the following statements about the relationship between transition planning and project management is INCORRECT?

A. Service transition should adopt program and project management best practice.

B. Simple transitions may not require any project management.

C. Multiple releases and deployments should be managed as a program, with each significant deployment run as a project.

D. Where unavoidable, transition planning should interface with project management; however, project management is a different framework, so to avoid confusion, this should happen only exceptionally.

10. Which of these statements about transition planning and support is/are correct?

    1. Transition planning and support identifies and manages risks in accordance with the risk management framework adopted by the organization.

    2. Transition planning and support ensures that repeatable processes are adopted by all engaged in the transition.

    A. 1 only

    B. 2 only

    C. Both

    D. Neither

Chapter
24

Service Transition Processes: Service Asset and Configuration Management

---

THE FOLLOWING ITIL INTERMEDIATE EXAM OBJECTIVES ARE DISCUSSED IN THIS CHAPTER:

✓ The service transition process of service asset and configuration management is discussed in terms of

- Purpose
- Objectives
- Scope
- Value
- Policies
- Principles and basic concepts
- Process activities, methods, and techniques
- Triggers, inputs, outputs, and interfaces
- Critical success factors and key performance indicators
- Challenges
- Risks

The syllabus covers the managerial and supervisory aspects of service transition processes. It excludes the day-to-day operation of each process and the details of the process activities, methods, and techniques as well as its information management. More detailed process operation guidance is covered in the intermediate service capability courses. More detail on the courses included in the ITIL exam framework can be found at www.axelos.com/qualifications/itil-qualifications. Each process is considered from the management perspective. Each process is considered from the management perspective. That means at the end of this section of the book, you should understand those aspects that would be required to understand the process and its interfaces, oversee its implementation, and judge its effectiveness and efficiency.

Service Asset and Configuration Management

We spent some time in the previous chapter discussing change management. In many ways, service asset and configuration management (SACM) is the companion process to change management; each depends upon the other for success. Without configuration management, those involved in the change management process would struggle to understand the implications of any change because they would lack the information regarding the CIs and their interrelationships. Without the discipline of change management, those involved in the service asset and configuration management process would struggle to develop and maintain an accurate CMS because changes might happen without any notification or documentation.

Purpose

The purpose of the SACM process is to ensure that the assets required to deliver services are properly controlled and that accurate and reliable information about those assets is available when and where it is needed. This information includes details of how the assets have been configured and the relationships between assets.

Objectives

The objectives of service asset and configuration management are as follows:

- To ensure that IT assets are managed and properly cared for throughout their lifecycle by identifying, controlling, recording, reporting, auditing, and verifying all configuration items, including versions, baselines, and constituent components and their attributes and relationships.

- To work with change management to ensure that only authorized components are used and only authorized changes are made.

- To account for, manage, and protect the integrity of CIs throughout the service lifecycle.

- To ensure the integrity of CIs and configurations required to control the services by establishing and maintaining an accurate and complete configuration management system (CMS).

- To include information regarding the historical, planned, and current state of services and other CIs in the CMS.

- To ensure that the other service management processes have accurate configuration information to allow informed decision-making—for example, to authorize changes and releases or to resolve incidents and problems by providing an accurate CMS. This process helps improve the performance of all the other processes.

Service assets that need to be managed in order to deliver services are known as configuration items (CIs).

Scope

The scope of SACM includes management of the complete lifecycle of every CI. It ensures that changes to all CIs are controlled and that releases are authorized. The relationship between items is recorded to build a model of each service. Included within the scope are the interfaces to internal and external service providers where shared assets and CIs need to be controlled.

Configuration management depends upon having a close interface with the organization's asset management. Asset management covers the full lifecycle management of IT and service assets and the maintenance of an asset inventory. However, asset management is not about the relationships between CIs and how they work together to deliver a service.

Value to the Business

Often the value to the business can be shown by the impact of poor configuration management, for example, service outages, fines, correct license fees, and failed audits. Accurate SACM enables better forecasting by the provision of information to the right people at the right time, which will assist with the management of change. It will also assist in the compliance to governance standards and the ability to assess the cost of services. The process provides visibility of accurate representations of a service, release, or environment that enables better forecasting and planning of changes, which in turn enables better assessment, planning, and delivery of changes and releases. Providing accurate CI information helps ensure that incidents and problems are resolved within the service level targets. By being able to track CIs and their status, the service provider will be able to ensure better adherence to standards or legal and regulatory obligations. Changes can be traced from requirements to implementation, and the costs of a service can be identified from the information showing all the CIs that make up that service. Finally, the business benefits from reduced cost and time to discover configuration information when it is needed and can be assured that the fixed assets that are under the control of the service provider are under proper stewardship too.

Policies, Principles, and Basic Concepts

Modern businesses functions require complex configurations of items to support the business services. For example, a person in an office in the United Kingdom may use a PC attached to the company network but may be accessing a financial system running in a completely different part of the world, such as the United States. A change to the network or the financial system might have an impact on this person and the business process they support. Many services may run on different virtual servers hosted on the same physical computer; changes to the physical server could impact all of these services.

Policies

The first step is to develop and maintain the SACM policies that set the objectives, scope, principles, and critical success factors (CSFs) for what is to be achieved by the process. These policies are often considered with the change and release and deployment management policies because they are closely related. The policies will be based on the organization's business drivers, on contractual and service management requirements, and on compliance to applicable laws, regulations, and standards.

Principles

The main policy sets out the framework and key principles against which assets and configurations are developed and maintained. Some of the typical principles include ensuring that service asset and configuration management operations costs and resources are commensurate with the potential risks to the services. Also included is the need to deliver governance requirements, such as software asset management, Sarbanes-Oxley, ISO/IEC 20000, ISO/IEC 38500, or COBIT, and the need to deliver the capability, resources, and warranties as defined by SLAs and contracts. Services provided must be available, reliable, and cost-effective. Adequate asset and configuration information must be provided to internal and external stakeholders and to other processes. The need for traceability and auditability must also be supported by this process.

Another principle is that there is a requirement for clear economic and performance criteria for interventions that reduce costs or optimize service delivery. An example would be specifying the age at which PCs should be replaced based on cost of maintenance of older models. Also included is the application of whole-life cost appraisal methods and moving from "find and fix" reactive maintenance to "predict and prevent" proactive management. Other common principles are using CSI to optimize the service levels, assets, and configurations; migration to a common CMS architecture; and using increased automation to reduce errors and costs.

Basic Concepts

Let's take a few minutes to remind ourselves of some of the basic concepts and definitions for this process. You should remember these from your Foundation level course.

- A service asset is any resource or capability that could contribute to the delivery of a service.

- A configuration item, or CI, is a service asset that needs to be managed in order to deliver an IT service.

- All CIs are service assets, but many service assets are not CIs.

- A configuration record contains the attributes of a CI, including the relationships between it and other CIs.

- Configuration records are stored in a configuration management database (CMDB) and managed with a configuration management system (CMS).

- The service knowledge management system (SKMS) is a set of tools and databases that are used to manage knowledge, information, and data. We cover the SKMS in the chapter on knowledge management, Chapter 26, "Service Transition Processes: Change Evaluation and Knowledge Management."

The Configuration Model

Service asset and configuration management delivers a model of the services, assets, and the infrastructure by recording the relationships between configuration items, as shown in Figure 24.1.

FIGURE 24.1   Example of a logical configuration model

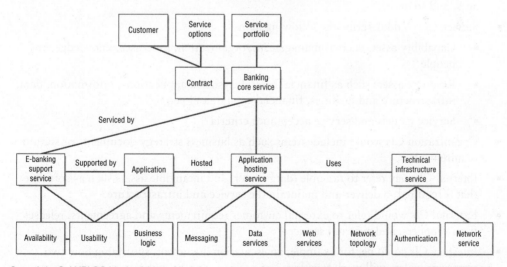

The configuration model enables other processes to access valuable information, as in these examples:

- To assess the impact and cause of incidents and problems

- To assess the impact of proposed changes

- To plan and design new or changed services

- To plan a technology refresh or a software upgrade or to migrate service assets to different locations and service centers

- To optimize asset utilization and costs and reuse assets by understanding which CIs make up each service

As we said previously, a configuration item (CI) is a service asset that needs to be managed in order to deliver an IT service. Configuration records should hold useful details of the attributes of the CI. Maintaining such information can be a significant administrative overhead, so care should be taken to include only information for which the value provided by the information is greater than the cost of gathering and maintaining it. Configuration items may vary widely in complexity, size, and type, ranging from an entire service or system (including all hardware, software, documentation, and support staff) to a single software module or a minor hardware component. Configuration items may be grouped and managed together; for example, a set of components may be grouped into a release.

Examples of Different CI Types

We usually think of CIs in terms of hardware, software, and network components, and indeed, the majority of CIs will fit into these categories. Configuration items include anything we want to manage and control, so we may also include other CI types:

- Service lifecycle CIs, which could include plans, business cases, service design packages, and so on.

- Service CIs could describe the following items:

  - Capability assets such as management, organization, processes, knowledge, and people

  - Resource assets such as financial capital, systems, applications, information, data, infrastructure and facilities, financial capital, and people

  - Service models and service acceptance criteria

- Organization CIs would include items such as business strategy documents or statutory requirements.

- Internal CIs may refer to tangible (data center) and intangible assets such as software that is required to deliver and maintain the service and infrastructure.

- External CIs would refer to external customer requirements and agreements, releases from suppliers, and external services.

- Interface CIs could be, for example, an escalation document, specifying how two service providers will work together.

Service asset and configuration management uses the configuration management system (CMS) to manage the CI data. (Chapter 29, "Technology Considerations for Service Transition," discusses the use of tools in this area in more detail.) The CMS holds all the information about CIs within scope. A service CI will include attributes such as supplier, cost, purchase date, and renewal date for licenses and maintenance contracts; the related documentation, such as SLAs and underpinning contracts, is held in the SKMS.

Figure 24.2 shows the relationship between configuration records, stored in the CMS, and the actual CIs, which may be stored in the SKMS or may be physical assets outside the SKMS.

FIGURE 24.2 Example of relationships between the CMS and SKMS

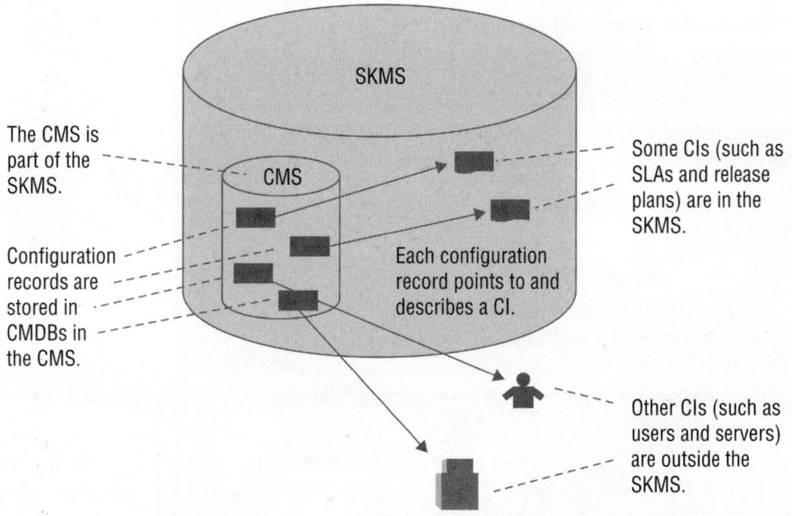

SKMS

The CMS is part of the SKMS.

CMS

Configuration records are stored in CMDBs in the CMS.

Each configuration record points to and describes a CI.

Some CIs (such as SLAs and release plans) are in the SKMS.

Other CIs (such as users and servers) are outside the SKMS.

All CI changes must be authorized by change management, and all updates must include updates to the relevant configuration records. The CMS is also used for a wide range of purposes outside of service asset and configuration management, such as fixed asset financial reporting. It maintains the relationships between all service components and may also include records for related incidents, problems, known errors, changes, and releases. Alternatively, these may be held in the SKMS, but show the link to the associated CI. The CMS may either link to corporate data about employees, suppliers, locations and business units, customers, and users or hold copies of this information.

In Figure 24.3 you can see an example of the application of the architectural layers of the CMS. We shall look at this in more detail in Chapter 26, when we consider knowledge management. The CMS may include data from configuration records stored in several physical CMDBs, which come together at the information integration layer to form an integrated CMDB. The integrated CMDB may also incorporate information from external data sources such as an HR database or financial database. The presentation layer of the CMS will contain different views and dashboards to fit the requirements of different groups of people needing access to configuration information. In addition to a view suitable for staff responsible for SACM, views may be provided that are suitable for those involved in change management and release and deployment management or for staff in technical and application management functions or the service desk. The CMS will provide access to data in asset inventories wherever possible rather than duplicating data.

FIGURE 24.3 Example of the application of the architectural layers of the CMS

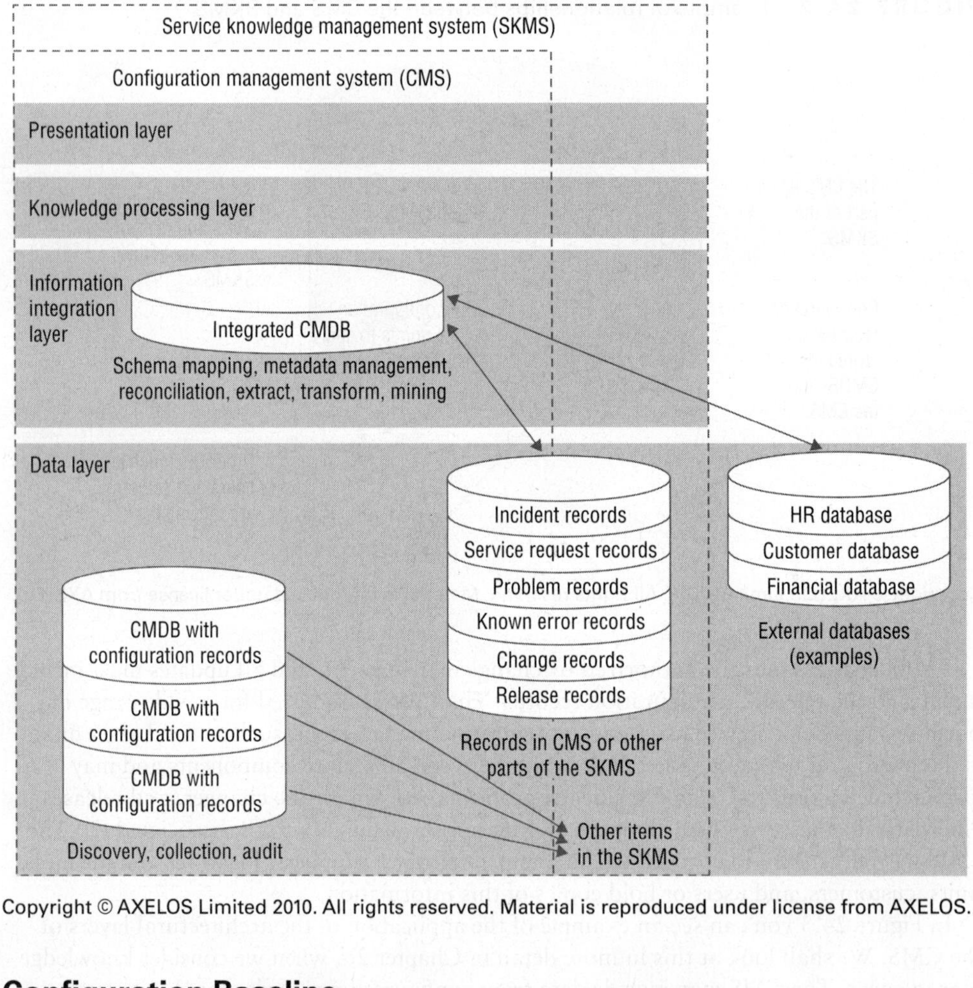

Configuration Baseline

A configuration baseline is a formally reviewed and agreed configuration of a service, product, or infrastructure. It captures the structure, contents, and details of a configuration and represents a set of configuration items that are related to each other. It is used to mark a milestone in the development of a service or to build a service component from a defined set of inputs. It can also be used to change or rebuild a specific version at a later date, to assemble all relevant components in readiness for a change or release, or to provide the basis for a configuration audit and back-out.

Snapshot

A snapshot is the current state of a CI, process, or other set of data recorded at a particular point in time. This is useful when problem management needs to analyze evidence about the time incidents actually occurred. It also facilitates system restores and supports security scanning software because any changes from the previous snapshot are obvious.

Asset Management

Organizations need to manage their fixed assets because they have a financial value. The process includes identifying and naming each asset and recording its owner. This information would be stored in an asset register, including details of the purchase cost, depreciation, and net book value of each asset. The process has to also safeguard the assets from interference and carry out audits to ensure their integrity. The major difference between asset management and configuration management is that asset management is concerned with the financial aspects of each individual asset, whereas configuration management is concerned with each item's relationship with other items and in the provision of the service; an asset of very low financial value may play a key role in the provision of a service.

Outsourced service providers may manage some of the organization's CI assets and carry out some or all of the same activities – tracking, naming, labeling, protecting, and auditing.

Software Asset Management

Additional risks are involved when managing software assets compared to other asset types. The risks include too few or too many licenses, loss of evidence of purchase, and inadvertent breaches of terms and conditions. Software asset management (SAM) manages the software, licenses, and activation codes.

Effective SAM is dependent on the use of appropriate tools, including a CMS and a definitive media library (DML). We look at the DML next.

Secure Libraries and Secure Stores

The DML is a secure library holding the definitive authorized versions of all media CIs. It consists of one or more software libraries or file-storage areas containing the master copies of all controlled software in the organization. This includes purchased software (with the license documents) and software developed on site and master copies of the relevant controlled documentation. The DML will also include a physical store (e.g., a fireproof safe) to hold master copies. Only authorized media should be accepted into the DML, and that is strictly controlled by SACM. The DML is a foundation for release and deployment management.

An area should also be set aside for the secure storage of definitive hardware spares. Details of these components, their locations, and their respective builds and contents should be comprehensively recorded in the CMS.

Electronic assets in the DML are held within the SKMS, and every item in the DML is a CI. Figure 24.4 shows the relationship between the DML and a CMDB in the CMS.

FIGURE 24.4 The relationship between the definitive media library and the configuration management system

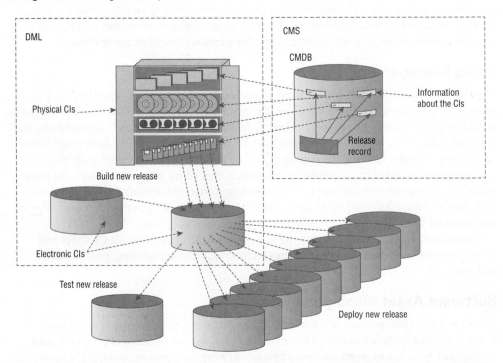

Decommissioning Assets

Assets are decommissioned for a number of reasons, including when a service is retired and the assets used for that service are no longer needed, when a technology refresh replaces old assets, when hardware failure results in components being replaced, and when reduced capacity requirements free up components.

The detailed steps to be taken when decommissioning assets should be documented in a service design package in the same way as for any other service transition. These steps should include redeploying, reusing, or selling the assets where appropriate to minimize waste and, where this is not possible, ensuring that the disposal meets the required environmental standards. The data stored on decommissioned assets must be removed and managed in accordance with the information security policy. If the equipment is leased, it should be returned, and maintenance contracts on decommissioned equipment should be canceled. Finally, the asset's status in the CMS should be updated and the fixed asset management process informed so that the asset records can be updated.

Process Activities, Methods, and Techniques

Before we start looking at the service asset and configuration management process activities, let's see how these activities work together. In Figure 24.5, you can see the high-level activities for service asset and configuration management in this example of an activity model.

FIGURE 24.5   Typical service asset and configuration management activity model

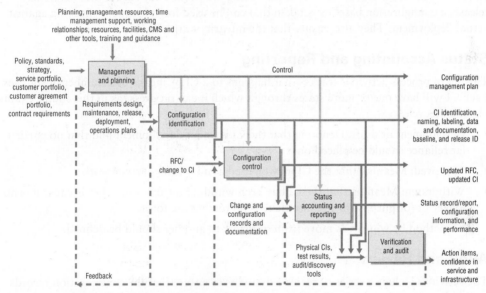

The service asset and configuration management activities include management and planning, configuration identification, configuration control, status accounting and reporting, and verification and audit. We shall look at each of them in turn.

Management and Planning

The level of service asset and configuration management required will vary between organizations, so there is no standard template. The management team should decide what level is required for the particular service or project and how this level will be achieved and document it in a SACM plan. There may be several SACM plans, one for each project, service, or group of services. These plans define the specific SACM activities within the context of the overarching SACM strategy.

Identification

The configuration identification process activities include defining and documenting the criteria for selecting CIs and their components and then selecting them according to the criteria. Each CI is then assigned a unique identifier. The relevant attributes of each CI are specified, including its relationship to other CIs, and the owner responsible for each CI is identified. The date from which each CI is placed under control of SACM is recorded.

Configuration Control

The configuration control activities ensure that no CI is added, modified, replaced, or removed without an appropriate procedure being followed. They ensure that before a release, a configuration baseline is taken that can be used for subsequent checking against actual deployment. They also ensure that the integrity of the DML is maintained.

Status Accounting and Reporting

This set of process activities tracks what happens to a CI by means of a number of statuses. Each CI will have one or more states through which it can progress, as in this simple example of a lifecycle:

- Development or draft: Denoting that the CI is under development and that no particular reliance should be placed on it

- Approved: Meaning that the CI may be used as a basis for further work

- Withdrawn: Meaning that the CI has been withdrawn from use, either because it is no longer fit for purpose or because there is no further use for it

  The method by which CIs move from one state to another should be defined.

Audit and Review

The activities include a series of reviews or audits to ensure that the configuration records match the actual situation—that CIs and their documentation actually exist as stated in the CMS. The audits aim to verify the existence of CIs and their documentation and to confirm that they are configured correctly, especially when a release is planned. Any unregistered and unauthorized items that are discovered should be investigated and corrective action taken to address possible issues with circumventing of procedures by some staff. All exceptions should be logged and reported, and records of the audit should be created to support future compliance checking.

Triggers, Inputs and Outputs, and Process Interfaces

Now let's look at the triggers, inputs and outputs, and process interfaces for service asset and configuration management. Let's look first at the triggers for this process.

Triggers

Updates to asset and configuration information are triggered by updates from the change and release and deployment processes. Other triggers are purchase orders, acquisitions, and service requests.

Inputs

Inputs to service asset and configuration management include the designs, plans and configurations contained in service design packages, and the RFCs and work orders from change management. Other inputs are the configuration information collected by discovery tools and audits and the organization's fixed asset register.

Outputs

Outputs include new and updated configuration records, snapshots and baselines, audit and status reports, and updated asset information for inclusion in the fixed asset register. The information output by the process regarding the attributes and relationships of configuration items is used by all the other service management processes.

Interfaces

SACM provides the single virtual repository of configuration data and information for IT service management, so it interfaces with every other process and activity to some extent. Perhaps the most important interface is that with change management, where it is used for impact assessment and also ensures that changes to CIs are captured, which is critical if SACM is to work effectively.

Other important interfaces include the interfaces with the following processes:

- Financial management, where it captures key financial information such as cost, depreciation methods, owner, maintenance and repair costs
- IT service continuity management, where it provides information regarding critical assets to be protected
- Incident and problem management, where it provides key diagnostic information and data to the service desk and helps identify problem causes
- Availability management, where it helps in the detection of points of failure by showing CI relationships

There is also a close relationship with the business process of asset management.

KPIs and CSFs

As with all processes, the performance of SACM should be monitored and reported, and action should be taken to improve it. As you have seen, SACM plays an essential role in providing many other processes with the information they require, so success or failure in implementing this process will have an indirect impact on customers. As discussed previously, each CSF should have a small number of KPIs that will measure its success, and each organization may choose its own KPIs. The *ITIL Service Transition* core volume lists a number of CSFs and corresponding KPIs. We shall just look at a couple of these now.

- Critical success factor: "Accounting for, managing, and protecting the integrity of CIs throughout the service lifecycle."

    - KPI: Improved accuracy in budgets and charges for the assets utilized by each customer or business unit

    - KPI: Increase in reuse and redistribution of underutilized resources and assets

    - KPI: Reduction in the use of unauthorized hardware and software, nonstandard and variant builds that increase complexity, support costs, and risk to the business services

    - KPI: Reduced number of exceptions reported during configuration audits

- Critical success factor: "Establishing and maintaining an accurate and complete configuration management system (CMS)."

    - KPI: Reduction in business impact of outages and incidents caused by poor service asset and configuration management

    - KPI: Increased quality and accuracy of configuration information

    - KPI: Improved audit compliance

    - KPI: Shorter audits because quality configuration information is easily accessible

    - KPI: Fewer errors caused by people working with out-of-date information

Challenges

Challenges to SACM include persuading technical support staff to adhere to the process when making changes to CIs. They often regard the process as a hindrance to a fast and responsive support service. Attracting and justifying funding for service asset and configuration management can be difficult because it is invisible to the customer. Another challenge is defining the optimal level of data to be gathered and managed—discovery tools may collect vast quantities of data that is not required but needs to be managed. Finally, due to its invisible nature, management may not appreciate the key support it provides to all other processes and therefore fail to provide the level of commitment and support required, especially when enforcing the process.

Risks

Risks to successful SACM include regarding it as technically focused and not appreciating what it delivers indirectly to the business. The accuracy of the information may degrade if the process and that of change management are not enforced. Errors found in audits must not only be corrected, but also investigated to identify poor adherence to the processes, which should then be addressed by management. An inaccurate CMS will lead to incorrect decisions based on faulty data. Too wide a scope will entail cost with little benefit; too narrow a scope will also fail to deliver any real benefit.

Summary

This chapter explored the service transition process of service asset and configuration management. We examined how this process is responsible for providing accurate information to many other processes. We looked at how the information about configuration items and their relationships with each other is gathered and maintained, and at the repository for this information, the CMS.

We also examined the importance of this process to the business and to the IT service provider.

Exam Essentials

Understand the purpose of service asset and configuration management. Be able to explain that the purpose of the service asset and configuration management process is to capture accurate and reliable information about the assets that make up our services.

Understand the objectives of service asset and configuration management. SACM objectives are about maintaining accurate information on configurations items and services. It is important to understand that this will enable informed decision-making across many processes.

Understand the scope of service asset and configuration management. SACM covers all service assets and configuration items that make up services and how the configuration items are identified and recorded as part of the configuration management system (CMS).

Know the different types of CIs. The different types of CIs are hardware CIs, internal and external CIs, service CIs, and service lifecycle CIs. Be able to give examples of each.

Understand the concept of attributes. Be able to suggest common attributes for different CI types.

Understand the use of configuration models. Configuration models show the dependencies and relationships between CIs to provide a model of the services, assets, and infrastructure.

Understand how the information held in the configuration management system (CMS) is used by other processes. Be able to provide examples.

Be able to explain the concept and use of a configuration baseline. A configuration baseline is used to capture the state of the infrastructure at a specific point to be reviewed and agreed on and used for trending, comparison, and planning.

Understand the difference between a baseline and a snapshot.   A snapshot is a capture of the infrastructure at a point in time, but it may contain errors and inaccuracies because it is not reviewed and finalized.

Be able to explain the use and contents of the definitive media library (DML).   The DML is a specific secure area set aside for the management of software media. It may consist of physical and electronic stores for master copies of licensed or authorized software in use in the live environment and the associated documentation.

Be able to list and explain the five main activities of SACM.   The activities are planning, identification, control, status accounting, and verification and audit.

Review Questions

You can find the answers to the review questions in the appendix.

1. Which of these statements is NOT part of the purpose of the SACM process?

    A. Control the assets that make up services.

    B. Manage the changes to service assets.

    C. Identify service assets.

    D. Capture accurate information about service assets.

2. SACM is a process that supports which of the following stages of the service lifecycle?

    1. Service strategy

    2. Service design

    3. Service transition

    4. Service operation

    5. Continual service improvement

       A. 1, 3, and 5

       B. 2, 3, and 4

       C. 2, 3, 4, and 5

       D. 1, 2, 3, 4, and 5

3. Which of these statements *best* describes a configuration record?

    A. Any resource or capability that could contribute to the delivery of a service.

    B. A service asset that needs to be managed in order to deliver an IT service.

    C. A record showing the attributes of a CI, including the relationships between it and other CIs. It is stored in a configuration management database.

    D. Categorization of the CIs that make up the services.

4. The configuration management system (CMS) is composed of four separate layers. Which option includes the correct identification of those layers?

    A. Presentation, knowledge processing, information integration, data

    B. Presentation, information integration, configuration item, data

    C. Presentation, knowledge processing, configuration item, configuration database

    D. Presentation, configuration item, configuration database, knowledge model

5. Which of the following statements concerning the value of the CMS to the business is INCORRECT?

    A. It helps prevent unnecessary purchases of licences or equipment by identifying spare items that can be reused.

    B. It ensures that the service desk staff have the knowledge they require to resolve incidents.

    C. It prevents the organization from being fined for not being able to prove that all of its software is legal.

    D. It helps prevent failed changes by allowing an accurate impact assessment.

6. Which of the following is NOT a potential danger when implementing SACM?

    A. Examining the related CIs for every change may slow down the change management process.

    B. Staff may not realize the importance of the process, and fail to follow the process consistently, leading to inaccuracies in the CMS.

    C. The cost of maintaining the level of detail being gathered may not be matched by the benefits of having the information.

    D. Ineffective change management may make maintaining an accurate CMS impossible.

7. Identify the correct word for the blanks in the following statements from the list provided.

    A _____ is any resource or capability that could contribute to the delivery of a service. A _____ is a service asset that needs to be managed in order to deliver an IT service. A _____ contains a set of _____ of a CI, including the relationships between it and other CIs. Configuration records are stored in a _____ and managed with a _____ .

    1. CMDB

    2. Configuration record

    3. Baseline

    4. CMS

    5. Unique identifier

    6. CI

    7. SKMS

    8. Service asset

    9. DML

    10. Attribute

        A. 8, 7, 3, 10, 4, 1

        B. 3, 2, 5, 7, 6, 10

        C. 6, 8, 3, 10, 1, 4

        D. 8, 6, 2, 10, 1, 4

8. Which of the following are benefits of a configuration model?

    1. Enables the impact and cause of incidents and problems to be assessed.

    2. Enables the impact of proposed changes to be assessed.

    3. Helps when planning and designing new or changed services.

    4. By understanding which CIs make up each service, asset utilization and costs can be optimized and assets reused.

    A. 1, 3, and 4 only

    B. All of the above

    C. 3 and 4 only

    D. 2, 3, and 4 only

9. Which of the following is not a valid example of a service CI?

    A. Management, organization, processes, knowledge, and people

    B. A service design package

    C. Financial capital, systems, applications, information, data, infrastructure and facilities, financial capital, and people

    D. Service models and service acceptance criteria

10. Which of the following statements is TRUE?

    A. A snapshot is a formally reviewed and agreed configuration of a service, product, or infrastructure.

    B. The detailed steps to be taken when decommissioning assets should be documented in a service design package.

    C. If an organization has effective asset management, there is little advantage in implementing SACM.

    D. Software asset management (SAM) should be managed separately from service asset and configuration management (SACM).

Chapter 25

Service Transition Processes: Release and Deployment Management and Service Validation and Testing

---

THE FOLLOWING ITIL INTERMEDIATE EXAM OBJECTIVES ARE DISCUSSED IN THIS CHAPTER:

✓ Release and deployment management and service validation and testing are discussed in terms of

- ■ Purpose
- ■ Objectives
- ■ Scope
- ■ Value
- ■ Policies
- ■ Principles and basic concepts
- ■ Process activities, methods, and techniques
- ■ Triggers, inputs, outputs, and interfaces
- ■ Critical success factors and key performance indicators
- ■ Challenges
- ■ Risks

The syllabus covers the managerial and supervisory aspects of service transition processes. It excludes the day-to-day operation of each process and the details of the process activities, methods, and techniques as well as its information management. More detailed process operation guidance is covered in the intermediate service capability courses. More details on the courses included in the ITIL exam framework can be found at www.axelos.com/qualifications/itil-qualifications. Each process is considered from the management perspective. That means that at the end of this section of the book, you should understand those aspects that would be required to understand each process and its interfaces, oversee its implementation, and judge its effectiveness and efficiency.

Release and Deployment Management

A release may include many different types of service assets and involve many people. Release and deployment management ensures that responsibilities for handover and acceptance of a release are defined and understood. It ensures that the requisite planning takes place, and controls the release of the new or changed CIs.

Purpose

The purpose of the release and deployment management process is to plan, schedule, and control the build, test, and deployment of releases and to deliver new functionality required by the business while protecting the integrity of existing services. This is an important process because a badly planned deployment can cause disruption to the business and fail to deliver the benefits of the release that is being deployed.

Objectives

The main objective of release and deployment management ensures that the purpose is achieved by delivering plans and managing the release effectively to meet the agreed standards. It aims to ensure that release packages are built, installed, tested, and deployed efficiently and on schedule and the new or changed service delivers the agreed benefits. An important aspect of release and deployment is that it also seeks to protect the current services by minimizing any adverse impact of the release on the existing services. It aims to satisfy the different needs of customers, users, and service management staff.

The objectives of release and deployment management include defining and agreeing on plans for release and deployment with customers and stakeholders and then creating and testing release packages of compatible CIs. Another objective is to maintain the integrity of the release package and its components throughout transition. All release packages should be stored in and deployed from the DML following an established plan. They should also be recorded accurately in the CMS.

Other objectives of release and deployment management include ensuring that release packages can be tracked, installed, tested, verified, and/or uninstalled or backed out and that organization and stakeholder change is managed. The new or changed service must be able to deliver the agreed utility and warranty.

The process ensures that any deviations, risks, and issues are recorded and managed by taking the necessary corrective action. Customers and users are able to use the service to support their business activities because release and deployment ensures that the necessary knowledge transfer takes place as part of the transition. It also ensures that the required knowledge transfer takes place to enable the service operation functions to deliver, support, and maintain the service according to the required warranties and service levels.

Scope

The scope of release and deployment management includes the processes, systems, and functions to package, build, test, and deploy a release into production and establish the service specified in the service design package before final handover to service operations.

It also includes all the necessary CIs to implement a release. These may be physical, such as a server or network, or virtual, such as a virtual server or virtual storage. Other CIs included within the scope of this process are the applications and software. As we said previously, training for users and IT staff is also included, as are all contracts and agreements related to the service.

You should note that release and deployment is responsible for ensuring that appropriate testing takes place; the actual testing is carried out as part of the service validation and testing process. Release and deployment management also does not authorize changes. At various stages in the lifecycle of a release, it requires authorization from change management to move to the next stage.

Value to the Business

A well-planned approach to the implementation and release and deployment of new or changed services can make a significant difference in the overall costs to the organization. The release and deployment process delivers changes faster and at optimum cost and risk while providing assurance that the new or changed service supports the business goals. It ensures improved consistency in the implementation approach across teams and contributes to meeting audit requirements for traceability.

Poorly designed or managed release deployment may force unnecessary expenditure and waste time.

Policies, Principles, and Basic Concepts

Release and deployment management policies should be in place. The correct policies will help ensure the correct balance between cost of the service, the stability of the service, and its ability to change to meet changing circumstances.

The relative importance of these different elements will vary between organizations. For some services, stability is crucial; for other services, the need to implement releases in order to support rapidly changing business requirements is the most important, and the business is willing to sacrifice some stability to achieve this flexibility. Deciding on the correct balance for an organization is a business decision; release and deployment management policies should therefore support the overall objectives of the business.

These policies can be applicable to all services provided or apply to an individual service, which may have a different desired balance between stability, flexibility, and cost.

Release Unit

The term *release unit* describes the portion of a service or IT infrastructure that is normally released as a single entity according to the organization's release policy. The unit may vary, depending on the different type(s) of service asset or service component being released, such as software or hardware.

In Figure 25.1, you can see a simplified example showing an IT service made up of systems and service assets, which are in turn made up of service components. The actual components to be released on a specific occasion may include one or more release units and are grouped together into a release package for that specific release. Each service asset will have an appropriate release-unit level. The release unit for business-critical applications may be the complete application in order to ensure comprehensive testing, whereas the release unit for a website might be at the page level.

FIGURE 25.1   Simplified example of release units for an IT service

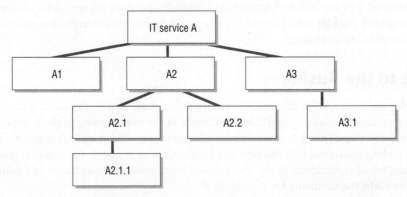

Ease of deployment is a major deciding factor when specifying release units. This will depend on the complexity of the interfaces between the release unit and the rest of the services and IT infrastructure.

Releases should be uniquely numbered, and the numbering should be meaningful, referencing the CIs that it represents and a version number—for example, Payroll-System v.1.1.1 or Payroll-System v.2.0. It is common for the first number to change when additional functionality is being released, whereas the later numbers show an update to an existing release.

Release Package

A release package is a set of configuration items that will be built, tested, and deployed together as a single release. It may be a single release unit or a structured set of release units such as the one shown in Figure 25.1. Release packages are useful when there are dependencies between CIs, such as when a new version of an application requires an operating system upgrade, which in turn requires a hardware change. In some cases, the release package may include documentation and procedures.

Figure 25.2 shows how the architectural elements of a service may be changed from the current baseline to the new baseline with releases at each level. The release teams need to understand the relevant architecture to plan, package, build, and test a release to support the new or changed service. For example, the technology infrastructure needs to be ready— with service operation functions prepared to support it with new or changed procedures— before an application is installed.

FIGURE 25.2 · Architecture elements to be built and tested

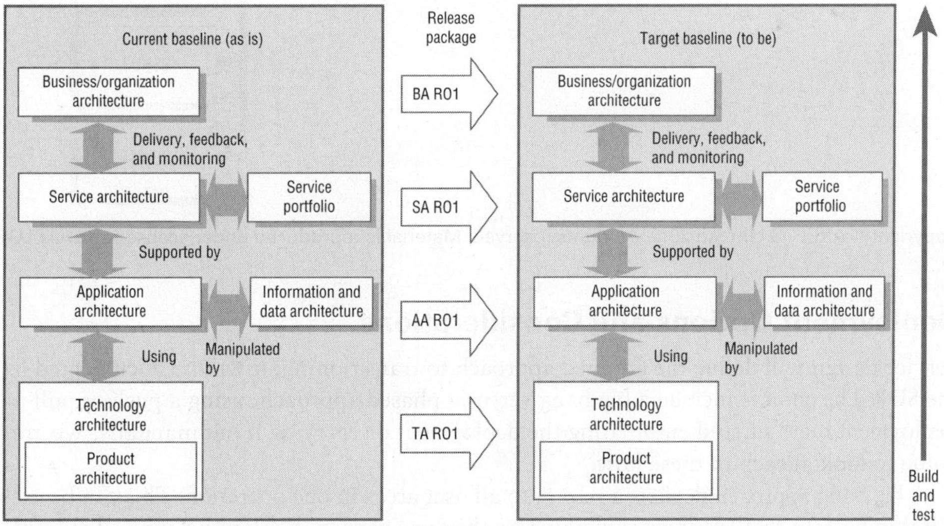

The example in Figure 25.3 shows an application with its user documentation and a release unit for each technology platform. The customer service asset is supported by two supporting services: SSA for the infrastructure service and SSB for the application service. These release units will contain information about the service, its utilities and warranties, and release documentation.

FIGURE 25.3   Example of a release package

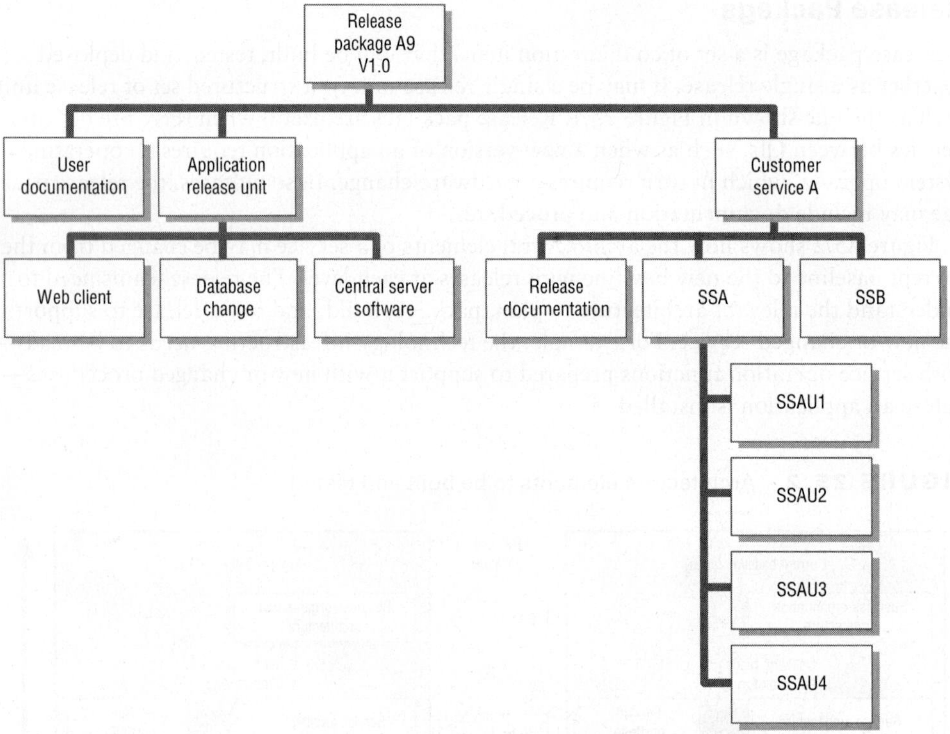

Deployment Options and Considerations

Service design will define the adopted approach to transitioning; it will be documented in the SDP. The choices include a big bang versus a phased approach, using a push or pull deployment method, and automating the deployment or carrying it out manually. We are going to look at each of these now.

A big bang approach deploys a release to all user areas in one operation. This can be useful if it is important that everyone is working on the same version, but it will have a significant impact should the deployment fail. A phased approach deploys the release to different parts of the user base in a scheduled plan. This is less risky but takes longer, and it will mean that there will be more than one version running concurrently.

Using a push mechanism to deploy the release means that the components are deployed from the center and the recipient cannot "opt out" of receiving them. A pull mechanism allows users to choose if and when they want to download the new release.

An automated approach to deployment will help to ensure repeatability and consistency and may be the only practical option if the deployment is to hundreds or thousands of CIs. However, the automated approach requires the distribution tools to be set up, and this may not always be justified. If a manual mechanism is used, the greater risk of errors or inefficiency should be considered.

Release and Deployment Models

As with other processes, the use of predefined models in release and deployment can be a useful way of achieving consistency in approach, no matter how many people are involved. The release and deployment models would contain a series of preagreed and predefined steps or activities to provide structure and consistency to the delivery of the process. Also included would be the exit and entry criteria for each stage, definitions of roles and responsibilities, controlled build and test environments, and baselines and templates. All the supporting systems and procedures would be defined in the model with the documented handover activities.

Process Activities, Methods, and Techniques

There are four phases to release and deployment management, shown in Figure 25.4. Let's look at each one in turn:

- The first phase is release and deployment planning. During this phase, the plans for creating and deploying the release are drawn up. This phase starts when change management gives the authorization to begin planning for the release and ends with change management authorization to build the release.

- This then marks the start of the second stage, release build and test. During this phase, the release package is built, tested, and checked into the DML. This phase ends with change management authorization for the baselined release package to be checked into the DML by service asset and configuration management. This phase happens only once for each release. Once the release package is in the DML, it is ready to be deployed to the target environments when authorized by change management.

- During the deployment phase, the release package is deployed to the live environment. This phase ends with the handover to the service operation functions and early life support. There may be many separate deployment phases for each release, depending on the planned deployment options.

- The final phase is the review and close phase. During this phase, experience and feedback are captured, performance targets and achievements are reviewed, and lessons are learned. These activities may result in additions to the CSI register. Note how it is change management that controls when the release takes place, with multiple trigger points for the release and deployment management activity. This does not require a separate RFC at each stage.

FIGURE 25.4   Phases of release and deployment management

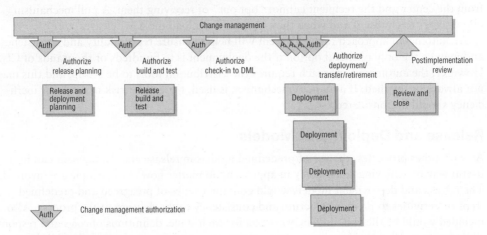

Let's look at each of these phases in a little more detail.

The plan release and deployment phase will include plans for all aspects of this phase; the plans will be mostly drawn up during service design and approved by change management. The plans must include not only the release and deployment plans themselves, but also the plans for pilot releases; the plans for building, testing, and packaging the release; and detailed deployment plans. Logistical considerations and financial plans must also be included. As part of this phase, the criteria for whether an activity has passed or failed to meet the required standard will be decided.

Next, let's consider the build and test phase. This phase includes writing the release and build documentation, ensuring that the necessary contracts and agreements are in place, and obtaining the necessary configuration items and components. These items will all need to be tested. The release packages will then need to be built, and this is an opportunity to make sure build management procedures, methodologies, tools, and checklists are in place to ensure that the release packages are built in a standard, controlled, and reproducible way. This will help to ensure that the output of this activity matches the solution design defined in the service design package. The final activity in this phase is the building and management of the test environments. The test environments must be controlled to ensure that the builds and tests are performed in a consistent, repeatable, and manageable manner. Failure to control the test environments can jeopardize the testing activities and could necessitate significant rework. Dedicated build environments should be established for assembling and building the components to create the controlled test and deployment environments.

The definitive version of the release package (authorized by change management) must be placed in the DML. The release package must always be taken from the DML to deploy to the service operation readiness, service acceptance, and live environments.

The entry criteria for the plan and prepare for deployment phase include all stakeholders being confident that they are ready for the deployment and that they accept the deployment costs and the management, organization, and people implications of the release. The deployment includes activities required to deploy, transfer, or decommission/retire services or service assets. It may also include transferring a service or a service unit within an organization or between organizations as well as moving and disposal activities.

An example of the deployment activities that apply to the deployment for a target group is shown in Figure 25.5. Note the actions taken at each stage, the authorizations obtained from change management at different stages, and the baselines taken at key points.

FIGURE 25.5   Example of a set of deployment activities

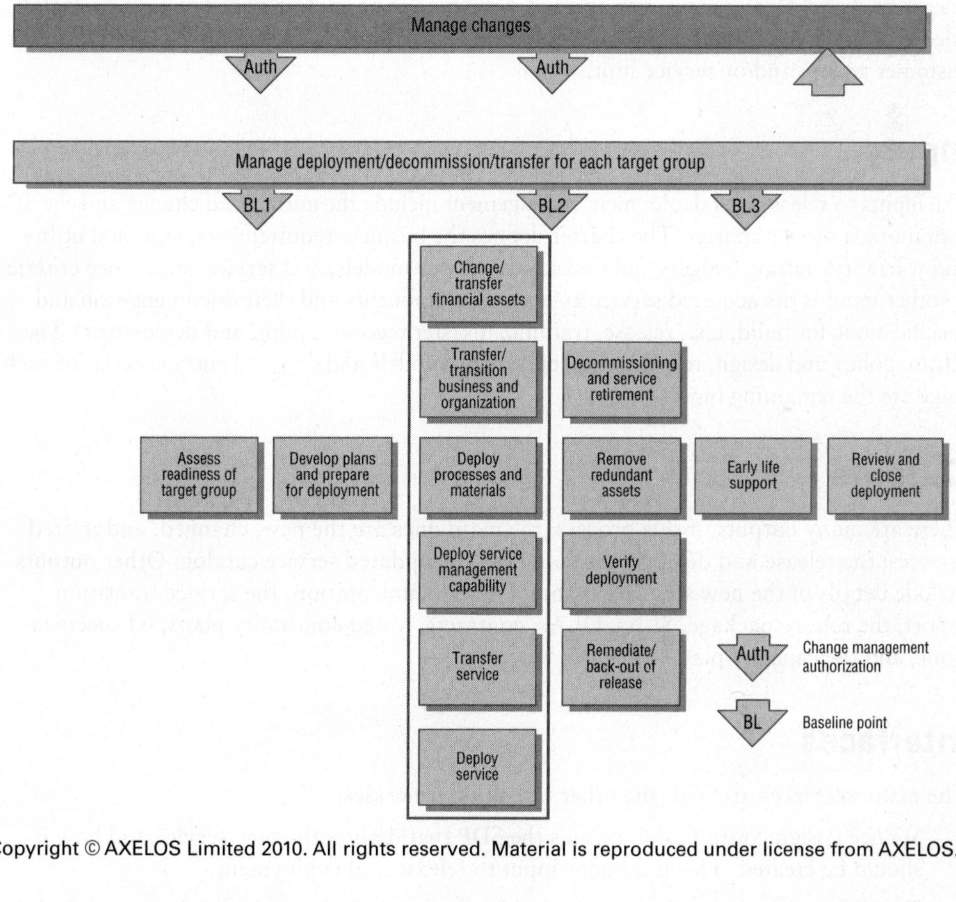

When the deployment activities are complete, it is important to verify that users, service operation functions, other staff, and stakeholders are capable of using or operating the

service as planned. This is a good time to gather feedback on the deployment process to feed into future improvements.

Successful confirmation of the deployment verification triggers the early life support for the deployment group. If it's unsuccessful, a decision may be made to remediate or back out of the release.

Now let's look at the triggers, inputs, outputs, and process interfaces for release and deployment management.

Triggers

We'll look first at the triggers for this process. Release and deployment management is triggered by the receipt of an authorized change to plan, build, and test a production-ready release package. Deployment is triggered by the receipt of an authorized change to deploy a release package to a target deployment group or environment, for example, a business unit, customer group, and/or service unit.

Inputs

The inputs to release and deployment management include the authorized change and the SDP containing a service charter. The charter defines the business requirements, expected utility and warranty, outline budgets and timescales, service models, and service acceptance criteria. Another input is the acquired service assets and components and their documentation and specifications for build, test, release, training, disaster recovery, pilot, and deployment. The release policy and design, release, and deployment models and exit and entry criteria for each stage are the remaining inputs.

Outputs

There are many outputs of this process; the main ones are the new, changed, and retired services; the release and deployment plan; and the updated service catalog. Other outputs include details of the new service capability and documentation, the service transition report, the release package, SLAs, OLAs, contracts, tested continuity plans, CI specifications, and the capacity plan.

Interfaces

The main interfaces are with the other transition processes:

- Service design coordination creates the SDP that defines the new service and how it should be created. This is a major input to release and deployment.

- Transition planning and support provides the framework in which release and deployment management will operate, and transition plans provide the context for release and deployment plans.

- Change management is tightly integrated with release and deployment. Change authorizes the release and deployment work. Release and deployment plans form part of the change schedule.

- Service asset and configuration management provides essential data and information from the CMS and provides updates to the CMS.

- Service validation and testing coordinates its actions with release and deployment to ensure that testing is carried out when necessary and that builds are available when required by service validation and testing.

Critical Success Factors and Key Performance Indicators

As with all processes, the performance of release and deployment management should be monitored and reported, and action should be taken to improve it. And as with the other processes we have discussed, each critical success factor (CSF) should have a small number of key performance indicators (KPIs) that will measure its success, and each organization may choose its own KPIs.

Let's look at two examples of CSFs for release and deployment management and the related KPIs for each.

The success of the CSF "Ensuring integrity of a release package and its constituent components throughout the transition activities" can be measured using KPIs that measure the trends toward increased accuracy of CMS and DML information when audits take place. Other relevant KPIs for this CSF would be the accuracy of the proposed budget and reducing the number of incidents due to incorrect components being deployed.

The success of the CSF "Ensuring that there is appropriate knowledge transfer" can be measured using KPIs that measure a falling number of incidents categorized as "user knowledge," an increase in the percentage of incidents solved by level 1 and level 2 support, and an improved customer satisfaction score when customers are questioned about release and deployment management.

Challenges

Challenges for release and deployment management include developing standard performance measures and measurement methods across projects and suppliers, dealing with projects and suppliers where estimated delivery dates are inaccurate, and understanding the different stakeholder perspectives that underpin effective risk management. The final challenge is encouraging a risk management culture where people share information and take a pragmatic and measured approach to risk.

Risks

The main risks in release and deployment include a poorly defined scope and an incomplete understanding of dependencies, leading to scope creep during release and deployment management. The lack of dedicated staff can cause resource issues. Other risks include the circumvention of the process, insufficient financing, poor controls on software licensing and other areas, ineffective management of organizational and stakeholder change, and poor supplier management. There may also be risks arising from the hostile reaction of staff to the release. Finally, there is a risk that the application or technical infrastructure will be adversely affected, due to an incomplete understanding of the potential impact of the release.

Service Validation and Testing

The underlying concept behind service validation and testing is quality assurance—establishing that the service design and release will deliver a new or changed service or service offering that is fit for purpose and fit for use.

Purpose

The purpose of the service validation and testing process is to ensure that a new or changed IT service matches its design specification and will meet the needs of the business.

Objective

The objectives of service validation and testing are to ensure that a release will deliver the expected outcomes and value within the projected constraints and to provide quality assurance by validating that a service is "fit for purpose" and "fit for use." Another objective is to confirm that the requirements are correctly defined, remedying any errors or variances early in the service lifecycle. The process aims to provide objective evidence of the release's ability to fulfil its requirements. The final objective is to identify, assess, and address issues, errors, and risks throughout service transition.

Scope

The service provider has a commitment to deliver the required levels of warranty as defined within the service agreement. Throughout the service lifecycle, service validation and testing can be applied to provide assurance that the required capabilities are being delivered and the business needs are met.

The testing activity of service validation and testing directly supports release and deployment by ensuring appropriate testing during the release, build, and deployment activities. It ensures that the service models are fit for purpose and fit for use before being authorized as live through the service catalog. The output from testing is used by the change evaluation process to judge whether the service is delivering the service performance with an acceptable risk profile.

Value to the Business

The key value to the business and customers from service testing and validation is in terms of the established degree of confidence it delivers that a new or changed service will deliver the value and outcomes required of it and the understanding it provides of the risks.

Successful testing provides a measured degree of confidence rather than guarantees. Service failures can harm the service provider's business and the customer's assets and result in outcomes such as loss of reputation, loss of money, loss of time, injury, and death.

Policies, Principles, and Basic Concepts

Now we'll look at the policies and principles of service validation and testing and the basic concepts behind it. The policies for this process reflect strategy and design requirements. The following list includes typical policy statements:

- All tests must be designed and carried out by people not involved in other design or development activities for the service.
- Test pass/fail criteria must be documented in a service design package before the start of any testing.
- Establish test measurements and monitoring systems to improve the efficiency and effectiveness of service validation and testing.

Service validation and testing is affected by policies from other areas of service management. Policies that drive and support service validation and testing include the service quality policy, the risk policy, and the service transition, release management, and change management policies.

Inputs from Service Design

A service is defined in the SDP. This includes the service charter defining agreed utility and warranty for the service, so the SDP is a key input to service validation and testing. The SDP also defines the service models that describe the structure and dynamics of a service delivered by service operation. The model can be used by service validation and testing to develop test models and plans.

The service design package defines a set of design constraints (as shown in Figure 25.6) against which the service release and new or changed service will be developed and built. Validation and testing should test the service at the boundaries to check that the design constraints are correctly defined and, particularly if there is a design improvement, to add or remove a constraint.

FIGURE 25.6 Design constraints driven by strategy

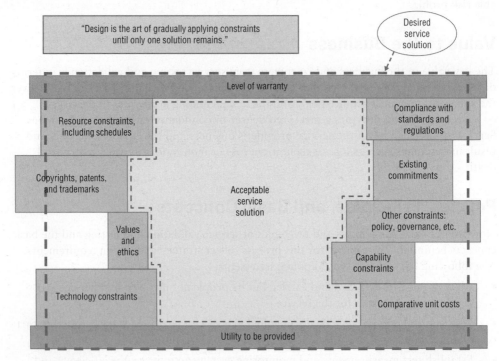

Service Quality and Assurance

Assurance of the service is achieved through a combination of testing and validation against an agreed standard, providing objective evidence that the service meets the defined requirements. Early in the service lifecycle, it confirms that customer needs, specified in the service charter, are translated correctly into the service design as service level requirements and constraints. Later in the service lifecycle, testing is carried out to assess whether the actual performance is achieved in terms of utility and warranty.

Policies that drive and support service validation and testing include service quality policy, risk policy, service transition policy, release policy, and change management policy. ITIL defines four quality perspectives: the level of excellence, value for money, conformance to specifications, and meeting or exceeding expectations.

The risk policy will influence the degree and level of validation and testing of service level requirements, utility, and warranty, that is, availability risks, security risks, continuity risks, and capacity risks.

The type and frequency of releases will influence the testing approach. Should a policy of frequent releases (such as once a day) be adopted, this will drive requirements for reusable test models and automated testing. The change management policy will define the testing to be done and ensure that it is integrated into the project lifecycle to support the aim of reducing service risk. Other aspects of the policy will ensure that feedback from testing is captured and that automation is introduced where possible.

A test strategy defines the overall approach to organizing testing and allocating testing resources. It is agreed with the appropriate stakeholders to ensure that there is sufficient buy-in to the approach. Early in the lifecycle, the service validation and test role needs to work with service design and service change evaluation to plan and design the test approach using information from the service package, service level packages, the SDP, and the interim evaluation report.

A test model includes a test plan, information on what is to be tested, and the test scripts that define how each element will be tested. A test model ensures that testing is executed consistently in a repeatable way that is effective and efficient. It provides traceability back to the requirement or design criteria and an audit trail through test execution, evaluation, and reporting.

Levels of Testing and Test Models

Because testing is directly related to the building of the service assets and products that make up services, each one of the assets or products should have an associated acceptance test. This will ensure that the individual components will work effectively prior to use in the new or changed service. Each service model should be supported by a reusable test model that can be used for both release and regression testing in the future. Testing models should be introduced early in the lifecycle to ensure that there is a lifecycle approach to the management of testing and validation.

Testing determines if the service meets the functional and quality requirements of the end users by executing defined business processes in an environment that simulates the live operational environment. The entry and exit criteria for testing are defined in the service design package. Testing should cover business and IT perspectives; testing from the business perspective is basically acceptance testing, with users testing the application, system, and service. Operations and service improvement testing tests if the technology, processes, documentation, staff skills, and resources are in place to deliver the new or changed service.

The diagram in Figure 25.7, sometimes called the service V-model, maps the types of tests to each stage of development. Using the V-model ensures that testing covers business and service requirements, as well as technical ones, so that the delivered service will meet customer expectations for utility and warranty. The left-hand side shows service requirements down to the detailed service design. The right-hand side focuses on the validation activities that are performed against these specifications. At each stage on the left-hand side, there is direct involvement by the equivalent party on the right-hand side. It shows that service validation and acceptance test planning should start with the definition of the service requirements. For example, customers who sign off on the agreed service requirements will also sign off on the service acceptance criteria and test plan.

FIGURE 25.7   Example of service lifecycle configuration levels and baseline points

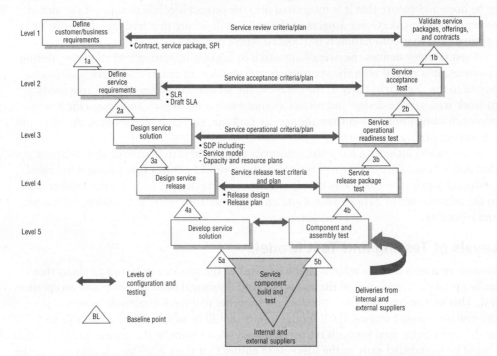

Types of Testing

There are many testing approaches and techniques that can be combined to conduct validation activities and tests. Examples include modeling or simulating situations where the service would be used, limiting testing to the areas of highest risk, testing compliance to the relevant standard, taking the advice of experts on what to test, and using waterfall or agile techniques. Other examples involve conducting a walk-through or workshop, a dress rehearsal, or a live pilot.

Functional and service tests are used to verify that the service meets the user and customer requirements as well as the service provider's requirements for managing, operating, and supporting the service. Functional testing will depend on the type of service and channel of delivery. Service testing will include many nonfunctional tests. They include testing for usability and accessibility, testing of procedures, and testing knowledge and competence. Testing of the warranty aspects of the service, including capacity, availability, resilience, backup and recovery, and security and continuity, is also included.

Process Activities, Methods, and Techniques

There are seven phases to service validation and testing, shown in Figure 25.8. The basic activities are as follows:

- Validation and test management
- Plan and test design
- Verify test plan and test design
- Prepare test environment
- Perform tests
- Evaluate exit criteria and report
- Test cleanup and closure

The test activities are not undertaken in a sequence; several may be done in parallel; for example, test execution begins before all the test design is complete. Figure 25.8 shows an example of a validation and testing process; it is described in detail in the following list.

FIGURE 25.8   Example of a validation and testing process

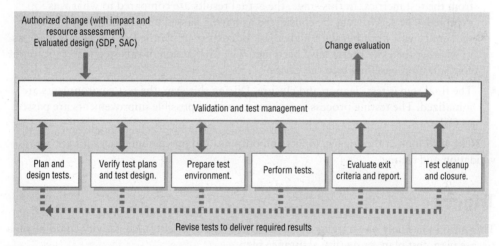

- The first activity is validation and test management, which includes the planning, control, and reporting of activities through the test stages of service transition. Also included are managing issues, mitigating risks, and implementing changes identified from the testing activities because these can impose delays.

- The next step, plan and design tests, starts early in the service lifecycle and covers many of the practical aspects of running tests, such as the resources required, any supporting services (including access, security, catering, and communications services), agreeing on the schedule of milestones, handover and delivery dates, agreeing on the time for consideration of reports and other deliverables, specifying the point and time of delivery and acceptance, and any financial requirements.

- The third step is to verify the test plan and test design, ensuring that the testing included in the test model is sufficient and appropriate for the service and covers the key integration points and interfaces. The test scripts should also be checked for accuracy and completeness.

- The next step is to prepare the test environment using the services of the build and test environment staff; use the release and deployment management processes to prepare the test environment where possible. This step also includes capturing a configuration baseline of the initial test environment.

- Next comes the perform tests step. During this stage, the tester carries out the tests using manual or automated techniques and records findings during the tests. In the case of failed tests, the reasons for failures must be fully documented, and testing should continue if at all possible. Should part of a test fail, the incident should be resolved or documented (e.g., as a known error) and the appropriate retests should be performed by the same tester.

- The next step is to evaluate the exit criteria and the report, which has been produced from the test metrics. In this stage, the actual results are compared to what was expected. The service may be considered as having passed or failed or it may be that the service will work but with higher risk or costs than planned. A decision is made as to whether the exit criteria have been met. The final action of this step is to capture the configuration baselines into the CMS.

- The final step is test cleanup and closure. During this step, the test environments are initialized. The testing process is reviewed, and any possible improvements are passed to CSI.

Next we'll look at the trigger, inputs and outputs, and process interfaces for service validation and testing.

Trigger

This process has only one trigger, a scheduled activity. The scheduled activity could be on a release plan, test plan, or quality assurance plan.

Inputs

A key input to this process is the service design package. This defines the agreed requirements of the service, expressed in terms of the service model and service operation plan. The SDP, as we have discussed previously, contains the service charter, including warranty and utility requirements, definitions of the interface between different service providers, acceptance criteria, and other information. The operation and financial models, capacity plans, and expected test results are further inputs.

The other main input consists of the RFCs that request the required changes to the environment within which the service functions or will function.

Outputs

The direct output from service validation and testing is the report delivered to service evaluation. This sets out the configuration baseline of the testing environment, identifies what testing was carried out, and the results. It also includes an analysis of the results (for example, a comparison of actual results with expected results) and any risks identified during testing activities.

Other outputs are the updated data and information and knowledge gained from the testing along with test incidents, problems, and known errors.

Interfaces

Service validation and testing supports all of the release and deployment management steps within service transition. It is important to remember that although release and deployment management is responsible for ensuring that appropriate testing takes place, the actual testing is carried out as part of the service validation and testing. The output from service validation and testing is then a key input to change evaluation. The testing strategy ensures that the process works well with the rest of the service lifecycle, for example, with service design, ensuring that designs are testable, and with CSI, managing improvements identified in testing. Service operation will use maintenance tests to ensure the continued efficacy of services, while service strategy provides funding and resources for testing.

Critical Success Factors and Key Performance Indicators

As with all processes, the performance of service validation and testing should be monitored and reported, and action should be taken to identify and implement improvements to the process. Each critical success factor (CSF) should have a small number of key performance indicators (KPIs) that will measure its success, and each organization may choose its own KPIs.

Let's consider two examples of CSFs for service validation and testing and the related KPIs for each.

The success of the CSF "Achieving a balance between cost of testing and effectiveness of testing" can be measured using KPIs that measure:

- The reduction in budget variances and in the cost of fixing errors
- The reduced impact on the business due to fewer testing delays and more accurate estimates of customer time required to support testing

The success of the CSF "Providing evidence that the service assets and configurations have been built and implemented correctly in addition to the service delivering what the customer needs" can be measured using KPIs that measure both the improvement in the percentage of service acceptance criteria that have been tested for new and changed services and the improvement in the percentage of services for which build and implementation have been tested separately from any tests of utility or warranty.

Challenges

The most frequent challenges to effective testing are based on other staff's lack of respect and understanding for the role of testing. Traditionally, testing has been starved of funding, and this results in an inability to maintain an adequate test environment and test data that matches the live environment, with not enough staff, skills, and testing tools to deliver adequate testing coverage. Testing is often squeezed due to overruns in other parts of the project so the go-live date can still be met. This impacts the level and quality of testing that can be done. Delays by suppliers in delivering equipment can reduce the time available for testing.

All of these factors can result in inadequate testing, which, once again, feeds the commonly held feeling that it has little real value.

Risks

The most common risks to the success of this process are as follows:

- A lack of clarity regarding expectations or objectives

- A lack of understanding of the risks, resulting in testing that is not targeted at critical elements

- Resource shortages (e.g., users, support staff), which introduce delays and have an impact on other service transitions

Summary

This chapter explored two more processes in the service transition stage, release and deployment management and service validation and testing. We examined how the release and deployment management process ensures that the required planning for the release is carried out, and the release activities are managed to minimize the risk to existing services. We also learned how the service validation and testing ensures that the release is fit for use and fit for purpose.

We examined how each of these processes supports the other and the importance of these processes to the business and to the IT service provider.

Exam Essentials

Understand the purpose of release and deployment management.   Release and deployment management ensures that releases are planned, scheduled, and controlled so the new or changed services are built, tested, and deployed successfully.

Understand and be able to list the objectives of release and deployment management.   The objectives of release and deployment are to ensure successful transition of a new or changed service into production, including the management of issues and risks. It also ensures that knowledge transfer is completed for both recipients and support teams.

Understand the scope of release and deployment management.   The scope of release and deployment management covers all aspects of packaging, building, and testing the release (including managing all CIs that are part of the release) to deploy the release into production.

Be able to explain the contents of a release policy.   The release policy describes the manner in which releases will be carried out, provides definitions for release types, and specifies the activities that should be managed under the control of the process.

Be able to list the four phases of release and deployment management.   The four phases of release and deployment are release and deployment planning, release build and test, deployment, and review and close. All four phases should be triggered by authorization from the change management process.

Understand and be able to list the objectives of service validation and testing.   The objectives of service validation and testing are to ensure that a release will deliver the expected outcomes and value and to provide quality assurance by validating that a service is fit for purpose and fit for use. The process aims to provide objective evidence of the release's ability to fulfil its requirements.

Understand the dependencies between the service transition processes of release and deployment management, service validation and testing, and change evaluation.   Release and deployment management is responsible for ensuring that appropriate testing takes place, but the testing is carried out in service validation and testing. The output from service validation and testing is then a key input to change evaluation.

Be able to list the typical types of testing used in service validation and testing. The main testing approaches used are as follows:

- Simulation
- Scenario testing
- Role playing
- Prototyping
- Laboratory testing
- Regression testing
- Joint walk-through/workshops
- Dress/service rehearsal
- Conference room pilot
- Live pilot.

Be able to describe the use and contents of a test model.   A test model includes a test plan, what is to be tested, and the test scripts that define how each element will be tested. A test model ensures that testing is executed consistently in a repeatable way that is effective and efficient. It provides traceability back to the requirement or design criteria and an audit trail through test execution, evaluation, and reporting.

Review Questions

You can find the answers to the review questions in the appendix.

1. Which of the following is the correct definition of a release package?

   A. A set of configuration items that will be built, tested, and deployed together

   B. A portion of a service or IT infrastructure that is normally released as a single unit

   C. One or more changes to an IT service that are built, tested, and deployed together

   D. A repeatable way of dealing with a particular category of release

2. The release and deployment process covers a concept called early life support. What is meant by early life support?

   A. Early life support refers to the end of the project lifecycle and the management of the postimplementation project review.

   B. Early life support refers to the handover between service transition and service operation, ensuring support for the new or changed service in the initial stages of operation.

   C. Early life support refers to the introduction of new processes into the operational environment, using service transition processes to ensure a complete integration of the new processes.

   D. Early life support refers to the step in the release and deployment process where the project team delivers the documentation of the infrastructure to the service management team.

3. Which of these statements does NOT describe a recommended part of a release policy?

   A. A unique identification structure or naming convention to ensure that releases can be easily identified and tracked

   B. Definitions of the roles and responsibilities required for the management of the release throughout all its stages

   C. Definition of the configuration management system naming convention

   D. Use of the definitive media library for all software asset releases

4. Which of these is NOT one of the phases of the release and deployment process?

   A. Release and deployment planning

   B. Deployment

   C. Review and close

   D. Verification and audit

5. Early life support is an important concept in the release and deployment management process. In which phase of the release and deployment process does early life support happen?

   A. Release build and test

   B. Review and close

    C. Deployment

    D. Release deployment and planning

6. Which of the following is NOT provided as part of a test model?

    A. A test plan

    B. A list of what is to be tested

    C. Test scripts that define how each element will be tested

    D. A test report

7. Which is the correct order of actions when a release is being tested?

    A. Perform tests, design tests, verify test plan, prepare test environment, test cleanup and closure, and evaluate exit criteria and report

    B. Design tests, perform tests, verify test plan, prepare test environment, evaluate exit criteria and report, and test cleanup and closure

    C. Design tests, verify test plan, prepare test environment, perform tests, evaluate exit criteria and report, and test cleanup and closure

    D. Verify test plan, design tests, prepare test environment, evaluate exit criteria and report, perform tests, and test cleanup and closure

8. Where are the entry and exit criteria for testing defined?

    A. The SKMS

    B. The CMS

    C. The KEDB

    D. The SDP

9. The diagram mapping the types of test to each stage of development to ensure that testing covers business and service requirements as well as technical ones is known as what?

    A. DIKW

    B. The service V-model

    C. The test plan

    D. The test strategy

10. Which of the following are valid results of an evaluation of the test report against the exit criteria?

    1. The service will work but with higher risk than planned.

    2. The service Passed.

    3. The service Failed.

    4. The service will work but with higher costs than planned.

        A. 2 and 3 only

        B. 2 only

        C. All of the above

        D. 1, 2, and 4 only

Chapter

26

Service Transition Processes: Change Evaluation and Knowledge Management

---

THE FOLLOWING ITIL INTERMEDIATE EXAM OBJECTIVES ARE DISCUSSED IN THIS CHAPTER:

✓ Change evaluation and knowledge management are discussed in terms of

- Purpose
- Objectives
- Scope
- Value
- Policies
- Principles and basic concepts
- Process activities, methods, and techniques
- Triggers, inputs, outputs, and interfaces
- Critical success factors and key performance indicators
- Challenges
- Risks

The ITIL Service Transition examination syllabus covers the managerial and supervisory aspects of service transition processes. It excludes the day-to-day operation of each process and the details of the process activities, methods, and techniques as well as its information management. More detailed process operation guidance is covered in the service capability courses. Each transition process is considered from the management perspective. That means at the end of this section of the book, you should understand those aspects that would be required to understand each process and its interfaces, oversee its implementation, and judge its effectiveness and efficiency.

Change Evaluation

Before a transition can be closed, it needs to be reviewed to ensure that it has achieved its purpose with no negative side effects. Successful completion of the change evaluation ensures that the service can be formally closed and handed over to the service operation functions and CSI.

An evaluation report is prepared that lists the deviations from the service charter/SDP and includes a risk profile and recommendations for change management.

Purpose

The purpose of the change evaluation process is to understand the likely performance of a service change and how it might impact the business, the IT infrastructure, and other IT services. The process provides a consistent and standardized means of assessing this impact by assessing the actual performance of a change against its predicted performance. Risks and issues related to the change are identified and managed.

Objectives

The objectives of change evaluation include setting stakeholder expectations correctly and providing accurate information to change management to prevent changes with an adverse impact and changes that introduce risk being transitioned unchecked. Another objective is to evaluate the intended and, as much as possible, the unintended effects of a service change and provide good-quality outputs to enable change management to decide quickly whether or not a service change is to be authorized.

Scope

Effective change management means that every change must be authorized by a suitable change authority at various points in its lifecycle. Typical authorization points include before build and test starts, before being checked into the DML, and before deployment to the live environment. The decision on whether or not to authorize the next step is made based on the evaluation of the change resulting from this process. The evaluation report provides the change authority with advice and guidance. The process describes a formal evaluation suitable for use for significant changes; each organization will decide which changes need formal evaluation and which will be evaluated as part of change management.

Value to the Business

Change evaluation is concerned with value. Effective change evaluation will judge whether the resources used to deliver the benefit that results from the change represent good value. This information will encourage a focus on value in future service development and change management. CSI can benefit enormously from evaluation regarding possible areas for improvement within the change process itself and the predictions and measurement of service change performance.

Policies, Principles, and Basic Concepts

Let's look at some of the key policies that apply to the change evaluation process. The first is that service designs or service changes will be evaluated before being transitioned. Second, although every change must be evaluated, the formal change evaluation process will be used only on significant changes; this requires, in turn, that criteria are defined to identify which changes are "significant."

Change evaluation will identify risks and issues related to the new or changed service and to any other services or shared infrastructure. Deviation from predicted to actual performance will be managed by the customer accepting the change with the deviation, rejecting the change, or introducing a new change to correct the deviation. These three are the only outcomes of change evaluation allowed.

The principles behind change evaluation include committing to identifying and understanding the consequences of both the unintended and intended effects of a change, as far as possible. Other principles include ensuring that each service change will be fairly, consistently, openly, and, wherever possible, objectively evaluated and ensuring that an evaluation report is provided to change management to facilitate decision-making at each authorization point.

The change evaluation process uses the Plan-Do-Check-Act (PDCA) model to ensure consistency across all evaluations. Using this approach, each evaluation is planned and then carried out in multiple stages, the results of the evaluation are checked, and actions are taken to resolve any issues found.

Figure 26.1 shows the change evaluation process and its key inputs and outputs. You can see the inputs that trigger the evaluation activity and the interim and final evaluation reports that are outputs of the process. Where performance does not meet the requirement, change management is responsible for deciding what to do next.

FIGURE 26.1   Change evaluation process flow

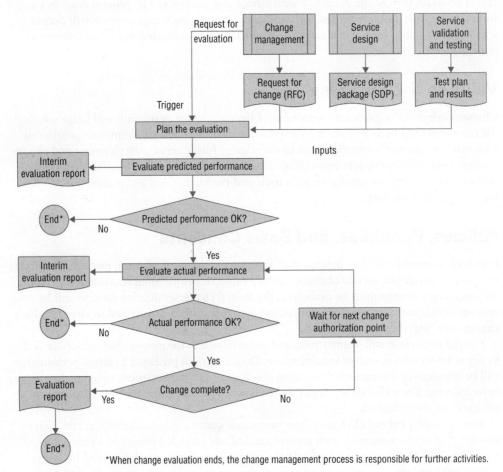

*When change evaluation ends, the change management process is responsible for further activities.

Evaluation Plan

Evaluation of a change should ensure that unintended effects as well as intended effects of the change are understood. Unintended effects will often be negative in terms of impact on other services, customers, and users of the service. Intended effects of a change should match the acceptance criteria. Unintended effects are often not seen until the pilot stage or even until live use; they are difficult to predict or measure.

Evaluation Report

The evaluation report contains the following sections:

- Risk profile, which explains the remaining risk left after a change has been implemented and after countermeasures have been applied

- Deviations report, which describes the difference between predicted and actual performance following the implementation of a change

- Qualification and validation statement (if appropriate), which is a statement of whether the IT infrastructure is appropriate and correctly configured to support the specific application or IT service

- Recommendation, which is a recommendation to change management to accept or reject the change based on the other factors within the evaluation report

Now let's look at the trigger, inputs and outputs, and process interfaces for change evaluation.

Trigger

Let's look first at the trigger for this process. The trigger for change evaluation is receipt of a request for evaluation from change management.

Inputs

Inputs to change evaluation are the service design package (which includes the service charter and service acceptance criteria), a change proposal, an RFC, a change record, and detailed change documentation. Other possible inputs are discussions with stakeholders and the test results and report.

Outputs

The outputs from change evaluation are interim and final evaluation report(s) for change management.

Interfaces

Change evaluation interfaces with a number of other processes. The main interfaces are as follows:

- Transition planning and support. Change evaluation works with transition planning and support to ensure that appropriate resources are available when needed and that each service transition is well managed.

- Change management. There is a critical interface with change management. The processes of change evaluation and change management must be tightly integrated, with clear agreement on which types of change will be subject to formal evaluation. The time required for this evaluation must be included when planning the change. In addition, it is change management that triggers change evaluation, and change management is dependent upon receiving the evaluation report in time for the CAB (or other change authority) to use it to assist in their decision-making.

- Service design coordination. This process provides the information about the service that change evaluation requires, in the form of a service design package.

- Service level management or business relationship management. Change evaluation may need to work with these processes to understand the impact of any issues that arise and to agree on the use of customer resources to perform the evaluation.

- Service validation and testing. This process provides change evaluation with information; the two processes must coordinate activities to ensure that required inputs are available in sufficient time.

Critical Success Factors and Key Performance Indicators

As with the other processes, the performance of change evaluation should be monitored and reported, and action should be taken to improve it. Here are two examples of CSFs for change evaluation and the related KPIs for each.

- Critical success factor: "Stakeholders have a good understanding of the expected performance of new and changed services."

  - KPI: The reduction in incidents reported when a new or changed service fails to deliver the required utility or warranty

  - KPI: Increased customer satisfaction with new or changed services

- Critical success factor: "Change management has good-quality evaluations to help them make correct decisions."

  - KPI: Increased percentage of evaluations delivered within the agreed timeframe

  - KPI: Reduced number of changes that fail or need to be backed out

  - KPI: Increased change management staff satisfaction when surveyed

Challenges

Challenges to change evaluation include developing standard performance measures and measurement methods across projects and suppliers, understanding the different stakeholder perspectives that underpin effective risk management for the change evaluation activities, and understanding (and being able to assess) the balance between managing risk and taking risks because this affects the overall strategy of the organization and service delivery. A further challenge is to measure and demonstrate less variation in predictions during and after transition.

The remaining challenges to change evaluation include taking a pragmatic and measured approach to risk and communicating the organization's attitude toward risk and approach to risk management effectively during risk evaluation. Finally, change evaluation needs to meet the challenges of building a thorough understanding of risks that have impacted or may impact successful service transition of services and releases and encouraging a risk management culture where people share information.

Risks

The most common risks to the success of this process include a lack of clear criteria for when change evaluation should be used and unrealistic expectations of the time required. Another risk is that staff carrying out the change evaluation have insufficient experience or organizational authority to be able to influence change authorities. Finally, projects and suppliers who fail to deliver on the promised date cause delays in scheduling change evaluation activities.

Knowledge Management

The ability to deliver a quality service or process relies to a significant extent on the ability of those involved to respond to circumstances. How effectively they are able to do this depends on their knowledge and experience. Service transition is about change, and change requires new information to be learned if staff are to be effective.

Purpose

The purpose of the knowledge management process is to share perspectives, ideas, experience, and information; to ensure that these are available in the right place at the right time to enable informed decisions; and to improve efficiency by reducing the need to rediscover knowledge.

Objectives

The major objective of knowledge management is to insure that knowledge, information, and data is gathered, analyzed, stored, shared, used, and maintained throughout the service provider organization. The knowledge is managed through the service knowledge management system (SKMS), which provides controlled access to knowledge, information, and data appropriate for each audience. Having this available will have the following results:

- It will reduce the need to rediscover knowledge, so the service provider can be more efficient—able to deliver improved quality of service and achieve increased satisfaction while reducing cost.

- It will ensure that staff have a clear understanding of the value and benefits realized from the use of those services.

- It will improve management decision-making by providing reliable and secure knowledge, information, and data.

Scope

Knowledge management is relevant to all lifecycle sectors, not just service transition. The main scope of the process includes oversight of the management of knowledge and the information and data from which that knowledge derives. Excluded from the process is the capture, maintenance, and use of asset and configuration data, which, as you saw earlier, is the responsibility of the service asset and configuration management process.

Value to the Business

Knowledge management is important for all stages of the lifecycle, for all roles. It is particularly important for the transition of services because there is a strong focus on management of knowledge transfer as part of transition. This will enable the business to use the delivered service effectively.

Effective knowledge management delivers conformance with legal and other requirements, such as company policy and procedures. It provides documented requirements for retention and disposal of each category of data, information, and knowledge and ensures that data, information, and knowledge is current, complete, valid, and available to the people who need it when they need it. It also ensures that procedures are in place for the safe disposal of knowledge that is no longer required.

Policies, Principles, and Basic Concepts

Let's now look at the policies, principles, and basic concepts that underpin knowledge management.

Policies

Knowledge management policies guide staff in the behaviors needed to make knowledge management effective. Policy statements typically include the following items:

- A secure and convenient way of storing and accessing the knowledge should be defined.

- Access should be available to all staff to assist them in supporting the services provided.

- All policies, plans, and processes must be reviewed at least once per year.

- All knowledge and information should be created, reviewed, approved, maintained, controlled, and disposed of following a formal documented process.

Data to Information to Knowledge to Wisdom

Knowledge management is typically displayed within the data, information, knowledge, wisdom (DIKW) model, as shown in Figure 26.2. You should remember this from your Foundation studies.

FIGURE 26.2 The flow from data to wisdom

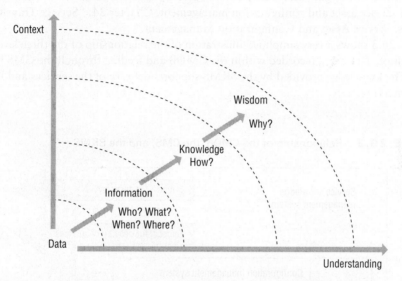

Let's look at the model, and examine what is meant by each of these concepts:

- Data is a set of discrete facts. Most organizations capture significant amounts of data in highly structured databases such as service management and service asset and configuration management tools/systems and databases.

- Information provides context to data. An example of information is the average time to close priority 2 incidents. This information is created by combining data from the start time, end time, and priority of many incidents.

- Knowledge is composed of the tacit experiences, ideas, insights, values, and judgements of individuals. Knowledge puts information into an "ease of use" form, which can facilitate decision-making. An example of knowledge is that the average time to close priority 2 incidents has increased by about 10 percent since a new version of the service was released.

- Wisdom makes use of knowledge to create value through correct and well-informed decisions. Wisdom involves having the contextual awareness to provide strong common-sense judgement. An example of wisdom is recognizing that the increase in time to close priority 2 incidents is due to poor-quality documentation for the new version of the service.

The Service Knowledge Management System

The service knowledge management system (SKMS) holds all the knowledge relating to IT service management. This knowledge is underpinned by a large quantity of data gathered by various processes and held in the SKMS. One very important example is the configuration management system (CMS), which forms part of the SKMS. The CMS describes the attributes and relationships of configuration items, many of which are themselves knowledge, information, or data assets stored in the SKMS. We covered the CMS in the chapter about service asset and configuration management, Chapter 24, "Service Transition Processes: Service Asset and Configuration Management."

Figure 26.3 shows a very simplified illustration of the relationship of the three levels, with configuration data being recorded within the CMDB and feeding through the CMS into the SKMS. The knowledge provided by the SKMS supports delivery of the services and informed decision-making.

FIGURE 26.3   Relationship of the CMDB, the CMS, and the SKMS

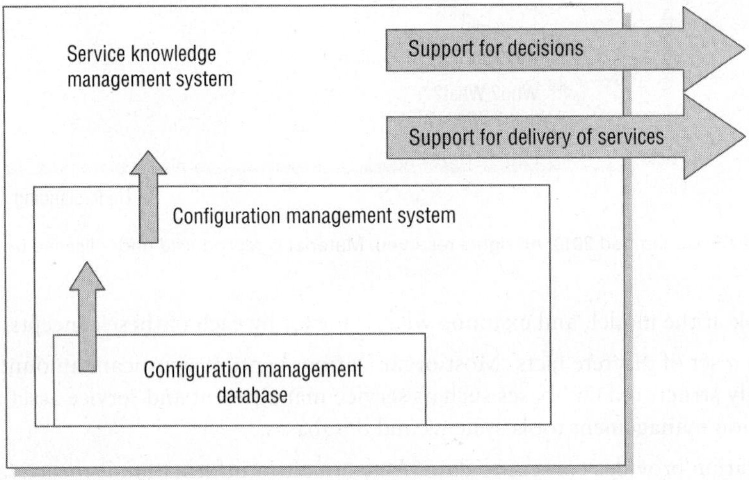

The SKMS will contain many different types of data, information, and knowledge, including the service portfolio, the CMS, the DML, SLAs and OLAs and contracts, the information security policy, the supplier and contract management information system (SCMIS), budgets, and cost models. Many of these knowledge and information assets are configuration items. Changes to CIs must be under the control of the change management process, and details of their attributes and relationships will be documented in the CMS. Figure 26.4 shows examples of information that should be in an SKMS.

FIGURE 26.4 Examples of data and information in the service knowledge management system

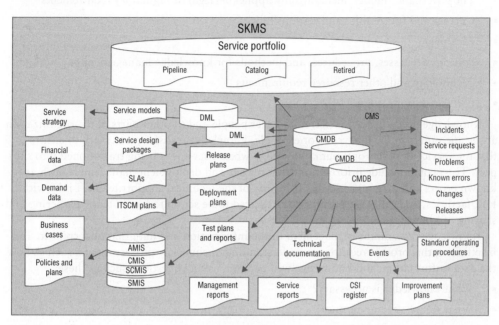

A knowledge management strategy is required. In the absence of an organizational knowledge management approach, action is required to establish the process within transition or IT service management. The strategy will address the governance model, roles and responsibilities, ongoing funding, policies, processes, procedures, methods and technology for knowledge management, performance measures, and how knowledge is to be identified, captured, and maintained.

Process Activities, Methods, and Techniques

An overall strategy for knowledge management is required. If the organization as a whole has no such strategy, it may be left to those responsible for IT service management as a whole or for service transition to impose knowledge management in their areas. The strategy should ensure that knowledge is shared with as wide a scope as practicable, covering direct IT staff, users, third-party support, and others likely to contribute to or make beneficial use of the knowledge.

If an organization has such a strategy, however, IT service management should be designed to fit within that overall organizational approach.

In either case, the strategy should address the following:

- The governance model, including any applicable legal or regulatory requirements
- Current and future roles and responsibilities
- Funding
- Policies, processes, procedures, and methods for knowledge management
- Technology and other resource requirements
- Performance measures

Knowledge needs to be transferred to other people and to other parts of the organization at specific points in the lifecycle. For example, knowledge transfer takes place to ensure that the service desk has optimum knowledge when a service is being transitioned into support. This would include information from release and deployment management such as known errors and diagnostic scripts from any of the technical support teams. Links with HR, facilities, and other supporting services need to be set up to facilitate the gathering and sharing of knowledge.

Knowledge rests on the management of the information and data that underpins it. To be efficient, this process requires an understanding of some key process inputs, such as how the data, information, and knowledge will be used, asking questions such as these:

- What knowledge is necessary?
- What do we need to monitor?
- What data is available?
- What is the cost of capturing and maintaining data?
- Does its value justify the cost?

We also need to consider applicable policies, legislation, standards, intellectual property rights, and copyright issues. Using the service knowledge management system reduces the costs of maintaining and managing the services.

Triggers

Now let's look at the triggers, inputs and outputs, and process interfaces for knowledge management. Let's look first at the triggers for this process. Knowledge management has many triggers relating to every requirement for storing, maintaining, and using knowledge, information, or data within the organization. For example, any of the following actions could trigger the need to store or retrieve knowledge:

- Business relationship management storing the minutes of a customer meeting
- Updates to the service catalog or service portfolio
- Modification of a service design package
- The creation of a new or updated capacity plan
- The receipt of an updated user manual from a supplier

- The creation of a customer report
- Updates to the CSI register

Inputs

Inputs to knowledge management include all knowledge, information, and data used by the service provider as well as relevant business data.

Outputs

The key output of knowledge management is the knowledge required to make decisions and to manage the IT services; this knowledge is maintained within an SKMS. The success of knowledge management depends in part on the participation of the relevant staff. For example, frontline operations staff will use the information about known errors to help when supporting users; they will also be responsible for gathering a lot of the data that will be stored in the SKMS, such as incident records. Problem management staff will be key users of incident data, while transition staff will capture data to be fed back to CSI and design.

Interfaces

Knowledge management has interfaces to every other service management process in every stage of the lifecycle. The SKMS can only be truly effective if all processes and activities use it to store and manage their information and data so that the maximum value can be extracted.

Critical Success Factors and Key Performance Indicators

As with the other processes, the performance of knowledge management should be monitored and reported, and action should be taken to improve it. Here are two examples of CSFs for knowledge management and the related KPIs for each.

- Critical success factor: "Availability of knowledge and information that helps to support management decision-making."
    - KPI: Increased number of accesses to the SKMS by managers
    - KPI: Increased percentage of SKMS searches by managers that receive a rating of good
- Critical success factor: "Successful implementation and early life support operation of new and changed services with few knowledge-related errors."
    - KPI: Reduction in the number of incidents and problems categorized as knowledge related
    - KPI: The increased percentage of successful service transitions

Challenges

Implementing knowledge management can be challenging. Challenges include justifying the effort needed to create a repository for existing knowledge, information, and data. There may be a perception that knowledge management is interfering in the work of other teams who manage their own information. The final challenge is persuading all the stakeholders of the benefits that a more cooperative and holistic approach to knowledge management can bring.

Risks

The risks to successful knowledge management are as follows:

- The emphasis could be on tools rather than on the creation of value.
- There could be insufficient understanding of what knowledge, information, and data are needed by the organization.
- There may be doubt as to the value of the process, leading to insufficient investment in the tools and people needed to support the SKMS.
- Without a clear knowledge management strategy, effort may be concentrated on knowledge capture with insufficient attention to knowledge transfer and reuse.
- The process may lose credibility if the knowledge and information that is stored and shared is out of date and irrelevant.
- If the benefits are not clear, stakeholders are unlikely to give the support and commitment the process requires.

Summary

This chapter explored the last two of the processes in the service transition stage, change evaluation and knowledge management. We examined how the change evaluation process evaluates the SDP and service acceptance criteria, and provides a report and a recommendation to change management whether the change should be authorized. We also considered how the knowledge management process ensures that those involved in providing the service have all the information they need to be effective, and to make decisions regarding the service.

We examined how each of these processes supports the other and the importance of these processes to the business and to the IT service provider.

Exam Essentials

Understand the purpose of change evaluation.   Change evaluation enables us to understand the likely performance of a service change and how it might impact the business, the IT infrastructure, and other IT services. It provides a consistent and standardized means of assessing this impact by assessing the actual performance of a change against its predicted performance.

Be able to explain the objectives of change evaluation. The objectives of change evaluation include setting stakeholder expectations correctly and preventing changes from being accepted into the live environment unless it is known that they will behave as planned. Another objective is to provide good-quality outputs to enable change management to decide quickly whether or not a service change is to be authorized.

Understand which changes go through the formal change evaluation process and the production of an evaluation report. Only those changes the organization has deemed important enough or risky enough to require a report will go through the formal change evaluation process; simpler changes will not, except through the change review process.

Be able to list and explain the main process interfaces with change evaluation. The major interfaces are with the following processes:

- Transition planning and support. To ensure that appropriate resources are available when needed.

- Change management. There must be agreed criteria for evaluation and time allowed for its completion. Change management is dependent upon receiving the evaluation report in time for the CAB (or other change authority) to use it to assist in their decision-making.

- Service design coordination. Provides the service in the service design package.

- Service level management or business relationship management. To agree on the use of customer resources to perform the evaluation.

- Service validation and testing. Provides change evaluation with information; the change evaluation and service validation and testing processes must coordinate activities to ensure that required inputs are available in sufficient time.

Understand the purpose of knowledge management. Knowledge management shares perspectives, ideas, experience, and information in the right place at the right time to enable informed decisions, reducing the need for knowledge rediscovery.

Understand the objectives of knowledge management. The objectives of knowledge management are to ensure that we have mechanisms for capturing and sharing knowledge to improve the quality of our services and decision-making.

Be able to describe the scope of knowledge management. Knowledge management extends across the whole of the service lifecycle, and included in the scope is the information interaction with customer and users. Excluded is the management of the CIs relating to knowledge.

Be able to describe the DIKW model. DIKW is data to information to knowledge to wisdom. This ensures that we add context and understanding to the communications we provide to the organization we support.

- Data is a set of discrete facts.

- Information provides context to data.

- Knowledge is composed of the tacit experiences, ideas, insights, values, and judgements of individuals.

- Wisdom makes use of knowledge to create value through correct and wellinformed decisions.

Be able to describe the role and purpose of the SKMS.   SKMS is the overarching system for the management of knowledge relating to service management. It integrates all the existing data sources from our service management processes and enables the DIKW structure for knowledge management across the whole of the service lifecycle.

Review Questions

You can find the answers to the review questions in the appendix.

1. Which option is an objective of change evaluation?
    A. Provide assurance that a release is fit for purpose.
    B. Optimize overall business risk.
    C. Provide quality assurance for a release.
    D. Set stakeholder expectations correctly.

2. Which is NOT a factor considered by change evaluation?
    A. Actual performance of a service change
    B. Cost of a service change
    C. Predicted performance of a service change
    D. Likely impact of a service change

3. What may be included in an evaluation report?
    1. A risk profile
    2. A deviations report
    3. A recommendation
    4. A qualification statement
        A. 1 and 2
        B. 2 and 3
        C. 1, 2, and 3
        D. All of the above

4. Which is the BEST description of a performance model?
    A. A performance benchmark
    B. Predefined steps for delivering good performance
    C. A representation of a service used to predict performance
    D. A framework used to manage the performance of a process

5. Which process triggers change evaluation activity?
    A. Change management
    B. Transition planning and support
    C. Release and deployment management
    D. Service validation and testing

6. Which of the following is NOT a permitted outcome of change evaluation in the event of deviation from the predicted?

   A. The customer accepts the change with the deviation.

   B. The customer is unhappy with the change but receives a discount on the price of the service as compensation.

   C. The customer rejects the change.

   D. The service provider introduces a new change to correct the deviation.

7. Which of the following statements is TRUE?

   A. Release and deployment is responsible for ensuring that appropriate testing takes place.

   B. Change evaluation carries out the testing.

   C. Service validation is responsible for ensuring that appropriate testing takes place.

   D. The output from service validation is a key input to change evaluation.

8. Match each of the DIKW concepts with its definition.

   1. Data

   2. Information

   3. Knowledge

   4. Wisdom

       A. Composed of tacit experiences, ideas, insights, values, and judgements

       B. A set of discrete facts

       C. Creates value through correct and well-informed decisions

       D. Gives context to data

9. The knowledge management process maintains and updates a tool used for knowledge management. What is this tool called?

   A. The service management tool

   B. The knowledge base for service management

   C. The service knowledge management system

   D. The service management database

10. An important focus for the service lifecycle is the capture and management of knowledge relating to IT service provision. How does the process of knowledge management work in the service lifecycle?

   A. Knowledge management is solely concerned with the transfer of knowledge when new or changed services are implemented.

   B. Knowledge management is used across the lifecycle stages of continual service improvement and service operation to ensure that improvements are managed effectively.

   C. Knowledge management is used solely in the service operation stage of the lifecycle to ensure that operation issues are managed efficiently.

   D. Knowledge management is used across the whole service lifecycle to ensure that appropriate knowledge is delivered to enable informed decision-making.

Chapter

27

Managing People through Service Transitions

THE FOLLOWING ITIL INTERMEDIATE EXAM OBJECTIVES ARE DISCUSSED IN THIS CHAPTER:

✓ **The concepts of service transition relating to**

- Managing communications and commitment
- Managing organizational and stakeholder change
- Organizational roles and responsibilities
- Organizational readiness
- Stakeholder Management

In this chapter, we will consider the concepts of service transition as a whole, how communication affects the success of a transition, the management of organizational and stakeholder change, the importance of roles and responsibilities, readiness to accept a change, and stakeholder management. You will be expected to be able to analyze and apply these concepts as presented in the exam.

Management of Communication and Commitment

One of the major traditional weaknesses in service transition has been the inability to deliver sufficient prompt understanding of the implications, benefits, and usage of IT services.

Communication is central to any service transition change process. The greater the change, the greater the need for clear communication about its delivery and proposed effects. Communications need to be targeted at the right audience, and the messages and benefits need to be clearly and consistently communicated.

There are likely to be a wide variety of people impacted by a service change, and the communication required needs to be at the appropriate level and the appropriate time. Those who are in support of the transition may need less communication, as will those who are in opposition, but with those who fall between those two extremes, effort should be spent to ensure effective communication.

Two-way communication channels will ensure that feedback is provided and is valuable. Managing the stakeholders may involve a significant resource requirement.

It is important that the service transition team members are capable of understanding the impact of their work on others and therefore tailoring their own approach to the stakeholder audience. Ultimately, the service transition team's goal is to build enthusiasm and commitment to the change while ensuring that all stakeholders are clear about how the changes will impact them and what will be expected of them in the coming months.

After establishing the strategies that will promote positive change enablers, and having understood the level of commitment within the organization, service transition must ensure that there is a detailed communications plan that will target information where it will be most effective. When information is announced during a service transition change, the following considerations should be made for each statement you need to communicate:

- What is the objective of the communication, and what are the desired outcomes?

- How formal and robust does the communication plan need to be? Some transitions will need a fully integrated and documented communication plan, but a more simple approach may be appropriate for smaller transitions.

- How should the information be delivered—all at once or divided into segments and released over a period of time? If it is going to be released in segments, what are the components, and what is the sequence of timing for the communication message delivery?

- What should the tone of each message be? What tone and style should be used to convey the message? Upbeat? Cautious? Optimistic?

- What actions could be taken before the communication to increase the understanding and the acceptance of the information given?

- How and when will groups be involved during the cascading of the communication information to other levels in the organization?

- Are the communications successful in overcoming the particular communication barriers on this service transition (for example, cultural differences)?

- Is there consideration to address the communication needs of other stakeholders in the project (for example, decision-makers, opinion leaders, system users, and internal and external regulatory bodies)?

- How will success of the communication be measured?

In Figure 27.1, you can see the key elements that need to be considered for a communication strategy. The main factors of setting a vision, identifying and maintaining sponsorship, and building partnerships form the frame of the strategy.

FIGURE 27.1   Example of a communication strategy and plan contents

Communication strategy

Setting a vision of the business objectives

Identifying and maintaining sponsorship

Communication plan

✔ Ownership
✔ Style
✔ Delivery mechanisms
✔ Competencies—skills, training
✔ Other related ongoing activities
✔ Audiences—internal and external
✔ Involve staff at all levels (stakeholder and operations)
✔ Timescales
✔ Critical success factors
✔ Monitor audience feedback
✔ Ensure that the right message meets the right people at the right time!

Removing barriers of resistance—building partnerships

Methods of Communication

There are many mechanisms for communicating during service transition, and indeed at any time. Using multiple communication means will help people understand the overall message. Let's explore some of these, starting with workshops.

Workshops

Workshops deliver a clear and consistent message to the target audience on the overall service transition approach; this will generally be useful at the start of any communication strategy in order to build understanding, ownership, and even excitement across the teams.

Newsletters

Organization, business unit, or IT newsletters can be used to reinforce any messages already delivered; however, care needs to be taken that this approach is used as reinforcement rather than as the first time that employees see the communication cascade.

Training Sessions

As part of the service transition, roles or processes may change; this requires targeted training, which should be planned to give sufficient time for employees to come to grips with any new ways of working.

Team Meetings

Team meetings give support to team leaders from the service transition team, who will ensure at their own weekly meetings that they can reinforce any messages. Employees' questions may be better understood at these lower-level meetings—people are more comfortable because they are used to this method of communication with colleagues with whom they work daily.

Organizational Meetings

Meetings of the whole organization, which may be face-to-face or use video or audio technology, depending on the size and type of organization, that are supported from the top of the organization.

One-to-One Meetings

In one-to-one meetings, key stakeholders make time to visit staff in their work environment (floor walks), to set a positive example of the support by senior management, and allow employees to ask questions pertinent to themselves.

Question and Answer (Q&A) Feedback

Employees can raise anonymous questions and receive feedback on any concerns they may have using Q&A feedback postings on boards or in mailboxes.

Other Communication Methods

Further communication methods include using the corporate intranet and other training approaches:

- Simulation games. These can be a practical and fun way of trying out a new method of working.

- Consistent reinforcement memos from the senior stakeholders, emphasizing key information or giving an update on the implementation activities. This will keep the service transition alive for those people not actually involved at all stages.

- Posters/road maps. Good-quality colorful communications on office walls showing implementation activities, progress, or general updates are a positive way of keeping communications alive and delivering a consistent message.

- Pay advice notes. Key communications attached to pay slips can ensure a practical communication update that reaches 100 percent of staff.

- Encapsulated reference cards. Small credit–card–sized documents (for example a Z-CARD) holding key information and expected to be carried by staff in their wallets or purses.

Communication Models

Models help to communicate expectations for each service or each type of change. Figure 27.2 is an example of a change model used to transition services from an organization to an external service provider (outsource). This is an example of a total organizational change, where there will be changes in management, processes, and staffing, although many staff may transfer into the new service provider organization. Having access to a set of service, change, and transition models in a form that is easy to communicate will help to set expectations during the service transition.

FIGURE 27.2   Example of service transition steps for outsourcing

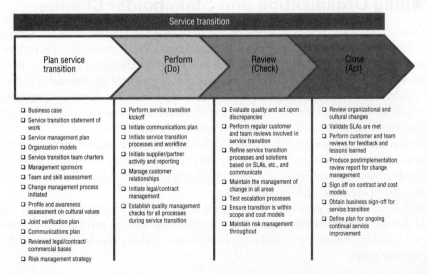

Motivation and the Importance of Communication

People need to be kept up-to-date with the progress of change, good or bad, if they are to be motivated to make it happen. In their 1980 book, *Work Redesign*, Hackman and Oldham described the state of affairs when people try to do well because they find the work satisfying as "internal motivation." The concept is defined in Table 27.1.

TABLE 27.1   Job characteristics that motivate people

The essential characteristics of the job	Benefit for the employees	The result if all these characteristics are present
Feedback from the job	Knowledge of the actual results of work activities	High internal work motivation
Autonomy	Experienced responsibility for outcomes of work	
Skill variety	Experienced meaningfulness of the work	
Task identity		
Task significance		

People will be mobilized and engaged if they can see progress. Short-term wins should be communicated and progress celebrated.

Managing Organization and Stakeholder Change

Service transition's basic role is building on the basis of agreed design from the service design lifecycle stage to implement a new or changed service. Without change, progress does not happen. A change of any significance may be an organizational change, ranging from moving a few staff to work from new premises to major alterations in the nature of how the business works. Change is an inevitable and important part of organizational development and growth. Change can occur in incremental phases or suddenly, affecting part of or the whole organization, its people, and its culture.

Organizational change efforts fail or fall short of their goals because changes and transitions are not led, managed, and monitored efficiently across the organization and throughout the change process. These gaps in key organizational activities often result in resistance, dissatisfaction, and increased costs.

We will cover in more detail the involvement of service transition in managing organizational change. It includes assurance of the organization change products from service design, stakeholder management and communications, and approaches to cope with change during transition.

Emotional Cycle of Change

To facilitate the acceptance of change, it is important to understand the emotional stages a person experiences. For all significant changes, individuals will go through this process.

Appropriate communication through these stages of transition will drive the energy of individuals from low to high, obtaining involvement and generating a more positive attitude as the change takes place. As emphasized, this is a pattern followed by individuals, and different people will pass through these typical phases at different speeds, so understanding where individuals are on this curve and supporting them and helping them progress through the stages can be a significant resource commitment for service transition. It is important to understand that the individual will be thinking of themselves throughout a significant change, so any communication will be viewed from this personal perspective. Figure 27.3 illustrates this emotional cycle.

FIGURE 27.3   The emotional cycle of change

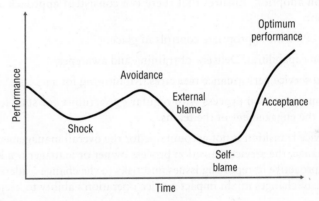

Effective Management of Change

There are five important ingredients of change: necessity, vision, plan, resources, and competence. If there is no necessity established, then there is likely to be a lot of resistance from the people involved. If there is no vision, there will be confusion among the employees. If there is no plan, there will be disorganization in the activities and transition. If there is a lack of resources, the employees may experience frustration. And if there is no competence, there may be a fear of failure among the employees.

Therefore, it is extremely important to pay adequate attention and establish management commitment to take adequate care of these requirements of the change.

Organization, Roles, and Responsibilities

It is the responsibility of the managers and executives of the organization to manage the change and transition.

A clear, strategic vision coming from management and/or executives is imperative to drive and maintain the change.

There needs to be understanding of potential resistance to change as well as open communications to enable change to be handled and responded to in an appropriate manner so that transitions can be effective. This is especially the case if a change is on a scale that is significant enough to affect the organization as a whole.

Service Transition's Role in Organizational Change

Organizational change is always a challenge. The following factors drive successful change initiatives at the organization level:

- Leadership for the change. This shows management support and commitment.

- Organization adoption. Ensures that there is a consistent approach across the organization.

- Governance. Puts the appropriate controls in place.

- Organization capabilities. Delivery of training and awareness.

- Business and service performance measures. Monitoring for success.

- A strong communication process with regular opportunity for staff feedback. Continuing the engagement of the teams.

Although service transition is not accountable for the overall management of business and technical change, the service transition process owner or manager is a key stakeholder and needs to be proactive in reporting issues and risks to the change leaders—for example, when the volume of changes might impact service operation's ability to keep the services running.

Let's look at the concept of organizational adoption in some more detail. Organizational adoption is a subset of change management practice. It typically happens at two levels: individual and organizational.

It is important to understand the culture of the organizations and the people involved. This will often be quite diverse across different business units and geographies. Business culture may be different depending on the industry, geography, and other factors. The culture of the customer, the service provider and IT organization, and the supplier will all have an impact on the management of the change, as will the requirements and attitudes of individual people, especially those managers in senior roles and champions of the change.

Cultural and organizational assessment and change design are the responsibility of strategy and design. However, most significant service transitions will have an effect on working practices and so require a change in the behavior and attitudes of many teams and stakeholder groups. Understanding the organizational change elements of a transition is therefore vital. The assessment of the likely risks and success is an important element of the transition as a whole. Service transition will be involved early in the lifecycle to ensure that risks and success are assessed and incorporated into the design and build of the organizational change.

Service transition must be actively involved in changing the mindsets of people across the lifecycle to ensure that they are ready to play their role in service transition. This includes the following people:

- Service transition staff
- Customers
- Users
- Service operation functions
- Suppliers
- Key stakeholders

Service transition will focus on simple messages at any one time to ensure that there is consistency in the implementation of the changes. For example, service transition would be interested in helping people to understand the need for knowledge and effective knowledge transfer. It is important to ensure that people understand the importance of making decisions at the right speed/within the appropriate time frame and to complete and review configuration baselines in a timely manner. Transition will ensure that in the future the lifecycle can apply more effective risk assessment and management methods for transitions and follow the deadlines for submitting changes and releases.

Service design will perform the assessment of the capability and capacity of the IT organization to transition the new or changed services. Service transition has a quality assurance role to check that the organization and stakeholders are ready for the change, and it will raise any issues and risks related to organizational change that are identified, such as issues raised during testing, pilots, deployment, and early life support.

Service transition is also responsible for ensuring that the organizational change happens according to the plans. This will include verifying that the change is still relevant in current circumstances and that it delivers the predicted organization structure, capabilities, and resources.

Achieving successful service transition requires organized, competent, and well-motivated people to build, test, deploy, and operate the service.

Because successful service transitions rely on changing the organization and people, it is important to focus on such aspects as competency assessment and development, recruiting, skills development, knowledge transfer, team building, process improvements, and resource deployment. If there is a gap in capability, then service transition will provide input into the relevant area (for example, project management, service design, or continual service improvement).

For successful service transition, an organization needs to determine the underlying values and drivers that enable effective management of change. In Table 27.2 are examples of the cultural aspects and questions to determine those values.

TABLE 27.2   Understanding the culture of the parties involved

Cultural aspect	Question
Language	Is there a common language or shared language(s)?
	Does the language inhibit and reinforce boundaries or facilitate effective change and knowledge transfer?
	Is the organizational language style mostly formal or informal?
Change	Does the organization appear to resist change or is it constantly evolving?
Communication	What are the preferred modes of communication?
	What is the content and style of internal communications?
	Where does official and unofficial communication happen?
	Are communication channels open and democratic or closed and hierarchical?
	How is knowledge and experience shared?
	Are rumors and gossip prevalent?
Knowledge flow	How do people describe the way knowledge and information is transferred around the organization?
	How easy is it to find what you need to know when you need it?
	How easy is it to find the right person with the right experience?
Communities	Are there identifiable communities within the organization?
	Is there a community leader (e.g., a problem management community leader)?
	What is the structure and function of these communities?
Networks	Are an individual's networks generally well developed?
	What kind of information is exchanged by these people?
Working environment	Does the working environment create the right conditions for knowledge transfer and integrated working (e.g., close physical proximity, electronic tools)?
	How are desks configured?
	How are communal areas used?
History	How does the organization see its own history?
	Is it valued and used or quickly forgotten?
	How does the organization value past experiences? For example, do people still refer back to their old company after a merger?

Cultural aspect	Question
Meetings	Are meetings seen as productive? How are they managed? Are they effective? Does everyone feel safe to speak? How is opinion or criticism handled? How is output captured or taken forward?
Rewards and motivations	How are individuals/teams rewarded or recognized for sharing knowledge/information and experience?
	What motivates people in the organization?
	What else might be blocking engagement of an individual/team (e.g., other major change, major incident handling)?
Time	What are the attitudes of individuals, teams, and the organization to time (e.g., busy or relaxed; punctual, rigid, and unchanging or flexible)?

It is important to understand any potential language barriers and whether the organization is able to accept change. Transition will need to plan the appropriate communication and knowledge flow and needs to understand the impact of communication and knowledge transfer.

Service transition needs to be aware of the structure of the organization in terms of communities, networks, and the working environment. Understanding the history of the organization will also be important because the history may inform the future.

It's important to understand communication mechanisms. Does the organization use meetings effectively, or is there a better way of managing communication?

Does the organization use rewards and motivations, and how is time organized?

All of these factors can make a difference to the success of service transition.

Planning and Implementing Organizational Change

Strategy and design play their part in managing organizational change. An organization's age and size affect its structure. During a service transition, changes in roles, processes, and relationships must be made or problems will arise. Understanding the different phases of development of the stakeholder organizations helps service transition to manage the stakeholders and users better.

Frequently, plans and designs for managing change are not balanced, and the organization and people side of change is omitted. Within IT organizations, project managers often focus on the technical activities rather than on the changes required for the organization or individuals. It is important that project plans are reviewed to ensure that the organizational change activities are included.

To manage organizational change, it is important that the stakeholders and teams understand what is required and can answer these questions:

- What are the business and organizational strategic drivers, personalities, and policy changes?
- What issues does the proposed change solve?
- What will the new or changed service deliver and what does it look like?
- How do current objectives need to be modified?
- What are the objectives of the change as defined by management, and how will success be judged throughout the levels of the organization?
- What are the processes, templates, decision points, and systems to be used, and what level of reporting data is required for the decisions to be made?
- Who will be involved and who will no longer be involved?
- Who will be affected within and outside the organization?
- What are the constraints (type, range, and flexibility) and what is the time slot, equipment, staff, and supplier availability?
- What is the planned timescale?
- Who or what can help in planning the implementation?
- What skills and measures should be considered?
- How will "normal" life be affected?
- What will the consequential changes be, for example, to business methods?

As part of quality assurance and implementation, the stakeholders and IT teams can be sampled to understand and clarify their expectations about these aspects and in this way be monitored for transition success.

Organizational Change Products

The change in the organization from the current state to a new state can require the adjustment of a combination of elements. This will enable the organizational transformation. The required service is defined in the service design package. Remember, service strategy and design assist with managing organizational change during service transition. These are examples of work products that are typically outputs from service strategy and service design.

There may be a stakeholder map, which allows service transition to understand who is involved and their relative importance and engagement. The current organization and capability assessment, along with the required competency model and competency assessments, will support transitional activity. It is important to understand the constraints (including organization, capability, and resources).

The service management process models, policies, processes, and procedures should also be referred to throughout the transition. This should include the role and responsibility definitions from, for example, a RACI (responsible, accountable, consulted, informed) matrix.

This will help with relationship management and support the communication plan. There should also be a supplier framework, especially where multiple suppliers are involved.

Service transition will check that organizational change products and services are fit for purpose. For large-scale changes, such as mergers and acquisitions and outsourcing, this should include validation of the approach to career development for staff. For example, are succession plans being built? Do individuals have an understanding of their progression prospects?

It is also important to carry out performance evaluation at the organization, team, and individual level. Are regular reviews conducted? Is there a formal template for documentation, and is there demonstration of a consistent approach?

Is there a net benefit to people affected by the change in terms of rewards and compensation?

Where there is a shortfall in any roles required, is there a fair and consistent process for selection, including the process of internal movement as well as selection from the external market?

There may be localized or corporate governance requirements, such as relevant laws and agreements. These could include, for example, the European Union Acquired Rights Directive (ARD), the UK Transfer of Undertakings regulations (TUPE), or agreements with works councils and trade unions.

There are a number of work products that are typically delivered from the build stage on which the service transition team depend. Some examples are organization models, providing detail on the new or changed organizational structure; the career development structure; any reward and compensation structure; and structures relating to performance measurement and evaluation.

There should also be a competency model detailed design, incorporating the competency list, matrix of activity, job roles and definitions, and staffing and competency requirements.

For the individual, there should be an assessment, including competency, performance, and learning needs.

Education and training is an important output from the build stage. There should be a plan for the approach to use for learning, testing the courses efficacy and how they will support and enhance performance.

Assessing Organizational Readiness for Change

Part of transition should be the assessment of the organization's readiness for change. Table 27.3 shows a typical approach to understanding the organizational capability and can be used to assess the role and skill requirements.

TABLE 27.3 Organizational role and skills assessment checklist

Check	Evidence
Is there an assessment of the number of staff required and their current skill levels?	Plan
Is there a documented vision/strategy to address any risks in each area (e.g., for resource shortfalls, start hiring actions, subcontract, or outsource the whole area)?	Vision/strategy

TABLE 27.3   Organizational role and skills assessment checklist *(continued)*

Check	Evidence
Have the generic roles and interactions throughout the service transition been reviewed?	Roles and responsibilities interaction matrix
Are the specific roles and measures defined?	Performance measures by role
Have the skills for each area—i.e., content, application, technical, and business—been defined?	Skills requirements for each area
Is there an assessment of the organization's personnel against the requirements?	Assessment report
Have personnel from areas in the organization other than the areas covered by the service transition been considered?	Assessment report
Have the requirements for both development and maintenance that support the business needs been considered?	Requirements
Has the level of risk that relates to the support available for certain areas been documented? Also the areas that cannot be supported and the assumptions that apply to the analysis?	Risk assessment report

You can see the check that is required and where the evidence for it can be found. For example, staff numbers and skills will be evidenced in the plan. The vision and strategy will identify any risks and should be a specific documented output. Roles and responsibilities should be captured, including measures and skills. The assessment report will show the personnel requirements for transition and beyond. Risk assessments and requirements capture will be another important area in the assessment for organizational readiness for change.

Monitoring Progress of Organizational Change

To enable a service transition program to be effective and successful, regular checks/surveys should be performed throughout many different levels of the organization. The results of any survey should be useful in determining the progress made through service transition. This will include the status of employee commitment and any areas for improvement. This will also serve as a useful tool at various milestones within the transition journey.

Employees are encouraged to feel that their opinions count at a critical time as they go into the service transition program. This is where positive engagement of the new processes can be increased by "taking the majority with you," as the acceptance of the transition spreads throughout the teams affected by it.

Monitoring is, of course, only the first part of a series of actions. The responses obtained must be analyzed and understood. Where required, issues should be addressed and fixed as soon as possible. Respondents to the survey must be kept informed of changes that result from their feedback. Only in this way can staff have confidence that their feedback matters and achieves improvements.

Often, improvements will be identified in the postimplementation review of the service change and can feed into the CSI register.

Organization and People in Sourcing Changes

A change in sourcing of IT services is one of the most significant, and often most traumatic, kinds of organizational change. Several different effects on staff will need to be considered, planned, and prepared for.

The impact of employee shock can be significant. There could be a morale issue caused by transition of staff replaced by the sourcing function. Sourcing is best done in an open atmosphere where all the options are clear and identified. Communication will be critical to ensuring that staff are not undermined by the transition.

Another major change is the way business is conducted. Keeping the relationship between business and service provider professional is vital. Sharing "everything" with an external service provider may lead to distrust if it is not presented in the correct terms. Care must be taken to ensure that information is passed to the service provider on a need-to-know basis.

Location change may also be extremely disruptive if not handled carefully during transition. There are a number of possible locational sourcing options, from local sourcing (remaining in the same geographic location as the business) to offshore sourcing (where the service provider is in a specific location). Combinations are becoming common, with different functions, or aspects of functions, delivered in different fashions. The cultural and organizational issues relating to the change in location need to be addressed to guarantee a successful service transition.

Linking of sourcing activities throughout the organization happens when there are multiple sources provided from different areas across the organization. Every aspect of the sourcing operation must be linked to the appropriate area/group within the business. These links need to be identified, established, and tested early on or the sourcing relationship will not be efficient.

Methods, Practices, and Techniques for Managing Change

The requirement to manage organizational change needs to be taken into account when the methods, practices, and techniques are chosen.

Kotter's Eight Steps

One approach is to use Dr. John P. Kotter's eight steps to transform your organization (see Table 27.4).

TABLE 27.4   Kotter's eight steps to transform your organization

Leading change: eight steps	Core challenge	Desired behavior
1. Establish a sense of urgency.	Get people "out of the bunker" and ready to move.	People start telling each other, "Let's go. We need to change things!"
2. Create a guiding coalition.	Get the right people in place with the trust, emotional commitment, and teamwork to guide the difficult change process.	A group powerful enough to guide large changes (with members that work well together) influences others to accept change.
3. Develop a vision and strategy.	Get the guiding team to create the right vision and strategies to guide action in all of the remaining stages of change. This requires moving beyond number crunching to address the creative and emotional components of vision.	The guiding team develops the right vision and strategy for the change effort.
4. Communicate the change vision (and communicate it over and over again).	Get as many people as possible acting to make the vision a reality.	People begin to buy in to the change, and this shows in their behavior.
5. Empower broad-based action.	Remove key obstacles that stop people from acting on the vision.	More people feel able to act, and do act, on the vision.
6. Create short-term wins.	Produce enough short-term (quick) wins fast enough to energize the change helpers, enlighten the pessimists, defuse the cynics, and build momentum for the effort.	Momentum builds as people try to fulfil the vision while fewer and fewer resist change.
7. Consolidate gains and produce more change.	Continue with wave after wave of change, not stopping until the vision is a reality, no matter how big the obstacles.	People remain energized and motivated to push change forward until the vision is fulfilled—fully realized.
8. Anchor new approaches in the culture.	Create a supporting structure that provides roots for the new ways of operating.	New and winning behavior continues despite the pull of tradition, turnover of change leaders, etc.

Further detail on John. P. Kotter's eight steps to transform your organization is described in *ITIL Continual Service Improvement* core volume. These are iterative stages, and at each communication event, people's understanding needs to be checked.

Organizational Change Strategies

Organizational change strategies include a number of different approaches. In 1979, Kotter and Leonard A. Schlesinger suggested the following strategies that work well in practice.

The first is education and commitment beginning in the early planning activities. The discussions generated around the pros and cons of the plan will help to dispel skepticism about the need for change and forge strong alliances that can be used as a change agent. Next is participation and involvement. Allowing people to participate in the change normally overcomes resistance, but it needs to be supported by education and commitment. Facilitation and support is critical to the success of transition and organizational change. Managers should be ready to respond positively when fears and anxieties about the change are expressed. Talking through the issues and performing a skills gap analysis may be sufficient, but at other times training in the new processes will be necessary, preferably prior to implementation.

Negotiation and agreement are commonly part of any organizational change. Change is easier to implement if you have agreement; gaining agreement suggests negotiation, so managers should be prepared to negotiate, formally if necessary. Involvement with unions or works councils and HR will be needed, especially if negative impact on individuals is expected.

It is sometimes necessary to strike deals with those who oppose change to gain their participation. This approach should be used with the caveat that it is likely to cause problems later on, but manipulation and co-option are valid strategies. There are occasions when explicit and implicit coercion is the appropriate tactic. It will come with associated costs, similar to the directive approach of "act now explain later."

Techniques to Overcome Individuals' Resistance to Change

Rosabeth Moss Kanter identified 10 reasons why people will resist change and optional strategies that will promote positive change enablers.

Briefly, the 10 reasons and the strategies supporting them are as follows:

- Loss of control. Moving from one state to another can feel like losing control, which can be mitigated by involving people in decision-making and planning.

- Excessive personal uncertainty. This simply requires an explanation for the individual of the personal impact of the proposed change.

- Avoiding surprises. People need time to absorb a new plan.

- The difference effect. As people lose sight of the familiar, maintaining familiar settings or approaches where possible will mitigate this effect.

- Loss of face. The individual is concerned about a loss of competence. Early engagement in the new approach will help to ensure that the individual feels empowered.

- Fear about competence. The lack of belief that a change can be made. Again, early engagement is key, providing training in advance of the change.

- Ripples. Other areas of an organization are affected by a change that is not directly applicable to them. This should be picked up in the planning stage.

- Increase in workload. This is an obvious concern, because most people will be reluctant to have their workload increased, but it should be considered and addressed by rewarding additional effort where possible.

- Past resentments. These can have associations to a new change, but old grievances should be addressed as part of the transition.

- Real threats. Real threats do exist in change and should not be denied, but they should be explained and individuals should be engaged in the solution.

Stakeholder Management

Stakeholder management is a crucial success factor in service transition. The new or changed service must support and deliver stakeholder requirements to be considered successful, and the active involvement of stakeholders will increase the likelihood of delivering as required. Failure to properly identify all stakeholder groups makes it almost inevitable that many of those affected will be unaware of proposed changes and unable to register their concerns and wishes, nor will they be able to be supportive.

Stakeholder Management Strategy

The stakeholder management strategy from service design sets out who the stakeholders are and what their interests and influences are likely to be. It is important to understand how the project or program will engage with them, what information will be communicated, and how feedback from the stakeholders will be processed.

It is helpful for service transition if stakeholders are listed under categories such as "users/ beneficiaries" and "providers." Each category can then be broken down further if necessary. Categories should be recognizable groups rather than abstract ones, for example, an organizational location rather than a belief system. Some categories may identify the same individuals, but it is often useful to differentiate between stakeholders "wearing different hats." You can see examples of stakeholders in Figure 27.4.

Stakeholders inevitably have different areas of interest in the overall change; for example, some will be concerned with how the change will affect their working environment, while others will want to influence changes in the way customers are handled.

A stakeholder map is a useful way of plotting the various stakeholders against their interests in the service transition and its activities and outcomes. Service transition should

FIGURE 27.4 Potential stakeholders

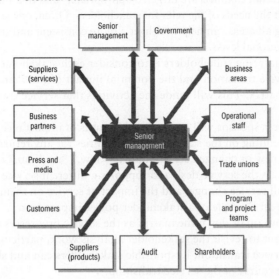

work with service design to ensure that there is an accurate and relevant stakeholder map or equivalent. Figure 27.5 provides an example of a stakeholder map.

A stakeholder analysis helps to ensure that there is sufficient understanding of the stakeholder requirements and the stakeholders' interest in, and impact on, the change. Stakeholders' positions (in terms of influence and impact) may be rational and justifiable or emotional and unfounded. However, they must all be taken into account because, by definition, stakeholders can affect the change process and hence the service transition. The stakeholder analysis helps

FIGURE 27.5 Example of a stakeholder map

Stakeholders	Strategic direction	Financial	Operational changes	Interface with customers	Public safety	Competitive position
Business partner	●	●		●		●
Project teams			●			
Customers		●		●	●	
Press and media						●
Trade unions			●			
Staff	●		●			
Regulatory bodies		●			●	

to ensure that communication channels are targeted appropriately and that messages, media, and levels of detail reflect the needs of the relevant stakeholders. Often, one larger communication approach covering all areas can help to deliver a more consistent and stronger message than by operating at functional levels.

One technique for analyzing stakeholders is to consider each stakeholder in terms of their importance to service transition and the potential impact of the change on them and "plot" them on a matrix. This will guide the activities that service transition should adopt.

For example, a business sponsor will have a "high" status of importance to the overall service change, and depending on the scale and opportunities for any return on their investment, the impact of the new or changed service may be "low," "medium," or "high."

Someone who works on the service desk and supports a different service will have a low importance to the overall service change, and the impact of service on them will be low. In Figure 27.6, you can see an example of a stakeholder power impact matrix.

Stakeholders may move up or down the matrix as the service progresses through the lifecycle, so it is important to revisit the stakeholder analysis work, particularly during the detailed planning for service transition. Responsible stakeholders can and should enhance and potentially alter the course of the service transition.

FIGURE 27.6 Power impact matrix

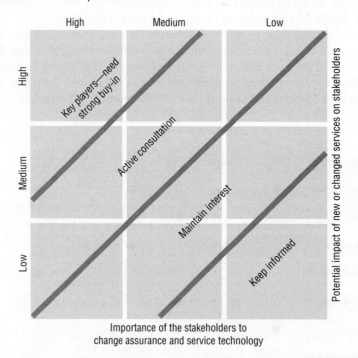

During the service lifecycle, stakeholders may come and go. Key stakeholders, such as the change sponsors, should (hopefully!) remain constant throughout. But sufficient records and documentation will be maintained to enable effective handover in the event that individuals are replaced: "sufficient" is adjudged in accordance with business risk and cost.

Some stakeholders will be able to participate in advisory or assurance roles, some will be important in assessing the realization of the benefits, and others will have an audit perspective.

The planning chart shows the current commitment level of individuals and groups and how that commitment must change if the transition is to be successful. You can see an example of this in Figure 27.7.

Each individual is rated with an O to indicate their current position and an X to indicate the degree of commitment needed from them. Sometimes they need to step back; for example, the departing director of customers shown in the chart in Figure 27.7 would need to hand over the leadership role.

FIGURE 27.7   Example of a planning commitment chart

Key players	Not committed	No resistance	Helps it happen	Makes it happen
Departing director of customers		X ⬅———————		O
Chair of board of service provider		O ——————————➤		X
New director of service provider				OX
Customer	O ———➤ X			
Your managers		O ———➤ X		
Your staff	O ——————————➤ X			
Service strategy team				OX
Suppliers	O ——————————➤ X			
Service operation staff		O ———➤ X		

Summary

This brings us to the end of this chapter, in which we reviewed the concepts relating to managing communication and commitment in service transition.

The chapter included an exploration of how to manage organizational and stakeholder change, including organizational roles and responsibilities and readiness. By exploring techniques such as John P. Kotter's eight steps to managing organizational change, we can support the change that is required by the business during periods of service transition. It is also important to ensure that the organization is ready for the change, so we reviewed the concept of organizational readiness.

Stakeholder management is very important during transition, and in this chapter we reviewed some techniques for analysis of stakeholder engagement with stakeholder maps and commitment charts.

Exam Essentials

Understand the importance of managing communication in transition. Communication is important throughout the lifecycle and especially when introducing new ideas or concepts in a new service.

Be able to explain and describe the commitment required in service transition. This is important not only for the service provider, but also for the customers, users, and all aspects of the business.

Understand the importance of service transition in organizational and stakeholder change. Although any organizational change will be managed by the business, changes involving IT should be supported by service transition. It is important to recognize the importance of stakeholders and to keep the stakeholders engaged and interested.

Be able to explain and describe the necessary organization roles and responsibilities relating to service transition. Leadership of transition and the roles relating to implementing transition are very important to its success.

Understand the importance of organizational readiness to the success of transition. Be able to explain the role of service transition in assessing the readiness of an organization to accept the transition.

Be able to explain and expand on the management of stakeholders. In terms of setting and meeting expectations, stakeholder management is important in the success of any transition. Make sure you understand the role of service transition in managing stakeholders according to their importance and influence.

Review Questions

You can find the answers to the review questions in the appendix.

1. Which group of people should have regular communication during a service transition?

    A. The IT steering group

    B. The service management team

    C. The stakeholders of the transition

    D. The release managers of the transition

2. Which of these are suggested as suitable communication methods during transition?

    1. Email

    2. Workshops

    3. Newsletters

    4. Faxes

    5. Team meetings

    6. Question and answer sessions

        A. 1, 2, 3, 4

        B. 2, 3, 5, 6

        C. 1, 3, 5, 6

        D. 2, 4, 5, 6

3. What is the benefit of using a communication model to support transition?

    A. It provides a consistent and clearly understood communication path.

    B. It ensures that results of testing and deployment are captured.

    C. It can be used to manage releases and ensure that there is an audit trail.

    D. It engages customer stakeholders when service providers do not need to experience the same communication.

4. What is meant by the term *emotional cycle of change*?

    A. The term refers to the various states a person goes through when experiencing change in an organization.

    B. The term refers to the service lifecycle stages.

    C. The term refers to the change management process for all IT changes.

    D. The term refers to the process for managing emotions of a senior manager during the service lifecycle.

5. Which of these correctly identifies factors that will be important in management of organizational change?

   1. Leadership for the change
   2. Organization adoption
      A. Neither statement
      B. Both statements
      C. Statement 1 only
      D. Statement 2 only

6. Which of these items can be described as change products from service transition's engagement in organizational change?

   1. A strategic plan for business development
   2. Policies, processes, and procedures
      A. Neither statement
      B. Both statements
      C. Statement 1 only
      D. Statement 2 only

7. What is the purpose of using a survey during service transition?
   A. To inform the business of the changes that are taking place
   B. To engage the stakeholders in the change and seek their opinions
   C. To capture the results of performance measurement
   D. To deliver a plan for transition

8. Which of these is most likely to be considered a challenge for people in organizational change?
   A. Policies relating to quality assurance
   B. Policies relating to release packages
   C. Managing IT resources
   D. Employee shock

9. Which of these are stages in Kotter's eight steps to transform your organization?
   A. People, process, policies, and procedures
   B. People, products, partners, and processes
   C. Empowering broad-based action and create short-term wins
   D. Developing products for organizational change

10. True or False? Service transition is supported by stakeholder management.
    A. True
    B. False

Chapter 28

Organizing for Service Transition

THE FOLLOWING ITIL INTERMEDIATE EXAM OBJECTIVES ARE DISCUSSED IN THIS CHAPTER:

✓ **The roles, responsibilities, and organizational structures for service transition:**

- Organizational development
- Role of technical and application management functions in service transition
- Organizational context for transitioning a service
- Service transition roles and responsibilities
- The relationship of service transition to other lifecycle phases

In this chapter, we will review the roles, responsibilities, and organizational structures that support service transition activities. We will look at the concept of organizational development and explore the role of functions in the transition. We will also review how service transition interacts with the rest of the service lifecycle.

Organizational Development

There is no single best way to organize, and the best practices described in ITIL need to be tailored to suit individual organizations and situations. Those making changes will need to take into account resource constraints and the size, nature, and needs of the business and customers. The starting point for organizational design is strategy, but it may be deployed or introduced during transition.

Technical and application management provide the technical resources and expertise to manage the whole service lifecycle, and practitioner roles within service transition may be performed by members of these functions. In smaller organizations, one person or group can perform multiple functions—for example, a technical management department could also incorporate the service desk function.

Small Organizations

Each organization should consider all of the roles that it requires and how they can be combined within its organizational constraints to create a structure that meets its needs. Figure 28.1 shows an example of a structure for a small organization.

FIGURE 28.1 Example of service transition organizational structure for a small organization

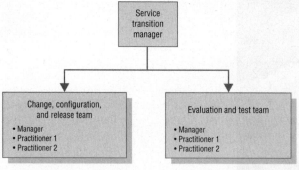

In this example of a small organization, there is a service transition manager who is the process owner, process manager, and process practitioner for transition planning and support.

The change, configuration, and release (CCR) manager is the process owner and the process manager for change management, service asset and configuration management (SACM), release and deployment management, and knowledge management. The CCR manager has a small team of practitioners who carry out specific activities for these processes.

The evaluation and test manager is the process owner and the process manager for change evaluation and for service validation and test. This manager also has a small team of practitioners.

Larger Organizations

In Figure 28.2, you can see the structure for a larger organization.

FIGURE 28.2 Example of service transition organizational structure for a larger organization

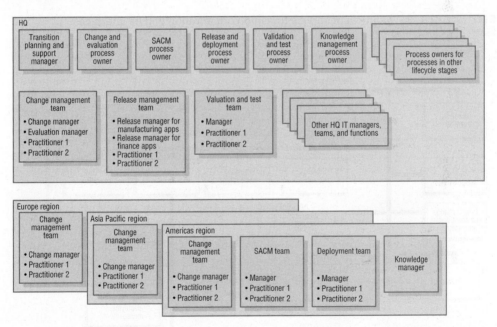

In this example for service transition in a larger organization, there is a central HQ organization, which includes all process owners as well as a change management team, release managers for each category of business application, and a validation and test team.

Each geographical area has its own process managers and practitioners for change management, SACM, and deployment and a knowledge manager.

Organizational Context for Transitioning a Service

Often a transition involves agencies or parties outside of the organization. If this is the case, then the other organizational units and third parties need to have clearly defined interface and handover points with service transition. This is necessary to ensure the delivery of the defined deliverables within the agreed schedule.

Service design has set the requirements for the service assets and components. Programs, projects, service design, and suppliers are responsible for the delivery of the service assets and components. The service components will include service level agreements (SLAs) and contracts in addition to initiating any changes that affect a service release or deployment.

Service transition will receive changes, service assets, and components from these third parties. An example of a service transition organization and its interfaces is shown in Figure 28.3.

FIGURE 28.3 Example of service transition organization and its interfaces

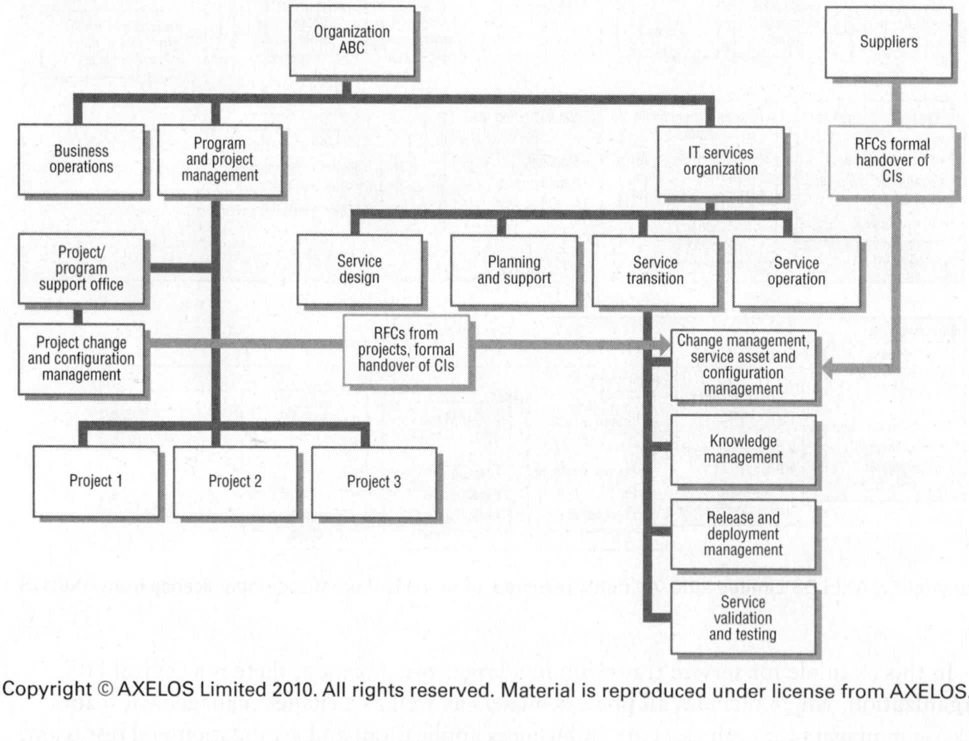

The interfaces to projects and business operations need to be clearly defined during service transition. Throughout the service lifecycle, there must be clear interaction and understanding of responsibility by all. It is critical that project teams have a clear understanding of service design, transition and operations requirements, and objectives of delivery and vice versa.

It is still often the case that projects and programs will work in isolation from service transition and operations, on the assumption that they have no part to play in the ongoing service delivery. Similarly, transition and operations can ignore ongoing project activity, or perhaps not be informed of that activity. Early engagement is critical to continued success of transitional activity; projects cannot be dealt with at a future date. It is important that there is cooperation, understanding, and mutual respect between project teams and service transition teams. In this way, new, changed, and ongoing delivery of services to the customer will be optimized.

Figure 28.4 shows the suggested interaction between programs, projects, and service management elements. The assumption is that the organization has a program and project director responsible for overall management of programs and projects and a service provider director responsible for all aspects of service management.

FIGURE 28.4 Organizational interfaces for a service transition

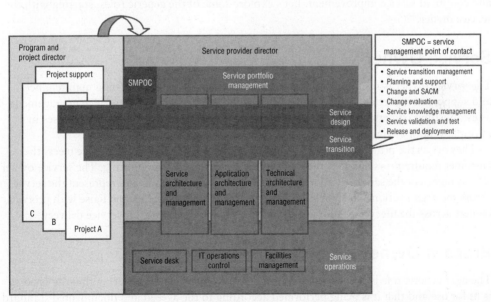

Service Transition Roles and Responsibilities

Service transition requires a number of roles. The framework provides guidelines and examples of role descriptions. These are not exhaustive or prescriptive, and in many cases roles will need to be combined or separated. Organizations should apply this guidance to suit their own requirements of structure and responsibility.

You will remember from your Foundation course that a role is a set of responsibilities, activities, and authorities granted to a person or team. A role is defined in a process or function. One person or team may have multiple roles. Sometimes roles are confused with job titles, but they are not the same. Each organization will define appropriate job titles and job descriptions that suit its needs, and individuals holding these job titles can perform one or more of the required roles.

Roles fall into two main categories: generic roles such as process manager and process owner and specific roles that are involved within a particular lifecycle stage or process.

A commonly used generic term is that of service manager for any manager within the service provider. It's often used to refer to a business relationship manager, a process manager, or a senior manager with responsibility for IT services overall. A service manager is often assigned several roles, such as business relationship management, service level management, and continual service improvement. Let's explore some of the generic roles, starting with the service owner.

Service Owner

The service owner is responsible for the initiation, transition, and ongoing maintenance and support of a particular service. Service ownership is as critical to service management as establishing ownership for processes that cross multiple departments or processes in a multiple-vendor environment.

They act as the prime customer contact and make sure delivery of the service meets the customer requirements and that there is effective reporting and monitoring. The service owner should represent the service at all meetings (such as service reviews) and represent the service across the organization. They will also identify service improvements and liaise with process owners across the lifecycle. They are accountable to the IT director for service delivery.

Process Owner

The next generic role is process owner. This role is responsible for ensuring that the process is fit for use and that it is being performed according to the agreed and documented standard and meets the process aims.

The process owner will define the strategy, policy, and standards and assist with process design. It is their responsibility to ensure that the process can be carried out by making sure relevant documentation is available and current. The process owner will assist with the design and maintenance of the process, including input into service improvement. Ensuring that the process is carried out requires the provision of education, resources, awareness, and training. The process should be regularly audited for effectiveness and efficiency.

Process Manager

The process manager role is accountable for the operational management of a process. There may be several process managers for one process, for example, regional change managers. The process manager role is often assigned to the person who carries out the process owner role, but the two roles may be separate in larger organizations.

The process manager is accountable for working with the process owner to plan and coordinate all process activities, ensuring that all activities are carried out as required throughout the service lifecycle. The process manager will appoint staff to the required roles and manage the resources assigned to the process. Obviously the process manager will be required to work with service owners and other process managers to ensure that services run smoothly. The role will also be involved in monitoring and reporting on process performance and identifying improvement opportunities for both service and process. This will require collaboration with the CSI manager.

Process Practitioner

A process practitioner is responsible for carrying out one or more process activities. In some organizations, and for some processes, the process practitioner role may be combined with the process manager role; in others there may be large numbers of practitioners carrying out different parts of the process.

The process practitioner's responsibilities typically include carrying out one or more activities of a process. It is important that the process practitioner has an understanding of how their role contributes to the overall delivery of service and creation of value for the business. They will work with other stakeholders, such as their manager, coworkers, users, and customers, to ensure that their contributions are effective. The practitioner is responsible for making sure inputs, outputs, and interfaces for their activities are correct and creating or updating records to show that activities have been carried out correctly.

This concludes the review of the generic process roles. We will now move onto reviewing the specific roles associated with the service transition processes.

Service Transition Manager

Many organizations will have a person with the job title service transition manager. This job typically combines the roles of transition planning and support process owner and transition planning and support process manager. So we will now consider each of these roles.

Transition Planning and Support Process Owner

First let's look at the transition planning and support process owner. Their responsibilities will include carrying out the generic process owner role and setting the scope and policies for service transition. They will also oversee the overall design of all service transition processes to ensure that they will work together to meet the transition needs of the business.

Transition Planning and Support Process Manager

The transition planning and support process manager's responsibilities typically include carrying out the generic process manager role and managing and coordinating the functions that are involved in service transition. The manager will be responsible for budgeting and accounting for service transition activities and resources, including requests for resources. They will act as the prime interface for senior management for service transition planning and reporting. The process manager will also be responsible for coordinating service transition activities across projects, suppliers, and service teams (working with project managers and other personnel as required). This should ensure that the final delivery of each service transition meets the agreed customer and stakeholder requirements specified in the service design package.

Transition Planning and Support Process Practitioner

The transition planning and support practitioner's responsibilities typically include maintaining and integrating plans for specific service transition. This will require the maintenance and monitoring of progress for service transition changes, issues, risks, and deviations. It should include tracking progress on actions and mitigation of risks as well as maintaining records and providing management information on resource use, project/service transition progress, and budgeted and actual spending. The practitioner will also be responsible for communicating with stakeholders.

Change Management Process Owner

The change management process owner's responsibilities typically include the responsibilities of the generic process owner role for the change management process. They are responsible for designing the change authority hierarchy and criteria for allocating RFCs to change authorities. They will also be responsible for designing change models and workflows. The process owner will work with other process owners to ensure that there is an integrated approach to the design and implementation of change management, service asset and configuration management, release and deployment management, and service validation and testing.

Change Management Process Manager

The change management process manager's responsibilities include the responsibilities of the generic process manager role and planning and managing support for change management tools and processes. They are responsible for maintaining the change schedule and projected service outage. The role is also responsible for coordinating interfaces between change management and other processes, especially service asset and configuration management and release and deployment management.

Change Initiator

Many different people in the organization may carry out the role of change initiator; it is not usually carried out by people who work in change management. Each change should have only a single change initiator, and they are responsible for identifying the requirement for a change. They will then be expected to complete and submit a change proposal if appropriate and complete and submit an RFC. They will be expected to attend CAB meetings, if invited, to provide further information about the RFC or change proposal and then review change when requested by change management, specifically before closure.

Change Practitioner

The change practitioner's responsibilities include verifying that RFCs are correctly completed and allocated to appropriate change authorities based on defined criteria. They will also submit requests for evaluation to trigger the change evaluation process. It is the practitioners responsibility to formally communicate decisions of change authorities to affected parties. Because there will potentially be many different teams engaged in the delivery of a change (including build and test), the practitioner is responsible for monitoring and reviewing their activities to ensure that the work is carried out correctly. This will be carried out as part of the release and deployment management process for a change that is part of a release. The practitioner will also be responsible for publishing the change schedule and projected service outage and ensuring that they are available when and where needed.

Change Authority

There will normally be different change authorities for each category of change. The change authority's responsibilities include reviewing specific categories of RFC and formally authorizing changes at agreed points in the change lifecycle. The change authority will participate in change reviews before changes are closed, including attending CAB meetings to discuss and review changes when required.

CAB Member

In many organizations, the CAB is the change authority for some categories of change. In other organizations, the CAB is just an advisory body. Some CAB members may also be change authorities for other specific categories of change.

The CAB member's responsibilities include participating in CAB meetings as the authorized representative for a particular group or function. They are expected to prepare for CAB meetings by circulating RFCs within their own group and coordinating feedback. They will then be required to review RFCs and recommend whether they should be authorized. Other activities include reviewing successful and failed changes and unauthorized changes. As part of the process, CAB members will be responsible for reviewing the change schedule and providing information to help identify conflicts or resource issues and for reviewing the projected service outage and providing feedback on the impact of planned outages.

CAB Chair

If there is a single change advisory board (CAB), the CAB chair will almost always be the change manager. If there are multiple CABs, there may be multiple change managers, each chairing a different CAB.

The CAB chair's responsibilities include deciding who should attend CAB meetings and then planning, scheduling, managing, and chairing CAB meetings. They will also be responsible for selecting RFCs, based on the change policy, for review at CAB meetings. These RFCs should be circulated in advance of CAB meetings to allow prior consideration. The CAB chair is also required to select successful and failed changes for review at CAB meetings.

If there is an emergency change, the CAB chair has the responsibility of convening the emergency change advisory board (ECAB) meetings for consideration of emergency changes.

SACM Process Owner

The SACM process owner's responsibilities include carrying out the generic process owner role for the SACM process. This involves agreeing on and documenting the scope for SACM, including the policy for determining which service assets should be treated as configuration items. The role will be required to work with other process owners to ensure that there is an integrated approach to the design and implementation of SACM, change management, release and deployment management, and knowledge management.

SACM Process Manager

The SACM process manager's responsibilities include carrying out the generic process manager role for the SACM process. They are specifically accountable to the organization for stewardship of the organization's fixed assets that are under the control of IT. The role is responsible for defining the service assets that will be treated as configuration items and then ensuring that configuration data is available when and where it is needed to support other service management processes. The process manager is also responsible for planning and managing support for SACM tools and processes as well as coordinating interfaces between SACM and other processes, especially change management, release and deployment management, and knowledge management.

Configuration Analyst

The configuration analyst role will often be combined with the role of the SACM process manager or that of the configuration librarian, depending on the size, structure, and culture of the organization. The responsibilities include proposing the scope for service asset and configuration management and supporting the process owner and process manager in the creation of principles, processes, and procedures. The analyst will also assist in defining the structure of the configuration management system, including CI types, naming conventions, required and optional attributes, and relationships. Once this has been decided, the analyst will also have the responsibility for training staff in SACM principles, processes, and procedures and performing configuration audits.

Configuration Librarian

A configuration librarian is the custodian of service assets that are registered in the configuration management system. They are responsible for controlling the receipt, identification, storage, and withdrawal of all supported CIs. This should include maintaining status information on CIs and providing it as required. They are also responsible for normal housekeeping activities, such as archiving superseded CIs and assisting in conducting configuration audits.

The librarian is responsible for identifying, recording, storing, and distributing information about issues relating to service asset and configuration management.

Release and Deployment Process Owner

There are a number of release and deployment management roles that need to be performed in support of the release and deployment management process. These roles are not job titles, and each organization will have to define appropriate job titles and job descriptions for its needs. Many of these roles are combined in an organization.

The release and deployment management process owner's responsibilities include carrying out the generic process owner role for the release and deployment management process. They will be responsible for designing release models and workflows. The process owner should also work with other process owners to ensure that there is an integrated approach to the design and implementation of change management, service asset and configuration management, release and deployment management, and service validation and testing.

Release and Deployment Process Manager

To avoid conflicts of interest, it is important that this role is not assigned to the person responsible for service validation and testing.

The release and deployment management process manager's responsibilities include carrying out the generic process manager role for the release and deployment management process. They are responsible for planning and coordinating all resources needed to build, test, and deploy each release, including resources from other functions such as technical management or application management. This is a matrix management approach; the manager will not assume line management responsibility for the staff. The release and deployment manager is responsible for planning and managing support for release and deployment management tools and processes. They also ensure that change authorization is provided before any activity that requires it, for example, before a release is checked in to the definitive media library (DML) and before it is deployed to a live environment. The process manager is responsible for coordinating interfaces between release and deployment management and other processes, especially change management, SACM, and service validation and testing.

Release Packaging and Build Practitioner

In smaller organizations, this role may be combined with the role of the release and deployment management process manager. It may also be combined with the role of the deployment practitioner, and in some organizations, it may be carried out by personnel working for the technical management or application management functions.

The release packaging and build practitioner's responsibilities include assisting in the design of the release package during the service design stage of the service lifecycle and in conjunction with personnel from other teams and functions. They will also establish the final release configuration, which should include knowledge, information, hardware, software, and infrastructure. The practitioner role is responsible for building and testing the release prior to independent testing, and that should include establishing and reporting outstanding known errors and workarounds. If appropriate, the practitioner will also provide input to support change authorization for check-in of the release to the DML.

Deployment Practitioner

This role is often combined with the role of release packaging and build practitioner. It may also be carried out by personnel from the technical management or application management functions.

The deployment practitioner's responsibilities include helping to plan the deployment during the service design stage of the service lifecycle and in conjunction with personnel from other teams and functions. They will then ensure that all deployment activity has been authorized by change management. The practitioner is responsible for carrying out the final physical delivery of the deployment.

The practitioner role is responsible for coordinating release documentation and communications, including training for support teams and customers, and updating and distributing service management and technical release notes providing technical and application guidance and support throughout the release process, including known errors and workarounds. This role is also responsible for providing feedback on the effectiveness of the release as well as recording and reporting deployment metrics to ensure that these are within agreed SLAs.

Early Life Support Practitioner

This role will often be carried out by personnel from the technical management or application management functions. It may also be combined with the roles of release packaging and build practitioner or deployment practitioner.

The early life support practitioner's responsibilities include providing IT service and business functional support from deployment to final acceptance and to ensure delivery of appropriate support documentation. The practitioner will provide release acceptance for provision of initial support, including support to assist the service desk in responding to incidents and errors detected within a new or changed service. As part of early life support, the practitioner should be adapting and perfecting elements that evolve with final usage, such as user documentation, support documentation (including service desk scripts) and data management (including archiving).

One of the key activities and responsibilities for the early life support practitioner is embedding activities for a new or changed service and dealing with the final transition of the service-to-service operation and continual service improvement. They should also be monitoring incidents and problems and undertaking problem management during release and deployment, raising RFCs as required. The responsibilities should also include providing initial performance reporting and undertaking service risk assessment based on performance.

Build and Test Environment Manager

This role will often be carried out by personnel from the technical management or application management functions. It may be combined with the deployment practitioner role.

Build and test environment manager responsibilities include ensuring that service infrastructure and application are built to design specification as well as planning the acquisition, build, implementation, and maintenance of ICT infrastructure. It is important that the build and test environment manager is responsible for ensuring that all components are from controlled sources.

They are also responsible for developing an integrated application software and infrastructure build and delivering appropriate build, operations, and support documentation for the build and test environments. They are there to manage the building, delivery, and maintenance of required test environments.

Service Validation and Testing Process Owner

The service validation and testing process owner's responsibilities include carrying out the generic process owner role for the service validation and testing process. This role will be responsible for defining the overall test strategy for the organization. They will work with other process owners to ensure that there is an integrated approach to the design and implementation of change management, change evaluation, release and deployment management, and service validation and testing.

Service Validation and Testing Process Manager

To avoid conflicts of interest, it is important that this role is not assigned to the person responsible for release and deployment management.

The service validation and testing process manager's responsibilities include carrying out the generic process manager role for the service validation and testing process. The manager will assist with the design and planning of test conditions, test scripts, and test data sets during the service design stage of the service lifecycle to ensure appropriate and adequate coverage and control throughout the transition.

The manager should be responsible for allocating and overseeing test resources, ensuring that test policies are adhered to, and verifying tests conducted by release and deployment management or other teams. They are responsible for managing test environment requirements and planning and managing support for service testing and validation tools and processes. The service validation and testing manager provides management reporting on test progress, test outcomes, success rates, issues, and risks.

Service Validation and Testing Process Practitioner

The service validation and testing practitioner's responsibilities include conducting tests as defined in the test plans and designs and documented in the service design package. The practitioner should be responsible for recording, analyzing, diagnosing, reporting, and managing test events, incidents, problems, and retest, depending on agreed criteria. They will also be responsible for administering test assets and components.

Contribution of Other Roles to Service Validation and Testing

A number of other roles play a significant part in service validation and testing.

Change management personnel ensure that tests are developed that are appropriate for the authorized changes and that agreed testing strategy and policy are applied to all changes.

Developers and suppliers establish the root cause of test failures. For complex situations, this may require collaboration between testing staff and development, build, or supplier personnel.

Service design personnel design tests as an element of the overall design. For many services, standard tests will exist, possibly defined in a service transition model or a release and deployment model.

Customers and users perform acceptance testing. These roles should be able to cover the full range of user profiles and requirements and adequately sign off on the conformance of a new or changed service against the agreed requirements. They will already have played a major role in helping to design the acceptance-testing approaches during the service design stage of the service lifecycle.

Change Evaluation Process Owner

The change evaluation process owner's responsibilities include carrying out the generic process owner role for the change evaluation process. They are responsible for working with other process owners to ensure that there is an integrated approach to the design and implementation of change management, change evaluation, release and deployment management, and service validation and testing.

Change Evaluation Process Manager

The change evaluation process manager's responsibilities include carrying out the generic process manager role for the change evaluation process. They are also responsible for planning and coordinating all resources needed to evaluate changes. The manager should make sure change evaluation delivers evaluation reports and interim evaluation reports in time to ensure that change authorities are able to use them to support their decision-making.

Change Evaluation Process Practitioner

The change evaluation process practitioner's responsibilities include using the service design and the release package to develop an evaluation plan as an input to service validation and testing. The role also includes establishing risks and issues associated with all aspects of the service transition (for example, through risk workshops). The practitioner should create an evaluation report as input to change management.

Knowledge Management Process Owner

In many organizations, this role will be combined with the knowledge management process manager role, and in very small organizations, both process owner and process manager roles may be combined with roles from service asset and configuration management.

The knowledge management process owner's responsibilities include carrying out the generic process owner role for the knowledge management process. The manager is responsible for creating the overall architecture for identification, capture, and maintenance of knowledge within the organization.

Knowledge Management Process Manager

The knowledge management process manager's responsibilities include carrying out the generic process manager role for the knowledge management process. The manager is responsible for ensuring that all knowledge items are made accessible to those who need them in an efficient and effective manner. This will include planning and managing support for knowledge management tools and processes and encouraging people throughout the service provider to contribute knowledge to the service knowledge management system (SKMS). The knowledge manager should act as an adviser to business and IT personnel on knowledge management matters, including policy decisions on storage, value, worth, and so on.

Knowledge Management Process Practitioner

In many organizations, the person carrying out this role is called a knowledge librarian. The knowledge management process practitioner's responsibilities include identifying, controlling, and storing any information that is deemed to be pertinent to the services provided and is not available by other means. This process is not intended to duplicate existing knowledge.

The manager (or librarian) is responsible for maintaining controlled knowledge items to ensure that they are current, relevant, and valid. Part of the role will be monitoring publicity regarding knowledge information to ensure that information is not duplicated and that the SKMS is recognized as a central source of information.

Knowledge Creator

The knowledge creator role may be carried out by many different people in the organization. Creation and sharing of knowledge is often written into the job descriptions of people in many different roles within IT and the business.

Service Transition Relationship with Other Lifecycle Stages

Service transition is presented as a discrete lifecycle step, but this should not be taken to imply that it can stand alone. Service transition exists to deliver the concepts documented within the stages from service design to service operation for day-to-day management, and so without design and operations, it has no purpose.

Upstream Relationships for Service Transition

Service transition takes its shape and input from the strategy set by the organization and from the new or changed services it is charged with bringing into live operation, that is, by the output of the service design stage. Its very nature is therefore dependent on its relationship with "upstream areas."

Logical Staff Mobility

Service operation staff will be involved in design and operation tasks directly via population of the service knowledge management system. The updates will be the experiences detected during service operation stages, such as through the incident-problem-error cycles. Capturing this information will drive informed and correct decision-making processes, which should facilitate more effective service transition. You can see this represented in Figure 28.5, showing the flow of experience.

FIGURE 28.5   Flow of experience

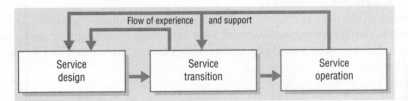

To retain and make effective use of experience, staff may well find themselves allocated (fully or partially) from service operation functions to support a design exercise and then follow that service through service transition. They may then, via early life support activities, move into support of the new or changed services that they have helped design and implement into the live environment.

Expert advice on transition (as with design and operation) will also provide expert input to the development and maintenance of service strategy. This is known as *logical staff mobility* because staff are engaged in more than one lifecycle stage.

Many of the capabilities of a service that require testing and acceptance with transition are established, and the approach and measures to be adopted are set within the service design stage of the lifecycle.

Downstream Process and Procedure Influence

Many elements initiated or perfected during service transition will be established and become key elements within service operation.

During transition testing, incidents will be detected that reveal errors within the new or changed service. The nature and identified resolution of these errors will provide direct input to the service operation procedures for supporting the new or changed service in live use. Service transition input is likely to affect most areas of the service operation stage.

Testing will share processes with service operation, possibly with some variations in procedure, for example, to accommodate the differing requirements and risk environments of analyzing and rectifying errors in testing and live environments.

Where testing detects errors in a new or changed service that are not significant enough to prevent the release of the service, the errors are released into the live known error database, and notification is passed to continual service improvement via the SKMS, of which CSI will make extensive use.

Summary

In this chapter, we explored the roles and responsibilities associated with the service transition lifecycle stage. This included the generic roles service owner, process owner, process manager, and process practitioner.

We explored the roles as they relate to the processes of transition planning and support management, change management, service asset and configuration management, release and deployment management, knowledge management, change evaluation, and service validation and testing.

Exam Essentials

Understand the roles associated with service transition.   Service transition has a broad scope, and the roles associated with each process are many and varied, but they are all based on the generic roles of process owner, manager, and practitioner.

Be able to explain and describe the roles associated with each process in the service transition stage.   This includes the roles for the following processes:

- Transition planning and support
- Change management
- Service asset and configuration management
- Knowledge management
- Change evaluation
- Service testing and validation
- Release and deployment management

Understand the importance of upstream and downstream experiences.   The service transition lifecycle stage does not stand alone, as with all the lifecycle stages. It is important to understand the flow of experiences across the lifecycle.

Review Questions

You can find the answers to the review questions in the appendix.

1. True or False? There is no single best practice approach to organization?
   - **A.** True
   - **B.** False

2. Which of these combinations would NOT be appropriate for a small organization?
   - **A.** Transition planning and support roles combined
   - **B.** Change, SACM, and release processes combined
   - **C.** Evaluation and service validation and test processes combined
   - **D.** Multiple change and release managers

3. Which of these roles is identified as a generic role in the transition lifecycle stage?
   - **A.** Change manager
   - **B.** Release and deployment manager
   - **C.** Process manager
   - **D.** Transition and support manager

4. Which of these roles is identified as being responsible for service transition teams?
   - **A.** Change manager
   - **B.** Service transition manager
   - **C.** Service manager
   - **D.** Transition and support manager

5. Which of these lifecycle stages has an interface to service transition?
   - **1.** Service strategy
   - **2.** Service design
   - **3.** Service operation
   - **4.** Continual service improvement
     - **A.** 2 and 3 only
     - **B.** 2, 3, and 4 only
     - **C.** 2 only
     - **D.** 1, 2, 3, and 4

6. According to ITIL, who is responsible for identifying improvements to a process?
   - **1.** The service owner
   - **2.** The process improvement manager

3. The process manager

4. The process owner
   A. 1 and 2 only
   B. 4 only
   C. All of the above
   D. 3 and 4 only

7. Which of these statements is not true?
   A. There may be several process practitioners for each process.
   B. There may be several process managers for each process.
   C. There may be several process owners for each process.
   D. Every process must have a process manager.

8. Which role should update process documentation following a change to the process itself?
   A. The process manager
   B. The change manager
   C. The process owner
   D. The knowledge manager

9. Which members of the organization are likely to be knowledge creators?
   A. Customers
   B. Users
   C. Service provider
   D. Anyone in the organization

10. True or False? The release and deployment manager has no relationship to any other process managers in the service transition lifecycle stage.
    A. True
    B. False

Chapter

29

Technology Considerations for Service Transition

THE FOLLOWING ITIL INTERMEDIATE EXAM OBJECTIVES ARE DISCUSSED IN THIS CHAPTER:

✓ **The role of technology in the service transition lifecycle stage:**

- Incorporating technology into design

- Mechanisms for maintaining and maximizing technology

- Specific tools applicable throughout the service transition processes and service lifecycle, including knowledge management tools, collaboration, and the configuration management system

In this chapter, we review the role of technology in the service transition lifecycle stage and how it can be applied through the use of tools. We will look at some of the specific tools in use as part of a service transition, including those that are used across the whole of the service lifecycle.

Technology Considerations

Technology has a major role to play in service transition, as it does throughout the lifecycle. It is important that the use of supporting technology is part of the design for service transition and that mechanisms for maintaining and maximizing benefit from technology are in place. All organizations should be aware that when the selection and implementation of tools to support service transition takes place, wider issues such as green IT and sustainability should be taken into consideration. Technology choices should also reflect the need to support future types of configuration items (CIs) as well as those currently in use.

There are two ways in which service transition is supported by technology. The service transition lifecycle stage has some processes and policies that are specific to managing the service transition stage itself, and there will be technology used to support those processes. Then there are the processes and policies that support the entire lifecycle, which require enterprise-wide tools for the broader systems and processes within which service transition delivers support.

Technology Throughout Service Transition

Technology is used throughout the service lifecycle, and some of the technology specifically applied during service transition will support the whole of the service lifecycle.

IT service management systems are many and varied in type and use and include enterprise frameworks that provide integration capabilities for connecting the CMS or tools. System, network, and application management tools are widely used to support service transition activities. They will assist in a number of processes, for example, distribution and deployment of software. During the transition stage, service dashboards and reporting tools will be used. As transitions progress, particularly during early life support, the transition teams are able to use them to monitor potential operational performance.

IT service management technology and tools are used throughout the service lifecycle, and service transition will benefit from them. A key system, based in the process of knowledge management, is the service knowledge management system (SKMS) and collaborative content management and workflow tools. Use will be made of other tools during service transition, such as data mining tools to extract, load, and transform data. Throughout the transition stage, measurement and reporting systems will be widely used as part of the transition processes. Testing is greatly enhanced by the use of test management and testing tools and database and test data management tools. The use of tools such as copying and publishing tools and deployment and logistics technologies, systems, and tools is a major part of the release and deployment process.

The processes of change management, service asset and configuration management (SACM), and release and deployment management have many support tools that can help to make them more efficient. They may come in a variety of combinations, and each organization will have to understand its requirements and select tools that are appropriate for its needs. This is extremely important because, although most tools share some basic functionality, there may be specific needs within the service environment. These tools include configuration management systems and tools; version control tools; and visualization, mapping, and graphical representations with drill-down functionality. They are commonly used to support the processes, just as document management systems are used to support the service management approach.

As transitions progress during the realization of designs during testing, tools such as requirements analysis and design tools and systems architecture and computer-aided software engineering (CASE) tools can facilitate impact analysis from a business perspective. Additionally, database management audit tools to track physical databases and discovery and audit tools (also called inventory tools) are useful in the management of CIs as part of configuration management.

Build and release tools (which provide listings of input and output CIs) and installation and deinstallation tools (which provide listings of CIs installed) are part of the processes of release and deployment management and service asset and configuration management. Distribution and installation tools and comparison tools (software files, directories, databases) are also useful for the release and deployment process.

Listing and configuration baseline tools (e.g., full directory listings with date/time stamps and checksums) and detection and recovery tools (where the build is returned to a known state) are all part of the management of service transition processes. Output and data management can be greatly supported by compression tools (to save storage space). Output and performance measurement will also require reporting tools, including those that access objects from several databases, providing integrated reports across systems.

Technology Throughout the Service Lifecycle

There are a number of specific tools that support processes across the service lifecycle:

- Knowledge management tools
- Collaboration
- Configuration management systems

Knowledge Management Tools

Knowledge management tools address the requirements of maintaining records and documents electronically.

> Records are distinguished from documents by the fact that they function as evidence of activities rather than evidence of intentions. For example, a change record captures the actions that have been carried out during a change.
>
> Documentation—examples of which include policy statements, plans, procedures, service level agreements, and contracts—shows the intent to do something. A service transition policy that states all changes will be managed under the change control process is an example of documentation.

The knowledge management tools supporting the processes include document management, records management, and content management. Used in collaboration, these tools provide the structure and functionality of the service knowledge management system (SKMS). Organizations may take the approach that there needs to be a single service management tool that hosts the SKMS, but this severely limits the capability of the concept. Instead, success should be built on the capability to integrate many different sources to provide a complete approach to the capture and management of knowledge in all its forms.

Document Management

Document management defines the set of capabilities to support the storage, protection, classification, searching, retrieval, maintenance, archiving, and retirement of documents and information.

Records Management

Records management defines the set of capabilities to support the storage, protection, classification, searching, retrieval, maintenance, archiving, and retirement of records.

Content Management

Content management provides the capability that manages the storage, maintenance, and retrieval of documents and information on a system or website. The result is often a knowledge asset represented in written words, figures, graphics, and other forms of knowledge presentation.

Web publishing tools, web conferencing, wikis, and blogs are examples of knowledge services that directly support content management. Other examples include word processing, data and financial analysis, presentation tools, flowcharting, and content management systems (codify, organize, version control, document architectures). Of course, there are also publication and distribution tools, which support the management of knowledge distribution.

Collaboration

Collaboration is the process of sharing tacit knowledge and working together to accomplish stated goals and objectives. This approach is supported by shared calendars and tasks and threaded discussions in email. Organizations now find the use of instant messaging, incorporating electronic whiteboards, and video- or teleconferencing a key part of the collaboration approach. The introduction of these tools supports a more mobile workforce. It also enables working remotely and is valuable in supporting international or global organizations.

Successful transitions rely on the organization having a collaborative approach to information and knowledge. Without this approach, the necessary integration of the many aspects of a transition will be much harder to achieve.

Communities

It is now more common for groups of people spread across time zones and in different countries to communicate, collaborate, and share knowledge using communities. The communities are typically facilitated through an online medium such as an intranet or extranet, and the community often acts as the integration point for all knowledge services provided to its members.

The tools required to support this collaborative approach include community portals; focus groups; and online events, podcasts, and Internet shows. Other technologies include email alias management. There is a need to be cautious regarding intellectual property, best practices, work examples, and template repositories, particularly where the community is engaging third-party organizations as part of the support structure. It is important to remember, though, that communities are a vital part of knowledge sharing in a diverse support model.

It's often difficult to encourage sharing in a collaborative community. To break down the historic view of "knowledge is power," where individuals retain their knowledge to ensure they are still perceived as being indispensable, sharing knowledge can be encouraged by using reward programs.

Workflow Management

Workflow management is another broad area of knowledge services. It provides systemic support for managing knowledge assets through a predefined workflow or process. Workflow applications provide the infrastructure and support necessary to implement a highly efficient process to accomplish specific types of tasks. Many knowledge assets today go through a workflow process that creates, modifies, augments, informs, or approves aspects of them.

Typical workflow services provided within this service category include workflow design, routing objects, event services, gatekeeping at authorization checkpoints, and state transition services.

Service management tools include workflow capability that can be configured to support these requirements, and this will be specific to the organizational needs.

Configuration Management System

Many organizations have some form of configuration management in operation, but it is often maintained in individual files, spreadsheets, or even paper-based solutions. Although this approach may be manageable on a small scale, for large and complex infrastructures, configuration management will operate more effectively when supported by a software tool that is capable of maintaining a configuration management system (CMS).

The configuration management system contains details about the attributes and the history of each configuration item (CI) and details of the important relationships between CIs. It is often a federated system comprising a number of configuration management databases (CMDBs).

In an integrated system with a number of data sources, ideally the data sources should be connected. This includes sources such as the definitive media library (DML), and the connections between a CMDB and the DML should be captured in the CMS.

The CMS should assist in preventing changes from being made to the IT infrastructure or service configuration baseline without valid authorization via change management. Wherever possible, the authorization record should automatically "drive" the change. It is important that, as far as possible, all changes be recorded on the CMS at least by the time they are implemented. The status (e.g., live, archive, etc.) of each CI affected by a change should be updated automatically if possible. This activity and capture of information should be integrated with the main service management system or the configuration management system where the effort of integration is beneficial. It is tempting to spend time and effort integrating systems so that updates take place automatically, but careful consideration should always be given to the cost of any customization of tools. There are also implications of what will happen in the future, when upgrades are needed to the systems in the integrated setup. The integration should always be justified in terms of cost and effort, which can be managed through use of the service lifecycle approach. For example, the following questions should be answered: Does it benefit the organization and support the strategy? Has the design been costed and scoped to meet the requirements? Can it be transitioned successfully, and will it be beneficial and effective in operation? Will it support continual improvement and upgrade?

Design of the CMS

When designing a configuration management system, it is important to consider the functionality that will be needed by the organization, such as the ability to integrate multiple data sources based on open standards or known interfaces and protocols. There will need to be sufficient security controls to limit access to a need-to-know basis and support for CIs of varying complexity (e.g., entire systems, releases, single hardware items, and software modules).

The CMS is all about the relationships between the CIs, and it should be simple to add or delete CIs while automatically maintaining the relationships and history of the items.

The more automation for version controls, data validation, and management of relationships there is within a tool, the more effective the system will be. Ease of use is critical for encouraging accurate updates of records and the management and use of configuration baselines. If the system does not make changes and entries easy for the operators, they are unlikely to keep the information up-to-date. Use of discovery tools and other automated approaches to populating the information can be especially useful. Some software systems will have this as a feature; others will require integration with different tools. This feature is particularly useful when managing software CIs and version control for patching.

There may be CIs that are not discoverable by tools, and where this is the case, manual upload and maintenance will be required. It is necessary to make sure the CMS supports the integration with other processes. As changes are made (discoverable or not), the database of CIs must be updated accurately for the data to retain its usefulness to the organization. Processes such as incident and problem management are reliant on this accuracy, as are the warranty processes (availability, capacity, security, and continuity) for planning and correct management of the IT estate.

Another extremely important factor in the design of the CMS is the output data. How it will be used, who will be using it, and how data will be captured and managed are all critical issues for the output data. As a result, the reporting capability from the CMS is very important. All forms of reporting should be included: graphical output, standard reports, hierarchy mapping, and the relationships between items to support impact analysis.

Summary

This brings us to the end of this chapter, in which we reviewed the concepts relating to technology in service transition.

We discussed specific tools that are applicable throughout the service transition processes and service lifecycle, including knowledge management tools, collaboration, and the configuration management system.

Exam Essentials

Understand the importance of technology in service transition. Technology is important throughout the lifecycle, and especially when introducing new ideas or concepts in a new service.

Be able to describe the use of technology in service transition. Using technology in service transition is important not only for the service provider, but also for the customers, users, and all aspects of the business. Technology in this context includes the service management tool, which in its turn, is the repository of the SKMS and CMS.

Understand the importance of specific toolsets in service transition processes and across the lifecycle. It is important to understand the transition toolsets and how they are used throughout the service lifecycle. For example, you should know how other processes use the configuration management system.

Be able to explain the use of tools relating to service transition. Know the tools that are used for testing or software distribution and how they relate to the service transition processes such as release and deployment management.

Review Questions

You can find the answers to the review questions in the appendix.

1. Which of these statements is/are correct?

    1. Service transition is supported by enterprise-wide tools that support the broader systems and processes within which service transition delivers support.

    2. Service transition is supported by tools targeted more specifically at supporting service transition or parts of service transition.

    A. Statement 1 only

    B. Statement 2 only

    C. Both statements

    D. Neither statement

2. Which of the following tools is/are knowledge management tools?

    1. Document management

    2. Records management

    3. Content management

    A. 1 only

    B. 1 and 2 only

    C. 2 and 3 only

    D. 1, 2, and 3

3. Which of these are included as collaborative knowledge sharing tools?

    1. Definitive media library

    2. Shared calendars and tasks

    3. Threaded discussions

    4. Event management

    5. Video- and teleconferencing

    A. 1 and 4 only

    B. 2, 3, and 5 only

    C. 1, 2, 3, and 5 only

    D. 1, 2, 3, 4, and 5

4. What is the relationship between the CMS (configuration management system) and the SKMS (service knowledge management system)?

    A. The SKMS is part of the CMS.

    B. The SKMS has no relationship to the CMS.

    C. The CMS is part of the SKMS.

    D. The SKMS and the CMS are the same thing.

5. True or False? The CMS holds information about relationships between configuration items.
   A. True
   B. False

6. Which of these statements is correct?
   1. The CMS is part of the CMDB.
   2. A CMDB is part of the CMS.
      A. Neither statement
      B. Both statements
      C. Statement 1 only
      D. Statement 2 only

7. What is the relationship between discovery tools and the CMS?
   A. There is no relationship between discovery tools and the CMS.
   B. Discovery tools can be used to populate data in the CMS.
   C. Discovery tools are the only source of data capture for the CMS.
   D. The CMS is used to populate data in discovery tools.

8. What is the main reason for the use of communities in organizations?
   A. Groups of people can be organized effectively.
   B. Ensuring teams understand their structures.
   C. Creating a team-building experience.
   D. Groups of people spread across time zones and country boundaries can communicate, collaborate, and share knowledge.

9. Which of these four options is the most important consideration for design of a CMS?
   A. Incident management process documentation
   B. A robust change management process
   C. Sufficient security controls to limit access to the CMS on a need-to-know basis
   D. Clear transition policies for the service transition lifecycle stage

10. True or False? Workflow management is a key part of knowledge management.
   A. True
   B. False

Chapter 30

Implementation and Improvement of Service Transition

THE FOLLOWING ITIL INTERMEDIATE EXAM OBJECTIVES ARE DISCUSSED IN THIS CHAPTER:

- ✓ The key activities in the introduction of service transition

- ✓ How to adopt an integrated approach to service transition processes

- ✓ Implementing service transition in a virtual or cloud environment

The learning objective for this chapter is to gain sufficient knowledge of service transition principles, techniques, and relationships to be able to understand how these are applied to ensure new, modified, or retired services meet the expectations of the business.

The Key Activities in the Introduction of Service Transition

Unless setting up an entirely new service provider organization (in what is known as a greenfield situation), we are seldom in the position of implementing service transition processes from scratch; even badly run organizations will some process for introducing new services, however inadequate. In the vast majority of cases, we shall be attempting to improve current processes. The ITIL *Continual Service Improvement* publication provides guidance on assessing the current approach to service transition processes and establishing the most effective and efficient improvements to make, prioritized according to the business benefit. The syllabus for the ITIL CSI Intermediate exam, which covers this guidance, is covered in Part 5 of this book, in Chapters 43–50. The CSI approach to implementing improvements, as shown in Figure 30.1, should be used. We have seen this diagram before; the CSI approach applies to all stages of the service lifecycle.

FIGURE 30.1   Steps to improving the service transition processes

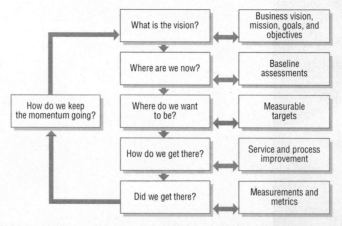

Introducing new or improved service transition processes will mean a significant organizational change. It should also improve the services delivered by the service provider. Logically, the guidance on delivering new or changed services contained in the ITIL Intermediate Service Transition course (which is covered in this section of the book) applies to introducing service transition itself. Although, as we have said, this is seldom carried out from scratch, implementing improvements to service transition is itself a service transition exercise. It will result in a change to how services are delivered by the service provider, and as with any transition, this carries a risk of disruption unless done carefully.

The key activities in the introduction of service transition are as follows:

- Justifying service transition
- Designing the service transition components
- Introducing the components to the organization
- Delivering the service (business as usual)

We are going to look at each of these in turn, but first you should note that the preceding list conforms to the usual service lifecycle; the justification stage is strategy, the design stage is design, introduction of components is transition, and business as usual is operation. Once implemented, the process will be subject to continual service improvement.

Justifying Service Transition

Effective service transition is essential if the service provider is to deliver quality services to the business. Transition delivers the design into day-to-day operations. If service transitions are executed successfully, the processes behind that delivery are invisible to customers; this means that they do not understand the importance of ensuring that these processes are properly resourced. A failed service transition will highlight a lack of or inadequate processes, but the challenge is to show the business how important they are, without having to "prove" it through a failed transition. To win the support of stakeholders for the implementation or improvement of service transition, the service provider must show them the benefits of such an initiative. The benefits should be quantified as far as possible, showing the balance between the impact to the business (negative and positive) and the cost. The negative impact of delayed implementation should be emphasized.

To justify improvement, the service provider may need to provide evidence of the costs that have resulted from previous failed changes, such as budget overruns and the number and impact of errors found in live running that could have been detected during test transition.

Designing Service Transition

The design of service transition should ensure that all the required legislative standards and policies are incorporated. Examples of such requirements include Sarbanes-Oxley regulations and/or the rules governing organizations responsible for the management of credit card payments.

Relationships

The new or changed IT service will often be there to support new business practices. In many situations, service transition must work together with parts of the organization that are transitioning other elements of a business change, such as HR, facilities management, education, and training. The processes should facilitate these relationships. The implementation of the business change can involve many parties, so it is essential that ownership of each component of the overall service is clear.

In addition to these other internal support services, service transition includes working with other stakeholders:

- Program and project management. Many large transitions involve specialist project and program management staff, using processes frameworks such as PRINCE2 or the PMBOK Guide. Service transition will form part of the overall project and will need to adhere to the requirements of the project management framework in terms of reporting and agreeing on the deliverables and milestones.

- Internal development teams and external suppliers. Service transition will need to choose a method of raising defects such as errors found during testing with these groups.

- Customers/users. It is essential that customers and users are communicated with properly to manage their expectations and to let them know what will be happening and when. This process can be helped by formulating a strategic stakeholder contact map. Often this communication will be routed through business relationship management or service level management.

- IT stakeholders. These could include staff involved in IT service continuity management, network management, security, and other areas as appropriate.

- Non-IT stakeholders within the organization such as facilities management, HR, and physical security.

- External stakeholders, such as landlords and regulatory bodies.

Budget and Resources

Although service transition provides an overall net benefit to the organization in that it saves the disruption and expense of failed changes, it has to be funded itself. The service transition strategy needs to address who provides the funding and the level of funding that is required. For example, service transition requires an infrastructure including testing environments, a CMS, and an SKMS.

The costing of transition objectives must be an integral part of design, whatever the funding mechanism may be, and will involve service transition and customers working with design.

The responsibility for the provision of the resources required by service transition must also be decided. These resources will include staff, test data, and network resources. The maintenance of the test environment is a significant cost item, but failure to fund this adequately or to provide the staff resources required will lead to inadequate testing, with the consequential risk of failed changes.

Introduction of the Components to the Organization

Careful consideration should be given to the introduction of service transition to existing projects. It will be practical to introduce these processes only when the project is at the transition stage, rather than attempting to "retrofit" the desired practices at an earlier stage. When bringing existing projects into the new process, the conversion from old to new process should be considered. This transition from one process to another needs to take place without risking the successful transition of the project. The conversion from old to new should be designed (and tested where possible) as part of the design responsibility.

Cultural Change

Even if procedures already exist, formalizing them may meet with resistance and will involve a degree of cultural change.

The support of service transition staff and those supporting and being supported by service transition need to understand why the changes to procedures are being made, the benefits to themselves and to the organization, and how their roles will change. A cultural change program is required that addresses all stakeholders. This should continue throughout and after transition to ensure that the changed attitudes are firmly embedded.

Risk and Value

As with all transitions, decisions around transitioning should be made only with a full understanding of the expected risks and benefits. Alienation of support staff, excessive costs to the business, and unacceptable delays to business benefits are all examples of possible risks. Measures of the benefits resulting from service transition might include customer and user satisfaction, reduced incident and failure rates for transitioned services, and reduced cost of transitioning.

The risks and beneficial values require a baseline of the current situation if the changes are to be measurable.

Delivering the Service (Business as Usual)

During the initial period immediately after the new processes are introduced, there should be extra support provided to ensure that staff have the guidance they need until the processes are fully understood and embedded. This early life support is a feature of all types of service transition. Following the successful introduction of service transition processes, the processes should be used for all transitions. Reporting the benefits of each transition should help to win over those who were previously unconvinced because in operation these benefits can be proved. There will be a need to adjust the processes over time to better fit the requirements, and this should be done in conjunction with continual service improvement.

An Integrated Approach to Service Transition Processes

The processes involved in the service transition stage of the service lifecycle are inter-independent. The relationships between them are complex, and it is not possible to design and implement them separately. The diagram in Figure 30.2 is a simplified example of the steps that might be required for a single service transition.

FIGURE 30.2   An example of a path through the processes that might be required for a single service transition

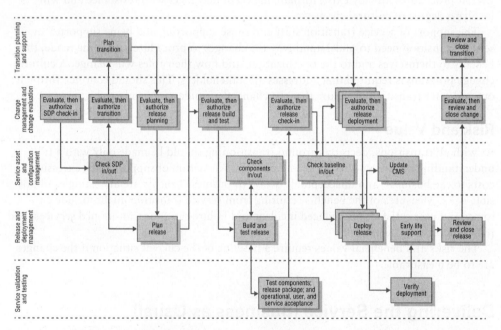

An integrated plan for introduction or improvement of service transition processes must consider how the processes fit together and the roles and responsibilities of all those involved. It must match the inputs, outputs, and triggers of each process step with the corresponding steps in other processes. Such a plan would include the following items:

▪ A clear understanding of how the processes will work together in practice for different types of transition.

▪ Each required input will be the output of another process step.

- Each activity should have accountable and responsible roles defined and people to fill those roles.

- The critical success factors (CSFs), key performance indicators (KPIs), and metrics should work together to support the objectives of the organization.

- Any improvements to one process will still integrate with other processes, including where those processes have been improved.

Implementing Service Transition in a Virtual or Cloud Environment

Implementing virtualization or cloud architectures will have an impact on how an organization manages the design, implementation, and operation of service transition. These technologies pose particular challenges due to the dynamic nature of the environments involved. They often require rapid provisioning of new virtual servers or migration of virtual servers between hosts to support changing workloads. Many activities such as the following examples will be automated:

- The creation, deployment, and retirement of virtual servers

- Adding physical resources to increase capacity to an existing virtual server

- Moving a virtual server from one physical server to another to allow maintenance activities

The automation required in virtual and cloud environments can be an opportunity but may also cause difficulties when implementing service transition processes. The challenges will need to be understood, and the processes need to be designed to work under such circumstances. This may necessitate more sophisticated tools, which will then need to integrate with the existing tools.

Configuration information is particularly challenging in this environment because configurations are so dynamic. The service provider might choose to document all allowed configurations and identify preferred configurations for use by the incident, problem, and change management processes as well as others. Alternatively, it may be sufficient to document the high-level configuration and use discovery tools to identify the current state when needed. Factors, such as the agreed warranty for the service and the specific service levels, will need to be considered when deciding which of these approaches is appropriate. The virtual or cloud architecture may also require the creation of new configuration item (CI) types, release models, change models, and standard changes. In addition, managing this technology will require different tools, activities, authorities, roles, and responsibilities. Adopting cloud or virtual architecture will therefore require new operational level agreements and underpinning contracts. There may be changes required to change, release, and deployment processes to ensure that they work in both physical and virtual environments. Where external services are used, the supplier management process becomes even more important because the services using the cloud architecture are likely to be business critical.

The service asset and configuration process may actually become easier if an organization uses a public cloud because most of the underlying complexity will be managed by the external service provider. The organization still needs to carry out service asset and configuration management, but the CIs are likely to be at a much higher level.

Summary

This chapter covered the implementation and improvement of service transition in an organization.

We explored the following topics:

- The key activities in the introduction of service transition

- How to adopt an integrated approach to service transition processes

- Implementing service transition in a virtual or cloud environment

Exam Essentials

Be able to list the other stakeholders involved in service transition.   Successful transition requires understanding who is affected and building the required relationships with affected groups, whether these are in the business, external to the organization, or other service provider teams.

Be able to explain and describe the four key activities in the introduction of service transition.   It is important to understand that the organization needs to know why service transition is necessary and the benefits it will bring. Also, the introduction of the process is like any other transition; it must be designed, and the introduction must be planned so that it goes smoothly. Finally, it needs to be embedded.

Understand the interrelationships and dependencies between the different service transition processes.   Know why the processes need to be introduced together and the importance of an integrated approach, such that the outputs of one process provide the required inputs for the next.

Be able to describe the particular challenges of implementing service transition in a cloud or virtual environment.   Understand how some aspects may be easier, due to automation or the level of management provided by the external supplier, and some may be more challenging, due to the dynamic nature of such environments.

Review Questions

You can find the answers to the review questions in the appendix.

1. Which of these statements is/are correct?
    1. Introducing new or improved service transition processes will mean a significant organizational change.
    2. Introducing or improving service transition is itself a service transition exercise.
        A. Statement 1 only
        B. Statement 2 only
        C. Both statements
        D. Neither statement

2. Which of these are valid activities for service transition involvement?
    1. Justification for the implementation (strategy)
    2. Design of the service transition components (design)
    3. Introduction of the new or changed components to the organization (service transition)
    4. Running in normal mode (service operation)
        A. 1 only
        B. 1 and 2 only
        C. 2 and 3 only
        D. 1, 2, and 3

3. Justification for service transition may require evidence of poor transition. Which of these are examples of evidence of poor transition?
    1. Cost of failed changes
    2. The actual costs of transitions exceeding the budget
    3. The discovery of errors during live running, instead of during the test phase
        A. 1 and 2 only
        B. 2 and 3 only
        C. 1, 2, and 3
        D. 1 and 3 only

4. Which of these is a key consideration for justifying service transition?
    A. Well-designed services are easier to transition and operate.
    B. Strategic planning is a key part of the lifecycle.
    C. It is difficult to "retrofit" new practices.
    D. Operational services require precise design.

5.   True or False: An integrated plan for introduction or improvement of service transition processes should be based on an understanding of how the processes fit together.

   A.   True

   B.   False

6.   Which of the following shows the correct order of the steps in the CSI approach, together with the correct matching inputs?

   A.   Where do we want to be? (measurable targets); what is the vision? (business vision, mission, goals, and objectives); how do we get there? (service and process improvements); where are we now? (baseline assessments); did we get there? (measurements and metrics); how do we keep the momentum going?

   B.   What is the vision? (measurable targets); where are we now? (measurements and metrics); where do we want to be? (business vision, mission, goals, and objectives); how do we get there? (service and process improvements); did we get there? (baseline assessments); how do we keep the momentum going?

   C.   What is the vision? (business vision, mission, goals, and objectives); where are we now? (baseline assessments); where do we want to be? (measurable targets); how do we get there? (Service and process improvements); did we get there? (measurements and metrics); how do we keep the momentum going?

   D.   Where do we want to be? (baseline assessments); what is the vision? (business vision, mission, goals, and objectives); how do we get there? (service and process improvements); where are we now? (measurable targets); did we get there? (measurements and metrics); how do we keep the momentum going?

7.   Which of the following are possible challenges when seeking support and funding to introduce or improve service transition?

   1.   The business is not aware of what happens during service transition.

   2.   The service transition processes are regarded as introducing delay at the end of a project without any obvious benefit because the business presumes that the service would have worked properly without them.

   3.   The cost benefit of effective service transition is only apparent following a failed transition due to poor or absent processes.

   4.   Errors that should have been found during testing but become apparent during live operation are blamed on the operation stage rather than the transition stage, therefore making it harder to convince stakeholders that support and funding for transition are necessary.

   A.   2, 3, and 4 only

   B.   1, 2, and 3 only

   C.   All of the above

   D.   1, 3, and 4 only

8.   Service transition may require liaison with other stakeholders. Which of the following are among possible stakeholders listed within the *ITIL Service Transition* publication?

   1.   Regulatory bodies

   2.   Landlords

3. HR

4. Project management

5. Suppliers

6. Business relationship managers

    A. None of the above

    B. 1, 4, 5, and 6 only

    C. 1, 2, 3, and 5 only

    D. All of the above

9. Which of the following statements about the introduction of service transition processes is/are TRUE?

    1. Service transition processes should be introduced to all projects, wherever they are in the service lifecycle.

    2. Service transition processes should be implemented one at a time to ensure that each is accepted and embedded before the next process is introduced.

    3. The introduction of service transition processes involves an element of risk.

    4. IT staff will usually welcome the introduction of service transition processes because it will make their job easier.

    5. Service transition processes should be based on best practice and therefore will not need to be amended after introduction; such amendments should be avoided because they will cause confusion.

    A. 1, 3, and 5 only

    B. 3 only

    C. 2 and 4 only

    D. 1, 2, and 5 only

10. Which of the following statements about implementing service transition in a virtual or cloud environment is/are TRUE?

    1. Configuration management can be more difficult due to the dynamic nature of the environment.

    2. The configuration process may actually become easier if an organization uses a public cloud because most of the underlying complexity will be managed by the external service provider.

    A. Both

    B. Only 1

    C. Only 2

    D. Neither

Chapter

31

Challenges, Critical Success Factors, and Risks

THE FOLLOWING ITIL INTERMEDIATE EXAM OBJECTIVES ARE DISCUSSED IN THIS CHAPTER:

✓ The challenges facing service transition

✓ Measurement through analyzing critical success factors

✓ Potential implementation risks that could affect services currently in transition and being planned

✓ External factors that affect the approach to service transition

In this chapter, we review the challenges, critical success factors, and risks relating to transitions. These concepts will enable you to manage transitions more effectively by understanding the issues you may face, how to measure for success, and to put in place mitigation actions to reduce the risk to the transition.

Service Transition Challenges

Challenges for service transition are driven by the complexity of provision because organizations now deal with a large variety of customers, users, programs, projects, suppliers, and partners. This provides a challenge in managing a large stakeholder group because transition affects everybody. The relationships with customers, suppliers, users, and projects are often complicated and need to be managed as a transition moves into operation.

Ensuring that transition processes can integrate with other business processes (for example, finance, HR, and procurement) is also a challenge. There may also be insufficient knowledge of the dependencies on legacy systems, making impact analysis difficult, and this may have a significant effect on the introduction of new systems and services.

A major challenge is to address the balance between maintaining a stable live environment and being responsive to the business needs for changing the services and achieving a balance between pragmatism and bureaucracy. Transition is perfectly placed to support this, and it is one of the reasons that this lifecycle stage is so important and must not be ignored or cut short.

Many of the challenges relate to cultural change, such as creating an environment that fosters standardization, simplification, and knowledge sharing. Service transition must persuade the business that it is an enabler of business change and, therefore, an integral component of the business change programs. It is made easier if the challenge of finding process champions is achieved. This can create a culture that encourages people to collaborate and work effectively together.

Developing standard performance measures across projects and suppliers and ensuring that the quality of delivery and support matches the business use of new technology is a significant challenge for all organizations. Effective use of the service transition processes requires protecting the service transition time and budget from being impacted by events earlier in the service lifecycle.

Risk management is the source of several challenges, including understanding different stakeholder perspectives on risk. This reflects the complexity of managing organizations with varied structures. During transition, it's important to achieve the optimum balance between managing risk and taking risks and to provide effective reporting in relation to risk management and corporate governance.

Some organizations will be driven by the requirements and reporting required by Sarbanes-Oxley, ISO/IEC 20000, ISO/IEC 38500, and COBIT (if applicable). These standards and governance requirements both support and provide challenges to the success of service transition as a lifecycle stage.

Critical Success Factors

Service provision, in all organizations, needs to be matched to current and rapidly changing business demands. The objective is to continually and cost-effectively improve the quality of service while ensuring that it is aligned to the business requirements. To meet this objective, certain critical success factors need to be considered for service transition.

It is necessary to understand and manage the different stakeholder perspectives that underpin effective risk management within an organization. Establishing and maintaining stakeholder buy-in and commitment and having clearly defined relationships and interfaces with program and project management is vital to the success of a transition. Equally important is maintaining these contacts and managing all the relationships during service transition.

Another critical success factor is the integration of service transition with the other service lifecycle stages and the processes and disciplines that impact service transition. It is important to ensure that the dependencies among the legacy systems, new technology, and human elements are clearly understood. Legacy systems are often overlooked but can have a significant impact on the introduction of new services.

Here are some additional critical success factors necessary for successful service transition:

- Automating processes to eliminate errors
- Managing knowledge
- Developing good-quality systems, tools, processes, and procedures
- Exploiting the cultural and political environment
- Understanding the technical configurations and dependencies
- Understanding the processes, procedures, skills, and competencies required for service transition
- Having a workforce with the necessary knowledge and skills, appropriate training, and the right service culture
- Ensuring clear accountabilities, roles, and responsibilities
- Encouraging a knowledge-sharing culture

It is important for service transition to deliver change with less variation in time, cost, and quality predictions during and after transition. This should ensure improved customer and user satisfaction, which is critical for continued successful transitions.

If it cannot be demonstrated that the benefits of establishing and improving the service transition practice and processes outweigh the costs, then there will be a significant impact on the credibility of transition. This should be supported by effective communication of the organization's attitude to risk during service transition activities and by building a thorough understanding of risks that have impacted or may impact successful service transition of services in the service portfolio.

Service Transition Risks

New service transition practices should not be implemented without recognizing the potential risk to services currently in transition and releases that are planned. A baseline assessment of current transitions and planned projects will help service transition to identify implementation risks.

Particular risks include the change in accountability, responsibilities, and practices of existing projects (for example, project teams not keeping operational teams up-to-date with progress on a particular activity) that demotivate the workforce, leading to alienation of some key support and operations staff. There may be additional unplanned costs to services in transition due to unforeseen circumstances, which is a risk, as is resistance to change and circumvention of the processes due to perceived bureaucracy. Another implementation risk is incurring excessive costs to the business by being overly risk averse.

Uncontrolled knowledge sharing, allowing people to have access to information they should not have, is another implementation risk. A lack of maturity and integration of systems and tools may result in people "blaming" technology for other shortcomings. There may be poor integration between the processes, causing a silo approach to delivering IT service management (ITSM), with no integration between processes. Finally, the loss of productive hours presents a risk, as do higher costs, loss of revenue, and perhaps even business failure as a result of poor service transition processes.

Service Transition under Difficult Conditions

In some circumstances, service transitions will be required under atypical or difficult conditions. These conditions may come about as a result of shortness of time or lack of money or people, or at least people with the right skills. There may be factors outside of service transition's control, such as internal political difficulty, the threat of redundancy, or outsourcing. The corporate culture may be riven with internal rivalries and competitiveness between managers. There may even be other external factors, such as extreme weather, political instability, the aftermath of a disaster, or new legislation.

In some cases, it might be possible to predict these adverse conditions, but it is often the case that they occur during the lifecycle of the transition. When this happens, reaction must take place during the transition stage.

Risk Management

There may be occasions when speed is more important than accuracy or smoothness. This is effectively a risk management decision, and general risk management principles apply. In time-critical situations, implementation of a new or changed service may be more important than a degree of disruption.

Some of the key factors that assist with delivering success in this context are the empowerment of staff to take appropriate levels of risk. It is essential to know the absolute cutoff date/time by which a service transition must deliver. If a "safety margin" has been built in, the service may be delivered earlier to meet the new timeline requirements, complete with errors that could have been removed before the actual deadline.

Similarly, assuming that there is some margin when none exists means missing deadlines. Being open and honest is the best policy in this situation.

Achieving early delivery depends on knowing which components must be available at the cutoff date and which could be added later. This requires an understanding of the dependencies for the whole project or program. Knowing which users/customers/locations must be in place at the cutoff date is also essential. Finally, you must understand what actually happens if you fail. Again, honesty is often the best policy here. Consider the business impact as well as cost, health and safety, embarrassment, and reputation. If a deadline is missed, is it just embarrassing or will huge penalties be involved? Will there be other implications?

In a crisis, follow the rules of crisis management:

- Rule 1: Don't panic.

- Rule 2: A good crisis manager makes decisions instantly and acts on them confidently. If these decisions later turn out to have been correct, so much the better, but speed is often more important than efficiency when managing a crisis situation.

- Rule 3: Accept that decisions won't be perfect and that people should not be blamed for making the best decision they can under difficult circumstances.

Success in these circumstances will rely heavily on the trust that is put in the people making the decisions. If a blame culture exists, then there is likely to be hesitancy in decision-making, whereas if the culture is one of empowerment, then a crisis may be handled more effectively.

Proven and reliable processes, procedures, and channels for authorization and control will be important as well. There must be agreed actions if the channels don't function—for example, increased delegated authority, escalation, and alternative support channels.

Restricted Resources

When resources are in short supply, a key aspect here is deciding what to measure and sticking to that decision and the framework for delivery.

It will be necessary to identify the most important factors—speed, low cost, or something else? These then need to be addressed in a practical manner. This may require some hierarchy of factors or qualification of the way in which they are applied. For example, it must be done within a certain time frame, but only if it remains below a certain cost.

Good communication, management structure, and integration with stakeholders are vital in this circumstance so that all the necessary decisions can be made with the correct authority and within the required timescales.

Safety-Critical Services and High-Risk Environments

Increasingly, IT services directly support or actually deliver services on which lives depend, such as hospital and emergency services and air traffic control. In these circumstances, extra security and foolproof approaches are required. This sort of environment favors accuracy over speed and requires rigorous testing as well as sign-off at the appropriate level and the ability to veto a change on safety grounds. Consider NASA and the go/no-go decisions by individual teams when a space rocket is launched.

Working with Difficult Customers

Of course, there is no such thing as a bad customer, but often there are customers who are unclear of their role and so act in a way that prevents rather than supports successful implementation. They may get more involved in the delivery than the end result, or make decisions based on their own experience and needs, not the overall business need. These kinds of situations can often be improved by awareness and education of all parties involved in the transition. Business relationship managers may be able to help too, but this is another area of cultural change, which needs to be carefully addressed.

Nothing can replace a good relationship with customers during transition. Although each of the lifecycle stages provides guidance on best practice, and service transition is no different, there is nothing that can be specifically applied without understanding the context of the organization. Employing transition leaders with experience and skill in managing transitions and who are sympathetic to the culture of the organization is a vital part of the success of any implementation.

Summary

In this chapter we discussed the following topics:

- The challenges facing service transition
- Measurement through analyzing critical success factors
- Potential implementation risks that could affect services currently in transition and being planned
- External factors that affect the approach to service transition

Exam Essentials

Understand the challenges faced by service transition.   Understand the variety of challenges that are facing service transition, including those involving the business, suppliers, and other stakeholders.

Understand how service transition challenges may be overcome using ITIL best practice.   Understand how to address the challenges of service transition by implementing best practice through service transition processes.

Understand the critical success factors that need to be in place if successful service transition is to take place.   Understand the importance of clearly defined objectives with measurable targets. Be able to list some CSFs for service transition.

Know the risks encountered in the service transition stage, in particular the danger that the importance of this stage may not be recognized.   Understand the risk that service transition's importance may often be overlooked, resulting in too little time or resources being spent, which can cause increased costs and delays later.

Understand and be able to explain the challenges of working with customers and stakeholders.   Understand the challenges of managing customers in all circumstances and the ways in which stakeholders need to be managed.

Explain the use of risk management as part of service transition.   Consider the elements of risk management and crisis management and the difficulties that may arise during a transition, and be able to explain how to deal with them.

Review Questions

You can find the answers to the review questions in the appendix.

1. Which of these statements is/are correct?
   1. One of the significant challenges for service transition is managing a complex stake-holder group.
   2. There is a challenge in integrating service transition with the business processes.
      A. Statement 1 only
      B. Statement 2 only
      C. Both statements
      D. Neither statement

2. Which of these statements reflects a major challenge for service transition?
   1. There must be a balance between the cost of design and the length of time it takes to complete it.
   2. There must be a balance between maintaining a stable live environment and being responsive to the business needs for changing the services.
   3. There must be a balance between the need to restore service and the requirement to identify root cause of failures.
      A. 2 only
      B. 1 and 2 only
      C. 2 and 3 only
      D. 1, 2, and 3

3. Which of these are included as challenges to service transition implementation?
   1. Business strategy
   2. Cultural change
   3. Risk management
      A. 1 and 3 only
      B. 2 and 3 only
      C. 1, 2, and 3
      D. 3 only

4. What guidance does ITIL provide regarding performance measures across projects, providers, and suppliers for service transition?
   A. The performance measures do not matter for service transition.
   B. The performance measures are used only during the operational lifecycle stage.

   C. The performance measures should be standardized for use in service transition.

   D. The performance measures are applicable only during service design.

5. True or False? A critical success factor for service transition is to engage and maintain stakeholder buy-in to the transition.

   A. True

   B. False

6. Which of these statements is a critical success factor for service transition?

   1. Automating processes to eliminate errors

   2. Managing knowledge

   3. Developing good-quality systems, tools, processes, and procedures

   4. Exploiting the cultural and political environment

      A. 1, 3, and 4 only

      B. 2 and 4 only

      C. 1, 2, and 3 only

      D. 1, 2, 3, and 4

7. What is the most important key factor for demonstrating the success of service transition?

   A. Demonstrating that change authorization is important

   B. Demonstrating that changes are delivered with less variation in time, cost, and quality predictions

   C. Demonstrating that release and deployment is important in the testing and delivery of new services

   D. Demonstrating that knowledge management supports the delivery of transitions

8. Which of these are included in the guidance for service transition in difficult conditions?

   1. Risk management

   2. Restricted resources

   3. Design constraints

   4. Crisis management

      A. 1 and 2 only

      B. 2 and 3 only

      C. 1, 2, and 4 only

      D. 1, 2, 3, and 4

9. Which of these is NOT a rule of crisis management?

    A. Accept that decisions may not be perfect.

    B. Don't panic.

    C. Authorize all funding as part of the process.

    D. Make instant decisions and follow them through confidently.

10. True or False? Certain environments require specific transitional handling, including a go/no-go decision on the final delivery.

    A. True

    B. False

Service Operation

PART

IV

Chapter

32

Introduction to the Service Operation Lifecycle Stage

THE FOLLOWING ITIL INTERMEDIATE EXAM OBJECTIVES ARE DISCUSSED IN THIS CHAPTER:

✓ **The main purpose and objective of service operation**

✓ **The scope of service operation**

✓ **The context of service operation and the service lifecycle**

✓ **Service operation's value to the business**

✓ **Service operation fundamentals**

Service operation's main aim is to deliver and manage services at agreed levels to business *users* and *customers*. The service operation stage is when the service is actually being delivered, and it's often a much longer stage than the previous stages of strategy, design, and transition. It is the most visible part of the lifecycle to the business. We will cover the purpose, objectives, and scope of this lifecycle stage and the context of service operation within the service lifecycle. We'll examine the value it provides to the business and discuss the fundamental concepts and definitions involved in this lifecycle stage.

Understanding the Purpose, Objectives, and Scope of Service Operation

The output from service strategy, design, and transition becomes visible in service operation. It is in the operational stage that the service—which was originally considered in strategy, put together in design, and rolled out in transition—actually delivers the benefit that the business requires. It is also a much longer stage of the lifecycle than the first three stages; the service should continue to meet the business requirement for months or even years.

Most IT staff are involved (to a greater or lesser extent) in the service operation stage. They may contribute to other lifecycle stages, but their main focus is the delivery of the operational services.

Service operation is a critical stage of the service lifecycle. After all, the best strategy will fail if the service is badly managed, and good design is of limited value if the service is not run effectively. Transition can be successful only if the environment into which the service is being transitioned is ready to receive it and takes responsibility for managing it. Finally, service improvements will not be possible without reliable metrics from monitoring performance and other data. Service operation gathers the measurements used for *baselines* and for measuring success of improvements, so consistent, systematic measurements are a key element of service operation.

The staff working in this stage of the service lifecycle need to have *processes* and support tools in place to enable them to do their job—monitoring tools that allow them to have an overall view of service operation and delivery so they can detect failures and resolve them quickly. They also need service management tools to ensure that the correct workflow takes place for each process and the necessary information is easily accessible. This may entail monitoring elements of the service supplied by external providers.

As services may be provided, in whole or in part, by one or more *partner/supplier* organizations, the service operation view of the end-to-end service needs to encompass external aspects of service provision, including managing cross-organizational workflows.

The Purpose of Service Operation

The purpose of the service operation stage of the service lifecycle is to deliver the service at the level that was agreed to through the *service level management* process. This includes performing all the activities required to deliver the service as well as managing the technology used to deliver the service (such as applying updates, backing up data, and so on).

Service operation must deliver the service effectively, but also has to ensure that the cost of that delivery is within the operational costs that formed part of the original business case. Should a service be operated at a higher cost than was originally envisaged, the benefits that were planned, such as cost savings, may never be realized.

Service operation staff members must view the service as a whole and be given the tools they need to evaluate whether the delivery meets the standard required. It is a common error to have staff members concentrate on individual aspects of a service or to ignore those parts of the service provided by third parties, losing sight of the end-to-end service as it appears to the customer. Technology can be used to spot deviations from expected service or *response levels* very quickly, allowing remedial action to be put in place immediately.

The Objectives of Service Operation

The objectives of service operation follow on from its purpose. Service operation is what the customer sees and experiences. Their perception of the quality of the service provision is based on their experience, not on the design or implementation of the service, which may or may not have been done well. It is important to remember that service operation is far more than just managing the components that make up the service. It is in service operation that it all comes together . . . or all falls apart! So the first objective is to maintain business satisfaction and confidence in IT through effective and efficient delivery and support of the service as agreed in the service level agreement (SLA); this ensures that the business receives the level of service it expects. The second objective supports the first; it is to minimize the impact of service *outages* on day-to-day business activities—by finding, preventing, and resolving *incidents* and *problems* that could impact the business. Some service outages are inevitable; service operation will work to reduce both the number and impact of outages. The service operation process of problem management aims to reduce the recurrence of incidents that disrupt business activities, while incident management aims to resolve those incidents that do occur as quickly as possible.

Service operation is also responsible for controlling *access* to IT services. The final objective is to protect the services from unauthorized access. The access management process ensures that only authorized users can have access to the services provided.

The Scope of Service Operation

The scope of service operation, described in the ITIL framework, includes the "processes, functions, organization, and tools" that are used to deliver and support the agreed services. This lifecycle stage is responsible for performing the critical day-to-day activities and processes that ensure the service meets the business requirement and enables the business to achieve its objectives. It also collects the performance data that will be required by continual service improvement to identify and track improvement opportunities. The *ITIL Service Operation* publication provides guidance on the successful management of the following:

The Services Themselves This includes all the activities required to deliver the services consistently within the agreed service levels. These activities may be carried out by the service provider, an external supplier, or the user or customer of a particular service.

The Service Management Processes These include the service operation processes of *event*, incident, problem, access management, and request fulfilment. (We will be looking at the service operation processes in Chapter 34, "Service Operation Processes: Incident and Problem Management," Chapter 35, "Service Operation Processes: Request Fulfilment," Chapter 36, "Service Operation Processes: Event Management," and Chapter 37, "Service Operation Processes: Access Management.") In addition to these processes, service operation is responsible for carrying out activities associated with processes that originated in other lifecycle stages. Figure 32.1 shows these processes. *Capacity management*, for example, is a design process; however, the day-to-day monitoring and *tuning* of capacity takes place in service operation. Another example is *service level management*, which is a process that is undertaken as part of service design; once it's operational, however, the monitoring and reporting of the service performance takes place during the operation phase. A process such as *strategy* management for IT services is outside of the scope of service operation because it is concerned with longer-term planning and improvement activities, but another service strategy process, financial management for IT Services, is included as the day-to-day management of *budgets* and takes place in operation. It is essential, therefore, that all of the processes that occur during the operation phase work effectively and efficiently. Continual service improvement (CSI) also depends on service operation producing the required information to allow improvement opportunities to be identified, baselines to be taken, and the success of any improvements measured.

Figure 32.1 shows how service operation is responsible for activities in processes from the other lifecycle stages.

The Technology Delivering IT services depends on the use of appropriate technology such as networks, desktops, servers, databases, and monitoring tools. Service operation is responsible for managing the technology that delivers the services.

FIGURE 32.1 Service operation involvement in other lifecycle processes

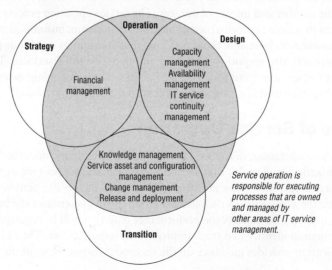

Strategy

Operation

Design

Financial management

Capacity management
Availability management
IT service continuity management

Knowledge management
Service asset and configuration management
Change management
Release and deployment

Transition

Service operation is responsible for executing processes that are owned and managed by other areas of IT service management.

The People   Despite automation, service operation depends on the actions of the support staff members to ensure that the service runs as it should. Their management of the technology and processes is the key to successful service delivery.

The Context of Service Operation and the Service Lifecycle

Service operation needs to be considered within the context of the whole service lifecycle. Each area of the *lifecycle* addresses a particular set of challenges that need to be addressed for successful service management, and each stage has an impact on all of the others. The service lifecycle diagram in Figure 32.2 shows the five areas of the lifecycle.

Stages of the lifecycle work together as an integrated system to support the ultimate objective of service management, which is to deliver business value. Every stage is interdependent, as shown in Figure 32.3. In particular, note the interdependence of service operation to each of the other lifecycle stages.

FIGURE 32.2   The ITIL service lifecycle

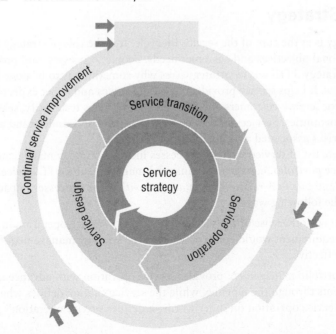

FIGURE 32.3 Integration across the ITIL service lifecycle

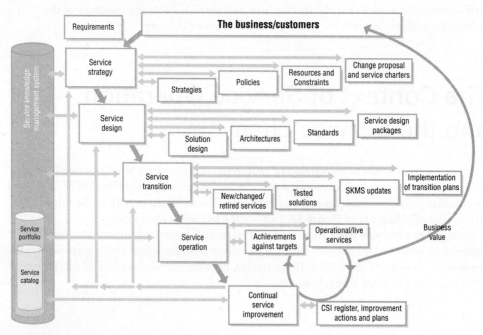

Service Strategy

Service strategy is at the core of the service lifecycle. It is the role of strategy to understand the organizational objectives and customer needs. People, processes, and products should support the strategy. ITIL service strategy asks why something is to be done before thinking of how. It helps service providers to set objectives and to set expectations of performance for serving customers and markets. It also helps to identify, select, and prioritize opportunities. Service strategy ensures that providers understand and can handle the costs and risks associated with their service portfolios.

The complete list of service strategy processes includes strategy management for IT services, *service portfolio* management, financial management for IT services, *demand* management, and *business relationship management*. These processes impact service operation in the following ways:

- The success or otherwise of the services provided in service operation in meeting the business requirement would confirm whether the strategy management for IT services has been effective.

- Service portfolio management provides service operation with advance notice of future requirements through the pipeline, while the service catalog defines what is to be provided by service operation (in other words, it defines service operation's scope).

- If demand management has been successful, service operation will be able to cope with the level of demand for the service, and any fluctuations in that demand, and will have techniques available to affect the levels of demand where required.

- Both financial management for IT services and business relationship management are strategic processes that take place during the service operation lifecycle stage; managing budgets and liaising with the business at a senior level are ongoing activities that touch all areas of the lifecycle.

Service Design

Service design turns strategic ideas into deliverables. The design must always consider the strategy, to ensure that services are designed with the business objectives in mind. Design considers the whole IT organization and how it will deliver and support the services, turning the service strategy into a plan for delivering the business objectives. Requirements from service operation processes, people, and tools must be taken into account to ensure that the design will work in the operational environment. Remember, design includes changes to existing services.

The complete list of service design processes includes design coordination, *service catalog* management, service level management, *availability* management, *capacity* management, *IT service continuity* management, *information security* management, and *supplier* management. Through these processes, design ensures that both the *utility* and the *warranty* of the new or changed service is considered in design, covering the continuity of the service, its achievement of service levels, and conformance to security standards and regulations.

- Design coordination is responsible for ensuring that the service operation requirements are included in the design and that an operations plan exists.

- The service catalog, as stated previously, defines the scope of service operation because it provides information about all operational services.

- Service operation provides the monitoring and metrics needed to manage the delivery of the availability and capacity targets and identify areas of concern.

- The reporting against service level targets and any actions required to deliver a service improvement plan take place as part of service operation.

- IT service continuity plans are tested regularly as part of operations, and any invocation of the plan would be to ensure that service operation is able to continue to deliver the required services to the business.

- Information security provides the policies that access management implements in operation.

- Supplier management is dependent upon the metrics from live operational services to know whether the suppliers are providing the contracted services.

Service Transition

Service transition provides guidance for developing and improving *capabilities* for introducing new and changed services into supported environments. The value of a service is identified in strategy, and the service is designed to deliver that value. Service transition ensures that the value is realized; it does so by enabling the necessary changes to take place without unacceptable risks to existing services. It enables the implementation of new services, and the modification of existing services, to ensure that the services provided deliver the service strategy of achieving the business objectives and that the benefits of the service design are fully realized. Service transition also introduces the *service knowledge management system*, which ensures that knowledge is stored and made available to all stages of the service lifecycle and that lessons are learned and decisions are backed with factual data, leading to improved efficiency and effectiveness over time.

The complete list of service transition processes includes transition planning and support, change management, *service asset* and configuration management, *release and deployment management*, *service validation and testing*, *change evaluation*, and *knowledge management*. Each process has a role to play to ensure that beneficial changes can take place and, as a consequence, the service can be introduced and will work as transitioned.

- Service asset and configuration management provides service operation with detailed knowledge of how configuration items are combined to deliver the service, showing the relationships and dependencies between these items.

- Release and deployment management ensures that the changes are delivered into the live environment without disrupting the existing services.

- Service validation and testing provides quality assurance, establishing that the service design and release will deliver into service operation a new or changed service or service offering that is fit for purpose and fit for use.

- Change evaluation checks the actual performance and outcomes of the new or changed service in service operation against the predicted performance and outcomes. Successful completion of the change evaluation ensures that the service can be formally closed and handed over to the service operation functions and CSI.

- Knowledge management provides knowledge base articles that can be of great use to incident, problem, and request processes.

Service Operation

Service operation, the subject of this section, describes best practice for managing services in supported environments. It includes guidance on achieving *effectiveness*, *efficiency*, stability, and security in the delivery and support of services to ensure value for the customer, the users, and the service provider. Without this, the services would not deliver the value required, and the achievement of business objectives would become difficult or impossible.

The service operation stage is therefore critical to delivering the design and, in doing so, achieving the service strategy. Service operation provides detailed guidance for delivering the service within the agreed service levels by tackling issues both proactively through problem and event management and reactively through incident management. It provides those delivering the service with guidance on managing the availability of services, controlling demand, optimizing capacity utilization, scheduling operations, and avoiding or resolving service incidents and managing problems. It includes advice on shared services, utility computing, web services, and mobile commerce. By delivering the services to the agreed levels, service operation enables the business to use the services to achieve its business objectives.

The complete list of service operation processes includes *event management, incident management, request fulfilment, problem management,* and *access management.* We shall be considering each of these later. Each process has a role to play to ensure the delivery of services within the agreed service levels. Service operation also describes the four service operation functions: the *service desk, technical management, IT operations management,* and *application management.* Each function is responsible for managing its own area of delivery across all stages of the lifecycle.

Continual Service Improvement

The final stage of the lifecycle is *continual service improvement (CSI).* CSI ensures that the service provider continues to provide value to customers by ensuring that the strategy, design, transition, and operation of the services is under constant review. Feedback from any stage of the service lifecycle can be used to identify improvement opportunities for any other stage of the lifecycle. This ensures that opportunities for improvement are recognized, evaluated, and implemented when justified. These may include improvements in the quality of the service or the capabilities of the service provider. It may be developing ways of doing things better, or doing them at the same level but more efficiently. Improvements may be major or small and incremental. CSI enables every new operation to incorporate lessons from previous operations.

CSI ensures that feedback from every lifecycle stage is captured, analyzed, and acted upon. Service operation is the source of information regarding the performance of services, and so the service operation lifecycle stage is an important source of information for CSI. Many of the improvement initiatives driven by CSI will directly affect service operation processes, products, and people; improvements to other lifecycle stages may lead indirectly to improved operational performance.

The CSI approach to improvement is based on establishing a baseline and checking to see whether the improvement actions have been effective. It uses the *Plan-Do-Check-Act (PDCA)* cycle, together with service measurement, demonstrating value with metrics, and conducting maturity assessments. The seven-step improvement process provides a framework for these approaches.

The Value Service Operation Delivers to the Business

Service operation is responsible for running the new service, and for fixing any unforeseen flaws. The service must run efficiently if the cost of the service is to be less than the benefit to the business. The ITIL framework offers guidance on the best practices that can be used in the various lifecycle stages, and following this advice can deliver real benefits. In the area of service operation, the following benefits can be achieved from following best practices:

- Financial savings from reduced downtime as a result of the implementation of the service operation processes of problem and incident management. Problem management will reduce the frequency of failures so that less time (and therefore money) is wasted by the business not being able to work. It will ensure that skilled IT staff members concentrate their efforts on identifying and removing the *root cause* of the incident, thus preventing recurrence. Meanwhile, efficient incident management ensures that the service is restored as soon as possible, often by service desk staff members using defined *work-arounds*. This both speeds up the service restoration and reduces costs, the latter because the more expensive IT staff members are not called on to resolve simple incidents.

- Service operation includes the production of management information regarding the efficiency and effectiveness of the service delivery. This is used by other processes to target, justify, and implement continual service improvement initiatives. Technology may be used to automate this report generation, reducing the cost of production.

- By carrying out the access management activities, service operation ensures that the business is able to meet the goals and objectives of the organization's security policy by ensuring that IT services will be accessed only by those authorized to use them; services are protected from unauthorized access in accordance with the organization's security policy.

- Service operation also provides a quick and effective access to standard services through request fulfilment. This improves the productivity of users by enabling quick access to the services and equipment they need for optimum efficiency while maintaining control over expenditure. Technology may be used to provide users with a self-service facility to reset passwords, order standard items, or log incidents through a web portal. This offers an efficient and cost-effective means of providing these services.

- By using technology to automate routine tasks, based on the information provided by the event management process, service operation reduces the number of staff members required to operate the service. This means as the number of users grows and the complexity of the services increases, the number of people needed to support the users remains broadly the same. This reduces costs and frees up technical staff members to concentrate on identifying improvements and new opportunities. Automation also delivers a more reliable and consistent service.

- Service operation also provides the operational results and data that is then used by other ITIL processes as evidence of the need for service improvements (answering the "Where are we now?" question) or to justify investment in service improvement activities. It also provides the data required to answer the "Did we get there?" question.

Service Operation Fundamentals

Finally, we are going to look at some of the fundamentals of service operation. These include how service operation provides business value and optimizes service operation performance. We will then look at the processes and functions within service operation.

How Service Operation Provides Business Value   Each stage in the service lifecycle provides value to business, but as we have said already, it is in the service operation stage that the customer sees the actual value of the service. In addition to the day-to-day running of the services, service operation needs to meet other challenges if it is to continue to deliver business value. These challenges center on the reluctance to invest in this stage of the lifecycle. Service operation needs to deliver the service within the projected cost in order to deliver the *return on investment (ROI)*, but once the project has been delivered, there may be little or no budget allocated for the costs of ongoing management of services, such as to fix design flaws or unforeseen requirements, because this is outside of the original project scope.

Most organizations never undertake a formal review of operational services for design and value. Incident and problem management are expected to resolve issues, but if the design is fundamentally flawed, this is not identified.

Service operation may struggle to be awarded the necessary budget for tools or improvement actions (including training) that would improve efficiency because they are not directly linked to the functionality of a specific service. Attempts to optimize the service or to use new tools to manage it more effectively are seen as successful only if the service has been very problematic in the past; otherwise, any action is perceived as "fixing services that are not broken."

Optimizing Service Operation Performance   Service operation is optimized in two ways. First, there are the long-term incremental improvements. Service operation processes, technologies, functions, and outputs are analyzed over time and a decision made about whether improvement is needed and, if so, how best to implement it through service design and transition. The improvements are logged in the CSI register and designed and transitioned into service. Typical examples include the deployment of a new set of tools, changes to process designs, and reconfiguration of the infrastructure.

Second, there are the short-term ongoing improvements; these are the improvements made to working practices within the processes, functions, and technologies that underpin service operation. They are generally smaller improvements that are implemented without any change to the fundamental nature of a process or technology. Examples include tuning, workload balancing, personnel redeployment, and training.

Functions and Processes in Service Operation

Now let's look at the functions and processes in service operation—you should remember this from your Foundation course.

Process   A *process* is defined as "a set of coordinated activities combining resources and capabilities to produce an outcome that creates value for the customer."

Function   A *function* is "a unit of an organization specialized to perform certain types of work and responsible for specific outcomes."

 WARNING   A process and a function may have the same name, such as capacity management, which is a process but may also be the name of a team of people.

A process for dealing with incidents comprises the coordinated activities of logging the call, prioritizing it, diagnosing it, and so on. The outcome that creates value is the user (hopefully) being able to work again. The service desk that carries out this process is a function. It is a specialized group that is responsible for carrying out activities within a process—for example, providing a fix to an incident. Make sure you understand the difference!

We will now examine the processes in service operation briefly. We shall be looking at these in more detail in later chapters.

Event Management   This process is concerned with having useful notifications about the status of the IT infrastructure and services. Event management sets up rules to ensure that events are generated so that they can be monitored, captured, and acted upon if necessary.

Incident Management   The purpose of incident management is to return normal IT service to users as quickly as possible. This may prompt the question, How do we define *normal service*? The answer is that it is the level of service specified, and agreed to, in the SLA. The goal is to minimize the adverse impact of incidents on the business, and thus on service quality and business productivity. The objective of incident management is to ensure that the best possible levels of business-aligned service quality are maintained.

Problem Management   The responsibility of problem management is to manage the lifecycle of problems, which includes monitoring and reviewing the process in addition to managing problems to their conclusion. Problem management is about the prevention and reduction of incidents, solving and removing their root cause. At the very least, if an incident cannot be prevented, then the impact to the business should be reduced through the provision of work-arounds provided through the known error database.

Request Fulfilment   The objectives of the request fulfilment process is to log and fulfil standard requests for users in a simple, efficient way. For a request to qualify, a predefined approval and qualification process must exist. Request fulfilment also provides information to users about the availability of services and how to obtain them. Users can request and receive the service or the software/hardware they require to use the service. Request fulfilment is also the channel for general information, complaints, and comments.

Access Management   Access management is responsible for putting the policies of availability and information security management into day-to-day practice. It is essential to control access to protect an organization's data and intellectual property while at the same time enabling authorized users to have the access they need. Access management is not responsible for ensuring that this access is available at all agreed times—this is provided by availability management.

Now we will look briefly at the service operation functions. Again, we will be examining these in more detail later, in Chapter 39, "Organizing for Service Operation."

The Service Desk   The service desk not only provides incident resolution and request fulfilment directly, it is also the single point of contact for the rest of IT. It provides a straightforward interface and ensures that more complex incidents and requests are allocated to the appropriately skilled people.

Technical Management   This refers to the various groups, departments, or teams that provide technical expertise and overall management of the IT infrastructure for an organization. Technical management provides detailed technical skills and the resources needed to support the ongoing operation of the IT infrastructure and plays an important role in the design, testing, release, and improvement of IT services.

Operations Management   Operations management's role is to execute the ongoing activities and procedures required to manage and maintain the IT infrastructure, thus delivering and supporting IT services at the agreed levels. It has two subfunctions. The first is *IT operations control*, which is usually staffed by shifts of operators who carry out routine operational tasks and centralized monitoring and control activities, usually using an operations bridge or network operations center. The other subfunction is *facilities management*. It refers to the management of the physical IT environment, usually data centers or computer rooms. In many organizations, technical and application management are colocated with IT operations in large data centers.

Application Management   The final function is application management, which is responsible for managing applications throughout their lifecycle. The application management function may be performed by any department, group, or team involved in managing and supporting operational applications. Application management should also play a significant role in the design, testing, and improvement of applications that form part of IT services. It makes recommendations about whether it is best to source applications from third parties or to develop them internally. Finally, it focuses on the ongoing management and maintenance of applications that takes place once applications have been deployed.

Summary

This chapter covered the purpose, objectives, and scope of service operation and how this lifecycle stage delivers value to the organization. We looked at service operation within the context of the service lifecycle and considered the fundamentals of service operation, including its processes and functions. We covered which processes from other lifecycle stages require service operation action. In the following chapters, we will be examining the service operation processes of incident management, problem management, access management, request fulfilment, and event management.

Exam Essentials

Understand that the purpose of the service operation lifecycle phase is to deliver the services that have been designed and transitioned as efficiently as possible. During this stage, faults that were not detected during transition will be identified and resolved, and the delivery of the service will be optimized.

Understand service operation's place in the service lifecycle. Understand the impact each of the other lifecycle stages has on service operation. Know the inputs from these other stages into service operation and the outputs from service operation into the rest of the lifecycle.

Understand the responsibility of service operation to deliver the services in line with the SLAs that have been agreed with the business. The transition stage should have validated the SLA targets through testing and piloting the service; it is the responsibility of service operation to continue to meet the SLA targets during the operational stage of the service lifecycle.

Understand the role played by service operation in ensuring that the services deliver business value. By delivering the services efficiently and within service targets, service operation ensures that the business benefits from the service as planned.

Understand the key functions and processes of service operation. Be able to name and describe the four service operation functions: technical management, application management, IT operations management, and the service desk. Be able to name the five service operation processes: incident management, request fulfilment, access management, problem management, and event management.

Review Questions

You can find the answers to the review questions in the appendix.

1. Service operation includes which of the following activities?

    A. Testing the service

    B. Rolling out the service

    C. Deciding whether to retire the service

    D. Optimizing the service

2. Many processes from other lifecycle stages also take place during the operation stage. Which of the following processes does not have an operational element to it?

    A. IT service continuity management

    B. Availability management

    C. Design coordination

    D. Service level management

3. One stage of the service lifecycle is commonly termed CSI. What does the abbreviation *CSI* stand for?

    A. Coordination of service improvements

    B. Continuous service improvement

    C. Centralized service improvement

    D. Continual service improvement

4. Which of the following is the correct list of functions described in ITIL?

    A. Technical management, facilities control, service desk

    B. Technical management, operations management function, service desk

    C. Infrastructure management, desktop support, application management, service desk

    D. Infrastructure management, service desk, application development

5. Which of the following statements is FALSE?

    A. Financial management is the responsibility of service strategy.

    B. Service operation does not need to be concerned with the financial aspects of the services it provides.

    C. Design must be carried out within the financial constraints set by service strategy.

    D. CSI will attempt to find ways of providing the same services, at the same level, at a reduced cost.

6. Match the activities to the following functions.

    1. Activity: Console management

    2. Activity: Identifying functional and manageability requirements for application software

    3. Activity: Providing a single point of contact

4. Activity: Designing and managing the infrastructure

    a.   Function: Service desk

    b.   Function: Technical management

    c.   Function: Application management

    d.   Function: Operations management

        A.   1d, 2a, 3c, 4b

        B.   1d, 2c, 3a, 4b

        C.   1a, 2b, 3c, 4d

        D.   1b, 2c, 3d, 4a

7. What are the two processes carried out by the service desk?

    1.   Incident management

    2.   Design coordination

    3.   Request fulfilment

    4.   Change management

        A.   1 and 3

        B.   2 and 4

        C.   All of the above

        D.   3 and 4

8. Which of the following is NOT a stage in the service lifecycle?

    A.   Continual service improvement

    B.   Service design

    C.   Service optimization

    D.   Service strategy

9. The service operation stage is concerned with which of the following?

    1.   The services being delivered

    2.   The service management processes

    3.   The technology used to deliver the services

    4.   The people involved in delivering the services

        A.   1 and 3

        B.   2 and 4

        C.   All of the above

        D.   3 and 4

10. Which of the following processes are NOT service operation processes?

1. Event management

2. Risk management

3. Request fulfilment

4. Strategy management for IT services

    A. 1 and 3

    B. 2 and 4

    C. All of the above

    D. 3 and 4

Chapter 33

Service Operation Principles

THE FOLLOWING ITIL INTERMEDIATE EXAM OBJECTIVES ARE DISCUSSED IN THIS CHAPTER:

✓ **The knowledge, interpretation, and analysis of service operation principles**

- All aspects related to operations are covered, including achieving balance in service operations, providing good service, involvement in other lifecycle stages, and operational health.

✓ **The concepts of how to achieve balance in service operation**

✓ **The challenges of providing service**

✓ **The involvement of service operation in the rest of the lifecycle**

✓ **The assessment of the operational health of the department**

✓ **The communication, documentation, and inputs and outputs required for service operation**

To meet the learning outcomes and examination level of difficulty, you must ensure that you are able to understand and describe the various concepts described in this chapter. We explore the service operation principles and the lifecycle inputs.

Service Operation Principles

In this chapter, we are going to explore the basic guiding principles of service operation. The challenges in service operation can vary from month to month, and often from day-to-day. It is the responsibility of service operation to deliver the agreed level of service, but the environment in which it does this is forever changing. New demands, financial restrictions, and new business priorities combine to force adaptations to how the service is delivered. Responding to these challenges, without risking the existing service delivery, is a key concern of service operation's management.

Achieving Balance in Service Operation

Services are viewed differently by the providers of the service (the internal view) and those who use them (the external view). Users neither understand nor care about the details of what technology is used to deliver or manage the services. All they care about is the service meeting their requirements (utility and warranty).

It is the responsibility of IT operations to care about the way the IT components and systems are managed to deliver the services. It is also important for service operations to understand why and when a service is valued by the customer. Due to the increasing complexity of IT, this often leads to multiple teams managing their own areas of the total solution. They concentrate on achieving good performance and availability of "their" systems. This approach is commonly represented by teams specializing in specific technologies, such as the network support team or a specific application support team. We need to support an approach that allows for a balance between the external and internal focus (Figure 33.1).

Both the external and internal views are valid, relevant, and necessary. It is important to achieve a balance between the two because an organization that focuses on one extreme or the other will not achieve value. Too far to the right and often promises are made that can't be met; too far to the left and expensive technical solutions are delivered, which results in little value for the customer.

FIGURE 33.1   Achieving a balance between external and internal focus

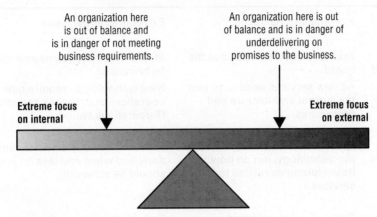

In Table 33.1, you will see examples of extreme internal and external focus.

TABLE 33.1   Examples of extreme internal and external focus

	Extreme internal focus	Extreme external focus
Primary focus	Performance and management of IT infrastructure devices, systems, and staff, with little regard to the end result on the IT service.	Achieving a high level of IT service performance with little regard to how it is achieved.
Metrics	Focus on technical performance without showing what this means for services.	Focus on external metrics without showing internal staff how these are derived or how they can be improved.
	Internal metrics (e.g., network uptime) reported to the business instead of service performance metrics.	Internal staff are expected to devise their own metrics to measure internal performance.
Customer/ user experience	High consistency of delivery, but only delivers a portion of what the business needs.	Poor consistency of delivery.
		"IT consists of good people with good intentions but cannot always execute."
	Prefers to have a standard set of services for all business units.	Reactive mode of operation.
		Prefers to deliver customized services upon request.

TABLE 33.1   Examples of extreme internal and external focus *(continued)*

	Extreme internal focus	Extreme external focus
Operations strategy and design	Standard operations across the board. All new services need to fit into the current architecture and procedures.	Multiple delivery teams and multiple technologies. New technologies require new operations approaches and often new IT operations teams.
Procedures and manuals	Focus purely on how to manage the technology, not on how its performance relates to IT services.	Focuses primarily on what needs to be done and when and less on how this should be achieved.
Cost strategy	Cost reduction achieved purely through technology consolidation. Optimization of operational procedures and resources. Business impact of cost cutting often only understood later. ROI calculations are focused purely on cost savings or "payback periods."	Budget allocated on the basis of which business unit is perceived to have the most need. Less articulate or vocal business units often have inferior services because there is not enough funding allocated to their services.
Training	Training is conducted as an apprenticeship, where new operations staff have to learn the way things have to be done, not why.	Training is conducted on a project-by-project basis. There are no standard training courses because operational procedures and technology are constantly changing.
Operations staff	Specialized staff, organized according to technical specialty. Staff work on the false assumption that good technical achievement is the same as good customer service.	Generalist staff, organized partly according to technical capability and partly according to their relationship with a business unit. Reliance on "heroics," where staff go out of their way to resolve problems that could have been prevented by better internal processes.

It is a very common occurrence that operational departments have to respond to sudden requirements for changes, sometimes under extreme pressure. In Figure 33.2, you can see the balance between stability and responsiveness.

FIGURE 33.2   Achieving a balance between focus on stability and responsiveness

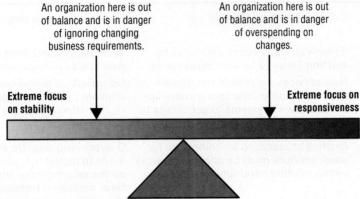

An organization here is out of balance and is in danger of ignoring changing business requirements.

An organization here is out of balance and is in danger of overspending on changes.

Extreme focus on stability

Extreme focus on responsiveness

An area of the business may suddenly require additional IT services, more capacity, and faster response times, perhaps due to winning new business. Service operation must be able to respond to this type of change without impacting other services. This is a continual balance for most IT departments because being responsive will often make services unstable, but not responding is perceived as being a block by the business. Many IT organizations are unable to achieve this balance and focus on either the stability of the IT infrastructure or the ability to respond to changes quickly.

In Table 33.2, you will see some examples of the extremes of focus.

TABLE 33.2   Examples of extreme focus on stability and responsiveness

	Extreme focus on stability	Extreme focus on responsiveness
Primary focus	Technology. Developing and refining standard IT management techniques and processes.	Output to the business. Agrees to required changes before determining what it will take to deliver them.
Typical problems experienced	IT can demonstrate that it is complying with SOPs and operational level agreements (OLAs), even when there is clear misalignment to business requirements.	IT staff are not available to define or execute routine tasks because they are busy on projects for new services.

TABLE 33.2 Examples of extreme focus on stability and responsiveness *(continued)*

	Extreme focus on stability	Extreme focus on responsiveness
Technology growth strategy	Growth strategy based on analyzing existing demand on existing systems. New services are resisted and business units sometimes take ownership of "their own" systems to get access to new services.	Technology purchased for each new business requirement. Using multiple technologies and solutions for similar solutions, to meet slightly different business needs.
Technology used to deliver IT services	Existing or standard technology to be used; services must be adjusted to work within existing parameters.	Overprovisioning. No attempt is made to model the new service on the existing infrastructure. New, dedicated technology is purchased for each new project.
Capacity management	Forecasts based on projections of current workloads. System performance is maintained at consistent levels through tuning and demand management, not by workload forecasting and management.	Forecasts based on future business activity for each service individually and do not take into account IT activity or other IT services. Existing workloads not relevant.

Another guiding principle for IT departments is balancing cost and quality, which is a common concern for organizations. What are the consequences of being too far one way or the other? In Figure 33.3, you can see the balance between cost and quality.

FIGURE 33.3 Achieving a balance between focus on cost and quality

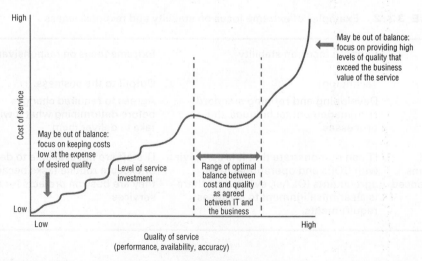

Different services will require a different balance. For example, the business may wish to prioritize high availability on a mission-critical service over that of an administrative tool. Service operation has to understand what is the correct balance for each service. Achieving the correct balance is important. Overemphasizing quality results in IT services that overdeliver at a higher cost and may lead to pressure to reduce the price of services. Overemphasizing cost may mean that although IT delivers on or under budget, they are risking the business through substandard IT services. In Table 33.3, you can see some examples of extreme focus on quality and cost.

TABLE 33.3   Examples of extreme focus on quality and cost

	Extreme focus on quality	Extreme focus on cost
Primary focus	Delivering the level of quality demanded by the business regardless of what it takes.	Meeting budget and reducing costs.
Typical problems experienced	Escalating budgets. IT services generally deliver more than is necessary for business success. Escalating demands for higher-quality services. Use of more support resources and other service assets than necessary to fulfil service demands.	IT limits the quality of service based on its budget availability. Escalations from the business to get more service from IT.
Financial management	IT usually does not have a method of communicating the cost of IT services. Accounting methods are based on an aggregated method (e.g., cost of IT per user).	Financial reporting is done purely on budgeted amounts. There is no way of linking activities in IT to the delivery of IT services.

Figure 33.4 shows delivering to an optimal level while balancing cost and quality.

Early improvements in quality may be achieved at relatively low cost, or savings may be made that do not affect quality. Once these have been made, however, further quality increases or cost savings get increasingly difficult to achieve—improved quality becomes very expensive, or savings have a big impact on quality. Consider the costs involved in improving availability from 90 percent to 95 percent as opposed to improving it from 95 percent to 99 percent, or think about the effect of cutting costs by reducing staff below a critical level. It must be a business decision to take on the cost of improving quality, so engagement with the business is vital. Think of the example of an Internet shop with no high street presence. The cost of high availability might be expensive, but at certain peak times of year, the amount of trade completed online may be worth the expenditure.

FIGURE 33.4   Balancing quality and cost

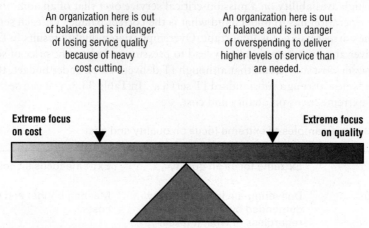

An organization here is out of balance and is in danger of losing service quality because of heavy cost cutting.

An organization here is out of balance and is in danger of overspending to deliver higher levels of service than are needed.

Extreme focus on cost

Extreme focus on quality

A reactive organization does not act unless it is prompted to do so by an external driver, for example, a new business requirement, an application that has been developed, or escalation in complaints made by users and customers. By then it may be too late to deliver the change in the required timescale. In Figure 33.5, you can see the balance between being reactive and being proactive.

FIGURE 33.5   Achieving a balance between being too reactive and too proactive

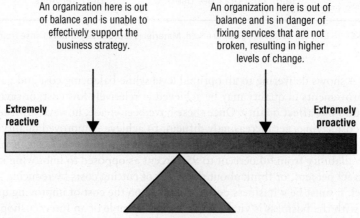

An organization here is out of balance and is unable to effectively support the business strategy.

An organization here is out of balance and is in danger of fixing services that are not broken, resulting in higher levels of change.

Extremely reactive

Extremely proactive

A proactive organization is always looking for ways to improve the current situation. It will continually scan the internal and external environments, looking for signs of potentially impacting changes. This is often shown by monitoring thresholds, identifying the potential risk of failure, and looking for a preventative approach to issues. Proactive behavior is usually seen as positive, but being too proactive can be expensive and can result in staff being distracted.

Table 33.4 shows examples of extremely reactive and proactive behavior.

TABLE 33.4   Examples of extremely reactive and proactive behavior

	Extremely reactive	Extremely proactive
Primary focus	Responds to business needs and incidents only after they are reported.	Anticipates business requirements before they are reported and problems before they occur.
Typical problems experienced	Preparing to deliver new services takes a long time because each project is dealt with as if it is the first. Similar incidents occur again and again because there is no way of trending them. Staff turnover is high and morale is generally low because IT staff keep moving from project to project without achieving a lasting, stable set of IT services.	Money is spent before the requirements are stated. In some cases, IT purchases items that will never be used because they anticipated the wrong requirements or because the project is stopped. IT staff tend to have been in the organization for a long time and tend to assume that they know the business requirements better than the business does.
Capacity planning	Wait until there are capacity problems and then purchase surplus capacity to last until the next capacity-related incident.	Anticipate capacity problems and spend money on preventing them—even when the scenario is unlikely to happen.
IT service continuity planning	No plans exist until after a major event or disaster. IT plans focus on recovering key systems but without ensuring that the business can recover its processes.	Overplanning (and overspending) of IT recovery options. Usually immediate recovery is provided for most IT services, regardless of their impact or priority.
Change management	Changes are often not logged, or they are logged at the last minute as emergency changes. Not enough time for proper impact and cost assessments. Changes are poorly tested and controlled, resulting in a high number of incidents.	Changes are requested and implemented even when there is no real need, i.e., a significant amount of work done to fix items that are not broken.

Providing Good Service

It is important to remember that a user's experience is not solely based on the technical aspects of service provision. Service operation management must consider the service as well. When highly technical staff are impatient with users, the overall service is perceived as poor in the users' eyes. Polite, helpful staff will not fully compensate for a deficient service. Being polite and helpful is essential, but a vacuous "have a nice day" approach that is not backed up with a quality service is of no use either.

Operational Staff Involvement in Other Lifecycle Stages

It can be argued that service operation is the most important stage in the lifecycle, but without the others, operation will struggle to be successful. The lifecycle works best when there is integration between the lifecycle stages.

Operational Involvement in Service Strategy

IT operation staff play an important assistance role in supporting service strategy activities. Assistance activities might include, for example, identifying and communicating current operation capabilities, workforce levels, and operational staff skills to those developing IT strategies along with identifying existing operational risk. It will also include gathering and identifying IT operational costs and the high-level impacts of chosen IT strategies on current operational activities. Service operation should also be involved in identifying operational constraints that may impact IT strategies, such as workforce union restrictions or inadequate physical environment capabilities and the operational risks for IT strategies being considered.

Operational Involvement in Service Design

One key to achieving balance in service operation is an effective set of service design processes. These will provide IT operations management, technical management, application management, and the service desk with a clear definition of IT service objectives and performance criteria. It will enable linkage of IT service specifications to the performance of the IT infrastructure and the definition of operational performance requirements.

Service design will also provide a mapping of services and technology and the ability to model the effect of changes in technology and changes to business requirements. Design will also deliver appropriate cost models (e.g., customer or service based) to evaluate return on investment and cost reduction strategies.

The nature of IT operations management involvement should be carefully positioned. Service design is a stage in the service lifecycle that uses a set of processes, not a function independent of service operation. As such, many of the people involved in service design may come from IT operations management, technical management, and application management.

Service operation involvement in service design activities should be strongly encouraged. This should include providing information and requirements for the operational phase as well as input to the operational acceptance tests and critical success factors from an operational viewpoint for sign-off. Staff should also be measured on their involvement in service design activities, and such activities should be included in job descriptions and roles whenever possible. This will help to ensure continuity between business requirements and technology design and operation, and it will also help to ensure that what is designed can also be operated.

Operational Involvement in Service Transition

IT operations management staff should be involved during service transition to ensure that service delivery is consistent and that both business and manageability requirements are met. Manageability activities might include training to learn how to operate a new service or to explain changes in how an existing service is currently operated.

It is important that service operation participates and reviews the operational acceptance tests and takes part in transition planning to identify the impact of transition activities on current operation activities.

Service operation should be involved in transition tasks such as moving applications and other components from their development environment to the live environment, and it should benefit from and engage with the provision of early life support activities for new services or major changes that have been released to the live environment.

Service operation should also take active participation in quality assurance activities such as validating operational readiness of a new service or a major change to the live environment.

Operational Involvement in Continual Service Improvement

Service operation staff should be involved in supporting CSI activities and identifying improvement opportunities for inclusion in the CSI register. There will be many instances where service operation provides support and information to CSI, such as ensuring that operational data is made available to personnel involved in CSI activities. Service operation staff will also be involved in validating accuracy of operational data used to identify improvement opportunities.

Service operation should take part in assessing the impact of proposed improvement actions on existing operation activities. The operational teams will be responsible for executing operational tasks to support service monitoring, measurement, and reporting activities. It is important that operational staff identify and promote operational issues and concerns to CSI staff and that they identify and propose improvements that can enhance the performance and quality of the IT services being delivered.

Operational Health

Using the concept of operational health is a useful way to understand how we can monitor the overall performance of a service by choosing the key elements and monitoring those. Deciding what to measure should be part of service design. Rather than pulse, blood pressure, and heart rate, we measure bandwidth, disk utilization, and memory.

Full checks are required to deal with potential issues, especially in conjunction with proactive problem, capacity, availability, and IT service continuity management.

Operational health is dependent on the ability to prevent incidents and problems by investing in reliable infrastructure and through good availability design and proactive problem management.

Operational health is also identifying faults and localizing them so they have minimal impact on the service, which may also involve self-healing systems.

Self-healing systems include a number of different features, and their cost will depend on the capability and features they provide. This may make them prohibitive for smaller organizations, but the value of their capability should be judged according to their value, not simply their cost.

Self-healing often includes resilience designed and built into the system, for example, multiple redundant disks or multiple processors. This protects the system against hardware failure because it is able to continue operating using the duplicated hardware component. Software, data, and operating system resilience is also designed into the system. Mirrored databases (where databases are duplicated) and disk-striping technology (where optimization of space is carried out automatically) are often used for this purpose.

The ability to shift processing from one physical device to another without any disruption to the service is another approach used by self-healing systems. This could be a response to a failure or because the device is reaching high utilization levels (some systems are designed to distribute processing workloads continuously, which is known as virtualization).

Built-in monitoring utilities enable the system to detect events and to determine whether they represent normal operations or not. A correlation engine (which allows consolidation of monitoring system output) will enable the system to determine the significance of each event and also to determine whether there is any predefined response to it.

A set of diagnostic tools, such as diagnostic scripts, fault trees, and a database of known errors and common workarounds, can be used to support the systems in use. These are used as soon as an error is detected to determine the appropriate response, which may include the ability to generate a call for human intervention by raising an alert or generating an incident.

Communication

Much of the success of service operation depends on successful communication. Everyone complains about information overload and that "no one tells us anything." It is important to ensure that there is suitable and sufficient communication between the various operational teams and between the teams and other units and departments. This should include communication both within and outside of the IT department.

We need to be aware of the danger of reporting for reporting's sake, however, and question the nature and purpose of all our communications. Many organizations waste considerable time and resources producing reports with no clear purpose. It's important to consider what is appropriate and what is overkill. We need to discuss with the recipients what they actually need and the format and frequency of communication.

Some communication concerns regular business-as-usual updates. Other communications may be urgent notifications or updates that may need immediate action. The difference between these should be clear—there is a danger otherwise that urgent communications may be lost in a myriad of routine updates!

The communication of strategy and design to the service operation teams is essential if they are to understand what is required from them in operation. Similarly, new or changed processes must be clearly communicated to affected parties if they are to be followed.

It is important to understand the nature and type of communications that are required, so let's look at some examples.

Meetings

Some organizations suffer from "meeting paralysis"—constantly attending meetings uses up time and resources and prevents real progress. As with reporting, the necessity for a meeting should be considered, and the format, duration, frequency, and attendees should be scrutinized to ensure that the meeting is fulfilling its purpose.

For example, daily or weekly operations meetings are a common method of sharing information between support teams. Departmental, group, or team meetings for a wider audience and customer meetings tailored for the nontechnical consumer audience are also typical.

Training is another important part of communication; the education and awareness of teams, customers, and users are vital for the success of system usage.

Documentation

The presence of relevant, complete, and up-to-date documentation is essential for successful service operation, ensuring consistency in the implementation of processes and a common understanding of requirements.

Having the correct level of documentation is an ongoing challenge for service operation teams. Too much and it is an unmanageable overhead; too little and it does not fulfil its purpose. Out-of-date documentation is arguably worse than no documentation at all!

Process documentation must include not only service operation processes, but other life-cycle processes where there is service operation involvement. It is essential to allocate the necessary time and resources to creating and maintaining documentation.

Designating key documentation as configuration items and using change management to make sure documents affected by a change are identified and updated ensures that documentation remains up-to-date. It also ensures that version control is maintained.

Consider the many different documents that are required in service operation, from technical manuals to plans and processes. Service operation staff should be involved across the lifecycle in the preparation of any documentation that has an impact on or engagement with service operation.

Service Operation Inputs and Outputs

There are other processes that will be executed or supported during service operation but are driven during other stages of the service lifecycle.

Service Strategy

An example of a service strategy process that is executed during the service operation stage is the financial management for IT services process.

Other inputs from service strategy include the strategic vision, mission, and plans. Operation will in turn provide risks and cost information to support strategic decision-making.

Service Design

Examples of the design processes that interface to service operation include capacity and availability management; these processes also rely on operational data for forecasting, planning, and monitoring. Other process interfaces include service catalog management, which identifies the live IT services that are to be delivered, and IT service continuity, which assures the recovery of live services.

Service level management drives the targets that operation needs to manage and support the required service performance. Information security management is also key when you consider the process interfaces between service operation and service design as well as guidance and policy for security incidents and access management.

The inputs and outputs to and from service operation and service design are shown in table 33.5. They include items such as service level agreements (SLAs), operational level agreements (OLAs), service design packages, and details of the required utility and warranty. Service operation provides inputs into service performance measures for availability and capacity, among others.

Service Transition

Service transition processes have close connections with service operation. For example, change management is a major process that should be closely linked to service asset and configuration management and release and deployment management. Service operation is also reliant on knowledge management, so there are close relationships between these two lifecycle stages.

Transition provides new or changed services, known errors, and change information into the operation stage. Service operation provides feedback on the success and quality of transitions as well as involvement in operational testing.

Continual Service Improvement

Continual service improvement has a close relationship with all the lifecycle stages, but service operation is where the improvement is most obviously seen, through service reporting and measurement.

The lifecycle stages of CSI and service operation provide inputs and outputs to each other. This includes the exchange of information about the results of customer satisfaction and service reports and data used to develop these reports.

Table 33.5 summarizes the service operation inputs and outputs.

TABLE 33.5   Service operation inputs and outputs by lifecycle stage

Lifecycle stage	Service operation inputs (from the lifecycle stages in the first column)	Service operation outputs (to the lifecycle stages in the first column)
Service strategy	Vision and mission	
	Service portfolio	Operating risks
	Policies	Operating cost information for total cost of ownership (TCO) calculations
	Strategies and strategic plans	
	Priorities	Actual performance data
	Financial information and budgets	
	Demand forecasts and strategies	
	Strategic risks	
Service design	Service catalogue	Operational requirements
	Service design packages, including:	Actual performance data
	Details of utility and warranty	RFCs to resolve operational issues
	Operations plans and procedures	
	Recovery procedures	Historical incident and problem records
	Knowledge and information in the SKMS	
	Vital business functions	
	Hardware and software maintenance requirements	
	Designs for service operation processes and procedures	
	SLAs, OLAs, and underpinning contracts	
	Security policies	

TABLE 33.5 Service operation inputs and outputs by lifecycle stage *(continued)*

Service transition	New or changed services	RFCs to resolve operational issues
	Known errors	
	Standard changes for use in request fulfilment	Feedback on quality of transition activities
	Knowledge and information in the SKMS (including the configuration management system)	Input to operational testing
		Actual performance information
		Input to change evaluation and change advisory board meetings
	Change schedule	
Continual service improvement	Results of customer and user satisfaction surveys	Operational performance data and service records
	Service reports and dashboards	Proposed problem resolutions and proactive measures
	Data required for metrics, key performance indicators (KPIs) and critical success factors (CSFs)	Knowledge and information in the SKMS
	RFCs for implementing improvements	Achievements against metrics, KPIs, and CSFs
		Improvement opportunities logged in the continual service improvement register

Summary

This chapter covered the interpretation and analysis of service operation principles. All aspects related to operations were covered, including achieving balance in service operations, providing good service, service operation's involvement in other lifecycle stages, and operational health.

We explored how to achieve balance in service operation and the challenges of providing service. We looked at the involvement of service operation in the rest of the lifecycle.

We considered the assessment of the operational health of the IT department and the communication, documentation, and inputs and outputs required for service operation.

Exam Essentials

Understand the concept of achieving balance in service operation.   Review the balance between cost and quality, internal and external focus, stability and responsiveness, and being reactive and being proactive for service operations.

Be able to explain and expand on the concept of providing good service.   Good service should be adopted to suit the business requirements of the organization.

Review and understand the involvement of service operation in other lifecycle stages.   Review the engagement in service strategy, service design, service transition, and continual service improvement.

Understand and expand on the concepts of operational health, communication, documentation, and service operation inputs and outputs.   These are all key factors in the delivery of service, assessing the state of the service, and being able to communicate this to the business. It is important to be able to expand on the inputs and outputs of the service operation stage.

Review Questions

You can find the answers to the review questions in the appendix.

1. True or False? The concept of good service is based solely on technical considerations because the equipment and the technology are the most important factors for the user.

   A. True

   B. False

2. The guidance contained in the *ITIL Service Operation* publication discusses the need to achieve balance. Which of the following is NOT one of the areas mentioned where balance must be achieved?

   A. Balance between internal and external focus

   B. Financial management and delivery against service requirements

   C. Providing good-quality knowledge and information about services and service assets

   D. Reactive and proactive approaches to support

3. Which of these is a way in which service operation interacts with the service strategy lifecycle stage?

   A. Service operation drives the choices of service strategy because it is necessary to make sure the service desk is the center of the strategic approach.

   B. Service operation contributes to service strategy by providing information about the operational constraints that may influence or affect strategy.

   C. Service operation has no input to service strategy because the strategy drives the lifecycle and has no requirement for input from other lifecycle stages.

   D. Service operation is the only input to service strategy because the technical operational requirements must override all other considerations.

4. Which of these statements is/are correct?

   1. The business does not care about how efficient the service is as long as it works.

   2. How we deliver the service can matter as much as *what* we deliver.

      A. Statement 1 only

      B. Statement 2 only

      C. Both statements

      D. Neither statement

5. Which of these statements describes a reactive organization?

   1. Primary focus – Responds to business needs and incidents only after they are reported.

   2. Primary focus – Anticipates business requirements before they are reported and problems before they occur.

      A. Statement 1 only

      B. Statement 2 only

    C. Both statements

    D. Neither statement

6. The ITIL framework talks about operational health. To what does this refer?

    A. The contribution of staff sickness to outages

    B. The availability of the network

    C. The management of the staff schedules

    D. The overall performance of a service

7. If an organization is primarily concerned with meeting budgets and reducing costs, it is considered to be _____ .

    1. extremely cost focused

    2. extremely quality focused

        A. Statement 1 only

        B. Statement 2 only

        C. Both statements

        D. Neither statement

8. Which of these statements is/are correct?

    1. Communication between internal and external providers is not necessary because it is covered by regular contractual meetings.

    2. Communication between IT and the business is not required because it is covered by regular service review meetings.

        A. Statement 1 only

        B. Statement 2 only

        C. Both statements

        D. Neither statement

9. Which of these processes is most involved with the proactive management of operational services?

    A. Incident management

    B. Request fulfilment

    C. Problem management

    D. Access management

10. True or False? Service operation has inputs and outputs from all the other service lifecycle stages.

    A. True

    B. False

Chapter

34

Service Operation Processes: Incident and Problem Management

THE FOLLOWING ITIL INTERMEDIATE EXAM OBJECTIVES ARE DISCUSSED IN THIS CHAPTER:

✓ Incident management and problem management are discussed in terms of

- Purpose
- Objectives
- Scope
- Value
- Policies
- Principles and basic concepts
- Process activities, methods, and techniques
- Triggers, inputs, outputs, and interfaces
- Critical success factors and key performance indicators
- Challenges
- Risks

Service Operation
Processes:
and Proble

The syllabus for the intermediate service operation exam covers the managerial and supervisory aspects of service operation processes. It excludes the information management aspects of the processes and the day-to-day operation of each process, including details of the process activities, methods, and techniques. More detailed process operation guidance is covered in the service capability courses. Each process is considered from the management perspective. That means at the end of the chapters covering the service operation processes (Chapters 34–37), you should understand the aspects that would be required to understand each process and its interfaces, oversee its implementation, and judge its effectiveness and efficiency.

Incidents and Problems: Two Key Service Management Concepts

The two processes of *incident* management and *problem* management are among the most important of all the ITIL processes. They are often the first to be implemented by an organization that has decided to adopt the ITIL framework. The differentiation between incident management and problem management is important, and an organization that has adopted both of these processes has made a major advance toward improving its services and its service management.

Both these processes are carried out by every IT service provider, whether they are called by these names or not. All service providers fix faults as quickly as possible when they occur (incident management) and try to ascertain why the fault occurred so that it can be prevented from happening again (problem management). Many organizations do not differentiate between the two processes, however, and problem management in particular may not be carried out in a consistent fashion. A failure to appreciate the difference between problems and incidents may result in delayed service restoration following an incident and in allowing incidents to recur, causing business disruption each time.

ITIL provides guidance for the best approach to these two key processes. Effective incident management will improve *availability*, ensuring that users are able to get back to work quickly following a failure. Problem management will improve the overall quality and availability of services by reducing recurring incidents and preventing incidents from happening in the first place (and as such, works in conjunction with continual service improvement);

it also makes best use of skilled IT staff, who are freed from resolving repeat incidents and are able to spend time preventing them instead.

Incident Management

In ITIL terminology, an *incident* is defined as an unplanned interruption to an IT service, a reduction in the quality of an IT service, or a failure of a configuration item (CI) that has not yet impacted an IT service (for example, failure of one disk from a mirror set). We can easily think of examples of unplanned interruptions to an IT service: server crash, hardware failure, and so on. A good example of a reduction in the quality of the IT service is when a service is running so slowly that it is impacting the organization's ability to achieve its objectives. An example of a failure that has yet to impact the IT service could be the failure of a disk in a storage device with a RAIDed configuration. This is treated as an incident even though the storage device is still usable. The point is that the failure of one disk means that the storage is no longer protected from the failure of another disk. If another disk fails, the device will fail, and the data on it will be inaccessible.

This definition of an incident is important because the incident is an interruption to service and restoring the service or improving the quality of the service to agreed levels resolves the incident. Note that incident resolution does not include understanding why the fault occurred or preventing its *recurrence*; these are matters for problem management. By understanding this distinction, you can see that resolving an incident does not require the skills that resolving a problem requires. If the service can be restored by a simple reboot, then the user can be instructed to do this by the service desk staff, and the service desk staff can use known error workarounds and knowledge base articles to resolve commonly occurring incidents. In both of these examples, it is not necessary to involve the more skilled (and therefore more expensive) second-line technicians. From the user and business perspectives, the focus is on being able to get back to work, and there is little interest in the cause of the failure. Repeat occurrences will impact their work and increase the number of calls to the service desk, so an investigation of the cause, and the permanent resolution of the underlying problem, will be required, but this can take place without impacting the users.

The incident management process is responsible for progressing all incidents from when they are first reported until they are closed. Some organizations may have dedicated incident management staff, but the most common approach is to make the service desk responsible for the process.

Sometimes the resolution of an incident is possible only by understanding the cause and fixing the underlying fault. When a hardware or network failure occurs due to a failed hardware component where there is no resilience, the component will need to be replaced or repaired before service can be restored. In the majority of incidents, however, service can be restored to the individual user without a permanent problem resolution.

The Purpose of Incident Management

The purpose of *incident management* is to restore normal service operation as quickly as possible and minimize the adverse impact on business operations, thus ensuring that agreed levels of service quality are maintained. *Normal service operation* is defined as an operational state where services and CIs are performing within their agreed service and operational levels, that is, as agreed in the SLA.

As explained, by focusing on service restoration, incident management enables the business to return to work quickly, thus ensuring that the impact on business processes and deadlines is reduced.

The Objectives of Incident Management

The objectives of the incident management process are as follows:

- Use standardized methods and models for managing incidents. This means that incidents should be handled in a consistent way regardless of service, technology, or support group. This enables the business and the service provider management to have clear expectations of how any particular incident will be handled. Also, in the case of repeat incidents, the logging and resolution can be proceduralized using incident models, thus ensuring both consistency and rapid restoration of service.

- Increase visibility and communication of incidents. This allows the business to track the progress of the incidents reported and ensures that all IT staff have access to the information relating to an incident.

- Enhance business perception of IT. All IT service providers will suffer incidents, but the way in which they respond can enhance their reputation; a well-designed incident management process should enhance the reputation of IT to the business by demonstrating a professional, effective approach.

- Align activities with business needs by ensuring that incidents are prioritized based on their importance to the business.

- Maintain user satisfaction.

All incidents must be efficiently responded to, analyzed, logged, managed, resolved, and reported. By carrying out these tasks in an efficient and effective manner and by ensuring that affected customers are updated as required, the IT service provider aims to improve customer satisfaction, even though a fault has occurred. At all times during the incident management process, the needs of the business must be considered; business priorities must influence IT priorities.

The Scope of Incident Management

Incident management encompasses all incidents: all events have a real or potential impact on the quality of the service. Incidents will mostly be logged as the result of a user contacting the service desk, but event management tools may report an incident following an alert (see the discussion of event management in Chapter 36, "Service Operation Processes: Event Management"); often there will be a link between the event system and incident management tool so that events meeting certain criteria can automatically generate an incident log. Third-party suppliers may notify the service desk of a failure, or technical staff may notice that an error condition has arisen and log an incident.

As discussed, not all events are incidents; many are informational or a confirmation that a component is functioning correctly.

Requests may be logged and managed at the service desk, but it is important to differentiate between these requests and incidents; in the case of requests, no service has been impacted. Problem management seeks to reduce the number of incidents over time, whereas the IT service provider may want to handle increasing numbers of requests through the service desk and the request fulfillment process as a quick, efficient, and customer-focused method of dealing with them.

The Value of Incident Management to the Business

Efficient incident management delivers several benefits to the business. It reduces the cost of incident resolution by resolving incidents quickly, using less-skilled staff. Where incidents need to be escalated, the resolution is faster (because the relevant information required will have been gathered and an initial diagnosis will have been made). Faster incident resolution means a faster return to work for the affected users, who are once again able to exploit the functionality of the service to deliver business benefits. Effective incident management improves the overall efficiency of the organization because nonproductive users are a cost to the company.

Incident *prioritization* is based on business priorities, which ensures that resources are allocated to maximize the business benefit. The data gathered by the service desk about the numbers and types of incidents can be analyzed to identify training requirements or potential areas for improvement.

As highlighted in the discussion of the service desk in Chapter 39, "Organizing for Service Operation," incident management is one of the most visible processes as well as one that all users understand the need for. It is therefore one of the easier areas to improve because an improved incident resolution service has easily understood benefits for the business.

Incident Management Policies

Next we consider some of the policies that support effective incident management.

Policy: Incidents and their status must be communicated in a timely and effective way. Users must be kept informed of the progress of incidents that affect them, and the information they are given must make sense to them—most users don't understand technical jargon, so it should not be used. This policy shows that incident management is not solely about resolving the incident. The business needs information about the status of open incidents so that it can make decisions about what to do to minimize the business impact. This is one of the key responsibilities of the service desk.

Policy: Incidents must be resolved in timescales that are acceptable to the business.   We should remember that IT is the servant of the business. Service level management will determine what timescales are acceptable and must ensure that the necessary *operational level agreements* and *underpinning contracts (UCs)* are in place to support them. To achieve the resolution within the required timescales requires the allocation of sufficient and appropriate resources to work on the incident, with access to the necessary technology and tools such as the *known error* database and configuration information.

Policy: Customer satisfaction must be maintained at all times.   Customer satisfaction is not only about meeting *SLA* targets. Users and customers will be dissatisfied if support staff are rude or patronizing, even if IT meets or exceeds all of its incident-related targets.

Policy: Incident processing and handling should be aligned with overall service levels and objectives.   Incidents should not be handled to suit the convenience or priorities of IT; incident management activities should support service levels and objectives by prioritizing those activities based on actual business need.

Policy: All incidents should be stored and managed in a single management system.   Using a single system provides a definitive recognized source for incident information and supports reporting and investigation efforts. Status and detailed information on incidents should be recorded and updated on a timely basis in incident records.

Policy: All incidents should be categorized in a standard way.   Standardized *categorization* enables useful analysis and reporting; it speeds up troubleshooting by making it easier to find other occurrences of a fault within the incident database or the *known error database (KEDB)*. It makes identification of trends easier. For incident management to be effective, there must be a well-defined and communicated set of incident classification categories. The tool can be programmed to discourage the entry of nonstandard categories.

Policy: Incident records should be audited on a regular basis.   The incident database is a rich source of information about what is happening in the infrastructure and about the difficulties being experienced by the business, but its usefulness depends on it being accurate and complete. We have already considered the importance of consistency in data entry; this policy ensures that the guidelines for data entry are being followed by auditing incident records for accuracy and completeness. Any issues discovered should be noted and acted upon.

Policy: All incidents should use a common format.   Staff should record the information that the service provider has deemed to be necessary in a standard format. This helps both the management of a live incident and later reporting and analysis.

Policy: Use a common and agreed-upon set of criteria for prioritizing and escalating.   This ensures that customer needs are handled consistently across all services and components rather than being dependent on the opinion of whoever logs the incident.

Principles and Basic Concepts for Incident Management

ITIL describes a number of principles and basic concepts to keep in mind when implementing the incident management process. They are covered in the following sections.

Timescales

Time is of the essence in incident management because every incident represents some loss or deterioration of service. Every aspect of the process needs to be optimized to produce the fastest end result. Service level agreements, operational level agreements, and underpinning contracts with measurable targets will define how long a support group or third party has to complete each step. When an incident is passed to a support group for investigation, a clock starts ticking—that group has a certain amount of time, defined in the OLA, to complete its work. If the incident is passed to a third party, the timescales set in the underpinning contracts would apply. These OLA and contract *target* timescales support the achievement of the SLA target.

Service management toolsets should be configured to capture how long it takes to log and escalate an incident, how many incidents are resolved within the first few minutes without requiring escalation, and how long support teams take to respond to and to fix incidents. These times should be monitored, and steps should be taken to identify bottlenecks or underperforming teams so that improvement actions can be taken. The tools can be used to automate timescales and escalate an incident as required based on predefined rules. The tools can also use alarms to warn when incidents are nearing a breach of the SLA. Care needs to be taken in organizations that cross time zones to make sure the clock is monitoring the appropriate time zone as well as the targeted time.

Incident Models

Many incidents have happened before and may well happen again. For this reason, many organizations will find it helpful to predefine standard *incident models* and apply them to appropriate incidents when they occur. A model is a predefined way of carrying out a commonly required task. ITIL recommends models for a number of processes, such as incident, request, and change processes. An incident model describes the steps needed to investigate and resolve a particular type of incident. The benefit of these models is that they speed up the resolution of recurring incidents as well as ensure consistency in handling them. Most service management tools have the capability to store multiple models; when one of these incidents occurs, it is logged using the appropriate prestored model. The incident can then be handled using the model. The tool can also automate many of the model steps, such as automatic assignment to the correct support group, escalations, and so on.

Incidents that would require specialized handling can be treated in this way (for example, security-related incidents can be routed to information security management, and capacity- or performance-related incidents would be routed to capacity management). Using incident models will help ensure consistency of approach and will speed up resolution.

A typical incident model should include the following contents:

- The steps required to handle the incident, including the timescales, chronological order, and any dependencies they might have

- Details of who is responsible for each step, and the escalation contacts

- Precautions to be taken, such as backing up data, or steps required to comply with health- and safety-related guidelines, such as isolating equipment from the power supply

- In the case of security- and capacity-related incidents, any steps to be taken to preserve evidence

Major Incidents

All incidents should get resolved as quickly as possible, but some incidents are so serious, with such an impact on the business, that they require extra attention. The first step is to agree on exactly what is a *major incident*. Some organizations will define all priority one incidents as major; others may restrict priority one incidents to those whose impact will be felt by the external customers. In this definition, an incident with a major impact within the organization would not normally be classed as major. An incident that (for example) prevents customers from ordering goods from the organization's website and that is therefore affecting both revenue and reputation would be included. The definition must align with the priority scheme to avoid confusion.

The purpose of defining an incident as a major incident is so that it can receive special focus. Specific actions to be undertaken are defined in advance so that when the major incident occurs, everyone knows what they are expected to do. The following typical actions might be defined:

- Notification of key contacts within the service provider organization and the business as soon as the major incident is declared.

- Regular updates posted through agreed channels. This would include who should be updated (which could be all users and IT or business management contacts) and the content and frequency of the updates. The agreed channels might include, for example, an intranet announcement, email, and telephone calls.

- Recorded greeting on the service desk phones to inform callers that the incident has occurred and is being dealt with to reduce the number of calls being handled by the desk.

- Appointment of a major incident manager (this may be the service desk manager) and a separate team to focus on resolving the incident.

NOTE   While the service desk manager is managing the incident, another manager can be appointed to head up the team; they would then report progress to the incident manager. This is necessary to avoid a situation in which the two roles, that of managing the situation and keeping stakeholders informed and that of pursuing a solution, are in conflict.

As with any incident, some major incidents can be resolved without understanding the cause (perhaps by restarting a server); some require the underlying cause to be understood. In the second case, problem management would become involved. It is essential, however, that the focus of incident management remains on restoring service as quickly as possible.

As we discuss in Chapter 39, a major responsibility of the service desk is communicating with the users; this is particularly true in the case of major incidents. Regular updates should be provided. The service desk staff members are also accountable for ensuring that the incident record is kept up-to-date throughout the incident, although it may be the technicians in other teams who actually enter the information. An accurate record is essential during an incident so that there is no confusion; it will also be used after the incident is resolved as part of the major incident review. Regular updates showing the steps taken and whether they were successful will allow improvements to be identified for future events.

Incident Status

Incident management tracks incidents through their lifecycle, using status codes and moving from when the incident is identified through diagnosis and resolution and finally closure. Incident management will remind resolving groups of the associated target times, making sure no incident is forgotten or ignored.

Most service management toolsets will allow a number of statuses to be defined for each incident to facilitate progress tracking. The following statuses are typical:

Open   The incident has been identified and logged. A service desk analyst may be working on it, or the service desk may be considering which second-line team it should be escalated to. Incidents resolved by the first-line team may move directly from Open to Closed because the service desk analyst obtains the user confirmation that the incident has been satisfactorily resolved.

Assigned   This may mean the incident has been sent to a support team but not allocated to a particular individual.

Allocated or In Progress   This is usually defined as when a support technician has been allocated the call.

On Hold   This status is sometimes used when the user is not available or doesn't have the time to test the resolution. It is used to "stop the target clock," because the service provider cannot do anything further to resolve the incident without the user.

On Hold status should be used with caution; support staff may be tempted to use it when they are too busy to work on the incident or when they are awaiting the actions of a third-party supplier. This is not its purpose, and using it in this way distorts reporting against OLAs and UCs because the failure to provide the support and meet the target is hidden by the fact that the clock is stopped.

Resolved   This status indicates that the technician has completed their work but it has not been confirmed by the customer that it was successful. It is common to use the service management's automated email facility to automatically email the user when an incident is resolved, asking for a response within a certain timescale if the user is still not happy. If no reply is received, the incident is automatically closed.

- If the user is unhappy, the call is put back into In Progress, and further work is carried out to resolve it.

- The service desk should attempt to contact users to obtain permission to close calls before the automated closure, especially for high-impact incidents where the user may not be aware of the resolution.

Closed   This status confirms that the incident is over to the user's satisfaction. The incident management process has no further involvement, although problem management may now investigate the underlying cause.

Expanded Incident Lifecycle

The expanded incident lifecycle is used by the service design availability management process and within CSI. It breaks down and examines each step of the process to understand the reasons for the failed targets. For example, the diagnosis of the incident may ascertain very quickly that the resolution requires the restoration of data, which takes three hours; this information would be used to pinpoint where improvements should be made. Delays in any step of the lifecycle can be analyzed, and improvements can be implemented to speed up resolution; implementing a knowledge base or storing spare parts on site are two typical measures that are taken to shorten the diagnosis and repair steps.

Incident Management Process Activities, Methods, and Techniques

In the following sections, we'll take a high-level look at each of the activities in incident management. Figure 34.1 shows a diagram of the process flow.

Step 1: Incident Identification and Logging

First, the incident is identified and then logged. Many incidents will be reported to the service desk, which will log them. But not all calls to the service desk are related to incidents; some will be service requests, which are handled by the request fulfilment process. As Figure 34.1 shows, these are rerouted.

It is essential that incidents are resolved in the shortest possible time because each represents business disruption. Whenever possible, therefore, we should be trying to realize that an incident has occurred before the user notices or, failing that, before they have reported it to the service desk. Chapter 36 shows how monitoring tools can be used to identify failures. The event management process should link directly to incident management so that any incidents spotted are worked on immediately and resolved quickly. Where event management is not in place, incidents will be identified by users contacting the service desk.

FIGURE 34.1   Incident management process flow

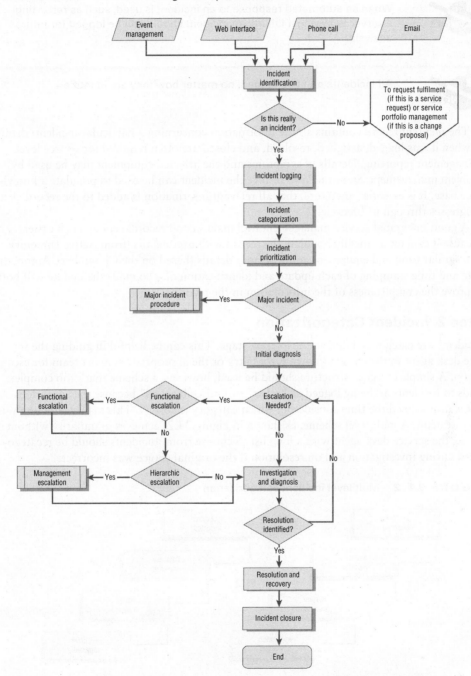

When an automated response to an incident is used, such as restarting a server following a failure, an incident should still be logged for future analysis.

All incidents must be logged, no matter how they are identified.

The *incident record* contains all the information concerning a particular incident; details of when it was logged, assigned, resolved, and closed are often required for service level management reporting. Details of symptoms and the affected equipment may be used by problem management. Steps taken to resolve the incident can be used to populate a knowledge base. It is essential, therefore, that all relevant information is added to the record as it progresses through its lifecycle.

A good integrated service management tool makes good recordkeeping much easier because it can automatically populate the record with user details (from Active Directory or a similar tool) and equipment and warranty details (based on the CI number). Automatic date and time stamping of each update and identification of who made the update will both improve the completeness of the information in the record.

Step 2: Incident Categorization

Incidents are categorized during the logging stage. This can be helpful in guiding the service desk agent to the correct known error entry or the appropriate support team for escalation. A simple category structure should be used, however; a scheme that's too complex leads to incidents all being logged as "other" or "miscellaneous" because the agent does not want to spend the time considering which category is correct. This makes later analysis very difficult. A multilevel scheme, as shown in Figure 34.2, achieves granularity without facing the service desk agent with a long list to choose from. Incidents should be recategorized during investigation and on resolution if the original choice was incorrect.

FIGURE 34.2   Multilevel incident categorization

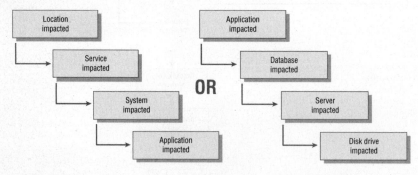

Categorization helps determine if a call is actually a request. This is especially useful when incidents and requests are logged via incident management.

Step 3: Incident Prioritization

Incidents need to be prioritized to ensure that the most critical incidents are dealt with first. It is often said that all users believe that their own incident is the highest priority, so it is important to agree during service level negotiations about what criteria should be used to decide priority. It is also imperative that incidents are prioritized consistently.

The ITIL framework recommends that two factors should be considered: business impact (effect the incident is having or will have on the business) and urgency (how quickly the business needs a resolution). Business impact can be assessed by considering a number of factors: the number of people affected, the criticality of the service, the financial loss being incurred, damage to reputation, and so on. Depending on the type of organization, other factors such as health and safety (for a hospital or a railway company or similar) and potential breach of regulations (financial institutions and so on) might be considered.

During the life of an incident, it may be necessary to adjust the priority of an incident if the assessment of the impact changes or a resolution becomes more urgent.

Deciding the priority must be a simple process because the incident has to be logged quickly. Employing service desk staff with good business knowledge and ensuring that they are trained to be aware of business impact will help to make a realistic assessment of business impact. Table 34.1 shows a simple but very effective way to determine priority.

Table 34.2 shows how the determination of priority made using the matrix in Table 34.1 can in turn be employed to set a target resolution time for the incident.

TABLE 34.1 Impact and urgency: a matrix for determining an incident's priority

Impact	Urgency		
	High	Medium	Low
High	1	2	3
Medium	2	3	4
Low	3	4	5

TABLE 34.2 Target resolution

Priority code	Description	Target resolution time
1	Critical	1 hour
2	High	8 hours

TABLE 34.2   Target resolution *(continued)*

Priority code	Description	Target resolution time
3	Medium	24 hours
4	Low	48 hours
5	Planning	Planned

Many organizations struggle with applying the prioritization rules when the user reporting the fault is in a senior position. Some organizations address this issue by formally recognizing the needs of VIPs for fast service and defining a special service level (gold service) for them within the SLA and documented in the service catalog.

Step 4: Initial Diagnosis

The initial diagnosis step refers to the actions taken at the service desk to diagnose the fault and, where possible, to resolve it at this stage. The service desk agent will use the known error database provided by problem management, incident models (covered earlier), and any other diagnostic tools to assist in the diagnosis and possible resolution. Where the service desk is unable to resolve the incident, the initial diagnosis will identify the appropriate support team for escalation.

Part of this stage is the gathering of information to assist the second-line technician in resolving the incident quickly. Again, sufficient time is required for this step; "saving" time by passing the incident to a second-line technician quickly but with sparse details is not helpful. The second-line technician will need to contact the customer to obtain the information, adding delay and frustration. Support teams should provide guidance to the service desk about the type and level of information they should be gathering.

Step 5: Incident Escalation

The ITIL framework describes two forms of escalation that may take place during incident management: functional escalation and hierarchic escalation.

Functional escalation takes place when the service desk is unable to resolve the incident; this may be realized immediately because of the type of incident, such as a server failure, or because the service desk agent may have spent the maximum time allowed under the organization's guidelines attempting to resolve the incident without success. It then needs to be passed to another group with a greater level of knowledge. The second-line support group that receives this escalated incident will also have a time limit for resolution, after which the incident gets escalated again to the next support level. Sometimes, as with the service desk, it is obvious that the incident will require a high level of technical knowledge, and in such a case the incident would be immediately escalated, without any attempt by second-line support staff to resolve it.

The service desk must know to whom the incident should be escalated to avoid unnecessary delays, so the service desk staff needs to have sufficient technical knowledge to be able to identify which incident goes to which team. Operational level agreements will specify the responsibilities of each group. There may be occasions when cooperation between support groups is required or the incident needs to be referred to third parties such as hardware maintenance companies. The OLAs and UCs should specify what should happen in these situations.

 Incident ownership remains with the service desk. Incidents may be escalated to support groups or third parties, but the service desk retains ownership of the incident, tracking progress, keeping users informed, and obtaining the user's agreement to its eventual closure. Accountability for incident resolution within agreed timescales is also with the service desk.

The second type of escalation is *hierarchic escalation*, which takes place for high-priority or major incidents. Hierarchic escalation consists of informing the appropriate level of management about the incident so that they are aware of it. This ensures that the management is able to make decisions that are required regarding prioritization of work, suppliers, and so on. In the case of a major incident, the IT director may be expected to brief the business directors about the progress of the incident; even if this is not the case, business managers may go directly to senior IT managers when a serious incident has occurred, so it is essential that the IT managers have been thoroughly briefed themselves.

It is also sometimes necessary to use hierarchic escalation when the incident is not progressing as quickly as it should or if there is disagreement among the support groups regarding assignment.

A good service management tool will be able to automatically escalate incidents, based on the SLA targets, and update the record with details. For example, a tool could be set to notify a team leader when 90 percent of the SLA target time had passed and to inform the team leader's line manager when the incident breached the target.

Step 6: Investigation and Diagnosis

The major activity that takes place for every incident is investigation and diagnosis. The incident will have undergone the initial diagnosis step (step 4, covered earlier); that step identifies whether the service desk can resolve the incident. The investigation and diagnosis stage here is different; it involves trying to ascertain what has happened and how the incident can be resolved.

The incident record should be updated to record what actions have been taken, and an accurate description of the symptoms, and the various actions taken, is required to prevent duplication of effort; the record will also be useful when the incident is reviewed, perhaps as part of problem management. Typical investigation and diagnosis actions would include gathering a full description of the issue and its impact and urgency, creating a timeline of events, identifying possible causes (such as recent changes), interrogating knowledge sources such as the known error database, and so on.

Step 7: Resolution and Recovery

Potential incident resolutions should be tested to ensure that they actually resolve the issue completely with no unintended consequences. This testing may involve the user. Other resolution actions might include the service desk agent or technician remotely taking over the user's equipment to implement a resolution or to show the user what they need to do in the future. Once the incident is resolved, it returns to the service desk for closure.

Step 8: Incident Closure

When the incident has been resolved and the service restored, the service desk will contact the user to verify that the incident can be closed. This is an important step because the fault may appear to be resolved to the IT department, but the user may still be having difficulties, especially if there were actually two incidents, with the symptoms of one being hidden by the other. The second incident would become apparent only after the first was resolved. The service desk may contact the user directly, or an email could be sent with a time limit, stating when the incident will be closed, as described earlier.

If the underlying cause of the incident is still unknown, despite the fact it has been resolved, a problem record may be raised to investigate the underlying cause and to prevent a recurrence. Finally, a user satisfaction survey is carried out.

Triggers for Incident Management

The incident management process is triggered by the notification of an incident. As already discussed, this could be from users, support staff or suppliers, or the event management process.

Inputs

The following information inputs are needed by incident management:

- Communication of events from event management.

- Information about CIs from the configuration management system (CMS). This information includes things like the location and configuration of hardware, CI status, software version numbers, and so on.

- Known errors and their workarounds from the known error database. This database contains details of workarounds that enable the rapid resolutions of some recurring incidents.

- Incidents and their symptoms.

- Recent changes and releases. Many incidents are related to changes that have unexpected side effects. The schedule of change provides information about recent and planned changes that can help with the diagnosis of incidents. Information about planned changes can also be useful, especially if the changes are to implement a fix to a recurring fault.

- Operational and service level objectives. Information in service level agreements provide resolution targets for incident management and also guidance on the impact and urgency of incidents affecting the service.

- Customer feedback.

- Criteria for prioritizing and escalating incidents.

Outputs

Information outputs from incident management are as follows:

- Resolved incidents and records of the resolution actions.

- Updated incident records with accurate incident detail and history.

- Updated incident classification once the cause is known; this is used by problem management.

- New problem records where the underlying cause of the incident has not been identified.

- Validation that problem resolution has been effective in stopping recurring incidents.

- Feedback on incidents related to changes and releases.

- Identification of affected CIs.

- Customer satisfaction feedback.

- Feedback on the effectiveness of event management activities.

- Incident and resolution history details to assist in assessing overall service quality.

- Incident models if the change has been seen before or is likely to be a regular recurrence.

- Management information.

- New incident classification types.

- Feedback on the achievement of SLA targets for incident management.

Interfaces between Incident Management and the Lifecycle Stages

Incident management is a key process that is carried out by all service providers. There are several links between the process and other processes both within service operation and within the service design stage.

Service Design

Several of the service design processes interface directly with the incident management process. These processes are among those we discussed previously; many of the process activities take place in the service operation lifecycle stage. Service level management interfaces with incident management because SLAs will contain incident targets; the other service design processes may result in incidents if the processes fail to prevent a security breach, a lack of capacity, or unplanned downtime.

Service Level Management   As you have seen, there are numerous links between incident and service level management (SLM). Incidents have target response and resolution times; these targets are set in the SLAs. Incident management in return provides the management information from the service management toolset to enable SLM to report on the success achieved in meeting these targets. Incident reporting enables SLM to identify failing services and to implement service improvement plans for them (in conjunction with continual service improvement).

Information Security Management, Capacity Management, and Availability Management   Incident management collects data on the number of security-related incidents and capacity issues. It provides the data on downtime that availability uses to calculate availability reports, and analysis of incident records helps availability management understand the weak points in the infrastructure that need attention. An efficient incident lifecycle also improves overall availability.

Service Transition

The service transition processes of service asset and configuration management (SACM) and change management interface with incident management; SACM provides useful information to the incident process, and changes may be the cause of incidents or the means by which incidents are resolved.

Service Asset and Configuration Management   Incident management uses SACM data to understand the impact of an incident because it shows the dependencies on each CI. It provides useful information regarding who supports particular categories of CI. By logging each incident against a CI and checking that the user of the CI is as recorded in the CMS, incident management helps keep the CMS accurate.

Change Management   Changes are often implemented to overcome incidents. Incidents may often be caused by changes. An important input into incident investigation is the change schedule; asking the question, What changed just before this incident occurred? can often highlight the cause of incidents. In the case of a major incident caused by a change, the decision may be made to back out of the change. Information identifying how many incidents were caused by changes should be fed back to change management to improve future changes.

Also, in some cases a fix to an incident may require an emergency change to be raised, to ensure that the CMS is kept up-to-date.

Service Operation

There is a strong interface between incident management and problem management. Access management issues may also cause incidents.

Problem Management   As you will learn when we discuss problem management later in this chapter, incident management and problem management have many links. Incident management provides the data on repeat incidents that problem management uses to identify underlying problems. The permanent resolution of these problems helps incident management by reducing the number of incidents that occur. The incident impact and urgency information helps problem management prioritize between problems.

Problem management provides known error information, which enables incident management to restore service.

Access Management   Incident management raises incidents following security breaches or unauthorized access attempts. This information can be used by access management to investigate access breaches. Failure to ensure that users are granted the access they require to do their job may result in incidents being reported because the user is greeted with an error message when attempting to carry out a task.

Critical Success Factors and Key Performance Indicators

Next we look at some examples of critical success factors (CSFs) for incident management and the key performance indicators (KPIs) that measure how successful they are.

Before we look at the CSFs and KPIs, take a minute to understand what these terms mean:

- A critical success factor is a high-level statement of what a process must achieve if it is to be judged a success. Normally a process would have only three or four CSFs. A CSF cannot be measured directly—that's what key performance indicators are for.

- A key performance indicator is a metric that measures some aspect of a CSF. Each CSF will have three or four associated KPIs.

The following CSFs are used for incident management:

- Critical success factor: "Resolve incidents as quickly as possible, minimizing impacts to the business."
  Two of the KPIs that measure this are:
  - The mean time to achieve resolution
  - The breakdown of incidents at each stage.
- Critical success factor: "Maintain user satisfaction with IT services."
  The key performance indicators that measure its success:
  - The average user/customer survey score (total and by question category)
  - The percentage of satisfaction surveys answered versus total number of satisfaction surveys sent.

Challenges

Incident management faces a number of challenges. First is the challenge of detecting incidents as early as possible. Comprehensive monitoring of the infrastructure plays a significant role here, but there are other things to be done. For example, user education—encouraging users to always report incidents—is important.

A very common challenge is that of persuading technical staff to log incidents that they encounter. Their automatic response is to fix the issue and move on, which is good, but information about trouble spots is often lost.

A poor or nonexistent problem management process will cause the workload on incident management to continue to rise because underlying errors are not being found and corrected. Also, the lack of documented known errors can have a negative effect on the service desk's ability to provide first-line fixes.

The lack of a configuration management system that holds accurate information about CIs and their relationships is another challenge. A comprehensive CMS would support the prioritization of incidents by linking CIs to services and provide valuable diagnostic information.

Finally, integrating the process with service level management would help the process to correctly assess the impact and priority of incidents and to define escalation procedures.

Risks

The risks faced by incident management include the failure to meet the challenges discussed in the preceding section. Another risk is insufficient resources in terms of numbers and capabilities of support staff, meaning that a process will be overwhelmed by incidents that cannot be handled within the agreed timescales.

A backlog of incidents resulting from inadequate support tools is also a risk. It is generally agreed that successful service management in general, and incident management in particular, needs good tools. Inadequate tools also produce the risk of inadequate information.

Finally, there is the risk of failing to meet agreed resolution times because the support staff are not properly incentivized by OLA targets that align with process objectives, or they are simply not aware of targets.

Problem Management

According to ITIL official terminology, a *problem* is defined as an underlying cause of one or more incidents. *Problem management* is the process that investigates the cause of incidents and, wherever possible, implements a permanent solution to prevent recurrence. Until such time as a permanent resolution is applied, it will also attempt to provide a workaround in the form of a known error record to enable the service to be restored and the incident to be resolved as quickly as possible. It is important to understand the differences between incidents and problems and to realize that an incident *never* becomes a problem, Each is held as a separate record. These records may be linked together in the ITSM tool.

A Mechanical Incident, Problem, and Workaround

One morning, as you leave your house to go to work, you find that your car will not start. You have an *incident*.

You have little mechanical knowledge, but you do know how to apply a *workaround*—to use jumper cables. You do this, the car starts, and your incident is over.

Every morning for a week, the same thing happens, and each time you apply the work-around to overcome the incident and restore service. The underlying *problem* could have several possible causes: a faulty battery, a mechanical fault preventing the engine from charging the battery, a light in the trunk left permanently on, and so on. The problem investigation has to be carried out by someone with a greater mechanical knowledge than you have.

On the weekend, you take the car to a mechanic, who diagnoses the root cause and applies a permanent resolution (replaces the battery, fixes the wiring, or whatever is required). Your car will now start each morning!

Many organizations make the mistake of thinking that problem management is not essential. Until and unless problem management is undertaken, incidents will recur, inconveniencing the business and occupying support staff time. Problem management will reduce incidents, freeing up more time to undertake more problem management. It is a virtuous circle; the more time spent on it, the more time is freed up by it.

Let's start by considering the definition of a problem. The definition used by ITIL is "the underlying cause of one or more incidents."

The use of the word *problem* is often misunderstood. Outside of service management, we might hear a total network failure described as a major problem. But service management would describe it as an incident, possibly a major incident. If we did not know why the network had failed, we would also have a problem. If we did know why the failure occurred, there would be no problem. So, a problem is a mystery—the mystery of why an incident occurred.

Purpose

The purpose of the problem management process is to document, investigate, and remove causes of incidents. It also provides another very useful benefit; by providing workarounds, it reduces the impact of incidents that occur and have no known permanent solution or have a permanent solution that no one is prepared to fund. It proactively identifies errors in the infrastructure that could cause incidents and provides a permanent resolution, thus preventing the incidents.

Objectives

Problem management aims to identify the root cause of incidents, to document known errors, and to take action to remedy them. Problem management has three simple objectives:

- First, it must prevent problems and resulting incidents from happening.

- Second, it should eliminate recurring incidents. This is a key objective. There are few things that will do more damage to a service provider's reputation than recurring incidents.

- The third objective is to minimize the impact of incidents that can't be prevented. The underlying fault can't always be fixed, or it may take some time to implement a fix, but problem management may be able identify a fast, reliable way of restoring service should the incident recur. This workaround would be documented in the known error database and used by service desk or other support staff. The scope of problem management includes diagnosis of the root cause of incidents and taking the necessary action in conjunction with other processes (such as change management and release and deployment management) to permanently remove them.

Problem management is also responsible for compiling information about problems and any associated workarounds or resolutions. By identifying faults, providing workarounds, and then permanently removing these faults, problem management reduces the number and the impact of incidents. It has a strong relationship with knowledge management because it is responsible for maintaining a known error database. Proactive problem management supports continual service improvement because it prevents future incidents from occurring and thus improves the quality of the service delivery.

There are important similarities and differences between the two principal service operation processes. The same service management tool will usually be used to track both incidents and problems, and a good tool will facilitate the linking of incident occurrences to specific problem records. Similar categories can be used, although the prioritization of problems may differ from that of the associated incidents; an incident may be a priority one due to its impact and urgency, but once a workaround is supplied, finding a permanent resolution may not be urgent. Problem management is sometimes a process of which the business is unaware. Once a workaround has been applied and an incident resolved, the user may think no more about it. Meanwhile, the IT service provider uses problem management to prevent recurrence. An effective workaround can take some of the pressure off support staff, allowing them to take the time to investigate the underlying cause, without being chased for a resolution because the service has been restored.

 Sometimes an incident cannot be resolved until the cause is known and remedied; a server fails and will not restart, for example, because of a hardware fault. In this situation, the problem resolution happens at the same time, not later.

Value

The value of problem management derives from the fact that it will diminish the number of incidents and their impact on the organization. Permanent fixes will tend to reduce the number of incidents, and the workarounds, documented in the known error database, enable fast resolution of recurring incidents. Together these mean higher availability of the services with all that implies.

Problem management improves the productivity of IT staff because they spend less time investigating and resolving repeat incidents because these are permanently resolved through problem resolutions.

Problem management identifies the underlying causes of incidents and is therefore able to devise an effective fix, or a workaround that always works. If the underlying cause is not known or is misunderstood, then there is a risk that any fix or workaround won't work. Last, the process reduces the impact of recurring incidents, which reduces associated costs.

Policies

The ITIL core guidance suggests three policies that support problem management:

Policy: Problems should be tracked separately from incidents.   The focus of each of the two processes is very different, especially as regards problem management's proactive activities.

Policy: All problems should be stored and managed in a single management system.   It is not a good idea for each technical team, for example, to have its own database of problems. There are many reasons a single management system is essential. For example, suppose the investigation of problems requires the use of scarce technical resources. To make the best use of those resources, we should prioritize activities by prioritizing problems. This becomes difficult or impossible if information about problems is scattered across many databases or spreadsheets.

Policy: All problems should subscribe to a standard classification schema that is consistent across the business enterprise.   The standard classification of problems provides faster access to investigation and diagnostic data and enables more effective analysis, particularly by proactive problem management. Notice that this policy says "across the business enterprise." In the case of a global enterprise, problems should be categorized in the same way wherever in the world they manifest themselves.

Principles and Basic Concepts

In the following sections, we'll present some examples of problem management policies.

Reactive and Proactive Aspects

Unlike incident management, which is entirely reactive (you cannot resolve an incident until it has occurred), problem management has both reactive and proactive features:

- Problem management will react to incidents and attempt to identify a workaround and a permanent resolution.

- Problem management will also proactively try to identify potential incidents and take action to prevent them from ever happening. This might include analysis of incident trends, such as intermittent but increasingly frequent complaints about poor response times, to identify a potential capacity issue. By working with capacity management, problem management can take proactive measures to provide sufficient capacity and avoid any major breaks in service. Event management reports can also be analyzed to the same end, in this case to prevent an incident before the user is aware of any issue.

- Problem management may assist in a major incident review, trying to identify how to prevent a recurrence.

The process steps for managing problems that are raised in reaction to incidents and for managing problems that are proactively identified are broadly similar. The main difference is the trigger for the process. Reactive activities take place as a result of an incident report and help prevent the incident from recurring or provide a workaround if avoidance is impossible; these activities complement the incident management process.

Proactive problem management analyzes incident records to identify underlying causes of incidents. It may be that analysis of previous incidents reveals a trend or pattern that was not apparent when each incident occurred. For example, users may complain of poor response periodically; it is only when all these complaints are analyzed that it becomes apparent that the poor response is always reported against the same module or from the same location. This would trigger a problem record to be raised to identify the common cause linking all these incidents.

Reactive and proactive problem management activities normally take place as part of service operation, but problem management is also closely related to continual service improvement. Where improvement opportunities are identified as a result of problem management, they should be entered into the CSI register.

Problem Models

Most problems are unique and can't be investigated in a predetermined way. But sometimes there are underlying issues that cannot be resolved—they are too difficult, the resolution is too costly, or they are outside our scope of action. For example, a badly designed application may, over time, experience intermittent incidents, each of which has a different specific cause, a different problem. A problem model might guide the investigation of problems in that application. It might describe how to collect and interpret relevant diagnostic information, for example.

Incidents vs. Problems

As we have said, problem management and incident management are closely related. Although incident management is not concerned with determining the underlying causes of the incidents it investigates, sometimes it is necessary to do that in order to resolve the incident. When that is the case, problem management should get involved. Determining the root cause might provide the workaround needed to close the incident. Potentially, problem management could get involved whenever an incident occurred that had no corresponding problem or known error record, but that would probably be overkill. Every organization should define criteria for determining when it's appropriate to involve problem management. It is very common, usual even, for problem management to be involved in the handling of major incidents.

Known Errors

When you examine the problem management process in detail, you will see that the process attempts to identify and document known errors, usually when the cause of the problem is known and a workaround is available but the permanent fix has yet to be applied. Known error records are used to document root causes and workarounds, allowing quicker diagnosis and resolution if further incidents do occur. Problem management is not the only source of known errors. Some will come from application development. It's often the case that a new application will go live in spite of known bugs in the software because they are not considered serious enough to delay the rollout. Where this is the case, the bugs should be documented in the known error database so that the information is available should there be in incident during live operation. These bugs might be discovered in development or during testing in service transition. A final source of known errors is the notifications received from suppliers when they discover issues in their products.

Workaround

A workaround is defined as a means of reducing or eliminating the impact of an incident or problem for which a full resolution is not yet available. Restarting a failed configuration item is an example of a workaround. Workarounds for problems are documented in known error records.

Process Activities, Methods, and Techniques

Next we consider some of the main problem management activities and the methods and techniques used.

When Is a Problem Raised?

Sometimes it is helpful to raise a problem record while the incident is still open. Each organization will decide on its own criteria for when a problem should be raised. For example, a problem might be raised when the support teams are sure the incident has been caused by a new problem because the incident appears to be part of a trend or because there is no match with existing known errors. The service desk or support teams may have resolved the incident without knowing the cause, and so there is a risk that the fault may recur. This is particularly true in the case of a major incident; the underlying cause needs to be identified as soon as possible to prevent future disruption to the business. (The problem diagnosis activity may take place in parallel with the incident resolution and may continue after the successful resolution until the underlying cause is identified and removed.) As already explained, it is also possible that suppliers may inform their customers of problems that they have identified.

As stated earlier, problem management is not an optional activity; it is fundamental to providing a consistent service in line with SLA commitments. By providing workarounds to enable resolution of incidents by the first-line staff, the organization makes better use of the more skilled and therefore more expensive second- and third-line staff, who are freed up to use their skills in problem investigation.

Process Activities

Now we are going to examine the problem management process step by step. Refer to Figure 34.3 as we discuss each activity.

FIGURE 34.3 The problem management process

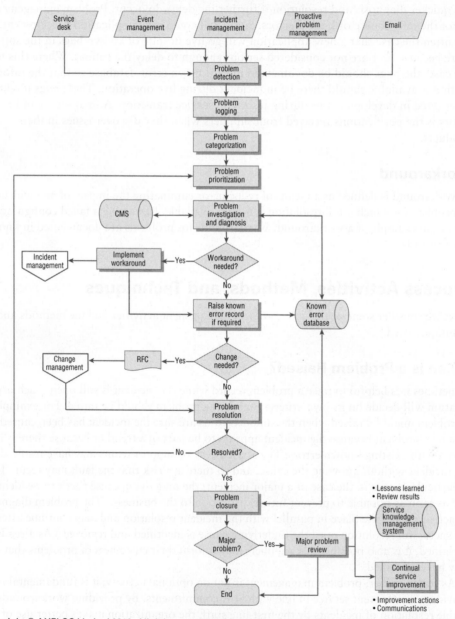

Step 1: Detecting Problems

The first step in the process is to identify that a problem exists. As we discussed previously, problems may be raised either reactively (in reaction to incidents) or proactively. In addition to the triggers identified earlier, a problem may also be identified as a result of alerts received as part of event management. The event monitoring tools may identify a fault before it becomes apparent to users and may automatically raise an incident in response.

As the diagram shows, problems can be identified in a number of ways, but they are all handled by a single problem management process and logged in a single database. A major source is the service desk acting for the incident management process. Any incident whose cause is unknown could trigger a problem investigation. In practice, few organizations will do that because of the very large number of problems that result. Most organizations are quite selective about the problems they log and investigate. This is supplemented by regular analyses of incident data, searching for recurring incidents that might have been missed. Potential problems can also be identified by event management and suppliers, and of course proactive problem management itself identifies problems.

Step 2: Logging Problems

Having identified that a problem exists, a problem record containing all the relevant information should be logged and time-stamped to provide a complete picture. Typical details would include who reported it and when, the service and equipment used, and a description of the incident or incidents and actions taken. The incident record number(s) and the priority and category would also be required.

Where possible, use the service management tool to link problem records with the associated incident records. Remember that the incident has not "become" a problem; the incident must continue to be managed to resolution whether the problem is resolved or not.

Step 3: Categorizing Problems

The problem is then categorized using the same system used by incident management, which allows incidents and problems to be more easily matched. For example, it might be possible to relate a number of types of incidents to a single common problem, which would bring a lot of extra diagnostic information.

The problem manager should emphasize the importance of accurate categorization to the service desk. The use of incident models can be very helpful here because they standardize the way common incidents are recorded. Enforcing categorization on incident resolution, as mentioned earlier, will also help ensure that incident categories are accurate.

Step 4: Prioritizing Problems

As with incidents, the priority of a problem should be based on the business impact of the incidents that it is causing and the urgency with which it needs to be resolved. The problem manager should also consider how frequently the incidents are occurring. It is possible that a "frozen screen" that can be resolved with a reboot is not a high-priority incident; if it is occurring 100 times a day, the combined impact to the business may be severe, so the problem needs to be allocated a high priority. The impact to the business must always be considered, so factors such as the cost of resolving the incident and the time this is likely to take will be relevant when assessing priority. It is likely that some problems are not considered important enough to spend resources on, especially if a reasonable and effective workaround has been identified.

Analyzing factors such as number affected, the duration of the downtime, and the business cost is known as pain value analysis. This technique can be useful in determining the business impact of a problem. Of course, circumstances change, new information is learned, and further incidents may occur, so the priority of a problem should be kept under review and changed if appropriate.

Step 5: Investigating and Diagnosing Problems

The next stage in the process is to investigate and diagnose the problem. The purpose of this stage is first to discover the root cause and then to determine a workaround and permanent fix. There may not be the resources to investigate every problem, so the priority level assigned to each will govern which ones get the necessary attention. It is important to allocate resources to problem investigation because until the problem is resolved, the incident will recur and resources will be spent on incident resolution.

Usually the task of investigating and diagnosing the problem is passed to the appropriate technical or application team; if it is unclear where the problem originates, it might be necessary to establish a team of technical specialists to investigate it. Sometimes it will be necessary to escalate a problem to a supplier.

The ITIL framework suggests a number of different problem-solving techniques, which are helpful in approaching the diagnosis logically. The CMS can be very helpful in providing CI information to help identify the underlying cause. It will also help in identifying the point of failure when several incidents are reported; the CMS may identify that all the affected CIs are linked to one "parent" CI. The fault affecting the "parent" configuration item is causing all those CIs attached to it to experience a loss of service. The KEDB may also provide information about previous, similar problems and their causes. Where a test environment exists, this can be used to recreate the fault and to try possible solutions.

Step 6: Identifying a Workaround

Although the aim of problem management is to find and remove the underlying cause of incidents, this may take some time; meanwhile, the incident or incidents continue, and the service is affected. When a user suffers an incident, the first priority is to restore the service so that the user can continue working. A priority of the process, therefore, is to provide a workaround to be used until the problem is resolved. A workaround is a means of reducing the impact of an error. This can be in the form of a circumvention, which is a way of working that avoids triggering incidents, or it may be a way of resolving incidents should they occur. At this point a known error should be raised and stored in the known error database.

The workaround does not fix the underlying problem, but it allows the user to continue working by providing an alternative means of achieving the same result. The workaround can be provided to the service desk to enable them to resolve the incidents while work on a permanent solution continues. The problem record remains open because the fault still exists and is continuing to cause incidents. The details of the workaround are documented within the problem record, and a reassessment of its priority may be carried out.

It is possible that IT or business management may decide to continue to use the workaround and suspend work on a permanent solution if one is not justified. A problem affecting a service that is due to be replaced, for example, may not be worth the effort and risk involved in implementing a permanent solution.

Of course it is not always possible to devise a workaround, and sometimes a workaround is not acceptable to the business—the fault must be fixed.

Step 7: Raising a Known Error Record

When problem management has identified and documented the root cause and workaround, this information is made available to support staff as a *known error*. Information about all known errors, including which problem record it relates to, is kept in the *known error database (KEDB)*. When repeat incidents occur, the support staff can refer to the KEDB for the workaround.

Although ITIL defines a known error as a problem with a cause that is known and a workaround that has been provided, in the real world, there may be times when a workaround is available even though the root cause is not yet known (for example, a reboot restores the service, but it's not known what causes the error). On other occasions, we may know the cause but not have a workaround because a change has to be implemented to fix the fault.

Sometimes a known error is raised before a workaround is available and sometimes even before the root cause has been fully identified. This may be just for information purposes; a workaround may be available that has not been fully proven. Rather than have a rigid rule about when a known error should be raised, a more pragmatic approach is advisable; a known error should be raised as soon as it becomes useful to do so.

Step 8: Problem Resolution

When problem management has identified a solution to the problem, it should be implemented to resolve the underlying fault and thus prevent any further incidents from disrupting the service. Implementing the resolution may involve a degree of risk, however, so the change management process will ensure that the risk and impact assessment of the RFC is satisfactory before allowing the change. The error might be in an application that is scheduled to be phased out in the near future, so the business may choose to accept the likely disruption temporarily rather than accept the cost and risk of a fix. Ultimately, the decision whether to go ahead with the resolution despite the risk is a business decision; the business damage being done by the problem may mean the business is prepared to accept the risk in order to have the fix implemented.

Problem Closure

When a permanent solution to the problem has been identified, tested, and implemented through the change management process, the problem record can be updated and closed. Any open incidents caused by the problem can be closed too. The KEDB should be updated to show that the problem is resolved so any future incidents will not have been caused by it; however, the information contained within the problem record may prove useful in addressing a future, similar problem.

Major Problem Review

Each organization must determine what constitutes a major problem, based on its own business priorities. Once a major problem is resolved, it is advisable to hold a formal review to learn from the experience. The review should be carried out in the immediate aftermath of events, when memories are fresh. It is led by the problem manager but should include the participation of everyone who played a role in the events under review.

The review is not only concerned with the failure that first triggered the major problem, but also with everything that happened and was done afterward. It takes a holistic view, in other words.

Specifically, the review asks the following questions:

- What did we do that was right? What did we do that made things worse?

- What could we do better in future?

- What can we do to prevent it from happening again?

- What proposals can we make for improvement?

These could involve making changes to processes or technology, requiring specific training for support or other staff, and requiring action by suppliers or changes to contracts.

A major problem review also has a significant role to play in rebuilding customer confidence, which will probably have suffered due to the major problem. The review should be conducted with this in mind, and it should be reflected in the resulting report. It might be useful to include a representative from the business in the review.

Figure 34.4 illustrates the way incident, problem, and change management activities are linked. It is largely self-explanatory, but note that an incident is closed when service is restored but a problem is closed only when a fix has been applied and is confirmed to be effective. Sometimes problem management cannot supply a workaround, so the incident stays open until the permanent fix is implemented.

FIGURE 34.4   How incidents, problems, and changes are linked

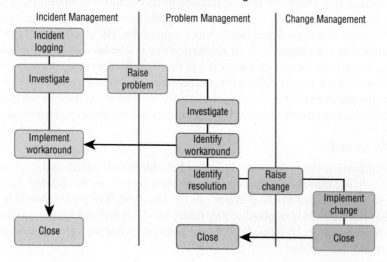

Triggers

Triggers for problem management will vary between organizations and include triggers for both reactive and proactive problem management.

Reactive problem management triggers include the identification of the need to determine the cause of one or more incidents by the service desk, resulting in a problem record being raised. The incidents may have been resolved, but the cause is unknown. The process of undertaking problem management should enable the identification and removal of the underlying cause, preventing any recurrence. Sometimes it is obvious that an incident, or incidents, has been caused by a major problem, so a problem record will be raised immediately.

Another trigger for reactive problem management is the result of incident analysis by a technical support group showing an underlying problem. Event monitoring tools may raise incidents automatically, and these may require a problem record to be raised. Finally, a supplier may inform the service provider that a problem exists and has to be resolved.

Proactive problem management triggers include analysis of incidents that have occurred, leading to a decision to raise a problem record to investigate what is causing them to occur. An analysis of trends may identify one or more underlying causes. When the cause is removed, recurrence can be prevented.

Another possible proactive trigger may result from continual service improvement; steps taken to improve the quality of a service may result in the need for a problem record to identify further possible improvement actions.

Trend analysis depends on meaningful and detailed categorization of incidents/problems and regular reporting of patterns and repeat occurrences of incidents. This can be helped by regular reporting on the "top ten" incidents.

Inputs

The incident database is a vital source of information for problem management because it contains information about current incidents and problems and is the basis of proactive problem management.

The configuration management system (CMS) provides information about the hardware and software components that underpin the IT services; this is essential for problem investigation and diagnosis. It also helps the process to prioritize problems appropriately by showing the links between components and services.

Problem management must assess whether a business case exists for the change request, which is required to implement a permanent fix to a problem; financial information is needed for this. Input from change management will provide feedback on progress and whether the changes are successful.

Finally in this list comes feedback from customers. If customers are unhappy about repeated recurrences of incidents interrupting their work, this would be both a trigger for and an input into problem management. Building and maintaining customer satisfaction is an essential objective of all service management activity, including problem management.

Outputs

Outputs from problem management include the obvious outputs such as updated problem records, requests for change, workarounds, and known error records. In addition, the process will output various reports. For example, a problem report might be discussed at a service review meeting. Reports of issues found should be referred to design teams and other processes. If reports include recommendations for improvement, they may be logged in the CSI register.

Interfaces between Problem Management and the Lifecycle Stages

Problem management is a key process that must be carried out if the service is to improve over time. There are several links between the process and other processes, both within the service operation area and across the service lifecycle.

Service Strategy

Problem management has a link with financial management for IT services to assess the financial impact of possible solutions or workarounds. This information can be used to decide whether a permanent resolution is financially justified.

Service Design

Problem management interfaces with several of the service design processes:

Availability Management   This process and problem management have a similar goal: to prevent downtime. The proactive activities undertaken by availability management are directly related to proactive problem management; availability attempts to proactively identify risks that could result in a loss of service and to take preventative action. Problem management can supply information to availability management about the success of any measures taken.

Capacity Management   Some performance problems can be caused by capacity issues. Capacity management will be involved in resolving these issues and also taking proactive measures to prevent capacity issues. Again, problem management can supply information about the success of any measures taken.

IT Service Continuity Management   If a significant problem is causing or will cause major disruption to the business, it may be necessary to invoke the IT service continuity management (ITSCM) plan until the issue is resolved. ITSCM also attempts to proactively identify risks that could result in a major loss of service and to take preventative action.

Service Level Management   The service level management process interfaces with problems in a different way. SLM is dependent on problem management to identify the root cause of incidents and resolve them in order to prevent downtime that could cause a service level target to be breached.

Service Transition

Problem management interfaces with several of the service transition processes:

Change Management   As discussed, changes may be the cause or solution to problems.

Service Asset and Configuration Management   Service asset and configuration management provides invaluable information to enable common factors to be identified across multiple incidents.

Release and Deployment Management   Release and deployment is involved in contributing to problem management's known error database, which is also related to knowledge management.

Knowledge Management   The last interface with service transition is with knowledge management. The workarounds developed by problem management are examples of the service knowledge that is the core concern of knowledge management. The service knowledge management system can be the basis of the known error database.

Service Operation

As we discussed in the section about incident management, the major relationship that problem and incident management have is with each other.

Continual Service Improvement

Problem management and continual service improvement have similar objectives; problem management activities can also be seen as CSI activities. The aims of CSI and problem management are very closely aligned. Both seek to drive out errors and improve service quality. As stated earlier, actions identified to resolve or prevent problems may be entered into the CSI register.

The seven-step improvement process can be used by CSI or problem management to identify and resolve underlying problems.

Critical Success Factors and Key Performance Indicators

The next topic that we'll discuss is that of the critical success factors (CSFs) for effective problem management and the key performance indicators (KPIs) that will show whether these CSFs are being achieved. The *ITIL Service Operation* publication provides three examples of critical success factors for problem management:

- Critical success factor: "Minimize the impact to the business of incidents that cannot be prevented."

   This CSF is concerned with workarounds and their effectiveness, so we need KPIs to evaluate this. Here are a couple of possible KPIs for this:

   - Number of errors added to the known error database. This is measuring the success of the process in identifying workarounds. Identifying workarounds is only beneficial if they are being used.

- Percentage of incidents resolved by the service desk. The assumption here is that the fix rate of the service desk will increase in line with an increasing number of known errors logged.

- Critical success factor: "Maintain quality of IT services through elimination of recurring incidents."

This is measuring the effectiveness of the process at eliminating the underlying causes of incidents through the provision of permanent fixes. You should be able to devise KPIs that support these CSFs. Two possible KPIs are as follows:

- The size of the problem backlog

- The number of repeat incidents

- Critical success factor: "Provide overall quality and professionalism of problem handling activities to maintain business confidence in IT capabilities."

This CSF is very much about the process itself rather than its direct impact on the quality of the IT services. There are many possible KPIs that would be relevant to this; let's consider just three examples.

- The percentage of major problem reviews completed. A best practice problem management process would conduct a formal review of every major problem. This KPI indicates whether that is being done. A KPI that tells us whether the reviews were being conducted in a timely manner would also be valuable.

- The average cost per problem. This refers to the cost of investigation and diagnosis; it would tell us if problem management is efficient.

- The backlog of outstanding problems and the trend—how effective is the process? This is an example of a KPI that might be used when the process is first established but discarded once the process is mature and has eliminated the backlog.

Challenges

Our next topic is the challenges faced by problem management. We've seen that problem management is dependent on the incident management process. This poses a number of challenges:

- The incident process must be mature enough to correctly identify possible problems and to gather sufficient information to enable problem management to diagnose the cause. A critical challenge is ensuring that the two processes have formal interfaces and common working practices.

- Problem resolution staff must have the skills and capabilities for problem solving.

- Ideally, a single tool should be used for problem and incident management. The tool should have the ability to relate incidents to problems and enable the determination of relationships between CIs to assist in problem diagnosis.

- A good working relationship between the second- and third-line staff working on problem support activities and first-line staff must be developed. Each must understand their role in the investigation of problems and that it is very much a team effort.

- Staff working on problem resolution must understand the impact of problems on the business. Understanding the business and the role of IT in supporting it is a common challenge across the lifecycle.

- The next challenge is the integration of activities with the CMS, which holds essential information about configuration items, their relationships, and their history.

- The final challenge is having staff with the necessary technical knowledge to investigate and diagnose problems. This requires the staff to be available to work on the problem. It can be difficult to release staff from other work to do problem management.

Risks

The final topic in this chapter is the risks facing problem management:

- Failing to meet any of the challenges listed in the preceding section is a risk.

- There may be simply too many problems to handle due to insufficient resources or because the criteria for raising problems are too loose.

- There may be a lack of information from incident management or from a CMS.

- The focus of operational level agreements may be on incident resolution, and so staff do not realize the importance of problem management.

Summary

This chapter explored the first two processes in the service operation stage, incident management and problem management. It covered the purpose, objectives, scope, and value of these processes. We examined how each of these processes supports the other and the importance of these processes to the business and to the IT service provider.

You learned about the high-level process activities, methods, and techniques. We discussed triggers, inputs, outputs, interfaces, critical success factors, and key performance indicators. Finally, we looked at the challenges and risks for these two processes.

In the following chapters, we look at the service operation processes of request fulfillment, event management, and access management and discuss some of the generic concepts and definitions associated with them.

Exam Essentials

Understand the purpose and objectives of incident management in reducing downtime by resolving incidents quickly. Describe the scope of incident management and basic concepts such as major incidents, incident models, and the importance of timely resolution.

Identify sources of incident reporting other than users reporting them to the service desk; for example, suppliers, support staff, and event management alerts are all possible sources. Understand that incident management is a reactive process. Be able to list and explain the interfaces that incident management has with other processes, especially problem management and service level management.

Understand that the aim of incident management is to restore service, not to identify the cause.   This focus on service restoration means that less-skilled staff are required to resolve incidents than are necessary to resolve problems. Be able to describe the differences between an incident, a problem, and a service request.

Explain how priority is calculated using business impact and urgency.   Understand what the terms *business impact* and *urgency* mean.

Be able to explain the concept of incident and problem models and their use.   Be able to describe the lifecycle of an incident and the use of the different statuses assigned to each stage. List the key information that would be recorded in an incident record. Describe the difference between the two types of escalation (hierarchic and functional) and when each is used.

Know the definition of a problem and the purpose, objectives, and scope of problem management.   A problem is the unknown, underlying cause of one or more incidents, and the aim of problem management is to find the cause of incidents and remove it to prevent recurrence. Be able to describe the relationship between problem management and other processes.

Understand the value of problem management.   List the ways in which problem management benefits the business, reduces downtime, and makes the best use of IT staff.

Understand the relationship between incidents, problems, and changes.   Understand that incidents are caused by problems and so will continue to recur until the problem is resolved, usually by implementing a change.

Understand the concepts of a workaround and a known error.   Explain why some problems might not be resolved, when it is not cost-effective to implement the fix, and when a workaround exists. Know how the known error database is used.

Review Questions

You can find the answers to the review questions in the appendix.

1. Which is the best description of an incident?

   A. An event that has significance and impacts the service

   B. An unplanned interruption to an IT service or a reduction in the quality of an IT service

   C. A fault that causes failures in the IT infrastructure

   D. A user error

2. When should an incident be closed?

   A. When the technical staff members are confident that it will not recur

   B. When desktop support staff members say that the incident is over

   C. When the user confirms that the service has been restored

   D. When the target resolution time is reached

3. Which of the following is NOT a satisfactory resolution to an incident?

   A. A user complains of poor response; a reboot speeds up the response.

   B. A user complains of poor response; second-line support runs diagnostics to be able to monitor it the next time it occurs.

   C. The service desk uses the KEDB to provide a workaround to restore the service.

   D. The service desk takes control of the user's machine remotely and shows the user how to run the report they were having difficulty with.

4. Incident management aims to restore normal service operation as quickly as possible. How is normal service operation defined?

   A. It is the level of service the user requires.

   B. It is the level of service the technical management staff members say is reasonable.

   C. It is the level of service defined in the SLA.

   D. It is the level of service that IT believes is optimal.

5. A service management tool has the ability to store templates for common incidents that define the steps to be taken to resolve the fault. What are these called?

   A. Major incidents

   B. Minor incidents

   C. Incident models

   D. Incident categories

6. Which incidents should be logged?

   A. Major incidents

   B. All incidents that resulted from a user contacting the service desk

   C. Minor incidents

   D. All incidents

7. What factors should be taken into consideration when assessing the priority of an incident?

   A. Impact and cost

   B. Impact and urgency

   C. Urgency and severity

   D. Severity and cost

8. Which of the following are types of incident escalation defined by ITIL?

   1. Hierarchic

   2. Management

   3. Functional

   4. Technical

      A. 1 and 4

      B. 1 and 3

      C. 1, 2, and 4

      D. All of the above

9. What is the best definition of a problem?

   A. An incident that the service desk does not know how to fix

   B. The result of a failed change

   C. The cause of one or more incidents

   D. A fault that will require a change to resolve

10. Problem management can produce which of the following?

   1. Known errors

   2. Workarounds

   3. Resolutions

   4. RFCs

      A. 1 and 4

      B. 1 and 3

      C. 1, 2, and 4

      D. All of the above

Chapter

35

Service Operation Processes: Request Fulfilment

THE FOLLOWING ITIL INTERMEDIATE EXAM OBJECTIVES ARE DISCUSSED IN THIS CHAPTER:

✓ **Request fulfilment is discussed in terms of its**

- Purpose

- Objectives

- Scope

- Value

- Policies

- Principles and basic concepts

- Process activities, methods, and techniques

- Triggers, inputs, outputs, and interfaces

- Critical success factors and key performance indicators

- Challenges

- Risks

Service Operation
Processes
Fulfilment

The service operation process we'll cover in this chapter is *request fulfilment*. This is the process for handling requests for standard services, equipment, or information. ITIL uses the expression *service request* to describe all those repeat, low-risk change/information requests that occur in any environment.

There is no absolute definition as to what will be classed as a request because this may vary from organization to organization. Many may, in fact, be small changes, falling under the definition of standard changes because they require a change to the configuration management system, such as equipment relocation or the installation of additional software. Service requests occur frequently, at a low cost, with an understood low risk. Examples of service requests that are not standard changes could include a password reset or information requests. Service requests are usually handled by a service desk, without a requirement for an RFC to be submitted.

The definition used by ITIL is "a formal request from a user for something to be provided—for example, a request for information or advice, to reset a password or to install a workstation for a new user."

Service requests relate to small-scale, clearly defined, and low-risk activities, such as the provision of a single workstation or supply of a toner cartridge. An important feature of what ITIL calls service requests is that they represent things that the service provider will be asked for repeatedly. They are all opportunities to provide the user with something they have asked for, and the request fulfilment process is used to handle them.

Many service requests require a change—the installation of a workstation, for example. If you think back to your Foundation studies, you may remember standard changes, which are low-risk, simple, preauthorized changes. The only changes that can be handled by the request fulfilment process are those for which a standard change exists. Be careful here though—not all standard changes are implemented through request fulfilment, and not all service requests involve standard changes. Requests for information or advice also fall within the scope of request fulfilment.

Purpose and Objectives

Request fulfilment is the process responsible for managing the lifecycle of all service requests from the users. The process has five objectives:

- To maintain customer and user satisfaction through efficient and professional handling of all service requests. We've learned that ensuring satisfaction involves not only meeting objective targets, but also the human aspects—treating requesters with respect, keeping them informed of progress, and so on.

- To provide a way for the user to make a request. This is normally through a web portal but the service desk could be used.

- To provide a way for users to find out what standard services are available to them and how they can request them. It can be surprising that, particularly in a large organization, users aren't even aware of everything the service provider can do for them.

- To source and deliver the tangible components of service—hardware, software, licenses, and so on.

- To assist with general information, complaints, or comments. So, the process should not only provide a means to submit a question, it should also ensure that the user gets a satisfactory response.

Request fulfilment provides an efficient way to supply standard equipment to users, once an item has been assessed and accepted as compatible with the infrastructure. The provision of such equipment can be preapproved and handled as a standard change. It can be added as a service within the service catalog, and all future requests of this type can be handled through this process. This encourages the users to request the standard equipment and software because it is the easiest and fastest to obtain. This is beneficial to IT because the equipment has been assessed as supportable and compatible with the infrastructure.

 Real World Scenario

Improving Efficiency by Providing a Standard Request Fulfilment Process

A hospital IT department handled requests for hardware and software from the hospital staff. Users would ask for equipment or software that they had seen advertised in magazines or at their local PC store. Often this equipment and software offered no benefit over the standard equipment and software in use in the rest of the organization. Each request was handled by the IT staff approaching several suppliers to find the best price and then informing the requester of the cost so that they could raise a purchase order. The money saved by sourcing the cheapest supplier did not cover the cost of the IT staff time it used. The process might be repeated several times a week for very similar requests because each was handled separately. When the purchase order was raised, the item would be ordered, and when it was delivered, the support staff would install it. Because each item could be different, the staff had to ensure that they were following the installation directions for the particular model or software. The IT department had to then support all these different items and manage the warranty agreements. Occasionally incidents would be caused because these nonstandard items were incompatible with a change. The whole process was expensive and took up considerable IT time. The process was slow, often taking three or four weeks from request to fulfilment, so users would sometimes circumvent it by buying and installing items themselves!

A new standard request fulfilment process was introduced to address these issues. Following discussion with the business, the IT department agreed on some standard software and a number of standard devices—a standard laptop and one for "power" users, a standard desktop PC, and a standard office printer. A small stock of each of these was bought and put in storage. Users now ordered from this short list, at a set price, supplying the purchase order at the time of order. The item was taken from stock and installed the same day, while the purchase order was used to replenish the stock. The new arrangement suited everybody; the user was happy to forego the ability to order any item in return for same-day installation, the IT staff had a simpler range of items to support, the IT management was happy to have a less labor-intensive process, and the finance department was pleased that the IT department was able to negotiate a good price from a single supplier in return for a steady stream of orders.

In addition to these benefits, the simpler process meant that the service desk was able to handle the request, assigning the installation to the desktop support team and ordering the replacement. The simple process was very suited to user self-service and became one of the first services offered to users on the new self-service portal.

Scope

The scope of request fulfilment will vary from one organization to another; it can include any requests that can be standardized and used where the organization has agreed to use it. Each request should be broken into agreed activities, each with a documented procedure. The procedures are then used to build the request models.

ITIL calls all these *service requests*; they are all opportunities to provide the user with something they have asked for, such as information, advice, a standard change, or access to an IT service (such as resetting a password or providing standard IT services for a new user), and as mentioned in the introduction to this chapter, the request fulfilment process is used to handle them.

ITIL Service Operation publication suggests that other sorts of requests, such as requests for building maintenance, may be handled together with IT requests. Take a moment to consider the advantages/disadvantages of this approach:

- Similar handling for both
- Expands single point of contact
- De-skills the (usually service desk) job

It will be up to each organization to decide and document which service requests it will handle through the request fulfilment process and which will have to go through other processes, such as business relationship management (BRM) processes for dealing with requests for new or changed services.

Value to the Business

The request fulfilment process benefits the business in a number of ways.

First, it improves the productivity of the business by giving its staff quick and effective access to the services they need to do their jobs. By providing a straightforward means of having its requests fulfilled, business staff can remain productive. Centralization encourages consistency and efficiency. Bureaucracy and delay is reduced, thus reducing the cost of fulfilment. Second, the process provides an efficient way to handle requests, again reducing bureaucracy. A formal process implies the centralization of sourcing and purchasing, enabling the service provider to standardize the hardware and software used, therefore reducing support costs. Central purchasing through approved suppliers can also reduce costs through economies of scale.

The standardized nature of request fulfilment means that it is an obvious candidate for self-help. Although not essential, automating the process with a *self-help* front end enables the requester to interface directly with the process and thus speeds up the fulfilment process. Typically, users can access a list of possible requests on a company external website or intranet. This ensures that the user provides all the necessary information and can be informed as to expected lead times (defined in the SLA).

Automation can simplify the logging of requests. It can also automate the fulfilment process, without the intervention of the service desk if there is a direct interface into the necessary systems. An example of such automated fulfilment is when you request and receive a password reset from an Internet shopping site such as Amazon, without any human intervention. Financial approval of requests can also be automated, with the request being sent to the appropriate budget holder for approval or rejection before fulfilment.

Next, we consider the policies, principles, and basic concepts of the request fulfilment process. Let's start with policies.

Policies

In this section, we'll consider some of the policies that support effective request fulfilment.

Policy: Process flows should be defined for each service request.   The first policy is that a process flow should be defined for the entire lifecycle of each service request. This will ensure that requests are satisfied effectively, efficiently, and consistently. Service designers should include new requirements for standard services in their design efforts.

Policy: Process should be owned by a single function.   A second policy is that there should be a single function that owns all service requests. This does not mean that there should be a single function for fulfilling the requests. Rather, the central function will monitor progress of requests and take action should progress be slow. This central function will also provide requesters with updates on progress where appropriate. Often the service desk takes this role.

Policy: Standard change process to be used where a change to a configuration item is involved.   Another policy is that if a request involves a change to a configuration item, then it must be implemented by a standard change. In other words, request fulfilment must follow normal change management procedures.

Policy: All service requests to be handled by a single system.   The fourth policy is that service requests should be handled by a single system. The parallel here is with incident management and the service desk.

Policy: All service requests to be authorized.   Policy five states that all requests must be authorized before they are fulfilled. Many requests incur costs, such as the purchase of hardware or a software license, and those costs must be authorized.

Policy: All service requests to be prioritized according to business criteria.   The next policy, policy six, is that the activity needed to fulfil a request must align with the needs and objectives of the business. In other words, each request must be prioritized using business criteria. Here is another parallel with incident management.

Policy: Users must be able to submit requests and obtain updates easily.   The last policy that we will discuss is that users must have a clear means of submitting a request and of getting an update on progress. This could be the single point of contact that is provided by the service desk for incidents. For request fulfilment, the point of contact could be the service desk or the web portal.

Principles and Basic Concepts

Many organizations use their existing incident management process (and tools) to handle service requests because key steps are often the same. In each case, the following questions need to be answered:

- Can the service desk deal with this?
- Would this impact negatively on incident handling?
- If not the service desk, who can deal with this?
- What are the timescales/agreed service levels?
- Is the user satisfied?

Separation of Requests and Incidents

Some organizations separate requests from incidents because incidents are unplanned and unwanted; a major aim of service management is to reduce the number of incidents, through improved design, problem management, and continual service improvement. In contrast, there may be a policy of increasing the number of items that can be dealt with through the request fulfilment process. The targets for incidents and requests may be very different: requests often have specified lead times, which are dependent on other factors (such as the user not being given access until they have attended a training course), whereas with incidents, the aim is to resolve each one as quickly as possible. Where there are a significant number of requests to be fulfilled, a separate process with a different record type should be used. This allows the service provided to be monitored and reported on in a more appropriate way than using incident reporting. Also, it is likely incidents will be given priority over requests, resulting in requests not meeting SLA targets because fixes take precedence. Similarly, if dealing with requests has an impact on incident resolution, the customer will be dissatisfied.

Request Models

The process needed to fulfil a request will vary depending upon exactly what is being requested, but it can usually be broken down into a set of activities that have to be performed. For each request, these activities should be documented into a *request model*. You encountered models when we studied incident management in Chapter 34, "Service Operation Processes: Incident and Problem Management." In this case, a request model defines how to handle a particular, frequently occurring request.

The model should define the sequence of actions that must be performed, who will perform them, and the required timescales for each of the steps as well as for the fulfilment of the complete request. Any *escalation* paths that may be required should also be included.

Menu Selection

The effectiveness of request fulfilment is hugely enhanced if it is supported by a software tool, and probably a tool that is web based. Such a tool should be provided with a menu of available services from which the user is able to select. The provision of all the required information can be enforced by using mandatory fields and providing drop-down lists of possible options. In addition, the tool should set the user expectations by showing lead times, costs, and so on.

Where organizations are already offering a self-help IT support capability to the users, it makes sense to combine this with a request fulfilment system as described.

Specialist web tools to offer this type of "shopping basket" experience can be used together with interfaces directly to the backend integrated ITSM tools used to manage the request fulfilment activities.

Request Status Tracking

The owner of requests must be able to track them through their lifecycle and report progress to the requester where appropriate. Each organization will choose the appropriate statuses for its needs, but let's consider the most common statuses that are used:

- Draft indicates that a request is being prepared for submission. For whatever reason, at the moment the requester is unable or unwilling to submit the request.

- In Review indicates a request that has been authorized but is now under review by the relevant fulfilment team. They could be planning a desktop installation, for example.

- Suspended indicates that fulfilment activity has been suspended. This may be because the fulfilment group is waiting for action or information from the requester.

The other common statuses—Waiting Authorization, Rejected, Cancelled, In Progress, Completed, and Closed—are self-explanatory.

Prioritizing and Escalating Requests

All service requests should be prioritized based on a standard set of criteria. This can be done by considering the impact and urgency of a request, as with incident management. Alternatively, an organization might have set lead times for different request types.

There are a variety of reasons for escalating a request. Perhaps the obvious one is that a request might not be fulfilled within agreed timescales. Escalation might also be required if the process is being misused by the business. For example, the relocation of up to five workstations might be a service request but more than five would require the submission of a change request. Some managers in the business might try to get around this limitation by submitting several requests, each for five workstations but amounting to a large number in total. The request owner should be on the alert for this and escalate in the agreed manner.

Approval

As you've seen, many requests will incur a cost that must be approved. Some requests will have a standard charge—a software license or a standard workstation, for example. In other cases, the fulfilment group must establish the cost in the context of what exactly has to be done, as with an equipment move, for example. The role within the business responsible for approving the spend should be identified within the request model. Financial approval can be automated, and it may take place before the request is seen by the service desk. Requests for standard cost items may be routed to the approver before arriving at the desk.

Sometimes other types of approval are needed. These may include *compliance* with the organization's policies, especially as regards information security, or *technical approval* to confirm that the request will work with the infrastructure. Request fulfilment must have the ability to define and check such approvals where needed. Procedures for obtaining required approvals should be included as part of the request fulfilment models to save time in processing the service request.

Coordination of Fulfilment Activity and Closure of the Request

A request, including fulfilment, can be handled in many ways. Some requests can be automated—password resets, for example. Where human intervention is needed, the request can be fulfilled by a dedicated fulfilment group, by the technical support teams, by suppliers, or by a combination of these. Remember, though, that ownership of requests should remain with one team—usually the service desk, unless a dedicated request team exists.

The service desk should monitor and chase progress and keep users informed throughout, regardless of the actual fulfilment source.

When the service request has been fulfilled, it must be referred back to the service desk for closure. The service desk should go through a closure process that checks to see whether the user is satisfied with the outcome.

Process Activities, Methods, and Techniques

Take a look at the process flow shown in Figure 35.1. Although you do not need to know the process flow in detail for the exam, an understanding of what is involved in fulfilling service requests will help you understand its objectives.

First we will look at the process flow and then discuss the high-level activities.

The diagram shows the complete request fulfilment process flow. You can see that it includes logging, categorizing, and prioritizing a request as you would an incident. It also includes some activities that are specific to this process. The request is logged and validated, categorized, and prioritized. Any necessary authorizations are then obtained, and the request is reviewed to ascertain who will fulfil it. The appropriate request model is then executed, and finally, the request is closed, with the requester's agreement. We'll look at each of these steps in turn.

Receiving the Request

The first activity is receiving the request. Most service requests are received either from the web portal or at the service desk, but they could come in by other routes, such as email or even as requests for change (RFCs). From the point of view of the service provider, the preferred route is through the web portal because this will reduce the calls to the service desk. Not all incoming requests will in fact be service requests; they could be incidents or change requests, in which case they must be routed to the appropriate process.

Logging the Request

When a request is received, it should be logged and allocated a unique reference number, and all necessary information should be recorded. The web portal should be designed to help the requester provide the necessary information. The request record should be updated as necessary as the request proceeds through its lifecycle with date and time stamping to maintain a track of what happened and when.

FIGURE 35.1 Request fulfilment process flow

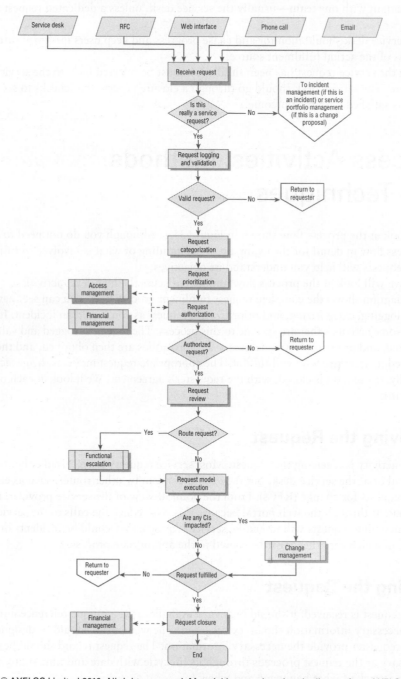

Validating the Request

The request is examined to confirm that it is valid; this includes making sure the request is within the scope of the IT services being offered. The web portal may help by restricting what can be logged to the available types of service requests. These tools ensure that the source of the request is valid and that only valid types of request are issued. Any requests that are invalid should be returned to the requester with an explanation; for example, the requested service might not be provided by the service provider.

Categorizing the Request

Categorizing the request will enable future analysis and reporting. As with the categorization of incidents, some thought should be given to the system employed. Requests could be categorized in a number of ways. For example, they could be categorized by activity, such as password reset or software installation. Another example is categorizing by the function that will fulfil the request.

Prioritizing the Request

Prioritization will be in line with business need, taking into account the impact and urgency of the request. A model such as was described previously for the prioritization of incidents could also be used here.

Authorizing the Request

We discussed the need for all requests to be authorized as one of the request policies. The degree of rigor needed here depends very much on the type of request. Requests that cannot be authorized should be returned to the requester.

Fulfilling the Request

After a request has been authorized, it is reviewed by the service desk and the appropriate fulfilment function is determined. In some cases, this will be the service desk itself; in others it might be a dedicated fulfilment team or even a supplier.

The request is then fulfilled by performing the actions specified in the appropriate request model. The request model can take a number of forms. In many organizations, it will simply be described in a written document; in others, a workflow tool will be used.

Completion and Closure of the Request

When the request has been fulfilled, it can be closed. Usually there will be a two-stage closure: the first stage simply records that, so far as the service provider is concerned, the fulfilment actions are complete; the second stage is the final closure, which should be performed only after consulting the requester.

If the service performed is chargeable, then at this point the appropriate charging mechanism is triggered. This might be sending a bill or registering a recharge. The service desk should check that the request documentation is up-to-date and that it is correctly categorized before final closure. Any updates to the CMS need to have been completed. This is also the time to conduct a satisfaction survey.

Triggers, Inputs, Outputs, and Interfaces

ITIL requires that every process should have a trigger and inputs to and outputs from the process activities. Each process will also have interfaces with a number of other processes.

Trigger

As previously explained, the request fulfilment process is triggered when a user submits a request. As you have seen, this may be directly to the service desk or via the web portal, where they can choose from a list of possible requests.

Inputs

The main input to the process is a request from the user. As you've seen, this can come by a variety of routes, each with its own format of information. Another significant input is the authorization form that may be required for some requests. Some requests may be logged as RFCs. Some requests will be for information, whereas others are for standard goods or services to be supplied.

Outputs

The following list includes examples of outputs from the process:

- Requests that have been authorized or rejected and those that are cancelled.

- Some requests may be rerouted as incidents. For example, a user requests a new laptop because their current machine keeps crashing. This could be rerouted to resolve the fault and thus save unnecessary expenditure on new equipment.

- Status reports may be output from the process.

- Where a standard change is required, an *RFC* may be raised.

- Some requests may be routed as changes because they are asking for nonstandard products or applications and need to be approved for use within the organization.

- The request should be updated as it is fulfilled.

- When the request is completed, the output will be a fulfilled request, which should then be closed.

- The final output is the update to the CMS when standard changes have been made.

Interfaces

Examples of primary interfaces with request fulfilment are as follows:

Financial Management for IT Services   Some requests may be chargeable, and financial approval may be required.

Service Catalog Management   The services that can be requested should be listed in the *service catalog.*

Release and Deployment Management   This will interface with request fulfilment when the request concerns the automatic deployment of new or upgraded components. In such cases, the release is predefined, built, and tested and deployed upon request.

Service Asset and Configuration Management   The CMS will need to be updated following any changes that may have been made as part of fulfilment activities. Where appropriate, software license checks/updates will also be necessary.

Change Management   Where a change is required to fulfil a request, it will need to be logged as an RFC and progressed through change management.

Incident and Problem Management   As discussed, requests may be handled using the incident management process. Where appropriate, it will be necessary to relate service requests issued by IT to any incidents or problems that created the need for the requests.

Access Management   This process may be involved with request fulfilment activities to ensure that those making requests are authorized to do so in accordance with the information security policy. Request fulfilment can act as the input to the access management process in relation to the creation and deletion of accounts.

Critical Success Factors and Key Performance Indicators

There are several possible critical success factors (CFSs) for request fulfilment, each of which will have key performance indicators (KPIs) to show whether the CSF is being achieved. Before we look at the CSFs and KPIs, we should take a minute to understand what these terms mean:

- A critical success factor, or CSF, is a high-level statement of what a process must achieve if it is to be judged a success. Normally, a process would have only three or four CSFs. A CSF cannot be measured directly; that's what key performance indicators are for.

- A key performance indicator, or KPI, is a metric that measures some aspect of a CSF. Each CSF will have three or four associated KPIs.

Here are some examples of CSFs and KPIs for request fulfilment:

- Critical success factor: "Requests must be fulfilled in an efficient and timely manner that is aligned to agreed service level targets for each type of request."

  Possible associated KPIs for this CSF are as follows:

  - The mean elapsed time for handling each type of service request
  - The number and percentage of service requests completed within agreed target times

  The first KPI relates to the requirement to fulfil requests in a timely manner and the second to meeting agreed targets. You may be able to think of other KPIs.

- Critical success factor: "Only authorized requests should be fulfilled."

  This could be measured by the following KPIs:

  - The percentage of service requests fulfilled that were appropriately authorized
  - The number of incidents related to security threats from request fulfilment activities

- Critical success factor: "User satisfaction must be maintained."

  The following examples would be relevant KPIs for this CSF:

  - The level of user satisfaction with the handling of service requests (as measured in some form of satisfaction survey)
  - The total number of incidents related to request fulfilment activities
  - The size of current backlog of outstanding service requests

Challenges

There are some common challenges encountered when implementing and running a request fulfilment process:

- Ensuring that the scope of the process is clearly defined by documenting the type of requests that will or will not be handled by this process and which requests need to go to change management.

- Providing an effective portal that will encourage users to submit requests there rather than calling the service desk. Clear targets must be agreed with the business for each type of request. These targets will be documented in the service level agreement.

- Reaching agreement with the business on where, when, and how authorization should be sought. It's important to adhere to normal budgetary controls in place within the organization.

- Agreeing on the costs for fulfilling requests, specifying whether they are to be recharged, and ensuring that service requests do not violate the information security policy.

- Providing the required level of information regarding the types of available requests in an easily accessible format, usually as part of the service catalog.

- Providing a documented request model with a predefined process flow for each of the services being requested to ensure that all requests follow a predefined standard fulfilment procedure.

- Making sure all service requests made through the web portal are processed in a timely manner to ensure customer satisfaction. Regular customer satisfaction surveys should be carried out.

Risks

There are five common risks faced by the request fulfilment process:

- A poorly defined or communicated scope will mean that users and IT staff will be unclear as to what the process will and won't handle.

- A poorly defined or implemented web portal will not be used. Users will continue to call the service desk and a major benefit of the process will be lost.

- Poorly designed or insufficiently resourced back-office fulfilment activities will mean that the process will not operate effectively or efficiently. Targets will not be met, backlogs will build up, and customer satisfaction will plummet.

- Inadequate monitoring capability will prevent metrics from being gathered, and as a result, performance won't be managed.

- Users may be reluctant to use a web-based tool if it is a new concept to the organization.

Summary

This chapter explored the next process in the service operation stage, request fulfilment. We discussed the key ITIL concepts of service requests and how the request fulfilment process can save time and money in expediting simple user requirements.

We examined the process in depth, covering its purpose, objectives, scope, and value. We considered its policies, principles, activities, and basic concepts and how its success might be measured. We also discussed what factors might work against a successful implementation.

Exam Essentials

Understand the purpose, objectives, and scope of request fulfilment.   Request fulfilment provides an efficient means of delivering services to customers, with low-risk requests and a defined fulfilment process. It can include IT and non-IT requests and be accessed through a self-help web portal.

Know how request fulfilment benefits the customer and the IT department. It provides the customer with an easy, efficient means of requesting services and enables the requests to be fulfilled by service desk and second-line staff with minimum bureaucracy.

Understand the use of request models. Because requests have a predefined fulfilment process, they are very well suited to the use of request models, which can be programmed into the service management toolset.

Understand the need for technical and financial approval. Although some requests are preauthorized, there may be occasions when authorizations are required. The usual corporate financial controls still apply, so the budget holder may need to approve, for example, the purchase of equipment. Technical authorization may be necessary as a confirmation that the request is compatible with the user's existing equipment.

Understand the use of a web portal and menu selection in implementing an efficient user interface. Request fulfilment can be greatly enhanced by providing the equivalent of an online shop, complete with "Add to Cart" facility. Users are familiar with this approach through Internet shopping, and it reduces the need for data entry at the service desk.

Review Questions

You can find the answers to the review questions in the appendix.

1. The request fulfilment process is suitable for which of the following?
    A. All requests, including RFCs
    B. Only requests that have been approved by the CAB
    C. Emergency requests for change, because the process will ensure a fast implementation
    D. Common, low-risk requests with a documented fulfilment procedure

2. Requests may be fulfilled by which of the following?
    1. Service desk staff
    2. Second-line staff
    3. Service level manager
    4. Business relationship manager
        A. 1 and 2
        B. All of the above
        C. 1 and 3
        D. 2 and 3

3. Which of the following statements is INCORRECT?
    A. Requests need to be authorized by the CAB.
    B. Requests need to be authorized by the budget holder when an expense will be incurred.
    C. Requests need to be authorized by technical management when technical compatibility is an issue.
    D. Requests which involve a change should be primarily preauthorized standard changes.

4. Which of the following could be defined as a service request?
    1. "Is the service available on weekends?"
    2. "How do I get training on this application?"
    3. "I need this application changed to include a web interface."
    4. "We have a new member of staff starting. Can you set them up on the system?"
        A. All of the above
        B. 3 and 4
        C. 1, 2, and 3
        D. 1, 2, and 4

5. Which of the following is the best description of a service request?

    A. A standard change

    B. A request from a user for information, for advice, for a standard change, or for access to an IT service

    C. An RFC

    D. The procurement process

6. Which of the following is NOT one of the objectives of the request fulfilment process?

    A. To provide a way for users to make requests through the service desk or web portal

    B. To provide a way for users to find out what standard services are available to them and how they can request them

    C. To assist with general information, complaints, or comments

    D. To understand and minimize the level of risk involved

7. Which of the following statements about request fulfilment are TRUE?

    1. The request fulfilment process and tools can be used for non-IT requests.

    2. The service desk should handle all requests, IT and others.

    3. A web portal can be a useful front end for users to access all types of service requests with automated authorization. Requests may then be forwarded to the appropriate department for resolution.

    4. A service catalog can be used to publicize the services available through the request process.

        A. 1, 2, and 4

        B. All of the above

        C. 1, 3, and 4

        D. 2 and 3

8. Requests can be handled using the incident management process rather than a separate request process. Which of the following statements about this approach is FALSE?

    1. It will always be more efficient to have a single process for incidents and requests.

    2. Reporting of trends may be confusing if requests are logged using the incident process.

    3. Incidents are time driven, whereas requests are more concerned with ensuring that all steps are carried out, and there may be a set lead time imposed for different request types, so each incident and request needs to be handled differently.

    4. The steps taken to log, assess, assign, and complete requests are exactly the same as those taken when managing incidents; if the number of requests is low, it can be easier to use a single process.

        A. 1 and 2

        B. 1 only

C. 2 and 3

D. 2 only

9. Which of the following process does NOT have an interface with request fulfilment?

   A. Service level management

   B. Access management

   C. Financial management

   D. Demand management

10. Which of the following is a possible risk for the request process?

   A. The budget for equipment purchase may be overspent due to multiple service requests for new devices.

   B. Users may try to use the request process to avoid the scrutiny of change management.

   C. The configuration management system might get out of step with the new and changed items being provided by the request process.

   D. Unnecessary items might be purchased when spare items are already in stock.

Chapter

36

Service Operation Processes: Event Management

THE FOLLOWING ITIL INTERMEDIATE EXAM OBJECTIVES ARE DISCUSSED IN THIS CHAPTER:

✓ **Event management is discussed in terms of its**

- Purpose
- Objectives
- Scope
- Value
- Policies
- Principles and basic concepts
- Process activities, methods, and techniques
- Triggers, inputs, outputs, and interfaces
- Critical success factors and key performance indicators
- Challenges
- Risks

Modern infrastructure management depends to a large extent on the use of event monitoring tools. These tools are able to monitor large numbers of configuration items simultaneously, identifying any issues as soon as they arise and notifying technical management staff. The process of event management is responsible for managing events throughout their lifecycle. Event management is one of the main activities of IT operations.

Definitions

To begin, let's consider some definitions from the *ITIL Service Operation* publication. These should be familiar from your Foundation course.

An *event* can be defined as any change of state that has significance for the management of a configuration item (CI) or IT service. Remember, an event is not necessarily an indication that something is wrong; it can merely be a confirmation that the system is working correctly. Many events are purely informational. Informational events could include notification of a user logging onto an application (significant because the use of the application may be metered) or a transaction completing successfully (significant because the notification of the successful completion may trigger the start of the next transaction).

An event that notifies staff of a failure or that a *threshold* has been breached is called an *alert*. An alert could be, for example, notification that a server has failed or a warning that the memory or disk usage on a device has exceeded 75 percent. If you consider these concepts in a non-IT environment, a car console may issue an event to say that the system has successfully connected to a Bluetooth device, or it might raise an alert (together with a beep or flashing light) to warn that a threshold has been breached and the car is now low on gas.

Effective service operation is dependent on knowing the status of the infrastructure and detecting any deviation from normal or expected operation. Event management monitors services for any occurrences that could affect their performance. It also provides information to other processes, including incident, problem, and change management.

There are two types of event monitoring tools:

- *Active monitoring tools* monitor configuration items or IT services by automated regular checks to discover the current status. The tool sends a message and expects a positive response within a defined time, such as sending a ping to a device. This is called polling of devices, and it is done to check that they are working correctly. Support staff will be notified of a failure to respond. Some tools will have *automated responses* to such situations, perhaps automatically restarting a device or rerouting data to avoid the faulty CI so that the service is not affected.

- *Passive monitoring tools* do not send out *polling* messages. They detect events generated by CIs and *correlate* them; that is, they identify related events. They rely on an alert or notification to discover the current status. Such notifications could include error messages.

Purpose

The purpose of event management is to detect events, understand what they mean, and take action if necessary.

Many devices are designed to communicate their status, and event monitoring will gather these communications and act upon any that need action. Some communications report operational information, such as "backup of file complete," "print complete," and so on. These events show that the service is operating correctly. They can be used to automate routine activities such as submitting the next file to be backed up or the next document to be printed. They may also be used to monitor the load across several devices, issuing automated instructions to balance the load depending on the events received. If the event is an alert, such as "backup failed," "printer jam," or "disk full," the necessary corrective steps will be taken. An incident should be logged in the case of a failure.

Objectives

Event management has the following objectives:

- It enables all significant changes of state for a CI or service to be detected. Event management should determine the appropriate control action for each event and ensure that they are communicated as necessary.

- The process provides the trigger for the automatic execution of many service operation processes and operations management activities. For example, a notification of a failure in the infrastructure would trigger the incident management process. By providing information when thresholds have been breached (for example, when a service has failed to respond within the agreed time), an event enables service level management to compare the actual operating performance against the SLA. The actual performance can also be compared to what was expected and planned for during the design stage.

- It triggers automated processes or activities in response to certain events. This may include automatically logging an incident in the service management tool in the event of a failure.

- Finally, the data gathered by event management forms the basis for service assurance and reporting and for comparing performance before and after a service improvement has been implemented.

Scope

Event management can be applied to any aspects of service management that need to be controlled and that could benefit from being automated. For example, the service management toolset automatically logs incidents in response to emails or events being received, escalates incidents when thresholds have been reached, and notifies staff of certain conditions (for example, a priority one incident being logged).

Configuration items can be monitored by event management tools; this monitoring can be for two different reasons:

▪ Some CIs will be monitored to make sure they are constantly available. An example of this is where action needs to be taken as soon as a CI such as a network device fails to respond to a ping.

▪ Other CIs may need to be updated frequently. This updating can be automated using event management, and the CMS can be automatically updated to show the new state.

Tracking licenses is another possible use for event management tools; licenses can be tracked to make sure there is no illegal use of an application by checking to see that the number of people using the software does not exceed the licenses held. This may also save money; by showing that there is less demand for concurrent use than was thought, the number of licenses can be reduced.

Monitoring for and responding to security events, such as detecting intruders, is another use; the tools can also be used to detect a denial of service attack or similar event.

Another use is the monitoring of *environmental conditions*. This might be for detecting a sudden increase in temperature in the server room or for other environmental changes.

Using Event Management to Preempt a Major Incident

A large transport organization installed event monitoring across its infrastructure, including monitoring the server room environments. A screen showing current events was installed at the service desk. On the second day after this was implemented, its value was proved. The service desk called the head office 150 miles away to ask the staff there to check the server room, because there were environmental alerts showing on the screen. The head office staff entered the server room to find that the air conditioning had failed and the room was extremely warm. Had the temperature increased much more, the servers would have failed, causing major disruption to the services. The head office staff members were able to avert the incident by using fans to lower the temperature until the air-conditioning engineer arrived to fix the fault.

Value

Event management offers many benefits to a business:

- Being able to carry out extensive monitoring without requiring a lot of staff. Using staff to monitor when errors may occur only occasionally would not be making best use of their skills.

- Errors would be identified faster, enabling an automated response, which would reduce downtime and its resultant costs to the business.

- Near-capacity situations would be identified before it is too late, giving time to take action.

- Event monitoring removes the need for repeated checks to be carried out on devices; it reduces effort by requiring responses only to exceptions.

- Event management, like other automation, takes place constantly, whereas staff may have other duties and may therefore miss something. It is also less error prone.

- Event management provides historical data to enable the identification of trends and potential problems.

Policies

Next, we consider suggested policies for event management.

The first policy states that event notifications should go to only those who have responsibility for acting on them. This means that a target audience must be identified for every event that we have chosen to handle—it is not acceptable to send a notification to everyone and hope that someone will do something.

The second policy relates to the centralization of event management. This ensures that notifications are handled consistently, that none are missed, and that none are handled by more than one person or team. It implies that a single rules engine will be used to process notifications, and of course that set of rules should be subject to change management.

The third policy provides guidance and constraints for the designers of new applications. There should be a common set of standards for events generated by applications. This will ensure consistency across applications and, of course, reduce the time to engineer event handling in new applications.

The next policy is that the handling of events should be automated as much as possible. The advantages of automation in general are well-known: reduced costs, fewer errors, and so on.

The fifth policy mandates the use of a standard classification scheme for events to ensure that similar types of events are handled in a consistent way.

The last policy states that all recognized events should at the very least be logged. This will provide a source of valuable information that might have a number of uses, for example, in problem investigation. A more sophisticated analysis of logged events might identify patterns of events that can be used to predict failures before they actually occur.

Principles and Basic Concepts

It is important to understand the difference between the two similar activities of monitoring and managing events. These are similar processes, but with specifically different emphasis.

Monitoring and Event Management

We need to monitor events, but monitoring covers more than events. Monitoring can be used, for example, to make sure devices are operating correctly, even without any events being generated. Monitoring actually looks for conditions that do not generate events.

Event management is about having useful notifications about the status of the IT infrastructure and services. Event management sets up rules to ensure that events are generated so they can be monitored, captured, and acted upon if necessary. Action is the key to event management.

The particular notifications themselves may be vendor specific. However, they are likely to use *Simple Network Management Protocol (SNMP)*, which is an Internet standard protocol for managing devices on IP networks. Devices that typically support SNMP include routers, switches, servers, workstations, printers, modem racks, and more. Because SNMP is an open standard, it makes interaction between different products simpler. Events must generate useful notifications. The time taken to create meaningful descriptions, with suggested actions, will save enormous effort later.

Event management can be enormously useful in managing large and complex infrastructures. It is often the case, however, that the full value of these tools is not realized. This is usually because there has been insufficient time spent making sure they are configured correctly to only notify staff of events for which they actually need notification. Failing to specify the correct thresholds, for example, will mean that far too many breaches are reported, causing staff to ignore them because they are seldom significant. Of course, this means that significant events are missed. If events are not filtered properly, the service management tool would be flooded with multiple spurious events, which would make it difficult to use its ability to automatically raise incidents.

Another important definition is that of an alert: An alert is a warning that a threshold has been reached, something has changed, or a failure has occurred. Alerts are often created and managed by system management tools and the event management process. Creating an alert when a disk or mailbox is nearly full is one such example.

Informational, Warning, and Exception Events

Some events indicate a failure that must be fixed, while others simply flag that something has happened and should be recorded. These are two types of event: the first is an *exception* and the second *informational*. There is a third type—a *warning* event. A warning event signifies unusual but not necessarily exceptional behavior. Warning events require further analysis to determine whether any action is required. Events will be handled according to their type.

Here are some examples of each type of event:

- Informational
  - A scheduled workload has completed.
  - A user has logged in to use an application.
  - An email has reached its intended recipient.
- Warning
  - A server's memory utilization reaches within 5 percent of its highest acceptable performance level.
  - The completion time of a transaction is 10 percent longer than normal.
- Exception
  - A user attempts to log on to an application with an incorrect password.

Notice that not all of these examples relate to a failure. (Failures would be alerts.) Some simply contain information, but information that for some reason it is important to record. For example, the business might want to maintain a record of who is using an application for audit purposes.

There are no definitive criteria for determining the type of an event; it depends very much on the specific situation of the organization. For example, an event might be that a previously unknown device has been detected on the network. Some organizations allow their staff to attach their own laptops to the corporate network, in which case the event would be informational. In a highly secure organization, it would almost certainly be treated as an exception.

Filtering

The next topic we'll examine is event filtering. We don't have complete control over the notifications that are generated by the configuration items. The manufacturers of hardware will have decided what notifications will be generated, and they may not have provided their customers with the ability to switch them off. A common experience when first beginning to monitor networks is that the monitoring tool is swamped by unrecognized and therefore unneeded notifications.

Filtering prevents the event management system from being overwhelmed by discarding notifications of events that have no significance to the organization.

There are four possible approaches to the problem:

- The first approach is to integrate event management into each service management process. What this means is that each process will identify the events that it is interested in.

- The next approach is to include event management requirements into the design of new services.

- A third approach is to use trial and error—evaluate notifications on a case-by-case basis and adjust the filtering accordingly.

- The final approach is to plan the introduction of event management within a formal project.

These approaches are not mutually exclusive; many organizations will adopt some hybrid of them.

Designing for Event Management

Successful event management in service operation requires analyzing and planning for what will be required. This should happen in the service design phase, although it will continue to be adjusted in service operation. Many organizations attempt and abandon event management, or they fail to achieve real value from it because this crucial design phase has been neglected.

The following questions should be asked when designing a service or planning the introduction of new technology:

- What needs to be monitored?

- What type of monitoring is needed?

- When should events be generated?

- What information should be communicated?

- Who are messages intended for?

- Who will respond to the event?

When event management is first established, these questions should be asked about the existing services and infrastructure. Stakeholders who must be consulted include the business, process owners, and operations management staff. Each of these groups will have monitoring requirements, and each could be involved in handling events when they occur.

Instrumentation

Instrumentation refers to specific ways to monitor and control the infrastructure and services. A number of practical issues need to be addressed when designing an event management system:

- How will events be generated? In the case of bought-in components, of course, this question is really, How *are* events generated?

- How will they be classified? This is not straightforward, and classifications can change over time.

- How will they be communicated and escalated? How exactly will the events get to the appropriate function? For example, how will an exception event trigger the incident management process? Ideally, this will be automated by integrating the event and incident management tools so that an incident will be logged automatically. Of course, this can only happen if the two tools have the necessary functionality.

- What data must be included in the event notification? What data will be needed for the event management system itself to interpret and make sense of the event, and what data will be needed by the function that will respond to the event? If the event relates to an error, then it should include necessary diagnostic information such as error messages and codes. Again, for bought-in software, this question is really, What data is included?

- Another question to be asked relates to the type of monitoring to use. Should it be active or passive?

- Where will event data be stored? There is likely to be a significant amount of event data, so the question of storage is important. Associated with this is the question of how long the data should be retained. This decision must be made on a case-by-case basis in consultation with the relevant stakeholders.

- How will supplementary data be gathered? In some cases, the event data alone will not be sufficient to evaluate the event. For example, it might be necessary to integrate the event management system with a CMDB.

Correlation Engine

As events are detected, the event management system must interpret and make decisions about how to handle them. This is done by software known as a *correlation engine*. The correlation engine allows the creation of rule sets that it will use to process events.

Using a correlation engine will enable the system to determine the significance of each event and also to determine whether there is any predefined response to an event. Patterns of events are defined and programmed into correlation tools for future recognition. The correlation engine can translate component-level events into service impacts and business impacts, as shown in Figure 36.1.

FIGURE 36.1   Correlation engine

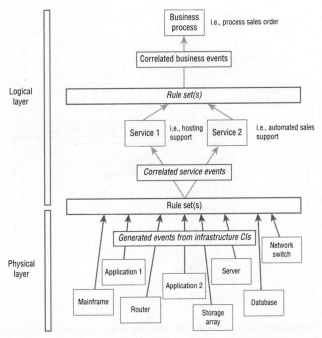

Process Activities, Methods, and Techniques

Next, we take a look at the event management process. The process steps are shown in Figure 36.2.

FIGURE 36.2   Event management process flow

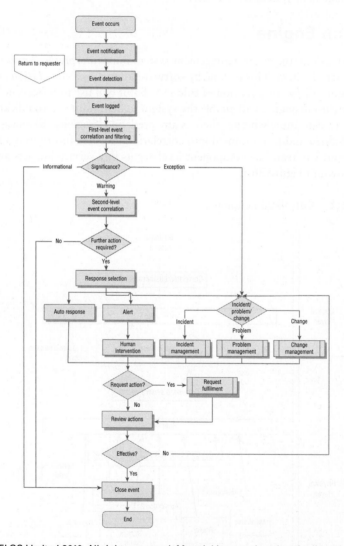

The initial sequence of activities in the event management process is as follows:

- An event occurs.
- The event notification is sent.
- The event is detected by the event management system and logged.
- First-level correlation and filtering takes place.

At this point, the event type (exception, warning, or informational) has been identified. No further processing is required for informational events. For exception events, one or more of the service management processes will be triggered. If the event concerns something that has broken and requires restoring to normal service levels, an incident should be raised. A problem record may be updated if another example of a fault under investigation occurs. The automated response to an event may include raising a change. Some events, such as a "toner low" message, may require a service request to be handled by the request fulfilment process.

Warning events will then enter second-level correlation, which identifies how to proceed. In some cases, the event will be treated as informational or as an exception. Other cases will trigger either an automated response or an alert for human intervention, as detailed in the following section.

Event Notification

Let's look at the initial process activities in a little more detail. Event notification refers to the communication of information about an event. You've already seen that some components will generate notifications independently, while others have to be prompted by polling.

Event Detection and Logging

Some events will be detected directly by the event management tool. Other events will be detected by a software agent running on the device being monitored. This agent then generates a notification that can be detected by the event management tool. All events are logged.

Correlation and Filtering

In first-level correlation, a decision about whether any further action is required is made, including whether the event has any significance to the organization. Correlation will determine whether an event is informational, a warning, or an exception. We discussed filtering earlier; this is necessary to stop staff being overwhelmed with events that do not require any action, or multiple reports of the same fault.

Informational events are closed at this point. Exception events will trigger one of the other service management processes. Warning events will go forward to second-level correlation.

Next, we consider the criteria that might be used by the second-level correlation engine to interpret an event:

- The number of similar events might be significant. For example, an event might notify us of an unsuccessful attempt to access our network. If this is just a single instance, we might treat it as informational, but if there have been 500 such attempts in the last 5 minutes, we might judge that we are the target of an organized attempt to break in.

- The number of devices generating similar events might be significant. It might indicate a widespread virus infection, for example.

- The data supplied with the event might indicate its significance.

- Events related to device utilization might be compared with a defined threshold.

The correlation engine determines whether the event requires some action or whether it can be treated as informational and closed.

Actions Taken

Some events indicate conditions that can be resolved automatically without human intervention. For example, if a file server is detected to be nearly full, then a script could be run that would free up space by archiving old data.

Some events will require human intervention—an alert from a smoke detector, for example. It's important that the alert is directed to the right person and that they know what to do.

Exception events will normally trigger the incident management process. Ideally, the event and incident management systems will be integrated so that an incident record can be raised automatically. A word of warning, however: This should be implemented only when you are happy that the filtering of events is working correctly. If this is not the case, your incident management system will be flooded with thousands of spurious incidents!

The problem management process might be triggered if the organization has a policy of always investigating the root causes of incidents that impact key services. Event management can support such a policy by automatically raising a problem record when it detects such an incident.

Change management can be triggered in two circumstances:

- First, if a previously unknown device is detected, an RFC should be raised, which can be progressed as appropriate by change management to have the device either added to the CMS or removed if required.

- The second circumstance is if a change is needed. For example, a server might need to be allocated more storage from a SAN.

Remember, sometimes it will be necessary to trigger a combination of these responses.

Review and Closure

There could be thousands of events each day, so it's unlikely that every one of them could be reviewed. It's sensible to review only what the service provider considers to be significant events. It is probably unnecessary to review events that have triggered other service management processes except to ensure that the triggers were effective.

Most events are neither opened nor closed but just logged in management systems or system logs. Many others can be closed automatically. For example, when a script is triggered to respond to an issue, the script itself could check that the corrective action has worked and generate an event to that effect.

Triggers, Inputs, Outputs, and Interfaces

We'll now consider the event management process triggers, inputs, outputs, and interfaces.

Triggers

Any type of change in state can trigger event management, and an organization should define which of these state changes need to be acted upon. Some examples are shown here:

- Exceptions to any level of CI performance defined in the design specifications or standard operating procedures.

- A breach of a threshold in an OLA could also generate an event.

- Any exceptions to a process, such as a failure to complete a process within the target time. An exception could also be a routine change that has been assigned to a build team or a business process that is being monitored by event management.

- The completion of an automated task or job could trigger the issuing of an event, as could a status change in a server or database CI.

- A user accessing a particular application or database could also cause an event to be issued if this is information that the business or the IT department wanted to know about. For example, IT may wish to track how often a service is being used to decide on the number of licenses required, or the business may wish to know how often a customer service representative needs to refer to the knowledge base to answer a query, as this might indicate a training requirement.

- The more usual trigger for an event, such as a situation in which a device, database, or application has reached a predefined threshold of performance.

Inputs

Inputs to event management usually come from service design and service transition. They include the examples listed here:

- Operational and service level requirements associated with events and their actions.

- Alarms, alerts, and thresholds for recognizing events.

- Event correlation tables, rules, event codes, and automated response solutions that will support event management activities.

- Roles and responsibilities for recognizing events and communicating them to those who need to handle them.
- Operational procedures for recognizing, logging, escalating, and communicating events.
- SLAs, which can be used by the correlation engine to determine the significance of an event or to identify a performance threshold.
- Rule sets that are provided by technical or application management staff based on the monitoring and management requirements. For example, the capacity management process would define the capacity thresholds that should generate an event.
- The roles and responsibilities of all those involved.
- Procedures for logging and escalating events as required.

Outputs

Outputs from event management are usually passed to other service management processes, such as incident management, change management, and request fulfilment. They include the examples listed here:

- Events that have been communicated and escalated to those responsible for further action
- Incident, problem, change, or request records required as a result of an event
- Event logs describing what events took place and any escalation and communication activities taken to support forensic, diagnosis, or further CSI activities
- Events that indicate an incident has occurred
- Events that indicate the potential breach of an SLA or OLA objective
- Events and alerts that indicate completion status of deployment, operational, or other support activities
- Populated service knowledge management system (SKMS) with event information and history

The most obvious output of the process is the events themselves. These should have been communicated and escalated to the appropriate people. Another output is a chronological event log describing what events took place and any escalation and communication activities taken. This may be useful information if further investigation is required or to spot possible improvement opportunities.

Some events output by event management will indicate that an incident has occurred, and others will warn of the potential breach of an SLA or OLA objective. Of course, as we have said, not all events show that something is wrong, and many events will just indicate successful completion of deployment or operational activities. The data output from event management can be used to populate the *SKMS* with the event information and history.

Interfaces between Event Management and the Lifecycle Stages

Finally, let's consider the interfaces event management has with the other lifecycle stages and their associated processes. Event management can interface with any process that requires monitoring and control, especially those that don't require real-time monitoring but do require some form of intervention following an event or group of events. First we'll consider how the process can even help the business directly.

Business Processes

The information provided by event monitoring may be used to help manage unusual occurrences with business processes.

Using Event Management to Preempt a Major Incident

Some years ago, a camera was mistakenly priced on a website at $59.99, when it should have been $599.99. Word spread through social media and thousands of orders were placed, which the company had to honor to avoid bad publicity. It took some time before anyone noticed, and then it was only when a staff member received an email from a friend. Event monitoring could have alerted the company to the unusual sales pattern very quickly, thus limiting the financial damage. Another similar example was an ATM that was filled with $20 notes in the $5 note holder. Queues formed as people withdrew cash from the machine, which was delivering four times the amount requested. In that situation, event management was in place, and the unusual pattern of multiple $5 withdrawals was spotted, and the machine was remotely closed down.

Service Design

Event management interfaces with a number of service design processes. Examples include the following:

- Service level management is the first such interface. Event management can be used to detect any potential impact on SLAs early so that action can be taken to resolve the fault to minimize that impact.

- Information security management may use event monitoring to monitor for unusual activity. This may be multiple login attempts or unusual activity for a business process, such as unusual spending on a credit card, which alerts the bank to a possible stolen card.

- Capacity and availability management define what events are significant, what the thresholds should be, and how to respond to them. Event management then responds to these events, improving the performance and availability of services.

Service Transition

Event management tools may also be used to support service transition processes:

- The service asset and configuration management process uses events to determine the current status of any CI. A discrepancy with the authorized baselines in the CMS will highlight an unauthorized change.

- Event management can determine the lifecycle status of assets. For example, an event could signal that a new asset has been successfully configured and is now operational.

- Knowledge management stores information obtained by event management in knowledge management systems. For example, patterns of performance information correlated with business activity is input into future design and strategy decisions.

- Event management interfaces with change management to identify conditions that may require a response or action.

Service Operation

Event management is a service operation process, and it interfaces with the other processes in that lifecycle stage:

- There is an obvious interface with incident and problem management because many alerts are results of failures and require an incident to be raised.

- By catching and logging each such occurrence, event management provides vital information to problem management about when and where the incidents are occurring.

- Finally, event management can be used by access management to detect unauthorized access attempts and security breaches.

Critical Success Factors and Key Performance Indicators

The next topics for discussion are critical success factors (CSFs) and key performance indicators (KPIs). Before we look at the CSFs and KPIs relevant to event management, we should take a minute to understand what these terms mean.

- A critical success factor, or CSF, is a high-level statement of what a process must achieve if it is to be judged a success. Normally, a process would have only three or four CSFs. A CSF cannot be measured directly–that's what key performance indicators are for.

- A key performance indicator, or KPI, is a metric that measures some aspect of a CSF. Each CSF will have three or four associated KPIs.

  Here are some examples of CSFs and KPIs for event management:

- Critical success factor: "Detect all changes of state that have significance for the management of CIs and IT services."Possible associated KPIs for this CSF include the following (notice that the first KPI is trying to gauge the success in detecting faults while the second is trying to measure the scope of the event management implementation):

- Number and ratio of events compared with the number of incidents
- Number and percentage of each type of event per platform or application versus total number of platforms and applications underpinning live IT services
- Critical success factor: "Ensure that all events are communicated to the appropriate functions that need to be informed or take further control actions."Associated KPIs might be as follows:
  - Number and percentage of events that required human intervention and whether this was performed
  - Number of incidents that occurred and percentage of them that were triggered without a corresponding event
- Critical success factor: "Provide the means to compare actual operating performance and behavior against design standards and SLAs."

The following KPIs would enable the CSF to be assessed:

- Number and percentage of incidents that were resolved without impact to the business (indicates the overall effectiveness of the event management process and underpinning solutions)
- Number and percentage of events that resulted in incidents or changes
- Number and percentage of events caused by existing problems or known errors (this may result in a change to the priority of work on that problem or known error)

Challenges

The following challenges could be encountered in event management:

- Lack of funding for tools and the effort needed to implement them successfully
- Establishing the correct level of filtering to avoid being flooded by events or having insufficient useful information
- Installing monitoring agents across the entire infrastructure
- Lack of time and funding for training to acquire the necessary skills to design and interpret events

Risks

The following risks are associated with event management; in many cases the risks are the result of failing to meet the challenges listed above.

- Failure to obtain adequate funding
- Ensuring the correct level of filtering
- Failure to maintain momentum in deploying the necessary monitoring agents across the IT infrastructure

If any of these risks are not addressed, they could adversely impact the success of event management.

Summary

This chapter explored the next process in the service operation stage, event management. It covered the use of event monitoring to manage large numbers of items and how automated responses to particular events may improve the delivery of services. It also explained the role of events in automating processes.

We discussed the key ITIL concepts of events and alerts and how event management can improve availability by preempting failures or reducing the time taken to identify them. Finally, we considered the technical and staff challenges of implementing this process.

Exam Essentials

Understand the purpose, objectives, and scope of event management.   Describe events (a change of state that has significance for the management of a CI) and alerts (a failure or breach of a threshold) and the difference between them. Be able to give examples of each.

Understand the role of event management in automation.   Describe passive and active monitoring and the difference between them. Be able to give examples of each. Understand the importance of filtering events and explain how effective event management can reduce downtime. Be able to explain automatic responses to certain types of events.

Know how event management benefits the customer and the IT department.   Understand the efficiency benefits to be gained by being able to have a small number of staff monitor huge numbers of CIs and services. Understand how improved availability through reduced downtime benefits the business.

Understand how event management can be used to monitor business events and environmental conditions.   Be able to explain how the process of event management can be applied beyond the technical IT environment.

Review Questions

You can find the answers to the review questions in the appendix.

1. For which of these situations would implementing automation by using event management be appropriate?
    1. Hierarchical escalation of incidents
    2. Speeding up the processing of month-end sales figures
    3. Notification of an "intruder detected" to local police station
    4. Running backups
        A. 3 and 4 only
        B. All of the above
        C. 2 and 3 only
        D. 1, 3, and 4 only

2. Event management can be used to monitor which of the following?
    1. Environmental conditions
    2. System messages
    3. Staff rosters
    4. License use
        A. 1 and 2 only
        B. 2 and 3 only
        C. 1, 2, and 4 only
        D. All of the above

3. Which of the following are types of event monitoring?
    1. Passive
    2. Virtual
    3. Active
    4. Standard
        A. 1 and 2 only
        B. 2 and 3 only
        C. 1 and 3 only
        D. All of the above

4. Which of the following is the best description of an alert?
    A. An unplanned interruption to a service
    B. The unknown, underlying cause of one or more incidents
    C. An event that notifies staff of a failure or that a threshold has been breached
    D. A change of state that has significance for the management of a CI

5. Which of the following describes an active monitoring tool?

A. A tool that correlates alerts generated from configuration items

B. A tool that allows the interconnection of configuration items in a single database

C. A tool that continually polls configuration items about their status

D. A tool that integrates with the active directory system to identify users

6. What is the correct way to handle an event?

1. Only the people or team responsible for handling events should be notified of an event.

2. All support teams should be notified of an event.

   A. Both are true.

   B. None are true.

   C. Only 1 is true.

   D. Only 2 is true.

7. Which of the following is NOT a type of event defined in ITIL?

A. Emergency

B. Exception

C. Warning

D. Informational

8. Which of the following does NOT describe a correlation engine?

A. Software that uses rule sets to process events

B. Software that uses rule sets to decide which changes should be approved

C. Software that uses rules to determine the significance of each event

D. Software that uses rules to determine the predefined response to each event

9. Which of the following describes the correct sequence of initial activities in the event management process?

A. Occurrence, detection, correlation, notification

B. Occurrence, notification, detection, correlation

C. Notification, occurrence, detection, correlation

D. Detection, occurrence, notification, correlation

10. Which of the following are valid inputs to the event management process?

1. OLA and SLA requirements associated with events and their actions

2. Alarms, alerts, and thresholds for recognizing events

3. Event correlation tables, rules, event codes, and automated response solutions

4. Roles and responsibilities for recognizing events and communicating them

5. SLAs used by the correlation engine to determine the significance of an event or to identify a performance threshold

6. Rule sets provided by technical or application management staff based on the monitoring and management requirements

   A. 1, 2, 4, and 6 only

   B. All of these are valid inputs

   C. 1, 3, 5, and 6 only

   D. 2, 3, 5, and 6 only

Chapter

37

Service Operation Processes: Access Management

THE FOLLOWING ITIL INTERMEDIATE EXAM OBJECTIVES ARE DISCUSSED IN THIS CHAPTER:

✓ Access management is discussed in terms of its

- ■ Purpose
- ■ Objectives
- ■ Scope
- ■ Value
- ■ Policies
- ■ Principles and basic concepts
- ■ Process activities, methods, and techniques
- ■ Triggers, inputs, outputs, and interfaces
- ■ Critical success factors and key performance indicators
- ■ Challenges
- ■ Risks

Access management is the process of granting *authorized* users the right to use a service while preventing nonauthorized users from gaining access. It is also sometimes referred to as *rights management* or *identity management*. Access requirements can change frequently, and service operation is responsible for granting access quickly, in line with the needs of the business, while ensuring that all requests are properly authorized.

Purpose

In Chapter 15, "Service Design Processes: Information Security Management and Supplier Management," we discussed information security management and its role in defining security policies. The process for implementing many of these policies is access management. This process provides users who have the required authorization with the ability to use the services they require. Ensuring that only authorized individuals are given access to data is a concern of every IT service provider; failure to carry this out correctly can be damaging and possibly breach legal or regulatory requirements. Consider the damage that could be done to an organization discovered to have allowed unauthorized access to medical or banking records because of poor access management processes.

Organizations need to ensure that access is managed not only when a new member of staff is appointed and set up with access to the systems, but also when the staff member leaves. A challenge many organizations face is keeping up-to-date with changing access requirements as a staff member moves between departments. Often new access rights are requested, but it's never determined whether the existing access rights are still required in the new position; therefore, the individual may amass significant rights over a period of years if this step is not carried out. It is dependent, in part, on the business informing the IT service provider of staff moving between departments; the IT provider should routinely query whether existing access is still required when additional access is requested.

There may also be occasions when access is restricted, perhaps, for example, during an investigation into suspected wrongdoing to prevent any evidence from being destroyed. Such requests would normally be made by senior management or human resources.

Objectives

The objectives of the access management process are to do the following:

- Manage access to services, carrying out the policies defined within information security management (see Chapter 15).

- Ensure that all requests for access are verified and authorized. This may include requests to restrict or remove access.

- Ensure that requests are dealt with efficiently, balancing the requirement for authorization and control with the need to be responsive to business requirements.

- Ensure (once access rights are granted) that the rights that have been granted are used in accordance with security policies. This might include, for example, Internet access for personal use. Although some personal use may be allowed, there are likely to be categories of websites that may not be accessed.

Scope

The scope of access management, as we have said, is the efficient execution of information security management policies. By carrying these out, the *confidentiality, integrity,* and *availability* (CIA) of the organization's data and intellectual property are protected. Confidentiality here means that only authorized users are able to see the data. Integrity means that the data is kept safe from corruption or unauthorized change. Access management ensures that the service is made available to the authorized user. This does not guarantee that it will always be available during service hours, which is the responsibility of availability management.

A request for access will often be made through the request management process. Some organizations will maintain a specialized team to carry out requests, but more commonly they are carried out by other functions. Technical and application management functions are involved, and a significant part of the process may be handled within the service desk. There should be a single coordination point to ensure consistency.

Value

The access management process provides a number of benefits to the business:

- First, by controlling access to services, it protects the confidentiality of the organization's information. Customer confidentiality, for example, is a significant concern for many organizations.

- A second benefit is that staff have the right level of access to perform their roles.

- A third benefit is that the process provides a means of tracking the use of services by users.

- Sometimes there may be a need to revoke access rights quickly—for example, if a user is suspected of criminal behavior. The process enables this to be done.

- Finally, the process will support regulatory and legal compliance not only by managing access, but also by being able to demonstrate that access is managed.

Policies

The *ITIL Service Operation* publication describes five useful policies for access management.

- The first policy is a formal statement of things we have already mentioned, especially that the management of access to services is led by the policies and controls defined by information security management. An implication of this is that if an unusual request for access is received, and it doesn't appear to fall within the guidelines laid down by information security management, then the request should be escalated to information security management. It cannot be granted at the discretion of access management.

- Another policy is that the use of services should be logged and tracked. *Tracked* here implies that access should be monitored in real time and events triggered as appropriate. There are also implications here for service designers—services must have the means of logging activity built into them.

- The third policy is that the process must keep the access rights up-to-date. In particular, it should modify rights as individuals change roles or leave the organization.

- The fourth policy is related to the second. It says that the process should maintain an accurate history of successful and unsuccessful attempts to access services. This information would be useful, for example, for later examination by auditors.

- The final policy is that escalation procedures should be defined for any events that threaten security.

Principles and Basic Concepts

We're now going to examine a number of basic access management concepts.

Access refers to the level and extent of a service's functionality or data that a user is entitled to use.

Identity refers to the information about a user that distinguishes them as an individual and verifies their status within the organization.

Rights, or *privileges*, refers to the actual settings whereby a user is provided access—for example, read, write, execute, change, and delete.

Service groups provide a means of simplifying the task of allocating rights. The idea behind service groups is that there are groups of users who will require exactly the same rights to the same set of services. Instead of rights being granted individually, a service group is created that has the required set of rights. Users are linked to the service group and will inherit the rights of the group.

Directory services refer to specific types of tools that are used to manage access and rights.

The High-Level Activities of the Access Management Process

You do not need to know the access management process in detail for the exam, but an understanding of the key points in managing access requests will help you understand the process. Figure 37.1 shows the Access Management process flow. We are going to look at each step of the process.

Request Access

A request for access can be made in a number of ways:

- The access request could be handled as a service request through the request fulfilment portal.
- It may result from the completion of a request form.
- If the change of access affects many users, a request for change will probably be used. For example, the transition of a new service will mean updating the access rights of everyone who will use the service.
- Another route is through an automated process. For example, each year a college or university will enroll possibly thousands of new students, and each of them must be granted access to student IT services. This is often done automatically by the student registration system when the student actually registers.
- The request may also come automatically from the HR system when a new member of staff is recorded or the status of an existing employee changes, such as when someone resigns or is transferred or promoted.

All requests, whether or not they are valid, are logged.

Verifying and Validating

The access request must then be verified. The identity of the requestor must be confirmed, and the access requirement must be judged as legitimate.

FIGURE 37.1 Access management process flow

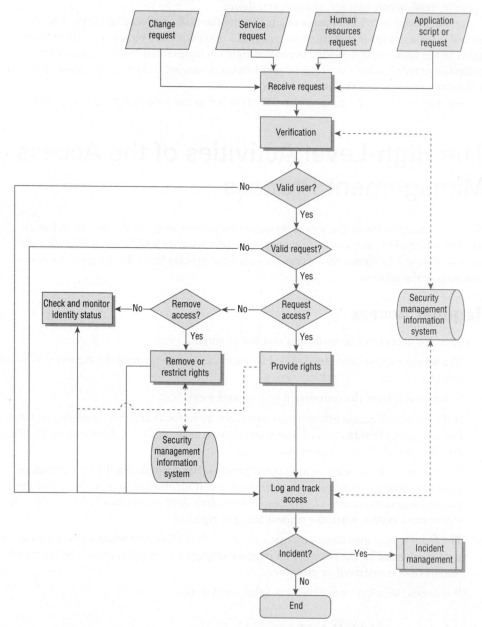

Usually, an existing user's username and password are accepted as proof of identity. In more secure environments, biometric data or physical identification devices can be used.

For new users, some physical evidence of identity will be required, such as official proof of identity (passport, driver's license).

New users include not only new permanent staff members, but also temporary and third-party users such as visitors, contract staff, and vendors. The organization will define how a request will be verified.

The second aspect of verification is checking that the request is legitimate; that is, the user is authorized to have the rights requested. This verification must be independent of the requester. A user cannot verify the legitimacy of their own request. Often a request will be verified by a line manager or HR. Requests that come by way of a request for change (RFC) will have been authorized through the change management process.

Some services will be available for use by anyone who requests them; there should be a policy that defines them. If the request is not valid, then it will be logged and returned to the requester. An incident may be raised to investigate why an invalid request was raised, if thought necessary. A valid request will be actioned appropriately.

Provide Access

The task of providing rights is often devolved to a specialist technical or application team that has the necessary knowledge and skills. This task can be automated by using access management tools that interface with multiple applications. This is only possible, of course, if the design of the applications included this as a requirement.

Access rights are associated with a role: a payroll clerk has the right to use the payroll system. Users can occupy multiple roles, each of which brings a set of rights, and sometimes these conflict with some enterprise policy such as the separation of duties. For example, it is usual practice to ensure that a person who places an order with a supplier is not able to authorize payment. Where a role conflict occurs, access management should escalate the issue to the appropriate stakeholder, who will be someone in the business area concerned. (For example, if the roles are within the finance department, the issue would be referred to the appropriate stakeholder in that department; if the roles are within the IT department, the appropriate IT manager would be consulted.)

Monitor Access

Once the access has been granted, the status of the user should be monitored to ensure that they still have a valid requirement for the access. In practice, this can be difficult to achieve. Access management should be notified of staff that leave so that their access can be revoked, and many organizations have robust procedures to ensure that this is done. Many organizations encounter difficulty in tracking the changing roles and accompanying access requirements of users, especially those who have been in the organization for many years. In this situation, new access requirements are added to existing rights, with no verification that the existing rights are still required. Consideration should be given to adding questions about existing access requirements to the access request form. The human resources department needs to be made aware of the importance of supplying information regarding changing job roles to access management in order to protect the organization's data. Access management should understand these different types of staff changes and determine how it will become aware of them. Ideally, this will be automated by an interface with the HR system. The failure to respond to changes in status is a common security issue. It leads, for example, to computer accounts remaining available for use even though the users have left the organization.

The tracking access activity might trigger a security incident if, for example, an unsuccessful attempt to access a service is made by a valid user.

Remove Access

The last activity that we'll look at is removing or restricting a user's rights. There are a number of circumstances when this might be necessary. Although in many cases the modification is permanent, such as in the case of dismissal or promotion, there may be situations where this is only temporary. For example, in some organizations, a user's computer account is suspended when they go on leave.

Access should be permanently revoked when a user leaves an organization; again, the human resources department needs to understand the importance of informing access management quickly in this situation.

Access management has to ensure that rights are not improperly used, which will require that access is logged and tracked. The degree of oversight required is determined when the service is designed and the appropriate logging mechanisms are provided. Should possible misuse be detected, the process must respond appropriately. This will usually entail raising a security incident and alerting stakeholders. In this situation, access may be temporarily revoked during the investigation, with access being restored if the misuse is deemed to have been an innocent mistake, or permanently revoked if it is found to be deliberate. The access management process may be required to provide a record of access, perhaps in the context of the investigation of criminal behavior.

Triggers, Inputs, Outputs, and Interfaces

Next we consider the triggers for the process, its inputs and outputs, and the interfaces it shares with other processes.

Triggers

Access management is triggered by a request for a user or users to access a service or group of services. This could originate from a number of circumstances.

The first possible trigger is an RFC, especially where a large number of access changes are required, perhaps as part of a rollout or project.

Another possible trigger is a service request. This is usually initiated through the service desk, or input directly into the request fulfilment system, and executed by the relevant technical or application management teams.

A request from human resources is another possible trigger. In this situation, human resources management personnel make the request through the service desk. These requests are usually as a result of hiring, promoting, relocating, termination, or retirement.

The final trigger may be a request from the manager of a department, who could be performing a human resources role or who could have made a decision to start using a service for the first time.

Inputs

The inputs to the process are those that relate to the triggers, such as these:

- Authorized RFCs and authorized requests to grant or terminate access rights
- The security policies of the enterprise
- Any information about the identity of users

Other inputs are the operational and service level requirements for granting access to services, performing access management administrative activities, and responding to events related to access management.

Outputs

The access management process has the following outputs:

- The provision of access to IT services in accordance with information security policies
- The access management records showing when access has been granted or denied and the reasons for the denial
- Timely communications concerning inappropriate access or abuse of services

Interfaces

The access management process interfaces with a number of other service management processes.

A key interface is the one with information security management. As already stated, access management acts under the guidance and instruction of information security management and plays an essential part in ensuring that the requirements of the information security policies are met.

Many requests for access will come from the change management process in the form of authorized requests for change or even standard changes.

It is through the service level management process that access requirements and criteria are agreed on with the business on a service-by-service basis.

The relationship of the process with IT service continuity management is interesting. Access requirements may need to be varied should the continuity plan be invoked. Also, there may be a need to grant temporary access when the plan is being tested.

Request fulfilment provides a route for users to submit access requests.

Critical Success Factors and Key Performance Indicators

The *ITIL Service Operation* publication suggests three critical success factors (CSFs) for access management.

The first is "Ensuring that the confidentiality, integrity, and availability of services are protected in accordance with the information security policy." The key performance indicators (KPIs) show whether the critical success factors are being achieved. The first KPI is percentage of incidents that involved inappropriate security access or attempts at access to services. You can see that this is measuring actual consequences of poor access management. The second KPI is the number of audit findings that discovered incorrect access settings for users who have changed roles or left the company. This is measuring the potential for security lapses caused by poor access management.

The second CSF for access management is "Provide appropriate access to services in a manner that's timely enough to meet business needs." The example KPI for this is percentage of requests for access that were provided within established SLAs and OLAs.

The last CSF for access management is "Provide timely communications about improper access or abuse of services." This, and the suggested KPI of a reduction in the average duration of access-related incidents (from time of discovery to escalation), are about ensuring that any issues are dealt with expeditiously.

Challenges

For access management to be successful, it must overcome a number of challenges. It must be able to do the following:

- Verify the identity of both the user and the approving person or body
- Verify that a user qualifies for access to a specific service
- Link multiple access rights to an individual user
- Determine the status of the user at any time, such as to assess if they are still employees

- Manage changes to a user's access requirements
- Restrict access rights to unauthorized users
- Keep a database of all users and the rights that they have been granted

Meeting these challenges requires a considerable effort.

Risks

Finally, we consider the risks faced by access management. Failure to meet any of the challenges described in the preceding section is a risk, of course. There are five additional risks:

- The first risk is a lack of appropriate supporting technologies, causing a reliance on error-prone manual involvement.
- Another risk is controlling access from "backdoor" sources such as application interfaces.
- A third risk is managing and controlling access to services by external third-party suppliers. Third parties may need access for a variety of legitimate reasons, but the access is often occasional and unplanned, which makes it difficult to manage.
- Lack of management support for the process is a risk for all service management processes. A particular issue here is that management can often see security controls as obstructing them and their staff from accomplishing their tasks and therefore do not support them.
- There is a risk that access controls will hinder the ability of users to conduct business.

Summary

This chapter explored the remaining process in the service operation stage, access management. It covered access management's purpose, objectives, scope, and value. We discussed policies, principles, and basic concepts; process activities, methods, and techniques; triggers, inputs, outputs, and interfaces; critical success factors and key performance indicators; and challenges and risks.

You learned about the key ITIL concepts of access, identity, rights, and service groups.

We discussed the importance of access management in preventing unauthorized access to data and some of the issues that arise in monitoring access rights.

Exam Essentials

Understand the purpose, objectives, and scope of access management.   Explain the relationship between access management and information security management. Access management is not just granting access, it is also restricting or removing it as required.

Understand the main process activities of access management.   Explain the following access management activities: requesting access, validating and verifying a request, providing a request and monitoring how it is used, and finally, where necessary, removing it.

Review Questions

You can find the answers to the review questions in the appendix.

1. Which of the following is the best description of access management?

   A. Access management enables authorized access to services and data. Information security management prevents nonauthorized staff from gaining access.

   B. Access management grants authorized users the right to use a service while preventing nonauthorized users from gaining access.

   C. Access management is responsible for setting security policies.

   D. Access management decides what services users should have access to.

2. Why is effective access management important for an organization?

   1. Because there may be legal requirements to require control over access to data.

   2. Because poor access management may lead to data that should have been protected being made available to unauthorized individuals, leading to negative press that could damage the reputation of the organization.

   3. Because effective access management will reduce costs.

   4. Because without it, potential customers may hesitate to deal with the organization, concerned that their data will not be protected.

   5. Because otherwise, deciding what access to allow will be an IT rather than a business decision.

      A. 1, 2, and 4 only

      B. 1, 4, and 5 only

      C. All of the above

      D. 1, 2, 4, and 5 only

3. Which of the following is NOT a challenge for access management?

   A. Verifying identity

   B. Validating access requests

   C. Tracking access rights when users change names (such as upon marriage) or have the same name as another user

   D. Tracking changes in requirements as users change jobs

4. When might access management reduce or remove access?

   1. If the user is on long-term leave

   2. If the user has left the organization

   3. If the user is under investigation for wrongdoing

   4. If the user has changed jobs within the organization

    A. All of the above

    B. 1, 3, and 4 only

    C. 2, 3, and 4 only

    D. 1, 2, and 3 only

5. Which of the following is the best description of why access management monitors the use of the access rights granted to users?

    A. To understand if users are accessing forbidden websites

    B. To ensure that the security policy is being adhered to

    C. To monitor users' personal emails

    D. To understand how often users attempt to breach security

6. When it's used in the context of access management, what does the acronym *CIA* stand for?

    A. Corruption, insecurity, and authorization

    B. Contingency, integration, and accessibility

    C. Configuration, integrity, and availability

    D. Confidentiality, integrity, and availability

7. Who might be involved in carrying out the access management process?

    1. A specialized team

    2. Technical and application management functions

    3. The service desk

    4. The information security process owner

        A. Any of the above

        B. 1, 2, and 3 only

        C. 1 and 2 only

        D. 1, 3, and 4 only

8. Which of the following is NOT an example of how a business benefits from the access management process?

    A. By controlling access to services, it protects the confidentiality of the organization's information.

    B. It defines the levels of protection required for different classes of data.

    C. It ensures that staff have the right level of access to perform their roles.

    D. It provides the means of tracking the use of services by users.

9. Which of the following is the correct definition for the term *identity*?

    A. The level and extent of a service's functionality or data that a user is entitled to use.

    B. The specific types of tool used to manage access and rights.

    C. The information about a user that distinguishes them as an individual and verifies their status within the organization.

D. The actual settings whereby a user is provided access—for example, read, write, execute, change, and delete. It provides the means of tracking the use of services by users.

10. Which of the following are valid triggers for the access management process?

   1. An RFC

   2. A service request

   3. A request from human resources

   4. A request from the manager of a department

      A. Any of the above

      B. 1, 2, and 3 only

      C. 1 and 2 only

      D. 1, 3, and 4 only

Chapter

38

Common Service Operation Activities

THE FOLLOWING ITIL INTERMEDIATE EXAM OBJECTIVES ARE DISCUSSED IN THIS CHAPTER:

✓ Service operation principles

✓ Techniques

✓ Relationships

✓ Application to the delivery and support of services at agreed levels

✓ To meet the learning outcomes and examination level of difficulty, you must ensure that you are able to understand, describe, identify, demonstrate, apply, distinguish, produce, decide, and analyze

- How the common activities of service operation are coordinated for the ongoing management of the technology that is used to deliver and support the services

- How monitoring, reporting, and control of the services contribute to the ongoing management of the services and the technology that is used to deliver and support the services

- How the operational activities of processes covered in other lifecycle stages contribute to service operation

- How IT operations staff should look for opportunities to improve the operational activities

This chapter focuses on a number of operational activities that ensure that technology is aligned with the overall service and process objectives. These are sets of specialized technical activities all aimed at ensuring that the technology required to deliver and support services is operating effectively and efficiently.

They are usually technical in nature, although the exact technology will vary depending on the type of services being delivered. This chapter focuses on the activities required to manage operational day-to-day delivery of IT services.

Common Service Operation Activities

It is important to remember that there is no "right" way of grouping and organizing the departments that perform these activities and services. In looking at these topics, we will not refer to names of departments.

These are typical technical activities involved in service operation. They do not represent any level of maturity but are usually all present in some form at all levels. They are just organized and managed differently at each level.

Sometimes they are carried out by a specialist team, sometimes shared between groups. For simplicity, we have listed the activities under the functional groups most likely to be involved in their operation, but many organizations will do things differently.

Smaller organizations usually assign groups of these activities (if they are needed at all) to single departments or even individuals.

We will not look in detail at the activities because they vary and change according to the technology in use. We will explore the importance and nature of technology management for IT service management.

Maturing Technology Management

As service operation matures, its focus moves from purely technical management of the infrastructure (as described in level 1 of Figure 38.1) to achieving control (described in level 2), followed next by consolidation and integration (described in level 3) and then mapping service provision to the business requirement (described in level 4).

FIGURE 38.1   Achieving maturity in technology management

Level 5	**Strategic contribution**	– IT is measured in terms of its contribution to the business. – All services are measured by their ability to add value. – Technology is subordinate to the business function it enables. – Service portfolio drives investment and performance targets. – Technology expertise is entrenched in everyday operations. – IT is viewed as a utility by the business.
Level 4	**Service provision**	– Services are quantified and initiatives aimed at delivering agreed service levels. – Service requirements and technology constraints drive procurement. – Service design specifies performance requirements and operational norms. – Consolidated systems support multiple services. – All technology is mapped to services and managed to service requirements. – Change management covers both development and operations.
Level 3	**Technology integration**	– Critical services have been identified together with their technology dependencies. – Systems are integrated to provide required performance, availability, and recovery for those services. – More focus on measuring performance across multiple devices and platforms. – Virtual mapping of configuration and asset data with single change management for operations. – Consolidated availability and capacity planning on some services. – Integrated disaster recovery planning. – Systems are consolidated to save cost.
Level 2	**Technology control**	– Initiatives are aimed at achieving control and increasing the stability of the infrastructure. – IT has identified most technology components and understands what each is used for. – Technical management focuses on achieving high performance of each component regardless of its function. – Availability of components is measured and reported. – Reactive problem management and inventory control are performed. – Change control is performed on "mission-critical" components. – Point solutions are used to automate those processes that are in place, usually on a platform-by-platform basis.
Level 1	**Technology-driven**	– IT is driven by technology and most initiatives are aimed at trying to understand infrastructure and deal with exceptions. – Technology management is performed by technical experts, and only they understand how to manage each device or platform. – Most teams are driven by incidents, and most improvements are aimed at making management easier—not to improve services. – Organizations entrench technology specializations and do not encourage interaction with other groups. – Management tools are aimed at managing single technologies, resulting in duplication. – Incident management processes start being created.

Finally, it matures to measuring services in terms of value to the business (described in level 5), and it becomes increasingly business-centric.

The diagram illustrates the steps involved in maturing from a technology-centric organization to an organization that harnesses technology as part of its business strategy. It further outlines the role of technology managers in organizations of differing maturity. The diagram is not comprehensive, but it does provide examples of the way in which technology is managed.

The following sections focus on technical management activities, but there is no single way of representing them. A less mature organization will tend to see each activity as an end in itself, not a means to an end. A more mature organization will tend to subordinate these activities to higher-level service management objectives. For example, the server management team will move from an insulated department, focused purely on managing servers, to a team that works closely with other technology managers to find ways of increasing their value to the business.

We begin by considering monitoring and control.

Monitoring and Control

The measurement and control of services is based on a continual cycle of monitoring, reporting, and subsequent action. We are going to explore this cycle because it is fundamental to the delivery, support, and improvement of services.

It is also important to note that, although this cycle takes place during service operation, it provides a basis for setting strategy, designing and testing services, and achieving meaningful improvement. It is also the basis for service level management measurement. Therefore, although monitoring is performed by service operation functions, it should not be seen simply as an operational matter. All stages of the service lifecycle will be involved in ensuring that measures and controls are clearly defined, executed, and acted upon.

Monitoring

Monitoring refers to the activity of observing a situation to detect changes that happen over time. In the context of service operation, this implies that tools will be used to monitor the status of key configuration items (CIs) and key operational activities. This should ensure that specified conditions are met or not met. In the case of the latter, this would lead to raising an alert to the appropriate group; for example, it would raise an alert to the network team if a key network device failed. This will assist with the management of the performance or utilization of a component or system and ensure that it is within a specified range as far as, for example, disk space or memory utilization.

Monitoring will also be concerned with the detection of abnormal types or unusual levels of activity in the infrastructure, such as potential security threats due to numerous unrecognized accounts trying to log in, and unauthorized changes, such as introduction of a software version or type not mandated within the organization. Monitoring can facilitate compliance with the organization's policies (such as flagging inappropriate use of email) and allows the organization to track outputs to the business and ensure that they meet quality and performance requirements. Monitoring data is also used to track any information used to measure key performance indicators (KPIs).

Reporting

Reporting refers to the analysis, production, and distribution of the output of the monitoring activity. In the context of service operation, this implies that tools will be used to collate the output of monitoring information that can be disseminated to various groups, functions, or processes.

The reports will be used to support the interpretation of the meaning of the monitoring information, and to determine where that information would best be used. It is an important aspect of monitoring and control to ensure that decision-makers have access to the information that will enable them to make decisions. This requires that the organization is able to route the reported information to the appropriate person, group, or tool.

Control

Control refers to the process of managing the utilization or behavior of a device, system, or service. It is important to note, however, that simply manipulating a device is not the same as controlling it. Control requires three conditions: First, the action must ensure that the outcome conforms to a defined standard or norm; second, the conditions prompting the action must be defined, understood, and confirmed; and third, the action must be defined, approved, and appropriate for these conditions.

When considered in the context of service operation, control usually implies that tools will be used to define what conditions represent normal or abnormal operations. Development of thresholds in toolsets will allow for the regulation of the performance of devices, systems, or services. Controls also support the measurement of availability by initiating corrective action, which could be automated (reboot a device remotely or run a script when triggered by a "self-healing" system) or manual (notification to operations staff of a status that needs attention).

Monitor Control Loops

The most common model for defining control is the monitor control loop. Although it is a simple model, it has many complex applications within IT service management (ITSM). The diagram in Figure 38.2 outlines the basic principles of control.

FIGURE 38.2   The monitor control loop

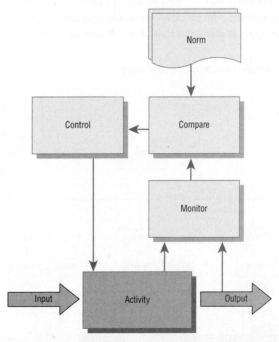

A single activity and its output are measured and compared using a predefined norm, or standard, to determine whether it is within an acceptable range of performance or quality. If not, action is taken to rectify the situation or to restore normal performance.

Typically, there are two types of monitor control loops, the open loop and the closed loop.

Open loop systems are designed to perform a specific activity regardless of environmental conditions. For example, a backup can be initiated at a given time and frequency and will run regardless of other conditions.

Closed loop systems monitor an environment and respond to changes in it. An example of this system would be the use of a closed loop in network load balancing. Monitoring will evaluate network traffic across a specific range. If network traffic exceeds this, the control system will begin to route traffic across a backup circuit. The monitor will continue to provide feedback to the control system, which will continue to regulate the flow of network traffic between the two circuits.

This example may help to clarify the difference. An open loop system would be used to solve capacity management through overprovisioning; a closed loop system would use a load balancer that detects congestion/failure and redirects capacity.

Complex Monitor Control Loop

Within the context of ITSM, the monitor control loop is often far more complex. The diagram illustrates a process consisting of three major activities. Each one has an input and an output, and the output becomes an input for the next activity.

In Figure 38.3, each activity is controlled by its own monitor control loop, using a set of norms for that specific activity. The process as a whole also has its own monitor control loop, which spans all the activities and ensures that all norms are appropriate and are being followed.

FIGURE 38.3 Complex monitor control loop

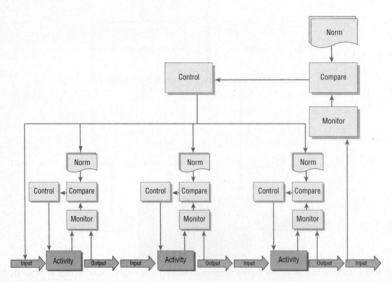

There is a double feedback loop. One loop focuses purely on executing a defined standard, and the second evaluates the performance of the process and also the standards whereby the process is executed.

This approach can be used to monitor the performance of activities in a process or procedure. Each activity and its related output can potentially be measured to ensure that problems with the process are identified before the process as a whole is completed. For example, in incident management, the service desk monitors whether a technical team has accepted an incident in a specified time. If not, the incident is escalated.

This can also measure the effectiveness of a process or procedure as a whole. In this case, the activity box represents the entire process as a single entity. For example, change management will measure the success of the process by checking whether a change was implemented on time, to specification, and within budget.

Finally the monitor control loop can also monitor the performance of a device. For example, the activity box could represent the response time of a server under a given workload.

To recap, we can use control loops to monitor a whole variety of areas—from processes to devices. We need to establish what the norm for output should be, and this is the major consideration for service management. Service management monitoring will be used to support the achievement of specific targets for process effectiveness and process outputs.

To define how to use the concept of monitor control loops in service management, the following questions need to be answered.

- How do we define what needs to be monitored?

- What are the appropriate thresholds for each of these?

- How will monitoring be performed (manual or automated)?

- What represents normal operation?

- What are the dependencies for normal-state service operation?

- What are the dependencies for monitoring and controlling?

- How frequently should the measurement take place?

- Do we need to perform active measurement to check whether the item is within the norm or do we wait until an exception is reported (passive measurement)?

- Is IT operations management the only function that performs monitoring?

- If not, how are the other instances of monitoring related to operations management?

- If there are multiple loops, which processes are responsible for each loop?

Although Figure 38.4 represents monitoring and control for the whole of ITSM, the control loop is used in service operation. Some may feel that it would be more suitably covered in ITIL service strategy. However, monitoring and control can effectively be deployed only when the service is operational. This means that the quality of the entire set of ITSM processes depends on how they are monitored and controlled in service operation.

FIGURE 38.4   The ITSM monitor and control loop

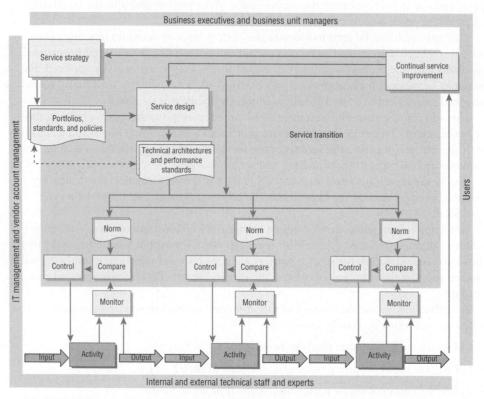

Internal and External Monitoring and Control

The definition of what needs to be monitored is based on understanding the desired outcome of a process, device, or system. IT should focus on the service and its impact on the business rather than just the individual components of technology. The first question that needs to be asked is, What are we trying to achieve?

If we consider internal monitoring and control, it is clear that most teams or departments are concerned about being able to execute effectively and efficiently the tasks that have been assigned to them. This type of monitoring and control focuses on activities that are self-contained within that team or department. For example, the service desk manager will monitor the volume of calls to determine how many staff need to be available to answer the telephone.

External monitoring and control is concerned with the monitoring that is addressing wider needs and requirements. Although each team or department is responsible for managing its own area, they do not act independently. Each team or department will also be controlling items and activities on behalf of other groups, processes, or functions. For example, the server management team will monitor the CPU performance on key servers and perform workload balancing so that a critical application is able to stay within performance thresholds set by application management.

If service operation focuses only on internal monitoring, it will have very well-managed infrastructure but no way of understanding or influencing the quality of services. If it focuses only on external monitoring, it will understand how poor the service quality is but will have no idea what is causing it or how to change it. In reality, most organizations have a combination of internal and external monitoring, but in many cases, these are not linked.

Defining Objectives for Monitoring and Control

It is common for organizations to start by asking the question, What are we managing? This will frequently lead to a strong internal monitoring system, with very little linkage to the real outcome or service that is required by the business. This may be because of the overall service management maturity of the organization.

Perhaps a better and more business-focused question would be, What is the end result of the activities and equipment that my team manages? Therefore, the best place to start when defining what to monitor is to determine the required outcome. But this will require a level of maturity, and it should start within the process of service level management.

The definition of monitoring and control objectives should ideally start with the service level requirements documents. These will specify how the customers and users will measure the performance of the service and are used as input into the service design processes. During service design, various processes will determine how the service will be delivered and managed. For example, capacity management will determine the most appropriate and cost-effective way to deliver the levels of performance required. The service design process will help to identify sets of inputs for defining operational monitoring, control norms, and control mechanisms.

All of this means that a very important part of defining what service operation monitors and how it exercises control is to identify the stakeholders of each service and their requirements.

Types of Monitoring Strategies

There are many different types of monitoring strategies and different situations in which each will be used. We have explored the concepts of internal and external monitoring. Now we'll briefly consider other monitoring types that are complementary to these high-level approaches.

Active monitoring is the ongoing "interrogation" of a device or system to determine its status. Because this type of monitoring is often resource intensive, it may be reserved to proactively monitor the availability of critical devices or systems. It can also be used as a diagnostic step for resolving an incident or diagnosing a problem.

Passive monitoring, which is more common, is generating and transmitting events to a "listening device" or monitoring agent. Passive monitoring depends on successful definition of events and instrumentation of the system being monitored. If the configuration of the tool is not correct, then events will not be captured and actions may not be taken.

Reactive monitoring is designed to request or trigger action following a certain type of event or failure. For example, degradation of server performance may trigger a reboot, or a system failure may generate an incident. Reactive monitoring is most commonly used for exceptions. But it can also be used as part of normal operations procedures—for example, a batch job completes successfully, which prompts the scheduling system to submit the next batch job.

Proactive monitoring is used to detect patterns of events that indicate that a system or service may be about to fail. Proactive monitoring is generally used in more mature environments where these patterns have been detected previously, often several times. Reactive and proactive monitoring could be active or passive.

In Table 38.1, you can see some example interactions between active and passive monitoring with reactive and proactive monitoring.

TABLE 38.1 Active and passive reactive and proactive monitoring

	Active	Passive
Reactive	Used to diagnose which device is causing the failure and under what conditions (e.g., pinging a device, or running and tracking a sample transaction through a series of devices) Requires knowledge of the infrastructure topography and the mapping of services to CIs Requires capability to simulate service workloads and demand volumes	Detects and correlates event records to determine the meaning of the events and the appropriate action (e.g., a user logs in three times with the incorrect password, which represents a security exception and is escalated through information security management procedures) Requires detailed knowledge of the normal operation of the infrastructure and services
Proactive	Used to determine the real-time status of a device, system, or service—usually for critical components or following the recovery of a failed device to ensure that it is fully recovered (i.e., it's not going to cause further incidents)	Event records are correlated over time to build trends for proactive problem management. Patterns of events are defined and programmed into correlation tools for future recognition.

Continuous Measurement vs. Exception-Based Measurement

Continuous measurement is focused on monitoring a system in real time to ensure that it complies with a performance norm. An example of this might be the availability of an application server for a specific percentage of agreed service hours. The difference between continuous measurement and active monitoring is that active monitoring does not have to be continuous. Continuous measurement is resource intensive and as a consequence is usually reserved for critical components or services. This may be reduced to a continuous regular sampling of data and extrapolation of the performance achieved over time, depending on the needs of the organization.

Exception-based measurement, as the name suggests, detects and reports against exceptions. For example, an event is generated if a transaction does not complete or if a predefined performance threshold is reached. This is more cost-effective and easier to measure, but it could result in longer service outages. Exception-based measurement is used for less critical systems or on systems where cost is a major issue. It is also used where IT tools are not able to determine the status or quality of a service and manual intervention is required. For example, manually checking a system for safety will be shown as the percentage of items that failed rather than focusing on success. It is important that both the OLAs and the SLA for the service being measured reflect that exception-based measurement is used because service outages are more likely to occur and users are often required to report the exception.

Performance vs. Output

There is an important distinction between the reporting used to demonstrate the achievement of service quality objectives and the reporting used to track the performance of components or teams or departments used to deliver a service.

IT managers often confuse these by reporting to the business on the performance of their teams or departments (e.g., number of calls taken per service desk analyst) as if that were the same thing as quality of service (e.g., incidents solved within the agreed time).

Performance monitoring and metrics should be used internally by the service management team to determine whether people, processes, and technology are functioning correctly and to standard.

Users and customers would rather see reporting related to the quality and performance of the service.

Although service operation is concerned with both types of reporting, the primary concern of this chapter is performance monitoring, whereas monitoring of service quality (or output-based monitoring) is discussed in detail in Part 5 of this book, which covers continual service improvement.

Monitoring in Test Environments

It's important to ensure, as with any IT infrastructure, that the test environment is subject to monitoring and control. A test environment consists of infrastructure, applications, and processes that have to be monitored, managed, and controlled just like any other environment. Like-for-like conditions must be reflected in the test environment, and it is important to define how it will be used, including replicating the monitoring systems and tools used in the operational environment.

It's also important to monitor items being tested. The results of testing need to be accurately tracked and checked. Any monitoring tools that have been built into new or changed services must also be tested.

Reporting and Action

It has been said that a report alone creates awareness but that a report with an action plan achieves results. Practical experience has shown that there is often more reporting in dysfunctional organizations than in effective organizations. This is because the reports are not being used to initiate predefined action plans but rather to shift blame for an incident or identify responsibility for an action.

Monitoring without control is considered to be irrelevant and ineffective. To be useful, monitoring should always be aimed at ensuring that service and operational objectives are being met. This means that unless there is a clear purpose for monitoring a system or service, it should *not* be monitored.

This also means that when monitoring is defined, so too should any required actions be defined. For example, being able to detect that a major application has failed is not sufficient. The relevant application management team should also have defined the exact steps that it will take when the application fails so it may be recovered.

In addition, it should be recognized that actions may need to be taken by different people. For example, a single event, such as an application failure, may trigger action by the application management team to restore service, by the users to initiate manual processing, and by management to determine how this event can be prevented in future.

Service Operation Audits

Regular audits must be performed on the service operation processes and activities to ensure that they are being performed as intended and that there is no circumvention. An audit will also establish if the processes are still fit for purpose or identify any required changes or improvements.

In an ideal situation, an organization's internal audit team should carry these out in the interest of keeping some form of independent element to the audits, but if this capability is not available, some organizations may choose to engage third-party consultants or audit and assessment companies so that an entirely independent expert view is obtained. Service operation managers may choose to perform such audits themselves.

Service operation audits are part of the ongoing measurement that takes place as part of CSI.

Measurement, Metrics, and Key Performance Indicators

We will now review the measurement, metrics, and key performance indicators.

Measurement

Measurement refers to any technique used to evaluate the extent, dimension, or capacity of an item in relation to a standard or unit.

- *Extent* refers to the degree of compliance or completion (e.g., are all changes formally authorized by the appropriate authority?).

- *Dimension* refers to the size of an item (e.g., the number of incidents resolved by the service desk).

- *Capacity* refers to the total capability of an item (e.g., the maximum number of standard transactions that can be processed by a server per minute).

Measurement only becomes meaningful when it is possible to measure the actual output or dimensions of a system, function, or process against a standard or desired level. This should be defined in service design and refined over time through CSI, but the measurement itself takes place during service operation.

Metrics

Metrics refers to the quantitative, periodic assessment of a process, system, or function together with the procedures and tools that will be used to make these assessments and the procedures for interpreting them.

This is an important definition because it not only specifies what needs to be measured, but also how to measure it, what the acceptable range of performance will be, and what action will need to be taken as a result of normal performance or an exception.

Key Performance Indicators

A key performance indicator (KPI) is a specific, agreed level of performance that will be used to measure the efficiency, effectiveness, and cost-effectiveness of a process, IT service, or activity. The KPIs are used to measure the critical success factors (CSFs) for a process. We explored the CSFs for the processes in earlier chapters.

Interfaces to Other Service Lifecycle Practices

There are a number of ways in which service operation activities interface into the other lifecycle stages. We have considered operational monitoring and reporting, but monitoring also forms the starting point for CSI, and there are some key differences in focus when monitoring is being used for CSI rather than service operation.

Quality is the key objective of monitoring for CSI. Monitoring will therefore focus on the effectiveness of a service, process, tool, organization, or CI. The emphasis is not on assuring real-time service performance; rather it is on identifying where improvements can be made to the existing level of service or IT performance.

Monitoring should focus on detecting exceptions and resolutions. For example, the CSI activities are not as interested in whether an incident was resolved but whether it was resolved within the agreed time and whether future incidents can be prevented.

Monitoring data can be quite large and voluminous if you're looking at the entire IT service infrastructure. Because the CSI activities are generally focused on targeted service improvements, requirements for specific subsets of monitoring data are likely to be needed for this analysis. The subsets of data can be determined by input from the business or obtained through improvements to technology.

This has two main implications: first, monitoring for CSI will change over time, and second, there needs to be a common process between service operation and CSI to agree on the requirements. For example, there may be interest in monitoring the email service one quarter and then moving on to look at human resources systems in the next quarter.

IT Operations

In the following sections, we are going to review the activities related to IT operations for management of the operational environment.

We will look at server and mainframe management and support and network management. An important operational activity relates to storage and archive, frequently supported by database administration. Directory services management is another key area, as are desktop and mobile device support and middleware management. Many organizations also provide Internet or web management as part of the operational activities. Facilities and data center management are also included in the operational activities.

Operations Bridge

The console management/operations bridge function handles a structured set of activities that centrally coordinates management of events, incidents, routine operational activities, and reporting on the status or performance of technology components.

Historically, it would have involved monitoring mainframe master consoles, but as technology moves on, we are much more likely to see monitoring of specific configuration items, server farms, and, indeed, virtual operations. As technology changes, so does the nature of this function. Whatever the items being managed and monitored, the operations bridge acts as a centralization of the observation, receiving feeds from disparate locations and systems.

If this function exists in an organization, it may be used as resilience for service desk functions or other support functions, because it is often a 24-hour operation (if required) and will provide after-hours support. Obviously, this function is separated into a specific team only where the organization warrants it due to size, complexity, or security requirements. Otherwise, this function is carried out within the scope of the technical support and service desk teams.

Job Scheduling

In large organizations with volumes of data processing to be completed each day, a solution may be to run batch processing overnight, and should this processing overrun, the following day's online services could be impacted.

Job scheduling aims to maximize overnight capacity and performance and has to factor in many variables, such as time sensitivity, critical and noncritical dependencies, workload balancing, and failure and resubmission. As a result, most operations rely on job scheduling tools that allow IT operations to schedule jobs for the optimal use of technology to achieve service level objectives.

The latest generation of scheduling tools allows for a single toolset to schedule and automate technical and service management process activities (such as change scheduling). While this is a good opportunity for improving efficiency, it also represents a greater single point of failure. Organizations using this type of tool will generally use other nonintegrated solutions as agents and also as a backup in case the main toolset fails.

Backup and Restore

Regularly backing up and restoring data is an essential service operation activity. It is important to establish what will be backed up, how often, how long it will be retained, and the time frame within which it will be required to be restored. During the earlier stages of the service lifecycle, the business will be asked for the requirements for data management, including backup and restore capability. These are all business decisions, and the backup regime will be designed as part of the overall solution during service design and tested during service transition. Requirements for backup and restoration are often regulatory and subject to audit, so the organization must agree on and document a traceable and defined approach.

Part of this definition and agreement is the recovery point objective. This describes the point to which data will be restored after recovery of an IT service. It may involve loss of data. For example, a recovery point objective of one day means that up to 24 hours of data may be lost. It is also necessary to agree on the recovery time objective. This describes the maximum time allowed for recovery of an IT service following an interruption. These agreements should be made through the service level management process and included in operational level agreements, contracts, and service level agreements.

Whatever arrangements are made, backups must be tested regularly to ensure not only that they have worked, but also that the data can be restored as agreed. This should be subject to the correct authorization, defined by the business requirements. This may form part of the continuity plan.

Print and Output Management

Although it may seem that print management is an old-fashioned concept, output management is not because electronic output is an important part of many organizational services. Many services consist of generating and delivering information in printed or electronic form. Ensuring that the right information gets to the right people, with full integrity, requires formal control and management. Print (physical) and output (electronic) facilities and services need to be formally managed because they often represent the tangible output of a service. The ability to measure that this output has reached the appropriate destination is therefore important; for example, it's important to measure data transfers between organizations, which is now the most common way of transferring financial information and payments.

Physical and electronic output often contains sensitive or confidential information. It is vital that the appropriate levels of security are applied to both the generation and the delivery of this output.

Those of us who have worked in IT for a number of years will remember times when organizations had a requirement for centralized bulk printing requirements, which IT operations had to handle. In addition to the physical loading and reloading of paper and the operation and care of the printers, other activities were needed. These included prenotification of large print runs and alerts to prevent excessive printing by rogue print jobs or the physical control of high-value stationery such as company checks or certificates. Some organizations will still have these requirements, but more commonly it is electronic output that concerns our IT teams.

IT may also be responsible for the management of the physical and electronic storage required to generate the output. In many cases, IT will be expected to provide archives for the printed and electronic materials.

Where appropriate, IT will have control of all printed material to adhere to data protection legislation and regulation such as the Health Insurance Portability and Accountability Act (HIPAA) in the United States and Financial Conduct Authority (FCA) in the United Kingdom.

Where print and output services are delivered directly to the users, it is important that the responsibility for maintaining the printers and storage devices is clearly defined in the SLA.

Server and Mainframe Management and Support

Successful management of servers and mainframes is essential for successful service operation. Servers and mainframes are used in many organizations to provide flexible and accessible services such as hosting applications and databases, operating high-volume transaction systems, running client/server services, providing storage, and print and file management.

The ways in which server and mainframe management teams are organized are quite diverse. In some organizations, mainframe management is a single, highly specialized team, whereas in others the activities are performed by several teams or departments, with engineering and third-level support provided by one set of teams and daily operations combined with the rest of IT operations. The support activities for servers are generally the same as those for mainframes. Although the technologies and skill sets needed to actually perform support activities are different, the types of activities are essentially similar.

The following procedures and activities must be undertaken by mainframe and server teams or departments. Remember that separate teams may be needed where different technology platforms are used (i.e., mainframe OS, UNIX, Wintel, etc.).

- Operating system support and maintenance of the appropriate operating system(s) and related utility software (e.g., failover software), including patch management and involvement in defining backup and restore policies

- License management for all server CIs, especially operating systems, utilities, and any application software not managed by the application management teams

- Third-level support for all incidents related to servers and/or server operating systems, including diagnosis and restoration activities. This will also include liaison with third-party hardware support contractors and/or manufacturers as needed to escalate hardware-related incidents.

- Advice to the business on the selection, sizing, procurement, and usage of servers and related utility software to meet business needs

- System security, including the control and maintenance of the access controls and permissions within the relevant server environment(s) as well as appropriate system and physical security measures. These include identification and application of security patches, access management, and intrusion detection.

- Definition and management of virtual servers. Server management will be required to set the standards for load balancing and virtual management and then ensure that workloads are appropriately balanced and distributed. They are also responsible for being able to track which workload is being processed by which server so that they are able to deal with incidents effectively.

- Provide information and assistance to capacity management to help achieve optimum throughput, utilization, and performance from the available servers

Other activities are also routine for the server and mainframe management team:

- Defining standard builds for servers as part of the provisioning process, and then building and installing new servers as part of ongoing maintenance or for the provision of new services

- Setting up and managing clusters, which are aimed at building redundancy, improving service performance, and making the infrastructure easier to manage

There is obviously a need for ongoing maintenance. This typically consists of replacing servers, or "blades," on a rolling schedule to ensure that equipment is replaced before it fails or becomes obsolete. This results in servers that are not only fully functional, but also capable of supporting evolving services.

Decommissioning and disposal of old server equipment is often done in conjunction with the organization's environmental policies for disposal.

There will be a requirement to provide interfacing to hardware (H/W) support, such as arranging maintenance, agreeing on time slots for work to be carried out, identifying H/W failure, meeting with H/W engineering, and providing assistance in writing batch and job scripts.

Network Management

Since almost all IT services require connectivity, network management's role in managing and maintaining the communications infrastructure is essential. Network management is responsible for the organization's own local area networks (LANs), metropolitan area networks (MANs), and wide area networks (WANs) and for liaising with third-party network suppliers. They are normally considered experts in the area of network administration.

Their role will include initial planning and installation of new networks or network components and maintenance and upgrades to the physical network infrastructure. This is done through service design and service transition.

Network management will usually provide third-level support for all network-related activities, including investigation of network issues and liaison with third parties as necessary. This also includes the installation and use of sniffer tools, which analyze network traffic, to assist in incident and problem resolution.

In most organizations, this team should also provide maintenance and support of network operating system and middleware software, including patch management and upgrades. They will also be responsible for monitoring network traffic to identify failures or to spot potential performance or bottleneck issues. Network management includes the reconfiguring or rerouting of traffic to achieve improved throughput or better balance in accordance with the definition of rules for dynamic balancing and routing.

Network security (in liaison with the organization's information security management process), including firewall management, access rights, and password protection, is another key aspect of this area.

Other activities include assigning and managing IP addresses, domain name systems, and dynamic host configuration protocol (DHCP) systems; managing firewalls and secure gateways; and managing Internet service providers (ISPs). Network management will also take on some responsibilities on behalf of information security management by implementing, monitoring, and maintaining intrusion detection systems. They will also be responsible for ensuring that there is no denial of service to legitimate users of the network.

As with all operational teams, network management will be required to update service asset and configuration management as necessary by documenting CIs, status, relationships, and so on.

Network management is also frequently responsible, often in conjunction with desktop support, for remote connectivity issues such as dial-in, dial-back, and virtual private network facilities provided to home workers, remote workers, or suppliers.

Some network management teams or departments will also have responsibility for voice/telephony, including the provision and support for exchanges, lines, circuits, Automated Call Distribution system (ACD), and statistical software packages and for Voice-over Internet protocol (VoIP), quality of service, and remote monitoring systems.

At the same time, many organizations see VoIP and telephony as specialized areas and have teams dedicated to managing this technology. Their activities will be similar to those described. If network management is managing VoIP as a service, they will need to be aware of and mitigate against any variations in bandwidth and utilization to optimize VoIP usage.

Remember, this is not a prescriptive description of a network management team, and each organization will have its own approach to structuring its teams and departments.

Storage and Archive

There is often a requirement to store data, sometimes for many years. This may be a requirement of the business or a legal or regulatory requirement. Managing the safe storage of data, and ensuring that it can be retrieved as required, is a service operation responsibility. One of the key things that needs to be considered is the change in technology over time because information may need to be stored through a number of technology iterations.

There are a variety of possible storage mechanisms that service operation needs to manage, sometimes by a specialized team. Such mechanisms include storage devices such as disks, controllers, tapes, and other media. Specific technologies include network attached storage (NAS), which is storage attached to a network and accessible by several clients. There are also storage area networks (SANs) designed to attach computer storage devices such as disk array controllers and tape libraries. In addition to managing the storage devices, a SAN will require the management of several network components, such as hubs, cables, and other hardware.

Other devices include direct attached storage (DAS), which is a storage device directly attached to a server, and content addressable storage (CAS), which is storage that retrieves information based on its content rather than location. The focus in this type of system is on understanding the nature of the data and information stored rather than on providing specific storage locations.

Database Administration

Regardless of what type of storage systems are being used, storage and archiving will require management of the infrastructure components as well as the policies related to where data is stored, how long it's stored, what form it's stored in, and who may access it. Specific responsibilities will include the definition of data storage policies and procedures and the file storage naming conventions, hierarchy, and placement decisions.

As part of service design, there should be involvement with defining an archiving policy and agreeing on the housekeeping practices of all data storage facilities and the data archiving rules and schedules. The storage teams or departments will also provide input into the definition of these rules and will provide reports on their effectiveness as input into future design.

It is important to ensure that the design, sizing, selection, procurement, configuration, and operation of all data storage infrastructures as well as planning for the maintenance and support for all utility and middleware data storage software are included early in the service lifecycle. This will include meeting with information lifecycle management team(s) or governance teams to ensure compliance with freedom of information, data protection, and IT governance regulations.

Retrieval of archived data as needed (e.g., for audit purposes, for forensic evidence, or to meet any other business requirements) is another required activity, as is the management of archiving technologies and, if needed, migration from one (outdated) technology to a newer archiving technology in order to be able to restore data over a long period of time (e.g., 10 years for legal requirements). The teams will also be expected to provide third-line support for storage- and archive-related incidents.

Database administration must work closely with key application management teams or departments—and in some organizations, the functions may be combined or linked under a single management structure. There are a number of different organizational options that can be adopted; for example, database administration can be performed by each application management team for all the applications under its control. Alternatively, there may be a dedicated department that manages all databases regardless of type or application.

Another option is to have several departments, each managing one type of database regardless of what application they are part of.

There is no defined approach. It is up to the organization to arrange database administration according to its requirements.

Database administration works to ensure the optimal performance, security, and functionality of databases that they manage. Database administrators (DBAs) typically have responsibilities that include creation and maintenance of database standards and policies and the initial database design, creation, and testing.

DBAs are also responsible for the management of database availability and performance (for example, resilience, sizing, and capacity volumetric information). Resilience may require database replication, which would be the responsibility of the DBAs, as well as ongoing administration of database objects such as indexes, tables, views, constraints, sequences, snapshots, stored procedures, and page locks to achieve optimum utilization. DBAs are responsible for the definition of triggers that will generate events, which in turn will alert DBAs about potential performance or integrity issues with the database. The role is also concerned with performing database housekeeping—the routine tasks that ensure that the databases are functioning optimally and securely (for example, tuning and indexing).

The team will also take responsibility for monitoring usage by keeping track of transaction volumes, response times, and concurrency levels. And they will generate reports; these could be reports based on the data in the database or reports related to the performance and integrity of the database.

The DBAs will assist with the identification, reporting, and management of database security issues, including audit trails and forensics. The DBAs' assistance will be engaged in designing database backup, archiving, and storage strategy and designing database alerts and event management. DBAs are also the providers of third-level support for all database-related incidents.

This is a particularly specialized area of IT management, but smaller organizations may not be able to justify the cost of such skills in-house, and this capability may be provided through a third party.

Directory Services Management

A directory service is a specialized software application that manages information about the resources available on a network and which users have access. It is the basis for providing access to those resources and for ensuring that unauthorized access is detected and prevented.

Directory services view each resource as an object of the directory server and assigns it a name. Each name is linked to the resource's network address so that users don't have to memorize confusing and complex addresses.

Directory services are a good source of data and verification for the CMS because they are usually maintained and kept up-to-date.

Directory services management refers to the process that is used. Its activities include working as part of service design and service transition and locating resources on a network. It is important to ensure that the status of these resources are tracked. Directory services management will also provide the ability to manage those resources remotely. This includes managing the rights of specific users or groups of users to access resources on a network. It is also concerned with the definition and maintenance of naming conventions to be used for resources on a network, including ensuring consistency of naming conventions and access control on different networks in the organization.

Directory services management may link different directory services throughout the organization to form a distributed directory service; that is, users will only see one logical set of network resources (this is called distribution of directory services).

This function is also responsible for monitoring events on the directory services, such as unsuccessful attempts to access a resource, and taking the appropriate action where required. It will also maintain and update the tools used to manage directory services.

It is another specialized area of expertise, but it may be combined with other technical management teams. Again, it is important to remember that not all organizations are large or complex enough to justify a team to manage these capabilities separately.

Desktop and Mobile Device Support

Because most users access IT services using desktops, laptops, and mobile computing devices, it is key that these are supported to ensure the agreed levels of availability and performance of services.

Desktop and mobile device support will have overall responsibility for all of the organization's desktop, laptop, and mobile device hardware, software, and peripherals. They will also manage desktop and mobile computing policies and procedures, such as licensing policies; use of laptops, desktops, and mobile devices for personal purposes; and USB lockdown.

As well as designing and agreeing on standard desktop and device images, this function will be responsible for service maintenance, including deployment of releases, upgrades, patches, and hotfixes (in conjunction with release and deployment management).

The design and implementation of desktop and mobile device archiving and rebuild policies (including policies relating to cookies, favorites, templates, personal data, and security) will also be managed by this function.

They will also provide third-level support of incidents related to desktops and mobile devices, including desk-side visits where necessary or replacing devices with reconfigured images and data when needed.

The function will take responsibility for the support of connectivity issues (in conjunction with network management) to home workers and mobile staff.

It is important to make sure configuration control and auditing of all desktop, laptop, and mobile device equipment is managed and maintained (in conjunction with service asset and configuration management and IT audit).

Middleware Management

Middleware is software that connects or integrates software components across distributed or disparate applications and systems. Middleware enables the effective transfer of data between applications and is therefore key to services that are dependent on multiple applications or data sources.

A variety of technologies are currently used to support program-to-program communication, such as object request brokers, message-oriented middleware, remote procedure calls, and point-to-point web services. Newer technologies are emerging all the time; for example, enterprise service bus (ESB) enables programs, systems, and services to communicate with each other regardless of the architecture and origin of the applications.

This is especially being used in the context of deploying service oriented architectures (SOAs).

Middleware management can be performed as part of an application management function (where it is dedicated to a specific application) or as part of a technical management function (where it is viewed as an extension to the operating system of a specific platform).

Functionality provided by middleware includes providing transfer mechanisms for data from various applications or data sources and sending work to another application or procedure for processing. It also includes transmitting data or information to other systems, such as sourcing data for publication on websites (e.g., publishing incident status information).

Middleware management will also be engaged in releasing updated software modules across distributed environments. The collation and distribution of system messages and instructions—for example, events or operational scripts that need to be run on remote devices—will also be part of this approach, as well as setting up multicast functionality with networks. Multicast is the delivery of information to a group of destinations simultaneously using the most efficient delivery route. This will require the management of queue sizes.

Middleware management is the set of activities that are used to manage middleware. These include working as part of service design and transition to ensure that the appropriate middleware solutions are chosen and that they can perform optimally when they are deployed. This will lead to the correct operation of middleware through monitoring and control, allowing the detection and resolution of incidents related to middleware.

Middleware management will also be responsible for maintaining and updating middleware, including licensing and installing new versions. This will include defining and maintaining information about how applications are linked through middleware.

Internet/Web Management

The Internet is increasingly important to most organizations as more and more conduct their business through it. A website may need to be updated regularly with prices, special offers, and other important information, and a failure could be catastrophic. (This is especially true for online retailers such as Amazon and Expedia who have no physical retail presence.)

Organizations with such a heavy dependence on the Internet will usually have a dedicated team for Intranet and Internet management. This team will be responsible for defining architectures for Internet and web services and specifying standards for development and management of web-based applications, content, websites, and web pages. This will typically be done during service design. The design, testing, implementation, and maintenance of websites will include the architecture of websites and the mapping of content to be made available.

The responsibilities of such a team or department incorporate both intranet and Internet management and are likely to include the management and operation of firewalls and secure gateways and secured subnetworks (e.g., the DMZ, or demilitarized zone) used to provide a secure perimeter between secured IT infrastructures and larger distrusted networks.

In many organizations, web management will include editing content to be posted as well as the maintenance of all web development and management applications.

Internet and web management is also responsible for meeting with and giving advice to web-content teams within the business. Content may reside in applications or storage devices, which implies close liaison with application management and other technical management teams.

Liaison with ISPs, hosts, and third-party monitoring or virtualization organizations will also be managed by this team. In many organizations, the ISPs are managed as part of network management.

They will also provide third-level support for Internet-/web-related incidents and support for interfaces with back end and legacy systems. This will often mean working with members of the application development and management teams to ensure secure access and consistent functionality.

Monitoring and management of website performance will include heartbeat testing, user experience simulation, benchmarking, on-demand load balancing, virtualization, website availability, resilience, and security. This will form part of the overall information security management of the organization.

Facilities and Data Center Management

Facilities management is the management of the physical environment of IT operations, usually located in data centers or computer rooms. In many respects, facilities management could be viewed as a function in its own right. However, in this section we review facilities management specifically as it relates to the management of data centers and as a subset of the IT operations management function.

Although data centers are often managed by general facilities management or office services departments (if these exist), they have specialized requirements regarding layout, heating and air-conditioning, planning the power capacity requirements, and so on. So, although data centers may be facilities owned by an organization, best practice would be to have them managed under the authority of IT operations. Where a general department carries it out, there should be a functional reporting line to IT.

The specific activities include building management, equipment hosting, and power management. It should also cover environmental conditions and safety and physical controls. Supplier management of the providers of the environment (when provided by an external organization) will also be part of this functionality.

Data Center Strategies

Managing a data center is far more than hosting an open space where technical groups install and manage equipment, using their own approaches and procedures. It requires an integrated set of processes and procedures involving all IT groups at every stage of the service lifecycle. Data center operations are governed by strategic and design decisions for management and control and are executed by operators. This requires a number of key factors to be put in place:

- *Data center automation* uses specialized automation systems that reduce the need for manual operators and monitor and track the status of the facility and all IT operations at all times.

- *Policy-based management* enables the rules of automation and resource allocation to be managed by policy rather than having to go through complex change procedures every time processing is moved from one resource to another.

- *Real-time services* should be provided 24 hours a day, 7 days a week.

- *Capacity management of environmental factors* include the physical environmental factors such as floor space, cooling, and power, which need to be managed in terms of their available capacities and workloads to ensure that shortfalls in these areas do not create incidents or generate unplanned costs.

- *Standardization of equipment* provides greater ease of management, more consistent levels of performance, and a means of providing multiple services across similar technology. Standardization also reduces the variety of technical expertise required to manage equipment in the data center and to provide services.

- *SOAs* define where service components can be reused, interchanged, and replaced very quickly and with no impact on the business. This will make it possible for the data center to be highly responsive in meeting changing business demands without having to go through lengthy and involved reengineering and re-architecting.

- *Virtualization* means that IT services are delivered using an ever-changing set of equipment geared to meet current demand. For example, an application may run on a dedicated device together with its database during high-demand times but be shifted to a shared device with its database on a remote device during nonpeak times, all automated. This will mean even greater cost savings because any equipment can be used at any time, without any human intervention except to perform maintenance and replace failed equipment. The IT infrastructure is more resilient because components are backed up by any number of similar components, any of which could take over a failed component's workload automatically. Remote monitoring, control, and management equipment and systems will be essential to manage a virtualized environment because many services will not be linked to any one specific piece of equipment.

- *Unified management systems* have become more important as services run across multiple locations and technologies. Today it is important to define what actions need to be taken and what systems will perform that action. This means investing in solutions that will allow infrastructure managers to simply specify what outcome is required and let the management system calculate the best combination of tools and actions to achieve the outcome.

Operational Activities of Processes Covered in Other Lifecycle Stages

In the previous sections, we looked at service operation activities. In the following sections, we'll cover the engagement of service operation in other lifecycle processes.

This will include the following processes from service transition:

- Change management
- Service asset and configuration management
- Release and deployment management
- Knowledge management.

In service design, we will consider the following operational activities:

- Capacity
- Availability
- Service continuity
- Information security
- Service level management

The service strategy processes covered are as follows:

- Demand management
- Financial management

Finally, we'll review the engagement of service operation in continual service improvement.

Change Management

Service operation staff will be involved with change management on a day-to-day basis. This includes using the change management process for standard, operational-type changes by raising and submitting requests for change (RFCs) as needed to address service operation issues. Operational staff will also participate in the change advisory board (CAB) or emergency change advisory board (ECAB) meetings to ensure that service operation risks, issues, and views are taken into account.

Obviously, there will be engagement from operational staff in implementing changes (or backing out changes) as directed by change management where they involve a service operation component or services. They will also assist with activities to move physical assets to their assigned locations within the data center.

Operational staff are also responsible for helping define and maintain change models relating to service operation components or services. They will receive change schedules and ensure that all service operation staff are made aware of and are prepared for all relevant changes. And finally, they will coordinate efforts with design activities to ensure that service operation requirements and concerns are addressed when planning and designing new or changed services.

Service Asset and Configuration Management

Service operation staff will be involved with certain aspects of service asset and configuration management (SACM) on a day-to-day basis. For example, they will inform service asset and configuration management of any discrepancies found between any CIs and the CMS and may be involved with making amendments necessary to correct discrepancies, under the authority of service asset and configuration management. Operational staff may also be tasked with labeling and tagging physical assets (e.g., serial numbers and bar codes) so they can be easily identified as well as assisting with audit activities to validate existence and location of service assets.

The responsibility for updating the CMS remains with service asset and configuration management, but in some cases operations staff might be asked, under the direction of service asset and configuration management, to update relationships, or even to add new CIs or mark CIs as "disposed" in the CMS if the updates are related to operational activities actually performed by operations staff. Operations staff may also assist service asset and configuration management activities by communicating changes in state or status with CIs impacted by incidents.

Release and Deployment Management

Service operation staff will be involved with release and deployment management on a day-to-day basis. They may also be under the direction of release and deployment management and be responsible for actual implementation actions regarding the deployment of new releases where they relate to service operation components or services.

It is important that operational staff participate in the planning stages of major new releases to advise on service operation issues.

Operational staff will manage the physical handling of CIs from/to the definitive media library (DML) as required to fulfil their operational roles, while adhering to relevant release and deployment management procedures, such as ensuring that all items are properly booked out and back in. They will also participate in activities to back out unsuccessful releases when they occur.

Knowledge Management

Relevant information (including data and metrics) should be passed up the management chain to other service lifecycle stages so that it can feed into the knowledge and wisdom layers of the organization's service knowledge management system (SKMS). It is vitally important that all data and information that can be useful for future service operation activities are properly gathered, stored, and assessed.

Key repositories of service operation, which have been frequently mentioned elsewhere, are the CMS and the KEDB, but the repositories must also include documentation from all of the service operation teams and departments, such as operations manuals, procedures manuals, work instructions, and other operational documentation.

Capacity Management

Although many of the capacity management activities are of a strategic or longer-term planning nature, there are a number of operational capacity management activities that must be performed on a regular ongoing basis as part of service operation.

Capacity and Performance Monitoring

All components of the IT infrastructure should be continually monitored (in conjunction with event management) so that any potential problems or trends can be identified before failures or performance degradation occurs. The components and elements to be monitored will vary depending upon the infrastructure in use. There are different kinds of monitoring tool needed to collect and interpret data at each level. For example, some tools will allow performance of business transactions to be monitored, while others will monitor CI behavior.

Event management needs to set up and calibrate alarm thresholds so that the correct alert levels are set and filtering is established as necessary to raise only meaningful events. Capacity management should be involved in helping specify and select any such monitoring capabilities and integrating the results or alerts with other monitoring and handling systems.

Event management must work with all appropriate support groups to make decisions on where capacity and performance alarms are routed and on escalation paths and timescales.

If there is a current or ongoing capacity or performance management issue and an alert is triggered or an incident is raised at the service desk, capacity management support personnel must become involved to identify the cause and find a resolution. Working together with appropriate technical support groups, and alongside problem management personnel, they must perform all necessary investigations to detect exactly what has gone wrong and what is needed to correct the situation.

When a solution, or potential solution, has been found for a capacity- or performance-related problem, any changes necessary to resolve it must be authorized via formal change management before implementation. If the fault is causing serious disruption and an urgent resolution is needed, the emergency change process should be used.

Capacity management has a role to play in identifying capacity or performance trends as they become discernible. Service operation should include activities for logging and collecting performance data and information relating to performance incidents to provide a basis for problem and capacity management trend analysis activities.

Large amounts of data are usually generated through capacity and performance monitoring. In any organization, it is likely that the monitoring tools used will vary greatly. In order to coordinate the data being generated and allow the retention of meaningful data for analysis and trending purposes, some form of central repository for holding this summary data is needed, such as a capacity management information system.

Modeling and/or sizing of new services and/or applications must, where appropriate, be done during the design and transition stages. However, the service operation functions have a role to play in evaluating the accuracy of the predictions and feeding back any issues or discrepancies.

Availability Management

During service design and service transition, IT services are designed and tested for availability and recovery. Service operation is responsible for actually making the IT service available to the specified users at the required time and at the agreed levels.

The IT teams, and particularly the users, are often in the best position to detect whether services actually meet the agreed requirements and whether the design of these services is effective. The actual experience of the users and operational functions during service operation can provide primary input into the ongoing improvement of existing services and the design.

However, there are a number of challenges with gaining access to this knowledge because most of the experiences of the operational teams and users are either informal or spread across multiple sources. The process for collecting and collating this data needs to be formalized.

There are three key opportunities for operational staff to be involved in availability improvement, because these are generally viewed as part of their ongoing responsibility:

- The review of maintenance activities and regular comparison of actual maintenance activities and times with the service design plans. This will highlight potential areas for improvement.

- Major problem reviews. Problems could be the result of any number of factors, one of which is poor design. Problem reviews therefore may include opportunities to identify improvements to the design of IT services, which will include availability and capacity improvement.

- Involvement in specific initiatives using techniques such as service failure analysis (SFA), component failure impact analysis (CFIA), and fault tree analysis (FTA) or as members of technical observation (TO) activities—either as part of the follow-up to major problems or as part of an ongoing service improvement plan (SIP), in collaboration with dedicated availability management staff. (These are fully explained in Chapter 13, "Service Design Processes: Service Level Management and Availability Management.")

There may be occasions when operational staff themselves need downtime of one or more services to enable them to conduct their operational or maintenance activities; this may have an impact on availability if not properly scheduled and managed. In such cases, they must liaise with SLM and availability management staff, who will negotiate with the business/users to agree on and schedule such activities, often using the service desk to perform this role.

IT Service Continuity Management

Service operation functions are responsible for the testing and execution of system and service recovery plans as determined in the IT service continuity plans for the organization. In addition, managers of all service operation functions must participate in key coordination and recovery teams as they have been outlined in those continuity plans.

Service operation needs to be involved in risk assessment, using its knowledge of the infrastructure and techniques such as CFIA and access to information in the CMS to identify single points of failure or other high-risk situations. It also needs to be involved in the execution of risk management measures, such as the implementation of countermeasures and increasing resilience to components of the infrastructures.

Operational staff will provide assistance in writing the actual recovery plans for systems and services under its control and participate in testing of the plans (such as involvement in off-site testing, simulations, etc.) on an ongoing basis under the direction of the IT service continuity manager. They will manage the ongoing maintenance of the plans under the control of the IT service continuity management and change management processes.

Operational staff need to participate in training and awareness campaigns to ensure that they are able to execute the plans and understand their roles in a disaster.

The service desk will play a key role in communicating with staff, customers, and users during an actual disaster and should also provide assistance with testing and execution of system and service recovery plans.

Information Security Management

Information security management has the overall responsibility for setting policies, standards, and procedures to ensure the protection of the organization's assets, data, information, and IT services. Service operation teams play a key role in executing these policies, standards, and procedures. As a consequence, they will work closely with the teams or departments responsible for information security management. It is important to separate the roles between the groups defining and managing the process and the groups executing specific activities as part of ongoing operation.

Key service operation team support activities can include policing and reporting, such as checking system journals, logs, and event/monitoring alerts, as well as intrusion detection and/or reporting of actual or potential security breaches.

Service operation staff are often first to detect security events and are in the best position to be able to shut down and/or remove access to compromised systems. Service operation staff may be required to escort visitors into sensitive areas and/or control their access. This will have to be established according to the requirements of the individual organization because it may not be considered appropriate for operational staff to be utilized in this way. They also have a role to play in controlling network access to third parties, such as hardware vendors dialing in for diagnostic purposes, for example.

Technical advice and assistance may be needed regarding potential security improvements (e.g., setting up appropriate firewalls or access/password controls). Technical support may also need to be provided to IT security staff to assist in investigating security incidents and producing reports or in gathering forensic evidence for use in disciplinary actions or criminal prosecutions. Event, incident, problem, and service asset and configuration management information can be relied on to provide accurate chronologies of security-related investigations.

Service operation staff are often responsible for maintaining operational security control by providing technical staff with privileged access to key technical areas (e.g., root system passwords and physical access to data centers and communications rooms). It is therefore essential that adequate controls and audit trails are kept of all such privileged activities to deter and detect security events.

All service operation staff should be screened and vetted to a security level appropriate to the organization in question. Suppliers and third-party contractors should also be screened and vetted—both the organizations and the specific personnel involved.

All service operation staff should be given regular and ongoing training of the organization's security policy and procedures. This should include the details of disciplinary measures in place. In addition, security requirements should be specified in the employee's contract of employment.

Service operation documented procedures must reference all relevant information relating to security issues extracted from the organization's overall security policy documents.

Service Level Management

Service level management (SLM) is the process responsible for negotiating SLAs and ensuring that they are enforced. It monitors and reports on service levels and holds regular customer reviews.

Incident management priorities and required resolution targets should be guided by service level targets. Problem management activities contribute to the improved attainment of service level targets by identifying root cause and instigating changes that are needed to improve performance. Service operation teams play a role in executing monitoring activities through the event management process that can provide early detection of service level breaches. SLM also maintains the agreements used by access management to provide access to services (such as the definition of criteria for which business users may be granted access), while request fulfilment activities may be bounded by agreed service targets.

Demand Management

Demand management is the name given to a number of techniques that can be used to modify demand for a particular resource or service. There are aspects of demand management that are of an operational nature, requiring short-term action. This can include controlling and managing access to a specific application with limited licenses.

There may be occasions when optimization of infrastructure resources is needed to maintain or improve performance or throughput. It may require moving a service or workload from one location or set of CIs to another, often to balance utilization or traffic or to carry out technical virtualization. Service operation would be responsible for setting up and using virtualization systems to allow movement of processing around the infrastructure to give better performance/resilience in a dynamic fashion.

It will only be possible to manage demand effectively if there is a good understanding of which workloads exist, so monitoring and analysis of workloads is therefore needed on an ongoing operational basis.

Financial Management for IT Services

Service operation staff must participate in and support the overall IT budgeting and accounting system and may be actively involved in a charging system that may be in place.

The service operation manager must also be involved in regular (at least monthly) reviews of expenditure against budgets as part of the ongoing IT budgeting and accounting process. Care should therefore be taken to ensure that IT is involved in discussing all cost-saving measures and contributes to overall decisions.

Improvement of Operational Activities

All service operation staff should be constantly looking for areas in which process improvements can be made to provide higher IT service quality in a more cost-effective way. Opportunities for improvement will be included in the CSI register for review and prioritization.

This may be covered by a range of different operational activities, such as automation of manual tasks. All tasks should be examined for their potential for automation to reduce effort and costs and to minimize potential errors. A judgement must be made on the costs of the automation and the likely benefits that will result.

It is important to review makeshift activities or procedures that were designed to be short term but that have become the "norm" because there are often efficiencies to be achieved.

Operational audits should be conducted of all service operation processes to ensure that they are working satisfactorily, and used to identify operational improvement opportunities. It is important to include education and training for service operation teams, who should understand the importance of what they do on a daily basis.

Summary

This brings us to the end of this chapter, during which we explored the activities of service operation, providing the knowledge, interpretation, and analysis of service operation principles, techniques, and relationships and their application to the delivery and support of services at agreed levels.

This included monitoring and control as it relates to event management and IT operations for management of the operational environment. We also looked at server and mainframe management and support and network management.

An important operational activity is related to storage and archive, which is often supported by database administration. Directory services management is another key area, as are desktop and mobile device support and middleware management. Many organizations also provide Internet or web management as part of the operational activities. Facilities and data center management are also included in the operational activities.

We looked at the service operation activities throughout the other lifecycle processes. In each lifecycle stage, service operation staff have an important part to play, and we explored some of the key processes in which they will be involved.

Exam Essentials

Understand and explain the uses of monitoring and control in service operation.   This includes the concepts of the monitor control loop and open and closed loop systems. Explain and expand on the nature of the various types of monitoring and measurement.

Understand how to apply the IT operations activities for service operation.   Understand the following:

- Server and mainframe management and support

- Network management

- Storage and archive

- Database administration

- Directory services management

- Desktop and mobile device support

- Middleware management

- Internet/web management

- Facilities and data center management

Understand the application of operational activities of processes covered in other lifecycle stages.   The engagement of service operation in the lifecycle is key for each stage because service operation is involved in all stages and processes. It is important to understand the involvement and be able to understand and apply this to each lifecycle stage.

Understand and expand on the improvement of operational activities.   Continual service improvement is based on the identification of improvement, and it is important to understand the mechanisms for managing improvement.

Review Questions

You can find the answers to the review questions in the appendix.

1. Measurement and control is a continuous cycle. Which of these is NOT part of that cycle?

    A. Monitoring

    B. Reporting

    C. Subsequent action

    D. Restoration

2. *Measurement* refers to any technique used to evaluate the extent, dimension, or capacity of an item in relation to a standard or unit. What is the definition ITIL applies to the term *extent*?

    A. The degree of compliance or completion (e.g., are all changes formally authorized by the appropriate authority?)

    B. The size of an item (e.g., the number of incidents resolved by the service desk)

    C. The total capability of an item (e.g., the maximum number of standard transactions that can be processed by a server per minute)

    D. The cost of the item (e.g., the amount of money spent on each item)

3. Which of these statements is/are correct?

    1. Monitoring is used to establish whether specific conditions are met or not met.

    2. Monitoring is also concerned with the detection of abnormal types or levels of activity.

    A. Statement 1 only

    B. Statement 2 only

    C. Both statements

    D. Neither statement

4. There are different types of monitoring. Which of these is the description for active monitoring?

    A. Active monitoring is the ongoing "interrogation" of a device or system to determine its status.

    B. Active monitoring is generating and transmitting events to a "listening device" or monitoring agent.

    C. Active monitoring is designed to request or trigger action following a certain type of event or failure.

    D. Active monitoring is used to detect patterns of events that indicate that a system or service may be about to fail.

5. In the monitor control loop, an activity and its output are compared to what?

    A. A predefined SLA

    B. A predefined OLA

    C. A predefined norm

    D. A predefined contract

6. In which stage of the service lifecycle is the ITSM monitor control loop based?

    A. In service operation, because this is where monitoring and control can take place

    B. In service design, because this is where the requirements for monitoring and control are defined

    C. In service strategy, because this is where the controls are agreed upon with the business

    D. In service transition, because this is where changes as a result of monitoring are managed

7. Which of these are common service operation activities?

    1. IT operations

    2. Design coordination

    3. Server and mainframe management and support

    4. Network management

    5. Service validation and testing

    6. Storage and archive

    7. Database administration

        A. 2, 5, 6, and 7

        B. 1, 3, 4, 6, and 7

        C. 1, 2, 5, and 7

        D. All

8. Service operation audits are an important part of the service operation lifecycle stage. Which of these statements about audits is/are correct?

    1. Regular audits must be performed on the service operation processes and activities to ensure that they are being performed as intended and that there is no circumvention.

    2. An audit will also establish if the processes are still fit for purpose or identify any required changes or improvements.

        A. Statement 1 only

        B. Statement 2 only

        C. Both statements

        D. Neither statement

9. True or False? Service operation is involved in activities in all of the other lifecycle stages.

    A. True

    B. False

10. Improvement is an important part of service operation. Which of these statements is/are correct about improvement in service operation?

   1. All service operation staff should be constantly looking for areas in which process improvements can result in higher IT service quality and/or be more cost-effective.

   2. Opportunities for improvement will be included in the CSI register for review and prioritization.

   A. Statement 1 only

   B. Statement 2 only

   C. Both statements

   D. Neither statement

Chapter

39

Organizing for Service Operation

THE FOLLOWING ITIL INTERMEDIATE EXAM OBJECTIVES ARE DISCUSSED IN THIS CHAPTER:

✓ **Service operation functions:**

✓ **Service desk**

- The service desk role
- Objectives
- Organizational structures
- Staffing options
- Efficiency and effectiveness metrics
- Issues and safeguards when outsourcing

✓ **Technical management**

- Technical management role
- Objectives
- Activities
- Organization
- Metrics
- Documentation

✓ **Application management**

- Application management role
- Objectives
- Activities
- Organization
- Metrics
- Documentation

✓ **IT operations management**

- ▪ Activities
- ▪ Organization
- ▪ Service operation roles
- ▪ Service operation structures

This chapter covers how the IT service provider organizes to deliver the services to the required standard. The service operation stage is when the service is actually being delivered, and often it takes much longer than the previous stages of strategy, design, and transition. We will cover the purpose, objectives, and scope for each function along with the value it provides to the business. We will look at the service operation functions identified in ITIL.

We will look at organizational structures later in this chapter. Before we start looking at the functions, however, it is important to remember that there can be a variety of structures, and some activities from technical and application management may be carried out, in part, by IT operations management.

When applied to an IT environment, operations management covers the aspect of the business that maintains and optimizes the IT services on a daily basis. In smaller organizations, this concept of separation in such detail may seem confusing; it may just be that everyone supporting the infrastructure is involved with the operations management function as well as the technical management function. It is important to remember that these are functions, not specific organizational structures.

The Service Desk Function

A *service desk* is a functional unit consisting of a dedicated number of staff members responsible for dealing with a variety of service activities, usually via telephone calls, web interface, or automatically reported infrastructure events. We will cover this function in detail because it plays a critical role in customer satisfaction. Although the service desk staff members do not have the same level of in-depth technical knowledge as the staff members in the other functions, their role is just as important.

The service desk function is the most visible of the four functions; every hour of every day, they come into contact with business users at all levels. A poor service desk can result in a poor overall impression of the IT department, while an efficient, customer-focused team can ensure customer satisfaction even when the service is operating below the agreed service level.

An essential feature of a service desk is that it provides a single point of contact (SPOC) for users needing assistance. It provides a single day-to-day interface with IT, whatever the user requirement. It provides a variety of services:

- Handles incidents, resolving as many as possible where the resolution is straightforward and within the service desk authority level

- Owns incidents that are escalated to other support groups for resolution

- Reports problems to the problem management process

- Handles service requests

- Provides information to users

- Communicates with the business about major incidents, upcoming changes, and so on

- Manages requests for change on the user's behalf if required

- Manages the performance of third-party maintenance providers, ensuring that they provide the agreed service as defined for the incident and request processes

- Monitors incidents and service requests against the targets in the SLA and provides reporting from the service desk tool to show the level of service achieved

- Updates the CMS as required

- Gathers availability figures based on incident data

Staffing

The service desk will use a service management tool and other technical resources to enable it to carry out its tasks and will follow defined processes (especially incident management and request fulfilment). Although these tools and processes are important, the people aspect of the service desk is critical. The interactions with the customers and users require good communication skills in addition to technical knowledge. Knowing the answer is only part of the job; explaining it in terms that users understand is essential.

Recruiting and retaining good service desk staff members is the key to customer satisfaction. This function often acts as an entry level to the other functions, providing staff members with an understanding of all the services, the technology that supports them, and the business impact of failure. This provides an excellent basis for future technical specialization.

Service desk staff members require a mix of technical knowledge and interpersonal skills. The technical knowledge may not be in depth, but it covers all the services provided by the IT service provider. The service desk analyst can be said to know a little about a lot of services rather than a lot about a few.

The ability to correctly prioritize incidents based on business impact and urgency requires that the service desk analyst has a good level of awareness about the business processes. Added to this knowledge is the requirement to be patient, helpful, assertive when dealing with support teams or third parties who are failing to meet targets, well organized, and calm under pressure.

Service desks are organized differently dependent upon the particular requirements of the organization. We cover various service desk structures later in the chapter in the section "Service Desk Organizational Structures." The skill level required may also vary; the service desk may be tasked with resolving a high proportion (75 percent to 80 percent) of incidents, or it may be limited to logging and escalating them for resolution by another team. Service desks are often outsourced to specialist providers; the decision to do this will be based on the overall IT strategy. If the decision is made to outsource, the third-party supplier's performance must be monitored and managed closely to ensure that this essential service is being provided to the highest standard.

Role

The provision of a single point of contact is accepted in many industries as being central to good customer service. Without a service desk, users would have to try to identify which IT support team they should approach. This could be confusing for users, leading to a delay in having their issue resolved. Technical staff members would waste time dealing with issues outside their specialist area or issues that could be dealt with by more junior staff members.

Providing a good service desk leads to a number of benefits:

- Increased focus of customer service

- Increased customer satisfaction

- Easier provision of support through the single point of contact

- Faster resolution of incidents and fulfilment of requests at the service desk, without the need for further escalation

- Reduced business impact of failures because of faster resolution

- More effective use of specialist IT staff members

- Accurate data (taken from the service desk tool) regarding the numbers and nature of incidents

Objective

As we have said already, the main objective of the service desk is to provide a single point of contact. The next most important objective is to restore service in the event of a failure. This may not mean a complete resolution of the incident; it may mean instead the provision of a workaround, to enable the user to continue working. Fulfilling a request, resetting a password, or answering a "How do I ....?" query all help the user get back to work as soon as possible.

The service desk also has the following responsibilities:

- Logging all incidents and requests with the appropriate level of detail

- Categorizing incidents and requests for future analysis

- Agreeing on the correct priority with the user based on impact and urgency (utilizing SLAs wherever possible for consistency)

- Investigating, diagnosing, and resolving incidents whenever possible

- Deciding upon the correct support team to escalate the incident to should the service desk be unable to resolve it

- Monitoring progress of the incident by support teams

- Communicating progress to the users
- Confirming closure of resolved incidents with the user
- Owning the incident on behalf of the user to ensure that it is progressed to resolution
- Carrying out surveys to ascertain the level of customer satisfaction

These are covered in more depth in the chapters on the incident (Chapter 34, "Service Operation Processes: Incident and Problem Management") and request (Chapter 35, "Service Operation Processes: Request Fulfilment") processes.

Service Desk Organizational Structures

The best structure for the service desk is dependent upon the size and structure of the organization. A global organization will have different needs from one with all its employees based in the same location. Here we look at the most common structures; the best option may be a combination of them. This will have been determined in service strategy.

Local Service Desk

This option provides a service desk colocated with the users it serves; an organization with three offices would have three local service desks. There are advantages with this approach in that the service desk is local, so it understands the local business priorities. Where the offices are spread across different countries, local service desks provide support in the language of the local users, work in the same time zone, have the same public holidays, and so on. This structure can also be useful when different locations have specialized support needs. The basic principle of a single point of contact is retained because, from the user perspective, they have only one number to call and are unaware of any other desks that may exist.

This is an expensive option because each new office location would require a new service desk too. Each desk needs sufficient staff to allow for annual leave, training, and sickness. At quiet times, there would be several service desk staff members spread across the various desks waiting for calls. There are potential issues with incidents and requests being logged in different languages; this makes incident analysis and problem identification difficult. Sharing knowledge is also more difficult: an incident that could be resolved by one service desk might be escalated by another because the resolution has not been shared between the desks. Resilience may be another issue. With local distributed desks, there may be the option of each desk providing cover for the others, but in reality this may be difficult to achieve.

To overcome these issues, IT management must ensure that information is shared effectively. Procedures need to be put in place to ensure that issues affecting more than one location are managed effectively without duplication of effort, each service desk assuming that another desk is responsible. Figure 39.1 shows the local structure.

FIGURE 39.1   Local service desk

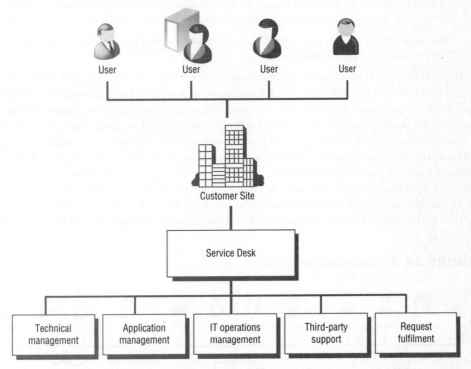

User   User   User   User

Customer Site

Service Desk

| Technical management | Application management | IT operations management | Third-party support | Request fulfilment |

Centralized Service Desk

A more common structure for service desks is that of a centralized service desk. In this model, all users contact the same service desk. This has the benefit of providing economies of scale because there is no duplication of provision. Specialist technology, such as intelligent call distribution or an integrated service management tool, may be justified for a centralized service desk but not when implementing this technology across many sites. There are no issues with confusion regarding ownership of major incidents, and knowledge sharing becomes much more straightforward. Offering a service at times of low demand is more cost-effective when only one service desk needs to be staffed.

Staff members on a centralized desk will gain more experience with particular incidents, which a local service desk may encounter only occasionally, leading to an increased ability to resolve these issues immediately. Where the centralized desk is supporting users in many countries, the language issue may be resolved by the following:

- Employing staff members with language skills and using technology to allocate calls requiring support in a particular language to staff members who have that language ability. Staff members would then log the call in the main language.

- Standardizing on one language; callers would need to report incidents in that language, and support would be provided in it. This option depends on the type of organization and whether its users may reasonably be expected to be able to converse in the language.

- Local super users may be required to support users without the necessary language ability and to log calls on their behalf.

To provide support to a global organization, a 24/7 service may be required. Where the resolution requires a physical intervention (unjamming a printer, for example), the service desk would require local support staff who could be assigned calls and be responsible for updating the incident records or could assist in the resolution of an issue at a remote site.

Consideration should also be given to maintaining service continuity because an event that affects a centralized service desk would impact support across the entire organization. A plan to provide the service from another location, possibly using different staff members, in the event of a disaster must be developed and tested in conjunction with IT service continuity management. There should also be plans in place to ensure the service desk's tool resilience in the event of disruption to the network or a power failure. This centralized structure is shown in Figure 39.2.

FIGURE 39.2   Centralized service desk

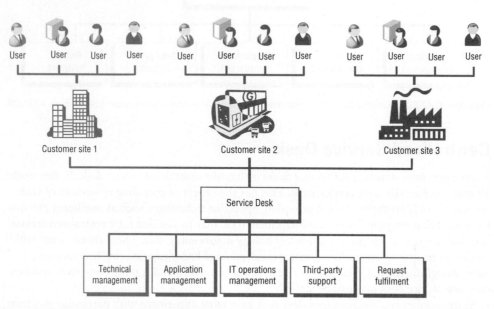

Virtual Service Desk

The third organizational option described by ITIL is that of a virtual service desk. This option consists of two or more service desk locations that operate as one desk. Calls and emails are distributed across the staff members as if they were in one centralized location. This ensures that the workload is balanced across all the desks. To the user, the virtual service desk appears as a single entity; the users may be completely unaware that this is not the case in reality. The virtual service desk retains the single point of contact principle.

The considerations we discussed earlier regarding knowledge sharing and clear ownership apply even more in this scenario, as does the need for all calls to be logged immediately. Users will become very frustrated if they call the service desk and explain an issue in detail only to find when they call for a second time that the service desk analyst can find no record of their first call. This is, of course, true for all service desks, but the difficulty of locating a "lost call" is increased in the virtual environment, where team members are not located together.

The ability to route calls to analysts with particular language knowledge or to adopt one language for all users can be considered, as with a centralized desk. Calls must be logged on one common system, using one language, because the next analyst to handle the incident may be in another location.

The virtual service desk structure allows for a variety of ways of working. Many call centers use home-based staff members, who log on to the service desk telephone system and are allocated calls. Extra staff members from other teams can supplement the core service desk staff members at busy times, without the users being aware. Many of us have had the experience of calling a local company, only to have the call answered offshore outside of normal hours or during busy times.

Offshoring support (providing support from another geographical location where staff members' costs may be lower) can be cost-effective but requires careful management to ensure consistency of service. Managers need to be culturally sensitive because users may become irritated by staff members behaving in a way in which they find unfamiliar.

 Real World Scenario

Offshore Support Difficulties

A large insurance company in the United Kingdom decided to offshore its service desk. Overseas staff members were recruited carefully, with tests to validate their language and technical skills. After some months, an analysis of telephone traffic showed that many customers were hanging up as soon as they realized that their call was being answered offshore. Focus groups of users were interviewed to try to understand why this was happening.

The answer was not the level of technical support but a combination of the lack of local knowledge and cultural issues. The offshore staff members had been coached in customer service and were putting the recommendations into effect, explaining to the user what they were doing, thanking the user after every piece of information was provided, and so on. The users were not used to this level of service and expressed a wish that "the service desk staff members just got on with the task and stopped talking about it!"

One benefit of a virtual structure is that it has built-in resilience; should one location go offline because of a major disruption affecting that location, the service would continue with little or no impact.

Figure 39.3 shows the virtual service desk structure.

FIGURE 39.3 Virtual service desk

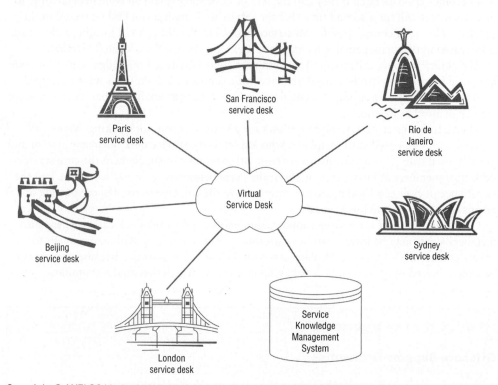

Follow the Sun

The fourth structure described within ITIL is known as *follow the sun*. This is a form of virtual service desk, but with this structure, the allocation of calls across the various desks is based on time of day rather than workload.

Follow the sun enables a global organization to provide support around the clock, without needing to employ staff members at night to work on the service desk. A number of service desks will each work standard office hours. The calls will be allocated to whichever desk or desks are open at the time the calls are made. Typically, this might mean a European service desk will handle calls until the end of the European working day, when calls will then be allocated to a desk or desks in North America. When the working day in North America finishes, calls are directed to another desk or desks in the Asia-Pacific region before being directed back to the European desk at the start of the next European working day.

This option is an attractive one for many global organizations, providing 24-hour coverage without the need for shift or on-call payments. The requirements for effective call logging, a centralized database, and a common language for data entry referred to earlier for the virtual structure apply equally here. Procedures for handoff between desks are also required to ensure that the desk that is taking over knows, for example, the status of any major incidents.

To the user, the single point of contact still applies; they have one number to call, no matter who answers it or where the service desk analyst may be located.

Specialized Service Desk Groups

Another possible variant on the previous structures is to provide specialist support for particular services. In this structure, a user may call the usual service desk number and then choose an option depending on the issue they have. Typically, the message would say, "Press 1 if the call is regarding system X, press 2 if it is regarding system Y, or hold for a service desk analyst if your call is in regard to anything else."

Although this approach can be useful, especially where in-depth knowledge is required to resolve a call, it is not popular with users when it expands to numerous options to choose from followed by yet more options.

There is a danger that the user does not always know what support they need and may choose the wrong option, leading to delay and frustration. For example, a printer may not print because of a hardware fault, a network issue, an application malfunction, or a user error. The user will not know which option to choose.

This specialist support option works best for a small number of complex services that require a level of both business and technical knowledge beyond what can reasonably be expected of a service desk analyst. Another possible reason to use this option is when the service contains confidential data. In this situation, the organization may wish to limit access to a small number of specialist support staff.

Service Desk Single Point of Contact

Building a single point of contact is an important part of the service desk communication. Regardless of the combination of options chosen to fulfil an organization's overall service desk structure, individual users should be in no doubt about who to contact if they need assistance or where they can access self-help support. A single telephone number (or a single number for each group if separate desks are chosen) should be provided and well publicized, as well as a single email address and a single web service desk contact page.

There are several ways to help publicize the service desk telephone number and email address and make them easily available when users are likely to need them, such as including the service desk telephone number on hardware CI labels attached to the components the user is likely to be calling about and printing service desk contact details on telephones. For PCs and laptops, there could be a customized background or desktop with the service desk contact details together with information such as IP address and OS build number in one corner.

Printing the service desk number on giveaway materials (pens, pencils, mugs, mouse pads, etc.) and prominently placing it on service desk Internet/intranet sites, as well as including it on calling cards or satisfaction survey cards left with users when a desk visit has been necessary are other ways to promote the service desk number. Repeating the details on all correspondence sent to users (together with call reference numbers) and placing the details on notice boards or physical locations that users are likely to regularly visit (entrances, canteens, refreshment areas, etc.) are important ways of maintaining the corporate presence of the service desk.

Service Desk Staffing

An organization must ensure that the correct number of staff are available at any given time to match the demand being placed upon the desk by the business. There is often a variety in the volumes of calls received by the service desk. An organization planning a new desk should attempt to predict the call arrival rate and profile and staff accordingly. Statistical analysis of call arrival rates of the current volumes or similar volumes will provide a good basis for understanding the requirements.

A common pattern of calls will be a peak in the mornings, with maybe another peak later in the day, around the early part of the afternoon. Each organization will be different, but it is common to find that there will be a recurring pattern. Staffing can then be adjusted to meet the demand.

A number of factors should be considered when choosing staffing levels, including customer service expectations and business requirements such as budget and call response times.

Self-help tools and automation of service request handling (e.g., password resets) will also have an impact on staffing levels, as will the size, relative age, design, and complexity of the IT infrastructure and service catalog. For example, staffing may be influenced by the number and type of incidents or the extent of customized software deployed instead of standard off-the-shelf software.

There are clearly some factors that have a direct impact on the staffing levels of the service desk, such as the number of customers and users speaking a different language and the technical skill levels of the staff and the types of calls handled. The duration of time required for call types (e.g., simple queries, specialist application queries, hardware, etc.) and whether or not local or external expertise is required for the volume and types of incidents and service requests are also factors.

Other factors will be the hours the service desk is taking calls, the after-hours support requirements, time zones to be covered, and locations to be supported (particularly if service desk staff also conduct desk-side support, given the travel time between locations). Understanding the pattern of requests (e.g., daily, end of the month) and the service level targets in place (response levels) will also have an impact, as will the type of responses required. There are a variety of contact mechanisms in use: telephone, email/voicemail/ video, online chat, texting, and online access/control. The skill levels and the level of training required for staff to support the processes and procedures will identify the requirements for development of the service desk.

These are factors to be considered before making any decision on staffing levels. These factors should also be reflected in the levels of documentation required. Service desks are often victims of their own success because the better the service, the more the business will use it.

A number of tools are available to help determine the appropriate number of staff for the service desk. These workload modeling tools are dependent on detailed local knowledge of the organization, such as call volumes and patterns and service and user profiles. Industry standards suggest 1,000 users equals 104 calls/day, but this may not fit all organizations.

The skill levels for the service desk will be dependent on the nature of the requirements of the business. A range of skill options is possible, starting from a call logging service only, where staff need only very basic technical skills, right through to a technical service desk where the organization's most technically skilled staff members are used. In the case of the former, there will be a high volume of calls to handle but a low resolution rate, while in the latter case this will be reversed.

The required skills level will often depend on target resolution times (agreed with the business and captured in service level targets), the complexity of the systems supported, and the business budget. There is a strong correlation between response and resolution targets and costs. Generally speaking, the shorter the target times, the higher the cost because more resources are required.

There is no rule about the way a service desk should be set up, but often organizations will start with a call logging approach, with technical skills in second-line and third-line support teams, and build up expertise at the service desk over time. Obviously, if there is an immediate requirement for highly skilled technical support at the first point of contact, this should be provided.

A way of improving the first-line skill set is to consider the physical location of the second- and third-line support teams. Closer proximity will enable and foster information exchange and enable the utilization of the more technical support personnel to provide support and backup for peak periods for the service desk.

However, second-line staff often have duties outside of the service desk, resulting in rosters having to be managed or second-line staff positions being duplicated. In addition, having to deal with routine calls may be demotivating for more experienced staff. A further potential drawback is that the service desk becomes really good at resolving incidents, whereas second-line staff should be focused on removing the root cause of incidents instead.

It is worth noting that although successful problem management will improve service desk performance by providing known error resolutions, in the longer term it may lead to a reduced first-time fix rate at the service desk. This is because, as recurrent faults are permanently fixed, the service desk is dealing with more complex and individual calls. A falling fix rate therefore does not necessarily mean that the service desk service is deteriorating.

Once the required skill levels have been identified, it is important to ensure that personnel with the correct balance of skills are on duty so that consistency is maintained.

Service desks will need necessary ongoing training and awareness programs to cover interpersonal skills, such as telephony, communication, active listening, and customer care skills. Business awareness and specific knowledge of the organization's business areas, drivers, structure, and priorities are critical for effective support.

Service awareness of all the organization's key IT services for which support is being provided is also essential for the effective support of the organization. Depending on the level of support provided, some diagnostic skills may be required, and the ability to use support tools and techniques will be important. All service desk staff are required to be trained on new systems and technologies prior to their introduction.

The service desk will need to be aware of the processes and procedures in the IT department, most particularly incident, request, change, and service asset and configuration management, but an overview of all ITSM processes and procedures is also valuable. Another useful skill is typing to ensure quick and accurate entry of incident or service request details.

To ensure that the service desk continues to perform as required, skill requirements and levels should be evaluated periodically and training records maintained. Careful formulation of staffing rotations or schedules should be maintained so that a consistent balance of staff experience and appropriate skill levels are present during all critical operational periods. It is important to have the correct blend of skills available.

Training

It is vital that all service desk staff are adequately trained before they are called upon to staff the service desk. This should include organizational induction and business awareness programs to ensure the staff are conversant with the organization they will support.

When starting on the service desk, new staff should initially "shadow" experienced staff (that is, sit with them and listen in on calls) before starting to take calls themselves with a mentor listening in and able to intervene and provide support where necessary. Mentoring is a useful technique to maintain training as the service desk personnel gain experience, and a mentor can be allocated for each service desk person as they progress through their career.

Service desk staff need training to keep their knowledge up-to-date and stay aware of new developments, services, and technologies. The timing of such events is critical so normal duties are not disrupted.

It is important to invest in the service desk to maintain a professional team. Traditionally, the service desk suffers from a high turnover of staff, but this can be mitigated by having staff progress into the organization rather than taking their knowledge away to a new company.

Staff Retention

It is very important that all IT managers recognize the importance of the service desk and the staff who work on it. High staff turnover is expensive because new staff have to be recruited and trained before they are fully effective. It is one of the common challenges in running a service desk. Any significant loss of staff can be disruptive and lead to inconsistency of service, so efforts should be made to make the service desk an attractive place to work.

Recognition of the importance of the service desk is vital, with reward packages, team-building exercises, and staff rotation to other activities (projects, second-line support, etc.). Good documentation and cross-training can support this approach.

The service desk can often be used as a stepping stone into other, more technical or supervisory/managerial roles. However, care is needed to ensure that proper succession planning takes place so that the desk does not lose key expertise in any area at one time.

Super Users

The introduction of super users throughout the user community to act as liaison points with IT in general and the service desk in particular can be beneficial, particularly for specific application expertise.

Super users can be given some additional training and used as a conduit for communications in both directions. It is important to note that super users should log all calls they deal with and not just those they pass on to IT. They will need access to, and training on how to use, the incident logging tools. This will ensure that valuable history regarding incidents and service quality is not lost.

They can also be used to cascade information from the service desk outward throughout their local user community, which can be useful in disseminating service details to all users very quickly.

It is important to ensure that the super users have the time and interest to perform the role. This will require commitment and support from their management.

Measuring Service Desk Performance

Metrics should be established so that service desk performance can be evaluated at regular intervals. This is important to assess the health, maturity, efficiency, and effectiveness of the service desk and recognize opportunities to improve its operations.

Metrics should not be viewed in isolation, and it is important to remember that metrics may drive behavior, for example isolated measures of call closure may result in poor quality of customer/user satisfaction, because the driver for the support analyst is to close the call, not ensure that the customer is satisfied with the result.

Typical service desk metrics include call-handling statistics and first-line resolution rates. The first-line resolution rate is the figure often quoted by organizations as the primary measure of the service desk's performance. It's also used for comparison with the performance of other service desks, but care is needed when making any comparisons to ensure that there is a "like-for-like" comparison in terms of the nature of the support delivered and the technical capability of the desk.

Other service desk metrics include average times to achieve a particular target, for example, the average time to resolve an incident (when resolved at first line).

It may be important to understand the average time to escalate an incident (where first-line resolution is not possible). This will show that the service desk staff are efficient and recognize their limitations, and it will identify where the user will be best served by the escalation of a call to more expert resources.

Service desks are bound by service targets. The user experience of IT is often only based on their contact with the service desk and measured with the service desk service targets. So the percentage of customer or user updates conducted within target times, as defined in SLA targets, may be the only measure on which the users base their perception of the whole IT department.

The average time to review and close a resolved call will demonstrate the efficiency of the service desk in handling their workload.

The number of calls broken down by time of day and day of week, combined with the average call-time metric, is critical in determining the staff required. There are no hard and fast rules about staffing levels for a service desk, so this analysis is vital to understand each organization's individual requirements.

Further general details on metrics and how they should be used to improve the quality of service is included in *ITIL Continual Service Improvement* core volume.

Customer/User Satisfaction Surveys

As well as tracking the "hard" measures of the service desk's performance, it is important to assess "soft" measures. These are expressed by how well the customers and users feel their calls have been answered, whether they feel the service desk operator was courteous and professional, and whether they instilled confidence in the user.

The only successful approach to soft measures is to obtain them from the users themselves. A common method for understanding the service desk issues is through a call-back telephone survey, in which an independent service desk operator or supervisor calls back a small percentage of users shortly after their incident has been resolved to ask their opinion of the support they have received.

This can be done as part of a wider customer/user satisfaction survey covering all of IT, or it can be specifically targeted at the service desk issues alone.

Care should be taken to keep the number of questions to a minimum so that users will have the time to cooperate. Survey questions should be designed so that the user or customer knows what area or topic the questions address and which incident or service they are referring to. To allow adequate comparisons of service over a given time period, the same percentage of calls should be selected in each period, and they should be rigorously carried out despite any other time pressures.

The service desk must act on low satisfaction levels and any feedback received.

Surveys are a complex and specialized area, requiring a good understanding of statistics and survey techniques, but it is not necessary to understand these as part of your studies of the *ITIL Service Operation* core volume.

Table 39.1 lists some typical examples of surveys.

TABLE 39.1   Survey techniques and tools

Technique/Tool	Advantages	Disadvantages
After-call survey Callers are asked to remain on the phone after the call and then asked to rate the service.	High response rate because the caller is already on the phone. Caller is surveyed immediately after the call, so they can easily recall their experience.	People may feel pressured into taking the survey, resulting in a negative service experience. The surveyor is seen as part of the service desk being surveyed, which may discourage open answers.
Outbound telephone survey Customers and users who have previously used the service desk are contacted sometime after their experience.	Higher response rate because the caller is interviewed directly. Specific categories of users or customers can be targeted for feedback (e.g., people who requested a specific service, or people who experienced a disruption to a particular service).	This method could be seen as intrusive if the call disrupts the users' or customers' work. The survey is conducted sometime after the user or customer used the service desk, so their perception may have changed.
Personal interviews Customers and users are interviewed personally by the person doing the survey. This is especially effective for customers or users who use the service desk extensively or who have had a very negative experience.	The interviewer is able to observe nonverbal signals as well as listen to what the user or customer is saying. Users and customers feel a greater degree of personal attention and a sense that their answers are being taken seriously.	Interviews are time consuming for both the interviewer and the respondent. Users and customers could turn the interviews into complaint sessions.
Group interviews Customers and users are interviewed in small groups. This is good for gathering general impressions and for determining whether there is a need to change certain aspects of the service desk (e.g., service hours or location).	A larger number of users and customers can be interviewed. Questions are more generic and therefore more consistent between interviews.	People may not express themselves freely in front of their peers or managers. People's opinions can easily be changed by others in the group during the interview.

TABLE 39.1   Survey techniques and tools *(continued)*

Technique/Tool	Advantages	Disadvantages
Postal/email surveys Survey questionnaires are mailed to a target set of customers and users. They are asked to return their responses by email or regular mail.	Either specific or all customers or users can be targeted. Postal surveys can be anonymous, allowing people to express themselves more freely. Email surveys are not anonymous but can be created using automated forms that make it convenient and easy for users to reply and increase the likelihood surveys will be completed.	Postal surveys are labor intensive to process. The percentage of people responding to postal surveys tends to be small. Misinterpretation of a question could affect the result.
Online surveys Questionnaires are posted on a website, and users and customers are encouraged via email or links from a popular site to participate in the survey.	The potential audience of these surveys is fairly large. Respondents can complete the questionnaire in their own time. The links on popular websites are good reminders without being intrusive.	The type and percentage of respondents cannot be predicted.

Service Desk Environment

The environment where the service desk is to be located should be carefully chosen. It is important to remember that the staff will often be expected to remain in a single location for long periods of time, and so, where possible, the facilities should be provided to take the working conditions into consideration.

If the organization can provide a location where the entire function can be positioned with sufficient natural light and overall space to allow adequate desk and storage space and room to move around if necessary, this will make the working environment much more acceptable.

Service desk staff should have easy access to the correct equipment to support their responsibilities, such as consoles, monitoring displays, and message boards to quickly gain a picture of any key operating or service events or issues that may be taking place. Because the service desk is often busy, potentially handling many different conversations at once, a quiet environment with adequate acoustic control so that one telephone conversation is not disrupted by another is essential.

The service desk can be a very stressful place to work, and thoughtful use of space, furniture, and assistive technology can be beneficial. Many organizations have discovered that the provision of pleasant surroundings and comfortable furniture to lighten the mood helps with the management of stress. Consider the use of a separate restroom and refreshment area nearby so that staff can take short breaks when necessary, without being away for too long. Breakout areas that encourage relaxation can be very helpful in maintaining service desk morale.

Placing the service desk at the heart of the department, not hidden away, will encourage collaborative working with second- and third-line colleagues.

Outsourcing the Service Desk

Outsourcing the service desk is a business decision, and the organization is ultimately responsible for the outcomes of the decision. There are some safeguards that are needed to ensure that the outsourced service desk works effectively and efficiently with the organization's other IT teams and departments and that end-to-end service management control is maintained.

Common Tools and Processes

In an outsourced environment, the service desk tools must not only support the outsourced service desk, they must support the customer organization's processes and business requirements as well. Some of the challenges of outsourcing involve access to tools—from in-house staff needing access to the outsourcer's tools and data to the outsourced support teams needing access to in-house tools and data.

The service desk will need access to several different types of data to be effective:

- All incident records and information
- Problem records and information
- Known error data
- Change schedule
- Sources of internal knowledge (especially technical or application experts)
- SKMS
- CMS
- Alerts from monitoring tools

There may be security issues in allowing staff from another organization such access. Integrating different tools can be challenging, but integrating processes of two very different organizations, with different maturity levels and different cultures, is very complex. Outsourcing is dependent on successful integration between the organizations.

It is important for the organization to understand the capability of the outsource partner. It may be incorrectly assumed that service management quality and maturity in an external outsource partner can be guaranteed by stating requirements in the procurement process for "ITIL conformance" or "ISO/IEC 20000 certification." These statements may indicate that a potential supplier uses the ITIL framework in its delivery of services to customers, or that it has achieved standards certification for its internal practices. This is not a guarantee that its approach to outsourcing is managed in the same way.

SLA Targets

When considering outsourcing arrangements, there may be issues with operational level agreements (OLAs) and underpinning contracts (UCs) in a mixed-sourced environment, which can be complex and, if not well handled, could impact service.

The important fact is that the user must receive a seamless service even when there are a number of outsourced organizations involved in the delivery of the service. It is essential that OLAs and UCs with internal and external providers of the component parts of the service are agreed and realistic and are actually achieved.

Good Communications

In this complex situation, good communication will happen only if it is planned; the OLAs and UCs can specify how this should be done.

It is essential that the service desk can communicate with the users and the support and fulfilment teams. This is more difficult if they are not colocated, and it can be very challenging if the service desk is offshored as well as outsourced.

Training in the customer organization's tools and methods of operation will help, especially if the service desk staff attend identical training as the end users do so they understand the capability of the users.

Offshored service desks need to concentrate on achieving good communication with the users, despite possible cultural and language issues. Training programs can help, especially understanding idiomatic use of the language in the customer market.

Ownership of Data

Another important factor for an outsourced environment is that the management of data be well defined because some cross-access is essential while other data has to be kept confidential.

Ownership of all data relative to users, customers, affected CIs, services, incidents, service requests, changes, and so on must remain with the organization that is outsourcing the activity, but both organizations will require access to it. Data that is related specifically to performance of employees of the outsourcing company (the company carrying out the work on behalf of the main organization) will remain the property of that company.

All reporting requirements and issues around ownership of data must be specified in the underpinning contract with the company providing the outsourcing service.

Other ITIL Functions

ITIL describes four main functions that are responsible for carrying out all the lifecycle processes. These are technical management, application management, IT operations management, and the service desk. We have reviewed the service desk, so now we will move on to the remaining functions. The IT operations management function is further divided into IT operations control and facilities management. We will cover each of these in turn and then look at where the responsibilities of each function overlap. It is important to remember that ITIL is not prescriptive and does not specify an organizational structure or specific names for teams within an organization. The responsibilities of the functions described here should be carried out, but each organization will have its own structure.

Technical Management

Whatever the name given to the team or teams in any particular organization (infrastructure support, technical support, network management, and so on), the function referred to in the ITIL framework as *technical management* is required to manage and develop the IT infrastructure. This function covers the groups or teams that together have the technical expertise and knowledge to ensure that the infrastructure works effectively in support of the services required by the business.

Role

The technical management function has a number of responsibilities:

- It is responsible for managing the IT infrastructure. This would include ensuring that the staff members performing this function have the necessary technical knowledge to design, test, manage, and improve IT services.

- Although we discuss this function under service operation, the function provides appropriately skilled staff members to support the entire lifecycle. Technical management staff members would be involved in drawing up the technical strategy and ensuring that the infrastructure can support the overall service strategy. Technical management staff members would also carry out the technical design of new or changed services and would be involved in planning and implementing their transition to the operational environment.

- Once the service is live, technical management provides technical support, resolving incidents, investigating problems, responding to alerts, and specifying any changes or updates required to have the service operate efficiently. Technical management staff members will identify service improvements and work with the CSI manager to design, test, and implement these improvements.

It is the responsibility of the manager or managers of this function to ensure the correct number of staff members, with the correct skills to carry out the required tasks. Specifying the numbers and skill levels required is discussed as part of the lifecycle stage strategy and detailed as part of the lifecycle stage of service design. Transition tests that the staff members are able to support the service as designed, and CSI identifies any improvements or training requirements. The technical manager must decide whether to employ new staff members with the correct skills, to train existing staff members, or to use short-term contract resources to meet a particular requirement. Larger organizations may have a team of subject-matter experts that can be called upon when required by subsidiary departments, without the need for those skills to be developed across the organization.

Most of the everyday operational support activities will be undertaken by the operations support staff members, but it is the responsibility of technical management, as the experts in the technology, to guide and support the operations staff members.

Objectives

The objectives of technical management are as follows:

- Providing the appropriate technical infrastructure to support the business processes. This should take account of the availability and capacity requirements, providing a stable resilient infrastructure at an affordable cost.

- Planning and designing the technical aspects of any new or changed service.

- Implementing these technical aspects and supporting them in the live environment, using the technical expertise that the function possesses to ensure that any issues that arise are swiftly resolved.

Generic Technical Management Activities

Technical management is involved in two types of activity. This includes activities that are generic to the technical management function as a whole. The other type of activity is linked to the processes that are performed by all three of the functions (technical, application, and IT operations management). We explored these as part of the review of operational activities in the previous chapter, which included activities such as monitoring, control and reporting, and the engagement of operational functions in the execution of other lifecycle processes (e.g., change management).

In this section, we will explore the activities that enable technical management to execute its role.

Technical management is responsible for identifying the knowledge and expertise required to manage and operate the IT infrastructure and to deliver IT services. This process starts during the service strategy stage, is expanded in detail in service design, and is executed in service transition and service operation. Ongoing assessment and updating of these skills is done during CSI. In this way, technical management operates throughout the service lifecycle.

This function is also responsible for documenting the skills that exist in the organization as well as skills that need to be developed. This will include the development of skills inventories and the performance of training needs analyses. Following this, it will be technical management that initiates training programs to develop and refine the skills in the appropriate technical resources and maintains training records for all technical resources.

The technical management function should have the appropriate skills to design and deliver training for users, the service desk, and other groups. Although training requirements must be defined in service design, they are executed in service operation. If there is no capability to actually deliver training, technical management will be responsible for identifying organizations that can provide it.

Technical management takes responsibility for managing the acquisition of skills that cannot be developed internally, for example, by recruiting or contracting additional resources. They also are responsible for acquisition of additional skills where there are insufficient people to perform the required technical management activities.

This function will also be involved in procuring skills for specific activities when the required skills are not available internally or in the open market or when it is more cost efficient to hire specialists.

During the service strategy and design stages, technical management will define the standards to be used in the design of new architectures and participate in the definition of technology architectures. As the repository of technical expertise, the function will also be responsible for research and development solutions that can help expand the service portfolio or be used to simplify or automate IT operations, reduce costs, or increase levels of IT service.

Additional activities for technical management include involvement in the design and build of new services. Technical management will contribute to the design of the technical architecture and performance standards for IT services. In addition, it will be responsible for specifying the operational activities required to manage the IT infrastructure on an ongoing basis.

Technical management will be participating in projects, not only during service design and service transition, but also for CSI or operational projects, such as operating system upgrades, server consolidation projects, and physical moves.

Modeling and workload forecasting are often done with technical management resources so that availability and capacity management for IT services meet the levels of service required by the business. This will also require assessing risk, identifying critical service and system dependencies, and defining and implementing countermeasures.

Technical management activities should include designing and performing tests for the functionality, performance, and manageability of IT services to support service transition activities. The function may also be engaged in managing suppliers; many technical management departments or groups are the only ones who know exactly what is required of a supplier and how to measure and manage them. For this reason, many organizations rely on technical management departments to manage contracts with suppliers of specific CIs. If this is the case, it is important to ensure that these relationships are managed as part of the SLM and supplier management processes.

It is obvious that as a function with service operation responsibilities, technical management will play a large role in the operational processes. For example, it will take the lead in defining and managing event management standards and tools. Technical management should also test event mechanisms during service transition and will also monitor and respond to many categories of events during service operation.

It is crucial that technical management departments or groups are integral to the performance of incident management. They receive incidents through functional escalation and provide second- and higher-level support. They are also involved in maintaining categories and defining the escalation procedures that are executed in incident management. They can provide scripts to ensure that correct incident details are captured and workarounds to assist the service desk in first-line resolution.

Technical management as a function provides resources that contribute to the execution of the problem management process. It provides technical expertise and knowledge that is used to diagnose and resolve problems. It also maintains relationships with the suppliers and their support teams that are used to escalate and follow up on technical issues, changes, incidents, and problems. They play an important part in defining coding systems that are used in incident and problem management (e.g., incident categories) and supporting problem management in validating and maintaining the known error database.

But as you have already seen, it is not only operational processes that gain value from this function; other lifecycle stages, such as service transition, will also benefit. Technical management will support the change management process where reliance on technical knowledge and expertise may be needed to evaluate changes and will assist with the deployment of releases.

In cooperation with application management, technical management will provide information for, and operationally maintain, the CMS and its data. This will be done to ensure that the correct CI attributes and relationships are created from the deployment of services and the ongoing maintenance over the life of CIs.

Technical management is involved in the CSI activities, identifying opportunities for improvement, particularly in highlighting areas for improvement and then helping to evaluate alternative solutions.

System and operating documentation needs to be maintained and kept up-to-date and properly utilized. This includes ensuring that all management, administration, and user manuals are up-to-date and complete and that technical staff are familiar with their contents. This needs to be done by those who have sufficient technical expertise, and the resources will often be provided through technical management.

Technical management will also be responsible for updating and maintaining data used for reporting on technical and service capabilities (for example, capacity and performance management, availability management, problem management) as well as for assisting financial management for IT services to identify the cost of technology and IT human resources used to manage IT services.

Many technical management departments, groups, or teams define the operational activities performed as part of IT operations management as well as performing the operational activities as part of an organization's IT operations management function.

Technical Management Organization

Technical management is not normally provided by a single department or group. It is usual to find one or more technical support teams or departments providing technical management and support for the IT infrastructure. In all but the smallest organizations, where a single combined team or department may have to cover everything, separate teams or departments may be needed for each type of infrastructure being used.

Because technical management consists of a number of technological areas, each of which may require a specific set of skills to manage and operate it, there may be a number of teams. Some skill sets are related and can be performed by generalists, whereas others are specific to a component, system, or platform.

The principle of technical management organizational structure is that people are grouped according to their technical skill sets and that these skill sets are determined by the technology that needs to be managed.

Technical Design and Technical Maintenance and Support

In the ITIL framework, technical management teams include both specialist technical architects and designers (who are primarily involved during service design) and specialist maintenance and support staff (who are primarily involved during service operation).

Many organizations see them as two separate teams or even departments. The challenge of a separated approach is that good design needs input from the people who are required to manage the solution, and good operation requires involvement from the people who designed the solution. In other words, support staff should be involved during the design or architecture of a solution.

If possible, it is advisable to introduce measures to support the technical function approach, so designers should be held accountable for their portion of the design flaws that create operational outages, and support staff should be held accountable for their contribution to the technical architecture.

Measuring Technical Management Performance

The performance metrics for technical management will largely depend on which technology is being managed, but some generic metrics are listed next.

Measurement of Agreed Outputs

The following outputs could be measured:

- Transaction rates and availability for critical business transactions
- Service desk training
- Problem resolutions recorded into the KEDB
- User measures of the quality of outputs as defined in the SLAs

Process Metrics

Technical management teams execute many service management process activities that will be measured:

- Response time to events and event completion rates
- Incident resolution times for second- and third-line support
- Problem resolution statistics
- Number of escalations and reason for those escalations
- Number of changes implemented and backed out

Technology Performance

These metrics are based on service design specifications and will typically be contained in OLAs or SOPs. Actual metrics will vary by technology but are likely to include the following:

- Utilization rates (memory or processor for server, bandwidth for networks)
- Availability of systems, network, devices, and other resources
- Accuracy of information and data that is being presented
- Performance (e.g., response times, queuing rates)

Mean Time between Failures of Specified Equipment

This metric is used to ensure that good purchasing decisions are being made and the equipment is being properly maintained (the latter when compared with maintenance schedules).

Measurement of Maintenance Activity

The following metrics provide information on maintenance activity:

- Maintenance performed per schedule
- Number of maintenance windows exceeded
- Maintenance objectives achieved (number and percentage)

Training and Skills Development

These metrics ensure that staff have the skills and training to manage the technology that is under their control:

- Achieved skills performance levels
- Number of calls and escalations to third-party or other internal subject-matter experts for additional help and support
- Percentage of incidents caused by skills issues

The areas of measurement include agreed outputs and process metrics. It will be important to measure technology performance, including the mean time between failures for specific equipment. Understanding the success of maintenance activity is equally important for this function. Because technical management will be responsible for training, it is important to measure the effectiveness of training and skills development.

Technical Management Documentation

Technical management is involved in drafting and maintaining several documents as part of other processes (e.g., capacity planning, change management, and problem management). There will be some documents that are specific to the technical management groups or teams, such as technical documentation for CIs (e.g., technical manuals and administration manuals).

During the design lifecycle phase, technical management will be part of the creation of maintenance schedules for the infrastructure. They will also maintain a skills inventory in line with the processes, architectures, and performance standards, which will enable the identification of training requirements. It is important to remember that skills inventories provide information about the capability of the department for the delivery of service as well as identifying training needs.

Operations Management

In business, the term *operations management* is used to mean the department, group, or team of people responsible for performing the organization's day-to-day operational activities, such as running the production line in a manufacturing environment or managing the distribution centers and fleet movements within a logistics organization. It is useful to consider IT operations management in the same way.

We will now explore the IT operations management function and how it contributes to service operation. We shall look at the IT operations management role and how to balance requirements. We will review the objectives, organization, metrics, and documentation relating to the function and how it supports service operation as a lifecycle stage.

The role of operations management is to carry out all the day-to-day activities that are required to deliver the services provided. The applications and technical management functions are the subject-matter experts in their respective fields and define what operational activities are to take place; operations management's role is to make sure these are done.

The service design stage defined the required service levels, and the transition phase carried out tests to ensure that they were achievable; operations management is responsible for ensuring that these service levels are met consistently. Although the primary focus is on stability and availability, operations management will seek to continually improve by implementing changes that will help protect the live service or by reducing costs and opportunities for human error by implementing automation of routine tasks.

The quality of the service delivered to the business is dependent on operations management. This role is divided into two parts, IT operations control and facilities management.

IT Operations Control

This part of operations management oversees the IT infrastructure. In larger organizations, this may be carried out as part of an operations bridge or network operations center (NOC). In these organizations, there are dedicated staff members monitoring operational events on consoles and reacting to them as necessary, often in a separate area from the rest of IT. In smaller organizations, the line between technical management and operations control may be more blurred, with operations control being carried out by the technical management team, who monitor the systems from their desks, perhaps with one or two wall-mounted plasma screens. Whichever arrangement is chosen depends upon what suits the organization, but it is important that there are clearly defined expectations to ensure that the operations control tasks are carried out to the level required.

The operations control tasks are as follows:

- The centralized monitoring and management of system events, as discussed, sometimes referred to as *console management*.

- The scheduling and management of batch jobs to carry out routine tasks such as database updates.

- Carrying out backups of data and ensuring that this data can be restored if and when required. This may include the backup of entire systems or the restoration of individual files that a user may have corrupted.

- Although most printing is now carried out directly by the users, there may be certain requirements for centralized printing; pay slips will need to be printed in a secure environment to ensure confidentiality, and large print volumes may make centralized printing more efficient. The printing and distribution of these and other electronic output is an operations control task.

- Management of the output from any control activities should also be undertaken, such as distribution.

- Operations control may also undertake maintenance activities, under the guidance of the technical or application management functions; this could include archiving data, applying system packs, updating virus signatures, and so on.

Facilities Management

The other part of operations management is *facilities management*. Staff members involved in this will be responsible for the physical IT environment. This would include the following:

- Ensuring that the necessary power is supplied (including any requirements for its quality, such as the prevention of power spikes) at operational and recovery sites.

- Operating and maintaining uninterruptible power supply (UPS) devices and generators. Facilities management is responsible for ensuring that these are available and for testing to ensure that they will work as designed in the event of a power failure. This role may cover just a server room in a smaller organization or one or more data centers for larger ones.

- Ensuring the maintenance of satisfactory air-conditioning/cooling for rooms housing IT equipment, whether this is a server room or a complete data center for either operational or recovery sites.

Many organizations have undertaken data center or server consolidation projects in recent years to take advantage of technical advances. The facilities management function would be responsible for managing any such projects. In the case where the data center management is carried out by a third party, it would be the responsibility of facilities management to ensure that the external service provider was carrying out the required tasks to the agreed standard and managing any exceptions utilizing the supplier management process.

To be effective, operations management needs to understand the technology and how it supports the services provided, although this level of knowledge will be less than that provided by the technical and application management functions. There is a risk that operations staff members do not interact with the business as part of their work and so may fail to appreciate the business impact of failures or to understand the business importance of services, thinking of them in purely technical terms. It is essential that they have adequate understanding of the business aspect; the information showing how technology supports the business is available in the SKMS, but specific training may be required to ensure that they have the necessary appreciation of the impact technology has on the business.

The importance of stability of services has been already mentioned; one way of maintaining that stability is to ensure that routine tasks are carried out consistently, no matter which staff members are on shift. This requires that properly documented procedures and technical manuals are available to operations staff members.

The performance of the operations management function should be measured against clear objectives based on the performance of the service, not merely of the technology. Delivering the service to the required level, within the agreed cost, is essential, so operations management should be able to demonstrate the effectiveness of what they do but also prove that they are operating at maximum efficiency. Operations management should always strive to optimize the use of existing technology and exploit new technical advances to provide the required level of service at the best cost.

Objectives

The objectives of IT operations management include continuing to provide stable services to enable the business to obtain the business benefits while also investigating possible improvements to enable the services to be provided more cost-effectively.

Service operation's other objectives are to overcome any failures that do occur as quickly as possible in order to minimize the impact to the business and to maintain service quality as new services are introduced.

Figure 39.4 illustrates that IT operations management is seen as a function in its own right but that, in the majority of organizations, staff from technical and application management groups form part of this function.

FIGURE 39.4 Service operation functions

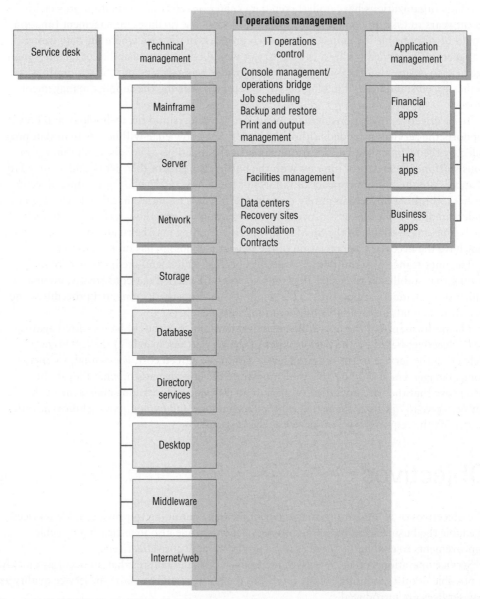

Some technical and application management departments or groups will manage and execute their own operational activities, whereas others will delegate these activities to a dedicated IT operations department.

Each organization is different and has its own requirements, so there is no single method for assigning activities because it depends on the maturity and stability of the infrastructure being managed. For example, technical and application management functions that are fairly new and unstable tend to manage their own operations. Groups where the technology or application is stable, mature, and well understood tend to have standardized their operations more. This will enable delegation of these activities.

Measuring IT Operations Management Performance

As with all lifecycle processes and functions, measurement plays an important part in understanding and maintaining effectiveness and efficiency. IT operations management performance is measured in terms of its effective execution of specified activities and procedures as well as its execution of process activities. This is an area in which there are numerous examples of measures that might be applied, but they should be tailored to the needs of the individual organization in measuring the true value that operations provides in business terms.

Examples of key metrics used to measure the performance of the IT operations function can include the percentage of scheduled jobs completed successfully on time or the number of exceptions to scheduled activities and jobs. Quantification of the number of data or system restores required will help understand the workload of the function, as will equipment installation statistics, including number of items installed by type, successful installations, and so on. This in turn will be used to identify and report on the cost of operational activities.

IT operations management executes many service management process activities. Its ability to do so will be measured as part of the process metrics where appropriate, and some examples are response times, resolution times, implementation timescales for changes and releases, and their success or failure. There will be financial process measures and measures relating to availability and capacity, all based on activities carried out by the IT operations function. The details of these measures are best considered as part of the processes and are covered in more detail in the relevant process areas across the lifecycle.

IT Operations Management Documentation

A number of documents are produced and used during IT operations management. In this section we provide a summary of some of the most important and do not include reports that are produced by IT operations management on behalf of other processes or functions.

The first set of documents are the standard operating procedures (SOPs). These documents represent the routine work for every device, system, or procedure. SOPs should also include specific security administration procedures covering all operational aspects of service, system, data, and physical security. They also outline the procedures to be followed if an exception is detected or if a change is required. SOP documents could also be used to define standard levels of performance for devices or procedures.

In some organizations, instead of listing detailed performance measures, the SOP documents are referred to in the OLA. A clause is inserted to refer to the performance standards in the SOP and how they will be measured and reported.

Any activity that is conducted as part of IT operations should be recorded in an operations log because they can be used to confirm the successful completion of specific jobs or activities or that an IT service was delivered as agreed. They are the basis for reports on the performance of the IT operations management teams and departments. The format of these logs is as varied as the number of systems and operations management teams or departments. They may also be used to support problem management, enabling research into the root cause of incidents.

Where required, IT operations will be responsible for managing shift patterns. Not all organizations will have a 24-hour operation, but where one does exist, shift schedules are used to outline the exact activities that need to be carried out during the shift. They will also list all dependencies and activity sequences. There will probably be more than one shift schedule; each team will have a version for its own systems. It is important that all schedules are coordinated before the start of the shift. This is usually done with the help of scheduling tools by a person who specializes in shift scheduling.

Shift reports are similar to operations logs, but they have additional functions to record major events and actions that occurred during the shift and to form part of the handover between shift leaders. They will be used to report exceptions to service maintenance objectives and identify uncompleted activity that might impact performance in the next service hours.

Operations schedules are similar to shift schedules but cover all aspects of IT operations at a high level. This schedule can include reviews of the forward schedule of change document and an overview of all planned change actions as well as information about maintenance, routine jobs, and additional work. It can also include information about upcoming business or vendor events. The operations schedule may be used as the basis for a daily operations meeting. It may also be used for IT operations managers to track progress and detect exceptions.

Applications Management

The final function described in the ITIL framework is *application management*. This function shares many features with the technical management function, although in this case it is the application software that is supported and managed throughout its lifecycle rather than the infrastructure. Application management and application development are not the same, and it is important to understand the differences between them:

- Application *management* is involved in every stage of the service lifecycle, from ascertaining the requirements through design and transition and then to operation and improvement.

- Application *development* is mostly involved in single, finite activities, such as designing and building a new service. We discuss this in more detail later in this chapter.

As with technical management, the application management function may be called something different in many organizations. Whichever teams of staff members are responsible for managing and supporting operational software applications is the application management function. As with technical management, this function may be split across a number of teams.

Application management may carry out some tasks as part of application development projects, such as design or testing. This is not the same as the work of application development itself.

Role

The application management function is involved in all applications. Even when the function has recommended purchase of the application from an external supplier, there is still a requirement for management activities to take place. These activities are very similar to those of the technical management function:

- It is responsible for managing the IT applications. This would include ensuring that the staff members performing this function have the necessary technical knowledge to design, test, manage, and improve IT services.

- It is the custodian of technical knowledge and expertise related to managing applications.

- Although we discuss this function under service operation, it provides appropriately skilled staff members to support the entire lifecycle. Application management staff members would be involved in drawing up the application strategy. They would carry out the design of new or changed applications and would be involved in planning and implementing their transition to the operational environment. Once the service is live, application management provides support, resolving incidents, investigating problems, and specifying changes or updates required to have the service operate efficiently. Application management staff members will identify service improvements and work with the CSI manager to design, test, and implement them.

Application management staffing and training responsibilities are the same as those identified for technical management, and the function similarly interacts with the other stages of the lifecycle.

Application management also performs other specific roles:

- Application support ensures that the operations management staff members are given the correct training to enable the applications to be run efficiently. They also contribute to the training for users so that the users can competently use the new or changed applications to support their business functions.

- As part of service design, application management may carry out a training needs analysis covering the service operation staff members and provide the required training, but this role is a continuous one, providing day-to-day support to the operations staff members.

Objectives

The objectives of application management are to do the following:

- Identify functional and manageability requirements for application software
- Help in the design of applications
- Assist in their deployment
- Support the applications in the live environment
- Identify and implement improvements

To be successful, application management must ensure that applications are well designed, taking account of both the utility and warranty aspects of service design. They must be able to deliver the right functionality at a reasonable cost if the business benefit is to be realized. The provision of the correct numbers of appropriately skilled staff members is essential so that these skills may be applied to resolve any application failures.

Application Management Principles

Application management is responsible for choosing whether to buy an application that supports the required business functionality or build the application specifically for the organization's requirements. The decisions are often made at a senior management level, perhaps by a chief technical officer (CTO) or steering committee, but they are dependent on information from a number of sources. This is covered as part of service design, but from an application management function perspective, there are a number of considerations that will require application management expertise and input.

Application management will explore the capability of existing technology to deliver the required functionality and, if it requires customization, consider the implications and cost to the organization. They will assist by providing application sizing and workload forecasts and specifying manageability requirements, ongoing operational costs, and the requirements for reporting or integration into other applications.

Another important aspect is identifying what skills will be required to support the solution and the impact of administration and security requirements.

Once a decision has been made to build, then a further decision has to be made on whether the development will be outsourced or built using employees. To achieve this, there must be recognition of the management of the requirements, the acceptance criteria, and management of the operational environment.

This will require a clear understanding of the operational model, which is the specification of the operational environment in which the application will eventually run when it goes live. The operational model should be used for testing and transition prior to live operation.

Application Management Lifecycle

There are many names for the lifecycle in which applications are developed and managed, including the software lifecycle (SLC) and software development lifecycle (SDLC), both of which are used by application development teams and their project managers. Examples of these lifecycle approaches are structured systems analysis and design methodology (SSADM), dynamic systems development method (DSDM), and rapid application development (RAD).

Although these are important for any organization, ITIL is primarily interested in the overall management of applications as part of IT services, whether the applications are developed in-house or purchased from a third party.

In Figure 39.5, you can see the six steps in the lifecycle, which applies to both developed and purchased software.

FIGURE 39.5   Application management lifecycle

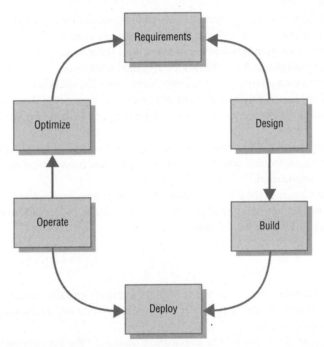

The software development lifecycle is a valid approach used by developers, especially third-party software companies. So there should be alignment between the development view of applications and the ongoing lifecycle management of those applications.

The basic lifecycle is used even for large third-party applications, like email, in that whatever the size of the application, it will need requirements, design, customization, operation, and deployment. Optimization is achieved through better management, improvements to customization, and upgrades.

The application management lifecycle is not an alternative to the service management lifecycle. Applications are part of services and have to be managed as such. Applications require a specialized focus at each stage of the service management lifecycle.

In the next sections, we'll review each step of the application management lifecycle.

Requirements

Obviously, as the name suggests, the requirements stage is the stage during which the requirements for a new application are gathered, based on the business needs of the organization. As you would expect, this stage is active primarily during the service design stage of the service lifecycle.

There are six types of requirements for any application, whether it is developed in-house, outsourced, or purchased.

The first is the functional requirements, which are specifically required to support a particular business function. Then we have the manageability requirements; the application is looked at from a service management perspective, and these requirements address the need for a responsive, available, and secure service and deal with issues such as deployment, operations, system management, and security. Next come the usability requirements that address the needs of the end user and result in features of the system that facilitate its ease of use. Architectural requirements are needed if a change to existing architecture standards is required.

Most applications will not be stand alone, so an important factor is to identify the interface requirements. These are needed where there are dependencies between existing applications or tools and the new application.

Finally, but not because they are less important, there are service level requirements. These specify how the service should perform, the quality of its output, and any other qualitative aspects measured by the user or customer.

Design

The design stage includes the design of the application itself and the design of the environment, or the operational model that the application has to run on, as the requirements are translated into specifications.

Architectural considerations for the application (design of the application architecture) and architectural considerations for the operation model (design of the system architecture) are strongly related and need to be aligned. Architectural considerations are the most important aspect of this stage because they can have an impact on the structure and content of both the application and the operational model.

In the case of purchased software, it is unlikely that an organization will be allowed direct input to the design of the software because it has already been built. However, it is important that application management is able to provide feedback to the software vendor about the functionality, manageability, and performance of the software. This should be part of the continual improvement of the software. A good vendor will be responsive to improvements but should ensure that there is a balance between being responsive and changing the software so much that it is disruptive or that it changes some basic functionality.

The design stage for purchased software should include the design of any customization that is required. It is important to evaluate the capability of future versions of the software to support importing and maintaining the customization. It is common to discover that with each successive upgrade, the actual time for release gets longer in order to reapply existing customization to the product.

Build

In this stage, both the application and the operational model are made ready for deployment. Application components are coded or acquired and then integrated and tested.

Testing is an integral component of both the build and deploy stages because it is a validation of the activity and output of those stages, even if different environments and staff are used. Testing in the build stage focuses on whether the application meets its functionality and manageability specifications. The test environment allows for testing the combination of application and operational models.

For purchased software, this will involve the actual purchase of the application, any required middleware, and the related hardware and networking equipment. If customization is required, a pilot implementation by the relevant application management team or department will need to be done here because the creation of tables, categories, and so on that will be used should be tested for success prior to full implementation.

Deploy

In the deploy stage, both the operational model and the application are deployed. The operational model is incorporated into the existing IT environment, and the application is installed on top of the operational model using the release and deployment management process, as described in *ITIL Service Transition*.

There is testing during this stage as well, although here the emphasis is on ensuring that the deployment process and mechanisms work effectively—for example, testing whether the application still performs to specification after it has been downloaded and installed. Specialized support for a new or changed IT service for a period of time after it is released is known as early life support (ELS). Support activities during this period can include review of KPIs, service levels, and monitoring thresholds and provision of additional resources for incident and problem management. ELS is covered in detail in *ITIL Service Transition*.

Operate

In the operate stage, the IT services organization operates the application as part of delivering a service required by the business.

It is important to understand that applications are not a service. It is common in many organizations to refer to applications as services, but applications are only one component of many needed to provide a business service. The performance of the application in relation to the overall service is measured continually against the service levels and key business drivers.

The operate stage is not exclusive to applications but exists for any product, technology, or service provision.

Optimize

During this stage, the results of the service level performance measurements are analyzed and acted upon. This is when possible improvements are discussed and developments are initiated if necessary. The two main strategies in this stage are to maintain and/or improve the service levels and to lower cost. This could lead to a repeat of the lifecycle or to justified retirement of an application.

An important thing to remember about the application management lifecycle is that the same application can reside in different stages of the lifecycle at the same time. This obviously requires strong version, configuration, and release control; for example, when the next version of an application is being designed and the current version is being deployed, the previous version might still be in operation in parts of the organization.

Some stages might take longer or seem more significant than others, but they are all crucial.

It is critical that information is passed along by those handling the application in one stage of its existence to those handling it in the next stage. Good communication is key as an application works its way through the stages of the lifecycle. It is also important that an organization monitors the quality of the application management lifecycle. Understanding the characteristics of every stage in the application management lifecycle is critical to improving the quality of the whole. Methods and tools used in one stage might have an impact on others, while optimization of one stage might have a negative impact on the whole.

Application Management Generic Activities

The exact nature of the role will vary depending upon the applications being supported, but application management teams or departments will be needed for all key applications. There are a number of generic activities, which we will briefly explore in this section.

Similar to technical management, the generic activities include the identification and provision of knowledge and expertise to manage and support the application and management of training to use or support the application.

Further activities will include recruiting or contracting resources with skills that cannot be developed internally. Resources will also need to be recruited when there are not enough people to perform the required application management activities.

Application management is responsible for designing and delivering end-user training. Training may be developed and delivered by either the application development or application management groups or by a third party, but application management is responsible for ensuring that training is conducted as appropriate. It is important to understand the staffing requirements and the most cost-effective way to provide them. This may include outsourcing for specific activities where the required skills are not available internally or in the open market or where it is more cost-efficient to do so.

During the definition of application architectures (as part of the service strategy processes), application management should help to define standards used in the design of new architectures. They should also play a major part in researching and developing solutions that can help expand the service portfolio or can be used to simplify or automate IT operations, reduce costs, or increase levels of IT service.

Application management should participate in the design and building of new services. All application management teams or departments will contribute to the design of the technical architecture and performance standards for IT services. They will also be responsible for specifying the operational activities required to manage applications on an ongoing basis.

In addition, application management may be used to participate in projects, not only during the service design process, but also for CSI or operational projects.

They will have responsibility for designing and performing tests for the functionality, performance, and manageability of IT services (bearing in mind that testing should be controlled and performed by an independent tester).

The design activity will include designing applications to meet the levels of service required by the business. Availability and capacity management are dependent on application management for design expertise and guidance to assess the appropriate level of resources that will meet business demand for applications. This means that modeling and workload forecasting are often done together by technical and application management resources.

Application management, like technical management, will be key in providing assistance in assessing risk, identifying critical service and system dependencies, and defining and implementing countermeasures.

Many application management departments or groups are relied on to manage contracts with suppliers of specific applications because they will have the required understanding and knowledge. If this is the case, it is important to ensure that these relationships are managed as part of the SLM and supplier management processes.

The application management function will be heavily involved in all of the operational processes, and they should be involved in the definition of event management standards and especially in the instrumentation of applications for the generation of meaningful events. The function will also be expected to provide resources that contribute to the execution of the problem management process. It is their technical expertise and knowledge that is used to diagnose and resolve problems. It is also their relationship with the vendors that is used to escalate and follow up with vendor support teams or departments. Other activities relating to incident and problem management include defining coding systems that are used in incident and problem management (e.g., incident categories) and providing resources to support problem management and the application development teams in validating and maintaining the known error database. Application management also provides scripts to the service desk to ensure good-quality incident capture and workarounds to facilitate first-time fixes.

Service transition will also make use of application management to support change management with technical application knowledge and expertise to evaluate changes. Many changes may be built by application management teams. They will also participate in release and deployment management activities. Application management is frequently the driver of the release and deployment management process for the applications they manage.

An important part of the function is assistance in defining, managing, and maintaining attributes and relationships of application CIs in the CMS and ensuring that they provide input into, and maintenance of, software configuration policies. They will also help in identifying opportunities for improvement and assist in the evaluation of alternative solutions.

Application management will be responsible for coordinating with development teams to ensure that a mechanism is in place to store and maintain documentation related to applications. This includes ensuring that all design, management, and user manuals as well as SOPs are up-to-date and complete and properly utilized on an ongoing basis. Application management also ensures that application management staff and users are aware of application documentation and familiar with its contents.

Another key area for this function is collaborating with technical management on performing training needs analysis and maintaining skills inventories.

The application management function is involved throughout the service lifecycle. They will assist financial management for IT services to identify the cost of the ongoing management of applications.

Many application management departments, groups, or teams also perform operational activities as part of an organization's IT operations management function, and they will be involved in defining the operational activities related to applications that will be performed as part of IT operations management.

Application bug tracking and patch management (coding fixes for in-house code, transports/patches for third-party code) are also part of the role, as is involvement in application operability and supportability issues such as error code design, error messaging, and event management hooks.

As part of service design, and in support of capacity and availability management processes, the function will be engaged in application sizing and performance, volume metrics, and load testing.

They will be involved in developing release policies and, of course, identification of enhancements to existing software, from both a functionality and manageability perspective.

Although all application management departments, groups, or teams perform similar activities, each application or set of applications has a different set of management and operational requirements. Each application was developed to meet a specific set of objectives, usually business objectives. For effective support and improvement, the group that manages an application needs to have a comprehensive understanding of the business context and how the application is used to meet the business objectives. The business objectives will be dependent on a number of factors, such as the purpose of the application. The understanding of the business objectives is often achieved by business analysts who are close to the business and responsible for ensuring that business requirements are effectively translated into application specifications. Business analysts should recognize that business requirements must be translated into both functional and manageability specifications. Another consideration is the functionality of the application. Each application is designed to work in a different way and to perform different functions at different times.

Not all applications run on the same platform, so technical management and application management will need to work together as they support the environment and the applications. Even applications that have similar functionality operate differently on different databases or platforms. Similarly, the type or brand of technology used will have an impact. These differences have to be understood to manage the application effectively.

Even though the activities to manage these applications are generic, the specific schedule of activities and the way they are performed will be different. For this reason, application management teams and departments tend to be organized according to the categories of applications they support.

For example, in larger organizations where a number of different applications are used for different aspects of financial management, there may be several departments, groups, or teams managing these applications (e.g., applications for debtors and creditors and age analysis, general ledger).

This approach can be used for a number of different applications, such as messaging and collaboration applications, human resources applications, manufacturing support applications, and applications for business functions such as sales and marketing, call centers, web portals, and online shopping.

Application Development vs. Application Management

As discussed earlier, application management and application development have separate aims and responsibilities. These two groups may work closely together or they may be quite separate, with different reporting structures and a different interface with the business. Application development, as we said earlier, is normally a finite activity to develop an application, and the team moves on to the next requirement when finished. Application management, on the other hand, remains involved throughout the lifecycle of the application. Here is a summary of the differences between them:

- Development focuses on the utility aspects, and most of its work is carried out on applications developed in-house. Management activities consider both warranty and utility and are carried out whether the application is internally developed or purchased.

- Development is concerned with functionality and does not consider how the application is to be operated or managed, whereas application management is concerned with how this functionality is to be delivered consistently.

- Development is often carried out as part of a project, with defined deliverables, costs, and handoff dates. This differs from application management, whose activities are ongoing throughout the service lifecycle and whose costs may not be separately identified.

- Developers may not have an understanding of what is required to manage and operate an application because they do not support the applications they have developed, instead moving on to the next development project. Similarly, application management staff members may have little involvement in development and therefore have less understanding of how applications are developed.

- Development staff members work to software development lifecycles. Application management staff members are often involved only in the operation and improvement stages of the service lifecycle.

Figure 39.6 shows the different roles of the application management and application development teams; the application development team is primarily concerned with the functionality of the application, whereas the application management team considers how the application infrastructure will support the application and how it will be built, deployed, and monitored in operation.

FIGURE 39.6 Role of teams in the application management lifecycle

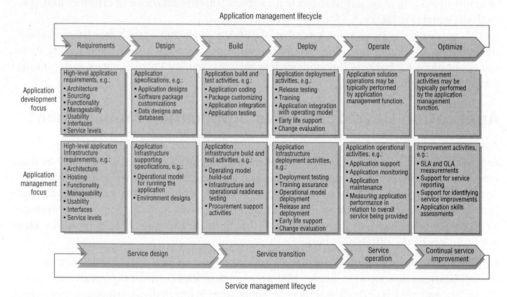

There is a growing tendency to end the division between the two teams because it is confusing for the business to understand. Ideally, this will mean a broadening of the development role to include considering how applications will operate, and it will mean more involvement in development for staff members who will be managing the application, as shown in Table 39.2.

TABLE 39.2 Application development vs. application management

	Application development	**Application management**
Nature of activities	One-time set of activities to design and construct application solutions.	Ongoing set of activities to oversee and manage applications throughout their entire lifecycle.
Scope of activities	Performed mostly for applications developed in-house.	Performed for all applications, whether purchased from third parties or developed in-house.
Primary focus	Utility focus. Building functionality for their customer. What the application does is more important than how it is operated.	Both utility and warranty focus. What the functionality is as well as how to deliver it. Manageability aspects of the application, i.e., how to ensure stability and performance of the application.
Management mode	Most development work is done in projects where the focus is on delivering specific units of work to specification, on time, and within budget. This means that it is often difficult for developers to understand and build for ongoing operations, especially because they are not available for support of the application once they have moved on to the next project.	Most work is done as part of repeatable, ongoing processes. A relatively small number of people work on projects. This means that it is very difficult for operational staff to get involved in development projects because that takes them away from their ongoing operational responsibilities.
Measurement	Staff are typically rewarded for creativity and for completing one project so that they can move on to the next project.	Staff are typically rewarded for consistency and for preventing unexpected events and unauthorized functionality (e.g., "bells and whistles" added by developers).
Cost	Development projects are relatively easy to quantify because the resources are known and it is easy to link their expenses to a specific application or IT service.	Ongoing management costs are often mixed in with the costs of other IT services because resources are often shared across multiple IT services and applications.

TABLE 39.2   Application development vs. application management *(continued)*

	Application development	Application management
Lifecycles	Development staff focus on software development lifecycles, which highlight the dependencies for successful operation but do not assign accountability for these.	Staff involved in ongoing management typically control only one or two stages of these lifecycles—operation and improvement.

Measuring Application Management Performance

Performance metrics for application management will largely depend on which applications are being managed, but some generic metrics are included here.

Measurement of Agreed Outputs

The following metrics could be used to measure agreed outputs:

- Percentage of users able to access the application and its functionality
- Percentage of reports and files that are transmitted accurately and on time to the users
- Percentage of availability for critical business transactions
- Number of capacity- and performance-related incidents compared to business transaction volumes
- Percentage of service desk staff with appropriate support skills
- Number of recorded problem resolutions in the known error database (KEDB)
- User measures of the quality of outputs as defined in the SLAs

Process Metrics

Application management teams execute many service management process activities. Their ability to do so will be measured as part of the process metrics, such as the following examples:

- Response time to events and event completion rates
- Incident resolution times for second- and third-line support
- Problem resolution statistics
- Number of escalations and reason for those escalations
- Number of changes implemented and backed out
- Number of unauthorized changes detected
- Number of releases deployed, total and successful, including releases for which adherence to the release policies of the organization are ensured

- Security issues detected and resolved
- Actual application transaction volumes and demand loads against capacity plan forecasts (where the team has contributed to the development of the plan)
- Tracking against SIPs
- Expenditure against budget

Application Performance

Application performance metrics are based on service design specifications and technical performance standards set by vendors and will typically be contained in OLAs or SOPs. Actual metrics will vary by application, but are likely to include the following measures as part of the suite of performance measures applied to application performance.

Response Times

Application availability is helpful for measuring team or application performance but is not to be confused with service availability, which requires the ability to measure the overall availability of the service and may use the availability figures for a number of individual systems or components. The following metrics are used to measure team performance:

- Integrity and accuracy of data and reporting
- Measurement of maintenance activity

The following metrics are application availability metrics:

- Maintenance performed per schedule
- Number of maintenance windows exceeded
- Maintenance objectives achieved (number and percentage)
- Measurement of project activity

Application management teams are likely to work closely with application development teams on projects, and appropriate metrics should be used to measure this, including these:

- Time spent on projects
- Customer and user satisfaction with the output of the project
- Cost of involvement in the project
- Training and skills development

These metrics ensure that staff have the skills and training to manage the applications that are under their control and will also identify areas where training is still required:

- A measure of the achieved skills by individuals, to meet the required skill levels
- Number of calls and escalations to third-party or other internal subject-matter experts for additional help and support
- Percentage of incidents caused by skills issues

Application Management Documentation

As you would expect, there are a number of documents produced and used during application management. The following sections provide a summary of some of the most important but do not include reports or documents produced by application management on behalf of other processes or functions.

Application Portfolio

Used primarily as part of service design, the application portfolio is a list (more accurately a system or database) of all applications in use within the organization and includes the following information:

- Key attributes of the application.

- Customers and users.

- Business purpose.

- Level of business criticality.

- Architecture (including the IT infrastructure dependencies)

- Developers, support groups, suppliers, or vendors.

- The investment made in the application to date. In this respect, the application portfolio can be used as an asset register for applications.

The purpose of the application portfolio is to analyze the need for and use of applications in the organization, and it forms part of the overall IT service portfolio. It can be used to link functionality and investment to business activity and is therefore an important part of ongoing IT planning and control. Another benefit of the application portfolio is that it can be used to identify duplication and excessive licensing of applications.

The Application Portfolio and the Service Catalog

The application portfolio should not be mistaken for the service catalog, and it should not be advertised as a list of services to customers or users. An application by itself is not a service. Applications are service assets and only one of the many components used to provide IT services.

The application portfolio should be used as a planning document by managers and staff who are involved with the development and management of the organization's applications. Other interested parties (for example, IT staff who may be tasked with managing the applications or the platforms on which the applications run) should also have access to the application portfolio.

The service catalog will focus on listing the services that are available rather than simply listing applications.

Application Requirements

There are two sets of documents containing requirements for applications: business requirements documents and application requirements documents.

Business Requirements Documents

Business requirements documents outline the utility and warranty conditions as well as any constraints for the required application. This will include the return on investment for the application as well as all related improvements to the business, and they outline what the business will do with the application. Business requirements documents will also include the service level requirements as defined by the service customers and users.

Application Requirements Documents

Application requirements documents are based on the business requirements and specify exactly how the application will meet them. They gather information that will be used to commission new applications or changes to existing applications. They can be used, for example, for the following purposes:

- To design the architecture of the application (specification of the different components of the system, how they relate to one another, and how they will be managed)

- To specify a request for proposal (RFP) for a commercial off-the-shelf (COTS) application

- To initiate the design and building of an application in-house

Requirements documents are usually owned as part of a project and as such are subject to document control for the project as part of the overall scope of the project.

Four different types of application requirements need to be defined:

- Functional requirements describe the things an application is intended to do and can be expressed as services, tasks, or functions the application is required to perform.

- Manageability requirements are used to define what is needed to manage the application or to ensure that it performs the required functions consistently and at the right level. Manageability requirements also identify constraints on the IT system. They drive design of the operational models and performance standards used in IT operations management.

- Usability requirements are normally specified by the users of the application and refer to its ease of use. Special requirements for handicapped users also need to be specified here.

- Test requirements specify what is required to ensure that the test environment is representative of the operational environment and that the test is valid (i.e., that it actually tests what it is supposed to).

Use Cases

Use cases are developed within service design and maintained by application management. For purchased software, the team that develops the functional specifications usually maintains the use case for that application. Use cases document the intended use of the application with real-life scenarios to demonstrate its boundaries and its full functionality. They can also be used as modeling and sizing scenarios.

Design Documentation

There is not a single design document. Design documentation is any documentation produced by application development or management. Because these documents are generally
owned and managed by the development teams, application management should ensure
that design documentation contains the following items:

- Sizing specifications
- Workload profiles and utilization forecasts
- Technical architecture
- Data models
- Coding standards
- Performance standards
- Software service asset and configuration management definitions
- Support requirements
- Environment definitions and building considerations (if appropriate)
- For third-party developed applications, documents that take the form of application
  specifications and are owned and managed by application management

Manuals

Application management is responsible for the management of manuals for all applications.
Although these are generated by the application development teams or third-party suppliers,
application management is responsible for ensuring that the manuals are relevant to the
operational versions of the applications.

Three types of manuals are generally maintained by application management:

- Design manuals contain information about the structure and architecture of the
  application. These are helpful for creating reports or defining event correlation rules.
  They could also help in diagnosing problems.
- Administration or management manuals describe the activities required to maintain
  and operate the application at the levels of performance specified in the design stage.
  These manuals will also provide detailed troubleshooting, known error and fault
  descriptions, and step-by-step instructions for common maintenance tasks.
- User manuals describe the application functionality as it is used by an end user. These
  manuals contain step-by-step instructions on how to use the application as well as
  descriptions of what should typically be entered into certain fields or what to do if
  there is an error.

Manuals and Standard Operating Procedures

Manuals should not be seen as a replacement for SOPs but as input into the SOPs. SOPs
should contain all aspects of applications that need to be managed as part of standard

operations. Application management should ensure that any such instructions are extracted from the manuals and inserted into separate SOP documentation for operations so that is it clear what needs to be done to maintain the application. It is also responsible for ensuring that these instructions are updated with every change or new release of the software.

Roles and Responsibilities in Service Management

There are many different ways to organize an IT department, and no two service providers are identical, so the exact configuration of roles within each organization will differ. Often two or more roles will be combined; in other organizations, a single role might be split. ITIL provides guidelines, not prescriptive rules, so each organization should consider what would best fit its own requirements.

We will first clarify what is meant by the term *role*. The official glossary defines it as follows:

> A set of responsibilities, activities and authorities assigned to a person or team. A role is defined in a process or function.

Within each of the processes we have covered, there are a number of roles. The role may be carried out by an individual or a team, and one person may have multiple roles. The person responsible for the availability management of the infrastructure may often also be fulfilling the capacity management role. It may be that capacity management is divided between a number of people, with one considering network capacity, another responsible for storage, and so on.

It is important to remember that although roles may be shared, or combined, there can be only one process owner for each process and one service owner for each service.

Often a job title will be the same as a role description; service level manager is one such example. Job titles are for each organization to decide, and it may be the case that the job of service level manager includes the role of service level manager, along with one or more other roles (such as supplier manager) within that particular organization.

It is also often true that one task carried out by an individual will touch several processes. A technician might submit a request for change to overcome a capacity issue that has been identified by problem management. The action may have been identified as desirable as part of a service improvement plan (SIP) that has been logged on the CSI register. The technician's action therefore involves several processes: problem, change, capacity, service level management, and continual service improvement.

Every process has its own specific roles. Here we will be looking at the generic roles that appear in all lifecycle stages.

Service Owner

Because every service interacts with so many processes, there is a danger that a service itself may no longer receive the required attention. To avoid this, ITIL recommends that each service should have a single service owner. This clarifies who is accountable for the service and ensures that there is a focus on the business processes that the service supports.

Whatever technology is used to deliver the service and regardless of whether aspects of the technology are provided in-house or are outsourced, the service owner remains accountable for delivering the service. This role is responsible to the customer for the service being developed, implemented, and maintained, but it is also accountable to the IT director or service management director for its delivery.

As we will examine, ITIL recommends that each process have an identifiable owner. Each process may affect many services, and it is the service owner of each who will ensure the service is delivered effectively and efficiently, whatever process is being carried out. Service owners will often own more than one service. For each service, they will carry out the following responsibilities:

- Ensuring that the service is delivered and supported to the required standards by working with all IT groups and process owners

- Ensuring that the customer's requirements are understood and that the tasks required to deliver them are implemented by working with the business relationship manager

- Communicating with the customer as required on all issues regarding the delivery of the service

- Using the service portfolio management process to define new service models and to evaluate the impact of any changes to existing services

- Ensuring that the service undergoes continual service improvement by identifying possible improvements and, with the customer's agreement, putting these forward as requests for change

- Ensuring that appropriate monitoring and reporting is taking place to enable an accurate view of the level of service being delivered

- Ensuring that the required levels of performance and availability are delivered

- Developing a thorough understanding of the components that make up the service and ensuring that the potential impact of their failure is realized

- Representing the service across the organization and attending service review meetings with the business

- Representing the service within IT and at change advisory board meetings and internal service reviews

- Being the escalation (notification) point for major incidents affecting the service

- Working with service level management to negotiate service level agreements that meet the customer requirements and operational level agreements that support the service provision at the agreed level

- Maintaining the service catalog entry

- Working with the CSI manager to identify improvements to be added to the CSI register and participating in the review and prioritization of these and their eventual implementation

As the owner of the service, this role is concerned with the impact of any process affecting the service. This means service owners should be considered stakeholders in these processes, with whatever level of involvement is appropriate.

For example, the service owner plays a major part in the major incident process and will attend or possibly run any crisis meetings. They will also be involved in investigating the root cause of problems affecting their service. The service owner will represent the service at CAB meetings and will be involved in discussions regarding if and when a release should go ahead. They will want to ensure that the service portfolio and catalog entries and configuration data held on their service is accurate.

As explained earlier, there will be a close relationship between the service level management process and the service owner who acts as the contact point for the service. The service owner will also liaise with the owners of the more technical processes, such as availability and capacity, to ensure that the data collected by these processes indicates that the performance and reliability of the services meets the agreed standard.

The service owner is responsible for ensuring that the IT service continuity management plan for their service is practical and that every element of the plan is in place. They will work with the ITSCM manager to make sure all aspects are considered. They will often attend rehearsals of the plan to observe it in action to confirm that nothing has been forgotten.

The service owner understands the costs involved in delivering the service and will work with the supplier manager and other managers to ensure that costs are controlled and value for money is achieved. In organizations where the business is charged for IT services, they will ensure that the recovery of costs takes place as agreed.

Finally, the service owner ensures that the service follows the information security management policies.

Process Owner

As you have seen, the service owner is the focus for one particular service, across all process areas. The process owner, in contrast, is accountable for a single process, whatever service it affects.

The process owner must ensure that the process works efficiently and effectively. Although the role may often be carried out by the same person who fulfils the process manager role, in larger organizations this is less likely. A global company may have a change management process owner and a number of process managers carrying out the process in different countries, for example. The process owner is accountable for ensuring that the process is fit for its purpose and is being carried out correctly by the process managers and practitioners. The role therefore has both a design and an enforcement aspect.

The process owner is accountable for the following:

- Developing the process strategy, policies, and standards
- Designing the process and amending it as required to implement improvements that make it more effective or efficient

- Designing the metrics for the process and ensuring that they provide the necessary information to judge the effectiveness and efficiency of the process

- Ensuring that the process is documented, that this documentation is available to those that require it, and that it is updated as needed

- Where the process has changed, ensuring that the process documentation is updated and the changes communicated to the process practitioners (those who actually carry out the process steps)

- Auditing the process activities to ensure adherence to the correct process

- Ensuring that the required resources are available to carry out the process and that the staff members involved have been trained to carry it out

- Communicating to the process technicians the importance of adhering to the documented process and explaining the implications for IT and the business of nonadherence

- As part of continual service improvement, reviewing the process strategy and the effectiveness of the process itself to identify possible improvements

- Where improvements to effectiveness or efficiency are identified, having these included in the CSI register and working with the CSI manager to review, prioritize, and implement them as appropriate

The process owner role is critical to the success of the process. In organizations where no such single point of ownership exists, those carrying out the process may decide to drop or amend steps in the process, and there is no one with the overall authority to prevent this. In global organizations, this can mean the process might develop regional variations. In addition to the danger of losing focus on the purpose of the process, this may invalidate the reporting from the process because each area may be inputting data differently.

Earlier in this volume, we discussed a generic process model. Without a process owner, there is no one with the responsibility of ensuring consistency in applying the process, and there is no one to ensure that the process output still matches the process objectives. Process documentation may not be updated because the responsibility for its upkeep would be unclear. Finally, there would be no one to assess the process and identify improvements.

Process Manager

The process owner is accountable for the success of the process but may often not be responsible for actually carrying it out. The responsibility for managing the day-to-day implementation of a process belongs to the process manager. In large or geographically spread-out organizations, there may be several process managers responsible for managing the implementation of the same process, each with a regional or infrastructure responsibility.

The process manager is accountable for the following:

- Liaising with the process owner to ensure that the process is implemented across all lifecycle stages as the process owner intended

- Ensuring that the right number of staff are assigned to the various roles within the process and that they understand what is required of them

- Working with other process managers and service owners to ensure that services are delivered as required

- Monitoring the process metrics to confirm that the process is working as designed

- As part of continual service improvement, reviewing the process performance to identify possible improvements

- Where improvements are identified, having them included in the CSI register and working with the CSI manager and process owner to review, prioritize, and implement them as appropriate

The role of process manager is important because it is the process manager who ensures that the process is carried out correctly day to day. The process manager may be distant from where the process actually occurs (working in the head office, while the process takes place in branch offices, for example). The process manager, or managers, will ensure that the staff members understand what is required of them and have been provided with the right resources and training to carry out the tasks. Because process managers are close to the process execution, they are in an ideal position to identify issues and possible improvements. The success of any improvement initiatives will depend heavily on the enthusiastic involvement of the process manager in ensuring that staff members adopt the improved process.

Process Practitioner

Depending on the process, there may be one or more people carrying out the process activities. In a small organization or for a simple process, this may be a single person, who is also likely to be the process manager. For a large organization or for a complex process, there may be many people, each carrying out parts of the process. The people involved in carrying out the process activities are the process practitioners.

The process practitioner is usually responsible for the following:

- Completing process activities to the required standard

- Understanding the importance of the process and their role within it and how they contribute to delivering the service

- Working with all the process stakeholders to ensure that the process inputs, outputs, and interfaces are working properly so that the process delivers the desired result

- Producing evidence, in the form of records that the process activities have been carried out correctly

- Identifying necessary improvements to the process or supporting tools

The process practitioner role is responsible for actually delivering the process activities. Under the guidance of the process manager (unless these roles are combined), the practitioner is responsible for carrying out the process as designed, consistently and efficiently.

It may be tempting to believe that the practitioner has nothing to contribute other than carrying out the activities; this is far from the truth. As a practitioner, the staff member will experience firsthand any issues with the process, such as tools that do not support the process effectively, bottlenecks in the process flow, or ambiguities in the documentation. The process manager and process owner should therefore seek out the views of practitioners when attempting to identify possible improvements.

Each role has its own purpose. Even where the roles are carried out by the same person, that person should attempt to consider each aspect of the roles. The practitioner has the advantage of daily interaction with the process but may be too close to it to see it objectively; the process manager is judged on the outcome of the process and so has a particular focus on the resources required to deliver these outcomes effectively and efficiently. They will monitor the process metrics closely to ensure that the outputs are being delivered on time and within budget. The manager will see only their own part of the process delivery, however. The process owner has the advantage of seeing the overall picture, comparing the delivery of the process in different locations and under different process managers. When the strengths and weaknesses of each perspective are understood, a complete picture of the process delivery can be achieved, and improvement initiatives can be gathered from each level.

Service Operation Process Roles

The *ITIL Service Operation* publication describes generic roles for each of the service operation processes, but because the generic responsibilities are comprehensive, we will cover only those elements specific for each process.

It is helpful to remember that any manager's job is to ensure that objectives are met and that activities are carried out. Each process will have a process manager role assigned to it.

The practitioners can be viewed in a similar way. The process activities are carried out by the practitioner. It is common to find the term *analyst* rather than *practitioner*, so each process often has an analyst role. We will begin with incident management and request fulfilment.

Incident Management/Request Fulfilment

For incident management there are three practitioner roles: first-, second-, and third-line analyst. The first-line analyst role is usually combined with the service desk analyst role. The others correspond to the levels of functional escalation, which means they reflect the levels of skill and seniority or experience in the supported technologies. Third-line analysts are often associated with the technical or application management functions.

For request fulfilment, it is not uncommon to have a specialized team supporting the process, but this will depend very much on the number and type of requests identified and managed under this process. Each organization will have to determine the most appropriate structure for dealing with requests, whether this is a dedicated team or part of the service desk function.

Remember, each process will have an owner carrying out generic ownership responsibilities and a manager focused on the management of the activities of the practitioners.

Problem Management

For problem management, there is one practitioner role, but this can be undertaken by any member of the organization that is involved in the investigation and resolution of problems. The problem analyst role is often undertaken by the functions of technical and application management due to the level of skill and understanding that is required to identify and correct the root cause of a failure.

Remember, each process will have an owner carrying out those generic responsibilities and a manager focused on the management of the activities of the practitioners.

Event Management

Event management is a process that makes use of the functional teams for the management of the process activity. Each organization will have to establish the structure it wishes to adopt to manage events.

The role of the service desk may be to receive and act on alerts generated by event management. If the enterprise has an operations bridge, it will usually receive these alerts.

Technical and application management participate in the design and implementation of monitoring facilities and the event handling tool, including automation. They might also respond to some alerts if there is no operations bridge.

If an operations bridge exists, it is usually the first responder to any alerts as part of the function of IT operations management.

Access Management

The service desk is the single point of contact, and it may be used by the users in the organization to request access and be kept informed of progress. In some cases, it is appropriate for the service desk to change access rights.

Technical and application management design and test the access mechanism and may be needed to change rights as necessary.

IT operations management in the form of an operations bridge may configure rights as necessary and will also respond to any alerts relating to misuse of rights.

Again, the structure of the support mechanism for the process will be specific to the organizational needs. In an organization with very high security controls around access, it is entirely possible that technical and application management will be the only areas with rights to grant or change access. In a less controlled environment, password resets may be carried out by service desk analysts or the request fulfilment team.

Technical and Application Management Roles

The technical and application management roles defined in *ITIL Service Operation* carry out the activities of these functions. If you understand what these functions do, then we don't think that the manager and analyst roles need any explanation.

A technical operator is a person who carries out routine day-to-day tasks related to the management of the infrastructure. If IT operations management exists as an organizational unit, then this role is carried out there.

IT Operations Management and Service Desk Roles

Many IT operations groups work some sort of shift system, often providing 24-hour coverage. The staff are organized into shifts, each with a shift leader who has a supervisory role.

IT operations analysts are skilled, experienced staff who are able to determine the best way of carrying out operational duties. For example, they would determine the best way to schedule the batch work.

The IT operator carries out the tasks defined for IT operations management.

The same considerations apply to the service desk, and there may also be a requirement for shift support patterns. Even when service desks are not based on a 24-hour shift pattern, they may still have a shift system to allow them to cover changing call volumes during the working day.

In addition to the dedicated staff at the service desk, super users based in the organizational business community can provide an element of functional support to the business. These individuals will need to receive appropriate training and will be required to log calls in the service management toolset, otherwise the health of the service in the business units may not be properly understood.

Many organizations will have the role of the duty manager to take responsibility during off-peak hours. These individuals will also require training and be required to log calls.

Organization for Functions

We have already examined some organizational structures for specific functions. In the following sections, we'll consider some specific organizational structures for all functions.

There are a number of ways of organizing service operation functions, and each organization will have to make its own decisions based on its scale, geography, culture, and business environment.

Organization by Technical Specialization

In this type of structure, departments are created according to technology and the skills and activities needed to manage that technology. This structure can work well, provided these groups are fully represented in the service design, testing, and improvement processes. It is shown in Figure 39.7.

FIGURE 39.7   IT operations organized according to technical specification (sample)

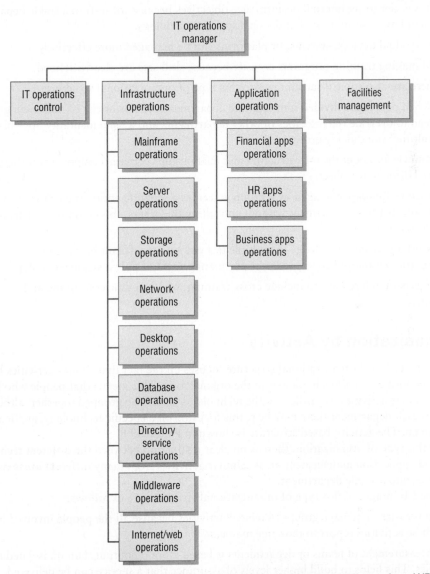

This structure also assumes that all technical and application management departments have clearly distinguished between their management activity and operations activity. It also requires that they have standardized these operational activities to maximize efficiency. This type of structure requires a significant level of maturity to manage effective communication, but there are a number of advantages to this structure:

- It is easier to set internal performance objectives because all staff in a single department have a similar set of tasks on a similar technology.

- Individual devices, systems, or platforms can be managed more effectively.

- Managing training programs is easier because skill sets are clearly defined.

There are also some disadvantages to this type of organizational structure:

- When people are divided into separate departments, the priorities of their own group tend to override the priorities of other departments and a "silo mentality" or "blame culture" can quickly grow.

- Knowledge about the infrastructure and relationships between components is fragmented and difficult to collect.

- Each technology managed by a group is seen as a separate entity. If a change is made by one team or department without consulting the others, this could be disastrous for the service.

- Work requiring knowledge of multiple technologies is difficult because most resources are trained for and concerned with the management of only a single technology.

Projects therefore have to include cross-training, which is time consuming and expensive.

Organization by Activity

The activity-based organizational structure focuses on the fact that similar activities have to be performed on all technologies in the organization. This means that people who perform similar activities, regardless of the technology, should be grouped together, although within each department there may be teams focusing on a specific technology, application, and so on. The activity-based structure is shown in Figure 39.8.

In this type of organization, there is no clear distinction between the different technical and application management areas. Similar activities from many different areas can be grouped into a single department.

The advantages of this type of organizational structure are as follows:

- It is easier to manage groups of related activities because all the people involved in these activities report to the same manager.

- Measurement of teams or departments is based more on output than on isolated activities. This helps to build higher levels of assurance that a service can be delivered.

FIGURE 39.8   A department based on executing a set of activities

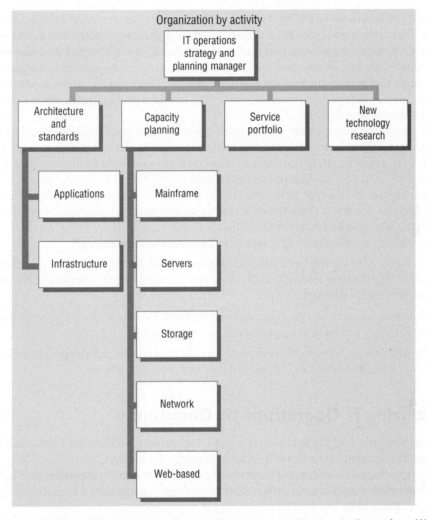

The activity-based structure has the following disadvantages:

- Resources with similar skills might be duplicated across different functions, which results in higher costs.
- Although measurement is based on output, it is still focused on the performance of internal activities rather than driven by the experience of the customer or end user.

Organizing to Manage Processes

Processes are used to overcome the "silo effect" of departments, not to create silos. However, it is not necessarily a good idea to structure the whole organization according to processes. There are a number of processes that may need a dedicated organizational structure for support and management. In process-based organizations, people are organized into groups or departments that perform or manage a specific process. This is similar to the activity-based structure, except that its departments focus on end-to-end sets of activities rather than on one individual type of activity.

If IT operations management is responsible for more than just IT operations, then this type of organizational structure may be used effectively. Process-based departments are really effective only when they are able to coordinate the execution of the process through the entire organization, not just in one department.

The advantage of this type of organizational structure is that processes are easier to define. Metrics of team or department performance and process performance are the same, effectively aligning internal and external metrics.

This type of organizational structure does have some disadvantages:

- When processes are used as a basis for organizational design, additional processes may need to be defined to ensure that the departments work together because there will still be external dependencies.

- While some aspects of a process can be centralized, there will always be a number of activities that will have to be performed by other groups.

- The relationship between the dedicated team or department and the people performing the decentralized activities is often difficult to define and manage.

Organizing IT Operations by Geography

Organizations can have physically distributed IT operations, and in some cases, each location needs to be organized according to its own particular context.

This type of structure is used when there are different regions or countries that use different technologies or provide a different set of services. A geography-based structure is shown in Figure 39.9.

Global organizations may have to organize according to regional variations in business models or organizational structures, in legislative regulations or standards, or in cultures and language.

The advantages of this type of organizational structure are as follows:

- Organizational structure can be customized to meet local conditions.

- IT operations can be customized to meet differing levels of IT service from region to region.

FIGURE 39.9 IT operations organized according to geography

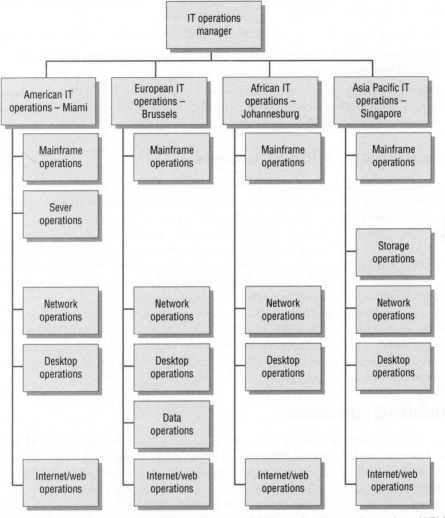

This type of organizational structure has the following disadvantages:

- Reporting lines and authority structures can be confusing. For example, does network operations report to the local data center manager or to a centralized network operations manager?

- Operational standards are difficult to impose, resulting in inconsistent and duplicated activities and tools. This can cause reduced economies of scale, which in turn increases the overall cost of operations.

- Duplication of roles, activities, tools, and facilities across multiple locations could be costly.

- Shared services, such as email, are more difficult to deliver because each regional organization operates differently.

- Communication with customers and inside IT will be more difficult because they are not colocated and it may be difficult for staff in one location to understand the priorities of customers or staff in another location.

Hybrid Organization Structures

It is unlikely that IT operations management will be organized using only one type of organizational structure. Some organizations use a technical specialization structure combined with some additional activity- or process-based structures.

The type of structure used will depend on a number of organizational variables, which may include the nature of the business and its requirements and expectations. Technology and architecture may be significant factors, as well as the stability of the current IT infrastructure and the availability of skills to manage it. Another factor may be the governance of the organization, which may be driven by external legislation.

Further considerations include the political and socioeconomic environment of the organization and its size, age, and maturity and the type and level of skills available to the organization. The organization's dependence on IT for business-critical activities, processes, and functions will have an effect, as will the participation of IT in the value chain and the relationship between IT and vendors.

Combined Functions

One final type of organization should be discussed. This structure incorporates IT operations, technical, and application management departments into a single structure. In this structure, the IT operations manager takes responsibility for all technical, application, and IT operations management. The centralized structure is shown in Figure 39.10.

The advantages of this organization structure are as follows:

- There is greater consistency and control between the more tactical and more operational technical management activities.

- It is easier to enforce the performance standards and technical architectures that are created in service design because the people who were involved in design are managing the activities of the people who are executing those activities.

- Because there is no duplication between location or activity, this structure is often more cost-effective.

The disadvantage of this organizational structure is that its scope makes it difficult to manage effectively in large organizations or in organizations with multiple data or operational centers.

FIGURE 39.10   Centralized IT operations, technical, and application management structure

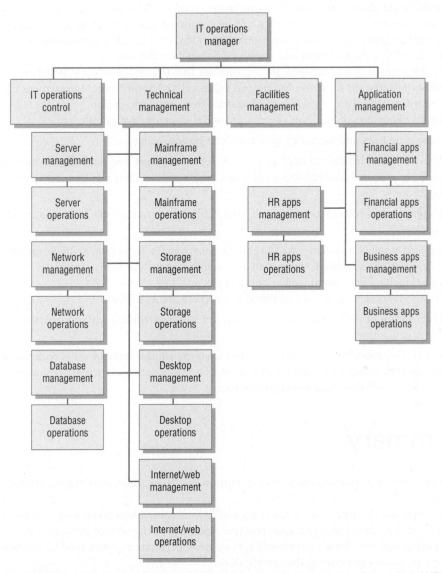

Organizing Application and Technical Management

Technical and application management organizations tend to be fairly straightforward. Technical management departments are usually based on the technology they manage, and application management departments are usually based on the applications and sets of applications they manage.

But there are alternatives, and they can be arranged in structures similar to those we have just considered. For example, they can be organized through a geographical approach, where the locations require local functional capability, or through a systems-based approach, linking the technical and application teams for the system.

The advantages of a geographical structure are that the organizational structure can be customized to meet local conditions and technical and application management can be customized to meet differing levels of IT service from region to region.

The disadvantages of this type of organizational structure are as follows:

- Reporting lines and authority structures can be confusing.

- Standards are difficult to impose, resulting in inconsistent and duplicated activities and tools, causing reduced economies of scale, which in turn increases the overall cost of operations.

- Duplication of roles, activities, tools, and facilities across multiple locations could be very costly.

The advantage of a system-based organization structure is that department members are focused on the success of the system as a whole rather than the performance of an individual technology component or application.

The disadvantages of this organizational structure are as follows:

- Duplication of skills and resources across several departments will increase the cost of the organization.

- Communication between staff who are managing similar technology is reduced, and this in turn reduces the amount of learning by experience and increases reliance on collaborative knowledge management tools.

Summary

In this chapter, we reviewed the service operation functions, roles, and organizational structures.

We explored the service desk function and how it contributes to service operation. We considered the role, objectives, and structures relating to the service desk, and potential staffing options. We also reviewed service desk performance metrics and the issues relating to in- or outsourcing the service desk.

We also looked at the function and how it contributes to service operation. We looked at the technical management role and the objectives, activities organization, metrics, and documentation relating to the technical management function.

The applications management function also contributes to service operation. We looked at the applications management role and the objectives and principles, and how applications management relates to the service lifecycle. We reviewed the activities of the function and the organization, metrics, and documentation relating to those activities.

Finally, we looked at the roles for service operation and the structures applicable to the organization based on its functions and requirements.

Exam Essentials

Understand the overlap between technical and application management functions and operations management.   Understand the role of the technical and application management functions in providing resources to the other lifecycle stages and in specifying the operational tasks that service operation staff members should carry out.

Explain the operations management function.   Understand the two areas of operations management: operations control and facilities management. Be able to think of examples of the responsibilities of each of these areas, such as monitoring environmental conditions (IT facilities management) and console management (operations control).

Know the role and importance of the service desk function.   Be able to list the skills and attributes that service desk staff members should possess, such as business awareness, technical awareness, customer focus, and so on. Be able to describe the different service desk structures of local, central, virtual, and follow the sun as well as when each might be used. Understand the advantages and disadvantages of each option.

Understand the roles and responsibilities of the service owner.   The service owner is accountable for ensuring the delivery of the service. The service owner will liaise with process owners to ensure that the service is delivered to the highest standard possible.

Understand the roles and responsibilities of the process owner, the process manager, and the process practitioner.   The process owner is accountable for the successful delivery of a process across all services and takes a lead role in ensuring that the process outcomes match the objectives.

There may be several process managers for each process, each responsible for managing the day-to-day implementation of the process by the process practitioners in their own geographical or infrastructure area.

The process practitioner is responsible for carrying out the process tasks under the direction of the process manager.

One person may be responsible for more than one of these roles, although there is a danger that process control may not be as strong when this is the case because of individuals being too close to the process to be objective. All roles have a responsibility to identify possible improvements in the process, but it is the process owner's responsibility to evaluate them and implement the ones that have value.

Review Questions

You can find the answers to the review questions in the appendix.

1. Service operation includes which of the following activities?

   A. Testing the service

   B. Rolling out the service

   C. Deciding whether to retire the service

   D. Optimizing the service

2. Many processes from other lifecycle stages also take place during the service operation stage. Which of the following processes does not fall into this category?

   A. IT service continuity management

   B. Availability management

   C. Service level management

   D. Design coordination

3. Which of the following is the correct list of service operation functions described in ITIL?

   A. Technical management function, facilities management function, service desk function

   B. Infrastructure management function, desktop support function, application management function, service desk function

   C. Technical management function, operations management function, application management function, service desk function

   D. Infrastructure management function, service desk function, application development function

4. Which of these activities is facilities management NOT responsible for?

   A. Maintaining air-conditioning to the required level in the server rooms

   B. Defining the infrastructure requirements to support the services

   C. Ensuring that the power supply at disaster recovery sites meets the requirement

   D. Testing the UPS and generators

5. Match the activities to the functions.

   1. Activity: Console management

   2. Activity: Identifying functional and manageability requirements for application software

   3. Activity: Providing a single point of contact

   4. Activity: Designing and managing the infrastructure

      a. Function: Service desk

      b. Function: Technical management

    c.   Function: Application management

    d.   Function: Operations management

       A.   1d, 2a, 3c, 4b

       B.   1d, 2c, 3a, 4b

       C.   1a, 2b, 3c, 4d

       D.   1b, 2c, 3d, 4a

6.   The service desk is NOT responsible for which of the following?

    A.   Providing a first point of contact

    B.   Resolving straightforward incidents

    C.   Preventing incidents from recurring

    D.   Providing updates to users

7.   The service desk carries out two processes. What are they?

    1.   Incident management

    2.   Design coordination

    3.   Request fulfilment

    4.   Change management

       A.   2 and 4

       B.   1 and 3

       C.   All of the above

       D.   3 and 4

8.   Which of the following should service desk staff members possess?

    1.   Specialist technical knowledge

    2.   Customer service skills

    3.   Technical ability

    4.   Business knowledge

       A.   1 and 2

       B.   2 and 3

       C.   All of the above

       D.   2, 3, and 4

9.   There are two elements to operations management. What are they called?

    A.   Facilities management, operations development

    B.   Facilities ownership, operations control

    C.   Console management, facilities management

    D.   Facilities management, operations control

10. Which of the following is NOT a service desk structure described in ITIL?
   A. Virtual
   B. Matrix
   C. Follow the sun
   D. Local

Chapter

40

Technology Considerations

THE FOLLOWING ITIL INTERMEDIATE EXAM OBJECTIVES ARE DISCUSSED IN THIS CHAPTER:

✓ **Service operation technology considerations:**

- The types of tools that would benefit service operation

- The generic requirements for service management tools

- The specific service operation process requirements for service management tools

- The use of tools and how they support the service lifecycle

This chapter brings all technology requirements together to define the overall requirements of an integrated set of service management technology tools for service operation. The same technology, with some possible additions, should be used for the other phases of IT service management (ITSM)—service strategy, service design, service transition, and continual service improvement—to give consistency and allow an effective ITSM lifecycle to be properly managed.

Tools can help the service operation and other processes to work more effectively. They should allow large amounts of repetitive work to be carried out quickly and consistently. Tools also provide a wealth of management information, leading to the identification of weaknesses and opportunities for improvement.

The use of tools will help standardize practices and both centralize and integrate processes.

Often organizations believe that by purchasing or developing a tool, all of their problems will be solved, and it is easy to forget that we are still dependent on the process, the function, and, most important, the people. Remember, "a fool with a tool is still a fool," and therefore training in the process and tool is imperative.

We are going to consider the generic requirements for such tools and the particular requirements needed to support the service desk function and the service operation processes of request fulfilment and event, incident, problem, and access management. It is important that the tool being used should support the processes, not the other way around.

Service Management Tools

We will begin by considering the generic requirements for IT service management tools. In this section, we look at a number of these requirements, which we would expect any good integrated toolset to offer.

The first two requirements are self-help functionality and a workflow engine.

You should be able to recall from the discussion of the release fulfilment process that we discussed the option for dealing with requests or simple incidents via self-help functionality. This might be restricted to the logging of requests and incidents, or it could allow them to be tracked and updated throughout their lifecycle. The advantage to providing a self-help facility is that requests and incidents can be logged at any time and this process is not dependent on service desk staff being available to answer the phone. This helps the service desk manage high volumes of calls if the less urgent ones are handled via a self-help, self-logging site. Self-help request tools can assist with password resets by, for example, requiring the user to validate their identity by answering previously set questions before the reset takes place. Additionally, a self-help request tool could download approved versions of requested software.

The next generic requirement is for a workflow or a process engine that can automate the steps of the process (assigning, escalating, etc.). It can also release work orders when prerequisite steps have been completed.

 Remember, the ITSM toolset is essential for many of the service management processes and functions and as such should be included in the IT service continuity provision.

The next generic requirement is for an integrated configuration management system (CMS).

The service management tool should be integrated with the CMS to allow the organization's configuration item (CI) information to be interrogated and linked to incident, problem, known error, and change records as appropriate.

Another generic requirement is for discovery/deployment/licensing technology tools; these are extremely helpful in verifying the accuracy of the CMS, especially with regard to license use. It is also very helpful if only changes since the last audit can be extracted and reported upon. The same technology can often be used to deploy new software to target locations; this is essential to enable patches, upgrades, and so on to be distributed to the correct users.

When implemented in conjunction with the self-help functionality previously mentioned, this facilitates the automation of the fulfilment of many service requests for software.

Another generic requirement is remote control. This allows the service desk analysts to take control of the user's desktop (under properly controlled security conditions) to do things such as conduct investigations and correct settings.

Some tools will store diagnostic scripts and other diagnostic utilities to assist with earlier diagnosis of incidents.

Good reporting is a requirement of any ITSM toolset. The tools hold enormous amounts of information about what is happening day to day. This data is helpful in planning ahead and tracking trends, but such reporting has to be flexible if it is to be useful. Standard reports and ad hoc reports should both be easily available.

Another generic requirement to consider is a dashboard facility. Dashboards are useful, both for day-to-day operations and for IT and business management to get a clear idea of real-time performance.

To facilitate greater business alignment, business applications and tools need to be able to interface with ITSM support tools to give the required functionality. An example of integration includes event management tools spotting unusual spending patterns on credit cards.

Software as a Service (SaaS) technologies offer hosted service management capabilities over the Internet. The advantages this offers include lower capital and start-up costs, faster implementation, and built-in service continuity.

However, it also means limited customization and changes to functionality, access restricted to vendor's hours of service availability, and licensing schemes that may become restrictive or expensive. There may also be limits on data storage size and possible security and access management constraints or risks. Finally, integration with other service management tools may be difficult or even impossible.

Each organization should review its requirements carefully so that it acquire the most appropriate toolset for its needs.

Tool Requirements for Service Operation Processes

In the following sections, we'll consider the requirements of each service operation process.

Event Management

The tool requirements for this process include an open interface with standard Simple Network Management Protocol (SNMP) agents to enable events from differing technologies to be managed together. The tool should be easy to deploy and should route all events to a single location. It should be able to be programmed to handle alerts differently, depending upon symptoms and impact, and to escalate events if they are not responded to within a set time period. It is essential that the tool should provide meaningful management information and a business user dashboard. It should also have a direct interface into the organization's incident management processes. Another possible capability would be the ability to use SMS messaging to escalate events to support staff.

Incident Management

Next, we will consider the specific tool requirements for incident management.

The first is the capability to log incidents quickly, often by using predefined "quick calls" for common incidents (also referred to as incident models), with preset categorization, prioritization, and assignment. Tracking and reporting of incidents must also be easy and efficient.

Another requirement is an integral CMS to allow automated relationships to be made and maintained between incidents, service requests, problems, known errors, workarounds, and all other CIs. The CMS should also be able to assist in determining priority, help investigation and diagnosis, and escalate to appropriate resolution teams within technical and application management.

A process flow engine is essential to allow processes to be predefined using target times to automate the workflow and escalation. So, for example, if a support team has not responded within 60 minutes to an incident assigned to them, the team leader is automatically informed.

An interface to event management should be in place, as previously discussed, to allow failures to be automatically raised as incidents, and a web interface can be set up to allow the use of self-help tools and self-logging of incidents and service requests.

An integrated known error database for recording and searching for diagnosed and/or resolved incidents and problems can help speed up future incident resolution.

Easy-to-use reporting facilities are needed to allow incident metrics to be produced, and diagnostic tools will help the service desk to resolve incidents at first contact. Reporting capabilities should enable efficient access to incident histories and summarizations of incidents by category, priority, status, and CIs impacted to provide data and support for reactive and proactive problem management activities.

Request Fulfilment

The specific requirements for request fulfilment include the ability to differentiate requests from incidents and the ability to link service requests to incidents or events that have initiated them. As previously mentioned, tools should include self-help capabilities to allow users to submit requests via a web-based, menu-driven selection process.

Otherwise, the facilities needed to manage service requests are very similar to those for managing incidents. They include predefined workflow control of request models, the ability to set and automate priority levels, automated escalation, and effective reporting.

Problem Management

Having a good ITSM tool is essential for effective problem management. A specific tool requirement for problem management is an integrated service management tool that differentiates between incidents and problems—and allows them to be linked.

Integration with change management is also required to allow request, event, incident, and problem records to be related to requests for change that have caused problems and to RFCs raised to resolve problems and incidents. There should be an integrated CMS to allow problem records to be linked to the components affected and the services impacted. Service asset and configuration management forms part of a larger service knowledge management system (SKMS), which includes links to many of the data repositories used in service operation.

An effective known error database (KEDB) will be an essential requirement to allow easy storage and retrieval of known error data. The ability to be able to link to vendor KEDBs is also a requirement.

Good reporting facilities are needed to ease the production of management reports and to allow drill-down capabilities for incident and problem analysis.

Access Management

The final service operation process, access management, requires integration with a number of technologies.

The first requirement is the ability to link to the technology used by human resources to validate the identity of users and to track their status. Another requirement is the ability to link to directory services. This technology enables technology managers to assign names to resources on a network and then provide access to those resources based on the profile of the user. Directory services tools also enable access management to create roles and groups and to link them to both users and resources.

Access management will use features in applications, middleware, operating systems, and network operating systems.

Changes to access requirements may be logged via a service request or be part of a work order from change management, so integration with these systems is very useful.

Access management also requires links to incident management in the case of suspected security incidents from people requesting access they should not have or inappropriate use of access.

Service Desk Function

In this section, we'll consider the requirements of the service desk, because in addition to the technology requirements for each process, the service desk function has some specific requirements.

The first requirement is for a known error database (already mentioned when we talked about the requirements of the incident and problem processes) to store details of previous incidents/problems and their resolutions so that recurrences can be more quickly diagnosed and fixed.

Diagnostic scripts should be developed, stored, and managed to allow service desk staff to pinpoint the cause of failures. This requires input from the technical and application management functions and suppliers who need to provide details of likely faults, the key questions to be asked, and details of the resolution actions to be taken.

We have already mentioned the importance of a self-help web interface so users can log their own incidents and requests and even obtain assistance, which will enable them to resolve their own difficulties. This should include the following features:

- FAQs
- Password change capabilities, including identity checking, without the need for service desk intervention
- Software fixes, downloads, and repairs
- Downloads of additional authorized software packages
- Advanced notice of planned downtime

Finally, it is often helpful for the service desk analysts to be able to take control of the user's desktop to allow them to, for example, conduct investigations or correct settings. Facilities to allow this level of remote control will be needed.

In addition to an integrated ITSM tool, the service desk needs the facilities offered by modern telephony services:

- An automated call distribution (ACD) system to allow a single telephone number. These systems provide extensive statistical reporting, providing insight into the busy times, average length of call, and so on.

- Interactive voice recognition (IVR) selection. These systems, which provide users with one or more menu selections, should be used with care. They should not have too many levels of options or offer ambiguous options.

- Computer Telephony Interface (CTI) software enables the caller to be identified from their telephone number and the incident record to then be automatically populated with their details extracted from the CMS.

- Voice over IP (VoIP) technology can significantly reduce telephony costs when dealing with remote and international users.

- Other possible facilities include cordless headsets, the ability to record calls for training purposes, and the ability to listen in on calls.

Service Management Tool Choice

There are many service management tools available, each with its own strengths and weaknesses, which makes choosing the right one difficult. To overcome this, you should define some objective selection criteria.

One simple method is MoSCoW analysis. This involves creating a detailed list of all your requirements and classifying each one as must have, should have, could have, or would like in future.

- *Must have* requirements are mandatory. Any tool that does not satisfy *all* of those requirements is rejected.

- *Should have* requirements are those that we expect but are not essential.

- *Could have* requirements are useful but not hugely important.

- And *Would like in future* requirements are those that we don't need right now but will need in future. For example, we're choosing a tool for incident management right now, but we'd like it to have problem management capability later.

You can then devise a scoring system based on this analysis, which would enable you to rank alternatives. It is possible to weight your decision, making a scoring system to ensure that you are getting the service management tool that delivers against your requirements.

Remember, the ITSM toolset is essential, but you are unlikely to get all of the requirements on your wish list. If you manage to get 80 percent of your requirements and the tool has some ability to be customized to meet your needs, then it probably is the best fit you can find.

Summary

This brings us to the end of the chapter. In this chapter, we reviewed the service operation requirements relating to tools such as the integrated service management tool.

We looked at the following topics:

- The types of tools that would benefit service operation in support of the processes and service desk function

- The generic requirements for service management tools

Exam Essentials

Understand the role of tools in supporting service operation.   This includes understanding how to select tools that are appropriate for organizational needs.

Explain the generic requirements that service operation has for toolsets and why they are important.   Understand the generic requirements that are applicable to service operation and how these tools will support the objectives of the lifecycle.

Understand the specific requirements for the individual service operation processes.   Be able to identify the requirements for the individual processes from service operation to ensure maximum efficiency from the toolset.

Explain the selection technique known as MoSCoW.   Understand what the acronym stands for (Must/Should/Could/Would) and be able to explain the use of each concept in tool selection.

Review Questions

You can find the answers to the review questions in the appendix.

1. Which of these statements about service management tools and technology is correct?
   A. Tools are useful but not essential.
   B. Tools assist good processes instead of replacing them.
   C. Tools can replace processes that do not function well.
   D. Tools define the processes we use by formalizing the steps in the design.

2. Which of these statements is/are correct?
   1. A CMS should be an integrated part of the service management tool.
   2. A service management tool without an SKMS is not a true service management tool.
      A. Statement 1 only
      B. Statement 2 only
      C. Both statements
      D. Neither statement

3. What is the first step when choosing a service management tool?
   A. Define the interfaces the tool will need to integrate with business tools.
   B. Understand the requirements for the tool.
   C. Decide how staff will be trained to achieve most from the tool.
   D. Research the available tools.

4. Which of these would be included in the generic requirements for a service management tool?
   1. Remote access capability
   2. Capability for integration with business tools
   3. Capability to link records such as incident and problem records
   4. Web-based access
      A. 1, 2, and 3
      B. 2, 3, and 4
      C. 1, 2, 3, and 4
      D. 1, 3, and 4

5. What is the MoSCoW technique used for?
   A. Categorization of requirements
   B. Categorizing incidents and problems
   C. Categorization of service desk components
   D. Designing the SKMS

6. Which of these is most likely to be part of a self-service portal?
    1. The ability to reset passwords
    2. The ability to log requests
    3. The ability to authorize a change request
    4. The ability to download approved software
        A. 1, 2, and 3
        B. 2, 3, and 4
        C. 1, 3, and 4
        D. 1, 2, and 4

7. Which of these considerations for reporting requirements for service management tools is important?
    A. Only industry-standard reports should be generated.
    B. No reporting capability should be integrated into the tool; it should be managed separately.
    C. There should be a good selection of generic reports.
    D. There should be a good selection of generic reports supported by easy generation of custom reports.

8. Management support is critical for successful service operation. What benefits are expected from management's commitment to technology and tools?
    A. Leadership, funding, and supporting commitment
    B. Higher first-time fix rate, reduced outages, and funding
    C. Improved customer satisfaction, reduced outages, and higher first-time fix rate
    D. Reduced outages, funding, and supporting commitment

9. Which of these statements is/are correct?
    1. The KEDB is an important part of problem management.
    2. The KEDB is an important part of incident management.
        A. Statement 1 only
        B. Statement 2 only
        C. Both statements
        D. Neither statement

10. True or False? A service management tool is a tool used to log records/tickets. No other tools are service management tools.
    A. True
    B. False

Chapter

41

Implementation of Service Operation

THE FOLLOWING ITIL INTERMEDIATE EXAM OBJECTIVES ARE DISCUSSED IN THIS CHAPTER:

- ✓ Managing change in service operation
- ✓ Service operation and project management
- ✓ Assessing and managing risk in service operation
- ✓ Operational staff in design and transition
- ✓ Planning and implementing service management technologies

The learning objective for this chapter is to gain sufficient knowledge to implement service operation. Upon completion of the chapter, you should understand the specific issues relevant to implementing service operation.

Managing Change in Service Operation

This chapter covers how the IT service provider manages changes within service operation. We start by considering the challenges of managing change in operations. The focus in the operational stage of the lifecycle is on protecting the live services, so changes in service operation must be absorbed without impacting stability. We will examine the many different triggers that cause changes to the live environment and consider how the changes are assessed before implementation. Finally, we will look at how changes can be measured to see if they are successful.

Change Triggers

There are many events that can trigger a change in the service operation environment:

- There may be a requirement to install or upgrade hardware, network, or application software.

- Changes or upgrades to system software, such as operating systems and utilities, also need to be handled with care.

- Regular updates to software, including patches and bug fixes, are also changes that need to be managed because they have the potential to have a serious impact on the environment if not implemented carefully.

- Often, changes in operation are the result of external factors such as those resulting from legislation, the need to conform to an external standard, or new governance rules. For example, a change in legislation could mean that records of transactions need to be kept for a longer period, which would impact archiving and storage requirements.

- A common reason for change in the service operation stage is the replacement of obsolete hardware or software. These items may still be functioning correctly but are no longer supported by the supplier and may be incompatible with future releases of other components and, therefore, need to be replaced.

- Other triggers for change in service operation are those driven by the business, which may need IT to support a new business initiative, such as providing a "reserve and collect" facility through an e-commerce website.

- Processes and procedures should be subject to continual service improvement; each change that results from these initiatives must be implemented without any adverse consequences. The same is true for any service management tool, whether it is being upgraded or replaced.

- Changes in staff can also be potentially disruptive, and care needs to be taken to ensure that the necessary knowledge transfer takes place so the service provided is not affected.

- A requirement for a change in agreed service levels or a change in the sourcing model (outsourcing service provision, changing an outsourcer, or insourcing a service previously outsourced) will need to be planned to ensure that it is implemented smoothly.

Service transition would be responsible for planning these changes, but service operation has to be ready to absorb them without them disrupting the services provided.

Change Assessment

All changes have a potential impact on operations. This is not always understood by nonoperations staff, so it is essential that service operation staff have an opportunity to assess all changes. It is not sufficient to involve operations staff at the CAB stage because it may be too late; fundamental decisions regarding the design of the new or changed service will have been made far earlier. It is unrealistic to think that a redesign could happen at such a late stage. To prevent this, it is essential that operation staff are consulted and informed much earlier, during the initial design stage, and remain involved throughout.

It is good practice for the change manager to inform all affected parties of the changes being assessed so that affected areas (in this case, the service operation area) can prepare a response showing the operational impact of the change and setting out any concerns. This can be distributed prior to the CAB meeting to inform the discussion.

Service operation staff need to be involved throughout the design and implementation of a change with an operational impact. Early involvement is necessary to ensure that the design takes account of operational issues and requirements; involvement in the later stages is necessary to ensure that the change is scheduled to avoid potential disagreements or particularly sensitive periods.

Measurement of Successful Change

The ultimate measure of a successful change made to service operation is that there are no unexpected variations or outages; the only visible effects are the benefits that result from the change, such as enhanced functionality, quality, or financial savings.

Service Operation and Project Management

The use of project management processes to manage changes is commonplace in other lifecycle stages, but there is often a disinclination to use these processes for operational changes. Service operation is generally viewed as "business as usual" and does include a project approach. In fact, project management processes are both appropriate and helpful for major infrastructure upgrades or the deployment of new or changed procedures; these significant tasks will benefit from the improved control and management of costs and resources delivered by project management. Using project management to manage these types of activity would deliver a number of benefits:

- A clear, agreed statement of the benefits to be delivered by the project.
- Greater visibility of tasks and their management, which enables other IT groups and the business to understand the contributions made by operational teams. This helps in obtaining funding for projects that have traditionally been difficult to cost justify.
- Greater consistency and improved quality of the deliverables.
- The achievement of objectives, leading to operational groups gaining credibility.

Assessing and Managing Risk in Service Operation

The overriding concern of service operation is to maintain stability; any threat to that stability has to be assessed and acted upon urgently. An obvious example of a situation in which service operation needs to carry out a risk and impact assessment is the risk to stability from a potential change. Service operation staff must assess the possible impact of the change and share this assessment with the CAB.

Risks Resulting from Changes

A change might be implemented despite the existence of known errors that become apparent during testing but were not considered serious enough to delay the change. The existence of such known errors poses a risk to operational stability; until the errors are resolved, incidents resulting from them can recur. The impact of these incidents and the effectiveness of the appropriate workaround for each (including the speed at which it overcomes the fault) must be assessed. The results of this assessment will feed into the prioritization of the problem. Having a proven workaround mitigates the risk to a certain extent because, although the fault will occur when the service is operational and will therefore impact the business, a quick fix can reduce the impact of the incident.

Every incident, whether reported through the incident and problem processes, through a warning from the supplier, or by event management, will be assessed for impact and urgency to calculate its priority. This assessment is also an assessment of the risk it poses to the business. Finally, new projects that will result in delivery into the live environment are assessed because there is a risk that they may impact other services.

Other Sources of Risk

There are other risks to operational stability that would require a risk assessment. The first is an environmental risk. Environmental risks would include the sorts of risks that are assessed as part of IT service continuity planning, such as fire and flood. There may also be political and commercial risks and risks related to industrial relations. Examples of these are the risks faced by drug companies that carry out testing on animals and therefore may be subject to sabotage by those opposed to this practice, the risk of strikes affecting operation, or even the risk of a competitor engaging in a price war, which would drive down the income received.

Suppliers may also constitute a source of risk. Their failure to deliver could affect the delivery of the overall service. Their ability to provide a service might also be affected by their own internal risks. This is particularly a problem if they are the sole supplier for a particular element of the service. Taking on new suppliers also involves some risk; without a known track record of reliable delivery, there is a risk that their service may not be satisfactory. Another major area of risk involves security; security-related incidents or events may result in either theoretical or actual risks. Finally, every new customer or service to be supported is both an opportunity to be successful and a potential risk for failure.

Operational Staff in Design and Transition

All IT groups will be involved during service design and service transition to ensure that new components or services are designed, tested, and implemented to provide the correct levels of functionality, usability, availability, and capacity. Additionally, service operation staff must be involved during the early stages of service design and service transition to ensure that when new services reach the live environment, they are fit for purpose from a service operation perspective and are "supportable" in the future.

In this context, *supportable* means that they will not negatively impact other services, processes, schedules, or operational working practices. They must also be capable of being operated by the current staff, at an understood cost. The support structure, including both the internal support teams and the support provided by third-party suppliers, must be clear and understood. There should be no unexpected costs after the service goes live, and contractual obligations must be clear and straightforward.

Note that change is not just about technology. There is also organizational change to consider, and the possibility that staff or users may be hostile to the change. It is possible to reduce the risk of people resisting change through a program of communication and training. Further details about organizational change are included in *ITIL Service Transition*.

Planning and Implementing Service Management Technologies

The final topic of this chapter is service management tools. A good service management tool can be very helpful for implementing processes based on the ITIL framework. Many organizations implement new tools to assist their implementation of new or improved processes. There are a number of factors that these organizations need to consider if the new tool is to be helpful and appropriate.

Licenses

The first factor to be considered is the type of license. There are usually a number of options, at different costs. Where tools are licensed on a modular basis, careful planning is needed to ensure that the right access is obtained to enable people to carry out their work with no unnecessary modules being purchased. Here are some possible options:

- Dedicated licenses. For this option, each named person has their own license. Dedicated licenses are suitable for staff that require frequent and prolonged use of a particular module. For example, service desk staff would need a dedicated license to use an incident management module.

- Shared licenses. These licenses can be shared between individuals; there is, however, a possibility that a staff member may not be able to access the tool because the license is already in use. Shared licenses are suitable for regular users who do not require constant access, such as second-line support staff. Careful calculation is required to ascertain the correct ratio of users to licenses. These licenses are more expensive than dedicated licenses, but fewer are required.

- Web licenses. These allow access via a web browser. Web licenses are usually suitable for staff requiring remote access or only occasional access. They usually cost a lot less than other licenses (they may even be free with other licenses). It is possible to provide sufficient access for a large number of occasional users by purchasing a small number of such licenses, as the number of concurrent users and therefore the number of licenses required will be low. In this way overall costs can be reduced further.

- On demand. Access to tools is provided when required (on demand), and the supplier charges for the access based on the time spent using the application. This can be attractive to smaller organizations or if the tools in question are very specialized and used relatively infrequently. A variation to this is the use of a specialist tool as part of a consultancy assignment (e.g., specialist capacity management tools); in such cases, the license fees are likely to be included in the consultancy fee.

- Agent/activity. A further variation in license options is software that is licensed and charged on an agent/activity basis. An example of this is simulation software (e.g., agent software that can simulate customer paths through a website to assess and report upon performance and availability).

In all cases, it is essential than sufficient investigation has been done to ensure that the costs are understood and agreed and that the organization remains legal in respect to having sufficient licenses.

Deployment

Many ITSM tools, particularly discovery and event monitoring tools, will require some client/agent software deploying to all target locations before they can be used. This will need careful planning and execution and should be handled through formal release and deployment management. Some deployment considerations are listed here:

- There should be careful scheduling and testing, and the deployment must be tracked so that it is clear which CIs have the software and which have yet to receive it.
- The CMS should be updated as the deployment progresses.
- It is often necessary to reboot devices for the client software to be recognized, and this needs to be arranged in advance to minimize service interruption.
- Special arrangements may be needed for portable equipment, which may not be present on site during deployment.
- The devices receiving the software must be checked in advance to ensure that they have sufficient storage and processing capacity to host and run the new software.
- The network capacity needs to be checked to ensure that it is capable of transmitting everything required.
- The best time to deploy a tool is dependent on the maturity level. A tool that is deployed too early shifts the focus of the improvement initiative away from the requirement to change processes and ways of working, and the whole improvement exercise then becomes merely a tool implementation.
- Training in the tool prior to deployment is necessary if benefits are to be realized.

Remember, a tool is usually not enough to make things work better. However, if it supports processes and the user has been trained to use it, a good tool can help staff carry out new processes.

Here are some further aspects of the deployment that must be considered:

- The type of introduction to be used. A decision must be made whether a "Big Bang" introduction or some sort of phased approach is to be adopted. Because most organizations will have live services to keep running during the introduction, a phased approach is more likely to be necessary.

- Transition between tools. If an older tool is being replaced, consideration must be given to the best way to transition between the old tool and the new tool. For example, the service desk should not be assigning an incident on a new tool to a team that has yet to transition from the old tool.

- Data migration. A decision needs to be made regarding what data needs to be migrated from the old tool to the new one. This may require reformatting, and so may need to be validated after migration, especially if the data is transferred electronically. A period of parallel running may be implemented instead, with the old tool being available in a read-only mode for an initial period alongside the new one so that historical data can be referenced if needed.

Complete details on the release and deployment management process can be found in Part 3 of this book, "Service Transition."

Summary

In this chapter, we discussed managing change in service operation and, in particular, the need to assess and manage risk. We looked at the involvement of operations staff in service design and service transition and aspects to consider when planning and implementing service management technologies within a company.

Exam Essentials

Understand the need to manage change within service operation so it can be implemented with the minimum adverse impact on the service and its users.   Understand the possible triggers for change and how and why changes are assessed and measured.

Explain how project management processes can help in the implementation of changes in service operation.   Understand the benefits of using project management processes to implement changes in service operation and the reasons why it might be resisted.

Know the risks that change poses to operational stability.   Understand how these risks might be managed.

Understand why service operation staff need to be involved in the design and transition stages.   In particular, understand what the concept of a service being supportable means and what is required for this to be the case.

Understand the license options available when implementing a new service management tool. Be able to describe the different options and give examples of when each would be appropriate.

Understand the deployment options available when implementing a new service management tool. Be able to describe the different options and give examples of when each would be appropriate.

Review Questions

You can find the answers to the review questions in the appendix.

1. Which of the following are valid triggers for making changes to live services?

    1. Legislative, conformance, or governance changes

    2. Obsolescence

    3. Changing business requirements

    4. Changes in management or personnel

        A. 1, 3, and 4 only

        B. 1, 2, and 3 only

        C. All of the above

        D. 1 and 2 only

2. Which of these statements is/are correct about the result of successful change in service operation?

    1. There may be limited unexpected variations or outage of service.

    2. The only visible effects should be the benefits.

        A. Statement 1 only

        B. Statement 2 only

        C. Both statements

        D. Neither statement

3. True or False? Service operation personnel should be involved during service design and service transition to ensure that new components or services are correctly designed, tested, and implemented.

        A. True

        B. False

4. How can a service management tool assist in service operation?

        A. It will define the processes to be used.

        B. It can help staff carry out new processes.

        C. It will improve customer satisfaction.

        D. It will reduce outages and improve the first-time fix rate.

5. Which of the following is NOT a benefit of using project management for complex operational changes?

        A. Provides a clear, agreed statement of the benefits to be delivered by the project.

        B. Project management would be funded by service transition and the project office, thus providing cost savings to service operation.

C. Gives greater visibility of tasks and their management, which enables other IT groups and the business to understand the contributions made by operational teams. This helps in obtaining funding for projects that have traditionally been difficult to cost justify.

D. Greater consistency and improved quality of the deliverables.

6. Which of these may be a trigger for changes to service operation?

   1. Changes driven by a business requirement

   2. Process or procedure improvements

   3. Enhancements to service management tools

   4. Staff changes

   5. Changes to required service levels

   6. Changes to the method of service provision

   A. 1, 2, 3, and 4 only

   B. 2, 4, and 6 only

   C. 1, 2, 4, and 6 only

   D. All of the above

7. Which of the following best describes when service operation staff should be involved in the design and implementation stages?

   A. Early in the design and implementation stages to ensure that the design takes account of operational issues.

   B. Transition hands over design and implementation to service operation staff during the early life support stage; service operation staff are not involved until that point.

   C. Toward the end of the design and implementation stage to ensure that the schedule for implementation does not clash with other operational priorities.

   D. Throughout the design and implementation process.

8. Which of these statements is/are correct about the management of change in service operation?

   1. A project management approach is appropriate for larger infrastructure changes.

   2. Changes should be managed in accordance with ITIL best practice guidelines.

   3. Project management should be adopted for all changes.

   4. Project management disciplines are inappropriate for operational changes, which are always "business as usual."

   A. Statement 2 only

   B. Statements 2 and 3 only

   C. Statements 1 and 2 only

   D. Statements 2 and 4 only

9. Which of the following is a potential risk in service operation?

1. Known errors may be introduced into the live environment through changes.

2. Suppliers may fail to deliver what is required, thus impacting the service being delivered.

3. Competitors may provide the same service at a lower cost, so that potential customers will purchase the service from these other providers. This would mean that there would be few or no customers for the service you are providing.

4. There may be a security breach, causing loss of confidence in the service provider.

   A. 2 only

   B. 2 and 4 only

   C. 1, 2, and 4 only

   D. All of the above

10. Which of the following is NOT a license option for service management tools?

   A. Dedicated

   B. Time limited

   C. Shared

   D. Web based

Chapter

42

Challenges, Critical Success Factors, and Risks

THE FOLLOWING ITIL INTERMEDIATE
EXAM OBJECTIVES ARE DISCUSSED
IN THIS CHAPTER:

✓ Service operation challenges

✓ Service operation critical success factors

✓ Service operation risks

Challenges Critical
Success Fa
and Risks

The learning objective for this chapter is to gain an
understanding of the challenges, critical success factors,
and risks of service operation. Upon completion of the chapter,
you should understand the specific issues relevant to service operation.

Service Operation Challenges

The following main challenges facing service operation management are expanded upon in
this chapter:

- Lack of engagement with development and project staff
- Justifying funding within service operations
- The differences between design and operational activities
- Ineffective service transition
- Ineffective service metrics
- The use of virtual teams
- Balancing internal and external relationships

Engagement with Development and Project Staff

The first challenge in service operation is to ensure the correct level of cooperation and
engagement between the service operation staff and the development and project teams.

The focus of the development and project teams is very different from that of service
operation staff. Staff involved in projects and development will focus on the development of
new applications or functionality and delivering it into the operational environment. Their
work has a defined end point, which is when the application or functionality is delivered.
Staff involved in service operation focus on the long-term operation of what has been
delivered.

While project staff consider that the delivery of a service on time and to budget is
paramount, operations staff care less about meeting a specific date than they do about how
well the service will run and what will be involved in supporting it.

Development and project staff may know very little about service management and
regard it as relevant only to operations. The ITIL framework makes it clear that service
management processes are involved from the very beginning of a service, as part of service

strategy, right through to design and transition. Service operation should be involved throughout the development of a new or changed service to ensure that the deliverable is supportable at the end.

These two areas of IT often work quite separately, and there may even be animosity between them. Development staff may see operations staff as introducing unnecessary delay into their project, while operations staff may feel that projects are "dumped" on them with little appreciation or consideration about how they are to be operated in the live environment.

Ensuring that this division is overcome is challenging, but it will mean that operational aspects are considered early enough in the development activities that they can be incorporated into the design fairly easily. Failure to achieve this would constitute a risk to the successful transition and operation of the new service.

Justifying Funding

Service operation managers face the challenge of justifying funding for their area. They may meet with resistance to their funding requests because money spent in this sphere is often regarded as infrastructure costs, with no clear benefit arising from the investment.

Service operation managers should be able to show how investment in the operations area can save the organization money as well as improve the quality of the service being delivered. Here are some examples:

- Reduced software license costs through the better management of licenses
- Fewer incidents and problems and faster resolutions due to effective problem management, leading to reduced support costs
- Improved processes, leading to better usage of existing resources and the elimination of duplication of activities
- Better customer retention from delivering higher levels of service consistently
- Improved utilization of existing infrastructure equipment and deferral of further expenditure as a result of better capacity management.

Differing Service Design and Service Operation Focus and Priorities

The differences between design activities and operational activities will continue to present challenges:

- Service design may tend to focus on one service at a time, whereas service operation tends to focus on delivering and supporting all services at the same time. Operation managers need to work closely with service design and service transition to provide the operation perspective.
- Service design will often be conducted in projects, while service operation focuses on ongoing, repeatable management processes and activities. This may mean that operational staff are unavailable to participate in service design project activities, although

as we just mentioned, their participation and engagement with development and project staff is essential if the new service is going to take account of operational issues.

- Once project staff have finished the design of one IT service, they could move onto the next project and not be available to provide support. Overcoming this challenge means ensuring that service operation staff are actively involved in design projects and participate in the early life support of services introduced in the operational environment.

- Success is measured differently for design and operation. Service design is measured by projects being on time and to budget, whereas service operation must ensure, through involvement in the design phase, that the service will operate as expected. If support and other costs are greater than expected in service operation, operational staff will blame the design, and service design staff will blame operations. Addressing this challenge requires service operation to be actively involved in the service transition stage of the lifecycle. The objective of service transition is to ensure that designed services will operate as expected. When the service operation manager is involved, operational aspects can be considered, allowing transition to understand and remedy issues before they become issues in the operational environment.

Other Challenges

- Ineffective service transition processes pose another challenge. Ensuring service operation personnel are involved in validation and testing is required in order that a decision to authorize changes is based on factual evidence. Good change management processes will ensure changes that do not meet expectation are denied.

- Choosing meaningful metrics can be challenging. What can be measured easily may not actually be a useful indication of the level of service being provided. For example, measuring the time taken to answer the phone on the service desk may be easy, but does not show whether the user then receives a good service. (The service design stage is responsible for ensuring that the appropriate metrics are included in the design of the service). Every service will produce its own measurements interpreting these to understand the level of service being provided may not be straightforward. Service level management can help to overcome this, but this requires involvement of operations staff.

Management of Staff

- The use of virtual teams can also present challenges. Hierarchical management structures do not fit increasingly complex organizations, so matrix management has developed in response, where employees report to different sources for different tasks. This makes allocating accountability difficult. Knowledge management and the use of RACI matrices will help in this situation.

- One of the most significant challenges faced by service operation managers is balancing many internal and external relationships. Most IT organizations today are complex, with an increased use of value networks, partnerships, and shared services models.

This increases the complexity of managing services, so investment in relationship management knowledge and skills is advisable to help deal with this challenge.

Critical Success Factors

Let us now consider some of the critical success factors for successful service operation:

- Visible ongoing management support, in relation to adherence to processes; appropriate ongoing funding of tools; and staff to support operational activities are essential for success.
- The support of the business is also important, to assist with formulating prioritization tables for incident management, ensuring that the users contact the service desk rather than approach support teams directly and providing the budget to fund operational activities.
- The existence of champions who lead others by their example and enthusiasm is another important factor. These may be senior managers, but champions can be at any level in the organization.
- Make sure there is sufficient staff resources to allow time to be spent implementing new processes and tools while ensuring that the day-to-day work does not suffer.
- Staff with the correct knowledge and skills is important. Staff need training and awareness of technical and service management aspects and may also require training in other areas, such as "soft skills," business awareness, and tool administration.
- Staff retention is important. Having invested in training, it is in the organization's interest to retain the trained staff, so it should try to develop career paths for these staff.

The final critical success factors that we consider are those surrounding the toolsets used:

- Using a tool that has been designed to support the processes described in ITIL makes the implementation and management of those processes much easier. Being able to link incidents and problems and to obtain information about configuration items and changes will support these processes, as will being able to report easily against KPIs.
- If a new tool is to be procured, evaluation against a set of defined criteria is required to ensure a good fit to requirements. The tools will also need to be configured and tested.
- The final critical success factor for tools is the ability to produce reports to show the effectiveness of the processes.

Service Operation Risks

In the last section of this chapter, we'll look at the risks service operation face. These include the absence of the critical success factors—for example, the visible support of management is a CSF, and the absence of that support is a risk.

The ultimate risk is the loss of critical IT services and the resultant damage to the business. In addition to financial loss, there may be extreme cases where the IT services affected are used for critical health or safety purposes when poor service operation poses a health and safety risk.

Other risks are as follows:

- Inadequate funding and resources. A clear business case needs to be made to secure adequate funding; inadequate funding will inevitably have an effect on the level of service that can be delivered. Once allocated, such funding must be reserved for its intended purpose and not spent on other items.

- Loss of momentum. Implementing best practice service management in service operation needs to become a permanent "business as usual" activity, not a short-term "flavor of the month." Without this clear message, staff may lose enthusiasm over time and revert to previous bad practices, seeing the move to best practice as purely temporary. An additional risk is that organizational changes may mean that the new best practice approach is dropped; again, this is the result of seeing the changes as temporary, to be replaced by the next initiative, rather than embedded.

- Loss of key personnel. This may be a significant risk for less mature organizations in which the loss of one or two key staff members can have a severe impact. This can be mitigated by ensuring that staff are cross-trained, thus reducing dependencies upon individuals. A more mature organization should have formalized knowledge transfer into processes, documents, and tools; this removes any dependency on a few knowledgeable people.

- Resistance to change or suspicion regarding the changes. This can be helped by education and training and better communication of the benefits of the changes. Often resistance to change is actually fear of change; providing staff with information as to how the changes will affect and possibly even benefit them in terms of job satisfaction and learning new skills may help to allay these fears and thus reduce resistance.

- Lack of management support. Middle managers may not see the overall vision or appreciate the hands-on benefits that more junior staff will gain. As stated previously, management support is a critical success factor for implementing best practice. Senior management must ensure that the middle managers understand both the benefits and the need for the changes, which deliver these benefits, to be visibly supported. Involving these managers in the appropriate stages and processes of service design and transition may help them to understand the benefits.

- Poor design. The success of each lifecycle stage is due, at least in part, to the quality of the inputs into that stage. A poor-quality design output from the design stage will impact both transition and operation. The implementation will never be really successful, and redesign will ultimately be necessary.

- Distrust. Service management can be viewed with suspicion by both IT and the business. While IT staff dislike the new controls it imposes on their work methods, the business may take the cynical view that IT is seeking more money without actually delivering any improvements. Overcoming this distrust and cynicism mean ensuring that the benefits are clearly articulated to stakeholders and then actually delivered.

- Differing customer expectations. Different customer and user groups may have differing expectations. One group may pay more for a superior service, but this higher level is resented by other groups. Clear service level management, and the involvement of business relationship management if required, will help overcome these issues. The solution is not to simply deliver improved service levels upon request if they are not required or funded.

Summary

In this chapter, we discussed service operation challenges, critical success factors, and risks. You have now completed all the material included in the syllabus for the service operation lifecycle course.

Exam Essentials

Understand the challenges faced by service operation staff when working with projects.   Understand the different drivers and priorities for project management and service operation staff and why they may lead to conflict. Understand why these two groups of staff must work together if both utility and warranty of the new service, and therefore its value, is to be delivered.

Understand the critical success factors that need to be in place if successful service operation is to take place.   Understand the importance of visible management support and the role played by other champions of the changes, at whatever level in the organization.

Understand why the involvement of the right people is a critical success factor.   Be able to explain the difference between the number of people involved (as a resource) and the skills and motivation of those involved (as a capability). As stated in this chapter, success requires the right number of staff with the right skills and knowledge.

Understand how implementing service operation disciplines successfully can lead to cost savings and ensure a return on investment.   Be able to list and describe possible savings, as detailed in this chapter, in the section describing the need to justify funding.

Know the risks encountered in the service operation stage, in particular the danger that the implementation of service management may lose momentum.   Understand how these risks might be mitigated.

Understand why there may be resistance to the new methods being adopted as part of the implementation of service management.   In particular, understand the possible reasons behind this resistance, the best way to tackle it, and the importance of visible management support in addressing the situation.

Review Questions

You can find the answers to the review questions in the appendix.

1. One of the key challenges of service operation is funding. Which of these statements is/are correct?
   1. Operational funding is often seen as infrastructure expenditure.
   2. Service operation projects often result in cost savings.
      A. Statement 1 only
      B. Statement 2 only
      C. Neither statement
      D. Both statements

2. With which lifecycle stages should service operation engage?
   A. Service design only
   B. Service design and service transition only
   C. Service design, service transition, and CSI only
   D. Service strategy, service design, service transition, and CSI

3. Visible support from which of the following is critical for successful service operation?
   1. Senior/middle management
   2. Business support
   3. Champions
   4. Suppliers
      A. 2 and 3 only
      B. 1, 2, and 3 only
      C. 1 and 2 only
      D. None

4. Which of the following factors are critical for staffing and retention and successful service operation?
   1. Clear career path
   2. Appropriate number of skilled staff
   3. Service management training
   4. Process training
      A. All
      B. 2 and 3 only
      C. 1, 2, and 3 only
      D. 1, 2, and 4 only

5. Which of the following is a source of risk for the service desk?

1. Inadequate funding and resources

2. Loss of key personnel

3. Resistance to change/suspicion

4. Lack of management support

    A. 1 and 4 only

    B. 1, 3, and 4 only

    C. All

    D. None

6. Service operation staff need to work with staff from other stages of the lifecycle. Which of the following statements describe why this a challenge?

1. Staff from service operation have a different focus than design or transition staff; they focus on long-term operations, whereas the other groups' involvement has a defined end point.

2. Operations staff are focused on delivery within the budget; development staff do not attach the same importance to this.

3. Project and development staff focus on meeting the delivery date; operations staff do not attach the same importance to this.

4. Development staff do not respect the skills of service operation staff.

5. Operations staff tend to focus on warranty aspects; project and development staff tend to focus on utility.

    A. 1 and 4 only

    B. 1, 3, and 5 only

    C. 3 and 5 only

    D. 3, 4, and 5 only

7. Service operation must show how investment in operations will show a financial return. Which of the following is NOT a financial benefit that would be a result of investment in service operations?

    A. Reduced software license costs through the better management of licenses

    B. More successful transitions due to more extensive testing

    C. Fewer incidents and problems and faster resolutions due to effective problem management, leading to reduced support costs

    D. Improved utilization of existing infrastructure equipment and deferral of further expenditure

8. Which of the following is NOT a challenge for service operation?

    A. Overcoming the difficulties in translating technology metrics into service metrics

    B. Defining requirements

    C. Ensuring thorough knowledge management

    D. Managing the increasingly complex balance between internal teams and external supplier relationships

9. Which of the following is NOT a critical success factor for service operation?

   A. Visible management support, especially support for adherence to processes

   B. The ability to translate strategic plans into tactical and operational plans that are executed by each organizational unit

   C. Sufficient staff resources

   D. Staff with the correct knowledge and skills

10. Which of the following is NOT a risk for service operation?

    A. Inadequate funding and resources

    B. Loss of momentum

    C. A clear definition of how things will be measured and reported

    D. Resistance to change/suspicion

Continual Service Improvement

PART V

Chapter

43

Introduction to the Continual Service Improvement Lifecycle Stage

THE FOLLOWING ITIL INTERMEDIATE EXAM OBJECTIVES ARE DISCUSSED IN THIS CHAPTER:

✓ The main purpose and objective and scope of continual service improvement

✓ Continual service improvement's value to the business

✓ The approach to continual service improvement

✓ The business questions to be asked to ensure that a CSI initiative is warranted

✓ The context of continual service improvement in the service lifecycle

✓ The inputs and outputs to CSI

In this chapter, we cover the purpose, objectives, and scope of this lifecycle stage and the value it provides to the business. We look at the approach to CSI, and the business questions that should be asked prior to undertaking a CSI initiative. We also examine the context of continual service improvement in relation to the other service lifecycle stages of service strategy, service design, service transition, and service operation. Finally, we look at CSI inputs and outputs.

The learning objective for this chapter is to achieve a full understanding of continual service improvement terms and core concepts.

Understanding the Purpose, Objectives, and Scope of Continual Service Improvement

This chapter reiterates concepts first introduced during your ITIL Foundation course regarding continual service improvement. It introduces the core concepts and terminology of continual service improvement. CSI's main aim is to ensure that IT services remain aligned to changing business needs; it is about looking for ways to improve effectiveness and efficiency in all stages of the ITIL service lifecycle.

Purpose

The purpose of the CSI stage of the lifecycle is to support the business by ensuring that the IT services provided meet its requirements. In most companies, there are business drivers that cause changes in behavior to meet market forces. Organizations that do not respond to outside forces or recognize the need to change will usually not survive the rigors of the marketplace. IT services support business processes, and as the business processes change, the IT services must change also to ensure that they still support the business. It is the job of CSI to identify and implement these improvements to IT services. These improvements may occur anywhere in the lifecycle; CSI looks for improvements in service strategy, service design, service transition, and service operation. CSI constantly tries to identify opportunities to improve service-effectiveness, process-effectiveness, and cost-effectiveness.

Metrics

Effective CSI requires every process or service to have metrics built in; the measurements can then be analyzed to identify improvement. Take a moment to consider the following sayings about measurements and management:

- You cannot manage what you cannot control.

- You cannot control what you cannot measure.

- You cannot measure what you cannot define.

Do you agree with these statements? If you cannot define the desired output and measure whether it has been achieved, then you cannot identify whether improvements are required. If you implement improvements, you cannot tell whether they have made the situation better.

That is why it is critically important to understand what to measure, why it is being measured, and what the successful outcome should be.

Why do we need to be continually improving? Let's consider what the outcome would be if we did not implement this constant appraisal of our services and processes and the subsequent amendments identified as necessary.

Most of us have experienced the one-off improvement exercises, where considerable effort and expense has been invested to improve something, but there has been no attempt to keep the improvements up-to-date with changing requirements later. The improvements may work well at first, but over time, they become less effective as changes to business requirements make them irrelevant. There may even be times when these supposed improvements actually start to impede the business objectives.

Changing Requirements

Consider the example of an organization where poor change management has caused excessive downtime. As part of a one-off improvement, the project and change management processes were strengthened, with strict rules implemented regarding defined deliverables, extensive testing of changes, and backing out of changes that do not work exactly as planned. This had an immediate benefit, with downtime as a result of changes reduced significantly.

Over the following couple of years, the business requirements changed rapidly, with a new emphasis on speed to market. What was now required from the IT service provider was a more agile approach to development and change management. Using agile methods enables an incremental and iterative approach with designers being free to respond to changes in requirements as they arise and make changes as the project progresses.

The IT service provider was no longer providing what the business required and in fact was actually preventing the business objectives from being achieved by slowing delivery of software enhancements that supported them. The service provider mistakenly thought that it had "fixed" project and change management and no further action was required. A CSI approach would have prevented this because it recognizes that the correct solution at one point may no longer be the optimum approach later, as circumstances change.

Objectives

Let's now look at the objectives for CSI. To achieve the purpose for this lifecycle stage, the *ITIL Continual Service Improvement* publication provides the following objectives:

- Review, analyze, prioritize, and recommend improvement opportunities in each lifecycle stage: service strategy, service design, service transition, and service operation as well as CSI. Regular activity of this type will move the improvement efforts from an ad hoc approach to a genuine improvement initiative.

- Review and analyze service level achievements according to the service level agreements in place.

- Identify and implement specific activities to improve IT service quality, including improvements to the effectiveness and efficiency of the enabling processes. The overall service quality is partially dependent on the quality of the processes. It can be tempting for IT services to assume that the only metrics that matter are those relating to the technology.

- Improve the cost-effectiveness of IT service delivery without negatively impacting customer satisfaction. Customer satisfaction is an important measure of the value of the service being delivered.

- Ensure that suitable and applicable quality management methods are in use to support the continual service improvement activities. The quality management methods in use should support the overall quality governance in place in the organization.

- Ensure that the processes in use have clearly defined objectives and measurements that produce identifiable and actionable improvements. This should be part of the controls around the processes in use throughout the service lifecycle.

- Understand what to measure, why it is being measured, and what the successful outcome should be. Recognizing exactly what is required will enable a better interpretation of the metrics and the behaviors they will drive.

Scope

There are four main areas that CSI needs to address. First is the overall health of IT service management (ITSM) as a discipline, and second is the continual alignment of the service portfolio with the current and future business needs. CSI will work with service strategy to ensure that the service portfolio remains relevant to the changing business requirements. Next it needs to consider the maturity and capability of the organization, management, processes, and people utilized by the services; where necessary, CSI will suggest and implement process improvements to ensure that the processes continue to deliver effectively and efficiently. Finally, it attempts to improve all aspects of the IT service and the service assets that support them.

It is CSI's responsibility to ensure that the ITSM processes continue to be followed after the initial novelty wears off—and despite day-to-day pressures. It is only by understanding how the improvements are to be carried out, and what the desired outcomes are, that you can deliver continual service improvement. The activities that support improvement are as follows:

- Reviewing the service performance targets and trends, using the available management information, to understand if the desired service levels are being met

- Reviewing process outputs to understand if the required performance is being achieved to enable the services

- Regularly carrying out maturity assessments on the processes in use to identify areas of concern or demonstrate improvement achievements

- Conducting compliance audits on the processes, ensuring that maturity is maintained

- Identifying and making proposals for improvements

- Conducting customer satisfaction surveys as required on a periodic basis

- Reviewing and understanding business trends and projections and maintaining awareness of business priorities

- Measuring and identifying the value created by continual service improvement initiatives

These activities will require ownership to ensure that they actually get done. Improvement activities should be planned and be part of a considered approach, managed by individuals who have appropriate authority to carry them out. It is important to make sure the processes and services are subject to a continual improvement strategy. This strategy should ensure that the improvement initiatives are achieving their targets and being kept up-to-date. Specific improvements that require changes should follow the change management process. It is easy for improvement programs to fade, so it is necessary for these activities to be monitored as part of the overall continual service improvement approach.

Value

The adoption of standard and consistent approaches to improving IT service quality will result in controlled, gradual, and maintainable improvement. Any improvements must, naturally, be cost-justified in terms of the return on the investment or, more appropriately, on the value of the investment.

When regular reviews of the business needs are employed and IT services remain aligned to them, the business can be assured of an acceptable level of support. Because IT services may be said to underpin the success of the majority of organizations, this assurance is critical for business confidence.

One of the key aspects of any improvement is cost, but it is not only the cost justification for the initiative; it is also the benefit that can be achieved in terms of cost. An improvement may be able to create cost savings in real terms or increase capability for additional workload. Because one of the most common themes of budget negotiations is the requirement to achieve more for the same or less than the previous year, this is a genuine long-term goal for organizations. Utilizing the techniques and approaches of continual service improvement will allow for a gradual and sustained increase in capability because the effectiveness and efficiency of the processes and services are managed.

But it is not only the processes and the services they support that are under the scrutiny of continual service improvement. It looks at all elements that enable the delivery of services to the business. This will include all resources, partners, technology, staff skills, training, and communications. The emphasis on a holistic approach to improvement means that true business benefits can be achieved by delivering cost-effective enhancements across the wider enterprise. For example, renegotiating contracts with third-party suppliers may deliver an ongoing benefit to the business.

To achieve these benefits, it is necessary to ensure that monitoring and reporting on performance across the service portfolio allows for the identification of improvement opportunities.

The Approach to Continual Service Improvement

As we have already stated, the ITIL guidance places a strong emphasis on the need for a continual approach to service improvement rather than doing this once and then never again. The process for improvement should be applied to all services and all processes throughout the service lifecycle. Improvements may not be simply achieving a higher level of service; it may also be the achievement of a reduction in cost for the same level of service. If the approach is adopted correctly, then the identification of improvement opportunities should become part of business-as-usual activities. There are many opportunities for CSI, and these opportunities should result in a constant cycle of improvement. The improvement sequence shown in Figure 43.1 is known as the CSI approach; it can be summarized in six stages. We are going to examine these one by one in the following sections.

FIGURE 43.1   Continual service improvement approach

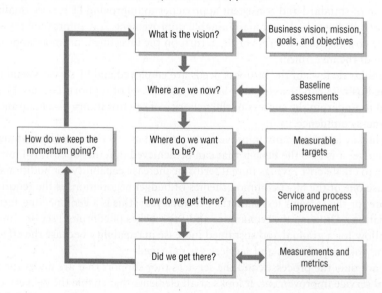

Stage 1: What Is the Vision?

There are key questions that need to be asked as part of implementing improvements. These are all covered by the continual service improvement approach. The first stage is to identify the vision that is driving the improvement initiative. Understanding the high-level focus of the business will allow for the alignment of the IT services and the business strategies. The IT service provider's vision must support the business vision, so this step is actually identifying the business vision and the IT vision that supports it.

Stage 2: Where Are We Now?

Stage 2 of the CSI approach is to assess the current situation to obtain an accurate, unbiased snapshot of where the organization is right now. This initial baseline assessment is essential; without it, we have no way of knowing whether we have been successful because we will have nothing to compare our postimprovement results with. If you have ever joined a gym to get fit, you know that the first action is to assess your current fitness level. This is documented, and another assessment is done after a few months to determine how much your fitness level has improved. This baseline assessment is an analysis of the current position in terms of the business, organization, people, processes, and technology. To ensure that the baseline is objective, external consultants may be used.

Stage 3: Where Do We Want to Be?

Stage 3 of the CSI approach is to decide where we want to be. Although we have already identified a vision, it is likely to be a high-level vision. By answering this question following the assessment of where the organization is currently, we are able to set measurable targets that will show an improvement on the results of the assessment. The full vision may be years away, but this step provides specific goals and a manageable time frame. So, our vision may be to provide extremely reliable services for all our customers, the assessment will show the services with the worst availability performance, and the targets set in this step would state explicitly the percentage of improvement in availability we must achieve for specific services across a defined time period. It is important that the targets set are challenging but achievable; setting targets that no one feels they have a chance of meeting will mean that CSI loses credibility and support. Remember also that these improvements take place alongside the provision of the usual service, so the amount of time and effort needed must be realistic.

Stage 4: How Do We Get There?

Stage 4 of the CSI approach is to define the steps to be taken to achieve the improvement targets we have defined. These steps will include improvements in service management processes and in the services provided. Other improvement actions may involve training staff and improving communication.

Stage 5: Did We Get There?

Stage 5 of the CSI approach assesses the success of the actions taken, asking, Did we get there? The results are compared with the original baseline taken in stage 2, and the extent of the improvement is compared with the target that was set in stage 3. We need to ensure that staff are complying with any new process requirements.

Stage 6: How Do We Keep the Momentum Going?

Finally, the process should ensure that the momentum for quality improvement is maintained and that changes become embedded in the organization. This stage involves ensuring that the improvement actions become the new business-as-usual way to operate. Because improvement must be continual, we also consider what actions should be taken next: Can we set new targets to move us closer to achieving the vision? Has the vision changed? What is the priority area for action? And so on.

The Business Questions to Ask to Ensure That a CSI Initiative Is Warranted

Next we consider the inputs into CSI received from the business. This business input is critically important because the purpose of CSI, as we have already discussed, is to ensure alignment between the business and IT. The business has a key role to play in setting priorities for CSI and participating in discussions on what improvement initiatives make sense and add the greatest value back to the business.

Using the CSI Approach

To help the business decide whether to support a CSI initiative, we would ask the same questions we asked in the CSI approach, except the emphasis would be placed on the business perspective.

What Is the Vision?   The IT service provider needs to understand the business vision and its long-term business aims. Often the business does not realize the importance of sharing its vision with IT.

Where Are We Now?   We need to establish an agreed objective baseline of data for services currently being delivered.

Where Do We Want to Be?   This is often expressed as business requirements.

How Do We Get There?   What actions should be taken to achieve the desired end result? These improvement initiatives will often include a mix of short-, medium-, and long-term plans. They should be logged in the CSI register.

Did We Get There?   This is assessed by reviewing service level achievements and performance against targets identified by the business requirements.

Proactive Improvement

Adopting an approach of continual service improvement does not mean that we have to wait for failures and then fix them through improvement initiatives. CSI does not need to wait until a service is operational to identify improvement opportunities. CSI is relevant for all lifecycle stages, so lessons learned from previous experience may lead to improvements in design or in planning and implementing a release. In this way, even new services can benefit from CSI, enabling the new services to avoid the same issues that have affected other services. CSI can therefore proactively prevent the potential flaws in new services.

The Context of Continual Service Improvement in the Service Lifecycle

In the remainder of this chapter, we shall look at continual service improvement and its relationships with the other lifecycle stages of service strategy, service design, service transition, and service operation. We shall also consider the inputs and outputs for this lifecycle stage.

Continual service improvement needs to be considered within the context of the whole service lifecycle. Each area of the lifecycle addresses a particular set of challenges that need to be addressed for successful service management, and each stage has an impact on all of the others. For CSI to be successful, it must provide improvement opportunities throughout the entire service lifecycle. Concentrating improvements on the service operation stage of the lifecycle may just treat a symptom of a problem instead of treating the problem itself. The cause may be in the service strategy, design, or transition stage of the service lifecycle.

There is much greater value to the business when service improvement takes a holistic approach throughout the entire lifecycle. The service portfolio is the "spine" that connects the lifecycle stages to each other. Figure 43.2 shows how the stages of the lifecycle work together as an integrated system to support the ultimate objective of service management for business value realization. All of the stages are interdependent. Let's look at how CSI interfaces with each one in turn, starting with strategy.

FIGURE 43.2   Integration across the service lifecycle

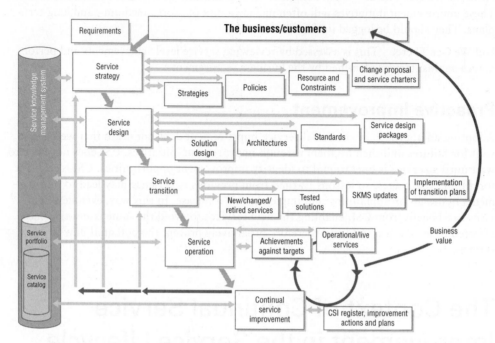

Service Strategy

Service strategy focuses on setting a strategic approach to service management as well as defining standards and policies that will be used to design IT services. It is at this stage of the lifecycle that standards and policies are determined around measuring and reporting for an enterprise-wide view of the organization, possibly utilizing a tool such as a balanced scorecard.

Service improvement opportunities could be driven by external factors such as new security or regulatory requirements, new strategies due to mergers or acquisitions, changes in technology infrastructure, or even new business services to be introduced. Feedback from the other core stages of the service lifecycle will also be important.

Service Design

Service design creates or modifies services and infrastructures that are aligned to the business needs. Design ensures that a customer-centric viewpoint is used throughout. It takes the strategy described in the first stage and transforms it through the design stage into deliverable IT services.

Service design is responsible for designing a management information framework that defines the need for critical success factors (CSF), key performance indicators (KPIs), and activity metrics for both the services and the ITSM processes.

New strategies, architecture, policies, and business requirements will drive the need for continual improvement within service design. Service design will also ensure that the success of improvements can be measured.

Service Transition

Service transition manages the transition of new or changed services into the production environment. Change and configuration management play major roles at this point in the lifecycle. This stage focuses on the best practices of creating support models and a knowledge base, managing workflow, and developing communication and marketing for use in the transitioning of services to production. As new strategies and designs are introduced, this provides an excellent opportunity for continual improvement.

Service transition is also responsible for defining the actual CSFs, KPIs, and activity metrics; creating the reports; and implementing the required automation to monitor and report on the services and ITSM processes.

Service Operation

Service operation provides best practice advice and guidance on all aspects of managing the day-to-day operation of an organization's IT services. Service operation is responsible for the monitoring and initial reporting related to the people, processes, and infrastructure technology necessary to ensure a high-quality, cost-effective provision of IT services that meet the business needs. Every technology component and process activity should have defined inputs and outputs that can be monitored. The results of the monitoring can then be compared against the norms, targets, or established service level agreements. When there is a discrepancy between what was actually delivered and what was expected, this becomes a service improvement opportunity.

Within the service operation stage of the lifecycle, internal reviews are performed to examine the results of the monitoring activity, what led to these results, and if necessary, recommendations for some level of fine-tuning.

Improvement throughout the Lifecycle

An organization can find improvement opportunities throughout the entire service lifecycle. There is no need to wait until a service or service management process is transitioned into the operations area to begin identifying improvement opportunities. Each lifecycle stage will provide an output to the next lifecycle stage. This same concept applies to CSI.

Figure 43.3 shows the interaction that should take place between each lifecycle stage. Take a moment to study it.

FIGURE 43.3   Continual service improvement and the service lifecycle

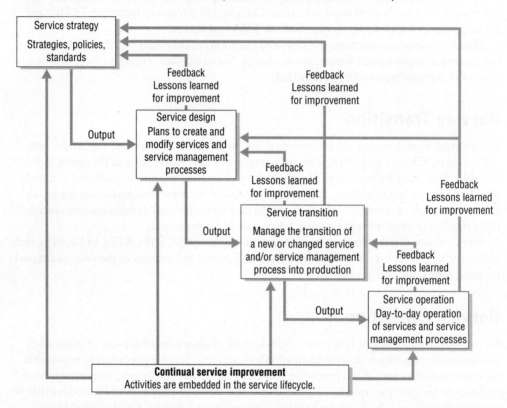

CSI Inputs and Outputs

We'll finish this chapter by considering the inputs to and outputs from CSI.

Service Strategy

We'll start by looking at the inputs from service strategy into CSI; these include the strategic vision and mission, policies, and plans. The service portfolio is another input into CSI. One possible improvement activity is to try and identify possible gaps in the services provided or services that are no longer required. The strategic priorities are an important input because the improvement initiatives suggested should be in line with them.

CSI can use financial information and budgets to see how money is currently being spent; possible areas for cost savings may be identified as a result. CSI can understand the current situation by studying the patterns of business activity and examining how current performance matches the KPIs and CSFs. Any improvement opportunities identified are logged in the CSI register.

CSI outputs to strategy would include the results of customer and user satisfaction surveys from business relationship management, feedback on strategies and policies, and input to business cases and the service portfolio. Financial information regarding improvement initiatives would be an essential output because they would form an input to budgets. Other outputs would be the data required for metrics, KPIs and CSFs, service reports, and requests for change (RFCs) for implementing improvements.

Service Design

CSI inputs from design include the service catalog and the service design packages with their details of utility and warranty. Other inputs into CSI are the knowledge and information contained in the SKMS. This information records the detailed design, measurements, processes, infrastructure, and supporting systems for each service. Service design is also responsible for the design for the seven-step improvement process and procedures. A key input is the record of achievements against metrics, KPIs, and CSFs because it will often highlight improvement opportunities. As with the other lifecycle stages, all improvement opportunities are logged in the CSI register.

CSI outputs to design would be the results of customer and user satisfaction surveys; input to design requirements; the data required for metrics, KPIs, and CSFs; and service reports. Another possible output would be any feedback on service design packages. Any possible improvement opportunities would also mean CSI would raise RFCs for implementing them.

Service Transition

CSI inputs from transition would be the reports from testing—a failed test may be an improvement opportunity. Change evaluation reports would highlight any improvements needed if a change did not result in all the desired benefits. The knowledge and information in the SKMS would be useful to CSI, and the performance measurements showing whether service level targets, KPIs, and CSFs have been achieved would show possible improvement opportunities to be logged in the CSI register.

CSI outputs to service transition would be the results of customer and user satisfaction surveys; input to testing requirements; and data required for metrics, KPIs, and CSFs. CSI may also provide input to change evaluation and change advisory board meetings and service reports. CSI would raise the RFCs for implementing improvements.

Service Operation

Finally, let's look at the inputs and outputs for CSI and service operation. The inputs to CSI would include operational performance data and service records (which would highlight weak areas), proposed problem resolutions and proactive measures (which would be improvement opportunities), the knowledge and information in the SKMS, and the achievements against metrics, KPIs, and CSFs. As with every other area, any improvement opportunities would be logged in the CSI register.

The CSI outputs to operation would be the results of customer and user satisfaction surveys; service reports and dashboards; the data required for metrics, KPIs, and CSFs; and the RFCs for implementing improvements.

Starting Improvement

At this point you may have concluded that all aspects of CSI must be in place before measurements and data gathering can begin. Nothing could be further from the truth. Improvement can start at any time. Although good data helps guide improvement, any data that can be gathered can form the starting point. Improving the information available can be one of the first CSI opportunities to be implemented. So don't wait until everything is in place because you will have missed opportunities that could have been followed up.

Summary

In this chapter, we looked at the purpose, objectives, and scope of continual service improvement and its value to the business. We also examined the CSI approach and the business questions to ask when evaluating a potential area for continual service improvement. Finally, we considered the context of CSI in relation to the other lifecycle stages of service strategy, service design, service transition, and service operation and the inputs and outputs to the CSI stage.

Exam Essentials

Understand the purpose of the continual service improvement stage of the lifecycle.   It is important to remember that the purpose of the CSI lifecycle stage is to maintain IT services in alignment with changing business needs, not simply to meet service targets.

Understand that CSI is not restricted to operational delivery.   Remember that the objectives and scope of CSI cover the whole of the service lifecycle, for both services and processes.

Understand that CSI is not about single initiatives but is a continual process.   Identifying improvement opportunities, large and small, and implementing the improvements should be a managed activity, carried out on a regular basis.

Be able to list and explain the stages of the CSI approach.   You need to remember the stages of the CSI approach and the questions that are asked at each stage.

Be able to explain the importance of measurement to CSI.   Understand the need for a baseline and for measurements to assess their success after the improvement actions have been carried out. Also, understand the need for longer-term measurements such as SLA reporting to identify downward trends, which would show a need for improvement.

Review Questions

You can find the answers to the review questions in the appendix.

1. Which of the following best describes the main aim of CSI?
    A. To ensure that IT services are delivered at minimum cost
    B. To ensure that IT services remain aligned to changing business needs
    C. To ensure that IT services are delivered at maximum quality
    D. To ensure that all improvement opportunities are identified and implemented

2. Which of the following statements is incorrect?
    A. You cannot manage what you cannot control.
    B. You cannot control what you cannot measure.
    C. You cannot measure what you cannot define.
    D. You cannot define what you cannot control.

3. Which areas of the service lifecycle are subject to CSI?
    A. Service design, service transition, service operation only
    B. Service strategy, service design, service transition, service operation only
    C. Service strategy, service design, service transition, service operation, and CSI
    D. Service design, service transition, service operation, and CSI only

4. Which of the following are the inputs into the "Where are we now?" step of the CSI approach?
    A. Business vision, mission, goals, and objectives
    B. Measurements and metrics
    C. Baseline assessments
    D. Service and process improvements

5. Which of these statements is/are correct about the purpose of the continual service improvement lifecycle stage?
    1. The purpose of CSI is to continue to support the business with IT services in the face of changing business needs.
    2. The purpose of CSI is to define the strategic approach for service management across the whole of the lifecycle.
        A. 1 only
        B. 2 only
        C. Both
        D. Neither

6. Which of these statements represents an objective of the continual service improvement lifecycle stage?

   A. Ensure that the changes to the services deliver the anticipated and required business value.

   B. Identify and implement specific activities to improve IT service quality.

   C. Identify the services and the customers who use them.

   D. Set the expectations for the performance and use of the new or modified services.

7. The *ITIL Continual Service Management* publication provides guidance in four main areas. Which of these is not one of the four areas?

   A. Continual alignment of the IT services with the current and future needs of the business

   B. The maturity and capability of the organization, management, processes, and people utilized by the services

   C. The development of a strategy that supports business organization improvements

   D. Continual improvement of all aspects of the IT service and the service assets that support them

8. What is the purpose of the continual service improvement (CSI) stage of the service lifecycle?

   A. The CSI stage is concerned with the management of improvement across the whole service lifecycle.

   B. The CSI stage considers only the improvements needed for the business outputs.

   C. The CSI stage focuses on improving the operational processes in the service lifecycle.

   D. The CSI stage manages the improvements between project management and live operational services.

9. What is the continual service improvement (CSI) approach?

   A. The CSI approach is used to manage processes in the operational environment.

   B. The CSI approach is focused on the delivery of quality management systems into IT.

   C. The CSI approach is used to manage improvement activity in line with business requirements.

   D. The CSI approach is focused on the introduction of projects into the operational environment.

10. Which of the following is NOT a valid reason for implementing CSI?

   A. To deliver a higher level of service to internal or external customers

   B. To be able to increase the charge for services provided

   C. To provide the same level of service but increase the profit margin on the provision of a service to external customers

   D. To reduce the time taken to carry out a process

Chapter

44

Continual Service Improvement Principles

THE FOLLOWING ITIL INTERMEDIATE EXAM OBJECTIVES ARE DISCUSSED IN THIS CHAPTER:

✓ CSI and organizational change

✓ Ownership

✓ CSI register

✓ External and internal drivers

✓ Service level management

✓ Knowledge management

✓ The Deming Cycle

✓ Service measurement

✓ IT governance

✓ Frameworks, models, standards, and quality systems

In this chapter, we explore how the principles of continual service improvement are adopted throughout the lifecycle. We review some specific relationships with continual service improvement and other lifecycle processes, and the relationship of continual service improvement with the Deming Cycle. We conclude the chapter by reviewing the role of continual service improvement and governance, and the use of standards and frameworks.

CSI and Organizational Change

In this chapter, we consider CSI principles and how the success of CSI depends upon an understanding of organizational changes, establishing clear accountability, and the influence of service level management.

Although service level management is a service design process, it has a close relationship with CSI, so it is necessary to understand the important elements of service level management.

This chapter also introduces tools such as the Deming Cycle (covered as part of the Foundation syllabus) and service measurement as used in conjunction with knowledge management and frameworks, models, standards, and quality systems to provide adequate governance.

Because service management is about how the staff of an IT service provider works to deliver the service, any improvements are likely to challenge current working practices. Staff may feel defensive and see the improvement initiative as a criticism of their work—if the change is to succeed, winning their support is essential. Many improvement initiatives fail to achieve lasting benefits because they have ignored this aspect of change.

Formal project management will help clarify the goals and measure success against them. Addressing the "soft" issues of staff resistance to change is essential. This should include looking at approaches to organizational change such as Dr. John P. Kotter's eight steps to transform your organization, which identifies and addresses common reasons for failure.

Ownership

To ensure that CSI retains the focus required, a manager should be appointed with specific responsibility for continual service improvement. Fundamental to CSI success is a manager who has ownership of the process. If there is no single point of ownership, improvements may be dropped due to pressure of other work. The CSI manager becomes the CSI owner and chief advocate. Their responsibilities include selling the benefits to the staff and maintaining focus on improvement. They must also ensure that there are sufficient resources and adequate tools. They are responsible for the ongoing CSI activities, such as monitoring, analyzing, and evaluating trends, and reporting as well as project-based service improvement.

CSI Register

Several initiatives or possibilities for improvement are likely to be identified. ITIL recommends keeping a CSI register to record all the improvement opportunities and ensure that they are categorized and tracked.

Each entry in the CSI register should be categorized as a small, medium, or large undertaking, and an assessment should be made as to whether they are "quick wins" or medium- or long-term improvements.

The projected benefits should be clearly stated, and this information will enable the suggested improvements to be prioritized. There is a danger that lower-priority improvements will never be addressed, so a system whereby the priority level is increased over time will ensure that these improvements reach the "top of the pile." Benefits should be assessed in terms of aspirational key performance indicator (KPI) metrics to ensure that priorities are based on the resulting business benefit.

The CSI register helps to ensure that all improvements are properly recorded, assessed, and tracked consistently. The benefits of improvements are also measured and captured here. It provides a coordinated, consistent view of the potentially many improvement activities. It is important to define the interface from the CSI register of initiatives with strategic initiatives and with processes such as problem management, capacity management, change management, and service level management. In particular, the service review meeting is likely to result in a number of requirements for improvement.

The CSI manager should have accountability and responsibility for the production and maintenance of the CSI register.

External and Internal Drivers

There are two major areas within every organization driving improvement: The first area includes aspects that are external to the organization, such as regulation, legislation, competition, external customer requirements, market pressures, and economics. The second area includes aspects that are internal to the organization, such as organizational structures, culture, new knowledge, new technologies, new skills, existing and projected staffing levels, and union rules.

In some cases these aspects may serve to hinder improvement rather than drive it forward. A SWOT analysis (examining strengths, weaknesses, opportunities, and threats) may be helpful in illuminating significant opportunities for improvement. The strengths and weaknesses focus on the internal aspects of the organization, while the opportunities and threats focus on aspects external to the organization.

Service Level Management

Adopting the service level management (SLM) process is a key principle of CSI. SLM is no longer optional because business demands that IT be driven by service requirements and outcomes. IT must become a trusted partner of the business because it is a core enabler of every critical business process.

SLM involves a number of steps to ensure that IT behaves as a provider of service. They will work with the business to identify service level requirements and understand the internal relationships within IT and how the groups within IT combine to deliver the service, documenting the relationships with operational level agreements. They will also ensure that external providers deliver their component of the overall service and that the underpinning contracts deliver what the business needs.

SLM is also responsible for identifying opportunities for improvement and feeding them into CSI.

Knowledge Management

The *ITIL Service Transition* volume explains knowledge management in detail, but it plays a key role in CSI.

Within each service lifecycle stage, data should be captured to enable knowledge gain and an understanding of what is actually happening, thus enabling wisdom. This is often referred to as the data, information, knowledge, wisdom (DIKW) structure. Gathering the data without a plan to analyze it is a common mistake. It is important to work through the steps of DIKW to achieve wisdom, which will lead to better decisions around improvement. This is shown in Figure 44.1.

FIGURE 44.1   Knowledge management leads to better IT decisions.

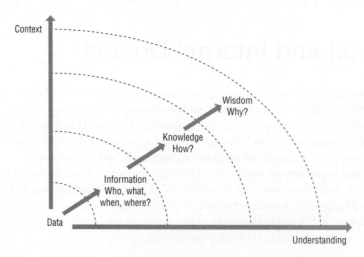

Data capture alone is not enough. The development of wisdom will lead to new approaches and methods and improvement. This applies both when looking at the IT services themselves and when drilling down into each individual IT process. Knowledge management is a mainstay of any improvement process.

The Deming Cycle

The Deming Cycle is covered in the Foundation syllabus. W. Edwards Deming advised large companies on quality improvement, and his advice has relevance for service management, especially CSI.

Deming's approach to quality improvement was encapsulated in the Deming Cycle, which translates very well to CSI. The four key stages of the cycle are Plan-Do-Check-Act (PDCA), after which a phase of consolidation prevents the improvement from slipping back to its original state.

The goal in using the Deming Cycle is steady, ongoing improvement. It is a fundamental tenet of CSI.

The PDCA cycle is critical at two points in CSI: implementation of CSI, when all four stages of the PDCA cycle are used, and for ongoing improvements, when CSI uses the check and act stages to monitor, measure, review, and implement initiatives.

The seven-step improvement process is covered later in more detail in Chapter 45, "The Seven-Step Continual Service Improvement Process." The seven-step continual service improvement process is an example of an implementation of the PDCA cycle, with each of the steps falling within one of the phases of the cycle: Plan, Do, Check, Act.

The cycle requires a process-led approach to management, where defined processes are in place, the activities are measured for compliance to expected values, and outputs are audited to validate and improve the process.

The PDCA cycle is a fundamental part of many quality standards, including ISO/IEC 20000.

Service Measurement

An important aspect of all CSI activity is the ability to measure. This can be achieved in a variety of ways, but it should always start with a baseline.

Baselines

Baselines must be established at the start of an improvement initiative. They act as markers or starting points for later comparison. They will also show if improvement is actually required because they will highlight which areas are failing to meet targets.

It is important that baselines are documented, recognized, and accepted throughout the organization. Baselines must be established at each level: strategic goals and objectives, tactical process maturity, and operational metrics and KPIs.

If a baseline is not initially established, the first measurement efforts will become the baseline. That is why it is essential to collect data at the outset, even if the integrity of the data is in question. It is better to have data to question than to have no data at all.

Why Do We Measure?

Basically, there are four reasons to monitor and measure:

- To validate—monitoring and measuring to validate previous decisions.

- To direct—monitoring and measuring to set direction for activities in order to meet set targets. It is the most prevalent reason for monitoring and measuring.

- To justify—monitoring and measuring to justify, with factual evidence or proof, that a course of action is required.

- To intervene—monitoring and measuring to identify a point of intervention, including subsequent changes and corrective actions.

The four basic reasons to monitor and measure lead to three key questions: Why are we monitoring and measuring? When do we stop? and Is anyone using the data? To answer these questions, it is important to identify which of the reasons is driving the measurement effort. Too often, we continue to measure long after the need has passed. Every time you produce a report, you should ask, Do we still need this?

Each organization should evaluate its own requirements and amend the register to suit its own purposes.

The Seven-Step Improvement Process

Fundamental to CSI is the concept of measurement. CSI uses the seven-step improvement process.

Which Steps Support CSI?

It is obvious that all the activities of the improvement process will assist CSI in some way. It is relatively simple to identify what takes places, but the difficulty lies in understanding exactly how it will happen. The improvement process spans not only the management organization, but also the entire service lifecycle. This is a cornerstone of CSI.

The seven-step improvement process shows the approach to measurement and how this relates to the PDCA cycle. The process is covered in detail in the next chapter, but this is a brief outline of each step.

Step 1: Identify the Strategy for Improvement

Identify the overall vision, the business need, the strategy, and the tactical and operational goals.

Step 2: Define What You Will Measure

Service strategy and service design should have identified this information early in the life-cycle. CSI can then start its cycle all over again at "Where are we now?" and "Where do we want to be?" This identifies the ideal situation for both the business and IT. CSI can conduct a gap analysis to identify the opportunities for improvement as well as answering the "How do we get there?" question.

Step 3: Gather the Data

To properly answer the "Did we get there?" question, you must first gather data (usually through service operation). Data is gathered based on identified goals and objectives. At this point, the data is raw and no conclusions are drawn.

Step 4: Process the Data

Here the data is processed in alignment with the specified CSFs and KPIs. This means that time frames are coordinated, unaligned data is rationalized and made consistent, and gaps in data are identified. The simple goal of this step is to process data from multiple disparate sources into an "apples to apples" comparison, which is turning the data into information. Once you have rationalized the data, you can begin analysis.

Step 5: Analyze the Information and Data

Here the data and information are analyzed to identify service gaps, trends, and the impact on business. It is the analyzing step that is most often overlooked or forgotten in the rush to present data to management.

Step 6: Present and Use the Information

Here the answer to "Did we get there?" is formatted and communicated in whatever way is necessary to present to the various stakeholders an accurate picture of the results of the improvement efforts. Knowledge is presented to the business in a form and manner that reflects its needs and assists in determining the next steps.

Step 7: Implement Improvement

The knowledge gained is used to optimize, improve, and correct services and processes. Issues have been identified and now solutions are implemented—wisdom is applied to the knowledge. The improvements that need to be made to improve the service or process are explained to the organization. Following this step, the organization establishes a new baseline and the cycle begins anew.

While these seven steps of measurement appear to form a circular set of activities, in fact, they constitute a knowledge spiral (see Figure 44.2).

FIGURE 44.2   Knowledge spiral—a gathering activity

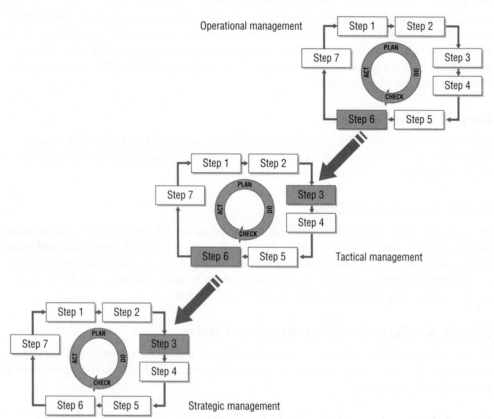

In actual practice, knowledge gathered and wisdom derived from that knowledge at one level of the organization becomes a data input to the next.

Governance

With the exposure of high-level corporate fraud in the early years of this century, IT was thrust into a new area of governance and is now subject to stricter legislative controls than in the past. An ever-increasing number of external regulations and external auditors are commonplace in large IT organizations.

IT can no longer mask its operations behind a veil of secrecy. It must run an organization that prides itself on its transparency.

Enterprise Governance

Enterprise governance is an emerging term to describe a framework that covers both the corporate governance and the business management aspects of the organization. In Figure 44.3, you can see the relationships that make up the view of enterprise governance.

FIGURE 44.3   Enterprise governance (source: CIMA)

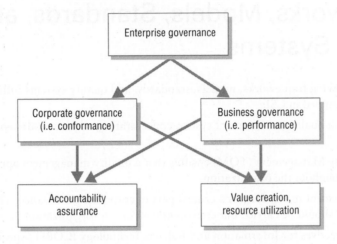

Achieving good corporate governance that is linked strategically with performance metrics will enable companies to focus all their energies on the key drivers that move their business forward.

This is a significant challenge as well as an opportunity. Much work has been carried out recently on corporate governance. The Chartered Institute of Management Accountants (CIMA) states that enterprise governance considers the whole picture to ensure that strategic goals are aligned and good management is achieved.

IT Governance

IT governance touches nearly every area detailed in Figure 44.3. On one hand, IT must now comply with new rules and legislation and continually demonstrate its compliance through successful independent audits by external organizations. On the other hand, IT is increasingly being called upon to do more with less and create additional value while maximizing the use of existing resources.

The corporate structure should support the adoption of governance from the director level down. It is important that this is driven from the top down because legislation often requires additional effort and spending over and above that which is required for standard operational activity.

Evidence must be provided to support the audit requirements, but there will still be a pressure for IT to deliver more, within boundaries of cost constraints. CSI should assist IT to improve effectiveness and efficiency, and there are some supporting standards and frameworks that complement these approaches.

Frameworks, Models, Standards, and Quality Systems

Each of the following frameworks, models, standards, and quality systems fully supports the concepts embodied in CSI:

- ISO 9000 is a quality management system concentrating on process-driven approaches to quality.

- Total Quality Management (TQM) ensures that a quality management approach is adopted throughout the organization.

- Risk management in any form is a crucial part of corporate governance. The management or risk should be carried out consistently across the organization.

- Control Objectives for Information and Related Technology (COBIT) specifically looks at the controls required to deliver service effectively.

- ISO/IEC 20000 and other ISO standards for IT are applicable to the delivery of IT services. ISO/IEC 20000 is the global international standard for service management delivery.

- ISO 14001 is the environmental management standard.

- Program and project management, including PRINCE 2 which is used to provide governance for projects.

- Skills Framework for the Information Age (SFIA) identifies the skills and capabilities for specific roles in service management.

- Capability Maturity Model Integration (CMMI) identifies the levels of maturity in processes and has been adapted for use in IT process assessment.

- ISO/IEC 27001 is the standard for information security management systems.

Which One Should I Choose?

Experience has shown that while each standard and framework in the preceding section may be complete in itself, none provides a total answer for IT management. In fact, there is a good deal of overlap between them, but for the most part, they are not competitive or exclusive but instead are complementary. Many organizations use a combination to manage and improve IT more effectively.

ISO/IEC 20000 (the IT service management standard) is most closely aligned with ITIL and is specifically aimed at IT service providers.

ISACA, in conjunction with the Office of Government Commerce (OGC), created a briefing paper titled "Aligning COBIT, ITIL and ISO17799 for Business Benefit." Other organizations have combined ITIL, CMMI, and Six Sigma as their formula for success.

Some organizations are unclear about which framework, model, standard, or quality system to choose, not wishing to go down the wrong path. It is important to realize that the decision is not "Which one should I choose?" but rather "What should I improve first?"

The greatest value from an effective CSI practice will be achieved by having a continuous monitoring and feedback loop as the service and ITSM processes move through the service lifecycle. It is important to look for improvement opportunities within service strategy, service design, service transition, and service operation.

Continual improvement should be integrated into the day-to-day culture of the organization.

Summary

In this chapter, we reviewed the importance of CSI in the context of organizational change and explored the importance of ownership of CSI activities. Ownership of activities is supported by the CSI register and ensuring ownership of the register to prioritize the improvements according to business need.

Improvements are driven by both internal and external drivers and must be supported throughout the service lifecycle by all processes, but especially by service level management. Knowledge management is also key to the management of improvement.

The Deming Cycle can be used as a driver for continual improvement and constant revision to continue to meet organizational needs. This requires use of measurement techniques to identify a baseline.

Governance and other supporting service management frameworks, standards, and quality systems will drive and support CSI in an organization and should be used appropriately according to the needs of the business.

Exam Essentials

Understand the principles of CSI.   Be familiar with the concepts involved in the practice of continual service improvement.

Be able to explain the importance of ownership in CSI.   It is important to understand the importance of ownership of the process of CSI as well as the maintenance of the CSI register and how it's used for prioritization.

Understand and expand on the drivers for CSI. There are both internal and external drivers for CSI, and it is necessary to know what they are and be able to differentiate between them for the exam.

Be able to explain and expand on the importance of service management processes in CSI. CSI does not simply take place as an afterthought; it is integral to the service lifecycle. Some processes are particularly critical, and you should be able to expand on the engagement of CSI with service level management and knowledge management processes.

Understand the use of the Deming Cycle within CSI. Plan-Do-Check-Act are integral parts of the improvement cycle. You should be able to describe and explain how each stage is important.

Know each of the steps in the seven-step improvement process. The CSI syllabus covers this in detail, but you should be able to identify each step and its importance to improvement.

Be able to explain the importance of service measurement in CSI. Measurement is vital for the improvement process, and you should be able to explain its importance and identify key aspects such as the use of a baseline.

Understand and explain the use of governance, frameworks, standards, and quality systems. You should be familiar with the frameworks that support CSI and understand their application.

Review Questions

You can find the answers to the review questions in the appendix.

1. How many steps does Kotter's transformation program have?
    A. Eight
    B. Seven
    C. Four
    D. Five

2. Which of these statements about the CSI register is/are correct?
    1. The register captures small, medium, and large improvements.
    2. The register is used to assist in prioritizing improvements.
    3. The register is managed by the customers.
    4. The register is part of the SKMS.
    5. The register is duplicated and managed as a set of databases across multiple sites.
        A. All
        B. 1, 2, 3, and 4
        C. 1, 3, and 5
        D. 1, 2, and 4

3. Which of these are external drivers?
    1. Culture and organizational structure
    2. Regulation and legislation
    3. Economics
    4. New knowledge, skills, and technologies
    5. Competition and market pressures
    6. Union requirements
        A. 2, 3, and 5
        B. 1, 3, and 6
        C. 4, 5, and 6
        D. 1, 2, and 3

4. Which of these are reasons to measure?
    1. To validate
    2. To direct
    3. To justify
    4. To intervene
        A. 1, 2, and 3
        B. 1, 2, 3, and 4

    C. 1 and 4

    D. 2 and 4

5. The knowledge spiral connects three approaches in service management. Which is the correct combination?

    A. Service level, availability, capacity

    B. Technical, application, operation

    C. Strategic, tactical, operational

    D. Design, transition, operation

6. Which of these statements is/are correct?

    1. CSI should be integrated with all stages of the service lifecycle.

    2. It is incorrect to combine ITIL with any other standards or frameworks because they do not complement one another.

    A. Statement 1 only

    B. Statement 2 only

    C. Both

    D. Neither

7. What is the importance of taking a baseline?

    A. It provides a goal for the end of an improvement project.

    B. It captures the starting point as a benchmark for an improvement project.

    C. It demonstrates the customer's perspective.

    D. It is only used in an operational context and has no importance in CSI.

8. Which process is concerned with the management of information in support of CSI?

    A. Knowledge management

    B. Service level management

    C. Demand management

    D. Change management

9. What is the final step of the seven-step improvement process?

    A. Gather data.

    B. Define the strategy for improvement.

    C. Implement corrective action.

    D. Analyze the data.

10. True or False? Continual service improvement should be a fundamental part of organizational change.

    A. True

    B. False

Chapter

45

The Seven-Step Continual Service Improvement Process

THE FOLLOWING ITIL INTERMEDIATE EXAM OBJECTIVES ARE DISCUSSED IN THIS CHAPTER:

✓ The seven-step continual service improvement process is discussed in terms of its

- Purpose

- Objectives

- Scope

- Value

- Policies, principles, and basic concepts

- Process activities, methods, and techniques

- Triggers, inputs, outputs, and interfaces

- How other processes play key roles in the seven-step improvement process

The Seven-Step Improvement Process

This chapter covers the seven-step improvement process, including its activities, interfaces, and inputs and outputs. It also covers how CSI integrates with the other stages of the ITIL service lifecycle and how other processes support the different steps in the seven-step improvement process.

Purpose

The purpose of the seven-step improvement process is to define and manage the steps needed to successfully implement improvements. This includes the identification and definition of the measures and metrics; the actions required for the gathering, processing, and analyzing data; how the results will be presented; and finally, the management of the implementation of the improvement.

Objectives

The objectives are as follows:

- Identify improvement opportunities for services, processes, and tools.

- Deliver cost reductions in the provision of services while maintaining the levels of service and outcomes the business requires. It will be important to ensure that cost reductions do not have a negative impact on the quality of service.

- Identify what needs to be measured, analyzed, and reported to establish improvement opportunities.

- Continually align and realign IT service provision with the required business outcomes, and monitor to ensure that service achievements meet the current business requirements.

- Understand what to measure and why it is being measured, and define the successful outcome.

    One of the important considerations for improvement is that it should be cost-effective. If the cost of implementing the improvement is not significantly outweighed by the benefit that will be achieved, it must be carefully assessed to ensure that it is actually worth the financial outlay. This means that each improvement opportunity will require justification. In the case of a small-scale improvement, this will be a simple report, but in the instance of a more significant activity, a full business case will be needed.

Scope

The seven-step improvement process is not designed to be utilized in isolation and will be fully effective only if it is applied across all aspects of IT service provision, including technology, services, processes, organization, and partners.

The scope should include analysis of the performance and capabilities of all of these aspects, including an assessment of the maturity of the processes enabling each service. It will also include making the best use of the technology available and exploiting the benefits of any new technology where it is cost justifiable and provides a measureable business benefit. Also within the scope are the organizational structures and capabilities of personnel, ensuring that the roles and responsibilities are appropriately allocated with the necessary skills.

Value to the Business

The seven-step improvement process delivers business value by ensuring that the services provided are aligned to the business requirements. It continually assesses the current situation against business needs and identifies opportunities to improve service provision for customers; it then ensures that the improvements take place whenever they are justified. By doing this, the service provided is constantly realigned to fit the business. The value of the seven-step improvement process is that by monitoring and analyzing the delivery of services, it will ensure that the current and future business outcome requirements can be met.

Where third-party suppliers are used to deliver part of the service, the seven-step improvement process provides value to the business by assessing partners to ensure that they are still delivering the level of service required. If the level of service or the value for money delivered is not at a sufficient level, a service improvement plan will be implemented. If insufficient improvement results, the supplier will be replaced. This ensures that the business obtains value for money from its suppliers.

Policies, Principles, and Basic Concepts

Many of the policies that support the seven-step improvement process are also found as a part of other processes, such as service level management (SLM), availability management, and capacity management. Here are examples of some of these policies:

- Monitoring requirements must be defined and implemented.

- Data must be gathered and analyzed and its integrity checked on a consistent basis.

- Trend reporting must be provided on a consistent basis.

- Service level achievement reports must be provided on a consistent basis.

- Internal and external service reviews must be completed on a consistent basis (in this case, *internal* means within IT and *external* means with the business).

These policies, when implemented, will assist in effective CSI. They will overcome the issue of inconsistent reporting or reporting based on poor data. Without consistent, reliable reporting, it is impossible to obtain a good baseline, preventing any meaningful comparisons against the baseline.

Other policies might include stating that all services must have either clearly defined service levels or, failing that, service targets. These are necessary to ascertain if the service is not being provided to the level required and therefore if a service improvement plan is required.

Another policy could be to ensure that all service management processes have defined critical success factors (CSFs) and key performance indicators (KPIs) to determine if there are gaps between the expected outcome and the real outcome.

A possible policy might specify when the reporting against targets needs to be done. This ensures that reporting is not an ad hoc activity but happens on predefined dates, ensuring that a proper comparison of results can be undertaken. Most organizations review service achievement and service management process results on a monthly basis. New services should initially be reviewed more frequently as part of early life support. This ensures that issues are addressed quickly. As the "teething problems" are sorted out, the service should become more stable, allowing early life support and frequent reporting to be replaced by the standard support and standardized reporting periods.

Additional policies suggested by ITIL include those that ensure that the CSI process itself is effective. The first of these is a statement that all improvement initiatives must use the formal change management process. This will help to make the changes more effective because they will be considered by members of the CAB and their impact will be assessed. This will help to avoid any unintended consequences from such initiatives.

The next policy states that all functional groups within IT have a responsibility for CSI activities. Most organizations do not have a dedicated CSI group, and so this ensures that everyone has a responsibility to support CSI activities. In other words, rather than leaving initiatives to an improvement department, every member of staff should be looking for ways to improve the service. The final policy states that roles and responsibilities will be documented, communicated, and filled within IT. Understanding who does what, and ensuring that all staff members have this understanding, is essential for identifying when someone has neglected to fulfil one of their duties.

It is a good idea to use a consistent template when defining the CSI policies. It should include the policy statement, the reason for the policy, and a definition of the benefits of the policy. If you have difficulty defining the reason for and benefits of a policy, it may not be needed. If you cannot monitor compliance, then the value of the policy must be in doubt.

Let's now look at a couple of key principles underpinning CSI. First, service providers, in competition with other providers, need to continually compare themselves to their competitors. They need to ensure that their offerings are competitively priced, of course, but equally important is comparing the services themselves; they should be examined to ensure that they still provide business value, that they are being delivered efficiently, and crucially, that the service provider is taking advantage of new technologies to enhance the services provided.

A basic concept of CSI is that it is *continual*. Improvements that are triggered only when someone reports a problem are not part of CSI. Approaching improvements in this reactive way often simply stops the recurrence of a single failure. CSI should be more proactive and all-encompassing. CSI pays ongoing and consistent attention to monitoring, analyzing, and reporting results with an eye toward improvement. Improvements can be incremental in nature but may also sometimes require a huge commitment to implement a new service or meet new business requirements.

In this chapter we are looking at the seven steps of improvement process in detail; it is important to realize that all seven steps must be carried out, and in the correct sequence. Missing a step puts us at risk of failing to achieve real improvement.

CSI is often seen as a luxury. On the contrary, it is essential that it is fully embedded and applied to all areas. Adequate staffing and tools are required to support CSI activities. Often small improvements can build the credibility of the process and thus make obtaining the necessary resources easier in the future.

It is important that we understand the difference between what should be measured and what can be measured. Start small—don't expect to measure everything at once. Understand the organizational capability to gather and process the data. As CSI proves its value, better monitoring can be put in place. The analysis of the data is where the real value comes in. It is through the analysis that improvement opportunities can be identified. Without this, there is no real opportunity to truly improve services or service management processes. We need to plan how and when the data will be reported and used. The right sort of reporting is essential; reporting is partly a marketing activity. IT managers should focus and report on the value added to the organization in addition to reporting on issues and achievements. As with any communication, it is imperative that the target audience is considered when presenting the information. Information presented in an engaging way, in an easy-to-understand format that illustrates issues relevant to the audience, is far more likely to engage their attention and enlist their support for improvement.

Finally, as we have said, it is essential to remember that improvement opportunities exist throughout the entire service lifecycle. There is no need to wait until a service or service management process is transitioned into the operations area.

Process Activities, Methods, and Techniques

Each step of the improvement process is designed to assist in the activity of CSI. The process makes it reasonably simple to see what takes place; the challenge is to implement this process to achieve the benefits in the live environment. The seven-step improvement process spans the entire service lifecycle and is the driving force behind continual service improvement. Refer to Figure 45.1 as we discuss each step.

FIGURE 45.1 The seven-step improvement process

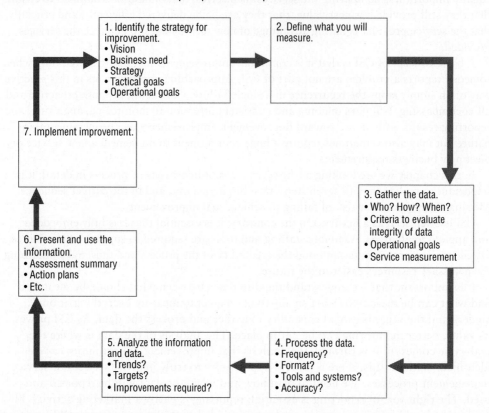

Step 1: Identify the Strategy for Improvement

In step 1, we identify the strategy for improvement. The questions we ask here are concerned with the establishment of the overall vision for the business. What are we attempting to achieve for the business? How can we support the overall business vision, objectives, and plans? What are the future plans for the business—short, medium, and long term? How do our IT services support these goals? This analysis will enable us to see where the business can best be aided by our efforts.

It will be necessary to review this step on a regular basis to ensure that we are continuing to align with the overall business objective. Meeting the requirements of the organization should be done by the best possible use of technology, delivering a cost-effective solution that enables the business processes at an appropriate level of cost and complexity.

Any initiative that is considered must be logged in the CSI register. If, after review of the business case or justification (through the change management process), it is rejected, the information can be archived so that we have a complete record of initiatives that have not been successful for later comparison.

Triggers and inputs for the improvement process are as follows:

- Business plans and strategy
- Service review meetings
- Vision and mission statements
- Corporate objectives
- Legislative requirements
- Governance requirements
- Customer satisfaction surveys
- CSI register

Step 2: Define What You Will Measure

This step is directly related to the goals that have been defined for measuring the services and service management processes to support the measurement and CSI activities.

In this step, it is necessary to define what you should measure, define and agree on what can actually be measured, and then carry out a gap analysis to finalize the actual improvement measurement plan.

In order to be effective, this step should focus on a few vital and meaningful measures that support qualitative and quantitative assessment of success. They should be usable and provide value to the improvement. IT is usually very capable of producing measures, but often the measures will deliver little value; too many measures will provide a confusing picture and will require rationalization.

Defining exactly what will be measured and the value that it will bring is an important early step. We need to ensure that we have the capability to capture the data and use the measurement. It should also be verified against the needs of the customer—it is not up to the IT department to decide what is of value.

The stages of the service lifecycle that support this step in the CSI process are service strategy and service design; we should have established the requirements for measurement in those stages. This step is complementary to the continual service management improvement approach, identifying how we will ascertain both "Where are we now?" and "Where do we want to be?" By using the gap analysis performed as part of this step, we are able to identify the requirements of the "How do we get there?" stage in the improvement approach.

This step has the following inputs:

- SLRs and targets
- Service review meeting
- Service portfolio and the service catalog
- Budget cycle
- Measurement results and reports (e.g., balanced scorecard)
- Customer satisfaction surveys
- Benchmark data

- Baseline data
- Risk assessments and risk mitigation plans

Step 3: Gather the Data

Gathering the data requires having monitoring in place. It is important to remember that for CSI data capture, we are less concerned with real-time monitoring and more interested in the exceptions, resolutions, and trends associated with the data produced. There are a number of ways in which we can carry out monitoring of our services, processes, and technology.

For technology monitoring, we can employ tools to automate the activity, and these will be part of the component- and application-based metrics measuring performance and availability.

Process measurement is a part of every service management process, and the data captured will assist in identification of improvement opportunities.

In Figure 45.2, you can see the tasks associated with this step. We need to ensure that as part of this step we answer the following questions:

- Who is responsible for monitoring and gathering the data?
- How will the data be gathered?
- When and how often will the data be gathered?
- What criteria will be used to evaluate the integrity of the data?

FIGURE 45.2   Monitoring and data collection procedures

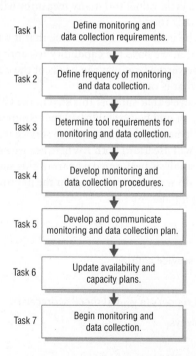

Task 1	Define monitoring and data collection requirements.
Task 2	Define frequency of monitoring and data collection.
Task 3	Determine tool requirements for monitoring and data collection.
Task 4	Develop monitoring and data collection procedures.
Task 5	Develop and communicate monitoring and data collection plan.
Task 6	Update availability and capacity plans.
Task 7	Begin monitoring and data collection.

It will be necessary to look at the data that is collected and verify that it makes sense in the context of the overall service provision. It is this step that enables us to answer the question, "Did we get there?" from the continual service improvement approach.

This step of the process includes the following inputs:

- New business requirements
- Existing SLAs
- Existing tools and monitoring capability
- Plans from service management processes (e.g., availability and capacity)
- Trend analysis reports
- CSI register
- Gap analysis reports (what you should/can measure)
- Customer satisfaction survey

Step 4: Process the Data

This step allows us to convert the data into the required format and audience. Figure 45.3 shows how it follows the trail from metric to KPI to CSF and back to the vision, if desired.

FIGURE 45.3   From vision to measurements

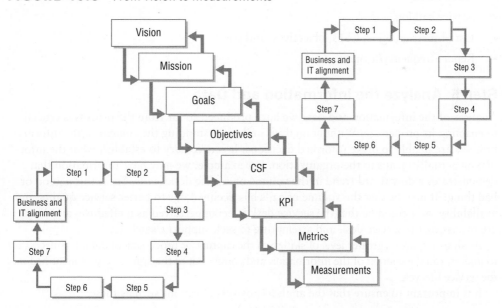

During this activity, it is common to use report-generating technology to assist with the processing of the data into information so that it can be analyzed. Processing the data into information allows for more successful analytical techniques and will encourage the use of an overall perspective on the measurement by associating data groups to an overall service.

When processing data, it is important to consider the following:

- The frequency of processing the data. This may be driven by the analysis requirements and the ability to capture trends.

- The format required for the output, which will also be affected by how the analysis is carried out and how the information will be used.

- The tools and systems that are used for data processing.

- The evaluation techniques we will use to verify the accuracy of the data.

Nearly all of the data captured for CSI is likely to be collected by automation, but there will be some elements that require manual capture. When processing the data, it is important to remember that data collected from a manual input may need greater effort in verification. Stressing the importance of accuracy in data entry to support teams and service management staff will help with the ability to process the data.

Inputs to processing data are as follows:

- Data collected through monitoring

- Reporting requirements

- SLAs/OLAs

- Service catalog

- List of metrics, KPIs, CSFs, objectives, and goals

- Report frequency/template

Step 5: Analyze the Information and Data

Analysis of the information and data we have produced so far from the process is crucial to enabling its proper use. Without analysis and understanding the context of the information, we are unable to make informed decisions. It is necessary to establish what the information actually means to the organization. For example, we may have information that demonstrates a downward trend in the volume of service desks calls. But is this a good or bad thing? It may be that the volume of calls has declined due to better service quality and availability, or it could be that the service desk is being perceived as ineffective, and users are bypassing the service desk and attempting to seek support elsewhere.

Analysis requires a greater level of skill than the capture or processing of data. It is necessary to understand the context of the information and compare it to the agreed targets identified in the service lifecycle.

It is important to ensure that the analysis answers questions such as these:

- Are operations running to plan? This could be a project plan or service management plans for availability, capacity, or continuity.

- Are targets agreed in SLAs being met?

- Does the information show any structural problems?

- Are improvements required?
- Are there any identifiable trends? Positive or negative?
- Is there an identifiable cause for the trends?

Reviewing the trends over a period of time is important for understanding the context and potential improvement opportunity.

The analysis should be shared with the IT managers and discussed in order to formulate plans for improvement opportunities. The output of the analysis can then be part of the presentation, which is the next step in the improvement process.

The inputs to this step are as follows:

- Results of the monitored data
- Existing KPIs and targets
- Information and perceptions from customer satisfaction surveys

Step 6: Present and Use the Information

In this step we present the answer to the question "Did we get there" from the continual service improvement approach. We present the knowledge, represented in the reports, monitors, action plans, reviews, evaluations, and opportunities, to the target audience.

Understanding the audience for the presentation is important so that we deliver the correct format. The format needs to be understandable and at the appropriate level of complexity for the audience, provide value, note exceptions to services, identify benefits, and allow the recipient to make an informed decision. The improvement opportunities identified could be at any stage of the service lifecycle: they may be strategic, tactical, or operational.

The reports should provide emphasis and highlight areas for action to be taken to implement improvements. It is too easy for IT departments to provide too much information to their target audience, without sufficient analysis. CSI should be providing useful and informative reports so that beneficial improvement initiatives can be introduced.

There are four common audience types:

- The customers. They require information on IT services and what will be done if the service provision has failed specific targets.

- Senior IT management. They often focus on CSFs and KPIs and the actual versus the predicted performance against targets. This may be presented in the form of a balanced scorecard.

- Internal IT. They are interested in KPIs and activity metrics to help plan and coordinate operational improvement activities.

- Suppliers. This group will be interested in KPIs and activity metrics related to their own service offerings and performance.

It is extremely important that we ensure that the information is presented in a meaningful way to the audience. For example, percentage figures for availability may not be useful for the customer because it is hard to relate a percentage to an actual outage event and understand the business impact that may have been felt.

Inputs to this step of the process are as follows:

- Collated information

- Format details (such as report templates)

- Stakeholder contact information

Step 7: Implement Improvement

The senior IT management then uses the knowledge presented in the previous step and combines it with previous experience to make an informed decision about an improvement initiative.

This stage may include a number of actions, from improvement activities to submitting a business case to justify an improvement. It will involve integration with other service management processes and other lifecycle stages and will include checking to make sure the improvement achieved its objective.

The decision-making process, applying wisdom to the knowledge provided, should be communicated across the organization, enabling the eventual improvement to be successfully implemented and understood by all stakeholders and practitioners.

After a decision to improve a service and/or service management process is made, the service lifecycle continues. CSI activities take place throughout the service lifecycle. A new baseline can be established, and the cycle will begin again.

This step includes the following inputs:

- Knowledge gained from presenting and using the information

- Agreed implementation plans

- CSI register

As we noted in Chapter 44, "Continual Service Improvement Principles," the seven steps appear to be a circular set of activities, but in fact the seven-step improvement process is actually part of a knowledge spiral.

In Figure 45.4, you can see the connection from the presentation of data from operational improvements into the capture of data for tactical improvements, which in turn will feed its presentation of data into strategic improvement activity.

DIKW and the Seven-Step Improvement Process

The definition of data, information, knowledge, and wisdom is covered under the process of knowledge management, which falls under service transition.

Figure 45.5 shows the association with DIKW throughout each of the seven steps of the improvement process. Each element of DIKW is associated with particular steps of the process as shown here:

- Data

    2. Define what you will measure.

    3. Gather the data.

FIGURE 45.4   Knowledge spiral—a gathering activity

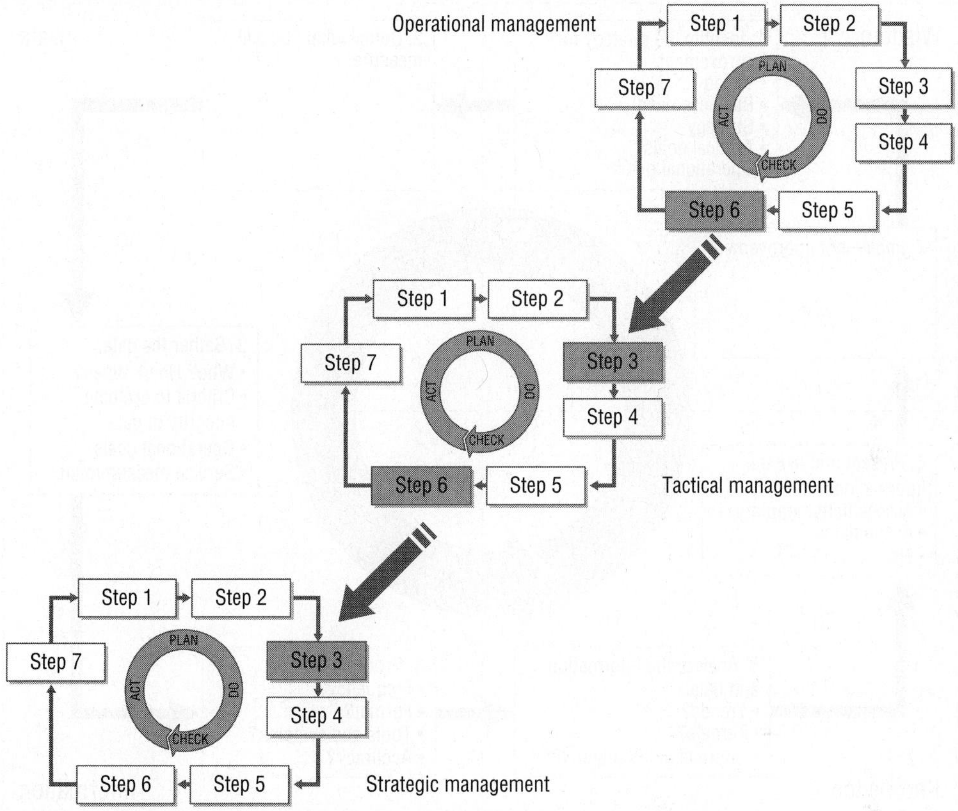

- Information
  4. Process the data.
- Knowledge
  5. Analyze the information and data.
  6. Present and use the information.
- Wisdom
  7. Implement improvement.
  1. Identify strategy for improvement.

FIGURE 45.5   The seven-step improvement process and DIKW

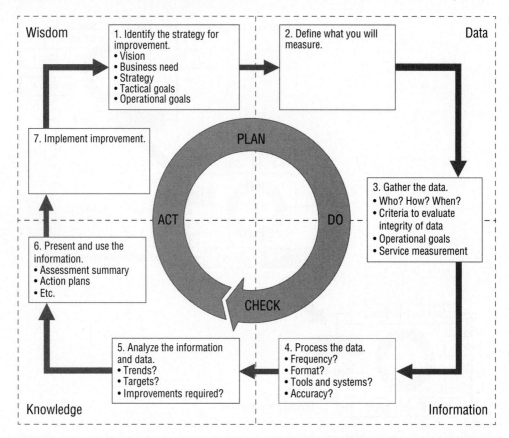

Data is quantitative, defined as numbers, characters, images, or other outputs. It is a collection of facts, whereas information is the result of processing and organizing raw data. Knowledge can be defined as information combined with experience, context, and interpretation. Wisdom is defined as the ability to make correct judgments and decisions.

The association between the processes of knowledge management and the seven-step improvement process ensures that the activities are captured as part of the overall management of knowledge in the service knowledge management system (SKMS).

PDCA and the Seven-Step Improvement Process

In Figure 45.6, you can see the integration of the seven-step improvement process and the Deming cycle.

FIGURE 45.6   The seven-step improvement process and the Deming Cycle

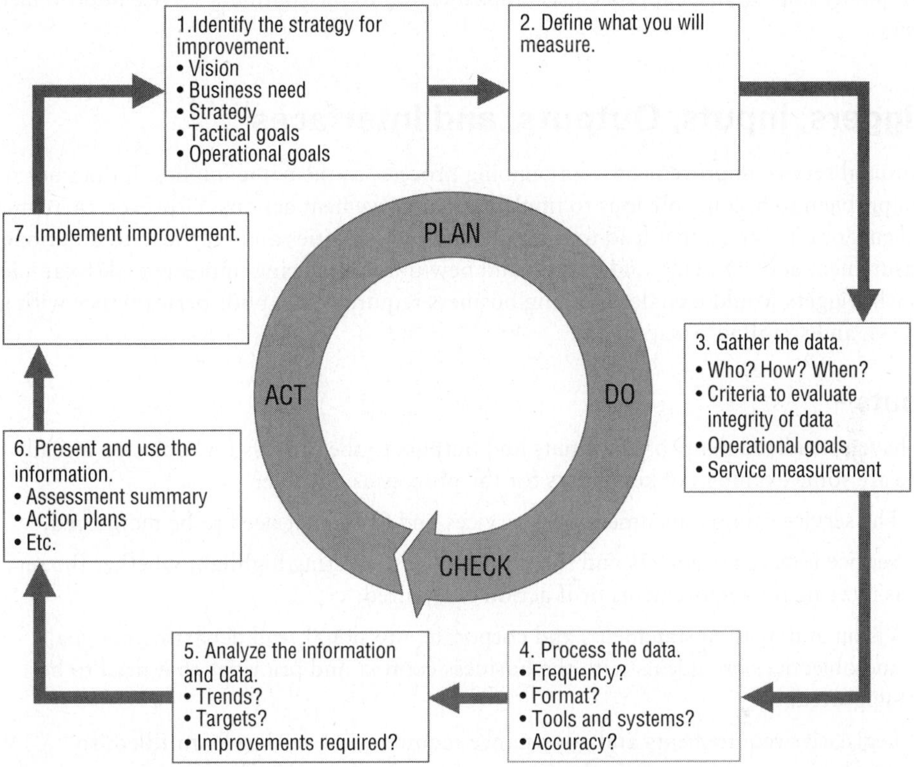

1.Identify the strategy for improvement.
- Vision
- Business need
- Strategy
- Tactical goals
- Operational goals

2. Define what you will measure.

7. Implement improvement.

PLAN

ACT

DO

CHECK

3. Gather the data.
- Who? How? When?
- Criteria to evaluate integrity of data
- Operational goals
- Service measurement

6. Present and use the information.
- Assessment summary
- Action plans
- Etc.

5. Analyze the information and data.
- Trends?
- Targets?
- Improvements required?

4. Process the data.
- Frequency?
- Format?
- Tools and systems?
- Accuracy?

The steps work together:

- Plan
  1. Identify the strategy for improvement.
  2. Define what you will measure.
- Do
  3. Gather the data.
  4. Process the data.
- Check
  5. Analyze the information and data.
  6. Present and use the information.
- Act
  7. Implement improvement.

We explored the Deming Cycle (PDCA) in the chapter covering CSI principles, Chapter 44. This quality improvement approach is complementary to the continual service improvement process.

Triggers, Inputs, Outputs, and Interfaces

Continual service improvement is an ongoing process, as the name implies. It does not wait for a problem to become obvious to implement improvement actions. However, there may be events or conditions that lead to a reevaluation of activities and may lead to additional measurement activity being undertaken and new initiatives being implemented. Examples of such triggers would include changing business requirements, poor performance with a process, and spiraling costs.

Inputs

We have considered many of the inputs and outputs to the process for each step already. Here are some examples of key inputs for the process as a whole:

- The service catalog documents the services and SLAs that need to be monitored.

- Service level requirements and the service review meeting highlight whether the service is meeting the requirements or if action is required.

- Vision and mission statements and corporate, divisional, and departmental goals and objectives provide us with the business context and priorities that need to be supported.

- Legislative requirements and governance requirements need to be fulfilled, so monitoring would be required to ensure that happens.

- Knowledge of the budget cycle is required if any new investment is likely to result from the CSI initiatives.

- Customer satisfaction surveys highlight possible areas of concern.

- The overall IT strategy, market expectations, and new technology drivers will help in the prioritization of possible improvements, while new opportunities to use flexible commercial models such as lease or rental of equipment rather than capital purchase may be considered as part of the improvement plan.

Outputs

The outputs from the CSI process include the data resulting from the monitoring, the analysis based on that data, and the presentation of the recommendations and proposed improvements.

Each stage has its own requirement for capturing improvement data. CSI is integrated with the improvements in every other lifecycle stage.

Strategy looks at the progress of strategies, standards, and policies and the decisions that have been made and implemented.

Design is concerned with the definition of the CSFs and KPIs chosen to support the business requirements and how effective these measurements are. It also evaluates projects and the service design to see whether the objectives have been met.

Service transition develops the procedures and criteria used during and after implementation, using data gathered on the actual release into production and comparing this to what was planned.

Service operation provides the data on the live services. Service operation staff are responsible for taking the component data and processing it in the format to provide an end-to-end perspective of the service achievements. Operation staff also identify incremental and large-scale improvement opportunities.

The Key Roles Played by Other Processes in the Seven-Step Improvement Process

As we previously stated, all processes contain an element of continual service improvement. All process owners should be comparing the output of their process with the desired output and making improvements to ensure that the output matches the requirement. Where the requirement is being met, process owners should be looking to improve the efficiency of the process. In the final part of this chapter, we are going to examine some of the ITIL processes that have key roles in the seven-step improvement process. Each process is required to deliver reports in the agreed format and to check that these are accurate.

Some processes play a key role in the gathering of data (step 3), others assist in the analysis of the data collected (step 6) or in implementing improvements (step 7). Many processes play a role in more than one step.

Gathering the Data (Step 3)

The third step of the seven-step process is gathering the data. All processes gather data to be able to compare their output with the desired end result. The processes listed here are particularly important for this step.

Service Level Management

The CSI and service level management processes have a particularly close connection. CSI will want to ensure that SLM has created measurable targets from which potential service improvements can be identified. Service level management helps to drive what to measure and provides regular reporting of service level achievements against the targets; these are important inputs into CSI and help in prioritizing improvements. When an organization has outsourced its service provision, it is essential that service improvement is included in the contract. If this is not done, the outsourcer will have no incentive to improve if they are already meeting the specified targets.

Service level management understands what data can be gathered and what is important to the business. This helps drive the requirements for monitoring and data collection. It ensures that the end-to-end service is monitored and reported on because that is what the business cares about. Because the service delivery may be impacted by the performance of suppliers or internal teams, SLM also gathers information about how well these groups are performing, which may highlight an area of concern to CSI. The SLM process also analyzes what the data means and whether there are any trends becoming apparent; this analysis will be very useful to CSI.

SLM supports the CSI data processing activity by ensuring that targets are measurable and by ensuring that the underpinning contracts and operational level agreements define the required measurements. Its end-to-end approach to measurement helps cross any departmental boundaries and ensures that the focus is on the service delivered.

Availability Management and Capacity Management

These processes support the data processing activities of CSI as follows:

- Ensuring that monitoring and data collection tool capabilities meet the requirements and that the availability and capacity plans are updated to reflect any changes to the requirements

- Defining roles and responsibilities for infrastructure monitoring and data collection activities, and ensuring that appropriately skilled staff are appointed to these roles

- Ensuring that the correct tools are in place to gather data

- Ensuring that the monitoring and data collection activities are consistently performed

- Processing the technical data and then working with SLM to provide service level data

- Processing data on KPIs, such as availability or performance measures

- Analyzing processed data for accuracy

Event Management, Incident Management, and the Service Desk

Event management, incident management and the service desk support the data processing activities of CSI:

- Incident management defines the monitoring required to automatically detect events and incidents; incident management may also, subject to defined criteria, automatically open or escalate incidents.

- Event management automatically monitors events and raises alerts as required; CSI activities may be required to correct the issue that prompted the alert.

- Identifying abnormal situations and conditions through monitoring enables issues to be predicted and possibly preempted, improving the service delivered.

- Incident management monitors and reports on response, repair, and resolution times. Including reports on service desk call volumes, the average time taken to answer telephone calls, call abandonment rates, and so on allows the performance of the service desk to be managed. For example, extra resources may be added to the desk if these measures start to show a downward trend.

- Incidents and service requests data shows who is accessing the service desk and the nature of the incidents.

- Data on KPIs such as MTRS (mean time to restore service) and percentage of incidents resolved within service targets is gathered by incident management, and any adverse trends can be identified quickly.

Information Security Management

Information security management contributes to monitoring and data collection as follows:

- Defining security monitoring and data collection requirements and then monitoring, verifying, and tracking the levels of security against the organizational security policies and guidelines

- Ensuring that security measures do not impede the data monitoring and collection from the perspective of confidentiality (accessible only to those authorized), integrity (data is accurate and not corrupted or not corruptible), and availability (data is available when needed).

- Measuring the response and resolution performance for security incidents, and analyzing any trends in security breaches

- Validating success of risk mitigation strategies

Financial Management for IT Services

Financial management for IT services monitors actual expenditures versus budget; it can also contribute useful data on how well cost or revenue targets are being achieved. Financial management for IT services can also provide information on the ongoing cost per service, for example. In addition, financial management for IT services will assist CSI in creating the budget and expenditure reports for the improvement initiatives. Importantly, it is this process that can provide the data to compute the ROI of the improvements.

Analyzing the Data (Step 5)

The fifth step of the seven-step process is analyzing the data. All processes use the data they collect to look for trends and possible improvements. The processes listed here are particularly important for this step.

Service Level Management

SLM supports the CSI data analysis activity as follows:

- Analyzing the service level achievements
- Analyzing trends to identify any pattern
- Identifying improvement opportunities
- Identifying the need to modify existing OLAs or UCs

Availability Management and Capacity Management

Availability management and capacity management support the CSI data analysis activity as follows:

- Analyzing and identifying trends in component and service performance data
- Identifying possible improvements in gathering and processing data
- Analyzing processed data for accuracy

Incident Management and the Service Desk

Incident management and the service desk support the CSI data analysis activity as follows:

- Documenting and reviewing incident trends on incidents, service requests, and telephony statistics over a period of time to identify consistent patterns

- Comparing results with agreed-to levels of service

- Identifying improvement opportunities

- Analyzing processed data for accuracy

Problem Management

Problem management plays a key role in analyzing data from other processes to identify trends and perform root cause analysis. Problem management's main purpose is to reduce incidents, but it should also help to define process-related problems.

Overall, problem management seeks to do the following:

- Perform root cause investigation into what is causing the identified trends

- Recommend improvement opportunities

Information Security Management

Information security management relies on the activities of other processes to help determine the cause of security-related incidents and problems. Information security management will submit requests for changes to implement corrections or new updates to, for example, the antivirus software. Other processes such as availability management (recoverability), capacity management (capacity and performance), and ITSCM (planning on how to handle crisis) will assist in planning longer term. In turn, information security management will play a key role in assisting CSI regarding all security aspects of improvement initiatives or for security-related improvements by doing the following:

- Documenting and reviewing security incidents for the current time period

- Comparing results with prior results

- Identifying the need for a SIP or improvements

- Analyzing processed data for accuracy

Presenting and Using the Information (Step 6)

The sixth step of the seven-step process is presenting and using the data. Each process will be involved in presenting and using the data it has gathered. The processes listed here are particularly important for this step.

Service Level Management

SLM presents information to the business on current service achievements and any trends that can be identified at regular service review meetings (internal and external), preparing and presenting the necessary reports. It updates the SLA monitoring (SLAM) chart and provides input into prioritizing improvement activities.

Availability Management, Capacity Management, Incident Management, Problem Management, and the Service Desk

These processes and the service desk all support the CSI presentation activity by preparing reports, providing input into prioritizing service improvement actions, and implementing incremental or fine-tuning improvements that do not require business approval. In each case, the improvement actions should reduce the number or duration of incidents, improving the service to the business.

Implementing Improvement (Step 7)

The last step of the seven-step process is implementing improvements. Each process uses the analysis of the data it has collected to identify improvement opportunities, which are logged in the CSI register and then implemented through CSI. The processes listed here are particularly important for this step.

Change Management

Implementing improvements will usually require a change to be made and for this change to go through the change management process. A request for change (RFC) will need to be raised, prioritized, and categorized according to the policies and procedures defined in the change management process. Release and deployment management, as a part of service transition, will then deploy the change to the live environment. Following the change, CSI will be involved in the postimplementation review, which will assess the success or failure of the change; in other words, whether it resulted in the required improvement.

Service Level Management

The SLM process often identifies improvements as part of the response to the reports presented at service reviews. SLM may need to work with problem management to identify underlying causes before the appropriate improvement actions can be ascertained. In each case, the improvement actions will be logged in the CSI register. Service level management will then be involved in reviewing and prioritizing the entries in the register. The process is also responsible for building appropriate service improvement plans (SIPs) to identify and implement the actions required to overcome the issue and restore service quality. SIP initiatives may address technical issues or issues such as training, system testing, and documentation. The nontechnical improvements require the involvement of the people involved if they are to become embedded. Of course, improvements do not take place one after the other; at any time, a number of them may be running in parallel to address issues with a number of services.

Some organizations establish an annual budget for improvement plans, which is held by service level management. It is important that, in situations where service delivery is outsourced to a third party, service improvement is included in the contract. As stated already, if this is not done, the outsourcer will have no incentive to improve if they are already meeting the specified targets.

Summary

This chapter considered the seven-step improvement process, including activities, interfaces, and inputs and outputs. It also covered how CSI integrates with the other stages of the ITIL service lifecycle and how other processes support the different steps in the seven-step improvement process.

Exam Essentials

Understand the purpose and objectives of the seven-step improvement process.   Be able to explain how the process gathers and analyzes data to highlight the required improvements, which it then implements.

Understand each step of the seven-step improvement process.   It is important for you to be able to explain the purpose of each step of this process. You need to understand why each step is required.

Understand how the seven-step improvement process interacts with the Deming Cycle.   Be able to explain which steps of the process correspond with each activity of the Deming Cycle (Plan-Do-Check-Act).

Understand how knowledge management interacts with the seven-step improvement process.   Be able to explain which steps of the process correspond with each step of the knowledge management data, information, knowledge, wisdom (DIKW) model.

Explain the role of the key processes of incident, problem, and availability management in the seven-step improvement process.   Understand that each process gathers data, which is then used by the CSI seven-step improvement process, and that the improvements identified need to be embedded within each process.

Understand the particular role of the service level management process in CSI.   Be able to explain the interaction between the service improvement plans of service level management and the CSI register.

Review Questions

You can find the answers to the review questions in the appendix.

1. How is the seven-step improvement process in the continual service improvement lifecycle stage used?

   A. The seven-step improvement process is used to manage improvement initiatives in line with business requirements.

   B. The seven-step improvement process is used to gather, analyze, and present data to assist in decision-making.

   C. The seven-step improvement process is used to format the improvement reports delivered to the business.

   D. The seven-step improvement process is used to manage the improvement program across the organization.

2. Which of the following is NOT a stated objective of the seven-step improvement process?

   A. Reduce cost of service without impacting quality.

   B. Improve service delivery by eliminating the root causes of incidents.

   C. Continually review service achievements.

   D. Understand measures and outcomes.

3. When should CSI take place?

   A. In response to a customer complaint.

   B. At the end of every project.

   C. Following a major incident.

   D. It should be an ongoing activity.

4. Which of the following statements about the seven-step improvement process is/are correct?

   A. The choice of which of the seven steps are required is the responsibility of the CSI manager.

   B. The process can start at any step, depending on the situation.

   C. The steps are *all* mandatory.

   D. The seven-step process takes place in the service operation stage because the data is not available until the service is live.

5. Step 5 (analyze the information and data) and step 6 (present and use the information) of the seven-step process align with which step of the Deming cycle?

   A. Plan

   B. Do

   C. Check

   D. Act

6. Which of the following is NOT a type of metric described in CSI?

   A. Technology

   B. Customer satisfaction

   C. Process

   D. Service

7. True or False? Continual Service improvement should always take action as soon as a report shows an example of a deterioration in service—before it becomes entrenched.

   A. True

   B. False

8. CSI will usually present data to four distinct groups, each with different interests. What are these four groups?

   A. Applications management, technical management, the customers, the IT steering group

   B. The customers, suppliers, senior IT managers, internal IT staff

   C. Senior IT managers, process owners, service owners, service level management

   D. Supplier management, service level management, senior IT managers, internal IT staff

9. The seven-step improvement process is mapped against the data, information, knowledge, wisdom structure from knowledge management. Which step(s) of the seven-step process align with the data part of the structure?

   A. 1 and 2

   B. 2 and 3

   C. 3

   D. 3 and 4

10. Put the seven steps of the CSI seven-step improvement process into the correct order.

   1. Analyze

   2. Identify

   3. Implement

   4. Process

   5. Gather

   6. Present

   7. Define

      A. 7, 5, 6, 3, 1, 2, 4

      B. 2, 7, 5, 4, 1, 6, 3

      C. 7, 2, 4, 5, 1, 6, 3

      D. 5, 2, 7, 1, 4, 3, 6

Chapter

46

Continual Service Improvement Methods and Techniques

THE FOLLOWING ITIL INTERMEDIATE EXAM OBJECTIVES ARE DISCUSSED IN THIS CHAPTER:

✓ **How to perform and interpret:**

- Assessments
- Gap analysis
- Benchmarking
- Service measurement
- Metrics
- Balanced scorecards
- SWOT analysis
- Service reports
- Return on investment

✓ **How CSI can use processes to support its activities:**

- Availability management
- Capacity management
- IT service continuity management
- Problem management
- Knowledge management

In this chapter we consider how to carry out some common CSI techniques. We also explore the use of measurement and metrics. The chapter also provides information on the support of continual service improvement from other service management processes.

Assessments

Assessments are formal mechanisms for comparing the operational process environment to performance standards for the purpose of measuring improved process capability and/or identifying potential shortcomings that could be addressed.

Assessments enable the sampling of particular elements of a process or organization that impact its efficiency and effectiveness. By conducting a formal assessment, an organization is demonstrating a significant commitment to improvement because assessments involve real costs, take up staff time, and require the management teams to be completely supportive and engaged in the activity.

Comparison of the operating environment to industry norms should be a relatively straightforward process. It is important to identify the "norm" that will be most effective for comparison. Assessments based on comparison to a maturity model have become common over the years.

A well-designed maturity assessment framework will evaluate all aspects of the process environment, people, processes, and technology. It will also cover factors that affect process effectiveness and efficiency in the organization, such as cultural factors, the process strategy and vision, governance, reporting and metrics, business and IT cooperation and alignment, and decision-making.

The initial step in the assessment process is to choose (or define) the maturity model and in turn the maturity attributes to be measured at each level.

A suggested approach is to turn to the best practice frameworks, such as CMMI, COBIT, ISO/IEC 20000, or the process maturity framework. These frameworks define maturity models directly or a model can be inferred. The frameworks are also useful in the definition of process maturity attributes.

When to Assess

Assessments can be carried out at any time, but it is good practice to associate an assessment to the improvement cycle (Plan-Do-Check-Act).

If we consider the Plan stage, there should be an assessment carried out as part of the project initiation. This is particularly important at the beginning of a process improvement initiative. When processes are being introduced, they should be assessed as part of the baseline for the improvement. Processes can be of many configurations and design, which increases the complexity of assessment data collection.

Planning can be a lengthy activity because incremental plans may be agreed on midstream during the project. Assessment taking place in the course of a process improvement—ensures that the project objectives are being met and can provide evidence that benefits are being achieved from the investment in time and resources.

When the process is in progress, we are part of the Do-Check stages. Assessment during a project—for example, at the conclusion of a project stage for process improvement—is important to validate the maturation of process and the process organization that was achieved through the efforts of the project team. Periodic reassessment following an improvement initiative will ensure that quality standards are maintained or further improvements are identified.

What to Assess and How

Setting the scope of the assessment is obviously a very important decision. A key consideration must be the objective of the assessment and what the expected future uses of the process assessments and assessment reports will be. Assessments can be targeted broadly at current processes or focussed on specific issues within the process environment.

There are three potential scope levels, namely process only; people, process, and technology; and a full assessment, including culture.

Process Only

The first of these is a process-only assessment of process attributes based on the general principles and guidelines of a process framework.

Process, People, and Technology

Extend the assessment of the process to include people and technology. This will mean that the skills and roles of management and practitioners involved with the processes will be included. It also includes the technology in place to support the processes.

Full Assessment

A full assessment extends the people, process, and technology assessment to include the whole organization supported by the service provider.

The full assessment will cover the culture of acceptance of the improvements within the organization and the ability of the organization to articulate a process strategy, which should include the vision for the process environment in the end. This will drive how the processes and functions are structured and the ability of the process governance to ensure that the process objectives are met. The strategy will define the alignment and cooperation between the business and IT in using the process framework.

A key part of this will also be the assessment of the reporting and metrics. The strategy will cover the capacity and capability across the business and IT of decision-making practices to improve processes over time. A full assessment will cover all of these aspects to give a complete review of the overall health of the IT organization.

How to Assess

Assessments can be conducted by the sponsoring organization or with the aid of a third party. Table 46.1 shows the pros and cons of these differing approaches.

TABLE 46.1 Pros and cons of assessment approaches

Pro	Con
Using external resources for assessments	
Objectivity	Cost
Expert ITIL knowledge	Risk of acceptance
Broad exposure to multiple IT organizations	Limited knowledge of existing environments
	Improper preparation affects effectiveness
Analytical skills	May not be there to see it through to the end to witness the results, good or not
Credibility	
Minimal impact to operations	
Performing self-assessments	
No expensive consultants	Lack of objectivity (internal agendas)
	Little acceptance of findings
Self-assessments available for free	Internal politics
	Limited knowledge or skills
Promotes internal cooperation and communication	Resource intensive
	Inability to see the wood for the trees; assessment often needs a fresh set of eyes
Good place to get started	
Internal knowledge of environment	Detracts from the day job; unless backfilled, could inadvertently reduce service effectiveness and efficiency during assessment
Can repeat exercise in future at minimal cost, using newly acquired skills	

The advantages of conducting a self-assessment are the reduced cost and the experiential learning of how to objectively assess relative performance and progress of an organization's processes. The downside is, of course, the difficulty associated with remaining objective and impartial.

Use of a third party can eliminate the lack of objectivity. There are a number of public "mini-assessments" that are available on various websites and provide a general perspective of maturity, but a more detailed assessment and resulting report can be produced by a firm specializing in an assessment practice. The increased cost of a third-party assessment can be balanced against the objectivity it provides and the experience that comes with performing assessments regularly.

Whether conducted internally or externally, the assessment should be reported using the levels of the maturity model. A best-practice reporting approach is to communicate assessment results in a graphical fashion. Graphs are an easy tool because they can fulfil multiple communication requirements; for example, they can be used to reflect changes or trends of process maturity over time or to compare the current assessment to standards or norms. It is often easier to provide a visual rather than textual report of the results because improvements can be seen at a glance. No graph should be unsupported by explanatory text; there needs to be a clear definition of the data, its source, and how it was used to produce the graphical output.

Advantages of Assessments

Assessments can provide an objective perspective of the current operational process state. This perspective can be compared to a standard maturity model and a process framework. Once a thorough assessment has been conducted, an accurate identification of any process gaps can be quickly completed, recommendations for remediation put forward, and action steps planned.

A well-planned and well-conducted assessment is a repeatable process. The assessment should be a useful management tool for measuring progress over time and establishing improvement targets or objectives.

Using an accepted industry-recognized maturity framework applied to a standard process framework allows an organization to compare its findings against a wider industry standard. This may be useful in promoting the organization for commercial tender.

An assessment provides information for the improvement cycle, answering the "Where are we now?" question and highlighting potential improvement areas.

Risks of Assessments

Of course there are risks to carrying out an assessment. It will only provide a snapshot of a specific state at a specific time. Dependent on the assessment mechanism used, you may be tying your organization into a particular vendor-specific choice of assessment and maturity framework. Occasionally, organizations find that the assessment and the achievement of the targets becomes an end in itself and the actual benefits and improvements that will help the organization are lost in the achievement of the maturity targets.

Improvement Strategy

An assessment can often become an end in itself when the strategy for the improvement initiative is unclear from the start. All improvement is worth pursuing but easily becomes unfocused when driven by a strategy that is not clear in its requirements for the deliverables at the end of the program or project. Improving for improving's sake is not going to provide sufficient structure to achieve desirable outcomes. There must be a desirable customer-focused end goal, and this can be linked to and identified with the assessment, but the assessment achievement should not be the goal in itself. The potential exception here would be the achievement of a standard such as ISO/IEC 20000, but even then, there must be a tangible benefit in achieving the accreditation for the whole organization.

All assessments take resource effort, both for the practitioners of the processes and the assessors. It is important to understand the impact of this and realistically schedule the right amount of time. This is one of the many challenging aspects for assessments, but it is often overlooked.

Whatever the results, any assessment will require some interpretation and will therefore be subject to the experience, attitude, and approach of the assessor. It is important to try to establish objectivity as much as possible, but this may not be possible.

Consideration of who carries out the assessment is also important, as is ensuring that objectivity is retained through subsequent repeated audits. This is a particular challenge if the same assessor is used or the assessment is carried out internally. Knowing what was previously in place will not necessarily show where any new improvements are needed or if something has relapsed to an earlier maturity level.

Assessment Considerations

In the CSI journey, the decisions as to what to improve are critical to the overall results that can be achieved. Any discussion on improvements has to begin with the services being provided to the business. This could lead to improvements of the service itself or to process improvements that support the business service.

Figure 46.1 shows the relationships between services, processes, and systems.

Service improvements are governed by the improvement lifecycle. The improvement lifecycle is modeled after the Deming Cycle of Plan-Do-Check-Act. The cycle establishes a clear pattern for continual improvement efforts. Assessment will be an important input into the planning and part of the output from the planning stages.

Value of Processes vs. Maturity of Processes

For service management process improvement projects, one of the questions should address how mature we need our processes to be. The answer is tied directly back to the business. In other words, how important a process is to the business.

FIGURE 46.1 The relationships between services, processes, and systems

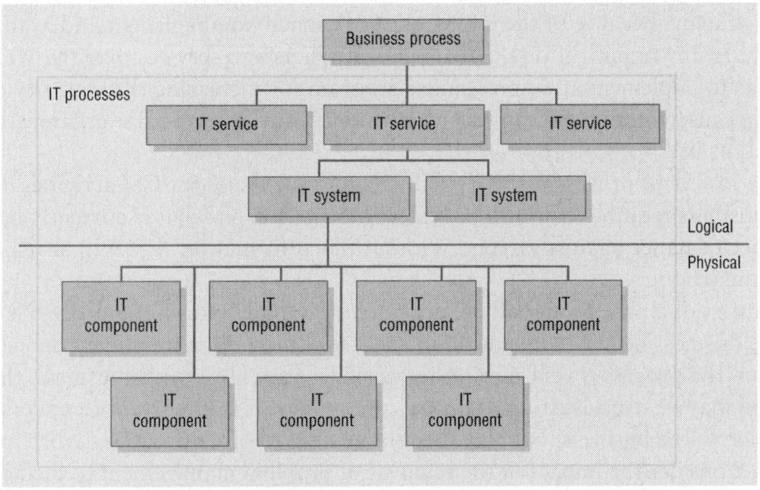

In Figure 46.2, you can see the value of a process mapped to the importance to the business using three examples—service level management (SLM), availability management (AM in the figure), and capacity management (CAP in the figure).

FIGURE 46.2 The value of a process versus the maturity of a process

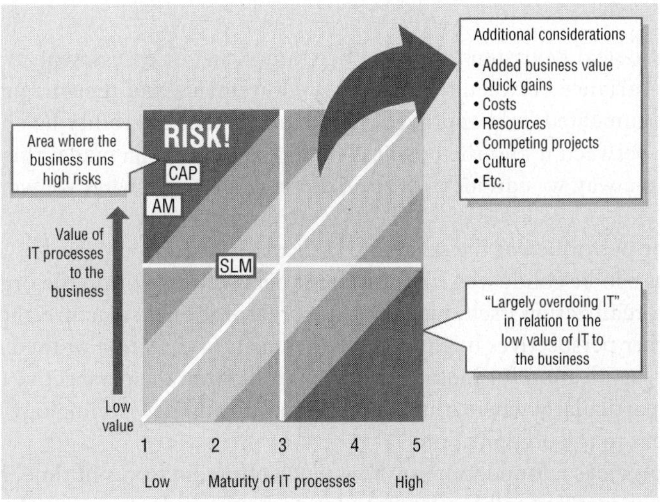

An assessment has shown that these processes are not very mature. This particular organization is changing its strategy for selling and delivering products and services to a web-based strategy. Because of the importance of capacity management and availability management to any organization that provides products and services over the Web, this company has to implement an improvement program for increasing the maturity of both processes, because without any improvement initiatives, this particular organization is putting itself at risk.

Having a low SLM process maturity will create some issues for CSI activities. SLM identifies new business requirements and provides information on what is currently being monitored and performance against targets. Without this information, CSI will have no baseline data for comparison.

The maturity of a process should ideally fall in the "safe" areas. If a process is immature but the business heavily depends on it, there is potentially a significant danger to the organization. If a process is very mature yet provides very little to the business, then an organization may be overinvesting resources and money. It is important to understand not only the value to the business, but also the relationship to other processes when making this assessment. Consider the impact of the removal of problem management to incident management, for example. A mature problem management process may be very proactive, and the benefit to the organization will be difficult to assess in business terms. But without it, the impact on incident management will definitely be adverse.

When CSI is looking at improving processes in support of IT services, it's critical to understand the value of processes to a business as well as their function in the lifecycle as a whole.

Gap Analysis

Gap analysis is a logical next step following benchmarking or assessment. A gap analysis requires that the variance between the business requirements and the current capability is determined, documented, and approved. Once the current capability has been identified, comparison between it and the business requirements can be made; this is the gap analysis. This is the way we can identify the difference between what we want and what we need.

Analysis can be performed at the strategic, tactical, or operational level of an organization. Gap analysis can be conducted from different perspectives within the organization, for example, the organization itself, including the organizational structure and capabilities of the people. Other perspectives might include the business direction or the business processes. There is a justification for looking at the analysis from the perspective of information technology, particularly where it is changing rapidly and new technology may provide a significant benefit to the organization.

Gap analysis provides a foundation for how much effort, in terms of time, money, and human resources, is required to have a particular goal achieved—for example, how to bring a service from a maturity level of 2 to 3.

Benchmarking

Benchmarking is a specific type of assessment and is a process used in management, particularly as part of strategic management. It is used in organizations to evaluate aspects of their processes in relation to best practice. One of the key aspects is that it enables a decision to be made on how to achieve best practice if there is an identified shortfall. Benchmarking may be a one-time event, but it is often treated as a continuous and repeatable process in which organizations continually seek to amend their practices, which supports the goals of CSI.

Benchmarking is actually a logical sequence of stages that an organization goes through to achieve continual improvement in its key processes. It involves cooperation with others because benchmarking partners can learn from each other where improvements can be made.

There are some key requirements for benchmarking success. First, it is necessary to ensure that there is sufficient management support at a senior level. Benchmarking should be objective and inclusive, gaining information from the business, internal IT, and external sources. It is very important to make sure an external view is considered as well as the internal organizational concerns. When completing comparisons, remember that it is necessary to compare processes, not outputs, across organizations. Processes may be the same, but the output may be very different dependent on the nature of the business undertaken or the industry sector being used as a comparison. If only the outputs from processes are compared, then there is a potential for missing improvements made in other industry sectors.

In addition, it is important to involve the process owners to ensure the support and buy-in by those who will be affected by any improvements. It is wise to set up benchmarking teams who will be instrumental in developing the culture within the organization. Individuals undertaking benchmarking will require some training and guidance. It is important to get assistance from an experienced in-house facilitator or an external consultant who will be able to provide experience in the chosen method.

It is important for organizations to plan their benchmarking process based on their own improvement needs, but it is necessary to understand that this may require measurement of other companies. A research organization may be a valuable benchmarking partner, for example, if target companies are competitors. Some cross-industry figures may be published by the international research organizations, but they will not necessarily include the assumptions and measurements a given organization needs.

Benchmarking is generally expected to be a process of comparing an organization's performance to industry-standard figures. This is often a challenge because having such benchmark figures available is often seen as the first hurdle in a benchmarking exercise. But benchmarks are relevant only when the comparison is of the same performance measures or indicators and with similar organizations in terms of size, industry, and geography.

Benchmarking Procedure

For benchmarking to be successful, it is important to identify your problem areas.

A range of research techniques may be required, such as informal conversations with customers, employees, suppliers, or focus groups to capture feedback. More formal approaches using marketing research and quantitative research can provide industry sector data. Internally, feedback can also be gained by using surveys and questionnaires. Often the result of a benchmarking activity will be process mapping and reengineering analysis. Quality control should be applied to variance reports to provide information on process achievements, and financial data will be used to understand the balance between cost and efficiency.

Benchmarking Costs

Benchmarking is a moderately expensive process, but most organizations find that it more than pays for itself. There are three main types of costs.

The costs associated with travel- and accommodation-related expenses for team members who need to travel to the site are known as visit costs. This is applicable for either internal or external assessors, but it is more likely when using an external organization because none of the team members will be based at the organization's sites.

Time costs will be significant if the assessment is to be completed thoroughly. Members of the benchmarking team will be investing time in researching problems and finding exceptional companies to study and on visits and implementation. This will take them away from their regular tasks for part of each day, so additional staff might be required.

Once benchmarking is part of business-as-usual practice, it is important to capture and manage the data collected. It is useful to create and maintain a database of similar best practices and the companies associated with each best practice.

Value of Benchmarking

Benchmarking can be seen as valuable only if the results are clearly communicated. This should include displaying the gaps, identifying the risks of not closing the gaps, and assisting with the prioritization of development activities and facilitating communication of this information.

Benchmarks show profiles of existing quality in the marketplace and industry sector. Demonstration of quality by comparison to benchmarks can motivate staff and aid retention. Achievement of a quality standard can be a source of pride and self-confidence in employees because it shows that they work in an efficient environment.

Customers will be able to see that the organization is a good IT service management provider.

Optimizing service quality is key to all IT organizations to maximize performance and customer satisfaction and provide value for money. Using a benchmark as a comparison allows organizations to demonstrate their achievement.

Benchmarking as a Lever

It is common to hear staff say, "The way we do it is the best because this is the way we've always done it."

Benchmarking is often a way to open an organization to new methods, ideas, and tools to improve their effectiveness. It can help break through resistance to change by demonstrating methods other than the ones currently employed and demonstrating evidence that others are using them successfully.

Benchmarking as a Steering Instrument

Benchmarking should be used as a management technique to improve performance. It is used to compare performance between different organizations or different units within a single organization undertaking similar processes.

It can be used as an ongoing method of measuring and improving products, services, and practices against the best that can be identified in any industry anywhere. It has been defined as "the search for industry best practices that lead to superior performance." Benchmarking can support management in driving the direction of organizational change.

Benchmarking Categories

An internal benchmark is where an organization sets a baseline at a certain point in time for the same system or department and then measures to see how it is doing today compared with the baseline originally set. This type of benchmark is often overlooked by organizations (service targets are a form of benchmark), but they can be as useful as comparing to external benchmarks by showing an improvement progression.

Other benchmarking categories are comparisons with industry norms provided by external organizations, direct comparisons with similar organizations, and comparison with other systems or departments within the same company.

Benefits

Using benchmark results should help deliver major benefits in achieving lower prices and higher productivity on the part of the service provider. This should include identifying efficiencies by comparing the costs of providing IT services and the contribution these services make to the business with what is achieved in other organizations. This helps the organization to identify areas for improvement.

Benchmarking will also demonstrate effectiveness in terms of actual business objectives realized compared with what was planned. To obtain the maximum benefit, it is necessary to look at economy, efficiency, and effectiveness rather than focusing on one to the exclusion of the others.

Who Is Involved?

Within an organization, there will be three parties involved in benchmarking. Each has a different perspective on the results of benchmarking and how to apply them.

- The customer or the business manager responsible for acquiring IT services to meet business objectives. The customer's interest in benchmarking would be, "How can I improve my performance in procuring services and managing service providers, and in supporting the business through IT services?"

- The user or consumer, namely anyone who uses IT services to support their work. The user's interest in benchmarking would be, "How can I improve my performance by utilizing IT?"

- The internal service provider who provides IT services to users under service level agreements negotiated with and managed by the customer. The provider's interest in benchmarking would be, "How can we improve our performance in the delivery of IT services that meet the requirements of our customers and are cost-effective and timely?"

There will also be participation from external parties:

- External service providers provide IT services to users under contracts and service level agreements negotiated with and managed by the customer.

- Members of the public are increasingly becoming direct users of IT services, and this is challenging when attempting to benchmark against their needs.

- It is important not to forget the input that will be required from benchmarking partners, that is, other organizations with whom comparisons are made in order to identify the best practices to be adopted for improvements.

What to Benchmark

Differences in benchmarks between organizations are normal. Each organization will have a slightly different setup; no two will be exactly the same. Direct comparison with similar organizations is most effective if there is a sufficiently large group of organizations with similar characteristics.

Benchmarking techniques can be applied at various levels, from relatively straightforward in-house comparisons to an industry-wide search for best practice. Benchmarking should follow the continual service improvement seven-step process to ensure that appropriate data is collected, analyzed, presented, and acted on.

Comparison with Industry Norms

ITIL is itself an industry-recognized best practice. The core publications provide documented guidance on benchmarking and process assessment. There are many organizations that provide IT service management consultancy and professional expertise in benchmarking, which may be useful to an organization. Use of maturity models is supported by a number of frameworks, and there is Capability Maturity Model Integration (CMMI), which is widely recognized.

Total cost of ownership (TCO), developed by Gartner, has become a key measurement of the effectiveness and efficiency of services. TCO is defined as all the costs involved in the design, introduction, operation, and improvement of services within an organization from its inception until retirement. TCO is often used to benchmark specific services in IT against other organizations, for example, managed service providers.

Benchmark Approach

Benchmarking will establish the extent of an organization's existing maturity with best practice and help in understanding how that organization compares with industry norms. Deciding what the key performance indicators (KPIs) are going to be and then measuring against them will give solid management information for future improvement and targets.

There are two basic approaches: either an internal benchmark, which is completed internally using resources from within the organization to assess the maturity of the service management processes against a reference framework, or an external benchmark, completed by an external third-party company. A third party will probably have its own proprietary models for the assessment of service management process maturity.

Viewed from a business perspective, benchmark measurements can help the organization to assess IT services, performance and spend against peer or competitor organizations, and best practice, both across the whole of IT and by appropriate business areas. There are a number of questions often asked about IT, such as: How does IT spending compare to other similar organizations—overall, as a percentage of revenue, or per employee? It is hard for an organization to understand whether or not it is spending too much compared to similar organizations for basic functions such as payroll or to compare spending across business units, locations, or processes. Competitors are unlikely to divulge details about spending on these types of services because it will be perceived as commercially confidential information. So a benchmarking activity against an agreed norm is often the only approach to support business understanding and justification of the costs of IT.

Benchmarking activities need to be aligned to the business. If carried out thoroughly, a benchmarking exercise, whether completed internally or externally, will incur significant costs. It is important that the benchmark is targeted to identify areas that will be of most value to the business.

The approaches to benchmarking can include an assessment of the cost and performance for internal service providers or the price and performance for external service providers. Or it can focus on the performance of processes against industry best practice. The comparison to industry sector or peer information relating to financial performance of IT is another assessment, as is effectiveness based on customer satisfaction ratings and business alignment.

Whichever approach is adopted, it is important that the context for benchmarking requires information about the organization's profile and complexity and relative comparators. An effective and meaningful profile contains four key components.

The company profile provides basic information. Company size, industry type, geographic location, and types of user are typical of data gathered to establish this profile.

There also needs to be an understanding of the current assets because the IT assets within the organization may include operational IT, desktop and mobile clients, peripherals, and network and server assets.

It is important to understand current best practices, including the policies, procedures, and/or tools that improve returns and their maturity and degree of usage. Understanding the organization includes information about the end-user community, the types and quantities of varied technologies in use, and how IT is managed.

There are a variety of IT benchmarking types available separately or in combination:

- Cost and performance for internal service providers
- Price and performance for external service providers
- Process performance against industry best practice
- Financial performance of high-level IT costs against industry or peers
- Effectiveness benchmarking, which considers satisfaction ratings and business alignment at all levels

Benchmarking will establish the extent of an organization's existing maturity with best practice and will help in understanding how that organization compares with industry norms.

Service Measurement

IT services have become integral for businesses of all sizes, private and public organizations, educational institutions, consumers, and the individuals working within these organizations. Without IT services, it is hard to see how any organization would be able to deliver their products and services in today's market. This has an impact on the expectations for availability, reliability, and stability because reliance on IT is paramount. It is why the integration of business and IT is so important, it is hard to think of a circumstance where they could be considered separately and an organization would still survive.

As a direct consequence, businesses require that IT services are measured, not just the performance of an individual component such as a server or application. IT must now be able to measure and report against an end-to-end service and understand how this service supports and enables the business to achieve its goals.

The seven-step improvement process discusses the need to define what you will measure after looking at the requirements and the ability to measure.

Most organizations will consider specific areas of measurement, the first being the availability of the service. It could be said that this is often the primary focus of the business in terms of understanding the support delivered by IT services. If the service is unavailable, then business may simply stop. Think for a moment about the impact of a web portal outage on an online retailer. Availability is critical to success.

Supporting availability is the reliability of the service. Service availability may be good, but if it is interrupted by minor outages on a repeated basis, this will not be satisfactory for the user experience. A service that is restored quickly and often may meet targets for availability overall, but the perception from the users will be negative. Reliability is a measure of continuous performance and will ensure that the business has trust in the services provided.

Measurement of overall performance is crucial to understanding the business impact of a service rather than its components. Measuring at the component level is necessary and valuable, but service measurement must go further. Service measurement will require someone to take the individual measurements and combine them to provide a view of the true customer experience.

Too often we provide a report against a component, system, or application but don't provide the true service level as experienced by the customer. In Figure 46.3, you can see how it is possible to measure and report against different levels of systems and components to provide a true service measurement. Even though the figure shows availability measuring and reporting, the same can apply for performance measuring and reporting.

FIGURE 46.3   Availability reporting

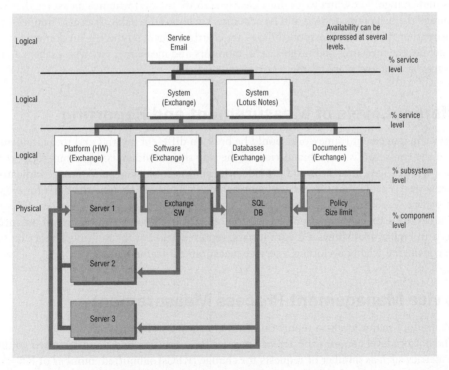

Design and Develop a Service Measurement Framework

It is always challenging for an organization to create a measurement framework that supports the business requirements. One of the key factors for this is the definition of what success looks like. We need to be mindful of both the past and the future; measurement should allow for the identification of future improvement as well as report on past performance.

Whether measuring one or multiple services, the following are key to a successful service measurement framework.

- The origins of the framework and defining what success looks like; in other words, what are we trying to achieve and how will we know when we've achieved it?
- Ensuring that we are building the framework and choosing measures that will provide us with information to make strategic, tactical, and/or operational decisions.

It is important to select measures that will deliver the data and information we need based on agreed targets within IT and the business.

There are some critical elements that should be included in a service measurement framework. For example, the framework should be integrated into business planning and focused on business and IT goals and objectives. It should support cost-effectiveness, with a balanced approach to the measures applied that can be sustained over a period of time and withstand change. The framework must clearly identify the performance measures that will encourage the behaviors desired and be accurate, timely, and reliable. It is also important to ensure that the roles and responsibilities are clearly defined, so there is no doubt about who defines the measures and targets, who monitors and measures, and who gathers and analyzes the data and prepares the reports.

Different Levels of Measurement and Reporting

A service management framework should be built on different metrics and measurements so that the end result is a combined view of the way the individual components support the overall service. This in turn should provide information to the key performance indicators, allowing us to ensure that targets are being achieved. This will then be the basis for creating a service scorecard and dashboard.

The service scorecard can then be used to populate an IT scorecard or overall balanced scorecard. Figure 46.4 shows a diagrammatic representation of the multiple levels that need to be considered when developing a service measurement framework.

Service Management Process Measurement

There are four major levels to report on. They are shown in Figure 46.5.

The bottom level contains the activity metrics for a process, and these are often volume-type metrics such as number of requests for change (RFCs) submitted, number of RFCs accepted into the process, number of RFCs by type, number approved, number successfully implemented, and so on.

FIGURE 46.4   Service measurement model

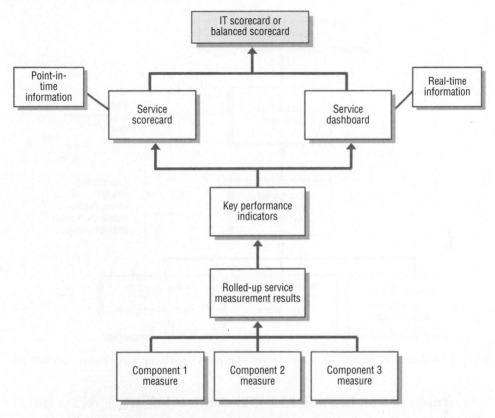

The next level contains the KPIs associated with each process. The activity metrics should feed into and support the KPIs. In turn, the KPIs will support the next level, which is the high-level goal such as improving service quality, reducing IT costs, or improving customer satisfaction.

Finally, this high-level goal will feed into the organization's balanced scorecard or IT scorecard. When first starting out, it is important not to pick too many KPIs to support the high-level goal(s). Additional KPIs can always be added at a later time.

Creating a Measurement Framework Grid

As a significant part of this approach, best practice recommends that the organization create a framework grid to set out the high-level goals and define which KPIs will support the goal, and also which category the KPI addresses.

FIGURE 46.5 Service management model

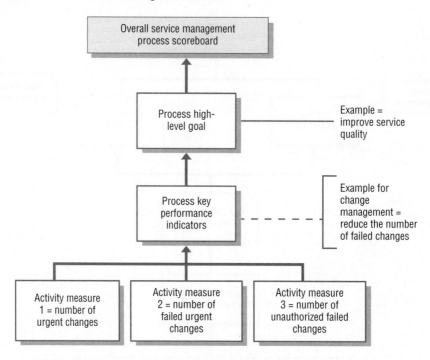

An example of this can be seen in Table 46.2, which is an extract from the CSI core publication.

TABLE 46.2 High-level goals and key performance indicators

High-level goal	KPI	KPI category	Measurement	Target	How and who
Manage availability and reliability of a service	Percentage improvement in overall end-to-end availability of services	Value Quality	End-to-end service availability based on the component availability that makes up the service AS 400 availability Network availability Application availability	99.995%	Technical managers Technical analyst Service level manager

In this example, the high-level goal relates to availability and reliability of a service, with a qualitative KPI to demonstrate a percentage improvement in overall availability. We can see the components measured and the desired target achievement as well as those responsible for the measurement.

When considering performance, it is important to recognize that there are different elements that combine to give an overall perception of achievement. These can be classified as compliance, quality, performance, and value.

- *Compliance* is a measure to demonstrate if we are doing something.

- *Quality* allows us to measure how well are we doing something.

- *Performance* demonstrates the speed and urgency of carrying out something; in other words, how fast or slow are we doing it.

- And last but by no means least, we have *value*, and this determines if what we are doing is making a difference.

Setting Targets

Targets set by management are quantified objectives to be attained. They may express the aims of the service or process at any level and provide the basis for identification of problems and early progress toward solutions and improvement opportunities.

It is important to recognize the variety of drivers for the service targets used in reporting. Some may be driven by business requirements or new policies or regulatory requirements. SLAs are also key drivers for targets, but it is necessary to ensure that service level management has verified the capability of the IT department to deliver on them.

Metrics

There are three types of metrics that are used to support the activities of service improvement. Making sure your metrics include all three types will ensure a well-rounded approach to measuring your services.

The three types that should be considered are technology, process, and service metrics:

- Technology metrics, measuring the response, availability, and performance of individual components, may not be easy for nontechnical folks to interpret, but combined with process metrics, they provide vital information for the measurement of end-to-end service.

- Process metrics relate to the quality, performance, value, and compliance for processes by capturing critical success factors associated with key performance indicators.

- Service metrics combine these to produce end-to-end service measures.

Metrics define what is to be measured, using a scale of measurement that has been agreed to as a clearly defined unit. Many business models use metrics at their base (CMMI, for example). Metrics are used to track trends, productivity, resources, and more. The most commonly tracked metrics are KPIs. Figure 46.6 shows the relationship between the overall vision and the measurements that prove it has been achieved.

FIGURE 46.6 From vision to measurement

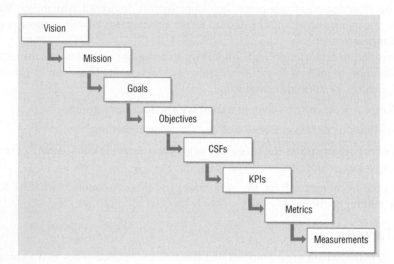

It is important to ensure that this relationship is recognized so that the measures that are applied support the achievement of the organizational vision.

How Many CSFs and KPIs?

It's a valid question—how many critical success factors and KPIs should we have?—and opinions on this are varied. The more KPIs there are, the more complex the reporting model and analysis required to interpret them will be.

Good practice suggests that CSFs should be supported by a number of associated KPIs, but there is no defined number for either. Even a very mature organization is unlikely to have more than five CSFs per process, with no more than five KPIs per CSF. But that still adds up to a potentially high number of metrics. So it is recommended that in the early stages of a CSI program, only two or three KPIs for each CSF are defined, monitored, and reported on. As the maturity of a service and service management process increases, further KPIs can be added.

Remember, KPIs will change over a period of time as their importance to the business and the maturity of the service provision alters, and this may have effect on other KPIs and processes. But the changes to KPIs must be carefully considered so that trending information or the value of the metric is not lost by too frequent alterations.

Qualitative KPIs

Qualitative KPIs are based on achievement of a quality-based CSF, such as improving service quality. In order to achieve the CSF, a specific KPI must be identified. In this example, the metrics required will be the customer satisfaction scores for handling incidents.

The measures needed to support this will be the incident handling survey score and the number of survey scores. It is important for a representative sample to be used for quality, so the number of survey scores should be captured. A sample from only one customer will not give a true representation of the facts.

Quantitative KPIs

Quantitative KPIs are based on achievement of a quantity-based CSF, such as reducing IT costs. In order to achieve the CSF, a specific KPI must be identified. For example, suppose the metrics required will be the costs of handling printer incidents at the start and end of the initiative and the cost of the improvement initiative itself.

There will be a number of measures to be considered for this KPI, including the costs associated with the salaries of the analysts working on the printers, costs of service calls to third parties, and the costs of developing any workaround for printers.

Is the KPI Fit for Use?

It is important to ensure that the KPI is fit for use. There are some key questions that should be addressed to ensure that your KPI will provide the information required.

How will the KPI help to achieve the goal? Does it provide any information on whether or not the goal will be achieved if we meet the target? Does the indicator provide enough information to establish a course of action? What is the required frequency of information? Is the KPI stable and accurate? Does it take into consideration external influences that may impact the results? Can it be changed to reflect different organizational circumstances? Can the performance indicator be measured now, and what would stop it from being measured?

It is also necessary to understand who will be managing the KPI: who is collecting the data, performing the analysis, interpreting the results, and producing and delivering the reports?

Tension Metrics

Tension metrics ensure that the team efforts stay in balance by measuring a combination of the elements that deliver a successful support team. There should be a balance of resources (the people and the money), the features (the product or service and the quality of that product or service), and the schedule (an element of timeliness).

Focusing on one factor above others will cause an imbalanced approach. For example, if too much focus is placed on delivering to a schedule, quality may be impacted by the increased speed to delivery. Similarly, concentrating too much on service quality may impact on the financial resources in use because high quality is costly and the end product needs to be cost justifiable.

Tension metrics are designed to measure a balanced approach so that if one measure drives a specific behavior, such as a service desk answering calls quickly, we have a measure in place to ensure that quality does not suffer to beat the time constraint. This is why there should always be a suite of measures in place; concentrating on any one aspect may harm the overall service.

Tension metrics should not cause conflict with goals or objectives but should ensure that the team maintains an overall focus on quality of service across all aspects of delivery.

Goals and Metrics

Goals and metrics are important for all stages of the lifecycle—from strategy, where the organization will decide on how IT will be funded; through design, where business requirements are translated into IT solutions; through transition, where they are made a reality; to operation, where the business finally sees the direct value of IT. Throughout the lifecycle, all stages must keep the business goals and requirements in mind, and these should be reflected in the goals and objectives for each stage.

Breaking Down Goals and Metrics

Best practice identifies three categories of metrics to be considered: financial metrics, learning and growth metrics, and organizational or process metrics.

Financial metrics include project costs or operational expenses, while learning and growth metrics may include increase in skill sets or certifications. Organizational or process metrics can be broken down further into product quality metrics and process quality metrics. Product quality metrics are the metrics supporting the contribution to the delivery of quality products. Process quality metrics are related to efficient and effective process management.

Using Organizational Metrics

Organizational metrics (including financial, learning and growth, and process metrics) are important for managing the overall service delivery and ensuring that teams and processes work successfully together to achieve the desired goal.

It is important to ensure that these are adopted to provide an overall approach for the organization, not just specific elements of IT. This is the relationship shown in the journey from vision to measurement.

Interpreting and Using Metrics

Results must be interpreted in the context of the objectives for the measures as well as any environmental or external factors. If results are considered out of context, they may be misinterpreted if extenuating factors have affected them. It is important to review the measures to ensure that the chosen indicators have worked and that the results are contributing to the overall objective of the service or process.

To make sure reports are useful and meaningful, it is important to ensure that the generated results are making sense. If the output does not show a probable or viable outcome, then investigation must take place into how this could have occurred. The investigation is not designed to identify blame but to rectify an error in reporting so the required results can be produced.

The following questions need to be answered to ensure that the results are verified properly:

- How did we collect this data?
- Who collected the data?
- What tools were used to collect the data?

- Who processed the data?
- How was the data processed?
- What could have led to the incorrect information?

Before starting to interpret results, you should always ensure that you have sufficient information about the data elements that have been used and the purpose of the results. It is important to understand the expected normal range for the results so that it is possible to identify any anomalous results or exceptions.

It is easy to jump to conclusions incorrectly; for example, a downward trend in calls opened at the service desk may be caused by a wide range of scenarios. There could have been a change in the way support is offered, perhaps by the introduction of self-service, or there could have been a failure in the telephone system. It should be noted if there have been any changes that might have triggered a set of results, and where insufficient information is available from simply reviewing the results, make sure the appropriate people are included in a discussion.

Using Measurement and Metrics

Metrics can be used for multiple purposes, and it is important to understand the objectives you are trying to achieve so that you select the correct purpose. For example, metrics can be used to validate a decision, such as whether you are supporting the strategy and vision of the business. They may also be used for justification, to answer the question, Do we have the right targets and metrics? Of course, we all understand that metrics can drive behaviors, so they can be used to direct and change people's actions based on factual data. Often metrics are used to identify when an intervention needs to take place or to take corrective actions such as identifying improvement opportunities.

As always, it is important to ensure that there is a balanced approach; focusing only on identification of improvement can have a negative impact on staff morale.

Service measurements and metrics should be used to drive decisions. Depending on what is being measured, the decision could be strategic, tactical, or operational.

CSI will have to manage many improvement opportunities, but often with only a limited budget to address them, so decisions must be made. Which improvement opportunities will support the business strategy and goals, and which will support the IT goals and objectives? What are the desired return on investment (ROI) and value on investment (VOI) opportunities? Note that the measures and metrics are always being reviewed against desired business goals and outcomes to ensure that IT continues to align with and meet business expectations.

Measures by themselves may tell the organization very little unless there is a standard or baseline against which to assess the data. Measuring only one particular characteristic of performance in isolation is meaningless unless it is compared with something else that is relevant. Measures of quality allow for measuring trends and the rate of change over a period of time. The following comparisons may be useful:

- Comparison of the assessment against the baseline or agreed standard. It is important to understand the criteria for any deviation from the standard so that you make only necessary improvements instead of responding to every discrepancy.

- Comparison against a target or goal in an SLA is important so there is a clear understanding of fluctuations in service quality. This will strengthen a relationship between service provider and customer by demonstrating engagement and forward planning.

- Comparison with other organizations is also helpful, but it is necessary to ensure that the strategy, goals, and objectives of other organizations align with yours.

- Comparison over time, such as day to day, week to week, month to month, quarter to quarter, or year to year, is a commonly used approach for trend analysis. Remember to ensure that you are still comparing relevant and appropriate data samples. If a measure has been altered, it may be that the comparison is no longer valid.

- Comparison between different business units and services allows the organization to ensure consistency across the enterprise as a whole.

Using measures and metrics is a powerful mechanism for the identification of improvements, and trend analysis can provide information to predict future performance.

It is also important to ensure that your measures take into consideration external factors, such as political influences or market forces outside of your organization.

Individual metrics and measures by themselves do not communicate very much from a strategic or tactical point of view. Some types of metrics and measures are often more activity based than volume based, but they have value from an operational perspective. They might include the services used and which customers are using those services. Understanding service usage both for the time of day and how often will help you understand the demand requirements, as will the medium through which it is accessed (for example, whether it's internal, external, or web based). At a lower level of granularity, the performance and availability of components also provides useful information on the quality of the service delivered.

Each of these measures by themselves will provide some information that is important to IT staff (particularly the technical management staff), but it is the examination of all the measurements and metrics together that delivers the real value.

It is important for someone to take responsibility for looking at these measurements as a whole and to analyze trends and interpret the meaning of the metrics and measures.

Creating Scorecards and Reports

CSI should assume responsibility for ensuring that the quality of service required by the business is provided within the imposed cost constraints. CSI is also instrumental in determining if IT is still on course with the achievement of planned implementation targets and, if not, plotting course corrections to bring it back into alignment.

Using techniques such as the balanced scorecard and SWOT analysis, CSI can measure and report on the success of improvement actions.

Service measurement information is used for three main purposes: to report on the service to interested parties, for comparison against targets, and to identify improvement opportunities.

Reports must be appropriate and useful for all those who use them, and typically there are three distinct audiences for service management reports. The business will be interested in evidence that IT is focused on delivering services on time and within budget. IT management will have an interest in the tactical and strategic results that support the business, and the operational and technical IT managers will make use of the tactical and operational metrics that support their activities. The operational managers will also be interested in technology domain measurements such as component availability and performance.

Many organizations make the mistake of creating and distributing the same report to everyone, but this does not provide value for everyone because of varied interests.

Creating Scorecards That Align to Strategies

Reports and scorecards should be linked to overall strategy and goals. Using a balanced scorecard approach is one way to manage this alignment. In Figure 46.7, there is an illustration of how the overall goals and objectives can be used to derive the measurements and metrics required to support the overall goals and objectives.

FIGURE 46.7   Deriving measurements and metrics from goals and objectives

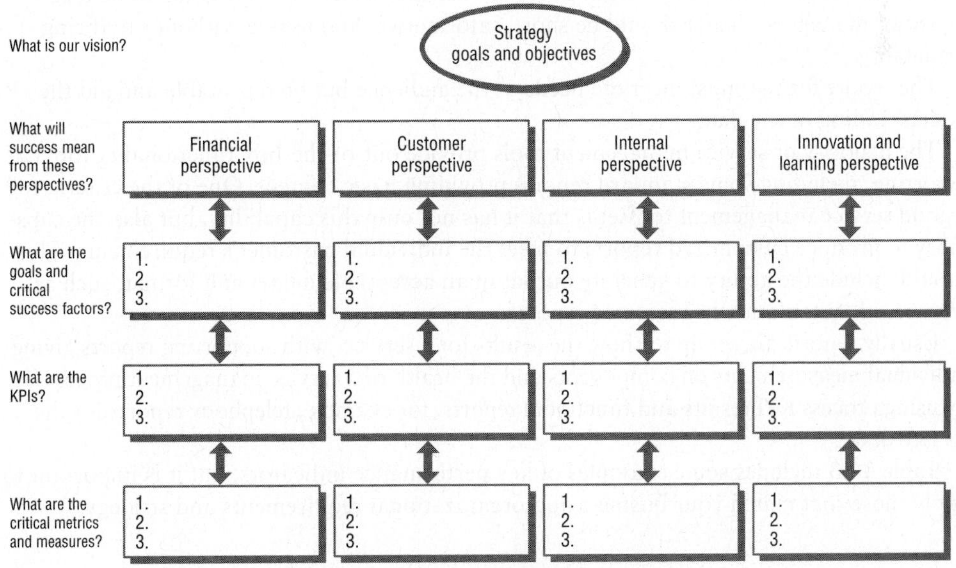

The arrows point both ways because the strategy, goals, and objectives will drive the identification of required KPIs and measurements, but it is also important to remember that the measures are input into KPIs and the KPIs support the goals in the balanced scorecard.

It is important to select the right measures and targets to be able to answer the question of whether the goals are being achieved and the overall strategy supported.

Creating Reports

When creating reports, it is important to know their purpose and the details required as well as the time frame to which they relate. Reports can be used to provide information for a single month, or a comparison of the current month with other months to provide a trend for a certain time period. Reports can be used to show whether service levels are being met or breached.

Before starting the design of any report, it is important to understand some key facts, which should be incorporated into the design. One of the first items to consider is the target audience. Most senior managers don't want a report that is 50 pages long. They like to have a short summary report and access to supporting details if they are interested.

Also important is understanding what the report will be used for because this will make a difference to the content and the way that it is presented and interpreted. Basic information about roles and responsibilities for the creation and production of the report and the frequency of reporting will also be part of the design. The audience will drive the information that is to be shared or exchanged. For example, if the report is going to be read by senior managers, then it should be short, informative, and usable without sacrificing readability.

The report format must meet the needs of the audience but be repeatable and aid the understanding of the data.

The majority of service management tools provide out-of-the-box functionality for reporting, including some standard reports providing basic content. One of the criteria for a good service management toolset is that it has not only this capability, but also the capability to produce customized reports to meet the individual customer's requirements. This should include the ability to generate output in an acceptable media and format, such as web-based, automatically generated reports.

Usually reports are set up to show the results for a service, with supporting reports giving individual measurements on components and the health of a service management process by using process KPI results and functional reports, for example, telephony reports for the service desk.

Table 46.3 includes some examples of key performance indicators, but it is important to apply those that match your business and organizational requirements and strategy.

TABLE 46.3   Sample key performance indicators

Process / Function	KPI / Description	Type	Progress indicator
Incident management	Incidents resolved within target time	Value	Meets/exceeds target times.
Incident management	% of incidents closed—first call	Performance	Service desk only; target is 80%.
Service desk	Abandon rate		Service desk with automatic call distribution (ACD). 5% or less goal (after 24 seconds).
Incident management	Count of incidents submitted by support group	Compliance	Consistency in number of incidents—investigation is warranted for (1) rapid increase, which may indicate infrastructure investigation, and (2) rapid decrease, which may indicate compliance issues.
Problem management	% of repeated problems over time	Quality	Problems that have been removed from the infrastructure and have reoccurred. Target is less than 1% over a 12-month rolling time frame.
Problem management	% root cause with permanent fix	Quality	Calculated from problem start date to permanent fix found. This may not include implementation of permanent fix. Internal target is fix 90% of problems within 40 days. External target is fix 80% of problems within 30 days. External target = third party/ vendor.
Problem management	% and number of incidents raised to problem management	Compliance	Sorted by infrastructure (internal and external) and development (internal and external).

TABLE 46.3   Sample key performance indicators *(continued)*

Process / Function	KPI / Description	Type	Progress indicator
Change management	% of RFCs success-fully implemented without back-out or issues	Quality	Grouped by infrastructure/ development.
Change management	% of RFCs that are emergencies	Performance	Sort by infrastructure or development and by emergency quick fix (service down) or business requirement.
Service asset and configuration management	Number of configuration item (CI) additions or updates	Compliance	CI additions or updates broken down by group—configuration management database (CMDB) or change modules.
Service asset and configuration management	Number of records related to CI	Performance	Number of associations grouped by process.
Release and deployment management	% of releases using exceptions	Value	Exceptions are criteria deemed mandatory—identify by groups.
Release and deployment management	% of releases bypassing process	Compliance	Identify groups bypassing release process.
Capacity management	Action required	Value	Number of services that require action vs. total number of systems.
Capacity management	Capacity-related problems	Quality	Number of problems caused by capacity issues sorted by group.

There are a wide variety of techniques used to measure IT and IT service effectiveness and efficiency, and they are often combined. CSI should be responsible for measurement of the quality of service (and corrections if the quality of service is below targets) while ensuring that IT is still operating within the financial constraints of the organization. CSI will measure progress, understand achievement against targets, and make corrections to improvements where required to remain on track.

It is tempting to allow reporting and measurement to become an end in itself because often the effort and analysis required for report generation requires a separate team of people within the department. CSI should ensure that the goal of reporting remains clearly focused on the progress toward the achievement of business goals and objectives and not simply chasing targets and producing statistics.

Setting Targets

The importance of setting the correct targets for your reports cannot be minimized. Targets set by management are quantified objectives to be attained. They express the aims of the service or process at any level and should provide the basis for the identification of problems and improvement opportunities.

It is as important as selecting the measures you will be using. Targets should be realistic but challenging based on the SMART principles (specific, measurable, achievable, relevant, and time-bound), and they should be easily understandable for those attempting to achieve them. Remember that the choice of measures and their targets can affect the behavior of those who are carrying out the work that is being measured. That is why it is always important to have a balanced approach.

A target that requires service desk staff to answer calls quickly will potentially drive them to clear callers off the line too quickly without resolution and to the detriment of the quality of the call response. It is important to provide a balanced approach and not rely on one target. A variety of targets will produce a holistic approach and maintain quality as well as meeting time-based requirements.

Once a target has been agreed, you must measure to provide a baseline so that improvement toward the target can be measured. Initially, it may not be necessary to report on this until a good statistical reference has been built to show progress.

Balanced Scorecard

Kaplan and Norton (in their paper published in the 1990s) documented the balanced scorecard technique, which involves the definition and implementation of a measurement framework covering four different perspectives: customer, internal business, learning and growth, and financial. These four linked perspectives provide a balanced scorecard to support strategic activities and objectives and can be used to measure overall IT performance. It is complementary to ITIL.

The balanced scorecard shares some common themes with the ITIL framework.

It looks at the client perspective of IT as a service provider, which is primarily documented in SLAs. It considers internal processes and operational excellence utilizing incident management, problem management, change management, service asset and configuration management, and release and deployment management as well as other IT processes and the successful delivery of IT projects. By considering learning and growth, the scorecard reviews business productivity, flexibility of IT, investments in software, professional learning, and development. Finally, the financial scorecard ensures that IT is aligned with business objectives, manages costs, manages risks, and delivers value. Financial management for IT services is the process used to allocate costs and calculate return on investment.

In Figure 46.8, you can see an example of an IT balanced scorecard, and in each sector a different aspect is reviewed.

In Customer: What do customers expect of IT provision?

For Internal (processes): What must IT excel at?

In Innovation (learning and growth): How does IT guarantee that the business will keep generating added value in the future?

And in Financial: What is the cost of IT?

FIGURE 46.8   IT balanced scorecard

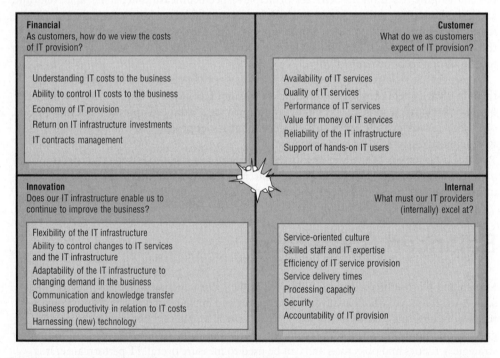

Financial
As customers, how do we view the costs of IT provision?

Understanding IT costs to the business
Ability to control IT costs to the business
Economy of IT provision
Return on IT infrastructure investments
IT contracts management

Customer
What do we as customers expect of IT provision?

Availability of IT services
Quality of IT services
Performance of IT services
Value for money of IT services
Reliability of the IT infrastructure
Support of hands-on IT users

Innovation
Does our IT infrastructure enable us to continue to improve the business?

Flexibility of the IT infrastructure
Ability to control changes to IT services and the IT infrastructure
Adaptability of the IT infrastructure to changing demand in the business
Communication and knowledge transfer
Business productivity in relation to IT costs
Harnessing (new) technology

Internal
What must our IT providers (internally) excel at?

Service-oriented culture
Skilled staff and IT expertise
Efficiency of IT service provision
Service delivery times
Processing capacity
Security
Accountability of IT provision

Cascading the Balanced Scorecard

Many organizations are structured around strategic business units (SBUs). Each business unit will focus on a specific group of products or services offered by the business. Once a balanced scorecard has been defined at the SBU level, it can be cascaded down through the organization.

Many organizations use scorecards in all departments, even at the board level, because for each strategic business-level measure and related target, business units or departments can define additional measures and targets that support the strategic goal and target. Action plans and resource allocation decisions can be made with reference to how they contribute to the strategic balanced scorecard.

The Balanced Scorecard and Measurement-Based Management

The Balanced Scorecard approach covers a number of important aspects, including customer-defined quality of service, continual improvement, employee empowerment, and measurement-based management and feedback.

The balanced scorecard is complementary to total quality management (TQM) and uses the same approach of feedback for internal business process outputs, but has an additional feedback loop for the outcomes of business strategies. This ensures a more complete approach to overall quality across the organization. To achieve this, metrics should be developed based on the priorities of the strategic plan. It is this plan that provides the key business drivers and criteria for metrics that managers most desire to watch. Services and processes can then be designed to collect information relevant to these metrics. Remember, metrics and measurements are part of the design of a service, as covered in the service design lifecycle stage.

Metrics are valuable because they provide a factual basis for defining feedback from some key areas. Strategic feedback shows the present status of the organization; information is gathered from many perspectives for decision-makers. Improvement requires input from diagnostics on a continuous basis, and performance trends can be tracked over time. It is always important to make sure the measures themselves are under continuous review because business requirements change and metrics should change to reflect this. Metrics should also be used to support forecasting methods, providing a quantitative input to the approach.

SWOT Analysis

SWOT stands for strengths, weaknesses, opportunities, and threats. This technique involves the review and analysis of four specific areas of an organization: the internal strengths and weaknesses and the external opportunities and threats.

The analysis allows action to be taken to exploit and capitalize on an organization's strengths while reducing, minimizing, or removing any weaknesses that have been identified. The external focus should encourage active engagement with opportunities while managing, mitigating, and eliminating threats.

SWOT analysis is a technique that can be applied quickly to a specific area of the business. It does not have to have an overall focus.

Purpose

SWOT analysis is a strategic planning tool. It is used to evaluate the strengths, weaknesses, opportunities, and threats associated with a project, business venture, or any other situation that requires decision-making.

How to Use SWOT Analysis

When SWOT analysis is used, the most important factor is to define the desired end state or objective. All the participants in the process must agree, and it must be clear and explicit. Without this clarity, the analysis will not be effective because each element is using the objective to define the specifics for each step. Because the subsequent actions following the analysis will be driven by the results, it is important to ensure that the objective is "SMART" (specific, measurable, achievable, relevant, and time-bound).

If we consider each step in turn, the analysis becomes clear as we define the action taking place. Strengths are the internal attributes that will be helpful in achieving the agreed objective, whereas weaknesses are internal attributes that will be harmful. The analysis then looks at external factors. Opportunities are those factors that will be helpful in achieving the agreed objective, and threats are external factors that will be harmful.

An accurate SWOT analysis is a useful planning tool, helping to answer questions such as, How can we use the strengths to our advantage? and How can we stop the weaknesses? Having a clear understanding of external factors is important; even if we are unable to change them, we may be able to adapt our practices to exploit them or mitigate against their impact.

Scope, Reach, and Range

A SWOT analysis can be performed at various levels throughout the organization. It can take place at an individual, departmental, divisional, or even corporate level. It is important to consolidate the results of the analyses, and this should be from the bottom up so that the lower levels of the hierarchy can be completed before the next is attempted.

For example, if the individual members of a functional team each perform a SWOT analysis to capture their individual perspective, the next SWOT analysis should be based on the team. Then multiple teams can perform the analysis until eventually the departmental level is reached. This would continue up to the corporate level.

It is also possible to conduct a SWOT analysis for a service or a process.

Common Pitfalls of a SWOT Analysis

It is important to align the SWOT analysis with the business vision, mission, goals, and objectives. If the end state of the analysis is not properly identified at the start, it may result in wasted resources and potentially failure. There are a number of common errors that can take place when carrying out a SWOT analysis.

One of the most common is conducting a SWOT analysis before defining and agreeing on the end state. Another common error is to confuse the external opportunities with the strengths in the internal organization. It is important to keep them separate. A further mistake is to confuse opportunities with possible strategies. SWOT is a description of conditions, while possible strategies define actions.

Creating a Return on Investment

For a return on investment (ROI) challenge, many factors need to be taken into consideration, one of which is the investment cost. This is the money an organization pays to improve services and service management processes. These costs will be, for example, internal resource costs, tool costs, and consulting costs. It is often easy to come up with these costs.

Another factor is what an organization can gain in a return. ROIs are often hard to define or quantify. Here are a few of the things that have to be considered when creating a return on investment (in addition to the cost of not implementing the improvement):

- The cost of downtime, including the loss of productivity and loss of revenue

- The cost of rework or redundant work, project work, and delayed implementation

- The cost of the operating environment, escalation of incidents, and hourly costs

It is important to understand the ROI the business will receive as a result of the improvements. Measuring availability is often a good way to understand the cost of lost productivity, the cost of not being able to complete a business transaction, or the true cost of downtime.

There are different approaches to measuring and reporting on availability. You can apply an analysis of the impact by minutes lost, which is a calculation of the duration of downtime multiplied by the number of customers impacted. This can be used to report on lost customer productivity. Then there is the impact by business transaction, which is a calculation based on the number of business transactions that could not be processed during the downtime. This measurement provides a better indication of business impact. Combining these can provide the true cost of downtime that has been agreed on.

Other areas of warranty—such as security, recoverability, and ensuring that there is sufficient capacity—also have to be taken into account.

For example, an insurance company not being able to write policies can easily translate to lost revenue. Internet companies providing goods and services online are also good examples for easily demonstrating lost revenue.

Establishing a Business Case

A business case needs to identify the reason for undertaking a service or a process initiative, including the specification of the data and evidence that needs to be provided to prove the costs and expected benefits.

It is important to remember that process redesign activities are complex and may be more costly than assumed. The same can be said for the impact of organizational change, and with the introduction of organizational and process change comes the potential requirement to improve competencies and tools, adding further cost to the improvement.

It is important not to limit the business case to return on investment but to include the value that a service improvement will bring to the organization. Value on investment can be measured as the improvement is implemented, whereas return on investment can really only be demonstrated once the implementation of the improvement has concluded. Working collaboratively with the business, it should be possible to identify the value the implementation brings to the business. Examples of business value measures include the time to market, customer retention, and the increase in organizational market share.

IT can demonstrate its contribution through gains in agility, managing and enhancing knowledge, and a reduction in costs and risk. IT should begin by defining the types of business values that each improvement will contribute.

Business Cases in a Data-Poor Environment

It is often the case that an organization that intends to carry out service improvements is doing so in a situation where the lack of process means that there is no evidence to prove the expected benefits, value on investment, or return on investment.

There is an approach that circumvents this situation by gaining approval to establish basic measurement capabilities as a means of gathering consistent data for future analysis. This may be as simple as ensuring that all IT staff record data in a consistent fashion or start measuring activities or outcomes that are not currently captured. After an agreed period of data capture, some evidence will exist to support (or perhaps not support) a process improvement initiative.

Another approach is to undertake a process maturity assessment of current processes, but this activity will identify only the absence of process and/or data. A process maturity assessment will not in itself provide the data to justify how much to spend on improving process. So often both approaches are used so that consistency is achieved with an understanding of how well processes are being followed, and from this, measures of value can be established.

It is important that once the decision to start capturing and reporting on data is made, an initial baseline is created so improvements can be measured against it.

Measuring Benefits Achieved

In the business case, we can identify estimated benefits, but eventually we need to measure achievements. These measurements show whether the improvement activity achieved the intended outcomes and should also consider whether the envisaged improvements were realized by measuring the benefits arising from the improvements. It is also important to demonstrate that the target ROI and the intended value-add was actually achieved (VOI).

Continual service improvement is cyclic, and the outcomes of measurements will lead to further process improvement actions being reevaluated.

It is important to ensure that enough time has passed before measuring the benefits. Some benefits will not be immediately apparent, and it is likely that benefits will continue to change over time as ongoing costs and ongoing benefits continue to change.

A further consideration in the measurement of benefits is that data quality and measurement precision pre- and postimprovement could be different. This may invalidate direct comparison, so there may be a requirement for the data to be normalized before validating benefits.

Service Reporting

Reporting should cover the purpose of the report, the intended audience, and its use. Once the data has been collected and analyzed, presentation is critical.

It is often the case that the majority of daily reports produced and delivered to the business are not used. They are much more appropriate for use by the internal IT team. Consider carefully the reports delivered to the business; trends and actions for improvement may be of more interest. Always ensure that reports are meaningful and appropriate for their audience.

Report content should be informative. It may be that the business will be more interested in a structure that reports on the actions taken. Reports on adherence to SLAs can be open to interpretation, whereas reports on future actions as well as the past will enable IT to promote its solutions to the issues the business may have experienced.

Reporting Policy and Rules

It is important to agree with the business on the policies and rules for the reports. Gain agreement in advance regarding the potential target audience, and then agree on what information the business requires about the service. During the design stage of the lifecycle, agreement should be sought on what is going to be measured and reported, including definitions of terms and boundaries. It is important to provide clarity on the mathematics used for all the calculations that are used. The scheduling and delivery mechanism for the reports and who will have access to them should be stipulated, as well as the attendees for the review and discussion meetings. It is good practice to agree on these elements in the design stage, but we should also remain flexible for alterations in the operations stage of the lifecycle.

Right Content for the Right Audience

It is important to ensure that the right content is provided for the right audience. It is good practice to apply the right policies for each target group because the needs of one customer may not be the same as another.

Once the framework, policies, and rules are in place, automating suitably styled reports is a task of translating flat historical data into meaningful business views. These will need to be annotated around the key questions, threats, mitigations, and improvements that have been identified in the report. Reports can then be presented via the medium of choice—for example, paper-based hard copies, online soft copies, web-enabled dynamic HTML, current snapshot whiteboards, and real-time portal/dashboards.

Simple and effective customizable and automated reporting is vital for an ongoing reporting schedule, which provides satisfactory reporting to the business.

It is also important to recognize that the initial schedule and content for reports may change over time as the business needs change. The end result should be targeted reporting that is clear, unambiguous, and relevant, delivered to the correct recipient in a medium and manner that promotes accessibility and use.

CSI and Other Service Management Processes

The CSI process makes wide use of methods and practices found in many of the other processes throughout the lifecycle of a service. This means that the outputs in the form of flows, matrices, statistics, and analysis reports provide valuable information about the service's design and operation. This information, combined with new business requirements, technology specifications, IT capabilities, budgets, trends, and possibly legislation is of great importance to CSI in enabling a determination of what needs to be improved and also how to prioritize it and suggest improvements if required.

Availability Management

Availability management's methods are part of the measuring process—gathering, processing, and analyzing activities. When the information is provided to CSI in the form of a report or a presentation, it becomes part of CSI's gathering activity.

When used by availability management, this activity provides IT with the business and user perspective about how failures and faults in the infrastructure and underpinning process and procedures impact the business operation. The use of business-driven metrics can demonstrate this impact in real terms and help quantify the benefits of improvement opportunities.

Component Failure Impact Analysis

Component failure impact analysis (CFIA) is the analysis of the impact to the business if a component fails. It identifies single points of failure, IT services at risk from failure of various configuration items (CIs), and the alternatives that are available should a CI fail. It should also be used to assess the existence and efficacy of recovery procedures for the selected CIs. The same approach can be used for a single IT service by mapping the component CIs against the vital business functions and users supported by each component.

When a single point of failure is identified, the information is provided to CSI. This information, combined with business requirements, enables CSI to make recommendations on how to address the failure.

Fault Tree Analysis

Fault tree analysis (FTA) is a technique that is used to determine the chain of events that cause a disruption of IT services. Using this technique, it is possible to construct detailed models of availability. It makes a representation of a chain of events and distinguishes between four types of events: basic events, resulting events, conditional events, and trigger events. Using Boolean algebra and notation (AND/OR statements), it is possible to indicate which part of the infrastructure, process, or service was responsible for the service disruptions. This information, combined with business requirements, enables CSI to make recommendations about how to address the fault.

Service Failure Analysis

Service failure analysis (SFA) is a technique designed to provide a structured approach to identify end-to-end availability improvement opportunities and deliver benefits to the user. Many of the activities involved in SFA are closely aligned with those of problem management. SFA should take an end-to-end view of the service requirements. It is therefore important to attempt to identify improvement opportunities that benefit the end user.

CSI and SFA work hand in hand because SFA identifies the business impact of an outage on a service, system, or process. This information, combined with business requirements, enables CSI to make recommendations about how to address improvement opportunities.

Technical Observation

A technical observation (TO) is a prearranged gathering of specialist technical support staff from within IT support. The TO's purpose is to monitor events as they occur, with the specific aim of identifying improvement opportunities within the current IT infrastructure. The TO is best suited to delivering proactive business and end-user benefits from within the real-time IT environment. The TO gathers, processes, and analyzes information about the situation. If the TO is included as part of the launch of a new service, system, or process, for example, a lot of the issues inherent to any new component will be identified and dealt with more quickly.

The Expanded Incident Lifecycle

The expanded incident lifecycle, as shown in Figure 46.9, provides a technique to help with the technical analysis of incidents affecting the availability of components and IT services.

FIGURE 46.9 The expanded incident lifecycle

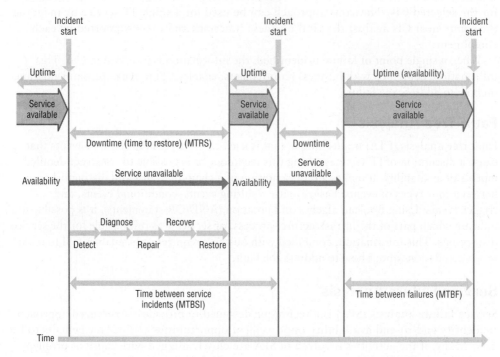

It is made up of two parts: time to restore service (also known as downtime) and time between failures (also known as uptime). There is a diagnosis part to the incident lifecycle as well as repair, restoration, and recovery of the service.

Using the other techniques in availability management, it is possible to review each element of the incident management process and apply to this review a continual service improvement activity to address issues in incident management. Management of infrastructure is often reliant on the information from the analysis of mean time between failures, mean time between system incidents, and the mean time to restore service.

Capacity Management

The capacity management process must be responsive to changing business requirements for processing capacity. New services are required, and existing services will require modification to provide extra functionality. Old services will become obsolete, freeing up capacity. Capacity management must ensure that sufficient hardware, software, and personnel resources are in place to support existing and future business capacity and performance requirements.

Similar to the availability management process, the capacity management process should play an important role in helping the IT support organization recognize where it can add value by exploiting its technical skills and competencies in a capacity context. Capacity management should use the continual improvement technique and apply this to technical capability. It is possible to do this either in small groups of technical staff or in a wider group within a workshop environment.

The information generated by the capacity management process should be made available to CSI through the capacity management information system (CMIS), a database that should form part of the service knowledge management system.

As you will remember from your Foundation course, capacity management has three subprocesses: business, service, and component capacity management.

Business Capacity Management

First we will look at business capacity management. A prime objective of the business capacity management subprocess is to ensure that future business requirements for IT services are considered and understood and that sufficient capacity to support the services is planned and implemented in an appropriate timescale.

New service level requirements from the business will drive new capacity requirements, as will improvements and requirements identified through its own investigation and analysis.

The information gathered in this subprocess allows CSI to answer the question, What do we need?

Service Capacity Management

A prime objective of the service capacity management subprocess is to identify and understand the IT services, their use of resources, working patterns, and peaks and troughs. In addition, the subprocess should ensure that the services can and do meet their SLA targets. This is another process, like availability management, that is concerned with end-to-end service provision and performance.

In this subprocess, the focus is on managing service performance as determined by the targets contained in the SLAs or SLRs.

The key to successful service capacity management is to preempt difficulties wherever possible. The information gathered here enables CSI to answer the question, What do we need?

Component Capacity Management

The component capacity management subprocess's prime objective is to identify and understand the capacity and utilization of each of the components of the IT infrastructure. This is where the technical management expertise will be utilized. This ensures the optimum use of the current hardware and software resources in order to achieve and maintain the agreed service levels.

As in service capacity management, the key to successful component capacity management is to preempt difficulties wherever possible.

It is important to understand how the three subprocesses tie together. Let's look at the example in Figure 46.10 and the requirements in Table 46.4.

FIGURE 46.10 Connecting business and service capacity management

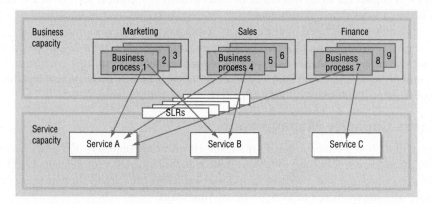

TABLE 46.4 Departmental requirements

	Marketing	Sales	Finance
Employees	15	40	5
Number of emails per day	100	200	50
Size of attachment	10 Mb	5 Mb	10 Mb
Frequency of large attachment	Infrequent	Very frequent (contracts)	Often
Requires remote access	No	Yes	Yes
Requires handheld computer	No	Yes	No

There are three services (A, B, and C) and three departments (Marketing, Sales, and Finance). Service A is used by all three departments. Service B is used only by Marketing and Sales. Service C is used only by Finance.

Each of the subprocesses will have a part to play in understanding the management of capacity in the organization. Changes in business focus should be communicated through business capacity management, but capacity planning is often carried out a year in advance, and it is very difficult to be accurate this far ahead, so it is important for business capacity management to be constantly informed of any changes by the organization. So if marketing provides business plans for an increase in sales, then this will have an impact on all three departments. Any of the services used will potentially be impacted. Marketing services will be required to take on greater capacity, while sales services will have a higher throughput, and so will the finance services as more sales go through.

It is also important for the activities in service capacity management to keep up with changes in service level requirements in real time, and these activities can be used to support the forecasting in business capacity management for the marketing department's predicted increase in sales.

Component capacity management is highly technical, but the reports and information it produces are used by service capacity management to continue to monitor the capacity capability of the service as a whole. Each of the subprocesses is important in managing the organizational requirements.

Workload and Demand Management

There are many different ways to influence customer behavior. Charging for services is an obvious option, but it is not always effective. People may still need to use the service and will use it regardless of the price.

Usage policies for the service is another way to influence customer behavior, by placing restrictions or limits on the service. You are probably familiar with restrictions such as amount of space allocated for email storage. Be careful because such policies may produce a negative effect, but regular reviews can be used to make sure the influencing mechanism is still having a positive effect.

For example, if an organization chooses to charge for every contact to the service desk, this could create negative behavior in that end users no longer call or email the service desk and instead call second-level support directly or turn to peer-to-peer support, which ultimately makes the cost of support go up, not down. However, if the goal is to move end users to a new self-service web-based knowledge system, then with a proper communication and education plan on using the new self-service system, this could be a positive influencing experience.

Business requirements change over time, and CSI should continue to review policies to ensure that they are still appropriate for business needs.

Capacity management uses a number of techniques to support the process.

Trend Analysis

Trend analysis of the data captured in service and component capacity management subprocesses will provide valuable information for the prediction and forecasting for capacity of services and components in the future. Problem management also uses trend analysis as a technique, but it relates to the historical view of trends for improving incident data.

Modeling

There is a wide range of modeling techniques applied in capacity management. Modeling is used to provide information on the "what if" scenario and is a useful tool for future prediction and forecasting based on potential situations.

Analytical models are representations of a computer system's behavior based on mathematical algorithms, for example, network queuing theory. Comparison to the actual performance is necessary to verify that the model is effective, and then variables can be changed to use the model for prediction.

Simulation involves the modeling of discrete events, such as transaction arrival rates, against a given hardware configuration. This type of modeling can be very accurate in sizing new applications or predicting the effects of changes on existing applications. It can also be very time consuming and therefore costly.

Improvements are gradual and incremental by nature. The first stage in modeling is to create a baseline model that accurately reflects the performance that is being achieved. When this baseline model is created, predictive modeling can be done. If the baseline model is accurate, then the accuracy of the result of the predicted changes can be trusted.

IT Service Continuity Management

IT service continuity management (ITSCM) allows an organization to manage IT risks through a process of identifying what is important to the stakeholder, mitigating against the risks the organization chooses to take, and ensuring that the business processes will continue to operate throughout a disruption. CSI reviews the requirements of the organization, and improvements should be managed through the change process to ensure that they are reflected in the continuity plans.

Business continuity management is concerned with the management of risks at an organizational level, which are then supported by the ITSCM plans. The BCM process involves reducing the risk to an acceptable level and planning for the recovery of business processes should a risk materialize and a disruption to the business occur.

Risk Management

Although not an ITIL-defined IT service management process, risk management is part of many IT service management processes.

Every organization manages its risk, but not always in a way that is visible, repeatable, and consistently applied to support decision-making. The task of risk management is to ensure that the organization makes cost-effective use of a risk process that has a series of well-defined steps. The aim is to support better decision-making through a good understanding of risks and their likely impact.

There are two distinct phases: risk analysis and risk management:

- Risk analysis is concerned with gathering information about exposure to risk so that the organization can make appropriate decisions and manage risk appropriately. Risk analysis involves the identification and assessment of the level (measure) of the risks calculated from the assessed values of assets and the assessed levels of threats to, and vulnerabilities of, those assets.

- Risk management involves having processes in place to monitor risks, access to reliable and up-to-date information about risks, the right balance of control in place to deal with those risks, and decision-making processes supported by a framework of risk analysis and evaluation. Risk management also involves the identification, selection, and adoption of countermeasures justified by the identified risks to assets in terms of their potential impact upon services if failure occurs and the reduction of those risks to an acceptable level.

A certain amount of risk taking is inevitable if an organization is to achieve its objectives. Effective management of risk helps to improve service performance by contributing to increased certainty and fewer surprises. It should also support better service delivery and more effective management of change. Managing and making more efficient use of resources by better management at all levels through improved decision-making should be a further effect of risk management. Organizational risk management should also reduce waste and fraud and deliver better value for money. By managing the risks of innovation, and also contingent and maintenance activities, risk management supports continual service improvement.

Problem Management

CSI and problem management are closely related because one of the goals of problem management is to identify and permanently remove errors that impact services from the infrastructure. This directly supports CSI activities of identifying and implementing service improvements.

Problem management also supports improvement activities through trend analysis and the targeting of preventive action. Although problem management activities are generally conducted within the scope of service operation, CSI takes an active role in the proactive aspects of problem management because it is here that the process is used to identify and recommend changes that will result in service improvements.

Knowledge Management

Knowledge management is a key support for CSI because capturing, organizing, assessing for quality, and using knowledge plays a large part in CSI activities. An organization has to gather knowledge and analyze what the results are in order to look for trends in service level achievements and the results and output of service management processes. This knowledge may be used to identify improvement opportunities for inclusion in the CSI register, which will then be reviewed and prioritized. It will also be used for contributing to service improvement plans and initiatives.

Knowledge management is constantly changing, in line with the technological advances in IT. The rate of change in the IT industry has opened up new opportunities for knowledge sharing and collaboration, not least of which is the extensive use of the Internet by corporations and end users. Staff turnover requires that corporate knowledge is captured centrally rather than being dependent on the individual because it is more common for individuals to change companies throughout their career.

Knowledge Management Concepts

Effective knowledge management enables a company to optimize the benefits of CSI by enhancing the organization's effectiveness through better decision-making enabled by having the right information at the right time. Knowledge management is key to facilitating learning through the exchange and development of ideas and individuals.

It supports the customer-supplier relationship because information and services are shared, expanding capabilities through collaborative efforts. In addition, it will improve business processes through sharing lessons learned, results, and best practices across the organization.

Knowledge management is key to the overall viability of an organization, from capturing the competitive advantage in an industry to decreasing cycle time and cost of an IT implementation. The approach to cultivating knowledge depends heavily on the makeup of the existing knowledge base and knowledge management norms for cultural interaction.

The identification of knowledge gaps and the resulting sharing and development of that knowledge must be built into CSI throughout the IT lifecycle. Throughout a CSI initiative, a lot of experience and information is acquired. It is important that this knowledge be gathered, organized, and accessible. To ensure the ongoing success of the program, knowledge management techniques must be applied.

Summary

In this chapter, we reviewed the methods and techniques used by CSI in the management of improvements.

We began by exploring the use of assessments and gap analysis to assist the start of improvements, to identify weak areas, and to demonstrate success. Benchmarking supports analysis, which enables a capture of the baseline for the improvement.

All improvements will need to be measured to prove they have been successful, so this chapter also explored the use of service measurement, metrics, and a balanced scorecard. We also considered the use of SWOT (strength, weakness, opportunity, and threat) analysis and how it can be used for identification of improvement.

Measurements must be shared with the appropriate audience, and in this chapter, we also looked at the use of service reports and demonstrating return on investment.

Finally, we explored the way in which other service management processes support the activities of CSI. These include availability management, capacity management, IT service continuity management, problem management, and knowledge management.

Exam Essentials

Understand the methods and techniques of CSI.   Be familiar with the methods involved in the practice of continual service improvement.

Be able to explain and expand on the importance of assessment in CSI.   It is important to understand the importance of assessment for CSI and the methods of assessment that can be used.

Understand and expand on the use of gap analysis for CSI.   You should be able to explain the use of gap analysis in the lifecycle stage of CSI and how it supports the delivery of improvement.

Be able to explain the importance of benchmarking in CSI.   Benchmarking is a vital part of any improvement and should be carried out regularly as part of an improvement program.

Understand the use of measurement within CSI.   This includes the use of service measurement and metrics in demonstrating success and tracking improvement. You should be able to identify the appropriate techniques and metrics for a given situation.

Know how to use a balanced scorecard.   Although a balanced scorecard does not originate as part of the ITIL framework, its use is complementary to and supportive of the CSI approach.

Be able to explain the importance of SWOT analysis in CSI.   SWOT analysis identifies the strengths, weaknesses, opportunities, and threats in an organization. You should be able to explain the use of SWOT analysis as part of CSI.

Understand and explain the use of service reports and ROI to support CSI.   To demonstrate the success of CSI, there must be measurement and suitable reporting. This includes justifying the return on investment in the improvement.

Understand and explain the support of other ITIL processes to CSI.   Understand and explain the use of other processes (availability, capacity, continuity, problem, and knowledge management) in the support of CSI processes.

Review Questions

You can find the answers to the review questions in the appendix.

1. What is the purpose of an assessment?
   1. To establish potential shortcomings
   2. To provide a comparison point for benchmarking
      A. Statement 1 only
      B. Statement 2 only
      C. Both
      D. Neither

2. Assessments require resources, but which of these is NOT an essential required resource?
   A. Real costs
   B. Staff time
   C. Management engagement
   D. Assessment tools

3. Maturity assessment frameworks evaluate which of the following elements?
   1. People
   2. Services
   3. Process
   4. Technology
      A. 1, 3, 4
      B. 2, 4
      C. 1, 3
      D. 3, 4

4. What is the commonly used acronym for the Deming Cycle?
   A. DCAP
   B. PDCA
   C. ACDP
   D. PADC

5. What is one of the purposes of benchmarking?
   A. Evaluate SLA performance in relation to SLRs
   B. Evaluate contract targets against SLA targets
   C. Evaluate processes in relation to best practice
   D. Evaluate change requests against expected outcome

6. Which of these are survey techniques that can help identify problem areas for improvement action?

 1. Informal conversations with customers, employees, suppliers

 2. Focus groups

 3. Automated monitoring

 4. Questionnaires

 5. Process mapping

 6. Quality control of variance reports

  A. 1, 2, 4, and 6

  B. 1, 3, 4, and 6

  C. 1, 2, 3, 4, and 5

  D. 1, 2, 3, 4, 5, and 6

7. Which of these internal and external personnel may be involved in benchmarking:

Internal organization

The customer

The user or consumer

Internal service provider

External partners

External service providers

Direct IT users (members of the public)

Benchmarking partners

 A. Only internal organizational personnel

 B. Only external partners

 C. Both internal and external

 D. Neither internal nor external

8. Which of these are basic measures used in service measurement?

 1. Availability

 2. Reliability

 3. Performance

 4. Security

  A. 1, 2, 4

  B. 2, 3, 4

  C. 1, 3, 4

  D. 1, 2, 3

9. Service targets may be driven by which of the following:

    1. Business requirements

    2. Regulatory requirements

    3. New policies

    4. Service level agreements

      A. 1, 2, 3

      B. 2, 3, 4

      C. 1, 2, 3, 4

      D. 1, 2, 3

10. Which of the following statements about the acronym SWOT is/are correct?

    1. *S* refers to external attributes that are helpful for achieving objectives.

    2. *W* refers to external attributes that are harmful for achieving objectives.

    3. *O* refers to external conditions that are helpful for achieving objectives.

    4. *T* refers to external conditions that are harmful for achieving objectives.

      A. None are correct.

      B. 1 only is correct.

      C. 1 and 2 are correct.

      D. 3 and 4 are correct.

Chapter

47

Organizing for Continual Service Improvement

THE FOLLOWING ITIL INTERMEDIATE EXAM OBJECTIVES ARE DISCUSSED IN THIS CHAPTER:

✓ The responsibilities, skills, and competencies for:

- Service owner

- Process owner

- Process manager

- Process practitioner

✓ The activities involved in the seven-step improvement process and the skills required

✓ Comparing the CSI manager role with other relevant roles

✓ How the responsibility model (RACI) can be used when defining roles and responsibilities in CSI

This chapter explores CSI in relation to the organization and revolves around the roles relevant to CSI and their responsibilities, skills, and competencies. We also review the nature of the activities and the skills required for the seven-step improvement process as well as how the authority matrices (RACI) are used by CSI.

Responsibilities, Skills, and Competencies

In the following sections, we consider the responsibilities, skills, and competencies for each of the generic roles defined in ITIL:

- Service owner
- Process owner
- Process manager
- Process practitioner

We then consider the roles specific to the seven-step improvement process:

- The seven-step improvement process owner
- The seven-step improvement process manager
- The reporting analyst

Generic Roles

Throughout the ITIL framework there is consistent use of some generic roles across all lifecycle stages. The first of these is the service owner.

Service Owner

Large organizations will have many specialist areas, each concerned with its own processes and capabilities. Providing a service to a customer requires many of these specialist silos to contribute part of that service. The service owner provides an end-to-end view, which ensures consistency across the service.

The service owner understands what the service needs to deliver and how it has been built to satisfy these requirements. As the representative of the service, they are involved in assessment of the impact of changes affecting the service, and they act as an escalation and communication point when it suffers a major incident.

By attending internal and external reviews, the service owner ensures that the service is delivered according to the customer requirements. This allows the role to identify the requirements for improvement and provide input to continual service improvement to work with IT to address any deficiencies that exist.

The service catalog process provides the business with information regarding the service, and maintaining this information with the service catalog process owner is another responsibility for the service owner.

The service owner interfaces with the underlying IT processes. They will have close associations with many of the processes:

Incident Management   The service owner is involved in or may actually chair the crisis management team for high-priority incidents impacting the service owned.

Problem Management   The service owner plays a major role in establishing the root cause and proposed permanent fix for the service being evaluated.

Release and Deployment Management   The service owner is a key stakeholder in determining whether a new release affecting a service in production is ready for promotion.

Change Management   The service owner participates in change advisory board decisions, approving changes to the services they own.

Asset and Configuration Management   The service owner ensures that all groups that maintain the data and relationships for the service architecture they are responsible for have done so with the level of integrity required.

Service Level Management   The service owner acts as the single point of contact for a specific service and ensures that the service portfolio and service catalog are accurate in relation to their service.

Availability and Capacity Management   The service owner reviews technical monitoring data from a domain perspective to ensure that the needs of the overall service are being met.

IT Service Continuity Management   The service owner understands and is responsible for ensuring that all elements required to restore their service are known and in place in the event of a crisis.

IT Financial Management   The service owner assists in defining and tracking the cost models in relations to how their service is costed and recovered.

Process Owner

The next generic role we look at is that of the process owner. The process owner role is accountable for ensuring that a process is fit for purpose. This role is often assigned to the same person who carries out the process manager role, but the two roles may be separate in larger organizations. The process owner role ensures that their process is performed according to the agreed and documented standard and meets the aims of the process definition.

The process owner has the following accountabilities:

- Sponsoring, designing, and change managing the process and its metrics
- Defining the process strategy
- Assisting with process design
- Defining appropriate policies and standards to be employed throughout the process
- Periodically reviewing the process strategy to ensure that it is still appropriate and makes changes as required
- Communicating process information or changes as appropriate to ensure awareness
- Providing process resources to support activities required throughout the service lifecycle
- Making improvements to the process

Process Manager

Working closely with the process owner, the process manager role is accountable for operational management of a process. There may be several process managers for one process, for example, regional change managers or IT service continuity managers for each data center. The process manager role is often assigned to the person who carries out the process owner role, but the two roles may be separate in larger organizations.

The process manager's accountabilities are as follows:

- Working with the process owner to plan and coordinate all process activities
- Ensuring that all activities are carried out as required throughout the service lifecycle
- Appointing people to the required roles
- Managing resources assigned to the process
- Working with service owners and other process managers to ensure the smooth running of services
- Monitoring and reporting on process performance
- Identifying improvement opportunities for inclusion in the CSI register
- Working with the CSI manager and process owner to review and prioritize improvements in the CSI register
- Making improvements to the process implementation

Process Practitioner

We have considered the generic roles of process owner and manager, and now we will review the practitioner role. A process practitioner is responsible for carrying out one or more process activities.

In some organizations, and for some processes, the process practitioner role may be combined with the process manager role; in others there may be large numbers of practitioners carrying out different parts of the process.

The process practitioner role typically includes the following responsibilities:

- Carrying out one or more activities of a process
- Understanding how the role contributes to the overall delivery of service and creation of value for the business
- Working with other stakeholders, such as their manager, coworkers, users, and customers, to ensure that their contributions are effective
- Ensuring that inputs, outputs, and interfaces for their activities are correct
- Creating or updating records to show that activities have been carried out correctly.

Next we examine the roles involved and the skills required for the implementation of the CSI seven-step improvement process and identify the activities involved.

Roles Specific to the Seven-Step Improvement Process

Next we consider the generic roles associated with the seven-step improvement process activities and the skills these roles require.

The Seven-Step Improvement Process Owner

The seven-step process needs a process owner, like any other process. Their responsibilities include all of the generic process owner responsibilities discussed previously. They work with the CSI manager, service owners, process owners, and functions to ensure that the seven-step improvement process is implemented throughout the service lifecycle.

The Seven-Step Improvement Process Manager

The seven-step process also needs a process manager, like any other process. Their responsibilities include all of the generic process manager responsibilities discussed previously. They would also be responsible for planning and managing support for improvement tools and processes and would maintain the CSI register. They ensure that the interfaces with other processes work smoothly.

The Reporting Analyst

The final generic role is that of reporting analyst. The reporting analyst is a key role for CSI and will often be shared with service level management. In Chapter 45, "The Seven-Step Continual Service Improvement Process," we discussed how critical the analysis of data is to successful service improvement. It is the responsibility of the reporting analyst to ascertain an accurate assessment of the end-to-end service, extracted from the various data sources reporting on components, systems, and subsystems.

The reporting analyst will also identify trends and establish whether they are positive or negative. This information is then used to present the data. The reporting analyst typically has the following responsibilities:

- Participating in CSI service level management meetings to ensure the validity of the reporting and to confirm the correct notification thresholds

- Consolidating data from multiple sources to obtain an end-to-end view

- Identifying and reporting trends and providing feedback on the trends, such as advising their likely impact

- Producing reports on service or system performance

The reporting analyst will require a number of key skills and competencies, including a good understanding of statistical and analytical principles and processes in addition to strong technical skills for the reporting tool(s). The reporting analyst should not be solely a number cruncher however; they require communication skills and the ability to translate technical requirements and specifications into easily understood reporting requirements.

The Activities Involved in the Seven-Step Improvement Process

We have already looked in detail at what is involved in the seven-step improvement process. The process is shown again in Figure 47.1.

FIGURE 47.1   The seven-step improvement process

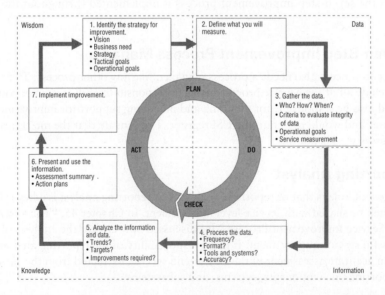

Figure 47.2 shows the four main activities undertaken as part of CSI. Each activity is different and will require different skill levels. Next we'll focus on the roles within each step.

FIGURE 47.2　Activities and skill levels needed for continual service improvement

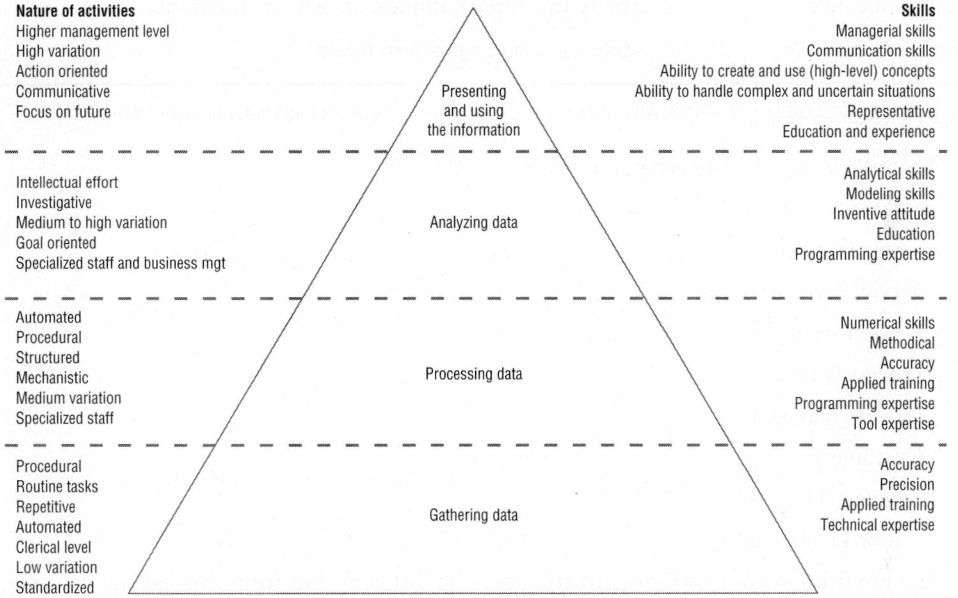

Nature of activities		Skills
Higher management level		Managerial skills
High variation		Communication skills
Action oriented		Ability to create and use (high-level) concepts
Communicative	Presenting and using the information	Ability to handle complex and uncertain situations
Focus on future		Representative
		Education and experience
Intellectual effort		Analytical skills
Investigative		Modeling skills
Medium to high variation	Analyzing data	Inventive attitude
Goal oriented		Education
Specialized staff and business mgt		Programming expertise
Automated		Numerical skills
Procedural		Methodical
Structured		Accuracy
Mechanistic	Processing data	Applied training
Medium variation		Programming expertise
Specialized staff		Tool expertise
Procedural		Accuracy
Routine tasks		Precision
Repetitive	Gathering data	Applied training
Automated		Technical expertise
Clerical level		
Low variation		
Standardized		

Roles and Skills in the Seven-Step Improvement Process

Let's look at the roles involved in each step of the process. Each of the seven steps requires specific skills to carry it out effectively.

Step 1: Identify the Strategy for Improvement

The decision on what should be measured has to be made at a senior level and by those in IT and the business who appreciate what is required to assist the business and to fulfil governance requirements. Some organizations may have a legal regulatory framework that they must abide by, for which they must provide evidence of compliance. Table 47.1 shows the type of activities required and the skills needed for this step.

TABLE 47.1   Skills involved in step 1 (identify the strategy for improvement)

Nature of activities	Skills
Senior management	Ability to create a high-level vision and strategy
High variation	Communication
Action oriented	Ability to create and use high-level concepts
Communicative	Ability to handle complex/uncertain situations
Focused on future	Ability to set longer-term goals

The following titles are typical of this role:

- Strategy manager
- Service owner
- Service level manager
- CSI manager
- Process owner
- Process managers
- Customers
- Business/IT analysts
- Senior IT managers

The job titles in your own organization may be different, but from this list you can see the types of people who should be involved in this step.

Step 2: Define What You Will Measure

The roles involved in step 2 must have a strong understanding of what can and should be measured. Measurement must always fit the capabilities of the information provider. Understanding what measurements the tools can provide, the skills of the staff who will have to specify the reports, and the processes in place are essential if the measurements are to be achievable. Table 47.2 shows the type of activities required and the skills needed for this step.

TABLE 47.2   Skills involved in step 2 (define what you will measure)

Nature of activities	Skills
Senior management	Managerial
High variation	Communication
Action oriented	Ability to create and use (high-level) concepts
Communicative	Ability to handle complex/uncertain situations

Nature of activities	Skills
Intellectual effort	Analytical
Investigative	Modeling
Medium to high variation	Inventive attitude

Typical titles of this role are as follows:

- Service manager
- Service owner
- Process owner
- Process managers
- Internal and external providers

Again, the job titles in your own organization may be different, but from this list, you can see the types of people who should be involved.

Step 3: Gather the Data

Those responsible for gathering the data will be those involved in the activities being measured. For example, the service desk staff will capture response and fix times, security staff will collect data on security breaches, and technical management will measure availability, capacity, and so on. Table 47.3 shows the type of activities required and the skills needed for this step.

TABLE 47.3   Skills involved in step 3 (gather the data)

Nature of activities	Skills
Procedural	Accuracy
Routine	Precision
Repetitive	Meticulous nature
Automated	Technical ability
Clerical	Ability to document

Step 4: Processing the Data

As with gathering the data, those responsible for processing it will be those involved in the activities being measured. For example, the service desk staff will produce the reports showing trends in response and fix times, security staff will do the same for security breaches, and technical management will process the data to produce reports on availability, capacity, and so on. Table 47.4 shows the type of activities required and the skills needed for this step.

TABLE 47.4 Skills involved in step 4 (processing the data)

Nature of activities	Skills
Automated	Numerical skills
Procedural	Methodical
Structural	Accuracy
Mechanistic	Meticulous nature
Medium variation	Programming skills
Specialized	Tool and technical skills and experience

Step 5: Analyzing the Data

The people who defined what could be measured are the right people to analyze the data. They will be individuals involved with providing the service (internal and external providers) and will understand the limitations of the tools, how the measurements are gathered, and any issues that may arise from this. Table 47.5 shows the type of activities required and the skills needed for this step.

TABLE 47.5 Skills involved in step 5 (analyzing the data)

Nature of activities	Skills
Intellectual	Analytical
Investigative	Modeling
Medium to high variation	Inventive attitude
Goal oriented	Ambitious
Specialized and business management	Programming skills

Here is a list of typical job titles for staff involved in this step. Again, the job titles in your own organization may be different, but from this list you can see the types of people who should be involved:

- Service owner
- Process owner
- Process managers
- Business/IT analysts
- Senior IT analysts
- Supervisors and team leaders

Step 6: Presenting and Using the Information

Service providers and key decision-makers will be responsible for presenting and using the information. They must understand the service and its processes to make use of the information. They must have the skills to present the information in a meaningful way so their audience understands what they are being told. The type of activities required and the skills needed for this step are shown in Table 47.6.

TABLE 47.6   Skills involved in step 6 (presenting and using the information)

Nature of activities	Skills
Higher management	Managerial
High variation	Communication
Action oriented	Ability to create and use (high-level) concepts
Communicative	Ability to handle complex/uncertain situations
Focused on future	Ambitious

Here are some typical titles of this role:
- CSI manager
- Service owner
- Service level manager
- Process owner
- Process managers
- Business/IT analysts
- Senior IT managers
- Internal and external providers
- Customers

Again, the job titles in your own organization may be different, but from this list you can see the types of people who should be involved in this step. Note the inclusion of the customers here among those who will process and use the information.

Step 7: Implementing Improvement

Anyone responsible for providing a service should always be trying to implement improvements to the service they provide (see Table 47.7).

TABLE 47.7   Skills involved in step 7 (implementing improvement)

Nature of activities	Skills
Intellectual effort	Analytical
Investigative	Modeling
Medium to high variation	Inventive attitude
Goal oriented	Ambitious
Specialized staff and business management	Programming skills

Typical titles of those with this role are as follows:

- CSI manager
- Service owner
- Service manager
- Service level manager
- Process owner
- Process managers
- Business/IT analysts
- Senior IT managers
- Internal and external providers

Again, the job titles in your own organization may be different, but from this list you can see the types of people who should be involved in this step.

Comparing the CSI Manager Role with Other Relevant Roles

There are similarities in responsibilities between a number of roles involved in continual service improvement.

The Roles

Here we consider the roles of CSI manager, business relationship manager, service level manager, and service manager.

CSI Manager

It is essential to assign someone the role of CSI manager to ensure that continual service improvement has the focus it needs. Without this key individual, improvement initiatives lose focus, get sidetracked, and eventually fail. Improvement becomes disjointed and ad hoc. The CSI manager ensures that improvement is continual.

The responsibilities of the CSI manager are extensive. The role combines working with IT and the business in the identification of improvement opportunities, communicating the vision to others so that they come on board, and then monitoring the success of each improvement plan. The manager must work with the other roles, such as service level manager, to devise the required improvement action plan.

The CSI manager also has an essential role to play in the seven-step improvement process, ensuring the production and analysis of data to identify deficiencies, baselining the current situation, and then monitoring the effectiveness of the improvement actions. The CSI manager is therefore critical to the success of this process.

It is their responsibility to ensure that the organization embeds improvement so that it becomes part of "business as usual." They must sell the concept at every opportunity, mentoring other staff and working with senior management to agree on priorities.

For such an important role to be successful, it is important that the person appointed has the necessary skills and authority. Possessing strong interpersonal skills is a necessity for a successful CSI manager. Much of the job requires building relationships with managers across the organization so that they feel that they are being consulted, not instructed. The CSI manager must act as a catalyst, ensuring that the various IT managers devote sufficient time and resources to the improvement plans. They must build strong relationships with the managers to ensure that improvement is accepted as part of every manager's job, not left to the CSI manager. Managers must be actively supportive of CSI, providing the required levels of commitment and resources if CSI is to work.

Business Relationship Manager

The objective of business relationship management is to establish and maintain a good relationship between the service provider and the customer based on understanding the customer and their business drivers. The customer's business drivers could require changes in SLAs and thus become input into service improvement opportunities. The chapters on service strategy in Part 1 of this book provide more detail on business relationship management and the role of business relationship managers.

Service Level Manager

The objectives of service level management are to define, document, agree on, monitor, measure, report, and review the level of IT services provided and instigate corrective measures whenever appropriate. It also is responsible for ensuring that specific and measurable targets are developed for all IT services and for monitoring and improving customer satisfaction with the quality of service delivered.

Service Manager

Service manager is a generic term for any manager within the service provider organization. The term is commonly used to refer to a business relationship manager, a process manager, or a senior manager with responsibility for IT services overall. A service manager is often assigned several roles, such as business relationship management, service level management, and continual service improvement.

Comparison

Business relationship managers, service level managers, service owners, and the CSI manager work together to deliver high-quality services. Together they embody the concepts of a service-oriented organization. These roles are crucial in ensuring that improvement happens. They stop improvements from being ad hoc and disjointed; they are responsible for ensuring that improvements take place as part of a structured program. Figure 47.3 shows how they work together to achieve this outcome.

FIGURE 47.3 Service management roles and customer engagement

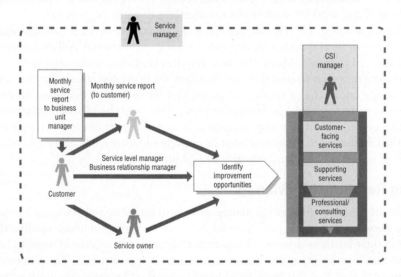

Table 47.8 compares the responsibilities of each of these roles:

- P = primary responsibility
- S = secondary responsibility
- Blank = no specific responsibility

TABLE 47.8   Skills involved in step 7 (implementing improvement)

Focus	CSI manager	Service level manager	Service owner	Business relationship manager
IT services	S	P	P	P
IT systems	S		P	
Processes	P	S	S	S
Customers	S	P	S	P
Technology	P	S	P	

Responsibilities	CSI manager	Service level manager	Service owner	Business relationship manager
Developing and maintaining the catalog of existing services		P	S	P
Developing and maintaining OLAs		P	S	
Gathering service level requirements (SLRs) from the customer	S	P	S	P
Negotiating and maintaining SLAs with the customer	S	P	S	S
Understanding underpinning contracts (UCs) as they relate to OLAs and SLAs	S	P	S	S
Ensuring that appropriate service level monitoring is in place	P	P	S	
Producing, reviewing, and evaluating reports on service performance and achievements regularly	P	P	P	P
Conducting regular meetings with the customer to discuss service level performance and improvement	S	P	S	S
Conducting yearly SLA review meetings with the customer	S	P	S	S

TABLE 47.8   Skills involved in step 7 (implementing improvement) *(continued)*

Responsibilities	CSI manager	Service level manager	Service owner	Business relationship manager
Ensuring customer satisfaction with the use of a customer satisfaction survey	S	P	S	P
Initiating appropriate actions to improve service levels through service improvement plans (SIPs)	P	P	P	P
Negotiating and agreeing on OLAs and SLAs	S	P	S	S
Ensuring the management of UCs as they relate to OLAs and SLAs	S	S	S	
Working with the service level manager to provide services to meet the customer's requirements	P		P	P
Appropriate monitoring of services or systems	P	P	S	
Producing, reviewing, and evaluating reports on service or system performance and achievement to the service level manager and the service level process manager	P	P	P	S
Assisting in appropriate actions to improve service levels (SIP)	P	P	P	P

Skills, knowledge, and competencies	CSI manager	Service level manager	Service owner	Business relationship manager
Relationship management skills	P	P	P	P
A good understanding of IT services and qualifying factors in order to understand how customer requirements will affect delivery	P	P	P	P

Skills, knowledge, and competencies	CSI manager	Service level manager	Service owner	Business relationship manager
An understanding of the customer's business and how IT contributes to the delivery of that product or service	P	P	P	P
Good communication skills	P	P	P	P
Good negotiation skills	P	P	P	P
Knowledge and experience of contract and/or supplier management roles	S	P	S	S
Good people management and meeting facilitating skills	P	P	P	P
Good understanding of statistical and analytical principles and processes	P	S	S	S
Good presentation skills	P	P	P	P
Good technical understanding and an ability to translate technical requirements and specifications into easily understood business concepts and vice versa	S	P	S	S
Innovative in respect to service quality and ways in which it can be improved within the bounds of the organization's limits (resource, budgetary, legal, etc.)	P	P	P	P
Good organizational and planning skills	P	P	P	P
Good vendor management skills	S	S	S	S

Using the RACI Model in CSI

The final part of this chapter looks at the RACI model. You should remember the RACI matrix from your Foundation studies. To summarize, RACI is a method of defining clear definitions of accountability and responsibility. Understanding the responsibilities and accountabilities is essential for effective service management. The activities involved in a process may take place across several organizational units. A RACI matrix helps to illustrate this, identifying key roles for a given process. RACI is an acronym for responsible, accountable, consulted, and informed. These are defined as follows:

Responsible   This is applied to the person or people responsible for correct execution, that is, for getting the job done.

Accountable   This is applied to the person who has ownership of quality and the end result. Only one person can be accountable for each task.

Consulted   This refers to the people who are consulted and whose opinions are sought. They have involvement through input of knowledge and information.

Informed   This refers to the people who are kept up-to-date on progress. They receive information about process execution and quality.

Remember the following points:

- Only one role can be accountable for a process/activity.

- Several people may be responsible for carrying the action out.

- Consultation and information provision may happen as part of the activity but are not essential to every step.

- Every activity must have someone accountable and at least one person responsible.

The RACI matrix provides an easy method of tracking who does what in each process. This can be useful to help understand who is responsible for what, especially because it is unusual to have CSI allocated to a full-time position. In this situation, we need to ensure that the other positions that take on part of this responsibility know what their role is and what their responsibilities are. These are not fixed and may vary over time as staff and organizational changes occur. The RACI matrix is also used to help define the communication required between the various parties involved in the improvement initiatives.

Table 47.9 shows a typical RACI matrix example, with no specific information about the individual activities. The rows represent the activities and the columns identify the people who make the decisions, carry out the activities, or provide input.

TABLE 47.9 An example of a simple RACI matrix

	IT director	Service level manager	Problem manager	Security manager	Service desk manager
Activity 1	AR	C	I	I	C
Activity 2	A	R	C	C	C
Activity 3	I	A		R	I
Activity 4	I	A	R	C	I

To build a RACI chart, the following steps are required:

- Identify the processes/activities.
- Identify and define the roles.
- Hold meetings with the relevant staff and assign the RACI codes.
- Identify any gaps or overlaps, for example, where there are multiple people responsible for a task or where no one has been defined as responsible. Ensure that each task has one, and only one, person accountable.
- Incorporate feedback.
- Ensure that people are adhering to the allocated roles.

Using the RACI approach is helpful in complex organizations where each function may be involved in many processes, resolving incidents, approving changes, specifying reporting, and so on. The RACI matrix makes the requirements on each team clear and explicit and ensures no "black holes."

One practical use for the RACI matrix is to define what should be included in operational level requirements. The clear statement of each internal team's involvement in the various tasks or activities, and the extent of that involvement, is an excellent starting point for these agreements. Operational level agreements are negotiated as part of service level management. Using RACI matrices to identify the responsibilities of a particular team across many processes helps identify what the OLA should include.

Another benefit of RACI is that it defines communication paths and responsibilities. The consulted/informed information captured in the RACI matrix ensures that the right people are consulted and that the required information flows to the correct people. Successful communication is central to effective CSI.

Summary

This brings us to the end of this chapter, in which we reviewed the organizational aspects of continual service improvement. We looked at the responsibilities, skills, and competencies for the generic roles of service owner, process owner, process manager, and process practitioner and for the roles specific to the seven-step improvement process—the owner of this process, the manager of this process, and the reporting analyst.

We examined the activities involved in the seven-step improvement process and compared the CSI manager role with other relevant roles. Finally, we considered how the responsibility model (RACI) can be used when defining roles and responsibilities in CSI.

Exam Essentials

Understand the responsibilities, skills, and competencies of the generic roles.   Be able to explain the differences between the process owner, the process manager, the process practitioner, and the service owner.

Be able to describe the roles specific to the seven-step improvement process.   Understand the roles of process owner, process manager, and reporting analyst for this process.

Be able to describe the activities involved in the seven-step improvement process.   Understand each step and the skills required to carry it out successfully. Be able to provide examples of typical job titles of the people who would be involved.

Be able to explain the differences in the roles of business relationship managers, service level managers, service owners, and the CSI manager.   Understand the particular responsibilities of each and how they complement each other.

Be able to explain how a RACI matrix is created.   Ensure that you understand the differences between responsible and accountable, and why there must be only one person accountable for each task.

Be able to explain how a RACI matrix helps in achieving continual service improvement.   Ensure that you understand how RACI clarifies who does what and who needs to be communicated with.

Review Questions

You can find the answers to the review questions in the appendix.

1. Which role "reviews and analyzes data from components, systems, subsystems, and services to understand the true end-to-end service delivery"?
   A. The CSI manager
   B. The event management process owner
   C. The reporting analyst
   D. The service level manager

2. What does the abbreviation RACI stand for?
   A. Responsible, advised, consulted, informed
   B. Responsible, accountable, consulted, informed
   C. Requested, accountable, consulted, interested
   D. Responsible, answerable consulted, involved

3. Match the description to the process role.
   1. Process owner
   2. Process manager
   3. Process practitioner
   X. Carries out the activity of the process
   Y. Ensures that the process can be carried out effectively
   Z. Ensures that the process is carried out effectively
   A. 1Z, 2Y, 3X
   B. 1Y, 2X, 3Z
   C. 1X, 2Y, 3Z
   D. 1Y, 2Z, 3X

4. Which of these is the best description of the role of service owner?
   A. Manages the process so that it is performed efficiently and meets the expectations of the business customer
   B. Ensures that the service produces the correct output
   C. Represents the service across the organization
   D. Represents the process at the change advisory board

5. Which of these is the responsibility of the CSI manager?
   A. Maintaining accurate information in the service catalog
   B. Sponsoring, designing, and managing changes to the process and its metrics
   C. Developing CSI practices, communication throughout the organization
   D. Ensuring that activities are carried out as required throughout the service lifecycle

6. Which of the following is NOT a possible benefit from using a RACI matrix?

   A. It makes the requirements for each team clear and explicit.

   B. It clarifies what can be promised in a service level agreement.

   C. It defines what should be included in operational level requirements.

   D. It defines communication paths and responsibilities.

7. Which generic role is responsible for "creating or updating records to show that activities have been carried out correctly"?

   A. Service owner

   B. Process owner

   C. Process manager

   D. Process practitioner

8. Which of the following skills and attributes are required for the role of reporting analyst?

   1. The ability to build trust with senior business managers

   2. A good understanding of statistical and analytical principles and processes

   3. An in-depth understanding of the technical infrastructure

   4. Strong technical skills in the reporting tool(s)

   5. Communication skills

   6. The ability to translate technical requirements and specifications into easily understood reporting requirements

   7. Customer-facing skills

      A. All of the above

      B. 2, 4, 5, and 6 only

      C. 1, 2, 4, 6, and 7 only

      D. 2, 3, 4, 5, and 6 only

9. Which of the seven steps require the ability to create, to use high-level concepts, and to handle complex/uncertain situations?

   1. Identify the strategy for improvement.

   2. Define what you will measure.

   3. Gather the data.

   4. Process the data.

   5. Analyze the information and data.

   6. Present and use the information.

   7. Implement improvement.

      A. All of the above

      B. 1, 2, and 6 only

      C. 1, 5, and 7 only

      D. 1, 5, and 6 only

10. Which of these shows the correct focus of the roles as far as customer focus is concerned (where P = primary responsibility, S = secondary responsibility, and blank = no specific responsibility)?

A. CSI manager - P, service level manager - P, service owner - S, business relationship manager - S

B. CSI manager - P, service level manager - P, service owner - blank, business relationship manager - S

C. CSI manager - blank, service level manager - P, service owner - blank, business relationship manager - P

D. CSI manager - S, service level manager - P, service owner - S, business relationship manager - P

Chapter 48

Technology Considerations

THE FOLLOWING ITIL INTERMEDIATE EXAM OBJECTIVES ARE DISCUSSED IN THIS CHAPTER:

- ✓ How tools can be used to assist some or all of the activities of CSI

- ✓ Holistic IT service management tools

- ✓ Specialist tools for managing:
    - Systems and networks
    - Events
    - Automated incident and problem resolution

- ✓ Performance management tools

- ✓ Statistical analysis tools

- ✓ Project and portfolio management tools

- ✓ Financial management tools

- ✓ Business intelligence/reporting tools

This chapter explores the technology and tools used to support CSI and how they would be implemented for CSI activities, such as performance, project, and portfolio management as well as service measurement and business intelligence reporting.

ITIL focuses on four areas—people, processes, products, and partners. In previous chapters, we examined the people and processes involved in CSI. Now we are going to look at the products. We have emphasized the importance of gathering and presenting data. The performance of IT services and service management processes needs to be monitored and reported. Modern service management tools can assist us in this, as can the other tools we will be looking at now.

Holistic IT Service Management Tools

IT systems have always supported the running of business processes; sophisticated tools are now available to help run IT itself. The range of tools available to assist in service management is vast. Some organizations use simple homegrown databases to manage incidents or changes. It is increasingly common for organizations to use dedicated, integrated toolsets designed to support the service management processes. These may even be marketed as ITIL conformant. It is important to remember that tools are a means to an end, not an end in themselves.

Often organizations believe that purchasing or developing a tool will solve all their problems, and it is easy to forget that we are still dependent on the process, the function, and, most important, the people. Remember, "A fool with a tool is still a fool."

We shall be looking at the following technology:

- Systems management toolsets that can monitor and control systems and infrastructure components

- Dedicated service management tools that manage process-based workflows, such as incident management

- Tools to support IT governance requirements

Output from these tools needs to be combined, collated, and analyzed collectively to provide the overall business intelligence required to effectively improve on the overall IT service provision. These tools can be thought of under a number of broad categories. We will start with IT service management suites.

IT Service Management Suites

Although it is possible to manage an IT department and its processes using spreadsheets and homebuilt access databases, it has become more common in recent years to recognize that managing this complex and essential part of the business requires investment in specialized tools, just as other areas of a business have their specialist tools that enable them to do things like automate accounting or manage inventory or resource utilization. IT service management suites provide an integrated toolset, allowing information regarding incidents, problems, changes, configuration items, and SLAs, for example, to be stored together. There are a wide variety of IT service management tools available, often offered using the Software as a Service (SaaS) model. Such tools can help support the implementation of ITIL processes; there are tools for just about every service management process, such as those supporting capacity and availability monitoring and automated event identification. The data provided by tools is a vital source for CSI. Capturing information, and linking the information together, is the major strength of these tools.

Tool Support for Incident/Problem Management

Data about the configuration items (CIs) involved can help in understanding the impact of incidents on affected services and thus help prioritize the incidents correctly. This information can also be used when designing incident models.

Having a tool that provides the ability to understand how changes are linked to CIs, which are then linked to incidents, which are in turn linked to problems, can provide us with possible root causes, show patterns of faults, and so on. This can be a very powerful aid to understanding what is going wrong and identifying possible improvement options.

Tool Support for Change

Toolsets that capture the CI data for changes, and provide a change schedule, help in identifying when changes have caused problems that led to incidents affecting the service. Modern tool capabilities include the ability to draw dynamic configuration relationships showing the changes, releases, incidents, and problems related to each CI. Tools can use the change schedule, projected service outage, and CMS and SLA data to automate risk assessment and reduce the workload of the change advisory board.

Tool Support for Service Asset and Configuration Management

Tools now offer extensive functionality in support of service asset and configuration management. Accurate CMS information is a critical data source for CSI.

Key tool functionality now available includes discovery and service dependency mapping capabilities, which offer a visual representation of the hierarchy and CI relationships. Tools often include auditing capabilities to streamline data verification and will allow different data sources or configuration management databases (CMDBs) to be federated into an overall CMS where appropriate.

Tool Support for Release

Tools are available to help in the release process by incorporating automatic software distribution and enforcing version numbering to control definitive software versions. They can often also automatically update CIs and track which CIs were updated.

Tool Support for Service Level Management

Tools can assist service level management by monitoring for breaches of thresholds for response to and resolution of incidents. This enables performance against service level agreements, operational agreements, and underpinning contracts to be monitored and the performance of internal and external suppliers to be tracked and reported. The tools will record response and fix times to enable service level reporting. ITSM toolsets can automate both hierarchical and functional escalation, speeding up resolution and reducing SLA breaches. Tools are also vital in supporting service reporting.

Tool Support for other Service Management Processes

ITSM tools can assist many service management processes:

- Availability management. ITSM tools will help by monitoring and reporting downtime.

- Service catalog management. ITSM tools will help by providing an online service catalog.

- Request fulfilment. ITSM tools will help by providing automated request authorization and fulfilment workflows.

- Release management. ITSM tools will help by automatically updating CMS data following a release.

- Continual service improvement will be helped by the extensive reporting capabilities of ITSM tools and the capture of baselines and trends. Such tools make it possible to highlight incidents that result in problems, changes that cause incidents, and releases that encapsulate certain changes. They provide all of the associated performance metric data that will feed the overall CSI initiatives. The right tool, properly configured, can be an enormous benefit to continual service improvement.

Remember, the ITSM toolset is essential for many of the service management processes and functions. There should be an IT service continuity plan in place to ensure that the toolset is available in the event of major disruption or disaster.

Specialist Tools

In addition to the integrated service management tool suites we have discussed, many other tools are commonly used by IT service providers to manage services. The data gathered by these tools is a major input to continual service improvement.

System and Network Tools

Complex infrastructures require effective system and network management tools; monitoring and controlling hundreds or thousands of CIs, understanding their interdependencies, and reporting on their performance would be impossible otherwise. Tools designed to manage the different technologies used can generate events to be captured and interpreted to show how the technology is performing. These tools can also be regarded as service management tools because they show the level of service being delivered in real time (using dashboards), provide data for several processes, and highlight issues for action before the users have become aware, thus helping reduce downtime.

Data produced by these tools will highlight incidents and provide input to availability (showing the mean time between failures and mean time to restore service, for example) and capacity management (by producing utilization reports). Many of these tools also have the capability to support release management and service asset and configuration management through their ability to deploy software updates and update the CMS to show that this has been done.

Event Management Tools

ITIL defines an event as any detectable or discernible occurrence that has significance for the management of the IT infrastructure or the delivery of IT services. Events are produced by many different systems; they are detected and analyzed by event management tools. These tools can use the information to evaluate the potential impact such an occurrence may have on the services being provided. By monitoring the levels of service being provided and warning of deterioration, event management tools enable action to be taken immediately, often before the customer is aware of any issue. Their ability to correlate multiple events (such as notification of a loss of connection from every CI downstream of a failure) means that the true cause is identified quickly. Speeding up the response to any issues improves the overall quality of the service.

Automated Incident and Problem Resolution

Automation of routine tasks can enhance the level of service being delivered. Tools work consistently and without breaks, unlike human staff. By identifying that an issue has occurred, matching the symptoms to a database of causes and recommended actions, and then implementing the resolution, all in a few seconds, these tools drastically reduce the time to resolve incidents. All of these actions can take place in the time a user would wait for their call to be answered at the service desk! These tools also collect huge amounts of data regarding the type and frequency of faults for later analysis by problem management and CSI.

Performance Management Tools

Powerful performance management tools gather huge amounts of data from a variety of sources; without such tools, collecting this data would otherwise be very time consuming, and it would be difficult to maintain consistency in the type of data collected and the frequency of collection. By populating the availability management information system (AMIS) and capacity management information system (CMIS) databases with current performance and historical data, trends can be identified by support staff, who can then take the necessary action in advance of an issue arising. The level of demand can be captured and compared to what was expected, and actual performance can be measured against targets; this data is then used to fine-tune the system to deliver the optimum service. The effects of the load-balancing and tuning can be monitored and trends can be predicted. The data also enables possible solutions to be modeled to help decide which course of action will deliver the greatest improvement.

These performance management tools are useful to CSI because the fine-tuning activities may be part of an overall improvement plan and their success or otherwise can be proved by the supplied data.

Statistical Analysis Tools

The vast amount of data provided by the various tools we have looked at in this chapter can present a real challenge. Data relating to a particular service will exist across many tools and needs to be correlated to provide the true picture. Although these various tools have reporting and analysis capabilities, the capabilities may be limited, and the analysis will certainly be restricted to the data provided by each separate tool. When all the raw data is captured into a single repository and statistical analysis tools are employed, complex calculations can be carried out, providing valuable information regarding the following items:

- The mean time to restore service
- The mean time between failures
- Service failure analysis
- Demand management
- Workload analysis
- Service modeling
- Application sizing

By using specialist analysis and reporting tools and analyzing data from several sources together, we are able to obtain real understanding of what is happening and the effect of any changes or improvement initiatives. Data can be grouped logically, and modeling can be used to predict future performance.

Project and Portfolio Management Tools

Specific tools are also available that can be used to assist with project and portfolio management. These tools are used to manage the business-related aspects of IT and can be used to support the management board approval process for strategic or major change projects. They support the registration, costing, resource management, portfolio visibility, and project management of new business functionality and the services and systems that underpin them.

They also help in assigning development tasks and provide useful data regarding resource utilization, changes, and release builds and provide financial management with information regarding the total cost of ownership.

Financial Management Tools

Many organizations spend millions of dollars on IT. The accounting and budgeting for this expenditure must align with the corporate financial processes and will require specialist financial management tools compatible with the business financial management tools.

Budgeting

IT management has the responsibility to ensure that sufficient financial resources are available to deliver the service, including provisions for contingencies. The budget must include day-to-day financial needs as well as longer-term strategic investments.

Accounting

IT must be able to justify its expenditure and show how this cost is outweighed by the business benefits that result. Understanding the total end-to-end cost of service provision is essential for input into business cases. All IT providers must budget and account for their expenditure.

Charging

Charging for IT services is optional; it will be a decision made by the business. If charging is to take place, financial management tools will enable the fair allocation of shared costs. When cost is calculated per CI, by usage, by resources used, or by any other method, the tools must interface with the service management tools that measure these elements. Data collectors gather the critical usage metrics for each of the technologies being measured, linking them to the costing information from the accounting software. The resulting information is used to allocate costs. To avoid disputes, it is essential that the charges can be justified and that the customers understand what they are being billed for. If queried, the IT service provider should be able to show how charges were calculated and the sources of the data that was used.

Business Intelligence/Reporting

The final area where tools can be beneficial that we consider here is the area of business intelligence and reporting. These tools can provide a common repository of all service information and business-related data (in addition to the technical data already discussed). The technology used to deliver IT services is increasingly complex, requiring powerful tools to administer, manage, improve, and ensure overall governance of IT service provision. Procuring the appropriate tools can reduce the administrative overhead of managing processes and improve the overall quality of IT service provision.

Summary

In this chapter, we looked at the technology required to support CSI. This included understanding the use of and value provided by tools. We considered specialist IT service management toolsets and tools used for system, network, and event management. We also looked at tools that provide automated incident and problem resolution and performance management capabilities. Finally, we examined statistical analysis tools, project and portfolio management tools, and those used for financial management for IT services and business intelligence and reporting.

In the next chapter, we will look at implementing continual service improvement.

Exam Essentials

Understand the role of tools in supporting continual service improvement.   This includes how system and network tools show the level of availability being delivered and how event management tools and automated incident management tools can invoke a response to a failure, thus reducing downtime and improving the level of service being delivered while gathering useful data for analysis by CSI.

Explain the capabilities that service management tool suites provide and how they support CSI and why they are important.   Understand the generic capabilities of integrated service management tool suites to gather and store information regarding incidents, problems, changes, configuration items, and SLAs. Understand the importance of this information being gathered together, such as identifying links between configuration items and problems, changes and incidents, and so forth.

Understand how specialist tools are used to support specific processes.   Be able to identify how performance management tools improve the level of service being delivered and how statistical analysis tools help process the data into useful information and knowledge, thus showing what improvement actions are required. Understand the tools used to support project and program management, financial management, and business intelligence and reporting, and how the data gathered by these tools helps identify areas for improvement, the cost of failure and of the improvement plan, and the reporting of the effect any actions that were taken have on the business.

Review Questions

You can find the answers to the review questions in the appendix.

1. Which of the following statements about tools is true?

    A. IT service management can be managed only by using an integrated toolset for all processes.

    B. A tool developed in-house will be preferable to a commercial tool.

    C. Software as a service is not appropriate for service management tools because every organization is different.

    D. Organizations will usually need to combine data from more than one tool to gain an overall view of performance.

2. Which of the following statements about integrated ITSM tools is incorrect?

    1. Integrated tools should be considered because they allow linkages between incidents, problems, changes, and configuration items.

    2. It is preferable to use individual tools for each process in order to be able to have the best available tool for each process.

    A. 1 only

    B. 2 only

    C. Both

    D. Neither

3. Which of the following is NOT a benefit of using automated tools?

    A. They work 24/7.

    B. They are faster than humans at identifying that an issue has occurred.

    C. They enforce adherence to the correct ITIL processes by the IT department staff.

    D. They can often be programmed to apply a resolution automatically.

4. Specialist tools may assist CSI in data gathering and analysis and other tasks. Which of the following specialist tools might be used to assist CSI?

    1. System and network tools

    2. Event management tools

    3. Business process automation tools

    4. Automated incident and problem resolution tools

    5. Performance management tools

    6. Statistical analysis tools

    7. Customer relationship management tools

    8. Project and portfolio management tools

    9. Financial management tools

    10. Business intelligence/reporting tools

       A.   1, 2, 3, 4, 5, 6, and 10 only

       B.   1, 2, 4, 5, 6, 8, 9, and 10 only

       C.   All of them

       D.   1, 2, 4, and 10 only

5.   Which of the following statements is true concerning the implementation of new tools?

       A.   The tool should be set up to carry out all the requirements from the start so that later changes are not required.

       B.   The tool should be intuitive, to cut training costs.

       C.   The reporting requirements must be considered when configuring the tool.

       D.   The tool should adhere strictly to ITIL guidelines.

6.   Which of the areas of service management known as the four *P*s is mostly concerned with tools?

       A.   People

       B.   Processes

       C.   Products

       D.   Partners

7.   Which term is used to describe integrated service management toolsets?

       A.   Centralized

       B.   Business process engineering

       C.   CRM

       D.   Holistic

8.   Which of the following is NOT an example of how tools can assist continual service improvement?

       A.   They can gather data that can be used as a baseline.

       B.   They can cut down the effort required to analyze large amounts of data to detect trends.

       C.   They can show linkages between incidents, CIs, changes, and so on.

       D.   They can make a decision regarding the prioritization of potential improvements.

9.   Which of the following statements concerning potential problems when using a variety of tools is/are true?

       1.   Each individual tool can produce only limited information.

       2.   The tools may each use a different basis for measurement, leading to conflicting results.

          A.   Both are true.

          B.   Only the first statement is true.

          C.   Only the second statement is true.

          D.   Neither are true.

10. Which of the following statements concerning the benefits of using tools is/are false?

A. Tools can improve service by detecting failures and automatically restarting the failing item or rerouting to avoid it.

B. Tools can help overcome the fact that an organization has poor processes.

C. Tools can gather data continuously, unlike people.

D. Tools can save staff time by automating routine tasks.

Chapter

49

Implementation of Continual Service Improvement

THE FOLLOWING ITIL INTERMEDIATE
EXAM OBJECTIVES ARE DISCUSSED IN
THIS CHAPTER:

✓ Critical implementation considerations and where to start

✓ The role of governance

✓ The effect of organizational change for CSI

✓ Communication strategies and planning

The learning objective for this chapter is to gain sufficient knowledge to implement continual service improvement.

Critical Considerations and Where to Start

ITIL considers implementing continual service improvement (CSI) to improve services and to improve the service management processes themselves. An organization with immature service management processes will struggle to implement the seven-step improvement process to improve services. The seven-step improvement process, as you have seen, depends to a large extent on having good data available. Immature processes usually have poor data quality if any at all. The following difficulties may be encountered when data is gathered:

- Processes may be poor or nonexistent.

- The data may be spread across many different tools, with different criteria for each regarding what is gathered.

- The monitoring that is carried out is often at a component or application level, not from an end-to-end service perspective.

- There is no central repository for data.

- There are no resources allocated to process and analyze the data.

- Reporting consists of too much data broken into too many segments to be meaningful or useful.

- There may be no reporting carried out at all.

Preparatory Steps

Before a program of CSI can be realistically started, the necessary foundations need to be put in place to overcome the issues listed in the preceding section.

Assign Roles

Before you start, you need to allocate the key roles to named individuals. These may be existing positions, with people already assigned, or they may be new. The individuals need to understand their responsibilities, especially if this is a new role. The key roles are as follows:

- CSI manager
- Service owner
- Reporting analyst
- Service level manager

The service level manager is going to be particularly important as the key interface between the business and IT.

Begin Monitoring and Reviewing

Improvement should be based on an agreed and documented baseline to enable and track the progress toward measurable targets. This means that monitoring and reporting on technology, process, and service metrics needs to be put into place.

Regular internal IT service review meetings should be held so that the IT service provider can evaluate performance and investigate any issues prior to meeting with the customer. This ensures that they can have a suggested improvement plan to present to the business's representatives when they meet with them.

Deciding Where to Start

Starting to implement CSI can be a daunting prospect. If there are too many areas needing attention, there is a danger that efforts may be spread too thin, meaning that no area gets the required level of attention and resources to affect a real change. There are a number of different approaches:

- The service approach
- The lifecycle approach
- The functional group approach

The Service Approach

The first approach is to choose just one service first and concentrate on it (expanding to other services later). The continual service improvement manager chooses a service with known issues and works with the service owner to compare the actual performance with what the business needs. The data should also be examined to identify any historical trends.

- The current monitoring should be reviewed to evaluate whether it is appropriate and sufficient. Limited component monitoring may be happening, for example, but no end-to-end monitoring. Although not ideal, the data that is available can be analyzed for trends, possible causes, and so on.
- Incident tickets should be reviewed to identify trends or consistently failing configuration items.

- Changes should also be reviewed to ascertain whether they have impacted the service.

- Report the findings and identify improvement opportunities.

Realistically, continual service improvement must start somewhere, even if this starting point is not ideal. If the data is very poor, then the first improvement to implement is to set up the necessary monitoring from that point forward. As better data becomes available, it can be analyzed to identify trends or repeated similar failures.

The Lifecycle Approach

An alternative answer to the "Where do we start?" question is to adopt a lifecycle approach. The success of each stage of the service lifecycle depends, in part, on the actions and outputs of the preceding stage; if service design does not document the service solution properly, it will be hard for service transition to thoroughly test it. Similarly, if service transition does not carry out effective knowledge transfer to service operations, the quality of support will suffer. Good information is needed for the staff involved in each stage to understand where they are weak and need to improve. It is the responsibility of staff involved in every stage to monitor, report, and analyze their activities and to identify improvement opportunities.

Ultimately, many issues with services can be traced back to failures in one of the lifecycle processes. The lifecycle stages cannot be examined using a linear approach because it will take some time to understand whether the strategy was correct. The key stages to be examined are design, transition, and operation. Each stage can feed back improvement suggestions to the preceding stage. By taking this approach, CSI can identify improvements to processes that will impact the eventual service quality before the service becomes live.

The Functional Group Approach

A third approach is known as the functional group approach. This approach is usually adopted if there is an obvious issue with a particular team, with many faults being traced back to their actions. There may be common issues across all services related to one particular group, so by addressing this, you will be improving all services. As a general rule, however, unless there is a real issue with a team, the end-to-end improvement process is preferable.

The Role of Governance

Next we consider the governance aspects of CSI. The growing importance of IT to the achievement of business goals means that IT service management strategy has moved from the purely operational focus of the past to tactical and strategic levels. The complexity of modern IT environments demands more formal processes and controls to be in place than previously. Increasingly, as we have discussed, service management tools are used to automate processes and gather data.

For some internal IT organizations, the move away from a technology management focus and a reactive approach to one based on proactive service management is difficult for the staff to adapt to; without this change of culture, however, the success of the move will be jeopardized. This change in focus is essential if the provider is to align more closely with the business and provide efficient and reliable management and delivery of core business services. Implementing IT service management process governance will support this transformation to a process- and service-based organization. It will also ensure that the organizational infrastructure necessary to manage process improvement initiatives is in place. Service management should become embedded as best practice within the organization and CSI treated as business as usual.

Successful implementation of IT service management requires a review of the organizational structure of the IT service provider in addition to the introduction of the required processes, policies, and controls. We discussed the roles required for continual service improvement in Chapter 47, "Organizing for Continual Service Improvement."

Business Drivers

IT service management processes and governance support current and future business plans as follows:

- They ensure that the actions and performance of IT support the organization's vision.
- By basing processes on best practice guidelines, the IT service provider is able to deliver the stability and reliability required; these processes also ensure that new services can be introduced smoothly and without any delay that could prevent the business from achieving its goals.
- Documented process policies, standards, and controls based on best practice will ensure compliance to internal audit and external regulatory and legislation requirements.
- They encourage a commitment to best practices.
- They assist in moving the IT organization from being technology focused to an enterprise IT services model. They ensure that this transformation can be achieved without risking the quality, reliability, and stability of the IT services provided.

Process Changes

Continual service improvement applies to all areas of IT; processes, people, technology, and management may all be affected. For CSI to be successful, it needs to become embedded within the organization—to become "business as usual." As we discussed previously, this may mean organizational changes and new processes and tools. Staff need to be taught to understand the importance of and relevance of CSI to their duties. Successful implementation of CSI will require a focus on people, processes, management, and technology aspects. Figure 49.1 identifies how CSI should take a holistic view to improvements.

FIGURE 49.1   Process reengineering changes everything

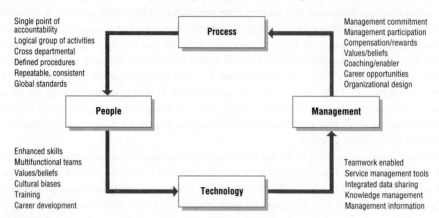

As we discussed, service management is not adopted by the IT department solely because it has benefits for IT. It is implemented because it ensures that the IT department can contribute more effectively to achieving the organization's goals. If you only focus on changing a process or technology, CSI will not be effective.

Effective service management should be recognized as central to achieving the organization's vision. Standard IT processes and a stable IT environment facilitate the implementation of new services, process standards and controls enable compliance with regulatory and legislation requirements, and the organization becomes committed to best practices.

COBIT

We looked at the COBIT framework in Chapter 44, "Continual Service Improvement Principles," along with other frameworks. COBIT is particularly useful when implementing continual service improvement. The maturity models in COBIT are useful when seeking to establish a benchmark, and they help drive improvement. COBIT helps to align goals and metrics to the business goals for IT, and these can then be used to create an IT management dashboard. Finally, the COBIT "monitor and evaluate" (ME) process domain defines the processes needed to assess current IT performance, IT controls, and regulatory compliance, all of which are required when deciding on improvement priorities.

The Effect of Organizational Change for CSI

Before we start talking about changing the culture of an organization, we should consider what is meant by this expression. Organizational culture is intangible. The employees know what behavior is expected of them, the values of the organization, and so forth without necessarily ever having been taught these things. There are tasks that everyone expects to be carried out and an accepted way to do so. For example, a CAB may approve a change without investigating the level of testing that has been carried out because adequate testing is custom and practiced throughout the IT organization.

Although intangible, the culture of an organization can sometimes be obvious to an outsider. In the days of mainframe computers, IBM was the largest and most successful of the mainframe suppliers. The IBM culture was focused on quality, with a very traditional approach to dress code. Suits, white shirts, and sober ties were the rule for the male members of staff, and females wore business suits. Many ex-IBM employees found it hard to wear a blue shirt to the office years after they had left the organization. Compare that culture with the laid-back approach to the dress code at Apple or Google. Their commitment to quality is as strong as IBM's was, but the more relaxed dress code is seen as an outward sign of their encouragement of creativity and "thinking outside the box." Other signifiers of the organizational culture include the different way authority is exercised and staff is communicated with. Are people told what to do and how to do it, consulted, or left to decide the best way to achieve the agreed outcome? Is the environment macho and competitive, or do staff feel able to admit that they are having difficulty with something, knowing they will be supported by others to achieve a successful outcome? Many IT organizations allow casual dress and are relaxed about timekeeping but expect staff to work late when required without payment.

We need to be aware of the organization's culture when implementing CSI because it may support change or resist it. Continual service improvement requires the staff to change how they do things. This also may be welcomed or resisted. People may treat CSI initiatives as criticism of their working practices, or they may be enthusiastic about trying the new approach. The support of senior management in changing behavior is critical. As employee behavior changes, the new methods become accepted as how things should be done; this becomes the organization's new culture.

It is important to remember that unless the behavior of staff is actually monitored to see if the tasks and activities are being done, there is little reason for an employee to change; they give lip service to the new methods by saying that they agree with them, but they don't actually change their behavior. This is why measurement and reporting—the Check part of Plan-Do-Check-Act is so important. There are two sayings to bear in mind about this:

- "What gets rewarded gets done." For example, bonus should be based on the required behavior changes.
- "You get what you inspect, not what you expect." Measurement and reporting are critical.

The Softer Aspects of Successful Organizational Change

Organizational change requires much more than issuing a new organizational chart, and behavioral change goes far beyond a new process manual. As we have discussed, unless the staff are on board, the change will be resisted, bad habits will resurface, and a year later, the issues that prompted the improvement initiative will still exist. Even worse, CSI will be seen as ineffective, something that can be ignored, which does not really change anything. This increases the risk of failure of future initiatives.

Successful organizational and cultural change is based on an awareness of the softer issues; staff need to be convinced of the value of the changes, so that they actively support them. They need to feel involved, empowered, and motivated. Guidance for addressing these issues can be found in John P. Kotter's Eight Steps to Transforming Your Organization described in his book *Leading Change* (Harvard Business School Press, 1996). This is one of the most well-known and successful approaches; it is used in conjunction with formal project management and has been found to significantly increase the chance of success.

Kotter's Eight Steps

Kotter identified the main reasons transformations of all types fail. The list here shows what needs to be in place to ensure success. The following actions need to be carried out:

- Establish a sense of urgency.

- Create a guiding coalition.

- Develop a vision and strategy.

- Communicate the change vision.

- Empower broad-based action.

- Create short-term wins.

- Consolidate gains and produce more change.

- Anchor new approaches in the culture.

The first five steps show the leadership actions required. We will now look at each of the steps in turn, and consider how they apply to CSI.

Step 1: Establish a Sense of Urgency

The first step is to establish a sense of urgency. Failure to do this is at the heart of many failed transformations. The staff need to understand that change is essential; asking "What if we do nothing?" can help them realize that unless something is done, nothing will get better, and in fact the situation may actually deteriorate because of the inevitable damage to the business that would occur. Examples of damage could include lost sales and therefore lost revenue from outages of business-critical systems or a reduction in the IT budget, which could ultimately lead to unwanted change such as downsizing or offshoring. Thinking about the consequences of inaction can be helpful when composing a business case for the initiative. Answering this question at all organizational levels, and considering the consequences of inaction of different stakeholders, will help people understand that this does affect them, and therefore it helps to win their support.

CSI initiatives must generate the belief that change is both necessary and inevitable—that the status quo is not an option. Staff can be involved in and influence the change, or not, but it will happen anyway.

Step 2: Create a Guiding Coalition

To lead the change, set up a small team made up of key individuals with experience who command respect, trust, and credibility. It is important to realize that team members need not all be senior managers; staff who are respected among their peers at lower levels of the organizational structure can be influential in winning support from the rest of the staff. A single champion cannot achieve success alone. Over time, the team may grow as more people come on board. The team must be totally convinced of the benefits of the change and prepared to spend time and effort convincing and motivating others to participate.

Step 3: Develop a Vision and Strategy

It is important that there is a shared vision of what is being attempted. Part of the job of the guiding coalition is to summarize this in a short vision statement that can be used to ensure that everyone is on board. A vision statement should do the following:

- Clarify the direction of the change.

- Motivate people to take action.

- Enable those actions to be coordinated.

- Outline the aims of senior management.

The vision statement also serves as a useful reference point when other suggestions are made. The suggestions can be analyzed to see whether they will help achieve the vision or whether they are a diversion from it. There is a danger otherwise that many different initiatives may be included, whether they complement or conflict with the original. This leads to confusion and ultimately failure. The vision statement needs to be simple and easy to communicate. The goals of CSI should be SMART (specific, measurable, achievable, relevant, and time-bound) and justified in terms relating to the business.

Step 4: Communicate the Change Vision

Communicating the vision in a way that builds support from the staff is essential. They will be thinking, "What is in this for me?" so make sure you make your message relevant to them. We look at how best to communicate the message later in this chapter.

Step 5: Empower Broad-based Action

Steps 1 to 4 are all aimed at creating enthusiasm and winning the stakeholders' and staff's support and commitment. Staff must feel part of the project, that it is being achieved by them, not that it is being done to them. This means they must both feel and be empowered to make the necessary changes. To be empowered means being enabled to do something, and the barriers preventing them from doing it are removed. They also need to understand what is to be done, so training and direction is important, and clear and unambiguous fixed goals need to be set. Finally, they need to have whatever tools are required to enable them to carry out the task. Remember, once people are empowered, they are accountable, so it is important for the CSI manager to ensure that the staff really understand what they need to do and are confident that they can carry it out successfully.

Step 6: Create Short-Term Wins

Kotter's sixth step concerns planning for and creating short-term wins. These early successes ensure that the initial enthusiasm among the staff is maintained, even in a large transformation project spread over many months. Early wins confirm that changes are happening and encourage the feeling of urgency and inevitability we talked about in step 1. An effective CSI manager will plan to have a mixture of changes to be implemented: quick wins, medium-term achievements, and the longer-term structural changes.

Many service management improvements take a long time to show results, so when the short-term wins are achieved, they should be communicated to everybody concerned to help maintain a feeling of forward motion and increasing momentum. It is important to include in the communication information about who benefits and how the changes support business goals. Short-term wins also help convince sceptics of the benefits of the implementation and ensure the continued support of influential stakeholders, who like to have something they can use to demonstrate progress. As more people become convinced by seeing these quick-win benefits delivered, they can join the guiding coalition. There is a saying that "nothing succeeds like success," which is very appropriate here—the successful delivery of benefits quickly builds momentum and morale and results in increased confidence when more challenging steps have to be taken.

Step 7: Consolidate Gains and Produce More Change

As we have discussed, successful short-term wins keep the momentum going and create more change. CSI should therefore address short-, medium-, and long-term wins. This ensures that changes are not just a flurry of quick wins but that these wins are followed by more fundamental medium- and long-term changes. Each type of gain (short-, medium- or long-term) has value:

- Short-term wins show that change is possible.
- Medium-term wins build confidence and help to develop new ways and practices.
- Long-term wins build CSI into all processes and embed cultural change.

This creates a culture of change by embedding changes into business as usual, avoiding the improvement being seen as "last year's buzzword."

Step 8: Anchor New Approaches in the Culture

The final step Kotter addresses is institutionalizing the change by anchoring the new approaches in the culture. This is the "holy grail" of continual service improvement; how do we make our changes business as usual? To institutionalize a change means to show how it has produced real benefits and to ensure that the improvements are embedded. Too often, CSI is regarded as a project, with the project team disbanded before this institutionalization has taken place; before long people may revert to old working practices. CSI must be a way of life, not a knee-jerk reaction to a specific failure.

Here are some ways of institutionalizing changes:

- Recruit staff with ITIL- or customer- and service-focused experience.
- Brief all new staff in the ways of working and train existing staff.

- Ensure that service goals and management reporting are matched to changing requirements.
- Make sure progress continues by ensuring that actions from meetings are carried out.
- Integrate new IT solutions into existing processes.

The proof of success is when staff defend "their" procedures and suggest improvements and service and process owners willingly promote the successful change.

Communication Strategies and Planning

The final topic in this chapter concerns communication. As you have seen, implementing and embedding CSI requires that staff understand what is required of them and why, and information about successful changes needs to be shared to build credibility in the process. So communication plays a key role in CSI.

Defining the Communications Plan

Effective communication requires a communications plan, which takes into account the culture of the organization. In some organizations, presentations or face-to-face meetings are the norm; in others, newsletters or email are.

Staff and stakeholders need to know of all changes to the processes they are involved in, the activities they carry out, and their roles and responsibilities. The goal of the communications plan is to build and maintain awareness, foster understanding, and encourage enthusiasm and support for the CSI program among key stakeholders. When developing a communication plan, remember that communication is not just a one-way process; feedback needs to be allowed, and responsibility needs to be assigned for providing responses to comments made at meetings.

Assigning Responsibility for the Communications Plan

The communications strategy and plan should include appointing an individual with the following responsibilities:

- Identifying the audience
- Designing and delivering communications to stakeholders
- Identifying communications opportunities and appropriate methods
- Developing a plan and milestones and covering who, what, why, where, and when
- Responding to feedback

Who Is the Messenger?

There are several key aspects to keep in mind when devising the plan. First, it is important to align the messenger with the message. Sometimes this will be the CIO; at other times it may be a service owner or process owner who should be doing the communicating.

What Is the Message?

Second, the purpose and objective of the message need to be defined and tailored to the target audience. Continually communicate the benefits of the CSI program as a whole, but address the WIIFM (what's-in-it-for-me) response from the audience.

Who Is the Target Audience?

Consider the target audience. For CSI, this could be senior management, mid-level managers, or the staff who will be tasked with performing CSI activities. The choice of the right messenger will depend on the target audience and the message; senior managers will expect to be briefed by one of their peers, whereas service desk staff would be intimidated by such a messenger, and the service desk manager or incident manager process owner may be more appropriate for them.

When and How Often?

You need to consider the timing and frequency of communications. Too early or too late will mean it is ineffective. The message needs to be repeated; a one-off communication is unlikely to really sink in. A schedule of what communications are planned, and when, will be an important part of your communications plan. Take a look at the sample in Table 49.1.

TABLE 49.1   Table for sample communication plan

Messenger	Target audience	Message	Method of communication	Date and frequency	Status
CIO	All of IT	CSI initiative is kicking off	Town hall meeting	Month/day	Planned

How Best to Communicate?

There are many methods open for how a message can be communicated. Methods such as emails, newsletters, notice boards, and the intranet will work well for some changes. Others will need the more personal approach of team meetings, personal briefings, and so on. These have the advantage of the presenter being able to judge how effective the communication has been and how well received; this information can be used to tailor the message in the future and/or show the need for additional means of communicating with the audience. For example, if there seems to be more information being provided than the audience can handle, the plan may be altered to split the meeting into two meetings or to provide a handout. Another advantage of meetings and briefings is that they allow feedback and thus make the communication a two-way process.

Provide a Feedback Mechanism

Finally, provide a feedback mechanism. Allow staff to ask questions and provide feedback on the change initiative. If the topic is sensitive, such as the effect the project may have on staff numbers, allow a method of anonymous feedback and questions. Make sure someone is assigned the responsibility for checking and ensuring that responses are provided to the questions/comments. Unless the question relates to a particular person, it is a good idea to publish all the questions received (without saying who submitted them) and the answers, because someone may have not raised an issue themselves but still wants to know the answer.

Summary

In this chapter, we have been looking at how to implement CSI successfully. In particular, we looked at the following topics:

- Critical considerations and where to start
- The role of governance
- The effect of organizational change for CSI
- Communication strategies and planning

Formalizing CSI within the organization requires an appropriate governance structure. CSI needs information to identify the need for improvement initiatives and to measure their success, so appointing staff to be responsible for trend evaluation, analysis reporting, and decision-making is essential. As we discussed in the preceding chapter, the implementation of CSI is dependent on having the necessary tools for monitoring and reporting. No CSI initiative will succeed without effective communications to ensure that the necessary behavior changes occur.

Exam Essentials

Understand why there may be resistance to the new methods being adopted as part of the implementation of continual service improvement.   In particular, understand the possible reasons behind this resistance, the best way to tackle it, and the importance of visible management support in addressing the situation.

Understand how the use of Kotter's eight steps may assist in achieving lasting cultural change.   Be able to list and describe the eight steps.

Understand the importance of communication in achieving improvement.   Be able to list possible audiences and different methods of communicating with them.

Be able to describe the contents of a typical communications plan. Understand how such a plan would be used.

Be able to list several ways in which IT service management processes and governance support current and future business plans. Understand how the COBIT framework can help monitor and measure whether this is happening.

Review Questions

You can find the answers to the review questions in the appendix.

1. Which of the following is NOT a prerequisite for starting the implementation of formal continual service improvement?

    A. Assign key roles

    B. Set up monitoring and reporting

    C. Prioritize the required improvements

    D. Schedule internal service reviews

2. Which of the following is NOT described in ITIL as an approach to implementing CSI?

    A. Functional approach

    B. Lifecycle approach

    C. Service approach

    D. Process approach

3. Which of the following are concerns when attempting to gather good-quality data to support CSI?

    1. Processes may be poor or nonexistent.

    2. The data may be spread across many different tools, with different criteria for each regarding what is gathered.

    3. Data from different tools is worthless; until the organization invests in one reporting tool to cover all processes, CSI will not be able to access the data it requires.

    4. The monitoring that is carried out is often at a component or application level but not from an end-to-end service perspective.

    5. There is no central repository for data.

    6. There are no resources allocated to process and analyze the data.

    7. The data may be limited to reports that show internal process performance; these are not relevant to CSI, which is concerned with customer-facing processes only.

    8. Reporting consists of too much data broken into too many segments to be meaningful or useful. There may be no reporting carried out at all.

    A. All of the above

    B. 1, 2, 4, 5, 6, and 8 only

    C. 1, 2, 4, 5, 6, 7, and 8 only

    D. 1, 2, 3, 7, and 8 only

4. Which of the following is one of Kotter's eight steps?

    A. Check.

    B. Where are we now?

    C. Establish a sense of urgency.

    D. Identify the strategy for improvement.

5. Who should be in the guiding coalition?

    1. Key individuals

    2. Senior managers

    3. Staff who are sceptical about the changes, so that they can be won over

        A. All of the above

        B. Key individuals only

        C. Senior managers only

        D. Senior managers and key individuals only

6. What purpose does a mission statement fulfil?

    1. Clarifies direction

    2. Motivates people to take action

    3. Coordinates actions

    4. Outlines the aims of senior management

        A. 1, 3, and 4 only

        B. 4 only

        C. All of the above

        D. 1, 2, and 4 only

7. Which of the following statements about the requirement for good-quality data and effective continual service improvement is incorrect?

    A. Without good data, we cannot accurately identify the areas most in need of improvement.

    B. Without good data, we cannot improve, so we should concentrate our actions on areas where good-quality data is available.

    C. Without good data, we cannot establish a baseline to measure improvement against.

    D. Without good data, we cannot build a business case for investment in improvements.

8. Which of the following is NOT essential to achieving cultural change?

    A. Enforcement

    B. Motivation

    C. Involvement

    D. Communication

9. Which of the following is NOT one of the four key roles that should be allocated to named individuals when CSI is being implemented?

    A. Process owner

    B. CSI manager

   C. Reporting analyst

   D. Service level manager

10. Which of the following best describes when CSI should be carried out?

   A. When issues become apparent, to save unnecessary effort and expense

   B. Prior to the negotiation or renegotiation of the service level agreement

   C. All the time

   D. When a service improvement plan has been agreed to at a service review

Chapter

50

Challenges, Critical Success Factors, and Risks

THE FOLLOWING ITIL INTERMEDIATE EXAM OBJECTIVES ARE DISCUSSED IN THIS CHAPTER:

✓ The challenges facing CSI

✓ The appropriate critical success factors for CSI

✓ The risks associated with implementing CSI

This chapter covers the last topic in the CSI syllabus. The learning objective for this chapter is to gain an understanding of the challenges facing CSI, the use of appropriate critical success factors (CSFs) for CSI, and the risks associated with implementing CSI.

Continual Service Improvement Challenges

CSI will be challenging for all organizations; some challenges will be unique to a particular organization, and some will be common to all. A major challenge will always be the introduction of cultural and behavioral changes across the organization, as we have discussed. Improvement using the seven-step improvement process requires a significant investment in resources and the appropriate tools. Attempting to implement CSI with inadequate resources, budget, and time is a major challenge. Another related challenge is when there is a history of overcommitting staff who are allocated with other work. This will inevitably lead to an inability to deliver on time or to budget; although this is damaging for any project, if CSI is still attempting to prove its value, it could be disastrous. It is essential that the managers responsible for allocating the resources understand the time commitment and the particular data-gathering and analysis skills that will be required.

Successful CSI, as we have discussed, means changing people's behavior, often against their will (at least initially). Job roles may change, there may be new tools to get used to, and effective reporting means that any failure to follow process becomes visible. If staff are resistant to the changes, it is essential that CSI has the commitment of senior managers, who will use their authority to ensure that the changes take place; management support is therefore a key critical success factor, and implementing CSI without it is a major challenge.

If the service management processes are immature, or missing, the information, monitoring, and measuring necessary for CSI is likely to be inadequate or missing completely. This presents a challenge to CSI in trying to answer the "Where are we now?" question. The CSI manager needs to start with what information is available and make processes and reporting an area for early improvement.

Another possible challenge is the existence of information and knowledge within the organization that is not captured, validated, and shared due to a lack of knowledge management. A lack of clear corporate objectives, strategies, policies, and business direction will make it difficult to identify CSI initiatives that support business objectives; similarly, a lack of IT objectives, strategies, and policies will make justifying CSI as a means of achieving the IT vision difficult.

If the IT provider does not have a good relationship with the business and has little communication with them, it will be difficult for them to appreciate business priorities and the impact of IT failures on the business. This in turn will make it difficult to prioritize actions; there is a danger that priorities will be set that suit the IT department rather than the business.

Another possible challenge when implementing CSI is staff resistance, as we discussed in Chapter 49, "Implementation of Continual Service Improvement," in the section covering the softer aspects of successful organizational change. Staff may feel that their current behavior and practices are being criticized and become defensive. The discussion in that chapter about achieving cultural change suggested some approaches to overcoming this challenge.

There may also be technical challenges—inadequate or nonexistent tools or tools so complex that no one wants to use them, even if they have the skills. Gathering monitoring data may be hampered if there are a large number of different types of technology to monitor. Finally, CSI initiatives may require suppliers to improve their performance. While service improvement plans may be agreed on at service level reviews, if targets have been missed, many suppliers see no need to improve as long as they are fulfilling the terms of the contract. Over time, these contracts should be changed to include a commitment to improvement, such as reducing downtime or costs by a stated percentage each year.

Critical Success Factors

Let us now consider some of the critical success factors (CSFs) for successful continual service improvement:

- The appointment of a CSI manager
- The adoption of CSI within the organization, with visible management commitment (meaning ongoing, visible participation in CSI activities)
- The provision of sufficient and ongoing funding for CSI activities
- Clear criteria for prioritizing improvement projects
- The adoption of the service lifecycle approach
- The commitment of sufficient time and resources to enable staff to be involved in the improvement activities alongside their "day job"
- The provision of the appropriate technology to support CSI activities, as discussed in Chapter 48, "Technology Considerations"
- The adoption of best practice service management processes

CSFs and KPIs

Organizations should identify appropriate process critical success factors based on their objectives for the process. Each CSF is followed by a typical key performance indicator (KPI) that supports the CSF. An organization should develop KPIs that are appropriate for its level of maturity, its CSFs, and its particular circumstances. KPIs should be monitored and improvement opportunities identified and logged in the CSI register.

It is important to understand that the seven-step improvement process is applied to processes, activities, and any other aspects of service provision that need improving. The success of the improvement is therefore measured by the KPIs for the process to which it has been applied; if the improvement to a process has been successful, the KPIs for that process would show the improvement.

So, for example, a possible CSF for CSI could be "All improvement opportunities identified." The KPIs used to measure this could be the improvement in defects—for example, 3 percent reduction in failed changes and 10 percent reduction in security breaches. These would actually be KPIs for change and security management, respectively.

Another CSF could be "The cost of providing services is reduced," and the KPI could be the decrease in overall cost of service provision—for example, 2.5 percent reduction in the average cost of handling an incident or a 5 percent reduction in the cost of processing a particular type of transaction. Again, they would be KPIs for the process that had been improved.

Continual Service Improvement Risks

In the last section of this chapter, we look at the risks in continual service improvement. We considered management of risk in Chapter 46, "Continual Service Improvement Methods and Techniques." Here we are considering the risks associated with the implementation of CSI as a process within an organization. The main risks are as follows:

- Being overambitious and trying to improve everything at once. Be realistic with time lines and expectations.

- Failing to discuss improvement opportunities with the business. The business has to be involved in improvement decisions that will impact them, and if they do not understand the reasons behind the actions being taken, they may even be hostile to the changes.

- Neglecting to focus on improving both services and service management processes.

- Failing to prioritize, leading to effort being spread too thin to be effective or emphasis given to areas that are not aligned to business priorities.

- Insufficient technology, making the essential data gathering difficult or impossible.

- Insufficient resources. The work involved in implementing CSI is considerable, and its success is at risk if insufficient resources are allocated.

- When improvements are made, failing to ensure that the required knowledge transfer regarding the new process takes place through education and training as close to the launch of improvements as possible. If this is not done, the staff will not know the new process and the benefits will not be achieved.

- Failing to perform all of the steps of the seven-step improvement process, leading to poor decisions on what and how to improve based on poor data.

- Taking on CSI initiatives randomly in an adhoc manner due to the absence of a formalized approach.

- Insufficient monitoring and analysis taking place, leading to difficulties in identifying the areas of greatest need.

- Staff resistance.

- Poor data hampering the production of a compelling business case for improvement, leading to a failure to achieve the necessary funding for improvement initiatives.

- Lack of ownership of the process.

- Focusing on IT improvements without clear understanding of business needs and objectives.

These risks are likely to affect the success of improvement initiatives that are carried out reactively, without any overall structure in place. The guidance given in the *ITIL Continual Service Improvement* core volume provides an alternative approach: a thought-out, logical process for gathering and analyzing data, identifying opportunities in line with business requirements, and following through so that the benefits are realized.

Summary

In this chapter, we discussed the following topics:

- Continual service improvement challenges

- Continual service improvement critical success factors

- Continual service improvement risks

Implementing CSI is not an easy task; changing attitudes and values never is. You should not wait to fix something when it is broken. You should spot the issue by analyzing the available data and proactively take the necessary steps to improve. Undertaking a SWOT analysis (examining strengths, weaknesses, opportunities, and threats) so that you understand the risks and challenges before you start to implement CSI is critical. You can then devise mitigation strategies for the risks and identify how to best overcome the challenges. Knowing the CSFs before undertaking CSI implementation will help manage the risks and challenges.

We have now completed the entire syllabus for the continual service improvement lifecycle stage course. This also marks the end of this book; we have now completed the entire syllabus for each of the Intermediate Lifecycle courses. If you have used this book to support your study of each of the intermediate lifecycle stages and have successfully passed each exam, you will now have enough credits to sit the final course "Managing Across the Lifecycle," the final step in your journey to become an ITIL Expert.

Exam Essentials

Understand the challenges faced by continual service improvement staff.   Understand the difficulties that may be encountered when attempting to analyze data to establish a benchmark if the tools are inadequate. Be able to describe the difficulties in achieving cultural change.

Understand the critical success factors that need to be in place if successful continual service improvement is to take place.   Understand the importance of visible management support and the involvement of the business in setting priorities.

Understand why the involvement of the right people is a critical success factor.   Be able to explain the difference between the number of people involved in CSI (as a resource) and the skills and motivation of those involved (as a capability). Success requires the right number of staff with the right skills and knowledge.

Know the risks encountered in the continual service improvement stage.   Understand how these risks might be mitigated, in particular the danger that the implementation of CSI may lose momentum.

Review Questions

You can find the answers to the review questions in the appendix.

1. Which of the following are common challenges when implementing CSI?

    1. Lack of management commitment

    2. Inadequate resources, budget, and time

    3. A lack of corporate objectives, strategies, policies, and business direction

    4. Poor supplier management and/or poor supplier performance

        A. 1, 2, and 3 only

        B. All of the above

        C. 1, 2, and 4 only

        D. 1 and 2 only

2. Which of the following statements describe risks to successful CSI?

    1. Failing to discuss improvement opportunities with the business

    2. Focusing entirely on improving services rather than service management processes

        A. Statement 1 only

        B. Both statements

        C. Neither statement

        D. Statement 2 only

3. Which of the following statements about the measurement of risk is/are true?

    1. A risk is measured by the impact it would have if it occurred.

    2. A risk is measured by the cost to overcome the situation, should it occur.

    3. A risk is measured by the cost to remove it.

    4. A risk is measured by how likely it is to happen.

        A. All of the above

        B. 1, 2, and 3 only

        C. 1, 2, and 4 only

        D. 1 and 4 only

4. Which of the following statements about measurement is correct?

    A. Measurements are meaningless without context.

    B. Measurements should be focused on measuring the achievement of internal goals.

    C. Measurements show day-to-day performance; they are not relevant to achievement of strategy.

    D. What is measured should remain consistent despite changes in strategy.

5. Which of the following are common challenges when CSI is implemented?

    1. Driving cultural and behavioral change

    2. Justifying the cost of CSI if data is poor

    3. Having adequate resources to support CSI initiatives

    4. Configuring the toolsets in place to deliver the required data to support improvement

        A. 1 and 2 only

        B. 1, 3, and 4 only

        C. 2, 3, and 4 only

        D. All of the above

6. The *ITIL Continual Service Improvement* publication considers the situation where "information and knowledge exists within the organization that is not captured, validated, and shared." Which of the following terms describes this?

    A. Risk

    B. CSF

    C. KPI

    D. Challenge

7. Which of the following may cause resistance to CSI from the IT staff?

    1. Changes to job roles

    2. Using new tools without adequate training

    3. More effective reporting makes their failure to follow the defined processes more visible

    4. Extra tasks to perform, in addition to the "day job"

        A. 2 and 4 only

        B. 2, 3, and 4 only

        C. All of the above

        D. 4 only

8. Which of the following is NOT a common challenge encountered by the service provider when setting priorities for CSI?

    A. Inadequate resources

    B. A lack of communication with the business

    C. Assessing the service performance by using only technical metrics that do not show the effect of IT failure on the business

    D. Service provider/IT department heads pushing their own priorities

9.   Which of the following is NOT a critical success factor for CSI?

   A.   Defining clear business-related criteria

   B.   Overambitious approach to implementation

   C.   Prioritizing improvement projects to match business needs

   D.   Resource allocation

10. What is measured by key performance indicators?

   A.   Risk

   B.   CSFs

   C.   Benefits

   D.   Challenges

Appendix

Answers to Review Questions

Chapter 1: Introduction to the Service Strategy Lifecycle Stage

1. C. Service transition provides guidance to ensure that the new or changed service meets the expectations agreed in service design.

2. D. Perspective is the vision and direction of the organization. Plans are how the service provider will transition from its current situation to its desired situation. Position is how the service provider intends to compete against other service providers in the market. Patterns are the ongoing, repeatable actions that a service provider will have to perform.

3. A, C, D, F. The purpose of the service strategy stage of the service lifecycle is to define the perspective, position, plans, and patterns that a service provider needs to be able to execute to meet an organization's business outcomes.

4. B. For services to provide true value to the business, they must be designed with the business objectives in mind. Design encompasses the whole IT organization, for it is the organization as a whole that delivers and supports the services. Service design is the stage in the lifecycle that turns a service strategy into a plan for delivering the business objectives.

5. C. The level of investment required to carry out the strategy is calculated using financial management for IT services. Availability management is part of service design, knowledge management is part of service transition, and the seven-step improvement process is used for continual service improvement.

6. D. The ITIL Service Operation core volume provides guidance on how to maintain stability in service operation, allowing for changes in design, scale, scope, and service levels. New models and architectures such as shared services, utility computing, web services, and mobile commerce to support service operation are described.

7. C. Service catalog management is part of service design. Problem management is a service operation process, service asset and configuration management is part of service transition, and service portfolio management is a responsibility of service strategy.

8. C. Whatever the strategy, and however well the resulting new or changed service is designed, unless it can be transitioned successfully, the value will not be realized. Attempting to implement an improvement that results in downtime due to a badly planned change could mean that the damage to the business outweighs any potential intended benefit. Service transition ensures that changes are controlled and managed so that this risk is minimized.

9. E. The ITIL service operation core guidance includes a detailed description of the four service management functions (technical management, applications management, operations management, and the service desk). The service knowledge management system (SKMS) is used throughout the lifecycle and described as part of knowledge management in the ITIL service transition core guidance. Plan-Do-Check-Act (PDCA) is primarily discussed in continual service improvement, and return on investment (ROI) is mostly considered in service strategy. Service level agreements are primarily discussed in service design.

10. B. Improvements may be to the level of service delivered or to the alignment of the service to business needs. They might not result in a cost saving but will deliver better value.

Chapter 2: Service Strategy Principles

1. D. The concepts link together as future versus present, operational effectiveness versus improvement in functionality, and launch versus ongoing.

2. C. An outcome is the result of carrying out an activity, following a process, or delivering an IT service. Business outcomes represent the business objectives of both the business unit and the service provider and involve internal customers. Customer outcomes are usually based on external service providers; the service provider's outcomes are based on the customer's outcomes but are different.

3. C. The service types described in service strategy are core, enabling, enhancing.

4. B. Economic value is based on the reference value perceived by the customer and the net difference that the service provider makes to the delivery.

5. A. This is the correct definition of utility and warranty.

6. E, C. The internal service provider is embedded in the business unit it serves.

7. B. This is the correct sequence for defining a service, starting with definition of the market. If you do not define the market first, you will not be able to provide the right service for the organization.

8. A. Options B and C are used for future planning. Only A is carried out after the investment has been made.

9. A, C, E, G, I. These are the basic elements of a business case, as discussed as part of financial management.

10. B, D, F, G, H. These are valid sourcing strategies as described in the sourcing strategy section of this chapter.

Chapter 3: Service Strategy Processes: Part 1

1. B. Securing the funding that is required for the provision of the agreed services is an objective of the financial management for IT services process, not the strategy management process.

2. D. *Service valuation* is defined as the ability to understand the costs of a service relative to its business value. The process responsible for identifying the actual costs of delivering IT services, comparing them with budgeted costs, and managing variance from the budget

is accounting within financial management for IT services. The framework that allows the service provider to determine the costs of providing services is the cost model, and the activity of predicting and controlling the spending of money is budgeting within financial management for IT services.

3. D. All service providers need to understand what funding they will require, using the budgeting process, and where the money has been spent, using the accounting process. Charging is the activity whereby payment is required for services delivered. For internal service providers charging is optional, and many organizations choose to treat their IT service provider as a cost center. External service providers must charge for their services, since this is where the organization obtains the revenue which keeps it in business.

4. B. Options A, C, and D are all business relationship management responsibilities. Option B describes a responsibility of service level management, not business relationship management.

5. D. The service portfolio should engage with all the lifecycle stages.

6. C. The *ITIL Service Strategy* publication states that the IT strategy document, the service management strategy document, and the strategy plans for each service are the documents that should always be included.

7. D. Managing by crisis, managing by reacting to customer demand, managing by extrapolation, managing by hope, and managing by best effort are all poor management strategies named in the *ITIL Service Strategy* publication.

8. D. Option A is incorrect as IT finances are a subset of the enterprise's finances, and the same rules and controls apply to it as to any other department. Option B is also incorrect as internal service providers may not necessarily charge for their services directly. Option C is incorrect as external service providers will not usually share this information, which would show their profit margins, to their customers. Option D is correct, as IT exists to serve the business, so all expenditure on IT must benefit the business directly or indirectly.

9. C. The others are objectives of business relationship management.

10. D. This is a key aspect of the purpose of service portfolio management. The other answers relate to the service design processes of capacity management, service level management, and availability management.

Chapter 4: Service Strategy Processes: Part 2

1. C. Patterns of activity are mechanisms for tracking business activity to deliver business outcomes, which show how the business will need to use business services.

2. B. Demand management is about matching supply to demand.

3. A. Demand management will use all of these information sources.

4. A. User profiles are based on the roles and responsibilities within an organization.

5. D. It is consumption that produces demand and production that consumes it in a highly synchronized pattern, not as stated in option D.

6. D. Services are designed to enable business activities, which in turn achieve business outcomes. Thus every time a business activity is performed, it generates demand for services. These patterns of business activity (PBAs) have to be properly defined and documented. ITIL guidance says that the following items need to be documented: classification, attributes, requirements, and service asset requirements.

7. D. Business relationship management has a strategic focus but not an operational focus.

8. A. Business relationship management will work with the business to build a business case for a new service. Service level management is only involved in ensuring that the service can be provided as required, not in whether it is the best use of investment funds.

9. A. Both are true statements and describe data repositories used by BRM.

10. B. Option B describes a situation that may be a trigger for CSI.

Chapter 5: Governance

1. B. Governance is an overarching area that ties business and IT together, defining common policies and rules that both business and IT need to do business.

2. C is 1 (direct), A is 2 (evaluate), and B is 3 (monitor). The direct activity relates to communicating the strategy, policies, and plans to, and through, management. Evaluate refers to the ongoing assessment of the organization's performance and its environment. In the monitor activity, the governors of the organization are able to determine whether governance is being fulfilled effectively.

3. D. ISO 20000 refers to IT service management. ISO 27001 refers to security. ISO 15504 refers to process assessment. ISO 38500 refers to corporate governance of IT.

4. A. Governance is expressed in a set of strategies, policies, and plans.

5. A. This statement is correct; policies should define boundaries for the organization.

6. A, B, C, D, E, F. All of these are principles covered in the ISO 38500.

7. C. IT governance must be part of the approach to corporate governance because IT is part of the organization and must abide by the same governance standards as the rest of the organization.

8. C. The final decision about the strategy, policies, rules, and plans and how they are enforced is made by the governors because they are accountable for governance. This

accountability may not be delegated to managers, who are required to comply with governance.

9. A, C, D, E. All but option B are valid discussion points at the IT steering group. Agreeing on corporate strategy is not appropriate for the IT steering group.

10. B, D, E, G. Options B, D, E, and G are the valid service strategy processes. Design coordination, IT service continuity management, and service level management are design stage processes, and service asset and configuration management is part of service transition.

Chapter 6: Organizing for Service Strategy

1. C, E. The rest are all service desk structures; centralized is both an organizational structure and a service desk structure.

2. D. The *ITIL Service Strategy* publication describes the sequence as moving through network, directive, delegation, coordination, and collaboration.

3. B. The *ITIL Service Strategy* publication describes the network stage as "Focused on rapid, informal, and adhoc delivery, reluctant to adopt formal structures."

4. A, B, C, D. Before deciding on the appropriate organizational design, the strategy and culture of the organization need to be considered, because there is a risk that the design will not enable the strategy or be resisted by the staff. Similarly, if the provider's organization will be structured by geography or aligned by customers, the process design will be guided by this criterion. Once key processes are understood, it is appropriate to begin organizational design.

5. C. The *ITIL Service Strategy* publication describes a role as a set of responsibilities, activities, and associated levels of authority granted to a person or team. A role is defined in a process or function.

6. C. The *ITIL Service Strategy* publication states that the service owner is accountable for the delivery of a specific service, and also that the role of service owner is critical to service management.

7. B. The *ITIL Service Strategy* publication identifies the financial management for IT services roles of process owner, process manager, and budget holder.

8. C. The service owner represents the service across the organization. It is the responsibility of the process manager to manage the process so that it is performed efficiently and produces the correct output. Although the service owner *does* represent the service at the change advisory board, option D says "represent the process."

9. A, C. It is the process owner's responsibility to ensure that everything is in place to enable the process to be carried out effectively, such as ensuring that staff are trained, the process

documentation is up to date, etc. The process owner is NOT responsible for ensuring that the process is actually carried out; this is the responsibility of the process manager.

10. A. Designing services to meet the patterns of business activity and being able to meet business outcomes is part of demand management responsibilities. Sizing applications, services, and systems is a key aspect of capacity management. Compiling and formulating the annual IT budgets to be scrutinized by the IT steering group is part of financial management responsibilities. Establishing and articulating business requirements for new services or changes to existing services is part of business relationship management responsibilities.

Chapter 7: Technology Considerations

1. B. Personalized service is *not* a benefit of service automation. All the other options are benefits.

2. B. Statements 1, 2, 4, 6, 7, and 8 are the techniques listed in the *ITIL Service Strategy* publication.

3. B. The *ITIL Service Strategy* publication describes service analytics as understanding patterns of information.

4. A. A fault is defined as an abnormal condition that requires action to repair, while an error is a single event. A fault is usually indicated by excessive errors. The behavior of a service is impacted by a combination of elements working together, so we need to understand the context to understand the actual relevance of any data. The simpler the process, the smaller the chance of error, so removing unnecessary steps may itself reduce performance variations because there are fewer steps to go wrong.

5. D. Technology-assisted describes a service encounter in which only the service provider has access to the technology, as when an airline representative uses a terminal to check in passengers.

6. B. There is no such technique as synthetic generation. All the other answers are techniques described in the *ITIL Service Strategy* publication.

7. C. All of these are listed in the *ITIL Service Strategy* publication as areas where service management may benefit from automation.

8. B. The greatest benefit often results from automating simple but frequent tasks. Complex tasks may be hard to automate because of the possibility of error, and the time saved may be minimal if they are infrequently used. So complex tasks may therefore be unsuitable for automation, and ITIL recommends that complex tasks should be simplified before automation is considered.

9. D. Service analytics will help convert data to information and then to knowledge, but no computer-based technology can provide wisdom. It requires people to provide evaluated understanding, to answer and appreciate the "why?" questions. So statement 1 is FALSE.

Service analytics does provide the linkage between components and the business process, the service model, so statement 2 is TRUE.

10. B. The items in the statement are listed as characteristics of service interfaces in the *ITIL Service Strategy* publication.

Chapter 8: Implementing Service Strategy

1. C. These are the four *P*s of service strategy, but they are also the four elements that service strategy should ensure are managed successfully.

2. D. Service strategy has an impact on all other stages of the lifecycle.

3. D. Both of these statements about the service strategy four *P*s are correct.

4. A. Defined services are captured in the service portfolio. The defined services include the pipeline, the catalog, and retired services.

5. C. The services are delivered to customers, and complementary to the service portfolio, this information is captured in the customer portfolio.

6. B. Testing the processes will be part of the service transition approach to implementing service strategy.

7. C. These are all valid constraints, as referenced in Figure 8.3, shown in Chapter 8.

8. A. Service models are a key factor in the development of services during design.

9. A. Patterns of business activity are explored as part of demand management.

10. B. Service design will consider business impact analysis in a number of processes during the design of services. Business impact analysis will help the teams judge where their efforts are best spent, especially where there is a resource conflict.

Chapter 9: Challenges, Critical Success Factors, and Risks

1. B. Measurements should not be focused on internal goals. They should be focused instead on customer satisfaction.

2. C. The ITIL glossary defines risk as "a possible event that could cause harm or loss, or affect the ability to achieve objectives. A risk is measured by the probability of a threat, the vulnerability of the asset to that threat, and the impact it would have if it occurred."

3. A. There is a risk that services fail to deliver the expected utility benefits; poor design causes poor performance. For example a change in the pattern of demand for a service could reduce the service's utility if it has not been designed to be scalable. This is defined as a design risk.

4. B. Accurate measurement is described as a challenge in the ITIL framework. Monitoring of discrete failures does not provide a picture of the customer experience. The failure to meet this challenge constitutes a risk to effective service management because inadequate or incomplete information impacts the quality of decision-making.

5. C. These are the challenges listed in the *ITIL Service Strategy* publication. The need to coordinate and prioritize many new or changed services is a service transition risk. If maturity levels of one process are low, it will be impossible to achieve full maturity in other processes, which is a service design risk. Lack of engagement with development and project staff is a service operation risk.

6. A, B, C, D. These are all essential elements of risk management.

7. C. These are among the methods listed as ways of preserving value.

8. B. Risk is normally seen as something to be avoided due to the possible negative consequences, but risks may also present opportunities. For example, underserved market spaces and unfulfilled demand are risks to be avoided, but they can also be seen as opportunities to be exploited. Organizations need to take risks but limit exposure to an acceptable level.

9. C. Appropriate responses are as follows: reducing the total cost of utilization (TCU), giving customers financial incentives to not switch to other options; differentiation, providing services that are unique, novel, or difficult for competitors to replicate; and consolidation, concentrating demand from several customers or customer groups onto a single service rather than offering a lot of diverse but similar services, thus reducing costs to help retain customers.

10. C. If the challenge of ensuring sufficient coordination is met, silos will not develop. Without the coordination, this would be a risk. Decision-makers have limited time, so they delegate roles and responsibilities to specialized teams and individuals. Specialization allows for development of in-depth knowledge, skills, and experience. However, increasing specialization requires a corresponding increase in the need for coordination. It is important to appreciate this increased need for coordination and to address it through cooperation and control between teams and individuals and with suppliers.

Chapter 10: Introduction to the Service Design Lifecycle Stage

1. A. Option A describes a purpose of the financial management for IT services process, which is part of service strategy, not service design.

2. C. These are all listed in the ITIL framework as goals of service design.

3. B. Risk management is not one of the five aspects.

The five aspects of service design are as follows:

- The design of the actual solution itself
- The service management system and tools that will be required to manage the service
- The management and technology architectures that the service will use
- The processes needed to support the service in operation
- The measurement systems, methods, and metrics that will be required

4. D. This is the ITIL glossary definition of a service design package.

5. C. The SACs are used to ensure that an IT service meets its functionality and quality requirements and that the IT service provider is ready to operate the new IT service when it has been deployed; the postimplementation review takes place *after* deployment.

6. C. Service portfolio management is a service strategy process. Service catalog management, service level management, and information security management are service design processes.

7. D. Service design does not impact the effectiveness of business processes. Options A, B, and C are benefits of effective service design.

8. D. Service design packages and updated service models are outputs to transition. Service strategy inputs are vision and mission, service portfolio, policies, strategies and strategic plans, priorities, and service charters.

9. B. These are some of the outputs from transition to design listed in the ITIL *Service Design* core volume.

10. C. All of the items mentioned except change schedule and the CMS are valid inclusions in a service design package.

Chapter 11: Service Design Principles

1. B. The service portfolio contains the service pipeline, service catalog, and retired services. The portfolio is part of the service knowledge management system. The SKMS includes the service portfolio and the configuration management system as well as other databases and information systems.

2. D. Warranty refers to the ability of a service to be available when needed, to provide the required capacity, and to provide the required reliability in terms of continuity and security. Warranty can be summarized as "how the service is delivered" and can be used to determine whether a service is "fit for use." Utility describes the functionality offered by a product or service to meet a particular need, "what the service does," and can be used to determine whether a service is able to meet its required outcomes, or is "fit for purpose." Removal of constraints is an aspect of utility.

3. D. The four *P*s of service design are the people, the processes, the products (the services, technology, and tools), and the partners (the suppliers, manufacturers, and vendors). Service design must consider each of the four *P*s to ensure a robust design that meets the requirements.

4. B. The three aspects to be balanced in a balanced design are functionality (the service or product and everything that is part of the service and its provision), resources (the people, technology, and money available for the effort), and schedule (the timescales for completion).

5. C. There are four separate technology domains that support components of every service, and design needs to address all four. They are infrastructure, environmental, data/information, and applications.

6. C. The service portfolio is made up of the service pipeline, the service catalog, and retired services.

7. B. When a design needs to be changed or any of the individual elements of the design need to be amended, consideration must be given to all aspects. This is called holistic service design. Holistic service design, therefore, involves all five aspects of design.

8. C. Option C is not a valid risk because it is utility that is about fitness for purpose. Spending insufficient time on warranty would not affect the service's fitness for use. The other options are all valid risks.

9. D. The design of a service must include the technology architectures that the service will use and details of the skills that the support staff will need to operate, support, and maintain the services. It also must include an understanding of which aspects will be supported internally and which by suppliers (and the OLAs and underpinning contracts that will be required to meet the required SLRs). It must include the details of the measurement systems, methods, and metrics that will be required to measure and monitor the service, and provide the necessary management information that will also be necessary. Governance and compliance requirements are inputs into defining the utility of the service, and the design will need to meet these requirements. These are in addition to the actual solution itself.

10. B. The business case will have been developed in strategy, and its development is not a service design activity. Evaluating the alternative solutions, procuring the preferred option, and developing it are all activities undertaken in service design.

Chapter 12: Service Design Processes: Design Coordination and Service Catalog Management

1. C. Option A is carried out by the manager of the service level management process. Option B is carried out by the transition planning and support process. Option D is completed by the IT steering group and senior management of the department.

2. A. The multi-view catalog shows all services that are used. The technical view shows the supporting services, and the business / customer catalog shows the customer facing services.

3. C. Option C describes the service catalog. Option A describes a service level agreement, option B the service portfolio, and option D a business case.

4. C. Strategic and retired services are not included in the service catalog.

5. B. The service catalog forms part of the service portfolio. The rest of the statements are false.

6. D. The design coordination process is not responsible for ensuring that the design meets the requirements, but it is responsible for ensuring that the solution is designed, providing a coordination point, and ensuring that the objectives of the service design stage are met.

7. D. The CMS and governance requirements are not part of the outputs from design coordination.

8. C. Option C is the only correct option because it is used to show which IT service supports each business process.

9. A. A connection can be drawn between the service catalog and the lifecycle processes because the service catalog refers to all the services provided to the organization and how they are delivered.

10. B. Design coordination is responsible for the coordination of the service design lifecycle stage, not the service operation stage.

Chapter 13: Service Design Processes: Service Level Management and Availability Management

1. A. The purpose of service level management is to ensure that there is a high-level relationship with customers to capture business demands. A high-level relationship with the customer is provided through the business relationship management process. The single point of contact for the users is the service desk. Service transition looks after the smooth transition of services.

2. B. Option A is an objective of change management, option C is an objective of the service desk, and option D is an objective of problem management.

3. C. AST stands for agreed service time, and DT stands for downtime.

4. D. Reliability, resilience, serviceability, and maintainability are all key concepts in availability management.

5. B. Utility is not included in the SLM requirements, and change records and configuration records are also out of scope.

6. C. You would not find a definition of business strategy in a service level agreement.

7. C. A strategic business plan and an internal finance agreement do not commonly support an SLA.

8. D. Option A describes an OLA, and option B describes an SLA. Option C is not a formal part of service level management.

9. B. VBF stands for vital business functions.

10. B. The service level monitoring chart is also known as a RAG chart—red, amber, and green.

Chapter 14: Service Design Processes: Capacity Management and IT Service Continuity Management

1. A. Service level management negotiates the targets for service level agreements.

2. A. The subprocesses of capacity management are business, service, and component capacity management.

3. B. Ensuring that the business has contingency plans in place in case of a disaster is the responsibility of the business, not IT service continuity management.

4. D. BIA stands for business impact analysis.

5. C. BCM and ITSCM are closely linked as described.

6. A = 1, B = 3, C = 2. Business capacity relates to business activities, service capacity to service performance, and component capacity to the technical infrastructure.

7. A. There are reactive and proactive elements to the process, to both plan and react to operational needs.

8. C. The number of incidents (4) is a KPI for incident management.

9. B. Risk management is part of service continuity management, not capacity management.

10. C. Testing takes place during implementation and ongoing operation.

Chapter 15: Service Design Processes: Information Security Management and Supplier Management

1. D. The business is responsible for defining the protection required for systems and data. Information security management ensures that it can be applied and implemented.

2. A. Security management information system (SMIS) is the information database associated with the information security management process.

3. D. Supplier management is concerned with external suppliers only.

4. C. Tactical is the other category, not trusted.

5. A. Although the rest of the options are part of information security management, the key purpose is to create a policy that will guide the other activities.

6. C. Suppliers are categorized according to the risk and impact to the achievement of business objectives and goals and their relative value and importance in providing the service.

7. C. Plan and maintain are both parts of the information security management approach, along with control, implement, and evaluation.

8. A. Service level agreements are often supported by third-party contracts and so there should be a close relationship between the processes.

9. A. Operational level agreements are internal agreements, not agreements with customers, and are not managed through supplier management.

10. C. Both statements are correct because the SCMIS is a repository for information relating to suppliers, such as supplier policies and contracts.

Chapter 16: Technology-Related Activities

1. B. Requirements engineering is the name given to the approach by which we ascertain, understand, and document the requirements of the business, users, and other stakeholders. This enables service design to understand what is required and ensures the traceability of changes to each requirement. The three stages of requirements engineering are elicitation, analysis, and validation.

2. C. A requirement is defined as a formal statement of what is needed—for example, a service level requirement, a project requirement, or the required deliverables for a process. The three categories of requirements are functional, management/operational, and usability.

3. D. All but market testing and outsourcing are valid methods for gathering requirements.

4. B. We need to know who will access the data and how and why this will be done. We need to maintain data quality and plan for its eventual disposal. If data is not managed effectively, resources will be wasted collecting and maintaining unnecessary data, or the data that is useful may not be available to those who need it. A data management process that establishes policies and standards will provide expertise and make it easier to handle the data aspects of new services. It will deliver all of the benefits listed in the question.

5. 1 and B, 2 and A, 3 and C. ITIL defines the data categories as follows: Tactical data is typically concerned with summarized data and historical data, operational data is necessary for the ongoing functioning of an organization, and strategic data is often concerned with longer-term trends and comparison with the outside world.

6. C. Option C does not describe one of the four areas. The missing area is the management of data standards and policies.

7. A. Customer satisfaction scores are not among the four types. The missing type is custom information provided by the applications.

8. C. *CASE* stands for *computer-aided software engineering.* Applications design may use CASE tools to specify requirements, draw design diagrams, or even generate complete applications or nearly complete application skeletons. These tools also provide a central location, generally called a repository, for storing and managing all the elements that are created during application development.

9. D. These are methods of describing functional requirements, that is, the utility to be provided.

10. C. Allowing insufficient time or failing to give priority to requirements gathering is the cause of most system errors; these will take far longer to fix later than gathering the requirements would have taken. It may even mean the project is unable to deliver.

Chapter 17: Organizing for Service Design

1. C. The service owner represents the service across the organization.

2. Process owner = (2) Ensures the process can be carried out effectively; Process manager = (3) Ensures that the process is carried out effectively; Process practitioner = (1) Carries out the activity of the process. The process owner is accountable for the process, the manager is responsible for the process management, and the practitioner will be responsible for carrying out the activity of the process.

3. A. The role of the service design manager often includes the process owner and manager roles for design coordination.

4. D. RACI stands for responsible, accountable, consulted, and informed. Option D describes the additional roles correctly.

5. B. Option B describes the role of the IT planner: the production and coordination of IT plans that will be used throughout the service lifecycle, but this takes place within service design.

6. A. Sizing applications, services, and systems is a key aspect of capacity management when the organization is designing and preparing for new or changed services.

7. C. Design coordination is responsible for the production of the service design package; the other processes contribute to its contents.

8. D. Service level management requires negotiating skills with the business to establish service level agreements that meet the requirements of both the business and IT.

9. C. Option A relates to supplier management, option B relates to information security management, and option D relates to ITSCM.

10. B. ITIL suggests adoption of a structure that supports the organizational needs, not necessarily the same one other organizations use.

Chapter 18: Technology Considerations

1. C. Stating the budget in advance would hamper negotiation later, which makes option C the incorrect statement. The other three statements are true.

2. A. Customization (but not configuration) will have to be repeated for each upgrade. Configuration would not affect supplier support obligations (customization might). Out-of-the box tools would mean standard training could be used. Processes should be defined before tool selection. The tool should follow the process, not vice versa.

3. C. *M* stands for *Must have* requirements, *S* stands for *Should have* requirements, *C* stands for *Could have requirements*, and *W* stands for *Would like in the future* requirements.

4. C. The steps in option C are in the correct order.

5. B. The use of a service design tool will not reduce testing time. All the other options show actual benefits of using a tool.

6. A. The tool should fit the process, not the other way around. It is acceptable if the tool fails to fit some process areas and some changes are made to the process as long as they are not major.

7. B. It is insufficient to just address the tool's capabilities and how it matches the process; due diligence should be carried out to ensure that the support offered is of the required standard.

8. C. All of the aspects that are listed should be considered.

9. D. These costs should all be included. If the tool is implemented but insufficient training or configuration is carried out, the capabilities of the tool will not be realized. Without good reporting, the data held in the tool will not be easily available, and so monitoring achievement against targets, monitoring of KPIs, and so on will be ineffective. Without time spent setting up the web portal, a major advance in terms of efficiency will not be realized because a poorly implemented portal will not be used by the customers. Failure to include these costs explains why so many operation initiatives fail; there is an attempt to deliver too much as business as usual rather than as a costed and funded project.

10. B. Training will still be required, but access to the service across a network to the supplier will simplify implementation and may reduce costs.

Chapter 19: Implementation and Improvement of Service Design

1. A. What is the vision? (Business vision, mission, goals, and objectives); Where are we now? (Baseline assessments); Where do we want to be? (Measurable targets); Did we get there? (Measurements and metrics).

2. C. All of the statements apply to business impact analysis.

3. B. SLM finds out the requirements prior to the start of the design. Design then attempts to ensure that the requirements are met by the design. The SLA is not agreed to and signed until design is complete because there may be reasons the SLRs may not be fully met in the design, such as cost or technical issues. These deviations will be negotiated during the design phase.

4. C. All of the approaches that are listed are valid.

5. D. These aspects of the review cover the people, processes, products, and partners—the four *P*s.

6. A. A balanced scorecard allows the business to prioritize what is important to achieve success.

7. B. Option B includes the correct steps for Six Sigma DMADV. Six Sigma is the problem solving approach that is complementary to the ITIL framework.

8. D. SMART stands for specific, measurable, achievable, realistic, and time-bound. These elements are identified to ensure that all objectives have a clear purpose, intent, and scope and can be achieved within a realistic timescale.

9. A. SWOT is used to identify the opportunities for improvement by investigating the elements that impact an organization.

10. D. All of these are the steps used in the Six Sigma DMAIC process, which is an improvement system for existing processes that fall below specification and need incremental improvement.

Chapter 20: Challenges, Critical Success Factors, and Risks

1. A. A critical success factor (CSF) describes something that must happen if an IT service, process, plan, project, or other activity is to succeed.

2. D. Key performance indicators (KPIs) are used to measure the achievement of each critical success factor. For example, the critical success factor "Protect IT services when making changes" could be measured by a key performance indicator such as reducing the number of changes that fail or that cause incidents over time measured as a percentage of all changes.

3. B. All the other KPIs are reporting on the success of cutting costs, speeding delivery, or improving quality; only option B is about reducing the impact of conflicting demands for resources.

4. B. The question includes the definition of a KPI in the official ITIL glossary and publications.

5. D. Testing is part of service transition. All of the other risks are valid service design risks.

6. B. A risk is measured by the probability of a threat, the vulnerability of the asset to that threat, and the impact it would have if it occurred.

7. D. This is a challenge. There may be an associated risk that, due to unclear or changing requirements, the design does not fulfil the requirements. A risk is the possible result of a challenge not being met successfully.

8. D. Market risks, such as sourcing decisions made by customers, are potential risks for all service providers, but they are a risk to service strategy, not design.

9. B. If speed and quality are most important, the cost will be high. If quality and cost are most important, the design will take more time. If cost and time are most important, quality will suffer.

10. D. KPIs are designed from the outset and collected regularly and at important milestones.

Chapter 21: Introduction to Service Transition

1. C. Option C is an objective of service strategy, not service transition.

2. C. It is design that turns strategy into deliverables (1), and it is in the service operations stage that the design is used in the real world and the strategy is realized (2).

3. D. Service transition covers the transfer of services, as described in options 1, 3, and 4. Producing a business case is a service strategy task. Terminating a supplier contract would involve a number of transition tasks, such as updating the CMS and supplier and contract management information system, putting an alternative supplier in place, or taking the service in house.

4. B. The purpose of service transition is to ensure seamless transition of designed services to meet the business expectations agreed in strategy.

5. A. Capacity plans are developed as part of service design in the capacity management process.

6. B. Change evaluation focus is strongly related to service transition because evaluation is part of ensuring that the release is fit for delivery into operation.

7. C. Both statements are correct.

8.   D. These are all approaches that can be managed under transition.

9.   C. Service transition supports the introduction of new services.

10.   A. As with all improvement activity across the lifecycle, service transition engages with CSI to ensure that improvements are made and prioritized according to business need.

Chapter 22: Service Transition Principles

1.   C. The management team is responsible for approving the formal transition policy.

2.   A. Transition emphasizes the need for controls, and governance is applicable across the whole service lifecycle, not just a specific stage.

3.   B. Changing business requirements may require course corrections in a current transition.

4.   A. Controls should be introduced as early as possible in the service lifecycle to support governance across the lifecycle.

5.   C. Statement 2 refers to capabilities.

6.   D. *Capability* refers to the ability of a service organization, person, process, application, configuration item, or IT service to carry out an activity.

7.   B. The items in option B are all strategy inputs to transition. Option A describes inputs from service design, option C from CSI, and option D from service operation.

8.   D. Although each of these policies will involve management of resource, the policies knowledge transfer and service transition, quality assurance, and plan release packages have other primary considerations. Proactively manage resources is primarily concerned with management of shared and specialist resources for transition.

9.   C. The policy relating to transition efficiency recommends reuse of existing processes and systems.

10.   A. Policies are used to provide guidance and management for the lifecycle stages.

Chapter 23: Service Transition Processes: Transition Planning and Support and Change Management

1.   C. It is important to note that transition planning and support is *not* responsible for detailed planning of the build, test, and deployment of individual changes or releases; these are part of change management and release and deployment management.

2. C. All of the options are valid start points for the change management process. A call to the service desk may require a change to fulfil the request or resolve the incident. A change proposal agrees to a major change in principle; this may then lead to several smaller changes being raised. A project initiation document will outline the changes that the project will deliver; change management will need to agree to each.

3. B. There are three different types of service change:

- Standard changes are low risk, relatively common, and follow a defined procedure. They are preauthorized.

- Emergency changes must be implemented as soon as possible (for example, to resolve a major incident or implement a security patch). These are normally defined as changes where the risk of *not* carrying out the change is greater than the risk of implementing it.

- All other changes are defined as normal changes.

4. C. Option C describes a critical success factor (CSF), not a key performance indicator (KPI).

5. A. Option A is the definition of a release package, option B describes a release unit, option C describes a release, and option D describes a release model.

6. A. Transition planning and support provides overall planning for service transitions and coordination of the resources they require.

7. C. Service asset and configuration management (SACM) is the process that manages the naming convention for the configuration management database. Release management is concerned with the release controls that are specified in the release policy; these would include release naming conventions, the use of the DML, and the roles and responsibilities of those involved.

8. D. The ECAB is responsible for emergency changes; it needs to be a small group because it needs to be contacted to make a decision quickly. The members are senior managers who agree whether the proposed change is workable (using the senior technical manager's assessment) and the risk is acceptable (the senior IT manager and the customer representative would decide upon this).

9. D. Although simple releases may need no more management than that provided by the change management process, more complex releases will require more detailed management and would benefit from the application of project management disciplines. Similarly, where there are several connected releases, using project management to treat each release as a project and linking each of these related projects together into a program will provide the required control and management. Using project management is helpful, not confusing.

10. C. These statements are both objectives of transition planning and support, ensuring that transitions are managed effectively.

Chapter 24: Service Transition Processes: Service Asset and Configuration Management

1. B. The purpose of SACM process is to identify and control the assets that make up services and maintain accurate information about these assets.

2. D. SACM is a process that supports all stages of the service lifecycle by providing information about the assets that make up services. The process is part of service transition, although the CMS is used across the lifecycle by many processes.

3. C. A configuration record captures the information about a configuration item and records the attributes and relationships. It is stored in the CMDB. Option A is a service asset, option B is a configuration item, and option D is an activity carried out in SACM.

4. A. The layers of the CMS are closely associated to the data, information, knowledge, wisdom (DIKW) model from knowledge management. The presentation layer allows for decision-making from the analysis and processing of data.

5. B. Although it may help provide background information for an incident, the CMS would not normally contain known error information that the service desk staff could use to resolve incidents.

6. A. When SACM has been successfully implemented, checking the related CIs for each change can be carried out quickly, and so will not slow down the change management process. It will actually benefit change management by allowing a more accurate impact analysis of the proposed change to be carried out, thus reducing risk. Failure of staff to carry out the process, because they are not aware of its importance, will endanger the accuracy of the CMS; staff need to understand the criticality of an accurate CMS through an awareness campaign. When implementing SACM, it is essential to ensure that the level of detail maintained matches the value of the information, as otherwise this process will not be cost-effective. Finally, without effective change management, effective SACM is impossible.

7. D. A service asset is any resource or capability that could contribute to the delivery of a service. A configuration item, or CI, is a service asset that needs to be managed in order to deliver an IT service. A configuration record is a set of attributes and relationships about a CI. Configuration records are stored in a configuration management database and managed with a configuration management system.

8. B. The configuration model enables other processes to access valuable information, as in the examples described in the question.

9. B. An SDP is an example of a service lifecycle CI, not a service CI. Service CIs include capability assets such as management, organization, processes, knowledge, and people. They

can also include resource assets such as financial capital, systems, applications, information, data, infrastructure and facilities, financial capital, and people. Also included are service models and service acceptance criteria.

10. B. Options A, C, and D are untrue. A snapshot is not formally reviewed, asset management alone does not provide information about relationships required for effective service management, and SAM is a subset of SACM.

Chapter 25: Service Transition Processes: Release and Deployment Management and Service Validation and Testing

1. A. Option B describes a release unit, Option C describes a release, and Option D describes a release model.

2. B. Early life support is the handover that takes place between service transition and service operation during the deployment phase of release and deployment. It ensures that the support of the deployment and development teams is still available as the new or changed service is introduced to the live environment.

3. C. SACM is the process that manages the naming convention for the configuration management system. Release management is concerned with the release controls that are specified in the release policy.

4. D. Verification and audit is a step in the SACM process.

5. C. Early life support takes place in the deployment phase, where the handover to service operation takes place.

6. D. The test report is not part of a test model.

7. C. The correct order is as follows: Design tests, Verify test plan, Prepare test environment, Perform tests, Evaluate exit criteria and report, Test cleanup and closure.

8. D. The exit and entry criteria for testing are defined in the service design package.

9. B. The left-hand side of the service V model shows service requirements down to the detailed service design. The right-hand side focuses on the validation activities that are performed against these specifications.

10. C. Any of the listed results are valid.

Chapter 26: Service Transition Processes: Change Evaluation and Knowledge Management

1. D. The objectives of change evaluation include setting stakeholder expectations correctly and providing accurate information to change management to prevent changes with an adverse impact and changes that introduce risk being transitioned unchecked. It also evaluates the intended and the unintended effects of a service change and provides good-quality outputs to enable change management to decide quickly whether or not a service change is to be authorized.

2. B. The purpose of the change evaluation process is to understand the likely performance of a service change and how it might impact the business, the IT infrastructure, and other IT services. The process assesses the actual performance of a change against its predicted performance.

3. D. These are the four sections of the report specified in *ITIL Service Transition*.

4. C. A model is a representation of a system, process, IT service, or configuration item that is used to help understand or predict future behavior.

5. A. The trigger for change evaluation is receipt of a request for evaluation from change management.

6. B. Options A, C, and D are the only permitted outcomes. If a discount were provided, it would have to be combined with the customer accepting the deviation.

7. D. Release and deployment management is responsible for ensuring that appropriate testing takes place, but the actual testing is carried out as part of the service validation and testing process. The output of service validation and testing is a key input to change evaluation and must be provided at an appropriate time and in a suitable format to enable changes to be evaluated in time for change management decision-making.

8. 1+B, 3+A, 4+C, 2+D. Knowledge management is typically displayed within the data, information, knowledge, wisdom (DIKW) model. The answer matches each of these concepts with its definition.

9. C. The tool is called the service knowledge management system (SKMS), and it's a repository for information, data, and knowledge relating to service management. This has important connections for managing information and knowledge throughout the whole service lifecycle.

10. D. Knowledge management is a process that has influence across the whole of the service lifecycle. It is used to capture and present ideas, perspectives, data, and information to all stages of the lifecycle, ensuring that the appropriate decisions can be made.

Chapter 27: Managing People through Service Transitions

1. C. It is important to ensure that all stakeholders are communicated with during the transition; this means both service provider and customer stakeholders.

2. B. Email and faxes are not recommended as communication methods. Email is too frequently received, and faxes are an old-fashioned approach to communication, and both are likely to be lost among many others of similar type.

3. A. Communication models support specific types of change with clearly understood, effective, and tested communication paths.

4. A. The emotional cycle of change reflects the path of an individual's experience of change from introduction to acceptance.

5. B. Both statements are correct. Leadership for the change shows management support and commitment. Organization adoption ensures that there is a consistent approach across the organization.

6. D. A business development plan would be owned by the business. Policies, processes, and procedures are considered to be change products.

7. B. It is important to engage the stakeholders and ensure that their opinions on the progress of the transition are used to inform it.

8. D. Employee shock in response to change is the most likely challenge.

9. C. Kotter's eight steps relate to actions that need to be taken to support transition.

10. A. Service transition requires the support and engagement of stakeholders and is therefore supported by stakeholder management.

Chapter 28: Organizing for Service Transition

1. A. Each organization must define its organizational roles to suit the needs of its own business. ITIL provides guidance and suggestions for specific processes, but the combination of roles and allocation of responsibility is dependent on the needs of the organization.

2. D. Small organizations are unlikely to have sufficient staff for multiple managers and are more likely to combine roles.

3. C. All the other options are specific process-based roles.

4. B. If the role of service transition manager exists within an organization (and this question assumes it does), then the person filling that role will be responsible for the service transition teams.

5. D. All lifecycle stages have an interface to the service transition lifecycle stage.

6. D. ITIL does not describe a role of process improvement manager. The process owner and manager roles have responsibility for identifying possible improvements.

7. C. ITIL specifies that the process owner is accountable for the process, and there can be only one person accountable.

8. C. Creating and maintaining the process documentation are the responsibilities of the process owner.

9. D. Anyone in the organization can be a knowledge creator.

10. B. The process managers in the service transition stage all work together.

Chapter 29: Technology Considerations for Service Transition

1. C. Transition is supported by tools related to specific processes and by enterprise-wide tools such as the configuration management system or knowledge management system.

2. D. All of these are knowledge management tools. Knowledge management incorporates many tools to support the process.

3. B. Shared calendars and tasks, threaded discussions, and video- and teleconferencing are knowledge sharing tools. Collaboration is important as part of knowledge management.

4. C. The CMS is part of the SKMS. The service knowledge management system should incorporate knowledge tools and systems, even if they are managed independently of the knowledge management process.

5. A. One of the key benefits of the CMS is that it holds information about the relationships between items.

6. D. The CMS is sometimes made up of a number of CMDBs.

7. B. Discovery tools can be used, but they are not the only source for data entry in the CMS.

8. D. Communities are often used to ensure collaboration across organizations.

9. C. Although all of these options would support the CMS, security controls for the CMS data is the most important when considering the design of the system.

10. A. Workflow is an important factor for knowledge management because it provides systemic support for managing knowledge assets through a predefined workflow or process.

Chapter 30: Implementation and Improvement of Service Transition

1. C. Even if procedures are mostly existing already, formalizing them may meet with resistance and will involve a degree of cultural change. It is also true that implementing improvements to service transition is itself a service transition exercise because it will result in a change to how services are delivered by the service provider, and as with any transition, this carries a risk of disruption unless done carefully. So the implementation has to be planned and tested like any other transition.

2. D. Service transition needs a degree of involvement in the justification and design activities to understand what the intended benefits of the transition are and how they are going to be achieved in the design. Service transition is responsible for the introduction activities, but once the period of early life support is completed, the activities required to run the service normally are the responsibility of service operation only; it is a key requirement of transition that it enables the service to be fully handed over to operations.

3. C. These are all proof of poor transition. Successful transition requires careful change management to ensure that changes are tested thoroughly to avoid the disruption and cost of failures resulting from changes. Discovering errors in live operation instead of during the testing stage means that the tests were poorly designed and did not reflect how the service would behave in operation. Transition also has a responsibility for ensuring that the service is delivered within budget and is able to run within the costs that were projected; if this is not the case, then the transition cannot be said to have been successful.

4. C. Well-designed services are indeed easier to transition, and the need for precise design for effective operations is also true, but these are justifications for design, not transition. Similarly, the importance of strategic planning is a justification for strategy, not transition. The difficulties encountered trying to retrofit new practices on existing services is a justification for using service transition processes to introduce the new practices.

5. A. An integrated plan for introduction or improvement of service transition processes must consider how the processes fit together because it must match the inputs, outputs, and triggers of each process step with the corresponding steps in other processes.

6. C. The answer shows the order of steps and the corresponding inputs, as illustrated in Figure 30.1.

7. C. These are all listed as possible challenges in the guidance contained within the *ITIL Service Transition* publication.

8. D. These are all possible groups that service transition may need to work with.

9. B. Based on the guidance within *ITIL Service Transition*, statement 3 is correct, and the other statements are false:

   Statement 3 is true because decisions around transitioning the transition service (as with all transitions) should only be made with a full understanding of the expected risks and benefits. Examples of possible risks include the alienation of support staff, excessive costs to the business, and unacceptable delays to business benefits.

Statement 1 is false because careful consideration should be given to the introduction of service transition to existing projects. It will be practical to introduce these process only when the project is at the transition stage rather than attempting to "retrofit" the desired practices at an earlier stage.

Statement 2 is false because the processes involved in the service transition stage of the service lifecycle are interdependent. The relationships between them are complex, and it is not possible to design and implement them separately.

Statement 4 is false because even if procedures already exist, formalizing them may meet with resistance and will involve a degree of cultural change. As stated above, staff resistance to change is a likely risk.

Statement 5 is false because there will be a need to adjust the processes over time to better fit the requirements, and this should be done in conjunction with continual service improvement.

10. A. Statement 1 is correct because configuration information is particularly challenging in a cloud environment because configurations are so dynamic. However, it may be sufficient to document the high-level configuration and use discovery tools to identify the current state when needed. Statement 2 is also correct because although the organization still needs to carry out service asset and configuration management, the CIs are likely to be at a much higher level.

Chapter 31: Challenges, Critical Success Factors, and Risks

1. C. Integration with the business processes and managing a complex stakeholder group are significant challenges for service transition.

2. A. Balancing the cost of design with the length of time it takes to complete it is applicable to service design, and the balance of service restoration to root cause investigation is applicable to service operation.

3. B. Cultural change and risk management are challenges of service transition. The impact of the business strategy would affect the service strategy lifecycle stage.

4. C. The performance measures should be standardized for use in service transition. Developing standard performance measures across projects and suppliers is a significant challenge for all organizations.

5. A. Establishing and maintaining stakeholder buy-in and commitment and having clearly defined relationships and interfaces with program and project management is vital to the success of a transition.

6. D. All of these are examples of critical success factors for service transition.

7. B. It is very important for service transition to demonstrate less variation in time, cost, and quality predictions during and after transition.

8. C. Design constraints are applicable in service design, but the others are all included in service transition.

9. C. During a crisis situation, it may not be possible to authorize funding as part of the process.

10. A. Increasingly, IT services directly support or actually deliver services on which lives depend. This sort of environment favors accuracy over speed and requires rigorous testing, sign-off at the appropriate level, and the ability to veto a change on safety grounds.

Chapter 32: Introduction to the Service Operation Lifecycle Stage

1. D. Rolling out and testing the service are service transition activities. Deciding whether to retire the service is the job of service strategy.

2. C. Design coordination happens only during the design stage, which includes coordinating all the design activities. The other processes take place in both the service design and service operation stages.

3. D. This stage of the lifecycle, which implements service improvements, is called continual service improvement in the ITIL publications.

4. B. The list in option B matches the list provided in the ITIL guidance.

5. B. Although service strategy is responsible for financial management, it is the responsibility of the other lifecycle stages to deliver within the budget allocated by strategy. If a service costs more to provide than was planned, it may fail to deliver the benefits that it was supposed to deliver.

6. B. Console management is undertaken by operations control (part of operations management), while it is the job of applications management to identify the functional and manageability requirements for application software. The service desk provides a single point of contact, and technical management designs and manages the infrastructure.

7. A. The service desk performs these two, customer-facing processes. The desk is not involved in design at all, and although it may attend the change advisory board meetings and approve changes, it is not responsible for change management.

8. C. The stage of the lifecycle in which service optimization takes place is service operation, not service optimization.

9. C. The service operation stage includes the services, processes, technology, and people within its scope.

10. B. Event management and request fulfilment are service operation processes (along with event, incident, and problem management). Risk management is not an ITIL process, and strategy management is a strategy process.

Chapter 33: Service Operation Principles

1. B. The user experience is not based solely on the technical aspects of service provision. Service operation management must consider the service as well, particularly customer service from a user perspective.

2. C. This is a purpose of the service asset and configuration management, which is part of service transition. The others are all part of the balance of operations discussed in this chapter.

3. B. It is important to ensure that service operation contributes to service strategy by, for example, identifying the operational risks for IT strategies being considered.

4. B. Options A, C, and D are wrong answers; the business *does* care about the efficiency of the service because inefficiency has implications for cost and quality.

5. A. An organization that responds only after something has been reported is reactive. Anticipation of issues demonstrates a proactive approach.

6. D. Operational health refers to the overall performance of a service, which is understood by monitoring and measuring to ensure that functions and processes are delivering correctly and targets are being met.

7. A. An organization that is focused on meeting budgets and reducing costs is extremely cost focused, but an organization focused on delivering the level of quality demanded by the business regardless of what it takes is focused on quality.

8. D. Communication is vital throughout service operation and should not be left until regular review meetings.

9. C. Problem management is most involved with proactive management of operational services, as it seeks to prevent incidents by identifying and resolving problems that could cause incidents before the incidents occur. The other processes react to incidents, service requests, or requests for new or changed access.

10. A. Service operation integrates with all other lifecycle stages.

Chapter 34: Service Operation Processes: Incident and Problem Management

1. B. Option B is the definition of an incident given in the ITIL framework. Option A refers to an event, and option C is a diagnosed problem.

2. C. The incident should not be closed until the user confirms that the service has been restored.

3. B. Option B does not restore the service to the agreed level or provide a workaround; the other options do this.

4. C. Option C is the definition of normal service operation given in the ITIL framework. Normal service operation is what the customer should expect because both sides have agreed on it in the SLA.

5. C. These are called incident models. A model is a repeatable way of dealing with a particular item, in this case a particular type of incident. It defines steps to be taken to resolve the incident along with timescales and escalation points. This speeds up logging and improves consistency.

6. D. All incidents should be logged to ensure that a true picture of the customer experience is achieved; this also allows the cumulative impact of minor incidents to be evaluated. It provides evidence as to when these incidents occur, which may be useful in diagnosing the underlying cause. Option B is incorrect because not *all* incidents will come from the user; they could come from event logs, suppliers, technical staff, and so on.

7. B. Priority within ITIL terms is always based on impact (effect on the business) and urgency (how quickly the business needs resolution).

8. B. Hierarchic escalation involves going up the chain of command to inform or gain additional resource. Functional escalation is going across increasing technical skill levels to speed up resolution.

9. C. A problem takes an unknown cause from one or more incidents, diagnoses the cause, and determines a permanent solution, where possible, thus turning an unknown into a known.

10. D. These are all potential outputs of problem management. Known errors and the associated workarounds are documented and passed to the service desk so that new incident occurrences can be resolved. An RFC may need to be raised to implement a permanent resolution.

Chapter 35: Service Operation Processes: Request Fulfilment

1. D. Only common, low-risk requests with a documented fulfilment procedure should be implemented using the request fulfilment process. Other changes require risk assessment through the change advisory board.

2.   A. Service desk staff fulfil many requests, with second-line staff carrying out installations, moves, and so on. Requests do not fall under the responsibilities of SLM or BRM.

3.   A. Requests do not need CAB approval. If a change is required to fulfil the request, it should usually be preauthorized because the level of risk is low and the fulfilment process known and defined. The usual financial controls still apply, so part of fulfilment may be obtaining the budget holder's agreement to the expenditure. Technical authorization may be required, as mentioned in the chapter.

4.   D. A request to change the functionality of a service by adding a web interface would require consideration of all of the implications and would need to be considered by the CAB. All the other options are examples of service requests.

5.   B. Option B is the definition of a service request provided in the ITIL guidance. A request might be for a standard change, but many requests are not. The procurement process is not necessarily involved in every request. An RFC is not required for a service request.

6.   D. The first three options are listed among the objectives of request fulfilment in the ITIL guidance. Requests are by definition low risk, so understanding and minimizing risk is part of change management, not request fulfilment.

7.   C. Although the request fulfilment process and tools may be used to simplify all sorts of non-IT requests, it does not follow that non-IT requests should be managed by the service desk. This is for the organization to decide; it may lead to a de-skilled service desk.

8.   B. Although the same process may be used, reporting will be complex due to the different goals of the processes—although we want to reduce the number of incidents over time, we may be encouraging users to log requests. So although the number of incidents may be reducing, this may be hard to measure if the number of requests logged this way is increasing. The ability to differentiate between requests and actual incidents is essential. There are similarities in the processes, but many differences too, such as the use of known errors and workarounds in incident management and the emphasis on time, whereas requests may have a set lead time. Each organization will need to assess whether it would be more efficient to have one process, so it cannot be said that it will always be more efficient to combine the two processes.

9.   D. Service level management interfaces with request fulfilment as this process will agree on target fulfilment times for various request types. Many requests will be to provide or remove access to services, and financial management rules may require financial approval of some requests. There is, however, no regular interface between request fulfilment and demand management.

10.   B. A well-designed request fulfilment process will include a process to check on the existence of spare equipment that can be reallocated to avoid the need to purchase a new item. The budget holder should still control expenditure, so the budget will not be spent unnecessarily. The process will also include steps to update the CMS. Users might try to use the request system to avoid change management; this needs to be resisted by checks in the process and communication of the rules to the user community.

Chapter 36: Service Operation Processes: Event Management

1. D. Situation 2 would not be helped by using events. Situation 1 would detect an alert that a time threshold or a priority condition existed and would carry out the escalation defined. Situation 3 would similarly respond to a particular event such as an alarm and would automatically notify the police station. Situation 4 could use the events signifying the successful backup of each file to automate the backup of the next file.

2. C. 1, 2, and 4 are all examples of where event management can be used. Heat and moisture content can be monitored through event management, and actions can be taken if they breach acceptable parameters. Licenses can be controlled by monitoring who is signing onto applications and raising an alert if the maximum legal number is breached. Staff rosters do not have changing conditions that could be monitored by the use of events.

3. C. The two types of event monitoring described in the chapter are passive and active. Passive monitoring waits for an error message to be detected, and active monitoring checks periodically on the "health" of the CI. The other two are not recognized by ITIL as event monitoring types.

4. D. Option C is the definition given in the chapter of an alert. Option A is the definition of an incident. Option B is the definition of a problem. Option D is the definition of an event.

5. C. Option A describes the correlation engine, Option B describes a CMDB, and Option D describes an access management tool. The definition given in Option C matches the explanation in the *ITIL Service Operation* publication.

6. C. Sending notification of every event to every support team would be inefficient. Part of setting up event management is defining who needs to know about specific types of event; the correct team can then be automatically notified, saving time and ensuring a consistent response.

7. A. ITIL does not define an emergency event type. Exception events indicate a failure that must be fixed, while informational events simply consist of a flag that something has happened and should be recorded. A warning event signifies unusual but not necessarily exceptional behavior.

8. B. The correlation engine allows the creation of rule sets that it will use to process events. This will enable the system to determine the significance of each event and also to determine whether there is any predefined response to that event. The correlation engine is not usually used for change management.

9. B. The initial sequence of activities in the event management process is as follows: an event occurs, the event notification is sent, the event is detected by the event management system and logged, and first-level correlation and filtering takes place.

10. B. All of these are valid inputs to event management.

Chapter 37: Service Operation Processes: Access Management

1. B. Option A is incorrect because security management does not prevent nonauthorized users from gaining access. Option C is incorrect because security management is responsible for setting security policies. Option D is incorrect because access management carries out the wishes of whoever is responsible for authorizing access (usually a business manager); it does not make the decision.

2. D. All of the statements except number 3 are correct. Organizations often have a legal requirement to protect data, and failure to do so may damage their reputation and lead to less business. The data belongs to the business, and effective access management is required to ensure that access is based on business reasons, not what IT thinks. Access management does not necessarily reduce costs.

3. C. Option C is not a valid challenge because access management will ensure that every user can be uniquely identified by using additional information such as employee number, date of birth, and so on, so a name change or the appointment of someone with the same name does not cause confusion. All the other options are challenges that access management has to meet.

4. A. Access management will remove or restrict access for staff on long-term leave because there is no valid reason for them to be accessing data. Any attempt to do so would raise suspicions. Access rights for those who have left the organization should be removed. It is poor practice to keep their access information available for the remaining staff to use; it should be adjusted if required to ensure a proper audit trail.

    If a user is under investigation for wrongdoing, their access should be reduced to prevent possible increased harm and to prevent any attempt on the part of the user to "cover their tracks." Finally, users moving within the organization should have their existing access reduced or removed and replaced with the access required for their new position.

5. B. Monitoring the use of the access rights granted to users helps to confirm that the security policies are being adhered to; the aim is not to find and punish those breaking the rules or to read personal emails but to be aware of breaches and raise awareness of the security policy.

6. D. Access management is the efficient execution of information security management policies that protect the confidentiality, integrity, and availability (CIA) of the organization's data and intellectual property. *Confidentiality* here means that only authorized users are able to see the data. *Integrity* means that the data is kept safe from corruption or unauthorized change. *Availability* refers to the service being available to the authorized user.

7. B. Organizations sometimes maintain a specialized team to carry out the requests, but more commonly it is carried out by other functions. Technical and application management functions are involved, and a significant part of the process may be handled within the service desk. There should be a single coordination point to ensure consistency. The information security process owner is NOT involved in carrying out access management.

8. B. It is the job of information security management to define the levels of protection required for different classes of data. All the other options provided are examples of business benefits of access management.

9. C. Option A refers to access, the level and extent of a service's functionality or data that a user is entitled to use. Option B refers to identity, the information about a user that distinguishes them as an individual and verifies their status within the organization. Option D refers to rights or privileges, which are the actual settings whereby a user is provided access. Finally, option B refers to directory services, which are specific types of tools that are used to manage access and rights.

10. A. These are all valid sources for access requests.

Chapter 38: Common Service Operation Activities

1. D. Options A, B, and C are all part of the measurement and control cycle. D is not because restoration is required after a failure and failure should not be continuous.

2. A. Option B is the definition of the dimension of an item, C is the capacity of an item, and D is the cost of an item.

3. C. Both of these statements are correct; monitoring is used for both of these purposes.

4. A. Active monitoring is the ongoing "interrogation" of a device or system to determine its status. Passive monitoring is generating and transmitting events to a "listening device" or monitoring agent. Reactive monitoring is designed to request or trigger action following a certain type of event or failure. Proactive monitoring is used to detect patterns of events that indicate that a system or service may be about to fail.

5. C. Options A, B, and D would measure against a target, not a control. A control is measured against a predefined norm.

6. A. Service operation is the only place where monitoring and control can be applied.

7. B. Design coordination and service validation and testing are processes from service design and service transition.

8. B. Both statements are correct. Audits must be completed regularly and should check if processes are fit for purpose.

9. A. Service operation is engaged in all other lifecycle stages.

10. C. Both statements are correct. Service operation should be looking for improvements, and these should be included in the CSI improvement register.

Chapter 39: Organizing for Service Operation

1. D. Testing and rolling out the service are part of the service transition stage, and the decision to retire the service is strategic.

2. D. Design coordination takes place solely within the service design lifecycle stage, whereas the other processes have elements of operational activity.

3. C. Option C includes the correct list of functions in service operation.

4. B. Defining the infrastructure requirements will be part of service design.

5. B. Option B correctly matches the activities and functions.

6. C. The problem management process is responsible for the prevention of incidents.

7. B. Design coordination is a process of service design, and change management is a process of service transition.

8. D. Specialist technical knowledge is more likely to be found in the technical or application management functions.

9. D. Facilities management and operations control are the two elements of operations management.

10. B. Matrix is not recognized as a service desk structure in the ITIL framework.

Chapter 40: Technology Considerations

1. B. Tools enable processes, not replace them, and although tools are used to support the processes, they should not define them.

2. A. Statement 2 is incorrect; a tool does not need to have a service knowledge management system to be a service management tool. However, having details of all CIs and being able to link incidents, problems, requests, and so on is incredibly useful.

3. B. The first step in selecting a toolset should be requirements gathering; if the requirements are not met, the tool may not function sufficiently to support the needs of the processes and teams.

4. C. All of the options are part of the generic requirements for a service management tool.

5. A. Must, Should, Could, Would (MoSCoW) technique is used to categorize requirements in the selection of a tool. For example, the tool must have the ability to link incident records to problem records.

6. D. The ability to authorize change requests is unlikely to be part of a self-service portal, but all of the rest are potentially standard capabilities.

7. D. Reporting is essential in service management. A good tool will have a selection of generic reports but should also provide the functionality to support tailored report requirements to support organizational needs.

8. A. Management should provide support and guidance throughout service management, and commitment is apparent if they provide the budget to enable training, obtain tools, and so on.

9. C. The KEDB (known error database) is important for both the processes of incident and problem management because this is where the information on root cause, workarounds, and resolutions is stored. Incident management can use it to improve its capability to fix incidents at first point of contact, and problem management will use the information to support raising changes and for trend analysis to understand underlying causes.

10. B. Telephony systems such as an ACD system may also be classified as a service management tool, not just a record/ticket logging system. It is important to remember that service management requires a suite of tools to support the processes effectively. For example, there should be monitoring systems for event and access management, which may be linked to an incident management system.

Chapter 41: Implementation of Service Operation

1. C. These are all valid triggers listed in the *ITIL Service Operation* core volume.

2. B. Statement 1 is incorrect; the aim of managing change is to ensure the benefits are delivered without any unexpected variation or outages. Statement 2 is correct, since if the change is successful, no such variations or outages will be visible to the customer; all they will notice is the benefits that have been delivered. Some technical changes may not be noticed by the customer at all, but will deliver a more robust service and reduce the likelihood of future outages.

3. A. Service operation personnel should be involved in design and transition to ensure that the end result is "supportable."

4. B. Processes are defined first; the tool is used to support them. Tools can facilitate process operation. Customer satisfaction is dependent upon many factors, and the tool alone is not likely to improve it. A service management tool will not reduce outages or increase first-time fix rates on its own, but using the tool correctly and optimizing data capture and knowledge share will assist the support teams.

5. B. Adopting project management does not mean that service operation does not have to fund the change. All other answers are benefits of using project management.

6. D. The six items in the question are all triggers for operational change listed in *ITIL Service Operation*.

7. D. Service operation staff need to be involved early in the process to ensure that the design takes into account operational issues, but their involvement is also needed later. Service operation staff also need to be involved late in the process to ensure that the schedule for implementation does not clash with other operational priorities. So staff involvement is necessary throughout the design and implementation process to ensure that all operational issues and possible impacts are dealt with.

8. C. ITIL and project management can be complementary; however, project management is not required for simple changes. Project management is useful where changes are large or complex. Not all operational changes are business as usual, and simple changes do not require project management.

9. D. These are all risks and should be mitigated using ITIL best practice.

10. B. Time limited is *not* a valid type of license. All the other terms are descriptions of possible licensing options.

Chapter 42: Challenges, Critical Success Factors, and Risks

1. D. As explained above, operational expenditure is seen as infrastructure costs and thus an overhead. It is not always understood that investment in operations can lead to cost savings. For example, investment in a knowledge base should improve first-contact resolution, saving the cost and delay of involving second- and third-line staff.

2. D. Service operation should engage with all lifecycle stages. This chapter has explained why involvement by design and transition is essential to ensure that the service can be operated as designed and the transition delivers a working system. Unless operations understand why a service is being deployed, and what it is meant to achieve, the focus will not be on achieving these aims. All stages of the lifecycle should engage with CSI.

3. B. Support from senior/middle management and the business is important when trying to implement changes in the face of opposition from some staff. Support from "champions" can help change how staff regard the changes. Support from suppliers is irrelevant; however, they can play a significant part in helping to deliver services.

4. A. All of these are CSFs for staff retention listed in *ITIL Service Operation*.

5. C. A successful service desk requires adequate funding because understaffing or insufficient tools will adversely impact the service to customers. Loss of key personnel, unless an effective knowledge base exists, could reduce the first-contact fix rate. Resistance to change could lead to second-line staff refusing to share knowledge to enable the service desk to resolve more incidents. This can be overcome with management support; if this is lacking, the service desk will struggle.

6. B. The focus of work in the operation stage of the lifecycle differs from the other stages because it concentrates on delivering a live service. Other staff work on projects with defined end dates, but operations staff seldom do; they are providing a continuous service. This means that operations staff are more concerned that the service works when delivered than about meeting a particular date. Operations staff are concerned with warranty because failure to meet warranty requirements will lead to problems delivering the live service; other areas, such a service design, are more concerned that the new capabilities work. However, all stages are concerned with sticking to the budget, and there is no evidence that operations staff are not respected.

7. B. Implementing best practice in configuration management will save money in preventing unnecessary license sales, problem management will reduce repeat incidents, and availability and capacity management will ensure the best utilization of the infrastructure. Better testing is a result of investment in transition, not operations.

8. B. Defining requirements is a challenge for service design, not service operation. Translating technical metrics into service metrics, sharing knowledge effectively, and managing suppliers and internal teams are all challenges listed in *ITIL Service Operation*.

9. B. Translating strategic plans into tactical and operational plans is a challenge for service design, not service operation. Ensuring that there is the right number of staff and that they have the necessary knowledge and skills are critical success factors for service operation, as is visual management support.

10. C. Inadequate funding, loss of momentum, and resistance to change are all risks listed in *ITIL Service Operation*. A clear definition of measurement and reporting is a critical success factor, not a risk.

Chapter 43: Introduction to the Continual Service Improvement Lifecycle Stage

1. B. To ensure that IT services remain aligned to changing business needs is the main objective of CSI according to the *ITIL Continual Service Improvement* core volume.

2. D. The first three statements are correct.

3. C. All areas, including CSI itself, are within the scope of CSI.

4. C. These are the inputs and outputs for each step of the process:

- What is the vision? (Business vision, mission, goals, and objectives)
- Where are we now? (Baseline assessments)
- Where do we want to be? (Measurable targets)
- How do we get there? (Service and process improvements)

- Did we get there? (Measurements and metrics)
- How do we keep the momentum going?

5. A. The second statement is the purpose of the service strategy lifecycle stage.

6. B. Options A and D are service transition objectives; option C is an objective of service strategy. CSI is concerned with the identification of improvement opportunities.

7. C. CSI provides guidance on service management improvements, not on business strategic planning.

8. A. The CSI stage applies across the whole of the service lifecycle and is key in the management of all improvements across all service stages.

9. C. The CSI approach is a set of steps that can be used to manage improvement initiatives in line with the requirements of the business.

10. B. Wanting to improve the level of service, being able to deliver it at a lower cost (thus improving the profit margin), and streamlining a process are all valid reasons for undertaking CSI. Increasing the cost of a service is not; CSI ensures that the service is provided to the agreed level, with no unnecessary costs or delays in that provision.

Chapter 44: Continual Service Improvement Principles

1. A. There are eight steps in Kotter's transformation program.

2. D. The register should not be managed by the customers. It should be managed on behalf of the customers by the CSI manager, and there should be a single register, not multiple registers to avoid duplication.

3. A. Regulation and legislation, competition and market pressures, and economics are all external drivers that come from outside the organization; the others are internal drivers.

4. B. To validate, direct, justify, and intervene are all reasons to measure.

5. C. The knowledge spiral connects strategic, tactical, and operational approaches.

6. A. ITIL complements other standards and frameworks, and CSI should work with all stages of the service lifecycle.

7. B. A baseline captures a starting point for improvement.

8. A. Knowledge management is concerned with the management of information.

9. C. Corrective action is the last step, but this corrective action may lead to further improvement.

10. A. CSI is an important part of all change in an organization and should be included as part of organizational change.

Chapter 45: The Seven-Step Continual Service Improvement Process

1. B. The seven-step improvement process is the process used as part of the CSI lifecycle stage to ensure that the correct data is gathered, analyzed, and presented to the correct audience to enable informed decision-making.

2. B. Improving service delivery by eliminating the root causes of incidents is the responsibility of problem management.

3. D. Service improvement must focus on increasing the efficiency, maximizing the effectiveness, and optimizing the cost of services and the underlying IT service management (ITSM) processes. The only way to do this is to ensure that improvement opportunities are identified throughout the entire service lifecycle.

4. C. All steps must be followed, and they must be followed in sequence. The process may be used at any stage of the service lifecycle.

5. C. The integration of the PDCA cycle and the seven-step improvement process is as follows:

   Plan

   1. Identify the strategy for improvement.
   2. Define what you will measure.

   Do

   3. Gather the data.
   4. Process the data.

   Check

   5. Analyze the information and data.
   6. Present and use the information.

   Act

   7. Implement improvement.

6. B. The three main types of metrics are technology, relating to component and application based metrics such as performance and availability; process, metrics captured as CSFs, KPIs, and activity metrics for monitoring the health of a process; and service, metrics used to assess the end-to-end service.

7. B. It is not advisable to take action based solely on a "snapshot" of a data point at a specific moment in time; an analysis of the data points over a period of time will show whether this is an ongoing issue requiring action or was a one-off occurrence.

8. B. There are usually four distinct audiences:

The customers: Their real need is to understand whether IT delivered the service they promised at the levels they promised and, if not, what improvements are being implemented to improve the situation.

Senior IT management: This group is often focused on the results surrounding CSFs and KPIs, such as customer satisfaction, actual versus planned costs, and achievement of revenue targets. Information provided at this level helps determine strategic and tactical improvements on a larger scale. Senior IT management often wants this type of information provided in the form of a balanced scorecard or IT scorecard format to see the big picture at one glance.

Internal IT: This group is often interested in KPIs and activity metrics that help them plan, coordinate, schedule, and identify incremental improvement opportunities.

Suppliers: This group will be interested in KPIs and activity metrics related to their own services and performance. Suppliers may also be targeted with improvement initiatives.

9. B. Step 2 (define what you will measure) and step 3 (gather the data) are aligned to the data part of the DIKW structure.

10. B. The order of the seven steps is as follows:

   1. Identify the strategy for improvement.

   2. Define what you will measure.

   3. Gather the data.

   4. Process the data.

   5. Analyze the information and data.

   6. Present and use the information.

   7. Implement the improvement.

Chapter 46: Continual Service Improvement Methods and Techniques

1. C. Both statements are correct.

2. D. Costs, staff, and management buy-in are essential, but there is no specific requirement for an assessment tool.

3. A. Maturity assessment frameworks evaluate people, processes, and technology. Services are made up of these elements but are not part of the maturity assessment.

4. B. The acronym commonly used is PDCA, which stands for Plan-Do-Check-Act.

5. C. Benchmarking is used as a comparison to best practice. The other three options are measurements that can be used in service management.

6. D. All of these are techniques that can help identify problem areas for improvement action.

7. C. All of the personnel listed may be involved in benchmarking.

8. D. These are basic measures used in service measurement.

9. C. All of these are drivers for service targets.

10. D. SWOT stands for strengths, weaknesses, opportunities, and threats. Strengths and weaknesses are both internal attributes, not external.

Chapter 47: Organizing for Continual Service Improvement

1. C. "The reporting analyst reviews and analyses data from components, systems and subsystems in order to obtain a true end-to-end service achievement." *(ITIL CSI* core volume, Chapter 6)

2. B. *RACI* is an acronym of the four levels of involvement in a process activity: responsible, accountable, consulted, informed.

- Responsible: The person or people responsible for getting the job done.
- Accountable: Only one person can be accountable for each task.
- Consulted: Involvement through input of knowledge and information.
- Informed: Receiving information about process execution and quality.

3. D. The process owner ensures the process can be carried out effectively, the process manager ensures that it is carried out effectively, and the process practitioner actually carries out the process activity.

4. C. The service owner is accountable for the delivery of a specific IT service and represents the service across the organization. The service owner is accountable to the customer for the initiation, transition, and ongoing maintenance and support of a particular service and accountable to the IT director or service management director for the delivery of the service.

5. C. The CSI manager is responsible for developing CSI practices and communication throughout the organization. The service owner is responsible for maintaining accurate information in the service catalog. The process owner is responsible for sponsoring, designing, and managing changes to the process and its metrics. The process manager is responsible for ensuring that activities are carried out as required throughout the service.

6. B. The RACI matrix shows who is responsible, accountable, consulted, or informed for each task in a process. It is the combination of OLAs and underpinning contracts that show what can be promised in an SLA.

7. D. The process practitioner is responsible for creating or updating records to show that activities have been carried out correctly. An example of a process practitioner is a service desk analyst who creates and updates incident and request records.

8. B. The reporting analyst does not need to have the ability to build trust with senior business managers; it is the CSI manager's role to build trust with senior IT and business managers. The reporting analyst does not need an in-depth understanding of the technical infrastructure, just an understanding of its reporting capabilities. Similarly, customer-facing skills are not required as their work is mostly internal, with the service provider.

9. B. These skills are required by those responsible for identifying the strategy for improvement (step 1), defining what to measure (step 2), and presenting and using the information (step 6).

10. D. Customer focus is a primary responsibility of the service level manager and business relationship manager; it is a secondary responsibility for the CSI manager and service owner.

Chapter 48: Technology Considerations

1. D. There is no single tool that can do everything.

2. B. Separate tools will make linking items difficult or impossible.

3. C. Tools support processes. Each organization will adopt and adapt the ITIL processes to suit its environment; the tool should be programmed to support the organization's processes. The tools themselves do not enforce adherence. Answers A, B, and D correctly describe the benefits of using such tools.

4. B. Business process automation tools and customer relationship management tools are not tools that would be used to assist service management. All the others are frequently used in service management.

5. B. However intuitive the tool is, training is always required to get the best use of the product. Reporting requirements should be considered from the beginning to ensure that the required data is captured. Requirements will change as processes mature, so one should expect the tool configuration to change over time. Strict adherence to ITIL is not necessary as long as the tool supports your processes.

6. C. Although tools may be involved in managing and automating processes, the area of service management that is mostly concerned with tools is products. This area involves the products and tools that may be used to assist in effective service management.

7. D. *Holistic* means that the tool deals with service management as a whole, not just some of its components. Integrated toolsets fit this definition. Business process engineering tools and customer relationship management (CRM) toolsets are specialist tools for those areas or activities; they are not service management tools. Finally, a tool may be centralized without being holistic; an event management tool may be operated centrally but only assists a single process, so it is not integrated.

8. D. The tools will provide data upon which a prioritization decision may be based, but the decision cannot be automated. It must be a matter for the service provider, based on the business benefits and priorities.

9. A. Both these statements are true.

10. B. Tools cannot replace the need for effective processes.

Chapter 49: Implementation of Continual Service Improvement

1. C. The decision regarding what to improve first can only be made when there is data to analyze and key people appointed to do it. The internal reviews will help inform the analysis.

2. D. The three approaches in ITIL are functional, lifecycle, and service.

3. B. Good data can be obtained from a combination of different tools, although the stakeholders need to agree on the criteria for what is gathered. CSI is concerned with the improvement of both customer-facing and internal processes because inefficient internal processes may increase cost and have an indirect negative impact on customer services.

4. C. Establish a sense of urgency is the first of Kotter's steps.

5. D. Senior management involvement is crucial to show that it is regarded as important. Key individuals who are not managers can still be influential among their peers. Only those who believe in the changes should be involved.

6. D. A mission statement does not coordinate actions.

7. B. Good data helps to direct and justify improvement actions, but ignoring failing areas because you lack the statistical data is wrong; the first step for improvement in these areas is to improve the quality of data being collected.

8. A. Cultural change means winning the hearts and minds of staff. Enforcement of a process does not mean that cultural change has taken place.

9. A. The four key roles are CSI manager, service owner, reporting analyst, and service level manager.

10. C. CSI must be continual. Reporting and reviewing should be embedded in every process, and improvement based on these reviews should be part of business as usual.

Chapter 50: Challenges, Critical Success Factors, and Risks

1.   B. These are all common challenges.

2.   B. The business has to be involved in improvement decisions that will impact them, and if they do not understand the reasons behind the actions being taken, they may even be hostile to the changes. CSI needs to include improvements to both services and service management processes. Poor service management processes will ultimately impact the business

3.   D. The cost to overcome the situation is already covered in the assessment of impact. Even if it is expensive to remove, a risk with a high chance of occurring and with a major impact will need to be mitigated.

4.   A. Measurements should be focused on customer satisfaction and should *not* be inwardly focused on measuring the achievement of internal goals. Achievement of the strategy should be able to be ascertained from day-to-day performance trends. If your strategy changes, the current measurements may be irrelevant and would therefore need to change.

5.   D. All of these are possible challenges.

6.   D. ITIL describes this as a challenge. There may be an associated risk that time is wasted re-creating knowledge that already existed but was not shared. Sharing of knowledge is a CSF for CSI; this could be measured by KPIs of "an expansion in the number of validated articles in the knowledgebase" and "increasing numbers of occasions when staff refer to the knowledge base and successfully obtain the information they require."

7.   C. These are all possible reasons CSI may be resisted. Adequate time and training needs to be provided, together with a cultural change program.

8.   A. If the IT provider does not have a good relationship with the business and has little communication with it, it will be difficult for them to appreciate business priorities. Similarly, technical metrics that do not show the impact of IT failures on the business will make it difficult to prioritize actions. Department heads within the service provider may try to use CSI as a means of implementing changes they think are important; there is a danger that priorities will be set that suit the IT department rather than the business. Inadequate resources may limit the improvements that can be made, but it does not stop them being prioritized.

9.   B. Option B describes a risk, not a CSF.

10.   B. KPIs measure critical success factors. A risk is the possible result if a challenge is not met successfully.

Index

Index

Note to the Reader: Throughout this index **boldfaced** page numbers indicate primary discussions of a topic. *Italicized* page numbers indicate illustrations.

D

S

U

Comprehensive Online Learning Environment

Register on Sybex.com to gain access to the comprehensive online interactive learning environment and test bank to help you study for your ITIL Intermediate Service Lifecycle certification.

The online test bank includes:

- **Assessment Test** to help you focus your study to specific objectives
- **Chapter Tests** to reinforce what you learned
- **Digital Flashcards** to reinforce your learning and provide last-minute test prep before the exam
- **Searchable Glossary** gives you instant access to the key terms you'll need to know for the exam

Go to `http://sybextestbanks.wiley.com` **to register and gain access to this comprehensive study tool package.**